# Color Oxford Dictionary and Thesaurus

**THIRD EDITION**

*Edited by*
Charlotte Livingstone

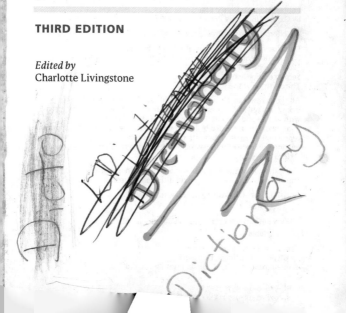

# OXFORD
UNIVERSITY PRESS

Great Clarendon Street, Oxford OX2 6DP

Oxford University Press is a department of the University of Oxford.
It furthers the University's objective of excellence in research, scholarship,
and education by publishing worldwide in

Oxford  New York

Auckland  Cape Town  Dar es Salaam  Hong Kong  Karachi
Kuala Lumpur  Madrid  Melbourne  Mexico City  Nairobi
New Delhi  Shanghai  Taipei  Toronto

With offices in

Argentina  Austria  Brazil  Chile  Czech Republic  France  Greece
Guatemala  Hungary  Italy  Japan  Poland  Portugal  Singapore
South Korea  Switzerland  Thailand  Turkey  Ukraine  Vietnam

Oxford is a registered trade mark of Oxford University Press
in the UK and in certain other countries

Published in the United States
by Oxford University Press Inc., New York

© Oxford University Press 2003, 2007, 2010

Database right Oxford University Press (makers)
First edition entitled *Color Oxford Dictionary, Thesaurus, and
Wordpower Guide*, 2003
Second edition 2007
Third edition 2010

British Library Cataloguing in Publication Data

Data available

Library of Congress Cataloging in Publication Data

Data available

Typeset in Frutiger and Parable
by Glyph International, Bangalore
Printed in China by C&C Offset Printing Co., Ltd

ISBN 978-0-19-957932-7
ISBN 978-0-19-957

# Contents

# Introduction

This brand-new edition of the *Color Oxford Dictionary and Thesaurus* provides you with both definitions and synonyms in convenient, multi-purpose entries. Whether you want to check the meaning of a word or find a range of alternative terms with the same meaning, you only need to look at one main entry. This unique, user-friendly feature means that finding the word you need is quick, easy, and convenient.

Since the last edition, the text has been revised and updated using the Oxford English Corpus, an enormous database containing billions of words of real English drawn from a wide variety of sources. The dictionary component provides up-to-date coverage of all of the words you need for everyday use, with definitions written in straightforward language and a clear, accessible style. The synonym sections work just like a thesaurus. Lists of alternative words are arranged in order of their closeness in meaning to the main entry word, with the closest one given first. Together with a center section containing information on word classes, punctuation, and a short guide to help you get the most out of the thesaurus, the *Color Oxford Dictionary and Thesaurus* is the ideal reference companion, in a handy size you can take anywhere.

# Guide to the dictionary and thesaurus

## 1. Structure of the entries

US variant spelling

headword

**axe** (US usu. **ax**) n. a chopping tool with a heavy blade.
• introduces new part of speech
• **v. (axed, axing) 1** reduce something by a large amount. **2** dismiss someone ruthlessly.

verb inflections

sense number

**heated** adj. impassioned or excited: *a heated debate.*

example of use

▷ SYNS introduces thesaurus section

▷ SYNS VEHEMENT, passionate, impassioned, animated, angry, furious, fierce.

core synonyms (in small capitals): the synonym closest in meaning to the headword

plural inflection

**woman** n. (pl. **women**) an adult human female. □ **womankind** women as a group.

□ introduces phrases section

■ introduces derivatives section

■ **womanhood** n. **womanly** adj.

▷ SYNS **1** LADY, girl, female; inf. bird, chick; US inf. dame. **2** GIRLFRIEND, sweetheart, partner, lover; wife, spouse.

label showing how term is used

## 2. Abbreviations used in the dictionary and thesaurus

| | | | |
|---|---|---|---|
| **abbr.** | abbreviation | **pl.** | plural |
| **adj.** | adjective | **poss. pron** | possessive pronoun |
| **adv.** | adverb | **p. p.** | past participle |
| **Austral.** | Australian | **pref.** | prefix |
| **comb. form** | combining form | **prep.** | preposition |
| **conj.** | conjunction | **pron.** | pronoun |
| **derog.** | derogatory | **Scot.** | Scottish |
| **esp.** | especially | **sing.** | singular |
| **exclam.** | exclamation | **sp.** | spelling |
| **hist.** | historical | **usu.** | usually |
| **inf.** | informal | **v.** | verb |
| **lit.** | literary | **var.** | variant |
| **n.** | noun | **vars.** | variants |
| **N. Engl.** | northern English | **v. aux.** | auxiliary verb |
| **offens.** | offensive | | |

Abbreviations that are in common use (such as *cm*, *RC*, and *USA*) appear in the dictionary itself.

## Note on trademarks and proprietary status

This dictionary includes some words which have, or are asserted to have, proprietary status as trademarks or otherwise. Their inclusion does not imply that they have acquired for legal purposes a non-proprietary or general significance, nor any other judgement concerning their legal status. In cases where the editorial staff have some evidence that a word has proprietary status this is indicated in the entry for that word by the label trademark but no judgement concerning the legal status of such words is made or implied thereby.

# Aa

**@** symb. 'at', used: **1** to show cost or rate per unit. **2** in Internet addresses between the user's name and the domain name.

**a** adj. **1** used when mentioning someone or something for the first time; the indefinite article. **2** one single. **3** per.

**AA** abbr. **1** Automobile Association. **2** Alcoholics Anonymous.

**aardvark** n. an African animal with a long snout.

**aback** adv. (**taken aback**) surprised.

**abacus** n. a frame with beads sliding on wires or rods, used for counting.

**abandon** v. **1** leave permanently. **2** give up. • n. lack of inhibition. ■ **abandoned** adj. **abandonment** n.
▷ SYNS v. **1** DESERT, leave, forsake, jilt. **2** GIVE UP, renounce, relinquish, forswear.

**abase** v. humiliate or degrade. ■ **abasement** n.

**abashed** adj. embarrassed or ashamed.
▷ SYNS EMBARRASSED, ashamed, shamefaced, mortified, humiliated.

**abate** v. become less intense.

**abattoir** n. a slaughterhouse.

**abbey** n. a building occupied by a community of monks or nuns.
▷ SYNS MONASTERY, CONVENT, priory, cloister, friary, nunnery.

**abbot** n. a man who is the head of a community of monks.

**abbreviate** v. shorten a word etc. ■ **abbreviation** n.
▷ SYNS SHORTEN, reduce, cut, condense, abridge, summarize, precis.

**ABC** n. **1** the alphabet. **2** the basic facts of a subject.

**abdicate** v. **1** renounce the throne. **2** fail to carry out a duty. ■ **abdication** n.
▷ SYNS **1** RESIGN, stand down, retire, quit. **2** GIVE UP, renounce, relinquish, waive, forgo, abandon, surrender.

**abdomen** n. the part of the body containing the digestive organs. ■ **abdominal** adj.

**abduct** v. kidnap. ■ **abduction** n.
▷ SYNS KIDNAP, carry off, run/make off with, seize.

**aberration** n. a deviation from what is normal. ■ **aberrant** adj.
▷ SYNS DEVIATION, anomaly, abnormality, irregularity, freak.

**abet** v. (**abetted, abetting**) assist in wrongdoing. ■ **abettor** n.

**abeyance** n. (**in abeyance**) in temporary disuse.

**abhor** v. (**abhorred, abhorring**) detest.

**abhorrent** adj. detestable. ■ **abhorrence** n.

**abide** v. **1** (**abide by**) accept or obey a rule or decision. **2** (**cannot abide**) dislike greatly.
▷ SYNS **1** *you must abide by the rules:* COMPLY WITH, obey, observe, follow, keep to, hold to, adhere to, stick to. **2** *I can't*

*abide smoke:* TOLERATE, bear, stand, put up with, endure.

**abiding** adj. lasting.

**ability** n. **1** the power to do something. **2** cleverness.
▷ SYNS **1** CAPACITY, capability, potential, power, facility, faculty. **2** TALENT, competence, proficiency, skill, expertise, aptitude, dexterity, knack; inf. know-how.

**abject** adj. **1** wretched. **2** completely without pride.

**abjure** v. renounce a belief or claim.

**ablaze** adj. blazing.

**able** adj. **1** capable of doing something. **2** talented.
■ **ably** adv.
▷ SYNS COMPETENT, capable, talented, skilful, skilled, clever, accomplished, gifted, proficient, expert, adept, adroit.

**ablutions** pl.n. the action of washing yourself.

**abnormal** adj. not normal.
■ **abnormality** n. **abnormally** adv.
▷ SYNS UNUSUAL, strange, odd, peculiar, uncommon, curious, queer, weird, unexpected, exceptional, irregular, atypical, anomalous, deviant, aberrant.

**aboard** adv. & prep. on board.

**abode** n. a house or home.

**abolish** v. put an end to formally. ■ **abolition** n.
▷ SYNS DO AWAY WITH, put an end to, end, stop, terminate, axe, scrap, quash, annul, cancel, invalidate, nullify, void, rescind, repeal, revoke.

**abominable** adj. causing revulsion. ■ **abominably** adv.
▷ SYNS HATEFUL, loathsome, detestable, odious, obnoxious, despicable, contemptible, disgusting, revolting, repellent, repulsive,

offensive, repugnant, abhorrent, foul, vile, horrible, nasty.

**abominate** v. lit. detest.
■ **abomination** n.

**aboriginal** adj. existing in a land from its earliest times.
• n. (**Aboriginal**) a member of one of the original peoples of Australia.

**Aborigine** n. an Australian Aboriginal.

**abort** v. **1** carry out the abortion of a fetus. **2** end prematurely because of a problem.

**abortion** n. an operation to end a pregnancy early.

**abortive** adj. unsuccessful.
▷ SYNS FAILED, unsuccessful, vain, futile, useless, fruitless.

**abound** v. be plentiful.

**about** prep. & adv. **1** concerning. **2** approximately. **3** surrounding. **4** in circulation. ▫ **about-turn** a reversal of direction or policy.

**above** adv. & prep. **1** at a higher level than. **2** more than.
▫ **above board** lawful.

**abracadabra** n. a magic formula.

**abrasion** n. **1** scraping or wearing away. **2** an area of scraped skin.

**abrasive** adj. **1** rough and used for polishing or cleaning. **2** harsh or unkind.
▷ SYNS CAUSTIC, cutting, harsh, acerbic, biting, sharp.

**abreast** adv. **1** side by side. **2** informed or up to date.

**abridge** v. shorten by using fewer words. ■ **abridgement** n.
▷ SYNS SHORTEN, cut down, condense, abbreviate, truncate, summarize, precis.

**abroad** adv. away from your home country.

**abrupt** adj. **1** sudden. **2** curt.
▷ SYNS **1** SUDDEN, quick, hasty, swift, rapid, precipitate, unexpected. **2** CURT, blunt, brusque, short, terse, brisk, unceremonious, rude.

**abscess** n. a swelling that contains pus.

**abscond** v. leave quickly and secretly.
▷ SYNS RUN AWAY, decamp, bolt, flee, take flight, take to your heels.

**abseil** v. climb down a rock face using a rope fixed at a higher point.

**absence** n. **1** the state of being absent. **2** lack.

**absent** adj. not present.
□ **absent yourself** stay away.
▷ SYNS AWAY, off, out, elsewhere, unavailable, lacking, gone, missing, truant.

**absentee** n. a person who is absent from work etc.
■ **absenteeism** n.

**absent-minded** adj. forgetful.
▷ SYNS FORGETFUL, distracted, preoccupied, inattentive, vague, scatterbrained.

**absolute** adj. **1** complete. **2** not limited. ■ **absolutely** adv.
▷ SYNS **1** COMPLETE, total, utter, out and out, outright, unqualified, unadulterated, unalloyed, downright, undiluted, consummate, unmitigated. **2** UNLIMITED, unrestricted, supreme, total, unconditional, full.

**absolution** n. formal forgiveness of sins.

**absolutism** n. the principle that the government should have unrestricted powers.

**absolve** v. clear of blame or guilt.

**absorb** v. **1** soak up.
**2** understand information.
**3** hold the attention of.
▷ SYNS **1** SOAK UP, suck up, sop up. **2** TAKE IN, assimilate, digest. **3** OCCUPY, engage, fascinate, captivate, engross, immerse, rivet.

**absorbent** adj. able to soak up liquid.

**absorbing** adj. very interesting.
▷ SYNS FASCINATING, gripping, interesting, captivating, engrossing, riveting, spellbinding, intriguing.

**absorption** n. the process of absorbing.

**abstain** v. **1** stop yourself from doing something. **2** choose not to vote. ■ **abstention** n.
▷ SYNS REFRAIN, decline, forbear, desist, avoid, eschew.

**abstemious** adj. not self-indulgent, esp. in eating and drinking.
▷ SYNS SELF-DENYING, self-restrained, moderate, temperate, abstinent, ascetic, puritanical.

**abstinence** n. abstaining, esp. from food or alcohol.

**abstract** adj. **1** relating to ideas or qualities rather than physical things. **2** (of art) not representing things pictorially.
• v. take out or remove. • n. a summary. ■ **abstraction** n.
▷ SYNS adj. THEORETICAL, conceptual, intellectual, metaphysical, philosophical.

**abstruse** adj. hard to understand.

**absurd** adj. ridiculous.
■ **absurdity** n.
▷ SYNS RIDICULOUS, foolish, silly, idiotic, stupid, nonsensical, senseless, inane, ludicrous,

laughable, preposterous, farcical, hare-brained, asinine; inf. daft, crazy.

**abundant** adj. plentiful.
■ abundance n.
▷ SYNS PLENTIFUL, ample, large, huge, copious, lavish, rich, profuse, teeming, overflowing, galore.

**abuse** v. 1 use badly or wrongly. 2 treat cruelly. 3 insult. • n. 1 cruel treatment. 2 misuse. 3 insulting language.
▷ SYNS v. 1 MISUSE, misapply, misemploy, exploit. 2 MISTREAT, maltreat, ill-treat, hurt, harm, molest, assault. 3 INSULT, swear at, curse, vilify, taunt. • n. 1 MISTREATMENT, maltreatment, ill-treatment; injury, hurt, harm; molestation, assault. 2 MISUSE, misapplication, mishandling, exploitation. 3 INSULTS, expletives, curses, swear words; swearing, cursing; invective, slander.

**abusive** adj. 1 very insulting. 2 cruel and violent.
▷ SYNS 1 INSULTING, rude, offensive, slanderous, libellous, derogatory, defamatory. 2 VIOLENT, brutal, cruel, harsh, oppressive.

**abut** v. (abutted, abutting) be next to or touching.

**abysmal** adj. very bad.

**abyss** n. a deep chasm.

**AC** abbr. alternating current.

**acacia** n. a tree or shrub with yellow or white flowers.

**academic** adj. 1 relating to education or study. 2 of theoretical interest only. • n. a scholar.
■ academically adv.
▷ SYNS adj. 1 EDUCATIONAL, scholastic, instructional; SCHOLARLY, studious, literary, well read,

intellectual, erudite, learned, cultured, highbrow, bookish, cerebral. 2 THEORETICAL, conceptual, hypothetical, speculative, conjectural. • n. SCHOLAR, lecturer, don, teacher, tutor, professor, fellow.

**academy** n. (pl. -ies) 1 a society of scholars or artists. 2 a school.

**accede** v. formal agree.

**accelerate** v. increase in speed.
■ acceleration n.
▷ SYNS SPEED UP, pick up speed, hasten, hurry, quicken.

**accelerator** n. a pedal on a vehicle for increasing speed.

**accent** n. 1 a distinctive way of pronouncing a language. 2 emphasis. 3 a written mark guiding pronunciation. • v. 1 emphasize. 2 (**accented**) spoken with an accent.
▷ SYNS n. 1 PRONUNCIATION, intonation, enunciation, articulation, inflection, tone, brogue. 2 STRESS, emphasis, accentuation, force, prominence, beat.

**accentuate** v. make more noticeable. ■ accentuation n.
▷ SYNS STRESS, highlight, emphasize, underline, draw attention to, heighten, point up, underscore, accent.

**accept** v. 1 agree to receive or do something offered. 2 believe to be valid or correct. 3 resign yourself to. ■ acceptance n.
▷ SYNS 1 RECEIVE, take; take on, undertake, assume, take responsibility for. 2 BELIEVE, credit, trust; inf. buy, swallow. 3 RESIGN YOURSELF TO, reconcile yourself to, tolerate, endure, put up with, bear, take, submit to.

**acceptable** adj. satisfactory.
■ acceptably adv.

▷ SYNS SATISFACTORY, adequate, passable, admissible, tolerable.

**access** n. **1** a way in. **2** the right or opportunity to use something or see someone. • v. **1** enter a place. **2** obtain data from a computer.
▷ SYNS n. **1** *a side access:* ENTRANCE, entry, way in; approach, means of approach. **2** *they were denied access:* ADMISSION, admittance, entry.

**accessible** adj. able to be reached or obtained.
■ accessibility n. accessibly adv.

**accession** n. **1** the reaching of a rank or position. **2** an addition.

**accessory** n. (pl. **-ies**) **1** something added as a supplement or decoration. **2** someone who helps in a crime.

**accident** n. **1** an unplanned event causing damage or injury. **2** chance. ■ accidentally adv.
▷ SYNS **1** MISHAP, misfortune, misadventure, disaster, tragedy, catastrophe, calamity. **2** CRASH, collision; inf. smash, pile-up. **3** CHANCE, fate, fortune, luck; inf. fluke.

**accidental** adj. happening by chance.
▷ SYNS CHANCE, unintentional, unintended, inadvertent, unexpected, unforeseen, unlooked-for, fortuitous, unplanned, unpremeditated.

**acclaim** v. praise enthusiastically. • n. enthusiastic praise.
■ acclamation n.
▷ SYNS v. PRAISE, applaud, cheer, celebrate, salute, honour, commend, hail, extol, laud. • n. PRAISE, commendation, honour, tribute, congratulations, applause, plaudits, bouquets.

**acclimatize** (or **-ise**) v. get used to new conditions.

**accolade** n. praise or honour.

**accommodate** v. **1** provide lodging for. **2** adapt to.
▷ SYNS HOUSE, put up, cater for, lodge, board, billet.

**accommodating** adj. willing to do as asked.
▷ SYNS OBLIGING, cooperative, helpful, considerate, unselfish, willing, hospitable, kind, agreeable.

**accommodation** n. a place to live.
▷ SYNS HOUSING, lodging, shelter, residence, house, billet, lodgings, quarters, digs.

**accompany** v. **1** go with. **2** play an instrumental part supporting a singer or instrument. ■ accompaniment n. accompanist n.
▷ SYNS ESCORT, go with, keep company, attend, usher, conduct, chaperone.

**accomplice** n. a partner in crime.
▷ SYNS PARTNER IN CRIME, accessory, collaborator, abetter, associate, henchman; inf. sidekick.

**accomplish** v. succeed in doing or achieving.
▷ SYNS ACHIEVE, carry out, fulfil, perform, attain, realize, succeed in, bring about/off, effect, execute.

**accomplished** adj. highly skilled.
▷ SYNS SKILLED, skilful, expert, gifted, talented, proficient, adept, masterly, polished, practised, capable, able, competent, experienced, professional, consummate.

**accomplishment** n.
**1** something achieved successfully. **2** a skill or special ability. **3** the successful achievement of a task.

**accord** v. be consistent with something. • n. agreement. □ **of your own accord** without being asked.

**according** adv. (**according to**) **1** as stated by. **2** in proportion to. ■ **accordingly** adv.

**accordion** n. a portable musical instrument with bellows and keys or buttons.

**accost** v. approach and speak to.

**account** n. **1** a description of an event. **2** a record of money paid or owed. **3** a credit arrangement with a bank or firm. • v. **1** explain. **2** make up.
▷ SYNS n. **1** STATEMENT, report, description, record, narration, narrative, story, recital, explanation, tale, version. **2** BILL, invoice, reckoning, tally, charges, debts.

**accountable** adj. obliged to account for your actions.
■ **accountability** n.

**accountant** n. a person who keeps or inspects financial accounts. ■ **accountancy** n.

**accoutrements** pl.n. equipment.

**accredited** adj. officially authorized.

**accrue** v. (**accrued, accruing**) accumulate.

**accumulate** v. **1** acquire more and more of. **2** increase.
■ **accumulation** n. **accumulative** adj.
▷ SYNS GATHER, collect, amass, stockpile, pile up, increase, accrue, store, hoard.

**accurate** adj. free from error.
■ **accuracy** n.
▷ SYNS CORRECT, right, true, exact, precise, factual, truthful, faultless, reliable, faithful, sound, authentic; inf. spot-on, bang-on.

**accuse** v. charge someone with an offence or crime.
■ **accusation** n.
▷ SYNS CHARGE, indict, arraign; blame, hold responsible, condemn, denounce; inf. point the finger at.

**accustom** v. make or be used to.

**accustomed** adj. customary; usual.
▷ SYNS *his accustomed style:* USUAL, customary, habitual, regular, established, normal, conventional, expected, familiar, common, traditional, ordinary, set, wonted.

**ace** n. **1** a playing card with a single spot. **2** inf. an expert. **3** (in tennis) a serve that an opponent is unable to return.

**acerbic** adj. harsh and sharp.
■ **acerbity** n.

**acetylene** n. a colourless gas, used in welding.

**ache** n. a dull continuous pain.
• v. suffer such a pain.
▷ SYNS n. PAIN, soreness, discomfort, throbbing, twinge, pang. • v. HURT, smart, sting, be sore/painful, pound, throb.

**achieve** v. succeed in doing, reaching, or gaining.
■ **achievable** adj. **achievement** n. **achiever** n.
▷ SYNS SUCCEED, accomplish, manage, carry out, complete, attain, gain, obtain, get, reach, win, bring off, effect, perform, fulfil.

**Achilles heel** n. a vulnerable point.

**acid** n. any of a class of substances that neutralize alkalis. • adj. **1** sour. **2** (of a remark) sharp or unkind. □ **acid rain** rain made acidic by pollution. ■ **acidic** adj. **acidity** n.

**acknowledge** v. **1** admit the truth of. **2** confirm receipt of. ■ **acknowledgement** n.
▷ SYNS ACCEPT, admit, concede, agree, allow, recognize, confess, grant, own up to, acquiesce to, accede to.

**acme** n. the height of perfection.

**acne** n. an eruption of pimples.

**acorn** n. the oval nut of the oak tree.

**acoustic** adj. relating to sound. • n. (**acoustics**) the qualities of a room that affect the way sound carries.

**acquaint** v. **1** make aware of. **2** (**be acquainted with**) know slightly.

**acquaintance** n. **1** a person you know slightly. **2** knowledge or familiarity.
▷ SYNS **1** FRIEND, contact, associate, colleague. **2** KNOWLEDGE, awareness, familiarity, understanding.

**acquiesce** v. agree.
■ **acquiescence** n. **acquiescent** adj.

**acquire** v. gain possession of.
▷ SYNS GET, obtain, gain, buy, purchase, come by, pick up.

**acquisition** n. **1** something acquired. **2** the act of acquiring.

**acquisitive** adj. eager to acquire things.

**acquit** v. **1** declare to be not guilty. **2** (**acquit yourself**) behave or perform.
■ **acquittal** n.
▷ SYNS CLEAR, exonerate, set free, free, release, discharge, let off.

**acre** n. a measure of land, 4,840 sq. yds (0.405 hectares).
■ **acreage** n.

**acrid** adj. bitter.
▷ SYNS BITTER, sharp, pungent, harsh, caustic.

**acrimonious** adj. angry and bitter. ■ **acrimony** n.
▷ SYNS ANGRY, bitter, bad-tempered, hostile, rancorous, spiteful, acerbic, acid, sharp, vitriolic, caustic.

**acrobat** n. a performer of spectacular gymnastic feats.
■ **acrobatic** adj. **acrobatics** n.

**acronym** n. a word formed from the initial letters of others.

**across** prep. & adv. **1** from side to side of. **2** on the other side of.

**acrylic** adj. (of a fabric, paint, etc.) made from acrylic acid (an organic acid).

**act** v. **1** do something. **2** behave. **3** perform in a play or film. • n. **1** something done. **2** a law made by parliament. **3** a section of a play. **4** an item in a variety show.
▷ SYNS v. **1** TAKE ACTION, take steps, move. **2** BEHAVE, conduct yourself, carry on. **3** PERFORM, play, appear as, portray, represent. • n. **1** ACTION, deed, feat, exploit, undertaking, achievement, step, move, operation. **2** LAW, statute, bill, decree, enactment, edict. **3** ROUTINE, performance, number, turn, item.

**acting** adj. temporarily doing another's duties.

▷ SYNS TEMPORARY, interim, provisional, stopgap, stand-in, fill-in, deputy, pro tem.

**action** n. **1** the process of doing something. **2** a thing done. **3** a lawsuit. **4** armed conflict.
▷ SYNS DEED, act, undertaking, feat, exploit, behaviour, conduct, activity.

**actionable** adj. giving cause for legal action.

**activate** v. cause to act or work. ■ activation n.
▷ SYNS **1** SET OFF, start, trigger, initiate. **2** STIMULATE, prompt, stir, energize, rouse, arouse, galvanize, fire, motivate.

**active** adj. **1** energetic. **2** functioning. ■ actively adv.
▷ SYNS **1** ENERGETIC, lively, busy, dynamic, enthusiastic, vigorous, sprightly, spry, animated; industrious, tireless, hard-working, committed. **2** WORKING, functioning, operative, in action.

**activist** n. a person who campaigns for change. ■ activism n.

**activity** n. **1** a particular pursuit. **2** lively action.
▷ SYNS **1** HOBBY, pastime, pursuit, interest, recreation, diversion, project, enterprise, undertaking. **2** MOVEMENT, action, bustle, excitement, liveliness, commotion, hurly-burly, animation, life, stir.

**actor** n. (fem. **actress**) a person who performs in a play or film.

**actual** adj. **1** existing in fact or reality. **2** current. ■ actuality n. actually adv.
▷ SYNS REAL, genuine, true, authentic, indisputable, factual, verified, confirmed, bona fide,

definite, unquestionable, tangible, in existence, living.

**actuary** n. (pl. **-ies**) an insurance expert who calculates risks and premiums.

**actuate** v. **1** activate. **2** motivate.

**acumen** n. shrewdness.

**acupuncture** n. medical treatment in which needles are inserted into the skin.

**acute** adj. **1** serious or severe. **2** sharp-witted. **3** (of an angle) less than 90°.
▷ SYNS **1** *an acute shortage:* SERIOUS, urgent, pressing, grave, critical. **2** *acute stomach pains:* EXCRUCIATING, sharp, severe, agonizing. **3** *his acute mind:* ASTUTE, shrewd, sharp, sharp-witted, quick, keen, penetrating.

**AD** abbr. Anno Domini (used to indicate that a date comes the specified number of years after the traditional date of Jesus's birth).

**adage** n. a saying expressing an accepted truth.

**adagio** adv. Music in slow time.

**adamant** adj. not changing your mind.
▷ SYNS DETERMINED, resolute, resolved, firm, unyielding, unshakeable, stubborn, intransigent.

**Adam's apple** n. the projection at the front of the neck.

**adapt** v. make or become suitable for new use or conditions. ■ adaptable adj. adaptation n.
▷ SYNS **1** GET USED, adjust, get accustomed, habituate yourself, get acclimatized, reconcile yourself, accommodate yourself. **2** ALTER, change,

modify, adjust, tailor, convert, remodel, restyle.

**adaptor** n. a device for connecting several electric plugs to one socket.

**add** v. **1** join to an existing item to increase or enlarge it. **2** say as a further remark. **3** put numbers together to calculate a total.
▷ SYNS **1** ATTACH, append, affix, include, incorporate, tack on. **2** TOTAL, count (up), reckon up, tot up.

**addendum** n. (pl. **-da**) a section added to a book.

**adder** n. a poisonous snake.

**addict** n. a person physically dependent on something, esp. a drug. ■ **addicted** adj. **addictive** adj.

**addiction** n. being addicted to something.
▷ SYNS DEPENDENCY, craving, habit, compulsion, obsession, enslavement.

**addition** n. **1** the act of adding. **2** a thing added.
▷ SYNS INCREASE, supplement, increment, adjunct, accessory, addendum, appendage, appendix, postscript, afterthought, attachment, extra.

**additional** adj. added or extra. ■ **additionally** adv.
▷ SYNS EXTRA, added, more, further, supplementary, other, new, fresh.

**additive** n. a substance added.

**addled** adj. (of an egg) rotten.

**address** n. **1** the details of where a person lives or where mail should be delivered. **2** a speech. • v. **1** write the address on mail. **2** speak to. **3** apply yourself to a task.

▷ SYNS n. **1** LOCATION, place, residence, home, house; formal abode, domicile, dwelling. **2** SPEECH, talk, lecture, oration, disquisition, discourse.

**adenoids** pl.n. the enlarged tissue between the back of the nose and the throat.

**adept** adj. very skilful.

**adequate** adj. satisfactory. ■ **adequacy** n.
▷ SYNS SATISFACTORY, passable, all right, average, competent, unexceptional, acceptable, unexceptionable, tolerable.

**adhere** v. **1** stick firmly. **2** follow or observe. ■ **adherence** n. **adherent** adj. & n.
▷ SYNS STICK, cling, bond; be fixed, be glued.

**adhesive** n. a sticky substance. • adj. sticky. ■ **adhesion** n.

**ad hoc** adv. & adj. for a particular occasion or purpose.

**adieu** exclam. goodbye.

**adjacent** adj. adjoining.
▷ SYNS NEIGHBOURING, adjoining, bordering, next, close, next door, touching, abutting.

**adjective** n. a word used to describe a noun.

**adjoin** v. be next to.

**adjourn** v. break off a meeting until later. ■ **adjournment** n.
▷ SYNS BREAK OFF, interrupt, suspend, discontinue, postpone, put off, delay, defer, prorogue.

**adjudge** v. decide judicially.

**adjudicate** v. act as judge of. ■ **adjudication** n. **adjudicator** n.

**adjunct** n. a non-essential supplement.

**adjust** v. **1** alter slightly. **2** adapt to new conditions. ■ **adjustable** adj. **adjustment** n.

▷ SYNS **1** MODIFY, alter, adapt, regulate, tailor, customize, tune, change, rearrange, remodel, rejig, fix, repair. **2** ADAPT, become accustomed, get used, reconcile yourself, accommodate yourself, get acclimatized, habituate yourself.

**adjutant** n. an army officer assisting in administrative work.

**ad-lib** v. (**ad-libbed**, **ad-libbing**) speak without preparing first. • adv. & adj. (also **ad lib**) spoken without preparation.

**administer** v. **1** organize or put into effect. **2** give out a drug or remedy.
■ administration n. administrative adj. administrator n.
▷ SYNS **1** MANAGE, direct, control, regulate, coordinate, run, organize, govern. **2** DISPENSE, issue, give, provide, distribute, hand out, dole out.

**admirable** adj. worthy of admiration. ■ admirably adv.
▷ SYNS COMMENDABLE, creditable, worthy, praiseworthy, laudable, meritorious, deserving, estimable, good, excellent, fine, exemplary, wonderful, marvellous.

**admiral** n. a naval officer of the highest rank.

**admiration** n. respect and warm approval.
▷ SYNS APPROVAL, regard, respect, praise, appreciation, commendation, approbation, esteem.

**admire** v. **1** respect highly. **2** look at with pleasure.
▷ SYNS RESPECT, look up to, think highly of, esteem, applaud, commend.

**admission** n. **1** entry to or permission to enter a place. **2** a confession. ■ admissible adj.
▷ SYNS **1** ADMITTANCE, entry, entrance, access. **2** CONFESSION, acknowledgement, acceptance, disclosure.

**admit** v. **1** confess to be true. **2** allow to enter. **3** accept as valid.
▷ SYNS ACKNOWLEDGE, confess, own up, concede, grant, accept, recognize, allow, reveal, disclose.

**admittance** n. admission.

**admittedly** adv. it must be admitted that.

**admonish** v. reprimand firmly. ■ admonition n.

**ad nauseam** adv. to an excessive extent.

**ado** n. commotion; fuss.

**adolescent** adj. & n. (a person) between childhood and adulthood. ■ adolescence n.
▷ SYNS TEENAGE, young, pubescent, immature, childish, juvenile, puerile.

**adopt** v. **1** bring up another's child as your own. **2** choose to follow a course of action.
■ adoption n. adoptive adj.
▷ SYNS ACCEPT, espouse, embrace, take on, assume, choose, approve, follow, support, back.

**adore** v. love or like very much. ■ adorable adj. adoration n.
▷ SYNS LOVE, be devoted to, dote on, cherish, treasure, think the world of; worship, idolize.

**adorn** v. decorate. ■ adornment n.
▷ SYNS DECORATE, embellish, ornament, enhance, beautify, deck, bedeck, trim.

**adrenal** adj. close to the kidneys.

**adrenalin** (or **adrenaline**) n. a stimulant hormone produced by the adrenal glands.

**adrift** adj. & adv. **1** drifting. **2** no longer fixed in position.

**adroit** adj. skilful.

**adulation** n. excessive flattery.

**adult** adj. fully grown. • n. an adult person or animal.
▷ SYNS adj. FULLY GROWN, grown-up, mature, of age, nubile.

**adulterate** v. make impure by adding a substance.
■ adulteration n.
▷ SYNS CONTAMINATE, taint, debase, doctor, dilute, water down, weaken.

**adultery** n. sexual infidelity to your wife or husband.
■ adulterer n. adulterous adj.

**advance** v. **1** move or put forward. **2** make progress. **3** lend money. • n. **1** a forward movement. **2** an improvement. **3** a loan. **4** (**advances**) a sexual approach. ■ advancement n.
▷ SYNS v. **1** MOVE FORWARD, proceed, forge ahead, gain ground, make headway, press on, push on. **2** PROGRESS, develop, evolve. **3** LEND, loan, provide, put up. • n. DEVELOPMENT, breakthrough, discovery, finding, progress, improvement, invention.

**advanced** adj. **1** far on in development or progress. **2** not basic.
▷ SYNS STATE-OF-THE-ART, modern, sophisticated, up-to-date, cutting-edge, new, the latest, pioneering, innovative, progressive, trendsetting.

**advantage** n. something that puts you in a favourable position. □ **take advantage of 1** exploit. **2** use.

▷ SYNS **1** BENEFIT, value, good point, asset, bonus, boon, blessing, virtue. **2** UPPER HAND, edge, superiority, dominance.

**advantageous** adj. good or useful in a particular situation.
▷ SYNS BENEFICIAL, helpful, useful, of use, profitable, worthwhile.

**advent** n. **1** an arrival. **2** (**Advent**) the time before Christmas.

**adventure** n. an exciting experience or undertaking.
■ adventurer n.
▷ SYNS EXPLOIT, deed, feat, escapade, venture, undertaking.

**adventurous** adj. open to or involving new or daring methods or experiences.
▷ SYNS DARING, brave, bold, courageous, heroic, enterprising, intrepid, daredevil.

**adverb** n. a word adding information about an adjective, verb, or other adverb.

**adversary** n. (pl. **-ies**) an opponent. ■ adversarial adj.

**adverse** adj. harmful or unfavourable.
▷ SYNS **1** UNFAVOURABLE, bad, disadvantageous, inauspicious, unpropitious; harmful, dangerous, injurious, detrimental; formal deleterious. **2** HOSTILE, unfavourable, antagonistic, unfriendly, negative.

**adversity** n. (pl. **-ies**) hardship.
▷ SYNS MISFORTUNE, bad luck, trouble, woe, affliction, disaster, sorrow, misery, hard times, tribulation.

**advertise** v. describe a product, service, etc. in the media to increase sales, or a vacancy to encourage applications.

▷ SYNS PUBLICIZE, promote, market, announce, broadcast; inf. plug, hype.

**advertisement** n. a notice or display advertising something.
▷ SYNS COMMERCIAL, blurb; flyer, poster; inf. ad, advert.

**advice** n. recommendations about what someone should do.
▷ SYNS GUIDANCE, help, counsel, suggestions, recommendations, hints, tips.

**advisable** adj. prudent or sensible.
▷ SYNS PRUDENT, sensible, wise, recommended, appropriate, expedient, judicious, politic.

**advise** v. 1 recommend that someone should do something. 2 inform. ■ adviser n. advisory adj.
▷ SYNS COUNSEL, give guidance, offer suggestions; recommend, suggest, urge, encourage, advocate.

**advocate** n. 1 a person who recommends a policy. 2 a person who speaks on behalf of another. • v. recommend.
■ advocacy n.
▷ SYNS n. SUPPORTER, champion, proponent, backer, spokesman, exponent, apologist. • v. RECOMMEND, advise, urge; support, back, argue for, favour, endorse, champion.

**aegis** n. protection or support.

**aeon** (US **eon**) n. a very long time.

**aerate** v. introduce air into.

**aerial** adj. 1 existing or taking place in the air. 2 by or from aircraft. • n. a wire for transmitting or receiving radio waves.

**aerobatics** n. spectacular feats by aircraft in flight.
■ aerobatic adj.

**aerobics** n. vigorous exercises designed to increase oxygen intake. ■ aerobic adj.

**aerodynamics** n. the science concerned with the movement of objects through the air.
■ aerodynamic adj.

**aeronautics** n. the study of aircraft flight.
■ aeronautical adj.

**aeroplane** n. a powered flying vehicle with fixed wings.

**aerosol** n. a pressurized can holding a substance for release as a fine spray.

**aerospace** n. the technology and industry concerned with flight.

**aesthete** (US **esthete**) n. a person who appreciates art and beauty.

**aesthetic** (US **esthetic**) adj. relating to beauty or its appreciation. • n. (**aesthetics**) the study of beauty and artistic taste. ■ aesthetically adv.

**afar** adv. far away.

**affable** adj. polite and friendly.
▷ SYNS FRIENDLY, agreeable, pleasant, amiable, good-natured, polite, civil, courteous.

**affair** n. 1 an event or series of events. 2 a matter that a person is responsible for. 3 a love affair.
▷ SYNS 1 EVENT, incident, happening, occurrence, episode, case. 2 BUSINESS, concern, responsibility, matter, problem. 3 RELATIONSHIP, love affair, romance, fling, involvement, liaison, intrigue.

**affect** v. 1 have an effect on. 2 pretend to feel or have.
▷ SYNS 1 ACT ON, influence, change, modify, transform. 2 MOVE, touch, upset, trouble,

disturb, distress. **3** ADOPT, assume; pretend, feign, fake, simulate; inf. put on.

**affectation** n. an artificial and pretentious manner.
▷ SYNS PRETENTIOUSNESS, pretence, artificiality, affectedness, pretension, posturing.

**affected** adj. artificial and designed to impress.
▷ SYNS UNNATURAL, contrived, artificial, pretentious, mannered, insincere, studied; inf. put-on.

**affection** n. love or liking.
▷ SYNS FONDNESS, liking, love, soft spot, warmth, attachment, tenderness, friendship.

**affectionate** adj. loving.
▷ SYNS LOVING, fond, caring, devoted, tender, doting, warm, friendly.

**affidavit** n. a written statement sworn on oath.

**affiliate** v. connect as a subordinate member or branch.
■ affiliation n.

**affinity** n. (pl. -ies) a close resemblance or attraction.
▷ SYNS **1** SIMILARITY, resemblance, likeness, correspondence, similitude. **2** LIKING, fondness, closeness, kinship, likemindedness, rapport.

**affirm** v. state firmly or publicly.
■ affirmation n.
▷ SYNS STATE, assert, declare, proclaim, maintain, confirm, attest, avow, swear, pronounce.

**affirmative** adj. saying that something is the case.

**affix** v. attach or fasten.

**afflict** v. cause suffering to.
■ affliction n.
▷ SYNS TROUBLE, burden, distress, worry, bother, oppress, torture, plague, rack, torment, beset, harass, bedevil, curse.

**affluent** adj. wealthy.
■ affluence n.

**afford** v. **1** have enough money or time for. **2** give or provide.

**afforestation** n. the planting of land with trees.

**affray** n. a public fight or riot.

**affront** n. an open insult.
• v. insult or offend.

**afloat** adv. & adj. **1** floating. **2** out of debt or difficulty.

**afoot** adv. & adj. going on.

**afraid** adj. **1** frightened. **2** regretful.
▷ SYNS **1** FRIGHTENED, scared, terrified, petrified, fearful, intimidated, nervous, alarmed, panicky. **2** SORRY, apologetic, regretful.

**afresh** adv. making a fresh start.

**aft** adv. at or towards the rear of a ship or aircraft.

**after** prep. **1** later than. **2** behind. **3** pursuing. • conj. & adv. in the time following an event. □ afterbirth the placenta discharged from the womb after a birth. after-effect an effect that occurs some time after its cause. afternoon the time between noon and evening. aftershave a scented lotion used after shaving. afterthought a thing thought of or added later. afterwards at a later time.

**aftermath** n. the results of an unpleasant event.
▷ SYNS EFFECTS, after-effects, consequences, repercussions, results.

**again** adv. **1** once more. **2** besides; too.

**against** prep. **1** in opposition or contrast to. **2** in or into contact with.

**agar** n. a substance obtained from seaweed, used to thicken foods.

**agate** n. a semi-precious stone.

**age** n. **1** the length of time that a person or thing has existed. **2** old age. **3** a historical period. **4** inf. a very long time. • v. (**aged**, **ageing**) grow older.
▷ SYNS n. **1** MATURITY, old age, advancing years, seniority, elderliness. **2** ERA, epoch, period, time.

**aged** adj. **1** of a specified age. **2** old.
▷ SYNS OLD, elderly, senior, in your dotage, long in the tooth.

**ageism** n. prejudice on grounds of age. ■ **ageist** n. & adj.

**ageless** adj. not growing or seeming to grow old.

**agency** n. (pl. **-ies**) **1** an organization providing a particular service. **2** action producing an effect.

**agenda** n. a list of things to be dealt with, esp. at a meeting.

**agent** n. **1** a person who acts on behalf of another. **2** a person or thing producing an effect.
▷ SYNS REPRESENTATIVE, middleman, go-between, broker, negotiator, intermediary, proxy, trustee, spokesman, spokeswoman.

**aggrandize** (or **-ise**) v. increase the power or importance of.

**aggravate** v. **1** make worse. **2** inf. annoy. ■ **aggravation** n.
▷ SYNS MAKE WORSE, worsen, exacerbate, intensify, inflame, compound, increase, heighten, magnify, add to.

**aggregate** n. **1** a whole combining several elements. **2** crushed stone used in making concrete. • adj. formed by combination. • v. combine or unite.

**aggression** n. hostile acts or behaviour. ■ **aggressor** n.

**aggressive** adj. showing aggression.
▷ SYNS HOSTILE, belligerent, combative, violent, argumentative, quarrelsome, warlike, antagonistic, provocative, pugnacious, bellicose, bullying.

**aggrieved** adj. having a grievance; resentful.
▷ SYNS RESENTFUL, indignant, affronted, offended, put out, piqued, annoyed.

**aghast** adj. filled with horror.

**agile** adj. nimble or quick-moving. ■ **agility** n.
▷ SYNS NIMBLE, lithe, limber, fit, supple, graceful, acrobatic, light-footed, quick-moving.

**agitate** v. **1** worry; disturb. **2** campaign to raise public concern. **3** stir briskly.
■ **agitation** n. **agitator** n.

**agitated** adj. worried or nervous.
▷ SYNS UPSET, worried, flustered, disconcerted, perturbed, unsettled, worked up, tense, nervous, on edge, edgy, jumpy.

**AGM** abbr. annual general meeting.

**agnostic** n. a person believing that nothing can be known about God's existence.
■ **agnosticism** n.

**ago** adv. in the past.

**agog** adj. eager and expectant.

**agonize** (or **-ise**) v. worry intensely.

**agonizing** adj. very painful or worrying.

▷ SYNS EXCRUCIATING, racking, very painful, acute, harrowing, searing.

**agony** n. (pl. **-ies**) extreme suffering.
▷ SYNS SUFFERING, anguish, pain, torment, torture.

**agoraphobia** n. extreme fear of open spaces. ■ **agoraphobic** n. & adj.

**agrarian** adj. of land or agriculture.

**agree** v. **1** have the same opinion. **2** be willing to do something suggested. **3** (**agree with**) be consistent with. **4** (**agree with**) be good for.
▷ SYNS **1** CONCUR, be of the same mind, see eye to eye. **2** CONSENT, accept, assent, acquiesce; allow; formal accede. **3** MATCH, correspond, accord, coincide, fit, tally.

**agreeable** adj. **1** pleasant. **2** willing to agree. ■ **agreeably** adv.

**agreement** n. **1** harmony in opinion. **2** an arrangement agreed between people.
▷ SYNS **1** ACCORD, concurrence, harmony, accordance, concord, unity. **2** CONTRACT, deal, settlement, pact, bargain, treaty, covenant.

**agriculture** n. the science or practice of farming.
■ **agricultural** adj.

**aground** adv. & adj. (of a ship) touching the sea bottom.

**ahead** adv. further forward in position or time.

**ahoy** exclam. a seaman's shout for attention.

**aid** v. & n. help.

**aide** n. an assistant.

**Aids** (or **AIDS**) abbr. acquired immune deficiency syndrome, a condition developing after infection with HIV, breaking down a person's immune system.

**ail** v. make or become ill.

**ailment** n. a slight illness.
▷ SYNS DISEASE, illness, sickness, disorder, complaint, malady, infirmity, affliction.

**aim** v. **1** point or direct towards. **2** try to achieve. • n. a purpose or intention.
▷ SYNS v. **1** POINT, direct, take aim, train, focus, zero in on. **2** PLAN, intend, resolve, wish, want, mean, propose, seek, strive, aspire, endeavour. • n. AMBITION, objective, object, end, goal, purpose, intention, intent, plan, target, hope, aspiration, desire, wish, design.

**aimless** adj. without a purpose. ■ **aimlessly** adv.

**ain't** contr. inf. **1** am not; is not; are not. **2** has not; have not.

**air** n. **1** the mixture of gases surrounding the earth. **2** an impression. **3** (**airs**) an affected and condescending manner. **4** a tune. • v. **1** express an opinion publicly. **2** expose to air to dry or ventilate. □ **airbag** a device in a car that fills with air in a collision to protect the driver. **airborne 1** carried by air or aircraft. **2** (of aircraft) in flight. **air conditioning** a system that cools the air in a building or vehicle. **aircraft** a machine capable of flight. **aircraft carrier** a warship acting as a base for aircraft. **airfield** an area for the take-off and landing of aircraft. **air force** a branch of the armed forces using aircraft. **air gun** a gun using compressed air to fire pellets. **airlift** an act of transporting supplies by

aircraft. **airline** a company providing an air transport service. **airliner** a passenger aircraft. **airlock 1** a stoppage of the flow in a pipe, caused by an air bubble. **2** an airtight compartment, used for entering or leaving a pressurized space. **airmail** mail carried overseas by aircraft. **airman** a member of an air force. **airplane** US an aeroplane. **airport** an airfield with facilities for passengers and goods. **air raid** an attack by aircraft. **airship** a large aircraft filled with gas that is lighter than air. **airspace** the part of the air above a country. **airstrip** a strip of ground where aircraft can take off and land. **airtight** not allowing air to enter or escape. **airwaves** the radio frequencies used for broadcasting. **airway 1** a regular route for aircraft. **2** a passage for air into the lungs. **airworthy** (of an aircraft) safe to fly.
▷ SYNS v. 1 EXPRESS, make known, voice, give vent to, vent, communicate, disclose, state, declare. 2 VENTILATE, aerate, freshen.

**airless** adj. stuffy.
▷ SYNS STUFFY, close, stifling, suffocating, muggy, oppressive, sultry.

**airy** adj. (-ier, -iest) **1** well ventilated. **2** delicate or light. **3** casual or dismissive. ■ **airily** adv.

**aisle** n. a passage between rows of seats.
▷ SYNS PASSAGEWAY, passage, gangway, walkway.

**ajar** adv. & adj. (of a door) slightly open.

**aka** abbr. also known as.

**akimbo** adv. with hands on hips.

**akin** adj. similar in nature or type.

**alabaster** n. a soft translucent mineral.

**à la carte** adj. & adv. ordered as separate items from a menu.

**alacrity** n. eager readiness.

**à la mode** adj. & adv. in fashion.

**alarm** n. **1** fear and anxiety. **2** a warning sound or device. **3** a warning of danger. • v. cause alarm to.
▷ SYNS n. 1 FEAR, apprehension, anxiety, consternation, panic, fright, trepidation. 2 SIREN, alert, bell, warning, signal. • v. FRIGHTEN, scare, panic, terrify, unnerve, dismay, disturb, startle, shock, upset, worry.

**alarmist** n. a person who causes excessive alarm.

**alas** exclam. an exclamation of sorrow.

**albatross** n. a large seabird.

**albino** n. (pl. **-os**) a person or animal born with white skin and hair and pink eyes.

**album** n. **1** a blank book for holding photographs, stamps, etc. **2** a collection of recordings issued as a single item.

**albumen** n. egg white.

**alchemy** n. a medieval form of chemistry, seeking to turn other metals into gold. ■ **alchemist** n.

**alcohol** n. **1** a colourless liquid found in intoxicating drinks such as wine, beer, and spirits. **2** drink containing this.

**alcoholic** adj. containing or relating to alcohol. • n. a person addicted to drinking alcohol. ■ **alcoholism** n.
▷ SYNS n. DRUNKARD, drunk, dipsomaniac, problem drinker, sot; inf. lush.

**alcove** n. a recess in a wall.

**alderman** n. hist. a member of a council below the rank of mayor.

**ale** n. beer.

**alert** adj. watchful; observant. • v. warn; make aware.
▷ SYNS adj. **1** WATCHFUL, vigilant, observant, wary, on your guard/ toes, circumspect, on the lookout. **2** SHARP, quick, quick-witted, bright, perceptive, keen; inf. on the ball. • v. WARN, advise, forewarn, inform, notify, tip off.

**alfresco** adv. & adj. in the open air.

**algae** pl.n. simple water plants with no true stems or leaves.

**algebra** n. a branch of mathematics using letters etc. to represent quantities.

**algorithm** n. a step-by-step procedure for calculation.

**alias** n. a false name. • adv. also called.

**alibi** n. evidence that an accused person was elsewhere when a crime was committed.

**alien** n. **1** a foreigner. **2** a being from another world. • adj. **1** foreign; unfamiliar. **2** extra-terrestrial.
▷ SYNS adj. FOREIGN, strange, unfamiliar, outlandish, exotic.

**alienate** v. cause to become unfriendly or unsympathetic.
■ alienation n.

**alight** v. **1** get off a train or bus. **2** (of a bird) land on. • adj. & adv. on fire.

**align** v. **1** bring into the correct position. **2** ally yourself.
■ alignment n.

**alike** adj. like one another. • adv. in the same way.

▷ SYNS adj. SIMILAR, the same, indistinguishable, identical, interchangeable, matching, twin.

**alimentary canal** n. the passage along which food passes through the body.

**alimony** n. money paid by a divorced person to their former spouse.

**alive** adj. **1** living; existing. **2** lively. **3** (**alive to**) aware of.
▷ SYNS **1** LIVING, breathing, live, animate; in existence, active, functioning. **2** ANIMATED, lively, full of life, alert, active, energetic. **3** (**alive to**) AWARE OF, conscious of, mindful of, sensitive to.

**alkali** n. any of a class of substances that neutralize acids. ■ alkaline adj.

**all** adj. the whole quantity or extent of. • pron. everything or everyone. • adv. completely. □ all clear a signal that danger is over. all right **1** unhurt. **2** satisfactory.

**allay** v. lessen fears.
▷ SYNS LESSEN, diminish, reduce, alleviate, calm, assuage, ease, quell, relieve, subdue, soothe, quieten, quiet.

**allegation** n. an unproven accusation.
▷ SYNS CHARGE, accusation, claim, assertion, contention, declaration.

**allege** v. declare without proof.
■ allegedly adv.
▷ SYNS CLAIM, assert, maintain, contend, declare, state, attest.

**alleged** adj. declared but not proved.
▷ SYNS SUPPOSED, claimed, declared, so-called, professed, stated.

**allegiance** n. loyal support.
▷ SYNS LOYALTY, faithfulness, fidelity, devotion, obedience; hist. fealty.

**allegory** n. (pl. **-ies**) a story etc. with a hidden or symbolic meaning. ■ allegorical adj.

**allegro** adv. Music briskly.

**alleluia** (or **hallelujah**) exclam. & n. praise to God.

**allergy** n. (pl. **-ies**) an abnormal sensitivity to certain foods, pollens, etc. ■ allergic adj.

**alleviate** v. ease pain or distress. ■ alleviation n.
▷ SYNS REDUCE, ease, lessen, diminish, relieve, allay, assuage, palliate, lighten, soothe, subdue, temper, soften.

**alley** n. (pl. **-eys**) a narrow street; a long enclosure for skittles or bowling.

**alliance** n. an association formed for mutual benefit.
▷ SYNS ASSOCIATION, union, coalition, partnership, affiliation, league, confederation, federation, syndicate, cartel, consortium.

**allied** adj. joined by an alliance.

**alligator** n. a reptile of the crocodile family.

**alliteration** n. the occurrence of the same sound at the start of adjacent words.

**allocate** v. allot or assign. ■ allocation n.

**allot** v. (**allotted**, **allotting**) distribute; give as a share.
▷ SYNS ALLOCATE, assign, give out, share out, distribute, award, apportion, grant, divide up, mete out, dole out, dish out.

**allotment** n. **1** a small piece of land rented for cultivation. **2** an allotted share.

**allow** v. **1** let someone do something. **2** provide or set aside. **3** acknowledge. **4** (**allow for**) take into account.
▷ SYNS PERMIT, let, give permission, authorize, consent, sanction, approve, license.

**allowance** n. **1** a permitted amount. **2** a sum of money paid regularly. □ make allowances be tolerant or lenient.
▷ SYNS **1** QUOTA, allocation, ration, portion, share. **2** PAYMENT, subsidy, remittance, grant.

**alloy** n. a mixture of chemical elements at least one of which is a metal.

**allude** v. refer briefly or indirectly. ■ allusion n.
▷ SYNS REFER TO, mention, touch on, suggest, hint at.

**allure** v. entice or attract.
• n. attractiveness.

**alluvium** n. a deposit left by a flood. ■ alluvial adj.

**ally** n. (pl. **-ies**) a country or person in alliance with another.
• v. side with; join or combine.
▷ SYNS n. PARTNER, associate, colleague, friend, confederate, supporter. • v. JOIN, unite, join forces, combine, band together, team up, collaborate, side, align yourself.

**almanac** (or **almanack**) n. **1** a calendar giving information on important dates, astronomical data, etc. **2** a book published yearly, containing information about that year.

**almighty** adj. **1** all-powerful. **2** inf. enormous.

**almond** n. an edible oval nut.

**almost** adv. very nearly.

**alms** pl.n. hist. money given to the poor.

**aloe** n. a plant with bitter juice.

**aloft** adv. high up; upwards.

**alone** adj. & adv. **1** on your own. **2** only.
▷ SYNS BY YOURSELF, on your own, unaccompanied, solo, single, isolated, solitary; lonely, friendless.

**along** prep. & adv. **1** moving or extending on. **2** in company with others.

**alongside** prep. close to the side of.

**aloof** adj. unfriendly and distant.
▷ SYNS DISTANT, unfriendly, unapproachable, remote, stand-offish, unsociable, reserved, stiff, cold, undemonstrative, unforthcoming.

**alopecia** n. abnormal hair loss.

**aloud** adv. audibly.

**alpaca** n. a llama with long wool.

**alpha** n. the first letter of the Greek alphabet (A, α). • adj. dominant within a group.

**alphabet** n. a set of letters in a fixed order representing the sounds of a language.
■ **alphabetical** adj. **alphabetically** adv.

**alpine** adj. of high mountains.

**already** adv. before this time; as early as this.

**Alsatian** n. a German shepherd dog.

**also** adv. in addition; besides.
▷ SYNS AS WELL, too, in addition, additionally, moreover, besides, to boot.

**altar** n. a table used in religious service.

**alter** v. make or become different.
▷ SYNS CHANGE, adjust, adapt, modify, revise, reshape, remodel, vary, convert, transform, amend, emend.

**alteration** n. a change or modification.
▷ SYNS CHANGE, adjustment, modification, adaptation, revision, amendment, reorganization, conversion, transformation.

**altercation** n. a noisy dispute.

**alternate** v. (cause to) occur in turn repeatedly. • adj. **1** every other. **2** (of two things) repeatedly following and replacing each other.

**alternative** adj. **1** available as another choice. **2** unconventional. • n. a choice or option.

**although** conj. despite the fact that.

**altitude** n. height above sea or ground level.

**alto** n. (pl. **-os**) the highest adult male or lowest female voice.

**altogether** adv. **1** in total. **2** completely. **3** on the whole.

**altruism** n. unselfishness.
■ **altruist** n. **altruistic** adj.

**aluminium** n. a lightweight silvery metal.

**always** adv. at all times; whatever the circumstances.

**Alzheimer's disease** n. a brain disorder which may affect older people.

**AM** abbr. amplitude modulation.

**a.m.** abbr. before noon.

**amalgam** n. **1** a blend. **2** an alloy of mercury with another metal.

**amalgamate** v. unite or combine. ■ **amalgamation** n.
▷ SYNS COMBINE, merge, unite, join, blend, integrate, fuse, join forces, link up.

**amass** v. heap up; collect.
▷ SYNS COLLECT, gather, accumulate, pile up, store up, hoard.

**amateur** n. a person who does something as a pastime rather than as a profession.
▷ SYNS NON-PROFESSIONAL, layman, dabbler, dilettante.

**amateurish** adj. incompetent or unskilful.
▷ SYNS INCOMPETENT, inept, unskilful, inexpert, unprofessional, clumsy, crude.

**amatory** adj. relating to love.

**amaze** v. overwhelm with wonder.
▷ SYNS ASTONISH, surprise, astound, startle, dumbfound, flabbergast, shock, stagger, stun, stupefy; inf. bowl over.

**amazement** n. a feeling of great surprise or wonder.
▷ SYNS ASTONISHMENT, surprise, shock, stupefaction, incredulity, disbelief.

**amazing** adj. 1 very surprising. 2 inf. very good or impressive.
▷ SYNS ASTONISHING, astounding, stunning, extraordinary, incredible, remarkable, sensational, fantastic, phenomenal, staggering, stupendous, unbelievable.

**Amazon** n. a tall, strong woman.

**ambassador** n. a senior diplomat representing their country abroad.
▷ SYNS DIPLOMAT, consul, envoy, emissary, representative, plenipotentiary.

**amber** n. 1 yellowish fossilized resin used in jewellery. 2 a yellowish colour.

**ambidextrous** adj. able to use either hand equally well.

**ambience** n. a place's atmosphere.

**ambiguous** adj. having two or more possible meanings.
■ ambiguity n.
▷ SYNS AMBIVALENT, equivocal, double-edged; obscure, unclear, vague, uncertain, enigmatic.

**ambition** n. a strong desire to achieve something.
▷ SYNS 1 DRIVE, enterprise, initiative, eagerness, determination; inf. get-up-and-go. 2 GOAL, aim, objective, desire, object, intent, purpose, design, target, wish, aspiration, dream.

**ambitious** adj. determined to succeed.
▷ SYNS FORCEFUL, enterprising, determined, aspiring, motivated, enthusiastic, committed, eager.

**ambivalent** adj. with mixed feelings. ■ ambivalence n.
▷ SYNS EQUIVOCAL, ambiguous, uncertain, doubtful, inconclusive, unclear, irresolute, in two minds, undecided.

**amble** v. & n. (walk at) a leisurely pace.

**ambulance** n. a vehicle equipped to carry sick or injured people.

**ambush** n. a surprise attack by people lying in wait. • v. attack in this way.

**ameba** US sp. of AMOEBA.

**ameliorate** v. make better.
■ amelioration n.

**amen** exclam. (in prayers) so be it.

**amenable** adj. 1 cooperative. 2 (**amenable to**) able to be affected by.
▷ SYNS 1 AGREEABLE, accommodating, cooperative, compliant, tractable, willing, acquiescent, biddable,

complaisant. **2** SUSCEPTIBLE, receptive, responsive.

**amend** v. make minor alterations in a text etc. □ make amends compensate for something. ■ **amendment** n.
▷ SYNS REVISE, alter, change, modify, adapt, adjust; edit, rephrase, reword.

**amenity** n. (pl. **-ies**) a useful or desirable feature of a place.
▷ SYNS FACILITY, service, convenience, resource, advantage.

**amethyst** n. a violet or purple precious stone.

**amiable** adj. likeable or friendly. ■ **amiability** n. **amiably** adv.
▷ SYNS FRIENDLY, agreeable, pleasant, charming, likeable, sociable, genial, congenial, good-natured.

**amicable** adj. friendly. ■ **amicably** adv.

**amid** (or **amidst**) prep. in the middle of.

**amino acid** n. an organic acid found in proteins.

**amiss** adj. not quite right. • adv. wrongly or badly.

**amity** n. formal friendly relations between people or countries.

**ammonia** n. a strong-smelling gas.

**ammonite** n. a fossil of a spiral shell.

**ammunition** n. a supply of bullets, shells, etc.

**amnesia** n. loss of memory.

**amnesty** n. (pl. **-ies**) a general pardon.
▷ SYNS PARDON, reprieve, pardoning; release.

**amoeba** (US **ameba**) n. (pl. **-bae** or **-bas**) a single-celled organism capable of changing shape.

**amok** (or **amuck**) adv. (**run amok**) be out of control.

**among** (or **amongst**) prep. **1** surrounded by. **2** being one of a larger group. **3** shared by; between.

**amoral** adj. not concerned about right or wrong.

**amorous** adj. showing sexual desire.
▷ SYNS LOVING, passionate, sexual, lustful, ardent.

**amorphous** adj. shapeless.
▷ SYNS SHAPELESS, formless, unstructured, nebulous, vague, indeterminate.

**amount** n. a total of anything; a quantity. • v. add up to; be equivalent to.
▷ SYNS n. QUANTITY, number, total, aggregate, sum, mass, weight, volume, bulk. • v. (**amount to**) ADD UP TO, total, come to, equal, make, correspond to.

**ampere** n. a unit of electric current.

**ampersand** n. the sign & (= and).

**amphibian** n. an animal able to live both on land and in water. ■ **amphibious** adj.

**amphitheatre** (US **amphitheater**) n. a semicircular unroofed building with tiers of seats round a central arena.

**ample** adj. **1** quite enough; plentiful. **2** large. ■ **amply** adv.
▷ SYNS ENOUGH, sufficient, adequate; plentiful, abundant, copious, lavish, bountiful, profuse, liberal, generous.

**amplify** v. **1** make louder. **2** add details to a statement. ■ **amplification** n. **amplifier** n.

▷ SYNS **1** BOOST, increase, intensify, heighten, magnify. **2** EXPAND, enlarge on, add to, elaborate on, fill out, flesh out, develop.

**amplitude** n. breadth; abundance.

**amputate** v. cut off a limb. ■ amputation n.

**amuck** = AMOK.

**amulet** n. something worn as a charm against evil.

**amuse** v. **1** cause to laugh or smile. **2** provide with entertainment. ■ amusing adj.
▷ SYNS **1** ENTERTAIN, divert, make laugh, regale with, delight, cheer, please. **2** OCCUPY, engage, entertain, busy, absorb, engross.

**amusement** n. **1** delight at being entertained. **2** something providing entertainment.
▷ SYNS **1** LAUGHTER, merriment, mirth, hilarity, fun, gaiety, pleasure, delight, enjoyment. **2** ENTERTAINMENT, interest, diversion, pleasure, recreation, pastime, hobby, sport, game.

**an** adj. the form of *a* used before vowel sounds.

**anachronism** n. something that seems to belong to another time. ■ anachronistic adj.

**anaconda** n. a large snake of South America.

**anaemia** (US **anemia**) n. lack of haemoglobin in the blood. ■ anaemic adj.

**anaesthesia** (US **anesthesia**) n.. insensitivity to pain, esp. as caused by an anaesthetic.

**anaesthetic** (US **anesthetic**) n. a drug or gas that stops you feeling pain.

**anaesthetist** (US **anesthetist**) n. a medical specialist who gives patients anaesthetics. ■ anaesthetize v.

**anagram** n. a word or phrase formed by rearranging the letters of another.

**anal** adj. of the anus.

**analgesic** n. a drug relieving pain.

**analogy** n. (pl. **-ies**) a comparison; a partial likeness. ■ analogous adj.

**analyse** (US **analyze**) v. examine in detail; psychoanalyse. ■ analyst n.
▷ SYNS STUDY, examine, investigate, review, evaluate, interpret, scrutinize, enquire into, dissect.

**analysis** n. (pl. **-ses**) a detailed examination or study. ■ analytic (or **analytical**) adj.
▷ SYNS STUDY, examination, investigation, scrutiny, enquiry, review, evaluation, interpretation.

**anarchist** n. a person who believes that government should be abolished. ■ anarchism n.

**anarchy** n. total lack of organized control; lawlessness. ■ anarchic adj.
▷ SYNS LAWLESSNESS, revolution, insurrection, chaos, disorder, mob rule.

**anathema** n. a detested thing.

**anatomize** (or **-ise**) v. examine the anatomy or structure of.

**anatomy** n. (pl. **-ies**) **1** the scientific study of bodily structure. **2** the bodily structure of a person, animal, or plant. **3** a detailed analysis. ■ anatomical adj. anatomist n.

**ancestor** n. a person from whom you are descended. ■ ancestral adj. ancestry n.

▷ SYNS FOREBEAR, forerunner, forefather, progenitor, predecessor, antecedent.

**anchor** n. a heavy metal structure for mooring a ship to the sea bottom. • v. moor with an anchor; fix firmly. □ **anchorage** a place where ships may anchor. **anchorman** a person presenting a live TV or radio programme.

▷ SYNS v. **1** MOOR, berth, make fast, tie up. **2** SECURE, fix, fasten, attach.

**anchovy** n. (pl. **-ies**) a small strong-tasting fish.

**ancient** adj. very old.

▷ SYNS VERY OLD, age-old, time-worn, time-honoured, archaic, antediluvian; early, prehistoric, primeval, primordial, immemorial, bygone, of yore.

**ancillary** adj. helping in a subsidiary way.

▷ SYNS SECONDARY, auxiliary, subsidiary, supplementary, additional, subordinate, extra.

**and** conj. used to connect words, clauses, or sentences.

**andante** adv. Music in moderately slow time.

**androgynous** adj. partly male and partly female in appearance.

**anecdote** n. a short, entertaining true story.

**anemia** US sp. of ANAEMIA.

**anemometer** n. an instrument for measuring wind speed.

**anemone** n. a plant with white, red, or purple flowers.

**anesthetic** etc. US sp. of ANAESTHETIC etc.

**anew** adv. **1** making a new start. **2** again.

**angel** n. **1** a supernatural being, messenger of God. **2** a kind person.

**angelic** adj. **1** relating to angels. **2** very beautiful, innocent, or kind.

▷ SYNS **1** HEAVENLY, divine, ethereal, holy. **2** INNOCENT, pure, virtuous, saintly, good.

**angelica** n. candied stalks of a fragrant plant.

**anger** n. a strong feeling of displeasure. • v. make angry.

▷ SYNS n. RAGE, fury, wrath, temper, annoyance, vexation, ire, exasperation, outrage, indignation, irritation, aggravation. • v. INFURIATE, enrage, incense, outrage, annoy, exasperate, antagonize, vex, irritate, aggravate.

**angina** (or **angina pectoris**) n. pain in the chest caused by inadequate supply of blood to the heart.

**angle** n. **1** the space between two lines or surfaces that meet; a corner. **2** a point of view. • v. **1** place obliquely; present from a particular viewpoint. **2** fish with a rod and line; try to get something by hinting. ■ **angler** n. **angling** n.

▷ SYNS **1** CORNER, intersection, bend, fork. **2** POINT OF VIEW, viewpoint, standpoint, opinion, position, slant.

**Anglican** adj. & n. (a member) of the Church of England.

**anglicize** (or **-ise**) v. make English in character.

**Anglo-** comb. form English or British.

**Anglo-Saxon** n. **1** a Germanic inhabitant of England between the 5th century and the Norman

Conquest. **2** the Old English language.

**angora** n. fabric made from the hair of a long-haired goat.

**angry** adj. (**-ier, -iest**) feeling or showing anger. ■ **angrily** adv.
▷ SYNS FURIOUS, enraged, incensed, outraged, wrathful, seething, raging, annoyed, irritated, exasperated, fuming, irate, indignant, vexed, heated; inf. apoplectic, mad, up in arms.

**angst** n. severe anxiety.

**anguish** n. severe physical or mental pain. ■ **anguished** adj.
▷ SYNS AGONY, suffering, pain, distress, torment, torture, misery, sorrow, grief, woe, heartache, tribulation.

**angular** adj. having angles or sharp corners.

**animal** n. a living being with sense organs, able to move voluntarily.
▷ SYNS CREATURE, beast, brute; (**animals**) wildlife, fauna.

**animate** v. **1** bring life or energy to. **2** make drawings into an animated film. • adj. living.

**animated** adj. lively.
▷ SYNS LIVELY, energetic, excited, enthusiastic, spirited, exuberant, vivacious, vibrant, cheerful, bright, ebullient, bubbly, eager, zestful, active, alive, sprightly, vigorous.

**animation** n. liveliness.
▷ SYNS LIVELINESS, vitality, vivacity, high spirits, energy, excitement, enthusiasm, ebullience, zest, exuberance, life, spirit, verve, sparkle.

**animosity** n. hostility.
▷ SYNS HOSTILITY, dislike, enmity, unfriendliness, resentment, antagonism, hate, hatred, loathing, antipathy, bitterness,

spite, bad blood, rancour, ill will, acrimony, malice, animus.

**animus** n. animosity.

**aniseed** n. the seed of the plant anise, used as flavouring.

**ankle** n. the joint connecting the foot with the leg.

**annals** pl.n. a historical record of events year by year.
▷ SYNS RECORDS, archives, history, chronicles, accounts, registers.

**annex** v. **1** take possession of. **2** add as an extra part. • n. a building attached or near to a main building. ■ **annexation** n.
▷ SYNS V. SEIZE, take over, conquer, appropriate, occupy.

**annihilate** v. destroy completely. ■ **annihilation** n.
▷ SYNS DESTROY, wipe out, exterminate, obliterate, eliminate, eradicate, liquidate, slaughter.

**anniversary** n. (pl. **-ies**) the date on which an event took place in a previous year.

**annotate** v. add explanatory notes to. ■ **annotation** n.

**announce** v. make known publicly. ■ **announcer** n.
▷ SYNS MAKE KNOWN, make public, publish, put out, report, state, reveal, declare, disclose, broadcast, proclaim, advertise, blazon.

**announcement** n. a public statement.
▷ SYNS STATEMENT, report, bulletin; declaration, proclamation, disclosure, publication, notification.

**annoy** v. make slightly angry.
▷ SYNS IRRITATE, anger, exasperate, infuriate, vex, irk, gall, pique, put out, antagonize, get on someone's nerves; inf. aggravate, nettle, bug.

**annoyance** n. **1** irritation or anger. **2** an annoying thing.
▷ SYNS **1** IRRITATION, exasperation, anger, ire, vexation, pique. **2** NUISANCE, pest, bother, irritant, trial; inf. pain, hassle, bind, bore.

**annoyed** adj. slightly angry.
▷ SYNS IRRITATED, exasperated, cross, vexed, peeved, riled, put out, disgruntled; inf. miffed, shirty.

**annoying** adj. causing annoyance.
▷ SYNS IRRITATING, infuriating, exasperating, maddening, trying, galling, troublesome, tiresome, irksome, bothersome, vexatious.

**annual** adj. yearly. • n. **1** a plant that lives for one year or one season. **2** a book published in yearly issues.
■ annually adv.

**annuity** n. (pl. **-ies**) a yearly allowance.

**annul** v. (**annulled, annulling**) cancel or declare invalid.
■ annulment n.
▷ SYNS CANCEL, nullify, declare null and void, invalidate, void, rescind, revoke, repeal.

**anodyne** adj. inoffensive but dull. • n. a painkilling medicine.

**anoint** v. apply water or oil to, esp. in religious consecration.

**anomalous** adj. differing from what is standard or normal.
▷ SYNS ABNORMAL, irregular, atypical, aberrant, exceptional, unusual, odd, eccentric, bizarre, peculiar.

**anomaly** n. (pl. **-ies**) something differing from what is standard or normal.

**anon** adv. old use soon.

**anonymous** adj. having a name that is not publicly known.
■ anonymity n.
▷ SYNS UNNAMED, unidentified, nameless, unknown, incognito, unsigned.

**anorak** n. a waterproof jacket with a hood.

**anorexia** (or **anorexia nervosa**) n. a condition characterized by an obsessive desire to lose weight. ■ anorexic adj. & n.

**another** adj. **1** an additional. **2** a different. • pron. another one.

**answer** n. **1** something said or written in response to a previous statement. **2** the solution to a problem. • v. **1** speak or act in response. **2** correspond to a description; satisfy a need. **3** (**answer for**) be responsible for. □ answering machine a machine that answers telephone calls and records messages.
▷ SYNS n. **1** REPLY, response, rejoinder, retort, riposte, comeback. **2** SOLUTION, remedy. • v. **1** REPLY, respond, react, come back, retort, rejoin. **2** SOLVE, remedy. **3** MEET, satisfy, fulfil, suit, measure up to, serve. **4** CORRESPOND TO, fit, match, conform to.

**answerable** adj. having to account for something.
▷ SYNS RESPONSIBLE, accountable, liable.

**ant** n. a small insect that lives in highly organized groups.
□ anteater a mammal that feeds on ants and termites.

**antagonism** n. open hostility.
▷ SYNS ANIMOSITY, hostility, enmity, antipathy, rivalry, friction, conflict.

**antagonist** n. an opponent or enemy.

**antagonize** v. make hostile.
▷ SYNS ANNOY, anger, irritate, alienate, offend, provoke.

**Antarctic** adj. & n. (of) regions round the South Pole.

**antecedent** n. **1** a thing that comes before another. **2** (**antecedents**) a person's ancestors. • adj. previous.

**antechamber** n. an anteroom.

**antedate** v. precede in time.

**antediluvian** adj. **1** of the time before the biblical Flood; **2** very old-fashioned.

**antelope** n. a deer-like wild animal.

**antenatal** adj. during pregnancy; before birth.

**antenna** n. **1** (pl. **-nae**) an insect's feeler. **2** (pl. **-nas**) an aerial.

**anterior** adj. further forward in position or time.

**anteroom** n. a small room leading to a main one.

**anthem** n. **1** a song chosen by a country to express patriotic feelings. **2** a piece of music to be sung in a religious service.
▷ SYNS HYMN, song, psalm, chant, chorale.

**anther** n. a part of a flower's stamen containing pollen.

**anthology** n. (pl. **-ies**) a collection of poems or other pieces of writing or music.
▷ SYNS COLLECTION, selection, compendium, treasury, miscellany.

**anthracite** n. a form of coal burning with little flame or smoke.

**anthrax** n. a serious disease of sheep and cattle.

**anthropoid** adj. (of apes) resembling a human in form.

**anthropology** n. the study of the origin and customs of human beings.
■ anthropologist n.

**anthropomorphic** adj. attributing human form or character to a god or animal.

**anti-** pref. opposed to; counteracting.

**antibiotic** n. a substance that destroys bacteria.

**antibody** n. (pl. **-ies**) a protein produced in the blood in re-action to harmful substances.

**anticipate** v. **1** be aware of and prepared for. **2** expect or look forward to. ■ anticipation n.
▷ SYNS **1** EXPECT, foresee, predict, be prepared for. **2** LOOK FORWARD TO, await, long for.

**anticlimax** n. a disappointing end to exciting events.
▷ SYNS LET-DOWN, disappointment, comedown, non-event, bathos; inf. washout, damp squib.

**anticlockwise** adj. & adv. in the direction opposite to clockwise.

**antics** pl.n. ridiculous behaviour.
▷ SYNS PRANKS, capers, escapades, high jinks, horseplay.

**antidote** n. a substance that counteracts the effects of poison.

**antifreeze** n. a substance added to water to prevent freezing.

**antihistamine** n. a drug used to treat allergies.

**antimony** n. a brittle metallic element.

**antipasto** n. (pl. **antipasti**) an Italian hors d'oeuvre.

**antipathy** n. (pl. **-ies**) strong dislike.

▷ SYNS DISLIKE, hostility, enmity, opposition, animosity, antagonism, aversion.

**antiperspirant** n. a substance that prevents or reduces sweating.

**antiphonal** adj. sung or recited alternately between two groups.

**Antipodes** pl.n. Australia and New Zealand. ■ Antipodean adj. & n.

**antiquarian** adj. relating to antiques and their study. • n. a person who studies antiques.

**antiquated** adj. very old-fashioned.

▷ SYNS OLD-FASHIONED, out of date, outmoded, outdated, behind the times, antediluvian, passé.

**antique** adj. belonging to the distant past. • n. an old and usu. valuable object.

**antiquity** n. (pl. -ies) 1 ancient times. 2 great age.

**anti-Semitic** adj. hostile to or prejudiced against Jews. ■ anti-Semitism n.

**antiseptic** adj. & n. (a substance) preventing infection.

▷ SYNS DISINFECTED, disinfectant, sterile, sterilized, sanitized.

**antisocial** adj. destructive or hostile to other members of society.

▷ SYNS 1 UNSOCIABLE, unfriendly, uncommunicative, misanthropic, reclusive. 2 DISRUPTIVE, disorderly, rude, unruly, objectionable, unacceptable.

**antithesis** n. (pl. -ses) an opposite; a contrast.

▷ SYNS OPPOSITE, reverse, converse, inverse, other extreme.

**antler** n. a branched horn of a deer.

**antonym** n. a word opposite to another in meaning.

**anus** n. the opening through which solid waste matter leaves the body.

**anvil** n. an iron block on which a smith hammers metal into shape.

**anxiety** n. an anxious feeling or state.

▷ SYNS WORRY, concern, apprehension, disquiet, uneasiness, nervousness, stress, tension, strain, misgiving, fear, fretfulness, angst.

**anxious** adj. 1 troubled and uneasy. 2 (**anxious to**) eager to.

▷ SYNS WORRIED, concerned, apprehensive, fearful, nervous, uneasy, disturbed, afraid, perturbed, agitated, edgy, troubled, upset, tense, overwrought, fretful; inf. nervy, jittery, on edge.

**any** adj. & pron. 1 one or some. 2 whichever or whatever you choose. □ anybody anyone. anyhow 1 anyway. 2 in a careless or disorderly way. anyone any person or people. anything a thing of any kind. anyway 1 used to emphasize something just said or to change the subject. 2 nevertheless. anywhere 1 in or to any place. 2 any place.

**AOB** abbr. any other business.

**aorta** n. the main artery carrying blood from the heart.

**apace** adv. swiftly.

**apart** adv. separately; to or at a distance; into pieces.

**apartheid** n. the former official system of racial segregation in South Africa.

**apartment** n. a flat; a set of rooms.

**apathetic** adj. not interested or enthusiastic.
▷ SYNS UNINTERESTED, indifferent, unenthusiastic, unconcerned, uninvolved, lukewarm.

**apathy** n. lack of interest or enthusiasm.

**ape** n. a tailless primate, e.g. a gorilla. • v. imitate or mimic.

**aperitif** n. an alcoholic drink taken before a meal.

**aperture** n. an opening, esp. one that admits light.
▷ SYNS OPENING, gap, hole, crack, slit, orifice, fissure.

**apex** n. the highest point or level.
▷ SYNS **1** TOP, peak, summit, tip, head, crest, crown, pinnacle. **2** HEIGHT, zenith, climax, culmination, acme.

**aphid** n. a small insect destructive to plants.

**aphorism** n. a short clever phrase which makes a true point.

**aphrodisiac** n. a substance arousing sexual desire.

**apiary** n. (pl. -ies) a place where bees are kept.

**apiece** adv. to, for, or by each.

**aplomb** n. self-possession or confidence.

**apocalypse** n. a catastrophic event. ■ apocalyptic adj.

**apocryphal** adj. of doubtful authenticity.

**apologetic** adj. admitting and showing regret for a wrongdoing.
▷ SYNS CONTRITE, sorry, remorseful, regretful, repentant, penitent, ashamed.

**apology** n. (pl. -ies) **1** a statement of regret for having done wrong or hurt someone. **2** (an apology for) a poor example of. ■ apologize v.

**apoplexy** n. **1** inf. extreme anger. **2** dated a stroke. ■ apoplectic adj.

**apostate** n. a person who renounces a former belief.

**apostle** n. **1** (Apostle) each of the twelve chief disciples of Jesus. **2** an enthusiastic supporter of an idea or cause.
▷ SYNS EVANGELIST, missionary, disciple, follower; advocate, proponent, propagandist, supporter.

**apostrophe** n. the sign ' used to show either possession or the omission of letters or numbers.

**appal** (US appall) v. (appalled, appalling) shock or greatly dismay someone.
▷ SYNS SHOCK, horrify, dismay, sicken, disgust, outrage, alarm, nauseate, revolt.

**appalling** adj. shockingly bad.
▷ SYNS SHOCKING, horrific, horrifying, terrible, dreadful, awful, ghastly, frightful, atrocious, hideous.

**apparatus** n. equipment for scientific or other work.
▷ SYNS DEVICE, instrument, contraption, mechanism, appliance, machine, gadget, tool; equipment, gear, tackle.

**apparel** n. formal clothing.

**apparent** adj. **1** clearly seen or understood. **2** seeming but not real. ■ apparently adv.
▷ SYNS **1** CLEAR, plain, obvious, evident, recognizable, noticeable, manifest, visible, unmistakable, patent. **2** SEEMING, ostensible, superficial, outward.

**apparition** n. a ghost.
▷ SYNS GHOST, phantom, spirit, spectre, wraith; inf. spook.

**appeal** v. 1 make an earnest or formal request. 2 refer a decision to a higher court. 3 seem attractive. • n. 1 an act of appealing. 2 attractiveness.
▷ SYNS v. 1 ASK, request, beg, plead, implore, entreat, call, beseech, petition. 2 INTEREST, tempt, fascinate, charm, engage, entice, enchant, beguile.
• n. 1 REQUEST, plea, call, application, entreaty, petition, cri de cœur, supplication. 2 ATTRACTION, interest, allure, temptation, charm, fascination, seductiveness.

**appear** v. 1 become visible. 2 seem.
▷ SYNS 1 TURN UP, show up, come into view, materialize, arrive. 2 OCCUR, materialize, be revealed, be seen, emerge, come to light, crop up. 3 SEEM, look, come across as. 4 PERFORM, act, take part, play.

**appearance** n. the way that someone or something looks or seems.
▷ SYNS 1 LOOK, air, aspect, mien. 2 IMPRESSION, show, semblance, guise.

**appease** v. pacify someone by agreeing to their demands.
■ appeasement n.
▷ SYNS PLACATE, pacify, mollify, conciliate, win over, propitiate.

**append** v. add at the end.

**appendage** n. a thing attached to something larger or more important.
▷ SYNS 1 ADDITION, attachment, addendum, adjunct, appurtenance. 2 LIMB, member, projection, protuberance.

**appendectomy** n. (pl. -ies) the surgical removal of the appendix.

**appendicitis** n. inflammation of the appendix.

**appendix** n. 1 a section at the end of a book, giving extra information. 2 a small closed tube of tissue attached to the large intestine.
▷ SYNS SUPPLEMENT, addition, addendum, postscript, codicil, coda, epilogue.

**appertain** v. formal relate to.

**appetite** n. desire, esp. for food.
▷ SYNS 1 HUNGER; taste, palate. 2 KEENNESS, eagerness, passion, desire, lust, hunger, thirst, yearning, longing, craving, relish; inf. yen.

**appetizing** (or -ising) adj. stimulating the appetite.
■ appetizer n.
▷ SYNS DELICIOUS, mouth-watering, tasty, succulent, palatable; inviting, tempting, appealing.

**applaud** v. express approval, esp. by clapping.
▷ SYNS 1 CLAP, cheer, give a standing ovation; inf. bring the house down. 2 PRAISE, admire, commend, congratulate, salute, acclaim, hail.

**applause** n. approval shown by clapping.
▷ SYNS CLAPPING, ovation, cheering.

**apple** n. a round fruit with firm juicy flesh.

**appliance** n. a piece of equipment for a specific task.
▷ SYNS DEVICE, gadget, instrument, apparatus, machine, mechanism, tool, implement, contraption.

**applicable** adj. appropriate; relevant. ■ applicability n.

▷ SYNS RELEVANT, appropriate, pertinent, apposite, apropos.

**applicant** n. a person who applies for something.
▷ SYNS CANDIDATE, interviewee, job-seeker, competitor, claimant, petitioner, supplicant.

**application** n. 1 a formal request. 2 sustained hard work. 3 the action of applying something. 4 a computer program designed for a particular purpose.
■ applicator n.

**applied** adj. put to practical use.

**apply** v. 1 make a formal request. 2 bring into operation or use. 3 be relevant. 4 spread over a surface. 5 (**apply yourself**) put all your efforts into a task.
▷ SYNS 1 PUT IN FOR, try for, request, ask for, seek, petition. 2 EXERT, administer, use, employ, exercise, utilize, bring to bear. 3 BE RELEVANT, relate, have a bearing, pertain, appertain. 4 PUT ON, rub in, cover with, spread, smear. 5 (**apply yourself**) CONCENTRATE, work hard, be industrious, exert yourself, devote yourself, persevere.

**appoint** v. 1 give a job or role to someone. 2 decide on a time or place. 3 (**appointed**) equipped or furnished.
▷ SYNS 1 NOMINATE, name, designate, install; select, choose, elect. 2 SET, fix, arrange, decide on, establish, settle on, determine, designate.

**appointment** n. an arrangement to meet; a job.
▷ SYNS 1 MEETING, engagement, date, arrangement, interview, rendezvous, assignation,

fixture; lit. tryst. 2 JOB, post, position, office, situation.

**apportion** v. share out.

**apposite** adj. appropriate; relevant.

**appraise** v. assess the quality or value of. ■ appraisal n.

**appreciable** adj. considerable. ■ appreciably adv.

**appreciate** v. 1 recognize the value of. 2 understand fully. 3 be grateful for. 4 rise in value. ■ appreciation n.
▷ SYNS 1 VALUE, treasure, admire, respect, rate highly, think a lot of. 2 RECOGNIZE, acknowledge, realize, know, be aware of, understand, comprehend.

**appreciative** adj. feeling or showing gratitude or pleasure.
▷ SYNS GRATEFUL, thankful, obliged, indebted.

**apprehend** v. 1 arrest. 2 understand.

**apprehension** n. 1 anxiety. 2 understanding.

**apprehensive** adj. worried or anxious.
▷ SYNS WORRIED, anxious, uneasy, on edge, nervous, frightened, afraid, fearful, concerned.

**apprentice** n. a person learning a craft. ■ apprenticeship n.
▷ SYNS TRAINEE, learner, pupil, student, beginner, novice, probationer, tyro.

**apprise** v. inform.

**approach** v. 1 come nearer to. 2 make a request or suggestion to. 3 start to deal with a task.
• n. 1 a way of dealing with something. 2 an initial proposal or request. 3 the action of approaching. 4 a path leading to a place.
▷ SYNS V. 1 MOVE TOWARDS, near, come near, close in on, gain on.

**2** SPEAK TO, sound out, make a proposal to, proposition, appeal to. **3** TACKLE, address, set about, make a start on, embark on.
• n. **1** METHOD, procedure, technique, modus operandi, style, way, means. **2** PROPOSAL, submission, application, appeal, overture, proposition.

**approachable** adj. easy to talk to.

**approbation** n. approval.

**appropriate** adj. suitable or proper. • v. take and use; set aside for a special purpose. ■ **appropriation** n.
▷ SYNS adj. SUITABLE, fitting, proper, right, apt, timely, opportune, seemly, becoming, correct, relevant, pertinent, apposite. • v. TAKE OVER, take possession of, seize, confiscate, requisition, annex, commandeer; steal, misappropriate.

**approval** n. **1** a good opinion of someone or something. **2** official permission or agreement.
▷ SYNS **1** APPROBATION, appreciation, liking, favour, admiration, respect, esteem. **2** ACCEPTANCE, agreement, consent, assent, permission; sanction, endorsement, ratification, authorization; inf. the OK, the go-ahead.

**approve** v. **1** regard as good or acceptable. **2** formally authorize or accept.
▷ SYNS **1** BE PLEASED WITH, think well of, like, hold with, admire, respect. **2** AGREE TO, accept, consent to, permit, pass, allow, sanction, authorize, endorse, ratify; inf. rubber-stamp.

**approximate** adj. almost but not quite exact. • v. be very similar. ■ **approximation** n.

▷ SYNS adj. ESTIMATED, rough, inexact, imprecise.

**approximately** adv. nearly; not exactly.
▷ SYNS ROUGHLY, about, around, circa, more or less, nearly, close/near to, in the region of, approaching, almost.

**après-ski** n. social activities following a day's skiing.

**apricot** n. an orange-yellow fruit resembling a small peach.

**April** n. the fourth month.

**apron** n. **1** a garment worn over the front of the body to protect clothes. **2** part of a theatre stage in front of the curtain. **3** an area on an airfield for manoeuvring and loading aircraft.

**apropos** adv. concerning.

**apt** adj. **1** appropriate. **2** (**apt to**) having a tendency to.
▷ SYNS **1** SUITABLE, appropriate, fitting, apposite, felicitous. **2** INCLINED, disposed, given, likely, liable, prone.

**aptitude** n. natural ability.
▷ SYNS TALENT, ability, gift, skill, flair, knack, capability, faculty.

**aqualung** n. a portable underwater breathing apparatus.

**aquamarine** n. a bluish-green gemstone.

**aquaplane** v. (of a vehicle) glide uncontrollably on a wet road surface.

**aquarium** n. (pl. **-riums** or **-ria**) a tank for keeping living fish etc.

**aquatic** adj. living or taking place in or on water.

**aqueduct** n. a structure carrying a waterway over a valley.

**aquiline** adj. like an eagle; curved like an eagle's beak.

**arabesque** n. a ballet position in which one leg is lifted and extended backwards.

**arable** adj. (of land) suitable for growing crops.

**arachnid** n. a creature of a class including spiders and scorpions.

**arbiter** n. a person with power to judge in a dispute.

**arbitrary** adj. not seeming to be based on a reason or plan.
■ arbitrarily adv.
▷ SYNS RANDOM, chance, unpredictable; casual, motiveless, irrational, illogical; capricious.

**arbitrate** v. officially settle a dispute.
▷ SYNS ADJUDICATE, judge, referee, umpire, mediate, negotiate.

**arbitrator** n. an impartial person chosen to settle a dispute. ■ arbitration n.
▷ SYNS ADJUDICATOR, judge, mediator, referee, umpire, arbiter, negotiator, intermediary, go-between.

**arboreal** adj. of or living in trees.

**arbour** (US **arbor**) n. a shady shelter under trees or a framework with climbing plants.

**arc** n. **1** part of a curve, esp. of the circumference of a circle. **2** a luminous electric discharge between two points.
▷ SYNS CURVE, crescent, semicircle, half-moon, arch, curvature.

**arcade** n. **1** a covered passage with arches along one or both sides. **2** a covered walk with shops along the sides. **3** an enclosed place containing games machines etc.

**arcane** adj. mysterious.

▷ SYNS SECRET, mysterious, recondite, enigmatic, abstruse, esoteric, cryptic.

**arch** n. a curved structure, esp. as a support; the inner side of the foot. • v. form an arch. • adj. affectedly playful or teasing.
□ archway an entrance or passageway under an arch.
▷ SYNS n. ARCHWAY, vault, span, bridge. • adj. PLAYFUL, mischievous, roguish, saucy, knowing.

**arch-** pref. chief or main.

**archaeology** (US **archeology**) n. the study of earlier civilizations through their material remains.
■ archaeologist n.

**archaic** adj. belonging to former or ancient times.

**archaism** n. an archaic word or phrase.

**archangel** n. an angel of the highest rank.

**archbishop** n. a chief bishop.

**archer** n. a person who shoots with a bow and arrows.
■ archery n.

**archetype** n. a typical example; an original model. ■ archetypal adj.
▷ SYNS PROTOTYPE, essence, quintessence, model, embodiment, pattern, original, standard, paradigm.

**archipelago** n. (pl. **-os** or **-oes**) a group of islands.

**architect** n. a designer of buildings.

**architecture** n. the design and construction of buildings.
■ architectural adj.

**archive** n. a collection of historical documents, data, etc.
■ archivist n.

**Arctic** adj. **1** of regions round the North Pole. **2** (**arctic**) inf. very cold.

**ardent** adj. passionate; enthusiastic.
▷ SYNS PASSIONATE, fervent, impassioned, eager, enthusiastic, intense, keen, zealous, vehement, fierce.

**ardour** (US **ardor**) n. passion; enthusiasm.

**arduous** adj. difficult and tiring.
▷ SYNS HARD, difficult, demanding, exhausting, laborious, strenuous, tiring, gruelling, punishing, tough, onerous, heavy, rigorous, back-breaking, taxing.

**area** n. **1** a part of a place, object, or surface. **2** the extent of a surface.
▷ SYNS **1** REGION, district, environment, vicinity, locality, zone, territory, neighbourhood, environs, terrain, sector, quarter, province, precinct. **2** SIZE, extent, expanse, measurement, space, square-footage, acreage.

**arena** n. a level area in the centre of an amphitheatre or sports stadium; an area of activity.

**argon** n. an inert gaseous element.

**arguable** adj. **1** able to be supported by reasons. **2** open to disagreement. ■ **arguably** adv.

**argue** v. **1** exchange conflicting views heatedly. **2** give reasons for an opinion.
▷ SYNS **1** QUARREL, row, disagree, squabble, bicker, fight, wrangle, have words. **2** CONTEND, maintain, hold, claim, assert, insist, reason, allege.

**argument** n. **1** a heated exchange of conflicting views. **2** a set of reasons given in support of an opinion.
▷ SYNS **1** QUARREL, row, disagreement, squabble, fight, altercation, dispute, wrangle, clash, difference of opinion; inf. tiff, barney. **2** REASONING, case, evidence, reasons, grounds.

**argumentative** adj. apt to argue.
▷ SYNS QUARRELSOME, disputatious, combative, belligerent, litigious.

**aria** n. a solo in an opera.

**arid** adj. dry or parched.
▷ SYNS DRY, dried up, waterless, parched, scorched, desiccated, barren, infertile, desert, lifeless, sterile.

**arise** v. **1** start to exist or be noticed. **2** lit. rise.
▷ SYNS COME TO LIGHT, appear, turn/crop up, emerge, occur.

**aristocracy** n. (pl. **-ies**) the hereditary upper classes. ■ **aristocrat** n.
▷ SYNS NOBILITY, peerage, upper class, gentry, high society, elite, ruling class.

**aristocratic** adj. of the aristocracy.
▷ SYNS NOBLE, titled, blue-blooded, upper class, well bred, refined, gracious, dignified.

**arithmetic** n. the use of numbers in calculation.

**ark** n. **1** (in the Bible) the ship built by Noah to escape the Flood. **2** a chest housing the holy scrolls in a synagogue.

**arm** n. **1** an upper limb of the body. **2** a raised side part of a chair. **3** a division of a company or organization. **4** (**arms**) weapons. • v. equip or supply with weapons; make a bomb ready to explode. □ **armchair** an

upholstered chair with side supports for a person's arms.
**armpit** the hollow under the arm at the shoulder.
▷ SYNS n. **1** LIMB, appendage, forelimb, member. **2** BRANCH, department, section, offshoot, division, sector. • v. EQUIP, supply, provide, issue with, furnish.

**armada** n. a fleet of warships.

**armadillo** n. (pl. **-os**) a mammal of South America with a body encased in bony plates.

**armament** (or **armaments**) n. military weapons.
▷ SYNS ARMS, weapons, weaponry, firearms, guns, munitions, ordnance.

**armistice** n. an agreement to stop fighting temporarily.

**armour** (US **armor**) n. a protective metal covering, esp. that formerly worn in battle.
■ **armoured** adj.

**armoury** (US **armory**) n. (pl. **-ies**) a place where weapons are kept.

**army** n. **1** an organized force for fighting on land. **2** a vast group.
▷ SYNS **1** ARMED FORCE, troops, soldiers, infantry, soldiery. **2** CROWD, horde, throng, swarm, pack, host, multitude, mob.

**arnica** n. a plant substance used to treat bruises.

**aroma** n. a pleasant smell.
■ **aromatic** adj.
▷ SYNS SMELL, scent, odour, fragrance, perfume, bouquet.

**aromatherapy** n. the use of essential plant oils for healing.

**arose** past of **ARISE**.

**around** adv. & prep. **1** on every side of. **2** in the vicinity of. **3** approximately. **4** to many places throughout an area; so as to encircle. **5** so as to face in the opposite direction.

**arouse** v. waken; stimulate.
▷ SYNS **1** WAKE (UP), awaken, waken, rouse. **2** CAUSE, stimulate, stir up, inspire, induce, provoke, whip up, foster, kindle.

**arpeggio** n. (pl. **-os**) the notes of a musical chord played in succession.

**arraign** v. accuse.

**arrange** v. **1** put into order. **2** organize; plan. **3** adapt a piece of music.
▷ SYNS **1** PUT IN ORDER, set out, sort, lay out, array, organize, position, group, tidy. **2** FIX, organize, plan, set up, schedule, settle on, determine.

**arrangement** n. **1** a plan for a future event. **2** an agreement. **3** the way in which something is arranged.
▷ SYNS **1** PREPARATION, plan, planning, provision. **2** AGREEMENT, deal, understanding, bargain, settlement, pact. **3** POSITIONING, layout, presentation, organization, order.

**arrant** adj. complete and utter.

**array** n. **1** a display or wide range. **2** an arrangement. **3** lit. fine clothing. • v. **1** arrange. **2** dress finely.
▷ SYNS n. RANGE, collection, selection, assortment, arrangement, line-up, display, presentation.

**arrears** pl.n. money owed and overdue for repayment.

**arrest** v. **1** seize someone by legal authority. **2** stop or delay. **3** (**arresting**) attracting attention. • n. the action of arresting someone.

▷ SYNS v. **1** APPREHEND, take into custody, take prisoner, put in jail, detain, seize; inf. nick. **2** STOP, halt, check, delay, slow down, stem, limit, impede; prevent, obstruct, block, hinder.

**arrive** v. reach the end of a journey; (of a particular moment) come. ■ **arrival** n.

▷ SYNS COME, appear, enter, show/turn up, make an appearance; inf. roll in/up.

**arrogant** adj. exaggerating your importance or abilities. ■ **arrogance** n.

▷ SYNS HAUGHTY, proud, conceited, self-important, pompous, bumptious, overbearing, superior, high-handed, imperious, overweening; inf. high and mighty, cocky.

**arrogate** v. take or claim for yourself without justification.

**arrow** n. a straight shaft with a sharp point, shot from a bow; a sign shaped like this.

**arsenal** n. a place where weapons are stored or made.

**arsenic** n. a brittle grey element with highly poisonous compounds.

**arson** n. the intentional and unlawful setting on fire of a building. ■ **arsonist** n.

**art** n. **1** the creation of something beautiful and expressive; paintings and sculptures. **2** (**arts**) subjects other than sciences; creative activities (e.g. painting, music, writing). **3** a skill. □ **artwork** illustrations to be included in a publication.

▷ SYNS **1** PAINTING, drawing, fine art, design. **2** SKILL, craft, talent, flair, aptitude, knack, facility, technique.

**artefact** (US **artifact**) n. a man-made object.

**artery** n. (pl. **-ies**) a large blood vessel carrying blood from the heart. ■ **arterial** adj.

**artful** adj. crafty.

▷ SYNS CUNNING, crafty, sly, devious, tricky, scheming, wily, clever, shrewd, canny, calculating.

**arthritis** n. a condition causing pain and stiffness in the joints. ■ **arthritic** adj.

**arthropod** n. an animal with a segmented body and jointed limbs (e.g. a crustacean).

**artichoke** n. a vegetable consisting of the unopened flower head of a thistle-like plant.

**article** n. **1** an individual object. **2** a piece of writing in a newspaper or journal. **3** a clause in an agreement.

▷ SYNS **1** THING, object, item, commodity, artefact. **2** STORY, piece, item, report, feature.

**articulate** adj. able to speak fluently and clearly. • v. **1** pronounce or express clearly. **2** (**articulated**) having sections connected by a flexible joint or joints. ■ **articulation** n.

▷ SYNS adj. ELOQUENT, fluent, lucid, expressive, silver-tongued; coherent, clear, comprehensible. • v. EXPRESS, put into words, voice, vocalize, state, say, utter.

**artifact** US sp. of **ARTEFACT**.

**artifice** n. a clever deception; skill.

**artificial** adj. not originating naturally; man-made. ■ **artificiality** n. **artificially** adv.

▷ SYNS **1** SYNTHETIC, imitation, fake, mock, ersatz, man-made, manufactured, fabricated.

**2** FALSE, feigned, affected, fake, unnatural, insincere, forced, sham, contrived, put-on, bogus, pseudo; inf. phoney.

**artillery** n. (pl. **-ies**) **1** large guns used in warfare. **2** a branch of an army using these.

**artisan** n. a skilled manual worker.

**artist** n. **1** a person who paints or draws. **2** a person who performs any of the creative arts.

**artiste** n. a professional entertainer.

**artistic** adj. **1** skilled in art. **2** of art or artists. ■ **artistically** adv.
▷ SYNS CREATIVE, imaginative, talented, gifted, cultured, cultivated; inf. arty.

**artistry** n. creative skill or ability.
▷ SYNS SKILL, art, talent, flair, creativity, proficiency, craftsmanship.

**artless** adj. simple and natural.
▷ SYNS INNOCENT, naive, simple, childlike, ingenuous, guileless.

**arty** adj. inf. pretentiously displaying your interest in the arts.

**as** adv. & conj. **1** used in comparisons to indicate extent or degree; used to indicate manner. **2** while. **3** because. **4** although. • prep. in the role or form of.

**asbestos** n. a soft fibrous mineral substance used to make fireproof material.

**asbestosis** n. a lung disease caused by inhaling asbestos particles.

**ASBO** abbr. antisocial behaviour order.

**ascend** v. rise; climb.
▷ SYNS CLIMB, go up, rise, mount, scale; take off, lift off, fly up.

**ascendancy** n. dominant power or influence.
▷ SYNS DOMINANCE, domination, supremacy, authority, power, control, command, rule, sovereignty.

**ascendant** adj. rising.

**ascension** n. **1** the act of ascending. **2** (**the Ascension**) the ascent of Jesus to heaven.

**ascent** n. **1** an act of ascending. **2** an upward slope.
▷ SYNS **1** CLIMB, scaling, conquest. **2** SLOPE, incline, gradient, hill.

**ascertain** v. find out.
▷ SYNS FIND OUT, establish, discover, work out, learn, determine, identify, confirm, verify.

**ascetic** adj. & n. (a person) abstaining from pleasures and luxuries. ■ **asceticism** n.
▷ SYNS ABSTEMIOUS, spartan, self-denying, frugal, austere, self-disciplined, strict, puritanical, monastic.

**ascorbic acid** n. vitamin C.

**ascribe** v. attribute.
▷ SYNS ATTRIBUTE, put down, assign, chalk up, impute, credit, accredit; lay at the door of, blame.

**asexual** adj. without sex.

**ash** n. **1** a tree with silver-grey bark. **2** powder that remains after something has burnt. □ **ashtray** a small container for tobacco ash and cigarette ends.

**ashamed** adj. feeling shame.
▷ SYNS SHAMEFACED, sorry, apologetic, embarrassed, sheepish, guilty, remorseful, mortified, contrite, penitent, repentant, rueful, chagrined.

**ashen** adj. pale as ashes; grey.
▷ SYNS PALE, white, pallid, wan, colourless, grey, ghostly.

**ashore** adv. to or on the shore.

**aside** adv. to or on one side.
• n. a remark made so that only certain people will hear.

**asinine** adj. silly.

**ask** v. 1 say something so as to get an answer or some information. 2 make a request. 3 invite someone.
▷ SYNS 1 ENQUIRE, query; question, interrogate, quiz. 2 REQUEST, seek, solicit, demand, call, appeal, apply; beg, implore, plead, beseech, supplicate. 3 INVITE, summon, bid.

**askance** adv. (**look askance at**) regard with disapproval.

**askew** adv. & adj. not straight or level.

**asleep** adv. & adj. in or into a state of sleep.
▷ SYNS SLEEPING, dozing, snoozing; inf. dead to the world, in the land of Nod.

**asp** n. a small poisonous snake.

**asparagus** n. a plant whose shoots are used as a vegetable.

**aspect** n. 1 a feature or part of something. 2 the appearance of something. 3 the direction in which a building faces.
▷ SYNS 1 FEATURE, facet, side, part, characteristic, element, detail, angle, slant. 2 APPEARANCE, look, expression, air, demeanour, cast, mien.

**aspen** n. a poplar tree.

**asperity** n. harshness.

**aspersions** pl.n. critical remarks.

**asphalt** n. a black tar-like substance mixed with gravel for surfacing roads.

**asphyxiate** v. suffocate.
■ asphyxiation n.

**aspic** n. a savoury jelly for coating cooked meat, eggs, etc.

**aspidistra** n. a plant with broad tapering leaves.

**aspiration** n. a hope or ambition.
▷ SYNS AIM, desire, ambition, goal, wish, hope, dream, longing, yearning.

**aspire** v. have a hope or ambition.
▷ SYNS DESIRE, hope, long, wish, dream, yearn, aim, seek.

**aspirin** n. a drug that relieves pain and reduces fever.

**aspiring** adj. ambitious to be or do something.
▷ SYNS WOULD-BE, hopeful, budding, potential, prospective; inf. wannabe.

**ass** n. 1 a donkey. 2 inf. a stupid person.

**assail** v. attack violently.
■ assailant n.

**assassin** n. a killer of an important person.
▷ SYNS MURDERER, killer, gunman; inf. hit man.

**assassinate** v. kill an important person by violent means.
■ assassination n.
▷ SYNS MURDER, kill, execute, slay, eliminate.

**assault** n. a violent attack.
• v. attack someone.
▷ SYNS v. ATTACK, strike, hit, punch, beat up, thump; inf. lay into, rough up.

**assemble** v. bring or come together; put together the parts of.

▷ SYNS **1** GATHER, collect, congregate, meet, rally, convene; round up, summon, muster, mobilize, marshal. **2** CONSTRUCT, build, erect, set up, piece/fit together, fabricate, manufacture, connect, join.

**assembly** n. an assembled group; assembling.
▷ SYNS GATHERING, meeting, crowd, group, congregation, throng, rally, convention.

**assent** n. agreement. • v. agree.
▷ SYNS n. AGREEMENT, consent, acceptance, approval, permission, sanction, acquiescence, approbation. • v. AGREE, accept, consent, comply, approve, acquiesce, concede, concur, accede.

**assert** v. **1** state or declare to be true. **2** exercise rights or authority. **3** (**assert yourself**) behave forcefully. ■ assertion n.
▷ SYNS DECLARE, state, maintain, contend, pronounce, insist, proclaim, claim, swear, affirm, aver.

**assertive** adj. confident and forceful.
▷ SYNS CONFIDENT, self-assured, assured, forceful, strong-willed, authoritative, dominant, pushy, decisive, determined.

**assess** v. calculate or estimate the value, importance, or quality of. ■ assessment n. assessor n.
▷ SYNS EVALUATE, judge, gauge, estimate, appraise, determine, weigh up, analyse, rate.

**asset** n. **1** a property with money value. **2** a useful or valuable thing or person.
▷ SYNS **1** ADVANTAGE, benefit, strength, strong point, forte, resource, blessing, boon, godsend. **2** (**assets**) WEALTH, money, resources, capital,

property, possessions, belongings, holdings, goods, valuables, estate, effects, chattels.

**assiduous** adj. showing great care and thoroughness.
■ assiduity n.

**assign** v. **1** give a task or duty to someone. **2** give someone a job or task. **3** provide with a value, date, etc.
▷ SYNS **1** ALLOCATE, give, set, charge with, entrust with. **2** APPOINT, select, delegate, commission, designate, name.

**assignation** n. a secret meeting, especially one between lovers.
▷ SYNS RENDEZVOUS, date, appointment, meeting; lit. tryst.

**assignment** n. a task assigned to someone.
▷ SYNS TASK, job, duty, mission, undertaking.

**assimilate** v. **1** take in and understand information. **2** absorb into a larger group. ■ assimilation n.
▷ SYNS **1** ABSORB, take in, understand, grasp, digest. **2** SUBSUME, incorporate, absorb, integrate; adopt, embrace, admit.

**assist** v. help or support.
▷ SYNS **1** HELP, aid, lend a hand, support, back up, abet, collaborate with, work with. **2** FACILITATE, expedite, spur on, promote, boost, benefit, encourage, advance, further.

**assistance** n. help or support.
▷ SYNS HELP, aid, support, backing, cooperation, collaboration.

**assistant** n. a helper; a person who serves customers in a shop.
▷ SYNS HELPER, subordinate, second-in-command, aide, deputy, number two, right-hand

man/woman, man/girl Friday; inf. sidekick.

**assizes** pl.n. hist. a county court.

**associate** v. 1 connect in your mind. 2 mix socially. 3 (**associate yourself**) be involved with something. • n. a work partner or colleague.

▷ SYNS v. 1 LINK, connect, relate, join. 2 MIX, socialize, keep company, fraternize, rub shoulders; inf. hobnob, hang out.

**association** n. 1 a group organized for a joint purpose. 2 a connection or link.

▷ SYNS FEDERATION, alliance, partnership, union, confederation, syndicate, coalition, league, cartel, consortium, club.

**assonance** n. the rhyming of vowel sounds.

**assorted** adj. of several sorts.

▷ SYNS VARIOUS, miscellaneous, mixed, varied, diverse, sundry, multifarious; old use divers.

**assortment** n. a varied collection.

▷ SYNS MIXTURE, mixed bag, selection, variety, collection, jumble, miscellany.

**assuage** v. soothe.

**assume** v. 1 accept as true without proof. 2 take responsibility or control. 3 begin to have. 4 pretend to have.

▷ SYNS 1 PRESUME, suppose, take it, take for granted, conjecture, surmise, conclude, think, believe, imagine, guess, gather. 2 ACCEPT, shoulder, bear, undertake, take on. 3 SEIZE, take, appropriate, acquire. 4 AFFECT, adopt, impersonate, put on, simulate, feign, fake.

**assumption** n. something assumed to be true.

▷ SYNS SUPPOSITION, presumption, belief, hypothesis, theory, conjecture, surmise, conclusion, guess, expectation, premise.

**assurance** n. 1 an assertion or promise. 2 self-confidence. 3 life insurance.

▷ SYNS 1 SELF-CONFIDENCE, self-assurance, poise, confidence. 2 PROMISE, guarantee, word, oath, pledge, bond.

**assure** v. tell confidently or promise.

▷ SYNS PROMISE, guarantee, give your word, swear, pledge, vow, declare, affirm, attest.

**assured** adj. confident; certain.

■ **assuredly** adv.

▷ SYNS 1 CONFIDENT, self-confident, self-assured, self-reliant, poised. 2 CERTAIN, definite, guaranteed, sure, confirmed.

**asterisk** n. a star-shaped symbol (*).

**astern** adv. behind or towards the rear of a ship or aircraft.

**asteroid** n. one of many small rocky bodies orbiting the sun between Mars and Jupiter.

**asthma** n. a chronic condition causing difficulty in breathing. ■ **asthmatic** adj. & n.

**astigmatism** n. a defect in an eye, preventing proper focusing.

**astonish** v. surprise greatly. ■ **astonishment** n.

▷ SYNS AMAZE, astound, stagger, stun, surprise, dumbfound, take aback, startle, stupefy, flabbergast.

**astound** v. amaze.

**astral** adj. of or from the stars.

**astray** adv. & adj. away from the proper path.

**astride** adv. & prep. with one leg on each side of.

**astringent** adj. 1 causing body tissue to contract. 2 sharp or severe. • n. an astringent lotion. ■ astringency n.

**astrology** n. the study of the supposed influence of stars on human affairs. ■ astrologer n. astrological adj.

**astronaut** n. a person trained to travel in a spacecraft.

**astronomical** adj. 1 of astronomy. 2 inf. very large. ■ astronomically adv.

**astronomy** n. the study of stars and planets and their movements. ■ astronomer n.

**astute** adj. shrewd.
▷ SYNS SHREWD, clever, quick, quick-witted, acute, canny, wily, cunning, artful; intelligent, perceptive, insightful, sagacious, wise.

**asunder** adv. lit. apart.

**asylum** n. 1 refuge or protection. 2 dated a mental institution.
▷ SYNS REFUGE, sanctuary, shelter, safety, protection, safe haven.

**asymmetrical** adj. lacking symmetry. ■ asymmetry n.
▷ SYNS UNEVEN, lopsided, askew, crooked, unbalanced, irregular, awry.

**at** prep. expressing: 1 location, arrival, or time. 2 a value, rate, or point on a scale. 3 a state or condition. 4 direction towards.

**ate** past of EAT.

**atheism** n. disbelief in the existence of a god or gods. ■ atheist n.

**atherosclerosis** n. damage to the arteries caused by a build-up of fatty deposits.

**athlete** n. a person who is good at athletics.

**athletic** adj. 1 strong, fit, and active. 2 of athletics. • n. track and field sports. ■ athleticism n.
▷ SYNS adj. 1 MUSCULAR, strong, well built, powerful, sturdy, robust, strapping, brawny; fit, in trim. 2 SPORTING, sports, gymnastic.

**Atlantic** adj. of the Atlantic Ocean.

**atlas** n. a book of maps.

**atmosphere** n. 1 the mixture of gases surrounding a planet; air. 2 a unit of pressure. 3 the feeling given by a place, situation, etc. ■ atmospheric adj.
▷ SYNS 1 AIR, sky, heavens, stratosphere, ether. 2 AMBIENCE, air, mood, feeling, spirit, character, tone, quality, flavour, aura, tenor.

**atoll** n. a ring-shaped coral reef enclosing a lagoon.

**atom** n. the smallest particle of a chemical element; a very small quantity. □ atom bomb a bomb deriving its power from atomic energy. ■ atomic adj.
▷ SYNS BIT, particle, scrap, shred, speck, fragment, jot, trace, iota, crumb, grain.

**atomize** (or **-ise**) v. reduce to atoms or fine particles. ■ atomizer n.

**atonal** adj. (of music) not written in any key.

**atone** v. make amends for a fault. ■ atonement n.
▷ SYNS MAKE AMENDS, compensate, make up for, pay, do penance, make good, expiate.

**atrocious** adj. 1 horrifyingly wicked. 2 very bad or unpleasant.

▷ SYNS **1** WICKED, brutal, cruel, barbaric, vicious, heinous, monstrous, vile, inhuman, ghastly, abominable, outrageous, despicable, sickening, horrifying, unspeakable. **2** APPALLING, dreadful, terrible, abysmal, execrable; inf. dire, rotten, lousy.

**atrocity** n. (pl. **-ies**) wickedness; a cruel act.
▷ SYNS OUTRAGE, crime, offence, horror, abomination, monstrosity, violation, evil.

**atrophy** v. **1** (of body tissue or an organ) waste away. **2** gradually become weaker. • n. the condition or process of atrophying.
▷ SYNS v. WASTE AWAY, wither, shrivel, decay, wilt, deteriorate, decline, degenerate.

**attach** v. **1** fasten or join. **2** regard as important. **3** (**attached to**) very fond of.
▷ SYNS **1** FASTEN, affix, join, stick, connect, tie, link, couple, pin. **2** ASCRIBE, assign, attribute.

**attaché** n. a person attached to an ambassador's staff. ▫ **attaché case** a small case for carrying documents.

**attached** adj. (**attached to**) fond of.

**attachment** n. **1** an extra part attached to something. **2** a computer file sent with an email.

**attack** n. a violent attempt to hurt or defeat a person; strong criticism; a sudden onset of illness. • v. make an attack on. ■ **attacker** n.
▷ SYNS n. **1** ASSAULT, offensive, raid, ambush, sortie, onslaught, charge, strike, invasion, foray, incursion. **2** CRITICISM, censure,

condemnation, denunciation, tirade, diatribe. **3** FIT, seizure, bout, spasm, convulsion, paroxysm. • v. **1** ASSAULT, assail, set on, beat up, strike, hit, punch; charge, pounce; inf. lay into, do over, rough up. **2** CRITICIZE, censure, condemn, denounce, pillory.

**attain** v. achieve. ■ **attainable** adj. **attainment** n.
▷ SYNS ACHIEVE, accomplish, gain, obtain, get, win, earn, acquire, reach, realize, fulfil, succeed in, bring off, secure, procure.

**attempt** v. try. • n. an effort.
▷ SYNS v. TRY, strive, endeavour, seek, aim, undertake, make an effort, have a go; inf. have a shot/crack. • n. TRY, go, effort, endeavour.

**attend** v. **1** be present at; accompany. **2** take notice. **3** (**attend to**) deal with. ■ **attendance** n.
▷ SYNS **1** BE PRESENT, appear, put in an appearance, turn up, visit, go to; inf. show up. **2** LOOK AFTER, take care of, care for, nurse, tend, see to, minister to. **3** ESCORT, accompany, chaperone, guide, conduct, usher, shepherd. **4** PAY ATTENTION, take notice/note, listen, concentrate, heed.

**attendant** n. an assistant; a person providing service in a particular place. • adj. accompanying.

**attention** n. **1** special care, notice, or attention. **2** a straight standing position in military drill.
▷ SYNS **1** CONSIDERATION, contemplation, deliberation, observation, scrutiny, thought, study, investigation. **2** NOTICE, awareness, observation, heed, recognition, regard. **3** CARE,

treatment, therapy, ministration.

**attentive** adj. paying attention; considerate and helpful.
▷ SYNS **1** ALERT, aware, watchful, awake, observant, vigilant, intent, focused, committed, heedful. **2** CONSIDERATE, thoughtful, helpful, conscientious, polite, kind, obliging.

**attenuate** v. make thin or weaker.

**attest** v. provide proof of; declare true or genuine.

**attic** n. a room in the top storey of a house.

**attire** n. formal or lit. clothes. • v. (**be attired**) be dressed.

**attitude** n. **1** a fixed way of thinking. **2** a position of the body.
▷ SYNS VIEW, point of view, opinion, viewpoint, outlook, belief, standpoint, frame of mind, position, perspective, stance, thoughts, ideas.

**attorney** n. (pl. **-eys**) US a lawyer.

**attract** v. draw someone in by offering something appealing; arouse interest or liking in.
■ **attraction** n.
▷ SYNS APPEAL TO, interest, fascinate, charm, captivate, entice, tempt, engage, bewitch, seduce, beguile, lure.

**attractive** adj. pleasing in appearance.
▷ SYNS GOOD-LOOKING, beautiful, handsome, pretty, lovely, stunning, striking, gorgeous, desirable, appealing, seductive, fetching, comely, prepossessing; inf. cute.

**attribute** n. a characteristic quality. • v. regard as belonging to or caused by. ■ **attributable** adj. **attribution** n.
▷ SYNS n. QUALITY, feature, characteristic, property, mark, sign, trait. • v. ASCRIBE, assign, put down to, credit, impute, chalk up.

**attrition** n. wearing away.

**attune** v. be receptive to and able to understand.

**atypical** adj. not characteristic of a group, type, or class.

**aubergine** n. a dark purple vegetable.

**auburn** adj. (of hair) reddish brown.

**auction** n. a public sale where articles are sold to the highest bidder. • v. sell by auction.
■ **auctioneer** n.

**audacious** adj. daring.
▷ SYNS BOLD, daring, fearless, brave, courageous, intrepid, valiant, plucky, reckless, daredevil.

**audacity** n. **1** a willingness to take risks. **2** impudence.
▷ SYNS **1** BOLDNESS, daring, fearlessness, bravery, courage. **2** IMPUDENCE, impertinence, insolence, cheek, effrontery, gall.

**audible** adj. loud enough to be heard. ■ **audibly** adv.

**audience** n. **1** a group of listeners or spectators. **2** a formal interview.
▷ SYNS **1** SPECTATORS, listeners, viewers, crowd, house, turnout, congregation. **2** INTERVIEW, meeting, hearing, consultation.

**audio** n. sound or the reproduction of sound. □ **audio-visual** using both sight and sound.

**audit** n. & v. (make) an official examination of accounts.
■ auditor n.

**audition** n. a test of a performer's ability for a particular part. • v. test or be tested in an audition.

**auditorium** n. (-riums or -ria) the part of a theatre or concert hall where the audience sits.

**auditory** adj. of hearing.

**auger** n. a boring tool with a spiral point.

**augment** v. add to or increase.
▷ SYNS INCREASE, add to, top up, supplement, enlarge, expand, multiply, extend, boost, amplify, swell, magnify.

**augur** v. be an omen.

**augury** n. a sign that shows what will happen in the future.
▷ SYNS SIGN, omen, portent, warning, prophecy.

**August** n. the eighth month.

**august** adj. majestic.
▷ SYNS DIGNIFIED, stately, majestic, noble, imposing, impressive, exalted, grand.

**auk** n. a northern seabird.

**aunt** n. the sister or sister-in-law of your father or mother.

**au pair** n. a foreign girl employed to look after children and help with housework in exchange for board and lodging.

**aura** n. the atmosphere surrounding a place or person.

**aural** adj. relating to the ear or hearing.

**au revoir** exclam. goodbye.

**aurora borealis** n. bands of coloured light seen in the sky near the North Pole; the northern lights.

**auspices** pl.n. (under the auspices of) with the support or protection of.

**auspicious** adj. being an omen of success.
▷ SYNS FAVOURABLE, promising, hopeful, encouraging, bright, rosy, fortunate, propitious, timely.

**austere** adj. 1 severe or strict. 2 very simple or plain.
■ austerity n.
▷ SYNS 1 SEVERE, stern, strict, harsh, dour, grim, cold, frosty, unfriendly; ascetic, abstemious, self-denying, self-disciplined, frugal, spartan, puritanical. 2 PLAIN, simple, basic, unadorned, unornamented, stark.

**authentic** adj. 1 known to be real and genuine. 2 based on facts; accurate. ■ authentically adv. authenticity n.
▷ SYNS 1 GENUINE, real, true, bona fide, actual, legitimate, valid; inf. the real McCoy. 2 TRUE, accurate, honest, reliable, dependable.

**authenticate** v. prove the authenticity of.
■ authentication n.
▷ SYNS VERIFY, validate, prove, confirm, substantiate, corroborate.

**author** n. the writer of a book etc.; an originator.
■ authorship n.
▷ SYNS WRITER, novelist, dramatist, playwright, poet, essayist, journalist.

**authoritarian** adj. demanding strict obedience.
▷ SYNS DICTATORIAL, domineering, tyrannical, strict, despotic, autocratic, imperious, high-handed, bossy.

**authoritative** adj. 1 reliably accurate or true. 2 commanding obedience and respect.
▷ SYNS 1 RELIABLE, accurate, authentic, sound, dependable, definitive, valid. 2 CONFIDENT, self-assured, assertive, commanding, masterful, lordly.

**authority** n. 1 the power to give orders and enforce obedience. 2 a person or organization with official power. 3 official permission. 4 a person with specialized knowledge.
▷ SYNS 1 POWER, jurisdiction, command, control, charge, rule, sovereignty, supremacy; influence, sway. 2 (**authorities**) OFFICIALS, officialdom, government, administration, establishment; inf. the powers that be. 3 RIGHT, authorization, power, mandate, prerogative, licence; permission, consent, sanction, assent, agreement, approval, clearance. 4 EXPERT, specialist, master, pundit.

**authorize** (or **-ise**) v. give official permission for.
■ authorization n.
▷ SYNS PERMIT, allow, agree to, consent to, approve, sanction, endorse, license.

**autism** n. a mental condition in which a person has difficulties with communication and relationships. ■ autistic adj. & n.

**auto-** comb. form 1 self. 2 a person's own.

**autobiography** n. (pl. **-ies**) the story of a person's life written by that person.
■ autobiographical adj.

**autocrat** n. a ruler with unrestricted power. ■ autocracy n. autocratic adj.

**autocue** n. trademark a device displaying a presenter's script on a television screen, unseen by the audience.

**autograph** n. a person's signature. • v. write your name in or on.

**automate** v. convert a machine etc. to automatic operation.
■ automation n.

**automatic** adj. functioning without human intervention; done without thinking. • n. an automatic machine or firearm.
■ automatically adv.
▷ SYNS adj. 1 AUTOMATED, mechanical, mechanized, electronic, computerized, robotic. 2 INSTINCTIVE, spontaneous, involuntary, unconscious, reflex, knee-jerk, unthinking, mechanical.

**automaton** n. (pl. **-tons** or **-ta**) a robot.

**automobile** n. US a car.

**automotive** adj. concerned with motor vehicles.

**autonomous** adj. independent; self-governing.

**autonomy** n. independence and freedom.
▷ SYNS INDEPENDENCE, freedom, self-government, self-determination, self-sufficiency, individualism.

**autopsy** n. (pl. **-ies**) a post-mortem.

**autumn** n. the season between summer and winter.
■ autumnal adj.

**auxiliary** adj. giving help or support. • n. (pl. **-ies**) a helper.
▷ SYNS adj. ADDITIONAL, supplementary, ancillary, extra, reserve, spare, backup.

**avail** v. formal (**avail yourself of**) use or take advantage of. • n. use or benefit.

**available** adj. ready to be used; obtainable. ■ availability n.
▷ SYNS OBTAINABLE, to hand, handy, unoccupied, vacant, at your disposal, ready, convenient, accessible.

**avalanche** n. a mass of snow pouring down a mountain.

**avant-garde** adj. new and experimental.

**avarice** n. greed for wealth.

**avaricious** adj. greedy for wealth.
▷ SYNS GREEDY, grasping, covetous, acquisitive, rapacious.

**avenge** v. take vengeance for. ■ avenger n.

**avenue** n. a wide road, usu. tree-lined; a method of approach.

**aver** v. (**averred, averring**) state as true.

**average** n. a value arrived at by adding several quantities together and dividing by the number of these; a standard regarded as usual. • adj. found by making an average; ordinary or usual.
▷ SYNS n. MEAN, median. • adj. 1 ORDINARY, usual, standard, normal, typical, regular. 2 MEDIOCRE, unexceptional, middling, run of the mill, undistinguished, ordinary, unremarkable.

**averse** adj. strongly disliking or opposed to.
▷ SYNS OPPOSED, hostile, antipathetic, unwilling, disinclined, reluctant, loath.

**aversion** n. a strong dislike.
▷ SYNS DISLIKE, distaste, hatred, repugnance, antipathy; reluctance, unwillingness.

**avert** v. turn away; ward off.
▷ SYNS DEFLECT, ward off, fend off, turn aside/away, parry, stave off, prevent.

**avian** adj. of birds. □ avian flu = BIRD FLU.

**aviary** n. (pl. **-ies**) a large cage or building for keeping birds.

**aviation** n. the practice or science of flying an aircraft. ■ aviator n.

**avid** adj. very interested or enthusiastic.
▷ SYNS KEEN, eager, enthusiastic, fervent, ardent, fanatical, zealous, passionate.

**avocado** n. (pl. **-os**) a pear-shaped tropical fruit.

**avoid** v. keep away from; refrain from. ■ avoidable adj. avoidance n.
▷ SYNS 1 EVADE, keep away from, steer clear of, dodge, give a wide berth to, sidestep; inf. duck, get out of. 2 ABSTAIN FROM, refrain from, eschew.

**avow** v. declare. ■ avowal n.

**avuncular** adj. kind towards a younger person.

**await** v. wait for; be in store for.
▷ SYNS WAIT FOR, expect, anticipate.

**awake** v. (**awoke, awoken, awaking**) wake. • adj. not asleep.

**awaken** v. awake.

**award** v. give by official decision as a prize or penalty. • n. something awarded; awarding.
▷ SYNS v. CONFER, give, grant, bestow, present, endow. • n. 1 PRIZE, trophy, decoration, medal, reward. 2 GRANT, scholarship, bursary.

**aware** adj. having knowledge or realization. ■ awareness n.

▷ SYNS CONSCIOUS, mindful, familiar, informed, acquainted.

**awash** adj. covered or flooded with water.

**away** adv. to or at a distance; into non-existence.

**awe** n. respect combined with fear or wonder. • v. fill with awe.

▷ SYNS n. WONDER, wonderment, amazement, admiration, respect.

**awesome** adj. 1 very impressive or daunting. 2 inf. excellent.

▷ SYNS BREATHTAKING, awe-inspiring, magnificent, impressive, imposing, dramatic, marvellous, amazing, stunning, stupendous.

**awful** adj. 1 extremely bad or unpleasant. 2 very great.
■ **awfully** adv.

**awhile** adv. for a short time.

**awkward** adj. 1 difficult to use, do, or handle; inconvenient; clumsy. 2 uncooperative. 3 embarrassing.

▷ SYNS 1 INCONVENIENT, difficult, troublesome, problematic. 2 UNWIELDY, cumbersome, unmanageable, bulky. 3 CLUMSY, ungainly, uncoordinated, graceless, gawky. 4 UNCOOPERATIVE, unhelpful, disobliging,

contrary, obstructive, perverse; inf. bloody-minded. 5 EMBARRASSING, uncomfortable, tricky, difficult.

**awl** n. a tool for making holes in leather or wood.

**awning** n. a canvas shelter.

**awoke**, **awoken** past & p.p. of AWAKE.

**AWOL** abbr. absent without leave.

**awry** adv. & adj. twisted to one side; wrong or amiss.

**axe** (US usu. **ax**) n. a chopping tool with a heavy blade. • v. (**axed**, **axing**) 1 reduce something by a large amount. 2 dismiss someone ruthlessly.

**axiom** n. an accepted general principle. ■ **axiomatic** adj.

**axis** n. (pl. **axes**) a line through the centre of an object, round which it rotates if spinning.

**axle** n. a rod passing through the centre of a wheel or group of wheels.

**ayatollah** n. a religious leader in Iran.

**aye** exclam. old use or dialect yes.

**azalea** n. a shrub with brightly coloured flowers.

**azure** n. a bright blue colour.

# Bb

**BA** abbr. Bachelor of Arts.

**babble** v. chatter indistinctly or foolishly. • n. babbling talk or sound.

▷ SYNS v. CHATTER, prattle, gabble, jabber.

**babe** n. a baby.

**babel** n. a confused noise.

**baboon** n. a large monkey.

**baby** n. (pl. **-ies**) a very young child or animal; a timid or childish person. • adj. miniature.

▷ SYNS n. INFANT, newborn, child, babe. • adj. MINIATURE, tiny, little, mini, dwarf.

**babyish** adj. childish and immature.
▷ SYNS CHILDISH, infantile, immature, juvenile, puerile.

**babysit** v. (-sat, -sitting) look after a child while its parents are out. ■ **babysitter** n.

**bachelor** n. **1** an unmarried man. **2** used in names of university degrees.

**bacillus** n. (pl. -li) a rod-shaped bacterium.

**back** n. **1** the rear surface of a person's body or the upper part of an animal's body. **2** the side or part furthest from the front. **3** a defending player in a team game. • adv. **1** at or towards the rear. **2** in or into a previous time, position, or state. **3** in return: *ring me back*. • v. **1** give support to. **2** move backwards. **3** lay a bet on. • adj. **1** at or towards the back. **2** relating to the past: *back numbers*. □ **back down** withdraw a claim or argument. **back out** withdraw from a commitment. **back up 1** support. **2** Computing make a spare copy of data or a disk.
▷ SYNS n. **1** SPINE, backbone, spinal column, vertebral column. **2** REAR, stern; end, rear end, tail end; reverse, other side. • v. **1** SUPPORT, uphold, sanction, endorse, champion; sponsor, finance, underwrite. **2** REVERSE, back off, retreat, withdraw, backtrack. • adj. **1** REAR, hind, end, hindmost, last. **2** PAST, old, previous, earlier.

**backbiting** n. spiteful talk.

**backbone** n. the column of small bones down the centre of the back.

**backdate** v. declare to be valid from a previous date.

**backdrop** (or **backcloth**) n. a painted cloth at the back of a theatre stage.

**backer** n. a supporter.
▷ SYNS SUPPORTER, champion; sponsor, promoter, patron, underwriter; inf. angel.

**backfire** v. **1** make an explosion in an exhaust pipe. **2** produce an undesired effect.

**backgammon** n. a board game played with draughts and dice.

**background** n. the back part of a scene or picture; the circumstances surrounding something.
▷ SYNS SURROUNDINGS, setting, context, circumstances, conditions, framework, environment.

**backhand** n. (in tennis etc.) a backhanded stroke.

**backhanded** adj. **1** performed with the back of the hand turned forwards. **2** expressed in an indirect or ambiguous way.

**backing** n. **1** support. **2** music or singing accompanying a pop singer.

**backlash** n. a hostile reaction.

**backlog** n. arrears of work.

**backpack** n. a rucksack.

**backside** n. inf. the buttocks.

**backslide** v. return to bad ways.
▷ SYNS RELAPSE, lapse, regress, weaken.

**backstage** adj. & adv. behind a theatre stage.

**backstroke** n. a swimming stroke performed on the back.

**backtrack** v. retrace your route; reverse your opinion.

**backward** adj. **1** directed towards the back. **2** having made less than normal progress. • adv. (also **backwards**) **1** towards the back or back towards the start. **2** in reverse.

**backwash** n. receding waves created by a ship etc.

**backwater** n. **1** a stretch of stagnant water on a river. **2** a place where change happens very slowly.

**backwoods** pl.n. a remote area.

**bacon** n. salted or smoked meat from a pig.

**bacteria** pl.n. (sing. **bacterium**) a group of microscopic organisms. ■ **bacterial** adj.

**bad** adj. **1** poor in quality. **2** unpleasant. **3** serious. **4** wicked. **5** harmful. **6** (of food) decayed.
▷ SYNS **1** POOR, inadequate, unsatisfactory, substandard, inferior, defective, deficient, faulty, incompetent, secondrate, inept, shoddy, awful, terrible, dreadful, frightful; inf. hopeless, lousy. **2** *bad weather:* UNPLEASANT, disagreeable, nasty, horrid, horrible, foul, appalling, atrocious. **3** *a bad accident:* SERIOUS, severe, grave, dangerous, disastrous, calamitous, dire. **4** *a bad character:* IMMORAL, wicked, evil, corrupt, sinful, criminal, depraved, villainous, dishonest, dishonourable, base. **5** *bad behaviour:* NAUGHTY, mischievous, unruly, wayward, disobedient. **6** *the meat's bad:* ROTTEN, decayed, mouldy, off, rancid, sour, putrid.

**bade** past of **BID**².

**badge** n. something worn to show membership, rank, etc.
▷ SYNS EMBLEM, crest, insignia; sign, mark, symbol.

**badger** n. a large burrowing animal with a black and white striped head. • v. pester.
▷ SYNS v. PESTER, bother, plague, nag, harass, torment, persecute.

**badly** adv. **1** in an unsatisfactory or undesirable way. **2** very intensely.

**badminton** n. a game played with rackets and a shuttlecock over a high net.

**baffle** v. be too difficult for; frustrate. ■ **bafflement** n.
▷ SYNS BEWILDER, bemuse, mystify, perplex, puzzle, confuse, confound, nonplus, floor, bamboozle; inf. flummox, stump.

**bag** n. **1** a flexible container; a handbag. **2** (**bags**) inf. a large amount. • v. (**bagged**, **bagging**) take or reserve for yourself.
▷ SYNS n. HANDBAG, shoulder bag; case, suitcase, grip, satchel, holdall, rucksack. • v. **1** CATCH, capture, shoot, kill, trap, snare, land. **2** GET, gain, acquire, obtain, reserve, secure, get hold of.

**bagatelle** n. **1** a board game in which balls are hit into numbered holes. **2** something unimportant.

**baggage** n. luggage.
▷ SYNS LUGGAGE, bags, cases, belongings, things.

**baggy** adj. (**-ier, -iest**) hanging in loose folds.

**bagpipes** pl.n. a musical instrument with pipes sounded by squeezing air from a bag.

**bail** (*see also* **BALE**) n. **1** money pledged as security that an accused person will return for trial. **2** each of two crosspieces resting on the stumps in cricket. • v. **1** (also **bale**) scoop water out of. **2** (**bail out**) obtain or allow the release of a person on bail; relieve by financial help.

**bailiff** n. a law officer empowered to seize goods for non-payment of fines or debts.

**bait** n. food put on a hook or in a trap to catch fish or other animals. • v. **1** taunt or tease. **2** place bait on or in.
▷ SYNS n. ENTICEMENT, lure, snare, trap, attraction, temptation, incentive, inducement, carrot. • v. TEASE, taunt, torment, plague, persecute, harass.

**baize** n. thick green woollen cloth.

**bake** v. cook or harden by dry heat. □ **baking powder** a mixture used to make cakes rise.

**baker** n. a person who bakes or sells bread. ■ **bakery** n.

**balaclava** n. a woollen cap covering the head and neck.

**balalaika** n. a Russian guitar-like instrument.

**balance** n. **1** an even distribution of weight. **2** a situation in which elements are in the correct proportions. **3** the difference between credits and debits in an account. **4** an amount still owed after paying part of a debt. **5** a device for weighing. • v. **1** be or put in a steady position. **2** compare.
▷ SYNS n. **1** STABILITY, steadiness, equilibrium, footing. **2** CORRESPONDENCE, equivalence, symmetry, equality, parity, proportion, evenness. **3** REMAINDER, rest, difference, residue.

• v. **1** STEADY, stabilize, poise. **2** WEIGH UP, compare, evaluate, assess. **3** COUNTERBALANCE, offset, counteract, compensate for, make up for.

**balcony** n. (pl. **-ies**) a projecting platform with a rail or parapet; the upper floor of seats in a theatre etc.

**bald** adj. **1** having no hair on the head; (of tyres) with the tread worn away. **2** without details. ■ **balding** adj.
▷ SYNS **1** HAIRLESS, bare, smooth. **2** PLAIN, simple, unadorned, straightforward, forthright, frank, direct, blunt, stark.

**bale** (see also **BAIL**) n. a large bound bundle of straw etc. • v. make into bales. □ **bale out** (or **bail out**) make an emergency parachute jump from an aircraft.

**baleful** adj. menacing. ■ **balefully** adv.

**balk** = BAULK.

**ball** n. **1** a rounded object used in games. **2** a throw or kick of the ball in a game. **3** a rounded part or thing. **4** a formal social gathering for dancing. □ **ball bearing** a ring of small metal balls reducing friction between moving parts of a machine, or one of these balls. **ballcock** a valve controlling the water level in a cistern. **ballpoint pen** a pen with a tiny ball as its writing point. **ballroom** a large room for formal dancing.
▷ SYNS SPHERE, globe, orb, globule.

**ballad** n. a song telling a story.

**ballast** n. heavy material placed in a ship's hold to steady it; coarse stones used as the base of a railway or road.

**ballet** n. an artistic dance form performed to music. ■ **ballerina** n.

**ballistics** n. the study of projectiles and firearms.

**balloon** n. **1** a small inflatable rubber bag used as a toy or decoration. **2** (or **hot-air balloon**) a large bag filled with hot air or gas to make it rise, with a basket for carrying passengers. • v. swell or increase.

**ballot** n. a vote recorded on a slip of paper; voting by this. • v. (**balloted**, **balloting**) ask to vote by ballot.
▷ SYNS n. VOTE, poll, election, referendum, plebiscite.

**balm** n. a fragrant ointment; a soothing influence.

**balmy** adj. (**-ier**, **-iest**) (of air or weather) pleasantly warm.

**balsa** n. lightweight wood from a tropical American tree.

**balsam** n. a scented resin used in perfumes and medicines.

**baluster** n. a short pillar in a balustrade.

**balustrade** n. a row of short pillars supporting a rail or coping.

**bamboo** n. a giant tropical grass with hollow stems.

**bamboozle** v. inf. cheat or deceive someone.

**ban** v. (**banned**, **banning**) forbid officially. • n. an order banning something.
▷ SYNS v. PROHIBIT, forbid, veto, outlaw, proscribe, interdict, bar, debar, exclude, banish. • n. PROHIBITION, veto, embargo, moratorium, boycott, bar, proscription.

**banal** adj. commonplace or uninteresting. ■ **banality** n.

▷ SYNS TRITE, clichéd, hackneyed, commonplace, unoriginal, unimaginative, stale, boring, dull, stock, stereotyped, platitudinous; inf. corny, old hat.

**banana** n. a curved yellow fruit.

**band** n. **1** a piece of material used as a fastener. **2** a stripe or strip. **3** a range of values within a series. **4** a group of musicians. **5** a group of people with a common purpose. □ **bandstand** a covered outdoor platform for a band playing music. **bandwagon** an activity or cause that has suddenly become fashionable or popular.
▷ SYNS **1** GROUP, troop, troupe, crowd, crew, gang, company, body, pack, bunch. **2** GROUP, orchestra, ensemble. **3** STRIPE, strip, line, belt, bar, streak, swathe.

**bandage** n. a strip of material for binding a wound. • v. bind with this.

**bandanna** n. a square of cloth worn on the head or around the neck.

**bandit** n. a member of a gang of robbers.
▷ SYNS ROBBER, thief, outlaw, looter, marauder, brigand; dated desperado.

**bandy** adj. (**-ier**, **-iest**) (of a person's legs) curving apart at the knees. • v. (**bandied**, **bandying**) spread an idea or rumour. □ **bandy words** exchange angry remarks.
▷ SYNS adj. bandy legs: BOWED, curved, bent, bow-legged. • v. **1** bandy words: EXCHANGE, swap, trade. **2** bandy rumours about: SPREAD, circulate, pass on, disseminate.

**bane** n. a cause of annoyance or misfortune.

**bang** n. 1 a sudden loud sharp noise. 2 a sharp blow. • v. 1 hit or put down forcefully or noisily. 2 make a banging noise.
▷ SYNS n. 1 CRASH, clang, thud, clunk; boom, blast, report, explosion. 2 BLOW, bump, knock, slap, punch, thump, smack, hit; inf. whack.

**banger** n. inf. 1 a sausage. 2 an old car. 3 a firework that explodes noisily.

**bangle** n. a bracelet of rigid material.

**banish** v. condemn to exile; dismiss from your presence or thoughts. ■ banishment n.
▷ SYNS 1 EXILE, expel, exclude, deport, expatriate, ostracize, eject, evict, outlaw, oust. 2 DISMISS, drive away, dispel, get rid of, suppress.

**banisters** (or **bannisters**) pl.n. the uprights and handrail of a staircase.

**banjo** n. (pl. **-os**) a guitar-like musical instrument with a circular body.

**bank** n. 1 a slope, esp. at the side of a river; a raised mass of earth etc. 2 a row of lights, switches, etc. 3 an establishment for safe keeping of money; a stock or store. • v. 1 build up into a mound or bank. 2 tilt sideways. 3 place money in a bank. 4 (**bank on**) rely on. □ bank holiday a public holiday. banknote a piece of paper money.
▷ SYNS n. 1 SLOPE, mound, embankment, hillock, incline, ridge, rise, pile, mass. 2 EDGE, shore, brink, side, margin, embankment. 3 STORE, reserve, supply, fund, stock, hoard, repository, pool, reservoir. 4 ROW, array, panel, tier.

**bankrupt** adj. & n. (a person) unable to pay their debts. • v. make bankrupt. ■ bankruptcy n.
▷ SYNS adj. & n. INSOLVENT, ruined, in liquidation, destitute, penniless; inf. broke, bust.

**banner** n. a flag; a piece of cloth bearing a slogan.
▷ SYNS FLAG, standard, pennant, pennon, colours, ensign, streamer.

**banns** pl.n. an announcement of a forthcoming marriage.

**banquet** n. an elaborate ceremonial meal.
▷ SYNS FEAST, repast, dinner; inf. blowout, spread.

**banshee** n. a spirit whose wail is said to foretell a death.

**bantam** n. a small chicken.

**banter** n. good-humoured joking. • v. joke in this way.
▷ SYNS n. REPARTEE, badinage, raillery, teasing, joking.

**bap** n. a large soft bread roll.

**baptism** n. a Christian ceremony of sprinkling with water as a sign of purification, usu. with name-giving. ■ baptize v.

**Baptist** n. a member of a Protestant sect believing in adult baptism by total immersion in water.

**bar** n. 1 a length of solid rigid material. 2 a stripe. 3 a counter or room where alcohol is served. 4 a barrier. 5 one of the short units into which a piece of music is divided. 6 (**the Bar**) barristers or their profession. 7 a unit of atmospheric pressure. • v. 1 fasten with bars. 2 forbid or exclude; obstruct. • prep. apart from. □ bar code a

pattern of printed stripes used as a machine-readable code.
▷ SYNS n. 1 BEAM, rod, pole, shaft, stake, stick, spar, rail. 2 BARRIER, obstacle, obstruction, impediment, hindrance, check, deterrent, problem, difficulty. 3 BAND, stripe, belt, strip, streak, line. 4 *bar of chocolate:* CAKE, slab, block, brick, wedge; ingot. 5 PUB, public house, inn, tavern. • v. 1 EXCLUDE, ban, banish, keep out, prohibit, forbid, outlaw, ostracize, proscribe. 2 BLOCK, obstruct, check, impede, prevent.

**barb** n. 1 a backward-pointing part of an arrow, fish hook, etc. 2 a wounding remark.

**barbarian** n. an uncivilized person.
▷ SYNS SAVAGE, brute, ruffian, hooligan, lout; inf. yob.

**barbaric** adj. 1 primitive. 2 savagely cruel. ■ **barbarity** n. **barbarous** adj.
▷ SYNS 1 UNCIVILIZED, primitive, wild, unsophisticated, crude, brutish. 2 CRUEL, brutal, savage, bestial, barbarous, vicious, ferocious.

**barbecue** n. an open-air party where food is cooked on a frame above an open fire; this frame. • v. cook on a barbecue.

**barbed** adj. having barbs; (of a remark) hurtful.

**barber** n. a men's hairdresser.

**barbiturate** n. a sedative drug.

**bard** n. lit. a poet.

**bare** adj. 1 not clothed or covered. 2 without the usual covering or contents. 3 without detail; basic. 4 just sufficient. • v. reveal. □ **bareback** on horseback without a saddle.

**barefaced** done openly and without shame.
▷ SYNS adj. 1 NAKED, nude, undressed, stripped; inf. starkers. 2 *a bare room:* EMPTY, unfurnished, plain, undecorated, austere. 3 *the bare facts:* BASIC, essential, fundamental, plain, simple, pure, stark, bald. 4 *a bare minimum:* MERE, minimum, paltry, meagre, scanty. • v. REVEAL, uncover, expose, lay bare; strip.

**barely** adv. only just.
▷ SYNS HARDLY, scarcely, just, narrowly, by the skin of your teeth.

**bargain** n. 1 an agreement where each side does something for the other. 2 something obtained cheaply. • v. 1 discuss the terms of an agreement. 2 (**bargain on/for**) rely on, expect.
▷ SYNS n. AGREEMENT, deal, pact, contract, arrangement, understanding, promise, pledge. • v. 1 NEGOTIATE, haggle, barter, argue. 2 (**bargain on/ for**) EXPECT, allow for, anticipate, be prepared for, take into account.

**barge** n. a large flat-bottomed boat used on rivers and canals. • v. (**barge in**) intrude.

**baritone** n. a male voice between tenor and bass.

**barium** n. a white metallic element.

**bark** n. 1 a sharp harsh sound made by a dog. 2 the outer layer of a tree. • v. 1 make a barking sound; say in a sharp commanding voice. 2 scrape skin off a limb accidentally.

**barley** n. a cereal plant; its grain.

**barmy** adj. (**-ier, -iest**) inf. crazy.

**barn** n. a large farm building for storing grain etc.

**barnacle** n. a shellfish that attaches itself to objects under water.

**barometer** n. an instrument measuring atmospheric pressure, used in forecasting weather. ■ **barometric** adj.

**baron** n. **1** a man belonging to the lowest rank of the British nobility. **2** an influential businessman. ■ **baronial** adj.

**baroness** n. **1** a baron's wife or widow. **2** a woman of the rank of baron.

**baronet** n. the holder of a hereditary title below a baron but above a knight.

**baroque** adj. of the ornate architectural or musical style of the 17th-18th centuries; complicated or elaborate.

**barque** n. a sailing ship.

**barrack** v. shout insults at a performer or speaker. • pl.n. (**barracks**) buildings for housing soldiers.

**barrage** n. **1** a continuous artillery attack. **2** a large number of questions or complaints. **3** an artificial barrier across a river.
▷ SYNS **1** BOMBARDMENT, shelling, salvo, volley; hist. broadside. **2** *a barrage of criticism:* TORRENT, stream, storm, deluge, flood, tide.

**barrel** n. **1** a cylindrical container with flat ends. **2** a tube forming part of a gun, pen, etc.
▷ SYNS CASK, keg, vat, butt, tun, hogshead.

**barren** adj. **1** (of land) not fertile. **2** unable to bear young. **3** bleak and lifeless.
▷ SYNS *barren land:* INFERTILE, unproductive, unfruitful, desert, arid, bare, bleak, desolate, lifeless, empty.

**barricade** n. a barrier. • v. block or defend with a barricade.
▷ SYNS n. see **BARRIER**. • V. BLOCK OFF, blockade, bar, obstruct; fortify, defend.

**barrier** n. something that prevents advance or access.
▷ SYNS **1** BAR, fence, railing, barricade, blockade, roadblock. **2** OBSTACLE, obstruction, hurdle, hindrance, impediment, bar, stumbling block.

**barring** prep. except for, apart from.

**barrister** n. a lawyer representing clients in court.

**barrow** n. **1** a two-wheeled cart pushed or pulled by hand. **2** a prehistoric burial mound.

**barter** v. exchange goods or services for other goods or services. • n. trading by bartering.
▷ SYNS v. SWAP, exchange, trade; haggle, bargain, negotiate.

**basalt** n. a dark volcanic rock.

**base** n. **1** the lowest part; a part on which a thing rests or is supported; a starting point. **2** headquarters; a centre of organization. **3** a substance capable of combining with an acid to form a salt. **4** each of four stations to be reached by a batter in baseball. **5** the number on which a system of counting is based. • v. make something the foundation or supporting evidence for. • adj. dishonourable; of inferior value.
□ **baseless** not based on fact; untrue. **baseball** a team game played with a bat and ball on a circuit of four bases, which a batter must run around to score.

▷ SYNS **n. 1** FOUNDATION, foot, bottom, support, stand, pedestal, plinth, rest, substructure. **2** BASIS, core, fundamentals, essence, essentials, root, heart, source, origin, mainspring. **3** HEADQUARTERS, centre, camp, station, post, starting point.
• v. **1** FOUND, build, support, rest, ground, construct, establish. **2** based in London: LOCATE, station, centre, situate, place.
• adj. IGNOBLE, dishonourable, mean, low, sordid, contemptible, shameful, shabby, despicable, unworthy, disreputable, unprincipled, immoral, evil, wicked, sinful.

**basement** n. a storey below ground level.

**bash** inf. v. hit violently. • n. a violent blow.

**bashful** adj. shy and easily embarrassed.

**basic** adj. **1** forming an essential foundation. **2** consisting of the minimum needed or offered.
■ **basically** adv.
▷ SYNS **1** FUNDAMENTAL, essential, intrinsic, primary, key, indispensable, vital. **2** PLAIN, simple, austere, spartan, unadorned, stark, minimal.

**basil** n. a sweet-smelling herb.

**basin** n. **1** a washbasin. **2** a round open container for food or liquid; a sunken place where water collects; an area drained by a river.
▷ SYNS BOWL, dish, pan, container, receptacle.

**basis** n. **1** a foundation or support. **2** a system of proceeding: on a regular basis.
▷ SYNS **1** FOUNDATION, base, grounding, support. **2** STARTING POINT, beginning, point of

departure, cornerstone, core, essence, heart, thrust. **3** a regular basis: FOOTING, position, arrangement, condition, status; system, way, method.

**bask** v. sit or lie in the sun for pleasure.
▷ SYNS LIE, laze, relax, sunbathe, lounge, loll; wallow, luxuriate, revel, delight, relish, lap up.

**basket** n. a container for holding or carrying things, made of interwoven cane or wire. □ **basketball** a team game in which goals are scored by throwing a ball through a hoop.

**bass**¹ adj. deep-sounding; of the lowest pitch in music. • n. the lowest male voice.

**bass**² n. (pl. **bass**) an edible fish.

**bassoon** n. a large bass woodwind instrument.

**bastard** n. **1** old use an illegitimate child. **2** inf. an unpleasant person.

**baste** v. **1** moisten with fat during cooking. **2** sew together temporarily with loose stitches.

**bastion** n. a projecting part of a fortified place; a stronghold.

**bat** n. **1** a wooden implement for hitting the ball in games. **2** a flying mammal that is active at night. • v. (**batted**, **batting**) **1** (in sport) take the role of hitting the ball. **2** hit with the flat of the hand. □ **batsman** a player who bats in cricket.

**batch** n. a set of people or things dealt with as a group.
▷ SYNS SET, group, lot, collection, bunch, quantity, pack.

**bated** adj. (**with bated breath**) in great suspense.

**bath** n. **1** a large tub filled with water for washing the body. **2** an act of washing in a bath.

**3** (also **baths**) a public swimming pool. • v. wash in a bath. □ **bathroom** a room with a bath, washbasin, toilet, etc.

**bathe** v. **1** wash by immersing the body in water. **2** take a swim. **3** soak or wipe gently with liquid. • n. a swim.
▷ SYNS v. **1** WASH, clean, cleanse, rinse, soak, wipe. **2** SWIM, go swimming, take a dip.

**baton** n. **1** a thin stick used to conduct an orchestra or choir. **2** a short stick passed from runner to runner in a relay race.
▷ SYNS STICK, rod, staff, wand.

**battalion** n. an army unit of several companies.

**batten** n. a long wooden or metal strip for strengthening or securing something.

**batter** v. hit hard and repeatedly. • n. **1** a mixture of flour, eggs, and milk or water, used in cooking. **2** a player batting in baseball.
▷ SYNS v. BEAT, hit, strike, bash, bludgeon, belabour, pound.

**battery** n. (pl. **-ies**) **1** a device containing and supplying electric power. **2** a group of big guns. **3** a set of similar or connected units of equipment; a series of small cages for intensive rearing of livestock. **4** an unlawful blow or touch.

**battle** n. **1** a prolonged fight between organized armed forces. **2** a long and difficult struggle. • v. fight or struggle with determination.
□ **battleaxe 1** a large axe used in ancient warfare. **2** inf. an aggressive woman. **battlement** a parapet with gaps for firing through. **battleship** a large, heavily armoured warship.

▷ SYNS n. CONFLICT, fight, clash, skirmish, fray, war, campaign, combat, action, hostilities, struggle.

**battlefield** n. the scene of a battle.
▷ SYNS BATTLEGROUND, front, combat zone, theatre of war.

**batty** adj. (**-ier, -iest**) inf. mad.

**bauble** n. a showy trinket or decoration.

**baulk** (or **balk**) v. be reluctant; hinder.

**bauxite** n. a mineral from which aluminium is obtained.

**bawdy** adj. (**-ier, -iest**) dealing with sex in an amusing way.
▷ SYNS RIBALD, risqué, racy, rude, earthy, suggestive, titillating, naughty, indecent; inf. raunchy.

**bawl** v. **1** shout. **2** weep noisily.
▷ SYNS **1** SHOUT, yell, roar, bellow, scream. **2** CRY, sob, weep, wail, whine, howl.

**bay** n. **1** part of the sea within a wide curve of the shore. **2** a recess. **3** a laurel, esp. a type used as a herb. • v. (of a dog) give a deep howling cry. • adj. (of a horse) reddish brown. □ **at bay** forced to face attackers.
▷ SYNS n. **1** COVE, inlet, gulf, basin, arm, bight, creek, fjord, estuary. **2** ALCOVE, recess, niche, opening, nook.

**bayonet** n. a stabbing blade fixed to a rifle.

**bazaar** n. **1** a market in an eastern country. **2** a sale of goods to raise funds.
▷ SYNS **1** MARKET, mart, souk. **2** FÊTE, fair, bring-and-buy sale.

**bazooka** n. a portable weapon firing anti-tank rockets.

**BBC** abbr. British Broadcasting Corporation.

**BC** abbr. before Christ (used to show that a date comes the specified number of years before the traditional date of Jesus's birth).

**be** v. 1 exist; occur; be present. 2 have a specified quality, position, or condition. • v.aux. used to form tenses of other verbs.

**beach** n. the shore. • v. bring on shore from water.
▷ SYNS n. SHORE, strand, seashore, sands, seaside.

**beacon** n. 1 a fire lit on a hill as a signal. 2 a light acting as a signal for ships or aircraft.

**bead** n. a small shaped piece of hard material pierced for threading with others on a string; a rounded drop of liquid.
▷ SYNS *beads of sweat:* DROP, droplet, globule, drip, blob, dot, dewdrop.

**beady** adj. (-ier, -iest) (of eyes) small, round, and observant.

**beagle** n. a small hound.

**beak** n. 1 a bird's horny projecting jaws. 2 inf. a magistrate or schoolmaster.

**beaker** n. 1 a tall plastic cup. 2 a glass container used in laboratories.
▷ SYNS CUP, mug, glass, tumbler.

**beam** n. 1 a long piece of timber or metal carrying the weight of part of a building. 2 a ray of light or other radiation. 3 a ship's breadth. • v. 1 send out radio signals. 2 shine brightly; smile radiantly.
▷ SYNS n. 1 BAR, spar, rafter, girder, support, boom, plank, board, joist, timber. 2 RAY, shaft, stream, streak, pencil, gleam. • v. 1 EMIT, radiate, shine,

broadcast, transmit, direct. 2 SMILE, grin.

**bean** n. an edible seed growing in long pods on certain plants; the seed of a coffee or cocoa plant.

**bear¹** n. a large, heavy mammal with thick fur.

**bear²** v. 1 carry; support; shoulder responsibilities etc. 2 endure or tolerate. 3 produce children, young, or fruit. 4 take a specified direction.
▷ SYNS 1 HOLD, support, carry, sustain, prop up, shoulder. 2 BRING, carry, transport, convey, fetch, deliver, move, take. 3 ENDURE, tolerate, abide, stand, cope with, stomach, put up with; formal brook. 4 PRODUCE, yield, give, supply, provide.

**bearable** adj. able to be endured.
▷ SYNS ENDURABLE, tolerable, supportable, sustainable.

**beard** n. a growth of hair on a man's chin. • v. boldly confront an important person.

**bearing** n. 1 a way of standing, moving, or behaving. 2 relevance. 3 a compass direction. 4 a device in a machine reducing friction where a part turns.
▷ SYNS 1 CARRIAGE, deportment, posture, stance, gait, demeanour, air, behaviour, manner. 2 RELEVANCE, pertinence, connection, significance, relation, application.

**beast** n. 1 a large animal. 2 an unpleasant person or thing.
▷ SYNS 1 ANIMAL, creature, brute. 2 BRUTE, monster, fiend, devil, ogre.

**beastly** adj. inf. very unpleasant.

**beat** v. **1** hit repeatedly. **2** move or pulsate rhythmically. **3** defeat or outdo. **4** mix cooking ingredients vigorously. • n. **1** an act of beating. **2** a main accent in music or poetry. **3** an area regularly patrolled by a policeman. ☐ **beat up** hit repeatedly.
▷ SYNS v. **1** HIT, strike, batter, thrash, slap, whip, cuff, cane, smack, thump, pound, flog; inf. bash, whack, clout, wallop. **2** PULSATE, throb, pound, palpitate, thump, vibrate. **3** DEFEAT, outdo, conquer, trounce, vanquish, overcome, subdue, outclass. **4** WHISK, whip, stir, blend, mix. • n. **1** PULSATION, vibration, throbbing, pounding, palpitation. **2** RHYTHM, tempo, metre, measure, time.

**beautician** n. a person who gives beauty treatments.

**beautiful** adj. **1** very pleasing to the senses. **2** excellent.
■ **beautifully** adv.
▷ SYNS LOVELY, attractive, pretty, gorgeous, ravishing, stunning, good-looking, exquisite; picturesque, scenic; Scot. & N. Engl. bonny; old use fair, comely.

**beautify** v. make beautiful.
▷ SYNS ADORN, embellish, decorate, prettify; inf. do up, titivate.

**beauty** n. **1** the quality of being very pleasing to the senses. **2** a beautiful person. **3** an excellent example.
▷ SYNS ATTRACTIVENESS, loveliness, prettiness, good looks, glamour; old use comeliness.

**beaver** n. an amphibious rodent that builds dams. • v. (**beaver away**) work hard.

**becalmed** adj. (of a sailing ship) unable to move through lack of wind.

**because** conj. for the reason that.
▷ SYNS SINCE, as, for the reason that, seeing that/as.

**beck** n. (**at someone's beck and call**) doing whatever someone asks.

**beckon** v. make a summoning gesture.
▷ SYNS GESTURE, signal, wave, gesticulate, motion.

**become** v. **1** turn into; begin to be. **2** suit; befit.
▷ SYNS **1** TURN INTO, grow into, develop into; grow, get, come to be. **2** SUIT, flatter, look good on; befit, behove.

**becoming** adj. (of clothing) looking good on someone.
▷ SYNS FLATTERING, fetching, attractive, elegant, stylish.

**bed** n. **1** a piece of furniture for sleeping on. **2** a flat base or foundation. **3** an area of ground where flowers are grown.
☐ **bedclothes** sheets, blankets, etc. **bedpan** a container used as a toilet by a bedridden person. **bedridden** confined to bed due to illness or old age. **bedrock** a layer of solid rock under soil; the central principles on which something is based. **bedroom** a room for sleeping in. **bedsit** (or **bedsitter**) a rented room combining a bedroom and living room. **bedsore** a sore caused by lying in bed in one position for a long time. **bedspread** a decorative bed covering. **bedstead** the framework of a bed.

**bedding** n. bedclothes.

**bedevil** v. (**bedevilled**, **bedevilling**; US **bedeviled**) cause continual trouble to.

**bedlam** n. a scene of uproar.

**bedraggled** adj. dishevelled and untidy.
▷ SYNS DISHEVELLED, untidy, unkempt, messy, disarranged.

**bee** n. an insect that produces honey. □ **beehive** a structure in which bees are kept. **make a beeline for** hurry straight to. **beeswax** wax produced by bees to make honeycombs, used in polishes etc.

**beech** n. a tree with smooth bark and glossy leaves.

**beef** n. meat from a cow, bull, or ox. • v. (**beef up**) inf. make stronger or larger. □ **beefburger** a fried or grilled cake of minced beef. **beefeater** a warder in the Tower of London.

**beefy** adj. (**-ier, -iest**) inf. muscular or strong.

**beep** n. a high-pitched sound made by electronic equipment or a car horn. • v. make a beep.

**beer** n. an alcoholic drink made from malt and hops.

**beet** n. a plant with a fleshy root used as a vegetable (**beetroot**) or for making sugar (**sugar beet**).

**beetle** n. an insect with hard wing covers.

**beetroot** n. the edible dark red root of a beet.

**befall** v. (**befell, befallen, befalling**) happen to.
▷ SYNS HAPPEN TO, occur, take place, come about, come to pass, transpire; lit. betide.

**befit** v. (**befitted, befitting**) be appropriate for.

**before** adv. & prep. & conj. during the time preceding; in front of; in preference to.
▷ SYNS 1 EARLIER, previously, beforehand, in advance, formerly, ahead. 2 PRIOR TO,

previous to, earlier than, in advance of, leading up to. 3 IN FRONT OF, in the presence of, in the sight of. 4 RATHER THAN, in preference to, sooner than.

**beforehand** adv. in advance.

**befriend** v. be supportive and friendly towards.

**befuddled** adj. confused.
▷ SYNS CONFUSED, bemused, dazed, bewildered, muddled, groggy.

**beg** v. (**begged, begging**) ask humbly for something; ask for food or money as charity.
▷ SYNS 1 PLEAD, entreat, ask, seek, beseech, implore, supplicate. 2 ASK FOR MONEY; inf. cadge, scrounge.

**beget** v. (**begot, begotten, begetting**) be the father of; give rise to.
▷ SYNS 1 FATHER, sire, spawn. 2 PRODUCE, give rise to, bring about, cause, result in, lead to.

**beggar** n. a person who lives by begging for food or money.
▷ SYNS TRAMP, vagrant, down-and-out; inf. scrounger, sponger.

**begin** v. 1 carry out or experience the first part of an action or activity. 2 come into being.
▷ SYNS 1 START, commence, set about, embark on, initiate, establish, institute, inaugurate, found, pioneer. 2 ARISE, emerge, appear, occur, happen, originate, materialize, spring up.

**beginner** n. a person just starting to learn a skill or take part in an activity.
▷ SYNS NOVICE, learner, trainee, apprentice, new recruit.

**beginning** n. the point at which something begins.
▷ SYNS 1 START, origin, commencement, outset, dawn, rise, birth,

inception, emergence, genesis. **2** PRELUDE, introduction, preface, opening.

**begonia** n. a plant with brightly coloured flowers.

**begrudge** v. feel envious; give reluctantly.

**beguile** v. charm or trick.
▷ SYNS CHARM, attract, delight, enchant, bewitch, please; lure, seduce, tempt, deceive, trick.

**behalf** n. (**on behalf of**) as the representative of; in the interests of.

**behave** v. **1** act in a specified way. **2** (also **behave yourself**) show good manners.
▷ SYNS **1** ACT, conduct yourself, acquit yourself. **2** BE GOOD, be polite, mind your manners.

**behaviour** (US **behavior**) n. a way of behaving.
▷ SYNS CONDUCT, actions, deportment, manners.

**behead** v. cut off the head of.

**behest** n. (**at the behest of**) at the request or order of.

**behind** adv. & prep. **1** in or to the rear of; following; less advanced than. **2** remaining after. **3** supporting. **4** late; in arrears.

**behold** v. (**beheld**, **beholding**) old use see or observe.

**beholden** adj. indebted.

**beige** n. a light fawn colour.

**being** n. **1** existence. **2** a living creature.
▷ SYNS **1** EXISTENCE, life, actuality, reality. **2** CREATURE, living thing, person, individual, human, mortal.

**belated** adj. coming late or too late.
▷ SYNS LATE, overdue, delayed, tardy, behind time.

**belch** v. noisily expel wind from the stomach through the mouth. • n. an act of belching.

**beleaguered** adj. in difficulties; under siege.

**belfry** n. (pl. **-ies**) a space for bells in a tower.

**belie** v. (**belied**, **belying**) contradict, fail to give a true idea of.

**belief** n. something believed; religious faith.
▷ SYNS **1** OPINION, judgement, view, thought, feeling, conviction, way of thinking, theory, notion, impression. **2** FAITH, creed, credo, doctrine, dogma, persuasion, tenet, teaching, ideology.

**believe** v. **1** accept as true or as speaking truth. **2** (**believe in**) have faith in the truth or existence of. **3** think or suppose.
■ **believer** n.
▷ SYNS **1** ACCEPT, be convinced by, trust; inf. swallow, buy, fall for. **2** THINK, hold, suppose, reckon, be of the opinion, imagine, understand.

**belittle** v. disparage.
▷ SYNS DISPARAGE, denigrate, run down, deprecate, make light of, detract from.

**bell** n. **1** a cup-shaped metal instrument that makes a ringing sound when struck. **2** a device that buzzes or rings to give a signal.

**belle** n. a beautiful woman.

**bellicose** adj. eager to fight.

**belligerent** adj. **1** aggressive. **2** engaged in a war.
■ **belligerence** n.

**bellow** n. a deep shout or noise. • v. make this sound.

**bellows** pl.n. a device for blowing air into a fire.

**belly** n. (pl. **-ies**) the abdomen; the stomach.

**belong** v. 1 (**belong to**) be owned by; be a member of. 2 be rightly placed or assigned; fit in a particular environment.
▷ SYNS 1 BE OWNED BY, be the property of. 2 BE A MEMBER OF, be in, be associated with, be affiliated to. 3 FIT IN, be suited, be at home, be accepted.

**belongings** pl.n. personal possessions.
▷ SYNS POSSESSIONS, effects, goods, property, chattels; inf. stuff, things.

**beloved** adj. dearly loved.
▷ SYNS LOVED, adored, dear, dearest, cherished, treasured, prized, precious, darling.

**below** adv. & prep. at a lower level than.

**belt** n. a strip of cloth or leather etc. worn round the waist; a long narrow strip or region. • v. 1 put a belt round. 2 inf. hit.
▷ SYNS n. 1 SASH, strap, girdle, waistband, cummerbund. 2 STRIP, stretch, band, region, zone, area, tract.

**bemoan** v. complain about.

**bemused** adj. bewildered.
▷ SYNS BEWILDERED, confused, puzzled, perplexed, baffled, befuddled, disconcerted.

**bench** n. 1 a long seat for several people; a long work table. 2 (**the bench**) the office of judge or magistrate. ▢ **benchmark** a standard against which things may be compared.

**bend** v. (**bent, bending**) make or become curved; stoop; distort rules. • n. a curve or turn.
▷ SYNS v. 1 CURVE, twist, turn, curl, veer, loop, wind. 2 STOOP, lean, crouch, bow, hunch. • n. CURVE,

corner, turn, twist, arc, loop, crook.

**beneath** adv. & prep. below or underneath; not worthy of.

**benefactor** n. a person who gives financial or other help.
▷ SYNS HELPER, supporter, sponsor, patron, backer, donor; inf. angel.

**benefice** n. an arrangement by which a Christian priest is paid and given accommodation in return for their duties.

**beneficial** adj. favourable or advantageous.
▷ SYNS ADVANTAGEOUS, favourable, profitable, helpful, useful, worthwhile, valuable, rewarding.

**beneficiary** n. (pl. **-ies**) a person who receives a benefit or legacy.

**benefit** n. 1 an advantage or profit. 2 a state payment to someone in need. • v. (**benefited, benefiting**; US **benefitted**) profit from something; give an advantage to.
▷ SYNS n. 1 ADVANTAGE, profit, reward; inf. perk, plus. 2 GOOD, welfare, well-being, advantage, convenience; aid, assistance, help, service. • v. 1 GAIN, profit, do well. 2 HELP, serve, aid, assist, advance, further, forward, boost, improve, better.

**benevolent** adj. kind and well meaning. ▪ benevolence n.
▷ SYNS KIND, kind-hearted, kindly, benign, generous, beneficent, magnanimous, humanitarian, altruistic, philanthropic, caring, compassionate.

**benign** adj. 1 kind. 2 (of a tumour) not malignant.

**bent** n. a natural talent. • adj. determined to do or get.
▷ SYNS n. TENDENCY, inclination, leaning, talent, gift, flair,

ability, aptitude, predilection, propensity, proclivity. • adj. DETERMINED, resolved, set, committed, fixated, insistent.

**benzene** n. a liquid obtained from petroleum and coal tar, used as a solvent, fuel, etc.

**bequeath** v. leave in your will.
▷ SYNS LEAVE, will, make over, pass on, hand down, transfer, donate, give.

**bequest** n. a legacy.
▷ SYNS LEGACY, inheritance, endowment.

**berate** v. scold.

**bereaved** adj. having recently had a relative or friend die.
■ bereavement n.

**bereft** adj. deprived; deserted and lonely.

**beret** n. a round flat cap with no peak.

**bergamot** n. an oily substance found in some oranges, used as a flavouring.

**beriberi** n. a disease caused by lack of vitamin B.

**berry** n. (pl. -ies) a small round juicy fruit with no stone.

**berserk** adj. out of control with anger etc.

**berth** n. **1** a place for a ship to tie up at a wharf. **2** a bunk or sleeping place in a ship or train. • v. moor at a berth.
▷ SYNS n. **1** MOORING, dock, quay, pier. **2** BUNK, bed, cot.

**beryl** n. a transparent green gem.

**beseech** v. (**besought**, **beseeching**) beg earnestly.
▷ SYNS IMPLORE, beg, entreat, plead with, appeal to, call on.

**beset** v. (**beset**, **besetting**) trouble persistently.

**beside** prep. **1** at the side of. **2** compared with. **3** (also **besides**) as well as. • adv. (**besides**) as well. □ beside yourself distraught.

**besiege** v. lay siege to.

**besmirch** v. damage someone's reputation.

**besotted** adj. infatuated.

**bespoke** adj. made to order.

**best** adj. of the highest quality; most suitable. • adv. **1** to the highest degree. **2** most suitably. • v. get the better of. • n. **1** (**the best**) that which is of the highest quality. **2** the highest standard that you can reach: *do your best.* □ best man a bridegroom's chief attendant.
▷ SYNS adj. FINEST, greatest, top, foremost, leading, pre-eminent, premier, prime, first, supreme, superlative, unrivalled, second to none, unsurpassed, peerless, matchless, unparalleled, ideal, perfect.

**bestial** adj. of or like a beast, savage. ■ bestiality n.
▷ SYNS SAVAGE, brutish, brutal, barbaric, cruel, vicious, violent.

**bestir** v. (**bestirred**, **bestirring**) (**bestir yourself**) exert yourself.

**bestow** v. award an honour, gift, etc.
▷ SYNS CONFER, grant, endow with, vest in, present, award.

**bet** v. **1** stake money on the outcome of a future event. **2** inf. feel certain. • n. an act of betting; the amount staked.
▷ SYNS v. WAGER, gamble, stake, risk, put/lay money, speculate. • n. WAGER, stake; inf. flutter.

**beta** n. the second letter of the Greek alphabet (Β, β). □ beta blocker a drug used to treat high blood pressure and angina.

**bête noire** n. (pl. **bêtes noires**) something greatly disliked.

**betide** v. lit. happen to.

**betoken** v. be a sign of.

**betray** v. act treacherously towards your country by helping an enemy; be disloyal to; reveal a secret. ■ **betrayal** n.

▷ SYNS BE DISLOYAL TO, break your promise to be, be unfaithful to, inform on, stab in the back; inf. do the dirty on, grass on, shop.

**betrothed** adj. engaged to be married. ■ **betrothal** n.

**better** adj. **1** more satisfactory or effective. **2** recovered from illness. • adv. **1** in a better way. **2** to a greater degree. • v. improve on.

**between** prep. & adv. **1** at, across, or in the space separating two things. **2** indicating a connection or relationship. **3** shared by; together with.

**bevel** n. a sloping edge. • v. (**bevelled**, **bevelling**; US **beveled**) give a sloping edge to.

**beverage** n. a drink.

**bevy** n. (pl. **-ies**) a large group.

**bewail** v. express great sorrow over.

**beware** v. be aware of danger.

**bewilder** v. puzzle or confuse. ■ **bewilderment** n.

**bewitch** v. cast a spell over; attract and delight.

**beyond** prep. & adv. at or to the far side of; outside the range or limits of; happening or continuing after.

**biannual** adj. happening twice a year.

**bias** n. **1** prejudice for or against a person or thing. **2** a direction diagonal to the weave of a fabric.

▷ SYNS PREJUDICE, partiality, partisanship, favouritism, unfairness, one-sidedness, bigotry, discrimination.

**biased** adj. prejudiced.

**bib** n. a covering put under a young child's chin to protect its clothes while feeding.

**Bible** n. the Christian or Jewish scriptures. ■ **biblical** adj.

**bibliography** n. (pl. **-ies**) a list of books about a subject or by a specified author. ■ **bibliographer** n. **bibliographical** adj.

**bicentenary** n. (pl. **-ies**) a 200th anniversary. ■ **bicentennial** adj. & n.

**biceps** n. a large muscle in the upper arm.

**bicker** v. quarrel about unimportant things.

**bicycle** n. a two-wheeled vehicle driven by pedals. • v. ride a bicycle.

**bid¹** n. **1** an offer of a price, esp. at an auction. **2** an attempt. • v. **1** offer a price for. **2** try to achieve something. ■ **bidder** n.

▷ SYNS n. **1** OFFER, tender, proposal. **2** ATTEMPT, effort, endeavour, try; inf. crack, stab.

**bid²** v. (**bid** or **bade**, **bidden**, **bidding**) **1** utter a greeting or farewell. **2** old use command.

**bide** v. (**bide your time**) wait patiently for an opportunity.

**biennial** adj. **1** happening every two years. **2** (of a plant) living for two years.

**bier** n. a movable stand for a coffin.

**bifocal** adj. (of a lens) made with two different areas, one for distant and one for close vision. • n. (**bifocals**) glasses with bifocal lenses.

**big** adj. (**bigger**, **biggest**) **1** large in size, amount, or extent. **2** important or serious. **3** older or grown-up.
▷ SYNS **1** LARGE, great, tall, high, huge, immense, enormous, colossal, massive, mammoth, vast, prodigious, gigantic, giant, monumental, gargantuan, king-size; inf. whopping, mega. **2** IMPORTANT, significant, major, momentous, weighty, far-reaching, critical.

**bigamy** n. the crime of marrying someone while already married to another person. ■ **bigamist** adj. **bigamous** adj.

**bigot** n. a prejudiced and intolerant person. ■ **bigotry** n.

**bigoted** adj. unreasonably intolerant.
▷ SYNS PREJUDICED, biased, one-sided, narrow-minded, discriminatory, intolerant, blinkered.

**bijou** adj. small and elegant.

**bike** n. inf. a bicycle or motorcycle. ■ **biker** n.

**bikini** n. a woman's two-piece swimming costume.

**bilateral** adj. **1** having two sides. **2** involving two parties.

**bile** n. **1** a bitter liquid produced by the liver. **2** anger.

**bilge** n. **1** a ship's bottom; water collecting there. **2** inf. nonsense.

**bilingual** adj. written in or able to speak two languages.

**bilious** adj. feeling sick.

**bill** n. **1** a written statement of charges to be paid. **2** a draft of a proposed law. **3** a programme of entertainment. **4** US a banknote.

**5** a poster. **6** a bird's beak.
□ **billboard** a hoarding for advertising posters. **billhook** a pruning tool with a curved blade.
▷ SYNS INVOICE, account, statement; US check; inf. tab.

**billet** n. a lodging for troops. • v. (**billeted**, **billeting**) place in a billet.

**billiards** n. a game played on a table, with three balls which are struck with cues into pockets at the edge of the table.

**billion** n. a thousand million or (less commonly) a million million.

**billionaire** n. a person owning assets worth at least a billion pounds or dollars.

**billow** n. a great wave. • v. rise or move like waves; swell out.

**bimbo** n. (pl. **-os**) inf. an attractive but unintelligent woman.

**bin** n. a container for rubbish; a large storage container. • v. (**binned**, **binning**) discard.

**binary** adj. **1** composed of or involving two things. **2** of a system of numbers with two as its base, using the digits 0 and 1.

**bind** v. **1** tie together; unite a group; secure a cover round a book; cover the edge of cloth. **2** tie up. **3** place under an obligation. • n. something irritating or tedious.
▷ SYNS v. TIE, fasten, secure, make fast, attach, strap, lash, tether.

**binding** n. **1** a book cover. **2** braid etc. used to bind an edge.

**binge** n. inf. a bout of excessive eating and drinking.

**bingo** n. a game using cards marked with numbered squares.

**binoculars** pl.n. an instrument with lenses for both eyes, for viewing distant objects.

**bio-** comb. form of living things.

**biochemistry** n. the chemistry of living organisms.
■ biochemist n.

**biodegradable** adj. able to be decomposed by bacteria.

**biodiversity** n. the variety of living things in an environment.

**biography** n. (pl. -ies) the story of a person's life. ■ biographer n. biographical adj.

**biology** n. the scientific study of living things. ■ biological adj. biologist n.

**bionic** adj. (of an artificial body part) electronically powered.

**biopsy** n. (pl. -ies) an examination of tissue taken from the body.

**bipartite** adj. involving two separate groups.

**biped** n. an animal that walks on two feet.

**biplane** n. an aeroplane with two pairs of wings.

**birch** n. a tree with thin, peeling bark.

**bird** n. 1 a feathered egg-laying animal, usu. able to fly. 2 inf. a young woman. □ bird flu a type of influenza that affects birds and can be fatal to humans.

**birdie** n. Golf a score of one stroke under par for a hole.

**biro** n. (pl. -os) trademark a ballpoint pen.

**birth** n. 1 the emergence of young from its mother's body. 2 the beginning of something. 3 a person's ancestry. □ birth control contraception. birthday the anniversary of the day on which a person was born. birthmark an unusual mark on the body which is there from birth. birthright a right or privilege possessed from birth.
▷ SYNS 1 CHILDBIRTH, delivery, nativity. 2 BEGINNING, emergence, genesis, dawn, dawning, rise, start. 3 ANCESTRY, lineage, blood, descent, parentage, family, extraction, origin, stock.

**biscuit** n. a small, flat, crisp cake.

**bisect** v. divide into two equal parts.

**bisexual** adj. & n. (a person) sexually attracted to both men and women.

**bishop** n. 1 a senior clergyman. 2 a mitre-shaped chess piece.

**bismuth** n. a metallic element.

**bison** n. (pl. bison) a wild ox.

**bistro** n. (pl. -os) a small informal restaurant.

**bit** n. 1 a small piece or quantity; a short time or distance. 2 the mouthpiece of a bridle. 3 a tool for drilling or boring. 4 Computing a binary digit.
▷ SYNS 1 PIECE, fragment, scrap, shred, crumb, grain, speck, snippet, spot, drop, pinch, dash, iota, jot, whit, atom, particle; inf. smidgen, tad. 2 MOMENT, minute, second; inf. jiffy, tick.

**bitch** n. 1 a female dog. 2 inf. a spiteful woman. • v. inf. make spiteful comments. ■ bitchiness n. bitchy adj.

**bite** v. (bit, bitten, biting) 1 cut into with the teeth. 2 take hold on a surface. 3 cause pain or distress. • n. 1 an act of biting; a wound made by this. 2 inf. a quick snack.

**biting** adj. (of wind) very cold; sharply critical.

**bitter** adj. **1** tasting sharp; not sweet. **2** resentful. **3** very distressing. **4** piercingly cold.
• n. beer flavoured with hops and slightly bitter.
■ bitterness n.
▷ SYNS adj. **1** ACRID, tart, sour, sharp, harsh, unsweetened. **2** RESENTFUL, embittered, rancorous, begrudging, spiteful, sour, jaundiced. **3** PAINFUL, distressing, upsetting, grievous, sad, tragic, harrowing, agonizing. **4** COLD, icy, freezing, biting, piercing, penetrating.

**bitumen** n. a black substance made from petroleum.

**bivouac** n. a temporary camp without tents or other cover.
• v. (**bivouacked**, **bivouacking**) camp in a bivouac.

**bizarre** adj. very strange or unusual.

**blab** v. (**blabbed**, **blabbing**) talk indiscreetly.

**black** adj. **1** of the very darkest colour. **2** marked by disaster or despair. **3** (of humour) presenting distressing situations in comic terms. **4** relating to people with dark-coloured skin. **5** (of tea or coffee) without milk. **6** hostile.
• n. **1** a black colour. **2** a black person. □ **black economy** unofficial and untaxed business activity. **black eye** a bruised eye. **black hole** a region in outer space from which matter and radiation cannot escape. **black magic** magic involving the summoning of evil spirits. **black market** illegal trading in goods that are officially controlled or hard to obtain. **in the black** not owing any money.

▷ SYNS adj. **1** JET, ebony, sable, inky, sooty, pitch-black, pitch-dark, raven. **2** DISASTROUS, bad, tragic, calamitous, fateful, grievous. **3** MACABRE, unhealthy, ghoulish, morbid, gruesome; inf. sick.

**blackball** v. exclude from membership of a club.

**blackberry** n. an edible dark berry growing on a prickly bush.

**blackbird** n. a European songbird, the male of which is black.

**blackboard** n. a dark board for writing on with chalk, used esp. in schools.

**blackcurrant** n. a small round edible black berry.

**blacken** v. **1** make or become black. **2** damage someone's reputation.

**blackguard** n. a dishonourable man.

**blackhead** n. a lump of oily matter blocking a pore in the skin.

**blackleg** n. a person who works while fellow workers are on strike.

**blacklist** n. a list of people considered untrustworthy or unacceptable.

**blackmail** v. extort money from someone by threatening to reveal compromising information. • n. the offence of doing this. ■ blackmailer n.

**blackout** n. **1** a period when all lights must be turned out during an enemy air raid. **2** a sudden failure of electric lights. **3** a short loss of consciousness. **4** an official restriction on the publishing of news. • v. (**black out**) lose consciousness.

**blacksmith** n. a person who makes and repairs things made of iron.

**bladder** n. a bag-like organ in the abdomen which stores urine for excretion.

**blade** n. the flattened cutting part of a knife or sword; the flat part of an oar or propeller; a long narrow leaf of grass.

**blame** v. hold responsible for a fault. • n. responsibility for a fault. ■ **blameworthy** adj.

▷ SYNS v. **1** ACCUSE, hold responsible, condemn. **2** ATTRIBUTE, ascribe, impute. • n. RESPONSIBILITY, accountability, guilt, fault, culpability, liability.

**blameless** adj. innocent of wrongdoing.

▷ SYNS INNOCENT, faultless, guiltless, irreproachable, unimpeachable, above reproach.

**blanch** v. **1** become white or pale. **2** immerse vegetables briefly in boiling water.

**blancmange** n. a jelly-like dessert, made with milk.

**bland** adj. **1** dull or uninteresting. **2** showing no emotion.

▷ SYNS **1** TASTELESS, insipid, flavourless. **2** DULL, boring, uninteresting, uninspired, uninspiring, unoriginal, unexciting, tedious, vapid.

**blank** adj. **1** not marked or decorated. **2** showing no interest, understanding, or reaction. • n. **1** a blank space. **2** a cartridge containing no bullet.

▷ SYNS adj. **1** BARE, plain, clean, unmarked, clear. **2** EXPRESSIONLESS, inscrutable, impassive, unresponsive, vacant, empty, uncomprehending, glazed, vacuous, emotionless, uninterested. **3** CONFUSED, baffled,

bewildered, at a loss, uncomprehending, puzzled, perplexed.

**blanket** n. a warm covering made of woollen or similar material. • adj. total and inclusive.

**blare** v. & n. (make) a loud harsh sound.

**blarney** n. charming and persuasive talk.

**blasé** adj. unimpressed with something through over-familiarity.

**blaspheme** v. speak disrespectfully about God or sacred things.

**blasphemous** adj. disrespectful towards God or sacred things.

▷ SYNS SACRILEGIOUS, profane, irreligious, impious.

**blasphemy** n. disrespectful talk about God or sacred things.

▷ SYNS SACRILEGE, profanity, irreligion; taking the Lord's name in vain.

**blast** n. **1** an explosion, or the rush of air spreading out from it. **2** a strong gust of wind. **3** a loud note on a whistle or horn. • v. **1** blow up with explosives. **2** (**blast off**) (of a rocket etc.) take off. **3** produce a loud sound.

▷ SYNS n. **1** EXPLOSION, detonation, discharge. **2** GUST, gale, wind, squall. **3** BLARE, roar, wail, hoot. • v. BLOW UP, bomb, dynamite, explode.

**blatant** adj. open and unashamed. ■ **blatantly** adv.

▷ SYNS FLAGRANT, barefaced, glaring, obvious, undisguised, unconcealed, open; shameless, unashamed, brazen, unabashed.

**blaze** n. **1** a bright flame or fire. **2** a bright light. **3** an outburst

or display. **4** a white mark on an animal's face. • v. burn or shine brightly.
▷ SYNS **n. 1** FIRE, conflagration, flames, inferno. **2** BEAM, gleam, shine, radiance, dazzle, flash, flare. • **v. 1** BURN, be on fire, flame, catch fire. **2** SHINE, dazzle, beam, flare, flash, glitter.

**blazer** n. a loose-fitting jacket, worn esp. by schoolchildren or sports players as part of a uniform.

**blazon** v. display or proclaim publicly.

**bleach** v. whiten by sunlight or chemicals. • n. a chemical used to bleach or sterilize.

**bleak** adj. cold and cheerless; not hopeful or encouraging.
▷ SYNS **1** DESOLATE, bare, barren, exposed, cold, unwelcoming, waste, desert, stark, windswept. **2** DISMAL, dreary, gloomy, depressing, discouraging, disheartening, miserable, hopeless.

**bleary** adj. (**-ier, -iest**) (of eyes) dull and unfocused.

**bleat** n. the cry of a sheep or goat. • v. utter this cry; speak or complain feebly.

**bleed** v. (**bled, bleeding**) leak blood or other fluid; draw blood or fluid from; extort money from.

**bleep** n. a short high-pitched sound. • v. make this sound, esp. as a signal. ■ **bleeper** n.

**blemish** n. a flaw or defect. • v. spoil the appearance of.
▷ SYNS **n.** DEFECT, flaw, fault, imperfection, blot, stain, mark, blotch. • **v.** SPOIL, mar, damage, injure, mark, stain, taint, disfigure, discolour, tarnish, blot.

**blend** v. **1** mix and combine. **2** (**blend in**) merge so as to be unnoticeable. • n. a mixture.
▷ SYNS **v.** MIX, combine, merge, meld, fuse, coalesce, mingle. • **n.** MIXTURE, mix, combination, amalgamation, amalgam, union, fusion, synthesis.

**blender** n. an appliance for liquidizing food.

**bless** v. **1** make holy. **2** ask God to protect. **3** (**be blessed**) have or be given something desired.
▷ SYNS CONSECRATE, sanctify, dedicate, make sacred.

**blessed** adj. **1** holy. **2** very welcome, much desired.
▷ SYNS **1** SACRED, holy, consecrated, hallowed, sanctified. **2** WELCOME, gratifying, much needed, wonderful, marvellous. **3** (**blessed with**) FAVOURED WITH, endowed with, having, lucky to have.

**blessing** n. **1** (a prayer for) God's favour and protection. **2** something you are very grateful for. **3** approval or support.
▷ SYNS **1** BENEDICTION, dedication, prayer, invocation. **2** GODSEND, boon, benefit, bonus, help, stroke of luck. **3** APPROVAL, permission, consent, sanction, backing, endorsement, assent, support, approbation; inf. go-ahead.

**blew** past of **BLOW**.

**blight** n. a disease or fungus that withers plants; a malignant influence. • v. affect with blight; spoil.
▷ SYNS **n. 1** DISEASE, fungus, infestation, canker. **2** AFFLICTION, scourge, bane, curse, plague, misfortune, trouble. • **v.** RUIN, destroy, spoil, wreck.

**blind** adj. **1** unable to see.
**2** lacking awareness,
judgement, or reason.
**3** concealed, closed, or blocked.
• v. **1** make blind. **2** stop from
thinking reasonably or clearly.
• n. **1** a screen, esp. on a roller,
for a window. **2** something
meant to hide your plans.
□ **blindfold** a piece of cloth used
to cover a person's eyes.
■ **blindness** n.
▷ SYNS adj. **1** SIGHTLESS, unsighted,
visually impaired, unseeing.
**2** OBLIVIOUS, unaware,
blinkered, uncritical,
unthinking, unreasoning,
mindless. • n. **1** SHUTTER, shade,
curtain, screen. **2** COVER,
pretext, camouflage,
smokescreen, front, facade.

**blink** v. open and shut your eyes
rapidly; shine unsteadily. • n. an
act of blinking; a quick gleam.

**blinkered** adj. having a limited
point of view.

**blinkers** pl.n. a pair of flaps
attached to a bridle to prevent a
horse from seeing sideways.

**blip** n. **1** a short high-pitched
sound. **2** a small flashing point
of light on a radar screen. **3** a
temporary change in an
otherwise steady situation.

**bliss** n. perfect happiness.
■ **blissful** adj. **blissfully** adv.

**blister** n. a bubble-like swelling
on the skin; a raised swelling on
a surface. • v. form blisters.

**blithe** adj. casual and carefree.

**blitz** n. **1** a sudden military
attack. **2** inf. a sudden and
concentrated effort.

**blizzard** n. a severe snowstorm.

**bloat** v. swell with fluid or gas.

**bloated** adj. swollen with fluid
or gas.

▷ SYNS SWOLLEN, distended, puffy,
inflated, enlarged.

**bloater** n. a salted smoked
herring.

**blob** n. a drop of liquid; a round
mass.
▷ SYNS DROP, droplet, globule, ball,
bead, spot, splash, blotch.

**bloc** n. a group of parties or
countries who combine for a
purpose.

**block** n. **1** a solid piece of material with flat surfaces on each
side. **2** a large building divided
into flats or offices. **3** a group of
buildings enclosed by roads.
**4** an obstacle. • v. prevent
movement, flow, or progress in
something. □ **block capitals**
plain capital letters.
▷ SYNS n. **1** CHUNK, hunk, lump,
wedge, slab, piece, bar.
**2** OBSTACLE, bar, barrier, impediment, hindrance, check,
stumbling block, deterrent.
• v. **1** CLOG, stop up, choke, plug,
obstruct, jam, close; barricade,
bar. **2** HINDER, prevent, hamper,
impede, check, stop, halt.

**blockade** n. the blocking of
access to a place, to prevent
entry of goods. • v. set up a
blockade of.

**blockage** n. an obstruction.

**blog** n. a weblog. • v. (**blogging**,
**blogged**) keep a weblog.
■ **blogger** n.

**bloke** n. inf. a man.

**blonde** adj. (also **blond**) fair-
haired; (of hair) fair. • n. a fair-
haired woman.

**blood** n. **1** the red liquid circulating in the arteries and veins.
**2** family background. • v. initiate in an activity. □ **bloodbath** a
massacre. **blood-curdling**
horrifying. **bloodhound** a large

dog used in tracking scents.
**bloodless** without violence or killing. **bloodshot** (of eyes) red from dilated blood vessels.
**blood sport** a sport involving the killing of animals.
**bloodstream** the blood circulating in the body. **blood vessel** a vein, artery, or capillary carrying blood through the body.
▷ SYNS n. *a woman of noble blood:* ANCESTRY, lineage, descent, parentage, family, birth, extraction, origin, stock, pedigree.

**bloodshed** n. the killing or wounding of people.
▷ SYNS KILLING, carnage, slaughter, murder, massacre, butchery, bloodletting, bloodbath.

**bloodthirsty** adj. taking pleasure in killing or violence.
▷ SYNS SAVAGE, cruel, murderous, ferocious, homicidal, vicious, brutal, barbaric, barbarous, violent.

**bloody** adj. (-ier, -iest) 1 covered in blood. 2 involving much violence or cruelty. • v. stain with blood. □ **bloody-minded** inf. deliberately uncooperative.

**bloom** n. 1 a flower. 2 the state or period of blooming. 3 a healthy glow in the complexion. • v. 1 produce flowers. 2 be healthy.
▷ SYNS V. 1 FLOWER, blossom, open. 2 FLOURISH, prosper, thrive, blossom.

**bloomers** pl.n. hist. women's loose knee-length knickers.

**blossom** n. flowers, esp. of a fruit tree. • v. open into flowers; develop and flourish.

**blot** n. a stain of ink etc.; an eyesore. • v. 1 make a blot on.
2 soak up with absorbent material. 3 (**blot out**) erase; obscure.
▷ SYNS n. 1 SPOT, smudge, blotch, stain, mark, blob, smear, splodge. 2 BLEMISH, imperfection, eyesore, defect, fault, flaw. • v. 1 MARK, stain, smudge, blotch, spatter. 2 (**blot out**) OBLITERATE, erase, efface, wipe out, delete; obscure, conceal, hide.

**blotch** n. a large irregular mark.
■ **blotchy** adj.

**blouse** n. a shirt-like garment worn by women.

**blow** v. 1 (of wind) move. 2 send out air through pursed lips.
3 play a wind instrument.
4 break open with explosives.
5 inf. spend or squander. • n. 1 an act of blowing. 2 a stroke with the hand or a weapon. 3 a shock or disappointment. □ **blowfly** a large fly which lays its eggs in meat. **blowout** the release of air or gas from a tyre, oil well, etc. **blowtorch** (or **blowlamp**) a portable device producing a hot flame, for burning off paint. **blow up** 1 explode. 2 begin to develop.
▷ SYNS V. 1 GUST, roar, bluster, blast, rush. 2 SWEEP, carry, drive, buffet, waft, whirl, whisk. 3 SOUND, toot, play. • n. 1 KNOCK, bang, hit, punch, smack; inf. whack, wallop, clout, bash. 2 SHOCK, surprise, calamity, catastrophe, disaster, upset, setback, bombshell.

**blowsy** adj. red-faced and slovenly.

**blowy** adj. windy.

**blubber** n. whale fat. • v. inf. sob noisily.

**bludgeon** n. a heavy stick used as a weapon. • v. strike with a bludgeon; coerce.

**blue** adj. 1 of the colour of the sky on a sunny day. 2 inf. unhappy. 3 inf. indecent. • n. 1 blue colour or material. 2 (**blues**) slow, sad music of black American origin. 3 (**the blues**) sadness or depression. □ **bluebell** a plant with blue bell-shaped flowers. **bluebottle** a large bluish fly. **blue-collar** (of work or a worker) manual. ■ **bluish** adj.

**blueprint** n. a technical drawing or plan; a model or prototype.
▷ SYNS DESIGN, plan, diagram, representation, prototype, model, pattern.

**bluff** n. 1 an attempt to deceive someone into believing that you know or will do something. 2 a steep cliff. • v. try to make someone believe that you know or will do something. • adj. frank and direct.
▷ SYNS v. PRETEND, sham; lie, dissemble. • adj. PLAIN-SPOKEN, straightforward, blunt, frank, direct, open, candid, forthright.

**blunder** v. move clumsily and uncertainly; make a mistake. • n. a stupid mistake.
▷ SYNS v. MAKE A MISTAKE, slip up, err, miscalculate, bungle. • n. ERROR, mistake, slip, miscalculation, faux pas, oversight, gaffe.

**blunt** adj. 1 without a sharp edge or point. 2 speaking or expressed plainly. • v. make or become blunt.
▷ SYNS adj. 1 DULL, unsharpened, rounded. 2 DIRECT, frank, straightforward, candid, forthright, bluff, outspoken,

brusque, abrupt, undiplomatic, tactless. • v. DULL, take the edge off, deaden, numb, dampen, lessen, reduce.

**blur** n. something perceived indistinctly. • v. (**blurred**, **blurring**) make or become indistinct.

**blurb** n. a short description written to promote a book, film, etc.

**blurred** adj. indistinct.
▷ SYNS INDISTINCT, blurry, fuzzy, hazy, misty, foggy, faint; unclear, vague, unfocused, obscure, nebulous.

**blurt** v. say abruptly or tactlessly.
▷ SYNS (**blurt out**) LET SLIP, blab, disclose, reveal, let out, divulge; inf. spill the beans, let on.

**blush** v. become red-faced from shame or embarrassment. • n. blushing.
▷ SYNS v. REDDEN, flush, colour, go red.

**blusher** n. a cosmetic giving a rosy colour to cheeks.

**bluster** v. 1 blow in gusts. 2 make aggressive but empty threats. • n. blustering talk.

**blustery** adj. (of weather) windy.
▷ SYNS WINDY, gusty, stormy, squally, wild, tempestuous.

**boa** n. a large snake that crushes its prey.

**boar** n. a wild pig; a male pig.

**board** n. 1 a long piece of sawn wood; a flat piece of wood or stiff material. 2 daily meals supplied in return for payment or services. 3 a committee. • v. 1 get on a ship, aircraft, train, or bus. 2 receive or provide accommodation and meals for payment. 3 cover or block with boards. □ **boarding school** a school in which the pupils live during term time. **boardroom** a room in which a board of directors meets. **on board** on or in a ship, aircraft, etc. ■ **boarder** n.

▷ SYNS n. **1** PLANK, beam, panel, slat, timber. **2** FOOD, meals, provisions, keep. **3** PANEL, committee, council, directorate. • v. **1** GET ON, go aboard, enter, embark, mount. **2** LODGE, stay, live, room.

**boast** v. **1** talk about yourself with excessive pride. **2** possess an impressive feature. • n. an act of boasting.

▷ SYNS v. **1** BRAG, show off, crow, gloat; inf. blow your own trumpet. **2** POSSESS, have, own, enjoy, pride itself on, benefit from.

**boastful** adj. showing excessive pride in yourself.

▷ SYNS CONCEITED, bragging, arrogant, full of yourself, cocky; inf. big-headed.

**boat** n. a vehicle for travelling on water.

**boater** n. a flat-topped straw hat.

**boatswain** n. a ship's officer in charge of equipment, etc.

**bob** v. (**bobbed, bobbing**) **1** move quickly up and down. **2** cut hair in a bob. • n. **1** a bobbing movement. **2** a hairstyle with the hair at the same length just above the shoulders. □ **bobsleigh** a sledge used for racing down an ice-covered run.

**bobbin** n. a small spool holding thread or wire in a machine.

**bobble** n. a small woolly ball as an ornament.

**bode** v. be a portent of.

**bodge** v. inf. make or repair badly.

**bodice** n. **1** the part of a dress above the waist. **2** a woman's sleeveless undergarment.

**bodily** adj. of the body. • adv. by taking hold of the body.

▷ SYNS adj. CORPOREAL, physical, corporal, fleshly; material, tangible.

**body** n. **1** the physical structure of a person or animal. **2** the main part. **3** a collection. **4** a group. □ **bodyguard** a person paid to protect an important person. **bodywork** the metal outer shell of a vehicle.

▷ SYNS **1** FIGURE, frame, form, physique, anatomy; torso, trunk; corpse, cadaver, carcass, remains. **2** ACCUMULATION, collection, quantity, mass, corpus. **3** ASSOCIATION, organization, group, party, company, society, circle.

**boffin** n. inf. a scientist.

**bog** n. **1** an area of soft, wet ground. **2** inf. a toilet. • v. become unable to make progress. ■ **boggy** adj.

▷ SYNS n. MARSH, swamp, mire, quagmire, morass; fen, wetland.

**bogey** n. (pl. **-eys**) **1** Golf a score of one stroke over par at a hole. **2** (also **bogy**) something causing fear.

**boggle** v. be amazed or alarmed.

**bogus** adj. false.

**Bohemian** adj. artistic and unconventional.

▷ SYNS UNCONVENTIONAL, eccentric, unorthodox, original, avant-garde, artistic, alternative; inf. offbeat, way-out.

**boil** v. bubble up with heat; heat liquid until it does this; cook in boiling water. • n. an inflamed swelling producing pus.

**boiler** n. a container in which water is heated.

**boisterous** adj. cheerfully noisy or rough.

▷ SYNS LIVELY, spirited, animated, playful, exuberant, frisky, unruly, rough, wild, irrepressible, undisciplined, rumbustious, uproarious, rowdy, noisy.

**bold** adj. **1** confident and courageous. **2** (of a colour or design) strong and vivid.

▷ SYNS **1** DARING, brave, adventurous, dauntless, courageous; plucky, intrepid, audacious, confident, fearless, valiant, heroic, valorous, undaunted, daredevil. **2** STRIKING, eye-catching, prominent, conspicuous, noticeable, vivid, bright, strong.

**bole** n. the trunk of a tree.

**bolero** n. (pl. **-os**) **1** a Spanish dance. **2** a woman's short open jacket.

**bollard** n. a short thick post.

**bolster** n. a long pad placed under a pillow. • v. support or prop.

▷ SYNS v. SUPPORT, prop up, shore up, hold up, reinforce, buttress, strengthen, aid, help.

**bolt** n. **1** a metal pin used with a nut to hold things together. **2** a sliding bar for fastening a door. **3** a flash of lightning. **4** a roll of fabric. • v. **1** fasten with a bolt. **2** run away. **3** eat food quickly.

▷ SYNS n. BAR, latch, lock, catch, fastening, pin, peg, rivet. • v. **1** LOCK, latch, bar, fasten, secure. **2** RUN, dash, sprint, dart, rush, hurtle, hurry, fly, flee, escape; inf. scarper. **3** GOBBLE, guzzle, wolf, gulp, devour.

**bomb** n. a device designed to explode and cause damage. • v. **1** attack with bombs. **2** inf. move quickly. **3** inf. be a failure. □ **bombshell** a great surprise or shock.

**bombard** v. attack with artillery; attack with questions etc. ■ **bombardment** n.

▷ SYNS ATTACK, shell, bomb, blitz, strafe, blast, pound, fire at, assault, assail, batter.

**bombastic** adj. using pompous words. ■ **bombast** n.

**bomber** n. an aircraft that carries and drops bombs; a person who places bombs.

**bona fide** adj. genuine.

**bonanza** n. a situation creating wealth or success.

▷ SYNS WINDFALL, bonus, stroke of luck; inf. jackpot.

**bond** n. **1** a thing used for fastening. **2** a force or feeling that unites people. **3** (**bonds**) ropes or chains used to restrain someone. **4** an agreement with legal force. • v. join securely.

▷ SYNS n. **1** CHAIN, fetter, shackle, manacle, restraint. **2** LINK, connection, tie, attachment, relationship, friendship, association. **3** CONTRACT, agreement, deal, pledge, promise, guarantee, word. • v. UNITE, join, bind, connect, attach, fasten, fix, secure, stick, glue, fuse.

**bondage** n. slavery or captivity.

**bone** n. each of the hard parts making up the vertebrate skeleton. • v. remove bones from.

**bonfire** n. a fire built in the open air.

**bongo** n. (pl. **-os** or **-oes**) each of a pair of small drums played with the fingers.

**bonnet** n. **1** a hat with strings that tie under the chin. **2** a hinged cover over the engine of a motor vehicle.

**bonny** adj. **(-ier, -iest)** Scot. & N. Engl. good-looking.

**bonsai** n. **(pl. bonsai)** an ornamental miniature tree or shrub; the art of growing these.

**bonus** n. an extra payment or benefit.
▷ SYNS GAIN, benefit, advantage, extra, plus, boon.

**bony** adj. very thin.
▷ SYNS THIN, angular, lean, skeletal, emaciated, cadaverous, gaunt; inf. scrawny.

**boo** exclam. an exclamation of disapproval; an exclamation to startle someone. • v. shout 'boo' at.

**boob** n. inf. **1** a blunder. **2** a breast.

**booby** n. **(pl. -ies)** inf. a stupid person. □ **booby prize** a prize given to the person who comes last in a contest. **booby trap** an object containing a hidden explosive device.

**boogie** v. **(boogied, boogieing)** dance to fast pop music.

**book** n. **1** a written or printed work consisting of pages bound in a cover. **2** a main division of a literary work. **3** **(books)** a set of records or accounts. • v. **1** reserve accommodation, a ticket, etc. **2** engage a performer for an event. **3** record details of an offender. □ **bookcase** a cabinet containing shelves for books. **bookkeeping** the keeping of records of financial transactions. **bookmaker** a person who takes bets and pays out winnings. **bookmark 1** a strip of card or leather to mark a place in a book. **2** a record of the address of a computer file, website, etc. enabling quick access by the user. **bookworm** inf. a person who loves reading.
▷ SYNS n. VOLUME, tome, work, title, publication. • v. RESERVE, charter, order, prearrange.

**booklet** n. a small thin book.
▷ SYNS LEAFLET, pamphlet, brochure.

**boom** v. **1** make a deep resonant sound. **2** have a period of prosperity. • n. **1** a booming sound. **2** a period of prosperity. **3** a long pole; a floating barrier.
▷ SYNS v. RESOUND, reverberate, rumble, thunder, bang, roar, crash. • n. **1** CRASH, bang, blast, rumble, roar, thunder, reverberation. **2** UPTURN, upsurge, improvement, growth, surge, increase, boost.

**boomerang** n. an Australian missile of curved wood that can be thrown so as to return to the thrower.

**boon** n. a benefit.

**boor** n. a rough, bad-mannered person.

**boorish** adj. bad-mannered.
▷ SYNS RUDE, crude, loutish, coarse, bad-mannered, uncivilized, uncouth, oafish, vulgar; inf. yobbish.

**boost** v. help or encourage. • n. a source of help or encouragement. ■ **booster** n.
▷ SYNS v. ENCOURAGE, help, assist, increase, raise, improve, promote, advance, support. • n. UPLIFT, spur, encouragement, stimulus; increase, upturn, rise, improvement, advance; inf. shot in the arm.

**boot** n. **1** an item of footwear covering both foot and ankle or lower leg. **2** a space at the back of a car for luggage. • v. **1** inf. kick hard. **2** start up a computer.

**bootee** n. a baby's woollen shoe.

**booth** n. **1** an enclosed compartment allowing privacy when telephoning etc. **2** a stall or stand.
▷ SYNS **1** CUBICLE, box, compartment, cabin. **2** STALL, stand, kiosk.

**bootleg** adj. smuggled or illicit. ■ **bootlegger** n.

**booty** n. loot.
▷ SYNS LOOT, plunder, haul, spoils, gains, pickings; inf. swag.

**booze** inf. v. drink alcohol. • n. alcoholic drink.

**border** n. a boundary, an edge; a flower bed round part of a garden. • v. **1** form a border to. **2** (**border on**) come close to being. □ **borderline** between two states or categories.
▷ SYNS n. EDGE, perimeter, verge, boundary, frontier, borderline, limit, margin, periphery, brink, fringe, rim. • v. **1** ADJOIN, abut, touch, join, be next to. **2** SURROUND, enclose, encircle, circle, edge, fringe, bound. **3** (**border on**) VERGE ON, approach, come close to, approximate, resemble.

**bore¹** past of BEAR.

**bore²** v. **1** make weary by being dull. **2** make a hole with a revolving tool. • n. **1** a tedious person or thing. **2** the hollow inside of a gun barrel.
■ **boredom** n.
▷ SYNS v. **1** STULTIFY, weary, tire, pall on, leave cold. **2** PIERCE, drill, cut; tunnel, mine, dig, sink.

**boring** adj. not interesting; tedious.

▷ SYNS TEDIOUS, dull, uninteresting, monotonous, dreary, humdrum, uninspiring, tiresome, wearisome.

**born** adj. **1** existing as a result of birth. **2** having a specified natural ability.

**borne** p.p. of BEAR.

**boron** n. a chemical element used in making steel.

**borough** n. a town or district with rights of local government.

**borrow** v. take something from someone, with the intention of returning it.

**borstal** n. the former name of an institution for young offenders.

**bosom** n. the breast.

**boss** inf. n. an employer; a person in charge. • v. give orders to in a domineering way.
▷ SYNS n. HEAD, chief, leader, manager, director, employer, supervisor, foreman, overseer; inf. gaffer.

**bossy** adj. (**-ier, -iest**) tending to give orders; domineering.
▷ SYNS DOMINEERING, overbearing, imperious, officious, high-handed, authoritarian, dictatorial.

**bosun, bo'sun** = BOATSWAIN.

**botany** n. the study of plants. ■ **botanical** adj. **botanist** n.

**botch** v. do a task badly.
▷ SYNS BUNGLE, make a mess of, do badly, mismanage; inf. mess up, screw up.

**both** adj., pron., & adv. the two.

**bother** v. **1** take the trouble to do something. **2** worry, disturb, or upset. • n. **1** trouble and fuss. **2** a cause of trouble and fuss.

▷ SYNS **v. 1** TAKE THE TIME, make the effort, go to the trouble. **2** DISTURB, trouble, inconvenience, pester, harass, plague, hound, annoy, irritate; worry, concern, perturb, distress; inf. hassle. • **n. 1** TROUBLE, effort, inconvenience, fuss; disturbance, commotion, disorder, uproar, fighting. **2** NUISANCE, annoyance, irritation, est, trouble, problem.

**bottle** n. a narrow-necked container for liquid. • v. **1** put in bottles. **2** (**bottle something up**) hide your feelings. ◻ **bottleneck** a narrow part of a road where congestion occurs.

**bottom** n. **1** the lowest or furthest point, part, or position. **2** the buttocks. • adj. in the lowest or furthest position.
■ **bottom**... s adj.
▷ SYNS **n.** BASE, foundation, basis, substructure, underpinning; underneath, underside, lower side, underbelly.

**botulism** n. a dangerous form of food poisoning.

**boudoir** n. a woman's bedroom or small private room.

**bouffant** adj. (of hair) standing out from the head in a rounded shape.

**bough** n. a main branch of a tree.

**bought** past & p.p. of BUY.

**boulder** n. a large rounded stone.

**boulevard** n. a wide street.

**bounce** v. **1** rebound. **2** move up and down repeatedly. **3** inf. (of a cheque) be returned by a bank when there is not enough money in an account for it to be paid. • n. **1** an act of bouncing. **2** lively self-confidence.

▷ SYNS **v. 1** REBOUND, spring back, ricochet. **2** BOUND, leap, jump, spring, bob, skip.

**bouncer** n. a person employed to eject troublemakers from a club etc.

**bound**[1] past and p.p. of BIND.

**bound**[2] v. **1** run with a leaping movement. **2** form the boundary of. • n. **1** a leap. **2** a boundary; a limitation. • adj. **1** heading in a specified direction. **2** (**bound to**) certain to.
▷ SYNS **v.** LEAP, jump, spring, skip, hop, vault, bounce. • adj. **1** CERTAIN, sure, destined, fated. **2** (**bound for**) HEADING FOR, going to, travelling towards, making for.

**boundary** n. (pl. **-ies**) a line marking the limit of an area.
▷ SYNS FRONTIER, border, borderline, limit, edge, dividing line, perimeter, margin, bounds, periphery, fringe.

**boundless** adj. unlimited.
▷ SYNS UNLIMITED, infinite, unbounded, unending, untold, inexhaustible, immeasurable, vast.

**bounty** n. **1** lit. generosity, or something given in large amounts. **2** a reward for capturing or killing someone.
■ **bounteous** adj. **bountiful** adj.
▷ SYNS GENEROSITY, munificence, altruism, largesse, benevolence, kindness, philanthropy.

**bouquet** n. **1** a bunch of flowers. **2** the perfume of wine.
▷ SYNS **1** BUNCH OF FLOWERS, spray, posy, nosegay, corsage. **2** SMELL, aroma, fragrance, scent, perfume, nose.

**bourbon** n. an American whisky made from maize.

**bourgeois** adj. conventionally middle-class.

**bout** n. **1** a period of exercise, work, or illness. **2** a boxing contest.
▷ SYNS **1** ATTACK, spell, fit, period, paroxysm. **2** MATCH, contest, fight, round, competition, encounter.

**boutique** n. a small shop selling fashionable clothes etc.

**bow**¹ n. **1** a knot tied with two loops and two loose ends. **2** a weapon for shooting arrows. **3** a rod with horsehair stretched between its ends, for playing a violin etc.

**bow**² v. bend the head and upper body as a sign of respect; bend with age or under a weight; submit. • n. **1** an act of bowing. **2** the front end of a ship.
▷ SYNS v. **1** CURTSY, bob, bend your knee, salaam. **2** SUBMIT, yield, give in, surrender, accept, capitulate.

**bowel** n. the intestine; the innermost parts.
▷ SYNS **1** INTESTINES, entrails, guts, viscera, insides. **2** INTERIOR, depths, inside, core, belly.

**bowl** n. **1** a round, deep dish or basin. **2** (**bowls**) a game in which heavy wooden balls are rolled as close as possible to a small white ball. **3** a heavy ball used in bowls or tenpin bowling. • v. **1** roll along the ground. **2** send a ball to a batsman. **3** move rapidly and smoothly. **4** (**bowl over**) knock down. **5** (**bowl over**) inf. impress or astonish.
▷ SYNS n. DISH, basin, container, vessel.

**bowler** n. **1** a person who bowls in cricket; a person who plays at bowls. **2** a hard felt hat with a rounded top.

**box** n. **1** a container with a flat base and sides and a lid. **2** an area enclosed by straight lines on a page or computer screen. **3** an enclosed area reserved for a group of people in a theatre, sports ground, etc. **4** a small evergreen shrub. • v. **1** put into a box. **2** fight with the fists as a sport. □ **box office** the place at a theatre or cinema where tickets are sold.
▷ SYNS n. CONTAINER, receptacle, case, crate, chest, coffer, casket, carton, pack.

**boxer** n. **1** a person who boxes as a sport. **2** a breed of dog resembling a bulldog.

**boxing** n. a sport in which contestants fight each other wearing big padded gloves.

**boy** n. a male child. □ **boyfriend** a person's regular male romantic or sexual partner. ■ **boyish** adj.
▷ SYNS YOUTH, lad, youngster, schoolboy, kid, stripling.

**boycott** v. refuse to deal with or trade with. • n. boycotting.
▷ SYNS n. BAN, embargo, veto, bar, prohibition, sanction, restriction.

**bra** n. a woman's undergarment worn to support the breasts.

**brace** n. **1** a strengthening or supporting part. **2** (**braces**) a pair of straps that pass over the shoulders and fasten to trousers to hold them up. **3** a wire device used to straighten the teeth. **4** a pair. • v. **1** make stronger or firmer. **2** (**brace yourself**) prepare for something difficult.
▷ SYNS v. **1** STRENGTHEN, support, reinforce, shore up, prop up,

buttress; fix, steady, secure, stabilize. **2** *brace yourself*: PREPARE, get ready, nerve, steel.

**bracelet** n. an ornamental band worn on the arm.

**bracing** adj. invigorating.
▷ SYNS INVIGORATING, refreshing, stimulating, energizing, reviving, restorative, fresh, brisk, crisp.

**bracken** n. a large fern.

**bracket** n. **1** any of the marks used in pairs to enclose and separate off words or figures, ( ), [ ], { }; a category of similar people or things. **2** a support for a shelf or lamp, projecting from a wall. • v. enclose in brackets; group together.

**brackish** adj. slightly salty.

**brag** v. (**bragged, bragging**) boast. ■ braggart n.

**braid** n. **1** a woven ornamental trimming. **2** a plait of hair. • v. **1** trim with braid. **2** plait.

**Braille** n. a system of representing letters etc. by raised dots which blind people read by touch.

**brain** n. the mass of soft grey matter in the skull, the centre of the nervous system in animals. □ brainchild a person's idea or invention. brainstorm **1** a moment in which you are unable to think clearly. **2** a group discussion to produce ideas. brainwash force someone to accept an idea or belief. brainwave a sudden clever idea. ■ brainy adj.

**brains** pl.n. intellectual ability.
▷ SYNS INTELLIGENCE, intellect, mind, cleverness, wit, brainpower, shrewdness, acumen.

**braise** v. fry lightly then stew slowly in a closed container.

**brake** n. a device for reducing speed or stopping motion. • v. stop or slow with a brake.

**bramble** n. a prickly shrub on which blackberries grow.

**bran** n. the ground inner husks of grain, sifted from flour.

**branch** n. **1** a part of a tree growing out from the trunk. **2** a division of a larger group. **3** a river, road, or railway extending out from a main one. • v. divide into branches.
▷ SYNS n. **1** BOUGH, limb, arm, offshoot. **2** DEPARTMENT, division, subdivision, section, subsection, part, wing. • v. FORK, divide, separate, bifurcate, split.

**brand** n. goods of a particular make; an identifying mark made on skin with hot metal. • v. mark with a brand; stigmatize. □ brand new completely new.
▷ SYNS n. MAKE, type, kind, sort, variety, line, trade name, trademark. • v. **1** STAMP, mark, burn, sear. **2** STIGMATIZE, mark out, label.

**brandish** v. wave or flourish.
▷ SYNS FLOURISH, wave, wield, raise, swing, display, shake.

**brandy** n. (pl. **-ies**) a strong alcoholic drink made from wine or fermented fruit juice.

**brash** adj. aggressively self-confident.

**brass** n. **1** a yellow alloy of copper and zinc. **2** a brass memorial plaque. **3** brass wind instruments.

**brassiere** n. a bra.

**brassy** adj. (**-ier, -iest**) **1** like brass. **2** bold and vulgar.

**brat** n. derog. a badly behaved child.

**bravado** n. confidence that is intended to impress.
▷ SYNS BOLDNESS, swagger, bluster, machismo, bragging, boasting.

**brave** adj. able to face and endure danger or pain. • v. face and endure bravely. • n. an American Indian warrior.
▷ SYNS adj. COURAGEOUS, valiant, fearless, intrepid, plucky, heroic, bold, daring, undaunted, lionhearted, spirited, dauntless, valorous.

**bravery** n. courage.
▷ SYNS COURAGE, fearlessness, pluck, boldness, intrepidity, daring, nerve, valour; inf. guts.

**bravo** exclam. well done!

**brawl** n. a noisy quarrel or fight. • v. take part in a brawl.
▷ SYNS FIGHT, scuffle, affray, fracas, skirmish, free-for-all, tussle, brouhaha.

**brawn** n. muscular strength.

**brawny** adj. physically strong; muscular.
▷ SYNS MUSCULAR, powerful, burly, strong, sturdy, strapping.

**bray** v. make a loud, harsh cry. • n. the cry of a donkey.

**brazen** adj. bold and shameless. • v. behave after doing wrong as if you have no need to be ashamed.
▷ SYNS adj. BOLD, shameless, unashamed, unabashed, defiant, barefaced, blatant, impudent, insolent, cheeky.

**brazier** n. a portable heater holding burning coals.

**Brazil nut** n. a large three-sided nut from a South American tree.

**breach** n. 1 a gap made in a wall or barrier. 2 an act of breaking a rule or contract. 3 a quarrel or disagreement. • v. 1 break through or make a hole in. 2 break a rule or agreement.
▷ SYNS n. 1 BREAK, split, crack, gap, hole, opening, rupture, fissure, fracture. 2 CONTRAVENTION, violation, infringement, infraction, transgression. 3 RIFT, schism, division, estrangement, split, break. • v. 1 BREAK THROUGH, burst, rupture. 2 BREAK, contravene, violate, infringe; defy, disobey, flout.

**bread** n. 1 food made of flour, water, and yeast mixed together and baked. 2 inf. money. ☐ bread-winner a person who earns money to support their family. on the breadline very poor.

**breadth** n. width, broadness.

**break** v. 1 separate into pieces as a result of a blow or strain. 2 stop working. 3 interrupt a sequence or course. 4 fail to observe a rule or agreement. 5 suddenly make or become public. 6 defeat. 7 beat a record. 8 (of a boy's voice) deepen at puberty. 9 (of the weather) change suddenly. • n. 1 a pause, gap, or short rest. 2 an instance of breaking, or the point where something is broken. 3 a sudden rush or dash. 4 inf. a chance. ☐ break down 1 stop working. 2 lose control of your emotions. break in force your way into a building. breakneck dangerously fast. breakwater a barrier built out into the sea to protect a coast etc. from waves.
■ breakable adj. breakage n.
▷ SYNS v. 1 SMASH, crack, shatter, split, burst, fracture, fragment, splinter, snap, disintegrate. 2 STOP WORKING, break down, go wrong, malfunction, crash;

inf. conk out, pack up. **3** STOP, pause, rest, discontinue, give up. **4** CONTRAVENE, breach, infringe; defy, violate, flout, disobey. **5** REVEAL, disclose, divulge, tell, impart, announce. **6** BEAT, surpass, exceed, better, top, cap, outdo. • n. **1** INTERRUPTION, gap, pause, interval, intermission; discontinuation, stop, breathing space, respite, rest; inf. breather. **2** BREACH, fracture, split, crack, fissure, gap, rupture.

**breakdown** n. **1** a failure or collapse. **2** a careful analysis.
▷ SYNS **1** FAILURE, collapse, disintegration. **2** ANALYSIS, classification, examination, investigation.

**breaker** n. a heavy sea wave that breaks on the shore.

**breakfast** n. the first meal of the day.

**breakthrough** n. a sudden important development or success.
▷ SYNS ADVANCE, leap forward, quantum leap, discovery, find, innovation, development, improvement, revolution.

**breast** n. the upper front part of the body; either of the two milk-producing organs on a woman's chest. □ **breastbone** the bone down the centre of the chest. **breaststroke** a swimming stroke in which the arms are pushed forwards and swept back while the legs are kicked out.

**breath** n. air drawn into and sent out of the lungs in breathing; a slight movement of wind. ■ **breathless** adj.

**breathalyser** (US trademark **Breathalyzer**) n. a device for measuring the amount of alcohol in a driver's breath.
■ **breathalyse** (US **-yze**) v.

**breathe** v. **1** take air into the lungs and send it out again. **2** say quietly.
▷ SYNS **1** INHALE, exhale, respire; puff, pant, gasp, wheeze. **2** WHISPER, murmur, sigh, say.

**breather** n. a pause for rest.

**breathtaking** adj. astonishing or impressive.
▷ SYNS SPECTACULAR, magnificent, awesome, awe-inspiring, amazing, astounding, exciting, thrilling, stunning.

**breech** n. the back part of a gun barrel.

**breeches** pl.n. trousers reaching to just below the knees.

**breed** v. (**bred, breeding**) produce offspring; keep animals for the offspring they produce; give rise to. • n. a variety of animals within a species; a sort.
■ **breeder** n.
▷ SYNS v. **1** REPRODUCE, procreate, multiply, give birth. **2** PRODUCE, bring about, give rise to, create, generate, stir up, engender, foster, arouse. • n. **1** VARIETY, type, kind, strain, stock, line. **2** STOCK, species, race, lineage, extraction, pedigree.

**breeding** n. good manners resulting from training or background.

**breeze** n. a light wind.

**breezy** adj. pleasantly windy.
▷ SYNS WINDY, blowy, blustery, gusty, fresh.

**brethren** pl.n. fellow Christians or members of a group.

**breve** n. (in music) a long note.

**brevity** n. briefness; conciseness.

▷ SYNS CONCISENESS, concision, pithiness, succinctness, incisiveness.

**brew** v. **1** make beer; make tea or coffee. **2** (of an unpleasant situation) begin to develop. • n. a liquid or amount brewed.
■ brewer n.
▷ SYNS v. **1** MAKE, prepare, infuse, ferment. **2** BE IMMINENT, loom, develop, be impending.

**brewery** n. a place where beer is made.

**briar** = BRIER.

**bribe** n. a gift offered to influence a person to act in favour of the giver. • v. persuade by this. ■ bribery n.
▷ SYNS n. INDUCEMENT, incentive; inf. backhander, sweetener. • v. BUY OFF, pay off, suborn.

**bric-a-brac** n. various objects of little value.

**brick** n. a block of baked or dried clay used to build walls. • v. block with a brick structure.
■ bricklayer n.

**bride** n. a woman at the time of her wedding. □ bridegroom a man at the time of his wedding. bridesmaid a girl or woman who accompanies a bride at her wedding. ■ bridal adj.

**bridge** n. **1** a structure providing a way across a river, road, etc. **2** the captain's platform on a ship. **3** the upper bony part of the nose. **4** the part on a stringed instrument over which the strings are stretched. **5** a card game for two pairs of players. • v. **1** be or make a bridge over. **2** reduce a gap between two groups or things.
▷ SYNS n. **1** VIADUCT, overpass, flyover. **2** BOND, link, tie, connection. • v. **1** SPAN, cross,

extend across, traverse, straddle. **2** REDUCE, lessen, narrow, connect, unite.

**bridle** n. a harness on a horse's head. • v. **1** put a bridle on; restrain. **2** show resentment or anger. □ bridleway (or bridle path) a path for horse riders or walkers.
▷ SYNS v. **1** RESTRAIN, curb, check, keep control of, govern, master, subdue. **2** BRISTLE, take offence, take umbrage, be affronted.

**brief** adj. **1** lasting only for a short time. **2** using few words. **3** (of clothes) not covering much of the body. • n. **1** a set of instructions about a task. **2** a summary of the facts in a case given to a barrister to argue in court. **3** (**briefs**) short underpants. • v. inform or instruct someone about a task.
■ briefly adv.
▷ SYNS adj. **1** CONCISE, succinct, short, pithy, incisive. **2** SHORT, fleeting, quick, momentary, passing. • v. INSTRUCT, inform, tell, prepare, prime; inf. fill in.

**briefcase** n. a case for carrying documents.

**briefing** n. a meeting for giving information or instructions.

**brier** (or **briar**) n. a prickly shrub.

**brigade** n. **1** an army unit forming part of a division. **2** inf. a group with a shared purpose or interest.

**brigadier** n. a British army officer next above colonel.

**brigand** n. a member of a gang of bandits.

**bright** adj. **1** giving out or reflecting much light; vivid. **2** intelligent. **3** cheerful; encouraging. ■ brightness n.

▷ SYNS **1** SHINING, brilliant, vivid, dazzling, sparkling, glittering, gleaming, radiant, glowing, shimmering, luminous. **2** INTELLIGENT, clever, smart, brainy, quick-witted. **3** PROMISING, encouraging, favourable, hopeful, auspicious, propitious.

**brighten** v. **1** make or become brighter. **2** make or become happier and more cheerful.
▷ SYNS **1** LIGHT UP, lighten, illuminate. **2** CHEER UP, gladden, enliven, animate; inf. perk up, buck up.

**brilliant** adj. **1** very bright or vivid. **2** very clever or talented. **3** inf. excellent. ■ **brilliance** n.
▷ SYNS **1** BRIGHT, shining, dazzling, gleaming, intense, radiant. **2** see **CLEVER**.

**brim** n. the edge of a cup or hollow; the projecting edge of a hat. • v. (**brimmed**, **brimming**) be full to the brim.
▷ SYNS n. RIM, lip, edge, brink.

**brine** n. water containing dissolved salt.

**bring** v. **1** carry or take to a place. **2** cause to be in a particular position or state. □ **bring up** rear a child.
▷ SYNS **1** FETCH, carry, bear, take, convey, transport, deliver; lead, guide, escort, conduct, usher. **2** CAUSE, produce, create, generate, precipitate, result in.

**brink** n. the edge of a steep place or of a stretch of water; the point just before an event or state. □ **brinkmanship** the pursuing of a dangerous course of action to the limits of safety before stopping.
▷ SYNS **1** EDGE, margin, limit, rim, boundary, fringe. **2** VERGE, threshold, point.

**brisk** adj. **1** active and energetic. **2** practical and efficient.
▷ SYNS **1** QUICK, rapid, fast, swift, speedy, energetic, lively, vigorous. **2** NO NONSENSE, decisive, businesslike; brusque, abrupt, short.

**brisket** n. a joint of beef from the breast.

**bristle** n. a short stiff hair.
• v. (of hair) stand upright as a result of anger or fear; show indignation.
▷ SYNS n. HAIR, stubble, whisker, prickle, spine, quill, barb.

**British** adj. of Britain or its people.

**Briton** n. a British person.

**brittle** adj. hard but easily broken.
▷ SYNS BREAKABLE, hard, crisp, fragile, delicate.

**broach** v. begin discussion of.
▷ SYNS INTRODUCE, raise, bring up, mention, touch on.

**broad** adj. **1** large from side to side. **2** not precise or detailed. **3** (of an accent) strong.
□ **broadband** a telecommunications technique which uses a wide range of frequencies, enabling messages to be sent simultaneously. **broad bean** a large flat green bean. **broadsheet** a large-sized newspaper. **broadside 1** a strongly worded criticism. **2** hist. the firing of all the guns on one side of a ship.
■ **broaden** v.
▷ SYNS **1** WIDE, large, extensive, vast, expansive, sweeping. **2** WIDE-RANGING, comprehensive, inclusive, encyclopedic, all-embracing. **3** GENERAL, non-specific, rough, approximate; loose, vague.

**broadcast** v. (**broadcast, broadcasting**) send out by radio or television; make generally known. • n. a broadcast programme. ■ **broadcaster** n.
▷ SYNS v. **1** TRANSMIT, relay, put on air, televise. **2** ANNOUNCE, make public, report, publicize, air, spread, circulate, disseminate. • n. PROGRAMME, show, transmission.

**broad-minded** adj. not easily shocked.
▷ SYNS OPEN-MINDED, liberal, tolerant, freethinking, permissive, unshockable.

**brocade** n. a fabric woven with raised patterns.

**broccoli** n. a vegetable with tightly packed green or purple flower heads.

**brochure** n. a booklet or leaflet giving information.
▷ SYNS BOOKLET, leaflet, pamphlet, handout, circular.

**brogue** n. **1** a strong shoe with ornamental perforated bands. **2** a strong regional accent, esp. Irish.

**broil** v. US grill meat or fish.

**broke** past of **BREAK**. • adj. inf. having no money.

**broken** p.p. of **BREAK**. • adj. (of a language) badly spoken by a foreigner.

**broker** n. an agent who buys and sells on behalf of others. • v. arrange a deal.

**bromide** n. a compound used to calm nerves.

**bromine** n. a dark red poisonous liquid element.

**bronchial** adj. relating to the tubes leading into the lungs.

**bronchitis** n. inflammation of the bronchial tubes.

**bronco** n. (pl. **-os**) a wild or half-tamed horse of the western US.

**brontosaurus** n. a large plant-eating dinosaur.

**bronze** n. a brown alloy of copper and tin; its colour. • v. make suntanned.

**brooch** n. an ornamental hinged pin fastened with a clasp.

**brood** n. young produced at one hatching or birth. • v. **1** think deeply about an unpleasant subject. **2** sit on eggs and hatch them.
▷ SYNS n. OFFSPRING, young, family, clutch, litter. • v. DWELL ON, worry, fret, agonize; think, ponder, contemplate.

**broody** adj. (**-ier, -iest**) **1** (of a hen) wanting to hatch eggs. **2** inf. (of a woman) wanting to have a baby. **3** thoughtful and unhappy.

**brook** n. a small stream. • v. tolerate, allow.
▷ SYNS n. STREAM, burn, beck, rivulet, runnel. • v. TOLERATE, stand, bear, allow.

**broom** n. **1** a long-handled brush. **2** a shrub with white, yellow, or red flowers. □ **broomstick** the handle of a broom, on which witches are said to fly.

**Bros** abbr. Brothers.

**broth** n. a thin meat or fish soup.

**brothel** n. a house where men visit prostitutes.

**brother** n. **1** the son of the same parents as another person. **2** a male colleague or friend. **3** a monk. □ **brotherhood** comradeship; a group linked by a shared interest. **brother-in-law** the brother of your husband or wife; the husband of your sister. ■ **brotherly** adj.

**brought** past and p.p. of **BRING**.

**brow** n. an eyebrow; a forehead; the summit of a hill.
□ **browbeat** intimidate.

**brown** adj. **1** the colour of rich soil. **2** suntanned. • v. make or become brown.

**browse** v. **1** read or look at in a leisurely way. **2** look at information on a computer. **3** feed on leaves, twigs, etc.
▷ SYNS SCAN, skim, glance, look, thumb, leaf, peruse.

**bruise** n. an injury that discolours skin without breaking it. • v. cause a bruise on.

**bruiser** n. inf. a tough brutal person.

**brunch** n. a meal combining breakfast and lunch.

**brunette** n. a woman with brown hair.

**brunt** n. the worst stress or chief impact.

**brush** n. **1** an implement with a handle and block of bristles or wire. **2** an act of brushing. **3** a brief encounter with something bad. **4** a fox's tail. **5** undergrowth. • v. **1** clean, smooth, or apply with a brush. **2** touch lightly.
▷ SYNS v. **1** SWEEP, clean, buff; groom, comb. **2** TOUCH, stroke, skim, graze, kiss.

**brusque** adj. curt and offhand.
▷ SYNS ABRUPT, curt, blunt, short, terse, gruff, offhand, discourteous.

**Brussels sprout** n. the edible bud of a kind of cabbage.

**brutal** adj. savage or cruel.
■ **brutality** n. **brutally** adv.
▷ SYNS SAVAGE, cruel, vicious, sadistic, violent, bloodthirsty, callous, murderous, heartless,
merciless, inhuman, barbarous, barbaric, ferocious.

**brute** n. a brutal person or large unmanageable animal. • adj. merely physical. ■ **brutish** adj.
▷ SYNS n. **1** ANIMAL, beast, creature. **2** SAVAGE, monster, sadist, fiend, devil.

**BSE** abbr. bovine spongiform encephalopathy, a fatal brain disease of cattle.

**BST** abbr. British Summer Time.

**bubble** n. a thin sphere of liquid enclosing air or gas; an air-filled cavity. • v. **1** contain rising bubbles. **2** show great liveliness.
▷ SYNS v. FIZZ, foam, froth, effervesce, boil, simmer.

**bubbly** adj. **1** containing bubbles. **2** cheerful and high-spirited.
▷ SYNS **1** FIZZY, foamy, frothy, effervescent, sparkling. **2** VIVACIOUS, lively, animated, excited, bouncy, ebullient.

**bubonic plague** n. a plague characterized by swellings.

**buccaneer** n. a pirate; an adventurer.

**buck** n. **1** the male of a deer, hare, or rabbit. **2** US & Austral. a dollar. • v. **1** (of a horse) jump with the back arched. **2** (**buck up**) inf. cheer up.

**bucket** n. an open container with a handle, for carrying liquid.
▷ SYNS PAIL, pitcher, scuttle.

**buckle** n. a device through which a belt or strap is threaded to secure it. • v. **1** fasten with a buckle. **2** crumple under pressure.
▷ SYNS n. CLASP, fastener, clip, catch, hasp. • v. **1** FASTEN, do up, strap, hook, clasp, clip. **2** BEND,

twist, contort, warp, crumple, distort.

**bucolic** adj. rustic.

**bud** n. a leaf or flower not fully open. • v. (**budded**, **budding**) form buds.
▷ SYNS n. SHOOT, sprout, floret. • v. SPROUT, shoot, germinate.

**Buddhism** n. an Asian religion based on the teachings of Buddha. ■ Buddhist adj. & n.

**budding** adj. beginning to develop or be successful.

**budge** v. move slightly.

**budgerigar** n. an Australian parakeet often kept as a pet.

**budget** n. a plan of income and expenditure; the amount of money someone has available. • v. allow or provide for in a budget.
▷ SYNS n. FINANCIAL PLAN, forecast, statement, account, allowance, allocation, quota.

**budgie** n. inf. a budgerigar.

**buff** n. **1** a fawn colour. **2** inf. an expert and enthusiast. • v. polish with soft material.
▷ SYNS n. FAN, enthusiast, aficionado, devotee, expert. • v. POLISH, shine, rub, burnish.

**buffalo** n. (pl. **buffaloes** or **buffalo**) a wild ox; a North American bison.

**buffer** n. something that lessens the impact of harmful effects.

**buffet**[1] n. a meal where guests serve themselves; a counter where food and drink are served.
▷ SYNS CAFE, cafeteria, snack bar.

**buffet**[2] v. strike repeatedly.
▷ SYNS BATTER, strike, pound, hit, lash.

**buffoon** n. a ridiculous but amusing person. ■ buffoonery n.

**bug** n. **1** inf. a germ or an illness caused by one. **2** a small insect. **3** an error in a computer program or system. **4** a hidden microphone. • v. **1** hide a microphone in. **2** inf. annoy.
▷ SYNS n. **1** GERM, virus; illness, disorder, infection, sickness. **2** INSECT; inf. creepy-crawly, beastie. **3** FAULT, error, defect, flaw, virus; inf. gremlin.

**bugbear** n. something feared or disliked.

**buggy** n. (pl. **-ies**) a small light vehicle; a lightweight folding pushchair.

**bugle** n. a brass instrument like a small trumpet. ■ bugler n.

**build** v. **1** construct by putting parts or material together. **2** (**build up**) establish gradually; increase. • n. bodily shape. ■ builder n.
▷ SYNS v. CONSTRUCT, make, erect, put up, assemble, set up, create, form. • n. PHYSIQUE, body, frame, shape.

**building** n. a house or similar structure. □ building society an organization that accepts deposits and lends money, esp. to people buying houses.
▷ SYNS STRUCTURE, construction, edifice, pile, erection.

**bulb** n. **1** the rounded base of the stem of certain plants. **2** the glass part giving light in an electric lamp. ■ bulbous adj.

**bulge** n. a rounded swelling. • v. form a bulge, swell.
▷ SYNS n. SWELLING, bump, protuberance, protrusion, lump. • v. SWELL, project, protrude, stick out, balloon, distend.

**bulimia** n. an eating disorder marked by bouts of overeating

followed by fasting or vomiting.
■ **bulimic** adj.

**bulk** n. **1** the mass or size of something large. **2** the greater part. **3** a large mass or shape. □ **bulkhead** a partition in a ship or aircraft.
▷ SYNS **1** SIZE, volume, dimensions, mass, magnitude, immensity. **2** MAJORITY, preponderance, main part.

**bulky** adj. (-ier, -iest) large and unwieldy.
▷ SYNS UNWIELDY, awkward, large, big, massive, hulking, weighty.

**bull** n. **1** the male of the ox, whale, elephant, etc. **2** a pope's official edict. □ **bulldog** a powerful dog with a flat wrinkled face. **bulldozer** a tractor with a device for clearing ground. **bullfighting** the sport of baiting and killing a bull. **bullseye** the centre of the target in archery and darts.

**bullet** n. a small piece of metal fired from a gun.

**bulletin** n. a short official statement of news.
▷ SYNS REPORT, announcement, statement, newsflash, message, communiqué, communication, dispatch.

**bullion** n. gold or silver in bulk or bars.

**bullish** adj. aggressively confident.

**bullock** n. a castrated bull.

**bully** n. (pl. **-ies**) a person who hurts or intimidates weaker people. • v. (**bullied**, **bullying**) intimidate.
▷ SYNS INTIMIDATE, coerce, browbeat, oppress, persecute, torment, terrorize, tyrannize, cow.

**bulrush** n. a tall reedlike plant.

**bulwark** n. **1** a defensive wall. **2** a ship's side above deck level.
▷ SYNS **1** RAMPART, embankment, fortification, bastion. **2** SUPPORT, defence, guard, protection, safeguard.

**bum** n. inf. **1** the buttocks. **2** a lazy or worthless person.

**bumble** v. move or act clumsily.

**bumblebee** n. a large bee.

**bumf** (or **bumph**) n. inf. printed information.

**bump** v. **1** knock or collide with. **2** travel with a jolting movement. • n. **1** a knock or collision; the dull sound of this. **2** a swelling or a raised area on a surface. **3** a jolt.
▷ SYNS v. **1** HIT, bang, strike, knock, crash into, collide with. **2** BOUNCE, jolt, shake, jerk, rattle. • n. **1** BANG, crash, thud, thump, knock, smash, collision. **2** LUMP, swelling, contusion, injury, bulge, protuberance.

**bumper** n. a horizontal bar at the front or back of a motor vehicle to lessen the damage in collision. • adj. unusually large or successful.

**bumpkin** n. an unsophisticated country person.

**bumptious** adj. conceited.

**bumpy** adj. uneven; full of bumps.
▷ SYNS ROUGH, uneven, rutted, potholed, pitted, lumpy.

**bun** n. **1** a small cake or bread roll. **2** a tight coil of hair at the back of the head.

**bunch** n. a number of things growing or fastened together; a group. • v. form or be formed into a bunch.
▷ SYNS n. **1** COLLECTION, cluster, batch, set, bundle, sheaf, clump. **2** BOUQUET, spray, posy, nosegay.

**3** GROUP, crowd, band, gang, flock, knot, cluster.

**bundle** n. a collection of things loosely fastened or wrapped together. • v. **1** make into a bundle. **2** move or push hurriedly.

▷ SYNS n. BUNCH, collection, heap, stack, parcel, bale, sheaf.
• v. **1** TIE, wrap, pack, parcel, roll. **2** PUSH, shove, hurry, hustle, manhandle.

**bung** n. a stopper for a jar or barrel. • v. **1** block up. **2** inf. throw or put.

**bungalow** n. a one-storeyed house.

**bungle** v. spoil by lack of skill. • n. a bungled attempt.

▷ SYNS v. BOTCH, mess up, make a mess of, mismanage, spoil, muff; inf. screw up.

**bunion** n. a painful swelling at the base of the big toe.

**bunk** n. a shelf-like bed.

**bunker** n. **1** a container for fuel. **2** a sandy hollow forming an obstacle on a golf course. **3** a reinforced underground shelter.

**bunting** n. **1** a bird related to the finches. **2** decorative flags.

**buoy** n. a floating object used as a navigation mark. • v. **1** keep afloat. **2** be cheerful and confident.

**buoyant** adj. **1** able to float. **2** cheerful.

**burden** n. something carried; an obligation causing hardship. • v. load; oppress.

▷ SYNS n. **1** LOAD, weight, cargo, freight. **2** RESPONSIBILITY, duty, obligation, onus, charge, care, worry, problem, trouble, difficulty, encumbrance.
• v. **1** LOAD, overload, be laden,

weigh down, encumber, hamper. **2** TROUBLE, worry, oppress, distress, afflict, torment, strain, tax, overwhelm.

**bureau** n. **1** a writing desk with drawers. **2** an office or department.

▷ SYNS **1** AGENCY, office, department, service. **2** DESK, writing desk.

**bureaucracy** n. (pl. **-ies**) government by unelected officials; excessive administration.
■ **bureaucrat** n. **bureaucratic** adj.

▷ SYNS OFFICIALDOM, administration, civil service, government; regulations, paperwork, red tape.

**burgeon** v. grow rapidly.

**burglar** n. a person who commits burglary. ■ **burgle** v.

▷ SYNS HOUSEBREAKER, intruder, thief, robber.

**burglary** n. the crime of entering a building illegally and stealing its contents.

▷ SYNS HOUSEBREAKING, breaking and entering, break-in, theft, robbery.

**burgundy** n. (pl. **-ies**) a red wine; a purplish red colour.

**burial** n. the burying of a corpse.

▷ SYNS FUNERAL, interment, entombment, obsequies.

**burlesque** n. a comically exaggerated imitation.

▷ SYNS PARODY, caricature, satire, lampoon; inf. send-up, spoof.

**burly** adj. (**-ier**, **-iest**) with a strong heavy body.

▷ SYNS WELL BUILT, muscular, brawny, thickset, stocky, beefy, sturdy, big, strong, strapping, hefty.

**burn** v. **1** (of a fire) flame or glow while using up a fuel. **2** harm or

destroy by fire. **3** feel a strong emotion. **4** (**burn out**) become exhausted through overwork. • n. an injury caused by burning.
▷ SYNS v. **1** BE ON FIRE, be alight, blaze, glow, smoulder. **2** SET FIRE TO, set alight, light, ignite, incinerate, scorch.

**burning** adj. **1** intense. **2** (of an issue) keenly discussed.
▷ SYNS **1** ON FIRE, blazing, ablaze, alight, smouldering. **2** INTENSE, eager, passionate, fervent, ardent, fervid. **3** IMPORTANT, crucial, significant, urgent, pressing, critical, vital, essential, pivotal.

**burnish** v. polish by rubbing.

**burp** inf. n. & v. (make) a belch.

**burr** n. a strong pronunciation of the letter 'r'.

**burrow** n. a hole dug by an animal as a dwelling. • v. dig a burrow.
▷ SYNS n. TUNNEL, hole, hollow, lair, den, earth, warren, set. • v. DIG, tunnel, excavate, mine, hollow out.

**bursar** n. a person who manages the finances of a college or school.

**bursary** n. (pl. **-ies**) a grant for study.

**burst** v. (**burst**, **bursting**) **1** break suddenly and violently apart. **2** force or be forced open. **3** be very full. **4** appear or come suddenly and forcefully. • n. **1** an instance of breaking. **2** a brief violent or energetic outbreak.
▷ SYNS v. **1** SPLIT, break open, rupture, shatter, explode, fracture, disintegrate, fragment. **2** RUSH, charge, dash, career, plough, hurtle.

**bury** v. (**buried**, **burying**) put or hide something underground;

cover or conceal; involve yourself deeply.
▷ SYNS **1** INTER, lay to rest, entomb. **2** CONCEAL, hide, cover, engulf.

**bus** n. (pl. **buses**; US **busses**) a large motor vehicle for public transport by road. • v. (**buses** or **busses**, **bussed**, **bussing**) travel or transport by bus.

**bush** n. **1** a shrub. **2** (**the bush**) wild or uncultivated country.
▷ SYNS **1** SHRUB; undergrowth, shrubbery. **2** WILDS, wilderness, backwoods.

**bushy** adj. (**-ier**, **-iest**) growing thickly.
▷ SYNS THICK, shaggy, dense, luxuriant, spreading.

**business** n. **1** a person's regular occupation. **2** commercial activity. **3** a commercial organization. **4** a person's concern.
■ **businessman** n. **businesswoman** n.
▷ SYNS **1** OCCUPATION, profession, work, line, career, job, trade, vocation, employment. **2** TRADE, commerce, dealing. **3** COMPANY, firm, corporation, enterprise, venture, organization. **4** CONCERN, affair, responsibility, problem, worry.

**businesslike** adj. efficient and practical.
▷ SYNS PROFESSIONAL, efficient, organized, methodical, systematic, well ordered, practical.

**busk** v. play music in the street for donations. ■ **busker** n.

**bust** v. inf. burst or break. • n. **1** a woman's breasts. **2** a sculpture of someone's head, shoulders, and chest. • adj. **1** broken. **2** bankrupt.

**bustle** v. make a show of activity or hurry. • n. excited activity.

▷ SYNS v. HURRY, rush, dash, scurry, scramble, run. • n. ACTIVITY, flurry, stir, movement, hustle, hurly-burly, commotion, excitement.

**busy** adj. **1** having a great deal to do. **2** occupied. **3** crowded or full of activity. ■ **busily** adv.
▷ SYNS **1** HECTIC, active, full, eventful, energetic, tiring. **2** ENGAGED, occupied, involved, working, hard at work, absorbed, engrossed; inf. on the go.

**busybody** n. an interfering person.
▷ SYNS MEDDLER, troublemaker, mischief-maker, gossip; inf. nosy parker.

**but** conj. **1** nevertheless. **2** on the contrary. **3** other than. • prep. except; apart from. • adv. only.

**butane** n. an inflammable gas used in liquid form as fuel.

**butch** adj. inf. ostentatiously and aggressively masculine.

**butcher** n. a person who cuts up and sells meat as a trade; a savage killer. • v. kill needlessly or brutally. ■ **butchery** n.

**butler** n. a chief manservant.

**butt** n. **1** the thick end of a tool or weapon. **2** a cigarette stub. **3** an object of criticism or ridicule. **4** a cask for holding liquid. • v. **1** push with the head. **2** (**butt in**) interrupt.
▷ SYNS n. **1** HANDLE, end, hilt, haft. **2** STUB, end, remnant; inf. dog end. **3** TARGET, victim, object, laughing stock. • v. **1** KNOCK, shove, bump, push. **2** INTERRUPT, intrude, interfere.

**butter** n. a fatty substance made from cream. • v. spread with butter. □ **buttercup** a plant with yellow cup-shaped flowers.

**buttermilk** the liquid left after butter has been churned.
**butterscotch** a sweet made with butter and brown sugar.

**butterfly** n. (pl. **-ies**) **1** an insect with four large wings. **2** a swimming stroke with both arms lifted at the same time.

**buttock** n. either of the two fleshy parts of the human body that form the bottom.
▷ SYNS (**buttocks**)BOTTOM, posterior, rump, backside, behind, hindquarters; inf. bum.

**button** n. **1** a disc sewn to a garment as a fastener. **2** a knob pressed to operate a device. • v. fasten with buttons.

**buttonhole** n. **1** a slit through which a button is passed to fasten clothing. **2** a flower worn in the buttonhole of a lapel. • v. accost and talk to.
▷ SYNS v. ACCOST, waylay, detain, take aside.

**buttress** n. a support built against a wall; something that supports. • v. reinforce or prop up.
▷ SYNS n. SUPPORT, prop, reinforcement, strut, stanchion, pier. • v. STRENGTHEN, support, reinforce, prop up, shore up, brace, underpin.

**buxom** adj. (of a woman) plump and large-breasted.

**buy** v. (**bought, buying**) obtain in exchange for money. • n. a purchase. ■ **buyer** n.
▷ SYNS v. PURCHASE, pay for, procure, get, acquire, obtain, come by. • n. PURCHASE, acquisition, bargain, deal.

**buzz** n. **1** a low, continuous humming sound. **2** an atmosphere of excitement and activity. **3** inf. a thrill. • v. **1** make a buzzing sound. **2** be full of activity. ■ **buzzer** n.

**buzzard** n. a large hawk.

**by** prep. **1** through the action of. **2** indicating extent or margin: *by far the best.* **3** indicating the end of a time period. **4** beside. **5** past and beyond. **6** during. • **adv.** so as to go past. □ **by and by** before long. **by and large** on the whole.

**bye** n. **1** a run scored from a ball not hit by the batsman. **2** the transfer of a competitor to a higher round in the absence of an opponent.

**by-election** n. an election of an MP to replace one who has died or resigned.

**bygone** adj. belonging to the past.
▷ SYNS PAST, former, previous, earlier, one-time, of old, antiquated, ancient, obsolete, outmoded.

**by-law** n. a regulation made by a local authority or corporation.

**bypass** n. a road taking traffic round a town; an operation providing an alternative passage for blood. • **v.** go past or round.

**by-product** n. something produced in the process of making something else.

**byre** n. a cowshed.

**bystander** n. a person standing near when something happens.
▷ SYNS ONLOOKER, spectator, eyewitness, witness, watcher, passer-by.

**byte** n. Computing a fixed number of bits (usually eight).

**byway** n. a minor road.

**byword** n. a famous or typical example; a familiar saying.

# Cc

**C** (or **c**) n. the Roman numeral for 100. • **abbr. 1** Celsius or centigrade. **2** cent(s). **3** (**c.**) century. **4** (**c** or **ca.**) (before a date or amount) circa. **5** (©) copyright.

**cab** n. **1** a taxi. **2** a compartment for the driver of a train, lorry, etc.

**cabal** n. a group involved in a plot.

**cabaret** n. entertainment provided in a nightclub etc.

**cabbage** n. a vegetable with thick green or purple leaves.

**cabin** n. a compartment in a ship or aircraft; a small hut.
▷ SYNS **1** HUT, shack, shed, chalet, lodge. **2** BERTH, compartment.

**cabinet** n. **1** a cupboard with drawers or shelves. **2** (**the Cabinet**) a committee of senior government ministers.

**cable** n. a thick rope of fibre or wire; a set of insulated wires for carrying electricity or signals. □ **cable car** a vehicle pulled by a moving cable for carrying passengers up and down mountains.

▷ SYNS ROPE, cord, hawser, line, guy; wire, lead.

**cache** n. a hidden store.

**cachet** n. prestige.

**cackle** n. the clucking of hens; a loud laugh. • v. give a cackle.

**cacophony** n. (pl. -ies) a discordant mixture of sounds. ■ cacophonous adj.

**cactus** n. (pl. -ti or -tuses) a fleshy plant, often with prickles, from a hot dry climate.

**cad** n. dated a dishonourable man.

**cadaver** n. a corpse.

**cadaverous** adj. very pale and thin.

▷ SYNS GAUNT, haggard, emaciated, skeletal, ashen, pale, wan, ghostly.

**caddie** (or **caddy**) n. a golfer's attendant carrying clubs.

**caddy** n. (pl. -ies) a small box for tea.

**cadence** n. the rise and fall of the voice in speech.

▷ SYNS RHYTHM, beat, tempo, lilt, intonation, modulation.

**cadenza** n. a difficult solo passage in a musical work.

**cadet** n. a young trainee in the armed forces or police.

**cadge** v. inf. ask for or get something without paying or working for it.

**cadmium** n. a silvery-white metal.

**Caesarean** (US **Cesarean**) n. an operation for delivering a child by cutting through the wall of the mother's abdomen.

**cafe** n. a small informal restaurant.

▷ SYNS CAFETERIA, snack bar, bistro, buffet, brasserie.

**cafeteria** n. a self-service restaurant.

**caffeine** n. a stimulant found in tea and coffee.

**caftan** = KAFTAN.

**cage** n. a structure of bars or wires, used for confining animals. • v. confine in a cage.

▷ SYNS n. PEN, enclosure, pound, coop, hutch, aviary.

**cagey** adj. inf. secretive or reticent.

**cagoule** n. a light hooded waterproof jacket.

**cahoots** pl. n. (**in cahoots**) inf. making secret plans together.

**cairn** n. a mound of stones as a memorial or landmark.

**cajole** v. coax.

▷ SYNS COAX, wheedle, persuade, prevail on, inveigle; inf. sweet-talk.

**cake** n. 1 a sweet food made from a baked mixture of flour, eggs, sugar, and fat. 2 a flat compact mass. • v. form a crust.

▷ SYNS n. 1 BUN, gateau, pastry. 2 BLOCK, bar, slab, lump, cube. • v. 1 CLOT, harden, solidify, congeal, coagulate. 2 COVER, coat, plaster, encrust.

**calamine** n. a soothing skin lotion.

**calamitous** adj. disastrous.

▷ SYNS DISASTROUS, catastrophic, devastating, cataclysmic, dire, tragic.

**calamity** n. (pl. -ies) a disaster.

▷ SYNS DISASTER, catastrophe, tragedy, misfortune, cataclysm.

**calcium** n. a whitish metallic element.

**calculate** v. 1 reckon mathematically; estimate. 2 intend or plan. ■ calculation n. calculator n.

▷ SYNS 1 WORK OUT, compute, determine, count up, figure,

reckon up, total. **2** ESTIMATE, gauge, judge. **3** DESIGN, plan, aim, intend.

**calculating** adj. ruthlessly scheming.

**caldron** US sp. of **CAULDRON**.

**calendar** n. a chart showing dates of days of the year.

**calf** n. (pl. **calves**) **1** the young of cattle, elephants, whales, etc. **2** the fleshy back of the human leg below the knee.

**calibrate** v. mark the units of measurement on or check the accuracy of a gauge.
■ **calibration** n.

**calibre** (US **caliber**) n. **1** degree of quality or ability. **2** the diameter of a gun, tube, or bullet.
▷ SYNS **1** BORE, gauge, diameter, size. **2** QUALITY, worth, stature, distinction, ability, merit, talent, capability, expertise.

**calico** n. a cotton cloth.

**caliper** (or **calliper**) n. **1** (also **calipers**) a measuring instrument with two hinged legs. **2** a metal support for a person's leg.

**call** v. **1** shout to attract attention. **2** summon. **3** telephone. **4** name or describe as. **5** pay a brief visit. • n. **1** an act of calling. **2** (**call for**) demand or need for. **3** the typical cry of a bird or animal. **4** a brief visit. □ **call centre** an office which handles large numbers of phone calls for an organization. **call for** necessitate. **call off** cancel.
■ **caller** n.
▷ SYNS v. **1** CRY, shout, yell, scream, roar. **2** SUMMON, send for, order. **3** TELEPHONE, phone, ring. **4** NAME, christen, baptize; designate, term, dub. • n. **1** CRY, shout, yell, scream, roar,

exclamation. **2** NEED, reason, occasion, justification; demand, desire.

**calligraphy** n. decorative handwriting.

**calling** n. a profession or occupation; a vocation.

**callous** adj. insensitive and cruel. • n. a patch of hardened skin.
■ **calloused** adj. **callousness** n.
▷ SYNS adj. INSENSITIVE, unfeeling, hard, heartless, hard-hearted, cold, uncaring, unsympathetic, merciless, pitiless.

**callow** adj. immature and inexperienced.
▷ SYNS IMMATURE, inexperienced, naive, unsophisticated; inf. wet behind the ears.

**calm** adj. **1** not excited or agitated. **2** not windy or disturbed by wind. • n. a calm condition. • v. make calm.
■ **calmness** n.
▷ SYNS adj. **1** COMPOSED, relaxed, collected, cool, controlled, self-controlled, self-possessed, tranquil, unruffled, serene, imperturbable, poised, level-headed, equable; inf. laid-back, unflappable. **2** STILL, windless, tranquil, quiet, peaceful.
• n. COMPOSURE, self-control, tranquillity, serenity, sangfroid, quietness, peace, peacefulness.
• v. **1** SOOTHE, quieten, pacify, placate. **2** COMPOSE YOURSELF, control yourself, cool down, get a grip.

**calorie** n. a unit of heat; a unit of the energy-producing value of food. ■ **calorific** adj.

**calumny** n. (pl. **-ies**) slander.

**calve** v. give birth to a calf.

**calypso** n. (pl. **-os**) a West Indian song with improvised words on a topical theme.

**cam** n. a projecting part on a wheel or shaft changing rotary to to-and-fro motion.

**camaraderie** n. comradeship.

**camber** n. a slight convex curve given to a surface, esp. of a road.

**cambric** n. thin linen or cotton cloth.

**camcorder** n. a combined video and sound recorder.

**came** past of **COME**.

**camel** n. a large animal with either one or two humps on its back.

**camellia** n. an evergreen flowering shrub.

**cameo** n. (pl. **-os**) **1** a piece of jewellery with a head carved in relief on a differently coloured background. **2** a small part played by a famous actor.

**camera** n. an apparatus for taking photographs or film pictures. ■ **cameraman** n.

**camisole** n. a woman's bodice-like undergarment with shoulder straps.

**camouflage** n. disguise or concealment by colouring or covering. • v. disguise or conceal in this way.
▷ SYNS n. DISGUISE, concealment, mask, screen, cover-up, front, facade, blind. • v. DISGUISE, hide, conceal, mask, screen, cloak, cover.

**camp** n. **1** a place with temporary accommodation in tents or huts. **2** a complex of buildings for holidaymakers. **3** the supporters of a particular party or viewpoint. • v. stay in a tent. • adj. exaggeratedly effeminate or theatrical. □ **camp bed** a portable folding bed.
■ **camper** n. **campsite** n.

▷ SYNS n. ENCAMPMENT, campsite, camping ground, bivouac.

**campaign** n. a connected series of military operations; an organized course of action to achieve a goal. • v. conduct or take part in a campaign.
■ **campaigner** n.
▷ SYNS n. **1** BATTLE, war, offensive, attack. **2** CRUSADE, drive, push, struggle, battle plan, strategy. • v. FIGHT, battle, work, crusade, strive, struggle.

**camphor** n. a strong-smelling substance used esp. in insect repellent.

**campus** n. the grounds of a university or college.

**can**¹ n. a cylindrical metal container. • v. (**canned, canning**) preserve in a can.

**can**² v.aux. (**can, could**) be able or allowed to.

**canal** n. **1** an artificial watercourse. **2** a duct in the body.

**canapé** n. a small piece of bread or pastry with a savoury topping.

**canary** n. (pl. **-ies**) a small yellow songbird.

**cancan** n. a lively high-kicking dance performed by women.

**cancel** v. **1** declare that something arranged will not take place; put an end to. **2** mark a ticket or stamp to prevent re-use. **3** (**cancel out**) offset or neutralize.
■ **cancellation** n.
▷ SYNS **1** CALL OFF, abandon, scrap, drop, axe. **2** ANNUL, invalidate, nullify, revoke, rescind, countermand, withdraw, quash. **3** (**cancel out**) COUNTERBALANCE, offset, counteract, neutralize.

**cancer** n. a malignant tumour; a disease in which these form. ■ **cancerous** adj.
▷ SYNS CARCINOMA, tumour, malignancy, growth.

**candelabrum** n. (pl. **-bra**) a large branched holder for several candles or lamps.

**candid** adj. frank. ■ **candidly** adv.
▷ SYNS FRANK, open, honest, truthful, direct, plain-spoken, blunt, straightforward, sincere, forthright.

**candidate** n. a person applying for a job, standing for election, or taking an exam. ■ **candidacy** n.
▷ SYNS APPLICANT, interviewee; contender, nominee, aspirant, possibility.

**candied** adj. encrusted or preserved in sugar.

**candle** n. a stick of wax enclosing a wick which is burnt to give light. □ **candlestick** a holder for a candle.

**candour** (US **candor**) n. frankness.
▷ SYNS FRANKNESS, honesty, truthfulness, openness, directness, sincerity.

**candy** n. (pl. **-ies**) US sweets.
□ **candyfloss** a mass of spun sugar on a stick.

**cane** n. a stem of a tall reed or grass; a length of cane used as a walking stick, for beating someone, etc. • v. beat with a cane.

**canine** adj. of dogs. • n. a pointed tooth between the incisors and molars.

**canister** n. a small metal container.

**canker** n. a disease of animals or plants.

**cannabis** n. a drug obtained from the hemp plant.

**cannelloni** pl.n. rolls of pasta with a savoury filling.

**cannibal** n. a person who eats human flesh. ■ **cannibalism** n.

**cannibalize** (or **-ise**) v. use parts from a machine to repair another.

**cannon** n. (pl. **cannon**) a large gun. • v. bump heavily into.

**cannot** v.aux the negative form of CAN².

**canny** adj. (**-ier, -iest**) shrewd.

**canoe** n. a light boat propelled by paddling. • v. (**canoed, canoeing**) go in a canoe. ■ **canoeist** n.

**canon** n. 1 a member of cathedral clergy. 2 a general rule or principle. 3 a set of writings accepted as genuine. ■ **canonical** adj.

**canonize** (or **-ise**) v. declare officially to be a saint. ■ **canonization** n.

**canopy** n. (pl. **-ies**) an ornamental cloth held up as a covering.

**cant** n. insincere talk; jargon.

**cantaloupe** n. a small round melon with orange flesh.

**cantankerous** adj. bad-tempered and uncooperative.

**cantata** n. a choral composition.

**canteen** n. 1 a restaurant for employees. 2 a case of cutlery.

**canter** n. a gentle gallop. • v. go at a canter.

**cantilever** n. a projecting beam or girder supporting a structure.

**canvas** n. a strong coarse cloth; a painting on this.

**canvass** v. 1 ask for votes. 2 propose a plan for discussion.

▷ SYNS **1** CAMPAIGN, electioneer, drum up support. **2** PROPOSE, suggest, discuss, debate.

**canyon** n. a deep gorge.
▷ SYNS RAVINE, gorge, gully, defile.

**cap** n. **1** a soft, flat hat with a peak; a cover or top; an upper limit. **2** an explosive device for a toy pistol. • v. (**capped, capping**) put a cap on; set an upper limit to.

**capable** adj. **1** able or fit to do something. **2** competent or efficient. ■ **capability** n.
▷ SYNS ABLE, competent, effective, efficient, proficient, accomplished, talented, adept, skilful, experienced, practised, qualified.

**capacious** adj. roomy.

**capacity** n. **1** the amount that something can contain. **2** ability to do something. **3** a role or function.
▷ SYNS **1** VOLUME, size, magnitude, dimensions, measurements, proportions. **2** ABILITY, capability, competence, proficiency, skill, talent. **3** POSITION, post, job, office; role, function.

**cape** n. **1** a sleeveless cloak. **2** a coastal promontory.

**caper** v. skip about in a lively way. • n. **1** inf. a light-hearted or dishonest activity. **2** an edible pickled flower bud.
▷ SYNS v. FROLIC, romp, skip, gambol, prance, dance.

**capillary** n. (pl. **-ies**) a very fine hairlike tube or blood vessel.

**capital** n. **1** the chief town of a country or region. **2** a capital letter. **3** money with which a business is started. **4** the top part of a pillar. • adj. **1** involving the death penalty. **2** inf. excellent. □ **capital letter** a large-sized letter used to begin sentences and names.
▷ SYNS n. ASSETS, wealth, finance, funds, principal, cash, savings, resources, means, reserves, property, wherewithal.

**capitalism** n. a system in which trade and industry are controlled by private owners for profit. ■ **capitalist** n.

**capitalize** (or **-ise**) v. **1** convert into or provide with capital. **2** write in capital letters or with a capital first letter. **3** (**capitalize on**) take advantage of.

**capitulate** v. surrender or yield.
▷ SYNS SURRENDER, yield, give in/up, back down, submit, cave in, relent.

**capon** n. a domestic cock fattened for eating.

**cappuccino** n. (pl. **-os**) coffee made with frothy steamed milk.

**caprice** n. a whim.

**capricious** adj. having sudden changes of mood.
▷ SYNS FICKLE, unpredictable, unreliable, impulsive, changeable, mercurial, volatile, erratic, wayward.

**capsize** v. (of a boat) overturn.
▷ SYNS OVERTURN, turn over, keel over, turn turtle.

**capstan** n. a revolving post or spindle on which a cable etc. winds.

**capsule** n. **1** a small gelatin case containing a dose of medicine. **2** a small case or compartment.
▷ SYNS PILL, tablet, lozenge.

**captain** n. a person commanding a ship or aircraft; the leader of a group or team; a naval officer next below rear admiral; an army officer next

below major. • v. be captain of.
■ **captaincy** n.

▷ SYNS n. **1** COMMANDER, master; inf.
skipper. **2** CHIEF, head, leader;
inf. boss.

**caption** n. a short title or heading; an explanation on an
illustration.

**captivate** v. attract and hold
the interest of.

▷ SYNS CHARM, delight, enchant,
bewitch, fascinate, beguile,
entrance, mesmerize, enthral,
enrapture.

**captive** adj. unable to escape.
• n. a person who has been
captured.

▷ SYNS adj. IMPRISONED, caged,
incarcerated, confined,
detained, interned; inf. under
lock and key. • n. PRISONER,
detainee, internee.

**captivity** n. imprisonment.

▷ SYNS IMPRISONMENT, detention,
confinement, internment,
incarceration.

**captor** n. a person who takes a
captive.

**capture** v. **1** gain control of by
force; take prisoner. **2** record
accurately in words or pictures.
**3** cause data to be stored in a
computer. • n. capturing.

▷ SYNS v. CATCH, arrest, apprehend,
take prisoner, take captive,
seize.

**car** n. a motor vehicle for a small
number of passengers; a railway
carriage or wagon.

**carafe** n. a glass bottle for
serving wine or water.

▷ SYNS FLASK, decanter, jug,
pitcher, bottle, flagon.

**caramel** n. brown syrup made
from heated sugar; toffee
tasting like this.

**carat** n. a unit of purity of gold; a
unit of weight for precious
stones.

**caravan** n. **1** a vehicle equipped
for living in, able to be towed by
a vehicle. **2** hist. a group travelling together across a desert.

**caraway** n. a plant with spicy
seeds used as flavouring.

**carbohydrate** n. an energy-
producing compound (e.g.
starch) in food.

**carbon** n. a chemical element
occurring as diamond, graphite,
and charcoal, and in all living
matter. □ **carbon copy** a copy
made with carbon paper; an
exact copy. **carbon dating** a
method of deciding the age of
something by measuring the
decay of radiocarbon in it.
**carbon dioxide** a gas produced
during respiration and by
burning carbon. **carbon monoxide** a poisonous gas formed
by the incomplete burning of
carbon. **carbon paper** paper
coated with carbon, used to
make copies of documents.

**carbonate** n. a compound releasing carbon dioxide when
mixed with acid.

**carbonated** adj. (of a drink)
fizzy.

**carbuncle** n. **1** a severe abscess.
**2** a polished red gem.

**carburettor** (US **carburetor**) n. a
device mixing air and petrol in a
motor engine.

**carcass** (or **carcase**) n. the dead
body of an animal.

▷ SYNS BODY, corpse, remains,
cadaver.

**carcinogen** n. a cancer-
producing substance.
■ **carcinogenic** adj.

**carcinoma** n. (pl. **-mata** or **-mas**) a cancerous tumour.

**card** n. **1** a piece of cardboard or thick paper. **2** a piece of card printed with information, greetings, etc. **3** a credit card. **4** a playing card. **5** (**cards**) any card game. • v. clean or comb wool with a wire brush or toothed instrument. □ cardboard stiff paper made from paper pulp.

**cardiac** adj. of the heart.

**cardigan** n. a sweater with buttons down the front.

**cardinal** adj. most important. • n. an important RC priest, having the power to elect the Pope. □ cardinal number a number denoting quantity rather than order (1, 2, 3, etc.).

**cardiograph** n. an instrument recording heart movements.

**cardiology** n. the branch of medicine concerned with the heart. ■ cardiologist n.

**care** n. **1** the provision of welfare and protection. **2** serious attention to avoid damage, risk, or error. **3** a feeling or cause for anxiety. • v. **1** feel concern or interest. **2** feel affection or liking. **3** (**care for/to do**) like to have or be willing to do. **4** (**care for**) look after.
▷ SYNS n. **1** SAFE KEEPING, supervision, custody, charge, protection, control, responsibility; guardianship. **2** CAUTION, circumspection, vigilance, heed, attention, thought. **3** WORRY, anxiety, trouble, stress, pressure, strain; sorrow, woe. • v. BE CONCERNED, trouble yourself, bother, mind, worry.

**career** n. an occupation undertaken for a long period of a person's life. • v. move swiftly or wildly.
▷ SYNS n. PROFESSION, occupation, job, vocation, calling, employment, line of work, métier.

**carefree** adj. light-hearted and free from worry.
▷ SYNS UNWORRIED, untroubled, blithe, airy, nonchalant, insouciant, happy-go-lucky, free and easy, easy-going, relaxed; inf. laidback.

**careful** adj. showing attention or caution. ■ carefully adv.
▷ SYNS **1** CAUTIOUS, alert, attentive, watchful, vigilant, wary, on your guard, heedful. **2** CONSCIENTIOUS, painstaking, meticulous, diligent, scrupulous, punctilious, methodical.

**careless** adj. showing insufficient attention or concern. ■ carelessly adv.
▷ SYNS **1** INATTENTIVE, thoughtless, negligent, unthinking, heedless, irresponsible, remiss. **2** SLAPDASH, shoddy, slipshod; inf. sloppy.

**carer** n. a person who looks after a sick or disabled person at home.

**caress** n. a gentle loving touch. • v. give a caress to.
▷ SYNS v. FONDLE, stroke, touch, pet.

**caretaker** n. a person employed to look after a building.
▷ SYNS JANITOR, concierge.

**careworn** adj. showing signs of prolonged worry.

**cargo** n. (pl. **-oes** or **-os**) goods carried by ship, aircraft, or motor vehicle.
▷ SYNS FREIGHT, load, consignment, goods, merchandise, shipment.

**caribou** n. (pl. **caribou**) a North American reindeer.

**caricature** n. a picture exaggerating someone's characteristics for comic effect. • v. portray in this way.
▷ SYNS n. CARTOON, parody, lampoon, burlesque, satire.

**caries** n. decay of a tooth or bone.

**carmine** adj. vivid crimson.

**carnage** n. great slaughter.
▷ SYNS SLAUGHTER, massacre, butchery, blood bath, holocaust, pogrom.

**carnal** adj. of the body or flesh.
▷ SYNS SEXUAL, sensual, erotic, lustful, lascivious, fleshly, bodily, physical.

**carnation** n. a plant with pink, white, or red flowers.

**carnival** n. a festival with processions, music, and dancing.
▷ SYNS FESTIVAL, celebration, fiesta, gala, festivity.

**carnivore** n. an animal feeding on flesh. ■ carnivorous adj.

**carol** n. a Christmas hymn.
• v. (**carolled, carolling**; US **caroled**) sing carols; sing joyfully.

**carotid artery** n. either of the two main arteries carrying blood to the head.

**carouse** v. drink and be merry.

**carousel** n. 1 a merry-go-round. 2 a conveyor system for baggage at an airport.

**carp** n. a freshwater fish.
• v. keep finding fault.

**carpenter** n. a person who makes or repairs wooden objects and structures.
■ carpentry n.

**carpet** n. a textile fabric for covering a floor; a covering.

• v. (**carpeted, carpeting**) cover with a carpet.

**carriage** n. 1 a horse-drawn passenger vehicle. 2 a passenger vehicle in a train. 3 the carrying of goods from one place to another. 4 a person's way of standing and moving. □ carriage clock a portable clock with a handle on top. carriageway the part of a road intended for vehicles.
▷ SYNS 1 COACH, car. 2 BEARING, deportment, posture, stance, comportment.

**carrier** n. 1 a person or thing carrying something. 2 a company that transports goods or people. □ carrier bag a plastic or paper shopping bag.

**carrion** n. dead decaying flesh.

**carrot** n. 1 a tapering orange root vegetable. 2 an incentive.

**carry** v. 1 transport, support and move; have on your person; transmit a disease. 2 support; assume responsibility. 3 entail a consequence. 4 take a process to a particular point. 5 approve a measure; gain the support of. 6 stock goods. 7 be audible at a distance. □ carry on continue. carry out put into practice.
▷ SYNS 1 CONVEY, transport, move, transfer, take, bring, fetch, bear, haul, lug. 2 SUPPORT, bear, sustain, hold up, shoulder. 3 INVOLVE, lead to, result in, entail.

**cart** n. a wheeled vehicle for carrying loads. • v. carry or transport. □ carthorse a large, strong horse. cartwheel a sideways handspring with the arms and legs extended.

**carte blanche** n. full power to do as you think best.

**cartel** n. a manufacturers' or producers' union to control prices.

**cartilage** n. the firm elastic tissue in the skeletons of vertebrates.

**cartography** n. map drawing. ■ cartographer n.

**carton** n. a cardboard or plastic container.
▷ SYNS BOX, container, package, packet, pack.

**cartoon** n. 1 a humorous drawing. 2 a film consisting of an animated sequence of drawings. ■ cartoonist n.
▷ SYNS 1 ANIMATION, comic strip. 2 CARICATURE, parody, lampoon, burlesque, satire.

**cartridge** n. 1 a case containing explosive for firearms. 2 a sealed cassette. □ cartridge paper thick strong paper.

**carve** v. cut hard material to make an object or pattern; cut meat into slices for eating.
▷ SYNS 1 SCULPT, sculpture, chisel, cut, hew, whittle, form, shape, fashion, mould. 2 ENGRAVE, etch, incise. 3 SLICE, cut up.

**cascade** n. a waterfall. • v. fall like a waterfall.
▷ SYNS n. WATERFALL, falls, cataract. • v. GUSH, pour, surge, spill, overflow, stream.

**case** n. 1 an instance of a particular situation. 2 a lawsuit; a set of arguments supporting a position. 3 a container or protective covering; a suitcase. 4 the form of a noun, adjective, or pronoun indicating its grammatical role in a sentence. • v. 1 enclose in a case. 2 inf. examine a building etc. in preparation for a crime. □ in case so as to allow for possible eventualities.
▷ SYNS n. 1 INSTANCE, occurrence, manifestation, demonstration, example, illustration, specimen. 2 SITUATION, position, state of affairs, circumstances, conditions, facts. 3 TRIAL, proceedings, lawsuit, action, suit. 4 CONTAINER, box, receptacle, canister, crate, carton, pack, suitcase, trunk.

**casement** n. a window opening on vertical hinges.

**cash** n. money in coins or banknotes. • v. 1 give or obtain notes or coins for a cheque etc. 2 (cash in on) take advantage of.
▷ SYNS n. MONEY, notes, coins, change; currency.

**cashew** n. an edible nut.

**cashier** n. a person employed to handle money. • v. dismiss from military service in disgrace.

**cashmere** n. fine soft wool from a breed of goat.

**casino** n. (pl. -os) a public building or room for gambling.

**cask** n. a barrel for liquids.
▷ SYNS BARREL, keg, vat, butt, tun.

**casket** n. 1 a small ornamental box for valuables. 2 US a coffin.

**casserole** n. a covered dish in which food is cooked and served; food cooked in this. • v. cook in a casserole.

**cassette** n. a small case containing a reel of magnetic tape or film.

**cassock** n. a long robe worn by clergy and choristers.

**cast** v. 1 throw forcefully. 2 cause light or shadow to appear on a surface. 3 direct your eyes or thoughts towards something. 4 register a vote. 5 shape molten metal in a mould. **6** give a part to an actor or allocate parts in a play or film. **7** leave aside or discard. **8** make a magic spell. • n. **1** the actors in a play or film. **2** an object made by casting molten metal. **3** (or **plaster cast**) a bandage stiffened with plaster of Paris to support and protect a broken limb. **4** appearance or character. □ **casting vote** a deciding vote when those on each side are equal. **cast iron** a hard alloy of iron and carbon cast in a mould. **cast-off** a discarded thing.

▷ SYNS v. **1** THROW, toss, fling, pitch, hurl, lob; inf. chuck, sling. **2** EMIT, give off, send out, shed, radiate, diffuse, spread. **3** DIRECT, shoot, throw, fling, send. **4** REGISTER, record, enter, file; vote. **5** MOULD, form, fashion, sculpt, model.

**castanets** pl.n. a pair of shell-shaped pieces of wood clicked in the hand to accompany Spanish dancing.

**castaway** n. a shipwrecked person.

**caste** n. each of the classes of Hindu society.

**castigate** v. reprimand severely. ■ **castigation** n.

▷ SYNS REBUKE, reprimand, scold, censure, upbraid, berate, admonish, chide, take to task, chastise.

**castle** n. a large medieval fortified building.

▷ SYNS FORTRESS, stronghold, fortification, citadel, keep.

**castor** (or **caster**) n. **1** a small swivelling wheel on a leg of furniture. **2** a small container with a perforated top for sprinkling sugar etc. □ **castor oil** an oil from the seeds of a

tropical plant, used as a laxative. **castor sugar** finely granulated white sugar.

**castrate** v. remove the testicles of. ■ **castration** n.

▷ SYNS NEUTER, geld, sterilize, cut.

**casual** adj. **1** relaxed and unconcerned. **2** happening by chance. **3** not regular or permanent: *casual work*. **4** not serious or formal. ■ **casually** adv.

▷ SYNS **1** INDIFFERENT, unconcerned, lackadaisical, blasé, nonchalant, insouciant, offhand; easy-going, free and easy, blithe, carefree, devil-may-care; inf. laid-back. **2** CHANCE, accidental, unplanned, unexpected, unforeseen, serendipitous. **3** RELAXED, informal, friendly, unceremonious.

**casualty** n. (pl. **-ies**) a person killed or injured in a war or accident.

▷ SYNS FATALITY, victim, loss.

**cat** n. a small furry domesticated animal; a wild animal related to this.□ **catcall** a whistle of disapproval. **catkin** a spike of small flowers hanging from a willow etc. **catnap** a short nap. **catseye** trademark each of a series of reflective studs marking the lanes of a road. **catwalk** a narrow platform along which models walk to display clothes.

**cataclysm** n. a violent upheaval or disaster.

**catacomb** n. an underground chamber with recesses for tombs.

▷ SYNS CRYPT, tomb, vault, sepulchre.

**catalogue** (US also **catalog**) n. a systematic list of items. • v. (**catalogued**, **cataloguing**) list in a catalogue.

▷ SYNS n. LIST, record, register, inventory, index, directory, archive.

**catalyst** n. a substance that aids a chemical reaction while remaining unchanged.

**catalytic converter** n. part of an exhaust system that reduces the harmful effects of pollutant gases.

**catamaran** n. a boat with parallel twin hulls.

**catapult** n. a device with elastic fitted to a forked stick for shooting small stones.
• v. hurl from or as if from a catapult.

**cataract** n. 1 a large waterfall. 2 an opaque area clouding the lens of the eye.
▷ SYNS WATERFALL, falls, cascade, rapids.

**catarrh** n. excessive mucus in the nose or throat.

**catastrophe** n. a sudden great disaster. ■ catastrophic adj.
▷ SYNS DISASTER, calamity, cataclysm, tragedy.

**catch** v. 1 seize and hold something moving. 2 capture. 3 surprise someone in the act of doing something wrong or embarrassing. 4 hear or understand. 5 become infected with an illness. 6 be in time to board a vehicle or see a person etc. • n. 1 an act of catching. 2 a device for fastening a door or window. 3 a hidden problem. 4 an amount of fish caught. □ catch out discover that someone has done something wrong. catchphrase a well-known phrase. catch up 1 reach those ahead of you. 2 do tasks which should have been done earlier.

▷ SYNS v. 1 SEIZE, grab, snatch, grasp, grip, clutch, hold; receive, intercept. 2 CAPTURE, apprehend, arrest, take prisoner; trap, snare; inf. nab, nick. 3 HEAR, make out, discern, perceive, understand, follow, grasp. 4 DISCOVER, find, come across, stumble on, surprise. 5 CONTRACT, get, pick up, develop, come down with.
• n. 1 LATCH, lock, fastener, clasp, hasp. 2 SNAG, disadvantage, drawback, problem, difficulty; trick, trap.

**catching** adj. infectious.
▷ SYNS CONTAGIOUS, infectious, communicable, transmittable, transmissible.

**catchment area** n. 1 an area from which rainfall drains into a river. 2 an area from which a hospital draws patients or a school draws pupils.

**catchy** adj. (-ier, -iest) (of a tune) pleasant and easy to remember.

**catechism** n. a series of questions and answers on the principles of a religion, used for teaching.

**categorical** adj. unconditional; absolute. ■ categorically adv.
▷ SYNS UNQUALIFIED, unconditional, unequivocal, unambiguous, definite, absolute, emphatic, positive, direct, conclusive, unreserved.

**category** n. (pl. -ies) a class of things. ■ categorize v.
▷ SYNS CLASS, group, classification, type, sort, kind, variety, grade, order, rank.

**cater** v. supply food; provide what is needed or wanted.
■ caterer n.

**caterpillar** n. the larva of a butterfly or moth.

**caterwaul** v. make a cat's howling cry.

**catharsis** n. (pl. **-ses**) a release of strong feeling or tension.
■ cathartic adj.

**cathedral** n. the principal church of a diocese.

**Catherine wheel** n. a rotating firework.

**catheter** n. a tube inserted into the bladder to extract urine.

**cathode** n. an electrode with a negative charge.

**catholic** adj. 1 all-embracing. 2 (**Catholic**) Roman Catholic.
■ Catholicism n.
▷ SYNS WIDE, broad, wide-ranging, all-embracing, comprehensive, all-inclusive, eclectic, diverse.

**cattery** n. (pl. **-ies**) a place where cats are boarded.

**cattle** pl.n. cows, bulls, and oxen.

**catty** adj. (**-ier, -iest**) spiteful.

**Caucasian** adj. 1 of peoples from Europe, western Asia, and parts of India and North Africa. 2 white-skinned.

**caucus** n. a group with shared interests within a political party.

**caught** past and p.p. of **CATCH**.

**cauldron** (US **caldron**) n. a large deep cooking pot.

**cauliflower** n. a cabbage with a large white flower head.

**causal** adj. relating to or acting as a cause.

**cause** n. 1 a person or thing that produces an effect. 2 a reason for doing something. 3 a principle or movement to support.
• v. make happen. ■ causation n.
▷ SYNS 1 SOURCE, origin, root, beginning; base, basis, foundation; agent, originator, author, creator. 2 REASON,

grounds, justification, call, need. 3 *devoted to the cause:* PRINCIPLE, ideal, belief; charity, movement. • v. BRING ABOUT, give rise to, lead to, result in, create, produce, engender, provoke, trigger, make happen, induce, foster.

**causeway** n. a raised road across low or wet ground.

**caustic** adj. 1 burning by chemical action. 2 sarcastic.
▷ SYNS 1 CORROSIVE, acid. 2 CUTTING, sarcastic, scathing, mordant, sharp, bitter, acerbic.

**cauterize** (or **-ise**) v. burn tissue to destroy infection or stop bleeding.

**caution** n. 1 care to avoid danger or error. 2 a warning.
• v. warn; reprimand.
▷ SYNS 1 CARE, wariness, circumspection, vigilance, heed, attention. 2 WARNING, reprimand.
• v. 1 WARN, advise, urge, counsel. 2 REPRIMAND, admonish, rebuke.

**cautionary** adj. conveying a warning.

**cautious** adj. having or showing caution.
▷ SYNS CAREFUL, wary, guarded, circumspect, chary, watchful, vigilant, attentive, heedful.

**cavalcade** n. a procession.
▷ SYNS PARADE, procession, cortège, march past.

**cavalier** adj. offhand or unconcerned. • n. a supporter of Charles I in the English Civil War.
▷ SYNS adj. OFFHAND, indifferent, casual, dismissive, insouciant, unconcerned.

**cavalry** n. (pl. **-ies**) mounted troops.

**cave** n. a hollow in a cliff or hillside. • v. **1** collapse. **2** yield.
▷ SYNS n. CAVERN, grotto, pothole, cavity.

**caveat** n. a warning.

**cavern** n. a large cave.

**cavernous** adj. huge, spacious, or gloomy.

**caviar** n. the pickled roe of sturgeon or other large fish.

**cavil** v. (**cavilled, cavilling;** US **caviled**) raise petty objections. • n. a petty objection.

**cavity** n. (pl. **-ies**) a hollow within a solid object.
▷ SYNS HOLE, hollow, crater, pit, gap, space.

**cavort** v. leap about excitedly.

**cayenne** n. a hot red pepper.

**CBE** abbr. Commander of the Order of the British Empire.

**cc** (or **c.c.**) abbr. **1** carbon copy or copies. **2** cubic centimetres.

**CD** abbr. compact disc.

**CD-ROM** n. a compact disc holding data for display on a computer screen.

**cease** v. come to an end; stop doing something. □ **ceasefire** a temporary truce.
▷ SYNS STOP, finish, quit, end, discontinue, suspend, terminate, desist, leave off, refrain from.

**ceaseless** adj. never stopping.
▷ SYNS ENDLESS, constant, continual, continuous, non-stop, perpetual, never-ending, incessant, relentless, unremitting, interminable, everlasting.

**cedar** n. an evergreen tree.

**cede** v. surrender territory etc.

**cedilla** n. a mark written under c (ç) to show that it is pronounced like an s.

**ceilidh** n. Scot. & Irish an informal gathering for traditional music and dancing.

**ceiling** n. the upper interior surface of a room; an upper limit.

**celebrate** v. mark or honour with festivities.
▷ SYNS **1** ENJOY YOURSELF, make merry, revel, party. **2** COMMEMORATE, honour, observe, keep, toast, drink to.

**celebrated** adj. famous.

**celebration** n. the action of celebrating; a social gathering held to celebrate something.
▷ SYNS **1** COMMEMORATION, observance, marking, keeping. **2** PARTY, festival, festivity; revelry, merrymaking, jollification.

**celebrity** n. (pl. **-ies**) a famous person; fame.
▷ SYNS STAR, superstar, personality, household name.

**celery** n. a plant with edible crisp stems.

**celestial** adj. of the sky; of heaven.

**celibate** adj. abstaining from sex. ■ **celibacy** n.
▷ SYNS CHASTE, pure, virginal, abstinent, self-denying.

**cell** n. **1** a small room for a prisoner or monk. **2** a microscopic unit of living matter. **3** a device for producing electric current chemically. ■ **cellular** adj.

**cellar** n. an underground room; a stock of wine.

**cello** n. (pl. **-os**) a bass instrument of the violin family. ■ **cellist** n.

**cellophane** n. trademark a thin transparent wrapping material.

**cellulite** n. lumpy fat under the skin, causing a dimpled effect.

**Celsius** n. a scale of temperature on which water freezes at 0° and boils at 100°.

**cement** n. a substance of lime and clay used to make mortar or concrete. • v. join with cement; unite firmly.

**cemetery** n. (pl. **-ies**) a burial ground other than a churchyard.
▷ SYNS GRAVEYARD, burial ground, churchyard, necropolis.

**censor** n. a person authorized to examine letters, books, films, etc., and suppress any parts regarded as socially or politically unacceptable. • v. examine and alter in this way.
■ censorship n.
▷ SYNS v. EXPURGATE, bowdlerize, cut, delete, edit.

**censorious** adj. severely critical.
▷ SYNS CRITICAL, disapproving, judgemental, moralistic, fault-finding, captious.

**censure** n. harsh criticism and rebuke. • v. criticize harshly.
▷ SYNS n. CRITICISM, blame, condemnation, denunciation, castigation, disapproval, reproof, reproach, rebuke, reprimand.
v. see CRITICIZE.

**census** n. an official count of the population.

**cent** n. a 100th of a dollar, euro, or other decimal currency unit.

**centaur** n. a mythical creature, half man, half horse.

**centenary** n. (pl. **-ies**) a 100th anniversary. ■ centennial adj. & n.

**center** etc. US sp. of CENTRE etc.

**centigrade** adj. measured by the centigrade scale of temperature.

**centimetre** (US **centimeter**) n. a 100th of a metre, about 0.4 inch.

**centipede** n. a small crawling creature with many legs.

**central** adj. of, at, or forming a centre; most important.
■ centrally adv.
▷ SYNS 1 MIDDLE, mid, mean. 2 MAIN, chief, principal, foremost, basic, fundamental, key, essential, primary, pivotal, core, cardinal.

**centralize** (or **-ise**) v. bring under the control of a central authority. ■ centralization n.

**centre** (US **center**) n. 1 a point or part in the middle of something. 2 a place devoted to a particular activity. 3 a point from which something spreads or to which something is directed. • v. 1 place in the centre. 2 (**centre on/around**) have as a major concern or theme.
▷ SYNS n. MIDDLE, heart, core, hub, nucleus, midpoint.

**centurion** n. a commander in the ancient Roman army.

**century** n. (pl. **-ies**) 1 a period of 100 years. 2 100 runs at cricket.

**ceramic** adj. made of pottery. • n. (**ceramics**) the art of making pottery.

**cereal** n. a grass plant with edible grain; this grain; breakfast food made from it.

**cerebral** adj. of the brain; intellectual. □ cerebral palsy a condition causing jerky, involuntary movements of the muscles.

**ceremonial** adj. of or used in ceremonies. ■ ceremonially adv.
▷ SYNS FORMAL, official, state, public; ritual, stately, courtly, solemn.

**ceremonious** adj. formal and grand.

**ceremony** n. (pl. **-ies**) a grand occasion on which special acts are performed; formal politeness.
▷ SYNS **1** RITE, ritual, observance; service, sacrament, liturgy. **2** POMP, protocol, formalities, decorum, etiquette.

**certain** adj. **1** definite or reliable. **2** feeling sure. **3** specific but not named: *certain people disagreed.*
▷ SYNS **1** SURE, confident, convinced, satisfied, persuaded. **2** ASSURED, inevitable, destined, inescapable, inexorable, unarguable. **3** DEFINITE, unquestionable, undisputed, reliable, dependable, infallible, foolproof.

**certainly** adv. of course; yes.

**certainty** n. (pl. **-ies**) conviction; definite truth or reliability; something that is certain.
▷ SYNS **1** CONFIDENCE, assurance, conviction, certitude. **2** INEVITABILITY, foregone conclusion.

**certifiable** adj. **1** able or needing to be officially recorded. **2** officially recognized as needing treatment for mental disorder.

**certificate** n. an official document attesting certain facts.
▷ SYNS CERTIFICATION, authorization, document, credentials, guarantee; licence, diploma.

**certify** v. (**certified**, **certifying**) declare or confirm formally; declare insane.
▷ SYNS VERIFY, guarantee, attest, validate, confirm, substantiate, endorse, vouch for, testify to, prove, demonstrate.

**certitude** n. a feeling of certainty.

**cervix** n. (pl. **-vices**) a necklike structure in the womb.
■ **cervical** adj.

**cessation** n. ceasing.
▷ SYNS END, finish, termination, conclusion, discontinuation.

**cesspool** (or **cesspit**) n. an underground tank for liquid waste and sewage.

**cf** abbr. compare.

**chafe** v. **1** make sore or wear away by rubbing. **2** warm by rubbing. **3** become impatient because of restrictions.

**chaff** n. corn husks separated from seed. • v. tease.

**chaffinch** n. a pink-breasted finch.

**chagrin** n. annoyance and embarrassment.
▷ SYNS ANNOYANCE, irritation, dissatisfaction, anger, vexation, displeasure; embarrassment, mortification, shame.

**chain** n. **1** a series of connected metal links; a connected series or sequence; a group of hotels or shops owned by the same company. **2** a unit of measurement (66 feet). • v. fasten with a chain. □ **chain reaction** a series of events in which each causes the next.
▷ SYNS n. **1** SHACKLE, fetter, manacle, bonds, coupling, link. **2** SERIES, succession, sequence, string, train, course.

**chair** n. **1** a movable seat for one person, usu. with a back and four legs. **2** the person in charge of a meeting or organization. **3** a post as a professor. • v. be in charge of a meeting. □ **chairlift** a series of chairs on a moving cable, for carrying passengers

up and down a mountain.
**chairman** (or **chairwoman**) a person in charge of a meeting or organization. **chairperson** a person in charge of a meeting.

**chalet** n. a Swiss hut or cottage; a small cabin in a holiday camp.

**chalice** n. a large goblet.

**chalk** n. white soft limestone; a piece of this or similar coloured substance used for drawing.

**challenge** n. **1** a demanding task or situation. **2** a call to someone to take part in a contest. **3** an objection or query. • v. **1** dispute or query something. **2** call on someone to fight or do something difficult. ■ **challenger** n.
▷ SYNS v. **1** QUESTION, dispute, call into question, disagree with, protest against, object to. **2** DARE, invite; stimulate, inspire, stretch, test, tax.

**challenging** adj. presenting a test of your abilities.
▷ SYNS STIMULATING, inspiring, testing, demanding, taxing.

**chamber** n. **1** a hall used for meetings of a council, parliament, etc. **2** old use a room. **3** (**chambers**) rooms used by a barrister. **4** an enclosed space or cavity. □ **chambermaid** a woman who cleans rooms in a hotel. **chamber music** music written for a small group of players.

**chameleon** n. a small lizard that changes colour according to its surroundings.

**chamois** n. **1** a small mountain antelope. **2** a piece of soft leather used for cleaning windows, cars, etc.

**champ** v. munch noisily.

**champagne** n. a sparkling white French wine.

**champion** n. **1** a person or thing that defeats all others in a competition. **2** a person who fights or speaks in support of another or of a cause. • v. support. ■ **championship** n.
▷ SYNS n. **1** WINNER, prizewinner, medallist, victor, title-holder. **2** SUPPORTER, defender, upholder, backer, advocate, proponent. • v. ADVOCATE, promote, defend, support, uphold, stand up for, back.

**chance** n. **1** a possibility or opportunity; a degree of likelihood. **2** development of events without planning or obvious reason. • v. **1** try something uncertain or dangerous. **2** happen; happen to do something. • adj. unplanned.
▷ SYNS n. **1** ACCIDENT, coincidence, luck, fate, destiny, fluke, providence, serendipity, fortuity. **2** POSSIBILITY, likelihood, prospect, probability, odds. **3** OPPORTUNITY, time, occasion, turn. • adj. ACCIDENTAL, fortuitous, adventitious, fluky, coincidental, serendipitous; unintentional, unintended, inadvertent, unplanned.

**chancel** n. the part of a church near the altar.

**chancellor** n. the government minister in charge of the nation's budget; a state or law official of various other kinds; the non-resident head of a university.

**chancy** adj. (**-ier, -iest**) inf. risky or uncertain.

**chandelier** n. a hanging light with branches for several bulbs or candles.

**change** v. **1** make or become different. **2** exchange for another. **3** move from one to another. **4** exchange a sum of money for the same sum in a different currency or denomination. • n. **1** the action of changing. **2** money returned as the balance of a sum paid. **3** coins as opposed to banknotes. □ **changeling** a child believed to have been exchanged by fairies for the parents' real child. **changeover** a change from one system etc. to another.

▷ SYNS v. **1** ALTER, adjust, amend, modify, refine, reorganize, vary, transform, transmute, metamorphose. **2** EXCHANGE, swap, switch, replace, substitute.
• n. **1** ALTERATION, modification, variation, adaptation, rearrangement, metamorphosis, transformation. **2** COINS, silver, coppers, cash.

**changeable** adj. likely to change, or able to be changed.
▷ SYNS VARIABLE, unpredictable, inconstant, varying, changing, fluctuating, irregular, erratic, inconsistent, unstable, fickle, capricious, volatile, mercurial.

**channel** n. **1** a band of frequencies used in radio and television transmission. **2** a means of communication. **3** a passage along which liquid flows. **4** a stretch of water joining two seas.
• v. (**channelled**, **channelling**; US **channeled**) direct towards a purpose or by a particular route.
▷ SYNS n. **1** *channels of communication:* MEDIUM, means, agency, route. **2** GUTTER, conduit, culvert, ditch, gully, trough. **3** PASSAGE, strait, waterway, fjord. • v. CONVEY, conduct, direct, send, pass on, transfer.

**chant** n. a monotonous song; a rhythmic shout of a repeated phrase. • v. say, shout, or sing in a chant.

**chaos** n. great disorder.
■ **chaotically** adv.
▷ SYNS DISORDER, disarray, disorganization, confusion, mayhem, bedlam, pandemonium, turmoil, tumult, uproar, disruption, upheaval, anarchy.

**chaotic** adj. in a state of complete confusion and disorder.
▷ SYNS DISORDERLY, in disarray, disorganized, confused, topsy-turvy, anarchic.

**chap** n. inf. a man.

**chapatti** n. a flat round piece of unleavened wholemeal bread.

**chapel** n. a small building or room used for prayers; a part of a large church with its own altar.

**chaperone** n. **1** a person who accompanies and looks after another person or people. **2** dated an older woman looking after an unmarried girl at social occasions. • v. accompany and look after.

**chaplain** n. a clergyman of an institution, private chapel, ship, regiment, etc. ■ **chaplaincy** n.

**chapped** adj. (of skin) cracked and sore.

**chapter** n. **1** a division of a book. **2** the canons of a cathedral.

**char** n. a woman employed to clean a private house.
• v. (**charred**, **charring**) become black by burning.

**character** n. **1** the distinctive qualities of someone or something; moral strength. **2** a person in a novel, play, or film; an individual and original person. **3** a printed or written letter or sign.

▷ SYNS **1** PERSONALITY, nature, disposition, temperament, temper, make-up. **2** STRENGTH, honour, integrity, moral fibre, fortitude, backbone. **3** ECCENTRIC, original, individual, one-off. **4** LETTER, sign, symbol, figure.

**characteristic** n. a feature typical of and helping to identify a person or thing.
• adj. typical of or distinguishing a person or thing.
■ **characteristically** adv.
▷ SYNS n. QUALITY, attribute, feature, trait, property, peculiarity, quirk, mannerism, idiosyncrasy, hallmark.
• adj. TYPICAL, distinctive, particular, special, peculiar, specific, idiosyncratic.

**characterize** (or **-ise**)
v. **1** describe the character of.
**2** be a characteristic of.
■ **characterization** n.
▷ SYNS PORTRAY, depict, describe, present, identify, categorize; typify, mark, distinguish.

**charade** n. **1** an absurd pretence. **2** (**charades**) a game involving guessing words from acted clues.
▷ SYNS PRETENCE, travesty, mockery, farce, parody, pantomime.

**charcoal** n. a black substance made by burning wood slowly.

**charge** n. **1** the price asked for goods or services. **2** an accusation. **3** responsibility and care; someone or something for which you are responsible. **4** a rushing attack. **5** the electricity contained in a substance. **6** a quantity of explosive. • v. **1** ask for a specified price from someone. **2** accuse formally. **3** entrust with a task or responsibility. **4** rush forward in

attack. **5** give an electric charge to. **6** load with explosive.
◻ **charge card** a credit card.
▷ SYNS n. **1** COST, rate, price, fee, payment, levy, toll. **2** ACCUSATION, allegation, indictment, arraignment. **3** ATTACK, assault, offensive, raid, strike, onslaught. **4** CARE, custody, responsibility, protection, safe keeping, guardianship.
• v. **1** ASK, levy, demand, exact; invoice. **2** ACCUSE, arraign, indict, prosecute, try. **3** ATTACK, storm, assault, rush, assail.
**4** ENTRUST, tax, burden, encumber, saddle.

**chargé d'affaires** n.
(pl. **chargés d'affaires**) an ambassador's deputy.

**charger** n. **1** a cavalry horse. **2** a device for charging a battery.

**chariot** n. a two-wheeled horse-drawn vehicle used in ancient times in battle and in racing.
■ **charioteer** n.

**charisma** n. the power to inspire devotion and enthusiasm in others. ■ **charismatic** adj.

**charitable** adj. **1** relating to charities. **2** lenient or kind.
■ **charitably** adv.·
▷ SYNS GENEROUS, philanthropic, magnanimous, munificent, bountiful, open-handed; liberal, lenient, tolerant, kind, understanding, broad-minded, sympathetic.

**charity** n. **1** an organization helping the needy; gifts or voluntary work for the needy.
**2** kindness and tolerance in judging others.
▷ SYNS **1** AID, welfare, handouts, largesse, philanthropy. **2** COMPASSION, humanity, goodwill, sympathy, tolerance,

generosity, kindness, altruism, humanitarianism, benevolence.

**charlatan** n. a person falsely claiming to be an expert.

**charm** n. **1** the power to attract, delight, or fascinate. **2** an act, object, or words believed to have magic power; a small ornament worn on a bracelet etc. • v. **1** delight; influence by personal charm. **2** control by magic. ■ **charming** adj.
▷ SYNS n. **1** ATTRACTION, appeal, allure, fascination, charisma. **2** AMULET, trinket, talisman, mascot. • v. DELIGHT, please, attract, captivate, fascinate, win over, bewitch, beguile, enchant, seduce, enthral, intrigue.

**chart** n. **1** a table, graph, or diagram; a map for navigators. **2** (**the charts**) a weekly list of the current best-selling pop records. • v. record or show on a chart.
▷ SYNS n. GRAPH, table, diagram, map, plan.

**charter** n. **1** an official document granting rights. **2** hiring an aircraft etc. for a special purpose. • v. **1** grant a charter to. **2** let or hire an aircraft, ship, or vehicle. □ **charter flight** a flight by an aircraft that has been hired for a specific journey.

**chartered** adj. (of an accountant, engineer, etc.) qualified according to the rules of an association holding a royal charter.

**chary** adj. cautious.

**chase** v. go quickly after in order to capture, overcome, or drive away. • n. a pursuit; hunting.
▷ SYNS v. PURSUE, run after; hunt, track, trail, tail.

**chasm** n. a deep cleft.

▷ SYNS ABYSS, ravine, gorge, canyon, crevasse, fissure, rift.

**chassis** n. (pl. **chassis**) the base frame of a vehicle.

**chaste** adj. **1** not having sex at all or not having sex outside marriage. **2** simple and undecorated.
▷ SYNS CELIBATE, abstinent, self-denying; innocent, virtuous, pure, undefiled, unsullied, virginal.

**chasten** v. subdue.
▷ SYNS SUBDUE, humble, deflate, put someone in their place.

**chastise** v. reprimand severely.

**chastity** n. the practice of refraining from all sex, or from sex outside marriage.
▷ SYNS CELIBACY, abstinence, self-denial; virtue, purity, innocence; virginity.

**chat** n. an informal conversation. • v. (**chatted**, **chatting**) have a chat. ■ **chatty** adj.
▷ SYNS n. TALK, gossip, conversation. • v. TALK, gossip, chatter; inf. natter.

**chateau** n. (pl. **-teaux**) a French castle or large country house.

**chattel** n. a movable possession.

**chatter** v. **1** talk quickly and continuously about unimportant matters. **2** (of teeth) rattle together. • n. chattering talk. □ **chatterbox** inf. a person who chatters.

**chauffeur** n. a person employed to drive a car.

**chauvinism** n. **1** extreme or unreasonable support for your own country or group. **2** the belief held by some men that men are superior to women. ■ **chauvinist** n. **chauvinistic** adj.

**cheap** adj. **1** low in price. **2** poor in quality. **3** worthless.

□ **cheapskate** inf. a miserly person. ■ **cheapen** v.

▷ SYNS **1** INEXPENSIVE, low-cost, economical, affordable, reasonable; cut-price, reduced, discounted. **2** POOR-QUALITY, inferior, shoddy, tawdry, second-rate; inf. tacky.

**cheat** v. act dishonestly or unfairly to win profit or advantage; deprive of something by trickery. • n. a person who cheats; a deception.

▷ SYNS v. **1** DECEIVE, trick, swindle, defraud, dupe, hoodwink, double-cross; inf. con. **2** *cheat death*: AVOID, elude, evade, dodge, escape. • n. SWINDLER, fraud, fake, charlatan, mountebank; inf. con man, phoney.

**check** v. **1** examine, test, or verify. **2** stop or slow the motion of. **3** Chess move a piece to a square where it directly attacks the opposing king. • n. **1** an inspection. **2** a control or restraint. **3** the exposure of a chess king to capture. **4** a pattern of squares or crossing lines. **5** US a restaurant bill. **6** US = CHEQUE. □ **check in** register at a hotel or airport. **checkmate** Chess a position from which a king cannot escape. **checkout** a point at which goods are paid for in a shop. **check out** pay a hotel bill before leaving. **checkpoint** a barrier where security checks are carried out on travellers.

▷ SYNS v. **1** EXAMINE, inspect, look over, scrutinize, test, monitor, investigate, study, vet. **2** STOP, halt, arrest, slow down; obstruct, inhibit, bar, impede, block, curb, delay, thwart. • n. EXAMINATION, inspection, scrutiny, test, investigation, study.

**checkers** etc. US sp. of CHEQUERS etc.

**cheek** n. **1** the side of the face below the eye. **2** rude or disrespectful remarks or behaviour. • v. speak rudely to.

**cheeky** adj. (**-ier, -iest**) mischievously impudent. ■ **cheekily** adv.

▷ SYNS IMPUDENT, impertinent, insolent, disrespectful, impolite, irreverent, forward; inf. saucy.

**cheep** n. a weak shrill cry like that of a young bird. • v. make this cry.

**cheer** n. **1** a shout of joy, encouragement, or praise. **2** cheerfulness. • v. **1** shout for joy, or in praise or encouragement. **2** make happier.

▷ SYNS n. **1** ACCLAIM, acclamation, applause, ovation; hooray, hurrah. **2** CHEERFULNESS, happiness, gladness, merriment, gaiety, joy, pleasure, jubilation, rejoicing, festivity, revelry. • v. **1** ACCLAIM, applaud, hail, clap. **2** BRIGHTEN, hearten, gladden, buoy up, enliven, uplift, perk up.

**cheerful** adj. **1** happy and optimistic. **2** bright and pleasant. ■ **cheerfully** adv.

▷ SYNS **1** HAPPY, glad, merry, joyful, jolly, jovial, animated, buoyant, light-hearted, carefree, gleeful, cheery, jaunty, optimistic, in good spirits, sparkling, exuberant, blithe, happy-go-lucky. **2** BRIGHT, sunny, pleasant, agreeable.

**cheerless** adj. gloomy or dreary.

**cheers** exclam. inf. **1** expressing good wishes before drinking. **2** thank you. **3** goodbye.

**cheery** adj. (**-ier, -iest**) cheerful.

**cheese** n. food made from pressed milk curds. □ **cheesecake** a rich sweet tart made with cream and soft cheese. **cheesecloth** thin, loosely woven cotton cloth. ■ **cheesy** adj.

**cheetah** n. a large, spotted, swift-moving wild cat.

**chef** n. a professional cook.

**chemical** adj. of or made by chemistry. • n. a substance obtained by or used in a chemical process. ■ **chemically** adv.

**chemist** n. 1 a person authorized to dispense medicines prescribed by a doctor. 2 a shop where medicines, toiletries, etc. are sold. 3 a scientist who studies chemistry.

**chemistry** n. 1 the branch of science concerned with the nature of substances and how they react with each other. 2 emotional interaction between people.

**chemotherapy** n. the treatment of cancer with drugs.

**chenille** n. a fabric with a velvety pile.

**cheque** (US **check**) n. a written order to a bank to pay out money from an account. □ **cheque card** a card guaranteeing payment of cheques.

**chequer** (US **checker**) n. 1 a pattern of squares of alternating colours. 2 (**checkers**) US the game of draughts.

**chequered** adj. 1 marked with a chequer pattern. 2 having frequent changes of fortune.

**cherish** v. 1 take loving care of. 2 cling to hopes etc.

▷ SYNS 1 TREASURE, prize, hold dear, love, adore, dote on, idolize, nurture, protect. 2 *cherish hopes:* HAVE, entertain, harbour, cling to.

**cherry** n. (pl. **-ies**) 1 a small soft round fruit with a stone. 2 a bright red colour.

**cherub** n. 1 (pl. **-bim**) an angelic being. 2 (in art) a chubby infant with wings. ■ **cherubic** adj.

**chervil** n. a herb with an aniseed flavour.

**chess** n. a game of skill for two players using 32 pieces on a chequered board.

**chest** n. 1 the upper front surface of the body. 2 a large strong box. □ **chest of drawers** a piece of furniture fitted with a set of drawers.

▷ SYNS 1 BREAST, thorax, sternum. 2 BOX, crate, case, trunk, container, coffer, casket.

**chestnut** n. 1 an edible brown nut. 2 a deep reddish-brown colour. 3 (**old chestnut**) a joke or story that has been repeated too often.

**chevron** n. a V-shaped symbol.

**chew** v. work or grind between the teeth. □ **chewing gum** flavoured gum used for prolonged chewing. ■ **chewy** adj.

▷ SYNS BITE, crunch, gnaw, masticate, champ.

**chic** adj. stylish and elegant.

▷ SYNS STYLISH, fashionable, smart, elegant, sophisticated.

**chicane** n. a sharp double bend on a motor-racing track.

**chicanery** n. trickery.

**chick** n. a newly hatched bird.

**chicken** n. 1 a domestic fowl kept for its eggs or meat. 2 inf. a

coward. • **adj**. inf. cowardly.
□ **chickenpox** a disease causing itchy red pimples.

**chicory** n. a plant whose leaves are eaten in salads and whose root can be used instead of coffee.

**chide** v. (**chided** or **chid**, **chidden**, **chiding**) rebuke.

**chief** n. a leader or ruler; the person with the highest rank. • **adj**. most important; highest in rank.
▷ SYNS n. **1** CHIEFTAIN, headman, ruler, leader, overlord. **2** HEAD, principal, director, manager, chairman, governor; inf. boss. • **adj. 1** HEAD, leading, principal, premier, highest, foremost, supreme, arch. **2** MAIN, principal, cardinal, key, primary, prime, central, fundamental, predominant, pre-eminent, overriding.

**chiefly** adv. mainly.

**chieftain** n. the chief of a clan or tribe.

**chiffon** n. a thin, almost transparent fabric.

**chihuahua** n. a very small smooth-haired dog.

**chilblain** n. a painful swelling caused by exposure to cold.

**child** n. (pl. **children**) a young human being; a son or daughter.
■ **childless** adj.
▷ SYNS BOY, girl, youngster, infant, baby, toddler, tot, adolescent, juvenile, minor; Scot. bairn; son, daughter; inf. kid, nipper.

**childbirth** n. the process of giving birth to a child.
▷ SYNS LABOUR, delivery, parturition; dated confinement.

**childhood** n. the state or period of being a child.

▷ SYNS YOUTH, early years/life, infancy, babyhood, boyhood, girlhood.

**childish** adj. like a child; silly and immature.
▷ SYNS IMMATURE, infantile, juvenile, puerile, irresponsible, foolish, silly.

**childlike** adj. innocent or simple.
▷ SYNS INNOCENT, unsophisticated, trusting, gullible, naive, ingenuous, guileless, artless, credulous.

**chill** n. **1** an unpleasant coldness. **2** a feverish cold. • **adj**. chilly.
• v. **1** make cold. **2** inf. relax.

**chilli** n. (pl. **-ies**) a small hot-tasting pepper.

**chilly** adj. **1** unpleasantly cold. **2** unfriendly.
▷ SYNS **1** COLD, cool, wintry, frosty, icy, raw, freezing. **2** UNFRIENDLY, unwelcoming, cold, cool, frosty.

**chime** n. the sound of a tuned set of bells; such a set. • v. **1** ring as a chime. **2** (**chime in**) interrupt.
▷ SYNS v. RING, peal, toll.

**chimney** n. (pl. **-eys**) a structure for carrying off smoke or gases from a fire or furnace.
□ **chimney breast** a projecting wall surrounding a chimney.

**chimpanzee** n. an African ape.

**chin** n. the protruding part of the face below the mouth.

**china** n. fine earthenware; things made of this.

**chinchilla** n. a small squirrel-like South American animal; its grey fur.

**chink** n. **1** a narrow opening, a slit. **2** the sound of glasses or coins striking together.
• v. make this sound.

▷ SYNS n. CRACK, gap, cleft, rift, slit, fissure, crevice, split, opening, aperture, cranny.

**chintz** n. glazed cotton cloth used for furnishings.

**chip** n. 1 a small piece cut or broken off something hard; a small hole left by breaking off such a piece. 2 a fried oblong strip of potato. 3 a counter used in gambling. • v. 1 cut small pieces off hard material. 2 (**chip in**) interrupt; make a contribution.
▷ SYNS n. 1 SHARD, flake, fragment, splinter, paring, sliver. 2 NICK, scratch, fault, flaw.

**chipmunk** n. a striped squirrel-like animal of North America.

**chipolata** n. a small sausage.

**chiropody** n. treatment of minor ailments of the feet.
■ chiropodist n.

**chiropractic** n. treatment of certain physical disorders by manipulation of the joints.
■ chiropractor n.

**chirp** n. a short sharp sound made by a small bird or grass-hopper. • v. make this sound.

**chirpy** adj. (-ier, -iest) inf. lively and cheerful.

**chisel** n. a tool with a sharp bevelled end for shaping wood, stone, or metal. • v. (**chiselled**, **chiselling**; US **chiseled**) cut with this.

**chit** n. a short written note.

**chivalrous** adj. (of a man) polite and gallant towards women.
▷ SYNS GALLANT, polite, courteous, gentlemanly, gracious, considerate, well mannered.

**chivalry** n. 1 an honourable code of behaviour which medieval knights were

expected to follow. 2 polite behaviour by a man towards women.

**chives** pl.n. a herb with thin onion-flavoured leaves.

**chivvy** v. (**chivvied**, **chivvying**) urge, nag, or pester.

**chlorinate** v. treat or sterilize with chlorine.

**chlorine** n. a poisonous green gaseous chemical element, used as a disinfectant.

**chloroform** n. a liquid used to dissolve things and formerly as an anaesthetic.

**chlorophyll** n. green pigment in plants which allows them to convert sunlight into energy.

**chock** n. a block or wedge for preventing a wheel from moving.

**chocolate** n. a dark brown sweet food made from cacao seeds; a drink made with this.

**choice** n. choosing; the right or opportunity to choose; a variety from which to choose; a person or thing chosen. • adj. of especially good quality.
▷ SYNS n. 1 SELECTION, election, choosing. 2 had no choice: ALTERNATIVE, option, possibility. 3 a wide choice: RANGE, variety, assortment. • adj. BEST, excellent, superior, first-rate, first-class, prize, prime, select, special, exclusive.

**choir** n. an organized band of singers, esp. in church.
■ choirboy n.

**choke** v. stop a person breathing by squeezing or blocking the windpipe; have difficulty breathing; clog or smother. • n. a valve controlling the flow of air into a petrol engine.

▷ SYNS v. **1** STRANGLE, asphyxiate, throttle, suffocate, smother, stifle. **2** CLOG, bung up, block, obstruct, plug, stop up.

**choker** n. a close-fitting necklace.

**cholera** n. a disease causing severe vomiting and diarrhoea.

**choleric** adj. easily angered.

**cholesterol** n. a fatty animal substance thought to cause hardening of the arteries.

**chomp** v. munch noisily.

**choose** v. (chose, chosen, choosing) select out of a number of things.
▷ SYNS SELECT, pick, decide on, opt for, plump for, settle on, agree on, elect; name, nominate, vote for.

**choosy** adj. (-ier, -iest) excessively fastidious.
▷ SYNS FUSSY, particular, finicky, pernickety, fastidious, hard to please.

**chop** v. **1** cut into pieces with a knife or axe. **2** strike with a short, heavy blow. **3** get rid of something or reduce it by a large amount. • n. **1** a thick slice of meat, usu. including a rib. **2** a downward cutting blow.
▷ SYNS v. CUT UP, dice, cube; fell, hew, split, lop.

**chopper** n. **1** a chopping tool. **2** inf. a helicopter.

**choppy** adj. (-ier, -iest) full of short broken waves.
▷ SYNS ROUGH, turbulent, stormy, squally.

**chopstick** n. each of a pair of sticks used as eating utensils in China, Japan, etc.

**choral** adj. for or sung by a choir.

**chorale** n. a simple, stately hymn tune.

**chord** n. a combination of notes sounded together.

**chore** n. a routine or irksome task.

**choreography** n. the composition of stage dances.
■ choreographer n.

**chorister** n. a member of a choir.

**chortle** n. & v. (give) a loud chuckle.

**chorus** n. **1** a group of singers; a group of singing dancers in a musical etc.; an utterance by many people simultaneously. **2** the refrain of a song. • v. say the same thing as a group.
▷ SYNS n. **1** CHOIR, ensemble, choristers. **2** REFRAIN.

**chose, chosen** past and p.p. of CHOOSE.

**chow** n. a long-haired dog of a Chinese breed.

**christen** v. admit to the Christian Church by baptism; name.
▷ SYNS BAPTIZE, name, call; dub, designate, style, term.

**Christian** adj. of or believing in Christianity. • n. a believer in Christianity. □ Christian name a person's first name.

**Christianity** n. the religion based on the teachings of Jesus Christ.

**Christmas** n. a festival (25 Dec.) commemorating Jesus's birth. □ Christmas tree an evergreen tree decorated at Christmas.

**chrome** n. a hard, bright, metal coating made from chromium.

**chromium** n. a metallic element that does not rust.

**chromosome** n. a threadlike structure carrying genes in animal and plant cells.

**chronic** adj. **1** constantly present or recurring; having a chronic disease or habit. **2** inf. very bad. ■ **chronically** adv.
▷ SYNS **1** PERSISTENT, long-lasting, long-standing, constant, continuing. **2** INVETERATE, confirmed, hardened.

**chronicle** n. a record of events. • v. record in a chronicle. ■ **chronicler** n.
▷ SYNS n. RECORD, account, history, story, description, annals, narrative, journal, archive, log.

**chronological** adj. following the order in which things happened. ■ **chronologically** adv.

**chronology** n. arrangement of events in order of occurrence.

**chrysalis** n. (pl. **-lises**) a form of an insect in the stage between larva and adult insect; the case enclosing it.

**chrysanthemum** n. a garden plant flowering in autumn.

**chubby** adj. (**-ier, -iest**) round and plump.
▷ SYNS PLUMP, tubby, fat, dumpy, stout, portly, rotund, roly-poly, podgy.

**chuck** v. **1** inf. throw carelessly; discard. **2** touch gently under the chin.

**chuckle** v. & n. (give) a quiet laugh.

**chuffed** adj. inf. pleased.

**chug** v. (**chugged, chugging**) move with the regular puffing sound of an engine running slowly.

**chum** n. inf. a close friend.

**chunk** n. a thick piece. ■ **chunky** adj.
▷ SYNS LUMP, piece, block, hunk, slab, wedge.

**church** n. **1** a building for public Christian worship. **2** (**Church**) a particular Christian organization. **3** (**the Church**) Christians as a whole. □ **churchwarden** either of two people elected by an Anglican congregation to take care of church property. **churchyard** an enclosed area surrounding a church.
▷ SYNS HOUSE OF GOD, place of worship, cathedral, chapel, abbey, minster.

**churlish** adj. ill-mannered or surly.
▷ SYNS RUDE, impolite, boorish, ungracious, ill-mannered, discourteous, surly, sullen.

**churn** n. a machine in which milk is beaten to make butter; a very large milk can. • v. **1** beat milk or make butter in a churn; move and turn violently. **2** (**churn out**) produce large quantities of something without thought or care.

**chute** n. a sloping channel down which things can be slid or dropped.

**chutney** n. (pl. **-eys**) a seasoned mixture of fruit, vinegar, spices, etc.

**CIA** abbr. (in the US) Central Intelligence Agency.

**ciabatta** n. an Italian bread made with olive oil.

**cicada** n. a chirping insect resembling a grasshopper.

**CID** abbr. Criminal Investigation Department.

**cider** n. an alcoholic drink made from apple juice.

**cigar** n. a cylinder of tobacco in tobacco leaves for smoking.

**cigarette** n. a roll of shredded tobacco in thin paper for smoking.

**cinch** n. inf. a very easy task; a certainty.

**cinder** n. a piece of partly burnt coal or wood.

**cinema** n. a theatre where films are shown; films as an art form or industry.
▷ SYNS FILMS, movies, motion pictures, the silver screen.

**cinnamon** n. a spice.

**cipher** (or **cypher**) n. **1** a code. **2** an unimportant person.

**circa** prep. approximately.

**circle** n. **1** a perfectly round plane figure. **2** a curved tier of seats at a theatre etc. **3** a group with similar interests or shared acquaintances.
• v. move in a circle; form a circle round.
▷ SYNS n. **1** RING, disc, hoop, band. **2** GROUP, set, crowd, ring, coterie, clique. • v. **1** REVOLVE, rotate, orbit, circumnavigate, wheel, whirl, swivel. **2** SURROUND, ring, encircle, enclose.

**circuit** n. **1** a roughly circular route returning to its starting point. **2** an itinerary regularly followed.

**circuitous** adj. long and indirect.
▷ SYNS WINDING, indirect, meandering, roundabout, twisting, tortuous, rambling, zigzag.

**circuitry** n. electric circuits.

**circular** adj. shaped like or moving round a circle. • n. a letter or leaflet sent to a large number of people.
▷ SYNS adj. ROUND, annular. • n. PAMPHLET, leaflet, flyer, advertisement.

**circulate** v. move around an area; pass from one place or person to another.
▷ SYNS SPREAD, communicate, broadcast, disseminate, publicize, advertise, put about.

**circulation** n. **1** circulating; the movement of blood round the body. **2** the extent to which something is known about or available; the number of copies sold of a newspaper.

**circumcise** v. cut off the foreskin of. ■ circumcision n.

**circumference** n. the boundary of a circle; the distance round something.
▷ SYNS PERIMETER, border, boundary, edge, rim, verge, margin.

**circumflex** n. the mark ^ over a letter.

**circumnavigate** v. sail completely round.

**circumscribe** v. restrict.

**circumspect** adj. cautious or wary.
▷ SYNS CAUTIOUS, wary, careful, chary, guarded, on your guard.

**circumstance** n. an occurrence or fact relevant to an event or situation.
▷ SYNS SITUATION, state of affairs, conditions, position, context, background, factors, occurrences, events, happenings; facts.

**circumstantial** adj. (of evidence) suggesting but not proving something.

**circumvent** v. find a way of avoiding a problem, obstacle, etc.

**circus** n. a travelling show with performing animals, acrobats, etc.

**cirrhosis** n. a disease of the liver.

**cirrus** n. (pl. **-rri**) a high wispy white cloud.

**cistern** n. a tank for storing water.

**citadel** n. a fortress overlooking a city.
▷ SYNS FORTRESS, fort, fortification, stronghold, bastion.

**citation** n. a quotation from a book or author; an official mention of a notable act.
▷ SYNS QUOTATION, quote, extract, excerpt, passage.

**cite** v. quote; mention as an example.
▷ SYNS QUOTE, mention, refer to, name, adduce, specify.

**citizen** n. **1** a person with full rights in a country. **2** an inhabitant of a city. ■ **citizenship** n.
▷ SYNS SUBJECT, national, native, passport-holder; inhabitant, resident, denizen.

**citrus** n. a fruit of a group that includes the lime, lemon, and orange.

**city** n. (pl. **-ies**) an important town; a town with special rights given by charter and containing a cathedral.
▷ SYNS TOWN, conurbation, metropolis, municipality.

**civic** adj. of a city or citizenship.

**civil** adj. **1** of citizens; not of the armed forces or the Church. **2** polite and obliging. □ **civil engineering** the design and construction of roads, bridges, etc. **civil servant** an employee of the **civil service**, government departments other than the armed forces. **civil war** war between citizens of the same country.
▷ SYNS POLITE, courteous, well mannered, well bred; cordial, pleasant, helpful, obliging.

**civilian** n. a person not in the armed forces.

**civility** n. (pl. **-ies**) politeness.

**civilization** (or **-isation**) n. **1** an advanced stage of social development; progress towards this. **2** the culture and way of life of a particular area or period.
▷ SYNS **1** DEVELOPMENT, advancement, progress, enlightenment, culture, refinement, sophistication. **2** SOCIETY, community, nation, people.

**civilize** (or **-ise**) v. bring to an advanced stage of social development.

**civilized** adj. polite and good-mannered.
▷ SYNS POLITE, courteous, well mannered, cultured, cultivated, educated, sophisticated, refined.

**cl** abbr. centilitres.

**claim** v. **1** demand as your right. **2** assert. • n. **1** a demand; a right to something. **2** an assertion. ■ **claimant** n.
▷ SYNS v. **1** REQUEST, ask for, apply for; demand, insist on. **2** PROFESS, maintain, assert, state, declare, allege, contend, hold, avow, affirm.

**clairvoyance** n. the supposed ability to see events in future or communicate with the dead. ■ **clairvoyant** n. & adj.
▷ SYNS SECOND SIGHT, psychic powers, ESP, extrasensory perception, telepathy, sixth sense.

**clam** n. a shellfish with a hinged shell.

**clamber** v. climb with difficulty.
▷ SYNS SCRAMBLE, climb, scrabble, shin.

**clammy** adj. (**-ier**, **-iest**) unpleasantly moist and sticky.

**clamour** (US **clamor**) n. a loud confused noise; a loud protest

or demand. • v. make a clamour.
■ **clamorous** adj.

▷ SYNS n. NOISE, uproar, racket,
row, din, shouting, yelling, commotion, hubbub, hullabaloo,
brouhaha.

**clamp** n. a device for holding
things tightly; a device attached
to the wheels of an illegally
parked car to immobilize it.
• v. **1** grip or fasten with a clamp;
fit a wheel clamp to a car.
**2** (**clamp down on**) suppress or
put a stop to.

**clan** n. a group of families with a
common ancestor.

**clandestine** adj. done secretly.

▷ SYNS SECRET, covert, surreptitious, furtive, cloak-and-
dagger.

**clang** n. & v. (make) a loud
ringing sound.

**clank** n. & v. (make) a sound like
metal striking metal.

**clap** v. (**clapped, clapping**)
**1** strike the palms of your hands
loudly together, esp. in
applause. **2** place your hand
somewhere quickly; slap
someone on the back. • n. **1** an
act of clapping. **2** a sharp noise
of thunder.

**claret** n. a dry red wine.

**clarify** v. **1** make more intelligible. **2** remove impurities from
fats by heating. ■ **clarification** n.

▷ SYNS EXPLAIN, clear up, throw
light on, simplify, elucidate.

**clarinet** n. a woodwind instrument. ■ **clarinettist** n.

**clarion call** n. a clear demand
for action.

**clarity** n. clearness.

**clash** v. come into conflict;
disagree or be at odds; be
discordant. • n. an act or sound
of clashing.

▷ SYNS v. FIGHT, contend, skirmish,
come to blows; quarrel,
wrangle, dispute, cross swords,
lock horns.

**clasp** n. a device for fastening
things, with interlocking parts;
a grasp or handshake. • v. grasp
tightly; embrace closely; fasten
with a clasp.

▷ SYNS n. CATCH, fastener,
fastening, clip, hook, buckle,
pin, hasp. • v. EMBRACE, hug,
squeeze, clutch, grip, grasp,
hold.

**class** n. **1** a set of people or
things with shared
characteristics; a standard of
quality; a social rank; a set of
students taught together.
**2** inf. impressive stylishness.
• v. assign to a particular
category. □ **classroom** a room in
which a class of students is
taught. ■ **classless** adj.

▷ SYNS n. **1** CATEGORY, group, sort,
type, kind, variety, classification, grade, denomination,
species, genus, genre. **2** RANK,
social stratum, level, echelon.
**3** QUALITY, excellence, stylishness, elegance, chic, sophistication. v. see CLASSIFY.

**classic** adj. **1** of recognized high
quality. **2** typical. **3** simple in
style. • n. **1** a classic author or
work etc. **2** (**Classics**) the study
of ancient Greek and Roman
literature, history, etc.
■ **classicist** n.

▷ SYNS adj. **1** DEFINITIVE, authoritative; outstanding, first-rate,
first-class, best, finest, excellent,
superior, masterly. **2** TYPICAL,
archetypal, quintessential,
vintage; model, representative,
perfect, prime, textbook.
**3** SIMPLE, elegant, understated;
traditional, timeless, ageless.

**classical** adj. **1** of ancient Greek and Roman civilization. **2** traditional in form and style.

**classify** v. **1** arrange systematically. **2** designate as officially secret. ■ **classification** n. **classified** adj.
▷ SYNS CATEGORIZE, class, group, grade, rank, order, sort, organize, codify, catalogue, systematize, bracket.

**classy** adj. (**-ier, -iest**) inf. stylish and sophisticated.

**clatter** n. & v. (make) a rattling sound.

**clause** n. **1** a single part in a treaty, law, or contract. **2** a distinct part of a sentence, with its own verb.
▷ SYNS SECTION, subsection, paragraph, article; proviso, stipulation.

**claustrophobia** n. extreme fear of being in an enclosed space. ■ **claustrophobic** adj.

**clavicle** n. the collarbone.

**claw** n. a pointed nail on an animal's or bird's foot.
• v. scratch or clutch with a claw or hand.
▷ SYNS n. NAIL, talon, pincer.
• v. SCRATCH, tear, scrape, lacerate, rip, maul.

**clay** n. stiff sticky earth, used for making bricks and pottery.

**clean** adj. free from dirt or impurities; not soiled or used; not indecent or obscene.
• v. make clean. ■ **cleaner** n. **cleanliness** n.
▷ SYNS adj. **1** UNSTAINED, spotless, unsoiled, hygienic, sanitary, disinfected, sterile, sterilized, washed, scrubbed. **2** *clean air:* PURE, clear, unpolluted, uncontaminated, untainted. **3** *a clean life:* GOOD, upright,

virtuous, decent, respectable, moral, upstanding, honourable. **4** *a clean piece of paper:* UNUSED, unmarked, blank, new.
• v. WASH, cleanse, wipe, sponge, scour, swab, launder, dust, mop, sweep.

**cleanse** v. make clean or pure.

**clear** adj. **1** easily perceived or understood. **2** transparent. **3** free of obstructions. **4** free from blemishes, doubts, or anything undesirable. • v. **1** free or become free from obstacles etc. **2** prove innocent. **3** get past or over. **4** give official approval for. **5** make as net profit.
■ **clearly** adv.
▷ SYNS adj. **1** *a clear day:* BRIGHT, cloudless, fine, sunny. **2** *clear water:* TRANSPARENT, translucent, limpid, pellucid, crystalline. **3** OBVIOUS, plain, evident, apparent, definite, indisputable, patent, manifest, incontrovertible. **4** *a clear account:* COMPREHENSIBLE, plain, intelligible, understandable, lucid, coherent. **5** *a clear road:* OPEN, empty, unobstructed, unimpeded, free. • v. **1** EMPTY, vacate, evacuate. **2** ACQUIT, absolve, exonerate. **3** JUMP, vault, leap, hurdle. **4** EARN, gain, make, net. **5** AUTHORIZE, sanction, permit, allow, pass, accept.

**clearance** n. **1** clearing. **2** official permission. **3** space allowed for one object to pass another.
▷ SYNS AUTHORIZATION, permission, consent, sanction, approval, endorsement.

**clear-cut** adj. easy to see or understand.
▷ SYNS DEFINITE, distinct, clear, precise, specific, explicit, unambiguous.

**clearing** n. a space cleared of trees in a forest.

**cleavage** n. **1** the space between a woman's breasts. **2** a marked difference or division.

**cleave**[1] v. (**cleaved** or **cleft** or **clove**, **cleft** or **cloven**, **cleaving**) split or divide.

**cleave**[2] v. lit. stick or cling.

**cleaver** n. a chopping tool.

**clef** n. a symbol on a stave in music, showing the pitch of notes.

**cleft** adj. split. • n. a split. □ **cleft lip** (or **palate**) a congenital split in the upper lip or the palate.
▷ SYNS n. SPLIT, crack, fissure, gap, crevice, rift.

**clematis** n. a climbing plant with showy flowers.

**clemency** n. mercy.
▷ SYNS MERCY, leniency, compassion, kindness, humanity, pity, sympathy.

**clement** adj. (of weather) mild.

**clementine** n. a small variety of orange.

**clench** v. close the teeth or fingers tightly.

**clergy** n. all the people ordained for religious duties, esp. those in the Christian Church.

**clergyman** (or **clergywoman**) n. a priest or minister.
▷ SYNS PRIEST, cleric, minister, chaplain, ecclesiastic, bishop, pastor, vicar, rector, parson, curate, deacon.

**cleric** n. a member of the clergy.

**clerical** adj. **1** of routine office work. **2** of clergy.
▷ SYNS **1** OFFICE, secretarial. **2** ECCLESIASTICAL, spiritual, priestly, pastoral, canonical.

**clerk** n. a person employed to do written work in an office.

**clever** adj. quick to learn and understand; showing skill.
▷ SYNS INTELLIGENT, bright, sharp, quick-witted, smart, gifted, talented, skilled, brilliant, able, capable, knowledgeable, educated; shrewd, wily, canny, astute, wily, canny.

**cliché** n. an overused phrase or idea. ■ **clichéd** adj.
▷ SYNS PLATITUDE, commonplace, banality, truism, old chestnut.

**click** n. a short sharp sound. • v. make or cause to make such a sound; press a button on a computer mouse.

**client** n. a person using the services of a professional person.
▷ SYNS CUSTOMER, buyer, purchaser, shopper, consumer, user, patron, regular.

**clientele** n. clients.

**cliff** n. a steep rock face on a coast. □ **cliffhanger** a story or event that is exciting because its outcome is uncertain.
▷ SYNS PRECIPICE, crag, bluff, escarpment, scarp, promontory, tor.

**climate** n. the regular weather conditions of an area. ■ **climatic** adj.

**climax** n. the most intense or exciting point; the culmination. ■ **climactic** adj.
▷ SYNS CULMINATION, high point, height, peak, pinnacle, summit, top, acme, zenith.

**climb** v. go up to a higher position or level. • n. an ascent; a route for ascent. ■ **climber** n.
▷ SYNS v. **1** GO UP, ascend, mount, scale, clamber up, shin up. **2** RISE, increase, shoot up, soar.

**clinch** v. settle conclusively. • n. a close hold or embrace.

▷ SYNS v. SETTLE, secure, conclude, seal, complete, confirm, wrap up.

**cling** v. (**clung**, **clinging**) hold on tightly; stick.
▷ SYNS **1** CLUTCH, hold on to, grasp, grip, clasp. **2** STICK, adhere, cohere.

**clinic** n. a place where medical treatment or advice is given.

**clinical** adj. **1** of or used in treatment of patients. **2** unemotional and efficient.

**clink** n. & v. (make) a sharp ringing sound.

**clip** n. **1** a device for holding things together or in place. **2** an act of cutting; an excerpt. **3** inf. a sharp blow. • v. **1** fasten with a clip. **2** cut with shears or scissors. **3** inf. hit sharply.
▷ SYNS n. **1** FASTENER, clasp, pin. **2** EXCERPT, cutting, snippet; trailer. • v. **1** CUT, crop, trim, snip, shear, prune. **2** PIN, staple, fasten, fix, attach.

**clipper** n. **1** a fast sailing ship. **2** (**clippers**) an instrument for clipping things.

**clipping** n. a newspaper cutting.

**clique** n. a small exclusive group.
▷ SYNS COTERIE, in-crowd, set, group, gang, faction, ring.

**clitoris** n. the sensitive organ just in front of the vagina.

**cloak** n. a loose sleeveless outer garment. • v. cover or conceal. □ cloakroom a room where coats and bags may be left; a room containing a toilet.

**clobber** inf. n. equipment; belongings. • v. hit hard.

**clock** n. an instrument indicating time. □ clockwise moving in the direction of the hands of a clock. clockwork a mechanism

with a spring and toothed gearwheels, used to drive a clock etc.

**clod** n. a lump of earth.

**clog** n. a wooden-soled shoe. • v. (**clogged**, **clogging**) block or become blocked.
▷ SYNS v. OBSTRUCT, block, jam, stop up, plug, bung up.

**cloister** n. a covered walk in a monastery etc.

**cloistered** adj. sheltered or secluded.
▷ SYNS SECLUDED, sheltered, protected, sequestered; solitary, reclusive.

**clone** n. a group of organisms or cells produced asexually from one ancestor; an identical copy. • v. produce a clone; make an identical copy of.

**close** adj. **1** near in space or time. **2** very affectionate or intimate. **3** airless or humid. **4** careful and thorough. • adv. so as to be very near; leaving little space. • v. **1** shut; cause to cover an opening. **2** bring or come to an end. **3** come nearer together. • n. **1** an ending. **2** a street closed at one end.
▷ SYNS adj. **1** NEAR, adjacent, neighbouring, adjoining. **2** *a close resemblance:* STRONG, marked, distinct, pronounced. **3** *close friends:* INTIMATE, dear, bosom, devoted, inseparable. **4** *close attention:* CAREFUL, rigorous, thorough, minute, detailed, assiduous, meticulous, painstaking, conscientious. **5** *close weather:* HUMID, muggy, airless, stuffy, sticky, oppressive. • v. **1** SHUT, slam, fasten, secure, lock, bolt, latch. **2** SEAL OFF, stop up, obstruct, block. **3** END, conclude, finish, terminate, wind up.

**closet** n. a cupboard or wardrobe. • adj. secret.
• v. (**closeted, closeting**) shut yourself away in private, esp. to talk to someone.
▷ SYNS adj. SECRET, unacknowledged, covert, private. • v. SHUT AWAY, sequester, cloister, seclude, confine, isolate.

**closure** n. closing or being closed.

**clot** n. 1 a thickened mass of liquid. 2 inf. a stupid person.
• v. (**clotted, clotting**) form clots.
▷ SYNS v. COAGULATE, set, congeal, solidify, thicken, curdle.

**cloth** n. woven or felted material; a piece of this for cleaning etc.
▷ SYNS FABRIC, material, textile, stuff.

**clothe** v. put clothes on or provide with clothes.
▷ SYNS DRESS, attire, garb, robe.

**clothes** pl.n. things worn to cover the body.
▷ SYNS GARMENTS, clothing, dress, attire, garb, apparel.

**clothing** n. clothes.

**cloud** n. 1 a visible mass of watery vapour floating in the sky; a mass of smoke or dust. 2 a state or cause of gloom.
• v. become full of clouds.

**cloudy** adj. 1 covered with clouds. 2 not clear or transparent.
▷ SYNS 1 OVERCAST, dark, grey, leaden, sunless. 2 MURKY, opaque, muddy, milky, turbid.

**clout** inf. n. 1 a blow. 2 influence.
• v. hit.

**clove**[1] past of **CLEAVE**[1].

**clove**[2] n. 1 a dried bud of a tropical tree, used as a spice. 2 any of the small bulbs making up a larger bulb of garlic.

**clover** n. a flowering plant with three-lobed leaves.

**clown** n. a person who does comical tricks. • v. perform or behave as a clown.

**club** n. 1 a group who meet for social or sporting purposes; an organization offering benefits to subscribers; a nightclub. 2 a heavy stick used as a weapon; a stick with a wooden or metal head, used in golf. • v. 1 strike with a club. 2 (**club together**) combine with others to do something.
▷ SYNS n. 1 CUDGEL, baton, truncheon, cosh, staff. 2 SOCIETY, group, association, organization, circle, league.

**cluck** n. the throaty cry of a hen.
• v. make a cluck.

**clue** n. something that helps solve a puzzle or problem.
▷ SYNS SIGN, lead, hint, indication, indicator, pointer, evidence, information, tip, tip-off.

**clueless** adj. unable to understand or do something.

**clump** n. a cluster or mass.
• v. 1 tread heavily. 2 form into a clump.
▷ SYNS n. CLUSTER, thicket, group, bunch, mass.

**clumsy** adj. (**-ier, -iest**) awkward and badly coordinated; tactless.
■ **clumsily** adv. **clumsiness** n.
▷ SYNS 1 AWKWARD, uncoordinated, ungainly, inept, maladroit, heavy-handed, inexpert, graceless, ungraceful.
2 TACTLESS, insensitive, undiplomatic, gauche, crass, ill-judged.

**clung** past and p.p. of **CLING**.

**cluster** n. a small close group.
• v. form a cluster.
▷ SYNS n. BUNCH, clump, group, crowd, knot, huddle. • v. GATHER, collect, assemble, congregate, group, huddle, crowd.

**clutch** v. grasp tightly. • n. 1 a tight grasp. 2 a mechanism that connects a vehicle's engine with the axle and the wheels. 3 a set of eggs laid at one time; chicks hatched from these.
▷ SYNS v. GRIP, grasp, clasp, cling to, hang on to, grab, seize.

**clutter** n. things lying about untidily. • v. cover with clutter.

**cm** abbr. centimetres.

**Co.** abbr. 1 Company. 2 County.

**co-** comb. form joint; mutual.

**c/o** abbr. care of.

**coach** n. 1 a long-distance bus; a railway carriage. 2 a private tutor; an instructor in sports. • v. train or teach.
▷ SYNS n. 1 BUS, dated charabanc. 2 INSTRUCTOR, trainer; teacher, tutor. • v. INSTRUCT, teach, tutor, school, drill, train.

**coagulate** v. change from liquid to semi-solid form.
▷ SYNS CONGEAL, clot, thicken, set, solidify, stiffen.

**coal** n. a hard black mineral burnt as fuel. □ **coalfield** a large area rich in underground coal.

**coalesce** v. form a single mass; combine.

**coalition** n. a temporary union of political parties.
▷ SYNS UNION, alliance, league, association, federation, bloc.

**coarse** adj. 1 composed of large particles; rough in texture. 2 crude or vulgar.
▷ SYNS 1 ROUGH, bristly, prickly, scratchy. 2 RUDE, ill-mannered, impolite, boorish, loutish, uncouth, crass. 3 VULGAR, indecent, obscene, crude, smutty, dirty, indelicate.

**coast** n. the seashore and land near it. • v. move easily without using power. □ **coastguard** an organization or person that keeps watch over coastal waters. **coastline** the land along a coast. ■ **coastal** adj.
▷ SYNS n. SHORE, seashore, coastline, seaside, seaboard.

**coaster** n. a mat for a glass.

**coat** n. a long outer garment with sleeves; the fur or hair covering an animal's body; a covering layer. • v. cover with a layer.
▷ SYNS n. 1 JACKET, overcoat. 2 FUR, hair, wool, fleece, hide, pelt. 3 LAYER, covering, coating, overlay, film, patina, veneer.

**coating** n. a covering layer.

**coax** v. persuade gently; manipulate carefully or slowly.
▷ SYNS CAJOLE, persuade, wheedle, inveigle, talk into, induce, prevail on.

**cob** n. 1 a sturdy short-legged horse. 2 a hazelnut. 3 the central part of an ear of maize. 4 a small round loaf. 5 a male swan.

**cobalt** n. a metallic element; a deep blue pigment made from it.

**cobble** n. a rounded stone formerly used for paving roads. • v. mend or assemble roughly.

**cobbler** n. a shoe-mender.

**cobra** n. a poisonous snake of Asia and Africa.

**cobweb** n. a spider's web.

**cocaine** n. a drug used as an illegal stimulant.

**cochineal** n. red food colouring.

**cock** n. a male bird. • v. **1** tilt or bend in a particular direction. **2** set a gun for firing.

**cockatoo** n. a crested parrot.

**cockerel** n. a young male fowl.

**cockle** n. an edible shellfish.

**cockpit** n. the compartment for the pilot in a plane, or for the driver in a racing car.

**cockroach** n. a beetle-like insect.

**cocksure** adj. overconfident.

**cocktail** n. a mixed alcoholic drink.

**cocky** adj. (**-ier, -iest**) conceited and arrogant.
▷ SYNS ARROGANT, conceited, vain, swollen-headed, cocksure.

**cocoa** n. a drink made from powdered cacao seeds and milk.

**coconut** n. a nut of a tropical palm.

**cocoon** n. a silky sheath round a chrysalis; a protective wrapping. • v. wrap in something soft and warm.

**cod** n. a large edible sea fish.

**coda** n. the final part of a musical composition.

**code** n. **1** a system of words or symbols used to represent others for secrecy; a sequence of numbers or letters for identification. **2** a set of laws or rules.
▷ SYNS **1** CIPHER, cryptogram. **2** SYSTEM, laws, rules, regulations.

**codeine** n. a painkilling drug.

**codify** v. (**codified, codifying**) arrange laws or rules into a code.

**coerce** v. compel by threats or force. ■ coercion n.

▷ SYNS FORCE, compel, pressure, pressurize, drive, bully, intimidate, terrorize, browbeat.

**coexist** v. exist together, esp. harmoniously. ■ coexistence n.

**coffee** n. a hot drink made from the bean-like seeds of a tropical shrub; a pale brown colour.

**coffer** n. **1** a small chest for holding valuables. **2** (**coffers**) financial resources.

**coffin** n. a box in which a corpse is placed for burial or cremation.

**cog** n. one of a series of projections on the edge of a wheel, engaging with those of another.

**cogent** adj. logical and convincing. ■ cogency n.
▷ SYNS CONVINCING, persuasive, compelling, forceful, effective, sound, powerful, strong, weighty, potent, influential, telling.

**cogitate** v. think deeply. ■ cogitation n.

**cognac** n. French brandy.

**cognition** n. gaining knowledge by thought or perception. ■ cognitive adj.

**cognizance** (or **-isance**) n. knowledge or awareness. ■ cognizant adj.

**cohabit** v. live together as man and wife. ■ cohabitation n.

**cohere** v. stick or hold together.

**coherent** adj. logical and consistent; able to speak clearly.
▷ SYNS LOGICAL, reasoned, reasonable, rational, consistent; clear, lucid, articulate; intelligible, comprehensible.

**cohesion** n. the holding together of something. ■ cohesive adj.

**cohort** n. a tenth part of a Roman legion; a group or set of people.

**coiffure** n. a hairstyle.

**coil** v. wind into rings or a spiral. • n. 1 something wound in a spiral; one ring or turn in this. 2 a contraceptive device inserted into the womb.
▷ SYNS v. LOOP, wind, spiral, curl, twist, snake, wreathe, entwine, twine.

**coin** n. a piece of metal money. • v. 1 make coins by stamping metal. 2 invent a word or phrase.

**coinage** n. 1 coins of a particular type. 2 a coined word or phrase.

**coincide** v. 1 happen at the same time or place. 2 be the same or similar.
▷ SYNS 1 OCCUR SIMULTANEOUSLY; clash. 2 AGREE, tally, match, correspond, concur.

**coincidence** n. 1 a remarkable instance of things happening at the same time by chance. 2 the fact of things existing together or being the same.
▷ SYNS ACCIDENT, chance, serendipity, fortuity, providence, fate, fluke.

**coincidental** adj. not planned or intentional.
▷ SYNS ACCIDENTAL, chance, fluky, unintentional, unplanned; fortuitous, serendipitous.

**coke** n. 1 a solid fuel made by heating coal in the absence of air. 2 inf. cocaine.

**colander** n. a bowl-shaped perforated container for draining food.

**cold** adj. 1 at or having a low temperature. 2 not affectionate or enthusiastic. 3 not prepared or rehearsed. • n. 1 low temperature; a cold condition. 2 an illness causing catarrh and sneezing. □ **cold feet** inf. loss of confidence. **cold-shoulder** treat with deliberate unfriendliness. **cold war** hostility between nations without fighting.
▷ SYNS adj. 1 CHILLY, cool, freezing, bitter, icy, chill, wintry, frosty, raw, perishing, biting, glacial, arctic; inf. nippy. 2 UNFRIENDLY, inhospitable, unwelcoming, forbidding, frigid, formal, stiff.

**cold-blooded** adj. 1 having a blood temperature varying with that of the surroundings. 2 unfeeling or ruthless.
▷ SYNS RUTHLESS, callous, inhuman, brutal, barbaric, heartless, merciless, hard-hearted.

**coleslaw** n. a salad of shredded raw cabbage in mayonnaise.

**colic** n. severe abdominal pain.

**collaborate** v. work in partnership. ■ **collaboration** n. **collaborator** n. **collaborative** adj.
▷ SYNS COOPERATE, join forces, unite, combine.

**collage** n. a picture formed by fixing various items to a backing.

**collapse** v. 1 fall down suddenly; fail and come to a sudden end. • n. collapsing; a sudden failure. ■ **collapsible** adj.
▷ SYNS 1 FALL DOWN, cave in, give way, crumple, subside. 2 FAINT, pass out, black out, swoon. 3 BREAK DOWN, fail, fold, fall through, founder, disintegrate.

**collar** n. 1 a band round the neck of a garment. 2 a band put round a dog's or cat's neck. • v. inf. seize.

**collate** v. collect and combine.

**collateral** adj. additional but subordinate. • n. security for repayment of a loan.

**colleague** n. a fellow worker in a business or profession.
▷ SYNS CO-WORKER, fellow-worker, associate, workmate, partner.

**collect** v. **1** bring or come together. **2** call for and take away. **3** find and keep items of a particular kind as a hobby. **4** (**collected**) calm.
■ collectable (or collectible) adj. & n. collector n.
▷ SYNS **1** GATHER, accumulate, pile up, stockpile, amass, store, hoard, save. **2** ASSEMBLE, congregate, converge, mass, flock together. **3** FETCH, call for, pick up.

**collection** n. a number of things that have been collected.
▷ SYNS **1** ACCUMULATION, pile, stockpile, stock, supply, heap, hoard. **2** DONATIONS, contributions, gifts.

**collective** adj. done by or belonging to all the members of a group. ■ collectively adv.
▷ SYNS JOINT, united, combined, shared, common, cooperative, collaborative.

**college** n. an educational establishment for higher or professional education; an organized body of professional people. ■ collegiate adj.
▷ SYNS UNIVERSITY, polytechnic, institute, school, academy.

**collide** v. hit when moving.
▷ SYNS CRASH; hit, bang into, smash into, cannon into, plough into.

**collie** n. a breed of dog often used as a sheepdog.

**colliery** n. (pl. -ies) a coal mine.

**collision** n. an instance when two or more things collide.
▷ SYNS CRASH, impact, accident, smash, pile-up.

**colloquial** adj. suitable for informal speech or writing.
■ colloquialism n. colloquially adv.
▷ SYNS CONVERSATIONAL, informal, everyday; idiomatic, demotic, vernacular.

**collude** v. cooperate secretly for a dishonest or underhand purpose. ■ collusion n.

**cologne** n. a light perfume.

**colon** n. **1** a punctuation mark (:). **2** the lower part of the large intestine. ■ colonic adj.

**colonel** n. an army officer next below brigadier.

**colonial** adj. of a colony or colonies. • n. an inhabitant of a colony.

**colonialism** n. a policy of acquiring or maintaining colonies.

**colonize** (or -ise) v. acquire as a colony; establish a colony in.
■ colonist n. colonization n.
▷ SYNS OCCUPY, settle, populate, people; take over.

**colonnade** n. a row of columns.

**colony** n. (pl. -ies) a country under the control of another and occupied by settlers from there; people of shared nationality or occupation living as a community; a community of animals or plants of one kind.
▷ SYNS **1** DEPENDENCY, territory, protectorate, satellite. **2** COMMUNITY, group, ghetto, quarter.

**coloration** (or colouration) n. colouring.

**colossal** adj. immense.
■ colossally adv.

**colour** (US **color**) n. the effect on something's appearance of the way it reflects light; pigment or paint; skin pigmentation as an indication of race. • v. put colour on; blush; influence. □ colour-blind unable to distinguish between certain colours.
▷ SYNS n. HUE, tint, shade, tone, coloration, colouring, pigmentation, pigment. • v. 1 TINT, dye, paint, stain. 2 INFLUENCE, affect, prejudice, bias, warp, distort.

**coloured** (US **colored**) adj. 1 having a colour. 2 offens. of non-white descent.

**colourful** (US **colorful**) adj. 1 full of colour. 2 vivid or lively. ■ colourfully adv.
▷ SYNS 1 BRIGHT, vivid, vibrant, rich, multicoloured, iridescent, psychedelic; gaudy. 2 GRAPHIC, lively, animated, dramatic, fascinating, stimulating.

**colourless** (US **colorless**) adj. without colour; dull.

**colt** n. a young male horse.

**column** n. 1 a round pillar. 2 a vertical division of a page; a regular section in a newspaper or magazine. 3 a line of people or vehicles.
▷ SYNS 1 PILLAR, post, support, upright, pilaster, obelisk. 2 LINE, file, queue, procession, train, cavalcade. 3 ARTICLE, piece, item, feature.

**columnist** n. a journalist who regularly writes a column of comments.

**coma** n. deep unconsciousness.

**comatose** adj. in a coma.

**comb** n. 1 an object with a row of teeth, used for tidying hair. 2 a chicken's fleshy crest. • v. tidy with a comb; search thoroughly.
▷ SYNS v. SEARCH, hunt through, scour, go over with a fine-tooth comb.

**combat** n. a battle or contest. • v. (**combated**, **combating**) try to stop or destroy. ■ combatant adj. & n.
▷ SYNS n. BATTLE, fighting, conflict, hostilities, action. • v. FIGHT, battle, tackle, attack, counter, resist, grapple with, struggle against, withstand.

**combative** adj. ready or eager to fight or argue.
▷ SYNS AGGRESSIVE, belligerent, pugnacious, bellicose, quarrelsome, argumentative, truculent.

**combination** n. combining or being combined; a set of united but distinct elements.
▷ SYNS 1 AMALGAMATION, amalgam, blend, mixture, mix, fusion, marriage, integration, synthesis, composite. 2 COOPERATION, collaboration, association, union, partnership, league.

**combine** v. join or unite. • n. 1 a combination of people or firms acting together. 2 (in full **combine harvester**) a combined reaping and threshing machine.
▷ SYNS v. 1 JOIN FORCES, unite, cooperate, get together, team up. 2 MIX, blend, fuse, merge, amalgamate, integrate, synthesize, join, marry.

**combustible** adj. capable of catching fire.
▷ SYNS FLAMMABLE, inflammable, incendiary, explosive.

**combustion** n. burning; rapid chemical combination with oxygen, involving the production of heat.

**come** v. (**came**, **come**, **coming**) move towards the speaker or a place or point; arrive; occur; pass into a specified state; originate from a specified place; have a specified place in an ordering. □ **come about** happen. **come across** find by chance. **comeback** a return to fame or popularity; a quick reply. **comedown** inf. a loss of status. **come off** be successful. **come round** recover consciousness. **comeuppance** inf. deserved punishment.
▷ SYNS **1** APPROACH, advance, draw near, bear down on, close in on. **2** ARRIVE, appear, turn up, materialize; inf. show up.

**comedian** n. (fem. **comedienne**) a humorous entertainer or actor.
▷ SYNS **1** COMIC, humorist. **2** WIT, wag, joker, clown.

**comedy** n. **1** an amusing film, play, or other entertainment.
▷ SYNS HUMOUR, wit, wittiness, fun, funny side.

**comely** adj. (**-ier**, **-iest**) old use attractive.

**comet** n. a mass of ice and dust with a luminous tail, moving around the solar system.

**comfort** n. a state of ease and contentment; relief of suffering or grief; a person or thing giving this. • v. make less unhappy. ■ **comforter** n.
▷ SYNS n. **1** EASE, well being, contentment, relaxation, cosiness; luxury, opulence. **2** SOLACE, consolation, support, reassurance. • v. CONSOLE, support, solace, reassure, cheer, soothe, hearten, uplift.

**comfortable** adj. **1** providing or enjoying physical or mental ease. **2** financially secure. ■ **comfortably** adv.
▷ SYNS **1** COSY, snug, homely, pleasant; inf. comfy. **2** AFFLUENT, prosperous, well-to-do, luxurious; untroubled, contented, happy.

**comic** adj. causing amusement; of comedy. • n. **1** a comedian. **2** a children's paper with a series of strip cartoons. ■ **comical** adj. **comically** adv.
▷ SYNS adj. FUNNY, humorous, amusing, droll, entertaining, hilarious.

**comma** n. a punctuation mark (,).

**command** n. **1** an order; authority; forces or a district under a commander. **2** the ability to use or control something. • v. give an order to; have authority over.
▷ SYNS n. **1** ORDER, instruction, decree, directive, edict, dictate, injunction, fiat, commandment. **2** CHARGE, control, authority, power, direction, leadership, rule. **3** *her command of English:* KNOWLEDGE, grasp, mastery. • v. **1** ORDER, tell, direct, instruct, charge, require. **2** BE IN CHARGE OF, control, lead, head.

**commandant** n. an officer in command of a military establishment.

**commandeer** v. seize for use.

**commander** n. a person in command; a naval officer next below captain.

**commandment** n. a rule to be strictly observed.

**commando** n. (pl. **-os**) a member of a military unit specially trained for making raids and assaults.

**commemorate** v. keep in the memory by a celebration or memorial. ■ commemoration n. commemorative adj.
▷ SYNS CELEBRATE, remember, honour, pay tribute to, salute, mark.

**commence** v. begin.
■ commencement n.
▷ SYNS BEGIN, start, initiate, inaugurate, embark on.

**commend** v. 1 praise publicly. 2 recommend.
■ commendation n.

**commendable** adj. deserving praise.
▷ SYNS ADMIRABLE, praiseworthy, laudable, creditable, worthy, meritorious.

**commensurate** adj. corresponding; in proportion.

**comment** n. an expression of opinion. • v. make a comment.
■ commentator n.
▷ SYNS n. REMARK, observation, statement. • v. SAY, observe, state, declare, remark, opine.

**commentary** n. 1 the making of comments; a set of notes on a text. 2 an account of an event, given as it occurs.
▷ SYNS 1 NARRATION, description, account, report, weblog, blog. 2 EXPLANATION, interpretation, analysis, critique, exegesis.

**commerce** n. all forms of trade and business.
▷ SYNS BUSINESS, trade, trading, dealing, buying and selling, traffic.

**commercial** adj. of or engaged in commerce; intended to make a profit. ■ commercially adv.

**commercialize** (or -ise) v. operate a business etc. so as to make a profit.
■ commercialization n.

**commiserate** v. express pity or sympathy. ■ commiseration n.

**commission** n. 1 an instruction, command, or duty. 2 a formal request for something to be designed or made. 3 a group of people given official authority to do something. 4 payment to an agent for selling something. 5 the position of officer in the armed forces.
• v. 1 order the production of something. 2 bring into working order.
▷ SYNS n. 1 TASK, job, project, mission, assignment. 2 PERCENTAGE, brokerage, share, fee; inf. cut. • v. ENGAGE, contract, employ, hire, appoint, book; order, authorize.

**commissionaire** n. a uniformed attendant at the door of a theatre, hotel, etc.

**commissioner** n. a member of a commission; a government official in charge of a district abroad.

**commit** v. 1 carry out a crime etc. 2 pledge to do something. 3 entrust; send to prison or psychiatric hospital.
■ committal n.
▷ SYNS 1 CARRY OUT, perpetrate, enact, do. 2 ENTRUST, trust, deliver, hand over, give, consign.

**commitment** n. 1 dedication to a cause or activity. 2 a promise. 3 an obligation.
▷ SYNS 1 DEDICATION, devotion, loyalty, allegiance. 2 PROMISE, pledge, undertaking, vow. 3 OBLIGATION, duty, responsibility, tie; task, engagement.

**committed** adj. dedicated to a cause, activity, etc.
▷ SYNS DEDICATED, enthusiastic, devoted, keen, passionate,

wholehearted, unwavering, ardent.

**committee** n. a group of people appointed for a particular function by a larger group.

**commode** n. a seat containing a concealed chamber pot.

**commodious** adj. roomy.

**commodity** n. (pl. **-ies**) an article to be bought and sold; something valuable.

**commodore** n. a naval officer next below rear admiral; a president of a yacht club.

**common** adj. **1** occurring, found, or done often; not rare. **2** ordinary or undistinguished. **3** generally or widely shared. **4** not well mannered. • n. a piece of open land for public use.
■ commonly adv.
▷ SYNS **adj. 1** ORDINARY, usual, familiar, average, normal, everyday, customary, conventional, typical, unexceptional, commonplace, run-of-the-mill, undistinguished, unsurprising. **2** WIDESPREAD, general, universal, popular, prevalent, prevailing, accepted; shared, public, communal, collective. **3** VULGAR, coarse, ill-bred, uncouth, unrefined, plebeian.

**commonplace** adj. ordinary. • n. a trite remark or topic.

**commonwealth** n. **1** an independent state. **2** a federation of states. **3** (**the Commonwealth**) an association of Britain and independent states formerly under British rule.

**commotion** n. confused and noisy disturbance.
▷ SYNS DISTURBANCE, uproar, disorder, tumult, pandemonium, rumpus, hubbub, fracas,

hullabaloo, row, furore, brouhaha, confusion, upheaval, disruption, turmoil, fuss; inf. to-do.

**communal** adj. shared among a group.
▷ SYNS COMMON, collective, shared, joint, general, cooperative.

**commune** v. communicate mentally or spiritually.
• n. a group of people sharing accommodation and possessions.

**communicable** adj. (of a disease) able to be passed on to other people.

**communicate** v. **1** exchange news and information; pass on information; transmit or convey. **2** (of two rooms) have a common connecting door.
■ communicator n.
▷ SYNS **1** CONVEY, tell, impart, relay, transmit, pass on, announce, report, recount, relate, present; spread, disseminate, promulgate, broadcast. **2** TALK, be in touch, converse, liaise.

**communication** n. **1** the action of communicating. **2** a letter or message. **3** (**communications**) means of sending information or travelling, such as telephone lines or roads.

**communicative** adj. talkative or willing to give information.
▷ SYNS TALKATIVE, chatty, open, frank, candid, expansive, forthcoming.

**communion** n. **1** the sharing of thoughts and feelings. **2** (also **Holy Communion**) a sacrament in which bread and wine are shared.

**communiqué** n. an official announcement or statement.

**communism** n. a political and social system based on common ownership of property.
■ communist n. & adj.

**community** n. (pl. **-ies**) **1** a group of people living together in one place or united by origin, interests, etc. **2** the people of an area as a group; society.

**commute** v. **1** travel regularly between your home and workplace. **2** make a sentence of punishment less severe.
■ commuter n.

**compact** adj. closely or neatly packed together; concise. • v. compress. • n. **1** a small flat case for face powder. **2** a pact or contract. □ compact disc a small disc on which music or other digital information is stored.
▷ SYNS adj. **1** DENSE, compressed, tightly packed, solid, firm, close. **2** CONCISE, succinct, terse, brief, pithy. **3** SMALL, neat, portable, handy.

**companion** n. a person living or travelling with another; a thing designed to complement another.
▷ SYNS ESCORT, friend, partner, confederate, colleague, associate, crony, comrade.

**companionship** n. fellowship or friendship.
▷ SYNS FRIENDSHIP, fellowship, closeness, togetherness, camaraderie, company.

**company** n. **1** being with other people; companionship; a group of people. **2** a commercial business. **3** a body of soldiers.
▷ SYNS **1** BUSINESS, firm, organization, corporation, conglomerate, consortium, concern, enterprise, house, establishment, partnership. **2** GROUP, band, party, body, troupe.

**comparable** adj. similar or able to be compared.
■ comparably adv.
▷ SYNS SIMILAR, alike, analogous, related, equivalent.

**comparative** adj. **1** involving or measured by comparison. **2** (of an adjective or adverb) expressing a higher degree of a quality (e.g. *braver*).
■ comparatively adv.

**compare** v. **1** assess the similarity of. **2** declare to be similar. **3** be of equal quality with something.
▷ SYNS **1** CONTRAST, measure against, juxtapose; liken, equate. **2** BEAR COMPARISON, be comparable, be on a par.

**comparison** n. **1** an instance of comparing things or people. **2** the quality of being similar or equivalent.
▷ SYNS **1** JUXTAPOSITION, correlation. **2** RESEMBLANCE, likeness, similarity, correspondence.

**compartment** n. a partitioned space.

**compass** n. **1** a device showing the direction of magnetic north. **2** range or scope. **3** (**compasses**) a hinged instrument for drawing circles.

**compassion** n. pity and concern.

**compassionate** adj. feeling or showing pity and concern.
▷ SYNS SYMPATHETIC, empathetic, understanding, caring, warm; considerate, kind, humane.

**compatible** adj. able to exist or be used together; consistent.
■ compatibility n.

▷ SYNS **1** WELL SUITED, like-minded, in tune. **2** CONSISTENT, in keeping, consonant.

**compatriot** n. a fellow countryman.

**compel** v. (**compelled**, **compelling**) force.
▷ SYNS FORCE, make, coerce, pressure, pressurize, constrain, oblige.

**compelling** adj. very interesting; very convincing.
▷ SYNS **1** FASCINATING, gripping, enthralling, mesmerizing. **2** CONVINCING, forceful, powerful, weighty, conclusive, cogent.

**compendium** n. (pl. **-dia** or **-diums**) a collection of information.

**compensate** v. **1** give payment to a person in recognition of loss, distress, or injury suffered. **2** reduce something bad by having an opposite effect.
▷ SYNS **1** RECOMPENSE, repay, reimburse, remunerate. **2** BALANCE OUT, counterbalance, counteract, offset, make up for, cancel out, neutralize.

**compensation** n. something given to compensate for loss, suffering, or injury.
▷ SYNS RECOMPENSE, repayment, reimbursement, indemnification.

**compère** n. a person who introduces performers in a variety show. • v. act as compère to.

**compete** v. try to gain or win something by defeating or being better than others.
▷ SYNS **1** TAKE PART, participate, play, enter, go in for. **2** *they had to compete with other firms:* CONTEND, vie, battle, struggle, strive against, challenge, take on.

**competent** adj. **1** having the necessary skill or knowledge. **2** acceptable and satisfactory.
■ competence n.
▷ SYNS CAPABLE, able, proficient, adept, accomplished, skilful, skilled, expert, efficient.

**competition** n. **1** an event in which people compete. **2** the activity of competing. **3** the people that you are competing with.
▷ SYNS CONTEST, match, game, tournament, championship, event, race.

**competitive** adj. involving competition; anxious to win.
▷ SYNS AMBITIOUS, combative, keen; ruthless, cut-throat.

**competitor** n. a person or organization that competes.
▷ SYNS **1** CONTESTANT, contender, challenger, participant. **2** RIVAL, opponent, adversary.

**compile** v. collect and arrange into a list or book.
■ compilation n.
▷ SYNS COLLECT, gather, accumulate, amass, assemble, put together, collate.

**complacent** adj. smug and self-satisfied. ■ complacency n.

**complain** v. express dissatisfaction or pain.
▷ SYNS GRUMBLE, moan, grouse, gripe, carp, whine.

**complaint** n. **1** an act of complaining. **2** an illness.
▷ SYNS **1** GRIEVANCE, criticism, protest, objection, grouse, grumble. **2** ILLNESS, disease, infection, disorder, ailment, sickness, malady.

**complement** n. **1** a thing that completes or improves

something else. **2** the full number required. • v. add to in a way that improves.
■ complementary adj.

**complete** adj. having all the necessary parts; finished; total or absolute. • v. make complete; fill in a form. ■ completion n.
▷ SYNS adj. **1** ENTIRE, whole, full, total; uncut, unabridged, un-expurgated. **2** FINISHED, done, concluded, ended, finalized. **3** ABSOLUTE, utter, out-and-out, downright, thorough, un-mitigated, unqualified, sheer.
• v. **1** FINISH, conclude, end, finalize; inf. wrap up. **2** ROUND OFF, finish off, crown, cap.

**completely** adv. totally; utterly.
▷ SYNS TOTALLY, utterly, absolutely, quite, thoroughly, wholly, altogether.

**complex** adj. made up of many parts; complicated or hard to understand. • n. **1** a complex whole; a group of buildings. **2** a set of unconscious feelings affecting behaviour.
■ complexity n.
▷ SYNS adj. COMPLICATED, difficult, intricate, convoluted, involved, elaborate, labyrinthine.

**complexion** n. the condition of the skin of a person's face; the general character of things.

**compliant** adj. obedient.
■ compliance n.

**complicate** v. make complicated.

**complicated** adj. consisting of many different, intricate, or confusing elements.

**complication** n. being complicated; a factor causing this; a secondary disease aggravating an existing one.

▷ SYNS DIFFICULTY, problem, obstacle, snag, catch, drawback, setback.

**complicity** n. involvement in wrongdoing.

**compliment** n. a polite expression of praise. • v. pay a compliment to.
▷ SYNS n. PRAISE, tributes, flattery, commendation, congratulations, accolades, plaudits, bouquets.
• v. CONGRATULATE, praise, commend, flatter, pay tribute to, salute, extol, laud.

**complimentary** adj. **1** expressing a compliment. **2** free of charge.
▷ SYNS CONGRATULATORY, admiring, approving, appreciative, flattering, laudatory.

**comply** v. **1** do what is requested or ordered. **2** meet specified standards.
▷ SYNS OBEY, observe, abide by, adhere to, conform to, follow, respect.

**component** n. one of the parts of which a thing is composed.
▷ SYNS PART, piece, element, bit, section, constituent, ingredient, unit.

**compose** v. **1** make up a whole. **2** create a work of music or poetry. **3** arrange in an orderly or artistic way. **4** (**composed**) calm and controlled.
■ composer n.
▷ SYNS **1** MAKE UP, constitute, form, comprise. **2** WRITE, create, devise, produce; pen, author.

**composite** adj. made up of parts.

**composition** n. **1** something's elements and the way it is made up; composing. **2** a musical or literary work.

▷ SYNS **1** STRUCTURE, make-up, organization, configuration, constitution, form, framework. **2** WORK, piece, opus.

**compost** n. decayed organic matter used as fertilizer.

**composure** n. calmness.

**compound** adj. made up of two or more elements. • n. **1** a compound substance. **2** a fenced-in enclosure. • v. **1** combine; make by combining. **2** make worse.
▷ SYNS n. BLEND, mixture, amalgam, combination, alloy, synthesis. • v. WORSEN, add to, exacerbate, aggravate, intensify, heighten.

**comprehend** v. **1** understand. **2** include. ■ **comprehension** n.
▷ SYNS UNDERSTAND, grasp, take in, follow, fathom.

**comprehensible** adj. able to be understood.
▷ SYNS UNDERSTANDABLE, clear, straightforward, intelligible, lucid.

**comprehensive** adj. including much or all. • n. a school providing secondary education for children of all abilities.
▷ SYNS adj. COMPLETE, all-inclusive, full, all-embracing, total, encyclopedic, wholesale, universal, exhaustive, detailed, thorough, broad, wide-ranging.

**compress** v. squeeze or force into less space. • n. a pad to stop bleeding or to reduce inflammation. ■ **compression** n. **compressor** n.
▷ SYNS v. COMPACT, squeeze, press together, crush, squash, flatten, cram, tamp.

**comprise** v. consist of.
▷ SYNS **1** CONSIST OF, contain, be composed of, encompass,

include. **2** MAKE UP, form, constitute, compose.

**compromise** n. an agreement reached by each side making concessions. • v. **1** make concessions so as to settle a dispute. **2** cause embarrassment or danger by reckless or indiscreet behaviour.
▷ SYNS n. AGREEMENT, understanding, settlement, deal, happy medium. • v. **1** MEET HALFWAY, make a deal, make concessions, give and take. **2** UNDERMINE, damage, harm, injure, jeopardize, discredit, dishonour.

**compulsion** n. forcing or being forced; an irresistible urge.
▷ SYNS **1** OBLIGATION, constraint, duress, coercion, pressure. **2** URGE, need, desire, drive; fixation, addiction, obsession.

**compulsive** adj. **1** resulting from or driven by an irresistible urge. **2** gripping.
▷ SYNS OBSESSIVE, uncontrollable, irresistible, overwhelming, urgent; obsessional, addicted, incorrigible, incurable.

**compulsory** adj. required by a law or rule.
▷ SYNS OBLIGATORY, mandatory, required, requisite, essential, statutory.

**compunction** n. guilt or regret.

**compute** v. calculate.

**computer** n. an electronic device for storing and processing data.

**computerize** (or **-ise**) v. convert to a system controlled by computer.

**comrade** n. a companion or associate. ■ **comradeship** n.

▷ SYNS FRIEND, companion, colleague, partner, associate, co-worker.

**con** v. (**conned, conning**) inf. trick or cheat. • n. inf. a confidence trick. □ pros and cons see PRO.

**concave** adj. curving inwards like the inner surface of a ball.

**conceal** v. hide or keep secret.
■ concealment n.
▷ SYNS HIDE, cover, obscure, screen, mask, disguise, camouflage.

**concede** v. 1 admit to be true. 2 admit defeat in a contest. 3 yield.
▷ SYNS ADMIT, acknowledge, accept, allow, grant, confess, recognize, own.

**conceit** n. excessive pride in yourself.
▷ SYNS PRIDE, vanity, egotism, self-importance, self-satisfaction, narcissism.

**conceited** adj. excessively proud.
▷ SYNS PROUD, vain, narcissistic, self-important, egotistical, self-satisfied, smug, boastful, arrogant; inf. big-headed.

**conceivable** adj. able to be imagined or grasped.
▷ SYNS CREDIBLE, believable, thinkable, imaginable, possible.

**conceive** v. 1 become pregnant. 2 imagine.

**concentrate** v. 1 focus all your attention. 2 gather together in a small area; make less dilute. • n. a concentrated substance.
▷ SYNS V. 1 FOCUS ON, put your mind to. 2 COLLECT, gather, crowd, mass, congregate.

**concentration** n. 1 the ability to concentrate. 2 a great deal of things gathered in one place. 3 the amount of a substance in a solution or mixture. □ concentration camp a camp for holding political prisoners.

**concentric** adj. having the same centre.

**concept** n. an abstract idea.
■ conceptual adj.

**conception** n. 1 the creation of a child in the womb. 2 the forming of a plan or idea. 3 a concept or idea.

**concern** v. 1 be about. 2 be relevant to; involve. 3 make anxious. • n. 1 anxiety. 2 something in which you are interested or involved. 3 a business or firm.
▷ SYNS V. 1 AFFECT, involve, apply to, touch. 2 WORRY, disturb, trouble, bother, perturb, distress. • n. 1 WORRY, anxiety, disquiet, distress, apprehension, perturbation. 2 RESPONSIBILITY, duty, job, task. 3 BUSINESS, company, firm, enterprise, organization, establishment.

**concerned** adj. anxious.

**concerning** prep. on the subject of.
▷ SYNS ABOUT, relating to, regarding, as regards, involving, with reference/respect to, re, apropos.

**concert** n. a musical entertainment.

**concerted** adj. done in combination.
▷ SYNS JOINT, combined, united, collective, collaborative, cooperative.

**concertina** n. a portable musical instrument with bellows and buttons.

**concerto** n. (pl. **-tos** or **-ti**) a musical composition for solo instrument and orchestra.

**concession** n. something granted; an allowance or reduced price.

**conch** n. a spiral shell.

**conciliate** v. 1 make calm and content. 2 try to bring the sides in a dispute together.
■ **conciliation** n. **conciliatory** adj.

**concise** adj. giving information clearly and briefly.
▷ SYNS SUCCINCT, brief, short, compact, condensed, terse, compressed, to the point, pithy, laconic.

**conclave** n. a private meeting.

**conclude** v. 1 end; settle finally. 2 reach an opinion by reasoning.
▷ SYNS 1 END, finish, cease, terminate, discontinue; inf. wind up. 2 DEDUCE, infer, gather, judge, conjecture, surmise.

**conclusion** n. 1 an ending. 2 an opinion reached.
▷ SYNS 1 END, finish, close, completion, termination, cessation. 2 DEDUCTION, inference, opinion, judgement, verdict.

**conclusive** adj. decisive; settling an issue.
▷ SYNS DECISIVE, definitive, certain, incontrovertible, unquestionable, categorical, irrefutable, convincing.

**concoct** v. prepare from ingredients; invent.
■ **concoction** n.
▷ SYNS INVENT, devise, think up, formulate, hatch, dream up.

**concord** n. agreement or harmony.

**concourse** n. a large open area at a railway station etc.

**concrete** n. a building material made from gravel, sand, cement, and water. • adj. having a material or physical form; definite. • v. cover or fix with concrete.
▷ SYNS adj. ACTUAL, real, definite, genuine, factual, substantial, solid, physical, visible, material, tangible, palpable.

**concubine** n. a woman who lives with a man as his wife but is not married to him.

**concur** v. (**concurred, concurring**) agree in opinion.

**concurrent** adj. existing or happening at the same time.
■ **concurrence** n. **concurrently** adv.

**concussion** n. temporary unconsciousness caused by a blow on the head.

**condemn** v. 1 express strong disapproval of; declare unfit for use. 2 sentence; doom.
■ **condemnation** n.
▷ SYNS 1 DENOUNCE, criticize, censure, deplore, castigate, revile. 2 SENTENCE, pass sentence on, convict. 3 DAMN, doom, destine.

**condensation** n. 1 droplets of water formed on a cold surface in contact with humid air. 2 condensing.

**condense** v. 1 make denser or briefer. 2 change from gas or vapour to liquid.

**condescend** v. 1 behave as if you are better than others. 2 do something you believe to be beneath you. ■ **condescension** n.
▷ SYNS 1 PATRONIZE, talk down to, look down on. 2 DEIGN, lower yourself, demean yourself, stoop, descend.

**condescending** adj. feeling or showing that you think you are better than other people.
▷ SYNS PATRONIZING, supercilious, disdainful, superior, lofty; inf. snooty.

**condiment** n. a seasoning for food.

**condition** n. **1** the state something is in. **2** something that is necessary if something else is to exist or occur. **3** (**conditions**) circumstances. • v. **1** influence or determine; train or accustom. **2** bring into the desired condition.
▷ SYNS n. **1** STATE OF AFFAIRS, situation, circumstances, position. **2** SHAPE, fitness, health, order, trim, fettle. **3** PROVISO, stipulation, prerequisite, requirement. **4** DISEASE, illness, disorder, complaint, problem, ailment, malady.

**conditional** adj. depending on one or more conditions being met.
▷ SYNS PROVISIONAL, dependent, contingent, limited, restricted, provisory.

**conditioner** n. a substance that improves the condition of hair, fabric, etc.

**condolence** n. an expression of sympathy.

**condom** n. a contraceptive device worn on a man's penis.

**condone** v. forgive or overlook a fault etc.
▷ SYNS ALLOW, tolerate, excuse, pardon, forgive, overlook, disregard.

**conducive** adj. contributing or helping towards.
▷ SYNS CONTRIBUTORY, helpful, favourable, useful, instrumental, advantageous, beneficial.

**conduct** v. **1** lead or guide; be the conductor of. **2** manage; carry out. **3** transmit heat or electricity. • n. behaviour; a way

of conducting business etc.
■ **conduction** n.
▷ SYNS v. **1** DIRECT, run, manage, administer, lead, organize, control, supervise, regulate. **2** SHOW, guide, lead, escort, accompany, take. • n. BEHAVIOUR, actions, performance.

**conductor** n. **1** a person who directs an orchestra's or choir's performance. **2** a substance that conducts heat or electricity. **3** a person collecting fares on a bus.

**conduit** n. **1** a channel for liquid. **2** a tube protecting electric wires.

**cone** n. **1** an object with a circular base, tapering to a point. **2** the dry scaly fruit of a pine or fir.

**confectionery** n. sweets and chocolates. ■ **confectioner** n.

**confederate** adj. joined by treaty or agreement. • n. an accomplice.

**confederation** n. a union of states or groups.

**confer** v. **1** grant a title etc. **2** have discussions.
▷ SYNS **1** BESTOW, present, award, grant, give. **2** TALK, consult, debate, deliberate, discuss, converse.

**conference** n. a meeting for discussion.
▷ SYNS MEETING, seminar, discussion, convention, forum, symposium.

**confess** v. acknowledge or admit; formally declare your sins to a priest. ■ **confession** n.
▷ SYNS ADMIT, acknowledge, own up, disclose, reveal, divulge, unburden yourself, come clean.

**confessional** n. an enclosed stall in a church for hearing confessions.

**confessor** n. a priest who hears confessions.

**confetti** n. bits of coloured paper thrown at a bride and bridegroom.

**confidant** n. a person in whom you confide.

**confide** v. tell someone about a secret or private matter.
▷ SYNS CONFESS, reveal, disclose, tell, divulge; open your heart.

**confidence** n. trust; certainty; belief in yourself; something told in secret. □ **confidence trick** a swindle achieved by gaining someone's trust.
▷ SYNS **1** BELIEF, faith, conviction, trust, credence. **2** SELF-ASSURANCE, poise, self-confidence, self-possession, aplomb.

**confident** adj. feeling confidence.
▷ SYNS **1** CERTAIN, sure, convinced, positive, optimistic, sanguine. **2** SELF-ASSURED, self-possessed, self-confident, poised; inf. together.

**confidential** adj. to be kept secret. ■ confidentiality n.
▷ SYNS SECRET, private, classified, off the record.

**configuration** n. an arrangement of parts.

**confine** v. keep within limits; shut in. • n. boundaries.
▷ SYNS v. **1** ENCLOSE, cage, lock up, imprison, detain, jail, shut up, intern, incarcerate, coop up. **2** RESTRICT, limit.

**confinement** n. **1** being confined. **2** dated the time of childbirth.

**confirm** v. **1** establish the truth of. **2** make definite. **3** (**be confirmed**) undergo the rite of confirmation.

▷ SYNS **1** CORROBORATE, verify, prove, validate, authenticate, substantiate; support, back up, bear out. **2** ASSURE, affirm, promise, guarantee.

**confirmation** n. **1** confirming or being confirmed. **2** a rite admitting a baptized person to full membership of the Christian Church.

**confiscate** v. take or seize by authority. ■ confiscation n.
▷ SYNS SEIZE, impound, take away, appropriate, commandeer.

**conflict** n. a fight or struggle; disagreement. • v. clash or disagree.
▷ SYNS n. **1** WAR, campaign, battle, fighting, confrontation, engagement, encounter, hostilities; warfare, combat. **2** DISPUTE, disagreement, dissension, clash; discord, friction, strife, antagonism, hostility, feud, schism. • v. CLASH, differ, disagree, be at odds/variance.

**conform** v. comply with rules, standards, or conventions.
▷ SYNS COMPLY WITH, abide by, obey, observe, follow, keep to, stick to.

**conformist** n. a person who behaves in an expected or conventional way.

**confound** v. surprise and confuse; prove wrong.

**confront** v. meet an enemy etc. face to face; face up to a problem. ■ confrontation n.
▷ SYNS FACE (UP TO), tackle, stand up to, challenge, take on, brave.

**confuse** v. **1** bewilder. **2** mix up or identify wrongly. **3** make muddled or unclear.
▷ SYNS **1** BEWILDER, puzzle, perplex, bemuse, baffle, nonplus; inf. flummox.

2 MUDDLE, mix up, obscure, cloud, complicate.

**confusion** n. 1 uncertainty or lack of understanding. 2 a situation or state of panic or disorder.
▷ SYNS 1 BEWILDERMENT, perplexity, bafflement, puzzlement, mystification, bemusement. 2 DISORDER, disarray, disorganization, chaos; turmoil, disruption, upheaval, muddle, mess.

**conga** n. a dance in which people form a long winding line.

**congeal** v. become semi-solid.
▷ SYNS SOLIDIFY, coagulate, thicken, clot, harden, gell.

**congenial** adj. pleasing to your tastes.
▷ SYNS AGREEABLE, pleasant, pleasing, genial, convivial, companionable, like-minded, friendly, sympathetic.

**congenital** adj. being so from birth.
▷ SYNS 1 HEREDITARY, inherited, innate, inborn. 2 INVETERATE, compulsive, chronic, incurable, incorrigible.

**conger eel** n. a large sea eel.

**congested** adj. 1 very crowded. 2 abnormally full of blood. 3 blocked with mucus.
■ congestion n.

**conglomerate** n. a number of things grouped together; a corporation formed from a merger of firms.
■ conglomeration n.

**congratulate** v. express pleasure at the good fortune of; praise the achievements of.
■ congratulation n.
▷ SYNS PRAISE, commend, applaud, salute, pay tribute to.

**congregate** v. flock together.
▷ SYNS GATHER, assemble, collect, mass, group, convene, converge, meet, crowd, cluster, throng.

**congregation** n. people assembled at a church service.

**congress** n. 1 a formal meeting between delegates. 2 (**Congress**) a national law-making assembly, esp. that of the US.

**conical** adj. cone-shaped.

**conifer** n. a tree bearing cones.
■ coniferous adj.

**conjecture** n. & v. (a) guess.
▷ SYNS GUESS, speculation, theory, surmise, inference.

**conjugal** adj. of marriage.
▷ SYNS MATRIMONIAL, nuptial, marital.

**conjugate** v. Grammar give the different forms of a verb.
■ conjugation n.

**conjunction** n. 1 a word such as 'and' or 'if' that connects others. 2 simultaneous occurrence.

**conjunctivitis** n. inflammation of the membrane connecting the eyeball and eyelid.

**conjure** v. produce as though by magic; summon or evoke.
■ conjuror n.

**connect** v. join or be joined; associate mentally; put into contact by telephone; (of a train, coach, or flight) arrive so that passengers are in time to catch another.
▷ SYNS 1 ATTACH, link, fix, couple, secure, tie. 2 ASSOCIATE, link, equate, bracket.

**connection** n. 1 a link or relationship. 2 (**connections**) influential friends or relatives. 3 a train, bus, etc. that connects with another.
▷ SYNS LINK, relationship, relation, association, correlation.

**connive** v. secretly allow. ■ **connivance** n.
▷ SYNS (**connive at**) OVERLOOK, disregard, condone, turn a blind eye to.

**connoisseur** n. an expert judge in matters of taste.

**connotation** n. an idea or feeling suggested by a word in addition to its literal meaning.
▷ SYNS OVERTONE, undertone, nuance, suggestion, implication.

**connote** v. (of a word) imply in addition to its literal meaning.

**conquer** v. overcome in war or by effort. ■ **conqueror** n.
▷ SYNS 1 DEFEAT, beat, vanquish, overpower, overthrow, subdue, rout, trounce, subjugate, triumph over, overwhelm, crush, quell, worst. 2 SEIZE, occupy, invade, annex, overrun.

**conquest** n. the action of conquering a territory or its people.
▷ SYNS 1 DEFEAT, overthrow, subjugation, rout; victory, triumph. 2 SEIZURE, occupation, possession, invasion, annexation.

**conscience** n. a sense of right and wrong guiding a person's actions.
▷ SYNS MORALS, principles, ethics, standards, scruples, qualms, compunction.

**conscientious** adj. diligent in your duty.
▷ SYNS DILIGENT, industrious, hardworking, painstaking, careful, meticulous, thorough, punctilious, dedicated, scrupulous, assiduous.

**conscious** adj. 1 awake and alert; aware. 2 intentional.
■ **consciousness** n.

▷ SYNS 1 AWAKE, aware, alert, sentient. 2 DELIBERATE, premeditated, intentional, intended, on purpose, calculated, voluntary.

**conscript** v. summon for compulsory military service. • n. a conscripted person.
■ **conscription** n.

**consecrate** v. make or declare sacred. ■ **consecration** n.
▷ SYNS SANCTIFY, bless, make holy.

**consecutive** adj. following in unbroken sequence.
▷ SYNS SUCCESSIVE, succeeding, following, in succession, in a row, running.

**consensus** n. general agreement.

**consent** v. agree; give permission. • n. permission; agreement.
▷ SYNS v. AGREE, assent, acquiesce, accede, allow, approve. • n. AGREEMENT, assent, acceptance, approval, permission, sanction; inf. go-ahead.

**consequence** n. 1 a result. 2 importance.
▷ SYNS RESULT, effect, outcome, aftermath, repercussion, upshot.

**consequent** adj. 1 resulting. 2 important. ■ **consequential** adj. **consequently** adv.
▷ SYNS RESULTING, resultant, subsequent, following, attendant.

**conservation** n. conserving; preservation of the natural environment. ■ **conservationist** n.
▷ SYNS PRESERVATION, protection, safe keeping, safeguarding, care, husbandry, upkeep, maintenance; ecology, environmentalism.

**conservative** adj. 1 opposed to change. 2 (of an estimate) purposely low. • n. a conservative person.

▷ SYNS **adj.** CONVENTIONAL, traditional, orthodox; cautious, unadventurous, old-fashioned, hidebound, reactionary.

**conservatory** n. (pl. **-ies**) a room with a glass roof and walls, built on to a house.

**conserve** v. protect from harm or overuse. • n. jam or marmalade.

▷ SYNS **v.** PRESERVE, protect, save, safeguard, keep, look after; sustain, prolong.

**consider** v. **1** think carefully about. **2** believe or think. **3** take into account.

▷ SYNS **1** THINK ABOUT, reflect on, weigh up, ponder, contemplate, deliberate over, mull over.
**2** BELIEVE, regard as, deem, hold to be, judge, rate.

**considerable** adj. great in amount or importance.
■ **considerably** adv.

▷ SYNS SUBSTANTIAL, sizeable, appreciable, fair, significant, handsome, decent, generous, large, ample.

**considerate** adj. careful not to hurt or inconvenience others.

▷ SYNS THOUGHTFUL, kind, helpful, attentive, solicitous, unselfish, compassionate, sympathetic, charitable, patient, generous, obliging, accommodating.

**consideration** n. careful thought; a factor taken into account in making a decision; being considerate.

**considering** prep. taking into account.

**consign** v. deliver or send; put for disposal.

**consignment** n. a batch of goods sent or delivered.

▷ SYNS DELIVERY, shipment, load, cargo, batch.

**consist** v. be composed of.

▷ SYNS BE COMPOSED OF, be made up of, comprise, contain, include, incorporate.

**consistency** n. (pl. **-ies**) **1** being consistent. **2** the degree of thickness or solidity of semi-liquid matter.

**consistent** adj. **1** unchanging. **2** not conflicting. ■ **consistently** adv.

▷ SYNS **1** CONSTANT, regular, unchanging, unvarying, steady, stable, uniform. **2** COMPATIBLE, consonant.

**consolation** n. **1** comfort received after a loss or disappointment. **2** a source of such comfort.

▷ SYNS COMFORT, solace; sympathy, commiseration; support, encouragement, reassurance.

**console**[1] v. comfort in time of sorrow.

**console**[2] n. a panel holding controls for electronic equipment.

**consolidate** v. **1** make stronger or more secure. **2** combine.
■ **consolidation** n.

**consommé** n. clear soup.

**consonant** n. a letter of the alphabet representing a sound made by obstructing the breath. • adj. in agreement.

**consort** n. a husband or wife, esp. of a monarch. • v. associate with someone.

**consortium** n. (pl. **-ia** or **-iums**) a combination of firms acting together.

**conspicuous** adj. easily seen; attracting attention.

▷ SYNS CLEAR, visible, obvious, evident, apparent, prominent, notable, noticeable, marked, plain, unmistakable, manifest, patent, striking, glaring, blatant, flagrant; obtrusive, showy, ostentatious.

**conspiracy** n. (pl. **-ies**) a secret plan made by a group.
▷ SYNS PLOT, scheme, machinations, intrigue, collusion.

**conspire** v. **1** plot secretly in a group to do something wrong. **2** (of events) combine to produce an effect as though deliberately. ■ **conspirator** n. **conspiratorial** adj.

**constable** n. a police officer of the lowest rank.

**constabulary** n. (pl. **-ies**) a police force.

**constant** adj. occurring continuously or repeatedly; unchanging; faithful. • n. an unvarying quantity.
■ **constancy** n.
▷ SYNS adj. **1** EVEN, regular, uniform, stable, steady, unchanging, fixed, consistent, unvarying. **2** CONTINUAL, unending, non-stop, sustained, incessant, endless, unceasing, persistent, interminable, unremitting, relentless.

**constellation** n. a group of stars.

**consternation** n. great surprise and anxiety or dismay.
▷ SYNS DISMAY, distress, anxiety, perturbation, alarm, surprise, astonishment, amazement.

**constipation** n. difficulty in emptying the bowels.
■ **constipated** adj.

**constituency** n. (pl. **-ies**) a body of voters who elect a representative.

**constituent** adj. being part of a whole. • n. **1** a voter in a constituency. **2** a part of a whole.

**constitute** v. be the parts of.

**constitution** n. **1** the principles by which a state is organized. **2** the general condition of the body. **3** the composition of something.

**constitutional** adj. of or in accordance with a constitution. • n. dated a regular walk taken to stay in good health.

**constrain** v. force or compel.

**constraint** n. a limitation or restriction.

**constrict** v. **1** make or become narrower or tighter. **2** restrict.
■ **constriction** n.

**construct** v. make by placing parts together. • n. an idea or theory.
▷ SYNS v. BUILD, make, assemble, erect, put up, manufacture, produce, fabricate, fashion.

**construction** n. **1** constructing; a thing constructed. **2** an interpretation.
▷ SYNS BUILDING, structure, edifice, framework.

**constructive** adj. (of criticism etc.) helpful or useful.
▷ SYNS USEFUL, helpful, productive, practical, valuable, worthwhile, beneficial.

**construe** v. interpret.

**consul** n. an official representative of a state in a foreign city.
■ **consular** adj. **consulate** n.

**consult** v. seek information or advice from. ■ **consultation** n. **consultative** adj.
▷ SYNS **1** CONFER, discuss, talk, deliberate. **2** ASK, call in, turn to.

**consultant** n. a specialist consulted for professional advice.

**consume** v. eat or drink; use up; (of fire) destroy; obsess.
▷ syns 1 EAT, drink, devour, swallow, ingest, gobble, guzzle. 2 USE, utilize, expend, deplete.

**consumer** n. a person who buys or uses goods or services.

**consummate** v. accomplish; complete a marriage by having sex. • adj. highly skilled.
■ consummation n.

**consumption** n. consuming.

**contact** n. touching; communication; an electrical connection; a person who may be contacted for information or help. • v. get in touch with. □ contact lens a small lens worn directly on the eyeball to correct the vision.
▷ syns n. TOUCH, proximity, exposure; communication, association, dealings. • v. COMMUNICATE WITH, get in touch with, approach, write to, phone, call, ring up, speak to.

**contagion** n. the spreading of a disease by close contact.

**contagious** adj. 1 (of a disease) spread by close contact between people. 2 having a contagious disease.
▷ syns CATCHING, infectious, communicable, transmissible.

**contain** v. 1 have within itself; include. 2 control or restrain.
▷ syns 1 HOLD, carry, accommodate, seat. 2 INCLUDE, comprise, take in, incorporate, involve. 3 RESTRAIN, hold in, control, keep in check, suppress, repress, curb, stifle.

**container** n. a receptacle; a metal box of standard design for transporting goods.

▷ syns RECEPTACLE, vessel, holder, repository.

**contaminate** v. pollute.
■ contamination n.
▷ syns POLLUTE, defile, corrupt, poison, taint, infect, sully.

**contemplate** v. 1 gaze at. 2 think about; meditate.
■ contemplation n.
▷ syns 1 THINK ABOUT, meditate on, consider, ponder, reflect on, muse on, dwell on, deliberate over, ruminate over. 2 HAVE IN MIND, intend, plan, propose, envisage. 3 LOOK AT, view, regard, examine, inspect, observe, scrutinize, survey, eye.

**contemplative** adj. showing or involving deep thought or meditation.
▷ syns THOUGHTFUL, pensive, reflective, meditative, ruminative, introspective, brooding.

**contemporary** adj. 1 living or occurring at the same time. 2 modern. • n. (pl. -ies) a person of the same age or living at the same time.
▷ syns adj. CURRENT, modern, present-day, up to date, latest, fashionable; inf. trendy.

**contempt** n. despising or being despised; disrespectful disobedience.
▷ syns SCORN, disdain, disgust, loathing, abhorrence, detestation, hatred.

**contemptible** adj. deserving contempt.
▷ syns DESPICABLE, deplorable, disgraceful, reprehensible, discreditable, mean, shameful, shabby.

**contemptuous** adj. showing contempt.
▷ syns SCORNFUL, disdainful, disrespectful, insulting, derisive,

insolent, mocking, condescending, superior, super-cilious, snide.

**contend** v. 1 struggle; compete. 2 assert. ■ **contender** n.

**content¹** adj. satisfied with what you have. • n. satisfaction. • v. satisfy.

**content²** n. (also **contents**) what is contained in something; the subject matter of a book etc.

**contented** adj. happy and satisfied.

▷ SYNS SATISFIED, content, pleased, happy, glad, gratified, at ease/ peace, serene, tranquil, un-worried, untroubled.

**contention** n. 1 disagreement. 2 an assertion.

**contentious** adj. causing disagreement.

**contentment** n. a state of happiness and satisfaction.

▷ SYNS SATISFACTION, contented-ness, happiness, pleasure, gratification, ease, comfort, peace, serenity, tranquillity.

**contest** v. compete for or in; oppose; argue about. • n. a struggle for victory; a com-petition.

▷ SYNS v. 1 COMPETE FOR, contend for, fight for, vie for, battle for, go for. 2 CHALLENGE, question, oppose, object to. • n. 1 see **COM-PETITION**. 2 STRUGGLE, battle, fight, tussle.

**contestant** n. a person who takes part in a contest.

▷ SYNS COMPETITOR, entrant, can-didate, contender, participant, rival, opponent, adversary.

**context** n. what precedes or follows a word or statement and fixes its meaning; circumstances.

▷ SYNS CIRCUMSTANCES, situation, conditions, state of affairs, background, setting, frame of reference, framework.

**continent¹** n. one of the earth's main land masses. ■ **continental** adj.

**continent²** adj. able to control the movements of the bowels and bladder. ■ **continence** n.

**contingency** n. (pl. **-ies**) a possible but unpredictable occurrence.

**contingent** adj. 1 subject to chance. 2 depending on other circumstances. • n. a body of troops contributed to a larger group.

**continual** adj. constantly or fre-quently recurring. ■ **continually** adv.

▷ SYNS 1 CONSTANT, continuous, unending, never-ending, un-remitting, relentless, un-relenting, unrelieved. 2 FREQUENT, repeated, recurrent, recurring, regular.

**continue** v. 1 keep happening or existing without stopping. 2 keep doing something. 3 carry on in the same direction. 4 start again after a break. ■ **continuation** n.

▷ SYNS 1 CARRY ON, proceed, go on, keep on, persist, persevere; stay, remain. 2 RESUME, re-commence, restart, return to, take up.

**continuous** adj. without interruptions or gaps. ■ **continuity** n.

▷ SYNS CONTINUAL, uninterrupted, unbroken, constant, ceaseless, incessant, sustained, unceasing, non-stop, unremitting, relent-less, endless, never-ending, perpetual, interminable.

**contort** v. force or twist out of normal shape. ■ **contortion** n. **contortionist** n.

**contour** n. an outline; a line on a map showing height above sea level.
▷ SYNS OUTLINE, silhouette, profile, figure, shape, form, line, curve.

**contra-** pref. against.

**contraband** n. smuggled goods.

**contraceptive** adj. & n. (a drug or device) used to prevent a woman becoming pregnant. ■ **contraception** n.

**contract** n. a formal agreement. • v. 1 make or become smaller or shorter. 2 make a contract. 3 catch an illness. ■ **contractor** n. **contractual** adj.
▷ SYNS n. AGREEMENT, arrangement, settlement, covenant, compact, understanding, bargain, deal. • v. 1 SHRINK, reduce, diminish, decrease, decline. 2 TENSE, tighten, flex. 3 CATCH, develop, get, go down with.

**contraction** n. making or becoming smaller; a shortened form of a word or words; a shortening of the womb muscles during childbirth.

**contradict** v. say that a statement is untrue or a person is wrong; conflict with. ■ **contradiction** n.

**contradictory** adj. 1 opposed or inconsistent. 2 containing inconsistent elements.
▷ SYNS OPPOSED, opposite, opposing, conflicting, incompatible, inconsistent, irreconcilable, contrary.

**contraflow** n. a flow (esp. of traffic) in a direction opposite to and alongside the usual flow.

**contralto** n. (pl. **-os**) the lowest female voice.

**contraption** n. a strange device or machine.
▷ SYNS DEVICE, machine, mechanism, gadget, contrivance; inf. gizmo.

**contrary** adj. 1 opposite in nature, tendency, or direction. 2 deliberately doing the opposite of what is desired. • n. the opposite.
▷ SYNS adj. 1 OPPOSING, opposite, contradictory, conflicting, contrasting, incompatible, irreconcilable, inconsistent, antithetical. 2 AWKWARD, wilful, perverse, obstinate, stubborn, headstrong, wayward, recalcitrant, refractory.

**contrast** n. a striking difference; a comparison drawing attention to this. • v. be strikingly different; point out the difference between two things.
▷ SYNS n. DIFFERENCE, dissimilarity, disparity, distinction, dissimilitude. • v. 1 COMPARE, juxtapose. 2 DIFFER, conflict, be at odds/ variance.

**contravene** v. break a rule etc. ■ **contravention** n.

**contribute** v. give to a common fund or effort; help to cause something. ■ **contributor** n.
▷ SYNS 1 GIVE, donate, provide, present, supply, bestow. 2 LEAD TO, be conducive to, help, play a part in.

**contribution** n. a gift or payment.
▷ SYNS DONATION, gift, offering, present, handout.

**contrite** adj. remorseful.
▷ SYNS PENITENT, repentant, remorseful, regretful, sorry, conscience-stricken, rueful.

**contrive** v. **1** plan or achieve skilfully. **2** manage to do.
■ contrivance n.

**contrived** adj. artificial or false.

**control** n. the power to direct, influence, or restrain something; a means of restraining or regulating; a standard for checking the results of an experiment.
• v. (**controlled, controlling**) have control of; regulate; restrain.
▷ SYNS n. **1** AUTHORITY, power, charge, management, command, direction, rule, government, supervision, jurisdiction, dominance, mastery, leadership, reign, supremacy. **2** LIMITATION, restriction, regulation, check, restraint, curb, brake. • v. **1** BE IN CHARGE OF, manage, head, direct, command, rule, govern, oversee, preside over. **2** REGULATE, restrain, keep in check, restrict, curb, hold back, contain, subdue, bridle.

**controversial** adj. causing controversy.
▷ SYNS DISPUTED, contentious, tendentious, at issue, debatable, moot, vexed.

**controversy** n. (pl. **-ies**) a prolonged and heated disagreement.
▷ SYNS DISPUTE, argument, debate, disagreement, dissension, contention, altercation, wrangle, war of words.

**contusion** n. a bruise.

**conundrum** n. a riddle or puzzle.

**conurbation** n. a large urban area formed where towns have spread and merged.

**convalesce** v. regain health after illness. ■ convalescence n. convalescent adj. & n.

**convection** n. the transmission of heat within a liquid or gas by movement of heated particles.
■ convector n.

**convene** v. call together; assemble. ■ convener (or **convenor**) n.
▷ SYNS CALL, summon, convoke; assemble, gather, meet.

**convenience** n. **1** freedom from effort or difficulty. **2** a useful or helpful thing. **3** a public toilet.

**convenient** adj. involving little trouble or effort; easily accessible.
▷ SYNS **1** SUITABLE, appropriate, fitting, favourable, advantageous, opportune, timely, well timed, expedient. **2** ACCESSIBLE, nearby, handy, at hand.

**convent** n. a community of nuns.

**convention** n. **1** a way in which something is usually done. **2** socially acceptable behaviour. **3** an agreement between states or countries. **4** a conference.
▷ SYNS CUSTOM, usage, practice, tradition, way, habit, norm; propriety, etiquette, protocol.

**conventional** adj. **1** based on or in accordance with convention. **2** not individual or adventurous. ■ conventionally adv.
▷ SYNS **1** ORTHODOX, traditional, established, accepted, mainstream, accustomed, customary; normal, standard, ordinary, usual. **2** CONSERVATIVE, traditionalist, conformist, bourgeois, old-fashioned, unadventurous.

**converge** v. come to or towards the same point.
▷ SYNS MEET, intersect, join.

**conversant** adj. (**conversant with**) having knowledge of.

**conversation** n. informal talk between people.
■ conversational adj.
▷ SYNS TALK, discussion, chat, dialogue, gossip, heart-to-heart, palaver; inf. natter.

**converse**[1] v. hold a conversation.

**converse**[2] adj. opposite. • n. the opposite. ■ conversely adv.

**convert** v. change from one form or use to another; cause to change an attitude or belief. • n. a person persuaded to adopt a new faith or other belief.
■ conversion n.
▷ SYNS V. CHANGE, turn, transform, metamorphose, transfigure, transmogrify, transmute; alter, modify, adapt.

**convertible** adj. able to be converted. • n. a car with a folding or detachable roof.

**convex** adj. curved like the outer surface of a ball.

**convey** v. transport or carry; communicate an idea etc.
▷ SYNS 1 TRANSPORT, carry, bring, fetch, take, move, bear, shift, transfer. 2 TRANSMIT, communicate, pass on, tell, relate, impart, reveal, disclose.

**conveyance** n. 1 transport; a means of transport. 2 the legal process of transferring ownership of property.
■ conveyancing n.

**conveyor belt** n. a continuous moving belt conveying objects.

**convict** v. officially declare guilty of a criminal offence. • n. a person convicted of a criminal offence and serving a prison sentence.

▷ SYNS V. FIND GUILTY, sentence.
• n. PRISONER, inmate; criminal, felon; inf. jailbird.

**conviction** n. 1 a firm belief; confidence. 2 convicting or being convicted.
▷ SYNS 1 CONFIDENCE, assurance, belief, certainty, certitude. 2 BELIEF, view, principle, opinion, thought, idea.

**convince** v. make a person feel certain that something is true.
▷ SYNS PERSUADE, satisfy, assure; induce, prevail on, talk round, win over.

**convincing** adj. able to convince.
▷ SYNS PERSUASIVE, powerful, strong, compelling, conclusive.

**convivial** adj. sociable and lively; friendly.
▷ SYNS FRIENDLY, genial, cordial, sociable, affable, amiable, congenial, agreeable, jolly, cheerful.

**convoluted** adj. complicated; intricately coiled.
■ convolution n.

**convoy** n. a group of ships or vehicles travelling together or under escort.
▷ SYNS GROUP, line, fleet, cortège, cavalcade, motorcade.

**convulse** v. suffer convulsions.

**convulsion** n. 1 a sudden uncontrolled movement of the body. 2 (**convulsions**) uncontrollable laughter.

**coo** n. & v. (make) a soft murmuring sound like a dove.

**cook** v. prepare food by heating; undergo this process. • n. a person who cooks. ■ cooker n. cookery n.

**cookie** n. US a sweet biscuit.

**cool** adj. 1 fairly cold. 2 calm; not enthusiastic or friendly. 3 inf.

fashionably attractive. • n. **1** low temperature. **2** inf. calmness.
• v. make or become cool.
■ **coolly** adv.
▷ SYNS adj. **1** CHILLY, fresh, refreshing, breezy, draughty; inf. nippy. **2** CALM, relaxed, composed, collected, self-possessed, level-headed, self-controlled, unperturbed, un-ruffled, serene. **3** ALOOF, distant, reserved, stand-offish, unfriendly, offhand, un-demonstrative, unwelcoming, uncommunicative, impassive.
• v. **1** CHILL, refrigerate.
**2** LESSEN, diminish, reduce, dampen.

**coop** n. a cage for poultry.
• v. (**coop up**) confine.

**cooperate** v. work together for a common end. ■ **cooperation** n.
▷ SYNS JOIN FORCES, unite, combine, collaborate, coordin-ate, pull together.

**cooperative** adj. helpful; in-volving mutual help; (of a busi-ness) owned and run jointly by its members. • n. a business run on this basis.
▷ SYNS adj. **1** JOINT, united, shared, combined, concerted, collective, collaborative. **2** HELPFUL, obli-ging, accommodating, willing.

**co-opt** v. appoint someone as a member of a committee.

**coordinate** v. arrange the elements of a complex whole to achieve efficiency; negotiate and work with others. • n. **1** Math. any of the numbers used to indi-cate the position of a point.
**2** (**coordinates**) matching items of clothing. ■ **coordination** n. **coordinator** n.
▷ SYNS v. ARRANGE, organize, order, synchronize, harmonize; cooperate, liaise, collaborate.

**coot** n. a waterbird.

**cop** n. inf. a police officer.

**cope** v. deal successfully with something.
▷ SYNS **1** MANAGE, succeed, survive, get by. **2** (**cope with**) HANDLE, deal with, take care of.

**copier** n. a copying machine.

**coping** n. the sloping top row of masonry of a wall.

**copious** adj. plentiful.
▷ SYNS ABUNDANT, plentiful, ample, profuse, extensive, generous, lavish.

**copper** n. **1** a reddish-brown metallic element; a coin containing this; its colour. **2** inf. a police officer.

**coppice** (or **copse**) n. a group of small trees and undergrowth.

**copse** n. a small group of trees.

**copulate** v. mate or have sex.
■ **copulation** n.

**copy** n. (pl. **-ies**) a thing made to look like another; a specimen of a book etc.; material for a newspaper or magazine article.
• v. (**copied**, **copying**) make a copy of; imitate. □ **copyright** the exclusive right to publish or record a work. **copywriter** a person who writes advertisements or publicity material.
▷ SYNS n. **1** REPRODUCTION, imi-tation, replica, likeness; counterfeit, forgery, fake.
**2** DUPLICATE, facsimile, carbon copy, photocopy. • v. **1** IMITATE, mimic, emulate, mirror, echo, ape, parrot; plagiarize. **2** REPRO-DUCE, replicate, forge, counter-feit.

**coquette** n. a woman who flirts.
■ **coquettish** adj.

**coracle** n. a small wicker boat.

**coral** n. a hard red, pink, or white substance built by tiny sea creatures; a reddish-pink colour.

**cord** n. **1** long thin flexible material made from twisted strands; a piece of this. **2** corduroy. ▷ SYNS STRING, rope, twine, cable, line, ligature.

**cordial** adj. warm and friendly. • n. a fruit-flavoured drink. ■ **cordially** adv.

**cordon** n. a line of police, soldiers, etc. enclosing something. • v. (**cordon off**) enclose with a cordon.

**cordon bleu** adj. of the highest class in cookery.

**corduroy** n. cloth with velvety ridges.

**core** n. the central or most important part; the tough central part of an apple etc., containing seeds. • v. remove the core from. ▷ SYNS n. CENTRE, heart, nucleus, nub, kernel, crux, essence, gist; inf. nitty-gritty.

**corgi** n. a small, short-legged breed of dog.

**coriander** n. a fragrant herb.

**cork** n. **1** a light substance obtained from the bark of a tree. **2** a bottle stopper. • v. stop up with a cork. □ **corkscrew** a device for pulling corks from bottles.

**corm** n. a bulb-like underground stem from which buds grow.

**cormorant** n. a large black seabird.

**corn** n. **1** wheat, oats, or maize; grain. **2** a small painful area of hardened skin, esp. on the foot. □ **cornflour** fine flour made from maize. **cornflower** a blue-flowered plant.

**cornea** n. the transparent outer covering of the eyeball.

**corner** n. a place or angle where two lines or sides meet; a remote area; a free kick or hit from the corner of the field in football or hockey. • v. **1** force into a position from which there is no escape. **2** drive round a corner. **3** obtain a monopoly of a commodity. □ **cornerstone** a vital part; a foundation. ▷ SYNS n. BEND, angle, curve, turn, crook; junction, intersection, crossroads, fork. • v. TRAP, capture, run to earth.

**cornet** n. **1** a brass instrument like a small trumpet. **2** a cone-shaped wafer holding ice cream.

**cornice** n. an ornamental moulding round the top of an indoor wall.

**cornucopia** n. a plentiful supply.

**corny** adj. (**-ier**, **-iest**) inf. sentimental; hackneyed.

**corollary** n. (pl. **-ies**) a proposition that follows logically from another.

**coronary** adj. of the arteries supplying blood to the heart. • n. (pl. **-ies**) a blockage of the flow of blood to the heart.

**coronation** n. the ceremony of crowning a king or queen.

**coroner** n. an officer holding inquests.

**coronet** n. a small crown.

**corpora** pl. of CORPUS.

**corporal** n. a non-commissioned officer next below sergeant. • adj. of the body.

**corporate** adj. shared by members of a group; united in a group.

**corporation** n. a large company or group of companies; a group elected to govern a town.

**corps** n. (pl. **corps**) a military unit; an organized body of people.

**corpse** n. a dead body.
▷ SYNS BODY, remains, cadaver, carcass.

**corpulent** adj. fat.
■ corpulence n.

**corpus** n. (pl. **-pora**) a collection of writings.

**corpuscle** n. a blood cell.

**corral** n. US an enclosure for cattle.

**correct** adj. 1 true; free from errors. 2 conforming to an accepted standard of behaviour. • v. mark or rectify errors in; put right. ■ correction n. correctly adv.
▷ SYNS adj. 1 RIGHT, accurate, true, exact, precise, unerring, faithful, strict, faultless, flawless; inf. spot on. 2 PROPER, suitable, appropriate, fit, fitting, seemly. • v. RECTIFY, amend, remedy, repair, emend.

**corrective** adj. correcting what is bad or harmful.

**correlate** v. have or bring into a dependent relationship.
■ correlation n.

**correspond** v. 1 be similar, equivalent, or in harmony. 2 write letters to each other.
▷ SYNS AGREE, concur, coincide, match, tally, correlate.

**correspondence** n. 1 a close link or similarity. 2 letters sent or received.

**correspondent** n. 1 a person who writes letters. 2 a person employed by a newspaper or TV news station to gather news and send reports.

**corridor** n. 1 a passage in a building or train giving access to rooms or compartments. 2 a strip of land linking two other areas.

**corroborate** v. support or confirm. ■ corroboration n.
▷ SYNS CONFIRM, verify, bear out, authenticate, validate, substantiate, uphold, back up.

**corrode** v. destroy a metal etc. gradually by chemical action.
■ corrosion n. corrosive adj.

**corrugate** v. 1 contract into wrinkles or folds. 2 (**corrugated**) shaped into alternate ridges and grooves. ■ corrugation n.

**corrupt** adj. 1 able to be bribed; immoral. 2 (of a text or computer data) full of errors. • v. make corrupt. ■ corruption n.
▷ SYNS adj. 1 DISHONEST, unscrupulous, dishonourable, untrustworthy, unprincipled, venal, fraudulent. 2 IMMORAL, depraved, wicked, evil, sinful, degenerate, perverted, dissolute, debauched, decadent. • v. 1 BRIBE, buy (off), suborn. 2 DEPRAVE, pervert.

**corset** n. a tight-fitting undergarment worn to shape or support the body.

**cortège** n. a funeral procession.

**cortex** n. (pl. **-tices**) the outer part of an organ, esp. that of the brain.

**cortisone** n. a hormone used in treating allergies.

**cosh** n. a thick heavy bar used as a weapon.

**cosine** n. Math. the ratio of the side adjacent to an acute angle (in a right-angled triangle) to the hypotenuse.

**cosmetic** n. a substance used to improve a person's appearance. • adj. improving the appearance; superficial.

**cosmic** adj. of the universe.

**cosmopolitan** adj. free from national prejudices; including people from all parts of the world. • n. a cosmopolitan person.
▷ SYNS adj. **1** INTERNATIONAL, global, universal; multicultural, multiracial. **2** SOPHISTICATED, urbane, worldly, worldly-wise, well travelled.

**cosmos** n. the universe.

**cosset** v. (**cosseted, cosseting**) pamper.

**cost** v. **1** (**cost, costing**) have as its price; involve the sacrifice or loss of. **2** (**costed, costing**) estimate the cost of. • n. what a thing costs.
▷ SYNS n. PRICE, charge, rate, value, quotation; payment, expense, outlay.

**costly** adj. expensive.
▷ SYNS EXPENSIVE, dear; exorbitant, extortionate; inf. steep.

**costume** n. a style of clothes, esp. that of a historical period; garments for a special activity.

**cosy** (US **cozy**) adj. **1** warm and comfortable. **2** not difficult. • n. (pl. **-ies**) a cover to keep a teapot or a boiled egg hot. ■ **cosily** adv. **cosiness** n.
▷ SYNS adj. COMFORTABLE, snug, warm, relaxed, homely; inf. comfy.

**cot** n. a child's bed with high sides.

**coterie** n. a select group.

▷ SYNS CLIQUE, set, crowd, circle, gang, club.

**cottage** n. a small simple house, esp. in the country. □ **cottage cheese** soft white lumpy cheese made from curds.

**cotton** n. a soft white substance round the seeds of a tropical plant; thread or fabric from cotton.

**couch** n. a sofa. • v. express in a specified way.

**cougar** n. US a puma.

**cough** v. expel air etc. from the lungs with a sudden sharp sound. • n. the act or sound of coughing; an illness causing coughing.

**could** past of CAN².

**coulomb** n. a unit of electric charge.

**council** n. a formal group meeting regularly for debate and administration; the body governing a town. ■ **councillor** n.

**counsel** n. **1** advice. **2** (pl. **counsel**) a barrister.
• v. (**counselled, counselling**; US **counseled**) **1** advise. **2** give professional help and advice to someone with psychological or personal problems.
■ **counsellor** n.

**count** v. **1** find the total of. **2** say numbers in order. **3** include. **4** regard as being. **5** be important. **6** (**count on**) rely on.
• n. **1** counting. **2** a total. **3** a point to consider. **4** a charge. **5** a foreign nobleman.
□ **countdown 1** the counting of seconds backwards to zero to launch a rocket. **2** the final moments before a significant event.
▷ SYNS v. **1** ADD UP, calculate, total, reckon up, tally, compute,

tot up. **2** REGARD, consider, think, hold, judge, deem. **3** MATTER, be of account, signify.

**countenance** n. a person's face or expression. • v. tolerate or allow.
▷ SYNS n. FACE, features, expression, look, visage, mien.

**counter** n. **1** a flat-topped fitment over which goods are sold or business transacted with customers. **2** a small disc used in board games. • adv. in the opposite direction; in conflict. • v. speak or act against.

**counteract** v. reduce or prevent the effects of.
▷ SYNS OFFSET, balance, counterbalance, neutralize, cancel out; prevent, thwart, frustrate, impede, hinder, hamper.

**counter-attack** n. & v. (make) an attack in reply to an opponent's attack.

**counterbalance** n. a weight or influence balancing or neutralizing another. • v. act as a counterbalance to.

**counterfeit** adj. not genuine; forged. • n. a forgery. • v. imitate fraudulently.
▷ SYNS adj. FAKE, forged, imitation, bogus, spurious, ersatz; inf. phoney. • n. FAKE, copy, forgery.

**counterfoil** n. a section of a cheque or receipt kept as a record by the person issuing it.

**countermand** v. cancel.

**counterpane** n. a bedspread.

**counterpart** n. a person or thing corresponding to another.
▷ SYNS EQUIVALENT, equal, opposite number, peer.

**counterpoint** n. Music a technique of combining melodies.

**counterproductive** adj. having the opposite of the desired effect.

**countersign** v. add a second signature to a document already signed by one person.

**countersink** v. insert a screw or bolt so that the head lies flat with the surface.

**countertenor** n. a male alto.

**countess** n. a count's or earl's wife or widow; a woman with the rank of count or earl.

**countless** adj. too many to be counted.
▷ SYNS INNUMERABLE, incalculable, infinite, limitless, untold, myriad.

**country** n. **1** a nation with its own government and territory. **2** land outside large towns. ☐ **countryside** the land of a rural area.
▷ SYNS **1** STATE, nation, realm, kingdom, province, principality. **2** LAND, territory, terrain; landscape, scenery, setting; countryside.

**county** n. (pl. **-ies**) a major administrative division of some countries.

**coup** n. **1** (also **coup d'état**) a sudden violent overthrow of a government. **2** a very successful action.

**coupe** n. a sports car with a fixed roof and a sloping back.

**couple** n. two people or things; a married or romantically involved pair. • v. fasten or link together.

**couplet** n. two successive rhyming lines of verse.

**coupling** n. a connecting device.

**coupon** n. a form or ticket entitling the holder to something.

**courage** n. the ability to control fear when facing danger or pain.
▷ SYNS BRAVERY, fearlessness, pluck, boldness, valour, daring, nerve, intrepidity; inf. guts.

**courageous** adj. brave.
▷ SYNS BRAVE, valiant, fearless, intrepid, plucky, bold, daring, undaunted, dauntless, lion-hearted, valorous.

**courgette** n. a small vegetable marrow.

**courier** n. **1** a person employed to deliver things quickly. **2** a person employed to guide and assist a group of tourists.

**course** n. **1** onward progress; a direction taken or intended; a procedure. **2** a series of lessons or treatments. **3** an area on which golf is played or a race takes place. **4** one part of a meal. • v. **1** move or flow freely. **2** pursue hares etc. with greyhounds. □ **of course** certainly; without doubt.
▷ SYNS n. **1** ROUTE, way, track, direction, path, line, tack, trajectory, orbit. **2** a course of action: WAY, method, approach, policy, plan, strategy. **3** in the course of the day: DURATION, passage, period, term, span. **4** an English course: CLASSES, lectures, curriculum, syllabus.

**court** n. **1** a body of people hearing legal cases; the place where they meet. **2** a courtyard; an area for playing squash, tennis, etc. **3** the home, staff, etc. of a monarch. • v. try to win the love or support of; risk danger etc. □ **court martial** (pl. **courts martial**) a court trying offences against military law. **courtship** the act or period of courting someone. **courtyard** an open area enclosed by walls or buildings.
▷ SYNS n. **1** LAW COURT, court of law, tribunal, bench, chancery, assizes. **2** ATTENDANTS, household, retinue, entourage, train, suite.

**courteous** adj. polite.
▷ SYNS POLITE, well mannered, civil, gracious, mannerly, well bred, civilized.

**courtesy** n. (pl. **-ies**) polite behaviour; a polite action.

**courtier** n. a sovereign's companion or adviser.

**courtly** adj. dignified and polite.

**cousin** (or **first cousin**) n. a child of your uncle or aunt. □ **second cousin** a child of your parent's cousin.

**cove** n. a small bay.
▷ SYNS BAY, inlet, fjord.

**coven** n. a gathering of witches.

**covenant** n. a formal agreement, esp. one to make regular payments to a charity. • v. make a covenant.

**cover** v. **1** be or place something over; conceal or protect in this way. **2** deal with a subject; report on for a newspaper etc. **3** be enough to pay for; protect by insurance. **4** travel over a distance. **5** keep a gun aimed at. **6** take over someone's job temporarily. **7** (**cover up**) conceal a thing or fact. • n. **1** a thing that covers; a wrapper, envelope, or binding of a book; a shelter or protection; a disguise. **2** protection by insurance. □ **coverlet** a bedspread. ■ **coverage** n. **cover-up** n.

▷ SYNS v. **1** PROTECT, shield, shelter, hide, conceal, veil; cake, coat, plaster, smother, daub, blanket, overlay, carpet, mantle, shroud. **2** DEAL WITH, involve, take in, contain, encompass, embrace, incorporate, treat. **3** REPORT, write up, describe.
• n. **1** COVERING, sleeve, wrapper, envelope, sheath, jacket, casing; awning, canopy, tarpaulin; lid, top, cap, veneer, coating, coat, layer, carpet, blanket, mantle, veil. **2** DISGUISE, front, camouflage, pretence, facade, smokescreen, pretext. **3** INSURANCE, protection, indemnity, indemnification.

**covert** adj. done secretly.
▷ SYNS SECRET, surreptitious, furtive, stealthy, cloak-and-dagger, clandestine.

**covet** v. (**coveted**, **coveting**) desire a thing belonging to another person. ■ **covetous** adj.
▷ SYNS DESIRE, want, wish for, long for, hanker after.

**cow** n. a fully grown female of cattle or certain other large animals (e.g. the elephant or whale). • v. intimidate.
□ **cowboy 1** a man on horseback who herds cattle in the western US. **2** inf. a dishonest or unqualified tradesman.

**coward** n. a person who lacks courage. ■ **cowardice** n.

**cowardly** adj. lacking courage.
▷ SYNS FEARFUL, timorous, fainthearted, spineless, lily-livered, craven, pusillanimous; inf. chicken, yellow.

**cower** v. crouch or shrink in fear.
▷ SYNS CRINGE, shrink, flinch, recoil, blench.

**cowl** n. a monk's hood or hooded robe; a hood-shaped covering on a chimney.

**cowslip** n. a wild plant with small yellow flowers.

**cox** n. a coxswain.

**coxswain** n. a person who steers a boat.

**coy** adj. pretending to be shy or embarrassed.
▷ SYNS COQUETTISH, arch, kittenish, shy, modest, demure, bashful.

**coyote** n. a North American wolf-like wild dog.

**coypu** n. a beaver-like aquatic rodent.

**cozy** US sp. of COSY.

**crab** n. a ten-legged shellfish.
□ **crab apple** a small sour apple.

**crabbed** adj. **1** (or **crabby**) bad-tempered. **2** (of handwriting) hard to read.

**crack** n. **1** a narrow opening between two parts of something which has split or been broken. **2** a sudden sharp noise. **3** a sharp blow. **4** inf. a joke. **5** inf. an attempt to do something. **6** a strong form of cocaine. • v. **1** break without separating. **2** give way under pressure or strain. **3** make a sudden sharp sound. **4** hit hard. **5** (of a voice) suddenly change in pitch. **6** solve a problem. **7** tell a joke. • adj. very good or skilful. □ **crackdown** a series of severe measures against something. **crackpot** inf. eccentric or impractical.
▷ SYNS n. SPLIT, break, chip, fracture, rupture; space, gap, crevice, fissure, breach, cleft, chink, cranny. • v. BREAK, split, fracture, splinter, snap.

**cracker** n. **1** a small explosive firework; a paper tube giving an explosive crack when pulled apart, containing a small gift. **2** a thin dry biscuit.

**crackers** adj. inf. crazy.

**crackle** v. make a series of light cracking sounds. • n. these sounds.

**cradle** n. a baby's bed on rockers; a place where something originates. • v. hold or support gently.
▷ SYNS n. **1** CRIB, cot, bassinet. **2** BIRTHPLACE, source, fount, wellspring. • v. HOLD, shelter, support, protect.

**craft** n. **1** an activity involving skill in making things by hand. **2** skill. **3** (pl. **craft**) a ship, boat, or aircraft. **4** cunning.
▷ SYNS **1** ACTIVITY, trade, occupation, profession, line of work, pursuit. **2** SKILL, art, talent, expertise, proficiency, ability. **3** VESSEL, ship, boat, aircraft.

**craftsman** n. a worker skilled in a craft. ■ craftsmanship n.

**crafty** adj. (**-ier**, **-iest**) cunning or using underhand methods. ■ craftily adv.
▷ SYNS CUNNING, artful, calculating, scheming, wily, shrewd, astute, canny, sharp, guileful, sly, devious.

**crag** n. a steep or rugged rock. ■ craggy adj.

**cram** v. **1** force into too small a space; overfill. **2** study intensively for an exam.
▷ SYNS STUFF, push, force, pack, ram, press, squeeze.

**cramp** n. **1** a painful involuntary tightening of a muscle. **2** a metal bar with bent ends for holding things together. • v. keep within too narrow limits.

**crane** n. **1** a large wading bird. **2** a machine for lifting and moving heavy objects. • v. stretch your neck to see something.

**cranium** n. (**-iums** or **-ia**) the skull.

**crank** n. **1** an L-shaped part for converting to-and-fro into circular motion. **2** an eccentric person. • v. turn a crank to start an engine. ■ cranky adj.

**cranny** n. (pl. **-ies**) a crevice.

**crash** v. **1** (of a vehicle) collide violently with something. **2** (of an aircraft) fall from the sky and hit the land or sea. **3** move loudly and forcefully. **4** Computing fail suddenly. • n. **1** an instance of crashing. **2** a sudden loud noise. • adj. rapid and concentrated. □ crash helmet a helmet worn to protect the head.
▷ SYNS v. COLLIDE WITH, bump into, smash into, plough into; hit, strike. • n. COLLISION, accident, smash; inf. pile-up.

**crass** adj. very stupid; insensitive.

**crate** n. a packing case made of wooden slats; a container divided into individual units for bottles.
▷ SYNS BOX, case, chest.

**crater** n. a bowl-shaped cavity; the mouth of a volcano.
▷ SYNS HOLE, hollow, pit, cavity, depression.

**cravat** n. a strip of fabric worn round the neck and tucked inside a shirt.

**crave** v. feel an intense longing for; ask earnestly for. ■ craving n.

**craven** adj. cowardly.

**crawl** v. **1** move on hands and knees or with the body close to the ground. **2** move very slowly. **3** (**crawling with**) be unpleasantly covered or crowded with. **4** inf. be very submissive or friendly so as to gain favour. • n. **1** a crawling movement or pace. **2** an overarm swimming stroke.
▷ SYNS v. CREEP, slither, squirm, wriggle, worm your way.

**crayfish** n. (pl. **crayfish**) a freshwater shellfish like a small lobster.

**crayon** n. a stick of coloured wax etc. for drawing.

**craze** n. a temporary enthusiasm.
▷ SYNS TREND, fashion, fad, vogue, enthusiasm, passion, obsession, mania.

**crazy** adj. **1** insane. **2** very foolish. **3** madly eager.
■ crazily adv.
▷ SYNS **1** MAD, insane, deranged, demented, lunatic, unbalanced, unhinged; inf. out of your mind, nuts, round the bend, barmy, bonkers. **2** FOOLISH, stupid, foolhardy, idiotic, irrational, unreasonable, illogical, senseless, absurd, impractical, silly, asinine, ludicrous.

**creak** n. a harsh squeak. • v. make this sound. ■ creaky adj.

**cream** n. the fatty part of milk; its yellowish-white colour; a thick lotion; the best part.
• v. **1** mash with milk or cream. **2** (**cream off**) take the best part of something. ■ creamy adj.
▷ SYNS n. LOTION, ointment, salve, unguent, liniment; moisturizer, emollient.

**crease** n. **1** a line made in cloth or paper by crushing or pressing. **2** a line marking the limit of the bowler's or batsman's position in cricket.
• v. make a crease in; develop creases.
▷ SYNS n. WRINKLE, furrow, line, fold, crinkle, ridge, corrugation.
• v. CRUMPLE, wrinkle, rumple, crinkle, ruck up, pucker.

**create** v. bring into existence; produce by what you do.
■ creation n. creator n.
▷ SYNS **1** PRODUCE, originate, design, establish, set up, invent, make, build, construct, develop, fabricate, found, form, mould, forge. **2** BRING ABOUT, engender, generate, lead to, result in, cause.

**creative** adj. involving or showing imagination and originality. ■ creativity n.
▷ SYNS INVENTIVE, imaginative, original, artistic, resourceful, ingenious.

**creature** n. an animal; a person.
▷ SYNS **1** ANIMAL, beast; US critter. **2** PERSON, human being, individual.

**crèche** n. a day nursery.

**credence** n. belief.

**credentials** pl.n. qualifications, achievements, etc.; documents attesting to these.
▷ SYNS DOCUMENTS, documentation, papers; references, certificates, diplomas.

**credible** adj. believable.
■ credibility n.
▷ SYNS BELIEVABLE, plausible, convincing, likely, conceivable.

**credit** n. **1** a system allowing customers to pay at a later date for services or goods supplied. **2** public recognition or praise. **3** a source of pride. **4** (**credits**) a list of the contributors to a film or television programme, displayed at the end. **5** an entry in an account recording a sum received. • v. **1** believe. **2** attribute something to. **3** add money to an account. □ **credit card** a plastic card allowing the holder to buy things and pay for them later.

▷ SYNS n. PRAISE, acclaim, commendation, acknowledgement, recognition, kudos, glory, respect, appreciation. • v. **1** BELIEVE, accept, trust; inf. buy, swallow, fall for. **2** ASCRIBE, attribute, assign, accredit, chalk up, put down.

**creditable** adj. deserving praise. ■ **creditably** adv.

▷ SYNS PRAISEWORTHY, commendable, laudable, meritorious, admirable, deserving.

**creditor** n. a person to whom money is owed.

**credulous** adj. too ready to believe things.

▷ SYNS GULLIBLE, over-trusting, naive, unsuspicious; inf. born yesterday.

**creed** n. a set of beliefs or principles.

▷ SYNS BELIEF, faith; principles, teaching, doctrine, ideology, dogma, tenets, credo.

**creek** n. a narrow inlet of water, esp. on a coast.

▷ SYNS INLET, bay, estuary, bight; Scot. firth.

**creep** v. **1** move slowly and cautiously. **2** progress or develop gradually. **3** (of a plant) grow along the ground or a wall etc. • n. **1** inf. an unpleasant person. **2** slow and gradual movement. **3** (**the creeps**) inf. fear or revulsion.

▷ SYNS v. TIPTOE, steal, sneak, slip, slink, sidle, edge, inch.

**creeper** n. a plant that grows along the ground or another surface.

**creepy** adj. (**-ier**, **-iest**) inf. frightening; disturbing.

**cremate** v. burn a corpse to ashes. ■ **cremation** n.

**crematorium** n. (pl. **-ria** or **-riums**) a place where corpses are cremated.

**Creole** n. a hybrid language.

**creosote** n. a dark brown oil used as a wood preservative.

**crêpe** n. **1** a fabric with a wrinkled surface. **2** a pancake.

**crept** past and p.p. of CREEP.

**crescendo** n. (pl. **-dos** or **-di**) a gradual increase in loudness.

**crescent** n. a narrow curved shape tapering to a point at each end; a curved street of houses.

**cress** n. a plant with small leaves used in salads.

**crest** n. **1** a tuft or outgrowth on a bird's or animal's head; a plume on a helmet. **2** the top of a slope or hill; a white top of a large wave. **3** a design above a shield on a coat of arms.

▷ SYNS **1** COMB, tuft, plume. **2** SUMMIT, top, peak, crown, brow. **3** BADGE, emblem, regalia, insignia, device, coat of arms.

**crestfallen** adj. sad and disappointed.

▷ SYNS DOWNCAST, dejected, glum, downhearted, disheartened, dispirited, despondent, disconsolate, disappointed, sad.

**cretin** n. inf. a stupid person.

**crevasse** n. a deep open crack esp. in a glacier.

**crevice** n. a narrow gap in a surface.

▷ SYNS FISSURE, cleft, crack, cranny, split, rift, slit, opening, gap, hole, interstice.

**crew¹** n. the people working on a ship or aircraft; a group working together. □ **crew cut** a very short haircut.

**crew²** past of CROW.

**crib** n. **1** a child's cot. **2** inf. a list of facts, often used to cheat in a test. **3** a rack for animal fodder. • v. (**cribbed**, **cribbing**) inf. copy dishonestly.

**cribbage** n. a card game.

**crick** n. a sudden painful stiffness in the neck or back.

**cricket** n. **1** an outdoor game for two teams of 11 players with ball, bats, and wickets. **2** a brown insect resembling a grasshopper. ■ **cricketer** n.

**crime** n. **1** an act that is illegal and can be punished by law. **2** illegal actions as a whole.

▷ SYNS **1** OFFENCE, unlawful act, felony, misdemeanour, misdeed, wrong. **2** LAW-BREAKING, wrongdoing, delinquency, criminality.

**criminal** n. a person guilty of a crime. • adj. of or involving crime. ■ **criminality** n. **criminally** adv.

▷ SYNS n. OFFENDER, lawbreaker, wrongdoer, felon, delinquent, malefactor, miscreant, culprit, villain; inf. crook. • adj. **1** UN-LAWFUL, illegal, illicit, lawless, felonious, delinquent, villain-ous, wicked, nefarious; inf. crooked, bent. **2** DEPLORABLE, scandalous, shameful, reprehensible.

**crimp** v. press into ridges.

**crimson** adj. & n. deep red.

**cringe** v. cower; feel embarrass-ment or disgust.

▷ SYNS COWER, shrink, flinch, recoil, shy away.

**crinkle** n. & v. (a) wrinkle.

**crinoline** n. a light framework formerly worn to make a long skirt stand out.

**cripple** n. offens. a disabled or lame person. • v. make lame; weaken seriously.

▷ SYNS V. DISABLE, incapacitate, lame, paralyse, immobilize.

**crisis** n. (pl. **-ses**) a time of intense danger or difficulty.

▷ SYNS EMERGENCY, disaster, catas-trophe, calamity, predicament, plight, extremity.

**crisp** adj. **1** firm, dry, and brittle. **2** cold and bracing. **3** brisk and decisive. • n. a thin slice of fried potato. □ **crispbread** a thin, crisp biscuit made from rye or wheat. ■ **crispy** adj.

▷ SYNS adj. **1** CRUNCHY, crispy, brittle. **2** INVIGORATING, bracing, fresh, refreshing. **3** BRISK, decisive, no-nonsense, brusque.

**criss-cross** adj. & adv. in a pattern of intersecting lines. • v. form a criss-cross pattern.

**criterion** n. (pl. **-ria**) a standard of judgement.

▷ SYNS MEASURE, standard, benchmark, yardstick, scale, touchstone, barometer.

**critic** n. **1** a person who expresses disapproval of someone or something. **2** a person who assesses the quality of literary or artistic works.

▷ SYNS **1** DETRACTOR, attacker. **2** RE-VIEWER, commentator, judge, pundit.

**critical** adj. **1** looking for faults. **2** of literary or artistic criticism. **3** of or at a crisis. ■ **critically** adv.

▷ SYNS **1** CENSORIOUS, dis-approving, disparaging,

derogatory, uncomplimentary, unfavourable, negative.
**2** CRUCIAL, decisive, pivotal, key, all-important, vital.
**3** DANGEROUS, grave, serious, risky, perilous, hazardous, precarious.

**criticism** n. the expression of disapproval.
▷ SYNS CONDEMNATION, censure, disapproval; attack, broadside; inf. flak.

**criticize** (or **-ise**) v. **1** find fault with. **2** analyse and evaluate.
▷ SYNS FIND FAULT WITH, censure, denounce, condemn, attack, lambaste, pillory, denigrate, cast aspersions on; inf. knock, pan.

**critique** n. an analysis and assessment.

**croak** n. a deep hoarse cry or sound like that of a frog. • v. make a croak.

**crochet** n. lacy fabric produced from thread worked with a hooked needle. • v. (**crocheted**, **crocheting**) make by or do such work.

**crock** n. **1** an earthenware pot. **2** inf. a weak person.

**crockery** n. household china.

**crocodile** n. **1** a large predatory amphibious tropical reptile. **2** a line of people walking in pairs.

**crocus** n. a small spring-flowering plant.

**croft** n. a small rented farm in Scotland. ■ **crofter** n.

**croissant** n. a rich crescent-shaped roll.

**crone** n. an old and ugly woman.

**crony** n. (pl. **-ies**) a close friend or companion.

**crook** n. **1** a hooked stick; an angle. **2** inf. a criminal. • v. bend a finger.

**crooked** adj. **1** not straight. **2** inf. dishonest.
▷ SYNS BENT, twisted, warped, contorted, misshapen; winding, twisting, zigzag; lopsided, askew, off-centre.

**croon** v. sing softly.

**crop** n. **1** a plant cultivated on a large scale for its produce; a group or amount produced at one time. **2** a pouch in a bird's gullet where food is broken up for digestion. **3** a very short haircut. • v. **1** cut or bite off. **2** (**crop up**) occur unexpectedly.
▷ SYNS n. HARVEST, yield, produce, vintage, fruits. • v. **1** CUT, trim, clip, shear, lop. **2** (**crop up**) HAPPEN, arise, occur, emerge, materialize.

**cropper** n. (**come a cropper**) inf. fall heavily; fail badly.

**croquet** n. a game played on a lawn with balls driven through hoops with mallets.

**croquette** n. a small ball of potato etc. fried in breadcrumbs.

**cross** n. **1** a mark or shape formed by two intersecting lines or pieces; an upright post with a transverse bar, formerly used in crucifixion. **2** an unavoidable affliction. **3** a hybrid; a mixture of two things. **4** a transverse pass of a ball. • v. **1** go or extend across; draw a line across; mark a cheque so that it must be paid into a named account. **2** intersect; mark with a cross. **3** cause to interbreed. **4** oppose the wishes of. • adj. annoyed. ◻ **crossbar** a horizontal bar between uprights.

**cross-breed** an animal produced by interbreeding. **cross-check** verify figures etc. by an alternative method. **cross-examine** question a witness called by the other party in a court of law. **cross-eyed** squinting. **crossfire** gunfire crossing another line of fire. **cross-reference** a reference to another place in the same book. **crossroads** a place where roads cross each other. **cross-section** a surface or shape revealed by cutting across something; a representative sample. **crosswise** (or **crossways**) in the form of a cross; diagonally. **crossword** a puzzle consisting of a grid of squares into which intersecting words are written according to clues.

▷ SYNS **n. 1** AFFLICTION, trouble, worry, burden, trial, tribulation, curse. **2** HYBRID, mixture, crossbreed; mongrel. • **v. 1** SPAN, pass over, bridge, traverse. **2** INTERSECT, meet, join, connect, criss-cross. **3** OPPOSE, resist, defy; obstruct, impede, hinder, hamper. • **adj.** ANNOYED, irritated, vexed, angry, irate, irascible, fractious, crotchety, querulous.

**crossing** n. a place where things cross; a journey across water; a place to cross a road, border, etc.

▷ SYNS **1** JUNCTION, crossroads, intersection. **2** JOURNEY, passage, voyage.

**crotch** n. the part of the human body between the legs.

**crotchet** n. a note in music equal to half a minim.

**crotchety** adj. irritable.

**crouch** v. stoop low with the legs tightly bent. • **n.** this position.

▷ SYNS **v.** SQUAT, bend, duck, stoop, hunch, hunker down.

**croup** n. an inflammation of the windpipe in children, causing coughing and breathing difficulty.

**croupier** n. a person in charge of a gambling table in a casino.

**crouton** n. a small piece of fried or toasted bread as a garnish.

**crow** n. **1** a large black bird. **2** a cock's cry. • **v.** (**crowed** or **crew**, **crowing**) (of a cock) make its loud cry; express triumph and glee.

**crowbar** n. an iron bar with a bent end, used as a lever.

**crowd** n. a large group. • **v.** fill completely or excessively; move or gather in a crowd.

▷ SYNS **n. 1** HORDE, throng, mob, mass, multitude, host, rabble, army, herd, flock, drove, swarm, troupe, pack; assembly, gathering, congregation. **2** AUDIENCE, house, turnout, gate, spectators. • **v. 1** GATHER, cluster, flock, swarm, throng, huddle. **2** SURGE, push/elbow your way, jostle; squeeze, pile, throng, cram, jam.

**crowded** adj. full; busy.

▷ SYNS FULL, busy, packed, teeming, swarming, crammed, thronged, populous.

**crown** n. **1** a monarch's ceremonial headdress. **2** (**the Crown**) the monarchy or reigning monarch. **3** the top or highest part. • **v. 1** place a crown on a new monarch. **2** rest on or form the top of. **3** be the climax of.

▷ SYNS **n. 1** CORONET, diadem, circlet. **2** MONARCH, sovereign, king, queen, monarchy, royalty. **3** TOP, crest, summit, apex, tip, peak. • v. **1** ENTHRONE, install. **2** CAP, round off, complete, perfect.

**crucial** adj. very important to the success or failure of something. ■ **crucially** adv.
▷ SYNS VITAL, essential, all-important, critical; decisive, pivotal, key.

**crucible** n. a container in which metals are melted.

**crucifix** n. a model of a cross with a figure of Jesus on it.

**crucify** v. (**crucified, crucifying**) put to death by nailing or binding to a cross.
■ **crucifixion** n.

**crude** adj. in a natural or raw state; roughly made; offensively coarse or rude. ■ **crudity** n.
▷ SYNS **1** UNREFINED, unprocessed, natural, raw. **2** ROUGH, primitive, simple, basic, rudimentary, makeshift, rough-and-ready.

**cruel** adj. (**crueller** or **crueler, cruellest** or **cruelest**) deliberately causing pain or suffering. ■ **cruelly** adv. **cruelty** n.
▷ SYNS BRUTAL, savage, inhuman, barbaric, barbarous, brutish, bloodthirsty, murderous, sadistic, wicked, evil, monstrous; callous, ruthless, merciless, pitiless, remorseless, uncaring, heartless, cold-blooded, unfeeling, unkind, inhumane.

**cruet** n. a set of containers for salt, pepper, etc. at the table.

**cruise** v. **1** sail for pleasure or on patrol. **2** travel at a moderate speed. • n. a voyage on a ship, as a holiday.

**cruiser** n. a fast warship; a motor boat with a cabin.

**crumb** n. a small fragment of bread etc.; a tiny piece.

**crumble** v. break into small fragments. • n. a baked pudding made with fruit and a crumbly topping. ■ **crumbly** adj.
▷ SYNS v. DISINTEGRATE, fall apart, fall to pieces, collapse, fragment, break up.

**crummy** adj. (**-ier, -iest**) inf. of poor quality.

**crumpet** n. a flat soft cake eaten toasted.

**crumple** v. crush or become crushed into creases; collapse.
▷ SYNS CRUSH, scrunch, squash, screw up, mangle; crease, rumple, wrinkle, crinkle.

**crunch** v. crush noisily with the teeth; make a muffled grinding sound. • n. **1** the sound of crunching. **2** inf. a crucial point or situation. ■ **crunchy** adj.
▷ SYNS v. BITE INTO, gnaw, champ, chomp, munch.

**crusade** n. **1** a medieval Christian military expedition to recover the Holy Land from Muslims. **2** a campaign for a cause. • v. take part in a crusade.
■ **crusader** n.
▷ SYNS n. CAMPAIGN, drive, movement, push, struggle, battle, war.

**crush** v. **1** press so as to squash, crease, or break. **2** defeat or subdue completely. • n. **1** a crowded mass of people. **2** inf. a short-lived feeling of love for someone.
▷ SYNS v. **1** SQUASH, squeeze, press, mash, compress, mangle, pound, pulverize, grind, pulp; crease, crumple. **2** PUT DOWN, defeat, suppress, subdue, overpower, quash, stamp out, extinguish.

**crust** n. a hard outer layer, esp. of bread. ■ **crusty** adj.

**crustacean** n. a creature with a hard shell (e.g. a lobster).

**crutch** n. 1 a support for a lame person. 2 the crotch.

**crux** n. the most important point.

**cry** v. 1 shed tears. 2 shout or scream loudly. • n. 1 a period of crying. 2 a shout or scream. 3 an animal's call.
▷ SYNS v. 1 WEEP, sob, wail, snivel, whimper, bawl, howl; inf. blubber. 2 CALL OUT, exclaim, yell, shout, bellow, roar. • n. CALL, exclamation, yell, shout, bellow, roar.

**cryogenics** n. a branch of physics dealing with very low temperatures.

**crypt** n. a room below the floor of a church.
▷ SYNS TOMB, vault, burial chamber, sepulchre, catacomb, mausoleum.

**cryptic** adj. mysterious or obscure in meaning.
▷ SYNS MYSTERIOUS, enigmatic, puzzling, perplexing, mystifying, obscure, arcane; ambiguous, elliptical.

**crystal** adj. a glass-like mineral; high-quality glass; a symmetrical piece of a solidified substance. ■ crystalline adj.

**crystallize** (or **-ise**) v. form into crystals; become definite in form; preserve fruit in sugar.

**cu.** abbr. cubic.

**cub** n. 1 the young of foxes, lions, etc. 2 (also **Cub Scout**) a member of the junior branch of the Scout Association.

**cubbyhole** n. a very small room or space.

**cube** n. 1 a solid object with six equal square sides. 2 the product of a number multiplied by itself twice. • v. 1 find the cube of a number. 2 cut into cubes. □ cube root a number which produces a given number when cubed. ■ cubic adj.

**cubicle** n. a small area partitioned off in a large room.

**cubism** n. a style of painting in which objects are shown as geometrical shapes. ■ cubist n.

**cuckoo** n. a bird that lays its eggs in other birds' nests.

**cucumber** n. a long green-skinned fruit eaten in salads.

**cud** n. food that cattle bring back from the stomach into the mouth and chew again.

**cuddle** v. hug lovingly; nestle together. • n. a gentle hug.
▷ SYNS v. HUG, embrace, clasp, hold tight; snuggle, nestle.

**cuddly** adj. pleasantly soft or plump.

**cudgel** n. a short thick stick used as a weapon. • v. (**cudgelled**, **cudgelling**; US **cudgeled**) beat with a cudgel.
▷ SYNS n. CLUB, cosh, stick, truncheon, baton.

**cue** n. 1 a signal to do something, esp. for an actor to begin a speech. 2 a long rod for striking balls in billiards etc. • v. (**cued**, **cueing**) give a signal to someone.
▷ SYNS n. SIGNAL, sign, indication, reminder, prompt.

**cuff** n. 1 a band of cloth round the edge of a sleeve. 2 a blow with the open hand. • v. strike with the open hand. □ cufflink a device for fastening together the sides of a shirt cuff. off the cuff inf. without preparation.

**cuisine** n. a style of cooking.

**cul-de-sac** n. a street closed at one end.

**culinary** adj. of or for cooking.

**cull** v. gather or select; select and kill animals to reduce numbers.

**culminate** v. reach a climax.
■ culmination n.

**culottes** pl.n. women's trousers styled to resemble a skirt.

**culpable** adj. deserving blame.
▷ SYNS GUILTY, in the wrong, at fault, blameworthy, to blame.

**culprit** n. a person who has committed an offence.
▷ SYNS GUILTY PARTY, offender, wrongdoer, miscreant, law-breaker, criminal, malefactor.

**cult** n. a system of religious worship; excessive admiration of a person or thing.
▷ SYNS 1 SECT, denomination, group, movement, church, per-suasion. 2 OBSESSION, fixation, mania, passion.

**cultivate** v. 1 prepare and use land for crops; produce crops by tending them. 2 develop a skill etc. by practice. 3 try to win the friendship or support of.
■ cultivation n.
▷ SYNS 1 TILL, farm, work, plough, dig. 2 WOO, court, pay court to, ingratiate yourself with, curry favour with.

**cultural** adj. relating to the arts.
■ culturally adv.
▷ SYNS ARTISTIC, aesthetic, intel-lectual.

**culture** n. 1 the arts and intel-lectual achievements as a whole. 2 an understanding or appreciation of this. 3 the art, customs, etc. of a particular country or society. 4 cells or bacteria grown for scientific study.
▷ SYNS 1 THE ARTS, the humanities; literature, music, painting, philosophy. 2 INTELLECTUAL AWARENESS, artistic awareness, education, enlightenment, discernment, discrimination, taste, refinement, sophisti-cation. 3 CUSTOMS, traditions, heritage; way of life, lifestyle, civilization.

**cultured** adj. well educated and able to appreciate art, litera-ture, music, etc.
▷ SYNS CULTIVATED, enlightened, civilized, educated, well read, artistic, knowledgeable, discerning, discriminating, refined, sophisticated.

**culvert** n. a drain under a road.

**cumbersome** adj. heavy and awkward to carry or use.

**cumin** n. a spice.

**cummerbund** n. a sash for the waist.

**cumulative** adj. increasing by additions.

**cumulus** n. (pl. -li) clouds formed in heaped-up rounded masses.

**cunning** adj. skilled at decep-tion; ingenious. • n. craftiness or ingenuity.
▷ SYNS adj. CRAFTY, wily, artful, guileful, devious, sly, scheming, calculating; shrewd, astute, clever, canny; deceitful, decep-tive, duplicitous.

**cup** n. a small bowl-shaped con-tainer with a handle for drinking from; a trophy shaped like this. • v. (cupped, cupping) form your hands into a cuplike shape.

**cupboard** n. a recess or piece of furniture with a door, in which things may be stored.

**cupidity** n. greed for gain.

**cur** n. a mongrel dog.

**curate** n. a member of the clergy who assists a parish priest.

**curator** n. a person in charge of a museum or other collection.
▷ SYNS KEEPER, caretaker, custodian, guardian, steward.

**curb** n. a means of restraint.
• v. restrain.
▷ SYNS v. RESTRAIN, check, control, contain, hold back, repress, suppress, moderate, dampen, subdue.

**curd** (or **curds**) pl.n. the thick, soft substance formed when milk turns sour.

**curdle** v. form or cause to form curds.

**cure** v. 1 restore to health; get rid of a disease or trouble etc. 2 preserve by salting, drying, etc. • n. a substance or treatment curing disease; restoration to health.
▷ SYNS v. 1 HEAL, remedy, rectify, put right, repair, fix. 2 PRESERVE, smoke, salt, dry. • n. REMEDY, antidote, treatment, therapy; panacea, nostrum.

**curfew** n. a law requiring people to stay indoors after a stated time; this time.

**curio** n. (pl. **-os**) an unusual and interesting object.

**curious** adj. 1 eager to learn or know something. 2 strange or unusual. ■ curiosity n.
▷ SYNS 1 INQUISITIVE; intrigued, interested, dying to know, agog. 2 see STRANGE.

**curl** v. form a curved or spiral shape. • n. a curled thing or shape; a coiled lock of hair.
▷ SYNS v. 1 SPIRAL, coil, bend, twist, wind, loop, twirl, wreathe; meander, snake. 2 CRIMP, perm.
• n. RINGLET, kink, wave, corkscrew.

**curler** n. a small tube round which hair is wound to make it curl.

**curlew** n. a wading bird with a long curved bill.

**curly** adj. having curls.
▷ SYNS CURLED, crimped, kinky, wavy, frizzy, permed.

**curmudgeon** n. a bad-tempered person.

**currant** n. 1 a dried grape used in cookery. 2 a small round edible berry.

**currency** n. (pl. **-ies**) 1 money in use in a particular area. 2 being widely used or known.

**current** adj. 1 belonging to the present time. 2 in general use.
• n. a body of water or air moving in one direction; a flow of electricity. ■ currently adv.
▷ SYNS adj. PRESENT, present-day, contemporary, modern; popular, prevailing, prevalent, accepted, common, widespread.
• n. FLOW, stream, tide, undercurrent, undertow; backdraught, slipstream, thermal.

**curriculum** n. (pl. **-la**) a course of study. □ curriculum vitae an outline of a person's qualifications and previous jobs. ■ curricular adj.

**curry** n. (pl. **-ies**) a savoury dish cooked with hot spices.

**curse** n. a call for harm to happen to a person or thing; something causing suffering or annoyance; an offensive word expressing anger. • v. utter a curse; afflict; swear.
▷ SYNS n. 1 MALEDICTION, the evil eye; inf. jinx. 2 SWEAR WORD, expletive, obscenity, oath, profanity, blasphemy.

**cursor** n. a movable indicator on a computer screen.

**cursory** adj. hasty and not thorough.
▷ SYNS HASTY, rapid, hurried, quick, perfunctory, casual, superficial, desultory.

**curt** adj. noticeably or rudely brief.
▷ SYNS TERSE, brusque, abrupt, clipped, monosyllabic, short; ungracious, rude, impolite, discourteous.

**curtail** v. cut short or reduce.
■ curtailment n.
▷ SYNS REDUCE, cut, decrease, lessen, trim; restrict, limit, curb; shorten, truncate.

**curtain** n. a piece of cloth hung as a screen, esp. at a window.

**curtsy** (or **curtsey**) n. (pl. **-ies**) a woman's movement of respect made by bending the knees.
• v. (**curtsied**, **curtsying**) make a curtsy.

**curvaceous** adj. (of a woman) having a shapely curved figure.

**curvature** n. curving; a curved form.

**curve** n. a line which gradually bends. • v. form a curve.
■ curvy adj.
▷ SYNS n. BEND, turn, loop, curl, twist, hook; arc, arch, bow, undulation, curvature.

**cushion** n. 1 a stuffed bag used for sitting or leaning on. 2 a support or protection. • v. lessen the impact of.
▷ SYNS v. 1 PILLOW, cradle, support, prop, rest. 2 SOFTEN, lessen, diminish, decrease, mitigate, dull, deaden.

**cushy** adj. (**-ier**, **-iest**) inf. pleasant and easy.

**cusp** n. 1 a pointed part where curves meet. 2 a point of

transition, esp. between astrological signs.

**custard** n. a sweet sauce made with milk and eggs or flavoured cornflour.

**custodian** n. a guardian or keeper.

**custody** n. 1 protective care. 2 imprisonment.
▷ SYNS 1 CARE, charge, guardianship, keeping, safe keeping, protection. 2 DETENTION, imprisonment, incarceration, confinement.

**custom** n. 1 the usual way of behaving or acting. 2 regular dealing by customers. 3 (**customs**) duty on imported goods.
▷ SYNS 1 TRADITION, practice, usage, way, convention, habit, wont; mores. 2 TRADE, business, patronage.

**customary** adj. usual.
■ customarily adv.
▷ SYNS USUAL, traditional, normal, conventional, familiar, accepted, routine, established, time-honoured, regular; accustomed, habitual, wonted.

**customer** n. a person buying goods or services from a shop etc.
▷ SYNS BUYER, purchaser, shopper, consumer, patron, client.

**customize** (or **-ise**) v. modify to suit a person or task.

**cut** v. 1 open, wound, divide, or shape by pressure of a sharp edge. 2 reduce. 3 intersect. 4 divide a pack of cards.
• n. 1 cutting. 2 an incision or wound. 3 a reduction. 4 a piece cut off. 5 inf. a share.
▷ SYNS v. 1 GASH, slash, lacerate, slit, nick; lance. 2 CARVE, slice, chop, sever, cleave. 3 TRIM, clip,

crop, snip, shear, dock, shave, pare, mow. **4** REDUCE, decrease, lessen, retrench, slash.
**5** SHORTEN, abbreviate, precis, summarize. • n. **1** GASH, laceration, slash, incision.
**2** CUTBACK, decrease, reduction. **3** SHARE, portion, percentage.

**cute** adj. attractive and endearing.

**cuticle** n. the skin at the base of a nail.

**cutlass** n. a short curved sword.

**cutlery** n. table knives forks, and spoons.

**cutlet** n. a lamb or veal chop from behind the neck; a flat cake of minced meat or nuts and breadcrumbs etc.

**cutter** n. **1** a person or thing that cuts. **2** a fast patrol boat or sailing boat.

**cutting** adj. (of remarks) hurtful. • n. **1** a passage cut through high ground for a railway etc. **2** a piece of a plant for replanting. **3** a piece cut out of a newspaper etc.
▷ SYNS **adj.** WOUNDING, hurtful, caustic, barbed, pointed, sarcastic, sardonic, sharp, mordant, snide, spiteful.

**cuttlefish** n. a sea creature resembling a squid, that squirts a black liquid when attacked.

**CV** abbr. curriculum vitae.

**cwt.** abbr. hundredweight.

**cyanide** n. a strong poison.

**cyclamen** n. a plant with pink, red, or white flowers.

**cycle** n. **1** a recurring series of events. **2** a bicycle or motorcycle. • v. ride a bicycle.
■ **cyclist** n.
▷ SYNS n. SERIES, sequence, succession, run; round, rotation.

**cyclic** (or **cyclical**) adj. recurring regularly.
▷ SYNS RECURRING, recurrent, regular, repeated.

**cyclone** n. a violent wind rotating around a central area.

**cygnet** n. a young swan.

**cylinder** n. an object with straight sides and circular ends.
■ **cylindrical** adj.

**cymbal** n. a brass plate struck against another or with a stick as a percussion instrument.

**cynic** n. a person who believes that people always act from selfish motives. ■ **cynicism** n.

**cynical** adj. **1** believing that people always act from selfish motives. **2** sceptical or doubtful.
■ **cynically** adv.
▷ SYNS SCEPTICAL, doubtful, distrustful, suspicious; pessimistic, negative, disenchanted, disillusioned, jaundiced.

**cypher** = CIPHER.

**cypress** n. an evergreen tree.

**cyst** n. a growth on the body containing fluid.

**cystic fibrosis** n. a hereditary disease, often resulting in respiratory infections.

**cystitis** n. inflammation of the bladder.

**czar** = TSAR.

# Dd

**D** n. (as a Roman numeral) 500.

**dab** v. (**dabbed**, **dabbing**) press lightly with something absorbent; apply with quick strokes. • n. a quick stroke; a small amount applied.

**dabble** v. **1** splash about gently or playfully. **2** work at something in a casual or superficial way.

**dachshund** n. a small dog with a long body and short legs.

**dad** (or **daddy**) n. inf. father.

**daddy-long-legs** n. inf. a long-legged flying insect.

**daffodil** n. a yellow flower with a trumpet-shaped central part.

**daft** adj. inf. silly or crazy.

**dagger** n. a short pointed weapon used for stabbing.

**dahlia** n. a garden plant with brightly coloured flowers.

**daily** adj. & adv. every day or every weekday.
▷ SYNS EVERYDAY, quotidian, diurnal.

**dainty** adj. **1** delicate, small, and pretty. **2** fastidious. ■ **daintily** adv. **daintiness** n.
▷ SYNS **1** PETITE, delicate, neat, exquisite, graceful, elegant, pretty, fine. **2** PARTICULAR, fastidious, fussy, choosy, finicky.

**dairy** n. (pl. **-ies**) a place where milk and its products are processed or sold.

**dais** n. a low, raised platform.

**daisy** n. (pl. **-ies**) a flower with many ray-like petals.

**dale** n. a valley.

**dally** v. (**dallied**, **dallying**) idle or dawdle; flirt. ■ **dalliance** n.
▷ SYNS DAWDLE, loiter, delay, linger, procrastinate, waste time; inf. dilly-dally.

**Dalmatian** n. a breed of dog with white hair and dark spots.

**dam** n. a barrier built across a river to hold back water. • v. (**dammed**, **damming**) build a dam across.

**damage** n. **1** harm or injury that reduces something's value, usefulness, or attractiveness. **2** (**damages**) money as compensation for injury. • v. cause damage to.
▷ SYNS n. **1** HARM, injury, destruction, impairment, vandalism, ruin, devastation. **2** (**damages**) COMPENSATION, recompense, restitution, redress. • v. HARM, injure, spoil, vandalize, destroy, wreck, ruin, mar, deface, mutilate, impair, sabotage.

**damask** n. a fabric woven with a pattern visible on either side.

**dame** n. **1** (**Dame**) the title of a woman with an order of knighthood. **2** US inf. a woman.

**damn** v. condemn to hell; condemn or criticize; swear at. • adj. (also **damned**) said to emphasize anger or frustration. ■ **damnable** adj. **damnation** n.

**damp** adj. slightly wet. • n. moistness. • v. **1** make damp. **2** restrain or discourage. ■ dampen v.
▷ SYNS adj. **1** MOIST, clammy, sweaty, dank. **2** RAINY, drizzly, humid, misty, foggy.

**damper** n. **1** something that depresses or subdues. **2** a pad silencing a piano string. **3** a metal plate controlling the draught in a flue.

**damson** n. a small purple plum.

**dance** v. **1** move rhythmically to music. **2** move in a quick and lively way. • n. **1** a series of steps and movements performed to music. **2** a social gathering at which people dance. ■ dancer n.
▷ SYNS v. CAPER, frolic, skip, prance, gambol, jig.

**dandelion** n. a wild plant with bright yellow flowers.

**dandruff** n. flakes of dead skin from the scalp.

**dandy** n. (pl. **-ies**) a man who pays excessive attention to his appearance. • adj. inf. excellent.

**danger** n. likelihood of harm or death; something causing this.
▷ SYNS **1** RISK, peril, hazard, jeopardy, precariousness. **2** CHANCE, possibility, threat.

**dangerous** adj. likely to cause harm or problems.
▷ SYNS **1** HAZARDOUS, perilous, risky, unsafe, precarious; inf. hairy. **2** MENACING, threatening, ruthless, violent, desperate, wild, savage.

**dangle** v. **1** hang so as to swing freely. **2** offer an incentive. ■ dangly adj.
▷ SYNS HANG, swing, sway, trail, droop, flap, wave.

**dank** adj. damp and cold.

**dapper** adj. neat and precise in dress or movement.

**dapple** v. mark with patches of colour or shade.

**dappled** adj. speckled.
▷ SYNS SPECKLED, spotted, mottled, flecked, variegated; piebald, pied, brindled.

**dare** v. be bold enough to do something; challenge to do something risky. • n. this challenge. □ daredevil a recklessly daring person.
▷ SYNS v. **1** RISK, hazard, venture. **2** CHALLENGE, defy, invite.

**daring** adj. bold. • n. boldness.
▷ SYNS adj. BOLD, adventurous, brave, courageous, intrepid, fearless, undaunted.

**dark** adj. **1** with little or no light. **2** of a deep colour. **3** (of skin, hair, or eyes) brown or black. **4** depressing or gloomy. **5** evil or sinister. • n. **1** absence of light. **2** night. □ dark horse a person about whom little is known. ■ darken v. darkness n.
▷ SYNS adj. **1** BLACK, pitch-black, jet-black, inky; shadowy, shady, murky, dim, cloudy, overcast. **2** SWARTHY, dusky, olive, black, ebony.

**darkroom** n. a darkened room for processing photographs.

**darling** n. a loved or lovable person or thing; a favourite. • adj. beloved or lovable.

**darn** v. mend a hole in fabric by weaving thread across it.

**dart** n. **1** a small pointed missile. **2** (**darts**) a game in which such missiles are thrown at a target. **3** a sudden run. **4** a tuck shaping a garment. • v. run suddenly.
▷ SYNS v. RUSH, dash, bolt, sprint, race, run, tear, fly, shoot, scuttle.

**dash** v. **1** run rapidly. **2** strike or throw violently against something; destroy hopes etc. • n. **1** a rapid run. **2** a small amount of liquid etc. added to something. **3** a punctuation mark (-) marking a pause or break in the sense or representing omitted letters. □ **dashboard** the instrument panel in a vehicle.
▷ SYNS v. **1** RUSH, run, hurry, race, sprint, tear, speed, fly, dart, bolt, shoot. **2** SHATTER, destroy, ruin, wreck. • n. BIT, pinch, drop, sprinkling, touch.

**dashing** adj. attractive and confident.
▷ SYNS HANDSOME, attractive, confident; stylish, smart, elegant, debonair.

**dastardly** adj. wicked.

**data** n. **1** facts used for reference or analysis. **2** information processed by a computer. □ **database** a set of data held in a computer.
▷ SYNS INFORMATION, facts, figures, details, statistics.

**date**¹ n. **1** a specified day of a month or year; the day or year of something's occurrence. **2** inf. a social or romantic appointment. • v. **1** establish the date of; originate from a specified date; mark with a date; become or show to be old-fashioned. **2** inf. have a date or regular dates with.
▷ SYNS n. **1** DAY, point in time. **2** MEETING, appointment, engagement, rendezvous, assignation, tryst. **3** PARTNER, escort, girlfriend, boyfriend.

**date**² n. a sweet, dark brown, oval fruit.

**dated** adj. old-fashioned.

▷ SYNS OUT OF DATE, outdated, old-fashioned, outmoded, antiquated; inf. old hat.

**daub** v. smear roughly.

**daughter** n. a female in relation to her parents. □ **daughter-in-law** a son's wife.

**daunt** v. intimidate or discourage. ■ **daunting** adj.
▷ SYNS INTIMIDATE, frighten, overawe, scare, dismay, unnerve, cow, dishearten, dispirit.

**dawdle** v. walk slowly; idle.
▷ SYNS LOITER, delay, linger, take your time, waste time, idle, dally, straggle.

**dawn** n. **1** the first light of day. **2** a beginning. • v. **1** (of a day) begin. **2** come into existence. **3** (**dawn on**) become evident to.
▷ SYNS n. DAYBREAK, break of day, sunrise; lit. cockcrow.

**day** n. **1** a period of 24 hours; the part of this when the sun is above the horizon; the part of this spent working. **2** a time or period. □ **daybreak** dawn. **daydream** a series of pleasant distracting thoughts. **daylight** the natural light of the day; dawn.
▷ SYNS **1** DAYTIME, daylight. **2** PERIOD, time, epoch, age, era, generation.

**daze** v. cause to feel stunned or bewildered. • n. a dazed state.
▷ SYNS v. STUN, stupefy, confuse, bewilder, dumbfound.

**dazzle** v. blind temporarily with bright light; impress with splendour. ■ **dazzling** adj.

**DC** abbr. direct current.

**deacon** n. **1** a Christian minister ranking below a priest. **2** (in some Protestant churches) a person who assists a minister.

**dead** adj. 1 no longer alive. 2 lacking sensation or emotion; lacking excitement. 3 no longer functioning. 4 complete. • adv. absolutely; exactly. □ dead end a road or passage that is closed at one end. dead heat a result in a race in which competitors finish at exactly the same time. deadline the latest time or date for completing something. deadpan expressionless.
▷ SYNS adj. 1 DECEASED, lifeless, gone, passed on/away, departed, defunct, extinct. 2 DULL, boring, tedious, uneventful, flat, uninspiring. 3 *dead silence*: COMPLETE, total, absolute, utter.

**deaden** v. make less intense; make numb.
▷ SYNS DESENSITIZE, numb, anaesthetize; reduce, blunt, dull, diminish, mitigate, alleviate.

**deadlock** n. a situation in which no progress can be made.
▷ SYNS STALEMATE, impasse, stand-off.

**deadly** adj. 1 causing death. 2 inf. very boring. • adv. extremely.
▷ SYNS adj. FATAL, lethal, mortal; toxic, poisonous.

**deaf** adj. wholly or partly unable to hear; refusing to listen.
■ deafen v. deafness n.

**deal** v. 1 distribute playing cards to players; hand out; inflict a blow or misfortune, etc. 2 engage in trade. 3 (**deal with**) take action about; have as a topic. • n. 1 a bargain or transaction. 2 treatment received. 3 fir or pine timber. □ a great deal a large amount.
▷ SYNS v. 1 TRADE, buy and sell, traffic. 2 DISTRIBUTE, share out, allocate, hand out, dole out, apportion. 3 ADMINISTER, deliver, give, inflict.

• n. AGREEMENT, transaction, arrangement, contract, bargain, understanding, settlement, pact.

**dealer** n. 1 a person who buys and sells goods. 2 a person who sells illegal drugs.
▷ SYNS TRADER, broker, retailer, wholesaler, supplier, distributor, merchant.

**dean** n. 1 a clergyman who is head of a cathedral chapter. 2 a university official.

**dear** adj. 1 much loved. 2 expensive. • n. a lovable person.
■ dearly adv.
▷ SYNS adj. 1 BELOVED, loved, adored, cherished. 2 EXPENSIVE, costly, overpriced, pricey.

**dearth** n. a scarcity or lack.
▷ SYNS LACK, scarcity, shortage, deficiency, insufficiency, paucity.

**death** n. the process of dying; the state of being dead; an end.
■ deathly adj.
▷ SYNS 1 DYING, demise, end. 2 KILLING, murder, massacre, slaughter.

**debacle** n. an utter and ignominious failure.
▷ SYNS FIASCO, disaster, catastrophe, failure, collapse.

**debar** v. (**debarred**, **debarring**) exclude.

**debase** v. lower in quality or value. ■ debasement n.
▷ SYNS DEGRADE, devalue, demean, disgrace, dishonour, shame, discredit, cheapen.

**debatable** adj. questionable.
▷ SYNS ARGUABLE, questionable, open to question, moot, disputable.

**debate** n. a formal discussion. • v. discuss formally; consider.

▷ SYNS n. DISCUSSION, dialogue, talk; argument, dispute, wrangle, conflict.

**debauched** adj. overindulging in sex, alcohol, or drugs.
■ debauchery n.
▷ SYNS DEGENERATE, dissipated, dissolute, immoral, decadent.

**debilitate** v. weaken.

**debility** n. physical weakness.

**debit** n. an entry in an account for a sum owing. • v. (**debited**, **debiting**) enter as a debit, charge.

**debonair** adj. having a carefree, self-confident manner.

**debrief** v. question to obtain facts about a completed mission.

**debris** n. scattered broken pieces or rubbish.
▷ SYNS RUBBLE, wreckage, detritus, rubbish, litter, waste, remains, ruins.

**debt** n. something owed; the state of owing something.
■ debtor n.
▷ SYNS 1 BILL, account, dues, arrears. 2 OBLIGATION, indebtedness.

**debunk** v. reveal a belief to be false.

**debut** n. a person's first appearance in a role. • v. perform in public for the first time.

**debutante** n. a young upper-class woman making her first formal appearance in society.

**decade** n. a ten-year period.

**decadent** adj. in a state of moral deterioration.
■ decadence n.

**decaffeinated** adj. with caffeine removed or reduced.

**decamp** v. go away suddenly or secretly.

**decant** v. pour liquid from one container into another to remove sediment.

**decanter** n. a bottle into which wine may be decanted before serving.

**decapitate** v. behead.
■ decapitation n.

**decathlon** n. an athletic contest involving ten events.

**decay** v. 1 rot. 2 become worse or weaker. • n. the state or process of decaying.
▷ SYNS 1 ROT, decompose, putrefy, spoil, perish, corrode. 2 DETERIORATE, degenerate, decline, go downhill, crumble, disintegrate.

**decease** n. death. ■ deceased adj.

**deceit** n. behaviour intended to mislead or deceive.
▷ SYNS DECEPTION, dishonesty, duplicity, double-dealing, fraud, treachery; inf. kidology.

**deceitful** adj. deliberately misleading or deceiving other people.
▷ SYNS DISHONEST, untruthful, insincere, false, untrustworthy, unscrupulous, unprincipled, two-faced, duplicitous, double-dealing, treacherous.

**deceive** v. 1 cause to believe something that is not true. 2 be sexually unfaithful to.
▷ SYNS TAKE IN, fool, delude, trick, hoodwink, dupe, swindle, cheat, double-cross; inf. con.

**decelerate** v. reduce speed.
■ deceleration n.

**December** n. the twelfth month.

**decent** adj. 1 conforming to accepted standards of propriety. 2 of an acceptable standard.

**3** inf. kind or generous.
■ **decency** n.
▷ SYNS **1** PROPER, correct, appropriate, seemly, fitting, suitable, tasteful, decorous, respectable. **2** *a decent salary:* SUFFICIENT, acceptable, reasonable, adequate, ample. **3** *a decent fellow:* HONEST, trustworthy, dependable, kind, thoughtful, obliging, helpful, generous, courteous, civil.

**deception** n. deceiving; a trick.

**deceptive** adj. misleading.
▷ SYNS MISLEADING, illusory, wrong, deceiving, unreliable.

**decibel** n. a unit for measuring the intensity of sound.

**decide** v. make up your mind; settle a contest or argument.
▷ SYNS MAKE UP YOUR MIND, resolve, determine, commit yourself; choose, opt, elect.

**decided** adj. having firm opinions; clear or definite.
■ **decidedly** adv.
▷ SYNS CLEAR, distinct, definite, obvious, marked, pronounced, unmistakable.

**deciduous** adj. (of a tree) shedding its leaves annually.

**decimal** adj. reckoned in tens or tenths. • n. a decimal fraction.
□ **decimal point** the dot used in a decimal fraction.

**decimate** v. kill or destroy a large proportion of.

**decipher** v. make out the meaning of a code or bad handwriting.

**decision** n. **1** a choice made after consideration. **2** the ability to decide quickly.
▷ SYNS CONCLUSION, resolution, judgement, verdict, pronouncement.

**decisive** adj. **1** very important for the outcome of a situation. **2** able to decide quickly.
■ **decisively** adv. **decisiveness** n.
▷ SYNS **1** DECIDING, conclusive, determining, critical, crucial, significant, influential. **2** RESOLUTE, firm, strong-minded, determined, unhesitating, purposeful.

**deck** n. **1** a floor of a ship or bus. **2** a pack of cards. **3** the part of a record player that holds and plays the records. • v. decorate.
□ **deckchair** a folding canvas chair.

**declaim** v. speak or say impressively. ■ **declamation** n. **declamatory** adj.

**declaration** n. **1** a formal statement. **2** an act of declaring something.
▷ SYNS **1** STATEMENT, announcement, proclamation, pronouncement. **2** ASSERTION, affirmation, avowal.

**declare** v. announce openly or formally; state firmly.
▷ SYNS PROCLAIM, announce, state, express; assert, maintain, affirm.

**decline** v. **1** decrease in size or number; lose strength or quality. **2** refuse politely. • n. a gradual decrease or loss of strength.
▷ SYNS v. **1** REFUSE, turn down, reject, rebuff. **2** LESSEN, decrease, dwindle, wane, fade, ebb, taper off, flag, deteriorate, diminish. • n. DECREASE, reduction, downturn, downswing, slump, deterioration.

**decode** v. convert from coded form into plain language.

**decompose** v. rot or decay.
■ **decomposition** n.

**decompress** v. reduce air pressure in or on.
■ decompression n.

**decongestant** n. a medicine used to relieve a blocked nose.

**decontaminate** v. free from radioactivity, germs, etc.
■ decontamination n.

**decor** n. the style of decoration used in a room.

**decorate** v. 1 make more attractive by adding extra items. 2 apply paint or wallpaper to. 3 give an award or medal to. ■ decorative adj. decorator n.
▷ SYNS 1 ORNAMENT, adorn, trim, embellish, festoon, garland. 2 REFURBISH, redecorate, renovate; inf. do up.

**decoration** n. 1 the act of decorating or the way something is decorated. 2 a decorative thing. 3 a medal or award.
▷ SYNS 1 ADORNMENT, ornamentation, embellishment. 2 ORNAMENT, trinket, bauble, knick-knack. 3 MEDAL, award, ribbon.

**decorous** adj. in good taste; polite and restrained.
▷ SYNS PROPER, seemly, decent, becoming, tasteful, fitting, correct, appropriate, suitable, polite, well mannered, genteel, respectable.

**decorum** n. correctness and dignity of behaviour.
▷ SYNS PROPRIETY, decency, correctness, seemliness, respectability, politeness, courtesy.

**decoy** n. a person or animal used to lure others into a trap.
• v. lure by a decoy.

**decrease** v. make or become smaller or fewer. • n. decreasing; the extent of this.

▷ SYNS v. LESSEN, reduce, drop, diminish, decline, dwindle, fall off; die down, abate, subside, tail off, ebb, wane. • n. REDUCTION, drop, decline, downturn, diminution.

**decree** n. an order given by a government or other authority.
• v. order by decree.
▷ SYNS n. 1 ORDER, edict, command, commandment, mandate, proclamation, dictum, fiat. 2 JUDGEMENT, verdict, adjudication, ruling. • v. ORDER, command, rule, dictate, pronounce, proclaim, ordain.

**decrepit** adj. made weak by age or use.
▷ SYNS DILAPIDATED, ramshackle, derelict, tumbledown, run down.

**decry** v. (**decried**, **decrying**) denounce publicly.

**dedicate** v. devote to a cause or task; address a book etc. to a person as a tribute.
■ dedication n.
▷ SYNS DEVOTE, commit, give, pledge.

**dedicated** adj. devoted to a task or purpose.
▷ SYNS COMMITTED, devoted, wholehearted, enthusiastic, keen, zealous, single-minded.

**deduce** v. reach a conclusion on the basis of available information.
▷ SYNS CONCLUDE, infer, reason, work out, surmise.

**deduct** v. subtract.

**deduction** n. 1 deducting; something deducted. 2 deducing; a conclusion deduced.
▷ SYNS 1 CONCLUSION, inference, supposition, surmise. 2 SUBTRACTION, removal.

**deed** n. **1** an action performed deliberately. **2** a legal document.
▷ SYNS ACT, action, feat, exploit, performance, undertaking, accomplishment, stunt, achievement.

**deem** v. consider to be of a specified character.

**deep** adj. **1** extending or situated far down or in from the top or surface. **2** intense or extreme. **3** profound. **4** low-pitched. ■ **deepen** v.
▷ SYNS **1** FATHOMLESS, bottomless, yawning, cavernous. **2** PROFOUND, extreme, intense, great, heartfelt, fervent, ardent, impassioned. **3** a deep voice: LOW, bass, rich, resonant, sonorous. **4** deep in thought: ENGROSSED, absorbed, preoccupied, rapt, immersed.

**deer** n. (pl. **deer**) a hoofed animal, the male of which usu. has antlers.

**deface** v. spoil or damage the surface of.
▷ SYNS SPOIL, disfigure, mar, damage, mutilate, vandalize.

**defame** v. attack the good reputation of. ■ **defamation** n. **defamatory** adj.
▷ SYNS SLANDER, libel, cast aspersions on, malign, insult, vilify, traduce, besmirch, defile.

**default** n. **1** failure to do something required by law. **2** an option adopted by a computer program when no alternative is specified. • v. fail to fulfil a legal obligation.

**defeat** v. win victory over; cause to fail. • n. defeating; being defeated.
▷ SYNS v. **1** BEAT, conquer, get the better of, vanquish, trounce,

overcome, overpower, overwhelm, crush, subjugate, subdue, quell. **2** BAFFLE, puzzle, perplex, confound, frustrate. • n. CONQUEST, rout, overthrow, subjugation.

**defeatist** n. a person who pessimistically expects or accepts failure. ■ **defeatism** n.

**defecate** v. discharge faeces from the body. ■ **defecation** n.

**defect** n. an imperfection. • v. desert your country or cause. ■ **defection** n. **defector** n.
▷ SYNS n. FAULT, flaw, imperfection, deficiency, shortcoming, weakness.

**defective** adj. imperfect or faulty.
▷ SYNS FAULTY, flawed, imperfect, malfunctioning.

**defence** (US **defense**) n. **1** the act of defending. **2** protective military measures or resources. **3** attempted justification. **4** the case presented by the party being accused or sued in a lawsuit.
▷ SYNS **1** PROTECTION, guard, shield, safeguard, shelter, fortification. **2** JUSTIFICATION, vindication, plea, explanation, excuse.

**defenceless** adj. without defence; completely vulnerable.
▷ SYNS VULNERABLE, helpless, exposed, powerless, unguarded, unprotected.

**defend** v. protect from attack; uphold by argument; represent a defendant. ■ **defender** n.
▷ SYNS **1** PROTECT, guard, safeguard, preserve, secure, shelter, screen, shield. **2** JUSTIFY, vindicate, argue for; support, back, stand by, stand up for.

**defendant** n. a person accused or sued in a lawsuit.

**defensible** adj. able to be defended.

**defensive** adj. **1** intended for defence. **2** sensitive to criticism.

**defer** v. **1** postpone. **2** yield to a person's wishes or authority. ■ deferral n.
▷ SYNS POSTPONE, put off/back, delay.

**deference** n. polite respect. ■ deferential adj.

**defiance** n. open disobedience.

**defiant** adj. openly disobedient.
▷ SYNS INTRANSIGENT, obstinate, uncooperative, recalcitrant; obstreperous, truculent, disobedient, insubordinate, rebellious, mutinous.

**deficiency** n. (pl. -ies) a lack or shortage; an imperfection. ■ deficient adj.
▷ SYNS **1** LACK, shortage, scarcity, want, dearth, insufficiency, paucity. **2** see DEFECT.

**deficit** n. **1** the amount by which something falls short. **2** an excess of money spent over money earned.

**defile** v. make dirty or impure.

**define** v. state precisely; give the meaning of; mark the boundary of.
▷ SYNS EXPLAIN, spell out, elucidate, describe, interpret, expound, clarify.

**definite** adj. clearly and firmly decided or stated; certain or unambiguous; with a clear shape or outline. □ definite article the word the. ■ definitely adv.
▷ SYNS **1** SPECIFIC, precise, particular, exact, clear, clear-cut, explicit, fixed, established, settled, confirmed. **2** CERTAIN,

sure, decided, positive, guaranteed, assured, conclusive.

**definition** n. a statement of precise meaning; distinctness or clearness of outline.

**definitive** adj. settling something finally and authoritatively.
▷ SYNS CONCLUSIVE, final, ultimate; positive, definite, authoritative.

**deflate** v. cause to collapse through release of air; make less confident.

**deflect** v. turn aside. ■ deflection n.
▷ SYNS TURN ASIDE, divert, parry, fend off, ward off, avert.

**deforest** v. clear of trees. ■ deforestation n.

**deform** v. spoil the shape of. ■ deformity n.

**deformed** adj. having a distorted shape or form.
▷ SYNS MISSHAPEN, distorted, malformed, contorted, twisted, crooked; disfigured, injured.

**defraud** v. swindle.
▷ SYNS CHEAT, swindle, rob; inf. rip off.

**defray** v. provide money to pay costs.

**defrost** v. remove ice from a refrigerator; thaw.

**deft** adj. skilful and quick.
▷ SYNS DEXTEROUS, adroit, skilful, skilled, adept, proficient, able, clever, expert, quick.

**defunct** adj. no longer existing or functioning.

**defuse** v. remove the fuse from an explosive; reduce the tension in a situation.

**defy** v. (**defied**, **defying**) resist or disobey; challenge.
▷ SYNS **1** DISOBEY, disregard, ignore, flout, contravene.

2 RESIST, stand up to, confront, face, meet head-on.

**degenerate** v. become worse physically, mentally, or morally. • adj. having degenerated. • n. a degenerate person.
■ **degeneracy** n. **degeneration** n. **degenerative** adj.
▷ SYNS v. DETERIORATE, decline, worsen, regress, slide.

**degrade** v. 1 treat disrespectfully or humiliate. 2 decompose.
■ **degradation** n.
▷ SYNS DEBASE, cheapen, demean, devalue, shame, disgrace, dishonour, humiliate, mortify.

**degree** n. 1 the extent to which something is true or present; a stage in a series. 2 a unit of measurement for angles or temperature. 3 an award given by a university or college.
▷ SYNS LEVEL, standard, grade, mark; amount, extent, measure; magnitude, intensity, strength; proportion, ratio.

**dehumanize** (or **-ise**) v. remove human qualities from.

**dehydrate** v. cause to lose a large amount of moisture.
■ **dehydration** n.

**deify** v. (**deified**, **deifying**) treat as a god. ■ **deification** n.

**deign** v. condescend.
▷ SYNS CONDESCEND, lower yourself, stoop, demean yourself.

**deity** n. (pl. **-ies**) a god or goddess.
▷ SYNS GOD, goddess, divinity.

**déjà vu** n. a feeling of having experienced a present situation before.

**dejected** adj. in low spirits.
■ **dejection** n.

**delay** v. make late; be slow; postpone. • n. delaying; time lost by delaying.
▷ SYNS v. 1 POSTPONE, put off/back, defer, hold over. 2 HOLD UP, detain, hinder, obstruct, hamper, impede. 3 LINGER, loiter, dawdle, dally, tarry; inf. dilly-dally. • n. HOLD-UP, wait; hindrance, obstruction, impediment.

**delectable** adj. delicious or delightful.

**delegate** n. a representative. • v. entrust a task etc. to someone.
▷ SYNS n. REPRESENTATIVE, agent, envoy, emissary. • v. PASS ON, hand over, transfer, entrust, assign, devolve.

**delegation** n. a group of representatives; delegating.
▷ SYNS DEPUTATION, legation, mission, commission.

**delete** v. cross out a word etc.
■ **deletion** n.
▷ SYNS ERASE, cross out, rub out, remove, take out, obliterate, efface.

**deleterious** adj. formal harmful.

**deliberate** adj. 1 intentional. 2 slow and careful. • v. engage in careful discussion or consideration. ■ **deliberation** n.
▷ SYNS adj. 1 INTENTIONAL, planned, calculated, studied, conscious, purposeful, wilful, premeditated. 2 CAREFUL, unhurried, cautious, steady, regular, measured.

**deliberately** adv. in a deliberate way.
▷ SYNS INTENTIONALLY, on purpose, by design, knowingly.

**delicacy** n. (pl. **-ies**) 1 the quality of being delicate. 2 a tasty, expensive food.

**delicate** adj. **1** fine or intricate. **2** fragile; prone to illness or injury. **3** requiring tact.
▷ SYNS **1** FINE, fragile, dainty, exquisite, slender, graceful, flimsy, wispy, gossamer. **2** FRAIL, sickly, weak, unwell, infirm, ailing. **3** CAREFUL, sensitive, tactful, discreet, considerate, diplomatic, politic. **4** DIFFICULT, awkward, tricky, sensitive, critical, precarious; inf. ticklish, touchy.

**delicatessen** n. a shop selling unusual or foreign prepared foods.

**delicious** adj. delightful, esp. to taste or smell.
▷ SYNS APPETIZING, tasty, delectable, mouth-watering, savoury, palatable, luscious.

**delight** n. great pleasure; a source of this. • v. please greatly; feel delight. ■ **delightful** adj.
▷ SYNS n. JOY, pleasure, happiness, bliss, ecstasy, elation, jubilation.

**delineate** v. outline. ■ **delineation** n.

**delinquent** adj. & n. (a person) guilty of persistent law-breaking. ■ **delinquency** n.

**delirium** n. **1** a disordered state of mind, esp. during fever. **2** wild excitement. ■ **delirious** adj.

**deliver** v. **1** take to an addressee or purchaser; make a speech etc.; aim a blow or attack. **2** rescue or set free. **3** assist in the birth of. ■ **delivery** n.
▷ SYNS **1** DISTRIBUTE, carry, bring, take, transport, convey, send, dispatch, remit. **2** SET FREE, save, liberate, free, release, rescue.

**3** AIM, give, deal, administer, inflict.

**dell** n. a small wooded hollow.

**delta** n. **1** the fourth letter of the Greek alphabet ($\Delta$, $\delta$). **2** an area of land where the mouth of a river has split into several channels.

**delude** v. deceive or mislead.

**deluge** n. a flood; a heavy fall of rain; a large quantity of something coming at the same time. • v. flood; overwhelm.
▷ SYNS n. FLOOD, downpour, inundation, spate, rush. • v. FLOOD, inundate, swamp, engulf, drown, overwhelm.

**delusion** n. a false belief or impression.
▷ SYNS MISCONCEPTION, illusion, fallacy, misapprehension, mistake, fantasy.

**de luxe** adj. of superior quality; luxurious.

**delve** v. search deeply.
▷ SYNS SEARCH, rummage, hunt through, investigate, probe, examine.

**demagogue** n. a political leader who wins support by appealing to popular feelings and prejudices.

**demand** n. **1** a firm request. **2** (**demands**) urgent or difficult requirements. **3** customers' desire for a product or service. • v. **1** ask for firmly. **2** need a quality etc.
▷ SYNS n. REQUEST, call, command, order; claim. • v. **1** ASK FOR, request, insist on, claim; order, command. **2** REQUIRE, need, necessitate, call for, involve.

**demanding** adj. requiring great skill or effort.

**demarcation** n. the marking of a boundary or limits.

**demean** v. lower the dignity of.

**demeanour** (US **demeanor**) n. the way a person behaves.
▷ SYNS AIR, attitude, appearance, manner; bearing, conduct, behaviour.

**demented** adj. mad.

**dementia** n. a mental disorder.

**demilitarize** (or **-ise**) v. remove military forces from.
■ demilitarization n.

**demise** n. death; failure.

**demobilize** (or **-ise**) v. release from military service.

**democracy** n. (pl. **-ies**) 1 a form of government in which the people vote for representatives to govern on their behalf. 2 a state governed in this way.
■ democrat n. democratic adj. democratically adv.

**demolish** v. pull or knock down; destroy. ■ demolition n.
▷ SYNS KNOCK DOWN, flatten, raze, level, bulldoze, destroy.

**demon** n. a devil or evil spirit.
■ demonic adj.

**demonstrable** adj. able to be proved or shown.
■ demonstrably adv.

**demonstrate** v. 1 clearly show to exist or be true. 2 show and explain how something works. 3 take part in a public demonstration.
■ demonstrator n.
▷ SYNS SHOW, indicate, establish, prove, confirm, verify; reveal, display, exhibit.

**demonstration** n. 1 proving; exhibiting. 2 a public protest.
▷ SYNS 1 EXHIBITION, exposition, presentation, display. 2 PROOF, confirmation, substantiation, verification. 3 PROTEST, march, rally, lobby, picket.

**demonstrative** adj. 1 showing feelings openly. 2 demonstrating something.

**demoralize** (or **-ise**) v. dishearten.
▷ SYNS DISCOURAGE, dishearten, dispirit, depress.

**demote** v. reduce to a lower rank or category. ■ demotion n.

**demur** v. (**demurred**, **demurring**) raise objections.
▷ SYNS OBJECT, take exception, protest, dissent, cavil.

**demure** adj. quiet, modest, and shy.
▷ SYNS MODEST, unassuming, quiet, reticent, bashful, shy, diffident, coy.

**den** n. a wild animal's lair; a person's small private room.

**denial** n. 1 a statement denying something. 2 refusal to accept something unpleasant.

**denigrate** v. criticize unfairly.
▷ SYNS DISPARAGE, belittle, deprecate, decry, cast aspersions on, malign.

**denim** n. 1 a strong cotton fabric. 2 (**denims**) trousers made of this.

**denizen** n. formal an inhabitant.

**denomination** n. 1 a branch of a Church or religion. 2 the face value of a coin or bank note. 3 formal a name.

**denominator** n. a number below the line in a vulgar fraction.

**denote** v. 1 be a sign of. 2 (of a word) have as a main meaning.
▷ SYNS INDICATE, signify, signal, represent, symbolize.

**denouement** n. the final outcome of a play or story.

**denounce** v. publicly condemn or criticize.

▷ SYNS CONDEMN, attack, criticize, censure, castigate, decry, inveigh against.

**dense** adj. **1** closely packed together. **2** stupid.
▷ SYNS CLOSE-PACKED, crowded, compressed, compact, thick, solid.

**density** n. the degree to which something is full or closely packed.

**dent** n. a hollow left by a blow or pressure. • v. mark with a dent; diminish or discourage.

**dental** adj. of teeth or dentistry.

**dentist** n. a person qualified to treat decay and malformations of teeth. ■ dentistry n.

**denture** n. a plate holding an artificial tooth or teeth.

**denude** v. strip of covering or property.

**denunciation** n. a public condemnation.

**deny** v. **1** say that something is not true. **2** prevent from having. **3** (**deny yourself**) go without something.
▷ SYNS REPUDIATE, reject, contradict, gainsay, refute, rebut.

**deodorant** n. a substance that prevents unwanted bodily odours.

**depart** v. leave. ■ departure n.
▷ SYNS LEAVE, go, withdraw, decamp, retire, retreat, set off/out, be on your way.

**departed** adj. dead.

**department** n. a section of an organization with a special function or concern. □ department store a large shop selling many kinds of goods.
■ departmental adj.

▷ SYNS SECTION, division, unit, branch, office, bureau, agency.

**depend** v. be determined by; rely on.
▷ SYNS (**depend on**) **1** BE DEPENDENT ON, hinge on, rest on, be contingent on. **2** RELY ON, count on, bank on, trust in.

**dependable** adj. reliable.
▷ SYNS RELIABLE, trustworthy, trusty, faithful, steadfast, steady, responsible.

**dependant** n. a person who depends on another for support.

**dependency** n. (pl. **-ies**) being dependent; a country controlled by another.

**dependent** adj. depending; controlled by another.
■ dependence n.
▷ SYNS **1** CONDITIONAL ON, contingent on, subject to, determined by. **2** RELIANT ON, supported by, sustained by.

**depict** v. represent in a picture or in words. ■ depiction n.
▷ SYNS PORTRAY, represent, illustrate, delineate, picture; describe, relate, detail.

**deplete** v. reduce the number of by overuse. ■ depletion n.
▷ SYNS EXHAUST, use up, consume, expend, drain, empty.

**deplorable** adj. shockingly bad.
■ deplorably adv.
▷ SYNS DISGRACEFUL, shameful, reprehensible, scandalous, shocking, despicable, contemptible, abominable, lamentable, dire.

**deplore** v. strongly disapprove of.

**deploy** v. move into position for action; utilize. ■ deployment n.
▷ SYNS **1** ARRANGE, position, dispose, distribute, station.

**2** USE, utilize, bring into play, have recourse to.

**depopulate** v. reduce the population of. ■ **depopulation** n.

**deport** v. remove a person from a country. ■ **deportation** n.
▷ SYNS EXPEL, banish, exile, expatriate, extradite.

**deportment** n. behaviour; bearing.

**depose** v. remove from power.

**deposit** n. **1** a sum of money paid into an account. **2** a first instalment in buying something. **3** a returnable sum paid when renting something, to cover possible loss or damage. **4** a layer of a substance that has accumulated. • v. **1** put down. **2** store for safe keeping. **3** pay as a deposit. **4** lay down a layer of a substance.
▷ SYNS n. **1** DOWN PAYMENT, advance payment, instalment. **2** ACCUMULATION, layer, covering, coating, sediment. • v. **1** PUT, place, set, drop. **2** STORE, stow, put away, lodge, bank.

**depository** n. (pl. **-ies**) a storehouse.

**depot** n. a storage area, esp. for vehicles; a bus or railway station.
▷ SYNS STATION, garage, terminus, terminal.

**deprave** v. corrupt morally. ■ **depravity** n.

**deprecate** v. **1** express disapproval of. **2** disclaim politely. ■ **deprecation** n.

**depreciate** v. diminish in value; belittle. ■ **depreciation** n.

**depredation** n. a harmful or damaging act.

**depress** v. **1** cause to feel dispirited. **2** press down.

**3** reduce the strength or activity of. ■ **depressant** adj.

**depression** n. **1** sadness or gloominess. **2** a long period of inactivity in trading. **3** pressing down; a hollow on a surface; an area of low atmospheric pressure. ■ **depressive** adj.
▷ SYNS **1** SADNESS, unhappiness, despair, gloom, dejection, despondency, melancholy, desolation. **2** RECESSION, slump, slowdown.

**deprive** v. prevent from using or enjoying something. ■ **deprivation** n.
▷ SYNS DISPOSSESS, strip, deny, divest, rob.

**depth** n. **1** distance downwards or inwards from a surface. **2** detailed treatment; intensity. **3** the deepest or most central part.

**deputation** n. a body of people sent to represent others.

**deputize** (or **-ise**) v. act as deputy.

**deputy** n. (pl. **-ies**) a person appointed to act as a substitute or representative.
▷ SYNS SUBSTITUTE, representative, stand-in, delegate, envoy, proxy, agent.

**derail** v. cause a train to leave the rails. ■ **derailment** n.

**deranged** adj. insane. ■ **derangement** n.

**derelict** adj. left to fall into ruin.
▷ SYNS ABANDONED, deserted, neglected, dilapidated, ramshackle, tumbledown, run-down, in disrepair.

**dereliction** n. **1** being derelict. **2** failure to do your duty.

**deride** v. mock scornfully.

▷ SYNS MOCK, ridicule, jeer at, scoff at, sneer at, make fun of, laugh at, scorn.

**derision** n. mockery or scorn.
■ derisive adj.

**derisory** adj. **1** ridiculously small or inadequate. **2** derisive.

**derivative** adj. imitating another artist, writer, etc.; not original. • n. something derived from another source.

**derive** v. obtain from a source; originate. ■ derivation n.

**dermatitis** n. inflammation of the skin.

**dermatology** n. the study of the skin and its diseases.
■ dermatologist n.

**derogatory** adj. disparaging.
▷ SYNS DISPARAGING, critical, disapproving, unflattering, insulting, defamatory.

**descant** n. a treble accompaniment to a main melody.

**descend** v. **1** move, slope, or lead down. **2** (**descend to**) do something shameful. **3** make an attack or unexpected visit. **4** (**be descended from**) have as an ancestor.
▷ SYNS GO DOWN, come down, drop, fall, sink, plummet, plunge; slope, dip, slant.

**descendant** n. a person descended from another.

**descent** n. descending; a downward slope; ancestry.
▷ SYNS **1** SLOPE, incline, dip, drop, gradient, declivity. **2** ANCESTRY, parentage, origins, lineage, extraction, heredity, stock, line, pedigree, blood.

**describe** v. give a description of.
▷ SYNS RECOUNT, relate, report, detail, tell, narrate, set out, portray, depict.

**description** n. **1** a statement of what a person or thing is like. **2** a kind or sort: *cars of all descriptions.* ■ descriptive adj.
▷ SYNS ACCOUNT, report, chronicle, narration, commentary, portrayal, depiction.

**desecrate** v. treat something sacred with violent disrespect.
■ desecration n.

**deselect** v. reject an MP as a candidate for re-election.
■ deselection n.

**desert**[1] n. a barren waterless area.
▷ SYNS WASTELAND, wilderness.

**desert**[2] v. **1** leave someone without help or support. **2** leave a place, making it seem empty. **3** illegally leave the armed forces. ■ deserter n. desertion n.
▷ SYNS ABANDON, leave, jilt, leave in the lurch, throw over; lit. forsake.

**deserted** adj. empty or abandoned.
▷ SYNS ABANDONED, empty, neglected, vacant, uninhabited, desolate, lonely.

**deserts** pl.n. what you deserve.

**deserve** v. be worthy of through your actions or qualities.
▷ SYNS MERIT, warrant, rate, justify, earn.

**deserving** adj. worthy of good treatment.

**desiccate** v. dry out moisture from.

**design** n. **1** a drawing that shows how a thing is to be made; a general form or arrangement; a decorative pattern. **2** an intention. • v. prepare a design for; plan or intend. ■ designer n.
▷ SYNS n. **1** PLAN, blueprint, drawing, sketch, outline,

map, diagram. **2** PATTERN, motif, style. **3** INTENTION, aim, purpose, plan, objective, goal, end, target, hope, desire, wish, aspiration. • v. **1** PLAN, outline, map out, draft. **2** CREATE, invent, originate, conceive. **3** INTEND, aim, plan, tailor, mean.

**designate** v. appoint to a position; officially assign a status to. • adj. appointed but not yet installed.
■ designation n.

**desirable** adj. **1** good-looking. **2** advisable or beneficial.
■ desirability n.

**desire** n. a feeling of wanting something strongly; sexual appetite; a thing desired. • v. feel a desire for.
▷ SYNS n. **1** WISH, want, fancy, longing, yearning, craving, hankering, aspiration. **2** LUST, passion. • v. WISH FOR, want, long for, yearn for, crave, ache for, set your heart on, hanker after, covet, aspire to.

**desirous** adj. desiring.

**desist** v. stop.

**desk** n. **1** a piece of furniture for working at. **2** a counter.
□ desktop **1** a computer suitable for use at a desk. **2** the working area of a computer screen.

**desolate** adj. bleak and lonely; very unhappy.
• v. make very unhappy.
■ desolation n.
▷ SYNS adj. **1** ABANDONED, deserted, barren, uninhabited, lonely, isolated, remote, cheerless, dismal, godforsaken. **2** SAD, unhappy, miserable, wretched, downcast, dejected, down-hearted, melancholy, depressed,

forlorn, despondent, distressed, bereft.

**despair** n. complete lack of hope. • v. feel despair.
▷ SYNS n. HOPELESSNESS, depression, despondency, pessimism, melancholy, misery, wretchedness.

**despatch** = DISPATCH.

**desperado** n. (pl. **-oes** or **-os**) a reckless criminal.

**desperate** adj. **1** hopeless; very bad or serious; made reckless by despair. **2** feeling an intense desire or need.
■ desperation n.
▷ SYNS URGENT, pressing, acute, critical, crucial, drastic, serious, grave, dire, extreme, great.

**despicable** adj. contemptible.

**despise** v. hate.
▷ SYNS HATE, detest, loathe, abhor, abominate, look down on, disdain, scorn.

**despite** prep. in spite of.

**despoil** v. lit. plunder.

**despondent** adj. dejected and discouraged. ■ despondency n.
▷ SYNS DOWNCAST, miserable, sad, disheartened, discouraged, de-jected, disconsolate, dispirited, downhearted, despairing, melancholy, woebegone.

**despot** n. a dictator. ■ despotic adj. despotism n.

**dessert** n. the sweet course of a meal.

**destabilize** (or **-ise**) v. make unstable or insecure.

**destination** n. the place to which a person or thing is going.

**destined** adj. **1** intended for a particular purpose. **2** bound for a particular destination.

▷ SYNS FATED, ordained, predestined, doomed, certain, sure, bound.

**destiny** n. (pl. **-ies**) **1** the events that will happen to a person. **2** the power believed to control future events; fate.

▷ SYNS FATE, providence, kismet; fortune, luck, chance, karma; future, lot.

**destitute** adj. very poor.
■ destitution n.

▷ SYNS PENNILESS, poor, impoverished, poverty-stricken, impecunious, indigent.

**destroy** v. **1** end the existence of something by badly damaging it. **2** kill an animal in a painless way. ■ destruction n. destructive adj.

▷ SYNS **1** DEMOLISH, knock down, level, raze, wreck, ruin, devastate, wreak havoc on. **2** KILL, put down, put to sleep, slaughter.

**destroyer** n. a fast warship.

**desultory** adj. without purpose or enthusiasm; moving at random between subjects.
■ desultorily adv.

**detach** v. separate or unfasten.
■ detachable adj.

▷ SYNS DISCONNECT, unfasten, remove, undo, separate, uncouple, loosen, free, disengage.

**detached** adj. **1** separate; not connected. **2** free from bias or emotion.

▷ SYNS DISPASSIONATE, disinterested, uninvolved, objective, unbiased, unprejudiced, impersonal, indifferent, aloof.

**detachment** n. **1** objectivity. **2** detaching. **3** a group sent on a military mission.

**detail** n. **1** a small individual fact or item; such items collectively.

**2** a small military detachment.
• v. **1** describe in detail. **2** assign to a special duty.

▷ SYNS n. ITEM, point, particular, factor, nicety, fact, element, aspect, circumstance, feature, respect, attribute, component, part, unit.

**detailed** adj. giving many details.

▷ SYNS FULL, comprehensive, exhaustive, thorough, itemized, precise, exact, specific, meticulous, painstaking.

**detain** v. keep in official custody; delay. ■ detainee n.

▷ SYNS **1** DELAY, hold up, keep, slow down, hinder, impede. **2** CONFINE, imprison, lock up, jail, incarcerate, hold.

**detect** v. discover the presence of. ■ detection n. detector n.

▷ SYNS **1** NOTICE, note, perceive, discern, make out, observe, spot, recognize, distinguish, identify, sense. **2** FIND OUT, discover, uncover, bring to light, expose, reveal.

**detective** n. a person whose job is to investigate crimes.

**détente** n. an easing of tension between nations.

**detention** n. **1** the state of being detained in custody. **2** the punishment of being kept in school after hours.

▷ SYNS CUSTODY, imprisonment, confinement, incarceration, internment, arrest.

**deter** v. (**deterred, deterring**) discourage from action.

▷ SYNS DISCOURAGE, dissuade, put off, scare off; prevent, stop.

**detergent** n. a liquid or powder used for removing dirt and grease.

**deteriorate** v. become worse.
■ **deterioration** n.
▷ SYNS WORSEN, decline, degenerate, sink, slip, go downhill.

**determination** n. **1** resolution or firmness of purpose. **2** establishing something.
▷ SYNS RESOLUTION, resolve, will power, persistence, tenacity, perseverance, single-mindedness, fortitude, dedication, doggedness.

**determine** v. **1** cause to occur in a particular way or be of a specific type. **2** firmly decide. **3** establish by research or calculation.
▷ SYNS **1** CONTROL, decide, regulate, direct, dictate, govern, affect, influence. **2** RESOLVE, decide, make up your mind, choose. **3** ASCERTAIN, find out, discover, establish, work out, learn.

**determined** adj. full of determination.
▷ SYNS FIRM, resolute, single-minded, steadfast, tenacious, strong-willed, dedicated, persistent, persevering, dogged, unwavering, stubborn, obdurate, intransigent.

**deterrent** n. something deterring or intended to deter.
▷ SYNS DISINCENTIVE, discouragement, restraint, curb, check.

**detest** v. dislike intensely.
■ **detestable** adj. **detestation** n.
▷ SYNS LOATHE, hate, abhor, despise, abominate.

**dethrone** v. remove from power.

**detonate** v. explode.
■ **detonation** n. **detonator** n.

**detour** n. a deviation from a direct or intended course.

**detract** v. cause to seem less valuable or impressive.
▷ SYNS TAKE AWAY FROM, diminish, reduce, lessen, lower, devalue.

**detractor** n. a person who criticizes something.

**detriment** n. harm.

**detrimental** adj. harmful.
▷ SYNS HARMFUL, damaging, injurious, hurtful, destructive, bad, unfavourable; formal deleterious.

**deuce** n. **1** a score of 40 all in tennis. **2** inf. (in exclamations) the Devil.

**devalue** v. reduce the value of; disparage. ■ **devaluation** n.

**devastate** v. cause great destruction to. ■ **devastation** n.
▷ SYNS DESTROY, ruin, lay waste to, ravage, demolish, wreck, flatten, obliterate.

**devastating** adj. very destructive; shocking and distressing.

**develop** v. **1** make or become larger, more mature, or more advanced; begin to exist or have. **2** make land etc. usable or profitable. **3** treat a film so as to make a picture visible.
■ **developer** n.
▷ SYNS **1** GROW, evolve, mature, improve, expand, spread, enlarge, advance, progress, flourish, prosper, make headway. **2** *a row developed*: BEGIN, start, come about, result, ensue, break out.

**development** n. **1** the action of developing. **2** a new stage in a changing situation. **3** an area with new buildings on it. **4** a new product or idea.
▷ SYNS **1** GROWTH, expansion, enlargement, evolution, spread, progress. **2** *new*

*developments:* EVENT, occurrence, incident, circumstance, situation. **3** *a housing development:* ESTATE, complex, site.

**deviant** adj. deviating from accepted standards.

**deviate** v. diverge from a route, course of action, etc. ■ **deviation** n.
▷ SYNS DIVERGE, branch off, turn aside, veer, swerve, drift, stray; digress.

**device** n. **1** a piece of equipment made for a particular purpose. **2** a plan or method.
▷ SYNS IMPLEMENT, gadget, tool, utensil, appliance, apparatus, instrument, machine, contraption; *inf.* gizmo.

**devil** n. an evil spirit; the supreme spirit of evil; a cruel person. □ **devil's advocate** a person who tests a proposition by arguing against it. ■ **devilish** adj.
▷ SYNS **1** DEMON, fiend, evil spirit. **2** SATAN, Lucifer, the Prince of Darkness.

**devilment** n. mischief.

**devilry** n. wickedness; mischief.

**devious** adj. underhand; (of a route) indirect.
▷ SYNS CUNNING, underhand, sly, crafty, wily, artful, scheming, calculating, deceitful, dishonest.

**devise** v. plan; invent.
▷ SYNS CREATE, invent, concoct, conceive, work out, formulate, compose, frame, think up, hatch.

**devoid** adj. (**devoid of**) entirely without.

**devolution** n. delegation of power esp. from central to local administration.

**devolve** v. transfer power to a lower level; (of duties) pass to a deputy.

**devote** v. give or use exclusively for a particular purpose.

**devoted** adj. showing devotion.
▷ SYNS COMMITTED, faithful, loyal, true, dedicated, staunch, devout, steadfast.

**devotee** n. an enthusiast; a worshipper.
▷ SYNS FAN, enthusiast, admirer, follower, adherent, disciple, supporter, fanatic.

**devotion** n. great love, loyalty, or commitment; religious worship; prayers. ■ **devotional** adj.
▷ SYNS LOVE, loyalty, commitment, allegiance, dedication, faithfulness, fidelity.

**devour** v. eat hungrily or greedily; consume or destroy; take in avidly.
▷ SYNS CONSUME, gobble, guzzle, wolf down.

**devout** adj. deeply religious; earnestly sincere.
▷ SYNS PIOUS, religious, godly, churchgoing, reverent, God-fearing.

**dew** n. drops of condensed moisture forming on cool surfaces at night.

**dexterity** n. skill. ■ **dexterous** (or **dextrous**) adj.

**diabetes** n. a disease in which sugar and starch are not properly absorbed by the body. ■ **diabetic** adj. & n.

**diabolical** adj. **1** (or **diabolic**) of or like the Devil. **2** *inf.* very bad. ■ **diabolically** adv.

**diadem** n. a crown.

**diagnose** v. make a diagnosis of.

**diagnosis** n. (pl. **-ses**) the identification of a disease or condition after observing its symptoms. ■ **diagnostic** adj.

**diagonal** adj. & n. (a line) joining opposite corners of a square or rectangle.
■ **diagonally** adv.
▷ SYNS CROSSWAYS, crosswise, slanting, slanted, sloping, oblique.

**diagram** n. a schematic drawing that shows the parts or operation of something.
▷ SYNS PLAN, picture, representation, drawing, sketch, outline, figure.

**dial** n. the face of a clock or watch; a similar plate or disc with a movable pointer; a movable disc manipulated to connect one telephone with another. • v. (**dialled, dialling;** US **dialed**) select or operate by using a dial or numbered buttons.

**dialect** n. a local form of a language.
▷ SYNS VERNACULAR, patois.

**dialogue** (US **dialog**) n. a conversation or discussion.
▷ SYNS CONVERSATION, talk, debate, discussion, discourse, parley, colloquy.

**dialysis** n. purification of blood by filtering it through a membrane.

**diameter** n. a straight line from side to side through the centre of a circle or sphere.

**diametrical** adj. 1 (of opposites) complete. 2 of or along a diameter.
■ **diametrically** adv.

**diamond** n. 1 a very hard clear precious stone. 2 a four-sided figure with equal sides and with angles that are not right angles; a playing card marked with such shapes.

**diaphanous** adj. almost transparent.

**diaphragm** n. 1 the muscular partition between the chest and abdomen. 2 a contraceptive cap fitting over the cervix.

**diarrhoea** (US **diarrhea**) n. a condition causing frequent fluid bowel movements.

**diary** n. (pl. **-ies**) a book for keeping a daily record of events or for noting appointments.
▷ SYNS JOURNAL, chronicle, memoir, record, log, weblog, blog, history, annals.

**diaspora** n. the dispersion of a people from their homeland, esp. the Jews from Israel.

**diatribe** n. a violent verbal attack.

**dice** n. (pl. **dice**) a small cube marked on each side with 1–6 spots, used in games of chance. • v. cut into small cubes.

**dichotomy** n. (pl. **-ies**) a division or contrast between two things.

**dictate** v. 1 say words aloud to be written or recorded. 2 give orders officiously; control or determine. • n. a command.
■ **dictation** n.
▷ SYNS v. ORDER, command, decree, ordain, direct, decide, control, govern.

**dictator** n. a ruler with unrestricted authority.
■ **dictatorship** n.
▷ SYNS DESPOT, autocrat, tyrant, oppressor.

**dictatorial** adj. 1 relating to a dictator. 2 insisting on total obedience.

▷ SYNS TYRANNICAL, despotic, overbearing, domineering, imperious, high-handed, authoritarian, peremptory, bossy.

**diction** n. a manner of uttering or pronouncing words.

**dictionary** n. (pl. -ies) a book that lists and gives the meaning of the words of a language.

**did** past of **do**.

**didactic** adj. meant or meaning to instruct.

**die¹** v. 1 cease to be alive; cease to exist; fade away. 2 (**be dying for** or **to**) inf. long for or to.
□ **diehard** a person who stubbornly supports something in spite of change or opposition.
▷ SYNS 1 EXPIRE, perish, pass on/away; inf. kick the bucket, snuff it. 2 COME TO AN END, disappear, vanish, fade, decline, ebb, dwindle, melt away, wane, wither.

**die²** n. a device for cutting or moulding metal or for stamping a design on coins etc.

**diesel** n. an oil-burning engine in which ignition is produced by the heat of compressed air; fuel used in this.

**diet** n. 1 the food that a person or animal usually eats. 2 a limited range or amount of food, eaten to lose weight or for medical reasons. • v. (**dieted**, **dieting**) keep to a special diet to lose weight. ■ **dietary** adj.

**dietitian** (or **dietician**) n. an expert in diet and nutrition.

**differ** v. 1 be unlike. 2 disagree.
▷ SYNS 1 VARY, contrast, diverge, deviate. 2 DISAGREE, conflict, clash, quarrel, argue.

**difference** n. 1 a way in which people or things are not the same. 2 a disagreement or dispute. 3 the remainder left after one value is subtracted from another.
▷ SYNS DISSIMILARITY, contrast, distinction, differentiation, disparity, variance, variation, divergence, deviation, imbalance, contradiction.

**different** adj. 1 not the same as another or each other. 2 separate. 3 new and unusual.
▷ SYNS DISSIMILAR, unlike, contrasting, divergent, differing, varying, disparate, incompatible, inconsistent, clashing, conflicting.

**differential** adj. of, showing, or depending on a difference; distinctive. • n. 1 an agreed difference in wage rates. 2 an arrangement of gears allowing a vehicle's wheels to revolve at different speeds when cornering.

**differentiate** v. distinguish between; make or become different. ■ **differentiation** n.

**difficult** adj. 1 needing much effort or skill to do, deal with, or understand. 2 hard to please.
▷ SYNS 1 a difficult job: HARD, demanding, laborious, onerous, burdensome, tough, strenuous, arduous, exhausting, tiring, wearisome, back-breaking. 2 a difficult problem: HARD, complex, complicated, problematic, puzzling, baffling, perplexing, knotty, thorny. 3 a difficult child: TROUBLESOME, demanding, unmanageable, contrary, recalcitrant, obstreperous, uncooperative.

**difficulty** n. 1 a problem. 2 a difficult situation.
▷ SYNS 1 PROBLEM, complication, snag, hitch, obstacle, hindrance,

hurdle, pitfall, impediment, barrier. **2** PREDICAMENT, quandary, dilemma, plight.

**diffident** adj. lacking self-confidence. ■ **diffidence** n.
▷ SYNS SHY, modest, bashful, un-confident, timid, timorous, self-effacing, unassuming, humble, meek.

**diffract** v. break up a beam of light into a series of coloured or dark-and-light bands.
■ **diffraction** n.

**diffuse** adj. **1** spread out over a large area. **2** not clear or concise. • v. spread over a wide area. ■ **diffusion** n.

**dig** v. **1** break up and move soil; extract from the ground in this way. **2** push or poke. **3** search for. • n. **1** digging; an excavation. **2** a sharp push or poke. **3** a cutting remark. **4** (**digs**) inf. lodgings. ■ **digger** n.
▷ SYNS **v. 1** CULTIVATE, turn over, work, till, harrow. **2** EXCAVATE, burrow, mine, quarry, hollow out, scoop out, tunnel, gouge. **3** POKE, nudge, prod, jab.

**digest** v. break down food in the body; absorb into the mind. • n. a methodical summary. ■ **digestible** adj. **digestion** n. **digestive** adj.

**digit** n. **1** any numeral from 0 to 9. **2** a finger or toe.

**digital** adj. involving computer technology; (of information) represented as a series of binary digits; (of a camera) pro-ducing images that can be stored in a computer; (of a clock) showing the time as a row of figures. ■ **digitally** adv.

**dignified** adj. showing dignity.
▷ SYNS FORMAL, grave, solemn, stately, noble, decorous, ceremonious, majestic, august, regal, imposing, grand, impres-sive.

**dignify** v. (**dignified**, **dignifying**) treat as important or deserving respect.

**dignitary** n. (pl. **-ies**) a person holding high rank or position.
▷ SYNS LUMINARY, worthy, notable, VIP, big name, leading light.

**dignity** n. (pl. **-ies**) **1** being worthy of respect. **2** a calm and serious manner.
▷ SYNS STATELINESS, nobility, solemnity, gravity, gravitas, decorum, propriety, majesty, regality, grandeur.

**digress** v. depart from the main subject temporarily.
■ **digression** n.

**dike** = DYKE.

**dilapidated** adj. in disrepair.
■ **dilapidation** n.
▷ SYNS RUN DOWN, ramshackle, in ruins, ruined, tumbledown, shabby, in disrepair, decrepit, neglected.

**dilate** v. make or become wider.
■ **dilation** n.

**dilemma** n. a situation in which a difficult choice has to be made.
▷ SYNS DIFFICULTY, problem, quandary, predicament, catch-22.

**dilettante** n. (pl. **-ti** or **-tes**) a person who dabbles in a subject for pleasure.

**diligent** adj. working or done with care and effort.
■ **diligence** n.
▷ SYNS ASSIDUOUS, industrious, conscientious, hard-working, painstaking, sedulous, meticu-lous, thorough, careful.

**dill** n. a herb.

**dilute** v. reduce the strength of fluid by adding water etc. • adj. diluted. ■ **dilution** n.

**dim** adj. **1** not bright or well lit. **2** indistinct. **3** inf. stupid. • v. (**dimmed**, **dimming**) make or become dim.
▷ SYNS adj. **1** FAINT, weak, feeble, dull; subdued, muted. **2** INDISTINCT, ill-defined, unclear, vague, shadowy, nebulous, blurred.

**dime** n. a 10-cent coin of the USA.

**dimension** n. **1** an aspect or feature. **2** a measurement such as length or breadth. ■ **dimensional** adj.
▷ SYNS **1** SIZE, extent, length, width, area, volume, capacity, proportions. **2** ASPECT, facet, side, feature, element.

**diminish** v. make or become smaller, weaker, or less.
▷ SYNS DECREASE, lessen, decline, subside, die down, abate, dwindle, fade, moderate, let up, ebb, wane, recede, reduce.

**diminutive** adj. tiny.
▷ SYNS SMALL, tiny, little, petite.

**dimple** n. a small dent, esp. in the skin.

**din** n. a loud annoying noise. • v. (**dinned**, **dinning**) impress information on someone by constant repetition.
▷ SYNS n. NOISE, uproar, row, racket, commotion, hullabaloo, hubbub, clamour, cacophony.

**dine** v. eat dinner. ■ **diner** n.

**dinghy** n. (pl. **-ies**) a small open boat or inflatable rubber boat.

**dingo** n. (pl. **-oes**) an Australian wild dog.

**dingy** adj. (**-ier**, **-iest**) dull and drab.

▷ SYNS DARK, dull, dim, gloomy, drab, dismal, dreary, cheerless, murky, dirty, grimy, shabby, seedy.

**dinner** n. the chief meal of the day; a formal evening meal. □ **dinner jacket** a man's jacket for formal evening wear.

**dinosaur** n. an extinct prehistoric reptile, often of enormous size.

**dint** n. (**by dint of**) by means of.

**diocese** n. a district under the care of a bishop.

**diode** n. a semiconductor allowing the flow of current in one direction only and having two terminals.

**dip** v. **1** put or lower briefly in or into. **2** move or slope downwards. **3** (of a level or amount) temporarily drop. • n. **1** a hollow. **2** an act of dipping. **3** a thick sauce in which pieces of food are dipped. **4** a brief swim.
▷ SYNS v. **1** IMMERSE, plunge, submerge, duck, dunk. **2** DESCEND, sink, subside, fall, drop, decline. • n. HOLLOW, basin, concavity, depression, slope, incline.

**diphtheria** n. an infectious disease with inflammation of the throat.

**diphthong** n. a compound vowel sound (as *ou* in *loud*).

**diploma** n. a certificate awarded on completion of a course of study.

**diplomacy** n. handling of international relations; tact.

**diplomat** n. **1** an official representing a country abroad. **2** a tactful person.

**diplomatic** adj. tactful.

▷ SYNS TACTFUL, sensitive, discreet, polite, careful, delicate, thoughtful, prudent, judicious, politic.

**dipper** n. 1 a diving bird. 2 a ladle.

**dipsomania** n. an uncontrollable craving for alcohol. ■ dipsomaniac n.

**dire** adj. extremely serious; very bad.

▷ SYNS TERRIBLE, dreadful, awful, appalling, frightful, horrible, atrocious, grim, cruel, disastrous, ruinous, calamitous, catastrophic.

**direct** adj. 1 straight, without interruptions or diversions; with nothing intervening or mediating; frank. 2 absolute: *the direct opposite*. • adv. in a direct way or by a direct route. • v. 1 control or manage; order. 2 aim in a particular direction; tell someone how to reach a place.

▷ SYNS adj. 1 STRAIGHT, undeviating; non-stop, uninterrupted, unbroken. 2 FRANK, straightforward, candid, open, honest, sincere, outspoken, forthright, matter-of-fact, blunt. 3 EXACT, complete, absolute, diametrical. • v. 1 GUIDE, steer, lead, conduct, usher. 2 MANAGE, lead, run, control, supervise, oversee. 3 AIM, point, train.

**direction** n. 1 a course along which someone or something moves; the way something faces. 2 control. 3 (**directions**) instructions. ■ directional adj.

**directive** n. an official instruction.

**directly** adv. 1 in a direct line or manner. 2 immediately.

**director** n. a person in charge of an activity or organization; a member of a board directing a business; a person who supervises acting and filming. ■ directorship n.

**directory** n. (pl. -ies) a book listing telephone subscribers etc.; a computer file listing other files.

**dirge** n. a mournful song.

**dirt** n. unclean matter; loose soil.

▷ SYNS 1 GRIME, dust, soot, muck, mud, filth, sludge, slime. 2 EARTH, soil, clay, loam.

**dirty** adj. (-ier, -iest) marked or covered with dirt; obscene; dishonourable or unfair. • v. (**dirtied**, **dirtying**) make dirty.

▷ SYNS adj. 1 UNCLEAN, filthy, stained, grimy, soiled, grubby, dusty, mucky, sooty, muddy, polluted, foul, tarnished. 2 OBSCENE, indecent, vulgar, smutty, coarse, rude. • v. SOIL, stain, muddy, blacken, smudge, smear, sully, pollute.

**disability** n. (pl. -ies) a physical or mental incapacity.

▷ SYNS HANDICAP, infirmity, impairment, affliction, disablement, incapacity.

**disable** v. impair the capacities or activity of; keep from functioning or from doing something.

**disabled** adj. having a physical disability.

**disabuse** v. disillusion.

**disadvantage** n. an unfavourable condition or position in relation to others; something diminishing your chances of success or effectiveness. ■ disadvantaged adj. disadvantageous adj.

▷ SYNS DRAWBACK, snag, downside, weakness, flaw, defect, fault, handicap, liability.

**disaffected** adj. discontented and no longer loyal.
■ disaffection n.

**disagree** v. 1 have a different opinion; be inconsistent. 2 (**disagree with**) make ill.
■ disagreement n.
▷ SYNS 1 TAKE ISSUE, dissent, be at variance, quarrel, argue, wrangle, dispute, debate. 2 DIFFER, vary, conflict, clash, contrast, diverge.

**disagreeable** adj. unpleasant; bad-tempered.
▷ SYNS UNPLEASANT, objectionable, horrible, nasty, offensive, obnoxious, off-putting.

**disallow** v. refuse to sanction.

**disappear** v. pass from sight or existence. ■ disappearance n.
▷ SYNS VANISH, be lost to view, fade away, melt away, evaporate.

**disappoint** v. fail to fulfil the hopes or expectations of.
■ disappointment n.
▷ SYNS LET DOWN, fail, dash someone's hopes, upset, sadden.

**disappointed** adj. sad or displeased because hopes have not been fulfilled.
▷ SYNS SADDENED, upset, disheartened, downhearted, downcast, depressed, despondent, dispirited, crestfallen.

**disapprove** v. consider to be bad or immoral. ■ disapproval n.
▷ SYNS OBJECT TO, dislike, deplore, frown on, criticize, censure, condemn, denounce.

**disarm** v. 1 deprive of weapons; reduce armed forces. 2 make less hostile; win over.
■ disarmament n.

**disarrange** v. make untidy.

**disarray** n. disorder or confusion.
▷ SYNS DISORDER, confusion, chaos, mess, muddle, shambles.

**disassociate** v. = DISSOCIATE.

**disaster** n. a sudden great misfortune or failure.
▷ SYNS CATASTROPHE, calamity, cataclysm, tragedy; accident, misfortune, misadventure.

**disastrous** adj. causing great damage.
▷ SYNS CATASTROPHIC, cataclysmic, calamitous, devastating, tragic, ruinous.

**disband** v. (of an organized group) break up.

**disbelieve** v. refuse or be unable to believe. ■ disbelief n.

**disburse** v. pay out money.

**disc** n. 1 a thin, flat round object; a record bearing recorded sound; a layer of cartilage between the vertebrae. 2 (**disk**) a device on which computer data is stored. □ disc jockey a DJ.

**discard** v. reject as useless or unwanted. • n. something rejected.
▷ SYNS v. THROW OUT/AWAY, dispose of, get rid of, jettison, dispense with, scrap, reject.

**discern** v. perceive with the mind or senses. ■ discernible adj. discernment n.
▷ SYNS SEE, notice, observe, perceive, make out, distinguish, detect, recognize.

**discerning** adj. having good judgement.
▷ SYNS DISCRIMINATING, astute, shrewd, perceptive, penetrating, judicious, sensitive, sophisticated.

**discharge** v. 1 dismiss or allow to leave. 2 allow liquid etc. to flow out. 3 pay a debt; fulfil an

obligation. • n. discharging; material flowing from something.
▷ SYNS v. **1** EMIT, exude, release, leak. **2** DISMISS, eject, expel; inf. fire, sack. **3** SET FREE, release, liberate. **4** CARRY OUT, perform, do, accomplish, fulfil, execute.

**disciple** n. a pupil or follower; one of the original followers of Jesus.
▷ SYNS APOSTLE, follower, acolyte, adherent, devotee, believer, advocate, proponent.

**disciplinarian** n. a person who enforces strict discipline.
▷ SYNS MARTINET, hard taskmaster, tyrant, slave-driver.

**discipline** n. **1** controlled and obedient behaviour; training and punishment producing this. **2** a branch of learning. • v. train to be orderly; punish.
■ **disciplinary** adj.
▷ SYNS CONTROL, self-control, self-restraint, strictness, regulation, direction, order, authority; training, teaching. • v. **1** CONTROL, restrain, regulate, govern, check, curb. **2** PUNISH, penalize; chastise, castigate, reprimand.

**disclaim** v. refuse to acknowledge.

**disclaimer** n. a denial of responsibility.

**disclose** v. reveal. ■ **disclosure** n.
▷ SYNS REVEAL, divulge, tell, impart, let slip.

**disco** n. (pl. **-os**) a place or party where people dance to pop music.

**discolour** (US **discolor**) v. make or become stained.
■ **discoloration** n.

**discomfit** v. (**discomfited**, **discomfiting**) make uneasy or embarrassed. ■ **discomfiture** n.

**discomfort** n. slight pain; slight unease or embarrassment.
▷ SYNS **1** PAIN, ache, soreness, tenderness, irritation. **2** UNEASE, embarrassment, discomfiture.

**disconcert** v. unsettle.
▷ SYNS UNSETTLE, take aback, perturb, discomfit, unnerve, nonplus, throw.

**disconnect** v. break the connection of; cut off the power supply of. ■ **disconnection** n.
▷ SYNS UNDO, detach, disengage, uncouple, unfasten, unplug.

**disconsolate** adj. very unhappy.

**discontent** n. dissatisfaction.

**discontented** adj. dissatisfied.
▷ SYNS DISSATISFIED, displeased, disgruntled, unhappy, disaffected; inf. fed up.

**discontinue** v. put an end to; cease.

**discontinuous** adj. having gaps or breaks.

**discord** n. **1** disagreement or quarrelling. **2** inharmonious sounds.
▷ SYNS DISAGREEMENT, conflict, friction, strife, hostility, antagonism.

**discordant** adj. (of a sound) harsh and unpleasant.
▷ SYNS DISSONANT, cacophonous, inharmonious, off-key, tuneless.

**discount** n. an amount of money taken off something's full price. • v. **1** reduce the price of. **2** disregard as unreliable.
▷ SYNS n. REDUCTION, rebate.
• v. DISREGARD, ignore, dismiss, overlook, pass over, take no notice of.

**discourage** v. dishearten; deter or dissuade.
■ **discouragement** n.

▷ SYNS **1** DISHEARTEN, dispirit, demoralize, cast down, unnerve, daunt, intimidate. **2** DISSUADE, put off, deter, talk out of.

**discourse** n. communication or debate; a treatise or lecture. • v. speak or write authoritatively.

▷ SYNS n. ADDRESS, speech, lecture, oration, sermon, homily; essay, treatise, dissertation, paper.

**discourteous** adj. impolite. ■ discourtesy n.

**discover** v. find; learn; be the first to find. ■ discovery n.

▷ SYNS **1** FIND, come across, locate, stumble on, bring to light, unearth. **2** FIND OUT, learn, realize, ascertain.

**discredit** v. (discredited, discrediting) damage the reputation of; cause to be disbelieved. • n. damage to a reputation. ■ discreditable adj.

▷ SYNS v. **1** DISGRACE, dishonour, compromise, stigmatize, smear, tarnish, taint. **2** DISPROVE, invalidate, refute.

**discreet** adj. unobtrusive; not giving away secrets.

▷ SYNS CAREFUL, circumspect, cautious, wary, guarded, sensitive, prudent, judicious, chary, tactful, reserved, diplomatic, muted, understated, delicate, considerate, politic, wise, sensible, sagacious.

**discrepancy** n. (pl. -ies) a difference or failure to match.

▷ SYNS INCONSISTENCY, disparity, deviation, variance, variation, difference, divergence, disagreement, dissimilarity, conflict.

**discrete** adj. separate and distinct.

**discretion** n. **1** being discreet. **2** freedom to decide something.

**discretionary** adj. done or used at a person's discretion.

**discriminate** v. **1** recognize a difference. **2** treat unfairly on the grounds of race, sex, or age. ■ discriminatory adj.

▷ SYNS DISTINGUISH, differentiate, tell apart.

**discriminating** adj. having good judgement.

**discrimination** n. **1** unfair treatment on the grounds of race, sex, or age. **2** good judgement or taste.

▷ SYNS **1** PREJUDICE, bias, intolerance, bigotry, favouritism; chauvinism, racism, sexism. **2** DISCERNMENT, taste, judgement, perception, acumen, insight, refinement, sensitivity.

**discursive** adj. (of writing) flowing and wide-ranging.

**discus** n. a heavy disc thrown in an athletic contest.

**discuss** v. talk or write about.

▷ SYNS TALK OVER, debate, consider, confer about; examine, explore, analyse.

**discussion** n. conversation or debate.

▷ SYNS CONVERSATION, talk, chat, dialogue, debate, discourse, consultation; exploration, analysis.

**disdain** v. & n. scorn.

**disdainful** adj. scornful.

▷ SYNS SCORNFUL, contemptuous, derisive, condescending, arrogant, proud, supercilious, haughty, superior.

**disease** n. an illness.

**diseased** adj. suffering from disease.

▷ SYNS SICK, ill, unhealthy, infected, septic.

**disembark** v. leave a ship, train, etc.

**disembodied** adj. (of a voice) with no obvious physical source.

**disembowel** v. (**disembowelled, disembowelling**; US **disemboweled**) take out the entrails of.

**disenchant** v. disillusion. ■ disenchantment n.

**disengage** v. detach; release.

**disentangle** v. free from tangles or confusion; separate.

**disfavour** (US **disfavor**) n. dislike or disapproval.

**disfigure** v. spoil the appearance of. ■ disfigurement n.
▷ SYNS MUTILATE, deface, deform, scar, spoil, mar, damage, injure, maim.

**disgrace** n. the loss of other people's respect. • v. bring disgrace on.
▷ SYNS n. SHAME, humiliation, dishonour, disrespect, scandal, ignominy, degradation, discredit, stigma.

**disgraceful** adj. shockingly unacceptable. ■ disgracefully adv.
▷ SYNS SCANDALOUS, outrageous, shocking, shameful, contemptible, despicable, reprehensible.

**disgruntled** adj. annoyed or resentful.
▷ SYNS DISSATISFIED, displeased, discontented, annoyed, irritated, vexed; inf. fed up.

**disguise** v. conceal the identity of. • n. a means of concealing your identity; being disguised.
▷ SYNS v. CAMOUFLAGE, cover up, conceal, dissemble, hide, screen, mask, veil, cloak.

**disgust** n. a feeling that something is very offensive or unpleasant. • v. cause disgust in. ■ disgusting adj.
▷ SYNS n. REVULSION, repugnance, abhorrence, loathing, detestation. • v. SICKEN, nauseate, revolt, repel; outrage, shock, appal, scandalize.

**dish** n. a shallow bowl, esp. for food; food prepared according to a recipe. • v. serve food. □ dishwasher a machine for washing dishes.
▷ SYNS n. PLATE, platter, bowl, basin, tureen, salver.

**dishearten** v. cause to lose hope or confidence.

**dishevelled** (US **disheveled**) adj. ruffled and untidy.
▷ SYNS UNTIDY, rumpled, messy, scruffy, bedraggled, tousled, unkempt.

**dishonest** adj. not honest. ■ dishonesty n.
▷ SYNS UNTRUTHFUL, deceitful, lying, two-faced; fraudulent, corrupt, treacherous, cunning, devious, underhand, dishonourable, unscrupulous, unprincipled, unfair, unjust.

**dishonour** (US **dishonor**) v. & n. disgrace.

**dishonourable** (US **dishonorable**) adj. bringing shame or disgrace.
▷ SYNS SHAMEFUL, disreputable, discreditable, ignominious, ignoble, blameworthy, contemptible, despicable, reprehensible, shabby, unseemly, unprincipled, unscrupulous.

**disillusion** v. rid of pleasant but mistaken beliefs. ■ disillusionment n.

**disincentive** n. something that discourages an action or effort.

**disinclined** adj. reluctant. ■ disinclination n.

**disinfect** v. clean by destroying harmful bacteria. ■ disinfectant n. disinfection n.

▷ SYNS STERILIZE, sanitize, clean, cleanse, purify, fumigate, decontaminate.

**disinformation** n. deliberately misleading information.

**disingenuous** adj. insincere.

**disinherit** v. prevent from inheriting.

**disintegrate** v. break into small pieces. ■ disintegration n.

▷ SYNS FALL APART, fall to pieces, break up, fragment, shatter, crumble.

**disinterested** adj. impartial.

▷ SYNS UNBIASED, unprejudiced, impartial, detached, objective, dispassionate, impersonal, neutral.

**disjointed** adj. lacking coherent connection.

▷ SYNS INCOHERENT, rambling, disconnected, disorganized, confused, muddled.

**disk** = DISC.

**diskette** n. Computing a small floppy disk.

**dislike** n. distaste or hostility. • v. feel dislike for.

▷ SYNS n. AVERSION, distaste, disapproval, disfavour, animosity, hostility, antipathy.

**dislocate** v. disturb the arrangement or position of; disrupt. ■ dislocation n.

**dislodge** v. remove from an established position.

**disloyal** adj. not loyal. ■ disloyalty n.

▷ SYNS UNFAITHFUL, faithless, false, inconstant, untrustworthy, treacherous, traitorous, perfidious, double-dealing, deceitful, two-faced.

**dismal** adj. gloomy; very bad. ■ dismally adv.

▷ SYNS GLOOMY, bleak, miserable, wretched, drab, dreary, dingy, cheerless, depressing, uninviting.

**dismantle** v. take to pieces.

**dismay** n. a feeling of shock and distress. • v. cause to feel this.

▷ SYNS n. CONSTERNATION, distress, anxiety, alarm, concern. • v. SHOCK, take aback, startle, alarm, disturb, perturb, upset, unsettle, unnerve.

**dismember** v. tear or cut the limbs from.

**dismiss** v. send away from your presence or employment; disregard. ■ dismissal n.

▷ SYNS DISCHARGE, get rid of, lay off, make redundant; inf. sack, fire.

**dismissive** adj. treating something as unworthy of consideration.

**dismount** v. get off a thing on which you are riding.

**disobedient** adj. not obedient. ■ disobedience n.

▷ SYNS INSUBORDINATE, rebellious, defiant, unruly, wayward, mutinous, wilful, uncooperative, naughty, obstreperous.

**disobey** v. disregard orders.

▷ SYNS DEFY, disregard, ignore, contravene, flout, infringe, violate.

**disorder** n. 1 untidiness. 2 a breakdown of discipline. 3 an ailment. ■ disorderly adj.

▷ SYNS 1 MESS, untidiness, chaos, muddle, clutter, confusion, disarray, disorganization, shambles. **2** DISTURBANCE, disruption, rioting, unrest. **3** DISEASE, complaint, affliction, illness, sickness, malady.

**disorganized** (or **-ised**) adj. not properly planned or arranged; muddled. ■ **disorganization** n.
▷ SYNS CONFUSED, disorderly, untidy, chaotic, jumbled, muddled, in disarray, unsystematic, haphazard, slapdash, careless; inf. hit-or-miss.

**disorientate** (or **disorient**) v. cause a person to lose their sense of direction.
■ **disorientation** n.

**disown** v. refuse to have any further connection with.
▷ SYNS RENOUNCE, repudiate, reject, abandon, forsake, deny, turn your back on.

**disparage** v. belittle; criticize.

**disparate** adj. very different in kind.

**disparity** n. a great difference.
▷ SYNS DISCREPANCY, inconsistency, difference, dissimilarity, contrast, gap.

**dispassionate** adj. unemotional and objective.

**dispatch** (or **despatch**) v. **1** send off to a destination or for a purpose. **2** complete a task quickly. **3** kill. • n. **1** sending off. **2** promptness. **3** an official report.
▷ SYNS v. SEND, post, mail, forward, transmit.

**dispel** v. (**dispelled**, **dispelling**) drive or clear away.

**dispensable** adj. not essential.

**dispensary** n. (pl. **-ies**) a place where medicines are dispensed.

**dispensation** n. **1** exemption. **2** distribution.

**dispense** v. **1** deal out; prepare and give out medicine. **2** (**dispense with**) do without; abandon.

**disperse** v. go or send in different directions; scatter.
■ **dispersal** n.
▷ SYNS BREAK UP, disband, separate, scatter, leave; dissipate, dissolve, vanish, melt away.

**dispirited** adj. dejected.
■ **dispiriting** adj.

**displace** v. take the place of; move from its place or home.
■ **displacement** n.
▷ SYNS DISLODGE, dislocate, move; replace, supplant.

**display** v. show or put on show. • n. displaying; something displayed.
▷ SYNS v. **1** SHOW, exhibit, present, lay/set out, array. **2** MANIFEST, evince, betray, reveal. • n. SHOW, exhibition, exhibit, presentation, demonstration; spectacle, parade, pageant.

**displease** v. irritate or annoy.
■ **displeasure** n.
▷ SYNS ANNOY, irritate, anger, put out, irk, vex, offend, pique, gall, exasperate.

**disposable** adj. **1** designed to be thrown away after use. **2** available for use.

**disposal** n. getting rid of something.

**dispose** v. **1** place or arrange. **2** make willing or ready to do something. **3** (**dispose of**) get rid of. ■ **disposed** adj.

**disposition** n. **1** a person's character; a tendency. **2** arrangement.

**disproportionate** adj. relatively too large or too small.

**disprove** v. show to be false.

▷ SYNS REFUTE, rebut, give the lie to, discredit, invalidate.

**disputable** adj. questionable.

**disputation** n. an argument or debate.

**dispute** v. argue or debate; question the truth of; compete for.
• n. a debate or disagreement.
▷ SYNS v. 1 DEBATE, argue, disagree, quarrel, wrangle, squabble.
2 QUESTION, challenge, contest, take issue with, impugn.
• n. ARGUMENT, quarrel, row, altercation, wrangle, squabble; debate.

**disqualify** v. (**disqualified, disqualifying**) cause or judge to be ineligible or unsuitable.
■ disqualification n.

**disquiet** n. uneasiness or anxiety.
▷ SYNS UNEASE, anxiety, agitation, worry, concern.

**disregard** v. pay no attention to. • n. lack of attention.
▷ SYNS v. IGNORE, take no notice of, discount, overlook, turn a blind eye to.

**disrepair** n. bad condition caused by lack of repair.

**disreputable** adj. not respectable.
▷ SYNS INFAMOUS, notorious, louche, dishonourable, dishonest, unprincipled, unsavoury, untrustworthy.

**disrepute** n. a bad reputation.

**disrespect** n. lack of respect.

**disrespectful** adj. showing disrespect.
▷ SYNS IMPOLITE, discourteous, ill-mannered, rude, uncivil, insolent, impertinent, impudent, cheeky.

**disrupt** v. interrupt the normal operation of an activity or process. ■ disruption n. disruptive adj.
▷ SYNS INTERRUPT, upset, disturb, interfere with, obstruct, impede, play havoc with.

**dissatisfied** adj. not pleased or contented. ■ dissatisfaction n.
▷ SYNS DISCONTENTED, displeased, disgruntled, disappointed, frustrated, unhappy, vexed, irritated, annoyed; inf. fed up.

**dissect** v. cut apart so as to examine the internal structure.
■ dissection n.

**dissemble** v. hide your feelings or motives.

**disseminate** v. spread widely.
■ dissemination n.
▷ SYNS SPREAD, circulate, distribute, disperse, communicate, publicize, promulgate, propagate.

**dissension** n. disagreement that gives rise to strife.

**dissent** v. disagree with a widely or officially held view.
• n. disagreement. ■ dissenter n.

**dissertation** n. a lengthy essay.

**disservice** n. an unhelpful or harmful action.

**dissident** n. a person who opposes official policy.
▷ SYNS DISSENTER, rebel, non-conformist.

**dissimilar** adj. unlike.
▷ SYNS DIFFERENT, distinct, disparate, contrasting, mismatched.

**dissimulate** v. conceal or disguise.

**dissipate** v. 1 dispel; fritter away. 2 (**dissipated**) living a dissolute life. ■ dissipation n.
▷ SYNS 1 DISPERSE, disappear, vanish, evaporate, dissolve.
2 SQUANDER, waste, fritter away, run through.

**dissociate** v. regard as separate; declare to be unconnected.
■ **dissociation** n.
▷ SYNS SEPARATE, set apart, isolate, detach, disconnect, divorce.

**dissolute** adj. indulging in immoral activities.

**dissolve** v. (of a solid) mix with a liquid and form a solution; disperse an assembly; end a partnership or agreement.
■ **dissolution** n.
▷ SYNS 1 LIQUEFY, melt, deliquesce. 2 END, bring to an end, terminate, discontinue, wind up, disband.

**dissuade** v. deter by argument.
▷ SYNS TALK OUT OF, discourage from, deter from, put off.

**distance** n. the length of space or time between two points; being far away; a far point or part; the full length of a race etc. • v. cause to be separate or dissociated.
▷ SYNS n. INTERVAL, space, span, gap, extent; length, width, breadth, depth; range, reach.

**distant** adj. far away; at a specified distance; cool and aloof.
▷ SYNS 1 FARAWAY, far-off, remote, out of the way, outlying, far-flung. 2 RESERVED, aloof, uncommunicative, remote, withdrawn, unapproachable, reticent, unfriendly, unresponsive; inf. stand-offish.

**distaste** n. dislike or disapproval.

**distasteful** adj. unpleasant or offensive.
▷ SYNS UNPLEASANT, disagreeable, undesirable, objectionable, offensive, obnoxious, unsavoury.

**distemper** n. 1 a disease of dogs. 2 a kind of paint for use on walls.

**distend** v. swell from internal pressure.

**distil** (US **distill**) v. (**distilled**, **distilling**) vaporize and condense a liquid so as to purify it; make alcoholic spirits in this way. ■ **distillation** n.

**distiller** n. a person or company that manufactures spirits.
■ **distillery** n.

**distinct** adj. 1 different in kind. 2 clearly perceptible.
■ **distinctly** adv.
▷ SYNS 1 DISCRETE, separate, different, unconnected, contrasting. 2 CLEAR, well defined, unmistakable, recognizable, visible, obvious, pronounced, prominent, striking.

**distinction** n. 1 a contrast or difference; difference in treatment or attitude. 2 excellence; an honour; a high grade in an exam.
▷ SYNS 1 CONTRAST, difference, dissimilarity, differentiation, division. 2 RENOWN, fame, celebrity, prominence, eminence, pre-eminence, merit, worth, greatness, excellence.

**distinctive** adj. characteristic and distinguishing.
▷ SYNS DISTINGUISHING, characteristic, typical, particular, special.

**distinguish** v. 1 perceive a difference; be a differentiating characteristic of. 2 discern.
■ **distinguishable** adj.
▷ SYNS 1 TELL APART, differentiate, discriminate. 2 SET APART, separate, characterize. 3 MAKE OUT, see, perceive, discern, pick out.

**distinguished** adj. dignified in appearance; worthy of great respect.
▷ SYNS EMINENT, renowned, well known, prominent, noted, famous, illustrious, celebrated, famed, respected, acclaimed, esteemed.

**distort** v. pull out of shape; misrepresent. ■ **distortion** n.
▷ SYNS MISREPRESENT, pervert, twist, falsify, misreport.

**distract** v. draw away the attention of.

**distraction** n. 1 something that distracts; an entertainment. 2 extreme distress and agitation.

**distraught** adj. very worried and upset.
▷ SYNS DISTRESSED, desperate, overwrought, frantic, hysterical, beside yourself.

**distress** n. unhappiness; pain; hardship. • v. make unhappy.
▷ SYNS n. 1 ANGUISH, suffering, pain, agony, torment, heartache, heartbreak; misery, wretchedness, sorrow, grief, woe, sadness, unhappiness, despair. 2 HARDSHIP, poverty, deprivation, privation, destitution, indigence, penury, need. • v. UPSET, pain, trouble, worry, disturb, sadden.

**distribute** v. divide and share out; spread over an area.
■ **distribution** n.
▷ SYNS GIVE OUT, deal out, dole out, hand out/round; allocate, allot, apportion, share out, divide up, parcel out; circulate, pass around, deliver.

**distributor** n. a firm supplying goods to retailers; a device in an engine for passing electric current to the spark plugs.

**district** n. a particular area of a town or region.
▷ SYNS AREA, region, locality, neighbourhood, sector, quarter, territory, zone, ward, parish.

**distrust** n. lack of trust. • v. feel distrust in. ■ **distrustful** adj.
▷ SYNS n. MISTRUST, doubt, suspicion, scepticism, wariness.

**disturb** v. 1 interrupt the rest or privacy of. 2 make anxious. 3 interfere with the arrangement of. 4 (**disturbed**) having emotional or mental problems.
■ **disturbance** n.
▷ SYNS 1 INTERRUPT, intrude on, distract, bother, trouble, pester, harass; inf. hassle. 2 PERTURB, trouble, concern, worry, upset, agitate, fluster, disconcert, dismay, unsettle.

**disunited** adj. not united.
■ **disunity** n.

**disuse** n. a state of not being used. ■ **disused** adj.

**ditch** n. a long narrow trench for drainage. • v. abandon.
▷ SYNS n. TRENCH, trough, channel, dyke, drain, gutter, gully, moat.

**dither** v. hesitate indecisively.

**ditto** n. (in lists) the same again.

**ditty** n. (pl. **-ies**) a short simple song.

**divan** n. 1 a bed consisting simply of a base and mattress. 2 a sofa without a back or arms.

**dive** v. plunge head first into water; swim under water using breathing apparatus; move quickly or suddenly downwards. • n. 1 an act of diving. 2 inf. a disreputable nightclub or bar.
▷ SYNS v. PLUNGE, plummet, nosedive, fall, drop, swoop, pitch.

**diver** n. a person who dives or swims under water; a diving bird.

**diverge** v. separate and go in different directions; be different from. ■ **divergence** n. **divergent** adj.
▷ SYNS SEPARATE, fork, branch off, bifurcate, divide, split, part.

**diverse** adj. of differing kinds.
▷ SYNS ASSORTED, various, miscellaneous, mixed, varied, heterogeneous, different, differing.

**diversify** v. (**diversified, diversifying**) make or become more varied; (of a company) enlarge its range of products. ■ **diversification** n.

**diversion** n. 1 diverting; an alternative route avoiding a closed road. 2 a recreation or entertainment.

**diversity** n. (pl. **-ies**) being varied; a wide range.

**divert** v. 1 turn from a course or route. 2 entertain; distract.

**divide** v. 1 separate into parts or from something else. 2 cause to disagree. 3 find how many times one number contains another; be divisible by a number without remainder.
• n. a wide difference between two groups.
▷ SYNS v. 1 SPLIT, cut up, halve, bisect; segregate, partition, separate. 2 BRANCH, fork, diverge, split in two. 3 SHARE OUT, allocate, allot, apportion, distribute, hand out, dole out.

**dividend** n. 1 a sum paid to a company's shareholders out of its profits. 2 (**dividends**) benefits.

**divider** n. 1 a thing that divides. 2 (**dividers**) measuring compasses.

**divine** adj. 1 of, from, or like God or a god. 2 inf. wonderful.
• v. discover by intuition or magic. ■ **divination** n. **diviner** n.
▷ SYNS adj. HEAVENLY, celestial, holy, angelic, saintly, seraphic, sacred.

**divinity** n. (pl. **-ies**) being divine; a god.

**divisible** adj. able to be divided.

**division** n. dividing or being divided; a dividing line or partition; one of the parts into which something is divided.
▷ SYNS 1 DIVIDING LINE, divide, boundary, borderline. 2 SECTION, subsection, subdivision, category, class, group, grouping, set. 3 BRANCH, department, unit.

**divisive** adj. tending to cause disagreement.

**divorce** n. the legal ending of a marriage. • v. legally end your marriage with.

**divorcee** n. a divorced person.

**divulge** v. reveal information.

**DIY** abbr. do-it-yourself.

**dizzy** adj. (**-ier, -iest**) feeling giddy. ■ **dizziness** n.
▷ SYNS LIGHT-HEADED, giddy, faint, shaky, weak at the knees, woozy.

**DJ** abbr. person who introduces and plays recorded pop music on radio or at a club.

**DNA** abbr. deoxyribonucleic acid, a substance storing genetic information.

**do** v. 1 carry out or complete; work at; deal with; provide or make. 2 act or proceed; fare. 3 be suitable or acceptable.
• v.aux. used to form the present or past tense, in questions, for emphasis, or to avoid repeating a verb just used. • n. (pl. **dos** or

**do's**) a party. □ **do away with** abolish. **do up 1** fasten. **2** *inf.* redecorate.

▷ SYNS **v. 1** PERFORM, carry out, undertake, execute, accomplish, discharge, achieve, implement. **2** SUFFICE, be sufficient, serve the purpose, fit/fill the bill. **3** *do him a favour:* GRANT, render, pay, give.

**Dobermann** (or **Dobermann pinscher**) n. a large breed of dog with powerful jaws.

**docile** adj. submissive or easily managed. ■ **docility** n.

▷ SYNS AMENABLE, compliant, tractable, manageable, accommodating, obedient, pliant, biddable, submissive.

**dock** n. **1** an enclosed body of water where ships are loaded, unloaded, or repaired. **2** an enclosure for the prisoner in a criminal court. **3** a weed with broad leaves. • v. **1** (of a ship) come into a dock. **2** (of a spacecraft) join with another craft in space. **3** deduct; cut short. □ **dockyard** an area where ships are repaired and built.

▷ SYNS n. PIER, quay, wharf, jetty, harbour, port, marina.
• v. DEDUCT, subtract, remove, take off; cut.

**docker** n. a labourer who loads and unloads ships in a dockyard.

**docket** n. a document listing goods delivered.

**doctor** n. **1** a person qualified to give medical treatment. **2** a person holding a doctorate. • v. **1** tamper with or falsify; adulterate. **2** *inf.* castrate or spay an animal.

▷ SYNS n. PHYSICIAN, GP, consultant, registrar.

**doctorate** n. the highest degree at a university. ■ **doctoral** adj.

**doctrinaire** adj. applying theories or principles rigidly.

**doctrine** n. a principle or the beliefs of a religious, political, or other group.

▷ SYNS CREED, credo, dogma, belief, teaching, ideology; tenet, maxim, canon, principle, precept.

**document** n. a piece of written, printed, or electronic material giving information or evidence. • v. record in written or other form. ■ **documentation** n.

▷ SYNS n. PAPER, certificate, deed, contract, record; licence, visa, warrant.

**documentary** adj. **1** consisting of documents. **2** giving a factual report. • n. (pl. **-ies**) a documentary film.

**dodder** v. totter because of age or frailty. ■ **doddery** adj.

**dodge** v. avoid by a quick sideways movement; evade. • n. an act of avoiding something.

▷ SYNS v. EVADE, avoid, elude, escape, give someone the slip; sidestep, get out of. • n. RUSE, ploy, scheme, stratagem, trick.

**dodgem** n. a small electric car driven in an enclosure at a funfair with the aim of bumping into other such cars.

**dodo** n. (pl. **-os**) a large extinct bird.

**doe** n. the female of the deer, hare, or rabbit.

**does** 3rd sing. of DO.

**doff** v. take off your hat.

**dog** n. a four-legged carnivorous wild or domesticated animal; the male of this or of the fox or wolf. • v. (**dogged, dogging**)

follow persistently. □ **dog collar**
inf. a white upright collar worn
by Christian priests. **dog-eared**
having worn or battered
corners. **dogfight** close combat
between military aircraft.
**dogfish** a small shark. **dogsbody**
inf. a person given menial tasks.
▷ SYNS n. HOUND, canine, mongrel,
puppy; inf. pooch, mutt.

**dogged** adj. very persistent.
▷ SYNS DETERMINED, tenacious,
single-minded, unflagging,
persistent, persevering, tireless.

**doggerel** n. bad verse.

**dogma** n. doctrines put forward
by authority to be accepted
without question.

**dogmatic** adj. firmly putting
forward your opinions and
unwilling to accept those of
others. ■ **dogmatically** adv.
▷ SYNS OPINIONATED, authoritarian, , dictatorial, uncompromising, unyielding,
inflexible, rigid.

**doily** n. (pl. **-ies**) a small ornamental lace or paper mat.

**doldrums** pl.n. a state of
inactivity or depression.

**dole** n. inf. unemployment
benefit. • v. (**dole out**)
distribute.

**doleful** adj. mournful.
■ **dolefully** adv.
▷ SYNS MOURNFUL, sad, sorrowful,
dejected, depressed, miserable,
disconsolate, woebegone.

**doll** n. a small model of a human
figure, used as a child's toy.

**dollar** n. the unit of money in
the USA and various other
countries.

**dollop** n. inf. a mass of something
soft.

**dolour** (US **dolor**) n. lit. sorrow.
■ **dolorous** adj.

**dolphin** n. a small whale with a
beak-like snout.

**dolt** n. a stupid person.

**domain** n. an area under a
person's control; a field of
activity.

**dome** n. a rounded roof with a
circular base; something shaped
like this.

**domestic** adj. of home or
household; of your own
country; domesticated.
■ **domestically** adv.

**domesticate** v. train an animal
to live with humans.
■ **domestication** n.

**domesticity** n. family life.

**domicile** n. a place of residence.

**dominant** adj. most important
or powerful. ■ **dominance** n.
▷ SYNS 1 ASSERTIVE, authoritative,
forceful, domineering,
commanding, controlling,
pushy. 2 CHIEF, main, leading,
principal, predominant,
paramount, primary.

**dominate** v. have a
commanding influence over; be
most influential or conspicuous
in; tower over. ■ **domination** n.
▷ SYNS 1 RULE, govern, control,
command, direct, preside over;
tyrannize, intimidate.
2 OVERLOOK, tower above, loom
over.

**domineering** adj. arrogant and
overbearing.
▷ SYNS OVERBEARING, authoritarian, autocratic, imperious,
high-handed, peremptory,
bossy, arrogant, dictatorial,
tyrannical.

**dominion** n. supreme power or
control; a ruler's territory.

**domino** n. (pl. **-oes**) a small
oblong piece marked with
0-6 pips, used in the game of

**dominoes**, where the aim is to match pieces with the same value.

**don** v. (**donned**, **donning**) put on. • n. a university teacher.

**donate** v. give as a donation.
▷ SYNS GIVE, contribute, present, grant, bestow.

**donation** n. something that is given to a charity.
▷ SYNS CONTRIBUTION, gift, present, grant, offering, handout.

**done** p.p. of **DO**. • adj. inf. socially acceptable.

**donkey** n. (pl. **-eys**) a long-eared animal of the horse family.

**donor** n. a person who gives or donates something.

**donut** US sp. of **DOUGHNUT**.

**doodle** v. scribble idly. • n. a drawing made in this way.

**doom** n. a grim fate; death or ruin. • v. destine to a grim fate.
□ **doomsday** the last day of the world's existence.
▷ SYNS n. DESTRUCTION, downfall, ruin, ruination, death.
• v. DESTINE, fate, condemn, predestine.

**door** n. a hinged, sliding, or re-volving barrier at the entrance to a room, building, etc.
□ **doorway** an entrance fitted with a door.
▷ SYNS DOORWAY, opening, portal, entrance, entry, exit.

**dope** inf. n. **1** an illegal drug. **2** a stupid person. • v. drug.

**dopey** (or **dopy**) adj. inf. half asleep; stupid.

**dormant** adj. temporarily inactive; in a deep sleep.
▷ SYNS SLEEPING, asleep, inactive, inert, latent, quiescent.

**dormitory** n. (pl. **-ies**) a bedroom for a number of people in a school etc.

**dormouse** n. (pl. **-mice**) a mouse-like animal that hibernates.

**dorsal** adj. of or on the back.

**dosage** n. the size of a dose.

**dose** n. an amount of medicine to be taken at one time; an amount of radiation received.
• v. give a dose of medicine to.

**dossier** n. a set of documents about a person or event.

**dot** n. a small round mark.
• v. (**dotted**, **dotting**) mark with dots; scatter here and there.
▷ SYNS n. SPOT, speck, fleck, speckle.

**dotage** n. senility.

**dote** v. be extremely and un-critically fond of. ■ **doting** adj.
▷ SYNS ADORE, love, idolize, worship, treasure.

**double** adj. **1** consisting of two equal or similar parts. **2** of twice the usual size. **3** for use by two people. • adv. twice as much.
• n. **1** a double quantity or thing. **2** a person very like another.
• v. **1** make or become double. **2** fold in two. **3** have two uses or roles. **4** (**double back**) go back in the direction you came from.
□ **double bass** the largest and lowest-pitched instrument of the violin family. **double-breasted** (of a coat) with fronts overlapping. **double chin** a chin with a roll of fat below. **double cream** thick cream with a high fat content. **double-decker** a bus with two decks. **double enten-dre** a word or phrase with two meanings, one of which is rude. **double glazing** two sheets of glass in a window, designed to

reduce heat loss. **double take** a second reaction to something unexpected, just after your first one. ■ **doubly** adv.

**double-cross** v. cheat or deceive.
▷ SYNS BETRAY, cheat, trick, deceive, hoodwink.

**doublet** n. hist. a man's short close-fitting jacket.

**doubt** n. a feeling of un-certainty. • v. **1** disbelieve or mistrust. **2** feel uncertain about.
▷ SYNS n. UNCERTAINTY, suspicion, scepticism, distrust, mistrust; reservations, misgivings. • v. DIS-BELIEVE, distrust, mistrust, suspect, question, query.

**doubtful** adj. feeling doubt; not known for certain; unlikely. ■ **doubtfully** adv.
▷ SYNS **1** IN DOUBT, uncertain, unsure. **2** SUSPICIOUS, distrustful, mistrustful, scep-tical. **3** DUBIOUS, uncertain, questionable, debatable.

**doubtless** adj. certainly.

**dough** n. **1** a thick mixture of flour and liquid, for baking. **2** inf. money. □ **doughnut** (US **donut**) a small fried cake or ring of sweetened dough.

**doughty** adj. brave and determined.

**dour** adj. stern or gloomy-looking.

**douse** v. **1** drench with a liquid. **2** extinguish a light.

**dove** n. **1** a bird with a thick body and short legs. **2** a person favouring negotiation rather than violence.

**dovetail** n. a wedge-shaped joint interlocking two pieces of wood. • v. fit together easily and neatly.

**dowager** n. a woman holding a title or property from her dead husband.

**dowdy** adj. (**-ier**, **-iest**) not smart or fashionable.
▷ SYNS FRUMPY, unfashionable, inelegant; inf. mumsy.

**dowel** n. a headless wooden or metal pin holding pieces of wood or stone together.

**down**[1] adv. **1** to, in, or at a lower place or position. **2** to or at a lower level of intensity; to a smaller size. **3** from an earlier to a later point in time or order. **4** in or into a worse or weaker position. **5** in writing. • prep. from a higher to a lower point of; at or to a point further along. • adj. **1** directed or moving downwards. **2** depressed. **3** (of a computer system) not functioning. • v. inf. **1** knock down. **2** swallow. □ **down and out** homeless and without money. **downbeat** gloomy; relaxed and low-key. **downfall** a loss of power or status. **downgrade** move to a lower rank or level. **down-hearted** sad or discouraged. **downhill** towards the foot of a slope; into a worsening situation. **downmarket** cheap and of poor quality. **down payment** an initial payment when buying something on credit. **downpour** a heavy fall of rain. **downsize** reduce the number of employees in a company. **downstairs** on or to a lower floor. **downstream** in the direction in which a stream or river flows. **down-to-earth** practical and realistic. **downtown** esp. US in, to, or towards the central area of a city. **downtrodden** oppressed.

down under inf. Australia and New Zealand.

**down**[2] n. 1 very fine soft furry feathers or short hairs.
2 (**downs**) chalk uplands.
■ downy adj.

**downcast** adj. 1 sad or depressed. 2 (of eyes) looking downwards.
▷ SYNS DESPONDENT, disheartened, dispirited, depressed, dejected, disconsolate, crestfallen, sad, gloomy, glum.

**download** v. copy data from one computer to another.
• n. a downloaded computer file.

**downright** adj. utter; completely as described.
▷ SYNS COMPLETE, total, absolute, utter, thorough, out-and-out.

**dowry** n. (pl. **-ies**) property or money brought by a bride to her husband on marriage.

**dowse** v. search for underground water or minerals by using a stick which dips when these are present.

**doyen** n. (fem. **doyenne**) the most important or highly regarded person in a particular field.

**doze** v. sleep lightly. • n. a short light sleep. ■ dozy adj.

**dozen** n. 1 a set of twelve.
2 (**dozens**) very many.

**Dr** abbr. Doctor.

**drab** adj. (**drabber**, **drabbest**) dull in colour.
▷ SYNS DULL, colourless, grey, dingy, dreary, cheerless, dismal, gloomy.

**draconian** adj. harsh or strict.

**draft** n. 1 a preliminary version of a piece of writing. 2 a written order to a bank to pay a specified sum. 3 US military

conscription. 4 US sp. of **DRAUGHT**. • v. 1 prepare a draft of.
2 US conscript for military service.
▷ SYNS n. OUTLINE, plan, skeleton, abstract, bare bones.

**drafty** US sp. of **DRAUGHTY**.

**drag** v. 1 pull along with effort.
2 trail along the ground. 3 (of time) pass slowly. 4 search the bottom of a lake etc. with nets or hooks. 5 move an image across a computer screen using a mouse. • n. 1 inf. a boring or tiresome person or thing. 2 the force exerted by air or water to slow down a moving object. 3 inf. an act of inhaling on a cigarette.
4 inf. women's clothes worn by a man.
▷ SYNS v. HAUL, pull, tug, heave, draw; trail, tow; inf. yank, lug.

**dragon** n. a mythical reptile able to breathe out fire.
□ dragonfly a long-bodied insect with two pairs of wings.

**dragoon** n. a cavalryman or (formerly) mounted infantryman. • v. force into action.

**drain** v. 1 draw liquid out of; become dry; draw off liquid by channels or pipes; flow away.
2 gradually deprive of strength or resources. 3 drink all the contents of. • n. 1 a channel or pipe carrying off water or liquid waste. 2 something that deprives you of energy or resources. ■ drainage n.
▷ SYNS v. 1 DRAW OFF, extract, remove, siphon off, pump out, bleed. 2 FLOW, pour, run; seep, leak, trickle, ooze. 3 USE UP, exhaust, deplete, sap. • n. CHANNEL, pipe, sewer, conduit.

**drake** n. a male duck.

**dram** n. a small drink of spirits.

**drama** n. a play; plays and acting; an exciting series of events.

**dramatic** adj. **1** of plays and acting. **2** exciting, striking, impressive. ■ **dramatically** adv.
▷ SYNS **1** THEATRICAL, stage, thespian. **2** EXCITING, action-packed, sensational, spectacular, thrilling, suspenseful, electrifying, stirring.

**dramatist** n. a writer of plays.
▷ SYNS PLAYWRIGHT, scriptwriter, screenwriter.

**dramatize** (or **-ise**) v. **1** present a novel etc. as a play or film. **2** cause to seem more exciting or serious. ■ **dramatization** n.

**drank** past of DRINK.

**drape** v. spread covers loosely over something.

**drastic** adj. having an extreme or violent effect.
▷ SYNS EXTREME, serious, desperate, radical; heavy, severe, harsh, draconian.

**draught** (US **draft**) n. **1** a current of air in a confined space. **2** an amount of liquid swallowed at one time. **3** (**draughts**) a game played with 24 round pieces on a chessboard. **4** the depth of water needed to float a ship. • adj. used for pulling loads. □ **draughtsman** a person who makes detailed technical plans or drawings. ■ **draughty** adj.

**draw** v. **1** create a picture or diagram by marking a surface. **2** pull; take out or from a store; take in breath. **3** attract. **4** finish a contest with scores equal. **5** pick lots to decide an outcome. **6** make your way: *draw near*. • n. **1** a lottery; an act of drawing lots. **2** a contest with equal closing scores.

**3** something that attracts. □ **drawbridge** a bridge hinged at one end so that it can be raised. **draw up** come to a halt; prepare a contract etc.
▷ SYNS v. **1** SKETCH, delineate, design, trace, portray, depict. **2** PULL, haul, drag, tug, yank, tow, trail, lug. **3** ATTRACT, interest, win, capture, lure, entice. **4** DRAIN, siphon off, pump out. • n. **1** LURE, attraction, pull, appeal, allure. **2** LOTTERY, raffle, sweepstake. **3** TIE, dead heat, stalemate.

**drawback** n. a disadvantage.
▷ SYNS DISADVANTAGE, catch, problem, snag, difficulty, trouble, hitch, stumbling block.

**drawer** n. **1** a lidless compartment sliding horizontally into and out of a piece of furniture. **2** a person who draws. **3** (**drawers**) knickers or underpants.

**drawing** n. a picture made with a pencil or pen. □ **drawing pin** a pin for fastening paper to a surface. **drawing room** a sitting room.
▷ SYNS PICTURE, sketch, illustration, portrayal, representation, depiction; diagram.

**drawl** v. speak slowly with prolonged vowel sounds. • n. a drawling manner of speaking.

**drawn** p.p. of DRAW. • adj. looking strained from tiredness or worry.

**dread** n. great fear. • v. fear greatly.
▷ SYNS n. FEAR, fright, terror, trepidation, foreboding.

**dreadful** adj. very bad or unpleasant. ■ **dreadfully** adv.
▷ SYNS **1** TERRIBLE, frightful, horrible, grim, awful, dire;

horrifying, alarming, shocking, distressing, appalling, harrowing; ghastly, fearful, horrendous. **2** NASTY, unpleasant, disagreeable, repugnant, revolting, distasteful, odious.

**dream** n. a series of pictures or events in a sleeping person's mind; something greatly desired; something unreal or impossible. • v. **1** have a dream while asleep; have an ambition or desire. **2** (**dream up**) invent or imagine something foolish or improbable.
▷ SYNS n. **1** VISION, nightmare, hallucination, fantasy; daydream, reverie. **2** AMBITION, aspiration, hope, goal, aim, objective, desire, wish.

**dreamy** adj. absorbed in a daydream.

**dreary** adj. (**-ier**, **-iest**) depressingly dull; gloomy. ■ **drearily** adv.
▷ SYNS DULL, uninteresting, uneventful, tedious, boring, humdrum, monotonous, wearisome.

**dredge** v. scoop up mud and objects from the bed of a river etc. ■ **dredger** n.

**dregs** pl.n. sediment at the bottom of a drink; the least useful, attractive, or valuable part.

**drench** v. wet all through.
▷ SYNS SOAK, saturate, wet through.

**dress** n. **1** a woman's or girl's garment with a bodice and skirt. **2** clothing. • v. **1** put clothes on. **2** put a dressing on. **3** decorate. **4** (**dress up**) put on smart or formal clothes. □ **dress rehearsal** a final rehearsal, in

full costume, of a dramatic production.
▷ SYNS n. **1** FROCK, gown, robe. **2** CLOTHES, clothing, garments, attire, costume, outfit, ensemble. • v. CLOTHE, attire, garb.

**dressage** n. exercises to show off a horse's obedience and deportment.

**dresser** n. a sideboard with shelves above it.

**dressing** n. **1** a sauce for salad. **2** a protective covering for a wound. □ **dressing down** inf. a scolding. **dressing gown** a loose robe worn when you are not fully dressed. **dressing table** a table topped by a mirror, used while dressing or applying make-up.

**dressy** adj. (**-ier**, **-iest**) (of clothes) smart or formal.

**drew** past of DRAW.

**dribble** v. **1** flow in drops; have saliva flowing from the mouth. **2** (in football etc.) move the ball forward with slight touches. • n. a thin stream of liquid; saliva running from the mouth.
▷ SYNS v. DROOL, slaver, slobber.

**dried** adj. past & p.p. of DRY.

**drier** n. = DRYER.

**drift** v. be carried by a current of water or air; go casually or aimlessly; pass gradually into a particular state. • n. **1** a drifting movement. **2** a mass of snow piled up by the wind. **3** the general meaning of a speech etc. □ **driftwood** pieces of wood floating on the sea or washed ashore.

**drifter** n. an aimless person.

**drill** n. **1** a tool or machine for boring holes or sinking wells. **2** training; repeated exercises.

• v. **1** bore a hole with a drill **2** train or be trained.

**drily** (or **dryly**) adv. in an ironically humorous way.

**drink** v. (**drank, drunk, drinking**) swallow liquid; consume alcohol, esp. to excess; express good wishes in a toast. • n. a liquid for drinking; alcohol. ■ **drinker** n.

▷ SYNS v. **1** SWALLOW, sip, swill, swig, quaff. **2** IMBIBE, tipple. • n. ALCOHOL, liquor, spirits; inf. booze.

**drip** v. (**dripped, dripping**) fall or let fall in small drops. • n. **1** a small drop of a liquid. **2** a device for slowly passing a substance into a patient's body through a vein. **3** inf. a weak person.

▷ SYNS DRIBBLE, trickle, drop, drizzle, leak.

**dripping** n. fat melted from roast meat.

**drive** v. **1** operate a motor vehicle. **2** carry in a vehicle. **3** carry or urge along. **4** make someone act in a particular way. **5** provide the energy to work a machine. • n. **1** a journey in a car. **2** a short private road leading to a house. **3** determination and ambition. **4** a natural urge. **5** an organized effort to achieve something. ■ **driver** n.

▷ SYNS v. **1** OPERATE, handle, manage, pilot, steer. **2** FORCE, compel, impel, make, prompt, spur. • n. **1** EXCURSION, outing, trip, jaunt; ride, run, journey. **2** DETERMINATION, ambition, motivation, enthusiasm, commitment, energy, vigour; inf. get-up-and-go.

**drivel** n. nonsense.

**drizzle** n. very fine drops of rain. • v. rain very lightly.

**droll** adj. strange and amusing.

**dromedary** n. a camel with one hump.

**drone** n. **1** a deep humming sound. **2** a male bee. • v. make a humming sound; speak monotonously.

**drool** v. **1** slaver. **2** show great pleasure or desire.

**droop** v. bend or hang down limply. ■ **droopy** adj.

**drop** n. **1** a small rounded mass of liquid. **2** a small drink. **3** an abrupt fall or slope. • v. **1** fall or let fall. **2** make or become lower or less. **3** give up a course of action. **4** set down a passenger or load. □ **droplet** a small drop of liquid. **drop off** fall asleep. **dropout** a person who lives an alternative lifestyle or has given up a course of study. **drop out** stop participating.

▷ SYNS n. **1** DROPLET, globule, bead, bubble, blob. **2** a drop in prices: DECREASE, fall, decline, reduction, cut, slump. **3** a steep drop: INCLINE, slope, descent, declivity. • v. FALL, descend, plunge, dive, plummet, tumble, dip, sink, pitch.

**droppings** pl.n. animal dung.

**dross** n. rubbish.

**drought** n. a very long period of little or no rainfall.

**drove**¹ past of **DRIVE**.

**drove**² n. **1** a flock of animals being herded along. **2** a large number of people.

**drown** v. **1** die or kill by submersion in water. **2** make inaudible by being much louder.

▷ SYNS FLOOD, submerge, inundate, deluge, swamp, engulf.

**drowse** v. be half asleep; doze.

**drowsy** adj. (**-ier, -iest**) sleepy. ■ **drowsily** adv. **drowsiness** n.

**drubbing** n. inf. a thorough defeat.

**drudge** n. a person who does laborious or menial work.
■ drudgery n.

**drug** n. **1** a substance used as a medicine. **2** an illegal substance taken for its effects on the body. • v. (drugged, drugging) give or add a drug to.
□ drugstore US a chemist's shop also selling toiletries etc.
▷ SYNS n. **1** MEDICINE, medication, remedy, cure, antidote. **2** NARCOTIC, stimulant, hallucinogen; inf. dope, gear.

**Druid** n. an ancient Celtic priest.

**drum** n. a round frame with a membrane stretched across, used as a percussion instrument; a cylindrical object.
• v. (drummed, drumming) play a drum; make a continuous rhythmic noise; tap your fingers repeatedly on a surface.
□ drumstick a stick used for beating a drum; the lower part of a cooked chicken's leg.
■ drummer n.

**drunk** p.p. of DRINK. • adj. unable to think or speak clearly from drinking too much alcohol. • n. a person who is drunk.
■ drunkard n. drunken adj. drunkenness n.
▷ SYNS adj. INTOXICATED, inebriated, merry, tipsy; inf. tiddly, plastered, paralytic, sloshed, tight. • n. DRUNKARD, alcoholic, dipsomaniac.

**dry** adj. **1** without moisture or liquid. **2** uninteresting. **3** (of humour) subtle and understated. **4** (of wine) not sweet. • v. **1** make or become dry; preserve food by removing its moisture. **2** (dry up) dry washed dishes; decrease and stop. □ dry-clean clean with chemicals without using water. dry rot a fungus that causes wood to decay. dry run inf. a rehearsal.
▷ SYNS adj. ARID, parched, dehydrated, desiccated, withered, shrivelled.

**dryer** (or **drier**) n. a device for drying things.

**dryly** = DRILY.

**dual** adj. composed of two parts; double. □ dual carriageway a road with a central strip separating traffic travelling in opposite directions.

**dub** v. (dubbed, dubbing) **1** give a film a soundtrack in a language other than the original. **2** give a nickname to. **3** confer a knighthood on.

**dubious** adj. **1** doubtful or hesitant. **2** probably not honest. **3** of uncertain value.
▷ SYNS **1** DOUBTFUL, uncertain, unsure, hesitant, undecided, irresolute, sceptical. **2** SUSPICIOUS, suspect, questionable, untrustworthy, unreliable; inf. dodgy.

**duchess** n. **1** a duke's wife or widow. **2** a woman holding a rank equivalent to duke.

**duchy** n. (pl. -ies) the territory of a duke.

**duck** n. **1** a waterbird with a broad blunt bill and webbed feet. **2** a female duck. **3** a batsman's score of 0. • v. **1** lower your head or body to avoid a blow or so as not to be seen. **2** push someone under water. **3** inf. avoid a duty. □ duckboards wooden slats forming a path over mud. duckling a young duck.

**duct** n. a channel or tube conveying liquid or air; a tube in the body through which fluid passes.
▷ SYNS PIPE, tube, conduit, channel, passage, canal, culvert.

**ductile** adj. (of metal) able to be drawn into fine strands.

**dud** inf. n. something that fails to work.

**dudgeon** n. deep resentment.

**due** adj. **1** expected or scheduled at a particular time. **2** owed or deserving something. **3** needing to be paid; owing. **4** proper or required. • n. **1** what is owed to or deserved by someone. **2** (**dues**) fees. • adv. directly:
□ due to **1** caused by. **2** because of.
▷ SYNS adj. **1** OWING, owed, payable, unpaid, outstanding. **2** DESERVED, merited, justified. **3** PROPER, correct, rightful, fitting, appropriate, apt.

**duel** n. a fight or contest between two people or sides. • v. (**duelled**, **duelling**; US **dueled**) fight a duel.

**duet** n. a musical composition for two performers.

**duffel coat** n. a heavy woollen coat with a hood.

**duffer** n. inf. an inefficient or stupid person.

**dug** past & p.p. of **DIG**.

**dugout** n. **1** an underground shelter. **2** a canoe made from a hollowed tree trunk.

**duke** n. a nobleman of the highest hereditary rank; a ruler of certain small states.
■ dukedom n.

**dulcet** adj. sounding sweet.

**dulcimer** n. a musical instrument with strings struck with hand-held hammers.

**dull** adj. **1** not interesting or exciting. **2** not bright, resonant, or sharp. **3** stupid. • v. make or become less intense, sharp, or bright. ■ dully adv.
▷ SYNS adj. **1** UNINTERESTING, boring, tedious, tiresome, wearisome, monotonous, flat, unimaginative, uninspiring, lacklustre. **2** dull colours: DRAB, dreary, sombre, faded, washed-out. **3** dull weather: OVERCAST, cloudy, gloomy, dreary, dark, leaden, murky, lowering. **4** a dull thud: MUTED, muffled, indistinct.

**dullard** n. a stupid person.

**duly** adv. as is required or appropriate; as might be expected.

**dumb** adj. **1** unable or unwilling to speak; silent. **2** inf. stupid. v. (**dumb down**) inf. make less intellectually challenging.
□ dumb-bell a short bar with weighted ends, lifted to exercise muscles.

**dumbfound** v. astonish greatly.
▷ SYNS ASTOUND, amaze, astonish, startle, stun, stagger.

**dummy** n. (pl. **-ies**) **1** a model or replica of a human being; a model of something used as a substitute. **2** a rubber teat for a baby to suck. □ dummy run a trial or rehearsal.

**dump** v. deposit as rubbish; put down carelessly; end a relationship with. • n. a site for depositing rubbish or waste; a temporary store; a dull or unpleasant place.
▷ SYNS v. DISPOSE OF, get rid of, discard, throw away/out,

scrap, jettison. • n. TIP, rubbish dump, scrapyard.

**dumpling** n. a ball of dough cooked in stew or with fruit inside.

**dun** adj. & n. greyish brown.

**dunce** n. a person slow at learning.

**dune** n. a mound of drifted sand.

**dung** n. animal excrement.

**dungarees** pl.n. overalls of coarse cotton cloth.

**dungeon** n. a strong underground cell for prisoners.

**dunk** v. dip food into soup or a drink before eating it.

**duo** n. (pl. **-os**) a pair of performers; a duet.

**duodenum** n. the part of the intestine next to the stomach. ■ **duodenal** adj.

**dupe** v. deceive or trick. • n. a duped person.

**duplicate** n. an exact copy. • adj. exactly like something speci-fied; having two identical parts. • v. make or be an exact copy of; do something again un-necessarily. ■ **duplication** n. **duplicator** n.
▷ SYNS n. COPY, photocopy, carbon copy; replica, reproduction. • adj. MATCHING, twin, identical, corresponding.

**duplicity** n. deceitful be-haviour.
▷ SYNS DECEIT, dishonesty, decep-tion, double-dealing, chicanery.

**durable** adj. hard-wearing. • pl.n. goods that can be kept without immediate consumption or replacement. ■ **durability** n.
▷ SYNS adj. LONG-LASTING, hard-wearing, strong, sturdy, tough.

**duration** n. the time during which a thing continues.

**duress** n. the use of force or threats.

**during** prep. throughout; at a point in the duration of.

**dusk** n. a darker stage of twilight.
▷ SYNS TWILIGHT, sunset, sundown, nightfall, gloaming.

**dusky** adj. darkish in colour.

**dust** n. fine particles of earth or other matter. • v. 1 wipe dust from the surface of. 2 cover lightly with a powdered substance. □ **dustbin** a large container for household rubbish. **dustman** a man employed to empty dustbins. **dustpan** a container into which dust and waste can be swept. ■ **dusty** adj.

**duster** n. a cloth for wiping dust from things.

**Dutch** adj. of the Netherlands. □ **Dutch courage** false courage obtained by drinking alcohol. **go Dutch** share expenses on an outing.

**dutiful** adj. obedient and conscientious. ■ **dutifully** adv.
▷ SYNS CONSCIENTIOUS, obedient, deferential, respectful, filial.

**duty** n. 1 a moral or legal obli-gation; a task that you are required to perform. 2 a tax on imports etc.
▷ SYNS 1 RESPONSIBILITY, obli-gation, commitment. 2 JOB, task, assignment, mission, function, charge, role.

**duvet** n. a thick soft bed quilt.

**dwarf** n. (pl. **dwarfs** or **dwarves**) 1 a mythical short human-like being. 2 an unusually small person. • v. cause to seem small by comparison.

**dwell** v. (**dwelt**, **dwelling**) 1 live as an inhabitant. 2 (**dwell on**) write, speak, or think lengthily about.

**dwelling** n. a house etc. to live in.

**dwindle** v. gradually become smaller or weaker.
▷ SYNS DIMINISH, decrease, decline, reduce, lessen, shrink.

**dye** n. a substance used to colour something. • v. (**dyed**, **dyeing**) colour something with dye.
▷ SYNS n. COLOUR, shade, tint, pigment.

**dying** present participle of DIE.

**dyke** (or **dike**) n. **1** a wall or embankment to prevent flooding. **2** a drainage ditch.

**dynamic** adj. **1** constantly changing or active. **2** full of energy and new ideas. **3** Physics of forces producing motion.
■ **dynamically** adv.
▷ SYNS ENERGETIC, vigorous, active, lively, spirited, forceful, powerful.

**dynamics** n. **1** the study of the forces involved in movement;

forces stimulating growth and change. **2** the variations in volume in a musical work.

**dynamism** n. the quality of being full of energy, vigour, or enthusiasm.

**dynamite** n. a powerful explosive. • v. blow up with dynamite.

**dynamo** n. (pl. **-os**) a small generator producing electric current.

**dynasty** n. (pl. **-ies**) a line of hereditary rulers.

**dysentery** n. a disease causing severe diarrhoea.

**dysfunctional** adj. **1** not operating normally. **2** unable to deal with normal relationships between people.

**dyslexia** n. a condition causing difficulty in reading and spelling. ■ **dyslexic** adj. & n.

**dyspepsia** n. indigestion.
■ **dyspeptic** adj. & n.

# Ee

**E** abbr. **1** east or eastern. **2** inf. the drug Ecstasy.

**each** adj. & pron. every one of two or more, taken separately. • adv. to or for each one individually.

**eager** adj. full of desire, interest, or enthusiasm.
▷ SYNS **1** KEEN, enthusiastic, avid; inf. raring. **2** LONGING, yearning, anxious, intent, agog, impatient.

**eagle** n. a large, keen-sighted bird of prey.

**ear** n. **1** the organ of hearing. **2** an ability to recognize and appreciate music or language. **3** the seed-bearing part of corn. □ **eardrum** a membrane in the ear which vibrates in response to sound waves. **earmark** choose for a particular purpose. **earphones** devices worn on the ears to receive communications or listen to a radio. **earring** a piece of jewellery worn on the ear. **earwig** a small insect with pincers at its rear end. **within** (or **out of**) **earshot** near enough (or too distant) to be heard.

**earl** n. a British nobleman ranking between marquess and viscount.

**early** adj. & adv. (**-ier, -iest**) before the expected time; near the beginning of a period or sequence.
▷ SYNS **1** ADVANCED, forward; premature, untimely. **2** AHEAD OF TIME, beforehand, in good time. **3** *early man:* PRIMITIVE, prehistoric, ancient.

**earn** v. get or deserve for work or merit; (of invested money) gain as interest.
▷ SYNS **1** GET, make, clear, bring in, take home, gross, net. **2** GAIN, win, achieve, secure, obtain, merit, deserve.

**earnest** adj. very serious.
▷ SYNS **1** SERIOUS, solemn, sober, staid. **2** HEARTFELT, wholehearted, sincere, fervent, ardent.

**earth** n. **1** (also **Earth**) the planet we live on. **2** soil. **3** electrical connection to the ground. • v. connect an electrical device to earth. □ **earthquake** a sudden violent movement in the earth's crust. **earthworm** a worm that burrows in the soil.
▷ SYNS n. SOIL, clay, loam, turf, ground.

**earthenware** n. pottery made of baked clay.

**earthly** adj. **1** relating to the earth or human life. **2** used for emphasis: *no earthly reason.*

▷ SYNS WORLDLY, temporal, mortal, human, material, carnal, fleshly, physical, corporeal.

**earthy** adj. (**-ier, -iest**) **1** like soil. **2** (of humour etc.) direct and uninhibited.

**ease** n. **1** lack of difficulty. **2** freedom from problems. • v. **1** make or become less severe or intense. **2** move carefully or gradually.
▷ SYNS n. **1** EFFORTLESSNESS, simplicity. **2** COMFORT, affluence, wealth, prosperity, luxury.
• v. RELIEVE, alleviate, mitigate, soothe, palliate, moderate, reduce, lighten, diminish, lessen.

**easel** n. a frame to support a painting, blackboard, etc.

**east** n. the direction in which the sun rises; the eastern part of a place. • adj. & adv. towards or facing the east; (of wind) from the east. ■ **easterly** adj. & adv. **eastern** adj. **eastward** adj.

**Easter** n. the Christian festival commemorating Jesus's resurrection.

**easy** adj. **1** achieved without great effort. **2** free from worries or problems. ■ **easily** adv.
▷ SYNS SIMPLE, uncomplicated, straightforward, undemanding, effortless, painless, trouble-free.

**easy-going** adj. relaxed in manner.
▷ SYNS RELAXED, even-tempered, carefree, happy-go-lucky, placid, tolerant, undemanding, amiable, good-natured, patient, understanding; inf. laid-back.

**eat** v. (**ate, eaten, eating**) chew and swallow food; use up resources; erode or destroy. ■ **eatable** adj.

▷ SYNS **1** CONSUME, devour, swallow, chew, munch, bolt, wolf, tuck into, ingest; inf. scoff. **2** ERODE, wear away, corrode; damage, destroy.

**eau de cologne** n. a delicate perfume.

**eaves** pl.n. the overhanging edge of a roof.

**eavesdrop** v. (**eavesdropped**, **eavesdropping**) listen secretly to a private conversation. ■ **eavesdropper** n.

**ebb** n. the movement of the tide out to sea. • v. **1** flow away. **2** decline.

**ebony** n. the hard black wood of a tropical tree. • adj. black as ebony.

**ebullient** adj. full of high spirits. ■ **ebullience** n.

**eccentric** adj. unconventional and strange. • n. an eccentric person. ■ **eccentrically** adv. **eccentricity** n.

▷ SYNS adj. ODD, strange, queer, peculiar, unconventional, idiosyncratic, quirky, weird, bizarre, outlandish; inf. offbeat.

**ecclesiastical** adj. of the Christian Church or clergy.

**echo** n. (pl. **-oes**) a repetition of sound caused by reflection of sound waves. • v. **1** reverberate or be repeated as an echo. **2** repeat someone's words.

▷ SYNS v. REVERBERATE, resonate, resound.

**éclair** n. a finger-shaped pastry cake with cream filling.

**eclectic** adj. taking ideas from a wide range of sources.

**eclipse** n. **1** the blocking of light from one planet etc. by another. **2** a loss of significance or power. • v. **1** (of a planet etc.) block the light from or to another.

**2** make less significant or powerful.

▷ SYNS v. OUTSHINE, overshadow, surpass, exceed, transcend.

**eco-friendly** adj. not harmful to the environment.

**ecology** n. (the study of) relationships of living things to each other and to their environment. ■ **ecological** adj. **ecologist** n.

**economic** adj. **1** of economics or the economy. **2** profitable.

**economical** adj. thrifty or avoiding waste. ■ **economically** adv.

▷ SYNS **1** THRIFTY, sparing, careful, prudent, frugal, penny-pinching, parsimonious. **2** CHEAP, inexpensive, low-cost.

**economics** n. the science of the production and use of goods or services; (as pl.) the financial aspects of a region or group. ■ **economist** n.

**economize** (or **-ise**) v. reduce your expenses.

▷ SYNS CUT BACK, cut costs, scrimp, save, retrench, tighten your belt.

**economy** n. (pl. **-ies**) **1** a country's system of using its resources to produce wealth. **2** being economical.

**ecosystem** n. a system of interacting organisms and their environment.

**ecstasy** n. **1** intense delight. **2** (**Ecstasy**) a hallucinogenic drug.

▷ SYNS BLISS, rapture, joy, elation, euphoria.

**ecstatic** adj. very happy or excited. ■ **ecstatically** adv.

▷ SYNS EUPHORIC, elated, rapturous, blissful, joyful, overjoyed, delighted, delirious, on cloud nine, in seventh heaven.

**eczema** n. a skin disease causing scaly itching patches.

**eddy** n. (pl. **-ies**) a circular movement in water or air etc. • v. swirl in eddies.

**edge** n. **1** the outer limit of an area or object; the area next to a steep drop. **2** the sharpened side of a blade; the narrow side of a thin, flat object. **3** a position of advantage. • v. **1** provide with a border. **2** move slowly and carefully. □ **on edge** tense or nervous.
▷ SYNS n. **1** BORDER, boundary, extremity, fringe, margin, side; lip, rim, brim, brink, verge; perimeter, circumference, periphery, limits, bounds. **2** ADVANTAGE, superiority, upper hand, ascendancy, whip hand. • v. CREEP, inch; sidle, steal, slink.

**edgy** adj. (**-ier**, **-iest**) tense and irritable.
▷ SYNS NERVOUS, tense, anxious, apprehensive, on tenterhooks, uneasy, jumpy; inf. uptight.

**edible** adj. suitable for eating.

**edict** n. an order issued by someone in authority.

**edifice** n. a large, imposing building.

**edify** v. (**edified**, **edifying**) improve the mind or character of. ■ **edification** n.

**edit** v. (**edited**, **editing**) prepare written material for publication; choose and arrange material for a film etc.
▷ SYNS CORRECT, emend, revise, rewrite, reword; shorten, condense, cut, abridge.

**edition** n. a version of a published text; all the copies of a text etc. issued at one time;

one instance of a regular broadcast programme.

**editor** n. a person responsible for the contents of a newspaper etc. or a section of this; a person who edits.

**editorial** adj. of an editor. • n. a newspaper article giving the editor's comments.

**educate** v. train the mind, character, and abilities of; teach.
▷ SYNS TEACH, instruct, tutor, school, coach, train; inform, enlighten.

**educated** adj. showing or having had a good education.
▷ SYNS INFORMED, literate, well read, knowledgeable, learned, enlightened, cultured.

**education** n. **1** the process of teaching, training, or learning. **2** the theory of teaching. ■ **educational** adj. **educationally** adv.

**EEC** abbr. European Economic Community.

**eel** n. a snakelike fish.

**eerie** adj. (**-ier**, **-iest**) mysterious and frightening. ■ **eerily** adv.
▷ SYNS UNCANNY, unearthly, ghostly, mysterious, strange, odd, weird, frightening; inf. spooky, scary.

**efface** v. rub out or obliterate; make inconspicuous.

**effect** n. **1** a change produced by an action or cause. **2** a state of being operative. **3** (**effects**) personal belongings. **4** (**effects**) lighting, sound, etc. used in a play or film. • v. bring about or cause.
▷ SYNS n. **1** RESULT, outcome, consequence, upshot, repercussions, ramifications, impact, aftermath.

**2** EFFECTIVENESS, success, influence, efficacy, power.

**effective** adj. **1** achieving the intended result; operative. **2** fulfilling a function in fact though not officially.
▷ SYNS SUCCESSFUL, effectual, efficacious, potent, powerful; helpful, beneficial, advantageous, valuable, useful.

**effectual** adj. effective.

**effeminate** adj. (of a man) feminine in appearance or manner. ■ effeminacy n.

**effervescent** adj. fizzy; vivacious or high-spirited.
■ effervesce v. effervescence n.
▷ SYNS BUBBLY, fizzy, frothy, foamy, sparkling, carbonated.

**efficacious** adj. effective.
■ efficacy n.

**efficient** adj. working well with no waste of money or effort.
■ efficiency n.
▷ SYNS WELL ORGANIZED, methodical, systematic, capable, competent, productive, businesslike; streamlined, cost-effective.

**effigy** n. (pl. **-ies**) a model of a person.
▷ SYNS STATUE, statuette, figurine, model, likeness, image.

**effluent** n. liquid sewage.

**effort** n. **1** a determined attempt. **2** the physical or mental energy needed to do something. ■ effortless adj.
▷ SYNS **1** ATTEMPT, try, endeavour; inf. shot, stab. **2** EXERTION, energy, work, application.

**effrontery** n. bold insolence.

**effusive** adj. expressing emotion in an unrestrained way.

▷ SYNS GUSHING, unrestrained, extravagant, fulsome, lavish, enthusiastic.

**e.g.** abbr. for example.

**egalitarian** adj. holding the principle of equal rights for all.
■ egalitarianism n.

**egg** n. **1** an oval or round object laid by a female bird, reptile, etc., containing an embryo. **2** an ovum. • v. (**egg on**) urge or encourage.

**ego** n. self; self-esteem.

**egocentric** adj. self-centred.

**egotism** n. the quality of being too conceited or self-absorbed.
■ egotist n.

**egotistic** adj. very conceited or self-centred. ■ egotistical adj.
▷ SYNS EGOCENTRIC, self-absorbed, self-centred, self-obsessed; narcissistic, vain.

**egregious** adj. outstandingly bad.

**eider** n. a large northern duck.
□ eiderdown a quilt filled with down or other soft material.

**eight** adj. & n. one more than seven; 8. ■ eighth adj. & n.

**eighteen** adj. & n. one more than seventeen; 18.
■ eighteenth adj. & n.

**eighty** adj. & n. ten times eight; 80. ■ eightieth adj. & n.

**either** adj. & pron. one or other of two; each of two. • adv. & conj. **1** as the first alternative. **2** likewise (used with negatives): *I don't like him and she doesn't either.*

**ejaculate** v. **1** eject semen. **2** say suddenly. ■ ejaculation n.

**eject** v. throw or force out.
■ ejection n. ejector n.
▷ SYNS EVICT, expel, throw out, force out, remove.

**eke** v. (**eke out**) make a supply etc. last longer by careful use; make a living laboriously.

**elaborate** adj. intricate or complicated. • v. develop in detail; add detail to.
■ elaboration n.
▷ SYNS adj. 1 COMPLICATED, detailed, complex, involved, intricate, convoluted. 2 ORNATE, fancy, showy, fussy, ostentatious, extravagant, baroque, rococo. • v. EXPAND ON, enlarge on, flesh out, add to.

**elan** n. energy and flair.

**elapse** v. (of time) pass.

**elastic** adj. going back to its original length or shape after being stretched or squeezed. • n. cord or material made elastic by interweaving strands of rubber etc. ■ elasticity n.
▷ SYNS adj. STRETCHY, stretchable, flexible, springy, pliant, pliable, supple.

**elated** adj. very happy and excited. ■ elation n.

**elbow** n. the joint between the forearm and upper arm. • v. strike or push with your elbow. □ elbow room enough space to move or work in.

**elder** adj. older. • n. 1 an older person. 2 a tree with small dark berries.

**elderly** adj. old.
▷ SYNS OLD, aged, ageing, ancient, long in the tooth, past your prime.

**eldest** adj. oldest.

**elect** v. choose by vote; decide on a course of action. • adj. chosen; elected but not yet in office.
▷ SYNS v. VOTE FOR, choose, pick, select; opt, decide.

**election** n. an occasion when representatives, office-holders, etc. are chosen by vote; electing or being elected.
▷ SYNS BALLOT, poll, vote, referendum, plebiscite.

**electioneering** n. campaigning to be elected to a political position.

**elective** adj. 1 using or chosen by election. 2 optional.

**elector** n. a person entitled to vote in an election. ■ electoral adj.

**electorate** n. the people entitled to vote in an election.

**electric** adj. of, producing, or worked by electricity. • n. (**electrics**) electrical fittings.

**electrical** adj. of electricity.
■ electrically adv.

**electrician** n. a person whose job is to deal with electrical equipment.

**electricity** n. a form of energy occurring in certain particles; a supply of electric current.

**electrify** v. (**electrified, electrifying**) charge with electricity; convert to the use of electric power.
■ electrification n.

**electrocute** v. kill by electric shock. ■ electrocution n.

**electrode** n. a solid conductor through which electricity enters or leaves a vacuum tube etc.

**electron** n. a subatomic particle with a negative electric charge.

**electronic** adj. having many small components, e.g. microchips, that control an electric current; concerned with electronic equipment; carried out using a computer.
■ electronically adv.

**electronics** pl.n. **1** the study of electrons or electronic devices. **2** electronic circuits or devices.

**elegant** adj. graceful and stylish. ■ **elegance** n.
▷ SYNS STYLISH, graceful, tasteful, artistic, fashionable, sophisticated, chic, smart, dashing, debonair.

**elegy** n. (pl. **-ies**) a sorrowful poem. ■ **elegiac** adj.

**element** n. **1** a basic part. **2** a substance that cannot be broken down into other substances. **3** earth, air, fire, and water, formerly thought to make up all matter. **4** a trace. **5** (**the elements**) weather. **6** a part that gives out heat in an electrical appliance. □ **in your element** in a situation or activity that suits you perfectly. ■ **elemental** adj.
▷ SYNS COMPONENT, constituent, part, piece, factor, feature, ingredient, unit, module.

**elementary** adj. dealing with the simplest facts of a subject.
▷ SYNS **1** BASIC, introductory, preparatory, fundamental, rudimentary. **2** EASY, simple, straightforward, uncomplicated.

**elephant** n. a very large animal with a trunk and ivory tusks.

**elevate** v. raise to a higher position or level.

**elevation** n. raising or being raised; altitude; a hill.

**elevator** n. US a lift.

**eleven** adj. & n. one more than ten; 11. ■ **eleventh** adj. & n.

**elf** n. (pl. **elves**) an imaginary small being with magic powers.
▷ SYNS FAIRY, pixie, sprite, goblin, hobgoblin, imp, puck.

**elicit** v. draw out a response.
▷ SYNS BRING OUT, draw out, obtain, evoke, call forth.

**eligible** adj. **1** qualified or having the right to something. **2** desirable as a marriage partner. ■ **eligibility** n.
▷ SYNS **1** ENTITLED, permitted, allowed, qualified, able. **2** DESIRABLE, suitable; available, single, unmarried, unattached.

**eliminate** v. get rid of; exclude. ■ **elimination** n.

**elite** n. a group regarded as superior and favoured.

**elitism** n. favouring of or dominance by a selected group. ■ **elitist** n. & adj.

**elixir** n. a liquid used for medicinal or magical purposes.

**elk** n. a large deer.

**ellipse** n. a regular oval shape. ■ **elliptical** adj.

**elm** n. a tree with rough serrated leaves.

**elocution** n. the skill of speaking clearly.

**elongate** v. lengthen.

**elope** v. run away secretly to get married. ■ **elopement** n.

**eloquence** n. fluent and persuasive use of language.

**eloquent** adj. fluent or persuasive.
▷ SYNS FLUENT, articulate, silver-tongued, expressive, persuasive, effective, lucid, vivid, graphic.

**else** adv. **1** in addition. **2** instead. □ **elsewhere** in or to another place. **or else** otherwise.

**elucidate** v. explain.

**elude** v. skilfully escape from; fail to be understood or achieved by.

▷ SYNS AVOID, dodge, evade, escape from, shake off, give someone the slip.

**elusive** adj. hard to find or achieve.

**emaciated** adj. abnormally thin. ■ emaciation n.

**email** n. **1** a message sent electronically from one computer user to another. **2** the system of sending emails. • v. send a message by email.

**emanate** v. originate from a source. ■ emanation n.

**emancipate** v. liberate or free from restrictions. ■ emancipation n.

**emasculate** v. make weaker or less effective. ■ emasculation n.

**embalm** v. preserve a corpse by using spices or chemicals.

**embankment** n. a bank or stone structure to keep a river from spreading or to carry a railway.

**embargo** n. (pl. **-oes**) an official ban on trade or another activity. • v. (**embargoed**, **embargoing**) impose an official ban on.
▷ SYNS n. BAN, bar, prohibition, proscription, veto, moratorium; boycott.

**embark** v. **1** board a ship. **2** (**embark on**) begin an undertaking. ■ embarkation n.

**embarrass** v. cause to feel self-conscious or ashamed. ■ embarrassment n.

**embarrassed** adj. feeling self-conscious or ashamed.
▷ SYNS MORTIFIED, red-faced, abashed, ashamed, shamefaced, humiliated, chagrined, awkward, self-conscious, sheepish.

**embassy** n. (pl. **-ies**) the official residence or offices of an ambassador.

**embattled** adj. beset by conflicts or problems.

**embed** (or **imbed**) v. (**embedded**, **embedding**) fix firmly in a surrounding mass.

**embellish** v. ornament; invent exciting details for a story. ■ embellishment n.
▷ SYNS DECORATE, adorn, ornament, beautify, enhance, trim, gild, festoon, deck.

**ember** n. a piece of burning coal or wood in a dying fire.

**embezzle** v. take company funds etc. fraudulently for your own use. ■ embezzlement n. embezzler n.
▷ SYNS STEAL, pilfer, misappropriate, filch, purloin.

**embittered** adj. resentful or bitter.

**emblem** n. a symbol or design used as a badge of something.
▷ SYNS CREST, insignia, badge, symbol, sign, representation, token, image, figure, mark.

**emblematic** adj. representing a particular quality or idea.

**embody** v. **1** give a tangible or visible form to. **2** include. ■ embodiment n.
▷ SYNS **1** PERSONIFY, represent, symbolize, stand for, typify, exemplify. **2** INCORPORATE, include, contain, encompass.

**embolism** n. obstruction of a blood vessel by a clot or air bubble.

**emboss** v. carve a raised design on.

**embrace** v. **1** hold someone closely in your arms. **2** accept or adopt; include. • n. an act of embracing.

▷ SYNS v. HUG, hold, cuddle, clasp, squeeze, enfold.

**embrocation** n. liquid for rubbing on the body to relieve aches.

**embroider** v. ornament with needlework; embellish a story. ■ embroidery n.

**embroil** v. involve in an argument or quarrel etc.

**embryo** n. (pl. **-os**) an animal developing in a womb or egg; something in an early stage of development.

**embryonic** adj. of an embryo; in a very early stage of development.

**emend** v. alter to remove errors. ■ emendation n.
▷ SYNS ALTER, change, edit, correct, revise, rewrite, improve, polish, refine.

**emerald** n. a bright green precious stone; its colour.

**emerge** v. come up or out into view; become known; recover from a difficult situation. ■ emergent adj.
▷ SYNS **1** APPEAR, surface, come out, materialize. **2** COME TO LIGHT, transpire.

**emergency** n. (pl. **-ies**) a serious situation needing prompt attention.
▷ SYNS CRISIS, accident, disaster, catastrophe, calamity.

**emery board** n. a strip of cardboard coated with a rough material, used for filing the nails.

**emigrate** v. leave one country and go to settle in another. ■ emigrant n. emigration n.

**émigré** n. an emigrant, esp. a political exile.

**eminence** n. fame or superiority; an important person.

**eminent** adj. famous or distinguished; outstanding. ■ eminently adv.
▷ SYNS IMPORTANT, great, distinguished, well known, celebrated, famous, renowned, noted, prominent, respected, esteemed, pre-eminent, outstanding.

**emissary** n. (pl. **-ies**) a person sent to conduct negotiations.

**emit** v. (**emitted**, **emitting**) send out light, heat, fumes, etc.; utter. ■ emission n.
▷ SYNS DISCHARGE, give out/off, issue, disgorge, vent, send forth, eject, spew out, emanate, radiate, exude, ooze, leak, excrete.

**emollient** adj. softening or soothing.

**emolument** n. a fee or salary.

**emotion** n. **1** a strong feeling. **2** instinctive feeling contrasted with reason.

**emotional** adj. of emotions; arousing or showing emotion. ■ emotionally adv.
▷ SYNS MOVING, touching, affecting, poignant, emotive, impassioned, heart-rending, tear-jerking, powerful.

**emotive** adj. arousing emotion.

**empathize** (or **-ise**) v. share and understand another's feelings.

**empathy** n. the ability to share and understand another's feelings.

**emperor** n. a male ruler of an empire.

**emphasis** n. (pl. **-ses**) special importance or prominence; stress on a sound or word; intensity of expression.

▷ SYNS PROMINENCE, importance, significance; stress, weight, accent, attention, priority.

**emphasize** (or **-ise**) v. stress; treat as important; make more noticeable.
▷ SYNS STRESS, underline, highlight, point up, spotlight; accent, accentuate, underscore.

**emphatic** adj. using or showing emphasis. ■ **emphatically** adv.
▷ SYNS FORCEFUL, vehement, firm, vigorous, forcible, categorical, unequivocal, definite, decided.

**emphysema** n. enlargement of the air sacs in the lungs, causing breathlessness.

**empire** n. a group of countries ruled by a supreme authority; a large organization controlled by one person or group.

**empirical** adj. based on observation or experiment rather than theory. ■ **empirically** adv.

**emplacement** n. a platform for a gun or battery of guns.

**employ** v. give work to; make use of. ■ **employer** n. **employment** n.
▷ SYNS **1** HIRE, engage, take on, recruit, appoint. **2** USE, make use of, utilize, apply, exercise, bring to bear.

**employee** n. a person employed.
▷ SYNS WORKER, member of staff; (**employees**) personnel, staff, workforce.

**empower** v. authorize or enable.
▷ SYNS AUTHORIZE, entitle, permit, allow, enable, license, qualify.

**empress** n. a female ruler of an empire; the wife of an emperor.

**empty** adj. **1** containing nothing; without occupants. **2** having no meaning or value. • v. make or become empty. ■ **emptiness** n.
▷ SYNS adj. **1** UNFILLED, vacant, unoccupied, uninhabited, hollow, void, bare, unadorned, blank. **2** MEANINGLESS, futile, ineffective, ineffectual, useless, insubstantial, idle, purposeless, aimless, worthless, valueless.
• v. VACATE, clear, evacuate; unload, void.

**emu** n. a large flightless Australian bird resembling an ostrich.

**emulate** v. match or surpass; imitate. ■ **emulation** n.

**emulsify** v. (**emulsified, emulsifying**) convert or be converted into emulsion.
■ **emulsifier** n.

**emulsion** n. **1** a mixture of two liquids in which particles of one are evenly distributed in the other. **2** a type of paint. **3** a light-sensitive coating on photographic film.

**enable** v. give the means or authority to do something.
▷ SYNS ALLOW, permit, equip, empower, facilitate, entitle, authorize, license.

**enact** v. **1** make into a law. **2** play a part or scene.
■ **enactment** n.

**enamel** n. **1** a glasslike coating for metal or pottery. **2** glossy paint. **3** the hard outer covering of teeth. • v. (**enamelled, enamelling**; US **enameled**) coat with enamel.

**enamoured** (US **enamored**) adj. fond.

**encampment** n. a camp.

**encapsulate** v. **1** symbolize or sum up. **2** summarize.

**encase** v. enclose in a case.

**enchant** v. delight; bewitch.
■ **enchanter** n. **enchantment** n.
**enchantress** n.

**enchanting** adj. delightful and
charming.
▷ SYNS CAPTIVATING, charming,
delightful, attractive,
appealing, engaging, irresistible, fascinating.

**encircle** v. surround.

**enclave** n. a small territory
wholly within the boundaries
of another.

**enclose** v. 1 shut in on all sides.
2 include with other contents.
▷ SYNS 1 SURROUND, circle, encircle, ring; shut in, confine,
fence in, wall in. 2 INCLUDE, put
in, insert.

**enclosure** n. 1 an enclosed area;
enclosing; fencing off land.
2 something placed in an envelope together with a letter.
▷ SYNS COMPOUND, yard, pen, ring,
fold, paddock, stockade, corral.

**encode** v. convert into a coded
form. ■ **encoder** n.

**encompass** v. 1 encircle.
2 include.

**encore** n. an extra performance
given in response to calls from
the audience.

**encounter** v. unexpectedly
meet or be faced with. • n. 1 an
unexpected meeting. 2 a confrontation.
▷ SYNS v. 1 MEET, run into; inf. bump
into. 2 EXPERIENCE, come up
against, face, confront. • n.
FIGHT, battle, clash, confrontation, engagement, skirmish.

**encourage** v. give hope, confidence, or stimulus to; urge.
■ **encouragement** n.
▷ SYNS 1 CHEER, rally, stimulate,
motivate, inspire, stir, hearten,
animate, invigorate, embolden.

2 URGE, persuade, exhort, spur
on, egg on. 3 PROMOTE, foster,
help, assist, support, aid, back,
boost, strengthen.

**encroach** v. intrude on
someone's territory or rights.
■ **encroachment** n.
▷ SYNS TRESPASS, intrude, invade,
infringe, infiltrate, impinge.

**encrust** v. cover with a crust of
hard material. ■ **encrustation** n.

**encumber** v. be a burden to.
■ **encumbrance** n.

**encyclopedia** (or **encyclo-
paedia**) n. a book containing
information on many subjects.
■ **encyclopedic** adj.

**end** n. 1 the point after which
something no longer exists or
happens; a furthest or final part
or point; a remnant. 2 death. 3 a
goal. • v. 1 bring or come to an
end. 2 (**end up**) eventually
reach a particular place or state.
□ **make ends meet** earn just
enough money to live on.
▷ SYNS n. 1 ENDING, finish, close,
conclusion, cessation, termination, completion, resolution,
climax, finale, culmination;
denouement, epilogue. 2 EDGE,
border, boundary, limit, extremity, margin, tip. 3 BUTT, stub,
remnant. 4 AIM, goal, purpose,
intention, objective, design,
aspiration, ambition, object.
5 DEATH, demise, expiry,
decease. • v. FINISH, stop, end,
cease, conclude, terminate, discontinue, break off; inf. wind up.

**endanger** v. cause danger to.
▷ SYNS THREATEN, put at risk,
jeopardize, imperil, risk.

**endear** v. make popular or well
liked.

**endearing** adj. inspiring
affection.

▷ SYNS CHARMING, appealing, lovable, engaging, winning, sweet, enchanting.

**endearment** n. words expressing love.

**endeavour** (US **endeavor**) v. & n. (make) an earnest attempt.
▷ SYNS TRY, attempt, strive, venture, struggle, essay.

**endemic** adj. commonly found in a specified area or people.

**ending** n. the final part.

**endless** adj. having or seeming to have no end or limit.
▷ SYNS UNLIMITED, infinite, limitless, boundless, inexhaustible, constant, continuous, unending, interminable.

**endorse** v. 1 declare approval of. 2 sign a cheque on the back. 3 record an offence on a driving licence. ■ **endorsement** n.
▷ SYNS SUPPORT, back, agree with, approve, favour, subscribe to, recommend, champion, uphold, affirm, sanction.

**endow** v. 1 provide with a permanent income or property. 2 (**be endowed with**) possess a desirable quality.
■ **endowment** n.

**endurance** n. the ability to endure something.
▷ SYNS TOLERANCE, stamina, staying power, perseverance, tenacity, fortitude, determination.

**endure** v. experience and survive pain or hardship; tolerate; last.
▷ SYNS 1 UNDERGO, go/live through, survive, withstand, weather. 2 LAST, live on, continue, persist, remain.

**enema** n. liquid injected into the rectum to empty the bowels.

**enemy** n. (pl. **-ies**) a person who is hostile to and seeks to harm another.
▷ SYNS ADVERSARY, opponent, foe, rival, antagonist.

**energetic** adj. possessing, showing, or requiring a great deal of energy. ■ **energetically** adv.
▷ SYNS ACTIVE, lively, vigorous, dynamic, brisk, spirited, animated, vibrant, sprightly, spry, tireless, indefatigable.

**energize** (or **-ise**) v. give energy to.

**energy** n. the strength and vitality needed for vigorous activity; the ability of matter or radiation to do work; power derived from physical resources to provide light, heat, etc.
▷ SYNS VIGOUR, strength, stamina, power, forcefulness, drive, enthusiasm, life, animation, liveliness, vivacity, vitality, spirit, fire, zest, exuberance, verve, effervescence, brio.

**enervate** v. cause to lose vitality.

**enfeeble** v. make weak.

**enfold** v. surround; embrace.

**enforce** v. compel obedience to a law etc.; force to happen or be done. ■ **enforceable** adj. **enforcement** n.
▷ SYNS 1 APPLY, implement, bring to bear, impose. 2 FORCE, compel, coerce, extort, exact.

**enfranchise** v. give the right to vote.

**engage** v. 1 occupy or involve; employ. 2 promise. 3 move part of a machine or engine into position. 4 (**engage in**) occupy yourself with.
▷ SYNS 1 EMPLOY, hire, take on. 2 CAPTURE, catch, grab, attract,

win; occupy, absorb, hold, engross, grip. **3** TAKE PART, participate in, join in, enter into, embark on, set about, tackle.

**engaged** adj. **1** having promised to marry a specified person. **2** occupied; in use.

**engagement** n. **1** a promise to marry a specified person. **2** an appointment. **3** engaging or being engaged. **4** a battle.

**engaging** adj. charming.

**engender** v. give rise to.
▷ SYNS CAUSE, produce, create, bring about, give rise to, lead to, arouse, generate, occasion.

**engine** n. a machine with moving parts that converts energy into motion; a railway locomotive.

**engineer** n. **1** a person skilled in engineering. **2** a person who controls an engine on an aircraft or ship. • v. **1** design and build. **2** arrange for something to happen.

**engineering** n. the application of science for the design and building of machines and structures.

**English** n. the language of England, used in many varieties throughout the world. • adj. of England or its language.

**engrave** v. carve a text or design on a hard surface.
■ engraver n. engraving n.

**engross** v. absorb the attention of.

**engulf** v. swamp.

**enhance** v. increase the quality, value, or extent of.
■ enhancement n.
▷ SYNS ADD TO, increase, heighten, improve, strengthen, boost, intensify, enrich, complement.

**enigma** n. a mysterious person or thing. ■ enigmatic adj.

**enjoy** v. **1** take pleasure in. **2** possess and benefit from. **3** (**enjoy yourself**) have a pleasant time. ■ enjoyment n.
▷ SYNS **1** TAKE PLEASURE IN, delight in, appreciate, like, love, relish, revel in, savour, luxuriate in. **2** HAVE, possess, benefit from, be blessed with.

**enjoyable** adj. giving pleasure.
▷ SYNS ENTERTAINING, amusing, delightful, pleasant, lovely, agreeable, pleasurable.

**enlarge** v. **1** make or become larger. **2** (**enlarge on**) say more about. ■ enlargement n.
▷ SYNS EXPAND, extend, add to, augment, amplify, supplement, magnify, widen, broaden, lengthen; distend, dilate, swell, inflate.

**enlighten** v. give greater knowledge or understanding to.
■ enlightenment n.
▷ SYNS INFORM, tell, notify, advise, apprise, update.

**enlist** v. enrol for military service; secure help or support.
▷ SYNS **1** ENROL, join up, sign up for, volunteer for. **2** OBTAIN, secure, get, procure, win.

**enliven** v. make more interesting or interested.
▷ SYNS BRIGHTEN UP, cheer up, hearten, stimulate, uplift, invigorate, revitalize, buoy up, revive, refresh.

**enmesh** v. entangle.

**enmity** n. hostility.

**enormity** n. (pl. **-ies**) **1** great wickedness. **2** great size.

**enormous** adj. very large.
▷ SYNS HUGE, immense, massive, vast, gigantic, colossal, mammoth, gargantuan,

mountainous, prodigious, tremendous, stupendous, titanic.

**enough** adj. & adv. & n. as much or as many as necessary.
▷ SYNS SUFFICIENT, adequate, ample.

**enquire** v. ask.

**enquiry** n. **1** an act of enquiring. **2** an official investigation.
▷ SYNS **1** QUESTION, query. **2** IN-VESTIGATION, examination, exploration, probe, inquest, hearing.

**enrage** v. make furious.
▷ SYNS MADDEN, infuriate, incense, exasperate, provoke, anger.

**enrich** v. enhance; make more rewarding, nourishing, etc.
■ enrichment n.

**enrol** (US **enroll**) v. (**enrolled, enrolling**) admit as or become a member.

**en route** adv. on the way.

**ensemble** n. a thing viewed as a whole; a group of performers.

**enshrine** v. preserve and respect.

**ensign** n. a military or naval flag.

**enslave** v. take away the freedom of.

**ensnare** v. snare; trap.

**ensue** v. happen afterwards or as a result.
▷ SYNS FOLLOW, result, develop, proceed, succeed, emerge; occur, happen, transpire, supervene.

**ensure** v. make certain.
▷ SYNS GUARANTEE, secure, assure, confirm, establish, verify.

**entail** v. involve as a necessary part or consequence.
▷ SYNS INVOLVE, require, call for, necessitate, demand, cause,

produce, result in, lead to, give rise to, occasion.

**entangle** v. tangle; entwine and trap. ■ entanglement n.

**entente** (or **entente cordiale**) n. friendly understanding between countries.

**enter** v. **1** go or come in or into; become involved in; register as a competitor. **2** record information in a book, computer, etc.
▷ SYNS **1** GO IN, set foot in, gain access to. **2** PENETRATE, pierce, puncture. **3** *enter into negotiations:* BEGIN, start, commence, embark on, engage in. **4** *entered the competition:* TAKE PART IN, participate in, go in for. **5** *enter your date of birth:* RECORD, register, put down, note, file, log.

**enterprise** n. a bold undertaking; a business activity.
▷ SYNS **1** VENTURE, undertaking, project, operation, endeavour, scheme, plan. **2** BUSINESS, company, firm, concern, organization, corporation, establishment.

**enterprising** adj. full of initiative.
▷ SYNS RESOURCEFUL, entrepreneurial, imaginative, ingenious, inventive, creative; quick-witted, clever, bright, sharp; enthusiastic, dynamic, ambitious, energetic.

**entertain** v. **1** amuse. **2** offer hospitality to. **3** consider an idea etc. ■ entertainer n.
▷ SYNS **1** AMUSE, divert, delight, please, charm, interest, beguile, engage, occupy, absorb. **2** CONSIDER, contemplate, countenance.

**entertainment** n. **1** the provision of amusement

or enjoyment. **2** an event or performance designed to entertain people.
▷ SYNS **1** AMUSEMENT, fun, enjoyment, recreation, diversion, pleasure. **2** SHOW, performance, production, spectacle.

**enthral** (US **enthrall**) v. (**enthralled, enthralling**) hold spellbound.

**enthralling** adj. fascinating.
▷ SYNS CAPTIVATING, enchanting, fascinating, bewitching, gripping, riveting, charming, intriguing, mesmerizing.

**enthuse** v. fill with or show enthusiasm.

**enthusiasm** n. eager liking or interest.
▷ SYNS EAGERNESS, keenness, fervour, ardour, passion, zeal, gusto, zest; commitment, devotion.

**enthusiast** n. a person who is full of enthusiasm for something.
▷ SYNS FAN, devotee, aficionado, lover, supporter, follower.

**enthusiastic** adj. having or showing great enthusiasm.
▷ SYNS KEEN, eager, avid, fervent, ardent, passionate, zealous; wholehearted, committed, devoted, fanatical.

**entice** v. attract by offering something pleasant; tempt.
▷ SYNS TEMPT, lure, seduce, inveigle, beguile, persuade, coax.

**entire** adj. complete.
▷ SYNS WHOLE, complete, total, full.

**entirely** adv. wholly; completely.
▷ SYNS COMPLETELY, absolutely, totally, wholly, utterly, altogether, thoroughly.

**entirety** n. (**in its entirety**) as a whole.

**entitle** v. give a person a right or claim. ■ **entitlement** n.
▷ SYNS **1** QUALIFY, authorize, allow, permit, enable, empower. **2** CALL, name, dub, designate.

**entity** n. (pl. **-ies**) a distinct and individual thing.

**entomology** n. the study of insects. ■ **entomologist** n.

**entourage** n. people accompanying an important person.
▷ SYNS RETINUE, escort, attendants, companions, followers; inf. groupies.

**entrails** pl.n. intestines.

**entrance¹** n. a door or passageway into a place; coming in; the right to enter a place.
▷ SYNS **1** WAY IN, entry, door, portal, gate; foyer, lobby, porch. **2** ADMISSION, admittance, right of entry, access, ingress.

**entrance²** v. fill with intense delight.

**entreat** v. ask earnestly or emotionally. ■ **entreaty** n.
▷ SYNS BEG, implore, plead with, beseech.

**entrench** v. establish firmly.

**entrepreneur** n. a person who is successful in setting up businesses. ■ **entrepreneurial** adj.

**entrust** v. make responsible for; place in a person's care.

**entry** n. (pl. **-ies**) **1** entering; an entrance. **2** an item entered in a record. **3** an item entered in a competition.

**entwine** v. twist together.

**enumerate** v. mention items one by one.

**enunciate** v. pronounce; state clearly. ■ **enunciation** n.

**envelop** v. (**enveloped**, **enveloping**) wrap up; surround.
▷ SYNS ENFOLD, cover, wrap, swathe, swaddle, cloak, surround.

**envelope** n. a paper holder for a letter, with a sealable flap.

**enviable** adj. desirable enough to arouse envy.

**envious** adj. full of envy.
▷ SYNS JEALOUS, covetous, green-eyed, grudging, begrudging, resentful.

**environment** n.
1 surroundings, setting. 2 the natural world. ■ **environmental** adj.
▷ SYNS SURROUNDINGS, habitat, territory, domain, milieu, situation, location, locale, background, conditions, circumstances, setting, context, framework.

**environmentalist** n. a person seeking to protect the natural environment.

**environs** pl.n. the surrounding districts, esp. of a town.

**envisage** v. imagine; foresee.
▷ SYNS PREDICT, foresee, anticipate, expect; imagine, visualize, picture, conceive of, think of, dream of.

**envoy** n. a messenger or representative.

**envy** n. discontent aroused by another's possessions or success; the object of this:
• v. (**envied**, **envying**) feel envy of.
▷ SYNS n. JEALOUSY, covetousness, resentment, bitterness. • v. COVET; begrudge, grudge, resent.

**enzyme** n. a protein formed in living cells and assisting chemical processes.

**eon** US sp. of AEON.

**epaulette** n. an ornamental shoulder piece on a uniform.

**ephemeral** adj. lasting only a short time.
▷ SYNS FLEETING, transitory, transient, momentary, brief, passing, fugitive.

**epic** n. a long poem, story, or film about heroic deeds or history.
• adj. of or like an epic; on a grand or heroic scale.

**epicentre** (US **epicenter**) n. the point on the earth's surface above the focus of an earthquake.

**epicure** n. a person who enjoys fine food and drink. ■ **epicurean** adj. & n.

**epidemic** n. an outbreak of a disease etc. spreading through a community.

**epidermis** n. the outer layer of the skin.

**epidural** n. a spinal anaesthetic affecting the lower part of the body, esp. used in childbirth.

**epigram** n. a short witty saying.

**epilepsy** n. a disorder of the nervous system, causing fits.
■ **epileptic** adj. & n.

**epilogue** n. a short concluding section of a book etc.

**episcopal** adj. of or governed by bishops.

**episode** n. an event forming one part of a sequence; one part of a serial. ■ **episodic** adj.
▷ SYNS 1 PART, instalment, chapter. 2 INCIDENT, occurrence, event, happening, experience, adventure, matter, affair.

**epistle** n. a letter.

**epitaph** n. words in memory of a dead person, esp. inscribed on a tomb.

**epithet** n. a descriptive word.

**epitome** n. a perfect example.
▷ SYNS PERSONIFICATION, embodiment, incarnation, essence, quintessence, archetype, model.

**epitomize** v. be a perfect example of.

**epoch** n. a long and distinct period of time.
▷ SYNS ERA, age, period, time.

**equable** adj. **1** calm and even-tempered. **2** free from extremes.

**equal** adj. **1** the same in quantity, size, value, or status. **2** evenly balanced. **3** (**equal to**) able to deal with. • n. a person or thing that is equal to another. • v. **1** be equal to. **2** match or rival. ■ **equality** n. **equally** adv.
▷ SYNS adj. IDENTICAL, alike, like, the same, matching, equivalent, corresponding. • n. EQUIVALENT, peer, counterpart, match, parallel.

**equalize** (or **-ise**) v. make equal; match an opponent's score.

**equanimity** n. calmness of mind or temper.
▷ SYNS COMPOSURE, self-control, self-possession, level-headedness, equilibrium, poise, aplomb, sangfroid, calmness, serenity, tranquillity, phlegm, imperturbability.

**equate** v. consider to be equal or equivalent.

**equation** n. a mathematical statement that two expressions are equal.

**equator** n. an imaginary line round the earth at an equal distance from the North and South Poles. ■ **equatorial** adj.

**equestrian** adj. of horse riding.

**equilateral** adj. having all sides equal.

**equilibrium** n. (pl. **-ria**) a balanced state.

**equine** adj. of or like a horse.

**equinox** n. the time of year when night and day are of equal length.

**equip** v. (**equipped**, **equipping**) supply with what is needed.
▷ SYNS PROVIDE, supply, furnish, issue, fit, kit, arm.

**equipment** n. the items needed for a particular activity.

**equitable** adj. fair and just.

**equity** n. **1** fairness or impartiality. **2** the value of the shares issued by a company.

**equivalent** adj. equal in amount, value, meaning, etc. • n. an equivalent thing. ■ **equivalence** n.
▷ SYNS adj. EQUAL, identical, the same; similar, comparable, corresponding, commensurate.

**equivocal** adj. ambiguous. ■ **equivocally** adv.
▷ SYNS AMBIGUOUS, indefinite, non-committal, vague, unclear; ambivalent, uncertain, unsure, indecisive.

**equivocate** v. use words ambiguously.

**era** n. a period of history.
▷ SYNS AGE, epoch, period, time, aeon; generation.

**eradicate** v. wipe out. ■ **eradication** n.
▷ SYNS ELIMINATE, get rid of, remove, obliterate; exterminate, destroy, annihilate, wipe out, stamp out, extinguish.

**erase** v. rub out. ■ **eraser** n.

▷ SYNS DELETE, rub out, remove, blot out, efface, obliterate.

**ere** prep. & conj. lit. before.

**erect** adj. upright; (of a body part) enlarged and rigid. • v. set upright; construct. ■ **erection** n.

**ermine** n. **1** a stoat. **2** the stoat's white winter fur.

**erode** v. wear away gradually. ■ **erosion** n.

▷ SYNS WEAR AWAY/DOWN, eat away, corrode, abrade, destroy.

**erotic** adj. of or arousing sexual desire. ■ **erotically** adv.

▷ SYNS AROUSING, stimulating, exciting, titillating, seductive, sexy, raunchy.

**err** v. (**erred, erring**) make a mistake; do wrong.

▷ SYNS MAKE A MISTAKE, blunder, miscalculate, slip up; misbehave, transgress.

**errand** n. a short journey to do a job for someone.

▷ SYNS TASK, job, chore, assignment.

**errant** adj. misbehaving.

**erratic** adj. happening or acting in an irregular way. ■ **erratically** adv.

▷ SYNS UNPREDICTABLE, inconsistent, changeable, irregular, fitful, varying, fluctuating, unreliable.

**erratum** n. (pl. **-ata**) an error in printing or writing.

**erroneous** adj. incorrect.

**error** n. a mistake; being wrong.

▷ SYNS MISTAKE, inaccuracy, miscalculation, blunder, slip-up, oversight; misprint, fallacy, misconception.

**erstwhile** adj. former.

**erudite** adj. learned. ■ **erudition** n.

**erupt** v. (of a volcano) eject lava; burst out; express an emotion violently. ■ **eruption** n.

**escalate** v. increase in intensity or extent. ■ **escalation** n.

▷ SYNS INCREASE, soar, shoot up, rocket; intensify, heighten, accelerate.

**escalator** n. a moving staircase.

**escapade** n. a piece of reckless or mischievous conduct.

▷ SYNS EXPLOIT, stunt, adventure, caper, antics.

**escape** v. get free; avoid danger; leak from a container; fail to be remembered by. • n. an act or means of escaping. ■ **escapee** n.

▷ SYNS v. **1** GET AWAY/OUT, run away, break free, break out, bolt, flee; inf. do a bunk. **2** AVOID, evade, dodge, elude; circumvent, sidestep. • n. BREAKOUT, getaway, flight.

**escapism** n. the habit of using fantasy or entertainment to distract yourself from unpleasant realities.

**escapologist** n. an entertainer whose act involves escaping from ropes and chains.

**escarpment** n. a steep slope at the edge of a plateau etc.

**eschew** v. lit. avoid or abstain from.

**escort** n. **1** a person, vehicle, or group accompanying another as a protection or honour. **2** a person accompanying a member of the opposite sex to a social event. • v. act as escort to.

▷ SYNS n. GUARD, entourage, retinue, convoy. • v. ACCOMPANY, guide, conduct, lead, usher.

**esophagus** US sp. of OESOPHAGUS.

**esoteric** adj. intended only for a few people with special knowledge or interest.
▷ SYNS ABSTRUSE, obscure, arcane, recondite, mysterious.

**ESP** abbr. extrasensory perception.

**especial** adj. special; particular.

**especially** adv. **1** more than any other; particularly, individually. **2** to a great extent.

**espionage** n. spying.

**esplanade** n. a promenade.

**espouse** v. support a cause.
■ espousal n.

**espy** v. (espied, espying) catch sight of.

**Esq.** abbr. Esquire, a courtesy title placed after a man's surname.

**essay** n. a short piece of writing.
• v. attempt.

**essence** n. **1** the quality which makes something what it is. **2** a concentrated extract.
▷ SYNS **1** QUINTESSENCE, soul, heart, core, substance.
**2** EXTRACT, concentrate, elixir.

**essential** adj. **1** absolutely necessary. **2** central to something's nature. • n. **1** something absolutely necessary. **2** (the essentials) the basic facts. ■ essentially adv.
▷ SYNS adj. **1** NECESSARY, important, indispensable, vital, crucial. **2** BASIC, fundamental, intrinsic, inherent, innate, elemental.

**establish** v. **1** set up. **2** make accepted by others. **3** find out facts.
▷ SYNS **1** SET UP, start, found, institute, create, inaugurate. **2** PROVE, show, demonstrate, confirm.

**establishment** n.
**1** establishing or being established. **2** an organization; its staff. **3** (the Establishment) the group in society who control policy and resist change.
▷ SYNS FIRM, business, company, concern, organization, enterprise, corporation, operation.

**estate** n. landed property; a residential or industrial district planned as a unit; property left at someone's death. □ estate agent a person who sells and rents out houses etc. for clients. estate car a car with a large storage area behind the seats and a rear door.
▷ SYNS **1** PROPERTY, lands, grounds. **2** ASSETS, holdings, capital, effects, possessions, wealth, fortune.

**esteem** v. think highly of.
• n. respect and admiration.
▷ SYNS v. RESPECT, admire, value, look up to, revere.

**esthete** etc. US sp. of AESTHETE etc.

**estimable** adj. worthy of esteem.

**estimate** v. make an approximate judgement of something's quantity, value, etc. • n. such a judgement. ■ estimation n.
▷ SYNS v. WORK OUT, calculate, assess, gauge, reckon, evaluate, judge.

**estranged** v. no longer friendly or loving.

**estrogen** US sp. of OESTROGEN.

**estuary** n. (pl. -ies) the mouth of a large river, affected by tides.

**etc.** abbr. et cetera, and other similar things.

**etch** v. **1** produce a picture by engraving a metal plate with acid.

**2** fix clearly in the mind.
■ **etching** n.

**eternal** adj. existing always; unchanging. ■ **eternally** adv.
▷ SYNS ENDLESS, everlasting, never-ending, immortal, deathless, undying, permanent; ceaseless, incessant, constant, continuous, unremitting, interminable, relentless, perpetual.

**eternity** n. (pl. **-ies**) unending time; a very long time.
▷ SYNS IMMORTALITY, the afterlife, the hereafter, heaven, paradise.

**ether** n. **1** the upper air. **2** a liquid used as an anaesthetic and solvent.

**ethereal** adj. **1** delicate and light. **2** heavenly or spiritual.

**ethic** n. **1** a moral principle or framework. **2** (**ethics**) moral principles.

**ethical** adj. of ethics; morally correct. ■ **ethically** adv.
▷ SYNS MORAL, honourable, upright, righteous, good, virtuous, decent, principled, honest, just.

**ethnic** adj. of a group sharing a common origin, culture, or language. ■ **ethnically** adv. **ethnicity** n.

**ethos** n. the characteristic spirit and beliefs of a community.

**etiquette** n. the rules of polite behaviour in a society.

**etymology** n. (pl. **-ies**) an account of a word's origin and development. ■ **etymological** adj.

**eucalyptus** n. an Australian tree whose leaves yield a strong-smelling oil.

**Eucharist** n. the Christian sacrament commemorating the Last Supper, in which bread and wine are consumed.

**eugenics** n. the science of controlling breeding to produce a healthier, more intelligent, etc. population.

**eulogy** n. (pl. **-ies**) a speech or work praising someone.
■ **eulogize** v.

**eunuch** n. a castrated man.

**euphemism** n. a mild expression substituted for an improper or blunt one.
■ **euphemistic** adj.

**euphoria** n. excited happiness.
■ **euphoric** adj.
▷ SYNS ELATION, happiness, joy, delight, glee, excitement, exhilaration, jubilation, exultation, ecstasy, bliss, rapture.

**eureka** exclam. a cry of joy on discovering something.

**euro** n. the basic unit of money in twelve states of the European Union.

**European** adj. of Europe or its people. • n. a European person.

**euthanasia** n. painless killing, esp. of someone with a terminal illness.

**evacuate** v. **1** send from a dangerous to a safer place. **2** empty. ■ **evacuation** n. **evacuee** n.
▷ SYNS LEAVE, abandon, vacate, quit, withdraw from.

**evade** v. escape or avoid.
▷ SYNS AVOID, dodge, escape, elude, shake off, sidestep.

**evaluate** v. assess the amount or value of. ■ **evaluation** n.
▷ SYNS ASSESS, appraise, weigh up, gauge, judge, rate, estimate.

**evangelical** adj. **1** a tradition within Protestantism emphasizing biblical authority. **2** of the gospel. **3** passionately supporting something.

**evangelist** n. any of the authors of the four Gospels; a person who tries to convert others. ■ **evangelism** n. **evangelistic** adj.

**evaporate** v. turn liquid into vapour; (of something abstract) disappear. ■ **evaporation** n.

**evasion** n. evading.

**evasive** adj. intending to avoid or escape something.
▷ SYNS EQUIVOCAL, prevaricating, elusive, ambiguous, non-committal, vague.

**eve** n. an evening, day, or time just before a special event.

**even** adj. 1 level. 2 equal in number, amount, or value. 3 regular or balanced. 4 exactly divisible by two. • v. make or become even. • adv. used for emphasis: *even faster.*
▷ SYNS adj. 1 FLAT, level, smooth, plane. 2 CONSTANT, steady, uniform, consistent, stable, regular. 3 TIED, level, all square, neck and neck.

**evening** n. the period of time at the end of the day.
▷ SYNS NIGHT, twilight, dusk, nightfall, sunset, sundown.

**event** n. something that happens; an organized social occasion; an item in a sports programme.
▷ SYNS 1 OCCASION, affair, occurrence, happening, episode, circumstance, phenomenon. 2 COMPETITION, contest, fixture, game, tournament, race.

**eventful** adj. full of exciting events.
▷ SYNS BUSY, action-packed, full, active, hectic, exciting.

**eventual** adj. ultimate or final. ■ **eventually** adv.

**eventuality** n. (pl. **-ies**) a possible event.

**ever** adv. 1 at any time. 2 always. □ **evergreen** a plant having green leaves throughout the year. **evermore** forever.

**everlasting** adj. lasting forever or a very long time.
▷ SYNS NEVER-ENDING, endless, eternal, perpetual, undying, abiding, enduring.

**every** adj. 1 each without exception. 2 indicating how often something happens: *every three months.* 3 all possible. □ **everybody** every person. **everyday** 1 daily. 2 ordinary. **everyone** every person. **everything** all things. **everywhere** in or to all places.

**evict** v. legally force to leave a property. ■ **eviction** n.
▷ SYNS EXPEL, eject, remove, throw out, turn out; inf. turf out.

**evidence** n. 1 information indicating whether something is true or valid. 2 information presented in a law court to support a case. • v. be evidence of.
▷ SYNS n. 1 PROOF, verification, confirmation, substantiation, corroboration. 2 TESTIMONY, statement, deposition, affidavit.

**evident** adj. obvious to the eye or mind.
▷ SYNS OBVIOUS, clear, apparent, plain, noticeable, visible, conspicuous, manifest, patent.

**evil** adj. morally bad; harmful; very unpleasant. • n. wickedness; something wicked.
▷ SYNS adj. 1 WICKED, wrong, bad, immoral, sinful, corrupt, nefarious, vile, base, iniquitous, heinous, villainous, malicious, malevolent. 2 BAD, harmful,

injurious, destructive, pernicious; formal deleterious.
• n. WICKEDNESS, wrong, wrongdoing, sin, immorality, vice, corruption, depravity, villainy.

**evoke** v. 1 cause someone to think of. 2 elicit a response.
■ evocation n. evocative adj.
▷ SYNS BRING TO MIND, conjure up, summon (up), elicit, kindle, stimulate, stir up, awaken, arouse.

**evolution** n. the process by which different kinds of animals and plants develop from earlier forms.
■ evolutionary adj.
▷ SYNS DEVELOPMENT, progress, growth, rise; natural selection, Darwinism.

**evolve** v. develop or work out gradually.
▷ SYNS DEVELOP, grow, progress, advance, mature.

**ewe** n. a female sheep.

**ex** n. inf. a former husband, wife, or partner.

**ex-** pref. former.

**exacerbate** v. make worse.
■ exacerbation n.
▷ SYNS AGGRAVATE, worsen, intensify, heighten, inflame.

**exact** adj. completely accurate; giving all details. • v. insist on and obtain.
▷ SYNS adj. PRECISE, accurate, correct, faithful, true, literal, strict. • v. REQUIRE, demand, insist on, impose; extract, wring, wrest.

**exacting** adj. demanding much effort or skill.

**exactly** adv. 1 without vagueness or discrepancy. 2 expressing total agreement.

**exaggerate** v. make something seem larger, better, etc. than in reality. ■ exaggeration n.
▷ SYNS OVERSTATE, overemphasize, overestimate, embellish, embroider, elaborate.

**exalt** v. regard or praise highly; raise in rank.

**exaltation** n. 1 extreme happiness. 2 praising; raising in rank.

**exam** n. an examination.

**examination** n. an inspection or investigation; a formal test of knowledge or ability.
▷ SYNS 1 STUDY, inspection, scrutiny, investigation, analysis, observation, consideration, appraisal. 2 EXAM, test, paper.

**examine** v. look at closely; test someone's knowledge or ability.
■ examiner n.
▷ SYNS STUDY, investigate, survey, analyse, review, consider, assess, appraise, weigh up, inspect.

**example** n. something seen as typical of its kind or of a general rule; a person or thing worthy of imitation.
▷ SYNS 1 SAMPLE, specimen, instance, case, illustration. 2 MODEL, pattern, ideal, standard, precedent.

**exasperate** v. annoy greatly.
■ exasperation n.
▷ SYNS ANGER, infuriate, annoy, irritate, madden, provoke, irk, vex, gall.

**excavate** v. make a hole by digging; dig something out; reveal buried remains by digging a site. ■ excavation n.

**exceed** v. be greater than; go beyond the limit of.
▷ SYNS SURPASS, beat, outdo, outstrip, outshine, transcend,

better, top, cap, overshadow, eclipse.

**exceedingly** adv. very.

**excel** v. (**excelled**, **excelling**) **1** be very good at something.
**2** (**excel yourself**) do better than you ever have.

**excellent** adj. extremely good.
■ **excellence** n.
▷ SYNS VERY GOOD, first-rate, first-class, high-quality, great, fine, superior, superb, outstanding, marvellous, splendid, brilliant, supreme, superlative, exemplary, consummate; inf. terrific, tremendous, fantastic.

**except** prep. not including.
• v. exclude.

**excepting** prep. except.

**exception** n. something that does not follow a general rule.
□ **take exception to** object to.

**exceptional** adj. very unusual; outstandingly good.
■ **exceptionally** adv.
▷ SYNS **1** UNUSUAL, uncommon, out of the ordinary, atypical, rare, anomalous, abnormal.
**2** OUTSTANDING, extraordinary, remarkable, phenomenal, prodigious.

**excerpt** n. an extract from a book, film, etc.
▷ SYNS EXTRACT, quote, citation, quotation, passage, piece, clip.

**excess** n. **1** an amount more than necessary, allowed, or desirable. **2** (**excesses**) outrageous behaviour. • adj. exceeding a limit.
▷ SYNS n. SURPLUS, glut, overabundance, surfeit, superfluity. • adj. SURPLUS, superfluous, redundant, unwanted.

**excessive** adj. too much.
▷ SYNS IMMODERATE, intemperate, overindulgent, unrestrained,

uncontrolled, lavish, extravagant; superfluous; unreasonable, disproportionate, exorbitant, extortionate.

**exchange** v. give something and receive another thing. • n.
**1** exchanging. **2** a brief conversation. **3** giving money for its equivalent in another currency.
**4** a building used for trading.
**5** a centre where phone lines are connected.
▷ SYNS v. TRADE, swap, change.

**exchequer** n. a national treasury.

**excise** n. duty or tax on certain goods and licences. • v. cut out or away. ■ **excision** n.

**excitable** adj. easily excited.
■ **excitability** n. **excitably** adv.
▷ SYNS TEMPERAMENTAL, emotional, highly strung, nervous, volatile, mercurial, tempestuous.

**excite** v. **1** make very enthusiastic and eager. **2** arouse sexually. **3** give rise to.
▷ SYNS **1** THRILL, exhilarate, animate, stimulate. **2** AROUSE, awaken, provoke, kindle, stir up.

**excitement** n. great enthusiasm and eagerness; a cause of this.
▷ SYNS **1** ANIMATION, enthusiasm, exhilaration, anticipation.
**2** THRILL, pleasure, delight, joy; inf. kick, buzz.

**exciting** adj. causing great enthusiasm and eagerness.
▷ SYNS THRILLING, exhilarating, stimulating, intoxicating, electrifying, gripping, dramatic.

**exclaim** v. cry out suddenly.
▷ SYNS CALL, cry, shout, yell.

**exclamation** n. a sudden cry or remark. □ **exclamation mark** a punctuation mark (!) indicating an exclamation. ■ **exclamatory** adj.

▷ SYNS CALL, cry, shout, yell, interjection.

**exclude** v. 1 prevent from being a part of something. 2 deliberately leave out. ■ **exclusion** n.

▷ SYNS KEEP OUT, shut out, bar, ban, prohibit.

**exclusive** adj. 1 excluding something. 2 limited to one or a few people; catering only for the wealthy. • n. a story published in only one newspaper. ■ **exclusivity** n.

▷ SYNS adj. SELECT, upmarket, elite, fashionable, chic, elegant, stylish.

**excommunicate** v. officially bar from membership of the Christian Church.
■ **excommunication** n.

**excrement** n. faeces.

**excrete** v. expel waste matter from the body. ■ **excretion** n. **excretory** adj.

**excruciating** adj. intensely painful or unpleasant.

▷ SYNS AGONIZING, unbearable, acute, searing, severe, intense.

**excursion** n. a short journey, esp. for pleasure.

**excuse** v. 1 justify or defend an action etc.; forgive. 2 exempt.
• n. a reason put forward to justify a fault etc.; a pretext.
■ **excusable** adj.

▷ SYNS v. 1 FORGIVE, pardon, exonerate. 2 LET OFF, exempt, release, relieve, free. • n.
1 EXPLANATION, reason, grounds, justification, defence, mitigation. 2 PRETEXT, pretence.

**execrable** adj. very bad or unpleasant.

**execute** v. 1 carry out an order; produce or perform a work of art. 2 put a condemned person to death. ■ **execution** n. **execitioner** n.

▷ SYNS 1 PUT TO DEATH, kill.
2 CARRY OUT, accomplish, bring off, achieve, complete.

**executive** n. a person or group with managerial powers, or with authority to put government decisions into effect.
• adj. having such power or authority.

**executor** n. a person appointed to carry out the terms of a will.

**exemplar** n. a typical example or good model.

**exemplary** adj. 1 providing a good example. 2 serving as a warning.

▷ SYNS PERFECT, ideal, model, faultless, impeccable.

**exemplify** v. (**exemplified**, **exemplifying**) serve as an example of. ■ **exemplification** n.

▷ SYNS TYPIFY, epitomize, symbolize, represent, illustrate, demonstrate.

**exempt** adj. free from an obligation etc. imposed on others. • v. make exempt.
■ **exemption** n.

▷ SYNS v. FREE, release, exclude, excuse, absolve, spare; inf. let off.

**exercise** n. 1 physical activity.
2 a task set to practise a skill.
3 the use of a power, right, etc.
• v. 1 use a power, right etc. 2 do physical exercise. 3 worry or puzzle.

▷ SYNS USE, employ, make use of, utilize, apply.

**exert** v. 1 apply a force, influence, etc. 2 (**exert yourself**) make an effort. ■ **exertion** n.

▷ SYNS **1** EMPLOY, exercise, use, make use of, utilize, apply, bring to bear. **2 (exert yourself)** MAKE AN EFFORT, try hard, strive, endeavour, struggle, do your best.

**exhale** v. breathe out; give off in vapour. ■ **exhalation** n.

**exhaust** v. **1** tire out. **2** use up completely. • n. **1** waste gases from an engine etc. **2** a device through which they are expelled. ■ **exhaustible** adj. **exhaustion** n.
▷ SYNS v. **1** TIRE, wear out, fatigue, drain, weary; inf. knacker. **2** USE UP, deplete, consume, finish.

**exhausting** adj. making you feel very tired.
▷ SYNS TIRING, wearying, wearing; gruelling, taxing, strenuous, arduous.

**exhaustive** adj. attending to every detail.
▷ SYNS COMPREHENSIVE, all-inclusive, complete, full, encyclopedic, thorough, in-depth; detailed, meticulous, painstaking.

**exhibit** v. put on show publicly; display a quality etc. • n. a thing on public show. ■ **exhibitor** n.
▷ SYNS v. **1** (PUT ON) DISPLAY, show, present, model, unveil. **2** SHOW, indicate, reveal, display, demonstrate, manifest, evince.

**exhibition** n. a public show; a display of a quality etc.
▷ SYNS DISPLAY, show, demonstration, presentation, exposition.

**exhibitionism** n. a tendency to behave in a way designed to attract attention.
■ **exhibitionist** n.

**exhilarate** v. make joyful or lively. ■ **exhilaration** n.

**exhort** v. urge or advise earnestly. ■ **exhortation** n.
▷ SYNS URGE, persuade, press, encourage, advise, counsel, entreat, enjoin.

**exhume** v. dig up a buried corpse.

**exigency** n. (pl. -ies) an urgent need or demand. ■ **exigent** adj.

**exile** n. banishment or long absence from your country or home, esp. as a punishment; an exiled person. • v. send into exile.
▷ SYNS n. EXPATRIATE, deportee, refugee, displaced person. • v. BANISH, deport, expatriate, expel, drive out.

**exist** v. be present somewhere; live. ■ **existence** n. **existent** adj.
▷ SYNS LIVE, breathe, draw breath, subsist, survive.

**exit** n. a way out; a departure. • v. go away.
▷ SYNS n. **1** WAY OUT, egress, door, doorway, gate, gateway. **2** DEPARTURE, withdrawal, leaving, retreat.

**exodus** n. a departure of many people.

**exonerate** v. show to be blameless. ■ **exoneration** n.

**exorbitant** adj. (of a price) unreasonably high.
▷ SYNS EXCESSIVE, unreasonable, extortionate, prohibitive, outrageous.

**exorcize** (or -ise) v. free a person or place of an evil spirit. ■ **exorcism** n. **exorcist** n.

**exotic** adj. belonging to a foreign country; attractively unusual or striking. ■ **exotically** adv.
▷ SYNS **1** FOREIGN, non-native, tropical. **2** STRIKING, colourful,

unusual, eye-catching, un-conventional.

**expand** v. 1 make or become larger; give a more detailed account. 2 become less reserved. ■ **expandable** adj. **expansion** n.
▷ SYNS GROW, enlarge, swell; extend, augment, broaden, widen, develop, diversify, build up; branch out, spread, proliferate.

**expanse** n. a wide area or extent.
▷ SYNS AREA, stretch, tract, sweep, region.

**expansive** adj. 1 covering a wide area. 2 genial and com-municative.

**expatiate** v. speak or write at length about a subject.

**expatriate** n. a person living outside their own country.

**expect** v. believe that a person or thing will come or a thing will happen; require or see as due; suppose or think.
▷ SYNS 1 SUPPOSE, assume, believe, imagine, think, presume, surmise, reckon. 2 ANTICIPATE, envisage, predict, forecast, hope for, look for, await. 3 DEMAND, insist on, require, ask for.

**expectant** adj. 1 filled with anticipation. 2 pregnant. ■ **expectancy** n.
▷ SYNS HOPEFUL, eager, excited, agog, in suspense, on tenterhooks.

**expectation** n. the belief that something will happen, or a thing that is expected to happen.
▷ SYNS ANTICIPATION, expectancy; assumption, supposition, calcu-lation, prediction.

**expedient** adj. advantageous rather than right or just. • n. a means of achieving something. ■ **expediency** n.
▷ SYNS adj. CONVENIENT, useful, pragmatic, advantageous, bene-ficial, helpful, politic, judicious, prudent. • n. MEANS, measure, stratagem, scheme, plan, con-trivance.

**expedite** v. help or hurry the progress of.

**expedition** n. a journey for a purpose; people and equipment for this.

**expeditious** adj. speedy and efficient.

**expel** v. 1 deprive of member-ship; force to leave. 2 force out breath etc.
▷ SYNS EVICT, banish, drive out, exile, throw out, expatriate, deport; inf. kick out.

**expend** v. spend; use up.

**expendable** adj. not causing serious loss if abandoned.

**expenditure** n. the expending of money etc.; an amount expended.

**expense** n. 1 money spent on something; something on which you spend money. 2 (**expenses**) the amount spent doing a job; reimbursement of this.
▷ SYNS COST, price, outlay, payment, expenditure, outgoings, charge, bill, overheads.

**expensive** adj. costing a great deal of money.
▷ SYNS OVERPRICED, exorbitant, steep, costly, dear, extortionate.

**experience** n. 1 practical involvement in an activity, event, etc. 2 knowledge or skill gained over time. 3 an event or

action from which you learn.
• v. undergo or be involved in.
▷ SYNS n. 1 SKILL, knowledge,
understanding, involvement,
participation, contact, acquaintance, exposure, observation.
2 EVENT, incident, occurrence,
happening, episode, adventure.
• v. UNDERGO, encounter, meet,
come across, go through, face.

**experienced** adj. having
knowledge or skill gained over
time.
▷ SYNS KNOWLEDGEABLE, skilful,
expert, proficient, trained,
capable, seasoned, practised.

**experiment** n. 1 a scientific
test to find out or prove
something. 2 a new course
of action with an uncertain
outcome. • v. perform
an experiment.
■ **experimentation** n.
▷ SYNS n. TEST, trial, investigation,
examination, observation,
assessment, evaluation.

**experimental** adj. based on
new ideas and not yet fully
tested. ■ **experimentally** adv.
▷ SYNS TRIAL, exploratory, pilot,
tentative, preliminary.

**expert** n. a person with great
knowledge or skill in a
particular area.
▷ SYNS AUTHORITY, specialist,
master, pundit, maestro, virtuoso, connoisseur; inf. buff.

**expertise** n. expert knowledge
or skill.

**expiate** v. make amends for.
■ **expiation** n.

**expire** v. 1 die; cease to be valid.
2 breathe out air.
▷ SYNS 1 RUN OUT, lapse, finish,
end, terminate. 2 see DIE.

**expiry** n. the end of the period
for which something is valid.

**explain** v. 1 make clear. 2 give a
reason for. ■ **explanatory** adj.
▷ SYNS 1 DESCRIBE, make clear,
spell out, clarify, elucidate.
2 ACCOUNT FOR, justify,
excuse.

**explanation** n. 1 a statement
or description that makes
something clear. 2 a reason or
justification.
▷ SYNS 1 DESCRIPTION, clarification,
interpretation, definition. 2 AC-
COUNT, justification, reason,
answer, excuse, defence.

**expletive** n. a swear word.
▷ SYNS SWEAR WORD, oath, curse,
obscenity, profanity.

**explicable** adj. able to be
explained.

**explicit** adj. clear and detailed.
▷ SYNS CLEAR, plain, exact, straightforward, detailed, specific, unambiguous.

**explode** v. 1 burst or shatter
violently. 2 suddenly express
emotion. 3 increase suddenly.
4 show a belief to be false.
▷ SYNS 1 BLOW UP, detonate, go off,
burst, erupt. 2 DISPROVE, refute,
debunk, give the lie to.

**exploit** v. 1 use unfairly. 2 make
full use of. • n. a daring act.
■ **exploitation** n.
▷ SYNS v. 1 TAKE ADVANTAGE OF,
abuse, misuse. 2 UTILIZE, make
use of, capitalize on; inf. cash in
on. • n. FEAT, deed, adventure,
stunt, achievement.

**explore** v. travel into a country
etc. in order to learn about it;
examine. ■ **exploration** n.
**exploratory** adj. **explorer** n.
▷ SYNS 1 TRAVEL OVER, traverse,
survey, inspect, reconnoitre.
2 INVESTIGATE, look into,
consider, research, study,
review.

**explosion** n. an act of exploding; a sudden increase.

**explosive** adj. & n. (a substance) able or liable to explode.

**exponent** n. a person who holds and argues for a theory etc.
▷ SYNS ADVOCATE, supporter, upholder, defender, champion, promoter, proponent, propagandist.

**exponential** adj. (of an increase) more and more rapid.

**export** v. send goods etc. to another country for sale. • n. exporting; an exported item.

**expose** v. leave uncovered or unprotected; subject to a risk etc.; allow light to reach film etc.
▷ SYNS 1 SUBJECT, lay open, put at risk, put in jeopardy. 2 UNCOVER, reveal, unveil, unmask, lay bare; discover, bring to light.

**exposé** n. a news report revealing shocking information.

**exposition** n. 1 an account and explanation. 2 a large exhibition.

**expound** v. explain in detail.

**express** v. 1 convey feelings etc. by words or gestures. 2 squeeze out liquid or air. • adj. 1 definitely stated; precisely identified. 2 travelling or operating at high speed. • n. a fast train or bus making few stops. • adv. by express train or special delivery service.

**expression** n. 1 expressing. 2 a look on someone's face conveying feeling. 3 a word or phrase.
▷ SYNS 1 UTTERANCE, articulation, voicing. 2 (TURN OF) PHRASE, term, idiom, saying. 3 LOOK,

countenance, appearance, air, mien.

**expressive** adj. conveying feelings etc. clearly.

**expropriate** v. (esp. of the state) deprive an owner of property. ■ expropriation n.

**expulsion** n. expelling or being expelled.

**expunge** v. wipe out.

**expurgate** v. remove unsuitable matter from a book etc. ■ expurgation n.

**exquisite** adj. 1 extremely beautiful and delicate. 2 acute; keenly felt.

**extemporize** (or -ise) v. speak, perform, or produce without preparation.

**extend** v. 1 make longer or larger. 2 reach over an area. 3 offer. 4 stretch out part of the body.
▷ SYNS 1 EXPAND, enlarge, increase, lengthen, widen, broaden. 2 CONTINUE, stretch, carry on, reach. 3 OFFER, give, proffer.

**extension** n. 1 a part added to and enlarging something. 2 extending. 3 an extra telephone.

**extensive** adj. large in area or scope.
▷ SYNS 1 LARGE, sizeable, substantial, spacious, considerable, vast. 2 BROAD, wide, wide-ranging, comprehensive, thorough, inclusive.

**extent** n. the area covered by something; scope or scale; the degree to which something is true.
▷ SYNS 1 AREA, size, expanse, length; proportions, dimensions. 2 DEGREE, scale,

level, magnitude, scope; breadth, reach, range.

**extenuating** adj. making an offence less serious or more forgivable.

**exterior** adj. on or coming from the outside. • n. an outer surface or appearance.
▷ SYNS adj. OUTER, outside, outermost, outward, external, surface.

**exterminate** v. destroy completely; kill. ■ extermination n.

**external** adj. of or on the outside. • n. an outward or superficial feature. ■ externally adv.

**externalize** (or **-ise**) v. express, see, or present as existing outside yourself.

**extinct** adj. with no living members; no longer active or alight. ■ extinction n.

**extinguish** v. put out a light or flame; put an end to.
■ extinguisher n.
▷ SYNS 1 PUT OUT, blow out, quench, smother, douse, snuff out. 2 DESTROY, end, remove, annihilate, wipe out, eliminate, eradicate.

**extol** v. (**extolled, extolling**) praise enthusiastically.

**extort** v. obtain by force or threats. ■ extortion n.

**extortionate** adj. (of a price) much too high.

**extra** adj. additional, more than is usual or expected. • adv. more than usually; in addition. • n. an additional item; a person employed as one of a crowd in a film.
▷ SYNS adj. ADDITIONAL, more, further, supplementary, added, other.

**extra-** pref. outside; beyond.

**extract** v. take out or obtain by force or effort; obtain by chemical treatment etc.; select a passage from a book etc. • n. a passage quoted from a book, film, etc.; the concentrated essence of a substance.
■ extractor n.
▷ SYNS v. 1 PULL OUT, prise out, remove, withdraw. 2 EXTORT, exact, wring, wrest. • n. EXCERPT, passage, citation, quotation.

**extraction** n. 1 extracting. 2 ancestry or origin.

**extradite** v. hand over an accused person for trial in the country where a crime was committed. ■ extradition n.

**extramarital** adj. occurring outside marriage.

**extramural** adj. for students who are not members of a university.

**extraneous** adj. 1 irrelevant. 2 of external origin.

**extraordinary** adj. very unusual or surprising.
■ extraordinarily adv.
▷ SYNS REMARKABLE, exceptional, amazing, astonishing, incredible, unbelievable, phenomenal; out of the ordinary, unusual, uncommon, rare, surprising.

**extrapolate** v. use a fact or conclusion valid for one situation and apply it to a different one.
■ extrapolation n.

**extrasensory perception** n. the supposed ability to perceive things by means other than the known senses.

**extraterrestrial** adj. of or from outside the earth or its atmosphere.

**extravagant** adj. **1** spending or using more than is necessary or can be afforded. **2** exceeding what is reasonable.
■ **extravagance** n.
▷ SYNS **1** SPENDTHRIFT, profligate, wasteful, lavish. **2** EXCESSIVE, immoderate, unrestrained, effusive, fulsome.

**extravaganza** n. a lavish spectacular display.

**extreme** adj. **1** very great or intense; reaching a very high degree; very severe; drastic or immoderate. **2** furthest or outermost. ● n. an extreme point; one end of a scale; a very high degree.
▷ SYNS adj. **1** UTMOST, maximum, supreme, great, acute, intense, severe, high, exceptional, extraordinary. **2** DRASTIC, serious, desperate, dire, harsh, tough, strict, rigorous, draconian. **3** RADICAL, extremist, immoderate, fanatical, revolutionary.

**extremely** adv. to or in the highest degree.
▷ SYNS VERY, exceptionally, especially, extraordinarily, tremendously, immensely, terribly; inf. awfully.

**extremist** n. a person holding extreme views. ■ **extremism** n.

**extremity** n. (pl. **-ies**) **1** extreme hardship. **2** the furthest point or limit. **3** (**extremities**) the hands and feet.

**extricate** v. free from a difficulty.

**extrovert** n. a lively sociable person.

**extrude** v. thrust or squeeze out.

**exuberant** adj. **1** full of high spirits. **2** growing profusely.
■ **exuberance** n.
▷ SYNS ELATED, exhilarated, cheerful, animated, lively, high-spirited, spirited, buoyant, effervescent, vivacious, excited, ebullient, enthusiastic, irrepressible, energetic.

**exude** v. **1** discharge slowly and steadily. **2** display a quality clearly.

**exult** v. feel or show delight.
■ **exultant** adj. **exultation** n.

**eye** n. **1** the organ of sight. **2** something compared to an eye in shape, position, etc. ● v. (**eyed**, **eyeing**) look at. □ **eyeball** the round part of the eye within the eyelids. **eyebrow** the strip of hair on the ridge above the eye socket. **eyelash** each of the hairs on the edges of the eyelids. **eyelet** a small round hole through which a lace can be threaded. **eyelid** either of the two folds of skin which cover the eye when closed. **eyeshadow** a cosmetic applied to the skin around the eyes. **eyesight** the ability to see. **eyesore** a very ugly thing. **eye-witness** a person who has seen something happen.

**eyrie** n. an eagle's nest.

# Ff

**F** abbr. Fahrenheit.

**f** abbr. Music forte.

**fable** n. a short story, often with a moral.

**fabled** adj. famous; legendary.

**fabric** n. **1** woven or knitted cloth. **2** the essential structure of a building etc.
▷ SYNS CLOTH, material, textile, stuff.

**fabricate** v. **1** invent a story etc. **2** construct. ■ **fabrication** n.
▷ SYNS MAKE UP, invent, concoct, think up, hatch, trump up.

**fabulous** adj. **1** extraordinarily great. **2** mythical. **3** inf. very good.
▷ SYNS **1** MYTHICAL, legendary, fairy-tale, fabled; imaginary, made-up. **2** (inf.) see **MARVELLOUS**.

**facade** n. the front of a building; an outward appearance, esp. a misleading one.

**face** n. **1** the front of the head; a person's expression. **2** an aspect. **3** a surface; a side of a mountain. **4** the dial of a clock. • v. **1** have your face or front towards; confront boldly. **2** put a facing on. □ **facecloth** a small cloth for washing the face. **faceless** remote and impersonal. **facelift** an operation to tighten the skin of the face. **lose** (or **save**) **face** suffer (or avoid) humiliation.
▷ SYNS **1** COUNTENANCE, visage, physiognomy, features; inf. mug. **2** EXPRESSION, look, appearance, air. • v. **1** LOOK ON TO, overlook,

give on to. **2** ENCOUNTER, meet, come up against, confront, withstand, cope with, deal with, brave.

**facet** n. **1** an aspect. **2** one of the sides of a cut gem.
▷ SYNS ASPECT, feature, element, side.

**facetious** adj. inappropriately humorous about serious subjects.
▷ SYNS FLIPPANT, frivolous, tongue-in-cheek, glib.

**facia** = FASCIA.

**facial** adj. of the face. • n. a beauty treatment for the face.

**facile** adj. misleadingly simple; superficial or glib.

**facilitate** v. make easy or easier. ■ **facilitation** n.

**facility** n. **1** a building, service, or piece of equipment provided for a particular purpose. **2** natural ability.
▷ SYNS **1** APTITUDE, talent, gift, flair, skill, knack, genius, ability, capability. **2** AMENITY, resource, service, convenience.

**facing** n. an outer covering; a layer of material at the edge of a garment for strengthening, etc.

**facsimile** n. an exact copy of a document etc.

**fact** n. something known to be true. □ **in fact** actually.
▷ SYNS **1** TRUTH, actuality, reality, certainty. **2** DETAIL, particular, point, item, piece of information.

**faction** n. an organized group within a larger one; dissension between such groups.
▷ SYNS GROUP, section, set, wing, branch, arm, contingent, camp, clique, coterie, caucus, cabal, splinter group.

**factor** n. 1 a circumstance that contributes to a result. 2 a number that divides into another number exactly.
• v. consider when making a decision.
▷ SYNS n. ELEMENT, part, component, ingredient, constituent, facet, aspect, characteristic, consideration.

**factory** n. (pl. **-ies**) a building in which goods are manufactured.

**factual** adj. based on or containing facts. ■ **factually** adv.
▷ SYNS TRUTHFUL, true, accurate, authentic, historical, genuine; true-to-life, correct, exact, honest, faithful, unbiased, objective, unvarnished.

**faculty** n. (pl. **-ies**) 1 a mental or physical power. 2 a department teaching a specified subject in a university or college.

**fad** n. a craze.
▷ SYNS CRAZE, mania, enthusiasm, vogue, fashion, trend.

**fade** v. lose colour, freshness, or vigour; disappear gradually.
▷ SYNS DWINDLE, diminish, die away, disappear, vanish, peter out, dissolve, melt away, wane.

**faeces** (US **feces**) pl.n. waste matter discharged from the bowels.

**fag** n. inf. 1 a tiring or tedious task. 2 a cigarette.

**faggot** n. 1 a tied bundle of sticks or twigs. 2 a ball of chopped seasoned liver etc., baked or fried.

**Fahrenheit** n. a temperature scale with the freezing point of water at 32° and boiling point at 212°.

**fail** v. 1 be unsuccessful; be unable to meet a particular standard. 2 neglect your duty; disappoint someone relying on you. 3 become weak; cease functioning. • n. a mark too low to pass an exam.
▷ SYNS v. BE UNSUCCESSFUL, fall through, founder, misfire, come to grief; inf. come a cropper.

**failing** n. a weakness or fault.
• prep. if not.
▷ SYNS n. FAULT, shortcoming, weakness, imperfection, defect, flaw, foible.

**failure** n. 1 lack of success. 2 an unsuccessful person or thing. 3 an act of failing.

**faint** adj. 1 indistinct or slight. 2 about to faint. • v. collapse unconscious. • n. the act or state of fainting. □ **faint-hearted** timid.
▷ SYNS adj. 1 INDISTINCT, unclear, vague, ill-defined, pale, faded. 2 SOFT, quiet, muted, low, weak, feeble, muffled. 3 a faint chance: SLIGHT, small, slim, slender, remote, unlikely. 4 DIZZY, giddy, light-headed; inf. woozy. • v. BLACK OUT, pass out, keel over, swoon.

**fair** adj. 1 treating people equally. 2 just or appropriate. 3 quite large. 4 (of hair) blonde. 5 (of weather) fine and dry.
• n. 1 a funfair. 2 a periodic gathering for a sale of goods. □ **fairground** an outdoor area where a funfair is held. **fairway** a part of a golf course between a tee and a green.
▷ SYNS adj. 1 JUST, impartial, unbiased, unprejudiced, objective, even-handed, equitable,

lawful, legal, legitimate.
**2** BLONDE, light, yellow, golden, flaxen. **3** FINE, dry, bright, clear, sunny. • **n. 1** FESTIVAL, carnival, fete, gala, funfair. **2** EXHIBITION, display, show, exposition, expo.

**fairly** adv. **1** justly. **2** moderately; quite.
▷ SYNS REASONABLY, quite, pretty, passably, moderately, rather, somewhat.

**fairy** n. (pl. **-ies**) an imaginary small being with magical powers. □ **fairy godmother** a benefactress providing help in times of difficulty.

**faith** n. reliance or trust; belief in religious doctrine. □ **faith healing** healing achieved with religious belief rather than medicine.
▷ SYNS **1** TRUST, belief, confidence, conviction, credence, reliance; optimism, hopefulness. **2** RELIGION, church, denomination, belief, creed, persuasion, teaching, doctrine.

**faithful** adj. **1** loyal. **2** true or accurate. ■ **faithfully** adv.
▷ SYNS **1** LOYAL, devoted, constant, dependable, true, reliable, staunch, steadfast, dedicated, committed. **2** ACCURATE, true, exact, precise, strict.

**faithless** adj. disloyal.

**fake** n. a person or thing that is not genuine. • adj. counterfeit. • v. make an imitation of; pretend.
▷ SYNS **n. 1** FORGERY, counterfeit, copy. **2** FRAUD, charlatan, impostor, sham, mountebank, quack; inf. phoney. • adj. COUNTERFEIT, forged, fraudulent, bogus, sham, imitation, false, pseudo, mock, simulated, artificial, synthetic, reproduction, ersatz;

assumed, affected, put-on, feigned, insincere; inf. phoney.

**falcon** n. a small long-winged hawk.

**falconry** n. the keeping and training of birds of prey.

**fall** v. **1** move downwards without control. **2** collapse to the ground. **3** hang or slope down. **4** become less or lower. **5** become. **6** be captured or defeated. • **n. 1** an act of falling. **2** something fallen. **3** (**falls**) a waterfall. **4** US autumn. □ **fallout** airborne radioactive debris. **fall out** quarrel. **fall through** (of a plan) fail.
▷ SYNS **v. 1** DROP, descend, sink, dive, plummet, cascade. **2** FALL DOWN/OVER, tumble, topple over, collapse. **3** DECREASE, decline, go down, diminish, dwindle, plummet, slump. • **n. 1** DOWNFALL, collapse, failure, decline, demise. **2** DECREASE, cut, dip, reduction, slump.

**fallacy** n. (pl. **-ies**) a mistaken belief; a false argument. ■ **fallacious** adj.
▷ SYNS MISCONCEPTION, mistake, misapprehension, delusion, misinterpretation.

**fallible** adj. liable to make mistakes. ■ **fallibility** n.

**fallow** adj. (of land) left unplanted to restore its fertility.

**false** adj. **1** not true or correct. **2** fake; artificial. **3** mistaken.
▷ SYNS INCORRECT, wrong, untrue, untruthful, fictitious, inaccurate.

**falsehood** n. a lie.

**falsetto** n. (pl. **-os**) a high-pitched voice.

**falsify** v. (**falsified, falsifying**) alter fraudulently. ■ **falsification** n.

▷ SYNS ALTER, doctor, tamper with, forge, distort.

**falter** v. lose strength or momentum; move or speak hesitantly.

**fame** n. the state of being famous. ■ **famed** adj.
▷ SYNS RENOWN, celebrity, stardom, popularity, prominence, eminence, stature; notoriety, infamy.

**familiar** adj. **1** well known. **2** having knowledge or experience. **3** friendly or informal. ■ **familiarity** n. **familiarize** v.
▷ SYNS **1** WELL KNOWN, recognized, accustomed, common, customary, everyday, ordinary, commonplace, habitual, usual, stock, routine, mundane, run-of-the-mill, conventional. **2** ACQUAINTED, knowledgeable, informed, conversant, well up, au fait.

**family** n. (pl. **-ies**) parents and their children; a person's children; a set of relatives; a group of related plants, animals, or things.
▷ SYNS **1** RELATIVES, relations, (next of) kin, kinsfolk, kindred, people; inf. folks. **2** CHILDREN, offspring, progeny; inf. kids. **3** ANCESTRY, parentage, pedigree, birth, descent, lineage, bloodline, stock, forebears, forefathers.

**famine** n. extreme scarcity of food.

**famished** adj. extremely hungry.

**famous** adj. known to very many people.
▷ SYNS WELL KNOWN, renowned, celebrated, famed, noted, prominent, eminent, great, illustrious, acclaimed; popular, legendary; notorious, infamous.

**fan** n. **1** a hand-held or mechanical device to create a current of air. **2** an enthusiastic admirer or supporter. • v. **1** cool with a fan. **2** spread from a central point.
▷ SYNS n. ADMIRER, follower, devotee, enthusiast, aficionado, supporter; inf. groupie.

**fanatic** n. **1** a person who holds extreme or dangerous political or religious opinions. **2** a person who is very enthusiastic about a hobby etc. ■ **fanaticism** n.
▷ SYNS EXTREMIST, militant, zealot, dogmatist, partisan, radical; inf. maniac.

**fanatical** adj. **1** holding extreme political or religious opinions. **2** obsessively concerned with something.
▷ SYNS **1** EXTREMIST, extreme, zealous, militant, dogmatic, radical, intolerant. **2** ENTHUSIASTIC, eager, keen, fervent, passionate, obsessive.

**fancier** n. a person with a special interest in something specified.

**fanciful** adj. imaginative; imaginary.

**fancy** n. **1** imagination; an unfounded idea. **2** a desire or whim. • adj. (**-ier, -iest**) ornamental, elaborate. • v. **1** imagine; suppose. **2** inf. feel a desire for something; be attracted to someone. □ **fancy dress** an unusual costume or design worn at a party.
▷ SYNS n. DESIRE, urge, wish; inclination, whim, impulse, notion; yearning, longing, hankering; inf. yen. • adj. ORNATE, elaborate, ornamental, decorative, ostentatious, showy, flamboyant; inf. flash, snazzy. • v. **1** THINK,

believe, suppose, imagine, reckon. **2** WISH FOR, want, desire, hanker after.

**fanfare** n. a short ceremonious sounding of trumpets.

**fang** n. a long sharp tooth; a snake's tooth that injects poison.

**fantasize** (or **-ise**) v. daydream.

**fantastic** adj. **1** hard to believe; bizarre or exotic. **2** inf. excellent. ■ **fantastically** adv.

**fantasy** n. **1** the imagining of improbable things. **2** an imagined situation. **3** fiction involving magic and adventure.
▷ SYNS **1** IMAGINATION, fancy, creativity, invention, make-believe. **2** DREAM, daydream, pipe dream.

**far** adv. **1** at, to, or by a great distance. **2** by a great deal. • adj. distant.
▷ SYNS adj. FARAWAY, far-flung, distant, remote, out of the way, outlying.

**farce** n. **1** a comedy involving ridiculous situations. **2** an absurd event.

**farcical** adj. absurd or ridiculous.
▷ SYNS RIDICULOUS, ludicrous, absurd, laughable, preposterous, nonsensical.

**fare** n. **1** the price charged for a passenger to travel; a passenger paying this. **2** food provided. • v. get on or be treated in a specified way.

**farewell** exclam. goodbye. • n. a parting.

**far-fetched** adj. unconvincing or unlikely.
▷ SYNS IMPROBABLE, unlikely, implausible, incredible, unbelievable.

**farm** n. a unit of land used for raising crops or livestock. • v. make a living by raising crops or livestock. □ **farmhouse** a farmer's house. **farmyard** an enclosed area round farm buildings. ■ **farmer** n.

**farrier** n. a person who shoes horses.

**farrow** v. give birth to piglets.

**farther**, **farthest** vars. of FURTHER, FURTHEST.

**fascia** n. **1** the instrument panel of a vehicle. **2** a nameplate over a shop front.

**fascinate** v. irresistibly interest and attract. ■ **fascination** n.
▷ SYNS CAPTIVATE, enchant, bewitch, enthral, entrance, hold spellbound, rivet, transfix, mesmerize, charm, intrigue, absorb, engross.

**fascism** n. a system of extreme right-wing dictatorship. ■ **fascist** n. & adj.

**fashion** n. **1** a manner of doing something. **2** a popular trend; producing and marketing styles of clothing etc. • v. make into a particular shape.
▷ SYNS n. **1** STYLE, vogue, trend, mode, taste, craze, rage, fad. **2** CLOTHES, couture; inf. rag trade. **3** WAY, manner, method, system, mode, approach.

**fashionable** adj. currently popular. ■ **fashionably** adv.
▷ SYNS STYLISH, up to date, contemporary, modern, in vogue, modish, popular, all the rage, trendsetting, smart, chic, elegant; inf. trendy, with it.

**fast**[1] adj. **1** moving or able to move quickly; working or done quickly. **2** (of a clock etc.) showing a time ahead of the correct one. **3** firmly fixed.

• adv. 1 quickly. 2 securely or tightly; soundly. ■ fastener n.

▷ SYNS adj. 1 QUICK, rapid, swift, speedy, brisk, hurried, breakneck, hasty, express, fleet; inf. nippy. 2 SECURE, fastened, tight, firm, closed, shut; immovable. • adv. QUICKLY, rapidly, swiftly, speedily, briskly, posthaste; inf. hell for leather, at a rate of knots.

**fast²** v. go without food. • n. a period without eating.

**fasten** v. close or do up securely; fix or hold in place.

▷ SYNS 1 ATTACH, fix, affix, clip, pin, tie, bind, tether, hitch, anchor. 2 BOLT, lock, secure, chain, seal; do up.

**fastidious** adj. attentive to details; very concerned about cleanliness.

▷ SYNS FUSSY, over-particular, finicky; scrupulous, painstaking, punctilious; inf. choosy, picky, pernickety.

**fat** n. an oily substance found in animals; a substance used in cooking made from this, or from plants. • adj. (fatter, fattest) excessively plump; substantial. ■ fatten v. fatty adj.

▷ SYNS adj. PLUMP, stout, overweight, obese, heavy, chubby, portly, corpulent, rotund, flabby, pot-bellied, paunchy, fleshy; inf. tubby, beefy, podgy, roly-poly.

**fatal** adj. causing death or disaster. ■ fatally adv.

▷ SYNS 1 MORTAL, deadly, lethal; terminal, incurable. 2 RUINOUS, disastrous, catastrophic, calamitous, cataclysmic.

**fatality** n. (pl. -ies) a death caused by accident or in war etc.

**fate** n. 1 a power thought to control all events. 2 the unavoidable events or outcome of a person's life. • v. be destined to happen in a particular way.

▷ SYNS n. 1 DESTINY, providence, chance, the stars, kismet. 2 future, destiny, lot, end. • v. PREDESTINE, preordain, destine.

**fateful** adj. leading to great usu. unpleasant events.

**father** n. a male parent or ancestor; a founder; a title of certain priests. • v. be the father of. □ father-in-law the father of your wife or husband. fatherland a person's native country. ■ fatherhood n. fatherly adj.

▷ SYNS n. PARENT, paterfamilias, patriarch; inf. dad, daddy, pop, pa, pater. • v. SIRE, beget.

**fathom** n. a measure (1.82 m) of the depth of water. • v. understand.

**fatigue** n. 1 tiredness. 2 weakness in metal etc., caused by stress. 3 (fatigues) soldiers' clothes for specific tasks. • v. tire or weaken.

▷ SYNS n. TIREDNESS, weariness, exhaustion, lethargy, lassitude, listlessness, enervation.

**fatuous** adj. silly.

▷ SYNS SILLY, foolish, stupid, senseless, inane, idiotic, ridiculous, asinine, vacuous, witless.

**fault** n. 1 a defect or imperfection. 2 responsibility for something wrong; a weakness or offence. 3 a break in layers of rock. • v. criticize. ■ faultless adj.

▷ SYNS n. 1 DEFECT, flaw, imperfection, blemish, failing, weakness, weak point, shortcoming. 2 MISDEED, wrongdoing, offence, misdemeanour, indiscretion, transgression, peccadillo.

**faulty** adj. not working.
▷ SYNS DEFECTIVE, malfunctioning, broken, out of order, damaged.

**faun** n. a Roman god of the countryside with a goat's legs and horns.

**fauna** n. the animals of an area or period.

**faux pas** n. (pl. **faux pas**) an embarrassing social blunder.

**favour** (US **favor**) n. 1 liking or approval. 2 a kind or helpful act. 3 favouritism. • v. like, approve of, or support.
▷ SYNS n. 1 SERVICE, good turn/ deed, kindness, courtesy. 2 AP-PROVAL, approbation, goodwill, kindness, benevolence. 3 BACKING, support, patronage. • v. 1 APPROVE OF, advocate, recommend, support, back, be in favour of. 2 PREFER, like, be partial to, go for.

**favourable** (US **favorable**) adj. 1 showing approval; giving consent. 2 advantageous.
■ **favourably** adv.
▷ SYNS 1 APPROVING, compli-mentary, commendatory, enthusiastic, positive. 2 ADVAN-TAGEOUS, in your favour, bene-ficial, helpful, good, promising, encouraging, auspicious, oppor-tune, propitious.

**favourite** (US **favorite**) adj. liked above others. • n. a favour-ite person or thing; a com-petitor expected to win.
▷ SYNS adj. BEST-LOVED, most-liked, favoured, preferred, chosen, pet. • n. FIRST CHOICE, pick; darling, pet; inf. blue-eyed boy.

**favouritism** (US **favoritism**) n. unfairly generous treatment of one person or group.

**fawn** n. 1 a deer in its first year. 2 light yellowish brown. • v. try to win favour by flattery.

**fax** n. a copy of a document which has been scanned and transmitted electronically; a machine for sending and re-ceiving faxes. • v. send someone a fax.

**FBI** abbr. (in the USA) Federal Bureau of Investigation.

**fear** n. an unpleasant sensation caused by nearness of danger or pain. • v. be afraid of. ■ **fearless** adj.
▷ SYNS n. FEARFULNESS, fright, terror, alarm, panic, trepidation, dread, nervousness, anxiety, worry, unease, foreboding.

**fearful** adj. 1 feeling or causing fear. 2 inf. very great. ■ **fearfully** adv.
▷ SYNS AFRAID, frightened, scared, terrified, apprehensive, alarmed, uneasy, nervous, panicky, anxious, worried.

**fearsome** adj. frightening.

**feasible** adj. able to be done.
■ **feasibility** n.
▷ SYNS PRACTICABLE, possible, achievable, attainable, workable, viable, reasonable, realistic, within reason.

**feast** n. a large elaborate meal; an annual religious celebration. • v. eat heartily.
▷ SYNS n. BANQUET, dinner, repast; inf. blowout, spread.

**feat** n. a remarkable achievement.
▷ SYNS DEED, act, action, exploit, achievement, accomplishment, performance, attainment.

**feather** n. each of the structures with a central shaft and fringe of fine strands, growing from a bird's skin.
■ **feathery** adj.

**feature** n. 1 a distinctive part of the face. 2 a noticeable attribute or aspect. 3 a newspaper article on a particular topic. 4 a full-length cinema film. • v. be a feature of or in.
▷ SYNS n. 1 CHARACTERISTIC, property, attribute, quality, trait, mark, peculiarity, idiosyncrasy; aspect, facet, side. 2 (**features**) FACE, countenance, visage, physiognomy; inf. mug. 3 ARTICLE, piece, item, report, story, column.

**febrile** adj. feverish; tense and excited.

**February** n. the second month.

**feces** US sp. of **FAECES**.

**feckless** adj. idle and irresponsible.

**fed** past and p.p. of **FEED**. □ **fed up** inf. annoyed or bored.

**federal** adj. of a system in which states unite under a central authority but are independent in internal affairs.
■ **federalism** n. **federalist** n.

**federate** v. unite on a federal basis.

**federation** n. a federal group of states.
▷ SYNS CONFEDERATION, league, alliance, coalition, union, syndicate, consortium, association.

**fee** n. a sum payable for professional advice or services, or for a privilege.

**feeble** adj. weak; ineffective.
■ **feebly** adv.
▷ SYNS 1 WEAK, frail, infirm, sickly, puny, delicate, ailing, helpless, debilitated, decrepit,
incapacitated, enfeebled. 2 INEFFECTUAL, unsuccessful, ineffective, unconvincing, implausible, flimsy.

**feed** v. (**fed**, **feeding**) give food to a person or animal; eat; supply with material or information. • n. food for animals; an act of feeding. □ **feedback** comments about a product or a person's performance; the return of part of the output of an amplifier to its input, causing a whistling sound.
▷ SYNS v. 1 NOURISH, sustain, cater for, provide for. 2 EAT, graze, browse.

**feel** v. 1 perceive or examine by touch. 2 give a specified sensation when touched. 3 experience an emotion or sensation. 4 have an opinion or belief. • n. 1 an act of touching. 2 the sense of touch. 3 an impression.
▷ SYNS v. 1 TOUCH, stroke, caress, fondle, handle, finger. 2 PERCEIVE, sense, notice, be aware of, be conscious of. 3 EXPERIENCE, undergo, go through, bear, endure, suffer. 4 THINK, believe, consider, hold, judge.

**feeler** n. 1 a long slender organ of touch in certain animals. 2 a tentative suggestion.

**feeling** n. 1 an emotional state or reaction. 2 (**feelings**) the emotional side of a person's character. 3 the ability to feel. 4 the sensation of touching or being touched. 5 a belief or opinion.
▷ SYNS 1 SENSATION, sense, awareness, consciousness; emotion, sentiment. 2 IDEA, suspicion, notion, inkling, hunch; presentiment, premonition.

**3** SYMPATHY, pity, compassion, understanding, concern, sensitivity, empathy, fellow feeling. **4** ATMOSPHERE, air, aura, feel, ambience, impression.

**feet** pl. of FOOT.

**feign** v. pretend.

**feint** n. a sham attack made to divert attention. • v. make a feint.

**feisty** adj. (-ier, -iest) inf. lively and spirited.

**felicitations** pl.n. congratulations.

**felicitous** adj. well-chosen or apt.

**felicity** n. (pl. -ies) **1** happiness. **2** a pleasing feature.

**feline** adj. of cats; catlike. • n. an animal of the cat family.

**fell**[1] past of FALL.

**fell**[2] n. a stretch of moor or hilly land, esp. in northern England. • v. cut or knock down.

**fellow** n. **1** inf. a man or boy. **2** an associate or equal. **3** a thing like another. **4** a member of a learned society or governing body of a college.

**fellowship** n. **1** friendly association with others. **2** a society.

**felon** n. a person who has committed a serious violent crime. ■ **felony** n.

**felt**[1] past and p.p. of FEEL.

**felt**[2] n. cloth made by matting and pressing wool. □ **felt-tip pen** a pen with a writing point made of fibre.

**female** adj. of the sex that can bear offspring or produce eggs; (of plants) fruit-bearing. • n. a female animal or plant.

**feminine** adj. of, like, or traditionally considered suitable for women. ■ **femininity** n.

**feminism** n. a movement or theory that supports the rights of women. ■ **feminist** n.

**fen** n. a low-lying marshy or flooded tract of land.

**fence** n. **1** a barrier enclosing an area. **2** inf. a dealer in stolen goods. • v. **1** surround with a fence. **2** practise the sport of fencing.

▷ SYNS n. BARRIER, railing, paling, barricade, stockade. • v. ENCLOSE, surround, encircle; shut in, confine, pen in.

**fencing** n. **1** the sport of fighting with blunted swords. **2** fences or material for making fences.

**fend** v. **1** (**fend for yourself**) support yourself. **2** (**fend off**) ward off.

▷ SYNS **1** (**fend for yourself**) TAKE CARE OF YOURSELF, support yourself, get by, cope, manage. **2** (**fend off**) WARD OFF, stave off, parry, turn aside, divert, deflect.

**fender** n. **1** a low frame bordering a fireplace. **2** US a vehicle's mudguard or bumper.

**feng shui** n. an ancient Chinese system of designing buildings and arranging objects to ensure a favourable flow of energy.

**fennel** n. an aniseed-flavoured plant.

**feral** adj. wild.

**ferment** v. break down chemically through the action of yeast or bacteria. • n. social unrest. ■ **fermentation** n.

**fern** n. a flowerless plant with feathery green leaves.

**ferocious** adj. fierce or savage. ■ **ferocity** n.

▷ syns FIERCE, savage, brutal, ruthless, cruel, merciless, vicious, barbarous, violent, barbaric, inhuman, bloodthirsty, murderous; wild, untamed, predatory, rapacious.

**ferret** n. a small animal of the weasel family. • v. (**ferreted**, **ferreting**) rummage.

**ferric** (or **ferrous**) adj. of or containing iron.

**ferry** n. (pl. **-ies**) a boat for transporting passengers and goods. • v. (**ferried**, **ferrying**) convey in a ferry; transport.

**fertile** adj. able to produce vegetation, fruit, or young; productive or inventive. ■ **fertility** n.

▷ syns 1 FRUITFUL, productive, rich, fecund. 2 INVENTIVE, creative, original, ingenious, resourceful, productive.

**fertilize** (or **-ise**) v. 1 introduce pollen or sperm into. 2 add fertilizer to. ■ **fertilization** n.

**fertilizer** (or **fertiliser**) n. material added to soil to make it more fertile.

**fervent** adj. showing intense feeling.

▷ syns PASSIONATE, ardent, impassioned, intense, vehement, heartfelt, emotional, fervid; zealous, fanatical, enthusiastic, avid.

**fervid** adj. fervent.

**fervour** (US **fervor**) n. intensity of feeling.

**fester** v. 1 make or become septic. 2 (of ill feeling) become worse.

**festival** n. 1 a day or period of celebration. 2 a series of concerts, plays, etc.

▷ syns CARNIVAL, gala, fête, fiesta, celebrations, festivities.

**festive** adj. of a festival.

▷ syns JOLLY, merry, joyous, joyful, happy, jovial, light-hearted, cheerful, jubilant.

**festivity** n. (pl. **-ies**) an event or activity celebrating a special occasion; celebration.

**festoon** n. a hanging chain of flowers or ribbons etc. • v. decorate with hanging ornaments.

▷ syns V. DECORATE, hang, drape, wreathe, garland, adorn, ornament, deck.

**fetch** v. 1 go for and bring back. 2 be sold for a specified price. 3 (**fetching**) attractive.

▷ syns 1 (GO AND) GET, bring, carry, convey, transport. 2 SELL FOR, realize, go for, bring in, yield.

**fete** n. an outdoor event to raise money for something, involving entertainments and sale of goods. • v. honour or entertain lavishly.

**fetid** (or **foetid**) adj. stinking.

**fetish** n. an object worshipped as having magical powers.

**fetlock** n. a horse's leg above and behind the hoof.

**fetter** n. a shackle for the ankles; a restraint. • v. put into fetters; restrict.

**fettle** n. condition.

**fetus** (or **foetus**) n. (pl. **-tuses**) an unborn baby of a mammal. ■ **fetal** adj.

**feud** n. a state of lasting hostility. • v. be involved in a feud.

▷ syns n. VENDETTA, conflict, rivalry, quarrel, argument, hostility, enmity, strife, discord, bad blood.

**fever** n. an abnormally high body temperature; nervous excitement. ■ **fevered** adj.

**feverish** adj. **1** having a fever.
**2** showing strong feelings of
nervous excitement or energy.
▷ SYNS **1** FEVERED, febrile, hot,
burning. **2** FRENZIED, frenetic,
agitated, excited, nervous,
overwrought, frantic, worked-
up, wild.

**few** adj. & n. not many.
▷ SYNS **1** NOT MANY, hardly any,
scarcely any, one or two, a
handful of, a couple of.
**2** SCARCE, rare, in short supply,
scant, thin on the ground.

**fez** n. (pl. **fezzes**) a high flat-
topped red cap worn by some
Muslim men.

**fiancé** n. (fem. **fiancée**) a person
to whom you are engaged to be
married.

**fiasco** n. (pl. **-os**) a total and
ludicrous failure.
▷ SYNS FAILURE, disaster, debacle,
catastrophe; inf. flop, washout.

**fib** n. a trivial lie. • v. (**fibbed**,
**fibbing**) tell a fib. ■ **fibber** n.

**fibre** (US **fiber**) n. **1** a threadlike
strand. **2** a substance formed of
fibres. **3** roughage in food.
**4** strength of character.
□ **fibreglass** a rigid plastic material containing glass fibres.
**fibre optics** the use of glass
fibres to send information in
the form of light. ■ **fibrous** adj.
▷ SYNS THREAD, strand, filament.

**fickle** adj. not loyal.
▷ SYNS CAPRICIOUS, changeable,
disloyal, volatile, mercurial,
flighty, giddy.

**fiction** n. literature describing
imaginary events and people; an
invented story. ■ **fictional** adj.
▷ SYNS **1** NOVELS, stories, creative
writing. **2** FABRICATION, lie,
untruth, falsehood, invention,
fib.

**fictitious** adj. imaginary or
invented.

**fiddle** inf. n. **1** a violin. **2** a
swindle. • v. **1** fidget with
something. **2** falsify figures etc.

**fiddly** adj. inf. awkward or
complicated.

**fidelity** n. faithfulness.
▷ SYNS FAITHFULNESS, loyalty,
commitment, constancy,
trustworthiness, dependability,
reliability; allegiance,
obedience.

**fidget** v. (**fidgeted**, **fidgeting**)
make small restless
movements. • n. a person who
fidgets.

**fidgety** adj. restless or impatient.
▷ SYNS RESTLESS, restive, on edge,
uneasy, nervous, nervy; inf.
twitchy, jittery.

**field** n. **1** an enclosed area of
open ground, esp. for pasture or
cultivation; a sports ground.
**2** an area rich in a natural
product. **3** a sphere of action or
interest. **4** all the competitors in
a race or contest. • v. **1** (in
cricket etc.) stop and return the
ball to prevent scoring. **2** put a
team into a contest. □ **field day**
an opportunity for successful
unrestrained action. **field
events** athletic contests other
than races. **field glasses** binoculars. **field marshal** an army
officer of the highest rank.
**fieldwork** practical research
done outside a laboratory or
office. ■ **fielder** n.
▷ SYNS n. **1** PASTURE, meadow,
paddock; lit. glebe, lea, mead.
**2** AREA, sphere, province,
department, subject, domain,
territory. **3** field of vision:
RANGE, scope, extent; limits.

**fiend** n. **1** an evil spirit; a cruel or mischievous person. **2** inf. a devotee or addict: *a fitness fiend*.
▷ SYNS **1** DEVIL, demon. **2** BRUTE, monster, beast, barbarian, sadist, ogre.

**fiendish** adj. cruel; extremely difficult.
▷ SYNS WICKED, cruel, vicious, evil, villainous; brutal, savage, barbaric, barbarous, inhuman, murderous, ruthless, merciless, dastardly.

**fierce** adj. violent or aggressive; intense or powerful.
▷ SYNS **1** FEROCIOUS, savage, wild, vicious, bloodthirsty, dangerous, aggressive, violent. **2** PASSIONATE, intense, powerful, ardent, strong, impassioned, fervent, fiery, fervid.

**fiery** adj. (-ier, -iest) **1** consisting of or like fire. **2** passionate.

**fiesta** n. (in Spanish-speaking countries) a festival.

**fifteen** adj. & n. one more than fourteen; 15. ■ **fifteenth** adj. & n.

**fifth** adj. & n. the next after fourth.

**fifty** adj. & n. five times ten; 50. □ **fifty-fifty** with equal shares or chances. ■ **fiftieth** adj. & n.

**fig** n. a soft, sweet pear-shaped fruit.

**fight** v. **1** take part in a violent physical struggle or war. **2** argue. **3** try hard to overcome or achieve. • n. an act of fighting.
▷ SYNS v. **1** BRAWL, grapple, scuffle, tussle, spar, wrestle; battle, war, take up arms. **2** QUARREL, argue, feud, bicker, squabble, fall out. **3** OPPOSE, contest, take a stand against, challenge, defy. • n. BRAWL, scuffle, tussle, skirmish;

battle, engagement, conflict, combat; quarrel, dispute, argument, feud.

**fighter** n. a person who fights; an aircraft designed for attacking others.

**figment** n. something that exists only in the imagination.

**figurative** adj. metaphorical.

**figure** n. **1** a number or numerical symbol. **2** bodily shape. **3** a well-known person. **4** a geometric shape. **5** a diagram or drawing. • v. **1** play a part. **2** calculate. **3** US inf. suppose or think. □ **figurehead 1** a leader without real power. **2** a carved statue at the front of a sailing ship. **figure of speech** an expression used for effect rather than literally.
▷ SYNS n. **1** NUMBER, numeral, digit, integer, symbol. **2** COST, price, amount, value, total, sum. **3** SHAPE, form, outline, silhouette. **4** BODY, physique, build, frame, proportions. **5** DIAGRAM, illustration, picture, drawing.

**figurine** n. a statuette.

**filament** n. a slender thread; a fine wire giving off light in an electric lamp.

**filch** v. inf. steal.

**file** n. **1** a folder or box for keeping documents. **2** a set of data in a computer. **3** a line of people or things one behind another. **4** a tool with a rough surface for smoothing things. • v. **1** place a document in a file; place on record. **2** march in a long line. **3** shape or smooth a surface with a file.
▷ SYNS n. **1** FOLDER, portfolio, document case. **2** DOSSIER, information, documents, records, data. **3** LINE, column, row,

string, chain, crocodile. • v.
**1** RECORD, categorize, classify, organize, store, archive.
**2** MARCH, parade, troop.

**filial** adj. of or due from a son or daughter.

**filibuster** n. a long speech which delays progress in a parliament etc.

**filigree** n. ornamental work of fine gold or silver wire.

**fill** v. **1** make or become full; stop up a cavity. **2** occupy; appoint someone to a vacant post. • n. as much as you want or can bear. □ **fill in 1** complete a form etc. **2** act as someone's substitute. **3** tell someone more details.
▷ SYNS v. **1** CROWD INTO, throng, squeeze into, cram into. **2** PACK, load, stack, supply, stock; replenish, top up. **3** STOP UP, block up, plug, seal, close, clog.

**filler** n. a thing or material used to fill a gap or increase bulk.

**fillet** n. a piece of boneless meat or fish. • v. (**filleted, filleting**) remove bones from.

**filling** n. a substance used to fill a cavity etc. • adj. (of food) satisfying hunger.

**fillip** n. a stimulus or incentive.

**filly** n. (pl. **-ies**) a young female horse.

**film** n. **1** a thin flexible strip of light-sensitive material for taking photographs. **2** a story told through a sequence of images projected on a screen. **3** a thin layer. • v. make a film of; record on film.
▷ SYNS n. **1** MOVIE, (motion) picture, video; inf. flick. **2** LAYER, coat, coating, covering, patina, skin.

**filmy** adj. (**-ier, -iest**) thin and almost transparent.

**filter** n. a device or substance that lets liquid or gas pass through but holds back solid particles; a device that absorbs some of the light passing through it; an arrangement allowing traffic to filter. • v. pass through a filter; move gradually in or out.
▷ SYNS v. STRAIN, sieve, sift, filtrate, purify, refine.

**filth** n. disgusting dirt; obscenity. ■ **filthiness** n.
▷ SYNS DIRT, muck, grime, mud, mire, slime, excrement, ordure, pollution.

**filthy** adj. disgustingly dirty.
▷ SYNS DIRTY, mucky, grubby, grimy, soiled, squalid, foul, polluted, contaminated, unwashed.

**filtrate** n. a filtered liquid.

**fin** n. a thin projection from a fish's body, used for propelling and steering itself; a similar projection to improve the stability of aircraft etc.

**final** adj. coming at the end of a series or process; allowing no dispute. • n. the last contest in a series; exams at the end of a degree course. ■ **finality** n. **finally** adv.
▷ SYNS adj. **1** LAST, closing, concluding, finishing, terminal, end, ultimate. **2** ABSOLUTE, conclusive, irrevocable, indisputable, decisive, definite, binding.

**finale** n. the closing section of a performance or musical composition.
▷ SYNS CLIMAX, culmination; end, ending, finish, close, conclusion, termination; denouement.

**finalist** n. a competitor in a final.

**finalize** (or **-ise**) v. decide on or conclude.
▷ SYNS COMPLETE, conclude, settle, work out, tie up, wrap up, put the finishing touches to, clinch, sew up.

**finance** n. management of money; money resources.
• v. fund.
▷ SYNS n. (**finances**) MONEY, funds, cash, resources, assets, capital, revenue, income. • v. PAY FOR, fund, subsidize, invest in, underwrite.

**financial** adj. to do with money.
▷ SYNS MONETARY, fiscal, pecuniary, economic.

**financier** n. a person engaged in financing businesses.

**finch** n. a small bird.

**find** v. 1 discover; learn. 2 work out or confirm by research etc. 3 declare a verdict. 4 (**find out**) detect; learn or discover.
• n. something found, esp. something valuable.
▷ SYNS v. 1 DISCOVER, come across, chance on, stumble on; come up with, hit on, bring to light, uncover, ferret out, locate, pinpoint, track down.
2 RECOVER, get back, retrieve. 3 GET, obtain, achieve, attain, acquire, gain, earn. 4 LEARN, realize, discover, observe, notice, note, perceive. 5 JUDGE, adjudge, declare, pronounce.

**finding** n. a conclusion reached after an inquiry etc.
▷ SYNS DECISION, conclusion, verdict, judgement, pronouncement, decree, ruling.

**fine¹** adj. 1 of very high quality; satisfactory; in good health. 2 bright and free from rain. 3 thin; in small particles; subtle.

▷ SYNS 1 EXCELLENT, first-class, first-rate, great, exceptional, outstanding, superior, magnificent, splendid, choice, select, prime, superb, rare; inf. top-notch. 2 ALL RIGHT, satisfactory, acceptable, agreeable, convenient, suitable; inf. OK. 3 WELL, healthy, fit, thriving, in the pink. 4 FAIR, dry, bright, clear, cloudless, sunny. 5 SHEER, light, lightweight, thin, flimsy, diaphanous, filmy, gauzy, transparent, translucent.

**fine²** n. a sum of money to be paid as a penalty. • v. punish with a fine.

**finery** n. showy clothes etc.

**finesse** n. delicate manipulation; tact.

**finger** n. each of the five parts extending from each hand; any of these other than the thumb; an object compared to a finger.
• v. touch or feel with the fingers. □ **fingerboard** a flat strip on the neck of a stringed instrument, against which the strings are pressed to vary the pitch. **fingerprint** a mark made by the pad of a person's finger, used for identification.

**finicky** adj. fussy; detailed and fiddly.

**finish** v. 1 bring or come to an end. 2 consume the whole or the remains of. 3 reach the end of a race etc. 4 (**finish off**) defeat or kill. 5 complete or put the final touches to. • n. 1 the final part or stage; the end of a race. 2 the way in which something is made; a surface appearance.
▷ SYNS v. 1 COMPLETE, end, conclude, close, terminate, round off; accomplish, carry out, discharge, do, get done;

stop, cease, discontinue; inf. wind up, wrap up, sew up. **2** USE UP, consume, exhaust, empty, drain, get through; inf. polish off. • n. END, completion, conclusion, close, cessation, termination, finale.

**finite** adj. limited.
▷ SYNS LIMITED, restricted, delimited, fixed.

**fiord** = FJORD.

**fir** n. an evergreen cone-bearing tree.

**fire** n. **1** the light, heat, etc. produced when something burns. **2** destructive burning. **3** wood or coal that is burning. **4** a gas or electrical heater. **5** passion. **6** the firing of guns. • v. **1** send a bullet or shell from a gun. **2** excite. **3** inf. dismiss from a job. **4** supply fuel to. □ **firearm** a rifle, pistol, or shotgun. **firebreak** a strip of open space to stop a fire from spreading. **fire brigade** an organized body of people employed to extinguish fires. **fire engine** a vehicle with equipment for putting out fires. **fire escape** a special staircase or apparatus for escape from a burning building. **firefly** a kind of beetle which glows in the dark. **fireman** a male firefighter. **fireplace** a recess at the base of a chimney for a domestic fire. **firework** a device containing chemicals that explode to produce spectacular effects. **firing squad** a group ordered to shoot a condemned person.
▷ SYNS n. **1** BLAZE, conflagration, inferno, flames, combustion. **2** PASSION, dynamism, energy, vigour, ardour, zeal, spirit, enthusiasm. • v. **1** SHOOT, let off, discharge. **2** STIMULATE, stir up, excite, arouse, rouse, inflame, inspire.

**firm** adj. not yielding when pressed or pushed; securely in place; (of a hold etc.) steady and strong; not giving way to argument, intimidation, etc. • adv. firmly. • v. make or become firm. • n. a business company.
▷ SYNS adj. **1** HARD, hardened, stiff, rigid, unyielding, solid, solidified, compacted, compressed, dense, set. **2** SECURE, stable, steady, strong, fixed, fast, immovable. **3** SETTLED, fixed, decided, definite, established, confirmed. **4** CONSTANT, enduring, abiding, long-standing, long-lasting, steadfast, devoted, staunch. **5** DETERMINED, resolute, resolved, unfaltering, unwavering, adamant, emphatic, insistent. • n. BUSINESS, company, concern, establishment, organization, corporation, conglomerate.

**firmament** n. the sky with the stars etc.

**first** adj. coming before all others in time, order, or importance. • n. **1** the first thing or occurrence; the first day of a month. **2** a top grade in an exam. • adv. before all others or another; before doing something else; for the first time. □ **first aid** basic treatment given for an injury etc. before a doctor arrives. **first-class** of the best quality; in the best category of accommodation; (of mail) delivered most quickly. **first-hand** directly from the original source. **first name** a personal name. **first-rate** excellent.
■ **firstly** adv.
▷ SYNS adj. **1** INITIAL, earliest, original, introductory, opening.

**2** BASIC, fundamental, rudimentary, key, cardinal, primary. **3** FOREMOST, principal, paramount, top, prime, chief, leading, main, major.

**firth** n. an estuary or narrow sea inlet in Scotland.

**fiscal** adj. of government finances.

**fish** n. (pl. **fish** or **fishes**) a cold-blooded vertebrate living wholly in water; its flesh as food. • v. try to catch fish; search or feel for something hidden; say something to elicit a compliment etc. □ **fisherman** a person who catches fish for a living or for sport. **fishmonger** a person selling fish for food. **fishnet** an open mesh fabric.

**fishery** n. (pl. **-ies**) a place where fish are reared commercially or caught in numbers.

**fishy** adj. (**-ier, -iest**) **1** like fish. **2** inf. arousing suspicion.

**fission** n. splitting, esp. of an atomic nucleus, with release of energy.

**fissure** n. a cleft.

**fist** n. a tightly closed hand. □ **fisticuffs** fighting with the fists.

**fit** adj. **1** suitable; right and proper; competent or qualified. **2** in good health. • v. **1** be the right size and shape for; be small or few enough to get into a space. **2** fix in place; join or be joined. **3** make or be appropriate; make competent. • n. **1** the way a garment etc. fits. **2** a sudden outburst of emotion, activity, etc.; a sudden attack of convulsions or loss of consciousness. ■ **fitness** n. **fitter** n.

▷ SYNS **adj. 1** WELL, healthy, in good health/shape, strong, robust, hale and hearty. **2** CAPABLE, able, competent, prepared, qualified, trained, equipped, eligible. **3** FITTING, proper, suitable, apt, appropriate. • v. **1** AGREE WITH, accord with, concur with, correspond with, match, tally with, suit, go with. **2** JOIN, connect, put together, fix, insert, attach. • n. **1** CONVULSION, spasm, paroxysm, seizure, attack. **2** BOUT, outburst, outbreak.

**fitful** adj. disturbed and erratic or restless. ■ **fitfully** adv.

**fitting** n. **1** a small part attached to furniture or equipment. **2** (**fittings**) items fixed in a house but removable when the owner moves. **3** an occasion of a garment being fitted. • adj. appropriate.

**five** adj. & n. one more than four; 5.

**fix** v. **1** fasten securely in position; direct the eyes or attention steadily. **2** repair. **3** agree on or settle. **4** inf. influence a result etc. dishonestly. **5** (**fix up**) organize; provide for. • n. **1** an awkward situation. **2** inf. a dose of an addictive drug. ■ **fixedly** adv.

▷ SYNS **v. 1** FASTEN, secure, attach, connect, join, couple, stick, glue, pin, nail, screw, bolt, implant, embed. **2** DECIDE ON, settle, set, agree on, arrange, determine, establish, name, specify. **3** REPAIR, mend, put right, patch up.

**fixate** v. (**fixate on** or **be fixated on**) be obsessed with.

**fixation** n. an obsession.

▷ SYNS OBSESSION, preoccupation, compulsion, mania; inf. thing.

**fixative** n. a substance used to fix or protect something.

**fixture** n. **1** a piece of equipment or furniture which is fixed in position. **2** a sporting event arranged to take place on a particular date.

**fizz** v. produce bubbles of gas with a hissing sound. • n. **1** the quality of being fizzy. **2** a fizzy drink.

**fizzle** v. **1** hiss or splutter feebly. **2** (**fizzle out**) end feebly.

**fizzy** adj. (**fizzier**, **fizziest**) (of a drink) containing bubbles of gas.
▷ SYNS BUBBLY, bubbling, sparkling, effervescent, carbonated, gassy.

**fjord** (or **fiord**) n. a narrow inlet of sea between cliffs, esp. in Norway.

**flabbergasted** adj. inf. very surprised.

**flabby** adj. (**-ier**, **-iest**) fat and limp. ▪ **flabbiness** n.

**flaccid** adj. soft, loose, and limp.

**flag** n. a piece of cloth attached by one edge to a staff or rope as a signal or symbol; a device used as a marker. • v. **1** mark or signal with a flag. **2** become tired or weak. ▢ **flagship** an admiral's ship; the most important product of an organization. **flagstone** a large paving stone.
▷ SYNS n. STANDARD, ensign, banner, pennant, streamer, colours. • v. **1** TIRE, weaken, wilt, droop. **2** FADE, decline, wane, diminish, ebb, decrease, dwindle.

**flagon** n. a large bottle for wine or cider.

**flagrant** adj. very obvious and unashamed.

▷ SYNS OBVIOUS, glaring, blatant, overt, shameless, barefaced, undisguised; shocking, scandalous, outrageous.

**flail** n. an implement formerly used for threshing grain. • v. thrash or swing about wildly.

**flair** n. natural ability.
▷ SYNS **1** ABILITY, aptitude, facility, skill, talent, gift, knack, instinct. **2** STYLE, panache, dash, elan, good taste, discrimination, discernment.

**flak** n. **1** anti-aircraft shells. **2** harsh criticism.

**flake** n. a thin, flat piece of something. • v. **1** come off in flakes; break food into flakes. **2** (**flake out**) inf. fall asleep from exhaustion. ▪ **flaky** adj.

**flambé** adj. (of food) served covered in flaming alcohol.

**flamboyant** adj. showy in appearance or manner.
▪ **flamboyance** n.

**flame** n. a hot, glowing quantity of burning gas coming from something on fire; an orange-red colour. • v. burn with flames; be bright.

**flamenco** n. (pl. **-os**) Spanish guitar music with singing and dancing.

**flamingo** n. (pl. **-os** or **-oes**) a wading bird with long legs and pink feathers.

**flammable** adj. able to be set on fire.

**flan** n. an open pastry or sponge case with filling.

**flange** n. a projecting rim.

**flank** n. a side, esp. of the body between ribs and hip; a side of an army etc. • v. be on either side of.

**flannel** n. **1** soft woollen or cotton fabric. **2** a facecloth.

**flap** v. (**flapped, flapping**) **1** move wings, arms, etc. up and down; flutter or sway. **2** inf. panic or be anxious. • n. **1** a piece of cloth, metal, etc., covering an opening and moving on a hinge. **2** a flapping movement. **3** inf. a panic.

**flapjack** n. a biscuit made with oats.

**flare** v. **1** blaze suddenly; burst into activity or anger. **2** grow wider towards one end. • n. **1** a sudden blaze; a device producing flame as a signal or illumination. **2** (**flares**) trousers with legs widening from the knee down.

**flash** v. **1** give out a sudden bright light. **2** display briefly or ostentatiously. **3** move or send rapidly. • n. **1** a sudden burst of bright light. **2** a sudden, brief show of wit, feeling, etc. **3** a device producing a brief bright light in photography. • adj. ostentatiously expensive, smart, etc. □ **flashback** a scene in a film or novel set in a time earlier than the main story. **flashpoint** a point at which anger or violence flares up.
▷ SYNS v. **1** GLARE, gleam, shine, glint, sparkle, flicker, shimmer, twinkle, glimmer, glisten. **2** SHOW OFF, flaunt, flourish, display, parade.

**flashy** adj. (**-ier, -iest**) ostentatiously smart, expensive, etc.

**flask** n. a narrow-necked bottle; a vacuum flask.

**flat** adj. **1** level and even. **2** not sloping. **3** not lively or interesting. **4** no longer fizzy. **5** (of a battery) having used up its charge. **6** (of a price) fixed. **7** firm and definite. **8** Music below true pitch. **9** (of a note) a semitone lower than a specified note. • adv. **1** so as to be flat. **2** inf. completely; absolutely. • n. **1** a set of rooms within a larger building, forming a home. **2** a flat part or area. **3** Music (a sign indicating) a note lowered by a semitone. □ **flatmate** a person with whom you share a flat. **flat out** as fast or as hard as possible. ▪ **flatten** v.
▷ SYNS adj. **1** LEVEL, horizontal, even, smooth, plane. **2** MONOTONOUS, boring, dull, tedious, uninteresting, unexciting. **3** a flat refusal: OUTRIGHT, direct, firm, definite, positive, explicit, categorical. **4** a flat fee: FIXED, set, invariable, regular, constant.

**flatter** v. compliment insincerely; cause to appear more attractive than is the case.
▷ SYNS COMPLIMENT, praise, fawn on; inf. sweet-talk, butter up, play up to.

**flattery** n. excessive or insincere praise.
▷ SYNS PRAISE, adulation, compliments, blandishments, blarney; inf. sweet talk.

**flatulent** adj. suffering from a build-up of gas in the digestive tract. ▪ **flatulence** n.

**flaunt** v. display ostentatiously.
▷ SYNS SHOW OFF, parade, display; inf. flash.

**flautist** n. a flute player.

**flavour** (US **flavor**) n. a distinctive taste; a special characteristic. • v. give flavour to. ▪ **flavouring** n.
▷ SYNS n. **1** TASTE, savour. **2** FLAVOURING, seasoning, tastiness, tang, piquancy,

spiciness, zest. **3** ATMOSPHERE, spirit, essence, nature, character, quality, feel, feeling, ambience.

**flaw** n. an imperfection.
■ **flawed** adj.
▷ SYNS FAULT, defect, imperfection, failing, shortcoming, blemish, weakness, weak spot, foible.

**flawless** adj. with no imperfections.
▷ SYNS PERFECT, unblemished, unmarked, undamaged, pristine, impeccable, immaculate, faultless.

**flax** n. a blue-flowered plant grown esp. for making cloth.

**flaxen** adj. lit. pale yellow.

**flay** v. **1** strip off the skin or hide of. **2** whip or beat.

**flea** n. a small jumping blood-sucking insect.

**fleck** n. a very small mark; a speck. • v. mark with flecks.

**fledged** adj. (of a young bird) having large enough wing feathers to fly.

**fledgling** (or **fledgeling**) n. a bird just fledged.

**flee** v. (**fled, fleeing**) run away.
▷ SYNS RUN AWAY/OFF, make off, take flight, bolt, take to your heels, decamp; inf. scarper, skedaddle, vamoose.

**fleece** n. a sheep's woolly hair. • v. inf. swindle. ■ **fleecy** adj.

**fleet** n. ships sailing together; vehicles or aircraft under one command or ownership. • adj. lit. swift and nimble.

**fleeting** adj. passing quickly.
▷ SYNS BRIEF, short-lived, transient, momentary, rapid, swift, transitory, ephemeral, evanescent, passing, fugitive.

**flesh** n. **1** the soft substance of animal bodies; the body as opposed to the mind or soul. **2** the pulpy part of fruits and vegetables. • v. (**flesh out**) add details to.

**fleshy** adj. (**-ier, -iest**) **1** plump. **2** thick and soft.

**flew** past of FLY.

**flex** n. a flexible insulated wire for carrying electric current. • v. bend; move a muscle so that it bends a joint.

**flexible** adj. able to bend easily; adaptable. ■ **flexibility** n.
▷ SYNS **1** BENDABLE, pliable, pliant, elastic, plastic, springy, supple. **2** ADAPTABLE, adjustable, open-ended. **3** COOPERATIVE, accommodating, amenable, easy-going.

**flick** n. **1** a quick, sharp, small movement. **2** inf. a cinema film. • v. move, strike, or remove with a flick.

**flicker** v. **1** burn or shine unsteadily. **2** occur or appear briefly. • n. **1** an unsteady light. **2** a brief or slight occurrence.

**flier** = FLYER.

**flight** n. **1** flying; a journey through air or space; the path of an object moving through the air; a group of birds or aircraft. **2** a series of stairs **3** feathers etc. on a dart or arrow. **4** running away.
▷ SYNS **1** AVIATION, flying, aeronautics. **2** ESCAPE, departure, exit, getaway, exodus.

**flighty** adj. irresponsible.

**flimsy** adj. (**-ier, -iest**) light and thin; fragile; unconvincing.
▷ SYNS **1** INSUBSTANTIAL, fragile, frail, makeshift, rickety, shaky, gimcrack. **2** THIN, light, fine, delicate, sheer, filmy,

diaphanous, transparent, gauzy.
**3** FEEBLE, weak, poor, inadequate, unconvincing,
implausible.

**flinch** v. make a nervous
movement in pain or fear;
shrink from something.
▷ SYNS WINCE, start, shy away,
recoil, draw back, blench.

**fling** v. (**flung**, **flinging**) throw or
move forcefully. • n. **1** a period
of enjoyment. **2** a brief sexual
relationship.

**flint** n. **1** a hard grey rock. **2** a
piece of flint or a metal alloy,
used to produce a spark.

**flip** v. (**flipped**, **flipping**) turn
over suddenly and swiftly.

**flippant** adj. not showing
proper seriousness.
▷ SYNS FRIVOLOUS, facetious, glib,
tongue-in-cheek, irreverent,
cheeky, disrespectful.

**flipper** n. a sea animal's limb
used in swimming; a large flat
rubber attachment to the foot
for underwater swimming.

**flirt** v. behave in a frivolously
amorous way. • n. a person who
flirts. ■ **flirtation** n. **flirtatious**
adj.
▷ SYNS v. CHAT UP, toy with, lead
on, tease. • n. COQUETTE, tease,
vamp.

**flirtatious** adj. liking to flirt
with people.
▷ SYNS COQUETTISH, flirty, kittenish, teasing, come-hither.

**flit** v. (**flitted**, **flitting**) move
swiftly and lightly.

**float** v. **1** rest or drift on the
surface of liquid; be supported
in air. **2** make a suggestion to
test reactions. **3** offer the shares
of a company for sale. **4** (of
currency) have a variable rate
of exchange. • n. **1** a thing

designed to float on liquid.
**2** money for minor expenditure
or giving change. **3** a small
vehicle.

**floatation** = FLOTATION.

**flock** n. **1** a number of animals or
birds together; a large number
of people; a congregation.
**2** wool or cotton material as
stuffing. • v. gather or go in a
group.
▷ SYNS n. **1** HERD, drove. **2** FLIGHT,
gaggle, skein. **3** CROWD, group,
throng, mass, host, multitude,
swarm, horde.

**floe** n. a sheet of floating ice.

**flog** v. (**flogged**, **flogging**) **1** beat
severely. **2** inf. sell.

**flood** n. an overflow of water on
a place usually dry; an
overwhelming quantity or
outpouring. • v. cover with flood
water; overflow; arrive in great
quantities; overwhelm.
▷ SYNS n. DELUGE, torrent, inundation, spate, overflow. • v.
**1** INUNDATE, deluge, immerse,
submerge, swamp, drown,
engulf. **2** OVERSUPPLY, saturate,
glut, overwhelm.

**floodlight** n. a lamp producing
a broad bright beam. ■ **floodlit**
adj.

**floor** n. **1** the lower surface of a
room. **2** a storey. **3** the right to
speak in a debate: *have the floor.*
• v. **1** provide with a floor. **2** inf.
knock down. **3** inf. baffle.
▷ SYNS n. STOREY, level, tier, deck.

**flooring** n. material for a floor.

**flop** v. **1** hang or fall heavily and
loosely. **2** inf. be a failure. • n. **1** a
flopping movement. **2** inf. a
failure.
▷ SYNS v. **1** COLLAPSE, slump, drop,
sink; droop, sag, dangle. **2** FAIL,
fall flat; inf. bomb.

**floppy** adj. (-ier, -iest) not firm or stiff. □ **floppy disk** a magnetic disk for storing computer data.

**flora** n. the plants of an area or period.

**floral** adj. of flowers.

**floret** n. each of the small flowers of a composite flower.

**florid** adj. **1** red or flushed. **2** over-elaborate.
▷ SYNS RED, ruddy, flushed, high-coloured, rubicund.

**florist** n. a person who sells flowers.

**floss** n. **1** a mass of silky fibres. **2** soft thread used to clean between the teeth.

**flotation** (or **floatation**) n. floating; the sale of shares in a company for the first time.

**flotilla** n. a small fleet.

**flotsam** n. floating wreckage.

**flounce** v. go in an impatient, annoyed manner. • n. **1** a flouncing movement. **2** a deep frill.

**flounder** v. move clumsily in mud or water; be confused or in difficulty. • n. a small flatfish.

**flour** n. fine powder made from grain, used in cooking. ■ **floury** adj.

**flourish** v. **1** grow vigorously; be successful. **2** wave dramatically. • n. a dramatic gesture; an ornamental curve; a fanfare.
▷ SYNS v. **1** BRANDISH, wave, wield, swing; display, exhibit, flaunt, show off. **2** THRIVE, develop, burgeon, bloom, blossom; succeed, prosper.

**flout** v. disobey a law etc. contemptuously.

▷ SYNS DEFY, break, disobey, violate, breach, ignore, disregard.

**flow** v. **1** move steadily and continuously in a current or stream. **2** move freely. **3** hang loosely. • n. a steady, continuous stream.
▷ SYNS v. RUN, course, glide, drift, circulate; trickle, seep, ooze, dribble, drip, spill; stream, swirl, surge, sweep, gush, cascade, pour, roll, rush. • n. CURRENT, stream, tide, spate, gush.

**flower** n. **1** the part of a plant where fruit or seed develops, usu. brightly coloured and decorative. **2** the best among a group of people. • v. produce flowers.
▷ SYNS n. **1** BLOOM, blossom, floweret, floret; annual, perennial. **2** BEST, finest, pick, cream, elite.

**flowery** adj. **1** full of flowers. **2** full of ornamental phrases.

**flown** p.p. of **FLY**.

**flu** n. influenza.

**fluctuate** v. vary irregularly. ■ **fluctuation** n.
▷ SYNS VARY, change, alter, swing, oscillate, alternate, rise and fall, go up and down, see-saw, yo-yo.

**flue** n. a smoke duct in a chimney; a channel for conveying heat.

**fluent** adj. speaking or spoken smoothly and readily. ■ **fluency** n.
▷ SYNS ARTICULATE, eloquent, silver-tongued, smooth-spoken.

**fluff** n. a soft mass of fibres or down. • v. **1** make something appear fuller and softer. **2** inf. bungle.

**fluffy** adj. resembling or covered with fluff.
▷ SYNS FLEECY, woolly, fuzzy, downy, furry, soft.

**fluid** adj. flowing easily; not fixed or settled. • n. a liquid. □ fluid ounce one-twentieth of a pint (about 28 ml). ■ fluidity n.
▷ SYNS adj. 1 LIQUID, liquefied, melted, molten, running, flowing. 2 SMOOTH, graceful, elegant, effortless, easy. 3 FLEXIBLE, open to change, adaptable, adjustable; unstable, fluctuating, shifting. • n. LIQUID, solution.

**fluke** n. a lucky accident.

**flummox** v. inf. baffle.

**flung** past and p.p. of FLING.

**flunkey** (or **flunky**) n. (pl. -eys or -ies) a uniformed male servant; a person who does menial work.

**fluorescent** adj. giving out bright light when exposed to radiation. ■ fluorescence n.

**fluoride** n. a compound of fluorine with metal.

**fluorine** n. a poisonous pale yellow gas.

**flurry** n. (pl. -ies) a short rush of wind, rain, or snow; a commotion.

**flush** v. 1 make or become red; blush. 2 clean or dispose of with a flow of water. 3 drive out from cover. • n. 1 a blush. 2 a rush of emotion. 3 an act of cleaning something with a rush of water. • adj. level with another surface.
▷ SYNS v. 1 BLUSH, turn red, redden, colour. 2 WASH, rinse, sluice, cleanse, clean.

**fluster** v. make agitated and confused. • n. a flustered state.
▷ SYNS v. AGITATE, unnerve, ruffle, unsettle, upset, disconcert, perturb, confuse, nonplus; inf. rattle, faze.

**flute** n. 1 a wind instrument consisting of a pipe with holes along it and a mouth hole at the side. 2 an ornamental groove.

**flutter** v. move wings hurriedly; wave or flap quickly; (of the heart) beat irregularly. • n. 1 a fluttering movement; a state of nervous excitement. 2 inf. a small bet.

**fluvial** adj. of or found in rivers.

**flux** n. a flow; continuous change.

**fly** v. 1 move through the air on wings or in an aircraft. 2 control the flight of or transport in an aircraft. 3 go or move quickly. 4 display a flag. 5 old use run away. • n. 1 a two-winged insect. 2 (also **flies**) a fastening down the front of trousers. □ flying saucer a disc-shaped flying craft, supposedly piloted by aliens. flying squad a group of police etc. organized to reach an incident quickly. flyover a bridge carrying one road or railway over another. flywheel a heavy wheel revolving on a shaft to regulate machinery. with flying colours with distinction.
▷ SYNS v. SOAR, glide, wheel, hover; take wing.

**flyer** (or **flier**) n. 1 a person or thing that flies. 2 a small printed advertisement.

**foal** n. a young horse or related animal. • v. give birth to a foal.

**foam** n. 1 a mass of small bubbles. 2 a bubbly substance prepared for shaving etc. 3 spongy rubber or plastic. • v. form or produce foam. ■ foamy adj.

▷ SYNS n. FROTH, bubbles, fizz, head, spume, lather, effervescence, suds.

**fob** n. a chain for a watch; a tab on a key ring. • v. (**fob off**) (**fobbed**, **fobbing**) give something inferior to someone; deceive into accepting.

**focaccia** n. a flat Italian bread made with olive oil.

**focal** adj. of or at a focus.

**fo'c'sle** = FORECASTLE.

**focus** n. 1 the centre of interest or activity. 2 clear visual definition; an adjustment on a lens to produce a clear image. 3 a point where rays meet. • v. 1 adjust the focus of; bring into focus. 2 concentrate.
▷ SYNS n. CENTRE (OF ATTENTION), central point, focal point, hub, pivot, nucleus, heart; cynosure. • v. AIM, point, turn; concentrate on, zero in on, centre on, pinpoint.

**fodder** n. food for animals.

**foe** n. an enemy.

**foetid** = FETID.

**foetus** = FETUS.

**fog** n. thick mist. • v. (**fogged**, **fogging**) become covered with mist; confuse. □ **foghorn** a device making a loud, deep sound as a warning to ships in fog. ■ **foggy** adj.
▷ SYNS n. MIST, smog, haze, murk; inf. pea-souper.

**fogey** n. (pl. -**eys** or -**ies**) an old-fashioned person.

**foible** n. a minor weakness or eccentricity.
▷ SYNS WEAKNESS, weak point, failing, shortcoming, flaw, quirk, idiosyncrasy, eccentricity.

**foil** n. 1 a very thin flexible sheet of metal. 2 a person or thing emphasizing another's qualities by contrast. • v. thwart or frustrate.
▷ SYNS v. THWART, frustrate, stop, defeat, block, baulk, prevent, impede, obstruct, hamper, hinder.

**foist** v. cause a person to accept an inferior or unwelcome thing.

**fold** v. 1 bend something thin and flat so that one part of it lies over another. 2 wrap; clasp. 3 mix an ingredient gently into a mixture. 4 inf. (of a business etc.) cease trading. • n. 1 a shape or line made by folding. 2 a pen for sheep.
▷ SYNS v. 1 DOUBLE UP, turn under/up, bend, tuck, crease, gather, pleat. 2 WRAP, enfold, clasp, embrace, envelop, hug, squeeze. 3 FAIL, collapse, go out of business, go bankrupt, go to the wall; inf. go bust, go under. • n. LAYER, pleat, crease, wrinkle, pucker, furrow, crinkle.

**folder** n. a folding cover for loose papers.

**foliage** n. leaves.

**folio** n. (pl. -**os**) 1 a sheet of paper folded once to form two leaves of a book. 2 a book made up of such sheets.

**folk** n. 1 inf. people in general. 2 inf. (**your folks**) your family. 3 (or **folk music**) traditional music. □ **folklore** the traditional beliefs and stories of a community.
▷ SYNS PEOPLE, populace, population, citizenry, public.

**follicle** n. a very small cavity containing a hair root.

**follow** v. 1 go or come after. 2 go along a route. 3 be a consequence or result. 4 act

according to instructions etc.
**5** accept as a leader, guide etc.
**6** understand or pay attention
to. **7 (follow up)** investigate
further. ■ **follower** n.
▷ SYNS **1** COME BEHIND, trail,
pursue, shadow, stalk, track; inf.
tail. **2** RESULT, arise, develop,
ensue, emanate, issue, proceed,
spring. **3** OBEY, observe, comply
with, heed, conform to, stick
to, adhere to. **4** UNDERSTAND,
comprehend, take in, grasp,
fathom. **5 (follow up)** INVESTI-
GATE, research, look into,
pursue.

**following** n. a body of believers
or supporters. • adj. **1** about to
be mentioned. **2** next in time.
• prep. as a sequel to.
▷ SYNS n. SUPPORTERS, fans,
admirers, devotees, public,
audience, patrons. • adj. NEXT,
ensuing, succeeding, sub-
sequent.

**folly** n. (pl. **-ies**) **1** foolishness; a
foolish act. **2** an impractical
ornamental building.

**foment** v. stir up trouble.
▷ SYNS INCITE, instigate, stir up,
provoke, arouse, encourage,
whip up, agitate.

**fond** adj. **1** liking someone or
something. **2** (of hope)
unlikely to be fulfilled.
■ **fondness** n.
▷ SYNS **1** ADORING, devoted, loving,
affectionate, caring, warm,
tender, doting, indulgent. **2** UN-
REALISTIC, foolish, naive,
deluded, vain.

**fondant** n. a soft sugary sweet.

**fondle** v. stroke lovingly.
▷ SYNS CARESS, stroke, pat, pet; inf.
paw.

**font** n. a basin in a church,
holding water for baptism.

**food** n. any substance that
people or animals eat or that
plants absorb to stay alive.
▷ SYNS NOURISHMENT, sustenance,
nutriment, fare, foodstuffs,
refreshments, meals,
provisions, rations; dated
victuals; inf. grub.

**fool** n. **1** a foolish person. **2** a
creamy fruit-flavoured
pudding. • v. trick or deceive;
behave in a silly or frivolous
way.
▷ SYNS n. **1** IDIOT, ass, halfwit,
blockhead, dunce, dolt,
simpleton; inf. numbskull, clot,
dimwit, moron, twit, berk,
muppet, airhead, bonehead.
**2** DUPE, laughing stock; inf.
sucker, mug. • v. TRICK, deceive,
hoax, dupe, take in, hoodwink,
delude, bamboozle; inf. con, kid,
have on.

**foolhardy** adj. recklessly bold.

**foolish** adj. lacking good sense
or judgement; ridiculous.
■ **foolishness** n.
▷ SYNS STUPID, silly, idiotic, mad,
unintelligent, dense, brainless,
mindless, obtuse, half-witted,
moronic, inane, absurd,
ludicrous, ridiculous,
laughable, fatuous, asinine,
senseless, irresponsible, ill-
advised; inf. thick, dim, dumb,
dopey; inf. crazy.

**foolproof** adj. unable to go
wrong or be misused.
▷ SYNS INFALLIBLE, certain, sure,
guaranteed, safe, dependable,
trustworthy, reliable.

**foolscap** n. a large size of paper.

**foot** n. (pl. **feet**) **1** the part of the
leg below the ankle. **2** the
bottom of something vertical.
**3** a measure of length = 12
inches (30.48 cm). **4** a unit of
metre in verse. • v. inf. pay a bill.

□ **foot-and-mouth disease** a contagious viral disease of livestock. **footfall** the sound of footsteps. **foothill** a low hill at the base of a mountain. **foothold 1** a place where you can put a foot down securely when climbing. **2** a secure position as a basis for progress. **footlights** a row of spotlights along the front of a stage. **footloose** free to do as you please. **footman** a uniformed manservant. **footnote** a note printed at the bottom of a page. **footpath** a path for walkers. **footprint** the mark left by a foot or shoe on the ground. **footstep** a step taken in walking. **footwear** shoes, boots, etc. **footwork** the manner of moving the feet in dancing and sport.

**footage** n. a length of film.

**football** n. a large round or elliptical inflated ball; a game played with this. ■ **footballer** n.

**footing** n. **1** a secure grip with your feet. **2** a position: *put us on an equal footing.*

**footling** adj. trivial.

**for** prep. **1** in support of; on behalf of. **2** to be received or used by. **3** relating to. **4** so as to get, have, or do. **5** in place of; as a price or penalty of. **6** over a period or distance. • **conj.** lit. because.

**forage** v. search for food. • n. fodder.

**foray** n. a sudden attack or raid.

**forbear** v. (**forbore, forborne, forbearing**) refrain from.

**forbearing** adj. patient or tolerant. ■ **forbearance** n.

**forbid** v. (**forbade, forbidden, forbidding**) order not to do something; refuse to allow.

▷ SYNS PROHIBIT, ban, bar, debar, outlaw, veto, proscribe, disallow.

**forbidding** adj. daunting or uninviting.

▷ SYNS **1** STERN, grim, hard, hostile, unfriendly, unwelcoming, offputting. **2** FRIGHTENING, ominous, threatening, menacing, sinister, daunting.

**force** n. **1** physical strength or energy. **2** violence or pressure. **3** influence or power. **4** a body of troops or police. **5** Physics a measurable influence causing movement. • v. **1** compel. **2** make a way through or into by force. **3** achieve by effort.

▷ SYNS n. **1** POWER, strength, energy, might, effort; impact, pressure. **2** COERCION, compulsion, duress, constraint, pressure, violence. **3** INFLUENCE, power, cogency, weight, effectiveness, validity. **4** UNIT, detachment, squad, group. • v. **1** COMPEL, coerce, make, pressure, pressurize, impel, oblige, constrain, press-gang. **2** PUSH, thrust, shove, drive, press.

**forceful** adj. powerful; assertive. ■ **forcefully** adv.

▷ SYNS **1** POWERFUL, vigorous, strong, dynamic, energetic, assertive. **2** PERSUASIVE, telling, convincing, compelling, effective, potent, cogent, valid.

**forceps** pl.n. pincers used in surgery etc.

**forcible** adj. done by force. ■ **forcibly** adv.

**ford** n. a shallow place where a stream may be crossed by wading or driving through. • v. cross a stream etc. in this way.

**fore** adj. & adv. in, at, or towards the front. • n. the front part.

**forearm** n. the arm from the elbow downwards. • v. arm or prepare in advance against possible danger.

**forebear** n. an ancestor.

**foreboding** n. a feeling that trouble is coming.

**forecast** v. (**forecast, forecasting**) predict future weather, events, etc. • n. a prediction. ■ **forecaster** n.
▷ SYNS v. PREDICT, foretell, foresee, prophesy, forewarn of, divine. • n. PREDICTION, prophecy, prognostication, augury, prognosis.

**forecastle** (or **fo'c's'le**) n. the forward part of certain ships.

**foreclose** v. take possession of property when a loan secured on it is not repaid. ■ **foreclosure** n.

**forecourt** n. an open area in front of a building.

**forefather** n. an ancestor.

**forefinger** n. the finger next to the thumb.

**forefront** n. the very front.

**forego** = FORGO.

**foregoing** adj. preceding.

**foregone conclusion** n. a predictable result.

**foreground** n. the part of a scene etc. that is nearest to the observer.

**forehand** n. (in tennis etc.) a stroke played with the palm of the hand turned forwards.

**forehead** n. the part of the face above the eyes.

**foreign** adj. of, from, or in a country that is not your own; relating to other countries; strange or out of place. ■ **foreigner** n.

▷ SYNS **1** OVERSEAS, distant, remote, alien, exotic. **2** STRANGE, unfamiliar, unknown, unheard of, odd, peculiar, curious.

**foreman** n. a worker supervising others; the president and spokesman of a jury.

**foremost** adj. most advanced in position or rank; most important. • adv. first; in the most important position.
▷ SYNS adj. LEADING, principal, premier, top, prime, primary, paramount, chief, main, supreme, highest.

**forensic** adj. of or used in law courts. □ **forensic medicine** medical knowledge used in police investigations etc.

**forerunner** n. a person or thing coming before and foreshadowing another.
▷ SYNS PREDECESSOR, precursor, antecedent, ancestor, forefather; harbinger, herald.

**foresee** v. (**foresaw, foreseen, foreseeing**) be aware of or realize beforehand. ■ **foreseeable** adj.

**foreshadow** v. be an advance sign of a future event etc.
▷ SYNS PRESAGE, bode, augur, portend, prefigure, indicate, mean, signal, signify, point to.

**foreshorten** v. show or portray an object as shorter than it is, as an effect of perspective.

**foresight** n. the ability to predict future events and needs.

**foreskin** n. the fold of skin covering the end of the penis.

**forest** n. a large area covered with trees and undergrowth.
▷ SYNS WOODLAND, wood(s), trees, plantation.

**forestall** v. prevent or foil by taking action first.
▷ SYNS PRE-EMPT, anticipate, intercept, thwart, frustrate, stave off, ward off, fend off, prevent, avert, foil.

**forestry** n. the science of planting and caring for forests.
■ forester n.

**foretaste** n. a sample or indication of what is to come.

**foretell** v. (**foretold**, **foretelling**) forecast.

**forethought** n. careful planning for the future.
▷ SYNS FORESIGHT, far-sightedness, anticipation, (forward) planning; prudence, care, caution.

**forever** adv. 1 for all time. 2 continually.
▷ SYNS ALWAYS, evermore, ever, for all time, until the end of time, eternally, until kingdom come.

**forewarn** v. warn beforehand.

**foreword** n. an introduction to a book.

**forfeit** v. lose property or a right as a punishment. • n. a punishment for wrongdoing.

**forge** n. 1 a blacksmith's workshop. 2 a furnace for heating metal. • v. 1 shape metal by heating and hammering. 2 make a fraudulent copy of.
■ forger n.
▷ SYNS v. FAKE, falsify, counterfeit, copy, imitate.

**forgery** n. a forged or copied item.
▷ SYNS FAKE, counterfeit, fraud, imitation, replica; inf. phoney.

**forget** v. 1 fail or be unable to remember. 2 (**forget yourself**) behave inappropriately.
▷ SYNS 1 FAIL TO REMEMBER, lose track of, overlook. 2 DISREGARD,

put out of your mind, ignore. 3 NEGLECT, omit, fail.

**forgetful** adj. tending to forget.
■ forgetfulness n.
▷ SYNS ABSENT-MINDED, vague, disorganized; inf. scatterbrained, scatty.

**forget-me-not** n. a plant with small blue flowers.

**forgive** v. (**forgave**, **forgiven**, **forgiving**) stop feeling angry or bitter towards or about.
▷ SYNS PARDON, absolve, exonerate, excuse.

**forgiveness** n. the action of forgiving or the state of being forgiven.
▷ SYNS PARDON, absolution, exoneration, clemency, mercy, reprieve, amnesty.

**forgiving** adj. willing to forgive.
▷ SYNS MERCIFUL, lenient, compassionate, magnanimous, understanding, humane, softhearted, forbearing, tolerant, indulgent.

**forgo** (or **forego**) v. (**forwent**, **forgone**, **forgoing**) give up; go without.
▷ SYNS DO/GO WITHOUT, waive, renounce, sacrifice, relinquish, surrender, abstain from, refrain from, eschew, give up.

**fork** n. a pronged implement for holding food or tool for digging; a point where a road, river, etc., divides; one of its branches. • v. 1 (of a road etc.) divide into two branches. 2 lift or dig with a fork. 3 (**fork out**) inf. give money. ■ forked adj.
▷ SYNS v. BRANCH, diverge, bifurcate, divide, split, separate.

**forlorn** adj. left alone and unhappy.

▷ SYNS UNHAPPY, sad, miserable, wretched, woebegone, disconsolate, dejected, despondent, downcast.

**form** n. **1** shape, appearance, or structure. **2** the way in which something exists. **3** correct behaviour. **4** a document with blank spaces for information. **5** a school class or year. **6** a bench. • v. create; shape; develop; constitute.
▷ SYNS n. **1** SHAPE, formation, configuration, structure, construction, arrangement, appearance, layout. **2** TYPE, kind, sort, variety, style, genre. **3** *in top form:* CONDITION, fitness, health, shape, trim, fettle. **4** *not good form:* MANNERS, polite behaviour, etiquette; inf. the done thing. • v. **1** MAKE, fashion, shape, model, mould, construct, build, assemble, produce, create. **2** DEVISE, formulate, think up, plan, draw up, hatch, develop, conceive, dream up. **3** SET UP, establish, found, institute, inaugurate. **4** TAKE SHAPE, appear, materialize, emerge. **5** COMPRISE, make up, constitute.

**formal** adj. **1** suitable for official or important occasions. **2** officially recognized. ■ **formalize** v. **formally** adv.
▷ SYNS **1** CEREMONIAL, traditional, conventional, ritualistic; solemn, stately; elaborate, dressy. **2** OFFICIAL, legal, authorized, approved.

**formality** n. (pl. **-ies**) **1** a thing done to follow customs or rules. **2** correct and formal behaviour.

**format** n. **1** the way something is arranged. **2** the shape and size of a book. **3** Computing a structure for the processing etc. of data. • v. (**formatted, formatting**) arrange in a format; prepare a disk to receive data.

**formation** n. forming or being formed; a structure or pattern.
▷ SYNS **1** ARRANGEMENT, pattern, order, grouping, configuration, structure, format, layout, disposition, design. **2** ESTABLISHMENT, institution, founding, creation, inauguration.

**formative** adj. influencing development.

**former** adj. **1** of an earlier period; mentioned first of two. **2** (**the former**) the first of two things to be mentioned.
▷ SYNS **1** PREVIOUS, ex-, preceding, late, sometime, erstwhile; prior, foregoing. **2** EARLIER, past, bygone, of yore.

**formerly** adv. in former times.

**formidable** adj. inspiring fear or awe; difficult to achieve.
■ **formidably** adv.
▷ SYNS **1** INTIMIDATING, daunting, alarming, frightening, fearsome, forbidding; inf. scary. **2** STRONG, powerful, impressive, mighty, great, redoubtable, terrific, indomitable, invincible. **3** DIFFICULT, arduous, onerous, tough, challenging.

**formula** n. (pl. **-lae** or **-las**) **1** symbols showing chemical constituents or a mathematical statement. **2** a fixed series of words for use on particular occasions.

**formulaic** adj. **1** containing a set form of words. **2** following a rule or style too closely.

**formulate** v. **1** create or devise. **2** express precisely.
■ **formulation** n.

▷ SYNS **1** DRAW UP, work out, plan, map out, compose, devise, think up, conceive, create, invent, design. **2** DEFINE, set down, specify, itemize, detail.

**fornicate** v. formal have sex outside marriage.
■ **fornication** n.

**forsake** v. **1** abandon. **2** give up.

**forswear** v. (**forswore, forsworn, forswearing**) renounce.

**forsythia** n. a shrub with bright yellow flowers.

**fort** n. a fortified building.

**forte** n. something at which a person excels. • **adv.** Music loudly.

**forth** adv. **1** outwards and forwards. **2** onwards from a point in time.

**forthcoming** adj. **1** about to occur or appear. **2** communicative.
▷ SYNS **1** FUTURE, coming, expected, imminent, impending. **2** COMMUNICATIVE, talkative, expansive, voluble, chatty, loquacious, open.

**forthright** adj. frank or outspoken.
▷ SYNS DIRECT, frank, open, candid, blunt, outspoken, plain-spoken, straightforward, honest.

**forthwith** adv. immediately.

**fortify** v. **1** strengthen against attack. **2** strengthen or invigorate. **3** increase the alcohol content or nutritive value of.
■ **fortification** n.
▷ SYNS **1** PROTECT, secure, strengthen; buttress, shore up. **2** INVIGORATE, energize, revive, refresh, restore.

**fortitude** n. courage in bearing pain or trouble.
▷ SYNS STRENGTH, courage, bravery, backbone, mettle,

spirit, strong-mindedness, tenacity, resilience, determination.

**fortnight** n. a period of two weeks.

**fortress** n. a fort or fortified town.

**fortuitous** adj. happening by chance.

**fortunate** adj. lucky.
■ **fortunately** adv.
▷ SYNS LUCKY, blessed, favoured, in luck; favourable, advantageous, happy, felicitous.

**fortune** n. **1** chance seen as affecting people's lives. **2** luck. **3** (**fortunes**) what happens to someone. **4** a large amount of money.
▷ SYNS **1** CHANCE, accident, luck, coincidence, serendipity, providence; fate, destiny. **2** WEALTH, riches, property, assets, means, possessions. **3** HUGE AMOUNT, mint, king's ransom; inf. packet, bomb.

**forty** adj. & n. four times ten; 40.
■ **fortieth** adj. & n.

**forum** n. a place or meeting where a public discussion is held.

**forward** adv. & adj. **1** in the direction you are facing or moving. **2** towards a successful end. **3** ahead in time. **4** in or near the front. • **adj.** bold or overfamiliar. • **n.** an attacking player in sport. • **v.** send on a letter etc. to another destination. ■ **forwards** adv.

**fossil** n. the remains of a prehistoric animal or plant that have hardened into rock.
□ **fossil fuel** fuel such as coal or gas, formed from the remains of living organisms. ■ **fossilize** v.

**foster** v. **1** encourage or help the development of. **2** bring up a child that is not your own.
▷ SYNS **1** ENCOURAGE, promote, further, stimulate, boost, advance, cultivate, help, aid, assist, support. **2** BRING UP, rear, raise, care for, look after, take care of, parent.

**fought** past and p.p. of FIGHT.

**foul** adj. **1** causing disgust; very bad; dirty. **2** wicked or obscene. • n. an action that breaks the rules of a game. • v. **1** make dirty. **2** commit a foul against. **3** (**foul up**) make a mistake with.
▷ SYNS adj. **1** DISGUSTING, revolting, repulsive, nauseating, sickening, loathsome, odious, abominable, offensive, nasty. **2** DIRTY, contaminated, polluted, adulterated, tainted, defiled, filthy, unclean. **3** BLASPHEMOUS, profane, obscene, vulgar, offensive, coarse, filthy, dirty, indecent, smutty. **4** ABHORRENT, detestable, hateful, despicable, contemptible, dishonourable, disgraceful, base, low, mean, sordid, vile, wicked, heinous, iniquitous, nefarious.

**found**[1] past and p.p. of FIND.

**found**[2] v. **1** establish an institution etc.; set on a base or basis. **2** melt and mould metal or glass.
▷ SYNS ESTABLISH, set up, institute, originate, initiate, create, start, inaugurate, endow.

**foundation** n. **1** a base or lowest layer; an underlying principle. **2** founding; an institution etc. that is founded.
▷ SYNS **1** BASE, bottom, substructure, bedrock, underpinning. **2** BASIS,
groundwork, principles, fundamentals, rudiments.

**founder** v. stumble or fall; (of a ship) sink; fail completely. • n. a person who has founded an institution etc.

**foundling** n. a deserted child of unknown parents.

**foundry** n. (pl. -ies) a workshop where metal or glass founding is done.

**fount** n. lit. a fountain; a source.

**fountain** n. an ornamental structure pumping out a jet of water. □ fountain pen a pen with a container supplying ink to the nib.
▷ SYNS SPRAY, jet, spout, well, fount.

**four** adj. & n. one more than three; 4. □ foursome a group of four people.

**fourteen** adj. & n. one more than thirteen; 14. ■ fourteenth adj. & n.

**fourth** adj. next after the third. • n. **1** a fourth thing, class, etc. **2** a quarter.

**fowl** n. a bird kept for its eggs or meat.

**fox** n. **1** a wild animal of the dog family with a bushy tail. **2** a cunning person. • v. inf. baffle or deceive. □ foxglove a tall plant with bell-shaped flowers. foxhound a hound trained to hunt foxes in packs. foxtrot a ballroom dance with slow and quick steps.

**foyer** n. an entrance hall of a theatre, cinema, or hotel.

**fracas** n. (pl. **fracas**) a noisy quarrel or disturbance.
▷ SYNS DISTURBANCE, altercation, fight, brawl, affray, rumpus, scuffle, skirmish, free-for-all.

**fraction** n. a number that is not a whole number; a small part or amount.

**fractious** adj. irritable; hard to control.

**fracture** n. a break, esp. in a bone; breaking. • v. break.
▷ SYNS n. BREAK, rupture, split, crack, fissure, cleft, rift, chink, crevice.

**fragile** adj. easily broken or damaged; delicate. ▪ **fragility** n.
▷ SYNS FLIMSY, breakable, frail, delicate, insubstantial, brittle, dainty, fine.

**fragment** n. a piece broken off something. • v. (cause to) break into fragments.
▪ fragmentation n.
▷ SYNS n. PIECE, part, particle, shred, chip, shard, sliver, splinter, scrap, bit, snip, snippet, wisp.

**fragmentary** adj. consisting of small disconnected or in-complete parts.
▷ SYNS INCOMPLETE, disconnected, disjointed, discontinuous, uneven, sketchy, patchy.

**fragrance** n. a pleasant smell. ▪ **fragrant** adj.
▷ SYNS SCENT, smell, perfume, aroma, bouquet.

**frail** adj. weak; fragile. ▪ **frailty** n.
▷ SYNS WEAK, infirm, ill, unwell, sickly, ailing, delicate, fragile.

**frame** n. **1** a rigid structure supporting other parts; a person's body. **2** a rigid structure surrounding a picture, window, etc. **3** a single exposure on a cinema film.
• v. **1** put or form a frame round. **2** construct. **3** inf. arrange false evidence against. ▫ **frame of mind** a particular mood.

**framework** a supporting structure.
▷ SYNS n. **1** STRUCTURE, framework, foundation, bodywork, chassis, skeleton, shell, casing, support. **2** BODY, physique, build, figure, shape, size.

**franchise** n. **1** authorization to sell a company's products. **2** the right to vote in public elections.

**frank** adj. honest in expressing your thoughts and feelings.
• v. mark a letter etc. to show that postage has been paid.
▷ SYNS adj. CANDID, direct, straight-forward, plain, plain-spoken, outspoken, blunt, open, sincere, honest, truthful, explicit.

**frankfurter** n. a smoked sausage.

**frankincense** n. a sweet-smelling gum burnt as incense.

**frantic** adj. wildly agitated or excited. ▪ **frantically** adv.
▷ SYNS DISTRAUGHT, overwrought, panic-stricken, panicky, beside yourself, at your wits' end, frenzied, wild, hysterical, frenetic, worked up, fraught, agitated.

**fraternal** adj. of a brother or brothers.

**fraternity** n. (pl. **-ies**) **1** a group of people with a common interest. **2** brotherhood.

**fraternize** (or **-ise**) v. associate with others in a friendly way.

**fraud** n. **1** criminal deception. **2** a person who deceives others.
▷ SYNS **1** DECEPTION, cheating, sharp practice, swindling, embezzlement, deceit, double-dealing, chicanery. **2** IMPOSTOR, fake, cheat, swindler, trickster, charlatan, quack; inf. phoney, con man.

**fraudulent** adj. involving fraud. ■ **fraudulence** n.
▷ SYNS DISHONEST, cheating, corrupt, criminal, deceitful, double-dealing; inf. crooked, shady.

**fraught** adj. **1** causing or suffering anxiety. **2** (**fraught with**) filled with.

**fray** v. (of fabric, rope, etc.) unravel or become worn; (of nerves) be strained. • n. a fight or conflict.

**frazzle** n. inf. an exhausted state. ■ **frazzled** adj.

**freak** n. **1** an abnormal person, thing, or event. **2** inf. an enthusiast for something specified. • adj. very unusual or unexpected. • v. react in a wild, shocked, or excited way.
▷ SYNS n. ABERRATION, abnormality, oddity, irregularity, anomaly; malformation, monstrosity, mutant. • adj. UNUSUAL, anomalous, aberrant, atypical, exceptional, unaccountable, unpredictable, unforeseeable, bizarre, queer, odd.

**freckle** n. a light brown spot on the skin. ■ **freckled** adj.

**free** adj. **1** costing nothing. **2** not confined or obstructed. **3** not in another's power. **4** not busy or in use. **5** (**free of/from**) not containing or affected by. **6** (**free with**) giving without restraint. • adv. at no cost. • v. set free. □ **a free hand** authority to do what you think fit. **freehand** drawn by hand without a ruler etc. **freehold** permanent ownership of land or property with the freedom to sell it when you wish. **freelance 1** self-employed and working for different companies. **2** (or **freelancer**) a freelance worker. **freeloader** inf.

a person who takes advantage of other people's generosity. **free-range** referring to farming in which animals are allowed to move around freely in natural conditions. **freewheel** ride a bicycle without pedalling.
■ **freely** adv.
▷ SYNS adj. **1** FREE OF CHARGE, complimentary, for nothing, gratis, on the house. **2** AT LIBERTY, at large, loose, unconfined, unfettered. **3** INDEPENDENT, self-governing, autonomous, sovereign, democratic. **4** AVAILABLE, unoccupied, at leisure, with time to spare; EMPTY, vacant. **5** WITHOUT, devoid of, lacking in, exempt from. • v. SET FREE, release, let go, liberate, turn loose, untie; rescue, extricate.

**freedom** n. **1** being free; independence. **2** unrestricted use. **3** honorary citizenship.
▷ SYNS **1** LIBERTY, emancipation, independence, autonomy, sovereignty, self-government. **2** SCOPE, latitude, flexibility, margin, elbow room, licence, free rein.

**Freemason** n. a member of an organization for mutual help, which holds secret ceremonies.

**freesia** n. a plant with fragrant flowers.

**freeze** v. (**froze, frozen, freezing**) **1** change or be changed from liquid to solid by extreme cold; (of weather etc.) be so cold that water turns to ice; feel very cold or die of cold. **2** preserve food etc. at a very low temperature. **3** become motionless; stop a moving image; hold prices or wages at a fixed level; prevent assets from being used. • n. 1 the freezing of prices etc. 2 inf. a very cold spell.

**freezer** n. a refrigerated container for preserving and storing food.

**freezing** adj. very cold.
▷ SYNS ICY, bitter, frosty, glacial, arctic, wintry, sub-zero, raw, biting.

**freight** n. goods transported in bulk. • v. transport goods.
▷ SYNS n. CARGO, load, consignment, lading, merchandise, goods.

**freighter** n. a ship or aircraft carrying mainly freight.

**French** adj. & n. (the language) of France. □ French dressing a salad dressing of oil and vinegar. French fries potato chips. French horn a brass wind instrument with a coiled tube. French window a window reaching to the ground, used also as a door.

**frenetic** adj. wild, agitated, or uncontrolled. ■ frenetically adv.

**frenzy** n. (pl. -ies) a state of wild excitement or agitation.
■ frenzied adj.
▷ SYNS MADNESS, mania, wildness, hysteria, delirium, dementedness, fever, tumult.

**frequency** n. (pl. -ies) 1 the rate at which something occurs. 2 frequent occurrence. 3 the number of cycles per second of a sound, light, or radio wave. 4 the waveband at which radio signals are transmitted.

**frequent** adj. happening or appearing often. • v. go frequently to, be often in a place.
▷ SYNS adj. 1 MANY, numerous, recurring, repeated, recurrent, persistent, continual. 2 REGULAR,

habitual. • v. VISIT, haunt, patronize.

**fresco** n. (pl. -os or -oes) a picture painted on a wall or ceiling before the plaster is dry.

**fresh** adj. 1 new or different. 2 (of food) recently made or obtained. 3 recently created. 4 (of water) not salty. 5 (of the wind) cool and fairly strong. 6 pleasantly clean or cool. □ fresher a first-year university student. freshwater of or found in fresh water; not of the sea. ■ freshen v.
▷ SYNS 1 NATURAL, unprocessed, raw. 2 NEW, brand new, recent, latest, up to date, modern, innovative, different, original, novel, unusual, unconventional, unorthodox. 3 ENERGETIC, vigorous, invigorated, lively, spry, sprightly; refreshed, rested, revived. 4 ADDITIONAL, more, further, extra, supplementary. 5 CLEAR, bright, cool, crisp, pure, clean, refreshing, bracing, invigorating.

**fret** v. (**fretted, fretting**) feel anxious. • n. each of the ridges on the fingerboard of a guitar etc.

**fretful** adj. distressed or irritable. ■ fretfully adv.

**fretwork** n. decorative designs cut into wood.

**friable** adj. easily crumbled.

**friar** n. a member of certain religious orders of men.

**fricassée** n. a dish of pieces of meat served in a thick sauce.

**friction** n. 1 rubbing; resistance of one surface to another that moves over it. 2 conflict of people who disagree.
▷ SYNS 1 ABRASION, attrition, rubbing, chafing, scraping,

rasping. **2** DISSENSION, dissent, disagreement, discord, strife, conflict, hostility, rivalry, animosity, antagonism, bad feeling.

**Friday** n. the day following Thursday.

**fridge** n. a refrigerator.

**fried** past and p.p. of FRY.

**friend** n. a person that you know well and like; a supporter of a cause or organization.
▷ SYNS COMPANION, comrade, playmate, intimate, confidante, alter ego, familiar; inf. mate, pal, chum; US inf. buddy.

**friendly** adj. (-ier, -iest) **1** kind and pleasant to others. **2** not harmful to a certain thing: eco-friendly. ■ **friendliness** n.
▷ SYNS AMIABLE, affable, warm, genial, agreeable, companionable, cordial, convivial, sociable, hospitable, neighbourly, outgoing, approachable, accessible, communicative, open, good-natured, kindly, benign; inf. matey.

**friendship** n. the relationship between friends.
▷ SYNS COMPANIONSHIP, intimacy, rapport, affinity, attachment, camaraderie, fellowship.

**frieze** n. a band of decoration round a wall.

**frigate** n. a small fast naval ship.

**fright** n. sudden great fear; a shock; a ridiculous or grotesque person or thing.
▷ SYNS **1** FEAR, terror, alarm, horror, dread, fearfulness, trepidation. **2** SCARE, shock.

**frighten** v. make afraid.
▷ SYNS SCARE, terrify, startle, petrify, shock, panic; inf. spook.

**frightful** adj. very bad or unpleasant; terrible. ■ **frightfully** adv.
▷ SYNS DREADFUL, terrible, awful, horrible, horrific, hideous, ghastly, gruesome, grisly, macabre, shocking, harrowing, appalling.

**frigid** adj. intensely cold; sexually unresponsive. ■ **frigidity** n.

**frill** n. **1** a gathered or pleated strip of material attached at one edge to a garment etc. for decoration. **2** inf. an unnecessary extra feature or luxury. ■ **frilled** adj. **frilly** adj.

**fringe** n. **1** an ornamental edging of hanging threads; front hair cut short to hang over the forehead. **2** the outer part of an area, group, etc. • adj. (of theatre etc.) unconventional. • v. give or form a fringe to.
▷ SYNS n. **1** BORDER, frill, ruffle, trimming, tassels, edging. **2** EDGE, border, perimeter, periphery, margin, rim, limits, outskirts.

**frisk** v. **1** leap or skip playfully. **2** feel over or search a person for concealed weapons etc. • n. a playful leap or skip.

**frisky** adj. (-ier, -iest) lively and playful.
▷ SYNS LIVELY, bouncy, playful, in high spirits, high-spirited, exuberant, perky, skittish; inf. full of beans.

**frisson** n. a sudden shiver of excitement.

**fritter** v. waste money or time on trivial things. • n. a fried batter-coated slice of fruit or meat etc.

**frivolous** adj. not serious. ■ **frivolity** n.

▷ SYNS FLIPPANT, facetious, glib, jokey, light-hearted, fatuous, inane.

**frizz** v. (of hair) form into a mass of tight curls. • n. such curls. ■ **frizzy** adj.

**frock** n. a woman's or girl's dress.

**frog** n. a small amphibian with long web-footed hind legs. □ **frogman** a diver with a rubber suit, flippers, and breathing equipment.

**frolic** v. (**frolicked, frolicking**) play about in a lively way. • n. such play.

**from** prep. **1** having as the starting point, source, material, or cause. **2** as separated, distinguished, or unlike.

**frond** n. a long leaf or leaflike part of a fern, palm tree, etc.

**front** n. **1** the part of an object that faces forward and is normally seen first. **2** the position directly ahead. **3** a battle line. **4** the forward edge of an advancing mass of air. **5** a false appearance or way of behaving. **6** a cover for secret activities. • adj. of or at the front. • v. **1** have the front towards. **2** place or be at the front of. **3** be the leader or presenter of. □ **frontage** the front of a building; a strip of land next to a street or waterway. **front runner** the contestant most likely to win.

▷ SYNS n. **1** FACADE, face, frontage, fore, forefront, foreground. **2** HEAD, beginning, top, lead. **3** SHOW, act, pretence. **4** COVER, blind, screen, disguise.

**frontal** adj. of or on the front.

**frontier** n. a boundary between countries.

▷ SYNS BORDER, boundary, limit, edge, rim, bounds.

**frontispiece** n. an illustration opposite the title page of a book.

**frost** n. small white ice crystals on grass etc.; a period cold enough for these to form. • v. cover or be covered with frost.

**frostbite** n. injury to body tissues due to exposure to extreme cold. ■ **frostbitten** adj.

**frosted** adj. (of glass) having its surface roughened to make it opaque.

**frosting** n. US sugar icing.

**frosty** adj. **1** cold with frost; covered with frost. **2** unfriendly. ■ **frostiness** n.
▷ SYNS **1** FREEZING, frozen, icy, glacial, frigid, arctic, wintry, bitter. **2** UNFRIENDLY, cold, unwelcoming, hostile.

**froth** n. & v. foam. ■ **frothy** adj.
▷ SYNS FOAM, fizz, lather, head, scum, effervescence, bubbles, suds, spume.

**frown** v. **1** wrinkle your forehead in thought or disapproval. **2** (**frown on**) disapprove of. • n. a frowning expression.
▷ SYNS v. **1** SCOWL, glare, glower, knit your brows, lour, look daggers. **2** DISAPPROVE OF, not take kindly to, take a dim view of, look askance at.

**froze**, **frozen** past and p.p. of **FREEZE**.

**fructose** n. a sugar found in honey and fruit.

**frugal** adj. economical; simple and costing little. ■ **frugally** adv.
▷ SYNS THRIFTY, economical, sparing, careful, cautious, prudent, abstemious.

**fruit** n. **1** the seed-containing part of a plant; this used as food. **2** (**fruits**) the product of labour. • v. produce fruit. □ fruit machine a coin-operated gambling machine.

**fruiterer** n. a shopkeeper selling fruit.

**fruitful** adj. producing much fruit or good results. ■ fruitfully adv.
▷ SYNS **1** FERTILE, fecund, prolific. **2** USEFUL, worthwhile, productive, well spent, profitable, advantageous, beneficial, rewarding, gainful.

**fruition** n. the fulfilment of a hope, plan, or project.
▷ SYNS FULFILMENT, realization, materialization, achievement, attainment, success, completion, consummation, maturation, maturity, ripening.

**fruitless** adj. producing little or no result.
▷ SYNS FUTILE, useless, vain, in vain, to no avail, worthless, pointless, ineffective, unproductive, profitless, unrewarding, unsuccessful, unavailing.

**fruity** adj. (-ier, -iest) like or containing fruit; (of a voice) deep and rich.

**frump** n. a dowdy woman. ■ frumpy adj.

**frustrate** v. prevent from achieving something or from being achieved. ■ frustration n.
▷ SYNS **1** DISCOURAGE, dishearten, dispirit, depress, dissatisfy, anger, annoy, vex, irritate, exasperate. **2** DEFEAT, thwart, obstruct, impede, hamper, hinder, check, block, foil, baulk, stymie, stop.

**fry**¹ v. (**fries, fried, frying**) cook or be cooked in very hot fat; be very hot. • n. a fried meal.

**fry**² n. (pl. **fry**) young fish.

**ft** abbr. foot or feet (as a measure).

**fuchsia** n. a plant with drooping flowers.

**fuddled** adj. unable to think clearly.

**fuddy-duddy** n. (pl. -duddies) inf. an old-fashioned person.

**fudge** n. **1** a soft sweet made of milk, sugar, and butter. **2** a makeshift way of dealing with a problem. • v. present or deal with in an inadequate and evasive way.

**fuel** n. material burnt as a source of energy; something that increases anger etc. • v. (**fuelled, fuelling**; US **fueled**) supply with fuel.

**fugitive** n. a person who is fleeing or escaping. • adj. passing or vanishing quickly.
▷ SYNS ESCAPEE, runaway, deserter, refugee, renegade.

**fugue** n. a musical composition using repeated themes in increasingly complex patterns.

**fulcrum** n. (pl. -cra or -crums) the point of support on which a lever pivots.

**fulfil** (US **fulfill**) v. **1** accomplish; satisfy, do what is required by a contract etc. **2** (**fulfil yourself**) develop and use your abilities fully. ■ fulfilment n.
▷ SYNS **1** ACCOMPLISH, carry out, execute, perform, discharge, complete. **2** ACHIEVE, realize, attain, consummate. **3** SATISFY, conform to, fill, answer, meet, comply with.

**full** adj. **1** holding or containing as much as is possible; having a lot of something. **2** complete. **3** plump; (of a garment) using much material in folds or gathers; (of a tone) deep and mellow. • **adv.** directly; very. □ **full back** (in football) a defender who plays at the side. **full-blooded** vigorous and hearty. **full-blown** fully developed. **full moon** the moon with the whole disc illuminated. **full stop** a dot used as a punctuation mark at the end of a sentence or abbreviation. ■ **fully** adv. **fullness** n.

▷ SYNS **adj. 1** FILLED, filled to the brim, brimming, overflowing, filled to capacity. **2** CROWDED, packed, crammed; inf. chock-a-block, jam-packed. **3** SATISFIED, sated, gorged, replete. **4** COMPLETE, entire, whole, comprehensive, thorough, exhaustive, detailed, all-inclusive, all-encompassing, extensive, unabridged. **5** WELL ROUNDED, plump, buxom, shapely, curvaceous, voluptuous. **6** BAGGY, voluminous, loose fitting, capacious.

**fulminate** v. protest strongly.

**fulsome** adj. excessively flattering.

**fumble** v. use your hands clumsily; grope about.

**fume** n. pungent smoke or vapour. • v. **1** emit fumes. **2** be very angry.

**fumigate** v. disinfect with chemical fumes. ■ **fumigation** n.

**fun** n. light-hearted amusement. □ **funfair** a gathering of rides, sideshows, etc. for entertainment. **make fun of** cause people to laugh at.

▷ SYNS AMUSEMENT, entertainment, recreation, relaxation, enjoyment, pleasure, diversion, play, playfulness, jollification, merrymaking.

**function** n. **1** the special activity or purpose of a person or thing. **2** an important ceremony. **3** (in mathematics) a relation involving variables; a quantity whose value depends on varying values of others. • v. perform a function; work or operate.

▷ SYNS n. **1** ROLE, capacity, responsibility, duty, task, job, post, situation, office, occupation, employment, business, charge, concern, activity. **2** SOCIAL EVENT, gathering, reception, party. • v. WORK, go, run, operate.

**functional** adj. of uses or purposes; practical and useful; working or operating. ■ **functionally** adv.

▷ SYNS **1** PRACTICAL, useful, serviceable, utilitarian, workaday. **2** WORKING, in working order, operative, in commission, in service.

**functionary** n. (pl. **-ies**) an official.

**fund** n. a sum of money for a special purpose; financial resources; a stock or supply. • v. provide with money.

▷ SYNS n. **1** RESERVE, collection, pool, kitty, endowment, foundation, grant. **2** (**funds**) MONEY, cash, capital, means, resources, savings. • v. FINANCE, pay for, sponsor, subsidize, endow.

**fundamental** adj. basic; essential. • n. a fundamental fact or principle. ■ **fundamentally** adv.

▷ SYNS **adj.** BASIC, rudimentary, elemental, underlying, primary, cardinal, prime, first, principal, chief, key, central, structural, organic, inherent, intrinsic, vital, essential, important, pivotal, indispensable, necessary.

**fundamentalist** n. a person who upholds a strict or literal interpretation of traditional religious beliefs.
■ **fundamentalism** n.

**funeral** n. a ceremony of burial or cremation.

**funereal** adj. solemn or dismal.

**fungicide** n. a substance that kills fungus.

**fungus** n. (pl. **-gi**) a plant without green colouring matter (e.g. a mushroom or mould).
■ **fungal** adj.

**funk** n. popular dance music with a strong rhythm. ■ **funky** adj.

**funnel** n. 1 a tube with a wide top for pouring liquid into small openings. 2 a chimney on a steam engine or ship. • v. (**funnelled**, **funnelling**; US **funneled**) guide through a funnel.

**funny** adj. 1 causing amusement. 2 puzzling or odd.
■ **funnily** adv.
▷ SYNS 1 AMUSING, comical, comic, humorous, hilarious, entertaining, diverting, hysterical, witty, riotous, droll, facetious, farcical, waggish. 2 PECULIAR, odd, strange, curious, weird, queer, bizarre, mysterious, suspicious, dubious.

**fur** n. 1 the short, soft hair of some animals. 2 the skin of an animal with fur on it. 3 a deposit on the inside of a kettle etc. ■ **furry** adj.

**furious** adj. very angry; intense or violent.

▷ SYNS 1 ENRAGED, raging, infuriated, livid, fuming, incensed, beside yourself; inf. mad, apoplectic. 2 VIOLENT, fierce, wild, intense, vehement, tumultuous, tempestuous, stormy, turbulent.

**furl** v. roll up and fasten a piece of fabric.

**furlong** n. an eighth of a mile.

**furlough** n. leave of absence.

**furnace** n. an enclosed fireplace for intense heating or smelting.

**furnish** v. 1 provide with furniture. 2 supply someone with something.

**furnishings** pl.n. furniture and fitments etc.

**furniture** n. movable articles (e.g. chairs, beds) for use in a room.
▷ SYNS FURNISHINGS, fittings, effects, movables, chattels.

**furore** (US **furor**) n. an outbreak of public anger or excitement.

**furrier** n. a person who deals in furs.

**furrow** n. a long cut in the ground; a groove. • v. make furrows in.
▷ SYNS n. 1 GROOVE, trench, channel, rut, trough, ditch, hollow. 2 SEE **WRINKLE**.

**further** adv. 1 at, to, or over a greater distance. 2 at or to a more advanced stage. 3 in addition. • adj. 1 (or **farther**) more distant in space. 2 additional. • v. help the progress of. □ **further education** education provided for people above school age but usu. below degree level.
▷ SYNS adj. ADDITIONAL, more, extra, supplementary, new, fresh. • v. ADVANCE, facilitate,

aid, assist, help, promote, encourage, foster.

**furtherance** n. assistance or advancement.

**furthermore** adv. moreover.

**furthest** (or **farthest**) adj. most distant. • adv. at, to, or by the greatest distance.

**furtive** adj. stealthy or secretive.

▷ SYNS SECRETIVE, secret, stealthy, surreptitious, clandestine, sneaky, shifty, covert, conspiratorial, sly.

**fury** n. (pl. **-ies**) wild anger; violence.

▷ SYNS 1 ANGER, rage, wrath, ire. 2 FIERCENESS, violence, ferocity, intensity, force, power.

**fuse** v. 1 blend metals etc.; become blended; unite. 2 (of an electrical appliance) stop working when a fuse melts. 3 fit an appliance with a fuse. • n. 1 a strip of wire placed in an electric circuit to melt and interrupt the current when the circuit is overloaded. 2 a length of easily burnt material for igniting a bomb or explosive. ■ **fusible** adj.

**fuselage** n. the body of an aeroplane.

**fusion** n. fusing; the union of atomic nuclei, releasing much energy.

**fuss** n. unnecessary excitement or activity; a vigorous protest. • v. show excessive concern about something.

▷ SYNS n. FLUSTER, agitation, excitement, bother, palaver, commotion, ado, worry; inf. to-do, flap, tizzy.

**fussy** adj. 1 hard to please. 2 full of unnecessary detail.

▷ SYNS PARTICULAR, over-particular, finicky, pernickety, fastidious, hard to please, difficult, demanding; inf. faddy, choosy, picky.

**fusty** adj. 1 smelling stale and stuffy. 2 old-fashioned.

**futile** adj. pointless. ■ **futility** n.

▷ SYNS USELESS, vain, in vain, to no avail, pointless, fruitless, unsuccessful, unprofitable, unavailing.

**futon** n. a Japanese padded mattress that can be rolled up.

**future** n. 1 time still to come; what may happen then. 2 a prospect of success. 3 (**futures**) goods or shares bought at an agreed price but paid for later. • adj. of time to come.

▷ SYNS adj. FORTHCOMING, coming; prospective, intended, planned, destined.

**futuristic** adj. with very modern technology or design.

**fuzz** n. 1 a fluffy or frizzy mass. 2 inf. the police.

**fuzzy** adj. 1 fluffy or frizzy. 2 indistinct.

▷ SYNS 1 DOWNY, frizzy, woolly, furry, fleecy, fluffy. 2 OUT OF FOCUS, unfocused, blurred, blurry, indistinct, unclear, ill-defined, misty, bleary.

# Gg

**G** (or **g**) abbr. **1** giga-. **2** grams. **3** gravity.

**gabble** v. talk quickly and indistinctly.

**gable** n. a triangular upper part of a wall, between sloping roofs.

**gad** v. (**gadded**, **gadding**) (**gad about**) inf. go from place to place enjoying yourself.

**gadget** n. a small mechanical device. ■ **gadgetry** n.

▷ SYNS APPLIANCE, device, tool, implement, apparatus, instrument, mechanism, invention, contraption; inf. gizmo.

**gaffe** n. an embarrassing blunder.

**gaffer** n. inf. **1** a boss. **2** an old man.

**gag** n. **1** something put over a person's mouth to silence them. **2** a joke. • v. (**gagged**, **gagging**) **1** put a gag on; deprive of freedom of speech. **2** retch.

**gage** US sp. of GAUGE.

**gaggle** n. **1** a flock of geese. **2** a noisy group.

**gaiety** n. the state of being light-hearted and cheerful.

**gaily** adv. **1** cheerfully. **2** thoughtlessly.

**gain** v. **1** obtain or secure. **2** reach a place. **3** increase in speed, value, etc. **4** (of a clock) become fast. **5** (**gain on**) get nearer to someone or something pursued. • n. an increase in wealth or value; something gained.

▷ SYNS v. **1** OBTAIN, get, acquire, secure, procure, attain, achieve, win. **2** REACH, arrive at, make. • n. **1** INCREASE, addition, rise, increment. **2** PROFIT, earnings, advantage, benefit, reward, yield, return, winnings, proceeds, dividend, interest; inf. pickings.

**gainful** adj. (of employment) useful and for which one is paid.

▷ SYNS PROFITABLE, rewarding, remunerative, lucrative, productive, beneficial, fruitful, advantageous, worthwhile, useful.

**gainsay** v. (**gainsaid**, **gainsaying**) deny or contradict.

**gait** n. a manner of walking or running.

**gala** n. **1** a social occasion with special entertainments. **2** a swimming competition.

**galaxy** n. (pl. -**ies**) a system of stars, esp. (**the Galaxy**) the one containing the sun and the earth. ■ **galactic** adj.

**gale** n. a very strong wind; a noisy outburst.

**gall** n. **1** bold impudence. **2** something very hurtful. **3** a sore made by rubbing. • v. make sore by rubbing; annoy. □ **gall bladder** an organ attached to the liver, storing bile. ■ **galling** adj.

**gallant** adj. brave; chivalrous. ■ **gallantry** n.

▷ SYNS **1** CHIVALROUS, gentlemanly, courteous, polite, attentive, gracious, considerate, thoughtful. **2** BRAVE, courageous, valiant, bold, daring, fearless, intrepid, heroic.

**galleon** n. a large Spanish sailing ship of the 15th-17th centuries.

**gallery** n. (pl. **-ies**) **1** a building for displaying works of art. **2** a balcony in a theatre or hall. **3** a long room or passage.

**galley** n. (pl. **-eys**) **1** an ancient ship, usu. rowed by slaves. **2** a kitchen on a boat or aircraft.

**gallivant** v. inf. go about looking for fun.

**gallon** n. a measure for liquids = 8 pints (4.55 litres).

**gallop** n. **1** a horse's fastest pace. **2** a ride at a gallop. • v. (**galloped, galloping**) **1** go at a gallop. **2** go fast.

**gallows** n. a framework with a noose for hanging criminals.

**galore** adv. in plenty.

**galoshes** pl.n. rubber overshoes.

**galvanize** (or **-ise**) v. **1** stimulate into activity. **2** coat iron or steel with zinc.

▷ SYNS ELECTRIFY, shock, stir, startle, jolt, spur, prod, stimulate, fire, energize, inspire.

**gambit** n. an opening move intended to secure an advantage.

**gamble** v. play games of chance for money; risk money etc. in hope of gain. • n. an act of gambling; a risky undertaking. ■ **gambler** n.

▷ SYNS v. BET, wager, stake money, lay money; inf. have a flutter.

**gambol** v. (**gambolled, gambolling**; US **gamboled**) jump about playfully.

**game** n. **1** a form of play or sport; a period of play with a closing score. **2** inf. a secret plan: *what's your game?* **3** wild animals hunted for sport or food. • adj. willing or eager. □ **gamekeeper** a person employed to breed and protect game.

▷ SYNS n. **1** PASTIME, diversion, recreation, entertainment, amusement, sport, play. **2** MATCH, contest, fixture, round, bout.

**gamma** n. the third letter of the Greek alphabet ($\Gamma$, $\gamma$). □ **gamma rays** electromagnetic radiation of shorter wavelength than X-rays.

**gammon** n. cured or smoked ham.

**gamut** n. the whole range or scope.

**gander** n. a male goose.

**gang** n. an organized group, esp. of criminals or workers. • v. form a group to intimidate someone.

▷ SYNS n. GROUP, band, company, crowd, pack, horde, mob.

**gangling** adj. tall and awkward.

**gangplank** n. a plank for walking to or from a boat.

**gangrene** n. decay of body tissue.

**gangster** n. a member of a gang of violent criminals.

▷ SYNS RACKETEER, crook, criminal, hoodlum, robber; US inf. hood, mobster.

**gangway** n. **1** a passage between rows of seats. **2** a movable bridge linking a ship to shore.

**gannet** n. a large seabird.

**gantry** n. (pl. **-ies**) an overhead framework supporting railway signals, road signs, a crane, etc.

**gaol** = JAIL.

**gap** n. a space or opening; an interval. ■ **gappy** adj.
▷ SYNS **1** OPENING, hole, aperture, cavity, space, breach, break, rift, fissure, cleft, chink, crack, crevice, cranny, orifice, interstice. **2** PAUSE, break, intermission, interval, interlude, lull, respite, breathing space. **3** DIFFERENCE, disparity; chasm, gulf.

**gape** v. open your mouth wide; be wide open.
▷ SYNS STARE, gaze, goggle; inf. gawk, rubberneck.

**garage** n. a building for storing a vehicle; an establishment selling petrol or repairing and selling vehicles.

**garb** n. clothing. • v. clothe.

**garbage** n. rubbish.
▷ SYNS WASTE, rubbish, refuse, litter, debris, junk, detritus; US trash.

**garble** v. confuse or distort a message etc.
▷ SYNS MIX UP, muddle, jumble, confuse, distort.

**garden** n. **1** a piece of cultivated ground by a house. **2** (**gardens**) ornamental public grounds. • v. tend a garden. ■ **gardener** n.

**gargantuan** adj. gigantic.

**gargle** v. wash the throat with liquid held there by breathing out through it. • n. an act of gargling; a liquid for this.

**gargoyle** n. a waterspout in the form of a grotesque carved face on a building.

**garish** adj. too bright and harsh.

▷ SYNS GAUDY, showy, loud, lurid, brassy, tawdry, tasteless; inf. flashy, flash.

**garland** n. a wreath of flowers as a decoration.

**garlic** n. an onion-like plant.

**garment** n. a piece of clothing.

**garner** v. gather or collect.

**garnet** n. a red semi-precious stone.

**garnish** v. decorate food. • n. something used for garnishing.

**garret** n. an attic.

**garrison** n. troops stationed in a town or fort. • v. guard a town etc. with a garrison.
▷ SYNS n. **1** TROOPS, soldiers, force, detachment, unit, brigade, platoon, squadron. **2** BARRACKS, base, fort, fortress, fortification, stronghold, camp, encampment.

**garrotte** (US **garrote**) n. a wire or a metal collar used to strangle a victim. • v. strangle with this.

**garrulous** adj. talkative.

**garter** n. a band worn round the leg to keep up a stocking.

**gas** n. (pl. **-ses**) **1** an airlike substance (not a solid or liquid); such a substance used as fuel. **2** US petrol. • v. (**gassed**, **gassing**) **1** attack or kill with poisonous gas. **2** inf. talk at length. □ **gas mask** a device worn over the face as protection against poisonous gas.

**gaseous** adj. of or like a gas.

**gash** n. a long deep cut. • v. make a gash in.
▷ SYNS v. CUT, slash, tear, lacerate, wound, gouge, slit.

**gasket** n. a piece of rubber etc. sealing a joint between metal surfaces.

**gasoline** n. US petrol.

**gasp** v. draw in breath sharply; speak breathlessly. • n. a sharp intake of breath.
▷ SYNS v. PANT, puff, puff and blow, gulp, choke, catch your breath, fight for breath, wheeze.

**gastric** adj. of the stomach.

**gastro-enteritis** n. inflammation of the stomach and intestines.

**gate** n. 1 a movable barrier in a wall or fence; an entrance. 2 the number of spectators paying to attend a sporting event. □ gatecrash go to a party without an invitation. gateway an opening closed by a gate; a means of access.
▷ SYNS BARRIER, turnstile; gateway, doorway, entrance, exit, opening.

**gateau** n. (pl. -aux or -aus) a large rich cream cake.

**gather** v. 1 come or bring together. 2 understand to be the case. 3 increase in speed, force, etc. 4 collect. 5 pull fabric into folds by drawing thread through it. • n. a small fold in a garment.
▷ SYNS v. 1 CONGREGATE, assemble, meet, come together, convene, converge, mass; summon, round up, muster, marshal. 2 UNDERSTAND, believe, hear, learn, infer, deduce, conclude, surmise.

**gathering** n. an assembled group.
▷ SYNS ASSEMBLY, meeting, convention, rally, congregation, group, crowd, throng.

**gauche** adj. socially awkward.
▷ SYNS AWKWARD, maladroit, inept, inelegant, graceless, unsophisticated.

**gaudy** adj. (-ier, -iest) tastelessly showy or bright. ■ gaudily adv.

**gauge** (US **gage**) n. 1 a measuring device; a standard measure of thickness etc. 2 the distance between the rails of a railway track. • v. estimate; measure.
▷ SYNS n. 1 METER, dial, scale. 2 SIZE, diameter, width, thickness, breadth; bore, calibre.

**gaunt** adj. lean and haggard.
▷ SYNS HAGGARD, drawn, cadaverous, skeletal, emaciated, skinny, bony, lean, scrawny.

**gauntlet** n. a glove with a long wide cuff. □ run the gauntlet be exposed to something dangerous or unpleasant.

**gauze** n. 1 thin transparent fabric. 2 fine wire mesh.

**gave** past of GIVE.

**gavel** n. a mallet used by an auctioneer or chairman to call for attention.

**gavotte** n. a French dance of the 18th century.

**gay** adj. 1 homosexual. 2 dated light-hearted; brightly coloured. • n. a homosexual person.

**gaze** v. look steadily. • n. a steady look.
▷ SYNS v. STARE, gape, goggle, eye; inf. gawp, rubberneck.

**gazebo** n. (pl. -os) a summer house with a wide view.

**gazelle** n. a small antelope.

**gazette** n. a journal or newspaper.

**gazetteer** n. an index of places, rivers, mountains, etc.

**GB** abbr. Great Britain.

**GBH** abbr. grievous bodily harm.

**GCE** abbr. General Certificate of Education.

**GCSE** abbr. General Certificate of Secondary Education.

**gear** n. **1** a set of toothed wheels working together to change the speed of machinery; a particular adjustment of these: *top gear.* **2** inf. equipment, belongings, or clothes. • v. **1** design or adjust the gears in a machine. **2** intend or direct to a particular purpose. □ **gearbox** a set of gears with its casing.
▷ SYNS n. **1** EQUIPMENT, tools, kit, apparatus, implements, tackle, appliances, utensils, supplies, accessories, paraphernalia, accoutrements. **2** BELONGINGS, possessions, things, luggage, baggage, effects; inf. stuff.

**geek** n. inf. **1** an awkward or unfashionable person. **2** an obsessive enthusiast. ■ **geeky** adj.

**geese** pl. of GOOSE.

**geisha** n. a Japanese hostess trained to entertain men.

**gel** n. a jelly-like substance. • v. (**gelling, gelled**) **1** (of jelly etc.) set or become firmer. **2** take definite form.

**gelatin** (or **gelatine**) n. a clear substance made by boiling bones and used in making jelly etc. ■ **gelatinous** adj.

**geld** v. castrate.

**gelding** n. a castrated horse.

**gelignite** n. an explosive containing nitroglycerine.

**gem** n. a precious stone; something of great beauty or excellence.

**gender** n. being male or female.

**gene** n. each of the factors controlling heredity, carried by a chromosome.

**genealogy** n. (pl. **-ies**) a line of descent; the study of family

pedigrees. ■ **genealogical** adj. **genealogist** n.
▷ SYNS FAMILY TREE, ancestry, pedigree, line, lineage, descent, parentage, birth, extraction, family, stock, bloodline, heritage.

**genera** pl. of GENUS.

**general** adj. **1** affecting or concerning all or most people or things. **2** not detailed or specific. • n. an army officer next below field marshal. □ **general election** an election of parliamentary representatives from the whole country. **general practitioner** a community doctor treating cases of all kinds. **in general 1** mostly. **2** as a whole.
▷ SYNS adj. **1** WIDESPREAD, common, prevailing, popular, public, wide. **2** COMPREHENSIVE, across-the-board, blanket, universal, inclusive, sweeping. **3** USUAL, customary, established, habitual, normal, conventional, typical, standard, regular. **4** BROAD, loose, rough, approximate, vague, inexact, imprecise.

**generality** n. (pl. **-ies**) a general statement; being general.

**generalize** (or **-ise**) v. **1** speak in general terms. **2** make generally available. ■ **generalization** n.

**generally** adv. in most cases.
▷ SYNS NORMALLY, in general, as a rule, by and large, mainly, for the most part, on the whole, usually, typically, ordinarily.

**generate** v. produce or bring into existence.
▷ SYNS CAUSE, give rise to, produce, create, engender, bring about, lead to.

**generation** n. **1** all the people born at roughly the same time; one stage in the descent of a family. **2** generating.

**generator** n. a machine converting mechanical energy into electricity.

**generic** adj. of a whole genus or group. ∎ **generically** adv.

**generous** adj. giving freely; large, plentiful. ∎ **generosity** n.
▷ SYNS **1** LIBERAL, magnanimous, benevolent, munificent, beneficent, bountiful, bounteous, open-handed, charitable, unstinting, free-handed; princely. **2** ABUNDANT, plentiful, lavish, ample, rich, copious.

**genesis** n. a beginning or origin.

**genetic** adj. of genes or genetics. • pl.n. (**genetics**) the study of inherited characteristics. ▢ genetic engineering manipulation of DNA to change hereditary features. ∎ **genetically** adv. **geneticist** n.

**genial** adj. kind and cheerful; (of climate etc.) pleasantly mild. ∎ **geniality** n. **genially** adv.
▷ SYNS AMIABLE, affable, friendly, congenial, amicable, convivial, agreeable, good-humoured, good-natured, pleasant, cordial, cheerful, cheery, kind, kindly, benign.

**genie** n. (pl. -ii) a spirit in Arabian folk lore.

**genital** adj. of animal reproduction or sex organs. • pl.n. (**genitals** or **genitalia**) the external sex organs.

**genitive** n. the grammatical case expressing possession or source.

**genius** n. (pl. -ses) exceptionally great intellectual or creative power; a person with this.

▷ SYNS **1** MASTERMIND, prodigy, virtuoso, master, maestro. **2** BRILLIANCE, intelligence, cleverness, brains, fine mind.

**genocide** n. deliberate extermination of a race of people.

**genre** n. a style of art or literature.

**genteel** adj. polite and refined, often affectedly so. ∎ **gentility** n.
▷ SYNS REFINED, respectable, decorous, well mannered, courteous, polite, proper, correct, seemly, well bred, ladylike, gentlemanly, dignified, gracious.

**Gentile** n. a non-Jewish person.

**gentle** adj. kind and mild; (of climate etc.) moderate. ∎ **gentleness** n. **gently** adv.
▷ SYNS **1** TENDER, kind, kindly, humane, benign, lenient, compassionate, tender-hearted, placid, sweet-tempered, mild, quiet, peaceful. **2** MODERATE, light, temperate, soft.

**gentleman** n. a well-mannered man; a man of good social position.

**gentry** n. people of good social position.

**genuine** adj. really what it is said to be.
▷ SYNS **1** REAL, authentic, true, pure, actual, bona fide, veritable, pukka; legitimate, lawful, legal, valid; inf. kosher. **2** SINCERE, truthful, honest, frank, candid, open, natural, unaffected, artless, ingenuous; inf. upfront.

**genus** n. (pl. **genera**) a group of similar animals or plants, usu. containing several species; a kind.

**geography** n. the study of the earth's physical features, climate, etc.; the features and

arrangement of a place.
■ **geographer** n. **geographical** adj.

**geology** n. the study of the earth's structure; the rocks etc. of a district. ■ **geological** adj. **geologist** n.

**geometric** adj. of geometry; (of a design) featuring regular lines and shapes. ■ **geometrical** adj. **geometrically** adv.

**geometry** n. the branch of mathematics dealing with lines, angles, surfaces, and solids.

**geranium** n. a cultivated flowering plant.

**gerbil** n. a rodent with long hind legs, often kept as a pet.

**geriatric** adj. of old people. • n. an old person.

**germ** n. **1** a microorganism causing disease. **2** a portion of an organism capable of developing into a new one. **3** an early stage of development.
▷ SYNS MICROBE, microorganism, bacillus, bacterium, virus; inf. bug.

**German** adj. & n. (a native or the language) of Germany.
□ German measles = **RUBELLA**. German shepherd a large breed of dog often used as guard dogs; an Alsatian.

**germane** adj. relevant.

**germinate** v. begin or cause to grow. ■ **germination** n.

**gestation** n. the period when a fetus is developing in the womb.

**gesticulate** v. make expressive movements with the hands and arms. ■ **gesticulation** n.

**gesture** n. **1** a movement designed to convey a meaning. **2** something done to display

good intentions etc., with no practical value. • v. make a gesture.
▷ SYNS n. SIGNAL, sign, wave, indication, gesticulation. • v. GESTICULATE, signal, motion, wave, indicate.

**get** v. **1** come to possess; receive; succeed in attaining. **2** fetch. **3** experience pain etc.; catch a disease. **4** bring or come into a specified state; arrive or bring somewhere. **5** persuade, induce, or order. **6** capture. □ getaway an escape. get-together a social gathering.
▷ SYNS **1** ACQUIRE, obtain, come by, secure, procure; buy, purchase. **2** RECEIVE, be sent, be given. **3** FETCH, collect, carry, transport, convey. **4** EARN, make, bring in, clear, take home. **5** *get cold:* BECOME, grow, turn.

**geyser** n. **1** a spring spouting hot water or steam. **2** a water heater.

**ghastly** adj. **1** causing horror. **2** inf. very unpleasant. **3** very pale.
▷ SYNS TERRIBLE, horrible, frightful, dreadful, awful, horrific, horrendous, hideous, shocking, appalling, grim, gruesome.

**gherkin** n. a small pickled cucumber.

**ghetto** n. (pl. -os) a part of a city occupied by people of a particular race, nationality, etc.

**ghost** n. an apparition of a dead person; a faint trace.
▷ SYNS **1** APPARITION, spectre, spirit, phantom, wraith; inf. spook. **2** SUGGESTION, hint, trace, glimmer, shadow.

**ghostly** adj. relating to or like a ghost.
▷ SYNS SUPERNATURAL, unearthly, spectral, phantom, eerie, weird, uncanny; inf. spooky.

**ghoul** n. an evil spirit; a person morbidly interested in death and disaster. ■ **ghoulish** adj.

**giant** n. (in fairy tales) a being of superhuman size; an abnormally large person, animal, or thing. • adj. very large.
▷ SYNS adj. GIGANTIC, enormous, huge, colossal, immense, vast, mammoth, gargantuan, titanic, towering.

**gibber** v. make meaningless sounds in shock or terror.

**gibberish** n. unintelligible talk; nonsense.

**gibbon** n. a long-armed ape.

**gibe** = JIBE.

**giblets** pl.n. the liver, heart, etc., of a fowl.

**giddy** adj. (-ier, -iest) having the feeling that everything is spinning; excitable and silly.
▷ SYNS DIZZY, faint, light-headed, unsteady; inf. woozy.

**gift** n. **1** something given or received without payment; a very easy task. **2** a natural talent or ability. • v. **1** give as a gift. **2** (**gifted**) having exceptional talent.
▷ SYNS n. **1** PRESENT, offering, donation, bonus; gratuity, tip; bequest, legacy. **2** TALENT, aptitude, flair, facility, knack, ability, faculty, capacity, skill, expertise, genius.

**gifted** adj. having exceptional talent.
▷ SYNS TALENTED, brilliant, clever, intelligent, able, accomplished, masterly, skilled, expert.

**gig** n. inf. a live performance by a pop group.

**gigantic** adj. very large.

**giggle** v. laugh quietly. • n. such a laugh. ■ **giggly** adj.
▷ SYNS v. TITTER, snigger, chuckle, chortle, laugh.

**gild** v. cover with a thin layer of gold or gold paint.

**gill** n. one-quarter of a pint.

**gills** n. the organ with which a fish breathes.

**gilt** adj. gilded. • n. gold leaf or paint used in gilding. □ **gilt-edged** (of an investment etc.) very safe.

**gimmick** n. a trick or device to attract attention. ■ **gimmicky** adj.

**gin** n. an alcoholic spirit flavoured with juniper berries.

**ginger** n. **1** a hot-tasting root used as a spice. **2** a light reddish-yellow colour. □ **gingerbread** cake flavoured with ginger.

**gingerly** adv. cautiously.

**gingham** n. cotton fabric with a checked or striped pattern.

**gingivitis** n. inflammation of the gums.

**ginseng** n. a medicinal plant with a fragrant root.

**Gipsy** = GYPSY.

**giraffe** n. a long-necked African animal.

**gird** v. lit. encircle with a belt or band.

**girder** n. a metal beam supporting a structure.

**girdle** n. a belt; an elastic corset. • v. surround.

**girl** n. a female child; a young woman. □ **girlfriend** a person's regular female romantic or

sexual partner; a woman's
female friend.
▷ SYNS YOUNG WOMAN, young lady,
miss; Scot. lass, lassie; inf. bird,
chick; lit. maid, maiden, damsel.

**giro** n. (pl. **-os**) a banking system
in which payment can be made
by transferring credit from one
account to another; a cheque or
payment made by this.

**girth** n. **1** the measurement
around the middle of
something. **2** a band under a
horse's belly holding a saddle in
place.
▷ SYNS CIRCUMFERENCE, perimeter,
width, breadth.

**gist** n. the general meaning of a
speech or text.
▷ SYNS ESSENCE, substance, core,
nub, crux, sense, meaning,
significance, thrust, import.

**give** v. **1** hand over; cause
someone to receive something;
devote to a cause; cause
someone to experience
something. **2** do; utter. **3** yield
under pressure. • n. elasticity.
□ **give in** acknowledge defeat.
**given name** a first name.
**give up** abandon hope or an
effort.
▷ SYNS v. **1** PRESENT, hand (over),
bestow, donate, contribute,
confer, award, grant, accord,
leave, will, bequeath, entrust,
consign, vouchsafe. **2** *give them
time:* ALLOW, permit. **3** *give
advice:* PROVIDE, supply,
furnish, proffer, offer.

**glacé** adj. preserved in sugar.

**glacial** adj. of or from glaciers;
very cold.

**glaciation** n. the formation of
glaciers.

**glacier** n. a mass or river of ice
moving very slowly.

**glad** adj. pleased or joyful.
■ **gladden** v.
▷ SYNS **1** HAPPY, pleased, delighted,
thrilled, overjoyed; gratified,
thankful; inf. chuffed, tickled
pink. **2** WILLING, eager, ready,
prepared. **3** JOYFUL, pleasing,
welcome, cheering, gratifying.

**glade** n. an open space in a
forest.

**gladiator** n. a man trained to
fight at public shows in ancient
Rome.

**gladiolus** n. (pl. **gladioli** or
**gladioluses**) a tall plant with
sword-shaped leaves.

**glamorize** (or **-ise**) v. make
something undesirable seem
attractive.

**glamorous** adj. attractive and
appealing.
▷ SYNS **1** BEAUTIFUL, elegant, chic,
stylish, fashionable. **2** EXCITING,
glittering, colourful, exotic; inf.
glitzy, jet-setting.

**glamour** (US **glamor**) n. an
attractive and exciting quality.
▷ SYNS **1** BEAUTY, elegance, style,
charisma. **2** EXCITEMENT, allure,
fascination, magic, romance,
mystique.

**glance** v. **1** look briefly. **2** strike
something and bounce off at an
angle. • n. a brief look.
▷ SYNS v. GLIMPSE, catch a glimpse,
peek, peep.

**gland** n. an organ that secretes
substances to be used or
expelled by the body.
■ **glandular** adj.

**glare** v. stare angrily or fiercely;
shine with a harsh dazzling
light; very obvious. • n. a fierce
stare; a harsh light.
▷ SYNS v. **1** SCOWL, glower, frown,
look daggers, lour, stare.
**2** DAZZLE, beam, blaze.

**glaring** adj. very obvious: *a glaring error.*

▷ SYNS OBVIOUS, conspicuous, unmistakable, inescapable, unmissable, striking, flagrant, blatant.

**glass** n. 1 a hard transparent substance. 2 a glass drinking container. 3 (**glasses**) a pair of lenses in a frame that rests on the nose and ears, used to correct eyesight. 4 a mirror. □ **glasshouse** a greenhouse.

**glasses** pl.n. spectacles.

▷ SYNS SPECTACLES, bifocals, sunglasses, lorgnette, pince-nez.

**glassy** adj. 1 resembling glass. 2 (of a person's eyes or expression) showing no interest or liveliness.

▷ SYNS 1 SHINY, glossy, smooth, clear, transparent, translucent. 2 GLAZED, blank, expressionless, empty, vacant.

**glaucoma** n. a condition causing gradual loss of sight.

**glaze** v. 1 fit or cover with glass. 2 coat with a glossy surface. 3 (of eyes etc.) lose brightness and animation. • n. a shiny surface or coating.

▷ SYNS n. GLOSS, varnish, lacquer, enamel, finish, lustre, shine.

**glazier** n. a person whose job is to fit glass in windows.

**gleam** v. shine brightly. • n. 1 a briefly shining light. 2 a brief or faint show of a quality.

▷ SYNS v. SHINE, flash, glint, glisten, glitter, flicker, shimmer, glimmer, sparkle, twinkle.

**glean** v. pick up grain left by harvesters; collect.

**glee** n. great delight. ■ **gleeful** adj.

**glen** n. a narrow valley.

**glib** adj. articulate but insincere or shallow.

**glide** v. move smoothly; fly in a glider. • n. a gliding movement.

**glider** n. an aeroplane with no engine.

**glimmer** n. a faint gleam. • v. gleam faintly.

**glimpse** n. a brief view of something. • v. catch a glimpse of.

▷ SYNS n. GLANCE, peek, peep. • v. CATCH SIGHT OF, spot, spy, make out, notice, discern.

**glint** n. a brief flash of light. • v. send out a glint.

**glisten** v. shine like something wet.

▷ SYNS SHINE, sparkle, twinkle, flicker, glint, glitter, gleam, glimmer, shimmer.

**glitch** n. inf. a sudden problem or fault.

**glitter** v. & n. sparkle.

▷ SYNS SPARKLE, twinkle, wink, glint, flash, gleam, shimmer, glimmer.

**gloat** v. exult in your own success or another's misfortune.

▷ SYNS RELISH, revel, glory, rejoice, exult, triumph, crow; inf. rub it in.

**global** adj. worldwide; of or affecting an entire group. □ **global warming** an increase in the temperature of the earth's atmosphere. ■ **globally** adv.

▷ SYNS 1 WORLDWIDE, international. 2 GENERAL, overall, comprehensive, universal, all-encompassing, all-inclusive; thorough, total, across the board.

**globalization** (or **-isation**) n. the process by which businesses

start to operate globally.
■ globalize v.

**globe** n. a ball-shaped object, esp. one with a map of the earth on it; the world.

**globetrotter** n. inf. a person who travels widely.

**globule** n. a small round drop.
■ globular adj.
▷ SYNS BEAD, drop, ball, droplet.

**glockenspiel** n. a musical instrument of metal bars or tubes struck by hammers.

**gloom** n. 1 semi-darkness. 2 depression or sadness.

**gloomy** adj. 1 dark or poorly lit. 2 causing or feeling depression or despair.
▷ SYNS 1 DARK, shadowy, murky, sunless, dim, dingy. 2 SAD, melancholy, unhappy, miserable, despondent, dejected, downcast, downhearted, glum, dispirited, depressed, pessimistic, morose.

**glorify** v. (glorified, glorifying) 1 praise highly; worship. 2 make something seem grander than it is.
■ glorification n.

**glorious** adj. having or bringing glory; beautiful or impressive.
▷ SYNS 1 ILLUSTRIOUS, celebrated, famous, acclaimed, distinguished, honoured; outstanding, great, magnificent, noble, triumphant. 2 WONDERFUL, marvellous, superb, sublime, lovely, beautiful; inf. super, great, fantastic, terrific, tremendous, heavenly, divine, fabulous.

**glory** n. (pl. -ies) fame, honour, and praise; beauty or splendour; a source of fame and pride. • v. take pride or pleasure in something.

▷ SYNS n. 1 DISTINCTION, fame, kudos, renown, honour, prestige, acclaim, praise, eminence, recognition. 2 SPLENDOUR, magnificence, grandeur, majesty, beauty. • v. EXULT, rejoice, delight, revel; boast, crow, gloat.

**gloss** n. 1 a shine on a smooth surface. 2 a type of paint. 3 a translation or explanation. • v. try to conceal a fault etc.

**glossary** n. (pl. -ies) a list of technical or special words with definitions.

**glossy** adj. shiny and smooth.
▷ SYNS SHINY, gleaming, smooth, lustrous, glistening, polished, glazed, silky, sleek.

**glove** n. a covering for the hand with separate divisions for fingers and thumb.

**glow** v. 1 give out steady light. 2 have a warm or flushed look. 3 (glowing) expressing great praise. • n. a glowing state.
□ glow-worm a beetle that gives out light.
▷ SYNS v. SHINE, gleam, glimmer, flicker. • n. GLEAM, glimmer, shine, radiance, light.

**glower** v. scowl.
▷ SYNS SCOWL, glare, frown, look daggers, lour.

**glowing** adj. expressing great praise.
▷ SYNS FAVOURABLE, enthusiastic, complimentary, admiring, rapturous; inf. rave.

**glucose** n. a form of sugar found in fruit juice.

**glue** n. a sticky substance used for joining things. • v. (glued, gluing) fasten with glue; attach closely.

▷ SYNS n. ADHESIVE, gum, fixative, paste. • v. STICK, paste, gum, fix, affix, seal.

**glum** adj. sad and gloomy.
▷ SYNS GLOOMY, melancholy, sad, despondent, miserable, dejected, downcast, downhearted, dispirited, depressed.

**glut** v. (glutted, glutting) supply or fill to excess. • n. an excessive supply.
▷ SYNS n. SURPLUS, excess, surfeit, overabundance, oversupply, saturation, superfluity.

**glutinous** adj. sticky.
▷ SYNS STICKY, viscous, viscid, tacky, gluey.

**glutton** n. 1 a greedy person. 2 a person who is eager for something challenging.
■ gluttonous adj. gluttony n.

**glycerine** (US **glycerin**) n. a thick sweet liquid used in medicines etc.

**GMT** abbr. Greenwich Mean Time.

**gnarled** adj. knobbly or twisted.

**gnash** v. grind your teeth.

**gnat** n. a small biting fly.

**gnaw** v. bite persistently at something hard.
▷ SYNS CHEW, munch, bite, champ, chomp, worry.

**gnome** n. an imaginary being like a tiny man.

**gnu** n. a large heavy antelope.

**go** v. 1 move or travel. 2 depart; (of time) pass. 3 pass into a specified state; proceed in a specified way: *the party went well.* 4 fit into or be regularly kept in a particular place. 5 function or operate. 6 come to an end; disappear or be used up. • n. 1 an attempt. 2 a turn to do something. 3 energy.

□ go-ahead inf. permission to proceed. go-between an intermediary or negotiator. go-cart (or go-kart) a miniature racing car. go off 1 explode. 2 (of food) become stale or bad.
▷ SYNS v. 1 MOVE, proceed, progress, walk, travel, journey. 2 LEAVE, depart, withdraw, retire, set off/out. 3 WORK, function, operate, run. 4 BECOME, grow, get, turn. 5 *her headache has gone:* STOP, cease, disappear, vanish, fade away, melt away. • n. TRY, attempt, turn, bid, endeavour, essay; inf. shot, stab, crack.

**goad** v. provoke to action. • n. 1 a stimulus to action. 2 a spiked stick for driving cattle.

**goal** n. 1 a structure or area into which players send the ball to score a point in certain games; a point scored. 2 an ambition or aim. □ goalkeeper (in football, hockey, etc.) a player whose role is to keep the ball out of the goal. goalpost either of the two upright posts of a goal.
▷ SYNS AIM, objective, end, purpose, ambition, target, design, intention, intent, aspiration.

**goat** n. a horned animal, often kept for milk.

**gob** n. inf. a person's mouth.

**gobble** v. 1 eat quickly and greedily. 2 (of a turkey) make a throaty sound.

**gobbledegook** n. inf. unintelligible language.

**goblet** n. a drinking glass with a stem and a foot.

**goblin** n. a mischievous ugly elf.

**God** n. 1 (in Christianity and some other religions) the creator and supreme ruler of the universe. **2** (**god**) a superhuman being or spirit. □ **God-fearing** earnestly religious.

**goddess** n. a female deity.

**godfather** n. **1** a male god-parent. **2** a head of an illegal organization, esp. the Mafia.

**godforsaken** adj. (of a place) remote or unattractive.
▷ SYNS WRETCHED, miserable, dreary, dismal, bleak, desolate, gloomy, deserted, neglected, remote, isolated.

**godmother** n. a female god-parent.

**godparent** n. a person who represents a child at baptism and takes responsibility for its religious education.

**godsend** n. a very helpful or welcome thing.
▷ SYNS BLESSING, boon, bonus, benefit, stroke of luck.

**goggle** v. stare with wide open eyes. • n. (**goggles**) close-fitting protective glasses.

**gold** n. a yellow metal of high value; coins or articles made of this; its colour; a gold medal (awarded as first prize). • adj. made of or coloured like gold. □ **goldfish** a small orange carp often kept in ponds and tanks. **gold leaf** gold beaten into a very thin sheet. **gold rush** a rush to a newly discovered goldfield. **goldsmith** a person who makes gold articles.

**golden** adj. **1** gold. **2** very happy. □ **golden jubilee** the 50th anniversary of a sovereign's reign. **golden wedding** the 50th anniversary of a wedding.

**golf** n. a game in which a ball is struck with clubs into a series of holes. ■ **golfer** n.

**gondola** n. a boat with high pointed ends, used on canals in Venice. ■ **gondolier** n.

**gone** p.p. of GO.

**gong** n. a metal plate that resounds when struck.

**goo** n. inf. a sticky wet substance. ■ **gooey** adj.

**good** adj. **1** having the right qualities; of a high standard. **2** morally right, polite, or obedient. **3** enjoyable or satisfying. **4** appropriate. **5** (**good for**) of benefit to. **6** thorough. • n. **1** morally correct behaviour. **2** something beneficial. **3** (**goods**) products, possessions, or freight. □ **good-for-nothing** worthless. **Good Friday** the Friday before Easter, commemorating the Crucifixion of Jesus. **goodwill** friendly feeling. ■ **goodness** n.
▷ SYNS adj. **1** FINE, superior, excellent, superb, marvellous, wonderful, first-rate, first-class; satisfactory, acceptable. **2** CAPABLE, proficient, able, accomplished, skilful, adept, expert. **3** VIRTUOUS, upright, moral, ethical, trustworthy, righteous, right-minded, honest, noble, exemplary; well behaved, well mannered, obedient, dutiful. **4** a good time: ENJOYABLE, pleasant, agreeable, pleasurable, delightful, nice, lovely; inf. fantastic, fabulous, terrific. **5** milk is good for you: WHOLESOME, healthy, nutritious, nourishing, beneficial. **6** a good reason: VALID, legitimate, genuine, authentic, sound, bona fide. • n. **1** VIRTUE, morality, honesty, integrity. **2** it's for your own good: BENEFIT, advantage, gain, profit, interest, well-being, welfare.

**goodbye** exclam. & n. an expression used when parting.
▷ SYNS FAREWELL, adieu, au revoir, ciao; inf. bye, cheerio, cheers, see you.

**goodly** adj. dated considerable in size or quantity.

**good-natured** adj. kind and unselfish.
▷ SYNS KIND, kind-hearted, kindly, warm-hearted, friendly, helpful, accommodating, amiable.

**goose** n. (pl. **geese**) a web-footed bird larger than a duck; the female of this. □ goose-step a way of marching in which the legs are kept straight.

**gooseberry** n. an edible berry with a hairy skin.

**gopher** n. an American burrowing rodent.

**gore** n. blood from a wound.
• v. pierce with a horn or tusk.

**gorge** n. a narrow steep-sided valley. • v. eat greedily.
▷ SYNS n. CHASM, canyon, ravine, defile, pass.

**gorgeous** adj. 1 beautiful. 2 inf. very pleasant.
▷ SYNS 1 BEAUTIFUL, attractive, lovely, good-looking, sexy; inf. stunning. 2 SPLENDID, magnificent, superb, impressive, wonderful, imposing, dazzling, breathtaking.

**gorilla** n. a large powerful ape.

**gorse** n. a wild evergreen thorny shrub with yellow flowers.

**gory** adj. covered with blood; involving bloodshed.
▷ SYNS BLOODY, bloodstained, grisly; violent, brutal, savage, sanguinary.

**gosling** n. a young goose.

**gospel** n. 1 the teachings of Jesus. 2 (**Gospel**) any of the first four books of the New Testament. 3 something regarded as definitely true.

**gossamer** n. a fine piece of cobweb.

**gossip** n. casual talk about other people's affairs; a person fond of such talk. • v. (**gossiped, gossiping**) engage in gossip.
▷ SYNS n. RUMOURS, scandal, tittle-tattle, hearsay, whispering campaign. • v. TITTLE-TATTLE, talk, whisper, tell tales.

**got** past and p.p. of GET.

**gouge** n. a chisel with a concave blade. • v. cut out with a gouge; scoop or force out.

**goulash** n. a rich stew of meat and vegetables.

**gourd** n. a hard-skinned fruit whose rind is used as a container.

**gourmand** n. a food lover; a glutton.

**gourmet** n. a connoisseur of good food and drink.

**gout** n. a disease causing inflammation of the joints.

**govern** v. conduct the policy etc. of a country, state, etc.; control or influence. ■ **governance** n. **governor** n.
▷ SYNS 1 RULE, preside over, reign over, control, be in charge of, command, lead, run, head. 2 DETERMINE, decide, regulate, direct, dictate, shape; affect, influence, sway.

**governess** n. a woman employed to teach children in a private household.

**government** n. the governing body of a state; the system by which a state is governed.
■ **governmental** adj.

▷ SYNS ADMINISTRATION, regime, parliament, ministry, executive, rule, leadership, command, control.

**gown** n. a long dress; a loose overgarment; an official robe.
▷ SYNS DRESS, frock, robe.

**GP** abbr. general practitioner.

**grab** v. (**grabbed**, **grabbing**) grasp suddenly; take greedily. • n. a sudden clutch or attempt to seize something.
▷ SYNS v. GRASP, seize, snatch, clutch, grip, clasp, take hold of.

**grace** n. 1 elegance of movement. 2 polite good will. 3 a short prayer of thanks for a meal. 4 mercy. 5 (**graces**) attractive qualities. • v. 1 honour by your presence. 2 make more attractive. ■ **graceless** adj.
▷ SYNS n. 1 ELEGANCE, poise, gracefulness, finesse; suppleness, agility, nimbleness, light-footedness. 2 *have the grace to apologize:* COURTESY, decency, (good) manners, politeness, decorum, respect, tact. 3 *say grace:* BLESSING, prayer, thanksgiving, benediction. • v. ADORN, decorate, ornament, embellish, enhance.

**graceful** adj. having or showing grace or elegance. ■ **gracefully** adv.
▷ SYNS ELEGANT, fluid, fluent, natural, neat; agile, supple, nimble, light-footed.

**gracious** adj. kind and pleasant, esp. towards inferiors.
▷ SYNS COURTEOUS, cordial, kindly, benevolent, friendly, amiable, considerate, pleasant, polite, civil, well mannered, chivalrous, charitable, obliging, accommodating, beneficent.

**gradation** n. a series of changes; a stage in such a series.

**grade** n. 1 a level of rank or quality. 2 a mark indicating the quality of a student's work. 3 US a class in school. • v. arrange in or allocate to grades.
▷ SYNS n. LEVEL, rank, standing, position, order, class, category, group. • v. CLASSIFY, class, categorize, sort, group, rank, evaluate, rate, value.

**gradient** n. a slope; the angle of a slope.
▷ SYNS SLOPE, incline, hill, rise, bank, acclivity, declivity.

**gradual** adj. taking place in stages over a long period. ■ **gradually** adv.
▷ SYNS PROGRESSIVE, steady, even, measured, unhurried, step-by-step, successive, continuous, systematic.

**graduate** n. a person who has a university degree. • v. 1 obtain a university degree. 2 change something gradually. ■ **graduation** n.

**graffiti** pl.n. words or drawings scribbled or sprayed on a wall.

**graft** n. 1 a shoot from one plant inserted into another to form a new growth. 2 living tissue transplanted surgically. 3 inf. hard work. • v. 1 insert or transplant as a graft. 2 inf. work hard.

**Grail** n. (in medieval legend) the cup or bowl used by Jesus at the Last Supper.

**grain** n. 1 small seed(s) of a food plant such as wheat or rice; these plants; a small hard particle; a very small amount. 2 the pattern of fibres in wood etc. □ **against the grain** contrary to your natural inclination.

▷ SYNS **1** PARTICLE, granule, bit, piece, scrap, crumb, fragment, speck, trace, mite, iota. **2** TEXTURE, weave, pattern, nap.

**gram** (or **gramme**) n. one-thousandth of a kilogram.

**grammar** n. **1** the whole system and structure of a language. **2** knowledge and use of the rules of grammar. **3** a book on grammar.

**grammatical** adj. conforming to the rules of grammar.
■ **grammatically** adv.

**gran** n. inf. grandmother.

**granary** n. (pl. **-ies**) a storehouse for grain.

**grand** adj. large and imposing; ambitious; excellent. • n. a grand piano. □ **grand piano** a large piano with horizontal strings. **grandstand** the main stand at a sports ground.
▷ SYNS adj. **1** IMPRESSIVE, imposing, magnificent, splendid, superb, palatial, stately, majestic, luxurious, lavish, opulent. **2** GREAT, noble, aristocratic, distinguished, august, illustrious, eminent, esteemed, venerable, pre-eminent, prominent, notable, renowned.

**grandad** n. inf. grandfather.

**grandchild** n. a child of your son or daughter.

**granddaughter** n. a female grandchild.

**grandeur** n. splendour.

**grandfather** n. a male grandparent.

**grandiloquent** adj. using pompous language.

**grandiose** adj. large and ambitious and intended to impress.

**grandma** n. inf. grandmother.

**grandmother** n. a female grandparent.

**grandpa** n. inf. grandfather.

**grandparent** n. a parent of your father or mother.

**grandson** n. a male grandchild.

**granite** n. a hard grey stone.

**granny** (or **grannie**) n. (pl. **-ies**) inf. grandmother.

**grant** v. **1** give or allow as a privilege. **2** admit to be true. • n. a sum of money given from public funds for a particular purpose. □ **take for granted 1** fail to appreciate or be grateful for. **2** assume to be true.
▷ SYNS v. **1** ALLOW, consent, permit; give, award, accord, bestow, confer, endow. **2** ACKNOWLEDGE, concede, accept, admit. • n. AWARD, endowment, allowance, subsidy, bursary; scholarship.

**granule** n. a small grain.
■ **granular** adj.

**grape** n. a green or purple berry growing in clusters, used for making wine. □ **the grapevine** the spreading of information through talk or rumour.

**grapefruit** n. a large yellow citrus fruit.

**graph** n. a diagram showing the relationship between quantities.

**graphic** adj. **1** of drawing, painting, or engraving. **2** giving a vivid description. • n. diagrams used in calculation and design; drawings.
■ **graphically** adv.
▷ SYNS adj. VIVID, explicit, striking, expressive, descriptive, colourful, lively, detailed.

**graphite** n. a form of carbon.

**graphology** n. the study of handwriting.

**grapple** v. 1 wrestle. 2 struggle to deal with.
▷ SYNS 1 FIGHT, wrestle, struggle, tussle, battle, brawl. 2 TACKLE, face, cope with, deal with, handle, confront, get to grips with.

**grasp** v. 1 seize and hold. 2 understand. 3 (**grasping**) greedy. • n. 1 a firm hold or grip. 2 an understanding.
▷ SYNS v. 1 GRIP, clutch, hold, clasp, grab, snatch, take hold of, seize. 2 UNDERSTAND, comprehend, follow, take in, perceive; inf. get.

**grass** n. 1 a plant with green blades; a species of this (e.g. a cereal plant); ground covered with grass. 2 inf. marijuana. 3 inf. an informer. □ **grasshopper** a jumping insect that makes a chirping sound. **grass roots** the ordinary people in an organization etc., rather than the leaders. ■ **grassy** adj.

**grate** n. a metal framework keeping fuel in a fireplace. • v. 1 shred finely by rubbing against a jagged surface. 2 make a harsh noise; have an irritating effect.
▷ SYNS v. 1 SHRED, mince, grind, granulate. 2 RASP, scrape, jar, scratch. 3 IRRITATE, annoy, rile, exasperate, chafe, set someone's teeth on edge.

**grateful** adj. thankful and appreciative. ■ **gratefully** adv.
▷ SYNS THANKFUL, appreciative, obliged, indebted, beholden.

**grater** n. a device for grating food.

**gratify** v. (**gratified, gratifying**) give pleasure to; satisfy wishes. ■ **gratification** n.

▷ SYNS PLEASE, delight, gladden, satisfy.

**grating** n. a screen of spaced bars placed across an opening.

**gratis** adj. & adv. free of charge.

**gratitude** n. the feeling of being grateful.
▷ SYNS GRATEFULNESS, thankfulness, thanks, appreciation, indebtedness.

**gratuitous** adj. uncalled for.
▷ SYNS UNPROVOKED, unjustified, uncalled for, unwarranted, unjustifiable, needless, unnecessary, superfluous.

**gratuity** n. (pl. **-ies**) a tip given to a waiter etc.

**grave**[1] n. a hole dug to bury a corpse. □ **gravestone** a stone slab marking a grave.

**grave**[2] adj. 1 causing anxiety or concern. 2 solemn.
▷ SYNS 1 SOLEMN, serious, sober, sombre, unsmiling, grim, severe, stern. 2 SERIOUS, important, significant, weighty, momentous, urgent, pressing, critical.

**gravel** n. small stones, used for paths etc.

**gravelly** adj. 1 like or consisting of gravel. 2 rough-sounding.

**graveyard** n. a burial ground.
▷ SYNS CEMETERY, burial ground, churchyard, necropolis.

**gravitate** v. be drawn towards.

**gravitation** n. movement towards a centre of gravity. ■ **gravitational** adj.

**gravity** n. 1 the force that attracts bodies towards the centre of the earth. 2 seriousness; solemnity.
▷ SYNS SOLEMNITY, seriousness, sombreness; importance,

significance, momentousness, weightiness.

**gravy** n. (pl. **-ies**) sauce made from the juices from cooked meat.

**gray** US sp. of **GREY**.

**graze** v. **1** eat grass in a field. **2** injure by scraping the skin. **3** touch lightly in passing. • n. a grazed place on the skin.
▷ SYNS v. SCRAPE, abrade, skin, scratch, chafe, bark.

**grease** n. a thick, oily substance used as a lubricant. • v. put grease on. □ **greasepaint** make-up used by actors.

**greasy** adj. covered with or like grease.
▷ SYNS OILY, fatty, buttery, oleaginous; slippery, slimy; inf. slippy.

**great** adj. **1** much above average in size, intensity, ability, quality, or importance. **2** inf. excellent. **3** (**great-**) (of a family relationship) one generation removed in ancestry or descent.
▷ SYNS **1** LARGE, big, extensive, expansive, broad, wide, sizeable, vast, immense, huge, enormous, colossal, gigantic; magnificent, imposing, impressive, grand, splendid, majestic, sumptuous. **2** PROMINENT, eminent, distinguished, illustrious, celebrated, renowned, notable, famous, famed, leading. **3** EXPERT, skilled, adept, accomplished, talented, masterly, brilliant, outstanding, first class, marvellous, superb. **4** *a great time:* see **EXCELLENT**.

**greatly** adv. very much.

**greed** n. excessive desire for food, wealth, power, etc.
▷ SYNS **1** GLUTTONY, voracity. **2** AVARICE, acquisitiveness, rapacity, covetousness, cupidity.

**3** DESIRE, hunger, craving, longing, eagerness.

**greedy** adj. having or showing greed.
▷ SYNS **1** GLUTTONOUS, voracious, ravenous; inf. piggish. **2** AVARICIOUS, acquisitive, grasping, covetous, materialistic.

**green** adj. **1** coloured like grass. **2** covered with grass. **3** (**Green**) concerned with protecting the environment. **4** inexperienced or naive. • n. **1** green colour. **2** a piece of grassy public land. **3** (**greens**) green vegetables. □ **green belt** an area of open land round a town. **greenfly** a green aphid. **greengrocer** a person selling fruit and vegetables.
▷ SYNS adj. **1** GRASSY, verdant, leafy. **2** ENVIRONMENTAL, ecological, conservation, eco-. **3** INEXPERIENCED, new, raw, naive, innocent, callow.

**greenery** n. green foliage or plants.

**greenhouse** n. a glass building for rearing plants. □ **greenhouse effect** the trapping of the sun's warmth in the earth's lower atmosphere. **greenhouse gas** a gas contributing to the greenhouse effect.
▷ SYNS HOTHOUSE, glasshouse, conservatory.

**greet** v. **1** welcome. **2** react to in a particular way.
▷ SYNS SAY HELLO TO, address, hail, acknowledge, welcome, meet, receive.

**greeting** n. a word or sign of welcome; a formal expression of good wishes.
▷ SYNS **1** HELLO, salute, salutation, acknowledgement, welcome. **2** (**greetings**) GOOD WISHES, best

wishes, regards, congratulations, compliments, respects.

**gregarious** adj. sociable.

**gremlin** n. a mischievous sprite blamed for mechanical faults.

**grenade** n. a small bomb thrown by hand or fired from a rifle.

**grew** past of **GROW**.

**grey** (US **gray**) adj. of the colour between black and white; dull or depressing. • n. a grey colour. □ **greyhound** a swift, slender breed of dog used in racing.
▷ SYNS adj. CLOUDY, overcast, dull, sunless, gloomy, dreary, dismal, cheerless, depressing.

**grid** n. a grating; a system of numbered squares for map references; a network of lines, power cables, etc. □ **gridiron** a metal grid for grilling food; a field for American football. **gridlock** a traffic jam affecting linked streets.

**grief** n. deep sorrow.
▷ SYNS SORROW, mourning, lamentation, misery, sadness, anguish, distress, heartache, heartbreak, desolation.

**grievance** n. a cause for complaint.
▷ SYNS 1 COMPLAINT, grumble, axe to grind, bone to pick; inf. grouse, gripe. 2 INJUSTICE, wrong, unfairness, injury, affront, insult.

**grieve** v. cause grief to; feel grief.
▷ SYNS 1 MOURN, lament, sorrow, weep and wail, cry, sob. 2 *it grieved her:* HURT, wound, pain, sadden, upset, distress.

**grievous** adj. very serious or distressing.

**griffin** (or **gryphon**) n. a mythological creature with an eagle's head and wings and a lion's body.

**griffon** n. 1 a small terrier-like dog. 2 a vulture.

**grill** n. 1 a device on a cooker that directs heat downwards. 2 food cooked using a grill. • v. 1 cook with a grill. 2 inf. interrogate.

**grille** (or **grill**) n. a framework of metal bars or wires.

**grim** adj. (**grimmer, grimmest**) stern or severe; forbidding; disagreeable.
▷ SYNS 1 STERN, forbidding, unsmiling, dour, formidable, harsh, stony; cross, surly, sour, ill-tempered; threatening, menacing. 2 *grim determination:* RESOLUTE, determined, firm, adamant, unyielding, unshakeable, obdurate, stubborn, unrelenting, relentless. 3 *a grim sight:* DREADFUL, horrible, horrendous, terrible, horrific, dire, ghastly, awful, appalling, frightful, shocking, unspeakable, grisly, hideous, gruesome.

**grimace** n. a contortion of the face in pain or amusement. • v. make a grimace.

**grime** n. ingrained dirt. ■ **grimy** adj.

**grin** v. (**grinned, grinning**) smile broadly. • n. a broad smile.

**grind** v. 1 crush into small particles or powder. 2 sharpen or smooth by friction. 3 rub together gratingly. 4 (**grind down**) treat harshly. • n. hard dull work. □ **grindstone** a revolving disc for sharpening or polishing.

▷ SYNS v. **1** CRUSH, pound, pulverize, mill, crumble. **2** SHARPEN, whet, hone, file; smooth, polish, sand.

**grip** v. **1** hold firmly. **2** hold the attention of. • n. **1** a firm hold. **2** understanding. **3** a part by which something is held.
▷ SYNS v. **1** GRASP, clutch, clasp, take hold of, clench, grab, seize. **2** ENGROSS, enthral, absorb, rivet, spellbind, fascinate, mesmerize. • n. **1** GRASP, hold. **2** UNDERSTANDING, comprehension, grasp, perception, awareness.

**gripe** v. inf. grumble. • n. **1** inf. a complaint. **2** colic pain.

**grisly** adj. (-ier, -iest) causing fear, horror, or disgust.

**grist** n. grain to be ground.

**gristle** n. tough inedible tissue in meat.

**grit** n. **1** particles of stone or sand. **2** inf. courage and endurance. • v. (**gritted**, **gritting**) **1** clench the teeth in determination. **2** spread grit on a road etc. ■ **gritty** adj.

**grizzle** v. inf. cry fretfully.

**grizzled** adj. grey-haired.

**groan** n. & v. (make) a long deep sound of pain or despair.
▷ SYNS MOAN, cry, whimper.

**grocer** n. a shopkeeper selling food and household goods.

**grocery** n. (pl. -ies) **1** a grocer's shop. **2** (**groceries**) a grocer's goods.

**grog** n. a drink of spirits mixed with water.

**groggy** adj. (-ier, -iest) inf. weak and unsteady.

**groin** n. **1** the place where the thighs join the abdomen. **2** US sp. of **GROYNE**.

**grommet** n. **1** a protective metal ring or eyelet. **2** a tube placed through the eardrum to drain the ear.

**groom** n. **1** a person employed to look after horses. **2** a bridegroom. • v. **1** clean and brush an animal; make neat and tidy. **2** prepare a person for a career or position.

**groove** n. a long narrow channel; a fixed routine. • v. cut grooves in.

**grope** v. feel about with your hands.
▷ SYNS FEEL, fumble, scrabble, search, hunt, rummage.

**gross** adj. **1** unattractively large. **2** vulgar. **3** inf. repulsive. **4** (of income etc.) without deductions. • n. (pl. **gross**) twelve dozen. • v. produce or earn as total profit.
▷ SYNS adj. **1** OBESE, corpulent, overweight, fat, bloated, fleshy, flabby. **2** COARSE, crude, vulgar, obscene, rude, lewd, dirty, filthy, smutty, blue, risqué, indecent, indelicate, offensive.

**grotesque** adj. ugly or distorted.
▷ SYNS MISSHAPEN, deformed, malformed, distorted, twisted, gnarled; ugly, unsightly, monstrous, hideous, freakish, unnatural, abnormal, strange, odd, peculiar.

**grotto** n. (pl. -oes or -os) a small cave.

**grouch** n. inf. a grumbler; a complaint. ■ **grouchy** adj.

**ground**¹ past & p.p. of GRIND.

**ground**² n. **1** the solid surface of the earth. **2** land of a specified type or used for a specified purpose. • v. **1** prevent an aircraft or a pilot from flying.

2 give a basis to. 3 instruct thoroughly in a subject.
□ **groundnut** a peanut. **ground rent** rent paid by the owner of a building to the owner of the land on which it is built. **groundsheet** a waterproof sheet used as the floor of a tent. **groundsman** a person employed to look after a sports ground. **groundswell** a build-up of public opinion.
▷ SYNS n. 1 EARTH, soil, turf; land, terrain; floor, terra firma. 2 PITCH, stadium, field, arena.

**grounding** n. basic training.

**groundless** adj. without basis or good reason.
▷ SYNS UNFOUNDED, unsubstantiated, unwarranted, unjustified, unjustifiable; irrational, illogical, unreasonable.

**grounds** pl.n. 1 land belonging to a large house. 2 reasons for doing or believing something. 3 dregs.
▷ SYNS 1 ESTATE, gardens, park, land, property, surroundings. 2 REASON, cause, basis, foundation, justification, rationale, occasion, pretext. 3 DREGS, deposit, lees, sediment.

**groundwork** n. preliminary work.
▷ SYNS PRELIMINARIES, preparations, spadework, planning.

**group** n. 1 a number of people or things placed or classed together. 2 a band of pop musicians. • v. form or put into a group; classify.
▷ SYNS n. 1 SET, lot, category, classification, class, batch, family, species, genus, bracket. 2 COMPANY, band, party, body, gathering, congregation, assembly, collection, bunch,
cluster, crowd, flock, pack, troop, gang, batch. 3 FACTION, set, coterie, clique. 4 SOCIETY, association, league, guild, circle, club. • v. 1 CLASSIFY, class, categorize, sort, grade, rank, bracket. 2 ASSEMBLE, collect, gather together, arrange, organize, marshal, range, line up, dispose.

**grouse** n. 1 a game bird. 2 inf. a complaint. • v. inf. grumble.

**grout** n. thin fluid mortar. • v. fill with grout.

**grove** n. a group of trees.

**grovel** v. (**grovelled, grovelling**; US **groveled**) crawl face downwards; behave humbly.
▷ SYNS ABASE YOURSELF, toady, fawn, curry favour, kowtow, lick someone's boots; inf. crawl.

**grow** v. 1 (of a living thing) develop and get bigger. 2 become larger or greater over a period of time. 3 become gradually or increasingly: *we grew braver*. 4 (**grow up**) become an adult. □ **grown-up** (an) adult.
▷ SYNS 1 LENGTHEN, extend, expand, stretch, spread, thicken, widen, fill out, swell, increase, multiply, proliferate. 2 DEVELOP, sprout, shoot up, germinate, bud, burgeon. 3 FLOURISH, thrive, prosper, succeed, make progress, develop. 4 *grow prettier*: BECOME, get, turn, wax. 5 *grow corn*: PRODUCE, cultivate, farm, propagate, raise.

**growl** v. make a low threatening sound as a dog does. • n. this sound.

**growth** n. the process of growing; something that grows or has grown; a tumour.

▷ SYNS **1** INCREASE, expansion, enlargement, development, proliferation, multiplication, extension. **2** TUMOUR, cancer, malignancy; lump, swelling, excrescence.

**groyne** (US **groin**) n. a solid structure built out into the sea to prevent erosion.

**grub** n. **1** the worm-like larva of certain insects. **2** inf. food. • v. (**grubbed**, **grubbing**) **1** dig the surface of soil. **2** rummage.

**grubby** adj. (**-ier**, **-iest**) dirty.
▷ SYNS DIRTY, filthy, grimy, soiled, mucky, stained.

**grudge** n. a feeling of resentment or ill will. • v. begrudge or resent.
▷ SYNS n. RESENTMENT, bitterness, ill will, pique, grievance, hard feelings, rancour, animosity, antipathy, disgruntlement. • v. BEGRUDGE, resent, envy, be jealous of.

**gruel** n. thin oatmeal porridge.

**gruelling** (US **grueling**) adj. very tiring.
▷ SYNS EXHAUSTING, tiring, wearying, taxing, demanding, arduous, laborious, backbreaking, strenuous, punishing, hard, difficult, harsh, severe.

**gruesome** adj. horrifying or disgusting.
▷ SYNS GRISLY, ghastly, frightful, horrible, horrifying, horrific, horrendous, awful, dreadful, grim, terrible, hideous, disgusting, repulsive, revolting, repugnant, repellent, macabre, sickening, appalling, shocking, loathsome, abhorrent, odious.

**gruff** adj. (of the voice) low and hoarse; (of a person) appearing bad-tempered.

**grumble** v. **1** complain in a bad-tempered way. **2** rumble. • n. **1** a complaint. **2** a rumbling sound.
▷ SYNS v. COMPLAIN, moan, protest, carp; inf. grouse, gripe, bellyache, whinge.

**grumpy** adj. (**-ier**, **-iest**) bad-tempered. ■ **grumpily** adv.
▷ SYNS BAD-TEMPERED, surly, churlish, crotchety, tetchy, testy, crabby, cantankerous, curmudgeonly; inf. grouchy.

**grunge** n. a style of rock music with a raucous guitar sound.

**grunt** n. a gruff snorting sound made or like that made by a pig. • v. make this sound.

**gryphon** = GRIFFIN.

**G-string** n. skimpy knickers consisting of a narrow strip of cloth attached to a waistband.

**guarantee** n. a formal promise to do something or that a thing is of a specified quality; something offered as security. • v. give or be a guarantee.
▷ SYNS n. **1** WARRANTY, warrant, covenant, bond, contract, guaranty. **2** PLEDGE, promise, assurance, word (of honour), oath, bond. • v. **1** UNDERWRITE, sponsor, support, vouch for. **2** PROMISE, pledge, give your word, swear.

**guarantor** n. the giver of a guarantee.

**guard** v. **1** watch over to protect or control. **2** take precautions. • n. **1** a person guarding or keeping watch. **2** a protective device. **3** a state of vigilance. **4** an official in charge of a train.
▷ SYNS v. PROTECT, defend, shield, secure, watch; patrol, police, keep safe. • n. SENTRY, sentinel, nightwatchman, lookout,

watch, guardian; warder, jailer, keeper.

**guarded** adj. cautious.
▷ SYNS CAREFUL, cautious, circumspect, wary, chary; inf. cagey.

**guardian** n. a person who guards or protects; a person legally responsible for someone unable to manage their own affairs.

**guava** n. a tropical fruit.

**guerrilla** (or **guerilla**) n. a member of a small independent group fighting against the government etc.

**guess** v. form an opinion without definite knowledge; think likely. • n. an opinion formed by guessing. □ guesswork guessing.
▷ SYNS v. 1 CONJECTURE, surmise, estimate, hypothesize, postulate, predict, speculate. 2 SUPPOSE, believe, think, imagine, suspect, dare say, reckon. • n. CONJECTURE, surmise, hypothesis, theory, supposition, speculation, estimate, prediction; inf. guesstimate.

**guest** n. 1 a person invited to someone's home or to a social occasion. 2 a person staying at a hotel. 3 an invited performer. □ guest house a small hotel.
▷ SYNS 1 VISITOR, caller, company. 2 RESIDENT, boarder, lodger, patron.

**guffaw** n. a loud, deep laugh. • v. give a loud, deep laugh.

**guidance** n. guiding; advice.
▷ SYNS 1 ADVICE, counsel, recommendations, suggestions, tips, hints, pointers. 2 DIRECTION, control, leadership, management, supervision, charge.

**guide** n. 1 a person who advises or shows the way to others. 2 an aid to deciding something. 3 a book of information, maps, etc. 4 a structure or mark to direct the movement or position of something. • v. act as a guide to. □ guidebook a book of information about a place. guideline a general rule or principle.
▷ SYNS n. 1 ESCORT, chaperone, courier, usher, attendant; adviser, counsellor, mentor, guru. 2 GUIDEBOOK, handbook, vade mecum, manual, directory. • v. 1 LEAD, conduct, show, usher, shepherd, direct, pilot, steer, escort, accompany, attend. 2 CONTROL, direct, manage, command, be in charge of, govern, preside over, superintend, supervise, oversee. 3 ADVISE, counsel.

**guild** n. 1 a medieval association of craftsmen or merchants. 2 an association of people for a common purpose.

**guile** n. clever but deceitful behaviour.

**guillotine** n. a machine for beheading criminals; a machine for cutting paper or metal. • v. behead or cut with a guillotine.

**guilt** n. 1 the fact of having committed an offence. 2 a feeling of having done something wrong.

**guilty** adj. (-ier, -iest) having committed an offence; feeling or showing guilt. ■ guiltily adv.
▷ SYNS 1 TO BLAME, blameworthy, culpable, at fault, responsible, errant, delinquent, offending. 2 REMORSEFUL, ashamed, conscience-stricken, shamefaced, regretful, contrite, repentant, penitent, rueful, sheepish, hangdog.

**guinea** n. a former British coin worth 21 shillings (£1.05).

**guinea pig** n. **1** a small domesticated rodent. **2** a person or thing used as a subject for an experiment.

**guise** n. a false outward appearance.
▷ SYNS LIKENESS, semblance, form; pretence, disguise, facade, front, screen.

**guitar** n. a stringed musical instrument. ■ **guitarist** n.

**gulf** n. **1** a large area of sea partly surrounded by land. **2** a deep ravine; a wide difference in opinion.
▷ SYNS **1** BAY, cove, inlet, bight. **2** DIVIDE, division, separation, gap, breach, rift, chasm, abyss.

**gull** n. a seabird with long wings.

**gullet** n. the passage by which food goes from mouth to stomach.

**gullible** adj. easily deceived. ■ **gullibility** n.
▷ SYNS CREDULOUS, over-trustful, unsuspecting, ingenuous, naive, innocent, inexperienced, green; inf. born yesterday.

**gully** n. (pl. **-ies**) a narrow channel cut by water or carrying rainwater from a building.

**gulp** v. swallow food etc. hastily or greedily. • n. the act of gulping; a large mouthful of liquid gulped.
▷ SYNS v. **1** SWALLOW, quaff, swill, swig. **2** BOLT, wolf, gobble, guzzle, devour, tuck into. • n. SWALLOW, mouthful, draught, swig.

**gum** n. **1** the firm flesh in which teeth are rooted. **2** a sticky substance exuded by certain trees; glue; chewing gum.
• v. (**gummed**, **gumming**) smear or stick together with gum.
□ **gumboot** dated a wellington boot. ■ **gummy** adj.

**gumption** n. inf. resourcefulness or spirit.

**gun** n. **1** a weapon that fires shells or bullets from a metal tube. **2** a device using pressure to discharge a substance.
• v. (**gunned**, **gunning**) shoot someone with a gun. □ **gunfire** repeated firing of a gun or guns. **gunman** a man who uses a gun to commit a crime. **gunpowder** an explosive mixture of saltpetre, sulphur, and charcoal. **gunship** a heavily armed helicopter. **gunsmith** a maker and seller of small firearms.

**gunge** n. inf. an unpleasantly sticky and messy substance.

**gung-ho** adj. too eager to fight.

**gunnel** = GUNWALE.

**gunner** n. an artillery soldier; a member of an aircraft crew operating a gun.

**gunrunner** n. a smuggler of firearms. ■ **gunrunning** n.

**gunwale** (or **gunnel**) n. the upper edge of a boat's side.

**gurgle** n. & v. (make) a low bubbling sound.

**guru** n. (pl. **-us**) a Hindu spiritual teacher; a revered teacher.

**gush** v. **1** flow in a strong, fast stream. **2** express excessive or insincere enthusiasm. • n. a strong, fast flow.
▷ SYNS v. **1** STREAM, rush, spout, spurt, surge, jet, well, pour, burst, cascade, flood, flow, run, issue. **2** ENTHUSE, wax lyrical, rave. • n. STREAM, outpouring, spurt, jet, spout, rush, burst, surge, cascade, flood, torrent, spate.

**gusset** n. a piece of cloth inserted to strengthen or enlarge a garment.

**gust** n. a sudden rush of wind, rain, or smoke. • v. blow in gusts. ■ **gusty** adj.

**gusto** n. enthusiasm and energy.

**gut** n. **1** the stomach or intestine. **2** (**guts**) inf. courage and determination. • v. **1** remove the guts from fish. **2** remove or destroy the internal parts of.
▷ SYNS n. STOMACH, belly, abdomen; intestines, entrails, viscera; inf. insides, innards.

**gutsy** adj. inf. brave and determined.

**gutter** n. **1** a trough round a roof, or a channel beside a road, for carrying away rainwater. **2** (**the gutter**) a very poor environment. • v. (of a flame) flicker.
▷ SYNS n. DRAIN, trough, trench, ditch, sluice, sewer, channel, conduit, pipe.

**guttural** adj. throaty or harsh-sounding.

**guy** n. **1** inf. a man. **2** an effigy of Guy Fawkes burnt on 5 Nov. **3** a rope fixed to the ground to secure a tent.

**guzzle** v. eat or drink greedily.

**gym** n. **1** a gymnasium. **2** gymnastics.

**gymkhana** n. a horse-riding competition.

**gymnasium** n. (pl. **-nasia** or **-nasiums**) a room equipped for physical training and gymnastics.

**gymnast** n. an expert in gymnastics.

**gymnastics** pl.n. exercises involving physical agility and co-ordination. ■ **gymnastic** adj.

**gynaecology** (US **gynecology**) n. the study of the physiological functions and diseases of women. ■ **gynaecological** adj. **gynaecologist** n.

**gypsum** n. a chalk-like mineral used in building etc.

**Gypsy** (or **Gipsy**) n. (pl. **-ies**) a member of a travelling people.

**gyrate** v. move in circles or spirals. ■ **gyration** n.
▷ SYNS ROTATE, revolve, wheel round, turn round, circle, whirl, pirouette, twirl, swirl, spin, swivel.

**gyroscope** n. a device used to keep navigation instruments steady, consisting of a disc rotating on an axis.

# Hh

**ha** abbr. hectares.

**haberdashery** n. sewing materials. ■ **haberdasher** n.

**habit** n. **1** a regular way of behaving. **2** inf. an addiction. **3** a monk's or nun's long dress.

▷ SYNS **1** CUSTOM, practice, wont, way, routine, matter of course, pattern, convention, norm, usage. **2** ADDICTION, dependence, weakness, obsession, fixation.

3 COSTUME, dress, garb, attire, clothes, clothing, garments.

**habitable** adj. suitable for living in.

**habitat** n. an animal's or plant's natural environment.

**habitation** n. a place to live in.

**habitual** adj. done regularly or constantly; usual. ■ **habitually** adv.
▷ SYNS **1** USUAL, customary, accustomed, regular, normal, set, fixed, established, routine, wonted, common, ordinary, familiar, traditional.
**2** CONFIRMED, addicted, chronic, inveterate, hardened, ingrained.

**habituate** v. accustom.
▷ SYNS ACCUSTOM, make used to, acclimatize, condition, break in, inure, harden.

**hack** v. **1** cut with rough or heavy blows. **2** gain unauthorized access to computer files. • n. **1** a writer producing dull, un-original work. **2** a horse for ordinary riding. □ **hacksaw** a saw with a narrow blade set in a frame. ■ **hacker** n.

**hackles** pl.n. the hairs on the back of an animal's neck, raised in anger.

**hackneyed** adj. (of a phrase etc.) overused and lacking impact.
▷ SYNS BANAL, trite, overused, tired, worn-out, stale, clichéd, platitudinous, unoriginal, unimaginative, stock; inf. corny.

**had** past and p.p. of HAVE.

**haddock** n. (pl. **haddock**) an edible sea fish.

**haemoglobin** (US **hemo-globin**) n. the red oxygen-carrying substance in blood.

**haemophilia** (US **hemophilia**) n. a condition in which blood fails to clot, causing excessive bleeding. ■ **haemophiliac** n.

**haemorrhage** (US **hem-orrhage**) n. heavy bleeding.

**haemorrhoid** (US **hemorrhoid**) n. a swollen vein at or near the anus.

**hag** n. an ugly old woman.

**haggard** adj. looking pale and exhausted.
▷ SYNS GAUNT, drawn, pinched, hollow-cheeked, exhausted, drained, careworn, wan, pale.

**haggis** n. a Scottish dish made from sheep's offal, oatmeal, etc.

**haggle** v. argue about the price or terms of a deal.

**hail** n. a shower of frozen rain; a shower of blows, questions, etc. • v. **1** pour down as or like hail. **2** call out to; welcome or acclaim. □ **hailstone** a pellet of hail.
▷ SYNS v. **1** GREET, salute, call out to, address. **2** see ACCLAIM.

**hair** n. **1** one of the fine thread-like strands growing from the skin. **2** strands of hair collect-ively. □ **haircut** an act of cutting a person's hair; a style of this. **hairdo** inf. a hairstyle. **hair-dresser** a person who cuts and styles hair. **hairgrip** a flat hairpin. **hairpin** a U-shaped pin for fastening the hair. **hairstyle** a way in which the hair is cut or arranged.
▷ SYNS **1** LOCKS, tresses. **2** FUR, wool, coat, fleece, pelt, mane.

**hair-raising** adj. very frightening.
▷ SYNS TERRIFYING, blood-curdling, spine-chilling, frightening; inf. scary.

**hairy** adj. **1** covered with hair. **2** inf. dangerous or frightening.
▷ SYNS HIRSUTE, shaggy, woolly, bushy, furry, fleecy; bristly, bearded, unshaven.

**halcyon** adj. (of a period) happy and peaceful.

**hale** adj. strong and healthy.

**half** n. (pl. **halves**) **1** each of two equal parts into which something is divided. **2** half a pint. • adj. & pron. an amount equal to a half. • adv. **1** to the extent of half. **2** partly. □ half a dozen six. half-and-half in equal parts. half board bed, breakfast, and evening meal at a hotel etc. half-brother (or half-sister) a brother (or sister) with whom you have only one parent in common. half-term a short holiday halfway through a school term. half-time the interval between two halves of a game. halfway at or to a point equal in distance between two others. half-witted inf. stupid.

**half-hearted** adj. not very enthusiastic.
▷ SYNS UNENTHUSIASTIC, cool, lukewarm, apathetic, indifferent.

**halibut** n. (pl. **halibut**) a large edible flatfish.

**halitosis** n. breath that smells unpleasant.

**hall** n. **1** the room or space inside the front entrance of a house. **2** a large room or building for meetings, concerts, etc.

**hallelujah** = ALLELUIA.

**hallmark** n. an official mark on precious metals to indicate their standard; a distinguishing characteristic.
▷ SYNS MARK, trademark, stamp, sign, badge, symbol, characteristic, indicator, indication.

**hallo** = HELLO.

**hallucinate** v. experience hallucinations.

**hallucination** n. the experience of seeing something which is not actually present.
▷ SYNS ILLUSION, delusion, figment of the imagination, vision, fantasy, mirage, chimera.

**halo** n. (pl. **-oes**) a circle of light, esp. one round the head of a sacred figure.

**halt** v. come or bring to a stop. • n. a temporary stop.
▷ SYNS v. STOP, terminate, block, end, finish, suspend, break off, impede, check, curb, stem. • n. STOP, stoppage, cessation, end, standstill, pause, interval, interlude, intermission, break, hiatus.

**halter** n. a strap round the head of a horse for leading or holding it.

**halting** adj. slow and hesitant.

**halve** v. **1** divide into two parts of equal size. **2** reduce by half.

**ham** n. **1** smoked or salted meat from a pig's thigh. **2** a bad actor. **3** inf. an amateur radio operator. □ ham-fisted clumsy.

**hamburger** n. a flat round cake of minced beef.

**hamlet** n. a small village.

**hammer** n. **1** a tool with a head for hitting nails etc. **2** a metal ball attached to a wire, thrown in an athletic contest. • v. hit or beat with a hammer; hit forcefully; impress an idea etc. on a person's mind.
▷ SYNS v. BEAT, batter, pound, hit, strike, bang.

**hammock** n. a hanging bed of canvas or netting.

**hamper** n. a basket used for food etc. on a picnic. • v. slow down or prevent the movement or progress of.
▷ SYNS v. HINDER, obstruct, impede, inhibit, delay, slow down, hold up, interfere with, handicap.

**hamster** n. a small domesticated rodent.

**hamstring** n. a tendon at the back of the knee.
• v. (**hamstrung, hamstringing**) **1** cripple by cutting the hamstrings. **2** severely restrict.

**hand** n. **1** the part of the arm below the wrist. **2** a pointer on a clock etc. **3** power or control. **4** help. **5** a manual worker. **6** a round of applause. **7** the cards dealt to a player in a game. **8** a unit of measurement of a horse's height. • v. give or pass to. ◻ **handbag** a small bag for personal items. **handbook** a book giving basic information. **handcuff** put handcuffs on. **handcuffs** a pair of lockable linked metal rings for securing a prisoner's wrists. **handout 1** a gift of money etc. to a needy person. **2** a piece of printed information given free of charge. **handshake** an act of shaking a person's hand. **handwriting 1** writing by hand. **2** a style of this.
▷ SYNS n. **1** FIST, palm; inf. mitt. **2** POINTER, indicator, needle. **3** WORKER, employee, operative, labourer.

**handful** n. **1** a few. **2** inf. a person hard to deal with or control.

**handicap** n. something that makes progress difficult; a disadvantage imposed on a superior competitor to equalize chances; a physical or mental disability. • v. (**handicapped, handicapping**) be a handicap to; place at a disadvantage.
▷ SYNS n. IMPEDIMENT, disadvantage, hindrance, obstruction, obstacle, encumbrance, check, block, barrier, stumbling block, constraint, restriction, limitation, drawback, shortcoming.

**handicraft** n. a decorative object made by hand.

**handiwork** n. (**your handiwork**) something that you have made or done.

**handkerchief** n. (pl. **-chiefs** or **-chieves**) a small square of cloth for wiping the nose etc.

**handle** n. a part by which a thing is held, carried, or controlled. • v. touch or move with the hands; deal with; manage. ■ **handler** n.
▷ SYNS n. SHAFT, grip, handgrip, hilt, haft, knob, stock.
• v. **1** TOUCH, feel, hold, finger, pat, caress, stroke, fondle. **2** COPE WITH, deal with, manage, tackle. **3** BE IN CHARGE OF, control, administer, direct, conduct, supervise, take care of. **4** DRIVE, steer, operate, manoeuvre. **5** DEAL IN, trade in, traffic in, market, sell, stock, carry.

**handlebar** n. a steering bar of a bicycle etc.

**handsome** adj. **1** good-looking. **2** striking or imposing. **3** (of an amount) large.
▷ SYNS **1** GOOD-LOOKING, attractive, striking; inf. dishy. **2** SUBSTANTIAL, considerable, sizeable, princely, large, big.

**handy** adj. **1** ready to hand; convenient; easy to use. **2** skilled with your hands. ◻ **handyman** a

person who does general building repairs. ■ **handily** adv.
▷ SYNS **1** TO HAND, at hand, within reach, available, accessible, near, nearby, close. **2** USEFUL, convenient, practical, serviceable, functional, user-friendly. **3** DEFT, dexterous, nimble-fingered, adroit, adept, skilful, skilled.

**hang** v. **1** suspend or be suspended from above. **2** kill by suspending from a rope tied round the neck. □ **hang-glider** an unpowered flying device consisting of a frame from which a person hangs in a harness. **hangman** a person who executes people by hanging.
▷ SYNS BE SUSPENDED, dangle, swing, sway; hover, float.

**hangar** n. a building for aircraft.

**hangdog** adj. shamefaced.

**hanger** n. a shaped piece of wood, metal, etc. to hang a garment on.

**hanging** n. a decorative piece of fabric hung on a wall.

**hangover** n. unpleasant after-effects from drinking too much alcohol.

**hang-up** n. an emotional problem.
▷ SYNS NEUROSIS, phobia, pre-occupation, fixation obsession, inhibition; inf. complex, thing, issue.

**hanker** v. feel a desire for or to do.
▷ SYNS YEARN, long, wish, hunger, thirst, ache.

**hanky** n. (pl. **-ies**) inf. a handkerchief.

**haphazard** adj. done or chosen at random.
▷ SYNS UNPLANNED, random, indiscriminate, chaotic,

unsystematic, disorganized, slapdash, careless, casual, hit-or-miss, arbitrary.

**hapless** adj. unlucky.

**happen** v. **1** take place; occur. **2** (**happen on**) find by chance. **3** (**happen to**) be the fate or experience of.
▷ SYNS OCCUR, take place, come about, transpire, materialize, arise, present itself, crop up.

**happening** n. an event or occurrence.
▷ SYNS OCCURRENCE, event, incident, episode, affair.

**happy** adj. **1** pleased or contented. **2** fortunate.
□ **happy-go-lucky** cheerfully casual. ■ **happily** adv. **happiness** n.
▷ SYNS **1** CHEERFUL, cheery, merry, in good/high spirits, joyful, light-hearted, jovial, gleeful, buoyant, carefree, blithe, smiling, glad, pleased, delighted, elated, ecstatic, blissful, euphoric, overjoyed, exuberant, in seventh heaven. **2** LUCKY, fortunate, advantageous, favourable, beneficial, opportune, timely, convenient, welcome, propitious, auspicious, fortuitous.

**harangue** v. lecture earnestly and at length.

**harass** v. worry or annoy continually; make repeated attacks on. ■ **harassment** n.
▷ SYNS **1** BOTHER, pester, annoy, provoke, badger, hound, torment, plague, persecute, nag, bedevil; inf. hassle. **2** HARRY, attack, assail, beleaguer, set upon.

**harbour** (US **harbor**) n. a place for ships to moor; a refuge.

• v. **1** keep a thought etc. in your mind. **2** shelter.

▷ SYNS n. **1** PORT, anchorage, dock, marina. **2** REFUGE, shelter, haven, sanctuary, retreat, asylum. • v. **1** SHELTER, shield, protect, conceal, hide. **2** NURSE, nurture, cherish, cling to, entertain, bear.

**hard** adj. **1** solid, firm, and rigid. **2** requiring effort. **3** harsh. **4** done with force. **5** not showing weakness. **6** (of information) reliable. **7** (of drink) strongly alcoholic. **8** (of a drug) very addictive. • adv. **1** with effort or force. **2** so as to be firm: *the cement set hard.* □ **hardback** a book bound in stiff covers. **hard-bitten** tough and cynical. **hardboard** board made of compressed wood pulp. **hard-boiled** (of eggs) boiled until the yolk and white are firm. **hard-headed** practical and unsentimental. **hard-hearted** unfeeling. **hard shoulder** an extra strip of road beside a motorway for use in an emergency. **hard up** inf. short of money. **hardware 1** the physical components of a computer. **2** tools and household implements. **hardwood** wood from broadleaved trees.

▷ SYNS adj. **1** FIRM, solid, rigid, stiff, compacted, compressed, strong. **2** ARDUOUS, strenuous, tiring, exhausting, back-breaking, gruelling, laborious, tough, difficult. **3** HARSH, grim, bad, bleak, dire, tough, rugged, austere, unpleasant. **4** FORCEFUL, violent, heavy, strong, powerful, sharp.

**harden** v. make or become hard or harder.

▷ SYNS SOLIDIFY, set, thicken, cake, congeal.

**hardly** adv. only with difficulty; scarcely.

▷ SYNS SCARCELY, barely, (only) just.

**hardship** n. poverty.

▷ SYNS ADVERSITY, deprivation, privation, want, need, destitution, poverty, suffering, affliction, pain, misery, wretchedness, tribulation, trials.

**hardy** adj. (**-ier, -iest**) capable of enduring cold or harsh conditions.

▷ SYNS HEALTHY, fit, strong, robust, sturdy, tough, rugged, vigorous.

**hare** n. a field animal like a large rabbit. • v. run rapidly. □ **hare-brained** wild and foolish.

**harelip** n. a cleft lip.

**harem** n. the women's quarters in a Muslim household; the women living in this.

**hark** v. **1** lit. listen. **2** (**hark back**) recall something from the past.

**harlequin** n. a character in traditional pantomime.

**harm** n. damage or injury. • v. cause harm to.

▷ SYNS n. HURT, injury, pain, suffering, trauma; damage, impairment. • v. HURT, injure, wound, maltreat, ill-treat, ill-use, abuse; damage, impair, spoil, mar.

**harmful** adj. causing harm.

▷ SYNS DAMAGING, injurious, detrimental, hurtful, destructive, dangerous, hazardous; formal deleterious.

**harmless** adj. not able or likely to cause harm.

▷ SYNS SAFE, innocuous, non-toxic.

**harmonica** n. a mouth organ.

**harmonious** adj. **1** tuneful. **2** pleasingly arranged. **3** free from conflict.
▷ SYNS **MELODIOUS**, tuneful, musical, sweet-sounding, mellifluous, dulcet. **2** **PEACEFUL**, friendly, amicable, cordial, amiable, congenial, united, cooperative, in tune, in accord, compatible, sympathetic.

**harmonium** n. a musical instrument like a small organ.

**harmonize** (or **-ise**) v. **1** add notes to a melody to form chords. **2** make consistent; go well together.
■ **harmonization** n.

**harmony** n. (pl. **-ies**) the combination of musical notes to form chords; pleasing tuneful sound; agreement; consistency.
■ **harmonic** adj.
▷ SYNS **1** **AGREEMENT**, accord, unanimity, cooperation, unity, unison, good will, amity, affinity, rapport, sympathy, friendship, fellowship, peace, peacefulness. **2** **COMPATIBILITY**, congruity, consonance, coordination, balance, symmetry. **3** **TUNEFULNESS**, melodiousness, mellifluousness.

**harness** n. straps and fittings by which a horse is controlled; fastenings for a parachute etc. • v. put a horse in harness; control and use resources.

**harp** n. a musical instrument with strings in a triangular frame. • v. (**harp on**) talk repeatedly about.

**harpoon** n. a spear-like missile with a rope attached. • v. spear with a harpoon.

**harpsichord** n. a piano-like instrument.

**harridan** n. a bad-tempered old woman.

**harrier** n. **1** a hound used for hunting hares. **2** a falcon.

**harrow** n. a heavy frame with metal spikes or discs for breaking up soil. • v. draw a harrow over soil.

**harrowing** adj. very distressing.
▷ SYNS **DISTRESSING**, traumatic, upsetting, shocking, disturbing, painful, agonizing.

**harry** v. (**harried**, **harrying**) harass.

**harsh** adj. disagreeably rough to touch, hear, etc.; severe or cruel; grim.
▷ SYNS **1** a harsh noise: **GRATING**, jarring, rasping, strident, raucous, discordant, dissonant; rough, unmusical, hoarse. **2** harsh colours: **GARISH**, gaudy, glaring, loud, bright, lurid. **3** harsh rule: **CRUEL**, brutal, savage, barbarous, despotic, tyrannical, ruthless, merciless, pitiless, relentless, unrelenting, inhuman, hard-hearted. **4** harsh measures: **SEVERE**, stringent, stern, rigorous, uncompromising, punitive, draconian. **5** harsh conditions: **AUSTERE**, grim, hard, inhospitable, bleak, spartan.

**harvest** n. the gathering of crops; a season's yield of a natural product. • v. gather a crop. ■ **harvester** n.
▷ SYNS n. **CROP**, yield, produce, vintage. • v. **GATHER**, reap, glean, pick.

**has** 3rd sing. of **HAVE**. □ **has-been** inf. a person who is no longer important.

**hash** n. **1** a dish of chopped reheated meat. **2** inf. hashish.

**hashish** n. cannabis.

**hassle** inf. n. annoying inconvenience. • v. harass or pester.

**hassock** n. a cushion for kneeling on in church.

**haste** n. hurry.
▷ SYNS SPEED, swiftness, rapidity, briskness.

**hasten** v. hurry; cause to go faster.

**hasty** adj. (-ier, -iest) hurried; acting or done too quickly.
■ hastily adv.
▷ SYNS **1** SWIFT, rapid, quick, fast, speedy, hurried, brisk. **2** IMPETUOUS, reckless, rash, precipitate, impulsive, unthinking.

**hat** n. a covering for the head.
□ hat-trick three successes in a row, esp. in sports.

**hatch**¹ n. an opening in a deck, ceiling, etc., to allow access.
□ hatchback a car with a back door that opens upwards.

**hatch**² v. emerge from an egg; devise a plot.
▷ SYNS DEVISE, concoct, contrive, plan, invent, formulate, conceive, dream up, think up.

**hatchet** n. a small axe.

**hate** n. hatred. • v. dislike greatly.
▷ SYNS v. LOATHE, detest, abhor, dislike, despise, abominate.

**hateful** adj. arousing hatred.

**hatred** n. intense dislike.
▷ SYNS HATE, loathing, detestation, abhorrence, dislike, aversion, hostility, ill will, enmity, animosity, antipathy, revulsion, repugnance.

**haughty** adj. (-ier, -iest) proud and looking down on others.
■ haughtily adv.

▷ SYNS ARROGANT, proud, conceited, self-important, vain, pompous, condescending, supercilious, patronizing, snobbish, disdainful; inf. snooty, high and mighty, stuck-up, hoity-toity.

**haul** v. **1** pull or drag forcibly. **2** transport by truck etc. • n. a quantity of goods stolen.
▷ SYNS V. DRAG, pull, tug, draw, heave, lug, tow.

**haulage** n. transport of goods.

**haulier** n. a person or firm transporting goods by road.

**haunch** n. the fleshy part of the buttock and thigh; a leg and loin of meat.

**haunt** v. (of a ghost) appear regularly at or to; linger in the mind of. • n. a place often visited by a particular person.
▷ SYNS V. **1** FREQUENT, patronize. **2** TORMENT, plague, disturb, trouble, worry, prey on someone's mind, weigh on, obsess.

**haute couture** n. high fashion.

**haute cuisine** n. high-class cookery.

**have** v. **1** possess; hold; contain. **2** experience; suffer from an illness etc. **3** cause to be or be done. **4** be obliged or compelled. **5** give birth to. **6** allow or tolerate. • v.aux. used with the past participle to form past tenses: *he has gone.*
▷ SYNS V. **1** OWN, possess, keep, use. **2** *he had a letter:* GET, receive; obtain, acquire, procure, secure, gain. **3** *the flat has five rooms:* CONTAIN, include, comprise, consist of. **4** *have some trouble:* EXPERIENCE, undergo, encounter, meet, face, go through.

**5** *have doubts:* FEEL, entertain, harbour, foster, nurse, cherish.

**haven** n. a refuge.
▷ SYNS REFUGE, shelter, sanctuary, asylum.

**haversack** n. a strong bag carried on the back or shoulder.

**havoc** n. great destruction or disorder.
▷ SYNS **1** DEVASTATION, destruction, damage, rack and ruin. **2** CHAOS, disorder, confusion, disruption, mayhem, disorganization.

**hawk** n. **1** a bird of prey. **2** a person who favours an aggressive policy. • v. offer items for sale in the street. ■ **hawker** n.

**hawthorn** n. a thorny tree with small red berries.

**hay** n. grass cut and dried for fodder. □ **hay fever** an allergy caused by pollen and dust. **haystack** (or **hayrick**) a large packed pile of hay.

**haywire** adj. out of control.

**hazard** n. a danger; an obstacle. • v. risk; venture.
▷ SYNS n. DANGER, peril, risk, jeopardy, threat, menace.

**hazardous** adj. dangerous.
▷ SYNS RISKY, dangerous, perilous, unsafe; inf. dicey.

**haze** n. thin mist.
▷ SYNS MIST, mistiness, fog, cloud, smog, vapour.

**hazel** n. **1** a tree with small edible nuts (**hazelnuts**). **2** light brown.

**hazy** adj. (**-ier**, **-iest**) misty; indistinct; vague. ■ **hazily** adv.
▷ SYNS **1** MISTY, foggy, cloudy, smoggy. **2** VAGUE, indefinite, fuzzy, faint, unclear, dim, indistinct.

**H-bomb** n. a hydrogen bomb.

**he** pron. the male previously mentioned.

**head** n. **1** the part of the body containing the brain, mouth, and sense organs. **2** a person in charge. **3** the front or top part. **4** a person considered as a unit: *six pounds a head.* **5** (**heads**) the side of a coin showing a head. • v. **1** be the head of. **2** give a heading to. **3** move in a specified direction. **4** (**head off**) intercept someone, forcing them to change direction. **5** (in football) hit the ball with your head. □ **come to a head** reach a crisis. **headache 1** a continuous pain in the head. **2** inf. a worry. **headdress** a decorative covering for the head. **headgear** hats, helmets, etc. **headhunt** approach someone employed elsewhere to fill a vacant post. **headland** a promontory. **headlight** (or **headlamp**) a powerful light at the front of a vehicle. **headline** a heading in a newspaper. **headlines** a summary of broadcast news. **headlong** with the head first; in a rash way. **headmaster** (fem. **headmistress**) a head teacher. **head-on** involving the front of a vehicle; directly confronting. **headphones** a pair of earphones. **headstone** a stone slab at the head of a grave. **headstrong** wilful and determined. **headway** progress. **headwind** a wind blowing from directly in front.
▷ SYNS n. **1** SKULL, cranium. **2** LEADER, chief, commander, director, manager, superintendent, principal, captain. **3** FRONT, beginning, start, top. • v. LEAD, run, supervise, be in charge of, control, command.

**header** n. a heading of the ball in football.

**heading** n. **1** word(s) at the top of written matter as a title. **2** a direction or bearing.

**headquarters** n. the place from which an organization or military operation is directed.
▷ SYNS HEAD OFFICE, base, HQ, command post, mission control.

**heady** adj. (**-ier, -iest**) intoxicating; exciting.

**heal** v. make or become healthy again; cure. ■ **healer** n.
▷ SYNS **1** CURE, remedy, treat. **2** RECONCILE, patch up, settle, mend, resolve.

**health** n. **1** the state of being free from illness. **2** mental or physical condition. □ **health farm** a place where people try to improve their health by dieting, exercise, etc.

**healthy** adj. (**-ier, -iest**) having or showing good health; producing good health.
■ **healthily** adv.
▷ SYNS **1** FIT, robust, strong, vigorous, flourishing, blooming, hale and hearty, in fine fettle; inf. in the pink. **2** BENEFICIAL, nutritious, nourishing, wholesome.

**heap** n. **1** a pile of a substance or a number of objects. **2** inf. a large amount or number. • v. **1** put in or form a heap. **2** load heavily with.
▷ SYNS n. PILE, stack, mound, mountain.

**hear** v. **1** perceive a sound with the ears. **2** be told about. **3** (**hear from**) be contacted by. **4** listen to. **5** judge a legal case.
□ **hearsay** information received which may be unreliable.

▷ SYNS **1** I heard he was dead: LEARN, find out, discover, gather, glean. **2** the judge heard the case: TRY, judge, adjudicate.

**hearing** n. **1** ability to hear. **2** an opportunity to state your case. **3** a trial in court. □ **hearing aid** a small amplifying device worn by a partially deaf person.
▷ SYNS INQUIRY, trial, inquest, investigation, tribunal.

**hearse** n. a vehicle carrying the coffin at a funeral.

**heart** n. **1** the muscular organ that keeps blood circulating. **2** the central or innermost part. **3** capacity for love or compassion. **4** courage or enthusiasm. □ **heart attack** sudden failure of the heart to function normally. **heartbeat** a pulsation of the heart. **heartburn** indigestion felt as a burning sensation in the chest. **heart-rending** very distressing. **heart-throb** a very good-looking famous man. **heart-to-heart** frank and personal.
▷ SYNS **1** ESSENCE, centre, crux, core, root. **2** COMPASSION, sympathy, empathy, humanity, fellow feeling, understanding. **3** ENTHUSIASM, courage, spirit, determination.

**heartache** n. worry or grief.
▷ SYNS SORROW, grief, sadness, anguish, pain, suffering, misery.

**heartbreak** n. overwhelming grief. ■ **heartbroken** adj.

**heartbreaking** adj. very upsetting.
▷ SYNS DISTRESSING, upsetting, heart-rending, harrowing, traumatic, agonizing, painful, sad, tragic.

**hearten** v. encourage.

**heartfelt** adj. deeply felt.

▷ SYNS SINCERE, genuine, earnest, profound, deep, wholehearted, honest.

**hearth** n. the floor or surround of a fireplace.

**heartless** adj. feeling no pity; very unkind.

▷ SYNS UNFEELING, unsympathetic, unkind, uncaring, cold, hard-hearted, cruel, callous, merciless, pitiless, inhuman.

**hearty** adj. (-ier, -iest) 1 vigorous; enthusiastic. 2 (of a meal or an appetite) large. ■ heartily adv.

**heat** n. 1 the quality of being hot; high temperature. 2 strength of feeling. 3 a preliminary round in a race or contest. • v. 1 make or become hot. 2 (**heat up**) become more intense. □ heatstroke a condition caused by excessive exposure to sun. heatwave a period of unusually hot weather. on heat (of female mammals) ready to mate. ■ heater n.

▷ SYNS n. 1 WARMTH, high temperature, humidity. 2 PASSION, intensity, vehemence, fervour, ardour; enthusiasm, excitement; anger.

**heated** adj. impassioned or excited: *a heated debate*.

▷ SYNS VEHEMENT, passionate, impassioned, animated, angry, furious, fierce.

**heath** n. flat uncultivated land with low shrubs.

**heathen** n. a person who does not believe in an established religion.

▷ SYNS PAGAN, infidel, idolater; unbeliever, atheist; heretic.

**heather** n. an evergreen shrub with purple, pink, or white flowers.

**heave** v. 1 lift or haul with great effort. 2 utter a sigh. 3 rise and fall like waves. 4 retch.

▷ SYNS LIFT, haul, tug, raise, hoist.

**heaven** n. 1 the place where God or the gods live. 2 a place or state of great happiness. 3 (**the heavens**) lit. the sky.

▷ SYNS 1 PARADISE, nirvana, the hereafter. 2 ECSTASY, bliss, rapture, joy.

**heavenly** adj. of heaven; of the sky; very pleasing.

▷ SYNS CELESTIAL, divine, holy, angelic, seraphic.

**heavy** adj. 1 of great weight. 2 thick or dense. 3 unusually large, forceful, or intense. 4 needing force or effort. 5 inf. serious or difficult. □ heavyweight 1 the heaviest weight in boxing etc. 2 inf. an influential person. ■ heavily adv.

▷ SYNS 1 WEIGHTY, hefty, substantial; unwieldy, cumbersome. 2 HARD, forceful, strong, powerful, violent, sharp. 3 ARDUOUS, strenuous, demanding, difficult, tough.

**heckle** v. interrupt a public speaker with aggressive questions or abuse. ■ heckler n.

**hectare** n. a unit of area equal to 10,000 sq. metres (2.471 acres).

**hectic** adj. full of frantic activity. ■ hectically adv.

▷ SYNS BUSY, active, frantic, frenetic, frenzied, manic, fast and furious.

**hedge** n. a barrier of bushes. • v. 1 surround with a hedge. 2 avoid making a definite statement or commitment. □ hedgehog a small mammal with a spiny coat. **hedgerow** bushes and trees bordering a field.

**hedonism** n. behaviour based on the belief that pleasure is the most important thing in life. ■ **hedonist** n.

**heed** v. pay attention to. ■ **heedless** adj.
▷ SYNS **v.** PAY ATTENTION TO, take notice of, listen to, take into account. • **n.** ATTENTION, notice, note, regard; consideration, thought, care.

**heel** n. **1** the back part of the foot. **2** part of a shoe supporting the heel. • v. **1** renew the heel on a shoe. **2** (of a ship) tilt to one side.

**hefty** adj. (**-ier, -iest**) large, heavy, and powerful.
▷ SYNS **1** HEAVY, burly, big, large, muscular, brawny, strapping, sturdy, beefy, strong, powerful, well built. **2** *a hefty bill:* SUBSTANTIAL, sizeable, huge, extortionate, stiff.

**heifer** n. a young cow.

**height** n. **1** measurement from base to top or foot to head; distance above ground or sea level. **2** being tall; a high place; the highest degree of something.
▷ SYNS **1** ALTITUDE, elevation; tallness, stature. **2** TOP, summit, peak, crest, crown, apex. **3** PEAK, zenith, apex, climax, pinnacle, apogee.

**heighten** v. make higher or more intense.
▷ SYNS **1** RAISE, lift, elevate. **2** INTENSIFY, increase, add to, augment, boost, strengthen, amplify, magnify, enhance.

**heinous** adj. very wicked.

**heir** n. (fem. **heiress**) a person entitled to inherit property or a rank. □ **heirloom** a valuable object that has belonged to a family for several generations.

**held** past and p.p. of HOLD.

**helicopter** n. an aircraft with horizontally rotating overhead rotors.

**helium** n. a light colourless gas that does not burn.

**helix** n. (pl. **-ices**) a spiral.

**hell** n. **1** a place of punishment for the wicked after death. **2** a place or state of great suffering. □ **hell-bent** recklessly determined. ■ **hellish** adj.

**hello** (or **hallo**, **hullo**) exclam. used as a greeting or to attract attention.

**helm** n. the tiller or wheel by which a ship's rudder is controlled.

**helmet** n. a protective head covering.

**help** v. **1** make something easier for someone. **2** improve a situation. **3** serve food or drink to. **4** (**help yourself**) take without asking first. **5** (**cannot help**) be unable to stop yourself doing. • n. a person or thing that helps.
▷ SYNS **v.** **1** ASSIST, aid, lend a hand, be of service; support, contribute. **2** SOOTHE, relieve, ease, alleviate, improve. • **n.** **1** ASSISTANCE, aid, support, advice, guidance, benefit, use, advantage. **2** RELIEF, alleviation, remedy, cure.

**helper** n. a person who helps.
▷ SYNS ASSISTANT, aide, deputy, auxiliary, supporter, right-hand man/woman, attendant.

**helpful** adj. giving help; useful. ■ **helpfully** adv.

▷ SYNS **1** USEFUL, of use/service, beneficial, valuable, advantageous, practical, constructive, productive, instrumental. **2** SUPPORTIVE, kind, obliging, accommodating, cooperative, neighbourly, charitable.

**helping** n. a portion of food served.
▷ SYNS PORTION, serving, ration, piece, plateful, share.

**helpless** adj. unable to manage without help; powerless.
▷ SYNS DEFENCELESS, unprotected, vulnerable, exposed; weak, incapable, powerless, impotent, dependent.

**helter-skelter** adv. in disorderly haste. • n. a spiral slide at a fair.

**hem** n. an edge of cloth turned under and sewn down. • v. **1** sew a hem on. **2** (**hem in**) surround and restrict.
▷ SYNS v. (**hem in**) SHUT IN, fence in, confine, constrain, restrict, limit, trap; surround, enclose.

**hemisphere** n. half a sphere; half of the earth.

**hemlock** n. a poisonous plant.

**hemp** n. **1** a plant with fibres used to make rope and cloth. **2** cannabis.

**hen** n. a female bird, esp. of a domestic fowl. ◻ hen night (or hen party) inf. an all-female celebration held for a woman about to get married. henpecked (of a man) nagged by his wife.

**hence** adv. **1** for this reason. **2** from now. ◻ henceforth (or **henceforward**) from this or that time on.

**henchman** n. a supporter or follower.

**henna** n. a reddish-brown dye.

**hepatitis** n. inflammation of the liver.

**heptagon** n. a geometric figure with seven sides.

**heptathlon** n. an athletic contest involving seven events.

**her** pron. the objective case of *she*. • adj. belonging to a female already mentioned.

**herald** v. be a sign of. • n. **1** a messenger. **2** a sign of something to come.

**heraldry** n. the study of coats of arms. ■ heraldic adj.

**herb** n. a plant used as a flavouring or in medicine. ■ herbal adj.

**herbaceous** adj. (of plants) soft-stemmed. ◻ herbaceous border a garden border containing plants which flower every year.

**herbivore** n. an animal feeding on plants. ■ herbivorous adj.

**herd** n. a group of animals feeding or staying together; a mob. • v. cause to move in a group. ◻ herdsman the owner or keeper of a herd of animals.
▷ SYNS n. FLOCK, pack, mob, crowd, throng, horde. • v. DRIVE, round up, shepherd, guide, lead.

**here** adv. in, at, or to this place, position, or point. ◻ hereabouts near this place. hereafter from now on; (**the hereafter**) life after death. hereby by this means. herein in this document etc.

**hereditary** adj. of or by inheritance.
▷ SYNS INHERITED, genetic, innate, inborn, inbred.

**heredity** n. inheritance of characteristics from parents.

**heresy** n. (pl. **-ies**) a belief, esp. a religious one, contrary to orthodox doctrine.

**heretic** n. a person believing in a heresy. ■ **heretical** adj.
▷ SYNS DISSENTER, nonconformist, apostate, free thinker, iconoclast, atheist, non-believer, pagan, heathen.

**herewith** adv. formal with this.

**heritage** n. inherited property; a nation's historic buildings etc.
▷ SYNS HISTORY, tradition, background, past; culture, customs.

**hermaphrodite** n. a creature with male and female sexual organs.

**hermetic** adj. airtight.
■ **hermetically** adv.

**hermit** n. a person living in solitude.
▷ SYNS RECLUSE, solitary, anchorite.

**hernia** n. a protrusion of part of an organ through the wall of the cavity containing it.

**hero** n. (pl. **-oes**) **1** a person admired for their courage or achievements. **2** the chief male character in a story.
■ **heroism** n.

**heroic** adj. very brave.
• pl.n. (**heroics**) brave behaviour.
■ **heroically** adv.
▷ SYNS adj. BRAVE, courageous, valiant, intrepid, bold, fearless, daring.

**heroin** n. a highly addictive drug.

**heroine** n. **1** a woman admired for her courage or achievements. **2** the chief female character in a story.

**heron** n. a long-legged wading bird.

**herring** n. an edible North Atlantic fish.

**hers** poss.pron belonging to her.

**herself** pron. the emphatic and reflexive form of *she* and *her*.

**hertz** n. (pl. **hertz**) Physics a unit of frequency of electromagnetic waves.

**hesitant** adj. uncertain or re-luctant. ■ **hesitancy** n.
▷ SYNS **1** UNCERTAIN, unsure, undecided, doubtful, dubious, sceptical, irresolute, indecisive, vacillating, wavering; diffident, timid, shy. **2** RELUCTANT, unwilling, disinclined.

**hesitate** v. pause doubtfully; be reluctant. ■ **hesitation** n.
▷ SYNS **1** DELAY, pause, hang back, wait, vacillate, waver, dither, shilly-shally, stall, temporize. **2** DEMUR, scruple, have misgivings, think twice.

**hessian** n. a strong coarse fabric.

**heterogeneous** adj. made up of people or things of various sorts. ■ **heterogeneity** n.

**heterosexual** adj. & n. (a person) sexually attracted to the opposite sex.

**hew** v. (**hewed**, **hewn** or **hewed**, **hewing**) chop or cut with an axe etc.
▷ SYNS CHOP, hack, cut, saw, lop; carve, sculpt, shape, fashion.

**hexagon** n. a geometric figure with six sides. ■ **hexagonal** adj.

**heyday** n. the time of someone's or something's greatest success.

**HGV** abbr. heavy goods vehicle.

**hiatus** n. (pl. **-tuses**) a break or gap in a sequence.

**hibernate** v. spend the winter in a sleep-like state.
■ **hibernation** n.

**hibiscus** n. a plant with large brightly coloured flowers.

**hiccup** (or **hiccough**) n. **1** a gulping sound in the throat. **2** inf. a minor setback.
• v. (**hiccuped**, **hiccuping**) make the sound of a hiccup.

**hide** v. **1** put or keep out of sight. **2** conceal yourself. **3** keep secret. • n. **1** a concealed shelter used to observe wildlife. **2** an animal's skin. □ **hideaway** (or **hideout**) a hiding place. **hidebound** unwilling to accept new ideas.
▷ SYNS v. **1** CONCEAL, secrete; obscure, block, cloud, shroud, veil, eclipse, camouflage. **2** CONCEAL YOURSELF, take cover, lie low, go to ground. **3** KEEP SECRET, conceal, cover up, mask, disguise.

**hideous** adj. very ugly.
▷ SYNS UGLY, unsightly, grotesque, monstrous, repulsive, repellent, revolting, gruesome, disgusting, ghastly.

**hiding** n. inf. a severe beating.

**hierarchy** n. a system with grades ranking one above another.
▷ SYNS RANKING, grading, ladder, pecking order.

**hieroglyphics** pl.n. writing consisting of pictorial symbols.

**hi-fi** adj. of high-fidelity sound.
• n. a set of high-fidelity equipment.

**higgledy-piggledy** adj. & adv. in complete confusion.

**high** adj. **1** extending far upwards. **2** of a specified height. **3** far above ground or sea level. **4** large in amount, value, or size. **5** great in status. **6** (of a sound) not deep or low. **7** inf. under the influence of drugs.
• n. **1** a high level. **2** an area of high atmospheric pressure. **3** inf. a euphoric state. • adv. at or to a high or specified level. □ **higher education** education at university etc. **high fidelity** the reproduction of sound with little distortion. **highland** (or **highlands**) an area of high or mountainous land. **high-rise** (of a building) with many storeys. **high school** a secondary school. **high-spirited** lively. **high-tech** involving advanced technology. **high tide** the tide at its highest level. **high time** at or past the time when something should happen.
▷ SYNS adj. **1** TALL, lofty, soaring, towering, big. **2** HIGH-RANKING, leading, top, powerful, important, prominent.

**highbrow** adj. intellectual or refined.
▷ SYNS INTELLECTUAL, scholarly, bookish, academic, cultured.

**high-handed** adj. using authority arrogantly.
▷ SYNS IMPERIOUS, domineering, overbearing, peremptory, arrogant, bossy, autocratic, tyrannical.

**highlight** n. **1** an outstandingly good part of something. **2** a bright area in a picture; a light streak in the hair.
• v. emphasize.

**highly** adv. **1** to a high degree. **2** favourably.
□ **highly strung** nervous and easily upset.

**highway** n. a public road; a main route. □ **highwayman** hist. a man who held up and robbed travellers.

**hijack** v. illegally seize control of a vehicle or aircraft in transit. • n. hijacking. ■ hijacker n.

**hike** n. 1 a long walk. 2 a sharp increase. • v. 1 go for a hike. 2 raise. ■ hiker n.

**hilarious** adj. very funny. ■ hilarity n.
▷ SYNS HYSTERICAL, uproarious, side-splitting.

**hill** n. a raised part of the earth's surface, lower than a mountain.
▷ SYNS 1 HILLOCK, knoll, hummock, tor, mound, mount. 2 SLOPE, incline, gradient, bank.

**hilt** n. the handle of a sword or dagger. □ to the hilt completely.

**him** pron. the objective case of *he*.

**himself** pron. the emphatic and reflexive form of *he* and *him*.

**hind**¹ adj. situated at the back.

**hind**² n. a female deer.

**hinder** v. delay or obstruct.
▷ SYNS HAMPER, obstruct, impede, inhibit, curb, delay, interfere with, set back, slow down, hold up; restrict, constrain, block, check, curtail, frustrate, handicap.

**hindrance** n. a difficulty or obstruction.
▷ SYNS IMPEDIMENT, obstacle, obstruction, hurdle, handicap, block, bar, barrier, drawback, snag, difficulty, stumbling block.

**hindsight** n. wisdom about an event after it has occurred.

**Hinduism** n. the principal religion and philosophy of India. ■ Hindu adj. & n.

**hinge** n. 1 a movable joint such as that on a door or lid. 2 (**hinge on**) depend on. • v. attach or join with a hinge.

**hint** n. a slight or indirect suggestion; a piece of practical information; a slight trace. • v. suggest or indicate.
▷ SYNS n. 1 CLUE, inkling, indication, intimation, mention; tip-off. 2 TIP, pointer, advice, help, suggestion. 3 TOUCH, trace, dash, soupçon, tinge, taste. • v. SUGGEST, insinuate, imply, indicate, allude to, intimate.

**hinterland** n. the area away from the coast or around a major town.

**hip** n. 1 the projection of the pelvis on each side of the body. 2 the fruit of a rose.

**hippopotamus** n. (pl. **-muses** or **-mi**) a large African river animal with a thick skin.

**hippy** (or **hippie**) n. (pl. **-ies**) a young person who rejects conventional clothes and lifestyles.

**hire** v. 1 purchase the temporary use of. 2 (**hire out**) grant temporary use of for payment. • n. hiring. □ hire purchase a system of purchase by payment in instalments.
▷ SYNS v. 1 RENT, lease, charter. 2 APPOINT, sign on, take on, engage, employ.

**hirsute** adj. hairy.

**his** adj. & poss.pron belonging to a male already mentioned.

**hiss** v. make a sharp sound as of the letter *s*, esp. in disapproval. • n. a hissing sound.

**historian** n. an expert on history.

**historic** adj. 1 important in the development of events. 2 relating to history.
▷ SYNS FAMED, notable, famous, celebrated, renowned, momentous, significant, important, consequential, memorable,

remarkable, epoch-making, red-letter.

**historical** adj. of or concerned with history; belonging to the past. ■ **historically** adv.
▷ SYNS DOCUMENTED, recorded, chronicled, archival, authentic, factual, actual; past, bygone.

**history** n. (pl. **-ies**) the study of past events; the past; someone's or something's past.
▷ SYNS **1** ANNAL, record, chronicle, account, narrative, report, memoir. **2** BACKGROUND, past, experiences, antecedents. **3** THE PAST, former times, bygone days, time gone by, antiquity.

**histrionic** adj. excessively theatrical in manner. • pl.n. (**histrionics**) theatrical behaviour.

**hit** v. **1** strike with the hand or an object. **2** come into sudden forceful contact with. **3** affect badly. **4** strike a target. • n. **1** an instance of hitting or being hit. **2** a success. **3** an instance of accessing a website. ■ **hitter** n.
▷ SYNS v. **1** STRIKE, smack, slap, punch, thump, thrash, batter, pummel, cuff, swat; inf. whack, wallop, bash, belt, clout, clobber. **2** RUN INTO, collide with, bang into, bump into.

**hitch** v. **1** move with a jerk. **2** hitchhike. **3** tether or fasten. • n. a temporary difficulty. □ **hitchhike** travel by getting free lifts in passing vehicles.

**hither** adv. to or towards this place.

**hitherto** adv. until this time.

**HIV** abbr. human immunodeficiency virus (causing Aids).

**hive** n. **1** a structure in which bees live. **2** (**hives**) a red, itchy rash. • v. (**hive off**) separate from a larger group.

**HMS** abbr. Her (or His) Majesty's Ship.

**hoard** v. save and store away. • n. a store, esp. of valuable things.
▷ SYNS v. STORE (UP), stock up, stockpile, put by, lay in, set aside, save, accumulate, amass, collect, gather, squirrel away; inf. stash away. • n. STORE, stockpile, supply, reserve, fund, cache, reservoir, accumulation; inf. stash.

**hoarding** n. a large board for displaying advertisements.

**hoar frost** n. white frost.

**hoarse** adj. (of a voice) rough and harsh.
▷ SYNS CROAKY, gruff, rough, throaty, harsh, husky, gravelly, rasping, guttural.

**hoary** adj. (**-ier**, **-iest**) grey with age; old and unoriginal.

**hoax** v. deceive jokingly. • n. a joking deception.
▷ SYNS v. TRICK, fool, deceive, hoodwink, delude, dupe, take in; inf. con. • n. PRACTICAL JOKE, prank, trick; fraud; inf. scam.

**hob** n. a cooking surface with hotplates.

**hobble** v. **1** walk lamely. **2** fasten the legs of a horse to limit its movement. • n. a hobbling walk.
▷ SYNS v. LIMP, stumble, totter, stagger.

**hobby** n. (pl. **-ies**) something done for pleasure in your spare time. □ **hobby horse 1** a stick with a horse's head, used as a toy. **2** inf. a favourite topic.
▷ SYNS INTEREST, pursuit, pastime, diversion, recreation.

**hobgoblin** n. a mischievous imp.

**hobnob** v. (**hobnobbed, hobnobbing**) mix socially.
▷ SYNS ASSOCIATE, fraternize, socialize, mingle, mix, consort.

**hock** n. 1 the middle joint of an animal's hind leg. 2 a German white wine.

**hockey** n. a field game played with curved sticks and a small hard ball.

**hocus-pocus** n. mystifying and often deceptive talk or behaviour.

**hod** n. 1 a trough on a pole for carrying mortar or bricks. 2 a tall container for coal.

**hoe** n. a tool for loosening soil or scraping up weeds. • v. (**hoed, hoeing**) dig or scrape with a hoe.

**hog** n. a castrated male pig reared for meat. • v. (**hogged, hogging**) inf. take or hoard selfishly.

**hoist** v. raise or haul up. • n. an apparatus for hoisting things.

**hoity-toity** adj. haughty.

**hold** v. 1 grasp, carry, or support. 2 contain. 3 have, own, or occupy. 4 keep or detain. 5 stay or keep at a certain level. 6 arrange and take part in. 7 consider to be of a particular nature. • n. 1 a grip. 2 a degree of control. 3 a storage space in a ship or aircraft. ◻ **holdall** a large, soft bag. **hold on** 1 wait. 2 endure. **hold out** resist, survive, or last. **hold up** 1 delay. 2 rob.
▷ SYNS v. 1 CLASP, clutch, grasp, grip, clench, cling to. 2 *the room holds 100 people:* TAKE, contain, accommodate, fit. 3 *he still holds a UK passport:* HAVE, own, possess, bear. 4 DETAIN, imprison, lock up, confine,

incarcerate. • n. 1 GRIP, grasp, clutch, clasp. 2 CONTROL, power, influence, authority, sway.

**holder** n. 1 a device for holding something. 2 a person who holds or possesses something.
▷ SYNS 1 CONTAINER, receptacle, case, cover, housing, sheath. 2 OWNER, possessor, bearer, keeper, custodian.

**holding** n. 1 land held by lease. 2 (**holdings**) stocks and property owned by someone.

**hole** n. 1 a hollow space or opening in a solid object or surface. 2 inf. an unpleasant or awkward place or situation. • v. make a hole in. ■ **holey** adj.
▷ SYNS n. 1 OPENING, aperture, gap, orifice, space, breach, break, fissure, crack, rift, puncture, perforation, cut, split, gash, slit, vent. 2 PIT, crater, cavity, pothole, depression, hollow.

**holiday** n. a period of re-creation. • v. spend a holiday.

**holistic** adj. treating the whole person rather than just particular isolated symptoms.

**hollow** adj. 1 empty inside; sunken; (of a sound) echoing. 2 worthless. • n. a cavity; a small valley. • v. make hollow.
▷ SYNS adj. 1 EMPTY, vacant, unfilled, void. 2 *hollow cheeks:* SUNKEN, deep-set, concave. 3 *hollow victories:* WORTHLESS, empty, pointless, meaningless, useless, futile, pyrrhic. • n. INDENTATION, depression, dip, hole, crater, cavern, pit, cavity, trough.

**holly** n. an evergreen shrub with prickly leaves and red berries.

**hollyhock** n. a tall plant with large showy flowers.

**holocaust** n. destruction or slaughter on a mass scale.
▷ SYNS GENOCIDE, mass murder, annihilation, massacre, slaughter, extermination, butchery, ethnic cleansing.

**hologram** n. a three-dimensional photographic image.

**holster** n. a leather case holding a pistol or revolver.

**holy** adj. **1** dedicated to God or a religious purpose. **2** morally and spiritually good.
■ holiness n.
▷ SYNS **1** SACRED, consecrated, hallowed, sanctified. **2** SAINTLY, godly, pious, religious, devout, God-fearing, spiritual.

**homage** n. things said or done as a mark of respect or loyalty.

**home** n. **1** the place where you live. **2** an institution for people needing special care. • adj. **1** of your home or country. **2** (of a match) played on a team's own ground. • adv. **1** to or at your home. **2** to the point aimed at. • v. (of an animal) return by instinct. □ home in on move or be aimed towards. home page the main page of an individual's or organization's Internet site.
▷ SYNS n. RESIDENCE, house; formal abode, dwelling, habitation.

**homeless** adj. having nowhere to live.
▷ SYNS OF NO FIXED ABODE, on the streets, vagrant, sleeping rough, destitute.

**homely** adj. **1** simple but comfortable. **2** US unattractive.
▷ SYNS COMFORTABLE, cosy, snug, welcoming, friendly, relaxed, informal.

**homeopathy** (or **homoe-opathy**) n. treatment of a disease by very small doses of a substance that would produce the same symptoms in a healthy person. ■ homeopathic adj.

**homicide** n. murder.
■ homicidal adj.

**homily** n. (pl. **-ies**) a talk on a moral or religious issue.

**homogeneous** adj. of the same kind. ■ homogeneity n.

**homogenize** (or **-ise**) v. **1** treat milk so that the cream does not separate. **2** make alike.

**homonym** n. a word spelt or pronounced the same way as another.

**homosexual** adj. & n. (a person) sexually attracted to people of your own sex.
■ homosexuality n.

**hone** v. sharpen a tool with a stone.

**honest** adj. **1** truthful and sincere. **2** fairly earned.
■ honestly adv. honesty n.
▷ SYNS **1** TRUTHFUL, sincere, frank, candid, forthright, open, straight; inf. upfront. **2** *an honest man:* UPRIGHT, honourable, principled, virtuous, good, decent, law-abiding, trustworthy, scrupulous.

**honey** n. a sweet substance made by bees from nectar. □ honeycomb a structure of six-sided wax compartments made by bees to store honey and eggs. honeydew a type of melon with sweet green flesh. honeymoon a holiday taken by a newly married couple; an initial period of goodwill. honeysuckle a climbing shrub with scented flowers.

**honk** n. the cry of a goose; the sound of a car horn. • v. make this noise.

**honorary** adj. **1** given as an honour. **2** unpaid.
▷ SYNS NOMINAL, titular, in name only; unpaid, unsalaried.

**honour** (US **honor**) n. **1** great respect. **2** honesty or integrity. **3** a privilege. • v. **1** regard or treat with great respect. **2** keep an agreement.
▷ SYNS n. **1** INTEGRITY, honesty, uprightness, high principles, morality, righteousness, high-mindedness, decency. **2** PRIVILEGE, distinction, prestige, glory, kudos, cachet; esteem, respect. • v. **1** ESTEEM, respect, admire, defer to; revere, venerate, worship; applaud, acclaim, praise, salute, pay tribute to. **2** FULFIL, observe, keep, follow, carry out, discharge.

**honourable** (US **honorable**) adj. honest; deserving honour.
■ **honourably** adv.
▷ SYNS HONEST, upright, ethical, moral, principled, upstanding, righteous, right-minded, virtuous, good, decent, fair, just, truthful, trustworthy, reliable, dependable.

**hood** n. **1** a covering for the head and neck. **2** a folding roof over a car. **3** US a car bonnet.

**hoodlum** n. a hooligan or gangster.

**hoodwink** v. deceive.

**hoody** n. **1** a hooded top. **2** inf. a youth wearing a hooded top.

**hoof** n. (pl. **hoofs** or **hooves**) the horny part of a horse's foot.

**hook** n. **1** a curved device for catching hold of or hanging things on. **2** a short punch made with the elbow bent. • v. catch or fasten with a hook.
■ **hooked** adj.

**hooligan** n. a violent young troublemaker.
▷ SYNS THUG, vandal, lout, delinquent, ruffian, tearaway, hoodlum; inf. yob.

**hoop** n. a rigid circular band.
▷ SYNS RING, band, circle, loop.

**hooray** exclam. hurrah.

**hoot** n. **1** an owl's cry; the sound of a hooter; a cry of laughter or disapproval. **2** inf. an amusing person or thing. • v. make a hoot.

**hooter** n. a siren, steam whistle, or horn.

**Hoover** n. trademark a vacuum cleaner. • v. (**hoover**) clean with a vacuum cleaner.

**hop**¹ v. **1** jump on one foot. **2** (of an animal) jump along. • n. **1** a hopping movement. **2** a short journey. □ **hopscotch** a children's game of hopping into and over marked squares.
▷ SYNS v. JUMP, leap, bound, spring, bounce, skip, caper.

**hop**² n. a plant used to flavour beer.

**hope** n. **1** a feeling of expectation and desire for something to happen. **2** a cause or source of hope. • v. expect and want to happen.
▷ SYNS n. **1** OPTIMISM, expectation, confidence, faith, belief. **2** ASPIRATION, desire, wish, ambition, dream. • v. EXPECT, anticipate; want, wish for, dream of.

**hopeful** adj. feeling or inspiring hope.
▷ SYNS **1** OPTIMISTIC, confident, positive, buoyant, sanguine; inf. upbeat. **2** ENCOURAGING, promising, heartening, reassuring, favourable.

**hopefully** adv. **1** in a hopeful way. **2** it is to be hoped.

**hopeless** adj. **1** without hope. **2** inadequate or incompetent.
▷ SYNS DESPAIRING, in despair, desperate, pessimistic, despondent, demoralized, wretched, defeatist.

**hopper** n. a container with an opening at the base for discharging its contents.

**horde** n. a large group or crowd.
▷ SYNS CROWD, throng, mob, mass, multitude, host, army, pack, gang, troop, drove, swarm, flock.

**horizon** n. **1** the line at which earth and sky appear to meet. **2** the limit of someone's knowledge or interests.

**horizontal** adj. parallel to the horizon. ■ horizontally adv.

**hormone** n. a substance produced in the body that controls the action of cells or tissues. ■ hormonal adj.

**horn** n. **1** a hard pointed growth on the heads of certain animals. **2** the substance of a horn. **3** a wind instrument. **4** a device sounding a warning. □ hornpipe a lively solo dance traditionally performed by sailors. ■ horned adj.

**hornet** n. a large wasp.

**horny** adj. (-ier, -iest) **1** of or like horn. **2** inf. sexually aroused.

**horoscope** n. a forecast of events based on the positions of stars.

**horrendous** adj. horrifying.

**horrible** adj. causing horror; very unpleasant. ■ horribly adv.
▷ SYNS **1** AWFUL, dreadful, terrible, horrific, horrifying, frightful, fearful, horrendous, shocking, gruesome, hideous, grim, ghastly, harrowing, abominable, appalling. **2** DISAGREEABLE,

nasty, unpleasant, obnoxious, odious, revolting, repulsive, loathsome, abhorrent, hateful, vile, insufferable.

**horrid** adj. horrible.

**horrific** adj. horrifying. ■ horrifically adv.

**horrify** v. (horrified, horrifying) fill with horror.
▷ SYNS SHOCK, appal, outrage, scandalize, disgust, revolt, repel, nauseate, sicken, offend.

**horror** n. intense shock and fear or disgust; a terrible event or situation.
▷ SYNS **1** TERROR, fear, alarm, fright, dread, panic, trepidation; loathing, disgust, revulsion, abhorrence. **2** ATROCITY, outrage.

**hors d'oeuvre** n. food served as an appetizer.

**horse** n. a four-legged animal used for riding. □ horse chestnut a brown shiny nut; the tree bearing this. horsefly a large biting fly. horseman (fem. **horsewoman**) a rider on horseback. horseplay boisterous play. horsepower a unit measuring the power of an engine. horseradish a hot-tasting root used to make a sauce. horseshoe a U-shaped strip iron band attached to a horse's hoof. on horseback riding on a horse.
▷ SYNS MOUNT, charger, cob, hack, nag.

**horticulture** n. the art of garden cultivation. ■ horticultural adj.

**hose** n. **1** (also **hosepipe**) a flexible tube for conveying water. **2** hosiery. • v. water or spray with a hosepipe.

**hosiery** n. stockings, socks, and tights.

**hospice** n. a hospital or home for the terminally ill.

**hospitable** adj. friendly and welcoming. ■ **hospitably** adv.
▷ SYNS WELCOMING, sociable, friendly, convivial, neighbourly, kind, warm, helpful, obliging, generous.

**hospital** n. an institution for the treatment of sick or injured people.
▷ SYNS CLINIC, infirmary, sanatorium, hospice.

**hospitality** n. friendly and generous entertainment of guests.

**hospitalize** (or **-ise**) v. send or admit to a hospital.

**host** n. **1** a person entertaining guests; a place providing facilities for visitors. **2** an organism on which another lives as a parasite. **3** a large number of people or things. • v. act as host at an event.
▷ SYNS n. PRESENTER, compère, master of ceremonies, MC, anchorman, anchorwoman.

**hostage** n. a person held captive to ensure that a demand is met.

**hostel** n. a place providing cheap accommodation for a particular group.

**hostelry** n. (pl. **-ies**) old use an inn or pub.

**hostess** n. a woman entertaining guests.

**hostile** adj. unfriendly; of an enemy.
▷ SYNS UNFRIENDLY, unkind, bitter, unsympathetic, malicious, vicious, rancorous, venomous; antagonistic, aggressive, confrontational, belligerent, truculent.

**hostility** n. hostile behaviour; acts of warfare.
▷ SYNS ANTAGONISM, unfriendliness, malevolence, malice, ill will, rancour, venom, hatred, enmity, animosity; aggression, belligerence.

**hot** adj. **1** having a high temperature. **2** producing an uncomfortable sensation of heat. **3** inf. popular. **4** showing strong emotion. • v. (**hotted**, **hotting**) become more exciting.
□ **hotbed** a place where an activity happens or flourishes. **hot dog** a hot sausage in a bread roll. **hotfoot** in eager haste. **hothead** a rash or quick-tempered person. **hothouse 1** a heated greenhouse. **2** an environment encouraging rapid development. **hotline** a direct phone line set up for a purpose. **hotplate** a flat heated surface on an electric cooker.
▷ SYNS adj. **1** HEATED, boiling, piping hot, sizzling; scalding, scorching, roasting, searing, sweltering, torrid, sultry. **2** SPICY, peppery, piquant, powerful.

**hotchpotch** n. a confused mixture.

**hotel** n. an establishment providing rooms and meals for tourists and travellers.

**hotelier** n. a hotel keeper.

**houmous** = HUMMUS.

**hound** n. a dog used in hunting. • v. harass.

**hour** n. **1** one twenty-fourth part of a day and night. **2** a point in time. **3** (**hours**) time fixed or set aside for work or an activity.
□ **hourglass** a device with two

connected glass bulbs containing sand that takes an hour to fall from the upper to the lower bulb.

■ **hourly** adj. & adv.

**house** n. 1 a building for people to live in. 2 a business. 3 a dynasty. 4 a law-making assembly. • v. 1 provide accommodation or storage space for. 2 encase. □ **houseboat** a boat that people can live in. **housebound** unable to leave one's house because of illness or old age. **housebreaking** breaking into a building to commit a crime. **householder** a person who owns or rents a house. **housekeeper** a person employed to manage a household. **house-trained** (of a pet) trained to be clean in the house. **house-warming** a party to celebrate moving into a new home. **housewife** a woman whose main occupation is looking after her family and the home. **housework** cleaning, cooking, etc. done in running a home. **on the house** at the management's expense.

▷ SYNS n. 1 RESIDENCE, abode, home, domicile, habitation. 2 FAMILY, clan, line, dynasty, lineage, ancestry. • v. ACCOMMODATE, lodge, put up, take in; shelter, harbour.

**household** n. a house and its occupants.

▷ SYNS FAMILY, house, occupants, clan.

**housing** n. 1 accommodation. 2 a rigid case enclosing machinery.

**hove** see **HEAVE**.

**hovel** n. a small squalid house.

**hover** v. 1 remain in one place in the air. 2 wait about

uncertainly. □ **hovercraft** a vehicle that travels over land or water on a cushion of air.

▷ SYNS 1 FLOAT, be suspended, hang. 2 LINGER, loiter, wait.

**how** adv. 1 by what means or in what way. 2 to what extent or degree. 3 in what condition.

**however** adv. 1 nevertheless. 2 in whatever way or to whatever extent.

**howl** v. & n. (make) a long loud wailing cry or sound.

▷ SYNS BAY, yowl, yelp, bark; cry, wail, bellow.

**howler** n. inf. a stupid mistake.

**h.p.** abbr. 1 hire purchase. 2 horse power.

**HQ** abbr. headquarters.

**HRH** abbr. Her (or His) Royal Highness.

**hub** n. 1 the central part of a wheel. 2 the centre of activity.

▷ SYNS CENTRE, core, heart, focus, focal point.

**hubbub** n. a confused noise of voices.

**hubris** n. arrogant pride.

**huddle** v. crowd into a small place. • n. a close group or mass.

▷ SYNS v. CROWD, throng, press, pack, cluster, herd, squeeze, gather, congregate.

**hue** n. a colour or shade.

▷ SYNS COLOUR, tone, shade, tint, tinge.

**hue and cry** n. public outcry.

**huff** n. a bad mood. • v. breathe heavily. ■ **huffy** adj.

**hug** v. 1 hold tightly in your arms. 2 keep close to. • n. an embrace.

▷ SYNS v. EMBRACE, cuddle, squeeze, hold tight.

**huge** adj. extremely large.

▷ SYNS ENORMOUS, immense, great, massive, colossal, vast, prodigious, gigantic, giant, gargantuan, mammoth, monumental, mountainous, titanic.

**hula hoop** n. a large hoop for spinning round the body.

**hulk** n. the body of an old ship; a large clumsy-looking person or thing.

**hulking** adj. inf. large and clumsy.

**hull** n. **1** the framework of a ship. **2** the pod of a pea or bean. • v. remove the hulls of beans, peas, etc.
▷ SYNS n. FRAMEWORK, body, frame, skeleton, structure.

**hullabaloo** n. inf. an uproar.

**hullo** var. of HELLO.

**hum** v. **1** make a low continuous sound; sing with closed lips. **2** be in a state of activity. • n. a humming sound.
▷ SYNS v. MURMUR, drone, vibrate, thrum, buzz, whirr, purr.

**human** adj. **1** of people. **2** showing kindness, emotion, etc. • n. a person.
▷ SYNS adj. **1** MORTAL, flesh and blood; fallible; physical, bodily. **2** COMPASSIONATE, humane, kind, considerate, understanding, sympathetic, tolerant.

**humane** adj. kind or merciful.
▷ SYNS KIND, compassionate, understanding, considerate, sympathetic, forgiving, merciful, charitable, humanitarian.

**humanism** n. the belief that people are able to live by reason rather than relying on religious faith. ■ humanist n.

**humanitarian** adj. promoting human welfare and reduction of suffering.

**humanity** n. **1** human nature; the human race. **2** kindness. **3** (**humanities**) arts subjects.

**humanize** (or **-ise**) v. make human or humane.

**humble** adj. **1** having a low opinion of your importance. **2** of low rank. **3** not large or elaborate. • v. cause to seem less important. ■ humbly adv.
▷ SYNS adj. **1** MEEK, deferential, respectful, submissive, self-effacing, unassertive, modest. **2** LOWLY, poor, undistinguished, mean, common, ordinary, simple, modest. • v. HUMILIATE, mortify, demean, shame.

**humbug** n. **1** hypocritical talk or behaviour. **2** a hard peppermint sweet.

**humdrum** adj. dull or commonplace.
▷ SYNS COMMONPLACE, routine, run-of-the-mill, unvaried, uneventful, ordinary, everyday, mundane, monotonous, dull, uninteresting, boring, tedious, prosaic.

**humerus** n. (pl. **-ri**) the bone in the upper arm.

**humid** adj. (of air) warm and damp. ■ humidity n.

**humidifier** n. a device for increasing the moisture in air.

**humiliate** v. cause to feel ashamed and foolish. ■ humiliation n.
▷ SYNS MORTIFY, shame, humble, disgrace, embarrass, discomfit, chasten, subdue, deflate, abash, abase, degrade, crush, demean.

**humility** n. a humble attitude of mind.
▷ SYNS HUMBLENESS, modesty, meekness, diffidence, lack of vanity/pride.

**hummock** n. a hump in the ground.

**hummus** (or **houmous**) n. a dip made from chickpeas.

**humorist** n. a writer or speaker noted for being amusing.

**humorous** adj. **1** causing amusement. **2** having or showing a sense of humour.
▷ SYNS FUNNY, amusing, entertaining, witty, comical, jocular, hilarious.

**humour** (US **humor**) n. **1** the quality of being amusing; the ability to perceive and enjoy this. **2** a state of mind. • v. keep a person contented by doing as they wish.
▷ SYNS n. **1** COMEDY, jokes, gags, wit, witticisms. **2** MOOD, temper, temperament, state of mind, disposition, spirits.

**hump** n. a rounded projecting part; a curved deformity of the spine. • v. hoist and carry.
■ humped adj.
▷ SYNS n. PROTRUSION, protuberance, projection, bulge, swelling, lump, bump, knob.

**humus** n. rich dark organic material in soil, formed by decay of dead leaves and plants.

**hunch** v. draw your shoulders up; bend your body forward.
• n. an intuitive feeling.
□ hunchback offens. a person with a hump on their back.
▷ SYNS n. FEELING, intuition, suspicion, inkling, impression, idea.

**hundred** n. ten times ten; 100.
□ hundredweight **1** a unit of weight equal to 112 lb (about 50.8 kg). **2** US a unit of weight equal to 100 lb (about 45.4 kg).
■ hundredth adj. & n.

**hung** past & p.p. of HANG. • adj. having no political party with an overall majority. □ hungover suffering from a hangover.

**hunger** n. **1** discomfort and weakness felt when you have not eaten for some time; lack of food. **2** a strong desire. • v. feel hunger. □ hunger strike refusal of food as a form of protest.
▷ SYNS n. **1** LACK OF FOOD, starvation, ravenousness. **2** LONGING, craving, yearning, desire, thirst, appetite, hankering, lust.

**hungry** adj. (**-ier, -iest**) feeling hunger. ■ hungrily adv.
▷ SYNS **1** FAMISHED, ravenous, starving, starved, empty.
**2** LONGING, yearning, craving, eager, keen, desirous, greedy, covetous.

**hunk** n. **1** a large thick chunk.
**2** inf. an attractive man.

**hunt** v. pursue wild animals for food or sport; pursue with hostility; search. • n. an act of hunting; a hunting group.
■ hunter n.
▷ SYNS v. **1** CHASE, pursue, stalk, track, trail, follow, shadow; inf. tail. **2** SEARCH FOR, look for, seek, try to find.

**hurdle** n. a portable fencing panel; a frame to be jumped over in a race; an obstacle or difficulty.
▷ SYNS **1** FENCE, barrier, railing, rail, bar. **2** OBSTACLE, hindrance, impediment, obstruction, stumbling block, snag, complication, difficulty, problem, handicap.

**hurl** v. throw violently.

**hurly-burly** n. bustling activity.

**hurrah** (or **hurray**, **hooray**) exclam. used to express joy or approval.

**hurricane** n. a violent storm with a strong wind.

**hurried** adj. done quickly or too quickly.
▷ SYNS QUICK, rapid, fast, swift, speedy; hasty, rushed, cursory, perfunctory.

**hurry** v. (**hurried, hurrying**) move or act with great or excessive haste. • n. hurrying.
■ **hurriedly** adv.
▷ SYNS v. BE QUICK, make haste, hasten, speed, run, dash, rush, sprint, scurry; inf. get a move on, step on it, hotfoot it.

**hurt** v. (**hurt, hurt, hurting**) cause pain, injury, or grief to; feel pain; offend. • n. injury, harm, or distress.
▷ SYNS v. **1** ACHE, smart, sting, throb, burn. **2** INJURE, wound, bruise, cut, scratch, lacerate, maim, damage, mutilate. **3** UPSET, sadden, grieve, distress, pain, cut to the quick. **4** HARM, damage, spoil, blight, mar, impair.

**hurtful** adj. causing mental pain or distress.
▷ SYNS UPSETTING, distressing, wounding, unkind, cruel, nasty, mean, spiteful, malicious.

**hurtle** v. move or hurl rapidly.

**husband** n. the man a woman is married to. • v. use economically.
▷ SYNS n. SPOUSE, partner, consort; groom, bridegroom.

**husbandry** n. **1** farming. **2** economical management of resources.

**hush** v. **1** make or become silent. **2** (**hush up**) stop from becoming known. • n. silence.
▷ SYNS v. SILENCE, quieten, shush, shut up. • n. QUIET, quietness, silence, stillness, peace, calm, tranquillity.

**husk** n. the dry outer covering of certain seeds and fruits.
• v. remove the husk from.

**husky** adj. (**-ier, -iest**) **1** (of a voice) low and hoarse. **2** big and strong. • n. (pl. **-ies**) an Arctic sledge dog. ■ **huskily** adv.

**hustings** n. a meeting for political candidates to address voters.

**hustle** v. push or move roughly.
• n. busy activity.

**hut** n. a small simple or roughly made house or shelter.
▷ SYNS SHED, lean-to, shack, cabin, shanty, hovel; Scot. bothy.

**hutch** n. a box-like cage for rabbits.

**hyacinth** n. a plant with fragrant bell-shaped flowers.

**hyaena** = HYENA.

**hybrid** n. the offspring of two different species or varieties; something made by combining different elements.

**hydrangea** n. a shrub with clusters of flowers.

**hydrant** n. a water pipe with a nozzle for attaching a fire hose.

**hydrate** v. cause to absorb or combine with water.

**hydraulic** adj. operated by pressure of fluid conveyed in pipes. • n. (**hydraulics**) the science of hydraulic operations.

**hydrocarbon** n. a compound of hydrogen and carbon.

**hydrochloric acid** n. a corrosive acid containing hydrogen and chlorine.

**hydroelectric** adj. using water power to produce electricity.

**hydrofoil** n. a boat with a structure that raises its hull out of the water when in motion.

**hydrogen** n. an odourless gas. □ hydrogen bomb a powerful nuclear bomb.

**hydrophobia** n. extreme fear of water; rabies.

**hyena** (or **hyaena**) n. a doglike African animal.

**hygiene** n. cleanliness as a means of preventing disease.

**hygienic** adj. free of the organisms which spread disease.
▷ SYNS SANITARY, clean, germ-free, disinfected, sterilized, sterile, aseptic, uncontaminated.

**hymen** n. the membrane partly closing the opening of the vagina of a virgin girl or woman.

**hymn** n. a song used in religious worship.

**hype** n. inf. intensive promotion of a product.

**hyperactive** adj. abnormally active.

**hyperbole** n. statements deliberately exaggerated for effect.

**hypermarket** n. a very large supermarket.

**hypertension** n. abnormally high blood pressure.

**hypertext** n. Computing a system allowing rapid movement between documents or sections of text.

**hyperventilate** v. breathe abnormally rapidly.
■ hyperventilation n.

**hyphen** n. a sign (-) used to join words together or mark the division of a word at the end of a line. ■ hyphenate v. hyphenation n.

**hypnosis** n. an induced sleep-like condition in which a person responds readily to commands or suggestions. ■ hypnotic adj.

**hypnotism** n. hypnosis.
■ hypnotist n.

**hypnotize** v. put into a state of hypnosis.
▷ SYNS MESMERIZE, entrance, enthral, spellbind, transfix, bewitch, captivate.

**hypochondria** n. the state of constantly imagining that you are ill. ■ hypochondriac n.

**hypocrisy** n. falsely pretending to be virtuous; insincerity.
▷ SYNS INSINCERITY, falseness, sanctimoniousness, dishonesty, cant, pietism.

**hypocrite** n. a person guilty of hypocrisy.

**hypocritical** adj. a person who claims to have higher moral standards than is the case.
▷ SYNS SANCTIMONIOUS, pious, self-righteous, holier-than-thou, insincere, two-faced.

**hypodermic** adj. injected beneath the skin. • n. a hypo-dermic syringe.

**hypotenuse** n. the longest side of a right-angled triangle.

**hypothermia** n. the condition of having an abnormally low body temperature.

**hypothesis** n. (pl. **-ses**) an idea not yet proved to be correct.
▷ SYNS THEORY, thesis, theorem, proposition, premise, postulate, supposition, assumption, conjecture, speculation.

**hypothetical** adj. supposed but not necessarily true.
■ hypothetically adv.
▷ SYNS THEORETICAL, speculative, notional, academic, suppositional.

**hysterectomy** n. (pl. **-ies**) the surgical removal of the womb.

**hysteria** n. extreme or uncontrollable emotion.
▷ SYNS FRENZY, feverishness, hysterics, delirium, derangement, panic, alarm.

**hysterical** adj. **1** affected by wildly uncontrolled emotion. **2** inf. very funny.

▷ SYNS OVERWROUGHT, out of control, frenzied, frantic, wild, beside yourself, delirious.

**hysterics** pl.n. **1** wildly emotional behaviour. **2** inf. uncontrollable laughter.

# Ii

**I** pron. used by a speaker to refer to himself or herself.

**ice** n. **1** frozen water. **2** an ice cream. • v. **1** decorate with icing. **2** (**ice over**) become covered with ice. □ **iceberg** a large mass of ice floating in the sea. **ice cream** a frozen dessert made with milk fat.

**icicle** n. a piece of ice hanging downwards.

**icing** n. a mixture of powdered sugar and liquid or fat used to decorate cakes.

**icon** n. **1** (also **ikon**) a sacred painting or mosaic. **2** Computing a graphic symbol on a computer screen.

**iconoclast** n. a person who attacks established traditions. ■ **iconoclasm** n.

**icy** adj. (**-ier, -iest**) covered with ice; very cold; very unfriendly. ■ **icily** adv. **iciness** n.
▷ SYNS **1** FREEZING, chilly, frigid, frosty, biting, raw, bitter, arctic, glacial. **2** FROZEN, glassy, slippery; inf. slippy.

**ID** abbr. identification.

**idea** n. **1** a thought or suggestion about a possible course of action. **2** a mental impression. **3** a belief.
▷ SYNS **1** CONCEPT, notion, thought, conception; plan, scheme, suggestion. **2** SENSE, suspicion, inkling, hunch. **3** THOUGHT, theory, feeling, belief, view, opinion.

**ideal** adj. satisfying your idea of what is perfect. • n. a person or thing regarded as perfect; an aim, principle, or standard. ■ **ideally** adv.
▷ SYNS adj. **1** PERFECT, consummate, supreme, flawless, exemplary, classic, archetypal, model. **2** UNATTAINABLE, Utopian, impracticable, ivory-towered, imaginary, romantic, fairy-tale. • n. **1** ARCHETYPE, model, pattern, exemplar, paradigm, yardstick. **2** PRINCIPLE, standard, value; morals, ethics.

**idealist** n. a person with high ideals. ■ **idealism** n.

**idealistic** adj. believing or reflecting a belief that ideals can be achieved.
▷ SYNS UTOPIAN, visionary, romantic, quixotic, unrealistic, impractical.

**idealize** (or **-ise**) v. regard or represent as perfect.

**identical** adj. the same; exactly alike. ■ identically adv.
▷ SYNS **1** THE SAME, the very same, one and the same, selfsame. **2** ALIKE, indistinguishable, corresponding, matching, twin.

**identify** v. (**identified, identifying**) recognize as being a specified person or thing; associate someone closely with someone or something else; feel sympathy for someone. ■ identifiable adj. identification n.
▷ SYNS **1** RECOGNIZE, single out, pick out, spot, point out, pinpoint, discern, distinguish, name. **2** ESTABLISH, find out, ascertain, diagnose. **3** RELATE TO, empathize with, sympathize with, feel for.

**identity** n. **1** who or what someone or something is. **2** being the same.
▷ SYNS **1** NAME, specification. **2** PERSONALITY, self, selfhood, individuality.

**ideology** n. (pl. **-ies**) ideas that form the basis of a political or economic theory.
■ ideological adj.
▷ SYNS DOCTRINE, creed, credo, teaching, dogma, theory, tenets, beliefs, ideas, principles, convictions.

**idiocy** n. (pl. **-ies**) extreme stupidity.

**idiom** n. a phrase whose meaning cannot be deduced from the words in it; an expression natural to a language.
▷ SYNS **1** PHRASE, expression, turn of phrase. **2** LANGUAGE, speech, usage, vocabulary, parlance, jargon; inf. lingo.

**idiomatic** adj. using idioms; sounding natural.
▷ SYNS COLLOQUIAL, informal, vernacular, conversational, natural.

**idiosyncrasy** n. (pl. **-ies**) a way of behaving distinctive of a particular person.
■ idiosyncratic adj.
▷ SYNS PECULIARITY, oddity, eccentricity, trait, mannerism, quirk, habit, characteristic, foible.

**idiot** n. a very stupid person.
■ idiotic adj.
▷ SYNS FOOL, ass, halfwit, blockhead, dunce, simpleton; inf. numbskull, dimwit, moron, twit, berk, muppet, bonehead.

**idle** adj. not employed or in use; lazy; aimless. • v. be idle; move slowly and aimlessly; (of an engine) run slowly in neutral gear. ■ idleness n. idly adv.
▷ SYNS adj. **1** LAZY, indolent, slothful, sluggish, shiftless. **2** INOPERATIVE, out of action, inactive, unused. **3** *idle hours:* EMPTY, unoccupied, vacant, spare, aimless.

**idol** n. an image worshipped as a god; an idolized person or thing.
▷ SYNS **1** ICON, effigy, graven image, fetish, totem. **2** HERO, heroine, star, celebrity, favourite, darling; inf. blue-eyed boy.

**idolatry** n. worship of idols.

**idolize** (or **-ise**) v. love or admire excessively.
▷ SYNS HERO-WORSHIP, worship, adore, dote on, lionize, revere, venerate.

**idyll** n. a happy or peaceful time or situation. ■ **idyllic** adj.

**i.e.** abbr. that is.

**if** conj. **1** on condition that; supposing that. **2** whether.

**igloo** n. a dome-shaped Eskimo snow house.

**ignite** v. set fire to; catch fire.
▷ SYNS **1** SET FIRE TO, light, set on fire, kindle, touch off. **2** CATCH FIRE, burn, burst into flames.

**ignition** n. igniting; a mechanism producing a spark to ignite the fuel in an engine.

**ignoble** adj. not honourable. ■ **ignobly** adv.

**ignominious** adj. deserving or causing public disgrace.
▷ SYNS HUMILIATING, undignified, embarrassing, mortifying, ignoble, inglorious.

**ignominy** n. public disgrace.

**ignorant** adj. lacking knowledge; rude or impolite. ■ **ignorance** n.
▷ SYNS **1** UNEDUCATED, unschooled, illiterate, benighted. **2** *ignorant of the law:* UNAWARE, unfamiliar, unconscious, unacquainted, uninformed, unenlightened; inf. in the dark.

**ignore** v. take no notice of.
▷ SYNS **1** DISREGARD, pay no attention to, take no notice of, brush aside, shrug off, turn a blind eye to, turn a deaf ear to. **2** SLIGHT, spurn, cold-shoulder, send to Coventry, cut.

**iguana** n. a large tropical lizard.

**ikon** = ICON.

**ill** adj. **1** not in good health. **2** bad or harmful: *ill effects.* • adv. badly or wrongly. • n. **1** a problem or misfortune. **2** harm. □ **ill-advised** unwise. **ill-gotten** obtained illegally or unfairly. **ill will** hostility.
▷ SYNS adj. UNWELL, sick, poorly, ailing, sickly, off-colour; nauseous, queasy.

**illegal** adj. against the law. ■ **illegality** n.
▷ SYNS UNLAWFUL, illegitimate, illicit, criminal, felonious, unauthorized, banned, forbidden, prohibited, proscribed, contraband, black-market, bootleg.

**illegible** adj. not readable.

**illegitimate** adj. **1** not allowed by law or rules. **2** born to parents not married to each other. ■ **illegitimacy** n.

**illicit** adj. unlawful or forbidden.

**illiterate** adj. unable to read and write; uneducated. ■ **illiteracy** n.

**illness** n. the state of being ill; a particular type of ill health.
▷ SYNS SICKNESS, ailment, disease, complaint, malady, disorder, affliction, indisposition, infection.

**illogical** adj. not logical. ■ **illogicality** n.
▷ SYNS IRRATIONAL, unreasonable, unsound, incorrect, invalid, erroneous, fallacious, faulty, flawed, specious, unscientific.

**ill-treat** v. treat badly or cruelly.
▷ SYNS MISTREAT, abuse, maltreat, misuse, harm, injure, damage.

**illuminate** v. light up; explain or clarify. ■ **illumination** n.

**illuminating** adj. making something easier to understand.
▷ SYNS INSTRUCTIVE, informative, enlightening, explanatory, revealing, helpful.

**illusion** n. a false belief; a deceptive appearance.

▷ SYNS **1** DELUSION, misapprehension, misconception, fantasy. **2** HALLUCINATION, figment of the imagination, mirage.

**illusionist** n. a conjuror.

**illusory** adj. based on illusion; not real.

▷ SYNS IMAGINED, imaginary, fanciful, fancied, unreal; false, mistaken, misleading.

**illustrate** v. supply a book etc. with drawings or pictures; make clear by using examples, charts, etc.; serve as an example of. ■ **illustrator** n.

▷ SYNS **1** DECORATE, adorn, ornament, embellish. **2** DEMONSTRATE, exemplify, show, display; explain, elucidate, clarify.

**illustration** n. a picture in a book etc.

▷ SYNS PICTURE, drawing, sketch, figure, plate, image.

**illustrious** adj. well known and respected.

**image** n. a picture or other representation; an optical appearance produced in a mirror or through a lens; a mental picture.

▷ SYNS LIKENESS, representation, depiction, portrayal, painting, picture, portrait, effigy, figure, statue, sculpture, bust.

**imagery** n. language producing images in the mind.

**imaginary** adj. existing only in the imagination, not real.

▷ SYNS UNREAL, non-existent, illusory, fanciful, chimerical; fictitious, fictional, mythical, made-up, invented.

**imagination** n. the ability to imagine or to plan creatively.

▷ SYNS CREATIVITY, vision, inventiveness, originality, ingenuity.

**imaginative** adj. having or showing creativity.

▷ SYNS CREATIVE, inventive, original, innovative, visionary, resourceful, ingenious.

**imagine** v. **1** form a mental image of. **2** suppose or assume. **3** believe something unreal to exist. ■ **imaginable** adj.

▷ SYNS **1** VISUALIZE, picture, envision, envisage. **2** ASSUME, presume, expect, suppose, think, believe, take it.

**imbalance** n. lack of balance.

**imbecile** n. a stupid person.

**imbed** = EMBED.

**imbibe** v. drink; absorb ideas.

**imbue** v. fill with feelings, qualities, or emotions.

**imitate** v. **1** follow as a model. **2** copy or mimic. ■ **imitative** adj.

▷ SYNS **1** COPY, emulate, follow, echo. **2** MIMIC, ape, impersonate, parody, mock, caricature; inf. send up, take off.

**imitation** n. **1** a copy. **2** the action of imitating. • adj. not real or genuine.

▷ SYNS n. **1** COPY, reproduction, replica, simulation, forgery. **2** IMPERSONATION, impression, parody, caricature; inf. take-off, spoof. • adj. ARTIFICIAL, synthetic, simulated, man-made, mock, fake, ersatz.

**immaculate** adj. spotlessly clean and tidy; free from blemish or fault.

**immaterial** adj. **1** having no physical substance. **2** of no importance.

**immature** adj. **1** not fully grown. **2** childish or irresponsible. ■ **immaturity** n.

▷ SYNS CHILDISH, juvenile, infantile, babyish, puerile, callow, jejune, inexperienced, unsophisticated.

**immeasurable** adj. too large or extreme to measure. ■ **immeasurably** adv.

**immediate** adj. **1** done or occurring without delay. **2** nearest in time, space, etc. ■ **immediacy** n.
▷ SYNS INSTANT, instantaneous, prompt, swift, speedy; sudden, abrupt, precipitate.

**immediately** adv. at once.
▷ SYNS RIGHT AWAY, straight away, at once, instantly, now, directly.

**immemorial** adj. extremely old.

**immense** adj. extremely great. ■ **immensity** n.
▷ SYNS HUGE, vast, massive, enormous, gigantic, colossal, giant, great, extensive, monumental, tremendous, prodigious, elephantine, titanic.

**immerse** v. **1** put completely into liquid. **2** involve deeply in an activity. ■ **immersion** n.
▷ SYNS **1** SUBMERGE, plunge, dip, dunk, duck, sink. **2** ABSORB, engross, occupy, engage, preoccupy, involve, bury.

**immigrant** n. a person who comes to live permanently in a foreign country.
▷ SYNS SETTLER, newcomer, incomer, migrant, non-native.

**immigration** n. the act of coming to live permanently in a foreign country. ■ **immigrate** v.

**imminent** adj. about to occur. ■ **imminence** n.
▷ SYNS IMPENDING, approaching, close at hand, near, coming, forthcoming, in the offing, on the horizon, on the way, brewing, looming.

**immobile** adj. not moving or unable to move. ■ **immobility** n. **immobilize** v.
▷ SYNS UNMOVING, motionless, still, static, stationary, at a standstill, stock-still, rooted to the spot.

**immolate** v. kill as a sacrifice.

**immoral** adj. morally wrong. ■ **immorality** n.
▷ SYNS BAD, wicked, evil, unprincipled, dishonest, unethical, sinful, corrupt, depraved, vile, base, degenerate, debauched, dissolute, indecent, lewd, licentious.

**immortal** adj. **1** living for ever. **2** deserving to be remembered forever. ■ **immortality** n. **immortalize** v.
▷ SYNS UNDYING, deathless, eternal, everlasting, imperishable, indestructible.

**immovable** adj. **1** unable to be moved. **2** unable to be changed.

**immune** adj. **1** resistant to infection. **2** not affected. **3** exempt or protected. ■ **immunity** n. **immunize** v.

**immure** v. confine or imprison.

**immutable** adj. unchangeable.

**imp** n. a small devil; a mischievous child.

**impact** n. **1** a collision. **2** a noticeable effect. ● v. **1** hit another object. **2** have a strong effect.
▷ SYNS n. **1** COLLISION, crash, smash, bump, knock. **2** EFFECT, influence; consequences, repercussions.

**impair** v. damage or weaken. ■ **impairment** n.
▷ SYNS WEAKEN, lessen, decrease, reduce, diminish, damage, mar, spoil, injure, harm, hinder, impede, undermine.

**impala** n. (pl. **impala**) an African antelope with lyre-shaped horns.

**impale** v. fix or pierce with a pointed object.

**impart** v. **1** communicate information. **2** give a quality to.
▷ SYNS COMMUNICATE, pass on, convey, transmit, relay, tell, make known, report.

**impartial** adj. not favouring one more than another.
■ impartiality n.
▷ SYNS UNBIASED, unprejudiced, neutral, disinterested, detached, objective.

**impassable** adj. impossible to travel on or over.

**impasse** n. a deadlock.

**impassioned** adj. strongly emotional.

**impassive** adj. not feeling or showing emotion.

**impatient** adj. **1** intolerant or easily irritated. **2** restlessly eager. ■ impatience n.
▷ SYNS **1** RESTLESS, restive, agitated, nervous, edgy. **2** EAGER, anxious, keen, yearning, longing. **3** IRRITABLE, testy, tetchy, snappy, querulous, peevish, short-tempered, intolerant.

**impeach** v. charge a public official with a serious crime.
■ impeachment n.

**impeccable** adj. faultless.
■ impeccably adv.

**impede** v. hinder.
▷ SYNS HINDER, obstruct, hamper, handicap, block, check, curb, bar, hold up/back, delay, interfere with, disrupt, slow down, thwart, frustrate, baulk, stop.

**impediment** n. **1** a hindrance. **2** a defect in speech.

▷ SYNS HINDRANCE, obstruction, obstacle, barrier, bar, block.

**impel** v. (**impelled**, **impelling**) force to do something.

**impending** adj. imminent.

**impenetrable** adj. **1** impossible to enter or pass through. **2** incomprehensible.

**imperative** adj. **1** essential or vital. **2** giving a command. **3** Grammar (of a verb) expressing a command. • n. an essential thing.

**imperceptible** adj. too slight to be noticed.
▷ SYNS UNNOTICEABLE, indiscernible, invisible; slight, small, subtle, faint, fine, negligible, microscopic, minute.

**imperfect** adj. **1** faulty or incomplete. **2** Grammar (of a tense) referring to a past action not yet completed. ■ imperfection n.
▷ SYNS FAULTY, flawed, defective, inferior, damaged, blemished, broken.

**imperial** adj. **1** of an empire or emperor. **2** (of measures) based on a non-metric system formerly used in the UK.
■ imperially adv.

**imperialism** n. the policy of having or extending an empire.
■ imperialist n.

**imperil** v. (**imperilled**, **imperilling**; US **imperiled**) endanger.

**imperious** adj. arrogantly giving orders.
▷ SYNS OVERBEARING, overweening, domineering, peremptory, arrogant, high-handed, assertive, commanding, authoritarian, dictatorial, bossy.

**impersonal** adj. **1** not showing or influenced by personal feeling. **2** lacking human feelings.

▷ SYNS ALOOF, distant, remote, unemotional, formal, stiff, businesslike.

**impersonate** v. pretend to be another person.
■ impersonation n.
▷ SYNS IMITATE, mimic, ape, mock, parody, caricature, masquerade as, pose as, pass yourself off as.

**impertinent** adj. disrespectful or rude. ■ impertinence n.
▷ SYNS INSOLENT, impudent, cheeky, rude, impolite, discourteous, disrespectful, bold, brazen, forward.

**imperturbable** adj. not easily upset or worried.

**impervious** adj. **1** impermeable. **2** (**impervious to**) unaffected by.

**impetuous** adj. acting or done quickly and recklessly.
▷ SYNS IMPULSIVE, hasty, hot-headed, rash, reckless, precipitate, foolhardy, incautious; spontaneous, impromptu, spur-of-the-moment, unthinking, unplanned.

**impetus** n. a moving or driving force.
▷ SYNS **1** MOMENTUM, energy, force, drive, power, propulsion. **2** STIMULUS, motivation, incentive, inducement, inspiration, encouragement, push, boost.

**impinge** v. make an impact; encroach.

**impious** adj. not reverent, esp. towards a god.

**implacable** adj. **1** unwilling to stop being hostile. **2** unstoppable.

**implant** v. insert tissue or a device into a living thing; fix an

idea in the mind. • n. something implanted.

**implausible** adj. not seeming probable.
▷ SYNS UNLIKELY, improbable, hard to believe, unconvincing, far-fetched, incredible, unbelievable.

**implement** n. a tool. • v. put into effect. ■ implementation n.
▷ SYNS n. TOOL, utensil, instrument, device, apparatus, gadget, contraption, appliance. • v. EXECUTE, carry out, perform, enact; fulfil, accomplish, bring about, achieve, realize.

**implicate** v. show or cause to be involved in a crime etc.

**implication** n. something implied; being implicated.
▷ SYNS SUGGESTION, inference, insinuation, innuendo, hint, intimation, imputation.

**implicit** adj. **1** implied but not stated. **2** absolute; total and unquestioning.
▷ SYNS **1** IMPLIED, indirect, unspoken, unstated, tacit, understood. **2** ABSOLUTE, complete, total, wholehearted, utter, unqualified, unconditional, unreserved, unquestioning.

**implore** v. beg earnestly.
▷ SYNS BEG, appeal to, entreat, plead with, beseech, ask, request, importune.

**imply** v. (**implied, implying**) convey without stating directly.
▷ SYNS INSINUATE, hint, suggest, intimate, make out.

**impolite** adj. bad-mannered or rude.

**import** v. bring goods into a country from abroad. • n. **1** an imported item. **2** the act of

importing. **3** implied meaning.
**4** importance.

**important** adj. **1** of great value
or significance. **2** having great
authority and influence.
■ **importance** n.
▷ SYNS **1** SIGNIFICANT, consequential, momentous, major, historic; critical, crucial, vital,
pivotal, urgent, essential, far-
reaching, serious, grave,
weighty. **2** POWERFUL, influential, high-ranking, prominent,
eminent, pre-eminent, notable,
distinguished, esteemed,
respected, prestigious.

**importune** v. make insistent
requests to.

**impose** v. **1** force something to
be done or accepted. **2** (**impose
on**) take unfair advantage of.
■ **imposition** n.

**imposing** adj. impressive.
▷ SYNS IMPRESSIVE, striking, grand,
splendid, majestic, spectacular.

**impossible** adj. **1** not able to
exist, occur, or be done. **2** very
hard to deal with.
■ **impossibility** n. **impossibly** adv.
▷ SYNS OUT OF THE QUESTION, inconceivable, unthinkable, unimaginable, impractical,
unattainable, unworkable.

**impostor** n. a person who
fraudulently pretends to be
someone else.
▷ SYNS FAKE, fraud, charlatan,
mountebank, trickster, cheat;
inf. con man.

**impotent** adj. **1** powerless. **2** (of
a man) unable to achieve an
erection. ■ **impotence** n.

**impound** v. take property into
legal custody.

**impoverish** v. cause to become
poor or weak.

**impracticable** adj. not able to
be put into practice.

**impractical** adj. not showing
realism or common sense; not
sensible or useful.
▷ SYNS UNREALISTIC, unworkable,
unfeasible, impracticable, non-
viable; unsuitable, inappropriate.

**imprecise** adj. not precise.
▷ SYNS INEXACT, approximate,
estimated, rough, inaccurate,
incorrect.

**impregnable** adj. safe against
attack.

**impregnate** v. **1** introduce
sperm or pollen into and fertilize. **2** saturate with a substance.

**impresario** n. (pl. **-ios**)
an organizer of public
entertainment.

**impress** v. **1** cause to feel
admiration. **2** make a mark
with a stamp etc. **3** (**impress
on**) cause to realize the
importance of.
▷ SYNS MAKE AN IMPRESSION ON,
influence, affect, move, stir,
rouse, inspire, excite.

**impression** n. **1** an idea,
feeling, or opinion. **2** an effect
produced on someone. **3** an imitation, done to entertain. **4** a
mark made by pressing.
▷ SYNS **1** FEELING, sense, suspicion,
hunch, inkling, fancy, notion,
idea, opinion. **2** IMPACT, effect,
influence. **3** IMPERSONATION,
imitation, mimicry, parody,
caricature; inf. take-off, send-up.
**4** MARK, indentation, dent,
outline, imprint.

**impressionable** adj. easily
influenced.
▷ SYNS SUGGESTIBLE, susceptible,
pliable, malleable, gullible,
ingenuous, naive.

**impressionist** n. an entertainer who impersonates famous people.

**impressionistic** adj. based on personal impressions.

**impressive** adj. inspiring admiration; grand or awesome.
▷ SYNS IMPOSING, striking, magnificent, splendid, spectacular, stirring, rousing, exciting, powerful, inspiring.

**imprint** v. make a mark on by pressure. • n. 1 a mark made by pressure. 2 a publisher's name etc. in a book.

**imprison** v. put into prison.
▷ SYNS PUT IN PRISON, jail, lock up, put under lock and key, incarcerate, confine, intern.

**imprisonment** n. the state of being imprisoned.
▷ SYNS CUSTODY, incarceration, internment, confinement, detention.

**improbable** adj. not likely to be true or to happen.
▷ SYNS UNLIKELY, doubtful, questionable, dubious, implausible, far-fetched, unconvincing, unbelievable, incredible.

**impromptu** adj. & adv. without preparation or rehearsal.
▷ SYNS UNREHEARSED, ad lib, unprepared, extempore, spontaneous, improvised, unscripted; inf. off-the-cuff.

**improper** adj. not conforming to accepted rules or standards; not decent or modest.
■ impropriety n.
▷ SYNS 1 UNSEEMLY, unbecoming, inappropriate, unsuitable, unethical. 2 INDECENT, off-colour, risqué, suggestive, smutty, obscene, lewd.

**improve** v. make or become better.

▷ SYNS AMELIORATE, amend, reform, rehabilitate, set/put right, correct, rectify, upgrade, revamp, modernize; progress, make progress, pick up, rally, look up.

**improvement** n. 1 the act of improving. 2 a thing that improves or is better than something.
▷ SYNS ADVANCE, development, upgrade, refinement, enhancement, progress; recovery, upswing.

**improvident** adj. not providing for future needs.

**improvise** v. perform drama, music etc. without preparation or a script; make from whatever materials are at hand.
■ improvisation n.

**impudent** adj. disrespectful.
■ impudence n.

**impugn** v. express doubts about the truth or honesty of.

**impulse** n. 1 a sudden urge to do something. 2 a driving force.
▷ SYNS 1 URGE, instinct, compulsion, drive. 2 STIMULUS, inspiration, stimulation, incentive, spur, motivation.

**impulsive** adj. acting or done without prior thought.
▷ SYNS IMPETUOUS, spontaneous, instinctive, unplanned, spur-of-the-moment; hasty, precipitate, rash, reckless, foolhardy, madcap, devil-may-care.

**impunity** n. freedom from punishment or injury.

**impure** adj. 1 mixed with unwanted substances. 2 morally wrong. ■ impurity n.

**impute** v. attribute a fault to someone. ■ imputation n.

**in** prep. 1 enclosed, surrounded, or inside. 2 during or within a period of time. **3** expressing a state or quality. **4** included or involved. **5** indicating the means of expression used. • adv. **1** so as to be enclosed, surrounded, or inside. **2** present at your home or office. **3** expressing arrival. • adj. inf. fashionable.

**inability** n. being unable to do something.

**inaccessible** adj. hard or impossible to reach or understand.

**inaccurate** adj. not accurate.
■ inaccuracy n.
▷ SYNS INEXACT, imprecise, incorrect, wrong, erroneous, faulty, imperfect, flawed, defective, unreliable; fallacious, false, mistaken, untrue.

**inaction** n. lack of action.

**inactive** adj. not active; not working or taking effect.
■ inactivity n.

**inadequate** adj. not of sufficient quantity or quality; incompetent. ■ inadequacy n.
▷ SYNS INSUFFICIENT, lacking, wanting, deficient, in short supply, meagre, scanty, scant, niggardly, scarce, sparse.

**inadmissible** adj. not allowable.

**inadvertent** adj. unintentional.
▷ SYNS ACCIDENTAL, unintentional, unpremeditated, unplanned, unconscious, unwitting, unthinking.

**inane** adj. silly.

**inanimate** adj. not alive; showing no sign of life.
▷ SYNS LIFELESS, insentient, insensate, dead, defunct.

**inappropriate** adj. unsuitable.
▷ SYNS UNSUITABLE, unfitting, out of place, unseemly, unbecoming, improper,
indecorous, inapposite, incongruous, out of keeping.

**inarticulate** adj. not expressed in words; unable to express ideas clearly.
▷ SYNS **1** UNINTELLIGIBLE, incomprehensible, incoherent, unclear, indistinct, mumbled. **2** TONGUE-TIED, lost for words.

**inattentive** adj. not paying attention.

**inaudible** adj. unable to be heard.

**inaugurate** v. introduce a policy etc.; admit formally to office. ■ inaugural adj. inauguration n.

**inauspicious** adj. not likely to lead to success.
▷ SYNS UNPROMISING, unpropitious, unfavourable, unfortunate, ominous.

**inborn** adj. existing from birth.

**inbred** adj. **1** produced by inbreeding. **2** inborn.

**inbreeding** n. breeding from closely related individuals.

**incalculable** adj. too great to be calculated or estimated.

**incandescent** adj. glowing with heat. ■ incandescence n.

**incantation** n. words or sounds uttered as a magic spell.

**incapable** adj. **1** not able to do something. **2** not able to care for yourself.
▷ SYNS INCOMPETENT, inept, inadequate, ineffective, ineffectual.

**incapacitate** v. prevent from functioning normally.

**incarcerate** v. imprison.
■ incarceration n.

**incarnate** adj. embodied, esp. in human form.

**incarnation** n. 1 embodiment, esp. in human form. 2 (**the Incarnation**) that of God as Jesus.

**incendiary** adj. designed to cause fire; tending to provoke conflict. • n. an incendiary bomb.

**incense**[1] n. a substance burnt to produce fragrant smoke.

**incense**[2] v. make angry.

**incentive** n. something that encourages action or effort.

**inception** n. the beginning of something.

**incessant** adj. not ceasing.
▷ SYNS UNCEASING, ceaseless, nonstop, endless, unending, neverending, everlasting, eternal, constant, continual, perpetual, continuous, uninterrupted, unbroken, unremitting.

**incest** n. sex between very closely related people.
■ incestuous adj.

**inch** n. a measure of length (= 2.54 cm). • v. move gradually.

**incidence** n. the rate at which something occurs.

**incident** n. an event, esp. one causing trouble.
▷ SYNS 1 EVENT, happening, occurrence, episode, experience, proceeding, occasion. 2 DISTURBANCE, commotion, scene, row, fracas, contretemps, skirmish, clash, conflict, confrontation.

**incidental** adj. 1 not essential. 2 occurring as a consequence of something else.
▷ SYNS SECONDARY, subsidiary, subordinate, minor, peripheral, inessential, non-essential, inconsequential, tangential.

**incidentally** adv. 1 used to introduce a further or unconnected remark. 2 as a chance occurrence.

**incinerate** v. burn to ashes.
■ incinerator n.

**incipient** adj. beginning to happen or develop.

**incise** v. make a cut in.
■ incision n.

**incisive** adj. clear and decisive.

**incisor** n. a sharp-edged front tooth.

**incite** v. urge on to action; stir up.
▷ SYNS 1 INSTIGATE, provoke, foment, whip up, stir up. 2 ENCOURAGE, urge, egg on, goad, spur, prod, stimulate, drive.

**incivility** n. rudeness.

**inclement** adj. (of weather) unpleasant.

**inclination** n. 1 a tendency; a liking or preference. 2 a slope or slant.
▷ SYNS TENDENCY, leaning, propensity, proclivity, predisposition, weakness, penchant, predilection, partiality, preference, affinity.

**incline** v. lean; bend. • n. a slope. □ inclined to having a tendency to.
▷ SYNS v. 1 TEND, lean, swing, veer. 2 BEND, slope, slant, bank, cant, tilt, lean, tip, list. • n. SLOPE, gradient, hill, declivity, descent, ascent, ramp, rise.

**include** v. 1 have as part of a whole. 2 make or treat as part of a whole.
▷ SYNS 1 INCORPORATE, comprise, encompass, cover, embrace, take in, contain. 2 ADD, allow for, count, take into account.

**inclusion** n. the act of including; a person or thing that is included.

**inclusive** adj. **1** including everything expected or required. **2** including the limits specified.

**incognito** adj. & adv. with your identity kept secret.

**incoherent** adj. disconnected; unclear or confused.
■ incoherence n.
▷ SYNS DISCONNECTED, disjointed, disordered, confused, unclear, mixed up, muddled, jumbled, garbled, rambling, unintelligible, inarticulate.

**income** n. money received as wages, interest, etc.
▷ SYNS SALARY, pay, earnings, wages, remuneration; takings, profits, revenue, proceeds.

**incoming** adj. coming in.

**incommunicado** adj. not allowed or not wishing to communicate with others.

**incomparable** adj. without an equal.
▷ SYNS INIMITABLE, unequalled, matchless, nonpareil, unrivalled, peerless, unparalleled, unsurpassed, superlative, supreme.

**incompatible** adj. conflicting or inconsistent; unable to exist together. ■ incompatibility n.
▷ SYNS UNSUITED, mismatched, ill-matched; irreconcilable, conflicting, discordant.

**incompetent** adj. lacking skill.
■ incompetence n.
▷ SYNS INCAPABLE, inept, inefficient, unqualified, useless, inadequate, deficient, inexpert, unskilful, bungling, amateurish.

**incomplete** adj. not complete.

**incomprehensible** adj. not able to be understood.
■ incomprehension n.

▷ SYNS UNINTELLIGIBLE, impenetrable, indecipherable, over your head, unfathomable, baffling, bewildering, mystifying, arcane, abstruse, recondite.

**inconceivable** adj. unable to be imagined; most unlikely.
▷ SYNS UNIMAGINABLE, unthinkable, incredible, unbelievable, impossible, out of the question.

**inconclusive** adj. not fully convincing.
▷ SYNS INDEFINITE, indeterminate, indecisive, undetermined, unsettled, unresolved, ambiguous.

**incongruous** adj. out of place.
■ incongruity n.
▷ SYNS OUT OF PLACE, inappropriate, discordant, jarring, out of keeping, at odds, strange, odd, unsuitable.

**inconsequential** adj. unimportant.

**inconsiderable** adj. of small size or value.

**inconsiderate** adj. not thinking of others' feelings.
▷ SYNS THOUGHTLESS, unthinking, uncaring, insensitive, tactless, uncharitable, unkind, ungracious, selfish.

**inconsistent** adj. not consistent. ■ inconsistency n.
▷ SYNS INCOMPATIBLE, out of keeping, contrary, at odds, at variance, in opposition, conflicting, in conflict.

**inconspicuous** adj. not noticeable.
▷ SYNS UNOBTRUSIVE, unnoticeable, ordinary, plain, unremarkable, undistinguished, unexceptional.

**inconstant** adj. **1** frequently changing. **2** disloyal.

**incontestable** adj. indisputable.

**incontinent** adj. unable to control your bladder or bowels. ■ incontinence n.

**incontrovertible** adj. undeniable.

**inconvenience** n. difficulty and discomfort; a cause of this. • v. cause inconvenience to. ▷ SYNS n. TROUBLE, bother, disruption, disturbance, problems, annoyance, difficulty; inf. hassle.

**inconvenient** adj. causing trouble or difficulty. ▷ SYNS AWKWARD, difficult, inopportune, unfortunate, troublesome, bothersome.

**incorporate** v. include as a part. ■ incorporation n. ▷ SYNS INCLUDE, embrace, absorb, integrate, assimilate, subsume, embody, encompass.

**incorrect** adj. **1** not right or true. **2** not in accordance with standards. ▷ SYNS WRONG, inaccurate, erroneous, mistaken, wide of the mark, inexact, false, fallacious.

**incorrigible** adj. not able to be reformed or improved. ▷ SYNS INVETERATE, habitual, hardened, incurable, hopeless, unrepentant.

**increase** v. make or become greater. • n. increasing; the amount by which a thing increases. ■ increasingly adv. ▷ SYNS v. GROW, expand, extend, multiply, intensify, heighten, mount, escalate, mushroom, snowball, spread; add to, enhance, build up, enlarge, augment, raise, strengthen, step up. • n. GROWTH, rise, enlargement, expansion,

extension, increment, addition, intensification, escalation.

**incredible** adj. unbelievable; very surprising. ▷ SYNS **1** UNBELIEVABLE, hard to believe, far-fetched, unconvincing, inconceivable, unimaginable, unthinkable, impossible. **2** EXTRAORDINARY, wonderful, great, supreme, tremendous, marvellous, amazing, magnificent, phenomenal, spectacular.

**incredulous** adj. feeling or showing disbelief. ■ incredulity n. ▷ SYNS DISBELIEVING, sceptical, cynical, distrustful, mistrustful, doubtful, dubious, unconvinced, suspicious.

**increment** n. an increase in a number or amount.

**incriminate** v. cause to appear guilty. ▷ SYNS IMPLICATE, involve, inculpate, inform against, blame, accuse, pin the blame on, point the finger at.

**incubate** v. hatch eggs by warmth; cause bacteria etc. to develop. ■ incubation n. incubator n.

**inculcate** v. fix ideas in someone's mind.

**incumbent** adj. forming an obligation or duty. • n. the holder of an office, esp. a rector or a vicar.

**incur** v. (**incurred**, **incurring**) bring something unpleasant on yourself.

**incursion** n. a sudden invasion or raid.

**indebted** adj. owing money or gratitude.

**indecent** adj. **1** not following accepted standards, esp. in

relation to sex. **2** inappropriate.
■ **indecency** n.
▷ SYNS **1** OBSCENE, pornographic, vulgar, dirty, filthy, lewd, salacious, offensive. **2** UNSEEMLY, unsuitable, inappropriate, improper.

**indecisive** adj. not decisive.
■ **indecision** n.
▷ SYNS IRRESOLUTE, hesitant, in two minds, wavering, vacillating, ambivalent, undecided, uncertain.

**indeed** adv. used to emphasize a statement.

**indefatigable** adj. untiring.
▷ SYNS TIRELESS, untiring, unflagging, persistent, tenacious, dogged, assiduous, industrious, indomitable, relentless.

**indefensible** adj. not able to be justified or defended.

**indefinite** adj. not clearly stated or fixed; vague; (of time) not limited. □ **indefinite article** the word *a* or *an*.
■ **indefinitely** adv.
▷ SYNS VAGUE, unclear, imprecise, inexact, ambiguous, ambivalent, equivocal, evasive; indeterminate, unspecified.

**indelible** adj. unable to be removed; unable to be forgotten.

**indelicate** adj. slightly indecent; tactless.
■ **indelicacy** n.

**indemnity** n. (pl. **-ies**) protection against penalties incurred by your actions; money paid as compensation.
■ **indemnify** v.

**indent** v. **1** start a line of text inwards from a margin; form recesses in a surface. **2** place an official order for goods etc.
■ **indentation** n.

**indenture** n. a written contract, esp. of apprenticeship.

**independence** n. the fact or state of being independent.
▷ SYNS **1** SELF-GOVERNMENT, autonomy, self-determination, sovereignty, self-rule, home rule. **2** FREEDOM, liberty, self-sufficiency, self-reliance.

**independent** adj. **1** not ruled or controlled by another. **2** not relying on another; not connected.
▷ SYNS **1** SELF-GOVERNING, autonomous, free, sovereign, self-determining, non-aligned. **2** SELF-SUFFICIENT, self-reliant, self-supporting, standing on your own two feet. **3** SEPARATE, unconnected, unrelated, distinct, different.

**indescribable** adj. too extreme, unusual, etc., to be described.

**indestructible** adj. unable to be destroyed.
▷ SYNS UNBREAKABLE, durable, imperishable, enduring, perennial, deathless, undying, immortal, everlasting.

**indeterminate** adj. not certain; vague.

**index** n. (pl. **indexes** or **indices**) **1** an alphabetical list of names, subjects, etc., with references. **2** an indicator of something.
• v. record in or provide with an index. □ **index finger** the forefinger.

**indicate** v. point out; be a sign of. ■ **indicative** adj.
▷ SYNS SHOW, demonstrate, point to, signal, signify, denote, betoken, suggest, imply; display, manifest, reveal, betray; make known, state, declare.

**indication** n. a sign or piece of information that indicates something.
▷ SYNS SIGN, signal, symptom, mark, demonstration, pointer, hint, clue, omen, warning.

**indicator** n. a thing that indicates; a flashing light on a vehicle showing when it is going to turn.

**indict** v. formally accuse of or charge with a crime.
■ indictment n.

**indifferent** adj. **1** having no interest or sympathy. **2** not very good. ■ indifference n.
▷ SYNS UNCONCERNED, apathetic, uninterested, unenthusiastic, unimpressed, detached, impassive, dispassionate, unresponsive, unmoved.

**indigenous** adj. native.

**indigent** adj. poor.
■ indigence n.

**indigestible** adj. difficult or impossible to digest.

**indigestion** n. discomfort caused by difficulty in digesting food.

**indignant** adj. feeling or showing offence and annoyance. ■ indignantly adv.
▷ SYNS AGGRIEVED, affronted, displeased, angry, irate, annoyed, offended, exasperated.

**indignation** n. anger aroused by something unjust.

**indignity** (pl. **-ies**) humiliating treatment or circumstances.

**indigo** n. a deep blue dye or colour.

**indirect** adj. not direct.
▷ SYNS **1** CIRCUITOUS, roundabout, meandering, winding, zigzag; tortuous. **2** OBLIQUE, inexplicit, implicit, implied.

**indiscreet** adj. too ready to reveal secrets. ■ indiscretion n.
▷ SYNS IMPRUDENT, unwise, incautious, injudicious, illadvised, ill-judged, foolish, impolitic, careless, tactless, insensitive, undiplomatic.

**indiscriminate** adj. done or acting at random; not making a careful choice.
▷ SYNS NON-SELECTIVE, unselective, undiscriminating, aimless, hitor-miss, haphazard, random, arbitrary, unsystematic, unthinking, casual, careless.

**indispensable** adj. essential.
▷ SYNS ESSENTIAL, vital, allimportant, crucial, imperative, key, necessary, requisite.

**indisposed** adj. **1** slightly ill. **2** unwilling. ■ indisposition n.

**indisputable** adj. undeniable.
▷ SYNS INCONTESTABLE, incontrovertible, undeniable, irrefutable, unquestionable, indubitable, certain, sure, definite, conclusive.

**indistinct** adj. unclear; obscure.
▷ SYNS **1** BLURRED, fuzzy, out of focus, bleary, hazy, misty, shadowy, dim, obscure, indefinite. **2** MUFFLED, muted, low, muttered, mumbled.

**indistinguishable** adj. unable to be told apart.

**individual** adj. **1** single; separate. **2** of or for one person. **3** striking or unusual. • n. a single person or item as distinct from a group; a person.
■ individuality n.
▷ SYNS **adj. 1** SINGLE, separate, discrete; independent, lone. **2** CHARACTERISTIC, distinctive, distinct, particular, peculiar, personal, personalized, special; original, striking, unique.

**individualist** n. a person who is very independent in thought or action. ■ individualism n.

**indoctrinate** v. teach someone to accept a set of beliefs uncritically. ■ indoctrination n.

**indolent** adj. lazy. ■ indolence n.

**indoor** adj. situated, used, or done inside a building.
■ indoors adv.

**indubitable** adj. impossible to doubt.

**induce** v. 1 persuade. 2 bring about. 3 bring on childbirth artificially.
▷ SYNS 1 PERSUADE, convince, prevail on, prompt, encourage, talk into. 2 BRING ABOUT, cause, produce, create, give rise to, generate, engender.

**inducement** n. an incentive or bribe.

**induct** v. introduce formally to a post or organization.

**induction** n. 1 inducting. 2 inducing childbirth. 3 reasoning by drawing a general rule from individual cases. ■ inductive adj.

**indulge** v. 1 satisfy a desire; allow someone to have what they want. 2 (**indulge in**) allow yourself something pleasant.
▷ SYNS PAMPER, spoil, mollycoddle, pander to, humour, go along with.

**indulgent** adj. allowing someone to do what they want or overlooking their faults.
■ indulgence n.
▷ SYNS GENEROUS, permissive, easy-going, liberal, tolerant, forgiving, lenient, soft-hearted, kind.

**industrial** adj. of, for, or full of industries. □ industrial action a strike or similar protest.

**industrial estate** an area of land developed for business and industry.

**industrialist** n. an owner or manager of an industrial business.

**industrialize** (or **-ise**) v. develop industries in a country or region on a wide scale. ■ industrialization n.

**industrious** adj. hard-working.
▷ SYNS HARD-WORKING, diligent, assiduous, conscientious, painstaking, indefatigable, tireless, unflagging; busy, active, energetic, vigorous.

**industry** n. (pl. **-ies**) 1 the manufacture of goods in factories; business activity. 2 hard work.

**inebriated** adj. drunk.

**inedible** adj. not fit for eating.

**ineffable** adj. too great or extreme to be described.

**ineffective** adj. not producing the desired effect.
▷ SYNS UNSUCCESSFUL, unproductive, fruitless, unprofitable, abortive, futile, useless, ineffectual, inefficient, inadequate; feeble, inept, lame.

**ineffectual** adj. ineffective; unable to deal with a role or situation.

**inefficient** adj. wasteful of time or resources.

**ineligible** adj. not eligible or qualified.

**inept** adj. lacking skill.
■ ineptitude n.
▷ SYNS INCOMPETENT, incapable, unskilled, inexpert, clumsy, awkward, maladroit, heavy-handed.

**inequality** n. (pl. **-ies**) lack of equality.

▷ SYNS DISPARITY, imbalance, variation, variability, difference, discrepancy, dissimilarity; unfairness, discrimination, bias, prejudice.

**inequitable** adj. unfair or unjust. ■ inequity n.

**inert** adj. without power to move; without active properties; not moving or taking action.

▷ SYNS UNMOVING, motionless, immobile, inanimate, still, stationary, static; dormant, sleeping; unconscious, comatose, lifeless, insentient; idle, inactive, sluggish, lethargic, torpid.

**inertia** n. **1** a tendency to do nothing or to remain unchanged. **2** a property by which matter remains still or continues moving unless acted on by an external force.

**inescapable** adj. unavoidable.

**inessential** adj. not essential.

**inestimable** adj. too great to be measured.

**inevitable** adj. unavoidable. ■ inevitability n.

▷ SYNS UNAVOIDABLE, inexorable, inescapable, ineluctable, fated, destined, predestined; assured, certain, sure.

**inexact** adj. not exact.

**inexcusable** adj. unable to be excused or justified.

**inexorable** adj. impossible to prevent; impossible to persuade.

**inexpensive** adj. not expensive.

**inexperienced** adj. lacking experience. ■ inexperience n.

▷ SYNS UNPRACTISED, untrained, unschooled, unqualified, unskilled, amateur, unseasoned; naive, unsophisticated, callow,

immature, green; inf. wet behind the ears.

**inexpert** adj. unskilful.

**inexplicable** adj. impossible to explain.

▷ SYNS UNACCOUNTABLE, incomprehensible, unfathomable, insoluble; baffling, puzzling, mysterious, strange, mystifying.

**infallible** adj. incapable of failing or being wrong. ■ infallibility n.

▷ SYNS **1** UNFAILING, foolproof, dependable, trustworthy, reliable, sure, certain, guaranteed. **2** UNERRING, faultless, flawless, impeccable, perfect.

**infamous** adj. having a bad reputation. ■ infamy n.

▷ SYNS NOTORIOUS, ill-famed, of ill-repute.

**infancy** n. babyhood or early childhood; an early stage of development.

**infant** n. a child during the earliest stage of its life.

▷ SYNS BABY, child, toddler; Scot. bairn.

**infantile** adj. of infants or infancy; very childish.

▷ SYNS CHILDISH, babyish, puerile, immature, juvenile.

**infantry** n. troops who fight on foot.

**infatuated** adj. feeling an intense passion for someone. ■ infatuation n.

**infect** v. **1** affect with an organism that causes disease. **2** contaminate.

▷ SYNS CONTAMINATE, pollute, taint, blight, poison.

**infection** n. **1** the process of infecting. **2** an infectious disease.

**infectious** adj. **1** (of disease) able to be transmitted through the environment. **2** likely to infect others.
▷ SYNS CONTAGIOUS, communicable, transmissible, catching.

**infer** v. (**inferred**, **inferring**) work out from evidence. ■ inference n.
▷ SYNS DEDUCE, conclude, work out, reason, surmise.

**inferior** adj. lower in status or quality. • n. an inferior person. ■ inferiority n.
▷ SYNS adj. **1** SECOND-CLASS, lower-ranking, subordinate, junior, lowly, humble, menial. **2** SECOND-RATE, substandard, low-quality, shoddy, poor, bad.

**infernal** adj. **1** of hell. **2** inf. irritating.

**inferno** n. (pl. **-os**) a raging fire; hell.

**infertile** adj. unable to have offspring; (of soil) not producing vegetation. ■ infertility n.

**infest** v. be present in a place in large numbers, esp. harmfully. ■ infestation n.
▷ SYNS OVERRUN, spread through, invade, swarm over, beset, plague.

**infidel** n. a person who does not believe in a religion.

**infidelity** n. (pl. **-ies**) unfaithfulness to your sexual partner.
▷ SYNS UNFAITHFULNESS, adultery, faithlessness, disloyalty, treachery, duplicity, deceit.

**infighting** n. conflict within an organization.

**infiltrate** v. make your way into a group etc. secretly and gradually. ■ infiltration n.

**infinite** adj. having no end or limit; very great.

▷ SYNS **1** BOUNDLESS, unbounded, unlimited, limitless, without end. **2** COUNTLESS, numberless, innumerable, immeasurable, incalculable, untold, inestimable, indeterminable.

**infinitesimal** adj. very small.
▷ SYNS TINY, minute, microscopic, minuscule, inappreciable, imperceptible.

**infinitive** n. the form of a verb not indicating tense, number, or person (e.g. *to go*).

**infinity** n. (pl. **-ies**) being infinite; an infinite number, space, or time.

**infirm** adj. weak from age or illness. ■ infirmity n.
▷ SYNS FEEBLE, enfeebled, weak, frail, debilitated, decrepit, ailing, ill, unwell, sick, poorly.

**infirmary** n. (pl. **-ies**) a hospital.

**inflame** v. **1** make something worse. **2** cause inflammation in.
▷ SYNS PROVOKE, incite, arouse, stir up, kindle, ignite.

**inflammable** adj. easily set on fire.

**inflammation** n. redness, heat, and pain in a part of the body.

**inflammatory** adj. arousing strong feeling or anger.

**inflate** v. **1** expand by filling with air or gas. **2** exaggerate. ■ inflatable n.
▷ SYNS BLOW UP, pump up, puff up/out, dilate, distend, swell.

**inflation** n. **1** the act of inflating. **2** a general increase in prices. ■ inflationary adj.

**inflect** v. **1** change the pitch of a voice in speaking. **2** Grammar change the ending or form of a word. ■ inflection n.

**inflexible** adj. **1** unable to be altered. **2** unwilling to change or compromise. **3** unable to be bent. ■ inflexibility n.
▷ SYNS **1** UNALTERABLE, hard and fast, unchangeable, immutable, unvarying, firm, fixed, entrenched. **2** STUBBORN, obstinate, intractable, intransigent, unbending, uncompromising, adamant.

**inflict** v. impose something painful or unpleasant on someone. ■ infliction n.
▷ SYNS ADMINISTER, deal out, mete out, deliver; impose, exact, wreak; foist.

**influence** n. power to produce an effect, esp. on character, beliefs, or actions; a person or thing with this power. • v. exert influence on. ■ influential adj.
▷ SYNS n. EFFECT, impact, control, sway, power, hold, authority; leverage; inf. clout. • v. AFFECT, have an effect on, sway, determine, guide, control, shape.

**influenza** n. a viral disease causing fever, muscular pain, and catarrh.

**influx** n. an arrival of large numbers of people or things.

**inform** v. give information to; reveal criminal activities to the authorities; showing knowledge or understanding. ■ informant n. informer n.
▷ SYNS **1** TELL, advise, apprise, notify, acquaint, brief, enlighten; inf. fill in. **2** (**inform on**) BETRAY, incriminate, inculpate; inf. grass on, rat on.

**informal** adj. relaxed; unofficial; casual. ■ informality n.
▷ SYNS CASUAL, unceremonious, unofficial, simple, unpretentious, everyday, relaxed, easy.

**information** n. facts told or discovered.
▷ SYNS DETAILS, particulars, facts, figures, statistics, data; knowledge, intelligence, news; inf. the low-down.

**informative** adj. giving information.
▷ SYNS INSTRUCTIVE, illuminating, enlightening, edifying, educational, revealing; newsy.

**infrared** adj. of or using radiation with a wavelength just greater than that of red light.

**infrastructure** n. the basic structural parts of something; roads, sewers, etc. regarded as a country's basic facilities.

**infrequent** adj. not frequent.
▷ SYNS RARE, occasional, irregular, sporadic, unusual, few and far between, intermittent; inf. once in a blue moon.

**infringe** v. break a rule or agreement; encroach. ■ infringement n.
▷ SYNS BREAK, disobey, violate, contravene, transgress, breach, disregard, defy, flout.

**infuriate** v. make very angry.

**infuse** v. **1** fill with a quality. **2** soak tea or herbs to bring out flavour. ■ infusion n.

**ingenious** adj. clever, original, and inventive. ■ ingenuity n.
▷ SYNS CLEVER, intelligent, smart, sharp, talented, brilliant, resourceful, inventive, imaginative, creative, original, subtle; crafty, wily, cunning.

**ingenuous** adj. innocent and unsuspecting.
▷ SYNS NAIVE, innocent, trusting, trustful, wide-eyed, inexperienced, green; open, sincere, honest, candid, artless, guileless.

**inglorious** adj. rather shameful.

**ingot** n. a brick-shaped lump of cast metal.

**ingrained** adj. deeply embedded in a surface or in a person's character.

**ingratiate** v. gain favour by flattery or trying to please.

**ingratitude** n. lack of gratitude.

**ingredient** n. any of the parts in a mixture.

**inhabit** v. live in as your home.
▷ SYNS LIVE IN, dwell in, reside in, occupy; people, populate.

**inhabitant** n. a person or animal that lives in or occupies a place.
▷ SYNS RESIDENT, dweller, occupier, occupant; local, native.

**inhale** v. breathe in air, smoke, gas, etc. ■ inhalation n.

**inhaler** n. a portable device used for inhaling a drug.

**inherent** adj. existing in something as a natural or permanent quality.
▷ SYNS 1 INTRINSIC, built-in, essential, basic, fundamental. 2 INNATE, inborn, congenital, natural.

**inherit** v. 1 receive property or a title from someone when they die. 2 have a characteristic passed on from parents or ancestors.

**inheritance** n. property or a title received on the death of the previous owner.
▷ SYNS LEGACY, bequest, endowment, birthright, heritage, patrimony.

**inhibit** v. restrain or prevent; cause inhibitions in.

▷ SYNS IMPEDE, hold back, prevent, stop, hamper, hinder, obstruct, interfere with, curb, restrict, restrain, constrain.

**inhibited** adj. unable to act naturally or express your feelings.
▷ SYNS SHY, reticent, self-conscious, reserved, repressed, insecure.

**inhibition** n. a feeling that makes you unable to act in a natural or relaxed way.

**inhospitable** adj. unwelcoming; (of a place) with a harsh climate or landscape.
▷ SYNS 1 UNWELCOMING, unfriendly, unsociable, discourteous, ungracious, cool, cold, aloof, unkind, unsympathetic, hostile, inimical. 2 BLEAK, bare, uninviting, desolate, lonely, empty.

**inhuman** (or **inhumane**) adj. brutal or cruel. ■ inhumanity n.

**inimical** adj. hostile; harmful.
▷ SYNS 1 HOSTILE, unfriendly, unwelcoming, antagonistic. 2 HARMFUL, injurious, detrimental, damaging; formal deleterious.

**inimitable** adj. impossible to imitate.

**iniquity** n. (pl. -ies) great injustice; wickedness.
■ iniquitous adj.

**initial** n. the first letter of a word or name. • v. (initialled, initialling; US initialed) mark or sign with initials. • adj. existing at the beginning.
▷ SYNS adj. FIRST, opening, early, primary, preliminary, introductory, inaugural.

**initiate** v. 1 cause a process etc. to begin. 2 admit to membership of a secret group;

introduce to a skill or activity.
■ **initiation** n.
▷ SYNS BEGIN, start, commence, open, institute, inaugurate, get under way, put in place, launch, originate, pioneer.

**initiative** n. **1** the capacity to invent and initiate ideas. **2** a position from which you can act to forestall others. **3** a fresh approach to a problem.
▷ SYNS ENTERPRISE, resourcefulness, inventiveness, originality, creativity, drive, dynamism, ambition.

**inject** v. **1** force liquid into the body with a syringe. **2** introduce a new element into a situation etc. ■ **injection** n.

**injunction** n. an authoritative order, esp. one made by a judge.
▷ SYNS COMMAND, instruction, order, ruling, direction, directive, dictate, decree.

**injure** v. cause injury to.
▷ SYNS HURT, harm, damage, wound; impair, spoil, mar, blight.

**injurious** adj. harmful.
▷ SYNS HARMFUL, bad, damaging, detrimental; formal deleterious.

**injury** n. **1** an instance of being harmed. **2** harm or damage.
▷ SYNS **1** wound, bruise, cut, gash, graze, lesion. **2** HARM, hurt, damage.

**injustice** n. **1** lack of justice. **2** an unjust act.
▷ SYNS UNFAIRNESS, unjustness, inequity; bias, prejudice, discrimination.

**ink** n. coloured liquid used in writing, printing, etc. • v. apply ink to. ■ **inky** adj.

**inkling** n. a slight suspicion.
▷ SYNS IDEA, notion, sense, impression, suggestion, indication, suspicion, hunch; hint, clue.

**inland** adj. & adv. in or towards the interior of a country.

**in-law** n. a relative by marriage.

**inlay** v. (**inlaid**, **inlaying**) decorate by embedding pieces of another material in a surface. • n. inlaid material or design.

**inlet** n. **1** an arm of the sea etc. extending inland. **2** a way in (e.g. for water into a tank).

**inmate** n. a person living in a prison or other institution.

**inn** n. a pub.

**innards** pl.n. inf. the stomach and bowels; the inner parts.

**innate** adj. inborn; natural.
▷ SYNS INBORN, inbred, congenital, hereditary, inherited, inherent, intrinsic, ingrained, natural.

**inner** adj. inside or nearer to the centre or inside.
■ **innermost** adj.
▷ SYNS INTERIOR, inside, central, middle.

**innings** n. (in cricket) a batsman's or side's turn at batting.

**innocent** adj. **1** not guilty. **2** having no experience of life. **3** not intended to offend. ■ **innocence** n.
▷ SYNS **1** GUILTLESS, blameless, in the clear, above suspicion, irreproachable. **2** NAIVE, ingenuous, trusting, credulous, inexperienced, unsophisticated, unworldly, artless.

**innocuous** adj. harmless.
▷ SYNS SAFE, harmless, inoffensive.

**innovate** v. introduce something new. ■ **innovation** n. **innovative** adj.

**innuendo** n. a remark indirectly referring to something.

▷ SYNS INSINUATION, implication, intimation, suggestion, hint, overtone, undertone.

**innumerable** adj. too many to be counted.

**inoculate** v. protect against disease with vaccines or serums. ■ inoculation n.

**inoperable** adj. unable to be cured by surgical operation.

**inoperative** adj. not functioning.

**inopportune** adj. happening at an unsuitable time.

**inordinate** adj. excessive.

**inpatient** n. a patient staying in a hospital during treatment.

**input** n. something put in or contributed for use or processing; supplying or putting in.

**inquest** n. a judicial investigation, esp. of a sudden death.

**inquire** v. make an inquiry.
▷ SYNS ASK, investigate, question, query, research, look into, examine, explore, probe, scrutinize, study.

**inquisition** n. an act of detailed or relentless questioning. ■ inquisitor n.

**inquisitive** adj. curious; prying.
▷ SYNS INQUIRING, questioning, curious, interested; intrusive, meddlesome, prying; inf. nosy.

**insalubrious** adj. unwholesome.

**insane** adj. 1 seriously mentally ill. 2 very foolish. ■ insanity n.

**insanitary** adj. dirty and unhygienic.

**insatiable** adj. impossible to satisfy.

**inscribe** v. write or carve words on a surface; write a dedication on or in.

**inscription** n. words inscribed.

**inscrutable** adj. impossible to understand or interpret.
▷ SYNS ENIGMATIC, impenetrable, unreadable, cryptic.

**insect** n. a small creature with six legs, no backbone, and a segmented body.

**insecticide** n. a substance for killing insects.

**insecure** adj. 1 not firmly fixed or attached. 2 lacking confidence.

**inseminate** v. insert semen into. ■ insemination n.

**insensible** adj. unconscious; numb.

**insensitive** adj. not sensitive. ■ insensitivity n.
▷ SYNS 1 HEARTLESS, uncaring, unfeeling, callous, tactless, thick-skinned, inconsiderate, thoughtless. 2 IMPERVIOUS, immune, oblivious, unaffected.

**inseparable** adj. impossible to separate or treat separately.

**insert** v. place, fit, or add into. • n. a loose page or section in a magazine. ■ insertion n.

**inset** n. a thing inserted. • v. (**inset**, **insetting**) insert.

**inshore** adj. & adv. at sea but near or towards the shore.

**inside** n. 1 an inner side, part, or surface. 2 (**insides**) inf. the stomach and bowels. • adj. on or in the inside. • prep. & adv. 1 situated or moving within. 2 within a specified time. □ inside out 1 with the inner side turned outwards. 2 thoroughly.

**insidious** adj. proceeding in a gradual and harmful way.
▷ SYNS STEALTHY, subtle, surreptitious, cunning, crafty, sly, wily.

**insight** n. intuitive perception and understanding.

**insignia** pl.n. symbols of authority or office; an identifying badge.

**insignificant** adj. of little importance or value.
■ insignificance n.
▷ SYNS UNIMPORTANT, trivial, trifling, negligible, inconsequential, petty.

**insincere** adj. saying things that you do not mean. ■ insincerely adv. insincerity n.
▷ SYNS UNTRUTHFUL, dishonest, deceptive, disingenuous, hypocritical, deceitful, duplicitous, double-dealing, two-faced, mendacious, false, fake, put-on, feigned.

**insinuate** v. 1 indirectly suggest something discreditable. 2 gradually move yourself into a favourable position.
■ insinuation n.
▷ SYNS IMPLY, hint, suggest, indicate, intimate.

**insipid** adj. lacking flavour, interest, or liveliness.

**insist** v. demand or state emphatically.
▷ SYNS MAINTAIN, assert, declare, contend, protest, swear, stress, reiterate.

**insistent** adj. insisting; forcing itself on your attention.
■ insistence n.
▷ SYNS PERSISTENT, determined, adamant, importunate, tenacious, dogged, unrelenting; urgent; emphatic, firm, assertive.

**insolent** adj. disrespectful and rude. ■ insolence n.
▷ SYNS IMPERTINENT, impudent, cheeky, rude, ill-mannered, impolite, disrespectful, insulting.

**insoluble** adj. 1 impossible to solve. 2 unable to be dissolved.

**insolvent** adj. unable to pay your debts. ■ insolvency n.
▷ SYNS BANKRUPT, penniless, impoverished, penurious, impecunious; inf. broke.

**insomnia** n. inability to sleep.
■ insomniac n.

**inspect** v. examine critically or officially.
▷ SYNS EXAMINE, check, look over, survey, scrutinize, vet, study, view, investigate, assess, appraise.

**inspection** n. the act of inspecting.
▷ SYNS EXAMINATION, check-up, survey, scrutiny, exploration, investigation.

**inspector** n. 1 a person who inspects. 2 a police officer above sergeant.

**inspiration** n. being inspired; a sudden brilliant idea; someone or something inspiring.
■ inspirational adj.
▷ SYNS 1 STIMULUS, stimulation, motivation, fillip, encouragement, goad, spur; muse, influence. 2 CREATIVITY, originality, inventiveness, genius, vision.

**inspire** v. stimulate to activity; encourage a feeling; cause to feel uplifted.
▷ SYNS 1 STIMULATE, motivate, encourage, influence, rouse, stir, energize, galvanize. 2 *she inspired affection:* AROUSE, awaken, prompt, kindle, produce.

**instability** n. lack of stability.

**install** v. place a person into office ceremonially; set in position and ready for use.
■ installation n.

**instalment** (US **installment**) n. one of the regular payments made to clear a debt paid over a period of time; one part of a serial.

**instance** n. an example; a particular case. • v. mention as an example.
▷ SYNS n. CASE (IN POINT), example, illustration, occasion, occurrence.

**instant** adj. happening or done immediately; (of food) quickly and easily prepared. • n. an exact moment; a very short time.
▷ SYNS adj. INSTANTANEOUS, immediate, prompt, rapid, swift, speedy; sudden, abrupt. • n. MOMENT, minute, second; juncture, point.

**instantaneous** adj. occurring or done instantly.

**instead** adv. as an alternative.

**instep** n. the middle part of the foot.

**instigate** v. bring about an action; urge to act.
■ instigation n.
▷ SYNS 1 SET IN MOTION, start, commence, begin, initiate, launch, institute, put in place, organize. 2 INCITE, encourage, urge, goad, provoke, spur on, push, motivate, persuade.

**instil** (US **instill**) v. (**instilled**, **instilling**) introduce ideas etc. into a person's mind gradually.

**instinct** n. an inborn impulse; a natural tendency or ability.
▷ SYNS 1 NATURAL FEELING, tendency, inclination, intuition, sixth sense. 2 TALENT, gift, ability, flair, aptitude, knack, bent.

**instinctive** adj. based on instinct.

▷ SYNS INTUITIVE, natural, innate, inborn, inherent; unconscious, subconscious, automatic, reflex, knee-jerk; inf. gut.

**institute** n. an organization for promotion of science, education, etc. • v. begin or establish.
▷ SYNS n. ORGANIZATION, establishment, institution, foundation, society, association.

**institution** n. 1 an important organization. 2 a home providing care for people with special needs. 3 an established law or custom.
■ institutional adj.

**instruct** v. 1 teach a subject or skill to. 2 give instructions to.
▷ SYNS 1 TELL, order, direct, command, charge, enjoin. 2 TEACH, educate, tutor, coach, train, school, drill, prime.

**instruction** n. 1 the process of teaching. 2 an order. 3 (**instructions**) an explanation of how to do or use something.
■ instructional adj.
▷ SYNS 1 TEACHING, education, coaching, training, schooling. 2 DIRECTIVE, direction, order, command, injunction, dictate, bidding.

**instructive** adj. informative.
▷ SYNS INFORMATIVE, educational, enlightening, illuminating, revealing, useful, helpful, edifying.

**instructor** n. a teacher or coach.
▷ SYNS TEACHER, tutor, coach, trainer.

**instrument** n. 1 a tool for delicate work. 2 a measuring device. 3 a device for producing musical sounds.

▷ SYNS IMPLEMENT, tool, appliance, apparatus, mechanism, utensil, gadget, contrivance, device.

**instrumental** adj. 1 important in achieving something. 2 performed on musical instruments.
■ instrumentalist n.

**insubordinate** adj. disobedient, rebellious.
■ insubordination n.
▷ SYNS DEFIANT, rebellious, mutinous, disobedient, refractory, recalcitrant, undisciplined, unruly, disorderly, wayward.

**insubstantial** adj. lacking reality or solidity.

**insufferable** adj. intolerable.

**insufficient** adj. not enough.
▷ SYNS INADEQUATE, deficient, in short supply, scarce, meagre, scant, scanty, at a premium.

**insular** adj. 1 of an island. 2 narrow-minded. ■ insularity n.
▷ SYNS NARROW-MINDED, provincial, parochial, blinkered; intolerant, prejudiced, biased, bigoted.

**insulate** v. 1 cover with material to prevent the passage of heat, sound, or electricity. 2 protect from something unpleasant.
■ insulation n.

**insulin** n. a hormone controlling the body's absorption of sugar.

**insult** v. speak or act so as to offend someone. • n. an insulting remark or act.
▷ SYNS v. ABUSE, slight, disparage, malign, defame, denigrate; offend, hurt. • n. JIBE, affront, slight, slur, dig.

**insuperable** adj. impossible to overcome.

**insupportable** adj. unbearable.

**insurance** n. 1 a contract to provide compensation for loss, damage, or death. 2 money paid by or to an insurance company. 3 a safeguard.

**insure** v. 1 protect by insurance. 2 ensure.
▷ SYNS INDEMNIFY, cover, underwrite, guarantee.

**insurgent** adj. rebellious.
• n. a rebel.

**insurmountable** adj. too great to be overcome.

**insurrection** n. a rebellion.

**intact** adj. undamaged.
▷ SYNS WHOLE, complete, entire, perfect, in one piece, unbroken, undamaged.

**intake** n. an amount of a substance taken into the body; people entering an establishment at a particular time.

**intangible** adj. not solid or real; vague and abstract.
▷ SYNS 1 IMPALPABLE, incorporeal, ethereal. 2 INDEFINABLE, indescribable, vague, subtle, elusive.

**integer** n. a whole number.

**integral** adj. necessary to make a whole complete.
▷ SYNS ESSENTIAL, necessary, indispensable, basic, fundamental, inherent, intrinsic, innate.

**integrate** v. combine parts into a whole; cause to be accepted in a social group. ■ integration n.
▷ SYNS COMBINE, amalgamate, merge, unite, blend, consolidate, intermingle, mix; incorporate, unify, assimilate.

**integrity** n. honesty.
▷ SYNS HONESTY, rectitude, virtue, probity, principle, morality, honour, decency.

**intellect** n. the ability to think logically and understand things.
▷ SYNS MIND, brain, intelligence, reason, understanding, thought.

**intellectual** adj. **1** of the intellect. **2** having a highly developed intellect. • n. an intellectual person.
▷ SYNS adj. **1** MENTAL, cerebral, cognitive. **2** INTELLIGENT, academic, educated, well read, erudite, learned, bookish, highbrow, scholarly, studious.

**intelligence** n. **1** the ability to gain and apply knowledge and skills. **2** secret information obtained about an opponent.
▷ SYNS INTELLECT, mind, brain, brainpower, reason, understanding, acumen, wit, cleverness; inf. nous.

**intelligent** adj. having great mental ability.
▷ SYNS CLEVER, bright, sharp, quick-witted, smart, perceptive, educated, knowledgeable.

**intelligentsia** n. educated and cultured people.

**intelligible** adj. able to be understood.
▷ SYNS UNDERSTANDABLE, comprehensible, clear, lucid, plain, straightforward, legible, decipherable.

**intend** v. **1** have as an aim or plan. **2** plan a particular use, role, or meaning for.
▷ SYNS PLAN, aim, propose, mean, be resolved, be determined.

**intense** adj. **1** great in force, strength, or degree. **2** very earnest. ■ intensity n.
▷ SYNS **1** EXTREME, great, acute, fierce, severe, strong, powerful, violent. **2** EARNEST, eager, keen, zealous, impassioned, passionate, vehement.

**intensify** v. increase in force, strength, or degree.
▷ SYNS ESCALATE, increase, step up, raise, strengthen, heighten, deepen, extend.

**intensive** adj. **1** involving much effort over a short time. **2** aiming to achieve maximum yields.
▷ SYNS THOROUGH, thoroughgoing, in-depth, exhaustive, complete; vigorous, strenuous, concentrated.

**intent** n. an aim, plan, or purpose. • adj. **1** (intent on) determined to do. **2** showing concentrated attention.
▷ SYNS adj. **1** BENT, set, determined, insistent, resolved, keen. **2** ATTENTIVE, absorbed, engrossed, enthralled, fascinated, rapt, focused.

**intention** n. an aim or plan.
▷ SYNS AIM, plan, purpose, intent, objective, goal.

**intentional** adj. done on purpose.
▷ SYNS DELIBERATE, wilful, purposeful, planned, calculated, conscious, premeditated, prearranged.

**inter** v. (interred, interring) bury a dead body. ■ interment n.

**interact** v. have an effect on each other. ■ interactive adj.

**intercede** v. intervene on someone's behalf.

**intercept** v. stop or catch between a starting point and destination. ■ interception n.
▷ SYNS CUT OFF, stop, head off, block, obstruct, impede, interrupt, waylay.

**interchange** v. **1** (of two people) exchange things.

**2** cause to change places. • n. **1** a process of interchanging. **2** a road junction built on several levels.

**intercom** n. an electrical device allowing one-way or two-way communication.

**intercontinental** adj. between continents.

**intercourse** n. **1** dealings between people or countries. **2** sexual intercourse.

**interest** n. **1** eagerness to know about something or someone. **2** the quality of arousing such a feeling. **3** a subject arousing enthusiasm or concern. **4** money paid for the use of money lent. **5** a person's advantage. **6** a share in a business. • v. make curious or attentive.
▷ SYNS n. **1** ATTENTIVENESS, attention, curiosity. **2** *a matter of interest:* CONCERN, consequence, importance, import, moment, significance, note, relevance. **3** HOBBY, pastime, diversion, amusement, pursuit. • v. APPEAL TO, attract, intrigue, amuse, entertain.

**interested** adj. not impartial.
▷ SYNS CONCERNED, involved, affected.

**interesting** adj. arousing curiosity or interest.
▷ SYNS ABSORBING, engrossing, fascinating, riveting, gripping, compelling, captivating, appealing, entertaining, stimulating, intriguing.

**interface** n. **1** a place where interaction occurs. **2** Computing a program or apparatus connecting two machines or enabling a user to use a program.

**interfere** v. **1** prevent from continuing or operating. **2** become involved in something without being asked.
▷ SYNS **1** HINDER, inhibit, impede, obstruct, check, block, hamper, handicap. **2** MEDDLE, butt in, intervene; inf. poke your nose in.

**interference** n. **1** the act of interfering. **2** disturbance to radio signals.

**interim** n. an intervening period. • adj. temporary.
▷ SYNS adj. TEMPORARY, provisional, stopgap, caretaker, acting.

**interior** adj. inner. • n. the inner part; the inside.

**interject** v. say something suddenly as an interruption.
■ interjection n.

**interlock** v. (of two things) fit into each other.

**interloper** n. an intruder.

**interlude** n. **1** an interval. **2** music or other entertainment provided during an interval.
▷ SYNS INTERVAL, intermission, break, pause, rest, respite, breathing space, hiatus.

**intermarry** v. (**intermarried**, **intermarrying**) (of people of different races or religions) marry each other.
■ intermarriage n.

**intermediary** n. (pl. **-ies**) a person who tries to settle a dispute.
▷ SYNS MEDIATOR, go-between, negotiator, arbitrator, middleman, broker.

**intermediate** adj. **1** coming between two things in time, place, etc. **2** having more than basic knowledge or skills.
▷ SYNS HALFWAY, in-between, middle, mid, midway, intervening, transitional.

**interminable** adj. lasting a very long time.
▷ SYNS ENDLESS, never-ending, everlasting, incessant, ceaseless, non-stop.

**intermission** n. an interval or pause.

**intermittent** adj. occurring at irregular intervals.
▷ SYNS FITFUL, spasmodic, irregular, sporadic, occasional, periodic, on and off.

**intern** v. confine as a prisoner.
■ internee n. internment n.

**internal** adj. 1 of the inside. 2 inside the body. 3 of affairs within a country. 4 used within an organization.
▷ SYNS 1 INNER, interior, inside, central. 2 DOMESTIC, home, civil.

**international** adj. 1 between nations. 2 agreed on or used by all or many nations. • n. a sports contest between players of different countries.
▷ SYNS adj. GLOBAL, worldwide, intercontinental, universal; cosmopolitan.

**internecine** adj. (of conflict) happening between members of a group.

**Internet** n. a global computer network.

**interplay** n. interaction.

**interpolate** v. interject; add to a text. ■ interpolation n.

**interpose** v. 1 place between one thing and another. 2 intervene between opponents.

**interpret** v. 1 explain the meaning of. 2 translate aloud the words of a person speaking a different language. 3 understand as meaning.
■ interpretation n. interpreter n.

▷ SYNS 1 EXPLAIN, elucidate, clarify. 2 TRANSLATE; decode, decipher. 3 UNDERSTAND, construe, take, regard.

**interrelated** adj. related to each other.

**interrogate** v. question closely or aggressively.
■ interrogation n.
▷ SYNS QUESTION, cross-examine, cross-question, quiz; inf. grill.

**interrogative** adj. in the form of or used in a question.

**interrupt** v. 1 break the progress or continuity of. 2 stop a speaker by saying or doing something. ■ interruption n.
▷ SYNS 1 SUSPEND, break off, discontinue, adjourn; stop, halt, end. 2 CUT IN, barge in, butt in, intervene.

**intersect** v. divide or cross by passing or lying across.
■ intersection n.
▷ SYNS 1 BISECT, cut in two, divide. 2 CROSS, criss-cross, meet.

**intersperse** v. place or scatter between or among other things.

**interval** n. 1 a period of time between events. 2 a pause. 3 a pause between parts of a play etc. 4 a difference in musical pitch.
▷ SYNS INTERMISSION, interlude, break.

**intervene** v. 1 become involved in a situation to improve or control it. 2 occur between events. ■ intervention n.
▷ SYNS INTERCEDE, involve yourself, step in; interfere, intrude.

**interview** n. a formal conversation with someone, designed to extract information or assess their suitability for a position. • v. hold an interview with.

**intestate** adj. not having made a valid will.

**intestine** n. a long tubular section of the alimentary canal between the stomach and anus. ■ intestinal adj.

**intimate**[1] adj. 1 close and friendly. 2 private and personal. 3 having a sexual relationship. 4 (of knowledge) detailed. • n. a close friend. ■ intimacy n.
▷ SYNS 1 CLOSE, dear, cherished, bosom. 2 *an intimate atmosphere:* INFORMAL, friendly, welcoming, warm, cosy. 3 *intimate details:* PERSONAL, private, confidential, secret.

**intimate**[2] v. state indirectly. ■ intimation n.
▷ SYNS IMPLY, suggest, hint, insinuate, indicate.

**intimidate** v. influence by frightening. ■ intimidation n.
▷ SYNS FRIGHTEN, scare, terrorize, threaten, browbeat, bully.

**into** prep. 1 to a point on or within. 2 expressing a change or result. 3 in the direction of. 4 concerning. 5 expressing division.

**intolerable** adj. unbearable.
▷ SYNS UNBEARABLE, unendurable, insufferable, insupportable.

**intolerant** adj. unwilling to accept ideas or behaviour different to your own. ■ intolerance n.
▷ SYNS BIGOTED, illiberal, narrow-minded, parochial, provincial, insular, small-minded, prejudiced, biased, partisan.

**intonation** n. the rise and fall of the voice in speaking.
▷ SYNS PITCH, tone, timbre, cadence, lilt, inflection.

**intone** v. chant, esp. on one note.

**intoxicate** v. 1 make drunk. 2 excite. ■ intoxication n.

**intractable** adj. hard to deal with or control.

**intranet** n. a computer network within an organization.

**intransigent** adj. stubborn. ■ intransigence n.

**intransitive** adj. Grammar (of a verb) not followed by a direct object.

**intravenous** adj. within or into a vein.

**intrepid** adj. fearless.

**intricate** adj. very complicated. ■ intricacy n.
▷ SYNS COMPLEX, complicated, convoluted, tangled, entangled, twisted; elaborate, ornate, detailed.

**intrigue** v. 1 arouse the curiosity of. 2 plot secretly. • n. a plot; a secret love affair. ■ intriguing adj.
▷ SYNS V. INTEREST, fascinate, attract, draw. • n. PLOT, conspiracy, scheme, machination.

**intrinsic** adj. existing in a thing as a natural or permanent quality; essential.
▷ SYNS INHERENT, innate, inborn, inbred, congenital, natural, basic, fundamental, integral.

**introduce** v. 1 make a person known to another; present to an audience. 2 bring into use. 3 insert. 4 occur at the start of.
▷ SYNS 1 PRESENT, make acquainted. 2 PREFACE, precede, lead into, start, begin. 3 BRING IN, originate, launch, inaugurate, institute, initiate, establish, found, put in place, set in motion, usher in, pioneer.

**introduction** n. introducing; an introductory part.

▷ SYNS FOREWORD, preface, preamble, prologue, prelude.

**introductory** adj. serving as an introduction.

▷ SYNS OPENING, initial, starting, first, preliminary; elementary, basic, rudimentary.

**introspection** n. concentration on your own thoughts and feelings. ■ introspective adj.

**introvert** n. an introspective and shy person. ■ introverted adj.

**intrude** v. come or join in without being invited or wanted. ■ intrusion n.

▷ SYNS ENCROACH, impinge, trespass, infringe, obtrude, invade, violate.

**intruder** n. a person who intrudes.

▷ SYNS TRESPASSER, interloper, invader; burglar, housebreaker.

**intrusive** adj. disturbing or unwelcome.

**intuition** n. the ability to understand or know something without conscious reasoning. ■ intuitive adj.

▷ SYNS INSTINCT, sixth sense, presentiment, feeling, hunch, inkling.

**inundate** v. flood; overwhelm.

▷ SYNS 1 FLOOD, deluge, swamp, submerge, engulf. 2 OVERWHELM, overload, snow under, bog down.

**inure** v. accustom to something unpleasant.

▷ SYNS HARDEN, toughen, season, condition, habituate, familiarize, accustom, acclimatize.

**invade** v. enter territory so as to conquer or occupy it; encroach on; overrun. ■ invader n.

▷ SYNS OCCUPY, conquer, capture, seize, take (over), annex; march into, overrun, overwhelm, storm, attack.

**invalid**[1] n. a person suffering from ill health.

**invalid**[2] adj. not valid.

▷ SYNS FALSE, untrue, inaccurate, faulty, fallacious, spurious; unsubstantiated, untenable, baseless, ill-founded, groundless.

**invalidate** v. make invalid.

**invaluable** adj. extremely useful.

▷ SYNS INDISPENSABLE, vital, irreplaceable, all-important, priceless, worth its weight in gold.

**invariable** adj. never changing.

**invasion** n. a hostile or harmful intrusion.

▷ SYNS 1 OCCUPATION, capture, seizure, annexation, takeover. 2 INTRUSION, encroachment, infringement, violation.

**invasive** adj. tending to invade; (of medical procedures) involving the introduction of instruments into the body.

**invective** n. abusive language.

**inveigle** v. persuade by trickery or flattery.

**invent** v. 1 create or design something new. 2 make up a false story, name, etc. ■ inventor n.

▷ SYNS 1 ORIGINATE, create, design, devise. 2 MAKE UP, fabricate, concoct, hatch, dream up.

**invention** n. 1 the act of inventing. 2 something invented. 3 creative ability.

**inventive** adj. creative and original.

▷ SYNS ORIGINAL, creative, innovative, imaginative, inspired, ingenious, resourceful.

**inventory** n. (pl. **-ies**) a detailed list of goods or furniture.

**inverse** adj. opposite or contrary.

**invert** v. put upside down or in the opposite position or order. ■ inversion n.

**invertebrate** n. an animal that has no backbone.

**invest** v. **1** use money, time, etc. to earn interest or bring profit. **2** confer rank or office on. **3** endow with a quality. ■ investor n.
▷ SYNS **1** PUT MONEY INTO, fund, subsidize. **2** SPEND, expend, put in, devote, contribute, donate, give.

**investigate** v. **1** inquire into. **2** research. ■ investigator n.
▷ SYNS INQUIRE INTO, research, probe, explore, scrutinize, study, examine.

**investigation** n. a formal inquiry or systematic study.
▷ SYNS EXAMINATION, inquiry, scrutiny, probe, research, exploration, study, review.

**investiture** n. investing a person with honours or rank.

**investment** n. **1** the act of investing. **2** something worth buying because it will be useful.

**inveterate** adj. habitual; firmly established.
▷ SYNS CONFIRMED, habitual, hardened, chronic, addicted, incorrigible.

**invidious** adj. liable to cause resentment.

**invigilate** v. supervise candidates during an exam. ■ invigilator n.

**invigorate** v. give strength or energy to.
▷ SYNS REVITALIZE, energize, refresh, revive, vivify,
rejuvenate, enliven, perk up, animate, galvanize, fortify, stimulate, exhilarate.

**invincible** adj. unconquerable.

**inviolable** adj. never to be broken or dishonoured.

**inviolate** adj. not violated; safe.

**invisible** adj. not able to be seen. ■ invisibility n.
▷ SYNS UNDETECTABLE, imperceptible, indiscernible, unseen, unnoticed, hidden, concealed.

**invite** v. **1** ask someone to come somewhere or do something. **2** ask for. **3** risk provoking. ■ invitation n.
▷ SYNS ASK FOR, request, call for, solicit, look for, seek, appeal for, summon.

**inviting** adj. pleasant and tempting.
▷ SYNS ATTRACTIVE, appealing, pleasant, agreeable, delightful, engaging, tempting, enticing, alluring, appetizing.

**invocation** n. invoking.

**invoice** n. a bill for goods or services. • v. send an invoice to.

**invoke** v. call for the help or protection of; summon a spirit.

**involuntary** adj. done without intention.
▷ SYNS **1** REFLEXIVE, reflex, automatic, mechanical, spontaneous, instinctive, unconscious, unthinking, unintentional. **2** UNWILLING, against your will, forced, compulsory, obligatory.

**involve** v. have as a part or consequence; cause to participate; require. ■ involvement n.
▷ SYNS **1** ENTAIL, imply, mean, require, necessitate. **2** INCLUDE, count in, cover, embrace, take in, incorporate, encompass, comprise, contain.

**involved** adj. 1 concerned in something; in a relationship with someone. 2 complicated.
▷ SYNS COMPLICATED, intricate, complex, elaborate, convoluted, knotty, tortuous, labyrinthine.

**inward** (or **inwards**) adv. towards the inside; into or towards the mind, spirit, or soul.

**iodine** n. a chemical used in solution as an antiseptic.

**ion** n. an electrically charged atom that has lost or gained an electron.

**iota** n. 1 a Greek letter (I, ι). 2 a very small amount.
▷ SYNS BIT, mite, speck, atom, jot, whit, particle.

**IOU** n. a signed paper given as a receipt for money borrowed.

**IQ** abbr. intelligence quotient, a number showing how a person's intelligence compares with the average.

**irascible** adj. hot-tempered.

**irate** adj. angry.

**ire** n. anger.

**iridescent** adj. shimmering with many colours.
■ iridescence n.

**iris** n. 1 the coloured part of the eyeball, round the pupil. 2 a plant with showy flowers.

**Irish** adj. & n. (the language of) Ireland.

**irk** v. annoy or irritate.
■ irksome adj.

**iron** n. 1 a strong hard metal; a tool made of this. 2 an implement with a heated steel base, used for smoothing clothes etc. 3 (**irons**) fetters. • v. 1 smooth clothes etc. with an iron. 2 (**iron out**) solve problems.

□ ironmonger a person selling tools and other hardware.

**ironic** adj. 1 expressing an idea with words that usually mean the opposite in order to be humorous or emphasize a point. 2 happening in the opposite way to what is expected.
▷ SYNS 1 SARCASTIC, sardonic, satirical, wry, mocking, scornful. 2 PARADOXICAL, odd, strange.

**irony** n. (pl. **-ies**) the expression of meaning through words which normally mean the opposite; a situation that is the opposite to what is expected.

**irradiate** v. 1 expose to radiation. 2 illuminate.
■ irradiation n.

**irrational** adj. not guided by reason.
▷ SYNS ILLOGICAL, unreasonable, groundless, unfounded, unjustifiable; ridiculous, silly, foolish, senseless.

**irrefutable** adj. impossible to disprove.

**irregular** adj. 1 not even or smooth. 2 contrary to rules or custom. ■ irregularity n.
▷ SYNS 1 ASYMMETRIC, lopsided, crooked. 2 UNEVEN, unsteady, shaky, fitful, variable, erratic, spasmodic, fluctuating, inconsistent. 3 IMPROPER, unethical, unprofessional, unacceptable, illegitimate.

**irrelevant** adj. not relevant.
■ irrelevance n.
▷ SYNS IMMATERIAL, unrelated, unconnected, extraneous, beside the point.

**irreparable** adj. unable to be repaired.

**irreplaceable** adj. impossible to replace.

**irrepressible** adj. impossible to control or subdue.

**irreproachable** adj. blameless or faultless.

**irresistible** adj. too strong or attractive to be resisted.
■ irresistibility n.
▷ SYNS **1** OVERWHELMING, overpowering, compelling, uncontrollable. **2** TEMPTING, alluring, enticing, seductive, captivating, enchanting, tantalizing.

**irresolute** adj. unable to make up your mind.

**irrespective** adj. (**irrespective of**) regardless of.

**irresponsible** adj. not showing a proper sense of responsibility.
■ irresponsibility n.
▷ SYNS UNDEPENDABLE, unreliable, untrustworthy, careless, reckless, rash, flighty, scatterbrained, thoughtless, incautious.

**irretrievable** adj. impossible to retrieve or put right.

**irreverent** adj. lacking respect.
■ irreverence n.
▷ SYNS DISRESPECTFUL, impertinent, cheeky, flippant, rude, discourteous, impolite.

**irreversible** adj. impossible to alter or undo.

**irrevocable** adj. unalterable.
▷ SYNS UNALTERABLE, unchangeable, fixed, settled, irreversible, immutable.

**irrigate** v. supply land with water by streams, pipes, etc.
■ irrigation n.

**irritable** adj. easily annoyed.
■ irritability n.
▷ SYNS BAD-TEMPERED, irascible, cross, snappy, testy, tetchy, touchy, crabbed, peevish, petulant, cantankerous, grumpy, grouchy, crotchety.

**irritate** v. **1** annoy. **2** cause to itch. ■ irritant n. irritation n.
▷ SYNS ANNOY, vex, provoke, irk, nettle, peeve, get on someone's nerves, exasperate, anger; inf. aggravate.

**Islam** n. the Muslim religion.
■ Islamic adj.

**island** n. a piece of land surrounded by water.
■ islander n.

**isle** n. an island.

**islet** n. a small island.

**isobar** n. a line on a map connecting places with the same atmospheric pressure.

**isolate** v. place apart or alone; separate from others or from a compound. ■ isolation n.
▷ SYNS SET APART, segregate, cut off, separate, quarantine.

**isolated** adj. **1** remote; lonely. **2** single; exceptional.
▷ SYNS **1** REMOTE, out of the way, off the beaten track, inaccessible, cut-off; secluded, solitary, lonely. **2** UNIQUE, lone, unusual, exceptional, untypical.

**isomer** n. each of two or more compounds with the same formula but a different arrangement of atoms.

**isosceles** adj. (of a triangle) having two sides equal.

**isotope** n. each of two or more forms of a chemical element differing in their atomic weight.

**ISP** abbr. Internet service provider.

**issue** n. **1** a topic or problem for discussion. **2** the action of supplying something; one edition of a magazine etc.

• v. 1 supply or give out.
2 publish.

▷ SYNS n. 1 MATTER, question, point, subject, topic; problem. 2 EDITION, number, copy, impression. • v. 1 PUT OUT, send out, release, announce, publish, distribute, circulate, broadcast. 2 EMANATE, emerge, pour, flow. 3 SUPPLY, provide, furnish, equip.

**isthmus** n. (pl. **-ses**) a narrow strip of land connecting two larger masses of land.

**it** pron. 1 the thing mentioned or being discussed. 2 used as the subject of an impersonal verb, as in *it is raining*. 3 used to identify someone, as in *hello, it's John here*.

**italic** adj. (of type) sloping to the right. • pl.n. (**italics**) italic type. ■ italicize v.

**itch** n. a tickling sensation in the skin causing a desire to scratch;

a restless desire. • v. feel an itch. ■ itchy adj.

**item** n. an individual article or unit.

▷ SYNS 1 ARTICLE, thing, object; element, constituent, component, ingredient. 2 POINT, detail, matter, particular.

**itemize** (or **-ise**) v. list; state the individual items of.

**itinerant** adj. travelling from place to place.

**itinerary** n. (pl. **-ies**) a planned route or journey.

**its** poss.pron of the thing mentioned; belonging to it.

**it's** contr. 1 it is. 2 it has.

**itself** pron. the emphatic and reflexive form of **it**.

**ivory** n. (pl. **-ies**) a hard creamy-white substance forming the tusks of an elephant etc.; its creamy-white colour.

**ivy** n. an evergreen climbing plant.

# Jj

**jab** v. (**jabbed**, **jabbing**) poke roughly with something pointed. • n. a rough poke; an injection.

▷ SYNS n. POKE, prod, dig, nudge, elbow, butt.

**jabber** v. talk rapidly, usu. unintelligibly.

▷ SYNS CHATTER, prattle, babble, gabble, prate, blather, rattle on.

**jack** n. 1 a portable device for raising heavy weights off the

ground. 2 a playing card next below queen. 3 an electrical connection with a single plug. 4 a small ball aimed at in bowls. • v. (**jack up**) raise with a jack.

**jackal** n. a doglike wild animal.

**jackass** n. 1 a male ass. 2 a stupid person.

**jackboot** n. a military boot reaching above the knee.

**jackdaw** n. a bird of the crow family.

**jacket** n. **1** a short coat. **2** an outer covering. **3** the skin of a potato.
▷ SYNS WRAPPING, wrapper, sleeve, cover, covering, sheath.

**jackknife** n. (pl. **-knives**) a large folding knife. • v. (of an articulated vehicle) fold against itself in an accident.

**jackpot** n. a large cash prize.

**jacuzzi** n. trademark a large bath with jets of water.

**jade** n. a hard bluish-green precious stone.

**jaded** adj. tired and bored.

**jagged** adj. having rough sharp projections.
▷ SYNS SERRATED, toothed, indented; spiky, barbed, uneven, rough, craggy.

**jaguar** n. a large spotted wild cat.

**jail** (or **gaol**) n. prison. • v. put into jail. ■ **jailer** (or **gaoler**) n.

**jam** n. **1** a spread made from fruit and sugar. **2** an instance of being blocked. **3** inf. a difficult situation. • v. **1** pack tightly into a space. **2** block through crowding. **3** become stuck. **4** block a radio transmission.
▷ SYNS V. STUFF, shove, force, ram, thrust, push, wedge, stick; press, cram, pack, crowd, squeeze, sandwich.

**jamb** n. the side post of a door or window.

**jamboree** n. a lavish or noisy party.

**jangle** n. a harsh metallic sound. • v. make or cause to make this sound; (of your nerves) be set on edge.

**janitor** n. the caretaker of a building.

**January** n. the first month.

**jar¹** n. a cylindrical glass or earthenware container.

**jar²** v. (**jarred**, **jarring**) strike with a painful shock; have a painful or disagreeable effect.
▷ SYNS **1** JOLT, jerk, shake, vibrate. **2** GRATE ON, irritate, set someone's teeth on edge.

**jargon** n. words or expressions developed for use within a particular group of people and hard for others to understand.
▷ SYNS SLANG, idiom, cant, argot.

**jasmine** n. a shrub with white or yellow flowers.

**jaundice** n. **1** yellowing of the skin due to a liver disorder. **2** bitterness or resentment. ■ **jaundiced** adj.

**jaunt** n. a short pleasure trip.
▷ SYNS TRIP, outing, excursion, expedition, mini break, tour, drive.

**jaunty** adj. (**-ier**, **-iest**) cheerful and self-confident. ■ **jauntily** adv.
▷ SYNS CHEERFUL, cheery, happy, merry, lively, perky, bubbly, buoyant, carefree, blithe.

**javelin** n. a light spear thrown in sport (formerly as a weapon).

**jaw** n. the bones forming the framework of the mouth.

**jay** n. a noisy bird of the crow family.

**jazz** n. a type of music involving improvisation, strong rhythm, and syncopation.

**jazzy** adj. (**-ier**, **-iest**) **1** in the style of jazz. **2** colourful and showy.

**jealous** adj. **1** envious of someone's success. **2** resentful of someone seen as a sexual rival. **3** very protective of your possessions. ■ **jealousy** n.

▷ SYNS **1** ENVIOUS, covetous, grudging, resentful, green-eyed. **2** SUSPICIOUS, distrustful, possessive.

**jeans** pl.n. denim trousers.

**jeep** n. trademark a small sturdy motor vehicle with four-wheel drive.

**jeer** v. laugh or shout rudely or scornfully. • n. a jeering shout.
▷ SYNS v. TAUNT, mock, ridicule, deride, jibe at, barrack, boo, scoff at, laugh at, sneer at.

**jell** v. = GEL.

**jelly** n. (pl. -ies) **1** a dessert made of a flavoured liquid set with gelatin. **2** a semi-solid substance. □ jellyfish a sea animal with a soft body and stinging tentacles.

**jemmy** n. (pl. -ies) a short crowbar.

**jeopardize** (or -ise) v. endanger.

**jeopardy** n. danger.
▷ SYNS RISK, danger, peril.

**jerk** n. **1** a sudden sharp movement. **2** inf. a stupid person. • v. move or raise with a jerk.
▷ SYNS v. **1** PULL, yank, tug, wrench. **2** JOLT, lurch, bump, bounce.

**jerkin** n. a sleeveless jacket.

**jerky** adj. moving in abrupt stops and starts.
▷ SYNS CONVULSIVE, spasmodic, fitful, shaky; inf. twitchy.

**jersey** n. (pl. -eys) a knitted woollen pullover with sleeves; machine-knitted fabric.

**jest** n. a joke. • v. make jokes.

**jester** n. a clown at a medieval court.

**jet¹** n. a hard black mineral; glossy black.

▷ SYNS STREAM, gush, spurt, spout, spray, rush, fountain.

**jet²** n. **1** a stream of water, gas, or flame from a small opening. **2** an engine or aircraft using jet propulsion. • v. (**jetted, jetting**) travel by jet aircraft. □ jet lag delayed tiredness etc. after a long flight.

**jetsam** n. goods jettisoned by a ship and washed ashore.

**jettison** v. throw or drop from an aircraft or ship.

**jetty** n. (pl. -ies) a landing stage etc. where boats can be moored.
▷ SYNS PIER, wharf, quay, dock, breakwater, groyne.

**Jew** n. a person of Hebrew descent or whose religion is Judaism. ■ Jewish adj.

**jewel** n. **1** a precious stone. **2** a highly valued person or thing. ■ jewelled adj.
▷ SYNS GEM, gemstone, precious stone.

**jewellery** (US **jewelry**) n. necklaces, rings, bracelets, etc. ■ jeweller n.

**jib** n. **1** a triangular sail in front of a mast. **2** the arm of a crane. • v. (**jibbed, jibbing**) be unwilling to do or accept.

**jibe** (or **gibe**) v. jeer. • n. a jeering remark.
▷ SYNS n. TAUNT, sneer, jeer, insult, barb; inf. dig.

**jiffy** n. inf. a moment.

**jig** n. **1** a lively dance. **2** a device that holds something and guides tools working on it. • v. (**jigged, jigging**) move up and down jerkily.

**jigsaw** n. **1** a picture cut into interlocking pieces that have to be fitted together. **2** a machine fretsaw.

**jilt** v. abandon a lover.
▷ SYNS ABANDON, walk out on, throw over, leave, forsake.

**jingle** v. make a ringing or clinking sound. • n. **1** this sound. **2** a simple rhyme, esp. one used in advertising.
▷ SYNS v. CLINK, chink, jangle, rattle, tinkle, ding, ring, chime. • n. DITTY, rhyme, refrain, limerick, tune.

**jingoism** n. chiefly derog. excessive patriotism.

**jinx** n. an influence causing bad luck.

**jitters** pl.n. inf. nervousness.
■ jittery adj.

**jive** n. a lively dance to jazz music. • v. dance in this style.

**job** n. a paid position of employment. **1** a task. □ jobcentre (in the UK) a government office providing information about available jobs.
■ jobless adj.
▷ SYNS **1** OCCUPATION, profession, trade, employment, vocation, career, position, post, situation, appointment. **2** TASK, assignment, undertaking, duty, chore, errand, responsibility, role.

**jockey** n. (pl. -eys) a person who rides in horse races. • v. manoeuvre to gain advantage.

**jockstrap** n. a protective support for the male genitals.

**jocular** adj. joking. ■ jocularity n.
▷ SYNS HUMOROUS, funny, amusing, witty, comic, comical, facetious, joking, playful, droll, entertaining.

**jodhpurs** pl.n. trousers worn for horse riding, fitting closely below the knee.

**jog** v. **1** run at a steady gentle pace. **2** knock slightly. • n. **1** a

spell of jogging. **2** a slight knock. ■ jogger n.
▷ SYNS v. **1** RUN, trot, lope. **2** NUDGE, prod, poke, push.

**joggle** v. shake slightly. • n. a slight shake.

**join** v. **1** link or become linked to. **2** unite to form a whole. **3** become a member of. **4** take part in. **5** (join up) enlist in the armed forces. • n. a place where things join.
▷ SYNS v. **1** CONNECT, unite, couple, attach, fasten, glue, fuse, weld, link, tie, bind. **2** MEET, touch, reach. **3** ENLIST, sign up, join up, team up. • n. JUNCTION, intersection, connection, joint, seam.

**joiner** n. a person who makes the wooden parts of a building.
■ joinery n.

**joint** n. **1** a join. **2** a structure in the body joining two bones. **3** a large piece of meat. **4** inf. a cannabis cigarette. **5** inf. a place of a specified kind. • adj. shared by two or more people. • v. cut into joints. ■ jointed adj. jointly adv.
▷ SYNS n. see JOIN. • adj. COMMON, shared, mutual, combined, collective, cooperative, united, concerted.

**joist** n. a beam supporting a floor or ceiling.

**joke** n. **1** something said or done to cause laughter. **2** a ridiculously inadequate person or thing. • v. make jokes.
▷ SYNS n. **1** JEST, witticism, quip, pun; inf. gag, wisecrack, crack. **2** PRACTICAL JOKE, prank, trick, jape. • v. TELL JOKES, jest, banter, quip.

**joker** n. **1** a person who jokes. **2** a playing card used as a wild card.

**jollification** n. time spent having fun.

**jollity** n. (pl. **-ies**) **1** lively activity. **2** cheerfulness.

**jolly** adj. **1** happy and cheerful. **2** lively and entertaining.
• v. encourage in a friendly way.
• adv. very.
▷ SYNS adj. HAPPY, cheerful, cheery, good-humoured, jovial, merry, joyful, light-hearted, buoyant, genial.

**jolt** v. **1** push or shake abruptly. **2** shock into action. • n. **1** a jolting movement. **2** a shock.
▷ SYNS v. **1** PUSH, jar, knock, bang, shake, jog. **2** BUMP, bounce, jerk, lurch, judder. **3** STARTLE, surprise, shock, shake, stun.

**joss stick** n. a thin stick that burns with a smell of incense.

**jostle** v. push roughly.
▷ SYNS PUSH, shove, elbow, barge, bang into.

**jot** v. (**jotted**, **jotting**) write quickly. • n. a very small amount.

**jotter** n. a notepad.

**joule** n. a unit of energy.

**journal** n. a daily record of events; a newspaper or periodical.
▷ SYNS **1** DIARY, notebook, log, logbook, weblog, blog, chronicle, record. **2** PERIODICAL, magazine, gazette, digest, newspaper, paper.

**journalist** n. a person employed to write for a newspaper or magazine. ■ journalism n.
▷ SYNS REPORTER, columnist, correspondent, reviewer; inf. hack.

**journey** n. (pl. **-eys**) an act of travelling from one place to another. • v. travel.
▷ SYNS n. TRIP, expedition, tour, trek, voyage, cruise, passage, odyssey, pilgrimage; travels, globetrotting.

**journeyman** n. a skilled worker employed by another.

**jovial** adj. cheerful and good-humoured. ■ joviality n.

**jowl** n. the lower part of the cheek.

**joy** n. **1** great happiness. **2** a cause of joy.
▷ SYNS DELIGHT, pleasure, jubilation, exultation, rejoicing, happiness, elation, euphoria, bliss, ecstasy, rapture.

**joyful** adj. feeling or causing great happiness.
▷ SYNS CHEERFUL, happy, elated, thrilled, delighted, pleased, gleeful, jubilant, ecstatic; inf. over the moon, on cloud nine.

**joyous** adj. very happy.

**joyriding** n. inf. the crime of stealing a vehicle and driving it very fast. ■ joyride n. joyrider n.

**joystick** n. **1** an aircraft's control lever. **2** a lever controlling the movement of an image on a screen.

**JP** abbr. Justice of the Peace.

**jubilant** adj. happy and triumphant. ■ jubilation n.

**jubilee** n. a special anniversary.

**Judaism** n. the religion of the Jews. ■ Judaic adj.

**judder** v. shake rapidly and forcefully.

**judge** n. **1** a public officer who decides cases in a law court. **2** a person who decides who has won a contest. **3** a person able to give an opinion. • v. **1** form an opinion about. **2** decide a case in a law court. **3** decide the winner of.
▷ SYNS n. **1** JUSTICE, magistrate, sheriff; inf. beak. **2** ADJUDICATOR, arbiter, assessor, examiner.

• v. 1 CONCLUDE, decide, consider, believe, think, deduce, surmise. 2 PRONOUNCE, decree, rule, find. 3 ASSESS, appraise, evaluate, examine, review.

**judgement** (or **judgment**) n. 1 the ability to make sound decisions. 2 an opinion or conclusion. 3 a decision of a law court or judge.
▷ SYNS 1 SENSE, discernment, perception, discrimination, reason, logic. 2 OPINION, view, conclusion. 3 VERDICT, decision, adjudication, ruling, decree, finding, sentence.

**judgemental** (or **judgmental**) adj. 1 of judgement. 2 too critical.

**judicial** adj. of a law court or judge. ■ judicially adv.

**judiciary** n. (pl. -ies) the whole body of judges in a country.

**judicious** adj. showing good judgement.
▷ SYNS WISE, prudent, politic, sagacious, shrewd, astute, sensible, sound, discerning, intelligent, smart, clever.

**judo** n. a Japanese system of unarmed combat.

**jug** n. a container with a handle and a lip, for holding and pouring liquids.
▷ SYNS PITCHER, carafe, decanter, jar, crock, ewer.

**juggernaut** n. a very large transport vehicle.

**juggle** v. 1 toss and catch several objects, keeping at least one in the air at any time. 2 do several things at the same time.
■ juggler n.

**jugular vein** n. any of several large veins in the neck.

**juice** n. 1 the liquid in fruits and vegetables. 2 (**juices**) fluid produced by the stomach.

▷ SYNS LIQUID, fluid, sap, extract, concentrate, essence.

**juicy** adj. 1 full of juice. 2 inf. interestingly scandalous.
▷ SYNS 1 SUCCULENT, moist; ripe. 2 SENSATIONAL, fascinating, scandalous, racy, risqué.

**ju-jitsu** n. a Japanese system of unarmed combat.

**jukebox** n. a coin-operated record player.

**July** n. the seventh month.

**jumble** n. an untidy collection.
• v. mix up in a confused way.
□ jumble sale a sale of second-hand goods.
▷ SYNS n. HEAP, muddle, mess, disarray, hotchpotch. • v. MIX UP, muddle, disorganize, disorder.

**jumbo** inf. adj. very large. • n. (pl. -os) (also jumbo jet) a very large airliner.

**jump** v. 1 push yourself off the ground with your legs and feet. 2 leap across. 3 move suddenly. 4 (**jump at**) accept eagerly. 5 pass abruptly from one thing to another. • n. 1 a jumping movement. 2 a sudden increase. 3 an obstacle to be jumped. □ jump the queue move ahead of your proper place in a queue.
▷ SYNS v. 1 LEAP, spring, bound, vault, hop; skip, caper, dance, prance. 2 START, flinch, recoil. • n. 1 LEAP, spring, bound, hop. 2 RISE, increase, upsurge; inf. hike. 3 HURDLE, fence, obstacle, barrier.

**jumper** n. 1 a pullover. 2 a person who jumps.

**jumpy** adj. (-ier, -iest) inf. anxious and uneasy.

**junction** n. 1 a join. 2 a place where roads or railway lines meet.

▷ SYNS **1** JOIN, joint, juncture, link, connection, seam, union. **2** CROSSROADS, crossing, intersection, interchange.

**juncture** n. **1** a particular point in time in the development of events. **2** a join.

▷ SYNS POINT, point in time, time, stage, period, critical point, crucial moment, moment of truth, turning point, crisis, crux, extremity.

**June** n. the sixth month.

**jungle** n. **1** a tropical forest; a mass of tangled vegetation. **2** a scene of ruthless struggle.

**junior** adj. **1** of younger people. **2** younger. **3** low or lower in status. • n. a junior person.

▷ SYNS **adj.** YOUNGER, minor, subordinate, lower, lesser, secondary.

**juniper** n. an evergreen shrub.

**junk** n. **1** inf. useless or discarded articles. **2** a flat-bottomed sailing boat used in China. ◻ **junk food** unhealthy food. **junk mail** unwanted advertising matter sent by post.

**junket** n. **1** inf. an extravagant trip paid for using public funds. **2** a dish of sweetened curds of milk.

**junkie** n. inf. a drug addict.

**junta** n. a military or political group ruling a country after seizing power.

**jurisdiction** n. the authority to administer justice or exercise power.

**juror** n. a member of a jury.

**jury** n. (pl. **-ies**) a group of people who have to give a verdict on a legal case.

**just** adj. **1** right and fair. **2** deserved. • adv. **1** exactly. **2** at the same moment. **3** very

recently. **4** by a small amount. **5** only.

▷ SYNS **adj. 1** FAIR, equitable, even-handed, impartial, unbiased, objective, neutral, disinterested, unprejudiced. **2** DESERVED, merited, rightful, due, fitting, appropriate, suitable.

**justice** n. **1** just behaviour or treatment. **2** legal proceedings. **3** a judge. ◻ **Justice of the Peace** a non-professional magistrate.

▷ SYNS JUSTNESS, fairness, fair play, fair-mindedness, equity, even-handedness, impartiality, objectivity, neutrality.

**justifiable** adj. able to be defended as right or reasonable. ■ **justifiably** adv.

▷ SYNS VALID, sound, well founded, legitimate, tenable, defensible, sustainable, warranted, reasonable, within reason, justified.

**justify** v. **1** show to be right or reasonable. **2** be a good reason for. **3** adjust lines of type to form straight edges. ■ **justification** n.

▷ SYNS **1** GIVE GROUNDS FOR, give reasons for, explain, account for, defend, vindicate. **2** WARRANT, be good reason for.

**jut** v. (**jutted, jutting**) extend out beyond.

▷ SYNS STICK OUT, project, protrude, bulge out, overhang.

**jute** n. rough fibre from the stems of a tropical plant.

**juvenile** adj. **1** of young people. **2** childish. • n. a young person or animal. ◻ **juvenile delinquent** a young person who regularly commits crimes.

▷ SYNS **adj.** CHILDISH, immature, puerile, infantile, babyish.

**juxtapose** v. place close together. ■ **juxtaposition** n.

# Effective English

This specially written guide gives you extra help with your writing and is divided into three main sections.

The first section, on word classes (nouns, verbs, etc.), explains the main categories of words in English and shows how nouns, verbs, and adjectives change according to how they are being used.

The second section, on punctuation, describes the tasks of the full stop, comma, apostrophe, etc. and shows how to use them correctly and in a way that makes your writing easy to understand.

In the last section, you can discover that it's easy to make a thesaurus work for you, to improve your writing and get better results.

## Contents

Further information on language can be found in these other books from Oxford University Press: the *Oxford A–Z of Grammar and Punctuation* (2004) by John Seely and the *Oxford A–Z of Spelling* (2004) by Catherine Soanes and Sheila Ferguson.

# Word classes

Words have many different tasks to do. Some describe actions (words like 'drive' and 'read'), others refer to people or things (words like 'boy', 'bucket', and 'dog'), while words like 'or' and 'because' connect other words together. Words can be grouped together according to the task they do. These groups or categories are called **parts of speech** or **word classes**. There are eight main word classes in English: noun, verb, adjective, adverb, pronoun, preposition, conjunction, and exclamation.

## Nouns

A noun is the name of a person or thing. There are two main kinds:

### Common nouns

Common nouns include the words for objects and creatures, for example:

> the red shoe     a horse galloped by

Common nouns can be either **singular** (*one horse*) or **plural** (*two*, *three*, or *lots of horses*). They don't begin with a capital letter unless they are the first word in a sentence.

You can also divide common nouns into two more kinds, **abstract nouns** and **collective nouns**.

Abstract nouns are words for qualities—things you can't see or touch, and things which have no physical reality:

> truth     danger     warmth     happiness

Collective nouns are words for groups of things or people:

> committee     herd     team     the government

## Proper nouns

Proper nouns are names, for example, of particular people, places, organizations, and events. They always begin with a capital letter:

> Jane    London    Marks and Spencer    the First World War

Proper nouns are always singular.

# Verbs

A verb tells you what a person or thing does or what happens. Verbs describe:

- an action, e.g. *run*, *hit*
- an event, e.g. *rain*, *happen*
- a situation, e.g. *be*, *have*, *seem*
- a change, e.g. *become*, *grow*

All verbs have a **subject**, which is the person or thing that comes before the verb:

>
> Joe    in    Joe ran home

In some sentences the verb has an **object** as well as a subject. The object tells you who or what is affected by the verb:

>
> the ball    in    Joe hit the ball

The basic form of a verb, which often appears with 'to', is called the **infinitive**:

> to laugh    to run    to happen

## Tenses

As well as telling you *what* someone does or *what* happens, verbs tell you *when* it happens or is done:

- present: *I laugh*
- future: *I will laugh*
- past: *I laughed*

These are examples of present, future, and past **tenses** of the verb *laugh*.

We can further divide the tenses up like this:

- the **simple present** tense: *the child laughs*
- the **present continuous** tense: *the child is laughing*
- the **past continuous** tense: *the child was laughing*
- the **simple past** tense: *the child laughed*
- the **present perfect** tense: *the child has laughed*
- the **past perfect** tense: *the child had laughed*

Different tenses of verbs are made either by adding *-ed* or *-ing* to the end of the verb, or by using words like *am*, *was*, *have*, *had*, and *will* (which are known as **auxiliary verbs**), or by doing both. Verbs whose tenses are formed in the normal way, like *laugh*, are called **regular** verbs. Some verbs, though, do not form tenses in the normal way. These are called **irregular** verbs. Verbs such as *sink*, *buy*, *creep*, and *take* are all irregular verbs:

| present | simple past | past participle |
|---------|-------------|-----------------|
| sink    | sank        | sunk            |
| buy     | bought      | bought          |
| creep   | crept       | crept           |
| take    | took        | taken           |

The **past participle** is the form of the verb that is used after *has*, *have*, *had*, *was* and *were* to refer to an action or event that happened in the past. Notice that the simple past tense and the past participle are always the same form in regular verbs (*the child laughed*; *the child had laughed*) but they are not always the same in irregular verbs. In this book the spellings used in the different tenses of irregular verbs are shown in the dictionary entry for each verb.

## Active and Passive

Depending on the way a sentence is worded, a verb is either **active** or **passive**. When the verb is active, the subject of the verb is doing the action. In these sentences the verb is active:

> she took the dog home    David bought the bike

When the verb is passive, its subject is affected by the action, rather than doing it. In these sentences the verb is passive:

the dog was taken home    the bike was bought by David

## Adjectives

An adjective is a word that tells us something about a noun. Here are some examples:

| | | | |
|---|---|---|---|
| red | Italian | large | sticky |
| clever | happy | wooden | old |

Most adjectives can be used both before the noun they describe:

the red house    a clever woman    an Italian city

and after a verb like *be*, *seem*, or *look*:

the house is red    she seems clever

Some adjectives can *only* be used before a noun:

the chief reason (you can't say 'the reason is chief')

These adjectives are called **attributive**.

Some can only be used after a verb:

the ship is still afloat (you can't say 'an afloat ship')

They are known as **predicative**.

### Comparing adjectives

Adjectives can have three different forms.

- The **positive** form gives a simple description, without making any comparisons with another person or thing:

he is tall    the book was interesting

- The **comparative** form compares one person or thing with another.

Short adjectives make the comparative by adding -*er* to the positive form:

| he is taller than me | today is warmer than yesterday |

Short adjectives which end in -*e* just add -*r* to the positive form:

| a larger box | a nicer taste |

Longer adjectives make the comparative by using the word 'more':

| the book was more interesting than the film |

● The **superlative** form compares one person or thing with every other member of their group.

Short adjectives make the superlative by adding -*est* to the positive form:

| he was the tallest boy in the class |

Short adjectives which end in -*e* just add -*st* to the positive form:

| the largest box |

Longer adjectives make the superlative by using the word 'most':

| the most interesting book I've ever read |

Some adjectives change their spellings when they make comparative and superlative forms with -*er* and -*est*:

● some words of one syllable that end in a single consonant (e.g. fat, big, or wet) double this final consonant: *he's fatter than he used to be*

● words ending in -*y* (e.g. happy or greedy) change the y to an *i* and add -*er* or -*est*: *the happiest day of her life*.

In this book, these comparative and superlative forms are shown in brackets in the dictionary entry for the adjective:

> **fat** adj (fatter, fattest)
> **happy** adj (happier, happiest)

## Adverbs

An adverb is used with a verb, an adjective, another adverb, or a whole sentence.

When it's used with a verb, an adverb can tell us:

- how something happens: *he walked quickly*
- where something happens: *I live here*
- when something happens: *they visited us yesterday*

It can make the meaning stronger or weaker:

- with a verb: *he really meant it*; *I almost fell asleep*
- with an adjective: *she is very clever*; *this is a slightly better result*
- with another adverb: *the boys nearly always get home late*

An adverb can also add to the meaning of a whole sentence:

> luckily, no one was hurt    he is probably our best player

Some words are both an adjective and an adverb:

> a fast horse (*adjective*)    he ran fast (*adverb*)
> a long time (*adjective*)    have you been here long? (*adverb*)

## Pronouns

Pronouns are used in place of nouns, often so that you don't have to repeat the noun:

| she | in | Kate was tired so she went to bed |
| him | in | Usha doesn't like him |
| that | in | that is a good idea |
| anything | in | anything can happen |

### Personal pronouns

Personal pronouns are used in place of nouns referring to

specific people or things:

|  | SINGULAR subject | object | PLURAL subject | object |
|---|---|---|---|---|
| first person | I | me | we | us |
| second person | you | you | you | you |
| third person | he/she/it | him/her/it | they | them |

## I or me?

Be careful with these two personal pronouns, as they are often used in the wrong place. If the pronoun is the subject of the verb, then you should use 'I':

> John and I went to the shops

If the pronoun is the object of the verb, then you should use 'me':

> Mum took John and me to the shops

**Tip:** If you're not sure which one to use, say the sentence to yourself using just 'I' or 'me' to find out which sounds right:

> I went to the shops (you'd never say 'me')
> Mum took me to the shops (you'd never say 'I')

## Prepositions

Prepositions are used in front of nouns or pronouns. They describe:

- the position of something: *the cat was under the chair*
- the time when something happens: *they arrived on Sunday*
- the way in which something is done: *we went by train*

## Conjunctions

Conjunctions (also known as **connectives**) are used to join words or parts of sentences together. There are two main kinds:

**Coordinating conjunctions** join items that are of equal importance:

| or | in | there's ice cream or frozen yoghurt |
| and | in | he plays football and goes swimming |

**Subordinating conjunctions** join additional items to the main part of a sentence:

| until | in | I waited at home until she arrived |
| because | in | he went to bed because he was tired |

## Exclamations

An exclamation (also called an **interjection**) is a word or phrase that expresses strong emotion, such as surprise, pleasure, or anger. Exclamations often stand on their own, rather than forming part of a sentence and they are often followed by an exclamation mark instead of a full stop:

| Ow! That hurt! | Hurrah! She's here at last |

Exclamations also express greetings or congratulation:

| Hello! | Well done, Anil |

Of course, many English words can be used in more than one word class. For example **place** can be a noun (*the church was a peaceful place*) or a verb (*place your hands on your knees*). The word **back** can be a noun (*he lay on his back*), an adjective (*the bike's back wheel*), or a verb (*back the car out of the drive*).

# Punctuation

Punctuation marks are essential when you are writing. They show the reader where sentences start and finish, and if they are used correctly they make your writing easy to understand. Here are the main types of punctuation mark with guidelines about how to use them.

## Full stop .

Full stops are used:

● to mark the end of a sentence that is not a question or an exclamation:

> I'm going to the cinema tonight.

● after initials and after some abbreviations:

> J. K. Rowling     p. 10 (page 10)     Sun. (Sunday)

● in website and email addresses:

> www.oup.com

## Comma ,

A comma marks a slight break between parts of a sentence. In particular it is used:

● to separate items in a list:

> I bought potatoes, peas, beans, and carrots.

The last comma in the list can be left out:

> I bought potatoes, peas, beans and carrots.

● to separate clauses in a sentence:

> After we had lunch, we went back to work.
> I'd been looking forward to seeing the film, but it was boring.

A **clause** is a group of words in a sentence that has its own verb. If the clause makes sense on its own, it is called a **main clause** (e.g. *we went back to work*). If the clause would not make sense on its own it is known as a **subordinate clause** (e.g. *after we had lunch*).

● before and after a clause beginning with 'who', 'which', or 'whom' that adds extra and non-essential information to a sentence:

> Mary, who has two young children, has a part-time job in the library.

But don't use a comma if the clause beginning with 'who', 'which', or 'whom' is necessary to the meaning of the sentence:

> Passengers who have young children may board the aircraft first.

● to separate the name of the person or people being addressed from the rest of the sentence:

> David, I'm here.

● after words that introduce direct speech (a speaker's words written down exactly as they were spoken), or after direct speech where there is no question mark or exclamation mark:

> Steve replied, 'No problem.'
> 'Here we are,' they said.

## Semicolon ;

The main task of the semicolon is to mark a break that is stronger than a comma but less strong than a full stop. It is used between two main clauses that balance each other and are too closely linked to be made into separate sentences:

> You could wait for him here; this would save you valuable time.
> The sun was already low in the sky; it would soon be dark.

## Colon :

A colon is used:

● between two main clauses, the second of which explains or follows from the first:

> It wasn't easy: to begin with I had to find the right house.

● to introduce a list of items:

> You will need: a tent, a sleeping bag, cooking equipment, and a rucksack.

● before a quotation and sometimes before direct speech:

> The headline read: 'Nuclear scientist goes missing'.

## Apostrophe '

An apostrophe is used:

**1.** to show that one or more letters or numbers have been missed out:

> it's (it is) raining          I haven't (have not) read it
> you can't (cannot) go     the summer of '88 (1988)

**2.** to show possession or belonging:

● 's is added to the end of singular nouns: *the girl's bag* (= the bag of the girl); *the cat's paw* (= the paw of the cat); *the waitress's apron* (= the apron of the waitress).

● ' on its own is added to the end of plural nouns that end with s: *my parents' car*; *the workers' salaries*.

● 's is added to the end of plural nouns that do not end with s: *the children's books*; *women's clothing*; *the men's final*. (Plural nouns that do not end with s are unusual in English.)

● 's is added to the end of singular names: *Gita's coat*; *James's house*.

You should **not** use an apostrophe in the possessive pronouns *hers*, *its*, *ours*, *theirs*, or *yours*:

> the choice is yours (not *your's*)   the cat hurt its paw (not *it's*)

Be careful to distinguish *its* meaning 'belonging to it' and *it's* meaning '*it is*'.

You also do **not** use an apostrophe to make plural nouns:

> two kilos of oranges (not *kilo's*)

**3.** when individual letters or numbers are referred to in plural form:

> mind your p's and q's   find all the number 7's

## Hyphen -

A hyphen is mainly used:

● to join two or more words so as to form a compound word:

> hard-hearted   mother-in-law

Nowadays most words formed from two nouns are written either as two words (e.g. credit card, text message) or as one word (e.g. website, database). Hyphens are less common than they used to be.

● to join a prefix to a proper name:

> half-Italian   pro-European

## Quotation marks ' ' or " "

Quotation marks or are used:

● to mark the beginning and end of direct speech (words written down exactly as they were spoken):

> 'That,' he said, 'is nonsense.'
> 'What time will they arrive?' she asked.

Note that when you are writing direct speech, you should start a new line for each change of speaker.

Effective English

- round a word or phrase that is being quoted or discussed:

> What does 'integrated circuit' mean?

Quotation marks are also called **inverted commas** or **speech marks**.

## Brackets ( ) [ ]

Round brackets (also called **parentheses**) are mainly used to separate extra information or a comment from the rest of a sentence:

> Zimbabwe (formerly Rhodesia) lies in south-east Africa.
> Mount Everest (8,848 m) is the highest mountain in the world.
> There are several books on the subject (see page 120).

Square brackets are mainly used to enclose words added by someone other than the original writer or speaker:

> He [the police officer] can't prove I did it.

## Exclamation mark !

An exclamation mark is used instead of a full stop at the end of a sentence to show that the speaker or writer is angry, enthusiastic, hurt, or surprised:

> Go away!     Ow!     We had a great time!

## Question mark ?

A question mark is used instead of a full stop at the end of a sentence to show that it is a question:

> Have you seen the film yet?

Note that it is not used at the end of a reported question:

> I asked you whether you'd seen the film yet.

## Dash —

A dash is used:

- to mark the beginning and end of an interruption in the flow of a sentence:

> My son—wherever he has gone—would like to meet you.

- to show other kinds of break in a sentence where a comma, semicolon, or colon would traditionally be used:

> The most important thing is this—don't rush the work.

Don't use a dash in this second way when you are writing formally.

# How to use a dictionary & thesaurus

## The Basics

Suppose you are writing a story and find that you are saying that there was *bad weather* and that someone had a *bad accident*, and you want to use a different word to *bad*. Just look up the adjective *bad* on page 48 of this book, and you will find this:

the word you have in mind →

**bad** adj. **1** poor in quality. **2** unpleasant. **3** serious. **4** wicked. **5** harmful. **6** (of food) decayed.
▷ SYNS **1** POOR, inadequate, unsatisfactory, substandard, inferior, defective, deficient, faulty, incompetent, secondrate, inept, shoddy, awful, terrible, dreadful, frightful; inf. hopeless, lousy. **2** *bad weather:* UNPLEASANT, disagreeable, nasty, horrid, horrible, foul, appalling, atrocious. **3** *a bad accident:* SERIOUS, severe, grave, dangerous, disastrous, calamitous, dire. **4** *a bad character:* IMMORAL, wicked, evil, corrupt, sinful, criminal, depraved, villainous, dishonest, dishonourable, base. **5** *bad behaviour:* NAUGHTY, mischievous, unruly, wayward, disobedient. **6** *the meat's bad:* ROTTEN, decayed, mouldy, off, rancid, sour, putrid.

→ words you can use instead

You can quickly see alternatives to make your writing more varied: you could say *foul* or *atrocious weather*, for example, or a *serious* or *disastrous* accident.

Read on to discover more about what is in a thesaurus.

## Difference between a thesaurus and a dictionary

Although some people use a thesaurus to try to find out the meaning of a word, a thesaurus is not the same as a dictionary. A thesaurus provides alternative words with a similar meaning, or 'synonyms', whereas a dictionary tells you what a word means.

### Dictionaries

A dictionary is a record of words in the English language. It provides an account of each word and includes at least some of these features:

- the spelling of the entry word, or 'headword'
- its pronunciation
- its word class, or 'part of speech': for example, whether it is a noun, verb, or adjective
- its different meanings
- different forms of the word ('inflections') that do not follow a standard pattern, such as *caught* as the past tense of *catch*, or *leaves* as the plural of *leaf*
- the history and origin of the word ('etymology')
- any words formed from it ('derivatives', such as *leafy*, formed from *leaf*)
- phrases and idioms containing the headword, such as *leaf through* at the entry for *leaf*
- information on how the word is used, e.g. whether it is formal or informal

> **leaf** n. (pl. **leaves**) **1** a flat green organ growing from the stem or root of a plant. **2** a single sheet of paper in a book; a very thin sheet of metal. • v. (**leaf through**) turn over the leaves of a book. ∎ **leafy** adj.

## Thesauruses

The purpose of a thesaurus is to provide you with 'synonyms'—words that have a similar meaning and could be used instead of one that you have in mind. For example, the words *foul* and *serious* are both synonyms for the word *bad*.

Some thesauruses also include other features, such as 'antonyms'—words which mean the opposite.

Remember that a thesaurus contains entries for only selected words. Unlike a dictionary, a thesaurus does not set out to describe every word in the English language systematically: it contains only words which have synonyms. Therefore you will not find entries for certain words—typically names for specific things—such as *giraffe* or *computer*.

# What's in a thesaurus?

## Word class

The first piece of information given after the headword is the 'word class' (or part of speech, as it is also known). Most words in a thesaurus are either nouns, verbs, adjectives, or adverbs. This is because those are the types of word most likely to have synonyms.

A **noun** is a word that names something. This could be a person (*woman, boy, Martin*), a thing (*building, tree, chair*), or an abstract concept such as an event, quality, or feeling (*birth, difficulty, happiness*). Some nouns, such as *clothes* or *earnings*, are always used in the plural; these are labelled **plural noun**.

A **verb** is a word that describes an action (*go, claim, put*) or a state (*be, live*) and is essential for forming a sentence.

An **adjective** is a word that describes a noun (*sweet, rich, green, technical*) and gives greater depth and interest to a sentence.

An **adverb** is a word that describes or 'modifies' a verb, such as *happily* or *obviously*.

Further word classes that you will come across occasionally in this thesaurus are:

A **preposition** is a word such as *after*, *in*, *to*, *on*, and *with*, which usually stands before a noun or pronoun and tells you how that noun relates to what has gone before.

A **conjunction** is a word such as *and*, *because*, *but*, *for*, *if*, *or*, and *when*, and is used to connect other words or parts of a sentence together.

An **exclamation** is a word, typically used on its own, expressing an emotion, such as *goodbye* or *sorry*.

Some words are used in more than one word class. For example, the word *place* can be either a noun (*a beautiful place*) or a verb (*place the tray in the oven*). If an entry has more than one word-class section, make sure you choose the right one for your needs.

For more detailed information and help, see page 2 of this section of the book.

### Senses

Many words have more than one meaning or 'sense'. Some entries are therefore divided into different senses. For example, the adjective *fair* is divided into three different senses in the thesaurus:

> **fair adj. 1** treating people
> equally. **2** just or appropriate.
> **3** quite large. **4** (of hair) blonde.
> **5** (of weather) fine and dry.
> • n. **1** a funfair. **2** a periodic
> gathering for a sale of goods.
> □ fairground an outdoor area
> where a funfair is held. fairway
> a part of a golf course between a
> tee and a green.
> ▷ SYNS **adj. 1** JUST, impartial,
> unbiased, unprejudiced, object-
> ive, even-handed, equitable,
> lawful, legal, legitimate.
> **2** BLONDE, light, yellow, golden,
> flaxen. **3** FINE, dry, bright, clear,
> sunny. • n. **1** FESTIVAL, carnival,
> fete, gala, funfair. **2** EXHIBITION,
> display, show, exposition, expo.

*Fair* can mean 'just' or 'impartial' (*a fair decision*), 'fair in colour' (*fair-haired*), or 'fine' or 'dry' (*fair weather*).

When you are looking at the different senses for a word, you can use the first synonym in each group (printed in **bold** type) to guide you to the meaning you want to express.

## Examples

Although very compact, the thesaurus section of this book still finds room for some examples when they are particularly useful in showing you how the headword is used and in guiding you to the correct sense.

For instance, the adjective *dull* has four senses in the thesaurus:

> **dull** adj. **1** not interesting or ex-
> citing. **2** not bright, resonant, or
> sharp. **3** stupid. • v. make or
> become less intense, sharp, or
> bright. ■ **dully** adv.
> ▷ SYNS **adj. 1** UNINTERESTING,
> boring, tedious, tiresome,
> wearisome, monotonous, flat,
> unimaginative, uninspired, un-
> inspiring, lacklustre. **2** *dull
> colours:* DRAB, dreary, sombre,
> faded, washed-out. **3** *dull
> weather:* OVERCAST, cloudy,
> gloomy, dreary, dark, leaden,
> murky, lowering. **4** *a dull thud:*
> MUTED, muffled, indistinct.

To find the right sense, first read the first synonyms and the example phrases and decide which is closest to the idea you wish to express: are you describing something just generally uninteresting or boring, a colour, the weather, or a sound? When you have chosen the right sense, look at the selection of synonyms that it contains.

## Synonyms

In this thesaurus, the first synonyms given in each group are the commonest and nearest to the meaning of the headword. However, you may have to read the whole list to find the synonym which is best suited to your needs. If you are not sure whether a word is the one you want, you should check its meaning in the dictionary part of the entry.

As well as thinking about meaning, you need to think about the style or tone when selecting a synonym. If you are writing an email to a friend you can be quite informal: you could describe music as being *cool*, for example. But in an essay, report, or review you need to use a more formal word, such as *marvellous* or *excellent*. If you wanted to use a more unusual word you could even try *sublime*—your thesaurus opens up all sorts of possibilities.

## Labels

Some words, like *good* and *bad*, can be used in any context. They are part of Standard English. But some words are only used in certain contexts; in this thesaurus they are labelled to show what the context is. There are two different types of label in this thesaurus: labels about level or style (register labels) and labels about where the word is used (geographical labels).

## Register labels

Register is the word used to describe the level of language—for example, whether it is *informal*.

Standard English is the language that we use in the company of people we are not that familiar with, in a workplace, to teachers, or indeed in any other 'business' situation, from speaking to a shop assistant to booking a holiday. It is the most accepted and established use of the language.

'Informal' language, on the other hand, is the language that you will use when you are with people that are close to you. When you are talking or writing to family and friends, you will automatically adopt this freer, chattier style. For example, the thesaurus entry for *steal* shows that synonyms such as *thieve*, *take*, and *appropriate* are Standard English, but that the alternatives *pinch*, *nick*, *swipe*, and *rip off* are informal, and so care must be taken to ensure they are used only in informal contexts.

**steal** v. **1** take dishonestly.
**2** move stealthily.
▷ SYNS **1** THIEVE, take, appropriate,
misappropriate, pilfer, purloin,
filch, embezzle; plagiarize;
inf. pinch, nick, swipe, rip off.
**2** SLIP, slide, tiptoe, sneak,
creep, slink, sidle.

Even if you have spoken English all your life, you may not always realize which category a word belongs to, so it is important to check that language is appropriate for the occasion.

## Finally...

We hope that this brief guide to a dictionary and thesaurus and its uses will help you to get the most from it. Take time to browse the pages of your thesaurus, and you will discover how easy it is to find your way around it. No doubt you will be drawn into the fascinating links and chains of words that it can weave.

A thesaurus serves many practical purposes, but you can also have fun just dipping into your personal treasure trove of words.

# Kk

**K** abbr. **1** kilobytes. **2** inf. thousand.

**kaftan** (or **caftan**) n. a long, loose dress or tunic.

**kale** n. a green vegetable.

**kaleidoscope** n. a tube containing coloured fragments reflected to produce changing patterns as the tube is rotated. ■ **kaleidoscopic** adj.

**kamikaze** n. (in the Second World War) a Japanese explosive-laden aircraft deliberately crashed on its target. • adj. reckless or suicidal.

**kangaroo** n. an Australian mammal with strong hind legs for jumping.

**kaput** adj. inf. broken.

**karaoke** n. entertainment in which people sing popular songs to pre-recorded backing tracks.

**karate** n. a Japanese system of unarmed combat.

**karma** n. (in Buddhism and Hinduism) a person's actions seen as affecting their future fate.

**kayak** n. a light covered canoe.

**kebab** n. pieces of meat etc. cooked on a skewer.

**kedgeree** n. a cooked dish of fish, rice, hard-boiled eggs, etc.

**keel** n. a structure running along the base of a ship. • v. (**keel over**) **1** capsize. **2** fall over.

**keen** adj. **1** eager and enthusiastic. **2** sharp. **3** quick to understand. **4** highly developed.
▷ SYNS **1** EAGER, enthusiastic, avid, ardent, fervent, committed, dedicated, conscientious; impatient, itching, dying, raring. **2** SHARP, acute; perceptive, astute, shrewd, penetrating, discerning.

**keep** v. **1** continue to have. **2** continue in a specified condition, position, or activity. **3** save for future use. **4** store in a regular place. **5** do something agreed. **6** cause to be late. **7** support financially. • n. **1** food and other essentials for living. **2** a strongly fortified structure in a castle. □ **keep up** move at the same rate as another.
▷ SYNS v. **1** RETAIN, save, hold on to; inf. hang on to. **2** CARRY ON, continue, maintain, persist. **3** COMPLY WITH, obey, observe, abide by, adhere to; fulfil, honour. **4** PROVIDE FOR, support, maintain, sustain; look after.

**keeper** n. a person who keeps or looks after something.
▷ SYNS CURATOR, custodian, caretaker, steward, guardian, administrator.

**keeping** n. (**in** (or **out of**) **keeping with**) fitting (or not fitting) in with.

**keepsake** n. a small item kept in memory of the person who gave it.
▷ SYNS MEMENTO, souvenir, reminder, remembrance, token.

**keg** n. a small barrel.

**kelp** n. a type of seaweed.

**kennel** n. 1 a shelter for a dog. 2 (**kennels**) a boarding place for dogs.

**kept** past and p.p. of **KEEP**.

**kerb** n. a stone edging to a pavement.

**kernel** n. 1 the softer part of a nut, seed, or fruit stone. 2 a central part.

**kerosene** n. paraffin oil.

**kestrel** n. a small falcon.

**ketchup** n. a thick tomato sauce.

**kettle** n. a container with a spout and handle, for boiling water. □ **kettledrum** a large bowl-shaped drum.

**key** n. 1 a piece of shaped metal for opening or closing a lock or turning a screw etc. 2 a lever pressed by the finger on a piano etc. 3 a button on a panel for operating a computer or typewriter. 4 a thing providing access or insight. 5 a system of related notes in music. 6 a list explaining the symbols used in a map or table. □ **keynote** 1 a central theme. 2 the note on which a musical key is based. **keypad** a set of buttons for operating an electronic device or phone. **keystone** 1 the central part of a policy or system. 2 the central stone at the top of an arch, locking it together. **keyword** 1 a significant word mentioned in an index. 2 a word used in a computer system to indicate a document's content.
▷ SYNS ANSWER, clue, solution, explanation.

**keyboard** n. a set of keys on a computer, typewriter, or piano. • v. key data. ■ **keyboarder** n.

**kg** abbr. kilograms.

**khaki** n. a dull brownish-yellow colour.

**kibbutz** n. a communal settlement in Israel.

**kick** v. 1 strike or propel with the foot. 2 inf. give up a habit. 3 (of a gun) spring back when fired. • n. 1 an act of kicking. 2 inf. a thrill. □ **kick-off** the start of a football match. **kick out** inf. force to leave.
▷ SYNS v. 1 BOOT, punt. 2 GIVE UP, stop, quit.

**kid** n. 1 inf. a child. 2 a young goat. • v. (**kidded**, **kidding**) inf. fool into believing.

**kidnap** v. (**kidnapped**, **kidnapping**; US **kidnaped**) take someone by force and hold them captive. ■ **kidnapper** n.

**kidney** n. (pl. **-eys**) either of a pair of organs that remove waste products from the blood and secrete urine.

**kill** v. 1 cause the death of. 2 put an end to. 3 pass time. • n. 1 an act of killing. 2 an animal killed by a hunter.
▷ SYNS v. 1 MURDER, put to death, execute, assassinate, dispatch, slaughter, butcher, massacre, exterminate; inf. bump off, do in. 2 DESTROY, put an end to, extinguish, ruin, wreck, dash, shatter.

**killer** n. a person or thing that kills.
▷ SYNS MURDERER, assassin, butcher, executioner, gunman; inf. hit man.

**killing** n. an act of causing death.
▷ SYNS MURDER, manslaughter, homicide, execution, slaughter, massacre, butchery, bloodshed, carnage, extermination.

**kiln** n. an oven for baking or drying things.

**kilo** n. (pl. **-os**) a kilogram.

**kilogram** n. a unit of weight or mass in the metric system (2.205 lb).

**kilohertz** n. a unit of frequency of electromagnetic waves, = 1,000 cycles per second.

**kilometre** n. 1,000 metres (0.62 mile).

**kilowatt** n. 1,000 watts.

**kilt** n. a knee-length skirt of pleated tartan cloth, tradition-ally worn by Highland men.

**kilter** n. (**out of kilter**) out of balance.

**kimono** n. (pl. **-os**) a loose Japanese robe worn with a sash.

**kin** (or **kinsfolk**) n. your relations. □ **kinship 1** blood relationship. **2** relationship based on similar characteristics. ■ **kinsman** n. **kinswoman** n.
▷ SYNS RELATIVES, relations, family, people, kindred, kith and kin, kinsfolk.

**kind** n. a class of similar people or things. • adj. considerate and generous. □ **in kind (of** payment) in goods etc., not money. ■ **kindness** n.
▷ SYNS n. SORT, type, variety, class, category, genus, species. • adj. CONSIDERATE, good-natured, kind-hearted, kindly, warm-hearted, caring, affectionate, warm, compassionate, sympa-thetic, understanding, ben-evolent, benign, altruistic, unselfish, generous, helpful, thoughtful.

**kindergarten** n. a school for very young children.

**kindle** v. light a fire; arouse a feeling.

▷ SYNS **1** LIGHT, set alight, set on fire, set fire to, ignite.
**2** STIMULATE, rouse, arouse, excite, stir, awaken, inspire, trigger, provoke.

**kindling** n. small pieces of wood for lighting fires.

**kindly** adv. **1** in a kind way. **2** please (used in polite requests). • adj. kind.
■ **kindliness** n.

**kindred** n. your relatives. • adj. similar in kind.
▷ SYNS adj. RELATED, connected, allied, like, similar, comparable, analogous.

**kinetic** adj. of movement.

**king** n. **1** the male ruler of a country. **2** the best or most important person or thing. **3** a playing card next below ace. **4** the most important chess piece. □ **kingpin** an important person or thing. **king-size** extra large.

**kingdom** n. **1** a country ruled by a king or queen. **2** each of the three divisions in which natural objects are classified.

**kingfisher** n. a colourful diving bird.

**kink** n. **1** a bend or twist in something straight. **2** a flaw. **3** a peculiar characteristic.
▷ SYNS **1** TWIST, corkscrew, curl, twirl, knot, tangle. **2** FLAW, defect, problem, snag, hitch. **3** QUIRK, eccentricity, foible, idiosyncrasy.

**kinky** adj. **1** inf. relating to or liking unusual sexual activities. **2** having kinks.

**kiosk** n. a booth where newspapers, tickets, etc. are sold, or containing a public phone.

**kip** n. inf. a sleep.

**kipper** n. a smoked herring.

**kirk** n. Scot. a church.

**kismet** n. destiny or fate.

**kiss** v. touch with the lips. • n. a touch with the lips. □ the kiss of life mouth-to-mouth resuscitation.

**kit** n. a set of equipment or clothes for a specific purpose. • v. (**kitted**, **kitting**) provide with appropriate clothing or equipment.

▷ SYNS n. 1 EQUIPMENT, tools, implements, instruments, utensils, gear, tackle, paraphernalia. 2 CLOTHES, clothing, garments, attire, outfit; strip.

**kitchen** n. a room where food is prepared.

**kite** n. 1 a light framework with fabric stretched over it, attached to a string for flying in the wind. 2 a large hawk.

**kith and kin** n. relatives.

**kitsch** n. art, objects, or design regarded as tasteless or too sentimental.

**kitten** n. a young cat.

**kitty** n. (pl. -**ies**) a communal fund.

**kiwi** n. a flightless New Zealand bird.

**klaxon** n. trademark an electric horn.

**kleptomania** n. a compulsive desire to steal. ■ **kleptomaniac** n.

**km** abbr. kilometres.

**knack** n. the ability to do something skilfully.

▷ SYNS TALENT, skill, aptitude, gift, flair, ability, capability, capacity, expertise, genius, facility.

**knacker** n. a person who buys and slaughters old horses, cattle, etc. • v. inf. 1 tire out. 2 damage.

**knapsack** n. a bag worn strapped on the back.

**knave** n. 1 old use a dishonest man. 2 a jack in playing cards.

**knead** v. press and stretch dough with the hands; massage.

**knee** n. 1 the joint between the thigh and the lower leg. 2 a person's lap. • v. (**kneed**, **kneeing**) hit with the knee. □ **kneecap** 1 the bone in front of the knee joint. 2 shoot in the knee as a punishment. **knee-jerk** automatic and unthinking. **knees-up** inf. a lively party.

**kneel** v. (**knelt** or **kneeled**, **kneeling**) rest on your knees.

**knell** n. the sound of a bell tolled after a death.

**knew** past of KNOW.

**knickers** pl.n. women's underpants.

**knick-knack** n. a small worthless ornament.

**knife** n. (pl. **knives**) a cutting instrument with a blade and handle. • v. stab with a knife.

**knight** n. 1 hist. a man of noble rank with a duty to fight for his king. 2 a man awarded a title and entitled to use 'Sir' in front of his name. 3 a chess piece shaped like a horse's head. • v. give the title of knight to. ■ **knighthood** n.

**knit** v. 1 make a garment from yarn formed into interlocking loops on long needles. 2 join together. 3 tighten the eyebrows in a frown. ■ **knitting** n.

▷ SYNS UNITE, unify, bond, fuse, join.

**knob** n. 1 a rounded lump. 2 a round door handle. ■ **knobbly** adj.

▷ SYNS BUMP, lump, protuberance, bulge, swelling, knot, nodule.

**knock** v. **1** hit noisily to attract attention. **2** collide with. **3** cause to move or fall by hitting. **4** make a hole etc. by hitting. **5** inf. criticize. • n. **1** a short sound made by a blow. **2** a blow. **3** a setback. □ knock-kneed having knees that bend inwards. knock out **1** make unconscious. **2** eliminate from a competition.

▷ SYNS v. **1** BANG, tap, rap, pound, hammer, hit, strike. **2** COLLIDE WITH, bump into, run into, crash into.

**knocker** n. a hinged device for knocking on a door.

**knoll** n. a small hill.

▷ SYNS HILLOCK, hill, hummock, mound, hump, barrow.

**knot** n. **1** a fastening made by tying a piece of string, rope, etc. **2** a tangled mass. **3** a hard mass in wood where a branch joins the trunk. **4** a small group of people. **5** a unit of speed of ships, aircraft, or winds. • v. **1** fasten with a knot. **2** tangle.

▷ SYNS n. *a knot of people:* CLUSTER, group, band, huddle, bunch. • v. TIE, fasten, secure, do up.

**knotty** adj. **1** full of knots. **2** very complex.

**know** v. **1** be aware of something. **2** be certain. **3** be familiar with. **4** have learned. □ know-how practical knowledge or skill.

▷ SYNS **1** BE AWARE, realize, be conscious. **2** BE FAMILIAR WITH, be conversant with, be acquainted with, understand, comprehend, have a grasp of, be versed in.

**knowing** adj. cunning; showing that you have secret knowledge: *a knowing look.*
■ knowingly adv.

**knowledge** n. **1** information and skills gained through experience or education. **2** the total of what is known.

▷ SYNS **1** LEARNING, education, scholarship, erudition, wisdom. **2** UNDERSTANDING, comprehension, grasp, command, mastery, skill, expertise.

**knowledgeable** adj. intelligent and well informed.

▷ SYNS **1** WELL INFORMED, educated, learned, erudite, scholarly, well read, cultured, cultivated, enlightened. **2** ACQUAINTED, familiar, au fait, conversant, experienced.

**knuckle** n. **1** a finger joint. **2** a joint of an animal's leg as meat. • v. (**knuckle under**) yield or submit.

**koala** n. a bearlike Australian tree-dwelling animal.

**Koran** n. the sacred book of Islam.

**kosher** adj. **1** (of food) prepared according to Jewish law. **2** inf. genuine or legitimate.

**kowtow** v. be very meek and obedient.

**krypton** n. a colourless, odourless gas.

**kudos** n. praise and honour.

**kung fu** n. a Chinese martial art.

# LI

**L** (or **l**) n. the Roman numeral for 50. • abbr. **1** learner driver. **2** (**l**) litres.

**lab** n. inf. a laboratory.

**label** n. a piece of card, cloth, etc., attached to something and carrying information about it. • v. (**labelled**, **labelling**; US **labeled**) attach a label to; put in a specified category.
▷ SYNS n. TAG, ticket, tab, sticker, marker. • v. CATEGORIZE, classify, describe, designate, brand, call, name, dub.

**laboratory** n. (pl. **-ies**) a room or building equipped for scientific work.

**laborious** adj. needing or showing much effort.
▷ SYNS HARD, heavy, difficult, arduous, strenuous, onerous, gruelling, tiring, wearying, wearisome.

**labour** (US **labor**) n. **1** work. **2** workers. **3** childbirth. • v. **1** work hard. **2** move or do with difficulty.
▷ SYNS n. **1** WORK, toil, exertion, effort, industry, drudgery. **2** WORKERS, employees, labourers, workforce, staff. **3** CHILDBIRTH, birth, delivery; formal parturition. • v. WORK, toil, slave, struggle, exert yourself.

**labourer** (US **laborer**) n. an unskilled manual worker.

**Labrador** n. a large dog.

**laburnum** n. a tree with hanging clusters of yellow flowers.

**labyrinth** n. a maze.
▷ SYNS MAZE, warren, network, web, entanglement.

**labyrinthine** adj. **1** like a labyrinth. **2** intricate and confusing.
▷ SYNS **1** MAZE-LIKE, winding, twisting, serpentine, meandering. **1** INTRICATE, complicated, complex, involved, tortuous, convoluted, elaborate.

**lace** n. **1** decorative fabric made by looping thread in patterns. **2** a cord used to fasten a shoe or garment. • v. **1** fasten with laces. **2** add alcohol to a dish or drink. ■ **lacy** adj.

**lacerate** v. tear flesh.
▷ SYNS CUT (OPEN), tear, gash, slash, rip, mutilate, hurt, wound, injure, maim.

**lachrymose** adj. tearful.

**lack** n. an absence or insufficiency of something. • v. be without or without enough of.
▷ SYNS n. ABSENCE, want, need, deficiency, dearth, shortage, scarcity, paucity.

**lackadaisical** adj. unenthusiastic or careless.

**lackey** n. (pl. **-eys**) **1** a servant. **2** a servile person.

**lacklustre** (US **lackluster**) adj. lacking energy or inspiration.

**laconic** adj. using few words.
▷ SYNS BRIEF, concise, succinct, pithy, terse, short.

**lacquer** n. a hard glossy varnish. • v. coat with lacquer.

**lacrosse** n. a game similar to hockey played using sticks with small nets on the ends.

**lad** n. a boy.

**ladder** n. **1** a set of bars between uprights, used for climbing up. **2** a series of stages by which progress can be made. **3** a strip of unravelled fabric in tights or stockings. • v. cause or develop a ladder.

**laden** adj. loaded.
▷ SYNS LOADED, burdened, weighed down, weighted, encumbered.

**ladle** n. a deep long-handled spoon. • v. serve with a ladle.

**lady** n. **1** a woman. **2** (**Lady**) a title used by peeresses and the wives and widows of knights. **3** a well-mannered woman;

**ladybird** n. a small flying beetle, usu. red with black spots.

**ladylike** adj. well-mannered.
▷ SYNS GENTEEL, polite, refined, well bred, decorous, proper, respectable, well mannered.

**lag** v. **1** fall behind. **2** cover a water tank etc. with insulating material. • n. a delay.
▷ SYNS V. FALL BEHIND, trail, bring up the rear, dawdle, hang back, straggle.

**lager** n. a light fizzy beer.

**laggard** n. a person who makes slow progress.

**lagging** n. material used to lag a boiler etc.

**lagoon** n. a saltwater lake beside the sea.

**laid** past & p.p. of **LAY**¹.

**laid-back** adj. easy-going and relaxed.

▷ SYNS RELAXED, easy-going, calm, free and easy, unexcitable, imperturbable; inf. unflappable.

**lain** p.p. of **LIE**².

**lair** n. a wild animal's resting place.

**laissez-faire** n. a policy of non-interference.

**laity** n. lay people, not clergy.

**lake** n. a large body of water surrounded by land.
▷ SYNS POND, tarn, pool, reservoir, lagoon; Scot. loch.

**lamb** n. **1** a young sheep. **2** an innocent or gentle person. • v. give birth to a lamb.

**lambaste** (or **lambast**) v. criticize harshly.

**lame** adj. **1** unable to walk normally. **2** unconvincing. • v. make lame.
▷ SYNS adj. **1** LIMPING, hobbling, halting, crippled. **2** WEAK, feeble, thin, flimsy, unconvincing.

**lamé** n. a fabric interwoven with gold or silver thread.

**lament** n. **1** an expression of grief. **2** a song or poem expressing grief. • v. feel or express grief or regret.
▷ SYNS V. **1** MOURN, grieve, sorrow, wail, weep, cry, keen. **2** COMPLAIN ABOUT, bemoan, bewail, deplore.

**lamentable** adj. very bad or regrettable.
▷ SYNS DEPLORABLE, regrettable, tragic, terrible, wretched, woeful, sorrowful, distressing, grievous.

**laminate** v. **1** cover with a protected layer. **2** make by sticking layers together. • n. laminated material.

**lamp** n. a device for giving light.

**lampoon** v. mock or ridicule.
• n. a mocking attack.

**lance** n. a long spear. • v. prick or cut open a boil etc.

**lancet** n. a surgeon's pointed two-edged knife.

**land** n. **1** the part of the earth's surface not covered by water. **2** an area of ground. **3** ground or soil used for farming. **4** a country or state. • v. **1** put or go ashore. **2** come or bring down to the ground. **3** inf. succeed in obtaining or achieving. **4** inf. put or end up in a difficult situation. □ **landfall** arrival on land after a sea journey. **landfill 1** the disposal of waste by burying it. **2** buried waste. **landlocked** surrounded by land. **landlubber** inf. a person unfamiliar with the sea or sailing. **landmark 1** an object or feature easily seen from a distance. **2** an event marking an important stage. **landmine** an explosive mine laid on or just under the surface of the ground. **landslide** (also **landslip**) **1** a fall of earth or rock. **2** an overwhelming majority of votes.
▷ SYNS n. **1** DRY LAND, terra firma; coast, coastline, shore. **2** GROUNDS, fields, property, acreage, estate. **3** COUNTRY, nation, state, realm, province, kingdom. • v. DISEMBARK, go ashore, alight, berth, dock; touch down, come to rest.

**landed** adj. owning land.

**landing** n. **1** coming or bringing ashore or to ground; a place for this. **2** a level area at the top of a flight of stairs.

**landlord** (or **landlady**) n. a person who rents out property to a tenant; a person who runs a pub.

**landscape** n. the scenery of a land area; a picture of this. • v. lay out an area attractively with natural-looking features.
▷ SYNS n. COUNTRYSIDE, scenery, country, panorama, perspective.

**lane** n. **1** a narrow road. **2** a division of a road for a single line of traffic. **3** a strip for each of the competitors in a race.

**language** n. **1** words and their use. **2** a particular system or style of this.
▷ SYNS **1** SPEECH, speaking, talk, discourse, communication, words, vocabulary. **2** TONGUE, dialect; inf. lingo.

**languid** adj. lacking energy.
▷ SYNS LANGUOROUS, unhurried, indolent, lazy, lethargic.

**languish** v. become weak or faint; live under miserable conditions.

**languor** n. tiredness or lack of energy. ■ **languorous** adj.

**lank** adj. (of hair) long, limp, and straight.
▷ SYNS LIMP, lifeless, dull, straggling, straight, long.

**lanky** adj. tall and thin.
▷ SYNS TALL, thin, spindly, gangling, gangly, lean, scrawny, gawky.

**lantern** n. a lamp enclosed in a metal frame with glass panels.

**lap** n. **1** a flat area over the thighs of a seated person. **2** one circuit of a racetrack. **3** a part of a journey. • v. **1** take up liquid with the tongue. **2** (of water) move against something with a gentle sound. **3** be one or more laps ahead of a competitor. □ **laptop** a portable computer.
▷ SYNS n. CIRCUIT, circle, leg, round.

**lapel** n. a flap folded back at the front of a coat etc.

**lapse** n. 1 a temporary failure of concentration, memory, etc.; a decline in standard. 2 the passage of time. • v. 1 (of a right or privilege) become invalid. 2 pass into an inferior state.
▷ SYNS n. 1 SLIP, error, mistake, blunder, failing, fault, failure, omission, oversight; inf. slip-up. 2 INTERVAL, gap, pause, intermission, interlude, hiatus, break. • v. 1 DECLINE, deteriorate, worsen, degenerate; inf. go downhill. 2 EXPIRE, run out, become void, become invalid.

**larch** n. a deciduous tree of the pine family.

**lard** n. pig fat.

**larder** n. a storeroom for food.

**large** adj. of great size or extent. □ at large 1 free to roam about. 2 as a whole. ■ largely adv. on the whole.
▷ SYNS BIG, great, sizeable, substantial, considerable, huge, vast, massive, immense, enormous, colossal, mammoth, gigantic, giant, fat, stout, strapping, burly.

**largesse** n. 1 generosity. 2 money or gifts.

**lark** n. 1 a skylark. 2 inf. something done for fun. • v. (lark about) inf. behave playfully.

**larva** n. (pl. -vae) an insect in the first stage of its life.

**larynx** n. the part of the throat containing the vocal cords.

**lasagne** n. a dish of pasta layered with meat and cheese sauce.

**lascivious** adj. lustful.
▷ SYNS LEWD, lecherous, lustful, licentious, libidinous, salacious, ribald.

**laser** n. a device emitting an intense narrow beam of light.

**lash** v. 1 beat with a whip. 2 beat against. 3 tie down. 4 (of an animal) move its tail quickly to and fro. • n. 1 an eyelash. 2 a blow with a whip. 3 the flexible part of a whip.

**lashings** pl.n. inf. a lot.

**lass** (or **lassie**) n. Scot. & N. Engl. a girl or young woman.

**lassitude** n. lack of energy.

**lasso** n. (pl. -sos or -soes) a rope with a noose for catching cattle.

**last** adj. 1 coming after all others. 2 most recent. 3 lowest in importance. • adv. on the last occasion before the present. • n. 1 the last person or thing. 2 the only remaining part. 3 a foot-shaped block used in making or repairing shoes. • v. 1 continue or be enough for a specified time. 2 remain usable. ■ lasting adj. lastly adv.
▷ SYNS adj. FINAL, closing, concluding, ending, ultimate, terminal. • v. CONTINUE, go on, carry on, keep on.

**latch** n. 1 a bar with a catch and lever, used to fasten a gate etc. 2 a lock that fastens when a door is closed. • v. fasten with a latch.

**late** adj. 1 arriving or happening after the proper or usual time. 2 far on in the day or night or a period. 3 dead. 4 recent. • adv. 1 after the proper or usual time. 2 far on in the day or night or a period.
▷ SYNS adj. 1 BEHIND SCHEDULE, overdue, delayed, tardy. 2 DECEASED, dead, departed.

**3** FORMER, recent, previous, preceding, past, prior.

**lately** adv. recently.

**latent** adj. existing but not active, developed, or visible.
▷ SYNS DORMANT, quiescent, inactive, hidden, concealed, undeveloped, unrealized, potential, possible.

**lateral** adj. of, at, to, or from the side(s).
▷ SYNS SIDEWAYS, sidelong, edgeways, indirect, oblique, slanting.

**latex** n. a milky fluid from certain plants, esp. the rubber tree.

**lath** n. (pl. **laths**) a narrow, thin strip of wood.

**lathe** n. a machine for holding and turning pieces of wood or metal while they are worked.

**lather** n. froth from soap and water; frothy sweat. • v. cover with or form lather.

**Latin** n. the language of the ancient Romans.

**latitude** n. **1** the distance of a place from the equator, measured in degrees. **2** freedom from restrictions.
▷ SYNS SCOPE, freedom, liberty, in-dependence, leeway, free rein, licence.

**latrine** n. a communal toilet in a camp or barracks.

**latte** n. frothy hot milk with espresso coffee added.

**latter** adj. **1** towards the end or in the final stages; recent. **2** (**the latter**) the second of two things to be mentioned. □ **latter-day** modern or recent. ■ **latterly** adv.

**lattice** n. a framework of crossed strips.

**laudable** adj. praiseworthy.

▷ SYNS PRAISEWORTHY, commend-able, admirable, meritorious, deserving, creditable, worthy.

**laugh** v. make sounds and facial movements expressing amusement. • n. the act or manner of laughing.
□ **laughing stock** a person who is ridiculed.
▷ SYNS V. CHUCKLE, chortle, guffaw, giggle, titter, snigger, be doubled up; inf. be in stitches, be creased up, fall about, crack up.

**laughable** adj. ridiculous.

**laughter** n. the act or sound of laughing.
▷ SYNS LAUGHING, chuckling, chortling, guffawing, giggling, tittering, sniggering; inf. hysterics.

**launch** v. send a ship into the water; send a rocket into the air; start an enterprise; introduce a new product.
• n. **1** the process of launching something. **2** a large motor boat.
▷ SYNS V. **1** FIRE, discharge, propel, throw, cast, hurl, let fly, blast off. **2** SET IN MOTION, get going, begin, start, embark on, initiate, instigate, institute, inaugurate, establish, put in place, set up, introduce.

**launder** v. **1** wash and iron clothes etc. **2** transfer illegally obtained money to conceal its origin.

**launderette** n. a place with coin-operated washing machines etc. for public use.

**laundry** n. (pl. **-ies**) a place where clothes etc. are washed; clothes etc. for washing.

**laurel** n. **1** an evergreen shrub. **2** (**laurels**) victories or honours gained.

**lava** n. flowing or hardened molten rock from a volcano.

**lavatory** n. (pl. **-ies**) a toilet; a room equipped with this.

**lavender** n. a shrub with fragrant purple flowers; light purple.

**lavish** adj. generous; luxurious and extravagant. • v. give generously.
▷ SYNS adj. **1** GENEROUS, liberal, bountiful, open-handed, un-stinting, unsparing, free. **2** SUMPTUOUS, luxurious, extravagant, expensive, opulent, grand, splendid. **3** ABUNDANT, copious, plentiful, liberal, prolific. • v. HEAP, shower, pour, give, bestow.

**law** n. **1** a rule or set of rules established by authority. **2** a statement of what always happens in certain circumstances. □ **lawsuit** a claim brought to a law court to be decided.
▷ SYNS **1** RULE, regulation, statute, act, decree, edict, command, order, ruling, directive; legislation, constitution. **2** PRINCIPLE, precept, credo, tenet, canon.

**law-abiding** adj. obedient to the laws of society.
▷ SYNS HONEST, honourable, upright, upstanding, good, virtuous, dutiful, obedient.

**lawful** adj. permitted or recognized by law.
▷ SYNS LEGAL, legitimate, licit, valid, permissible, allowable, rightful, proper, constitutional, legalized, authorized.

**lawless** adj. disregarding the law.
▷ SYNS **1** ANARCHIC, disorderly, unruly, insurgent, rebellious, insubordinate, riotous,

mutinous. **2** UNLAWFUL, illegal, illicit, illegitimate, criminal, felonious.

**lawn** n. an area of closely cut grass in a garden or park.

**lawyer** n. a person qualified in legal matters.
▷ SYNS SOLICITOR, barrister, advocate, counsel, Queen's Counsel, QC; US attorney.

**lax** adj. not strict or severe.
■ **laxity** n.
▷ SYNS SLACK, slipshod, negligent, remiss, careless, heedless, slapdash, casual; easy-going, lenient, permissive, indulgent, overindulgent.

**laxative** adj. & n. (a medicine) stimulating the bowels to empty.

**lay**¹ v. **1** put down carefully. **2** put down in position for use. **3** assign or place. **4** (of a bird) produce eggs. • adj. **1** not belonging to the clergy. **2** non-professional. □ **layabout** an idle person. **lay-by** a roadside area where vehicles may stop. **lay off** discharge workers temporarily.
▷ SYNS v. PUT, place, set, deposit, position; set out, arrange, dispose.

**lay**² past of LIE².

**layer** n. one of several sheets or thicknesses of a substance covering a surface. • v. arrange in layers.

**layette** n. an outfit for a newborn baby.

**laze** v. spend time idly.
▷ SYNS IDLE, loaf, lounge, loll, take it easy, relax, unwind.

**lazy** adj. (**-ier, -iest**) unwilling to work or use energy; done without effort or care.
■ **lazily** adv.

▷ SYNS IDLE, indolent, slothful, work-shy, sluggish, lethargic, languorous.

**lb** abbr. pounds (in weight).

**lbw** abbr. Cricket leg before wicket.

**lea** n. lit. an area of grassy land.

**leach** v. (of minerals etc.) be removed from soil by water passing through it.

**lead**¹ v. 1 cause to go with you. 2 be a route or means of access. 3 result in. 4 influence. 5 be in charge of. 6 be ahead of or superior to. 7 have a particular way of life. • n. 1 an example for others to follow. 2 a position of advantage. 3 the chief part in a play or film. 4 a clue. 5 a strap or cord for leading a dog. 6 a wire conveying electric current.

▷ SYNS v. 1 GUIDE, conduct, show, usher, escort, steer, shepherd. 2 RESULT IN, give rise to, bring on, provoke, contribute to. 3 CAUSE, induce, prompt, move, incline, persuade, make. 4 COMMAND, control, govern, run, manage, be in charge of, preside over. • n. 1 EXAMPLE, model, pattern. 2 FIRST PLACE, winning position, vanguard. 3 CLUE, tip-off, pointer. 4 LEASH, strap, rope.

**lead**² n. 1 a heavy grey metal. 2 graphite in a pencil. ■ **leaded** adj.

**leaden** adj. 1 heavy or slow-moving. 2 a dull grey colour.

**leader** n. 1 a person who leads. 2 a newspaper article giving editorial opinions. ■ **leadership** n.

▷ SYNS 1 RULER, head, chief, commander, director, governor, principal, captain, skipper, manager, overseer; inf. boss. 2 PIONEER, trendsetter, front

runner, innovator, trailblazer, originator.

**leading** adj. most important or in first place.

▷ SYNS MAIN, chief, top, principal, foremost, key, central, greatest, pre-eminent, star.

**leaf** n. (pl. **leaves**) 1 a flat green organ growing from the stem or root of a plant. 2 a single sheet of paper in a book; a very thin sheet of metal. • v. (**leaf through**) turn over the leaves of a book. ■ **leafy** adj.

**leaflet** n. 1 a printed sheet of paper giving information. 2 a small leaf of a plant.

▷ SYNS PAMPHLET, booklet, brochure, handbill, circular, flyer.

**league** n. 1 a group of people or countries united for a purpose; an association of sports clubs that compete against one another. 2 a class or standard: *in a league of his own.*

▷ SYNS ALLIANCE, confederation, federation, union, association, coalition, consortium, guild, corporation, cooperative, syndicate, group.

**leak** v. (of liquid, gas, etc.) pass through a crack; (of a container) lose contents through a crack or hole; disclose secrets or be disclosed. • n. a crack or hole through which contents leak; an instance of leaking. ■ **leakage** n. **leaky** adj.

▷ SYNS v. 1 SEEP OUT, escape, drip, ooze out; exude, discharge, emit, issue. 2 DISCLOSE, divulge, reveal, make known, impart, pass on, give away, let slip; inf. blab, spill the beans. • n. 1 DRIP, leakage, escape, seepage, discharge. 2 HOLE, opening, puncture, crack, fissure, gash, slit.

**lean**[1] v. 1 put or be in a sloping position; rest against something for support. 2 (**lean on**) depend on. □ **lean-to** a shed etc. against the side of a building.
▷ SYNS **1** BE SUPPORTED, be propped, recline. **2** INCLINE, bend, slant, tilt, slope, bank, list. **3** DEPEND, be dependent, rely, count, trust.

**lean**[2] adj. thin; (of meat) with little fat; (of a period) characterized by hardship.
▷ SYNS see THIN.

**leaning** n. a tendency or inclination.
▷ SYNS TENDENCY, inclination, bent, proclivity, propensity, penchant, predisposition, predilection, partiality, preference, bias, liking, fondness, taste.

**leap** v. 1 jump vigorously. 2 (**leap at**) accept eagerly. • n. a vigorous jump. □ **leap year** a year with an extra day (29 Feb.), occurring every four years.
▷ SYNS V. JUMP, bound, hop, skip, spring, vault, hurdle.

**leapfrog** n. a game in which each player vaults over another who is bending down.

**learn** v. (**learned** or **learnt**, **learning**) gain knowledge of or skill in; become aware of; memorize.
▷ SYNS **1** MASTER, grasp, take in, absorb, assimilate, pick up. **2** MEMORIZE, learn by heart, get off pat. **3** DISCOVER, find out, gather, hear, be informed, understand, ascertain, get word/wind of.

**learned** adj. having or showing great learning.

▷ SYNS ERUDITE, scholarly, well educated, knowledgeable, well read, cultured, intellectual, academic, literary, bookish.

**learner** n. a person who is learning a subject or skill.
▷ SYNS BEGINNER, trainee, apprentice, pupil, student, novice, tyro, neophyte.

**learning** n. knowledge obtained by study.

**lease** n. a contract allowing the use of land or a building for a specified time. • v. let out or rent by lease. ■ **leasehold** n.
▷ SYNS V. RENT (OUT), hire (out), charter; let out, sublet.

**leash** n. a dog's lead.
▷ SYNS LEAD, rope, cord, strap.

**least** adj. smallest in amount or degree; lowest in importance. • n. the least amount etc. • adv. in the least degree.

**leather** n. material made by treating animal skins.

**leathery** adj. tough like leather.

**leave** v. 1 go away from. 2 stop living at or working for. 3 go away without taking. 4 cause to be in a specified state: *leave the door open.* 5 allow to do without interfering. 6 deposit or entrust to someone. • n. 1 time absent from work or duty. 2 permission.
▷ SYNS V. **1** DEPART, go, withdraw, retire, make off, pull out, decamp; inf. push off, do a bunk, vamoose. **2** *he left his job:* GIVE UP, quit, resign, retire. **3** *he left her his money:* BEQUEATH, will, endow, hand down.
• n. **1** HOLIDAY, vacation, break, furlough, sabbatical. **2** PERMISSION, consent, authorization, sanction, dispensation.

**leaven** n. a substance causing dough to rise.

**lecherous** adj. showing sexual desire in an offensive way.
■ **lechery** n.
▷ SYNS LUSTFUL, licentious, lascivious, lewd, salacious, debauched.

**lectern** n. a stand with a sloping top from which a bible etc. is read.

**lecture** n. 1 an educational talk. 2 a lengthy reprimand. • v. 1 give a lecture. 2 reprimand.
■ **lecturer** n.
▷ SYNS n. 1 TALK, speech, address, discourse, presentation. 2 REPRIMAND, scolding, rebuke, reproach; inf. dressing-down, telling-off. • v. 1 SPEAK, talk, hold forth, teach. 2 REPRIMAND, scold, rebuke, reproach, remonstrate with, upbraid, berate.

**led** past & p.p. of LEAD¹.

**ledge** n. a narrow horizontal projection or shelf.
▷ SYNS SHELF, sill, mantel, mantelpiece, projection, overhang, ridge, step.

**ledger** n. a book used for keeping accounts.

**lee** n. shelter from the wind given by a hill, building, etc.
□ **leeward** (on) the side away from the wind. **leeway** the available amount of freedom to move or act.

**leech** n. a small bloodsucking worm.

**leek** n. a vegetable with an onion-like flavour.

**leer** v. look slyly, maliciously, or lustfully. • n. a leering look.

**lees** pl.n. sediment in wine.

**left¹** past & p.p. of LEAVE.

**left²** adj. & adv. of, on, or towards the side of the body which is on the west when you are facing north. • n. 1 the left side or region; the left hand or foot. 2 people supporting socialism or a more extreme form of socialism than others in their group.
▷ SYNS adj. & adv. 1 LEFT-HAND; port. 2 LEFT-WING, socialist, communist, radical, progressive.

**leg** n. 1 each of the limbs on which a person, animal, etc. stands or moves; a support of a table, chair, etc. 2 one section of a journey or contest.
▷ SYNS 1 LIMB, member, shank; inf. peg, pin. 2 PART, portion, segment, section, bit, stretch, stage, lap.

**legacy** n. (pl. -ies) something left to someone in a will, or handed down by a predecessor.

**legal** adj. of or based on law; authorized or required by law. □ **legal tender** currency that must, by law, be accepted as payment. ■ **legality** n. **legally** adv.
▷ SYNS LAWFUL, legitimate, licit, legalized, valid, right, permissible, permitted, allowed, authorized, sanctioned, licensed.

**legalize** v. make legal.
▷ SYNS DECRIMINALIZE, make legal, legitimize, permit, allow, authorize, sanction, license.

**legate** n. an envoy.

**legato** adv. Music smoothly and evenly.

**legend** n. 1 a story handed down from the past. 2 a very famous person. 3 an inscription, caption, etc.
▷ SYNS MYTH, saga, epic, (folk) story, (folk) tale, fable.

**legendary** adj. 1 described in legends. 2 famous.

▷ SYNS **1** MYTHICAL, fabled, traditional, storybook, fairy-tale. **2** FAMOUS, celebrated, acclaimed, illustrious, famed, renowned.

**legible** adj. clear enough to be read.

**legion** n. a division of the ancient Roman army; a huge crowd. • adj. very numerous.

**legislate** v. make laws. ■ legislative adj.

**legislation** n. laws collectively.

**legislature** n. the group that formulates a country's laws.

**legitimate** adj. **1** in accordance with a law or rule; justifiable. **2** born of parents married to each other. ■ legitimacy n. legitimize v.
▷ SYNS **1** LEGAL, lawful, licit, rightful, real, true, proper, authorized, permitted, allowed, sanctioned, licensed. **2** VALID, justifiable, reasonable, sound, admissible, well founded, sensible, bona fide.

**legume** n. a plant of the family bearing seeds in pods.

**leisure** n. time free from work.
▷ SYNS FREE TIME, spare time, time off, relaxation, recreation.

**leisurely** adj. & adv. unhurried.
▷ SYNS UNHURRIED, relaxed, easy, gentle, comfortable, restful, slow.

**lemming** n. a mouse-like Arctic rodent.

**lemon** n. **1** a yellow citrus fruit with acidic juice. **2** a pale yellow colour.

**lemonade** n. a lemon-flavoured fizzy drink.

**lemur** n. a nocturnal monkey-like animal of Madagascar.

**lend** v. (**lent**, **lending**) give something to someone for temporary use; provide money temporarily in return for payment of interest; add an effect to something. ■ lender n.
▷ SYNS **1** LOAN; advance. **2** IMPART, add, give, bestow, confer, provide, supply.

**length** n. **1** the measurement or extent from end to end; being long; the full extent; a piece of cloth etc. **2** an extreme effort: *go to great lengths.* ▫ lengthways (or **lengthwise**) in a direction parallel with a thing's length.
▷ SYNS **1** DISTANCE, extent, span, reach. **2** PERIOD, stretch, duration, term, span. **3** PIECE, section, measure, segment, swatch.

**lengthen** v. make or become longer.
▷ SYNS EXTEND, elongate, increase, prolong, draw out, protract.

**lengthy** adj. (**-ier**, **-iest**) very long.
▷ SYNS LONG, long-lasting, prolonged, extended, protracted, long-drawn-out.

**lenient** adj. merciful or tolerant.
▷ SYNS MERCIFUL, forgiving, sparing, compassionate, humane, forbearing, tolerant, indulgent, kind, easy-going.

**lens** n. a piece of glass or similar substance shaped for use in an optical instrument.

**Lent** n. the Christian period of fasting and repentance before Easter.

**lent** past and p.p. of LEND.

**lentil** n. a kind of bean.

**leopard** n. a large spotted wild cat.

**leotard** n. a close-fitting stretchy garment worn by dancers, gymnasts, etc.

**leper** n. a person with leprosy.

**leprosy** n. an infectious disease affecting the skin and nerves and causing deformities.

**lesbian** n. a homosexual woman.

**lesion** n. a region in an organ or tissue that is damaged by injury or disease.

**less** adj. & pron. not so much; a smaller amount of. • adv. to a smaller extent. • prep. minus.

**lessen** v. make or become less.
▷ SYNS **1** *aspirin will lessen the pain:* REDUCE, decrease, minimize, diminish, allay, assuage, alleviate, dull, deaden, take the edge off. **2** *the rain had lessened:* SUBSIDE, decrease, slacken, abate, die down, let up, ease off, tail off, ebb, wane.

**lesser** adj. not so great or important as the other.

**lesson** n. **1** a period of learning or teaching; something to be learnt by a pupil; an experience by which you can learn. **2** a passage from the Bible read aloud.
▷ SYNS **1** CLASS, seminar, tutorial, lecture. **2** EXAMPLE, warning, deterrent, message, moral.

**lest** conj. for fear that.

**let** v. **1** allow. **2** allow someone to use accommodation in return for payment. **3** used to express an intention, suggestion, or order: *let's go.* • n. **1** (in tennis etc.) a situation in which a ball is obstructed. **2** a period during which property is let. □ **let off** fire or explode a weapon, firework, etc.; excuse.
▷ SYNS v. **1** ALLOW, permit, authorize, sanction, grant, license,

assent to, consent to, agree to, give the go-ahead. **2** LET OUT, rent (out), lease, hire out, sublet.

**let-down** n. a disappointment.
▷ SYNS DISAPPOINTMENT, anticlimax, non-event; inf. washout, damp squib.

**lethal** adj. causing death.
▷ SYNS FATAL, deadly, mortal, death-dealing, murderous, killing; poisonous, toxic, virulent, destructive.

**lethargic** adj. having no energy or enthusiasm.
▷ SYNS SLUGGISH, slow, listless, languid, weary, enervated, fatigued, lazy, inactive.

**lethargy** n. a lack of energy or vitality.

**letter** n. **1** a symbol representing a speech sound. **2** a written message sent by post.
• v. inscribe letters on. □ **the letter of the law** the precise terms of a law or rule.
▷ SYNS n. **1** CHARACTER, sign, symbol. **2** MESSAGE, note, line, missive, epistle, dispatch.

**lettuce** n. a plant whose leaves are eaten in salads.

**leukaemia** n. a disease in which too many white blood cells are produced.

**level** adj. **1** flat, even, and horizontal. **2** at the same height or in the same relative position as something. • n. **1** a position on a scale. **2** a height reached. • v. **1** make or become level. **2** aim a gun. □ **level crossing** a place where a road and railway cross at the same level. **level-headed** sensible.
▷ SYNS adj. **1** FLAT, smooth, even, plane, flush, horizontal. **2** EVEN, uniform, regular, consistent,

constant, stable, steady, unchanging, unvarying. **3** EQUAL, on a level, neck and neck, level-pegging, side by side.
• n. POSITION, rank, standing, status, degree, grade, stage, standard.

**lever** n. a bar pivoted on a fixed point to lift something; a pivoted handle used to operate machinery; a means of power or influence. • v. lift or move with a lever.

**leverage** n. the action or power of a lever; power or influence.

**leveret** n. a young hare.

**leviathan** n. something of enormous size and power.

**levitate** v. rise and float in the air.

**levity** n. the flippant treatment of something serious.

**levy** v. (**levied**, **levying**) impose a tax, fee, or fine. • n. (pl. **-ies**) a tax; an act of levying a tax etc.

**lewd** adj. treating sexual matters in a crude, vulgar way.

**lexicon** n. a dictionary; a vocabulary.

**liability** n. (pl. **-ies**) **1** being legally responsible. **2** a debt. **3** a cause of difficulty.

**liable** adj. **1** held responsible by law; legally obliged to pay a tax etc. **2** likely to do something.
▷ SYNS **1** RESPONSIBLE, accountable, answerable; blameworthy, at fault. **2** APT, likely, inclined, disposed, predisposed, prone. **3** EXPOSED, subject, susceptible, vulnerable, in danger of.

**liaise** v. establish a cooperative link or relationship.

**liaison** n. **1** communication and cooperation. **2** a sexual relationship.

**liar** n. a person who tells lies.
▷ SYNS FIBBER, perjurer, false witness, deceiver.

**libel** n. a published false statement that damages a person's reputation.
• v. (**libelled**, **libelling**; US **libeled**) publish a libel against.
▷ SYNS n. DEFAMATION, denigration, vilification, disparagement, aspersions, calumny, slander, false report, slur, smear.
• v. DEFAME, vilify, blacken someone's name, denigrate, disparage, cast aspersions on, slander, traduce, slur, smear.

**libellous** adj. constituting libel.
▷ SYNS DEFAMATORY, disparaging, derogatory, false, untrue, scurrilous.

**liberal** adj. **1** tolerant; respecting individual freedom; (in politics) favouring moderate social reform. **2** generous. **3** (of an interpretation) not strict or exact.
▷ SYNS **1** TOLERANT, broad-minded, open-minded, enlightened, unprejudiced, indulgent, permissive. **2** GENEROUS, magnanimous, open-handed, unsparing, unstinting, munificent, bountiful. **3** COPIOUS, ample, abundant, lavish, plentiful, profuse.

**liberalize** (or **-ise**) v. make less strict.

**liberate** v. set free. ■ **liberator** n.
▷ SYNS SET FREE, free, release, let out, let go, discharge, set loose, rescue, emancipate.

**libertine** n. a man who lives an irresponsible immoral life.

**liberty** n. (pl. **-ies**) freedom; a right or privilege. □ **at liberty** free; permitted to do something. **take liberties**

behave with undue freedom or familiarity.

▷ SYNS FREEDOM, independence; autonomy, sovereignty, self-government, self-rule.

**libido** n. (pl. **-os**) sexual desire.

**librarian** n. a person who works in a library.

**library** n. (pl. **-ies**) a collection of books or records, films, etc. for consulting or borrowing.

**libretto** n. (pl. **-rettos** or **-retti**) the words of an opera.

**lice** pl. of LOUSE.

**licence** (US **license**) n. **1** an official permit to own or do something; permission. **2** freedom to do as you like.

▷ SYNS **1** PERMIT, certificate, credentials, document, documentation, pass. **2** PERMISSION, authority, right, authorization, leave, entitlement; liberty, freedom.

**license** v. grant a licence to or for.

▷ SYNS PERMIT, allow, authorize, sanction, entitle, let, empower.

**licensee** n. a holder of a licence.

**licentious** adj. sexually immoral.

**lichen** n. a low-growing dry plant that grows on rocks etc.

**lick** v. **1** pass the tongue over. **2** (of waves or flame) touch lightly. **3** inf. defeat. • n. **1** an act of licking. **2** inf. a quick application of paint etc.

**licorice** US sp. of LIQUORICE.

**lid** n. a hinged or removable cover for a box, pot, etc.; an eyelid.

▷ SYNS COVER, top, cap, covering.

**lie¹** n. a deliberately false statement. • v. (**lied**, **lying**) tell a lie.

▷ SYNS n. UNTRUTH, falsehood, fib, fabrication, invention; inf. whopper. • v. TELL A LIE, fib, perjure yourself.

**lie²** v. **1** have or put your body in a flat or resting position; be at rest on something. **2** be in a specified state; be situated. • n. the pattern or direction in which something lies. □ **lie-in** a prolonged stay in bed in the morning.

▷ SYNS v. **1** RECLINE, be recumbent, be prostrate, be supine, be prone, sprawl, rest, repose, lounge, loll. **2** BE SITUATED, be located, be placed, be positioned.

**lieu** n. (**in lieu**) instead.

**lieutenant** n. a rank of officer in the army and navy; a deputy or substitute.

**life** n. **1** the ability to function and grow. **2** the existence of an individual. **3** a particular type or aspect of existence. **4** living things and their activity. **5** vitality or energy. □ **lifeboat 1** a boat for rescuing people at sea. **2** a small boat on a ship for emergency use. **lifeguard** a person employed to rescue swimmers in difficulty. **life jacket** a buoyant or inflatable jacket for keeping a person afloat in water. **lifeless** dead or apparently dead; without living things; lacking energy. **lifeline** a rope thrown to rescue someone in difficulty in water; a thing essential for continued existence. **lifestyle** the way in which a person lives. **lifetime** the length of time that a person lives or a thing lasts.

▷ SYNS **1** EXISTENCE, being, living, animation. **2** LIVING THINGS, living creatures, fauna, flora.

**3** LIFETIME, days, lifespan, time on earth, existence.

**lifelike** adj. exactly like a real person or thing.
▷ SYNS REALISTIC, true-to-life, faithful, natural, vivid, graphic.

**lift** v. **1** raise; move upwards; make larger, louder, or higher. **2** pick up and move; remove legal restrictions etc. • n. **1** an apparatus for moving people and goods from one floor of a building to another. **2** an act or manner of lifting. **3** a free ride in a car etc. **4** a feeling of encouragement. □ **lift-off** vertical take-off of a spacecraft etc.
▷ SYNS v. PICK UP, uplift, hoist, heave up, raise (up), heft.

**ligament** n. a tough flexible tissue holding bones together.

**ligature** n. a thing used for tying; thread used in surgery.

**light**[1] n. **1** the natural energy that makes things visible. **2** a source of light. **3** understanding or enlightenment. • v. **1** provide with light. **2** ignite. **3** (**light up**) become animated. • adj. **1** well lit. **2** (of a colour) pale. □ **lighthouse** a tower with a powerful light to guide ships at sea. **light year** the distance light travels in one year, about 6 million million miles.
▷ SYNS n. ILLUMINATION, brightness, brilliance, radiance, luminescence, luminosity, incandescence, blaze, glare, glow, lustre. • v. **1** ILLUMINATE, brighten, irradiate. **2** SET FIRE TO, ignite, kindle. • adj. **1** BRIGHT, well lit, sunny. **2** PALE, pastel, subtle, bleached.

**light**[2] adj. **1** having a lot of light. **2** (of a colour) pale. **3** of little weight. **4** not heavily built. **5** relatively low in density or amount. **6** not serious or profound. □ **light-headed** dizzy and slightly faint. **light-hearted** cheerful or carefree.

**lightweight 1** a weight in boxing etc. between featherweight and welterweight. **2** inf. a person of little importance.
■ **lightly** adv.
▷ SYNS **1** LIGHTWEIGHT, easy to lift/carry, portable. **2** a light robe: FLIMSY, thin, delicate, floaty, gossamer. **3** light duties: EASY, simple, undemanding; inf. cushy. **4** light reading: ENTERTAINING, diverting, amusing, humorous, funny; frivolous, superficial, trivial.

**lighten** v. make or become lighter.
▷ SYNS **1** BRIGHTEN, light up, illuminate, irradiate; bleach, whiten. **2** REDUCE, lessen, decrease, diminish, alleviate, relieve.

**lighter** n. **1** a device for lighting cigarettes and cigars. **2** a flat-bottomed boat for carrying ships' cargoes ashore.

**lighting** n. a means of providing light; the light itself.

**lightning** n. a flash of bright light produced from cloud by natural electricity.

**like** prep. **1** similar to. **2** in a way similar or appropriate to. **3** such as. • v. **1** enjoy or find pleasant. **2** wish for. • conj. **1** in the same way that. **2** as if. • n. **1** a similar person or thing. **2** (**likes**) things that you like. • adj. similar.
▷ SYNS prep. **1** SIMILAR TO, the same as, identical to. **2** IN THE SAME WAY AS, in the manner of, in a similar way to. **3** SUCH AS, for example, for instance, namely, in particular. • v. BE FOND OF, be attracted to, be keen on, have a

soft spot for; enjoy, be partial to, love, adore, relish.

**likeable** (or **likable**) adj. pleasant.
▷ SYNS PLEASANT, nice, friendly, agreeable, amiable, genial, charming, engaging, pleasing, appealing, lovable.

**likelihood** n. a probability.
▷ SYNS PROBABILITY, chance, prospect, possibility.

**likely** adj. **1** probable. **2** promising. • adv. probably.
▷ SYNS adj. **1** PROBABLE, possible, to be expected, on the cards, odds-on. **2** APT, inclined, tending, liable, prone. **3** PROMISING, talented, gifted; inf. up-and-coming.

**liken** v. point out the likeness of one thing to another.
▷ SYNS COMPARE, equate, correlate, link, associate.

**likeness** n. resemblance; a copy or portrait.
▷ SYNS **1** RESEMBLANCE, similarity, sameness, similitude, correspondence, analogy. **2** PICTURE, drawing, sketch, painting, portrait, photograph, study, representation, image.

**likewise** adv. **1** also. **2** in a similar way.

**liking** n. a fondness.
▷ SYNS FONDNESS, love, affection, desire, preference, partiality, penchant, bias, weakness, soft spot, taste, predilection, inclination, proclivity.

**lilac** n. a shrub with fragrant purple or white flowers; pale purple.

**lilt** n. **1** a rise and fall of the voice when speaking. **2** a gentle rhythm in a tune. ■ **lilting** adj.

**lily** n. (pl. **-ies**) a plant with large flowers on a tall, slender stem.

**limb** n. an arm, leg, or wing; a large branch of a tree.
▷ SYNS **1** ARM, leg, wing, member, extremity, appendage. **2** BRANCH, bough.

**limber** adj. supple. • v. (**limber up**) exercise in preparation for athletic activity.

**limbo**[1] n. an uncertain period of waiting.

**limbo**[2] n. (pl. **-os**) a West Indian dance in which the dancer bends back to pass under a bar.

**lime** n. **1** a white substance used in making cement etc. **2** a green citrus fruit like a lemon; its colour. **3** a tree with heart-shaped leaves. □ **limelight** the focus of public attention. **limestone** a hard rock composed mainly of calcium carbonate.

**limerick** n. a humorous poem with five lines.

**limit** n. a point beyond which something does not continue; a restriction; the greatest amount allowed. • v. set or serve as a limit to.
▷ SYNS n. **1** BOUNDARY, border, bound, frontier, edge, perimeter, confines, periphery. **2** MAXIMUM, ceiling, limitation, restriction, check, restraint. • v. RESTRICT, curb, check, restrain, constrain, freeze, peg.

**limitation** n. a restriction.
▷ SYNS RESTRICTION, curb, restraint, control, check; impediment, obstacle, obstruction, bar, barrier, block, deterrent.

**limousine** n. a large luxurious car.

**limp** v. walk or proceed lamely or with difficulty. • n. a limping walk. • adj. not stiff or firm.

▷ SYNS **adj.** FLOPPY, droopy, soft, flaccid, flabby, loose, slack.

**limpet** n. a small shellfish that sticks tightly to rocks.

**limpid** adj. (of liquids) clear.

**linchpin** n. **1** a pin passed through the end of an axle to secure a wheel. **2** a person or thing vital to an enterprise.

**linctus** n. a soothing cough mixture.

**line** n. **1** a long narrow mark. **2** a row or series. **3** a course or channel. **4** a length of cord, wire, etc. **5** a phone connection. **6** a railway track or route. **7** a wrinkle. **8** a series of military defences. **9** an area of activity: *my line of work.* **10** (**lines**) an actor's part. • v. **1** be positioned along. **2** mark with lines. **3** cover the inner surface of. □ **linesman** (in sport) an official who assists the referee or umpire. **line-up** a group assembled for a purpose.

▷ SYNS n. **1** STROKE, dash, score, underline, slash, stripe, band, strip, belt. **2** ROW, file, column, queue, train, string, chain, procession. **3** WRINKLE, furrow, crease, crow's foot. **4** CORD, cable, wire, thread, string.

**lineage** n. ancestry.

**linear** adj. extending along a line; formed with straight lines; proceeding straightforwardly from one stage to another.

**linen** n. **1** cloth made of flax. **2** sheets, pillowcases, etc.

**liner** n. a passenger ship or aircraft.

**linger** v. stay longer than necessary; take a long time doing something.

▷ SYNS STAY, remain, wait/hang around, dawdle, loiter, dally, take your time, tarry, dilly-dally.

**lingerie** n. women's underwear.

**lingo** n. (pl. **-os**) inf. a language.

**linguist** n. a person who is skilled in languages or linguistics.

**linguistic** adj. of language. • n. (**linguistics**) the study of language.

**liniment** n. an embrocation.

**lining** n. a layer of material or another substance covering an inner surface.

**link** n. **1** a connection. **2** a means of communication. **3** a loop in a chain. • v. connect or join. ■ **linkage** n.

▷ SYNS n. CONNECTION, relationship, association; bond, tie, attachment, affiliation. • v. CONNECT, join, fasten, attach, bind, couple, yoke; associate, relate.

**linoleum** n. a smooth covering for floors.

**linseed** n. the seed of flax, a source of oil.

**lint** n. a soft fabric for dressing wounds.

**lintel** n. a horizontal timber or stone over a doorway.

**lion** n. a large wild cat.

**lip** n. **1** either of the fleshy edges of the mouth opening. **2** the edge of a container or opening. **3** inf. cheeky talk. □ **lip-read** understand speech from watching a speaker's lips. **lipstick** a cosmetic for colouring the lips.

▷ SYNS EDGE, rim, brim, verge, brink.

**liqueur** n. a strong sweet alcoholic spirit.

**liquid** n. a flowing substance like water or oil. • adj. **1** of or like liquid. **2** (of assets) easily converted into cash.
▷ SYNS n. FLUID, liquor, solution, juice, sap.

**liquidate** v. **1** close a company and sell its assets to pay its debts. **2** convert assets into cash.

**liquidity** n. a company's possession of liquid assets.

**liquidize** (or **-ise**) v. reduce to a liquid. ■ liquidizer n.
▷ SYNS PURÉE, liquefy, blend.

**liquor** n. **1** alcoholic drink. **2** juice from cooked food.

**liquorice** (US **licorice**) n. a black substance used in medicine and as a sweet.

**lisp** n. a speech defect in which *s* is pronounced like *th*. • v. speak with a lisp.

**lissom** adj. slim and supple.

**list** n. a number of connected items or names written as a series. • v. **1** make a list of. **2** include in a list. **3** (of a ship) lean to one side.
▷ SYNS n. CATALOGUE, inventory, record, register, roll, file, index, directory. • v. RECORD, register, enter, itemize, enumerate, catalogue, file, classify.

**listen** v. **1** pay attention to a sound. **2** take notice of advice or a request. ■ listener n.
▷ SYNS PAY ATTENTION, hear, attend, prick up your ears, be all ears.

**listless** adj. without energy or enthusiasm.
▷ SYNS LETHARGIC, enervated, spiritless, lifeless, inactive, inert, languid, apathetic, sluggish, torpid.

**lit** past & p.p. of **LIGHT**¹.

**litany** n. (pl. **-ies**) **1** a series of prayers. **2** a long list of complaints etc.

**liter** US sp. of **LITRE**.

**literal** adj. using or interpreting words in their most basic sense. ■ literally adv.
▷ SYNS WORD FOR WORD, verbatim, exact, precise, faithful, strict.

**literary** adj. of or associated with literature.
▷ SYNS WELL READ, learned, well educated, intellectual, cultured, highbrow, erudite, bookish.

**literate** adj. able to read and write. ■ literacy n.

**literature** n. great novels, poetry, and plays; books and printed information on a particular subject.
▷ SYNS **1** WRITTEN WORKS, writings, published works. **2** BROCHURES, leaflets, pamphlets, circulars, information, data.

**lithe** adj. supple or agile.
▷ SYNS AGILE, flexible, supple, limber, loose-limbed, lissom.

**lithium** n. a light metallic element.

**lithography** n. printing from a plate treated so that ink sticks only to the design. ■ lithograph n.

**litigate** v. take a dispute to a law court. ■ litigation n.

**litmus** n. a substance turned red by acids and blue by alkalis.

**litre** (US **liter**) n. a metric unit of capacity (1.76 pints) for measuring liquids.

**litter** n. **1** rubbish left lying about. **2** young animals born at one birth. **3** material used as bedding for animals or to absorb their excrement.

• v. make untidy by dropping litter.
▷ SYNS n. **1** RUBBISH, debris, refuse, junk, detritus, waste; US trash, garbage. **2** BROOD, young, offspring.

**little** adj. **1** small in size, amount, or degree. **2** young or younger. • n. & pron. **1** a small amount. **2** a short time or distance. • adv. **1** to a small extent. **2** hardly.
▷ SYNS adj. **1** SMALL, short, slight, petite, tiny, wee, miniature, diminutive; inf. pint-sized. **2** UNIMPORTANT, insignificant, minor, trivial, trifling, petty, paltry, inconsequential, negligible.

**liturgy** n. (pl. **-ies**) a set form of public worship. ■ **liturgical** adj.
▷ SYNS RITUAL, worship, service, ceremony, rite, observance, celebration, sacrament.

**live** v. **1** be or remain alive. **2** have your home in a place. **3** spend your life in a particular way. • adj. **1** living. **2** (of a broadcast) transmitted while it is happening. **3** connected to an electric current. **4** unexploded.
▷ SYNS adj. LIVING, alive, animate, vital.

**livelihood** n. a way of earning enough money to live on.
▷ SYNS LIVING, income, subsistence; work, employment, occupation, job.

**lively** adj. (**-ier, -iest**) full of energy or action. ■ **liveliness** n.
▷ SYNS **1** FULL OF LIFE, active, animated, energetic, vigorous, spirited, high-spirited, vivacious, exuberant, enthusiastic, buoyant, bouncy, perky, spry, sprightly. **2** a lively debate: ANIMATED, spirited, stimulating, heated. **3** a lively scene: BUSY, crowded, bustling, hectic.

**liven** v. make or become lively.

**liver** n. a large organ in the abdomen, secreting bile.

**livery** n. (pl. **-ies**) a distinctive uniform; a colour scheme in which a company's vehicles are painted.

**livestock** n. farm animals.

**livid** adj. **1** furiously angry. **2** dark blue-grey.

**living** adj. alive. • n. an income. □ **living room** a room for everyday use.
▷ SYNS adj. ALIVE, live, breathing, animate.

**lizard** n. a four-legged reptile with a long tail.

**llama** n. a South American animal related to the camel.

**load** n. **1** a thing or quantity carried; a weight or source of pressure. **2** the amount of electric current supplied by a source. **3** (**loads**) inf. a great deal. • v. **1** put a load in or on; burden. **2** put ammunition into a gun or film into a camera; put data into a computer. **3** bias towards a particular outcome. ■ **loaded** adj.
▷ SYNS n. **1** CARGO, freight, consignment, shipment, lorryload. **2** BURDEN, onus, encumbrance, weight, responsibility, duty, charge, obligation, strain, trouble, worry, pressure; cross, millstone, albatross. • v. **1** FILL (UP), charge, pack, stock; heap, stack, stuff, cram. **2** BURDEN, weigh down, saddle, charge, tax, encumber, overburden, overwhelm, trouble, worry.

**loaf** n. (pl. **loaves**) a piece of shaped and baked bread. • v. spend time idly. ■ **loafer** n.

▷ SYNS v. LAZE, lounge, loll, idle, hang about.

**loam** n. rich soil.

**loan** n. **1** money lent. **2** the act of lending. • v. lend.

**loath** adj. unwilling.
▷ SYNS RELUCTANT, unwilling, disinclined, averse, opposed, resistant.

**loathe** v. feel hatred and disgust for.
▷ SYNS HATE, detest, abhor, despise, abominate, dislike.

**loathing** n. intense dislike or disgust.
▷ SYNS HATRED, hate, detestation, abhorrence, antipathy, aversion, dislike, disgust, repugnance.

**loathsome** adj. arousing hatred or disgust.
▷ SYNS HATEFUL, detestable, abhorrent, repulsive, odious, repugnant, disgusting, revolting, nauseating, abominable, vile, horrible, nasty, obnoxious.

**lob** v. (**lobbed, lobbing**) throw or hit a ball slowly in a high arc. • n. a lobbed ball.

**lobby** n. (pl. **-ies**) **1** a porch, entrance hall, or anteroom. **2** a body of people seeking to influence legislation. • v. (**lobbied, lobbying**) seek to persuade an MP etc. to support your cause. ■ **lobbyist** n.

**lobe** n. the lower soft part of the ear.

**lobelia** n. a garden plant with blue or scarlet flowers.

**lobster** n. an edible shellfish with large claws.

**local** adj. of or affecting a particular area, or the area where a person lives. • n. **1** a person living in a particular area. **2** inf. a person's nearest pub. ■ **locally** adv.
▷ SYNS n. **1** INHABITANT, resident, parishioner. **2** PUB, public house, bar, inn, tavern.

**locale** n. the scene of an event.

**locality** n. (pl. **-ies**) the position of something; an area or neighbourhood.
▷ SYNS VICINITY, area, neighbourhood, district, region.

**localize** (or **-ise**) v. confine within an area.

**locate** v. discover the position of; situate in a particular place.
▷ SYNS **1** FIND, discover, identify, pinpoint, detect, track down, run to earth. **2** SITUATE, site, position, place, put, build, base, establish, station, settle.

**location** n. a place where something is situated; locating something.
▷ SYNS POSITION, place, situation, whereabouts, bearings, site, spot, point, scene, setting, venue, locale; formal locus.

**loch** n. Scot. a lake; an arm of the sea.

**loci** pl. of **LOCUS**.

**lock** n. **1** a device opened by a key for fastening a door or lid etc. **2** a section of a canal enclosed by gates, where the water level can be changed. **3** a wrestling hold. **4** a coil or hanging piece of hair. • v. **1** fasten with a lock. **2** shut into a locked place. **3** make or become fixed. □ **lockjaw** tetanus. **lockout** the exclusion of employees from their workplace during a dispute. **locksmith** a person who makes and repairs locks. **lock-up 1** a makeshift jail. **2** a garage etc. separate from other premises.

▷ SYNS n. **1** BOLT, catch, fastener, clasp, latch, hasp. **2** TRESS, strand, hank, curl, ringlet. • v. BOLT, fasten, secure, padlock.

**locker** n. a lockable cupboard or compartment.
▷ SYNS CUPBOARD, compartment, cabinet, chest, safe.

**locket** n. a small ornamental case worn on a chain round the neck.

**locomotion** n. the ability to move from place to place.

**locomotive** n. a self-propelled engine for moving trains.

**locum** n. a temporary stand-in for a doctor, clergyman, etc.

**locus** n. (pl. **loci**) a particular position.

**locust** n. a tropical grasshopper that devours vegetation.

**lodge** n. **1** a cabin for use by hunters, skiers, etc.; a gatekeeper's house; a porter's room at the entrance to a building. **2** the members or meeting place of a branch of certain societies. **3** a beaver's or otter's lair. • v. **1** live somewhere as a lodger. **2** present a complaint, appeal, etc. to an authority. **3** make or become fixed or embedded.
▷ SYNS v. **1** BOARD, have digs/lodgings, put up, reside, dwell. **2** REGISTER, submit, present, put forward, place, file, lay.

**lodger** n. a person paying for accommodation in another's house.

**lodging** n. **1** temporary accommodation. **2** (**lodgings**) a rented room or rooms in the same house as the owner.

**loft** n. a space under a roof. • v. hit, throw, or kick a ball in a high arc.

**lofty** adj. (**-ier, -iest**) very tall; noble or exalted.
▷ SYNS **1** TOWERING, soaring, tall, high. **2** NOBLE, exalted, grand, sublime, fine, high-minded.

**log** n. **1** a piece cut from a trunk or branch of a tree. **2** a systematic record; a logbook. **3** a device for gauging a ship's speed. **4** a logarithm. • v. **1** enter facts in a logbook. **2** (**log in/on** or **out/off**) begin or finish using a computer system. □ **logbook** a log of a ship or aircraft; a document recording details of a vehicle and its owner.
▷ SYNS n. *the ship's log:* LOGBOOK, record, register, journal, diary, ledger, account.

**loganberry** n. a large dark red fruit resembling a raspberry.

**logarithm** n. one of a series of numbers set out in tables, used to simplify calculations.

**loggerheads** pl.n. (**at loggerheads**) disagreeing or quarrelling.

**logic** n. a science or method of reasoning; correct reasoning.
▷ SYNS REASON, reasoning, judgement, wisdom, sense, good sense, common sense, rationality, rationale.

**logical** adj. of or according to logic; following naturally and sensibly; reasonable.
▷ SYNS **1** REASONED, well reasoned, rational, sound, cogent, coherent, clear. **2** REASONABLE, natural, understandable, predictable, unsurprising, likely.

**logistics** pl.n. the detailed organization of a large and complex exercise.

**logo** n. (pl. **-os**) a design used as an emblem.

**loin** n. the part of the body between the ribs and hip bone. □ loincloth a cloth worn round the hips.

**loiter** v. stand about idly.
▷ SYNS HANG AROUND, linger, wait, skulk; loaf, lounge, idle, waste time.

**loll** v. sit, lie, or stand in a relaxed way; hang loosely.

**lollipop** n. a large flat boiled sweet on a small stick.

**lolly** n. inf. **1** a lollipop. **2** money.

**lone** adj. solitary.
▷ SYNS SINGLE, solitary, sole, unaccompanied.

**lonely** adj. **1** solitary; sad because you lack friends. **2** (of a place) remote. ■ loneliness n.
▷ SYNS **1** FRIENDLESS, alone, isolated, lonesome, forlorn, unloved, with no one to turn to. **2** REMOTE, desolate, isolated, out of the way, off the beaten track, deserted, uninhabited, unfrequented, godforsaken.

**loner** n. a person who prefers to be alone.

**lonesome** adj. lonely.

**long** adj. of great or a particular length. • adv. **1** for a long time. **2** throughout a specific period. • v. have a strong wish. □ longhand ordinary hand-writing as opposed to shorthand etc. long shot a scheme or guess very unlikely to succeed. long-sighted able to see close things clearly. long-standing having existed for a long time. long-suffering bearing provocation patiently.

longways lengthways. long-winded long and boring.
▷ SYNS adj. LENGTHY, extended, prolonged, protracted, long-lasting, drawn-out, interminable. • v. YEARN, pine, wish, hanker, hunger, thirst, itch, crave.

**longevity** n. long life.

**longing** n. an intense wish.
▷ SYNS WISH, desire, yearning, craving, hunger, thirst, itch, lust, hankering; inf. yen.

**longitude** n. the distance east or west (measured in degrees on a map) from the Greenwich meridian.

**loo** n. inf. a toilet.

**look** v. **1** use or direct your eyes in order to see, search, or examine. **2** seem. **3** (**look after**) take care of. • n. **1** an act of looking. **2** appearance. **3** (**looks**) a person's attractiveness. □ lookout **1** a place from which to keep watch. **2** a person keeping watch.
▷ SYNS **v.** **1** GLANCE, gaze, stare, gape, peer, peep, peek; watch, observe, view, regard, eye, examine, study, inspect, scan, scrutinize, survey, contemplate, ogle; inf. gawp. **2** SEEM, appear, give the appearance of being, strike someone as. **3** FACE, overlook, front, give on to. • n. **1** GLANCE, view, examination, inspection, scan, survey, peep, peek, glimpse, gaze, stare; inf. dekko. **2** EXPRESSION, face, countenance, features, mien, appearance.

**lookalike** n. a person who looks very similar to another.
▷ SYNS DOUBLE, twin, living image, clone, doppelgänger; inf. spitting image, dead ringer.

**loom** v. appear, esp. close at hand or threateningly. • n. an apparatus for weaving cloth.
▷ SYNS v. APPEAR, emerge, take shape, materialize, be imminent, be on the horizon.

**loop** n. a curve that bends round and crosses itself. • v. form into a loop. □ **loophole** a way of evading a rule or contract.
▷ SYNS n. COIL, ring, circle, noose, spiral, curl, bend, curve.

**loose** adj. 1 not firmly fixed in place. 2 not tied up or shut in. 3 (of a garment) not fitting tightly. 4 not exact. • v. unfasten or set free. □ **loose-leaf** with each page removable.
▷ SYNS adj. 1 UNSECURED, unattached, untied, detached, unsteady. 2 FREE, at large, at liberty, on the loose. 3 BAGGY, roomy, oversized, slack, shapeless, sloppy. 4 VAGUE, inexact, imprecise, approximate, broad, general. • v. FREE, let loose, release, untie, unchain, unleash, unfasten.

**loosen** v. make or become loose.
▷ SYNS SLACKEN, relax, loose, let go, lessen, weaken.

**loot** n. goods taken from an enemy or by theft. • v. take loot.
▷ SYNS n. BOOTY, spoils, plunder, haul; inf. swag. • v. PLUNDER, pillage, rob, burgle, steal, ransack, sack, despoil.

**lop** v. (**lopped, lopping**) cut off branches from a tree.
▷ SYNS CUT, chop, hack, prune, sever, dock, clip, crop.

**lope** v. run with a long bounding stride.

**lopsided** adj. with one side lower, smaller, or heavier than the other.

**loquacious** adj. talkative.

**lord** n. 1 a nobleman. 2 the title of certain peers or high officials. 3 a master or ruler. • v. (**lord it over**) act in an arrogant and bullying way towards.

**lore** n. traditional knowledge.

**lorry** n. (pl. **-ies**) a large vehicle for transporting goods.

**lose** v. 1 have taken away; no longer have. 2 become unable to find. 3 fail to win. 4 waste an opportunity. ■ **loser** n.
▷ SYNS 1 MISLAY, misplace. 2 BE DEFEATED, be beaten, be trounced.

**loss** n. 1 the act of losing. 2 a person or thing lost. 3 sadness after losing a person or thing.

**lost** adj. 1 unable to be found or recovered. 2 unable to find your way.
▷ SYNS 1 MISSING, gone missing/astray, mislaid, misplaced. 2 OFF COURSE, disorientated, having lost your bearings, astray.

**lot** pron. & adv. (**a lot** or inf. **lots**) a large number or amount. • n. 1 inf. a group or set of people or things. 2 an item for sale at an auction. 3 each of a set of objects drawn at random to make a decision. 4 a person's situation in life. 5 a plot of land.

**lotion** n. a creamy liquid applied to the skin as a cosmetic or medicine.
▷ SYNS CREAM, salve, ointment, moisturizer, balm, emollient, lubricant, unguent, liniment, embrocation.

**lottery** n. (pl. **-ies**) a system of raising money by selling numbered tickets and giving prizes to holders of numbers drawn at random.

▷ SYNS DRAW, raffle, sweepstake, tombola.

**lotus** n. a tropical water lily.

**loud** adj. **1** making a lot of noise. **2** garish. □ **loudspeaker** a device that converts electrical impulses into sound.
▷ SYNS **1** NOISY, blaring, booming, deafening, resounding, thunderous, tumultuous, ear-splitting, piercing, raucous. **2** GARISH, gaudy, lurid, showy, flamboyant, vulgar, tasteless; inf. flashy.

**lounge** v. sit or stand about idly. • n. **1** a sitting room. **2** a waiting room at an airport etc.
▷ SYNS v. LAZE, lie, recline, relax, take it easy, sprawl, slump, loll, repose, loaf, idle, loiter, hang about. • n. SITTING ROOM, drawing room, living room; dated parlour.

**lour** (or **lower**) v. frown; (of clouds) look dark and threatening.

**louse** n. (pl. **lice**) a small parasitic insect.

**lousy** adj. (-ier, -iest) inf. very bad.

**lout** n. a rude or aggressive man or youth.
▷ SYNS HOOLIGAN, boor, oaf, ruffian; inf. yob.

**louvre** (or **louver**) n. each of a set of overlapping slats arranged to let in air but exclude light or rain.

**lovable** adj. inspiring love.
▷ SYNS ADORABLE, dear, sweet, cute, charming, lovely, delightful, captivating, enchanting, engaging, appealing, winsome, winning, endearing.

**love** n. **1** very strong affection. **2** sexual passion. **3** a beloved person or thing. **4** (in games) a score of zero. • v. **1** feel love for.
**2** like very much. □ **lovelorn** unhappy because of unrequited love. **make love** have sex.
■ **lovingly** adv.
▷ SYNS n. **1** AFFECTION, fondness, care, attachment, intimacy, devotion, adoration, passion, ardour, infatuation. **2** LIKING, appetite, penchant, weakness, partiality, enjoyment, relish.
• v. **1** BE IN LOVE WITH, adore, dote on, worship, idolize, treasure, prize, cherish, be devoted to, care for, hold dear. **2** LIKE, be addicted to, enjoy greatly, relish, delight in, be partial to, have a soft spot for.

**lovely** adj. (-ier, -iest) very beautiful or pleasant.
▷ SYNS **1** BEAUTIFUL, pretty, attractive, good-looking, adorable, charming, enchanting, engaging, gorgeous, ravishing. **2** DELIGHTFUL, pleasant, enjoyable, marvellous, wonderful, terrific, fabulous.

**lover** n. **1** a person in a sexual or romantic relationship with someone. **2** a person who enjoys a specified thing.
▷ SYNS **1** BOYFRIEND, girlfriend, mistress, partner, beloved, sweetheart. **2** DEVOTEE, admirer, fan, enthusiast, aficionado; inf. buff.

**loving** adj. showing love.
▷ SYNS AFFECTIONATE, fond, devoted, adoring, doting, caring, tender, warm; amorous, passionate.

**low** adj. **1** not high or tall or far above the ground. **2** below average in amount or strength. **3** inferior. **4** depressed. **5** not moral. • n. **1** a low point. **2** an area of low atmospheric pressure. • adv. at or into a low point. • v. (of a cow) moo.

□ **lowbrow** not intellectual or cultured. **low-key** not elaborate or ostentatious. **lowland** (also **lowlands**) low-lying country.
▷ SYNS **adj. 1** SHORT, small, little, squat, stunted. **2** INFERIOR, poor, inadequate, second-rate. **3** DEPRESSED, dejected, despondent, downhearted, downcast, gloomy, glum, miserable; *inf.* fed up, blue.

**low-down** n. the important facts.
▷ SYNS INFORMATION, data, facts, facts and figures; *inf.* info.

**lower¹** adj. less high. • v. let downwards; reduce the height, pitch, or degree of. □ **lower case** letters that are not capitals.
▷ SYNS **adj.** LESSER, subordinate, junior, inferior. • **v. 1** LET DOWN, take down, haul down. **2** SOFTEN, quieten, hush, tone down, muffle, turn down, mute. **3** REDUCE, bring down, lessen, cut, slash.

**lower²** verb see LOUR.

**lowly** adj. (**-ier, -iest**) of humble rank or condition.
▷ SYNS HUMBLE, low-born, plebeian; simple, plain, ordinary, modest, common.

**loyal** adj. firm and faithful in your support.
▷ SYNS FAITHFUL, true, devoted, constant, trusty, steadfast, staunch, dependable, reliable, unswerving; patriotic.

**loyalist** n. a person who is loyal, esp. while others revolt.

**loyalty** n. the state of being loyal.
▷ SYNS ALLEGIANCE, fidelity, faithfulness, devotion; patriotism.

**lozenge** n. **1** a small medicinal tablet that is sucked. **2** a diamond-shaped figure.

**LP** abbr. a long-playing record.

**LSD** n. a powerful hallucinogenic drug.

**lubricant** n. a lubricating substance.

**lubricate** v. oil or grease machinery etc. to allow smooth movement.

**lucid** adj. clearly expressed. ■ **lucidity** n.
▷ SYNS CLEAR, crystal-clear, comprehensible, intelligible, understandable, plain, simple, direct, vivid, graphic.

**luck** n. **1** good or bad things that happen by chance. **2** good fortune. ■ **luckless** adj.
▷ SYNS **1** FATE, fortune, destiny, chance, accident. **2** GOOD LUCK, good fortune, success, prosperity.

**lucky** adj. (**-ier, -iest**) having, bringing, or resulting from good luck. ■ **luckily** adv.
▷ SYNS **1** FORTUNATE, in luck, favoured, charmed, successful, prosperous. **2** PROVIDENTIAL, fortuitous, fortunate, advantageous, timely, opportune, expedient, auspicious, propitious.

**lucrative** adj. profitable.
▷ SYNS PROFITABLE, profit-making, moneymaking, well paid, gainful, remunerative.

**ludicrous** adj. ridiculous.
▷ SYNS ABSURD, ridiculous, stupid, laughable, risible, farcical, silly, nonsensical, preposterous, idiotic.

**lug** v. (**lugged, lugging**) drag or carry with great effort. • n. *inf.* an ear.

**luggage** n. suitcases and bags holding a traveller's possessions.

**lugubrious** adj. sad or gloomy.

**lukewarm** adj. only slightly warm; not enthusiastic.

**lull** v. send to sleep; cause to feel deceptively confident. • n. a period of quiet or inactivity.
▷ SYNS V. SOOTHE, quiet, hush, silence, calm, still, quell, assuage, allay, ease. • n. RESPITE, interval, break, hiatus, let-up, calm, quiet, quietness, tranquillity.

**lullaby** n. (pl. -ies) a soothing song for sending a child to sleep.

**lumbago** n. rheumatic pain in the lower back.

**lumber** n. 1 unwanted furniture. 2 US timber sawn into planks. • v. 1 move heavily and awkwardly. 2 burden with something unwanted. □ lumberjack a person who fells and cuts up trees.

**luminary** n. (pl. -ies) an eminent person.

**luminescence** n. light given off by a substance that has not been heated. ■ luminescent adj.

**luminous** adj. shining or glowing, esp. in the dark.
▷ SYNS BRIGHT, shining, brilliant, radiant, dazzling, glowing, luminescent, phosphorescent.

**lump** n. 1 a hard or solid mass. 2 a swelling. • v. treat as alike, without regard for differences. ■ lumpy adj.
▷ SYNS n. 1 MASS, chunk, hunk, wedge, piece, ball, knob, clod, wad. 2 BUMP, swelling, bulge, protuberance, growth, tumour.

**lunacy** n. 1 insanity. 2 great stupidity.

**lunar** adj. of the moon.

**lunatic** n. 1 a mentally ill person. 2 a very foolish person.
▷ SYNS MANIAC, madman, madwoman, psychopath; inf. loony, nutter, nutcase.

**lunch** n. a midday meal. • v. eat lunch.

**luncheon** n. lunch.

**lung** n. either of the pair of breathing organs in the chest.

**lunge** n. & v. (make) a sudden forward movement of the body.
▷ SYNS THRUST, dive, rush, spring.

**lurch** v. & n. (make) an unsteady swaying movement. □ leave in the lurch leave a person in difficulties.
▷ SYNS STAGGER, sway, reel, weave, stumble, totter.

**lure** v. entice. • n. 1 an enticement. 2 a bait used in fishing or hunting.
▷ SYNS V. TEMPT, entice, attract, inveigle, draw, seduce, beguile.

**lurid** adj. in glaring colours; vividly shocking or sensational.
▷ SYNS 1 BRIGHT, glaring, dazzling, fluorescent, vivid, showy, gaudy. 2 SENSATIONAL, exaggerated, graphic, explicit, unrestrained, shocking, startling; inf. juicy.

**lurk** v. wait in hiding to attack someone.
▷ SYNS SKULK, lie in wait, hide, loiter.

**luscious** adj. delicious; voluptuously attractive.
▷ SYNS JUICY, sweet, succulent, mouth-watering, tasty, appetizing, delicious, delectable; inf. scrumptious.

**lush** adj. (of grass etc.) growing thickly and strongly; rich or luxurious.

▷ SYNS **1** LUXURIANT, abundant, rich, profuse, dense, thick, overgrown, prolific, rank. **2** LUXURIOUS, sumptuous, grand, palatial, opulent, lavish, elaborate, extravagant; inf. plush.

**lust** n. **1** strong sexual desire. **2** a strong desire. • v. feel lust.

**lustful** adj. filled with lust.
▷ SYNS LECHEROUS, lascivious, libidinous, licentious, salacious, prurient.

**lustre** (US **luster**) n. a soft glow or shine; prestige or honour.
■ lustrous adj.

**lusty** adj. (**-ier, -iest**) strong and vigorous.

**lute** n. a guitar-like instrument with a rounded body.

**luxuriant** adj. growing profusely.
▷ SYNS LUSH, rich, abundant, profuse, dense, thick, riotous, overgrown, prolific.

**luxuriate** v. enjoy or indulge in as a luxury.

**luxurious** adj. very comfortable and elegant.
▷ SYNS OPULENT, sumptuous, expensive, costly, de luxe, grand, splendid, magnificent, palatial, well appointed, extravagant, fancy; inf. plush.

**luxury** n. (pl. **-ies**) great comfort and extravagance; something unnecessary but very pleasant.

▷ SYNS **1** OPULENCE, sumptuousness, grandeur, splendour, magnificence. **2** EXTRA, nonessential, frill, extravagance, indulgence, treat.

**lychee** n. a sweet white fruit with a brown spiny skin.

**Lycra** n. trademark an elastic fabric.

**lying** present participle of LIE[1], LIE[2].

**lymph** n. a colourless fluid containing white blood cells.
■ lymphatic adj.

**lynch** v. (of a mob) kill someone for an alleged crime without a legal trial.

**lynx** n. a wild animal of the cat family.

**lyre** n. a stringed instrument like a small harp, used in ancient Greece.

**lyric** adj. (of poetry) expressing the poet's feelings. • n. **1** a lyric poem. **2** (**lyrics**) the words of a song.

**lyrical** adj. resembling or using language suitable for lyric poetry; expressing yourself enthusiastically.
▷ SYNS EFFUSIVE, rapturous, ecstatic, euphoric, carried away, impassioned.

**lyricism** n. the imaginative expression of emotion in writing or music.

**lyricist** n. a person who writes lyrics.

# Mm

**M** n. (as a Roman numeral) 1,000. • **abbr. 1** motorway. **2** (**m**) metres; miles; millions.

**MA** abbr. Master of Arts.

**mac** n. inf. a mackintosh.

**macabre** adj. disturbingly concerned with death and injury.
▷ SYNS GRUESOME, grisly, gory, hideous, morbid.

**macadam** n. layers of broken stone used in road-making.

**macaroni** n. tube-shaped pasta.

**macaroon** n. a small almond biscuit.

**macaw** n. an American parrot.

**mace** n. **1** a ceremonial staff. **2** a spice.

**machete** n. a broad, heavy knife.

**Machiavellian** adj. elaborately cunning or deceitful.

**machinations** pl.n. clever scheming.

**machine** n. **1** a mechanical device for performing a particular task. **2** an efficient group of powerful people. • v. make or work on with a machine. □ **machine gun** an automatic gun firing bullets in rapid succession. **machine-readable** in a form that a computer can process.
▷ SYNS n. APPLIANCE, device, apparatus, instrument, tool, contraption, gadget, mechanism.

**machinery** n. machines; the parts of a machine; a system or structure.

**machinist** n. a person who works machinery.

**machismo** n. aggressive masculine pride.
▷ SYNS MASCULINITY, manliness, virility, chauvinism.

**macho** adj. aggressively masculine.

**mackerel** n. an edible sea fish.

**mackintosh** (or **macintosh**) n. a raincoat.

**macramé** n. the art of knotting cord in patterns.

**macrocosm** n. the universe; a large complex whole.

**mad** adj. **1** insane. **2** very foolish. **3** frantic. **4** inf. very enthusiastic. **5** inf. angry. ■ **madness** n.
▷ SYNS **1** INSANE, crazy, deranged, demented, out of your mind, lunatic, unhinged, psychotic; inf. mental, nuts, barmy, bonkers. **2** *a mad idea:* FOOLISH, stupid, foolhardy, idiotic, senseless, absurd, silly, ludicrous. **3** *a mad dash to get ready:* FRENZIED, frantic, frenetic, wild, hectic, manic. **4** *mad about jazz:* see ENTHUSIASTIC.

**madam** n. a polite form of address to a woman.

**madcap** adj. wildly impulsive.

**madden** v. make someone very annoyed.
▷ SYNS INFURIATE, exasperate, irritate, anger, annoy, enrage, incense, provoke.

**made** past and p.p. of **MAKE**.

**madman** (or **madwoman**) n.
1 a person who is mentally ill.
2 a foolish or reckless person.
▷ SYNS LUNATIC, maniac, psychopath; inf. loony, psycho.

**Madonna** n. the Virgin Mary.

**madrigal** n. a part-song for unaccompanied voices.

**maelstrom** n. a powerful whirlpool; a scene of confusion.

**maestro** n. (pl. **-tri** or **-tros**) a great musical conductor or composer; a master of any art.

**magazine** n. 1 an illustrated periodical. 2 a chamber holding cartridges in a gun, slides in a projector, etc. 3 a store for arms or explosives.
▷ SYNS PERIODICAL, journal, supplement.

**magenta** adj. & n. purplish red.

**maggot** n. a larva, esp. of the bluebottle.

**magic** n. 1 the supposed use of supernatural powers to make things happen. 2 conjuring tricks. • adj. using or used in magic. ■ magical adj.
▷ SYNS n. 1 SORCERY, witchcraft, wizardry, enchantment, the occult, voodoo. 2 SLEIGHT OF HAND, conjuring, illusion.

**magician** n. 1 a person with magic powers. 2 a conjuror.
▷ SYNS SORCERER, witch, wizard, enchanter, enchantress.

**magisterial** adj. 1 authoritative.
2 of a magistrate.

**magistrate** n. an official with authority to hold preliminary hearings and judge minor cases.

**magma** n. molten rock under the earth's crust.

**magnanimous** adj. noble and generous. ■ magnanimity n.

▷ SYNS GENEROUS, charitable, benevolent, kind, indulgent, bountiful, noble, altruistic, philanthropic, unselfish, selfless, self-sacrificing, merciful, forgiving.

**magnate** n. a wealthy influential business person.

**magnesium** n. a white metallic element that burns with an intensely bright flame.

**magnet** n. 1 a piece of iron that attracts iron and points north when suspended. 2 a powerful attraction.

**magnetic** adj. having the properties of a magnet. □ magnetic tape tape used in recording, computers, etc.

**magnetism** n. 1 the properties of magnetic substances.
2 charm and attraction.

**magnetize** (or **-ise**) v. make magnetic.

**magnificent** adj. 1 impressively beautiful, elaborate, or extravagant. 2 very good.
■ magnificence n.
▷ SYNS 1 SPLENDID, grand, impressive, resplendent, grandiose, imposing, striking, glorious, majestic, noble, stately, awe-inspiring, sumptuous, opulent, luxurious, lavish. 2 EXCELLENT, masterly, skilful, impressive, fine.

**magnify** v. (**magnified**, **magnifying**) 1 make an object seem larger than it is, esp. by using a lens. 2 make larger or stronger. ■ magnification n.
▷ SYNS 1 AUGMENT, enlarge, expand, amplify, intensify, heighten, boost, enhance.
2 EXAGGERATE, overstate, overemphasize, dramatize, embellish, enhance.

**magnitude** n. size; great size or importance.
▷ SYNS SIZE, extent, measure, proportions, dimensions, amplitude.

**magnolia** n. a tree with large white or pink flowers.

**magnum** n. a wine bottle of twice the standard size.

**magpie** n. a black and white bird of the crow family.

**maharaja** (or **maharajah**) n. hist. an Indian prince.

**mahogany** n. a very hard reddish-brown wood.

**maid** n. a female servant.

**maiden** n. old use a young unmarried woman. • adj. first of its kind: *a maiden voyage*. □ maiden name a woman's surname before she married.

**mail** n. 1 letters etc. sent by post. 2 email. 3 armour made of linked metal rings. • v. send by post or email. □ mail order the buying and selling of goods by post.
▷ SYNS n. POST, letters, parcels, correspondence.

**maim** v. inflict a permanent injury on.

**main** adj. greatest or most important. • n. a chief water or gas pipe or electricity cable. □ mainframe a large computer. mainland the main area of land of a country, not including islands. mainstay a thing on which something depends or is based. mainstream the ideas, attitudes, etc. shared by most people.
▷ SYNS adj. CHIEF, principal, head, leading, foremost, central, prime, primary, predominant, pre-eminent, paramount.

**mainly** adv. for the most part.

▷ SYNS MOSTLY, on the whole, largely, by and large, predominantly, chiefly, principally, generally, usually, as a rule.

**maintain** v. 1 cause to continue or remain in existence; keep repaired and in good condition; provide with financial support. 2 assert.
▷ SYNS 1 CONTINUE, keep up, carry on, preserve, prolong, sustain. 2 CARE FOR, look after, keep up, conserve, preserve. 3 SUPPORT, provide for, keep, finance, feed, nurture. 4 INSIST, hold, declare, assert, state, affirm, claim, contend.

**maintenance** n. 1 maintaining something. 2 money paid to a former spouse after a divorce.
▷ SYNS 1 UPKEEP, repairs, preservation, conservation, care. 2 ALIMONY, support, allowance, keep.

**maisonette** n. a flat on two storeys of a larger building.

**maize** n. a tall cereal plant bearing grain on large cobs; its grain.

**majestic** adj. stately and dignified, imposing.
▷ SYNS REGAL, royal, princely, noble, stately, awesome, lofty, distinguished, magnificent, grand, splendid, resplendent, glorious, impressive, imposing, proud.

**majesty** n. (pl. **-ies**) 1 impressive stateliness. 2 (**Majesty**) the title of a king or queen.

**major** adj. 1 important or serious. 2 Music (of a scale) having intervals of a semitone between the 3rd and 4th, and 7th and 8th notes. • n. an army officer next below lieutenant colonel. • v. US specialize in a subject at college.

▷ SYNS **adj. 1** GREATEST, best, leading, foremost, chief, outstanding, notable, eminent. **2** IMPORTANT, significant, crucial, vital, weighty.

**majority** n. **1** the greater number. **2** the number of votes by which one party defeats the opposition. **3** the age when a person is legally an adult.

▷ SYNS **1** MOST, bulk, mass, preponderance, lion's share. **2** COMING-OF-AGE, age of consent, adulthood, maturity.

**make** v. **1** form by combining parts. **2** cause. **3** force to do. **4** add up to. **5** earn money. **6** arrive at or achieve. • n. a brand of goods. ■ maker n.

▷ SYNS **v. 1** CONSTRUCT, build, assemble, put together, erect, manufacture, fabricate, create, form, fashion, model. **2** CAUSE, create, bring about, generate, effect. **3** FORCE, compel, pressurize, oblige, require. **4** make him president: APPOINT, designate, name, nominate, select, elect. **5** make money: ACQUIRE, obtain, gain, get, secure, win, earn. • n. BRAND, label, sort, type, variety.

**make-believe** n. fantasy or pretence. • adj. imitating something real.

▷ SYNS **n.** FANTASY, pretence, daydreams, play-acting, charade. • adj. IMAGINARY, feigned, made-up, fantasy, fictitious, mock; inf. pretend.

**makeshift** adj. temporary and improvised.

▷ SYNS TEMPORARY, rough and ready, improvised, provisional, stopgap.

**maladjusted** adj. unable to cope with normal life.

**maladroit** adj. clumsy.

**malady** n. (pl. **-ies**) an illness.

**malaise** n. a feeling of illness, discomfort, or uneasiness.

**malapropism** n. a comical confusion of words.

**malaria** n. a disease causing recurring fever.

**malcontent** n. a dissatisfied and rebellious person.

**male** adj. **1** of the sex that can fertilize or inseminate a female. **2** (of a plant) having stamens but not a pistil. • n. a male person, animal, or plant.

**malefactor** n. a wrongdoer.

**malevolent** adj. wishing harm to others. ■ malevolence n.

**malformation** n. a deformity. ■ malformed adj.

**malfunction** v. function faultily.

**malice** n. a desire to harm others.

▷ SYNS MALEVOLENCE, ill will, animosity, hostility, enmity, hatred, hate, spite, vindictiveness, rancour, bitterness.

**malicious** adj. intending or intended to do harm.

▷ SYNS SPITEFUL, malevolent, vindictive, hostile, malign, mean, hurtful.

**malign** adj. harmful or evil. • v. say unpleasant and untrue things about.

▷ SYNS **v.** SLANDER, libel, defame, smear, vilify, cast aspersions on, denigrate.

**malignant** adj. **1** (of a tumour) cancerous. **2** malevolent.

**malinger** v. pretend illness to avoid work.

**mall** n. a large enclosed shopping precinct.

**mallard** n. a wild duck.

**malleable** adj. able to be hammered or pressed into shape; easy to influence.

**mallet** n. a hammer, usu. of wood; an instrument for striking the ball in croquet or polo.

**malnutrition** n. weakness resulting from lack of nutrition.

**malodorous** adj. stinking.

**malpractice** n. illegal or improper professional behaviour.

**malt** n. barley or other grain prepared for brewing or distilling.

**maltreat** v. treat cruelly. ▪ maltreatment n.
▷ SYNS TREAT BADLY, mistreat, abuse, bully, harm, hurt, molest.

**mammal** n. an animal that produces milk and bears live young. ▪ mammalian adj.

**mammary** adj. of the breasts.

**mammoth** n. a large extinct elephant. • adj. huge.

**man** n. (pl. **men**) 1 an adult human male. 2 human beings. • v. (**manned**, **manning**) provide a place etc. with people to work in or defend it. □ manhole a covered opening giving access to a sewer etc. manpower the number of people available for work. manslaughter the crime of killing a person without meaning to do so. ▪ manhood n.

**manacle** n. a shackle for the wrists or ankles. ▪ manacled adj.

**manage** v. 1 be in charge of. 2 cope. 3 succeed in doing.
▷ SYNS 1 RUN, head, direct, control, preside over, lead, govern, rule, command, supervise, oversee, administer. 2 COPE, get along, survive, make do.

**manageable** adj. able to be managed without difficulty.
▷ SYNS 1 ACHIEVABLE, doable, practicable, possible, feasible. 2 COMPLIANT, tractable, controllable, docile, accommodating, amenable.

**management** n. 1 managing. 2 the people who manage a business.
▷ SYNS 1 RUNNING, charge, care, leadership, control, command, administration. 2 MANAGERS, employers, bosses, owners, proprietors, directors, directorate, administration.

**manager** n. (fem. **manageress**) a person in charge of a business etc. ▪ managerial adj.

**mandarin** n. 1 a senior influential official. 2 a variety of small orange. 3 (**Mandarin**) the literary and official form of the Chinese language.

**mandate** n. & v. (give) authority to perform certain tasks.

**mandatory** adj. compulsory.
▷ SYNS OBLIGATORY, compulsory, required, requisite, essential, imperative, necessary.

**mandible** n. a jaw or jaw-like part.

**mandolin** n. a musical instrument like a lute.

**mane** n. long hair on the neck of a horse or lion.

**maneuver** US sp. of **MANOEUVRE**.

**manful** adj. brave and resolute.

**manganese** n. a hard grey metallic element.

**mange** n. a skin disease affecting hairy animals.

**manger** n. an open trough for horses or cattle to feed from.

**mangle** n. a clothes wringer.
• v. damage by cutting or crushing roughly.
▷ SYNS v. MUTILATE, maul, butcher, disfigure, deform.

**mango** n. (pl. **-oes** or **-os**) a tropical fruit.

**mangrove** n. a tropical tree growing in swamps.

**manhandle** v. move forcibly or roughly.
▷ SYNS 1 MAUL, mistreat, abuse, treat roughly. 2 HEAVE, haul, push, shove, tug; inf. lug.

**mania** n. 1 violent madness. 2 an extreme enthusiasm for something.
▷ SYNS 1 FRENZY, violence, hysteria, derangement, dementia. 2 OBSESSION, compulsion, fixation, fetish, preoccupation, passion, enthusiasm.

**maniac** n. a person behaving wildly; a fanatical enthusiast.
■ maniacal adj.

**manic** adj. showing wild excitement; frantically busy; or of affected by mania.

**manicure** n. treatment to improve the appearance of the hands and nails. • v. apply such treatment.

**manifest** adj. clear and unmistakable. • v. show clearly; appear.
▷ SYNS adj. OBVIOUS, clear, plain, apparent, patent, noticeable, conspicuous, unmistakable, distinct, blatant.

**manifestation** n. a sign that something exists or is happening.

▷ SYNS 1 DISPLAY, demonstration, show, exhibition, presentation. 2 SIGN, indication, evidence, symptom, proof, testimony.

**manifesto** n. (pl. **-os**) a public declaration of policy.

**manifold** adj. many and varied.
• n. (in a machine) a pipe or chamber with several openings.

**Manila** n. brown paper used for envelopes.

**manipulate** v. 1 handle or control skilfully; treat a part of the body by moving it by hand. 2 control or influence someone unscrupulously.
■ manipulation n.
▷ SYNS 1 HANDLE, wield, ply, work. 2 INFLUENCE, control, exploit, manoeuvre, direct, guide. 3 JUGGLE, falsify, doctor, fiddle, tamper with.

**mankind** n. human beings as a whole.
▷ SYNS THE HUMAN RACE, man, humanity, humans, Homo sapiens, people.

**manly** adj. (**-ier**, **-iest**) brave and strong; considered suitable for a man.
▷ SYNS MASCULINE, macho, virile, muscular, strapping, rugged, tough.

**manna** n. something unexpected and welcome.

**mannequin** n. a dummy used to display clothes in a shop window.

**manner** n. 1 the way in which something is done or happens; a sort or kind. 2 a person's way of behaving towards others. 3 (**manners**) polite social behaviour.
▷ SYNS 1 WAY, means, method, approach, technique, procedure, methodology, fashion,

mode. **2** AIR, appearance, demeanour, bearing, behaviour, conduct. **3** KIND, sort, type, variety, form, nature, category.

**mannered** adj. **1** having manners of a specified kind. **2** stilted and unnatural.
▷ SYNS AFFECTED, unnatural, artificial, stilted, theatrical, pretentious.

**mannerism** n. a distinctive personal habit or way of doing something.
▷ SYNS HABIT, characteristic, trait, idiosyncrasy, quirk, foible.

**manoeuvre** (US **maneuver**) n. **1** a skilful movement. **2** a well planned scheme. **3** (**manoeuvres**) a large-scale military exercise. • v. **1** move with skill or care. **2** cleverly manipulate.
■ manoeuvrable adj.
▷ SYNS n. **1** MOVEMENT, move. **2** TRICK, stratagem, tactic, subterfuge, device, dodge, ploy, ruse, scheme. • v. STEER, guide, direct, work, move, manipulate.

**manor** n. a large country house, usu. with lands. ■ manorial adj.

**manse** n. a church minister's house.

**mansion** n. a large stately house.

**mantelpiece** n. the shelf above a fireplace.

**mantle** n. a loose cloak; a covering.

**mantra** n. a phrase repeated to aid concentration during meditation; a statement or slogan frequently repeated.

**manual** adj. of the hands; done or operated by the hands. • n. a handbook.

**manufacture** v. make or produce goods on a large scale

by machinery; invent a story. • n. the process of manufacturing. ■ manufacturer n.
▷ SYNS v. MAKE, produce, build, construct, assemble, create, fabricate, fashion, model, forge.

**manure** n. animal dung used as fertilizer.

**manuscript** n. a book or document written by hand or typed.

**many** pron. & adj. a large number of. • n. the majority of people.
▷ SYNS pron. & adj. A LOT, lots, numerous, innumerable, countless, scores, copious.

**map** n. a diagram of an area showing physical features, cities, roads, etc. • v. (**mapped**, **mapping**) **1** make a map of. **2** (**map out**) plan in detail.

**maple** n. a tree with broad leaves and winged fruits.

**mar** v. (**marred**, **marring**) disfigure; spoil.

**maraca** n. a container of dried beans etc., shaken as a musical instrument.

**marathon** n. **1** a long-distance running race. **2** a long, difficult task.

**maraud** v. go around stealing things or attacking people.
■ marauder n.

**marble** n. **1** crystalline limestone that can be polished and used in sculpture and building. **2** a small ball of coloured glass used as a toy.
■ marbled adj.

**March** n. the third month.

**march** v. walk in a regular rhythm or an organized column; walk purposefully; force to walk somewhere quickly.
• n. the act of marching; a

piece of music suitable for marching to.

▷ SYNS **v.** WALK, parade, process, step, pace, stride.

**marchioness** n. the wife or widow of a marquess; a woman with the rank of marquess.

**mare** n. the female of the horse or a related animal.

**margarine** n. a butter substitute made from vegetable oils or animal fats.

**margin** n. 1 an edge or border. 2 the blank border around the edges of a page. 3 an amount by which something is won.

▷ SYNS **1** EDGE, side, verge, border, perimeter, boundary, periphery. **2** LEEWAY, latitude, scope, allowance.

**marginal** adj. 1 in a margin. 2 of minor importance.
■ **marginally** adv.

▷ SYNS SLIGHT, small, tiny, minute, negligible.

**marginalize** (or **-ise**) v. treat as unimportant.

**marigold** n. a plant with golden daisy-like flowers.

**marijuana** n. cannabis.

**marina** n. a harbour for yachts and small boats.

**marinade** n. a flavoured liquid in which savoury food is soaked before cooking. • v. soak in a marinade.

**marinate** v. marinade.

**marine** adj. of the sea or shipping. • n. a soldier trained to serve on land or sea.

**mariner** n. a sailor.

**marionette** n. a puppet worked by strings.

**marital** adj. of marriage.

**maritime** adj. 1 of seafaring. 2 living or found near the sea.

▷ SYNS NAVAL, marine, nautical, seafaring.

**mark** n. 1 a small area on a surface different in colour from the rest. 2 something indicating position. 3 a symbol. 4 a distinguishing feature. 5 a point awarded for a correct answer. • v. 1 make a mark on. 2 write a word or symbol on an object to identify it. 3 show the position of. 4 give a mark to a piece of work. 5 pay attention to. 6 (in team games) stay close to an opponent to prevent them from gaining the ball.

▷ SYNS **n.** **1** STAIN, blemish, spot, blotch, smudge, scratch, scar, dent, chip. **2** MARKER, guide, pointer, landmark, signpost. **3** SIGN, symbol, indication, feature, token, evidence, proof. • **v.** **1** STAIN, smear, dirty, scratch, scar, dent. **2** LABEL, identify, initial, brand. **3** CORRECT, assess, evaluate, appraise, grade.

**marked** adj. clearly noticeable.

▷ SYNS PRONOUNCED, striking, clear, glaring, blatant, unmistakable, conspicuous, noticeable.

**marker** n. 1 an object used to indicated a position or route. 2 a broad felt-tip pen.

**market** n. 1 a place or gathering for the sale of provisions, livestock, etc. 2 demand for a commodity. • v. (**marketed**, **marketing**) advertise; offer for sale. □ **market garden** a small farm producing vegetables.
■ **marketable** adj.

**marking** n. the colouring of an animal's skin, feathers, or fur.

**marksman** n. a person skilled in shooting.

**marmalade** n. a jam made from oranges.

**marmoset** n. a small bushy-tailed monkey.

**maroon** n. a brownish-red colour. • v. leave stranded in a desolate place.
▷ SYNS V. ABANDON, desert, strand.

**marquee** n. a large tent used for a party or exhibition etc.

**marquess** n. a nobleman ranking between duke and earl.

**marquetry** n. inlaid work in wood, ivory, etc.

**marquis** n. a rank in some European nobilities.

**marriage** n. the legal union of a man and woman.
▷ SYNS MATRIMONY, wedlock, union, match.

**marrow** n. 1 a soft fatty substance in the cavities of bones. 2 a gourd used as a vegetable.

**marry** v. 1 enter into marriage. 2 join in marriage.
▷ SYNS WED, become man and wife; inf. tie the knot, get hitched.

**marsh** n. low-lying watery ground. ■ marshy adj.
▷ SYNS MARSHLAND, bog, swamp, mire, quagmire, fen.

**marshal** n. a high-ranking officer; an official controlling an event or ceremony.
• v. (**marshalled, marshalling**; US **marshaled**) arrange in proper order; assemble.
▷ SYNS V. ASSEMBLE, gather, collect, muster, arrange, deploy.

**marshmallow** n. a soft sweet made from sugar, egg white, and gelatin.

**marsupial** n. a mammal that carries its young in a pouch.

**martial** adj. of war; warlike.
▷ SYNS MILITANT, warlike, combative, belligerent, pugnacious.

**martinet** n. a person who exerts strict discipline.

**martyr** n. a person who undergoes death or suffering for their beliefs. • v. make a martyr of. ■ martyrdom n.

**marvel** n. a wonderful thing.
• v. (**marvelled, marvelling**; US **marveled**) feel wonder.
▷ SYNS n. WONDER, sensation, spectacle, phenomenon, miracle. • v. BE AMAZED, be awed, wonder.

**marvellous** (US **marvelous**) adj. amazing or extraordinary; very good.
▷ SYNS AMAZING, astounding, astonishing, awesome, breath-taking, sensational, remarkable, spectacular, phenomenal, excellent, splendid, wonderful, magnificent, superb, super, great, smashing, fantastic, terrific, fabulous; inf. ace, wicked.

**marzipan** n. an edible paste made from ground almonds.

**mascara** n. a cosmetic for darkening the eyelashes.

**mascot** n. an object believed to bring good luck to its owner.

**masculine** adj. of, like, or traditionally considered suitable for men. ■ masculinity n.
▷ SYNS MALE, manly, virile, macho, muscular, rugged.

**mash** n. a soft pulp of crushed matter; boiled, mashed potatoes. • v. beat into a soft mass.
▷ SYNS V. CRUSH, pulp, purée, squash.

**mask** n. a covering worn over the face as a disguise or protection. • v. cover with a mask; disguise or conceal.

▷ SYNS n. DISGUISE, cover, camouflage, veil, front, facade.
• v. DISGUISE, hide, conceal, cover up, camouflage, veil, screen.

**masochism** n. the enjoyment of your own pain. ■ **masochist** n.

**mason** n. a person who works with stone.

**masonry** n. stonework.

**masquerade** n. a pretence. • v. pretend.

**mass** n. 1 a amount of matter with no definite shape. 2 a large group. 3 (**masses**) a large amount. 4 the quantity of matter a body contains. 5 (**Mass**) a Christian service of the Eucharist. • adj. done by or affecting large numbers of people or things. • v. gather into a mass. □ **mass-produced** produced in large quantities in a factory.
▷ SYNS adj. WHOLESALE, universal, widespread, general, extensive. • v. ASSEMBLE, gather, collect.

**massacre** n. a brutal slaughter. • v. brutally kill many people.

**massage** n. rubbing and kneading of the body to reduce pain or tension. • v. 1 give a massage to. 2 manipulate figures to give a better result.
▷ SYNS v. RUB, knead, pummel, manipulate.

**masseur** n. (fem. **masseuse**) a person who provides massage professionally.

**massive** adj. large and heavy or solid.

**mast** n. a tall pole, esp. supporting a ship's sails.

**mastectomy** n. (pl. **-ies**) surgical removal of a breast.

**master** n. 1 a man in a position of authority, control, or ownership. 2 a person skilled in a particular activity. 3 a male teacher. 4 an original recording etc. from which copies are made. • adj. highly skilled.
• v. 1 gain complete knowledge or skill in. 2 gain control of. □ **mastermind** 1 a person who plans and directs a complex scheme. 2 be the mastermind of. **masterpiece** a work of outstanding skill. ■ **masterly** adj.
▷ SYNS n. LORD, ruler, governor, commander, captain, chief.
• v. 1 LEARN, grasp, understand; inf. get the hang of. 2 CONQUER, overcome, control, subdue, vanquish, defeat, curb.

**masterful** adj. 1 powerful and commanding. 2 very skilful.
▷ SYNS AUTHORITATIVE, powerful, controlling, domineering, dictatorial, overbearing, peremptory, high-handed.

**mastery** n. 1 thorough knowledge or great skill. 2 control or supremacy.

**masticate** v. chew.

**mastiff** n. a dog of a large, strong breed.

**masturbate** v. stimulate the genitals with the hand. ■ **masturbation** n.

**mat** n. a piece of decorative or protective material placed on a floor or other surface. ■ **matted** adj.

**matador** n. a bullfighter.

**match** n. 1 a contest in a game or sport. 2 a person or thing equal to another. 3 a short stick with a tip that ignites when rubbed on a rough surface. • v. 1 correspond. 2 be equal to. □ **matchmaker** a person who arranges marriages or relationships between others.

▷ SYNS v. **1** GO WITH, complement, coordinate, suit, correspond. **2** EQUAL, rival, compare with.

**mate** n. **1** inf. a friend. **2** an animal's sexual partner. • v. (of animals) have sex.

**material** n. **1** matter from which something is or can be made. **2** items needed for doing something. **3** cloth. • adj. **1** of the physical things. **2** essential or relevant.

▷ SYNS n. **1** MATTER, substance, stuff, constituents. **2** FABRIC, cloth, textiles.

**materialism** n. concentration on material possessions rather than spiritual values.
■ materialistic adj.

**materialize** (or **-ise**) v. appear, become visible; become a fact or happen.

▷ SYNS **1** HAPPEN, occur, come about, take place. **2** APPEAR, turn up, become visible, come to light, emerge.

**maternal** adj. of a mother; related through your mother.

**maternity** n. motherhood.

**mathematics** n. the science of numbers, quantities, and measurements. ■ mathematical adj. mathematician n.

**maths** (US **math**) n. mathematics.

**matinee** n. an afternoon performance in a theatre or cinema.

**matins** n. morning prayer.

**matriarch** n. the female head of a family or tribe.
■ matriarchal adj.

**matriculate** v. enrol at a college or university.

**matrimony** n. marriage.
■ matrimonial adj.

**matrix** n. (pl. **-trices** or **-trixes**) an environment in which something develops; a mould in which something is shaped.

**matron** n. **1** a woman in charge of domestic and medical arrangements at a school etc. **2** dated the woman in charge of nursing in a hospital.

**matt** adj. not shiny.

**matter** n. **1** physical substance or material. **2** a situation or affair; a problem or issue. • v. be important; be distressing or of concern to someone.

▷ SYNS n. **1** MATERIAL, substance, stuff. **2** no laughing matter: AFFAIR, business, situation, circumstance, event, occurrence, incident. **3** important matters: SUBJECT, topic, issue, point. • v. BE IMPORTANT, signify, count, be relevant.

**mattress** n. a fabric case filled with padding or springy material, used on or as a bed.

**mature** adj. fully grown or developed; not childish; (of a life assurance policy etc.) due for payment. • v. make or become mature. ■ maturation n. maturity n.

▷ SYNS adj. **1** ADULT, grown-up, full-grown, of age. **2** RIPE, ready.

**maudlin** adj. sentimental in a self-pitying way.

▷ SYNS MAWKISH, sentimental; inf. soppy.

**maul** v. wound by tearing and scratching.

**mausoleum** n. a magnificent tomb.

**mauve** adj. & n. pale purple.

**maverick** n. an unorthodox and independent-minded person.

▷ SYNS NONCONFORMIST, rebel, dissenter, dissident, eccentric.

**mawkish** adj. sentimental in a sickly way.

**maxim** n. a sentence giving a general truth or rule of conduct.
▷ SYNS APHORISM, proverb, adage, saying, axiom.

**maximize** (or **-ise**) v. make as great as possible.

**maximum** adj. & n. (pl. **-mums** or **-ma**) the greatest (amount) possible.
▷ SYNS HIGHEST, greatest, biggest, largest, topmost, most, utmost.

**May** n. the fifth month.

**may**[1] v.aux. used to express a wish, possibility, or permission.

**may**[2] n. hawthorn blossom.

**maybe** adv. perhaps.

**Mayday** n. an international radio distress signal used by ships and aircraft.

**mayhem** n. violent confusion and disorder.
▷ SYNS HAVOC, disorder, confusion, chaos, bedlam.

**mayonnaise** n. a cold creamy sauce made with eggs and oil.

**mayor** n. the head of the municipal corporation of a city or borough.

**mayoress** n. a female mayor; a mayor's wife.

**maze** n. a network of paths etc. through which it is hard to find your way.

**MBE** abbr. Member of the Order of the British Empire.

**MD** abbr. Doctor of Medicine; Managing Director.

**me** pron. the objective case of *I*.

**mead** n. an alcoholic drink made from honey and water.

**meadow** n. a field of grass.
▷ SYNS FIELD, pasture, paddock.

**meagre** (US **meager**) adj. scanty in amount.
▷ SYNS PALTRY, sparse, scant, inadequate, insufficient, insubstantial, skimpy, miserly, stingy.

**meal** n. **1** an occasion when food is eaten; the food itself. **2** coarsely ground grain.

**mealy-mouthed** adj. afraid to speak frankly.

**mean**[1] adj. **1** ungenerous; unkind; vicious. **2** of poor quality. ■ meanness n.
▷ SYNS **1** MISERLY, niggardly, parsimonious, penny-pinching, tight-fisted, stingy. **2** NASTY, disagreeable, unpleasant, unfriendly, offensive, obnoxious, bad-tempered, churlish, cantankerous.

**mean**[2] adj. & n. (something) midway between two extremes; an average.

**mean**[3] v. **1** convey or express; signify. **2** intend. **3** result in.
▷ SYNS **1** INDICATE, signify, express, convey, denote, designate, represent, symbolize, connote, imply, suggest. **2** INTEND, aim, set out, contemplate, desire, want, wish. **3** INVOLVE, entail, lead to, result in.

**meander** v. follow a winding course; wander in a leisurely way. • n. a winding bend in a river or road.
▷ SYNS v. WIND, zigzag, snake, curve.

**meaning** n. what is meant. ■ meaningful adj. meaningless adj.
▷ SYNS **1** DEFINITION, explanation, interpretation. **2** SIGNIFICANCE, point, value, worth, importance.

**means** n. a thing or method used to achieve a result; financial resources.
▷ SYNS WAY, method, expedient, manner, medium, channel, avenue, course.

**meantime** adv. meanwhile.

**meanwhile** adv. in the intervening period; at the same time.

**measles** n. an infectious disease producing red spots on the body.

**measly** adj. inf. meagre.

**measure** v. find the size, amount, etc. of something by comparison with a known standard; be of a specified size; take or give a measured amount. • n. **1** a course of action to achieve a purpose; a law. **2** a standard unit used in measuring; a certain quantity or degree. ■ measurable adj.
▷ SYNS v. CALCULATE, compute, estimate, quantify, evaluate, rate, assess, appraise, gauge, determine, judge. • n. **1** SIZE, dimension, proportions, magnitude, amplitude, mass, bulk, quantity. **2** SHARE, portion, division, quota, lot, ration, percentage. **3** take measures: ACTION, act, procedure, step, means, expedient.

**measured** adj. **1** with a slow steady rhythm. **2** carefully considered.

**measurement** n. measuring; a size etc. found by measuring.

**meat** n. animal flesh as food.

**meaty** adj. (-ier, -iest) **1** full of meat. **2** substantial or challenging.

**mechanic** n. a skilled workman who uses or repairs machines.

**mechanical** adj. **1** of or worked by machinery. **2** done without conscious thought.
▷ SYNS **1** AUTOMATED, automatic, motorized. **2** AUTOMATIC, unthinking, unconscious, involuntary, instinctive.

**mechanics** n. the study of motion and force; the science of machinery.

**mechanism** n. a piece of machinery; the way something works or happens.
▷ SYNS **1** MACHINE, apparatus, appliance, tool, device, instrument, contraption. **2** PROCESS, procedure, system, method, means, medium.

**mechanize** (or -ise) v. equip with machinery.

**medal** n. a coin-like piece of metal commemorating an event or awarded for an achievement.

**medallion** n. a pendant shaped like a medal.

**medallist** (US **medalist**) n. the winner of a medal.

**meddle** v. interfere in other people's affairs.

**media** pl. of MEDIUM. • pl.n. (**the media**) newspapers and broadcasting as providers of information.

**mediaeval** = MEDIEVAL.

**median** adj. in or passing through the middle. • n. a median point or line.

**mediate** v. act as peacemaker between opposing sides.
▷ SYNS ARBITRATE, negotiate, conciliate, intervene, intercede, umpire, referee.

**medic** n. inf. a doctor or medical student.

**medical** adj. of the science of medicine. • n. an examination to assess someone's health or fitness.

**medicate** v. treat with a medicine or drug.

**medication** n. drugs etc. for medical treatment; treatment with these.

**medicinal** adj. having healing properties.
▷ SYNS MEDICAL, therapeutic, curative, healing, remedial, restorative.

**medicine** n. the science of the prevention and cure of disease; a substance used to treat disease.
▷ SYNS MEDICATION, drug, remedy, cure.

**medieval** (or **mediaeval**) adj. of the Middle Ages.

**mediocre** adj. second-rate.
■ mediocrity n.
▷ SYNS INDIFFERENT, average, ordinary, commonplace, run-of-the-mill, tolerable, passable, adequate, unexceptional, inferior, second-rate, poor; inf. so-so.

**meditate** v. think deeply; focus your mind in silence for relaxation or religious purposes.
■ meditation n.
▷ SYNS CONTEMPLATE, think, muse, ponder, consider, concentrate, reflect, deliberate, ruminate.

**Mediterranean** adj. of the Mediterranean Sea.

**medium** n. 1 a means of doing or communicating something. 2 a substance through which something acts or is conveyed. 3 (pl. **-diums**) a person claiming to communicate between the dead and the living. 4 the middle state between two extremes. • adj. roughly halfway between extremes.

▷ SYNS n. 1 MEANS, agency, channel, avenue, instrument. 2 MEDIAN, midpoint, middle, centre, average, norm, standard.
• adj. MIDDLE, mean, median, midway, intermediate.

**medley** n. (pl. **-eys**) an assortment.

**meek** adj. quiet and obedient.
▷ SYNS DOCILE, humble, submissive, compliant, amenable, dutiful, deferential, weak, timid.

**meet** v. 1 come together at the same place and time. 2 be introduced to for the first time. 3 satisfy a requirement etc.
• n. a meeting.
▷ SYNS v. 1 ENCOUNTER, run into, come across, chance on, happen on; inf. bump into. 2 *the land and sea meet:* CONNECT, converge, touch, join, intersect. 3 *the committee met:* ASSEMBLE, gather, congregate, convene.

**meeting** n. an assembly for discussion.
▷ SYNS GATHERING, assembly, conference, convention; inf. get-together.

**megabyte** n. Computing a unit of information equal to one million bytes.

**megalith** n. a large stone, esp. as a prehistoric monument.

**megalomania** n. obsession with power or delusion about your own power.
■ megalomaniac adj. & n.

**megaphone** n. a funnel-shaped device for amplifying the voice.

**megapixel** n. a unit for measuring the resolution of a digital image, equal to $2^{20}$ or (strictly) 1,048,576 pixels.

**megawatt** n. a unit of power equal to one million watts.

**melancholy** n. great sadness or depression. • adj. sad or depressing.

**melanin** n. a dark pigment in the skin, hair, etc.

**meld** v. blend.

**melee** n. a confused fight; a disorderly crowd.

**mellifluous** adj. sweet-sounding.

**mellow** adj. smooth or soft in sound, taste, or colour; relaxed and cheerful. • v. make or become mellow.
▷ SYNS adj. GENTLE, easy-going, pleasant, amicable, amiable, good-natured, affable, genial, jovial, cheerful, happy.

**melodious** adj. tuneful; pleasant-sounding.
▷ SYNS MELODIC, musical, tuneful, harmonious, lyrical, dulcet, sweet.

**melodrama** n. a sensational play.

**melodramatic** adj. over-dramatic or exaggerated.
▷ SYNS EXAGGERATED, histrionic, overdramatic, overdone, theatrical.

**melody** n. (pl. **-ies**) sweet music; the main part in a piece of harmonized music.
■ melodic adj.
▷ SYNS TUNE, air, music, refrain, theme, song.

**melon** n. a large sweet fruit.

**melt** v. make or become liquid by heating; make or become less stern; vanish.
▷ SYNS DISSOLVE, thaw, defrost, soften.

**member** n. a person belonging to a particular group or society; a limb. ■ membership n.

▷ SYNS **1** ADHERENT, associate, fellow. **2** LIMB, appendage.

**membrane** n. a thin flexible skin-like tissue.

**memento** n. (pl. **-oes** or **-os**) a souvenir.

**memo** n. (pl. **-os**) a note sent within an organization.

**memoir** n. a written account of events etc. that you remember.

**memorabilia** pl. n. objects collected because of their links with people or events.

**memorable** adj. worth remembering, easy to remember.
▷ SYNS UNFORGETTABLE, momentous, significant, notable, noteworthy, important, consequential, remarkable, outstanding, striking, impressive.

**memorandum** n. (pl. **-da** or **-dums**) **1** a memo. **2** a formal report.

**memorial** n. an object or custom etc. established to commemorate an event or person.
▷ SYNS MONUMENT, statue, shrine.

**memorize** (or **-ise**) v. learn and remember exactly.

**memory** n. **1** the ability to remember things. **2** a thing remembered. **3** a computer's storage capacity.
▷ SYNS REMEMBRANCE, recollection, recall, reminiscence.

**men** pl. of MAN.

**menace** n. **1** something dangerous. **2** a threatening quality. • v. threaten.
▷ SYNS n. THREAT, danger, hazard, jeopardy.

**menagerie** n. a small zoo.

**mend** v. **1** repair. **2** improve a bad situation.
▷ SYNS REPAIR, fix, restore, renovate, darn, patch.

**menial** adj. lowly or degrading. • n. a person who does menial tasks. ■ menially adv.
▷ SYNS adj. LOWLY, humble, unskilled, routine, humdrum, boring. • n. SERVANT, domestic, drudge, underling; inf. dogsbody, skivvy.

**meningitis** n. inflammation of the membranes covering the brain and spinal cord.

**menopause** n. the time of life when a woman ceases to menstruate.

**menstruate** v. (of a woman) discharge blood from the womb each month. ■ menstrual adj.

**mental** adj. **1** of the mind. **2** inf. mad.

**mentality** n. (pl. -ies) a typical way of thinking.
▷ SYNS MIND SET, attitude, outlook, character, disposition, make-up.

**menthol** n. a peppermint-flavoured substance, used medicinally.

**mention** v. refer to briefly. • n. a reference to someone or something.
▷ SYNS v. **1** REFER TO, allude to, touch on, raise, broach. **2** SAY, state, remark, disclose, divulge, reveal. • n. REFERENCE, allusion, comment, remark.

**mentor** n. a trusted adviser.
▷ SYNS ADVISER, counsellor, guide, guru, teacher, tutor, coach, instructor.

**menu** n. (pl. -us) **1** a list of dishes available. **2** a list of options on a computer screen.

**mercantile** adj. of trade.

**mercenary** adj. working merely for money. • n. (pl. -ies) a professional soldier hired by a foreign army.
▷ SYNS adj. GRASPING, greedy, acquisitive, avaricious.

**merchandise** n. goods for sale.
▷ SYNS GOODS, wares, stock, commodities, produce.

**merchant** n. a wholesale trader. □ merchant navy commercial shipping.
▷ SYNS TRADER, dealer, wholesaler, seller, vendor, supplier.

**merciful** adj. showing mercy; giving relief from pain and suffering.
▷ SYNS LENIENT, clement, compassionate, forgiving, forbearing, humane, tender-hearted, kind, tolerant, generous, beneficent.

**merciless** adj. showing no mercy.
▷ SYNS RUTHLESS, remorseless, pitiless, unforgiving, unsparing, inhumane, inhuman, unsympathetic, heartless, harsh, cruel.

**mercurial** adj. liable to sudden changes of mood.

**mercury** n. a heavy silvery liquid metallic element.

**mercy** n. **1** pity or forgiveness shown to someone in your power. **2** something to be grateful for. □ at the mercy of in the power of.
▷ SYNS PITY, compassion, leniency, clemency, charity, forgiveness, kindness, indulgence.

**mere** adj. no more than what is specified. ■ merely adv.

**merge** v. combine into a whole; blend gradually.

▷ SYNS JOIN, amalgamate, unite, combine, incorporate, blend, fuse, mingle, mix, intermix.

**merger** n. the combining of two organizations into one.

**meridian** n. any of the great semicircles on the globe, passing through the North and South Poles.

**meringue** n. sugar and egg whites baked until crisp.

**merit** n. **1** excellence. **2** a good point or quality. • v. (**merited, meriting**) deserve.

▷ SYNS n. **1** EXCELLENCE, quality, worth, value. **2** GOOD POINT, advantage, asset, plus. • v. DESERVE, earn, be worth, warrant, rate, earn.

**meritorious** adj. deserving reward or praise.

▷ SYNS PRAISEWORTHY, laudable, commendable, admirable, estimable, creditable, worthy, deserving, excellent, exemplary, good.

**mermaid** n. a mythical sea creature with a woman's head and body and a fish's tail.

**merry** adj. **1** cheerful and lively. **2** inf. slightly drunk. ☐ merry-go-round a roundabout at a funfair. merrymaking lively celebration. ■ merriment n.

▷ SYNS CHEERFUL, cheery, high-spirited, light-hearted, carefree, joyful, jolly, convivial, happy.

**mesh** n. material made of a network of wire or thread; the spacing of the strands in this. • v. (of a gearwheel) engage with another; make or become entangled; be in harmony.

▷ SYNS n. NETTING, net, lattice, latticework, lacework.

**mesmerize** (or **-ise**) v. completely capture the attention of.

▷ SYNS HYPNOTIZE, spellbind, entrance, enthral, bewitch, captivate, enchant, fascinate.

**mess** n. **1** a dirty or untidy state. **2** a difficult or confused situation. **3** a room where members of the armed forces have meals. • v. **1** make untidy or dirty. **2** (**mess about**) behave in a silly or playful way.

▷ SYNS n. **1** UNTIDINESS, disorder, disarray, clutter, jumble, muddle, chaos. **2** PLIGHT, predicament, difficulty, trouble, quandary, dilemma, muddle, mix-up, confusion.

**message** n. **1** a spoken, written, or electronic communication. **2** a significant point or central theme. • v. send a message to.

▷ SYNS n. **1** COMMUNICATION, news, note, memo, email, letter, missive, bulletin, communiqué. **2** MEANING, idea, point, moral.

**messenger** n. the bearer of a message.

▷ SYNS COURIER, envoy, emissary, agent, go-between.

**messiah** n. a great leader or saviour.

**Messrs** pl. of **Mr**.

**messy** adj. **1** untidy or dirty. **2** confused and difficult.

▷ SYNS UNTIDY, dirty, disordered, scruffy, cluttered, chaotic, disorganized, in disarray.

**met** past and p.p. of **MEET**.

**metabolism** n. the process by which food is used for growth or energy. ■ metabolic adj.

**metal** n. a hard, shiny, solid material which conducts electricity and heat. ■ metallic adj.

**metallurgy** n. the study of the properties of metals.

**metamorphic** adj. (of rock) changed in form or structure by heat, pressure, etc.

**metamorphosis** n. (pl. **-ses**) a change of form or character. ■ metamorphose v.
▷ SYNS TRANSFORMATION, transfiguration, change, alteration, conversion, mutation.

**metaphor** n. the application of a word or phrase to something that it does not apply to literally (e.g. the *evening* of your life, *food* for thought). ■ metaphorical adj.

**metaphysics** n. the branch of philosophy dealing with the nature of existence and knowledge. ■ metaphysical adj.

**mete** v. (**mete out**) dispense justice, punishments, etc.

**meteor** n. a small body of matter from outer space appearing as a streak of light.

**meteoric** adj. of meteors; swift and brilliant.

**meteorite** n. a meteor fallen to earth.

**meteorology** n. the study of atmospheric conditions in order to forecast weather. ■ meteorologist n.

**meter** n. 1 a device that measures and records quantity, degree, or rate. 2 US sp. of METRE. • v. measure with a meter.

**methane** n. a flammable gas.

**method** n. 1 a way of doing something. 2 organization.
▷ SYNS 1 PROCEDURE, technique, system, practice, modus operandi, process, approach, way, manner, mode. 2 ORDER, organization, structure, plan, design.

**methodical** adj. orderly and systematic.

▷ SYNS ORDERLY, organized, systematic, structured, logical, efficient.

**Methodist** adj. & n. (a member of) a Protestant religious denomination based on the teachings of John Wesley.

**methodology** n. (pl. **-ies**) a system of methods used in an activity or study.

**meths** n. inf. methylated spirit.

**methylated spirit** n. a form of alcohol used as a solvent and for heating.

**meticulous** adj. careful and precise.
▷ SYNS CONSCIENTIOUS, careful, scrupulous, punctilious, painstaking, exacting, thorough, perfectionist, fastidious.

**metre** (US **meter**) n. 1 a metric unit of length (about 39.4 inches). 2 rhythm in poetry.

**metric** adj. of or using the decimal system of weights and measures, using the metre, litre, and gram as units.
□ metric ton a unit of weight equal to 1,000 kg (2,205 lb).

**metrical** adj. of or in poetic metre.

**metronome** n. a device used to indicate tempo while practising music.

**metropolis** n. the chief city of a country or region. ■ metropolitan adj.

**mettle** n. courage and strength of character.

**mew** v. (of a cat or gull) make a soft, high-pitched sound.

**mews** n. a set of stables converted into houses.

**mezzanine** n. an extra storey set between two others.

**mezzo** (or **mezzo-soprano**) n. a woman's singing voice between soprano and contralto.

**mg** abbr. milligrams.

**miaow** v. (of a cat) make its characteristic cry.

**miasma** n. an unpleasant or unhealthy atmosphere.

**mica** n. a mineral substance used as an electrical insulator.

**mice** pl. of **MOUSE**.

**microbe** n. a bacterium or germ.

**microchip** n. a miniature electronic circuit made from a tiny wafer of silicon.

**microcosm** n. a thing that has the features and qualities of something much larger.

**microfiche** (or **microfilm**) n. a piece of film containing miniature photographs of documents.

**microorganism** n. a micro-scopic organism.

**microphone** n. an instrument for picking up sound waves for transmitting or amplifying.

**microprocessor** n. an integrated circuit which can function as the main part of a computer.

**microscope** n. an instrument with lenses that magnify very small things, making them visible.

**microscopic** adj. too small to be seen without a microscope.
▷ SYNS INFINITESIMAL, minuscule, tiny, minute.

**microwave** n. an electro-magnetic wave of length between about 30 cm and 1 mm; an oven using such waves to heat food quickly.

**mid** adj. in the middle.

**midday** n. noon.

**middle** adj. **1** at an equal distance from. **2** medium in rank, quality, etc. • n. a middle point or position. □ middle age the part of life between youth and old age. middle class the social group between upper and working classes. middleman a person who buys goods from producers and sells them to consumers.
▷ SYNS adj. MID, medium, midway, halfway, central, median.
• n. CENTRE, midpoint, heart, core.

**middling** adj. average in size, amount, or rank.

**midfield** n. the part of a football pitch away from the goals.

**midge** n. a small biting insect.

**midget** n. a very small person.

**midnight** n. 12 o'clock at night.

**midriff** n. the front part of the body just above the waist.

**midst** n. the middle.

**midway** adv. halfway.

**midwife** n. a person trained to assist at childbirth.

**mien** n. a person's manner or bearing.

**might**[1] n. great strength or power.
▷ SYNS FORCE, power, strength, potency, toughness.

**might**[2] v.aux. **1** used to express possibility or make a sugges-tion. **2** used politely in questions and requests.

**mighty** adj. (-ier, -iest) very strong or powerful; very great.
• adv. very, extremely.
▷ SYNS adj. **1** FORCEFUL, powerful, strong, potent, tough, robust, vigorous. **2** HUGE, massive, vast, enormous, colossal, gigantic.

**migraine** n. a severe form of headache.

**migrant** adj. migrating. • n. a migrant animal; a person travelling in search of work.
▷ SYNS adj. MIGRATORY, wandering, nomadic, itinerant.

**migrate** v. (of animals) regularly move from one area to another each season.
■ migration n.

**mike** n. inf. a microphone.

**mild** adj. **1** not serious, severe, harsh, or extreme. **2** (of weather) fairly warm. **3** not strong in flavour. **4** gentle.
▷ SYNS **1** GENTLE, soft, warm, balmy. **2** BLAND, insipid, tasteless. **3** TENDER, gentle, sympathetic, placid, meek, docile.

**mildew** n. tiny fungi forming a coating on things exposed to damp.

**mile** n. a measure of length, 1760 yds (about 1.609 km). □ mileage a number of miles covered. milestone **1** a stone showing the distance to a particular place. **2** a significant event or stage.

**milieu** n. (pl. -lieus or -lieux) environment or surroundings.
▷ SYNS ENVIRONMENT, surroundings, setting, location.

**militant** adj. & n. (a person) prepared to take aggressive action. ■ militancy n.
▷ SYNS ACTIVIST, extremist, partisan.

**militarism** n. support for maintaining and using a military force. ■ militaristic adj.

**military** adj. of soldiers or the army or all armed forces. • n. the armed forces.

▷ SYNS n. ARMY, armed forces, services, militia, navy, air force.

**militate** v. be a factor preventing something.

**militia** n. a military force, esp. of trained civilians available in an emergency.

**milk** n. **1** a white fluid produced by female mammals to feed their young. **2** cow's milk. • v. **1** draw milk from. **2** exploit a person or situation.

**milky** adj. **1** containing milk. **2** having a soft white colour.
▷ SYNS WHITE, pale, creamy, ivory, alabaster.

**mill** n. **1** machinery for grinding specified material. **2** a building fitted with machinery for manufacturing. • v. **1** grind in a mill. **2** move about as a confused crowd. □ millstone **1** each of a pair of circular stones used for grinding grain. **2** a burden of responsibility.
▷ SYNS n. FACTORY, plant, foundry, works, workshop. • v. GRIND, pulverize, crush, powder.

**millennium** n. (pl. -iums or -ia) a period of 1,000 years.

**miller** n. a person who owns or works in a grain mill.

**millet** n. a cereal plant.

**milliner** n. a person who makes or sells women's hats.

**million** n. **1** one thousand thousand (1,000,000). **2** (millions) inf. very many. ■ millionth adj. & n.

**millionaire** n. a person who has over a million pounds, dollars, etc.

**millipede** n. a small crawling creature with many legs.

**milometer** n. an instrument measuring the distance in miles travelled by a vehicle.

**mime** n. acting with gestures without words. • v. act in mime.

**mimic** v. (mimicked, mimicking) imitate the voice or behaviour of. • n. a person skilled in mimicking. ■ mimicry n.
▷ SYNS v. IMITATE, copy, impersonate, ape, parody; inf. take off.

**mimosa** n. an acacia tree with yellow flowers.

**mince** v. 1 cut meat into very small pieces. 2 walk with short, quick steps and swinging hips. • n. minced meat. □ mincemeat a mixture of dried fruit, sugar, etc. mince pie a small pie containing mincemeat.

**mind** n. 1 the faculty of consciousness and thought. 2 the intellect or memory. 3 attention or will. • v. 1 be distressed or annoyed by. 2 remember to do. 3 watch out for. 4 take care of temporarily. 5 (minded) inclined to think in a particular way: liberal-minded. ■ minder n.
▷ SYNS n. 1 BRAIN, intelligence, intellect, brains, brainpower, wits, understanding, reasoning, sense. 2 ATTENTION, thoughts, concentration. • v. 1 OBJECT, care, be bothered, be annoyed, dislike, disapprove. 2 WATCH OUT FOR, look out for, beware of. 3 LOOK AFTER, take care of, attend to, watch.

**mindful** adj. conscious or aware of something.
▷ SYNS PAYING ATTENTION TO, heedful of, watchful of, careful of, wary of, chary of, cognizant of, aware of, conscious of, alert to, alive to, sensible of.

**mindless** adj. taking or showing no thought; not requiring thought or intelligence.

**mine**[1] adj. & poss.pron belonging to me.

**mine**[2] n. 1 an excavation for extracting coal etc. 2 an abundant source. 3 a bomb placed on or in the ground or water. • v. 1 obtain from a mine. 2 lay explosive mines on or in. □ minefield 1 an area planted with explosive mines. 2 a situation presenting hidden dangers. minesweeper a warship equipped for detecting and removing explosive mines.
▷ SYNS n. 1 COLLIERY, pit, quarry. 2 SOURCE, repository, store. • v. EXCAVATE, quarry, dig, extract.

**miner** n. a person who works in a mine.

**mineral** n. an inorganic natural substance. □ mineral water water naturally containing dissolved mineral salts.

**minestrone** n. soup containing vegetables and pasta.

**mingle** v. blend together; mix socially.
▷ SYNS 1 MIX, blend, combine, merge, unite, amalgamate, fuse. 2 CIRCULATE, socialize, hobnob, fraternize.

**miniature** adj. very small. • n. a miniature thing.
▷ SYNS adj. SMALL, mini, little, baby, pocket; inf. pint-sized.

**minibus** n. a small bus for about twelve people.

**minidisc** n. a small disk used for recording and playing back sound or data.

**minim** n. a note in music, lasting half as long as a semibreve.

**minimal** adj. very small, the least possible; negligible.
▷ SYNS MINIMUM, least, smallest, slightest, nominal, token.

**minimize** (or **-ise**) v. **1** reduce to a minimum. **2** represent as small or unimportant.
▷ SYNS **1** REDUCE, decrease, curtail, cut back. **2** BELITTLE, play down, deprecate, underestimate.

**minimum** adj. & n. (pl. **-ma**) the smallest (amount) possible.
▷ SYNS MINIMAL, lowest, smallest, least, slightest.

**minion** n. a lowly worker or assistant.

**minister** n. **1** the head of a government department; a senior diplomatic representative. **2** a member of the clergy. • v. (**minister to**) attend to the needs of. ∎ **ministerial** adj.

**ministrations** pl.n. the providing of help or care.

**ministry** n. (pl. **-ies**) **1** a government department headed by a minister. **2** the work of a minister of religion. **3** a period of government under one Prime Minister.

**mink** n. a small stoat-like animal, farmed for its fur.

**minnow** n. a small fish.

**minor** adj. **1** not important or serious. **2** Music (of a scale) having intervals of a semitone between the 2nd and 3rd, 5th and 6th, and 7th and 8th notes. • n. a person not yet legally of adult age.
▷ SYNS adj. SLIGHT, small, unimportant, insignificant, inconsequential, negligible, trivial, trifling.

**minority** n. (pl. **-ies**) **1** the smaller part of a group or class; a small group differing from or disagreeing with others. **2** being below the legal age of adulthood.

**minster** n. a large church.

**minstrel** n. a medieval singer and musician.

**mint**¹ n. a place authorized to make a country's coins. • v. make coins.

**mint**² n. a fragrant herb; peppermint, a sweet flavoured with this.

**minuet** n. a slow stately dance.

**minus** prep. **1** with the subtraction of. **2** (of temperature) falling below zero by. **3** inf. without. • adj. **1** (of a number) less than zero. **2** (after a grade) slightly below. • n. the sign (−).

**minuscule** adj. very small.

**minute**¹ n. **1** one-sixtieth of an hour or degree; a moment of time. **2** (**minutes**) a written summary of the proceedings of a meeting. • v. record in the minutes.

**minute**² adj. extremely small; very precise and detailed.
▷ SYNS TINY, minuscule, microscopic, miniature, little, small.

**minx** n. a cheeky girl or woman.

**miracle** n. a welcome event so extraordinary that it is attributed to supernatural causes; an outstanding example or achievement.
▷ SYNS WONDER, marvel, phenomenon.

**miraculous** adj. like a miracle; very surprising and welcome.
▷ SYNS AMAZING, astounding, remarkable, extraordinary, incredible, unbelievable, wonderful.

**mirage** n. an optical illusion caused by hot air.

**mire** n. a boggy area.

**mirror** n. a surface which reflects a clear image. • v. reflect.

▷ SYNS V. REFLECT, reproduce, imitate, copy, mimic, echo, parallel.

**mirth** n. amusement.
▷ SYNS GAIETY, merriment, cheerfulness, hilarity, glee, laughter.

**misadventure** n. an accident or unlucky occurrence.

**misanthrope** (or **misanthropist**) n. a person who dislikes people in general. ■ misanthropic adj.

**misapprehension** n. a mistaken belief.

**misappropriate** v. take dishonestly.

**misbehave** v. behave badly.
▷ SYNS BEHAVE BADLY, be naughty, be disobedient, get up to mischief; inf. act up.

**miscarriage** n. the birth of a baby or fetus before it can survive independently.

**miscarry** v. (**miscarried**, **miscarrying**) 1 have a miscarriage. 2 (of a plan) fail.

**miscellaneous** adj. assorted.
▷ SYNS VARIED, assorted, mixed, diverse, sundry, motley, indiscriminate, heterogeneous.

**miscellany** n. (pl. **-ies**) a collection of assorted items.
▷ SYNS ASSORTMENT, mixture, variety, collection, medley, potpourri, mix, mishmash.

**mischief** n. playful misbehaviour; harm or trouble caused by a person or thing.
▷ SYNS MISCHIEVOUSNESS, naughtiness, bad behaviour, misconduct, wrongdoing, delinquency.

**mischievous** adj. 1 full of mischief. 2 intended to cause trouble.

▷ SYNS NAUGHTY, bad, badly behaved, disobedient, troublesome; playful, teasing, impish, roguish.

**misconceived** adj. badly judged or planned.

**misconception** n. a wrong interpretation.

**misconduct** n. bad behaviour.

**miscreant** n. a wrongdoer.

**misdemeanour** (US **misdemeanor**) n. a wrongful act.

**miser** n. a person who hoards money and spends as little as possible. ■ miserly adj.

**miserable** adj. very unhappy; very small or inadequate.
▷ SYNS UNHAPPY, dejected, depressed, downcast, downhearted, despondent, desolate, gloomy, dismal, blue, melancholy, sad, forlorn.

**misery** n. (pl. **-ies**) great unhappiness or discomfort; a cause of this; someone who is always complaining.
▷ SYNS 1 DISTRESS, wretchedness, suffering, anguish, grief, sorrow, heartbreak, despair, depression, melancholy, woe, sadness, unhappiness.
2 TROUBLE, misfortune, adversity, hardship, affliction, ordeal, pain, burden, trial, tribulation.

**misfire** v. (of a gun or engine) fail to fire correctly; (of a plan etc.) go wrong.

**misfit** n. a person not well suited to their environment.

**misfortune** n. bad luck; an unfortunate event.
▷ SYNS BAD LUCK, setback, adversity, misadventure, mishap, blow, accident, disaster, affliction, trial, tribulation.

**misgivings** pl.n. feelings of doubt or worry.
▷ SYNS QUALMS, doubts, reservations, second thoughts; apprehension, uneasiness.

**misguided** adj. badly judged.
▷ SYNS MISTAKEN, deluded, erroneous, wrong, ill-advised, unwise, injudicious, imprudent, foolish.

**mishap** n. an unlucky accident.
▷ SYNS ACCIDENT, trouble, setback, reverse, misadventure, misfortune.

**misjudge** v. form a wrong opinion of; estimate wrongly.

**mislay** v. (**mislaid, mislaying**) lose temporarily.
▷ SYNS LOSE, misplace, miss.

**mislead** v. (**-led, -leading**) cause to form a wrong impression.
▷ SYNS MISINFORM, misdirect, delude, take in, deceive, fool, hoodwink, pull the wool over someone's eyes.

**mismanage** v. manage badly or wrongly.

**misnomer** n. a wrongly applied name or description.

**misogynist** n. a man who hates women. ■ misogyny n.

**misprint** n. an error in printing.

**Miss** n. the title of a girl or unmarried woman.

**miss** v. **1** fail to hit, reach, or catch; fail to catch; fail to see or hear; be too late for; fail to take an opportunity. **2** regret the absence of. **3** (**miss out**) omit. • n. a failure to hit or catch something.
▷ SYNS v. **1** SKIP, play truant from. **2** LET SLIP, pass up, overlook, disregard. **3** LONG FOR, pine for, yearn for, ache for.

**misshapen** adj. not having the normal shape.

▷ SYNS DEFORMED, distorted, warped, bent.

**missile** n. an object thrown or fired at a target.

**missing** adj. not present; not in its place.
▷ SYNS LOST, mislaid, misplaced, absent, gone astray.

**mission** n. **1** an important assignment. **2** a strongly felt aim or calling.
▷ SYNS **1** ASSIGNMENT, task, job, expedition, operation, project. **2** VOCATION, calling, pursuit, quest.

**missionary** n. (pl. **-ies**) a person sent to spread religious faith.

**missive** n. a letter.
▷ SYNS LETTER, message, communication, note, memo, memorandum, communiqué, dispatch.

**mist** n. water vapour near the ground or clouding a window etc. • v. cover or become covered with mist.

**mistake** n. **1** a thing that is incorrect. **2** an error of judgement. • v. **1** be wrong about. **2** (**mistake for**) confuse with.
▷ SYNS n. ERROR, fault, inaccuracy, slip, blunder, miscalculation, misunderstanding, oversight, faux pas.

**mister** var. of **MR**.

**mistletoe** n. a plant with white berries, growing on trees.

**mistreat** v. treat badly or unfairly.
▷ SYNS ILL-TREAT, maltreat, abuse, injure, harm, hurt, molest.

**mistress** n. a woman who has control of people or things; a female teacher; a married man's female lover.

**mistrust** v. feel no trust in. • n. lack of trust.
▷ SYNS v. DISTRUST, suspect, have reservations about, have misgivings, be wary, question, doubt.

**misty** adj. (-ier, -iest) full of mist; indistinct.
▷ SYNS HAZY, foggy, cloudy, blurred, indistinct, vague.

**misunderstand** v. (**misunderstood**, **misunderstanding**) fail to understand correctly.
▷ SYNS MISINTERPRET, misconstrue, misread; inf. get the wrong end of the stick.

**misunderstanding** n. 1 a failure to understand correctly. 2 a disagreement.
▷ SYNS 1 MISINTERPRETATION, misconception, misreading, misapprehension. 2 DISAGREEMENT, dispute, quarrel, argument, clash.

**misuse** v. 1 use wrongly. 2 treat badly. • n. wrong use.
▷ SYNS v. 1 ABUSE, squander, waste, dissipate. 2 MALTREAT, mistreat, ill-treat, abuse, manhandle, harm, hurt, bully, molest.

**mite** n. a very small spider-like animal; a small creature, esp. a child.

**mitigate** v. make less intense or severe. ■ mitigation n.
▷ SYNS ALLEVIATE, reduce, diminish, lessen, attenuate, allay, assuage, palliate, soothe, relieve, ease, soften, temper, mollify, moderate.

**mitre** (US **miter**) n. 1 the pointed headdress of bishops and abbots. 2 a join between pieces of wood that form a right angle.

**mitt** n. a mitten.

**mitten** n. a glove with no partitions between the fingers.

**mix** v. 1 combine or be combined. 2 make by combining ingredients. 3 (**mix up**) confuse or spoil the arrangement of. 4 meet people socially. • n. a mixture. ■ mixer n.
▷ SYNS v. 1 BLEND, combine, mingle, unite, join, amalgamate. 2 SOCIALIZE, mingle, associate. • n. MIXTURE, blend, combination, union, amalgamation, fusion.

**mixed** adj. consisting of different kinds, qualities, or elements.
▷ SYNS 1 ASSORTED, varied, miscellaneous, diverse, heterogeneous. 2 mixed reactions: AMBIVALENT, equivocal, contradictory, conflicting.

**mixture** n. something made by mixing.
▷ SYNS 1 COMPOUND, blend, mix, brew, concoction. 2 ASSORTMENT, variety, melange, collection, medley, potpourri, conglomeration, jumble, mix, mishmash.

**ml** abbr. millilitres.

**mm** abbr. millimetres.

**MMR** abbr. measles, mumps, and rubella (a vaccination given to children).

**mnemonic** adj. & n. (a verse etc.) aiding the memory.

**moan** n. a low mournful sound; a grumble. • v. give a moan; complain.
▷ SYNS n. GROAN, lament, lamentation, wail, whimper, whine. • v. 1 GROAN, wail, whimper, whine. 2 COMPLAIN, whine, carp; inf. grouse, gripe, whinge.

**moat** n. a deep wide water-filled ditch round a castle etc.

**mob** n. a large disorderly crowd; a group. • v. (**mobbed**, **mobbing**) crowd round in a disorderly or violent way.

▷ SYNS n. CROWD, horde, multitude, rabble, mass, throng, host, gang. • v. CROWD AROUND, surround, besiege, jostle.

**mobile** adj. able to move or be moved easily. • n. 1 an ornamental hanging structure whose parts move in currents of air. 2 (or **mobile phone**) a portable telephone.
■ mobility n.

**mobilize** (or **-ise**) v. assemble troops etc. for active service.

▷ SYNS MUSTER, rally, marshal, assemble, organize, prepare, ready.

**moccasin** n. a soft flat-soled leather shoe.

**mocha** n. a kind of coffee.

**mock** v. tease or ridicule; imitate scornfully. • adj. not genuine or real.

▷ SYNS v. RIDICULE, jeer, sneer, deride, scorn, make fun of, tease, taunt, insult.
• adj. IMITATION, artificial, simulated, synthetic, fake, sham, false, bogus, pseudo.

**mockery** n. (pl. **-ies**) ridicule; an absurd or unsatisfactory imitation.

▷ SYNS 1 RIDICULE, jeering, derision, contempt, scorn, disdain, jibe, insult. 2 PARODY, travesty, caricature, lampoon.

**mode** n. 1 a way of doing something. 2 the current fashion.

**model** n. 1 a three-dimensional reproduction, usu. on a smaller scale. 2 someone or something seen as an example of excellence. 3 a person employed to pose for an artist or display clothes by wearing them.

• adj. exemplary. • v. 1 make a model of; shape. 2 work as an artist's or fashion model.

▷ SYNS n. 1 REPLICA, representation, mock-up, copy, dummy, imitation. 2 PROTOTYPE, archetype, original, pattern, paradigm, sample, example. 3 STYLE, design, form, mark, version, type, variety, kind, sort. 4 IDEAL, paragon, perfect example, exemplar, epitome.

**modem** n. a device for transmitting computer data via a telephone line.

**moderate** adj. 1 average. 2 not politically extreme. • n. a person with moderate views. • v. make or become moderate.
■ moderation n.

▷ SYNS adj. AVERAGE, modest, medium, middling, adequate, fair, tolerable, passable.
• v. ABATE, let up, die down, calm down, lessen, decrease, diminish, weaken, subside.

**moderately** adv. to a certain extent.

▷ SYNS SOMEWHAT, quite, fairly, reasonably, to some extent.

**moderator** n. an arbitrator.

**modern** adj. of present or recent times; in current style.
■ modernity n.

▷ SYNS 1 CONTEMPORARY, present-day, present, current, 21st-century. 2 FASHIONABLE, in style, in vogue, modish, new, newfangled, fresh; inf. trendy, with-it.

**modernize** v. bring up to date with modern equipment, techniques, etc.

▷ SYNS UPDATE, renovate, remodel, revamp, refashion.

**modest** adj. 1 not boastful. 2 small or moderate. 3 not

showing off the body.
■ **modesty** n.
▷ SYNS **1** SELF-DEPRECATING, self-effacing, unassuming; shy, bashful, diffident, reserved. **2** SMALL, ordinary, simple, plain, humble, inexpensive, unostentatious, unpretentious.

**modicum** n. a small amount.

**modify** v. (**modified, modifying**) make minor changes to.
■ **modification** n.
▷ SYNS ALTER, change, adjust, adapt, revise, refine; inf. tweak.

**modish** adj. fashionable.

**modulate** v. **1** regulate. **2** vary in tone or pitch.

**module** n. a standardized part or independent unit forming part of a complex structure; a unit of training or education.
■ **modular** adj.

**mogul** n. inf. an important or influential person.

**mohair** n. yarn made from the fine silky hair of the angora goat.

**moist** adj. slightly wet.
■ **moisten** v.
▷ SYNS WET, damp, steamy, humid, dank, clammy.

**moisture** n. tiny drops of water making something damp.
▷ SYNS WATER, liquid, wetness, damp, humidity.

**moisturize** (or **-ise**) v. make skin less dry. ■ **moisturizer** n.

**molar** n. a back tooth.

**molasses** n. syrup from raw sugar.

**mold** etc. US sp. of MOULD etc.

**mole** n. **1** a small burrowing animal with dark fur. **2** inf. a spy within an organization. **3** a small dark spot on human skin.

**molecule** n. a group of atoms forming the smallest unit into which a substance can be divided. ■ **molecular** adj.

**molest** v. **1** assault sexually. **2** dated harass.

**mollify** v. (**mollified, mollifying**) cause to feel less angry.
▷ SYNS CALM, pacify, placate, appease, soothe.

**mollusc** n. an animal with a soft body and often a hard shell.

**mollycoddle** v. pamper.

**molt** US sp. of MOULT.

**molten** adj. liquefied by heat.

**moment** n. **1** a point or brief period of time. **2** importance.
▷ SYNS MINUTE, second, instant, point, time, juncture; inf. tick, jiffy.

**momentary** adj. lasting only a moment. ■ **momentarily** adv.
▷ SYNS BRIEF, short-lived, fleeting, passing, transient, transitory, ephemeral, temporary.

**momentous** adj. of great importance.
▷ SYNS CRUCIAL, critical, vital, decisive, pivotal, important, significant, consequential, fateful, historic.

**momentum** n. impetus gained by movement.
▷ SYNS IMPETUS, impulse, thrust, drive, power, energy, force.

**monarch** n. a king or queen.

**monarchist** n. a supporter of monarchy.

**monarchy** n. (pl. **-ies**) **1** government by a monarch. **2** a state ruled by a monarch.

**monastery** n. (pl. **-ies**) a community of monks.

**monastic** adj. of monks or monasteries.

**Monday** n. the day before Tuesday.

**monetary** adj. of money or currency.

**money** n. **1** coins and banknotes. **2** wealth. **3** payment or profit.
▷ SYNS CASH, capital, funds, finances, notes, coins, currency; inf. dough, lolly, bread, dosh.

**moneyed** adj. wealthy.

**mongoose** n. (pl. **-gooses**) a small carnivorous mammal of Africa and Asia.

**mongrel** n. a dog of no definite breed.

**monitor** n. **1** a person or device that monitors something. **2** a television used to view a picture from a camera or a display on a computer. **3** a school pupil with special duties. • v. keep under observation.
▷ SYNS n. DETECTOR, scanner, re-corder; observer, watchdog, overseer, supervisor.
• v. OBSERVE, watch, track, record, oversee.

**monk** n. a member of a male religious community.

**monkey** n. (pl. **-eys**) a small primate, usu. long-tailed and tree-dwelling. • v. (**monkeyed, monkeying**) behave mischievously; tamper with.

**monochrome** adj. done in only one colour or in black and white.

**monocle** n. a single lens worn at one eye.

**monogamy** n. the system of being married to only one person at a time.

**monogram** n. letters (esp. a person's initials) combined in a design.

**monograph** n. a scholarly study on a single subject.

**monolith** n. a large single upright block of stone.
■ **monolithic** adj.

**monologue** n. a long speech.

**monopolize** (or **-ise**) v. have exclusive control or the largest share of; keep to yourself.
▷ SYNS CORNER, control, take over, dominate.

**monopoly** n. (pl. **-ies**) exclusive control of the supply of a product or service.

**monotone** n. a level unchanging tone of voice.

**monotonous** adj. dull because lacking in variety or variation.
■ **monotony** n.
▷ SYNS UNVARYING, unchanging, repetitious, uniform, routine, humdrum, uninteresting, un-exciting, dull, boring, tedious.

**monsoon** n. a seasonal wind in South Asia; the rainy season accompanying this.

**monster** n. **1** a large, frightening imaginary creature. **2** a cruel person.
▷ SYNS FIEND, beast, brute, demon, dragon, ogre.

**monstrosity** n. (pl. **-ies**) a very large and ugly object.

**monstrous** adj. **1** large and ugly or frightening. **2** evil or wrong.
▷ SYNS **1** GROTESQUE, hideous, ugly, horrible, frightening. **2** see OUTRAGEOUS.

**month** n. **1** each of the twelve periods into which a year is divided. **2** a period of 28 days.
■ **monthly** adj. & adv.

**monument** n. an object com-memorating a person or event etc.; a structure of historical importance.

▷ SYNS MEMORIAL, statue, shrine, mausoleum, obelisk.

**monumental** adj. of great size or importance; of or serving as a monument.

**moo** v. (of a cow) make a long, deep sound.

**mooch** v. inf. pass your time aimlessly.

**mood** n. 1 a temporary state of mind. 2 a fit of bad temper.
▷ SYNS HUMOUR, temper, frame of mind.

**moody** adj. 1 having sudden changes of mood. 2 sulky or gloomy.
▷ SYNS TEMPERAMENTAL, volatile, capricious, changeable, unpredictable.

**moon** n. 1 the natural satellite of the earth. 2 a natural satellite of any planet. • v. behave dreamily.

**moonlight** n. light from the moon. • v. (**moonlighted**, **moonlighting**) inf. have two jobs.

**moor**[1] n. a stretch of open uncultivated land. □ **moorhen** a small black waterbird.

**moor**[2] v. fasten a boat to the shore or to an anchor. □ **mooring** (or **moorings**) a place where a boat is moored; the ropes for mooring it.

**moose** n. (pl. **moose**) an elk.

**moot** adj. uncertain or undecided: *a moot point*.
▷ SYNS DEBATABLE, doubtful, disputable, arguable, controversial, unresolved, undecided.

**mop** n. a pad or bundle of yarn on a stick, used for cleaning things; a thick mass of hair. • v. (**mopped**, **mopping**) clean with a mop; wipe your eyes, forehead, etc.; soak up liquid by wiping.

**mope** v. be unhappy and listless.

**moped** n. a low-powered motorcycle.

**moral** adj. 1 concerned with right and wrong behaviour. 2 virtuous. • n. 1 a moral lesson learned from a story etc. 2 (**morals**) standards of behaviour.
▷ SYNS n. LESSON, message, meaning, significance, point, teaching.

**morale** n. a feeling of confidence and satisfaction.
▷ SYNS CONFIDENCE, heart, spirit, hope, hopefulness, optimism.

**morality** n. 1 moral principles. 2 the extent to which an action is right or wrong.
▷ SYNS MORALS, standards, ethics, principles.

**moralize** (or **-ise**) v. comment on moral issues.

**morass** n. a boggy area; a complicated or confused situation.

**moratorium** n. (pl. **-riums** or **-ria**) a temporary ban on an activity.

**morbid** adj. 1 preoccupied with gloomy or unpleasant things. 2 of disease.
▷ SYNS GRUESOME, grisly, macabre, hideous, horrible.

**mordant** adj. (of wit) sharply sarcastic.

**more** n. & pron. a greater quantity or degree; an additional quantity. • adv. 1 to a greater extent. 2 again. □ **moreover** besides.
▷ SYNS n. & pron. EXTRA, addition, supplement, increase, increment. • adv. TO A GREATER EXTENT, further, longer.

**moreover** adv. besides.

▷ SYNS BESIDES, furthermore, what's more, in addition, also, as well, into the bargain, to boot.

**mores** pl.n. customs or conventions.

**morgue** n. a mortuary.

**moribund** adj. on the point of death.

**morning** n. the part of the day before noon or the midday meal.

**moron** n. inf. a stupid person.

**morose** adj. gloomy and unsociable.

**morphine** n. a painkilling drug made from opium.

**Morse code** n. a code of signals using short and long sounds or flashes of light.

**morsel** n. a small piece of food.
▷ SYNS BITE, nibble, bit, crumb, grain, piece, scrap, taste.

**mortal** adj. **1** subject to death. **2** causing death; lasting until death. • n. a human being.
▷ SYNS adj. **1** TEMPORAL, transient, ephemeral, impermanent, perishable, human, earthly, worldly, corporeal. **2** *mortal enemies*: DEADLY, sworn, irreconcilable, bitter, implacable.

**mortality** n. (pl. -ies) **1** the state of being mortal. **2** death. **3** the death rate.

**mortar** n. **1** a mixture of lime or cement with sand and water, for joining bricks or stones. **2** a bowl in which substances are pounded with a pestle. **3** a short cannon.

**mortgage** n. a loan using property as security. • v. pledge property as security for a loan.

**mortify** v. (**mortified**, **mortifying**) humiliate or embarrass.

▷ SYNS HUMILIATE, humble, disgrace, shame, abash, chasten, crush, discomfit, embarrass.

**mortise** (or **mortice**) n. a slot in one piece of wood to hold the end of another piece.

**mortuary** n. (pl. -ies) a place where corpses are kept temporarily.

**mosaic** n. a pattern or picture made with small pieces of coloured glass or stone.

**Moslem** adj. & n. = **MUSLIM**.

**mosque** n. a Muslim place of worship.

**mosquito** n. (pl. -oes) a bloodsucking insect.

**moss** n. a small green plant growing in damp places.
■ **mossy** adj.

**most** n. & pron. the greatest amount or number; the majority. • adv. **1** to the greatest extent. **2** very.

**mostly** adv. for the most part.
▷ SYNS ON THE WHOLE, largely, mainly, chiefly, predominantly.

**motel** n. a roadside hotel for motorists.

**moth** n. an insect like a butterfly, usu. active at night.
□ **mothball** a small ball of camphor for keeping moths away from stored clothes.

**mother** n. **1** a female parent. **2** the title of the head of a convent. • v. look after kindly and protectively.
□ **mother-in-law** the mother of your wife or husband. **mother-of-pearl** a pearly substance lining the shells of oysters. ■ **motherhood** n.

**motherly** adj. kind and protective.

▷ SYNS MATERNAL, protective, kind, caring, loving, affectionate, warm.

**motif** n. a pattern; a recurring feature or theme.

**motion** n. **1** moving; movement. **2** a formal proposal put to a meeting for discussion. • v. direct someone with a gesture.
▷ SYNS n. MOBILITY, locomotion, movement, travel, flow, action, activity.

**motionless** adj. not moving.
▷ SYNS UNMOVING, still, stationary, immobile, static, frozen.

**motivate** v. give a motive to; stimulate the interest of. ■ motivation n.
▷ SYNS MOVE, cause, lead, persuade, prompt, drive, impel, spur, induce, provoke, incite, inspire.

**motive** n. a person's reason for doing something.
▷ SYNS MOTIVATION, reason, rationale, grounds, cause, basis, occasion, incentive, inducement, influence, stimulus, spur.

**motley** adj. made up of a variety of different things.

**motocross** n. a motorcycle race over rough ground.

**motor** n. **1** a machine supplying power and movement for a vehicle or machine. **2** a car. • adj. **1** driven by a motor. **2** producing motion. • v. inf. travel by car. □ **motorbike** a motorcycle. **motorcycle** a two-wheeled vehicle powered by a motor. **motorcyclist** a motorcycle rider. **motorway** a road designed for fast long-distance traffic.

**motorist** n. a car driver.

**mottled** adj. patterned with irregular patches of colour.

▷ SYNS BLOTCHED, blotchy, speckled, spotted, marbled, flecked, dappled.

**motto** n. (pl. **-oes**) a short sentence or phrase expressing an ideal or rule of conduct.
▷ SYNS MAXIM, aphorism, adage, saying, axiom, precept.

**mould** (US **mold**) n. **1** a hollow container into which a liquid is poured to set in a desired shape. **2** a furry growth of tiny fungi. • v. **1** form into a particular shape. **2** influence the development of. ■ mouldy adj.
▷ SYNS v. SHAPE, form, fashion, model, create, carve, sculpt.

**moulder** (US **molder**) v. decay, rot away.

**moulding** (US **molding**) n. an ornamental strip of plaster or wood.

**moult** (US **molt**) v. shed old feathers, hair, or skin. • n. this process.

**mound** n. a pile of earth or stones; a small hill; a large pile.
▷ SYNS HILLOCK, knoll, rise, hummock, tump, embankment, bank, dune.

**mount** v. **1** go up stairs, a hill, etc.; get up on to a horse etc. **2** organize and set in process. **3** increase in number, size, or intensity. **4** fix on or in a support or setting. • n. **1** a support or setting. **2** a mountain.
▷ SYNS v. **1** ASCEND, go up, climb, scale. **2** STAGE, put on, prepare, organize, arrange. **3** INCREASE, grow, escalate, intensify.

**mountain** n. a mass of land rising to a great height; a large heap or pile.
▷ SYNS PEAK, height, pinnacle, fell, alp; Scot. ben; lit. mount.

**mountaineer** n. a person who climbs mountains.
■ **mountaineering** n.

**mountainous** adj. **1** full of mountains. **2** huge.

**mourn** v. feel or express sorrow about a dead person or lost thing. ■ **mourner** n.
▷ SYNS GRIEVE, sorrow, lament, bewail, bemoan.

**mournful** adj. sorrowful.

**mourning** n. **1** the expression of deep sorrow for someone who has died. **2** black clothes worn in a period of mourning.

**mouse** n. **1** (pl. **mice**) a small rodent with a long tail; a quiet timid person. **2** (pl. also **mouses**) a small rolling device for moving the cursor on a VDU screen.

**mousse** n. a frothy creamy dish; a soft gel or frothy preparation.

**moustache** (US **mustache**) n. hair on the upper lip.

**mousy** adj. **1** dull greyish brown. **2** quiet and timid.

**mouth** n. **1** the opening in the body through which food is taken in and sounds are made. **2** an opening or entrance. **3** the place where a river enters the sea. • v. **1** move the lips as if to form words. **2** say insincerely. □ **mouth organ** a small musical instrument played by blowing and sucking. **mouthpiece** the part of a musical instrument, telephone, etc. put in or against the mouth.
▷ SYNS n. **1** LIPS, jaws; inf. gob, trap. **2** OPENING, entrance, entry, inlet, aperture.

**move** v. **1** go in a specified direction; change or cause to change position; change your residence. **2** prompt to action; provoke emotion in. **3** make progress. **4** put to a meeting for discussion. • n. **1** an act of moving. **2** a calculated action or initiative. **3** a player's turn during a board game.
■ **movable** (or **moveable**) adj.
▷ SYNS v. **1** GO, walk, march, proceed, progress, advance. **2** CARRY, transport, transfer, shift. **3** TAKE ACTION, act, do something, get moving. **4** MOVE HOUSE, relocate, leave, go away. **5** moved by the performance: AFFECT, touch, impress, upset, disturb, disquiet. **6** moved to tears: PROVOKE, incite, rouse, excite, stimulate, motivate, influence, prompt, cause, induce. **7** move that he be sacked: PROPOSE, put forward, advocate, recommend, urge, suggest. • n. **1** MOVEMENT, motion, action, activity, gesture, gesticulation. **2** ACTION, act, deed, measure, step, manoeuvre, tactic, stratagem.

**movement** n. **1** an act of moving. **2** a group with a shared cause. **3** (**movements**) a person's activities during a particular period. **4** a main division of a musical work.
▷ SYNS **1** MOVE, motion, action, gesture, gesticulation. **2** a peace movement: CAMPAIGN, crusade, drive, group, party, organization, coalition, front.

**movie** n. US a cinema film.

**moving** adj. arousing pity or sympathy.
▷ SYNS **1** AFFECTING, touching, emotive, emotional, poignant, stirring, arousing, upsetting, disturbing. **2** MOVABLE, mobile, motile, unfixed. **3** the moving force: DRIVING, dynamic,

impelling, motivating, stimulating, inspirational.

**mow** v. (**mowed**, **mown**, **mowing**) cut down grass on an area of ground. ■ **mower** n.

**MP** abbr. Member of Parliament.

**mph** abbr. miles per hour.

**Mr** n. (pl. **Messrs**) the title prefixed to a man's name.

**Mrs** n. (pl. **Mrs**) the title prefixed to a married woman's name.

**MRSA** n. a strain of bacteria resistant to antibiotics.

**Ms** n. the title prefixed to a married or unmarried woman's name.

**much** pron. a large amount.
• adv. to a great extent; often.

**muck** n. dirt or mess; manure. ■ **mucky** adj.
▷ SYNS 1 DIRT, grime, filth, mud, slime, sludge; inf. gunk, gunge. 2 DUNG, manure, excrement, faeces.

**mucus** n. a slimy substance coating the inner surface of hollow organs of the body.

**mud** n. wet soft earth.

**muddle** v. confuse or mix up; progress in a haphazard way.
• n. a muddled state or collection.
▷ SYNS v. 1 CONFUSE, mix up, jumble, scramble, mess up. 2 CONFUSE, disorientate, bewilder, perplex, puzzle, baffle, nonplus, confound.

**muddy** v. 1 make something muddy. 2 make something difficult to understand.
▷ SYNS 1 DIRTY, soil, spatter. 2 *muddy the issue:* MAKE UNCLEAR, obscure, confuse, obfuscate, cloud.

**muesli** n. a breakfast cereal of oats, dried fruit, and nuts.

**muff** n. a tube-shaped furry covering for the hands.
• v. inf. bungle.

**muffin** n. 1 a flat bread roll eaten toasted with butter. 2 a small cake.

**muffle** v. 1 wrap for cover or warmth. 2 make a sound quieter.
▷ SYNS 1 WRAP, swathe, enfold, envelop. 2 DEADEN, dull, dampen, mute, soften, quieten, stifle, smother.

**muffler** n. a scarf.

**mug** n. 1 a large drinking cup with a handle. 2 inf. the face. 3 inf. a gullible person.
• v. 1 attack and rob in a public place. 2 (**mug up**) inf. learn a subject intensively. ■ **mugger** n.
▷ SYNS v. ASSAULT, attack, rob.

**muggy** adj. (**-ier**, **-iest**) (of weather) oppressively damp and warm.
▷ SYNS CLOSE, stuffy, sultry, oppressive, airless, humid.

**mulberry** n. a purple or white fruit resembling a blackberry.

**mulch** n. a mixture of wet straw, leaves, etc., spread on the ground to protect plants or retain moisture. • v. cover with mulch.

**mule** n. 1 the offspring of a female horse and a male donkey; a stubborn person. 2 a backless shoe. ■ **mulish** adj.

**mull** v. 1 (**mull over**) think over. 2 heat wine with sugar and spices.

**multicultural** adj. of or involving several cultural or ethnic groups.

**multifarious** adj. very varied.

**multinational** adj. & n. (a business company) operating in several countries.

**multiple** adj. having or involving many parts; numerous. • n. a quantity divisible by another a number of times without remainder.
▷ SYNS adj. SEVERAL, many, numerous, various.

**multiplicity** n. (pl. -ies) a large number; a great variety.

**multiply** v. (**multiplied, multiplying**) add a number to itself a specified number of times; (cause to) become more numerous. ■ **multiplication** n. **multiplier** n.
▷ SYNS **1** BREED, reproduce. **2** INCREASE, grow, accumulate, augment, proliferate.

**multitask** v. do several things at once; (of a computer) operate more than one program at the same time.

**multitude** n. a great number of things or people.
▷ SYNS CROWD, assembly, throng, host, horde, mass, mob.

**mum** inf. n. mother. • adj. silent: *keep mum*.

**mumble** v. speak indistinctly.

**mummy** n. (pl. -ies) **1** inf. mother. **2** a corpse embalmed and wrapped for burial, esp. in ancient Egypt.

**mumps** pl.n. a disease causing painful swellings in the neck.

**munch** v. chew vigorously.
▷ SYNS CHEW, chomp, masticate, crunch, eat.

**mundane** adj. dull or routine.
▷ SYNS COMMON, ordinary, everyday, workaday, usual, prosaic, pedestrian, routine, customary, normal, typical, commonplace.

**municipality** n. (pl. -ies) a self-governing town or district. ■ **municipal** adj.

**munificent** adj. very generous.

**munitions** pl.n. weapons, ammunition, etc.

**mural** n. a painting on a wall.

**murder** n. intentional unlawful killing. • v. kill intentionally and unlawfully.
▷ SYNS n. KILLING, slaying, manslaughter, homicide, slaughter, assassination, butchery, carnage, massacre. v. see KILL (1).

**murderer** n. a person who commits murder.
▷ SYNS KILLER, assassin, serial killer, butcher; inf. hit man.

**murderous** adj. capable of or involving murder or extreme violence.
▷ SYNS FATAL, lethal, deadly, mortal, homicidal, bloodthirsty.

**murk** n. darkness or fog.

**murky** adj. dark and gloomy; (of liquid) cloudy.
▷ SYNS DARK, dim, gloomy, dirty, muddy, dingy, dull, cloudy.

**murmur** n. a low continuous sound; softly spoken words. • v. make a murmur; speak or utter softly.
▷ SYNS n. WHISPER, undertone, mutter, mumble, burble, drone. • v. WHISPER, speak sotto voce, mutter, mumble, burble, drone.

**muscle** n. a strip of fibrous tissue able to move a part of the body by contracting; power or strength.

**muscular** adj. of muscles; having well-developed muscles.
▷ SYNS BRAWNY, strapping, well built, hefty, rugged, beefy, burly.

**muse** v. be deep in thought. • n. a poet's source of inspiration.

▷ SYNS v. THINK, meditate, ruminate, contemplate, reflect, deliberate, daydream.

**museum** n. a place where objects of historical or scientific interest are collected and displayed.

**mush** n. a soft pulp. ■ **mushy** adj.

**mushroom** n. an edible fungus with a stem and a domed cap. • v. spring up in large numbers.

**music** n. vocal or instrumental sounds arranged in a pleasing way; the written signs representing this.

**musical** adj. of or involving music; sweet-sounding. • n. a play with songs and dancing.
▷ SYNS adj. TUNEFUL, melodic, melodious, harmonious, dulcet.

**musician** n. a person who writes or plays music.

**musk** n. a substance secreted by certain animals or produced synthetically, used in perfumes.

**musket** n. a long-barrelled gun formerly used by infantry.

**Muslim** (or **Moslem**) adj. of or believing in Muhammad's teaching. • n. a believer in this faith.

**muslin** n. a thin cotton cloth.

**mussel** n. a bivalve mollusc.

**must** v.aux. expressing obligation, insistence, or certainty.

**mustache** US sp. of **MOUSTACHE**.

**mustard** n. a hot-tasting yellow paste.

**muster** v. 1 summon up a feeling. 2 bring troops together.

**musty** adj. smelling stale or mouldy.
▷ SYNS FUSTY, mouldy, stale, stuffy, airless, damp, dank.

**mutant** n. a living thing differing from its parents as a result of genetic change.

**mutate** v. change in form or nature.

**mutation** n. 1 a change in form. 2 a mutant.
▷ SYNS CHANGE, variation, alteration, transformation, metamorphosis.

**mute** adj. 1 not speaking. 2 unable to speak. • n. a device used to muffle a musical instrument. • v. muffle the sound of.
▷ SYNS adj. SILENT, speechless, wordless, taciturn; inf. mum.

**muted** adj. 1 quiet and soft. 2 not bright.
▷ SYNS 1 MUFFLED, faint, quiet, soft. 2 SUBDUED, subtle, delicate, understated.

**mutilate** v. severely injure or damage.

**mutinous** adj. rebellious.
▷ SYNS REBELLIOUS, insubordinate, insurgent, subversive, seditious, riotous.

**mutiny** n. (pl. **-ies**) a rebellion against authority, esp. by soldiers or sailors. • v. (**mutinied, mutinying**) rebel.
■ mutineer n.
▷ SYNS n. REBELLION, revolt, insurrection, insurgence, uprising.

**mutter** v. 1 say quietly and indistinctly. 2 grumble privately. • n. something muttered.

**mutton** n. the flesh of sheep as food.

**mutual** adj. 1 felt or done by two or more people equally. 2 shared by two or more people.

**muzzle** n. 1 the nose and mouth of an animal. 2 a guard fitted over an animal's muzzle to stop it biting. 3 the open end of the barrel of a gun. • v. 1 put a muzzle on. **2** prevent from expressing opinions freely.

**muzzy** adj. **1** confused or dazed. **2** blurred.

**my** adj. belonging to me.

**myopia** n. short-sightedness. ■ **myopic** adj.

**myriad** n. a vast number.

**myrrh** n. a resin used in perfumes and incense.

**myself** pron. the emphatic and reflexive form of *I* and *me*.

**mysterious** adj. difficult or impossible to explain or understand.
▷ SYNS ENIGMATIC, impenetrable, inscrutable, incomprehensible, inexplicable, unfathomable, obscure, arcane, cryptic, supernatural, uncanny, mystical, peculiar, strange, weird, curious, bizarre, mystifying, perplexing.

**mystery** n. (pl. **-ies**) a matter that remains unexplained; a story dealing with a puzzling crime.
▷ SYNS ENIGMA, puzzle, secret, riddle, conundrum.

**mystic** n. a person who seeks to obtain union with God by spiritual contemplation. • adj. mystical. ■ **mysticism** n.

▷ SYNS adj. SPIRITUAL, paranormal, transcendental, other-worldly, supernatural, occult, metaphysical.

**mystify** v. (**mystified, mystifying**) confuse or baffle.
▷ SYNS CONFUSE, bewilder, confound, perplex, baffle, nonplus, puzzle; inf. stump, bamboozle.

**mystique** n. an aura of mystery, glamour, or power.

**myth** n. a traditional tale containing beliefs about ancient times or natural events and usually involving supernatural beings.
▷ SYNS **1** LEGEND, saga, (folk) tale, story, fable, allegory, parable, fairy story. **2** FANTASY, delusion, invention, fabrication, untruth, lie.

**mythical** adj. **1** occurring in or relating to myths. **2** imaginary or not real.
▷ SYNS **1** LEGENDARY, mythological, fabled, fabulous, fairy-tale, storybook. **2** IMAGINARY, fictitious, make-believe, fantasy, invented, made-up; inf. pretend.

**mythology** n. myths; the study of myths. ■ **mythological** adj.

**myxomatosis** n. an infectious, usu. fatal disease of rabbits.

# Nn

**N** abbr. north or northern.

**naan** = NAN.

**nab** v. (**nabbed, nabbing**) inf. arrest; steal.

**nadir** n. the lowest point.

▷ SYNS THE LOWEST POINT, rock-bottom, the depths.

**nag** v. (**nagged, nagging**) scold continually; (of pain) be felt persistently.

• n. **1** a person who nags.
**2** inf. a horse.
▷ SYNS v. SCOLD, carp, pick on, keep on at, harp on at, henpeck, bully, chivvy. • n. SHREW, scold, harpy, termagant.

**nail** n. **1** a small metal spike used to join pieces of wood. **2** a thin hard layer over the tip of a finger or toe. • v. fasten with nails.

**naive** adj. lacking experience or judgement. ■ naivety n.
▷ SYNS INNOCENT, inexperienced, unsophisticated, unworldly, immature, artless.

**naked** adj. **1** without clothes. **2** without coverings. **3** not hidden.
▷ SYNS NUDE, bare, stripped, unclothed, undressed; inf. starkers, in the buff.

**namby-pamby** adj. feeble or cowardly.

**name** n. **1** the word(s) by which a person or thing is known. **2** a famous person. **3** a reputation. • v. **1** give a name to. **2** identify by name. **3** specify a time etc. □ namesake a person or thing with the same name as another.
▷ SYNS n. TITLE, designation, tag, nickname, sobriquet, label; inf. moniker, handle. • v. CALL, dub, label, term, title, christen, baptize.

**namely** adv. that is to say.

**nan**[1] n. inf. a person's grandmother.

**nan**[2] (also **naan**) n. a soft, flat Indian bread.

**nanny** n. (pl. -ies) a child's nurse.

**nanosecond** n. one thousand millionth of a second.

**nap** n. **1** a short sleep. **2** short raised fibres on the surface of some fabrics. • v. (**napped**, **napping**) have a short sleep.
▷ SYNS n. CATNAP, doze, rest, lie-down; inf. snooze, kip.

**napalm** n. a jelly-like form of petrol used in firebombs.

**nape** n. the back of the neck.

**naphtha** n. a flammable oil.

**napkin** n. a piece of cloth or paper used at meals to protect clothes or wipe the lips.

**nappy** n. (pl. -ies) a piece of material worn by a baby to absorb urine and faeces.

**narcissism** n. excessive self-admiration. ■ narcissistic adj.

**narcissus** n. (pl. -cissi) a daffodil with pale outer petals.

**narcotic** n. a drug causing drowsiness, or affecting mood or behaviour. • adj. of narcotics.

**narrate** v. give an account of. ■ narration n. narrator n.
▷ SYNS TELL, relate, recount, recite, describe, detail.

**narrative** n. a story.

**narrow** adj. **1** small in width. **2** limited in extent or scope. **3** only just achieved. *a narrow escape.* • v. make or become narrow. ■ narrowly adv.
▷ SYNS adj. SLENDER, slim, slight, attenuated, thin.

**narrow-minded** adj. unwilling to listen to or accept the views of others.
▷ SYNS INTOLERANT, illiberal, re-actionary, conservative, pro-vincial, insular, small-minded, prejudiced, bigoted.

**nasal** adj. of the nose.

**nascent** adj. just coming into existence.

**nasty** adj. **1** unpleasant. **2** spiteful. ■ nastily adv. nastiness n.

▷ SYNS UNPLEASANT, disagreeable, distasteful, disgusting, vile, foul, revolting, repellent, horrible, obnoxious, loathsome.

**natal** adj. of or from a person's birth.

**nation** n. a large group sharing the same culture, language, or history, and inhabiting a particular state or area.
▷ SYNS COUNTRY, state, land, realm, kingdom, republic, people, race.

**national** adj. **1** of a nation. **2** owned or supported by the state. • n. a citizen of a particular country. □ **national curriculum** an official curriculum of study to be taught in state schools. ■ **nationally** adv.
▷ SYNS adj. NATIONWIDE, country-wide, state, widespread. • n. CITIZEN, subject, native.

**nationalism** n. patriotic feeling; a policy of national independence. ■ **nationalist** n. & adj.

**nationality** n. (pl. -ies) **1** the status of belonging to a particular nation. **2** an ethnic group.

**nationalize** (or -ise) v. convert from private to state ownership. ■ **nationalization** n.

**native** adj. **1** born or belonging in a particular place. **2** inborn. • n. **1** a person born in a specified place. **2** a local inhabitant.
▷ SYNS adj. **1** INDIGENOUS, domestic, local. **2** native wit: INBORN, innate, natural, inherent, intrinsic.

**Nativity** n. (**the Nativity**) the birth of Jesus.

**NATO** abbr. North Atlantic Treaty Organization.

**natter** v. & n. inf. chat.

**natty** adj. inf. smart and fashionable. ■ **nattily** adv.

**natural** adj. **1** of or produced by nature; not man-made. **2** born with a particular skill or quality. **3** relaxed and unaffected. • n. a person with a natural skill or talent. □ **natural history** the study of animals or plants. ■ **naturally** adv.
▷ SYNS adj. **1** ORGANIC, pure, un-refined, unprocessed. **2** INNATE, inherent, inherent, intrinsic; born, instinctive, congenital. **3** UNAFFECTED, relaxed, genuine, open, real, authentic, unpretentious.

**naturalism** n. realism in art or literature. ■ **naturalistic** adj.

**naturalist** n. an expert in natural history.

**naturalize** (or -ise) v. make a foreigner a citizen of a country; introduce a plant or animal into a region where it is not native.

**nature** n. **1** the physical world with all its features and living things. **2** the typical qualities or character of a person or thing; **3** a kind or sort.
▷ SYNS **1** THE ENVIRONMENT, wildlife, the countryside. **2** CHARACTER, personality, disposition, temperament. **3** KIND, sort, type, variety, category, class.

**naturist** n. a nudist. ■ **naturism** n.

**naughty** adj. **1** disobedient or badly behaved. **2** inf. mildly indecent. ■ **naughtiness** n.
▷ SYNS BADLY BEHAVED, dis-obedient, defiant, unruly, wayward, delinquent, undisciplined, mischievous.

**nausea** n. a feeling of sickness.

**nauseate** v. cause to feel sick or disgusted.

**nauseous** adj. suffering from or causing nausea.
▷ SYNS **1** SICK, queasy, bilious. **2** DISGUSTING, revolting, repulsive, repellent, repugnant, offensive, loathsome, abhorrent, odious.

**nautical** adj. of sailors or navigation. □ **nautical mile** a unit of 1,852 metres (approx. 2,025 yds).
▷ SYNS MARITIME, naval, marine, seagoing, seafaring.

**naval** adj. of a navy.

**nave** n. the main part of a church.

**navel** n. the small hollow in the abdomen where the umbilical cord was attached.

**navigable** adj. able to be used by boats and ships.

**navigate** v. plan and direct the route of a ship, aircraft, etc.; travel along a planned route. ■ **navigation** n. **navigator** n.

**navy** n. (pl. **-ies**) **1** the branch of a country's armed forces which fights at sea. **2** (also **navy blue**) very dark blue.

**NB** abbr. note well.

**NE** abbr. north-east; north-eastern.

**near** adv. **1** at or to a short distance. **2** almost. • prep. **1** a short distance from. **2** on the verge of. • adj. **1** at a short distance away. **2** close to being: *a near disaster.* • v. draw near.
▷ SYNS adj. **1** CLOSE, nearby, at hand, accessible, within reach, neighbouring. **2** IMMINENT, in the offing, coming, impending, looming.

**nearby** adj. & adv. not far away.

**nearly** adv. almost.
▷ SYNS ALMOST, virtually, well-nigh, about, practically, roughly, approximately.

**neat** adj. **1** tidy or carefully arranged. **2** clever but simple. **3** undiluted. ■ **neaten** v.
▷ SYNS **1** TIDY, orderly, spick and span; smart, spruce, trim. **2** *a neat solution:* CLEVER, ingenious, inventive, imaginative.

**nebula** n. (pl. **-lae**) a cloud of gas or dust in space.

**nebulous** adj. having no definite form; vague.

**necessarily** adv. unavoidably.

**necessary** adj. **1** needing to be done or achieved, or to be present. **2** unavoidable.
▷ SYNS NEEDED, essential, required, requisite, vital, indispensable, imperative, mandatory, obligatory, compulsory.

**necessitate** v. make necessary.

**necessity** n. (pl. **-ies**) being necessary or unavoidable; something essential.

**neck** n. **1** the part connecting the head to the body. **2** a narrow connecting or end part. □ **neck and neck** level in a race. **necklace** a piece of jewellery worn round the neck. **neckline** the edge of a garment at or below the neck.

**necromancy** n. the supposed art of predicting the future by communicating with the dead.

**nectar** n. a fluid produced by flowers and made into honey by bees.

**nectarine** n. a kind of peach with a smooth skin.

**née** adj. born (used in stating a married woman's maiden name).

**need** v. **1** want something essential. **2** be obliged or required to. • n. **1** a situation in which something is necessary or must be done. **2** something needed. **3** poverty.
▷ SYNS v. REQUIRE, want, necessitate, demand, call for, lack.
• n. REQUIREMENT, want, prerequisite, requisite.

**needful** adj. necessary.

**needle** n. **1** a thin pointed piece of metal used in sewing or knitting. **2** a pointer on a compass or dial. **3** the thin leaf of a fir or pine tree. • v. inf. annoy. □ needlework sewing or embroidery.

**needless** adj. unnecessary.
■ needlessly adv.
▷ SYNS UNNECESSARY, uncalled-for, gratuitous, pointless, dispensable, expendable, inessential.

**needy** adj. (-ier, -iest) very poor.

**nefarious** adj. wicked or criminal.

**negate** v. **1** make ineffective. **2** deny the existence of.
■ negation n.

**negative** adj. **1** expressing denial, refusal, or prohibition; showing the absence of something. **2** (of a quantity) less than zero. **3** (of a battery terminal) through which electric current leaves. **4** not hopeful or favourable. • n. **1** a negative statement or word. **2** a photograph with lights and shades or colours reversed, from which positive pictures can be obtained.
▷ SYNS adj. PESSIMISTIC, defeatist, gloomy, cynical, jaundiced, critical, unhelpful.

**neglect** v. fail to give enough care or attention to; fail to do.
• n. neglecting or being neglected. ■ neglectful adj.
▷ SYNS v. **1** FAIL TO LOOK AFTER, abandon, forsake, leave alone. **2** LET SLIDE, shirk, be remiss/lax about. • n. NEGLIGENCE, neglectfulness, carelessness, heedlessness, laxity.

**negligee** n. a woman's light, thin dressing gown.

**negligence** n. lack of proper care or attention.

**negligent** adj. failing to take proper care.
▷ SYNS NEGLECTFUL, remiss, lax, careless, inattentive, thoughtless, unmindful, slack, sloppy.

**negligible** adj. too small to be worth taking into account.
▷ SYNS TRIVIAL, trifling, insignificant, paltry, petty, tiny, small, minor, inconsequential.

**negotiate** v. **1** reach agreement by discussion; arrange by such discussion. **2** get past an obstacle successfully.
■ negotiation n. negotiator n.
▷ SYNS BARGAIN, debate, parley, haggle.

**Negro** n. (pl. -oes) dated or offens. a black person.

**neigh** n. a horse's high-pitched cry. • v. make this cry.

**neighbour** (US **neighbor**) n. a person living next door or near to another. • v. be next or very near to. ■ neighbourly adj.

**neighbourhood** (US **neighborhood**) n. a district.
▷ SYNS DISTRICT, area, region, locality, quarter, precinct.

**neighbouring** adj. next to or very near.
▷ SYNS ADJACENT, adjoining, bordering; nearby, near, in the vicinity.

**neither** adj. & pron. not either.
• adv. 1 not either. 2 not also.

**nemesis** n. a means of deserved and unavoidable downfall.

**Neolithic** adj. of the later part of the Stone Age.

**neologism** n. a new word.

**neon** n. a gas used in fluorescent lighting.

**neonatal** adj. of the newly born.

**nephew** n. a son of your brother or sister.

**nepotism** n. favouritism shown to relatives or friends.

**nerve** n. 1 a fibre in the body along which impulses of sensation pass. 2 (**nerves**) nervousness. 3 courage and steadiness. 4 inf. impudence. □ get on someone's nerves inf. irritate someone.

**nervous** adj. 1 easily frightened. 2 anxious. 3 of the nerves.
▷ SYNS ANXIOUS, worried, apprehensive, on edge, edgy, tense, agitated, uneasy, jumpy, on tenterhooks, frightened, scared; inf. jittery, uptight.

**nest** n. 1 a structure in which a bird lays eggs and shelters its young. 2 a breeding place or lair. 3 a set of similar objects designed to fit inside each other. • v. 1 build or use a nest. 2 fit an object inside a larger one. □ nest egg a sum of money saved for the future.

**nestle** v. 1 settle comfortably. 2 (of a place) lie in a sheltered position.
▷ SYNS SNUGGLE, curl up, cuddle.

**net**¹ n. 1 open-meshed material of cord, twine, etc. 2 a piece of this for catching fish, etc. 3 (**Net**) the Internet.

• v. (**netted**, **netting**) catch in a net. □ netball a team game in which a ball has to be thrown into a high net.
▷ SYNS n. NETTING, mesh, fishnet, webbing. • v. CATCH, trap, snare, bag.

**net**² (or **nett**) adj. remaining after all deductions; (of weight) not including packaging.
• v. (**netted**, **netting**) obtain or yield as net profit.

**nether** adj. lower.

**netting** n. open-meshed fabric.

**nettle** n. a wild plant with leaves that sting when touched.
• v. annoy.

**network** n. 1 a system of intersecting lines. 2 a group of interconnected people or broadcasting stations, computers, etc. • v. keep in contact with others to exchange information.

**neural** adj. of nerves.

**neuralgia** n. a sharp pain along a nerve. ■ neuralgic adj.

**neurosis** n. (pl. **-oses**) a mental illness involving depression or obsessive behaviour.

**neurotic** adj. 1 of or caused by a neurosis. 2 excessively sensitive or obsessive.
▷ SYNS UNSTABLE, obsessive, fixated, oversensitive, hysterical, irrational.

**neuter** adj. 1 (of a noun) neither masculine nor feminine. 2 without developed sexual parts. • v. castrate or spay.
▷ SYNS adj. ASEXUAL, sexless.
• v. CASTRATE, geld, emasculate, spay.

**neutral** adj. 1 not supporting either side in a conflict. 2 without distinctive or positive characteristics. • n. a position of

a gear mechanism in which the engine is disconnected from driven parts. ■ **neutrality** n. **neutrally** adv.
▷ SYNS **adj.** IMPARTIAL, unbiased, unprejudiced, open-minded, non-partisan, disinterested, objective.

**neutralize** (or **-ise**) v. make neutral or ineffective.
▷ SYNS COUNTERACT, cancel, nullify, negate, annul, invalidate.

**neutron** n. a subatomic particle with no electric charge.

**never** adv. **1** not ever. **2** not at all.

**nevertheless** adv. in spite of this.

**new** adj. **1** made, discovered, or experienced recently. **2** not previously used or owned. **3** unfamiliar or different. **4** replacing a former one of the same kind.
• adv. newly. □ **newfangled** derog. newly developed and unfamiliar. **new moon** the moon seen as a thin crescent. **New Testament** the second part of the Christian Bible. **new year** the first days of January.
▷ SYNS **adj.** RECENT, up to date, latest, current, state-of-the-art, contemporary, modern, avant-garde.

**newcomer** n. a person who has recently arrived or is new to an activity.
▷ SYNS NEW ARRIVAL, incomer, settler, immigrant; stranger, outsider, foreigner, alien; beginner, novice, learner.

**newel** n. the post at the top or bottom of a stair rail.

**newly** adv. recently; afresh. □ **newly-wed** a recently married person.

**news** n. **1** new information about recent events. **2** (**the news**) a broadcast or published news report. □ **newsagent** a shopkeeper who sells newspapers, magazines, etc. **newsflash** a brief item of important news, interrupting other radio or television programmes. **newsgroup** a group of Internet users who exchange information about a subject. **newsletter** a bulletin issued periodically to the members of a society etc. **newsprint** cheap, low-quality paper used for newspapers. **newsreader** a person who reads the news on radio or television.
▷ SYNS REPORT, story, account, announcement, press release, communiqué, bulletin, information, word.

**newspaper** n. a daily or weekly publication containing news and articles.
▷ SYNS PAPER, journal, gazette, periodical; tabloid, broadsheet; inf. rag.

**newt** n. a small lizard-like amphibian animal.

**newton** n. a unit of force.

**next** adj. nearest in position or time. • adv. immediately afterwards. • n. the next person or thing. □ **next door** in or to the next house or room. **next of kin** a person's closest living relative(s).
▷ SYNS **adj. 1** FOLLOWING, succeeding, subsequent, upcoming, ensuing. **2** NEIGHBOURING, adjacent, adjoining, bordering.

**NHS** abbr. National Health Service.

**nib** n. the pointed end of a pen.

**nibble** v. take small quick or gentle bites at. • n. a small quick bite.

**nice** adj. 1 pleasant or enjoyable. 2 kind.
▷ SYNS GOOD, pleasant, enjoyable, pleasurable, agreeable.

**nicety** n. (pl. **-ies**) 1 a fine detail. 2 accuracy.

**niche** n. 1 a small hollow in a wall. 2 a role or job that suits someone.

**nick** n. 1 a small cut. 2 inf. prison. 3 inf. condition. • v. 1 make a nick in. 2 inf. steal.

**nickel** n. 1 a silver-white metallic element. 2 US a 5-cent coin.

**nickname** n. another name by which someone is known. • v. give a nickname to.

**nicotine** n. a poisonous substance found in tobacco.

**niece** n. a daughter of your brother or sister.

**niggardly** adj. not generous; mean.

**niggle** v. worry or annoy slightly. • v. a minor worry or criticism.

**nigh** adv. & prep. old use near.

**night** n. 1 the time from sunset to sunrise. 2 an evening. □ **nightcap** a hot or alcoholic drink taken at bedtime. **nightclub** a club open at night, with a bar and music. **nightdress** a loose garment worn by a woman or girl in bed. **nightfall** dusk. **nightlife** entertainment available at night. **nightshade** a plant with poisonous black berries. **nightshirt** a long shirt worn in bed. **nightspot** inf. a nightclub. ▪ **nightly** adj. & adv.

**nightie** n. inf. a nightdress.

**nightingale** n. a small bird with a tuneful song.

**nightmare** n. 1 a frightening dream. 2 a very unpleasant experience. ▪ **nightmarish** adj.

**nihilism** n. the belief that nothing has any value. ▪ **nihilist** n.

**nil** n. nothing; zero.

**nimble** adj. quick and agile. ▪ **nimbly** adv.
▷ SYNS AGILE, quick, sprightly, spry, skilful, deft.

**nimbus** n. (pl. **-bi** or **-buses**) a rain cloud.

**nincompoop** n. a stupid person.

**nine** adj. & n. one less than ten; 9. ▪ **ninth** adj. & n.

**nineteen** adj. & n. one more than eighteen; 19. ▪ **nineteenth** adj. & n.

**ninety** adj. & n. nine times ten; 90. ▪ **ninetieth** adj. & n.

**nip** v. (**nipped**, **nipping**) 1 pinch or bite sharply. 2 inf. go quickly. • n. 1 an act of nipping. 2 a sharp coldness. 3 a small drink of spirits.

**nipple** n. the small projection at the centre of each breast.

**nippy** adj. 1 nimble or quick. 2 chilly.
▷ SYNS ICY, chilly, bitter, raw.

**nirvana** n. (in Buddhism) a state of perfect happiness.

**nit** n. the egg of a human head louse. □ **nit-picking** petty criticism.

**nitrate** n. a substance formed from nitric acid.

**nitric acid** n. a very corrosive acid.

**nitrogen** n. a gas forming about four-fifths of the atmosphere.

**nitroglycerine** (or **nitro-glycerin**) n. a powerful explosive.

**nitty-gritty** n. inf. the most important details.

**no** adj. not any. • exclam. used to refuse or disagree with something. • adv. not at all. • n. (pl. **noes**) a decision or vote against something.

**no.** abbr. number.

**nobility** n. (pl. **-ies**) 1 being noble. 2 the aristocracy.

**noble** adj. 1 belonging to the aristocracy. 2 having admirable personal qualities. 3 impressive; magnificent. • n. a member of the aristocracy. □ **nobleman** (or **noblewoman**) a member of the aristocracy. ■ **nobly** adv.
▷ SYNS adj. 1 ARISTOCRATIC, blue-blooded, titled. 2 GOOD, virtuous, righteous, honourable. 3 MAGNIFICENT, splendid, grand, imposing, impressive, stately.

**nobody** pron. no person. • n. (pl. **-ies**) an unimportant person.

**nocturnal** adj. done or active at night. ■ **nocturnally** adv.

**nocturne** n. a short romantic piece of music.

**nod** v. 1 move your head down and up quickly to show agreement or as a signal. 2 let your head droop from drowsiness. 3 (**nod off**) inf. fall asleep. • n. an act of nodding.
▷ SYNS v. INCLINE, bob, bow, dip.

**node** n. 1 a point in a network where lines intersect. 2 a point on a stem where a leaf or bud grows out. 3 a small mass of tissue in the body.

**nodule** n. a small swelling or lump. ■ **nodular** adj.

**noise** n. 1 a sound, esp. a loud or unpleasant one. 2 disturbances interfering with an electrical signal.
▷ SYNS SOUND, din, hubbub, racket, uproar, commotion, pandemonium.

**noisy** adj. (**-ier**, **-iest**) full of or making much noise. ■ **noisily** adv.

**nomad** n. a member of a people that roams to find fresh pasture for its animals. ■ **nomadic** adj.
▷ SYNS ITINERANT, traveller, migrant, wanderer, vagabond, vagrant, tramp.

**nom de plume** n. (pl. **noms de plume**) a writer's pen name.

**nomenclature** n. a system of names used in a particular subject.

**nominal** adj. 1 existing in name only. 2 (of a fee) very small. ■ **nominally** adv.
▷ SYNS 1 IN NAME ONLY, titular, theoretical, self-styled. 2 TOKEN, symbolic, minimal.

**nominate** v. 1 put forward as a candidate. 2 formally specify. ■ **nomination** n. **nominee** n.
▷ SYNS NAME, propose, submit, recommend.

**nominative** n. the grammatical case used for the subject of a verb.

**non-** pref. not: *non-existent*.

**nonchalant** adj. calm and relaxed. ■ **nonchalance** n.
▷ SYNS CALM, composed, relaxed, unconcerned, cool, blasé, casual; inf. laid-back.

**non-committal** adj. not expressing a definite opinion.

**nonconformist** n. 1 a person who does not follow established practices. 2 (**Nonconformist**) a member of a Protestant Church not conforming to Anglican practices.

**nondescript** adj. lacking distinctive characteristics.

**none** pron. **1** not any. **2** no one. • adv. not at all: *none the wiser*.

**nonentity** n. (pl. **-ies**) an unimportant person.

**non-event** n. a very disappointing or uninteresting event.

**non-existent** adj. not real or present.

**nonplussed** adj. surprised and confused.
▷ SYNS SURPRISED, taken aback, disconcerted, confused, puzzled, perplexed, bewildered.

**nonsense** n. **1** words that make no sense. **2** foolish behaviour. ■ **nonsensical** adj.
▷ SYNS RUBBISH, gibberish, claptrap, balderdash; inf. drivel, twaddle, tripe, tosh, gobbledegook, poppycock, bilge.

**non sequitur** n. a statement that does not follow logically from what has just been said.

**non-stop** adj. & adv. not ceasing; having no stops on the way to a destination.
▷ SYNS INCESSANT, ceaseless, constant, continuous, continual, unbroken, relentless, persistent, endless, interminable.

**noodles** pl.n. pasta in narrow strips.

**nook** n. a secluded place.
▷ SYNS CORNER, cranny, recess, alcove, niche, crevice.

**noon** n. twelve o'clock in the day.

**no one** n. no person.

**noose** n. a loop with a knot that tightens when pulled.

**nor** conj. and not; and not either.

**norm** n. the usual or standard thing.

**normal** adj. usual, typical, or expected. ■ **normality** n. **normalize** v. **normally** adv.
▷ SYNS USUAL, ordinary, standard, average, common, commonplace, conventional, typical, regular, run-of-the-mill, everyday.

**north** n. **1** the direction to the left of a person facing east. **2** the northern part of a place. • adj. & adv. **1** towards or facing the north. **2** (of wind) from the north. ■ **northerly** adj. & adv. **northern** adj. **northward** adj. & adv. **northwards** adv.

**north-east** n., adj., & adv. (in or towards) the point or direction midway between north and east. ■ **north-easterly** adj. & n. **north-eastern** adj.

**northerner** n. a person from the north of a region.

**north-west** n., adj., & adv. (in or towards) the point or direction midway between north and west. ■ **north-westerly** adj. & n. **north-western** adj.

**nose** n. **1** the organ at the front of the head, used in breathing and smelling. **2** the front end of an aircraft etc. **3** a talent for finding something. • v. **1** look around or pry. **2** move forward slowly. **3** push the nose against something. □ **nosebag** a bag of fodder hung from a horse's head. **nosedive** a steep downward plunge by an aircraft.
▷ SYNS n. PROBOSCIS, snout, muzzle; inf. conk, hooter. • v. PRY, snoop, search, investigate.

**nosh** inf. n. food.

**nostalgia** n. longing for a better or happier time in the past. ■ **nostalgic** adj.

**nostril** n. either of the two external openings in the nose.

**nosy** adj. (**-ier, -iest**) inquisitive.
▷ SYNS INQUISITIVE, curious, interfering, meddlesome, intrusive.

**not** adv. used to express a negative.

**notable** adj. worthy of notice. • n. an eminent person. ■ **notably** adv.
▷ SYNS adj. NOTEWORTHY, remarkable, outstanding, important, significant, momentous, memorable, striking, impressive, uncommon, unusual, special, extraordinary.

**notary** n. (pl. **-ies**) an official authorized to witness the signing of documents.

**notation** n. a system of symbols used in music, mathematics, etc.

**notch** n. 1 a V-shaped cut or indentation. 2 a point on a scale. • v. 1 make notches in. 2 (**notch up**) score or achieve.

**note** n. 1 a brief written record. 2 a short message. 3 a banknote. 4 a musical sound of particular pitch and length, or a symbol representing this. • v. 1 notice. 2 write down. □ **notebook** a small book for writing notes in. **notepaper** paper for writing letters on. **noteworthy** interesting or important.
▷ SYNS n. 1 RECORD, notation, comment, jotting. 2 MESSAGE, letter, memo, epistle.
• v. 1 OBSERVE, perceive, behold, detect. 2 WRITE DOWN, record, register.

**noted** adj. well known.
▷ SYNS RENOWNED, well known, famous, prominent, celebrated, notable, eminent, distinguished, acclaimed.

**nothing** n. not anything; something unimportant; nought. • adv. not at all.

**notice** n. 1 attention or observation. 2 warning or notification. 3 a formal statement of the termination of a job or an agreement. 4 a sheet displaying information. • v. become aware of.
▷ SYNS n. ATTENTION, observation, awareness, regard, consideration. • v. OBSERVE, note, discern, see, detect, spot, perceive.

**noticeable** adj. easily seen or noticed. ■ **noticeably** adv.
▷ SYNS OBSERVABLE, visible, discernible, perceptible, distinct, evident, obvious, apparent, manifest, patent, plain, clear, conspicuous.

**notify** v. (**notified, notifying**) inform about something. ■ **notification** n.
▷ SYNS INFORM, tell, advise, apprise, warn, alert.

**notion** n. a belief or idea; an understanding. ■ **notional** adj.
▷ SYNS IDEA, belief, opinion, thought, impression, view, conviction, hypothesis, theory.

**notorious** adj. famous for something bad. ■ **notoriety** n.
▷ SYNS INFAMOUS, disreputable, dishonourable, scandalous.

**notwithstanding** prep. in spite of. • adv. nevertheless.

**nougat** n. a chewy sweet.

**nought** n. the figure 0; nothing.

**noun** n. a word that refers to a person, place, or thing.

**nourish** v. feed so as to keep alive and healthy.

**nourishment** n. food necessary for life and growth.

▷ SYNS FOOD, nutriment, nutrition, sustenance, provisions.

**nous** n. inf. common sense.

**nouveau riche** n. people who have recently become rich and make a display of their wealth.

**nova** n. (pl. **-vae** or **-vas**) a star that suddenly becomes much brighter for a short time.

**novel** n. a book-length story. • adj. new or unusual.
▷ SYNS adj. NEW, fresh, different, original, unusual, imaginative, inventive, unconventional, innovative.

**novelist** n. a writer of novels.

**novelty** n. (pl. **-ies**) 1 being new or unusual. 2 a small toy or ornament.

**November** n. the eleventh month.

**novice** n. 1 a beginner. 2 a probationary member of a religious order.
▷ SYNS BEGINNER, learner, newcomer, apprentice, trainee, student, pupil.

**now** adv. 1 at the present time. 2 immediately. • conj. as a result of the fact. □ nowadays at the present time, in contrast with the past.
▷ SYNS adv. AT PRESENT, at the moment, currently.

**nowhere** adv. not anywhere.

**noxious** adj. unpleasant and harmful.
▷ SYNS UNWHOLESOME, unhealthy, poisonous, toxic, harmful.

**nozzle** n. the vent or spout of a hosepipe etc.

**nuance** n. a subtle difference in meaning.

**nub** n. 1 the central point of a problem etc. 2 a small lump.

**nubile** adj. (of a young woman) sexually mature and attractive.

**nuclear** adj. of the nucleus of an atom or cell; using energy released in nuclear fission or fusion.

**nucleic acid** n. either of two substances, DNA or RNA, present in all living cells.

**nucleus** n. (pl. **-clei**) the central part or thing round which others are collected; the central portion of an atom, seed, or cell.
▷ SYNS CORE, kernel, centre, heart, nub.

**nude** adj. naked. • n. a naked figure in a picture etc. ■ nudity n.

**nudge** v. 1 prod with the elbow to attract attention. 2 push gently. • n. a light prod or push.
▷ SYNS v. PROD, elbow, poke, jab, push.

**nudist** n. a person who prefers to wear no clothes. ■ nudism n.

**nugget** n. a small lump of precious metal found in the earth.

**nuisance** n. an annoying person or thing.
▷ SYNS ANNOYANCE, inconvenience, bother, irritation, pest.

**null** adj. having no legal force.

**nullify** v. (**nullified, nullifying**) make legally null; cancel out the effect of. ■ nullification n.

**numb** adj. deprived of the power of sensation. • v. make numb.
▷ SYNS adj. WITHOUT FEELING, insensible, anaesthetized, paralysed, immobilized, frozen, dazed, stunned. • v. DEADEN, anaesthetize, paralyse, immobilize, freeze, daze, stun.

**number** n. 1 a quantity or value expressed by a word or symbol. 2 a quantity. 3 a single issue of a magazine. **4** an item in a performance. • v. **1** amount to. **2** give a number to. **3** count. □ **number plate** a sign on a vehicle showing its registration number.

▷ SYNS **n.** FIGURE, digit, numeral, unit, integer.

**numberless** adj. too many to count.

**numeral** n. a symbol representing a number.

**numerate** adj. having a good basic knowledge of arithmetic. ■ **numeracy** n.

**numerator** n. the number above the line in a vulgar fraction.

**numerical** adj. of a number or series of numbers. ■ **numerically** adv.

**numerous** adj. great in number.

▷ SYNS MANY, lots, innumerable, myriad, several, various.

**nun** n. a member of a female religious community.

**nunnery** n. (pl. **-ies**) a community of nuns.

**nuptial** adj. of marriage or a wedding. • n. (**nuptials**) a wedding.

**nurse** n. **1** a person trained to care for sick or injured people. **2** dated a person employed to look after young children. • v. **1** act as nurse to. **2** hold carefully. **3** harbour a belief or feeling. **4** feed a baby at the breast. □ **nursing home** a place providing accommodation and health care for old people.

▷ SYNS **v.** TAKE CARE OF, look after, tend, minister to.

**nursery** n. (pl. **-ies**) **1** a room for children. **2** a place where plants are grown for sale. □ **nursery rhyme** a traditional song or poem for children. **nursery school** a school for children between three and five.

**nurture** v. **1** care for and promote the growth or development of. **2** cherish a hope, belief, etc. • n. nurturing.

▷ SYNS **v.** BRING UP, care for, tend, raise, rear.

**nut** n. **1** a fruit with a hard shell round an edible kernel. **2** this kernel. **3** a small metal ring for screwing on to a bolt. **4** inf. (or **nutcase**) a mad person. **5** inf. the head. • adj. (**nuts**) inf. mad. □ **in a nutshell** in the fewest possible words. ■ **nutty** adj.

**nutmeg** n. a spice.

**nutrient** n. a nourishing substance.

**nutriment** n. nourishing food.

**nutrition** n. the process of eating or taking nourishment. ■ **nutritional** adj.

**nutritious** adj. full of nutrients.

**nuzzle** v. press or rub gently with the nose.

**NW** abbr. north-west; north-western.

**nylon** n. a light, strong synthetic fibre.

**nymph** n. **1** a mythological semi-divine maiden. **2** a young insect.

**nymphomania** n. uncontrollable sexual desire in a woman. ■ **nymphomaniac** n.

# Oo

**oaf** n. a stupid or clumsy man.

**oak** n. a large tree producing acorns and a hard wood.

**OAP** abbr. old-age pensioner.

**oar** n. a pole with a flat blade, used to row a boat.

**oasis** n. (pl. **-ses**) a fertile place in a desert.

**oast house** n. a building containing a kiln for drying hops.

**oat** n. 1 a cereal plant. 2 (**oats**) the edible grain of this.
□ oatcake an oatmeal biscuit. oatmeal ground oats.

**oath** n. 1 a solemn promise. 2 a swear word.
▷ SYNS 1 VOW, promise, pledge, word of honour. 2 SWEAR WORD, curse, expletive, profanity, obscenity.

**obdurate** adj. stubborn.
■ obduracy n.

**OBE** abbr. Order of the British Empire.

**obedient** adj. doing what you are told. ■ obedience n.
▷ SYNS COMPLIANT, biddable, acquiescent, deferential, governable, docile, submissive.

**obeisance** n. 1 respect. 2 a bow or curtsy.

**obelisk** n. a tall pillar set up as a monument.

**obese** adj. very fat. ■ obesity n.

**obey** v. 1 carry out an order. 2 behave in accordance with a law etc.

▷ SYNS ABIDE BY, comply with, adhere to, observe, conform to, respect, follow.

**obituary** n. (pl. **-ies**) a short biography of a person, published when they die.

**object** n. 1 a physical thing that can be seen or touched. 2 a purpose. 3 a person or thing to which an action or feeling is directed. 4 a noun acted on by a transitive verb or a preposition.
• v. express disapproval or opposition. ■ objector n.
▷ SYNS n. 1 THING, article, entity, item. 2 OBJECTIVE, aim, goal, target, purpose, end, intention, point. • v. PROTEST, oppose, take exception, demur, complain.

**objection** n. an expression of disapproval or opposition.
▷ SYNS PROTEST, protestation, complaint; opposition, disapproval, disagreement.

**objectionable** adj. unpleasant.

**objective** adj. not influenced by personal feelings or opinions; having actual existence outside the mind. • n. a goal or aim.
■ objectivity n.
▷ SYNS adj. UNBIASED, unprejudiced, impartial, neutral, disinterested, detached, fair, open-minded. n. see **OBJECT** (2).

**objet d'art** n. (pl. **objets d'art**) a small decorative or artistic object.

**obligated** adj. obliged or compelled.

▷ SYNS OBLIGED, compelled, required, forced.

**obligation** n. something you are legally or morally bound to do; the state of being bound in this way.

**obligatory** adj. compulsory.
▷ SYNS COMPULSORY, mandatory, necessary, essential, required, requisite, imperative, unavoidable.

**oblige** v. **1** make someone do something by law, necessity, or duty. **2** do something to help someone. **3** (**be obliged**) be grateful.

**obliging** adj. willing to help.

**oblique** adj. **1** slanting. **2** not explicit or direct.
▷ SYNS **1** SLANTING, sloping, inclined, angled, tilted, diagonal. **2** INDIRECT, implied, ambiguous, evasive, backhanded.

**obliterate** v. destroy completely. ■ obliteration n.
▷ SYNS DESTROY, wipe out, annihilate, demolish; erase, blot out, rub out, delete.

**oblivion** n. the state of being forgotten; the state of being unconscious or unaware.

**oblivious** adj. unaware.
▷ SYNS HEEDLESS, unaware, ignorant, blind, deaf, inattentive, absent-minded, unconcerned, preoccupied.

**oblong** n. & adj. (having) a rectangular shape.

**obnoxious** adj. very unpleasant.

**oboe** n. a woodwind instrument of treble pitch. ■ oboist n.

**obscene** adj. dealing with sexual matters in an offensive way. ■ obscenity n.

▷ SYNS INDECENT, pornographic, blue, off-colour, risqué, lewd, smutty, suggestive, vulgar, dirty, filthy, coarse, offensive, immoral, improper.

**obscure** adj. not discovered or known about; hard to see or understand. • v. conceal; make unclear. ■ obscurity n.
▷ SYNS adj. **1** UNCLEAR, indeterminate, opaque, abstruse, arcane, cryptic, mysterious, puzzling, confusing, unfathomable, incomprehensible, impenetrable, vague, indefinite, indistinct, hazy, ambiguous, blurred, fuzzy. **2** UNKNOWN, unheard-of, insignificant, minor, unimportant, unsung.

**obsequious** adj. servile or excessively respectful.
▷ SYNS SERVILE, subservient, submissive, slavish, fawning, grovelling, sycophantic, ingratiating.

**observance** n. the keeping of a law, custom, or festival.

**observant** adj. quick to notice things.
▷ SYNS ALERT, sharp, eagle-eyed, attentive, vigilant, watchful, on guard, intent, aware.

**observation** n. **1** watching carefully; noticing things. **2** a remark.
▷ SYNS **1** SCRUTINY, monitoring, surveillance, attention, consideration, study, examination. **2** REMARK, comment, statement, pronouncement.

**observatory** n. (pl. **-ies**) a building equipped for the observation of stars and planets.

**observe** v. **1** notice; watch carefully. **2** make a remark. **3** obey a rule; celebrate a festival.

▷ SYNS **1** SEE, notice, perceive, discern, detect, espy, behold, watch, view, spot, witness. **2** KEEP, obey, adhere to, abide by, heed, follow, comply with, respect. **3** CELEBRATE, commemorate, mark, remember, solemnize.

**observer** n. a person who observes.
▷ SYNS SPECTATOR, onlooker, watcher, viewer, witness.

**obsess** v. preoccupy to a disturbing extent.
▷ SYNS PREOCCUPY, prey on, possess, haunt, consume, plague, torment.

**obsession** n. **1** being obsessed. **2** a persistent thought. ■ **obsessive** adj.
▷ SYNS FIXATION, passion, mania, compulsion, fetish, preoccupation, infatuation; inf. hang-up.

**obsolescent** adj. becoming obsolete.

**obsolete** adj. no longer used or of use.
▷ SYNS DISCONTINUED, extinct, bygone, outmoded, antiquated, out of date, old-fashioned, dated, antique, archaic, ancient.

**obstacle** n. a thing that obstructs progress.
▷ SYNS BARRIER, obstruction, hurdle, stumbling block, impediment, hindrance, snag, difficulty.

**obstetrics** n. the branch of medicine dealing with childbirth. ■ **obstetrician** n.

**obstinate** adj. **1** refusing to change your mind. **2** hard to deal with. ■ **obstinacy** n.
▷ SYNS STUBBORN, unyielding, inflexible, intransigent, pig-headed, mulish, wilful,

recalcitrant, immovable, uncompromising, persistent, tenacious.

**obstreperous** adj. noisy and unruly.
▷ SYNS UNRULY, disorderly, rowdy, boisterous, rough, riotous, out of control, wild, undisciplined.

**obstruct** v. hinder the movement or progress of. ■ **obstruction** n. **obstructive** adj.
▷ SYNS BLOCK, barricade, bar, shut off, choke, clog, stop, hinder, impede, hamper, frustrate, thwart, curb.

**obtain** v. **1** get possession of. **2** formal be established or usual. ■ **obtainable** adj.
▷ SYNS GET, acquire, come by, procure, secure, gain, pick up.

**obtrude** v. be noticeable in an unwelcome way. ■ **obtrusive** adj.

**obtuse** adj. **1** slow to understand. **2** (of an angle) more than 90° but less than 180°. **3** blunt.

**obverse** n. the side of a coin bearing a head or main design; an opposite or counterpart.

**obviate** v. remove or prevent a need or difficulty.

**obvious** adj. easily seen or understood. ■ **obviously** adv.
▷ SYNS CLEAR, plain, visible, noticeable, perceptible, evident, apparent, manifest, patent, conspicuous, pronounced, transparent, prominent, unmistakable.

**occasion** n. **1** the time at which an event takes place; a special event; a suitable time or opportunity. **2** formal reason or cause. • v. cause.
▷ SYNS n. **1** TIME, juncture, point, instance, case, circumstance.

**2** EVENT, incident, occurrence, happening, episode, affair.

**occasional** adj. happening or done from time to time.
▷ SYNS INFREQUENT, intermittent, irregular, sporadic.

**occasionally** adv. sometimes.
▷ SYNS NOW AND THEN, from time to time, sometimes, once in a while, periodically.

**occidental** adj. of the countries of the West.

**occult** n. supernatural powers, practices, or phenomena.

**occupant** n. a person occupying a place. ■ occupancy n.

**occupation** n. **1** a job or profession. **2** occupying or being occupied. **3** a way of spending time.
▷ SYNS **1** JOB, profession, work, trade, employment, business, career, field. **2** INVASION, seizure, conquest, capture.

**occupational** adj. of a job or profession.

**occupy** v. **1** live in. **2** enter and take control of a place. **3** fill a space. **4** keep busy. ■ occupier n.
▷ SYNS **1** LIVE IN, inhabit; people, settle. **2** CAPTURE, seize, conquer, invade.

**occur** v. **1** happen. **2** be found or present. **3** (**occur to**) come into the mind of.
▷ SYNS **1** HAPPEN, take place, come about, materialize, transpire, arise, crop up. **2** BE FOUND, be present, exist, appear.

**occurrence** n. **1** an incident or event. **2** the fact of something happening or existing.
▷ SYNS **1** EVENT, incident, happening, affair, circumstance. **2** EXISTENCE, instance, appearance, frequency, incidence.

**ocean** n. a very large expanse of sea.

**ocelot** n. a wild cat found in South and Central America.

**ochre** (US **ocher**) n. pale brownish yellow earth, used as a pigment.

**o'clock** adv. used in specifying an hour.

**octagon** n. a geometric figure with eight sides.
■ octagonal adj.

**octane** n. a hydrocarbon present in petrol.

**octave** n. the interval of eight notes between one musical note and the next note of the same name above or below it.

**octet** n. a group of eight voices or instruments; music for these.

**October** n. the tenth month.

**octopus** n. (pl. **-puses**) a sea creature with eight tentacles.

**ocular** adj. of, for, or by the eyes.

**odd** adj. **1** strange or unexpected. **2** (of a number) not exactly divisible by two. **3** occasional. **4** separated from a set or pair. □ oddment an item or piece left over from a larger piece or set.
▷ SYNS STRANGE, peculiar, weird, bizarre, eccentric, queer, unusual, unexpected.

**oddity** n. (pl. **-ies**) **1** a strange person or thing. **2** being strange.

**odds** pl.n. **1** the ratio between the amounts staked by the parties to a bet. **2** the chances of something happening. □ at odds in conflict.

**ode** n. a poem addressed to a person or celebrating an event.

**odious** adj. hateful.
▷ SYNS ABHORRENT, hateful, offensive, disgusting, repulsive, vile,

unpleasant, disagreeable, loathsome, despicable, contemptible.

**odium** n. widespread hatred or disgust.

**odour** (US **odor**) n. a smell.
■ **odorous** adj.
▷ SYNS AROMA, smell, scent, perfume, fragrance, bouquet, stench, stink.

**odyssey** n. (pl. **-eys**) a long eventful journey.

**oesophagus** (US **esophagus**) n. the tube from the mouth to the stomach.

**oestrogen** (US **estrogen**) n. a hormone which produces female physical and sexual characteristics.

**of** prep. **1** expressing the relationship between a part and a whole. **2** belonging to; coming from. **3** indicating measurement, value, or age. **4** made from.

**off** adv. **1** away from a place. **2** so as to be separated. **3** so as to finish or be discontinued. **4** not working or connected. • prep. **1** away from. **2** leading away from. • adj. (of food) no longer fresh. □ **offbeat** inf. unconventional. **off colour** slightly unwell. **offcut** a piece of wood, fabric, etc. left after cutting a larger piece. **off-licence** a shop selling alcoholic drinks to be drunk elsewhere. **offline** not connected to a computer. **offload** unload. **off-putting** unpleasant or unsettling. **offshoot** a thing that develops from something else. **offshore** at sea some distance from land; (of the wind) blowing towards the sea from the land; made, situated, or registered abroad. **offside** (in football etc.) in a position on the field where playing the ball is not allowed.

**offal** n. the internal organs of an animal, used as food.

**offence** (US **offense**) n. **1** an illegal act. **2** a feeling of hurt or annoyance.
▷ SYNS **1** CRIME, misdemeanour, felony, wrongdoing, sin. **2** ANNOYANCE, resentment, indignation, displeasure.

**offend** v. **1** cause to feel hurt or annoyed. **2** do something illegal.
▷ SYNS **1** UPSET, affront, insult, hurt, wound, slight. **2** COMMIT A CRIME, break the law, do wrong.

**offender** n. a person who commits a crime or does something wrong.
▷ SYNS WRONGDOER, culprit, criminal, lawbreaker, miscreant, delinquent, sinner.

**offensive** adj. **1** causing offence. **2** used in attack. • n. a campaign to attack or achieve something.
▷ SYNS adj. INSULTING, rude, hurtful, wounding, abusive; unpleasant, disagreeable, nasty, distasteful.

**offer** v. **1** present for acceptance or refusal. **2** express willingness to do something. • n. **1** an expression of willingness to do or give something. **2** an amount offered. **3** a specially reduced price.
▷ SYNS v. **1** PUT FORWARD, proffer, present, propose, submit, suggest. **2** VOLUNTEER, step forward, show willing.

**offering** n. a gift or contribution.

▷ SYNS CONTRIBUTION, donation, gift, present.

**offhand** adj. rudely casual or abrupt. • adv. without previous thought.
▷ SYNS adj. CASUAL, careless, uninterested, dismissive, abrupt, unceremonious, cursory, impolite.

**office** n. 1 a room or building used for business or clerical work. 2 a position of authority.
▷ SYNS 1 PLACE OF WORK, place of business, workplace. 2 POST, position, role, function, responsibility.

**officer** n. 1 a person holding a position of authority, esp. in the armed forces. 2 a policeman or policewoman.

**official** adj. of or authorized by a public body or authority; formally approved. • n. a person holding public office.
■ **officially** adv.
▷ SYNS adj. AUTHORIZED, accredited, approved, certified, endorsed, sanctioned, recognized, accepted, legitimate, bona fide, proper.

**officiate** v. act as an official in charge of an event; perform a religious ceremony.
▷ SYNS TAKE CHARGE, preside, oversee, superintend, chair.

**officious** adj. bossy.
▷ SYNS SELF-IMPORTANT, dictatorial, domineering, interfering, intrusive, meddlesome; inf. pushy.

**offset** v. counteract by having an equal and opposite force or effect.
▷ SYNS COUNTERBALANCE, cancel out, counteract, compensate for, make up for.

**offspring** n. a person's child or children.
▷ SYNS CHILDREN, family, progeny, young, descendants, heirs, successors; inf. kids.

**often** adv. 1 frequently. 2 in many cases.
▷ SYNS FREQUENTLY, a lot, repeatedly, again and again.

**ogle** v. look lustfully at.

**ogre** n. (in stories) a man-eating giant; a terrifying person.

**oh** exclam. expressing surprise, delight, or pain, or used for emphasis.

**ohm** n. a unit of electrical resistance.

**oil** n. 1 a thick, sticky liquid obtained from petroleum. 2 a thick liquid that will not dissolve in water. 3 (**oils**) oil paints. • v. lubricate or treat with oil. □ **oilfield** an area where oil is found beneath the ground or the seabed. **oil paint** paint made by mixing pigment with oil. **oilskin** 1 heavy cotton cloth waterproofed with oil. 2 (**oilskins**) clothing made of oilskin.

**oily** adj. 1 containing or covered with oil. 2 insincerely polite or flattering.
▷ SYNS 1 GREASY, fatty, oleaginous. 2 UNCTUOUS, ingratiating, smooth-talking, flattering; inf. slimy.

**ointment** n. a cream rubbed on the skin to heal injuries etc.
▷ SYNS CREAM, lotion, salve, balm, liniment.

**OK** (or **okay**) adj. & adv. inf. all right.

**okra** n. the long seed pods of a tropical plant, eaten as a vegetable.

**old** adj. **1** having lived or existed for a long time or a specified time. **2** former. □ **old age** the later part of life. **old-fashioned** no longer fashionable. **Old Testament** the first part of the Christian Bible. **old wives' tale** a traditional but unfounded belief.
▷ SYNS **1** ELDERLY, aged, older, senior, ancient, decrepit, senile; inf. getting on, over the hill. **2** *the old days:* BYGONE, past, early, earlier, primeval, pre-historic. **3** *an old girlfriend:* FORMER, previous, ex-, past, earlier.

**olfactory** adj. of the sense of smell.

**olive** n. **1** a small oval fruit from which **olive oil** is obtained. **2** a greyish-green colour. • adj. (of skin) yellowish brown. □ **olive branch** an offer to restore friendly relations.

**ombudsman** n. an official who investigates complaints against organizations.

**omelette** n. a dish of beaten eggs cooked in a frying pan.

**omen** n. an event seen as a prophetic sign.
▷ SYNS PORTENT, sign, signal, token, warning, forecast.

**ominous** adj. giving the impression that trouble is imminent.
▷ SYNS THREATENING, menacing, gloomy, sinister, bad, un-promising, inauspicious, unfavourable, unlucky.

**omit** v. (**omitted**, **omitting**) **1** leave out or exclude. **2** fail to do. ■ **omission** n.
▷ SYNS **1** LEAVE OUT, exclude, except, miss, pass over, drop.

**2** FORGET, neglect, overlook, skip.

**omnibus** n. **1** a volume containing several works originally published separately. **2** dated a bus.

**omnipotent** adj. having un-limited or very great power. ■ **omnipotence** n.
▷ SYNS ALL-POWERFUL, almighty, supreme, invincible.

**omniscient** adj. knowing everything. ■ **omniscience** n.

**omnivorous** adj. eating both plants and meat.

**on** prep. **1** into contact with a surface, or aboard a vehicle. **2** about or concerning. **3** as a member of. **4** stored in or broadcast by. **5** in the course of. **6** at a point in time. **7** taking medication. • adv. **1** in contact with or covering something. **2** with continued movement or action. **3** taking place or being presented. **4** functioning. □ **oncoming** approaching. **online** controlled by or connected to a computer. **onlooker** a spectator. **onward** (or **onwards**) in a forward direction.

**once** adv. **1** on one occasion only. **2** formerly. □ **at once 1** immedi-ately. **2** simultaneously. **once-over** a rapid inspection or search.

**one** n. & adj. **1** the smallest whole number; 1. **2** single, or a single person or thing. **3** a certain. **4** the same: *of one mind.* • pron. **1** used to refer to a person or thing previously mentioned. **2** used to refer to the speaker, or to represent people in general. □ **one-sided 1** unfairly biased. **2** very unequal.

**onerous** adj. involving effort and difficulty.
▷ SYNS ARDUOUS, strenuous, difficult, hard, taxing, demanding, exacting, wearisome.

**oneself** pron. the emphatic and reflexive form of *one*.

**ongoing** adj. still in progress.
▷ SYNS IN PROGRESS, under way, continuing, developing.

**onion** n. a vegetable with a bulb having a strong taste and smell.

**only** adj. single or solitary. • adv. 1 with no one or nothing more besides. 2 no longer ago than. • conj. inf. except that.

**onomatopoeia** n. the use of words that sound similar to the thing described (e.g. *sizzle*).
■ onomatopoeic adj.

**onset** n. the beginning of something.
▷ SYNS START, beginning, commencement, arrival.

**onslaught** n. a fierce attack.
▷ SYNS ASSAULT, attack, raid, foray, push, thrust, blitz.

**onto** prep. on to.

**onus** n. a duty or responsibility.
▷ SYNS BURDEN, responsibility, liability, obligation, duty.

**onyx** n. a semi-precious stone like marble.

**ooze** v. 1 slowly seep out. 2 exude.

**opal** n. a semi-transparent precious stone.

**opalescent** adj. having small points of shifting colour.

**opaque** adj. impossible to see through; difficult to understand. ■ opacity n.

**open** adj. 1 not closed, fastened, or restricted. 2 not covered or protected. 3 undisguised. 4 frank and communicative. 5 expanded or unfolded. 6 not finally settled. • v. 1 make or become open. 2 establish or begin. □ opencast (of mining) near the surface, rather than from shafts. open house hospitality to all visitors. open-plan having few or no dividing walls. open to subject or vulnerable to. open verdict a verdict that a death is suspicious but the cause is unknown. ■ opener n. openly adv. openness n.
▷ SYNS 1 AJAR, unlocked, unbolted, unfastened, gaping, yawning. 2 EXPOSED, extensive, broad, sweeping, airy, uncluttered. 3 open hostility: OVERT, obvious, undisguised, unconcealed, blatant, clear, patent, conspicuous. 4 FRANK, candid, honest, forthright, direct, blunt. • v. UNLOCK, unbolt, unlatch; unwrap, undo, untie.

**opening** n. 1 a gap. 2 a beginning. 3 an opportunity.
▷ SYNS 1 GAP, aperture, space, hole, orifice, vent. 2 VACANCY, position, job, opportunity, chance.

**opera** n. a play in which words are sung to music. ■ operatic adj.

**operable** adj. 1 able to be used. 2 suitable for treatment by surgery.

**operate** v. 1 use or control a machine. 2 function. 3 perform a surgical operation.
▷ SYNS 1 USE, utilize, control, employ, handle. 2 WORK, run, function, go.

**operation** n. 1 functioning. 2 an act of surgery performed on a patient. 3 an organized action involving a number of people.

**operational** adj. **1** in or ready for use. **2** of the functioning of an organization.
▷ SYNS OPERATIVE, running, working, functioning, in use, usable.

**operative** adj. **1** functioning. **2** of surgery. • n. **1** a worker. **2** a secret agent.

**operator** n. a person who operates a machine; a person who works at the switchboard of a telephone exchange; a person who runs a business or enterprise.

**operetta** n. a short or light opera.

**ophthalmic** adj. of or for the eyes.

**opiate** n. a sedative containing opium.

**opine** v. formal express or hold as an opinion.

**opinion** n. a personal view not necessarily based on fact or knowledge; the views of people in general; a formal statement of advice by an expert.
▷ SYNS VIEW, belief, thought, standpoint, judgement, estimation, feeling, impression, notion, conviction.

**opinionated** adj. tending to state your views forcefully.

**opium** n. an addictive drug made from the juice of a poppy.

**opossum** n. a small tree-living marsupial.

**opponent** n. **1** a person who competes with another. **2** a person who disagrees with something.
▷ SYNS RIVAL, adversary, competitor, enemy, contender, challenger.

**opportune** adj. happening at a good or convenient time.

**opportunist** n. a person who exploits opportunities, esp. in an unscrupulous way.
■ opportunism n.

**opportunity** n. (pl. **-ies**) a set of circumstances making it possible to do something.
▷ SYNS CHANCE, favourable time; inf. break.

**oppose** v. **1** disagree with and try to prevent. **2** compete with.
▷ SYNS OBJECT TO, resist, withstand, defy, fight, dispute.

**opposite** adj. **1** facing. **2** totally different; contrasting. • n. an opposite person or thing. • adv. & prep. in an opposite position to.
▷ SYNS adj. **1** FACING, face-to-face. **2** OPPOSING, differing, different, contrary, contradictory, conflicting, discordant, incompatible.

**opposition** n. **1** resistance or disagreement. **2** a group of opponents. **3** (**the Opposition**) the main parliamentary party opposing the one in power. **4** a contrast or opposite.
▷ SYNS **1** HOSTILITY, resistance, defiance. **2** OPPONENT, rival, adversary, competition, antagonist, enemy, foe.

**oppress** v. govern or treat harshly; distress or make anxious. ■ oppression n. oppressor n.
▷ SYNS SUBJUGATE, suppress, crush, subdue, tyrannize, repress, persecute.

**oppressive** adj. **1** harsh and unfair; causing distress or anxiety. **2** (of weather) sultry and tiring.
▷ SYNS **1** TYRANNICAL, despotic, draconian, repressive, domineering, harsh, cruel, ruthless, merciless. **2** MUGGY,

close, airless, stuffy, stifling, sultry.

**opt** v. 1 make a choice. 2 (**opt out**) choose not to participate.

**optic** adj. of the eye or vision.

**optical** adj. of vision, light, or optics. □ **optical fibre** a thin glass fibre used to transmit signals. **optical illusion** something that deceives the eye by appearing to be other than it is.

**optician** n. a person who examines eyes and prescribes glasses etc.

**optics** n. the study of vision and the behaviour of light.

**optimal** adj. best or most favourable.

**optimism** n. a tendency to take a hopeful view of things. ■ **optimist** n.

**optimistic** adj. hopeful and confident about the future.
▷ SYNS POSITIVE, hopeful, confident, cheerful, buoyant; inf. upbeat.

**optimum** adj. & n. (pl. **-ma** or **-mums**) the best or most favourable (conditions, amount, etc.).
▷ SYNS BEST, ideal, perfect, peak, top, optimal.

**option** n. a thing that you may choose; the freedom or right to choose; a right to buy or sell something at a specified price within a set time.
▷ SYNS CHOICE, alternative, possibility, preference.

**optional** adj. not compulsory. ■ **optionally** adv.
▷ SYNS VOLUNTARY, discretionary, elective.

**opulent** adj. ostentatiously luxurious. ■ **opulence** n.
▷ SYNS LUXURIOUS, sumptuous; inf. plush, ritzy.

**opus** n. (pl. **opera**) a musical composition numbered as one of a composer's works.

**or** conj. used to link alternatives; also known as; otherwise.

**oracle** n. 1 (in ancient Greece or Rome) a priest or priestess who gave prophecy from the gods. 2 an authority which is always correct.

**oral** adj. 1 spoken not written. 2 of or done by the mouth. • n. a spoken exam. ■ **orally** adv.

**orange** n. a large round citrus fruit with reddish-yellow rind; its colour.

**orang-utan** (or **orang-utang**) n. a large ape.

**oration** n. a formal speech.

**orator** n. a skilful public speaker.

**oratorio** n. (pl. **oratorios**) a musical work on a religious theme for voices and orchestra.

**oratory** n. the art of public speaking. ■ **oratorical** adj.

**orb** n. a sphere or globe.

**orbit** n. 1 the curved path of a planet, satellite, or spacecraft round a star or planet. 2 an area of activity or influence. • v. (**orbited, orbiting**) move in orbit round.
▷ SYNS n. CIRCUIT, course, path, circle, revolution.

**orbital** adj. 1 of orbits. 2 (of a road) round the outside of a city.

**orchard** n. a piece of land planted with fruit trees.

**orchestra** n. a large group of people playing various musical instruments. ■ **orchestral** adj.

**orchestrate** v. 1 arrange music for an orchestra. 2 direct a

situation carefully or secretly.
■ **orchestration** n.

**orchid** n. a showy flower.

**ordain** v. 1 appoint ceremonially to the Christian ministry. 2 order or decree officially.

**ordeal** n. a painful or difficult experience.
▷ SYNS TRIAL, test, tribulation, suffering, affliction, torment, trouble.

**order** n. 1 the arrangement of people or things according to a particular sequence or method. 2 a state in which everything is in its right place. 3 a state of peace and obedience to law. 4 a command. 5 a request to supply goods etc. 6 a rank, kind, or quality. 7 a religious community. 8 a classifying category of plants or animals. • v. 1 give a command. 2 request that something be supplied. 3 arrange methodically. □ out of order not functioning.
▷ SYNS n. 1 *alphabetical order:* SEQUENCE, arrangement, organization, classification, categorization, grouping, system. 2 ORDERLINESS, tidiness, neatness, organization, symmetry, uniformity, regularity. 3 PEACE, control, law and order, calm. 4 *give orders:* COMMAND, instruction, directive, direction, decree, edict. • v. 1 COMMAND, instruct, direct, tell. 2 REQUEST, book, reserve, call for, requisition.

**orderly** adj. 1 neatly arranged. 2 well behaved. • n. 1 a hospital attendant. 2 a soldier assisting an officer. ■ **orderliness** n.
▷ SYNS adj. 1 NEAT, tidy, organized, shipshape. 2 WELL BEHAVED, disciplined, controlled, peaceful.

**ordinal number** n. a number defining a thing's position in a series, such as *first* or *second*.

**ordinance** n. a decree; a religious rite.

**ordinary** adj. normal or usual.
■ **ordinarily** adv.
▷ SYNS USUAL, normal, standard, conventional, typical, common, commonplace, customary, habitual, everyday, regular, routine, established, run-of-the-mill, unremarkable, unexceptional.

**ordination** n. ceremonial appointment to the Christian ministry.

**ordnance** n. mounted guns; military equipment.

**ore** n. solid rock or mineral from which a metal or mineral can be obtained.

**oregano** n. a herb.

**organ** n. 1 a body part with a specific function. 2 a keyboard instrument with pipes supplied with air by bellows. 3 a newspaper expressing particular views. ■ **organist** n.

**organic** adj. 1 of or derived from living matter. 2 produced without artificial chemicals. 3 of bodily organs. 4 (of development or change) continuous or natural.
■ **organically** adv.

**organism** n. an individual animal, plant, or life form.

**organization** n. organizing; a systematic arrangement; an organized group of people, e.g. a business.
▷ SYNS 1 ARRANGEMENT, regulation, coordination, categorization, administration, management. 2 see **COMPANY** (1).

**organize** (or **-ise**) v. **1** arrange in an orderly way. **2** make arrangements for.
▷ SYNS **1** ARRANGE, regulate, marshal, coordinate, systematize, standardize, sort, classify, categorize, catalogue. **2** ADMINISTRATE, run, manage.

**orgasm** n. a climax of sexual activity.

**orgy** n. (pl. **-ies**) **1** group sexual activity. **2** excessive indulgence in a specified activity.
■ **orgiastic** adj.

**orient** n. the countries of the East. • v. (or **orientate**) **1** position in relation to the points of a compass. **2** (**orient yourself**) find your position in relation to unfamiliar surroundings. **3** tailor to meet particular needs. ■ **oriental** adj. **orientation** n.
▷ SYNS v. ADAPT, adjust, familiarize, acclimatize, accustom, get your bearings.

**orifice** n. an opening.

**origami** n. the Japanese decorative art of paper folding.

**origin** n. **1** the point where something begins. **2** a person's ancestry or parentage.
▷ SYNS **1** BEGINNING, start, genesis, source, basis, root, derivation, provenance. **2** DESCENT, ancestry, parentage, pedigree, lineage, heritage, extraction.

**original** adj. **1** existing from the beginning. **2** inventive or novel. **3** not copied. • n. a model on which copies are based.
■ **originality** n. **originally** adv.
▷ SYNS adj. **1** FIRST, early, indigenous, aboriginal. **2** INNOVATIVE, inventive, creative, imaginative, new, novel, unusual, unconventional.

**originate** v. bring or come into being. ■ **originator** n.
▷ SYNS **1** ARISE, stem, spring, result, derive, start, begin, commence. **2** INVENT, dream up, conceive, initiate, create, formulate, inaugurate, pioneer, introduce, establish, found, develop.

**ornament** n. an object used as a decoration; decoration.
■ **ornamentation** n.
▷ SYNS KNICK-KNACK, trinket, bauble, accessory, decoration, adornment, embellishment, trimming.

**ornamental** adj. intended as decoration.
▷ SYNS DECORATIVE, fancy, ornate, attractive.

**ornate** adj. elaborately decorated.
▷ SYNS ELABORATE, decorated, embellished, fancy, ostentatious, showy.

**ornithology** n. the study of birds. ■ **ornithological** adj. **ornithologist** n.

**orphan** n. a child whose parents are dead. • v. make a child an orphan.

**orphanage** n. a place where orphans are cared for.

**orthodox** adj. **1** following traditional or accepted beliefs. **2** conventional. □ **Orthodox Church** the Eastern or Greek Church.
■ **orthodoxy** n.
▷ SYNS CONVENTIONAL, conformist, established, traditional, conservative, prevalent, popular.

**orthopaedics** (US **orthopedics**) n. the branch of medicine concerned with bones and muscles. ■ **orthopaedic** adj.

**oscillate** v. move or swing to and fro. ■ **oscillation** n.

**osier** n. willow with flexible twigs.

**osmosis** n. the passage of molecules through a membrane from a less concentrated solution into a more concentrated one. ■ osmotic adj.

**osprey** n. a large fish-eating bird.

**ossify** v. (ossified, ossifying) turn into bone; stop developing or progressing. ■ ossification n.

**ostensible** adj. apparent, but not necessarily true. ■ ostensibly adv.

▷ SYNS APPARENT, seeming, outward, alleged, claimed, supposed.

**ostentation** n. showy display intended to impress.

**ostentatious** adj. expensive or showy in a way intended to impress other people.

▷ SYNS SHOWY, flamboyant, conspicuous, pretentious, loud, overdone, extravagant; inf. flash, flashy, over the top, bling.

**osteopathy** n. the treatment of certain conditions by manipulating bones and muscles. ■ osteopath n.

**ostracize** (or -ise) v. exclude from a society or group. ■ ostracism n.

▷ SYNS COLD-SHOULDER, exclude, shun, spurn, avoid, boycott, reject, blackball, blacklist.

**ostrich** n. a large flightless African bird.

**other** adj. & pron. 1 used to refer to a person or thing different from one already mentioned or known. 2 additional. 3 alternative of two. 4 those not already mentioned. □ otherwise 1 in different circumstances.

2 in other respects. 3 in a different way.

▷ SYNS 1 DIFFERENT, alternative, distinct, separate. 2 MORE, further, additional. extra.

**otter** n. a fish-eating water animal.

**ottoman** n. a low upholstered seat without a back or arms.

**ought** v.aux. 1 expressing duty, desirability, or advisability. 2 expressing strong probability.

**ounce** n. a unit of weight, one-sixteenth of a pound (about 28 grams); a very small amount.

**our** adj. of or belonging to us.

**ours** poss.pron belonging to us.

**ourselves** pron. the emphatic and reflexive form of *we* and *us*.

**oust** v. force out.

**out** adv. & adj. 1 away from a place. 2 away from your home or office. 3 outdoors. 4 so as to be heard or noticed. 5 not possible. 6 at or to an end. 7 so as to be extinguished. • v. reveal the homosexuality of. □ out and out complete. out of date no longer current, valid, or fashionable.

**outback** n. a remote or sparsely populated area.

**outboard** adj. (of a motor) attached to the outside of a boat.

**outbreak** n. a sudden occurrence of war, disease, etc.

▷ SYNS ERUPTION, upsurge, outburst, start.

**outbuilding** n. an outhouse.

**outburst** n. a sudden release of feeling.

▷ SYNS ERUPTION, explosion, attack, fit, paroxysm.

**outcast** n. a person rejected by their social group.

**outclass** v. surpass in quality.
▷ SYNS SURPASS, outshine, eclipse, overshadow, outstrip, outdo, defeat.

**outcome** n. a consequence.
▷ SYNS RESULT, upshot, issue, conclusion, after-effect, aftermath.

**outcrop** n. a part of a rock formation visible on the surface.

**outcry** n. a strong protest.

**outdated** adj. no longer used or fashionable.
▷ SYNS OLD-FASHIONED, out of date, outmoded, dated, old, antiquated, passé.

**outdistance** v. get far ahead of.

**outdo** v. (outdid, outdone, outdoing) do better than.
▷ SYNS SURPASS, top, exceed, outstrip, outshine, eclipse, outclass, defeat.

**outdoor** adj. of or for use in the open air. ■ **outdoors** adv.

**outer** adj. 1 outside. 2 further from the centre or inside.
■ **outermost** adj.
▷ SYNS 1 OUTSIDE, outermost, outward, exterior, external, surface. 2 OUTLYING, distant, remote.

**outfit** n. a set of clothes.

**outgoing** adj. 1 sociable. 2 leaving an office or position. ● n. regular expenditure.
▷ SYNS adj. 1 EXTROVERT, demonstrative, friendly, affable, sociable, open, expansive, talkative, gregarious. 2 RETIRING, departing, leaving. ● n. EXPENSES, expenditure, outlay, costs, overheads.

**outgrow** v. (outgrew, outgrown, outgrowing) grow too large for; stop doing something as you mature.

**outhouse** n. a shed, barn, etc.

**outing** n. a brief journey.

**outlandish** adj. bizarre or unfamiliar.
▷ SYNS STRANGE, unfamiliar, odd, unusual, extraordinary, peculiar, queer, curious, eccentric, bizarre, weird; inf. wacky.

**outlast** v. last longer than.

**outlaw** n. a criminal who remains at large. ● v. make illegal.

**outlay** n. money spent.

**outlet** n. a way out; a means for giving vent to energy or feelings; a market for goods.

**outline** n. 1 a line showing a thing's shape or boundary. 2 a summary. ● v. draw or describe in outline; mark the outline of.
▷ SYNS n. 1 SKETCH, rundown, summary, synopsis. 2 CONTOUR, silhouette, profile, perimeter.

**outlook** n. a person's attitude to life; the prospect for the future.
▷ SYNS 1 VIEW, viewpoint, perspective, attitude, standpoint, interpretation, opinion. 2 VIEW, vista, panorama, aspect.

**outlying** adj. situated far from the centre.
▷ SYNS OUT-OF-THE-WAY, remote, distant, far-flung, isolated.

**outmoded** adj. old-fashioned.

**outnumber** v. exceed in number.

**outpatient** n. a person visiting a hospital for treatment but not staying overnight.

**outpost** n. a small military camp at a distance from the main army; a remote settlement.

**output** n. the amount of electrical power, work, etc. produced.

▷ SYNS PRODUCTION, productivity, yield, harvest.

**outrage** n. extreme shock and anger; an extremely immoral or shocking act. • v. cause to feel outrage.
▷ SYNS n. **1** ATROCITY, crime, horror, enormity. **2** OFFENCE, affront, insult, injury, abuse, scandal. **3** ANGER, fury, rage, indignation, wrath, annoyance, resentment, horror.

**outrageous** adj. shockingly bad or excessive.
▷ SYNS SHOCKING, scandalous, disgraceful, appalling, atrocious; exaggerated, improbable, preposterous, ridiculous.

**outright** adv. **1** altogether. **2** frankly. **3** immediately. • adj. **1** total. **2** frank and direct.

**outset** n. the beginning.

**outside** n. the external side or surface. • adj. **1** on or near the outside. **2** not belonging to a particular group. • prep. & adv. **1** on or moving beyond the boundaries of. **2** not being a member of.
▷ SYNS adj. EXTERIOR, external, outer, outdoor.

**outsider** n. **1** a non-member of a group. **2** a competitor thought to have little chance of success.
▷ SYNS STRANGER, foreigner, alien, immigrant, incomer.

**outsize** adj. exceptionally large.

**outskirts** pl.n. the outer districts.
▷ SYNS EDGES, fringes, suburbs, environs, outlying districts, borders.

**outspoken** adj. very frank.
▷ SYNS CANDID, frank, forthright, direct, blunt, plain-spoken.

**outstanding** adj. **1** conspicuous; exceptionally good. **2** not yet paid or dealt with.
▷ SYNS EXCELLENT, exceptional, superlative, pre-eminent, notable, noteworthy, distinguished, important, great.

**outward** adj. & adv. **1** on or from the outside. **2** out or away from a place. ■ **outwardly** adv. **outwards** adv.

**outweigh** v. be more significant than.

**outwit** v. (**outwitted**, **outwitting**) defeat by being cunning or crafty.
▷ SYNS GET THE BETTER OF, outsmart, trick, dupe, fool.

**ova** pl. of **ovum**.

**oval** n. & adj. (having) a rounded elongated shape.

**ovary** n. (pl. -ies) a female reproductive organ in which eggs are produced. ■ **ovarian** adj.

**ovation** n. enthusiastic applause.

**oven** n. an enclosed compartment in which things are cooked or heated.

**over** prep. **1** extending upwards from. **2** above. **3** expressing movement across. **4** higher or more than. **5** expressing authority or control. • adv. **1** expressing movement across. **2** beyond and falling or hanging from. **3** finished. **4** repeatedly.
• n. Cricket a sequence of six balls bowled from one end of the pitch.

**overall** n. a loose-fitting garment worn over ordinary clothes for protection. • adj. & adv. including everything; taken as a whole.
▷ SYNS adj. COMPREHENSIVE, universal, all-embracing,

inclusive, general, sweeping, blanket, global. • adv. ON THE WHOLE, in general.

**overawe** v. impress someone so much that they are silent or nervous.
▷ SYNS INTIMIDATE, daunt, unnerve, frighten, alarm, scare.

**overbalance** v. fall due to loss of balance.

**overbearing** adj. unpleasantly overpowering.

**overboard** adv. from a ship into the water.

**overcast** adj. cloudy.

**overcoat** n. a long, warm coat.

**overcome** v. 1 succeed in dealing with a problem. 2 defeat. 3 (of an emotion) overwhelm.
▷ SYNS CONQUER, defeat, beat, vanquish, overpower, overwhelm, master, subdue.

**overdose** n. & v. (take) a dangerously large dose of a drug.

**overdraft** n. an arrangement with a bank allowing you to take out more money than your account holds.

**overdrawn** adj. having taken more money from a bank account than it holds.

**overdrive** n. 1 a mechanism providing an extra gear above top gear. 2 a state of great activity.

**overdue** adj. not paid or arrived etc. by the required or expected time.
▷ SYNS 1 LATE, behind, delayed, belated, tardy. 2 UNPAID, owing, outstanding, in arrears.

**overgrown** adj. 1 covered with weeds. 2 having grown too large.

**overhang** v. hang outwards over something.
▷ SYNS STICK OUT, extend, project, protrude, jut out.

**overhaul** v. examine and repair. • n. an examination and repair.

**overhead** adj. & adv. above your head. • n. expenses incurred in running a business etc.

**overhear** v. (**overheard**, **overhearing**) hear accidentally.

**overjoyed** adj. very happy.

**overkill** n. an excessive amount of something.

**overlap** v. (**overlapped**, **overlapping**) extend over something so as to cover part of it; partially coincide. • n. a part or amount that overlaps.

**overleaf** adv. on the other side of a page.

**overload** v. put too great a load on or in. • n. an excessive amount.

**overlook** v. 1 fail to notice; disregard. 2 have a view over.
▷ SYNS 1 FAIL TO NOTICE, miss, neglect, ignore, disregard, omit, forget. 2 LOOK OVER, have a view of.

**overly** adv. excessively.

**overnight** adv. & adj. during or for a night.

**overpower** v. 1 defeat with greater strength. 2 overwhelm.

**overpowering** adj. very strong or powerful.
▷ SYNS OVERWHELMING, oppressive, unbearable, intolerable, unendurable.

**overrate** v. have too high an opinion of.

**overreact** v. react more strongly than is justified.

**override** v. (**overrode**, **overridden**, **overriding**) overrule;

be more important than; interrupt the operation of an automatic device.

**overriding** adj. more important than anything else.

▷ SYNS MOST IMPORTANT, predominant, principal, primary, paramount, chief, main, major, foremost, central.

**overrule** v. set aside a decision etc. by using your authority.

**overrun** v. (overran, overrun, overrunning) 1 occupy in large numbers. 2 exceed a limit.

**overseas** adj. & adv. in or to a foreign country.

**oversee** v. (oversaw, overseen, overseeing) supervise.
■ overseer n.

**overshadow** v. cast a shadow over; be more important or prominent than; distract attention from.

**oversight** n. an unintentional failure to do something.

▷ SYNS 1 CARELESSNESS, inattention, neglect, laxity, dereliction, omission. 2 MISTAKE, error, blunder, gaffe, fault, omission, slip, lapse.

**overspill** n. people moving from an overcrowded area to live elsewhere.

**overstep** v. (overstepped, overstepping) go beyond a limit.

**overt** adj. done or shown openly.

▷ SYNS OBVIOUS, undisguised, open, blatant, patent, manifest, noticeable, conspicuous.

**overtake** v. 1 pass while travelling in the same direction. 2 affect suddenly.

▷ SYNS PASS, go past, leave behind, outstrip.

**overthrow** v. (overthrew, overthrown, overthrowing) remove forcibly from power. • n. a removal from power.

**overtime** n. time worked in addition to normal working hours.

**overtone** n. an additional quality or implication.

▷ SYNS IMPLICATION, innuendo, hint, suggestion, insinuation, connotation.

**overture** n. 1 an orchestral piece at the beginning of a musical work. 2 (overtures) an initial approach or proposal.

**overturn** v. 1 turn upside down or on to its side. 2 reverse a decision etc.

**overview** n. a general survey.

**overweening** adj. showing too much confidence or pride.

**overwhelm** v. 1 bury beneath a huge mass. 2 overcome completely; have a strong emotional effect on.

▷ SYNS 1 OVERCOME, move, dumbfound, stagger, take aback. 2 INUNDATE, flood, engulf, swamp, overload, snow under.

**overwhelming** adj. very great or strong.

▷ SYNS 1 an overwhelming majority: VERY LARGE, enormous, immense, inordinate, massive, huge. 2 an overwhelming desire to laugh: UNCONTROLLABLE, irrepressible, irresistible, overpowering, compelling.

**overwrought** adj. in a state of nervous agitation.

**ovulate** v. discharge ova from the ovary. ■ ovulation n.

**ovum** n. (pl. ova) a female reproductive cell.

**owe** v. 1 be required to pay or repay money etc. in return for something received. **2** have something because of: *I owe him my life.*

**owing** adj. yet to be paid.
□ owing to because of.

**owl** n. a bird of prey with large eyes, usu. flying at night.

**own** adj. belonging to a specified person. • v. **1** possess. **2** admit. **3** (**own up**) confess. ■ owner n. ownership n.
▷ SYNS v. POSSESS, have, keep.

**ox** n. (pl. **oxen**) **1** a cow or bull. **2** a castrated bull.

**oxide** n. a compound of oxygen and one other element.

**oxidize** (or **-ise**) v. cause to combine with oxygen.
■ oxidation n.

**oxygen** n. a gas forming about 20 per cent of the earth's atmosphere.

**oxygenate** v. supply or mix with oxygen.

**oxymoron** n. a figure of speech in which apparently contradictory terms appear together (e.g. *a deafening silence*).

**oyster** n. an edible shellfish.

**oz** abbr. ounces.

**ozone** n. a strong-smelling, toxic form of oxygen.
□ ozone layer a layer of ozone in the stratosphere, absorbing ultraviolet radiation.

# Pp

**p** abbr. **1** penny or pence. **2** Music piano (softly).

**PA** abbr. **1** personal assistant. **2** public address.

**p.a.** abbr. per annum (yearly).

**pace** n. **1** a single step. **2** a rate of progress. • v. **1** walk steadily. **2** measure a distance by pacing. **3** (**pace yourself**) do something at a steady rate.
□ pacemaker **1** an artificial device for regulating the heart muscle. **2** a runner who sets the pace for others.
▷ SYNS n. **1** STEP, stride. **2** SPEED, rate, velocity.

**pachyderm** n. a large thick-skinned mammal, e.g. an elephant.

**pacific** adj. **1** peaceful. **2** (**Pacific**) of the Pacific Ocean.

**pacifist** n. a person totally opposed to war. ■ pacifism n.

**pacify** v. (**pacified**, **pacifying**) make calm. ■ pacification n.
▷ SYNS CALM DOWN, placate, appease, mollify, soothe, quieten.

**pack** n. **1** a cardboard or paper container and the items in it. **2** a set of playing cards. **3** a group of dogs or wolves. • v. **1** fill a bag with items for travel. **2** fill a container for storage etc. **3** cover, surround, or fill.
▷ SYNS n. **1** PACKET, package, carton. **2** GANG, crowd, mob, group, band, company, troop; inf. bunch. • v. **1** FILL, store, stow,

load, stuff, cram. **2** *people packing the stadium:* FILL, crowd, throng, mob, jam.

**package** n. **1** a parcel. **2** a set of proposals. • v. put into a box or wrapping.

**packed** adj. very crowded.
▷ SYNS CROWDED, full, crammed, jammed; inf. chock-full.

**packet** n. a small pack or package.

**pact** n. a formal agreement.
▷ SYNS AGREEMENT, treaty, deal, settlement, truce.

**pad** n. **1** a thick piece of soft material. **2** sheets of blank paper fastened together at one edge. **3** the fleshy underpart of an animal's foot. • v. **1** fill or cover with padding. **2** lengthen a speech etc. with unnecessary material. **3** walk softly or steadily.

**padding** n. soft material used as a pad.

**paddle** n. a short oar with a broad blade. • v. **1** propel with a paddle. **2** walk with bare feet in shallow water.

**paddock** n. a field or enclosure for horses.
▷ SYNS FIELD, meadow, pen, corral.

**padlock** n. & v. (fasten with) a detachable lock attached by a hinged hook.

**paediatrics** (US **pediatrics**) n. the branch of medicine which deals with children's diseases. ■ paediatric adj. paediatrician n.

**paedophile** (US **pedophile**) n. a person who is sexually attracted to children. ■ paedophilia n.

**paella** n. a Spanish dish of rice, seafood, chicken, etc.

**pagan** adj. & n. (a person) holding religious beliefs other than those of an established religion.
▷ SYNS HEATHEN, infidel, non-Christian.

**page** n. **1** a leaf of a book etc. **2** one side of this. **3** a boy attending a bride. **4** a young male attendant in a hotel. • v. summon over a public address system or by a pager.

**pageant** n. a public entertainment performed by people in costume. ■ pageantry n.
▷ SYNS DISPLAY, spectacle, extravaganza, show, parade.

**pager** n. a small device that bleeps or vibrates to summon the wearer.

**pagoda** n. a Hindu or Buddhist temple or other sacred building.

**paid** past & p.p. of PAY.

**pail** n. a bucket.

**pain** n. **1** physical discomfort caused by injury or illness. **2** mental suffering. **3** (**pains**) great care or trouble. • v. cause pain to. □ painkiller a medicine for relieving pain.
▷ SYNS n. **1** SUFFERING, agony, discomfort; soreness, ache, throb, twinge, pang. **2** SORROW, grief, heartache, sadness, unhappiness, distress, misery.

**painful** adj. affected with or causing pain.
▷ SYNS SORE, hurting, tender, aching, throbbing.

**painless** adj. **1** not causing pain. **2** involving little effort or stress.
▷ SYNS **1** PAIN-FREE, without pain. **2** EASY, trouble-free, effortless, simple, plain sailing; inf. child's play, a cinch.

**painstaking** adj. very careful and thorough.

▷ SYNS CAREFUL, thorough, assiduous, conscientious, meticulous, punctilious, scrupulous.

**paint** n. colouring matter for applying in liquid form to a surface. • v. apply paint to; depict with paint; describe. ■ painting n.

**painter** n. **1** a person who paints as an artist or decorator. **2** a rope attached to a boat's bow for tying it up.

**pair** n. **1** a set of two things or people. **2** an article consisting of two parts: *a pair of scissors.* • v. form a pair.
▷ SYNS n. COUPLE, duo, set, brace, two.

**paisley** n. a pattern of curved feather-shaped figures.

**pajamas** US sp. of PYJAMAS.

**pal** n. inf. a friend.

**palace** n. an official residence of a monarch, president, etc.

**palaeontology** (US **paleontology**) n. the study of fossil animals and plants.

**palatable** adj. **1** pleasant to taste. **2** acceptable.
▷ SYNS **1** TASTY, appetizing, delicious, mouth-watering. **2** PLEASANT, acceptable, agreeable.

**palate** n. **1** the roof of the mouth. **2** the sense of taste.

**palatial** adj. like a palace.
▷ SYNS LUXURIOUS, splendid, grand, magnificent, opulent, sumptuous, grand; inf. plush.

**palaver** n. inf. a fuss.

**pale** adj. **1** light in colour. **2** (of the face) having less colour than normal. • v. **1** turn pale. **2** seem less important.
▷ SYNS adj. **1** LIGHT, pastel, muted, soft; faded, bleached, washed-out. **2** WHITE, pallid, pasty, wan, colourless, anaemic, ashen.

**palette** n. a board on which an artist mixes colours; a range of colours used. ☐ palette knife a blunt knife with a flexible blade, for applying or removing paint.

**palindrome** n. a word or phrase that reads the same backwards as forwards, e.g. *madam.*

**paling** n. a fence made from pointed stakes; a stake.

**pall** n. a cloth spread over a coffin; a dark cloud of smoke. • v. come to seem less interesting. ☐ pall-bearer a person helping to carry a coffin at a funeral.

**pallet** n. **1** a straw mattress. **2** a portable platform on which goods can be lifted or stored.

**palliate** v. alleviate; make less severe. ■ palliative adj.

**pallid** adj. pale. ■ pallor n.

**palm** n. **1** the inner surface of the hand. **2** an evergreen tree of warm regions, with large leaves and no branches.

**palmistry** n. fortune-telling by examining the lines on the palm of a person's hand. ■ palmist n.

**palomino** n. (pl. **-os**) a golden-coloured horse with a white mane and tail.

**palpable** adj. able to be touched or felt. ■ palpably adv.
▷ SYNS UNMISTAKABLE, obvious, clear, plain, perceptible, noticeable.

**palpate** v. examine medically by touch.

**palpitate** v. (of the heart) throb rapidly. ■ palpitation n.

**palsy** n. dated paralysis.
■ **palsied** adj.

**paltry** adj. (of an amount) very small; petty or trivial.
▷ SYNS **1** *a paltry sum:* SMALL, meagre, trifling, minor, insignificant, derisory. **2** *a paltry excuse:* WORTHLESS, sorry, puny, petty, trivial.

**pampas** n. vast grassy plains in South America.

**pamper** v. treat very indulgently.
▷ SYNS SPOIL, cosset, indulge, mollycoddle.

**pamphlet** n. a small booklet or leaflet.
▷ SYNS LEAFLET, booklet, brochure, circular.

**pan** n. a metal container for cooking food in; the bowl of a toilet. • v. (**panned, panning**) **1** inf. criticize severely. **2** move a camera while filming to give a panoramic effect.

**panacea** n. a remedy for all kinds of diseases or troubles.

**panache** n. a confident stylish manner.
▷ SYNS STYLE, verve, flamboyance, zest, brio.

**panama** n. a straw hat.

**pancake** n. a thin, flat cake of fried batter.

**pancreas** n. a digestive gland near the stomach, which also produces insulin.

**panda** n. a bear-like black and white mammal.

**pandemonium** n. uproar.

**pander** v. indulge an unreasonable desire or bad habit.
▷ SYNS GRATIFY, indulge, humour, please, satisfy.

**pane** n. a sheet of glass in a window or door.

**panegyric** n. a speech or text of praise.

**panel** n. **1** a section in a door, vehicle, garment, etc. **2** a group of people assembled to discuss or decide something.
■ **panelled** (US **paneled**) adj. **panellist** (US **panelist**) n.

**pang** n. a sudden sharp pain.

**panic** n. sudden strong fear.
• v. (**panicked, panicking**) feel panic. ■ **panic-stricken** adj. **panicky** adj.
▷ SYNS n. ALARM, fright, fear, terror, horror, agitation, hysteria. • v. BE ALARMED, take fright, be hysterical, lose your nerve, overreact.

**pannier** n. **1** a bag fitted on a motorcycle or bicycle. **2** a basket carried by a donkey etc.

**panoply** n. (pl. **-ies**) a splendid display.

**panorama** n. a view of a wide area; a complete survey of a set of events. ■ **panoramic** adj.

**pansy** n. (pl. **-ies**) **1** a garden flower. **2** inf., derog. an effeminate or homosexual man.

**pant** v. breathe with short quick breaths.
▷ SYNS PUFF, huff, blow, gasp, wheeze.

**pantechnicon** n. dated a large van for transporting furniture.

**panther** n. a black leopard.

**pantomime** n. a theatrical show based on a fairy tale, involving slapstick comedy.

**pantry** n. (pl. **-ies**) a room or cupboard for storing food.

**pants** pl.n. **1** underpants or knickers. **2** US trousers.

**pap** n. soft, bland food.

**papacy** n. (pl. **-ies**) the position or role of the pope. ■ **papal** adj.

**paparazzi** pl.n. photographers who pursue celebrities to get pictures of them.

**papaya** n. a tropical fruit.

**paper** n. **1** material manufactured in thin sheets from wood pulp, used for writing on, wrapping, etc. **2** a newspaper. **3** a document. **4** an essay. **5** a set of exam questions. • v. cover with wallpaper. □ **paperback** a book bound in flexible card. **paperweight** a small, heavy object for keeping loose papers in place. **paperwork** routine work involving written documents.
▷ SYNS n. **1** NEWSPAPER, journal, gazette, broadsheet, tabloid; inf. rag. **2** ESSAY, article, dissertation, treatise, thesis, monograph, report, study.

**papier mâché** n. a mixture of paper and glue that becomes hard when dry.

**paprika** n. red pepper.

**papyrus** n. (pl. **papyri**) a material made in ancient Egypt from the stem of a water plant, used for writing on.

**par** n. Golf the number of strokes needed by a first-class player for a hole or course. □ **below par** not as good or well as usual. **on a par with** equal to in quality or importance.

**parable** n. a story told to illustrate a moral.

**paracetamol** n. a drug that relieves pain and reduces fever.

**parachute** n. a device used to slow the descent of a person or object dropping from a great height. • v. descend or drop by parachute.

**parade** n. a public procession; a formal assembly of troops; an ostentatious display; a promenade or row of shops. • v. march in a parade; display ostentatiously.
▷ SYNS n. PROCESSION, cavalcade, spectacle, pageant. • v. **1** MARCH, process. **2** *parade their wealth:* DISPLAY, show off, exhibit, flaunt.

**paradise** n. heaven; the Garden of Eden; an ideal place or state.

**paradox** n. a statement that seems self-contradictory but is in fact true. ■ **paradoxical** adj.
▷ SYNS CONTRADICTION, inconsistency, incongruity, anomaly, self-contradiction.

**paraffin** n. an liquid fuel obtained from petroleum.

**paragon** n. an apparently perfect person or thing.

**paragraph** n. a distinct section of a piece of writing, begun on a new line.

**parakeet** n. a small parrot.

**parallel** adj. **1** (of lines or planes) going continuously at the same distance from each other. **2** existing at the same time and corresponding. • n. **1** a person or thing similar to another; a comparison. **2** a line of latitude. • v. (**paralleled**, **paralleling**) be parallel or comparable to.
▷ SYNS adj. **1** SIDE BY SIDE, equidistant. **2** SIMILAR, like, analogous, comparable, equivalent, corresponding, matching. • n. COUNTERPART, equivalent, analogue, match, duplicate, equal. • v. BE SIMILAR TO, resemble, correspond to, compare with.

**parallelogram** n. a figure with four straight sides and opposite sides parallel.

**paralyse** (US **paralyze**) v. affect with paralysis.
▷ SYNS IMMOBILIZE, incapacitate, debilitate, disable, cripple.

**paralysis** n. loss of the ability to move part of the body.
■ paralytic adj.

**paramedic** n. a person trained to do medical work but not having a doctor's qualifications.

**parameter** n. a limit dictating the scope of a process or activity.
▷ SYNS LIMIT, limitation, restriction, boundary, guideline.

**paramilitary** adj. organized like a military force.

**paramount** adj. chief in importance.

**paranoia** n. 1 a mental condition in which a person has delusions of persecution etc. 2 unjustified mistrust of others.
■ paranoid adj.

**paranormal** adj. supernatural.

**parapet** n. a low wall along the edge of a balcony or bridge.

**paraphernalia** n. miscellaneous equipment.

**paraphrase** v. express in different words.

**paraplegia** n. paralysis of the legs and lower body.
■ paraplegic adj. & n.

**parasite** n. 1 an organism living on or in another. 2 a person living off others. ■ parasitic adj.

**parasol** n. a light umbrella used to give shade from the sun.

**paratroops** pl.n. troops trained to parachute into an attack.
■ paratrooper n.

**parboil** v. cook partially by boiling.

**parcel** n. 1 something wrapped in paper to be posted or carried. 2 something considered as a unit. • v. (**parcelled**, **parcelling**; US **parceled**) 1 wrap as a parcel. 2 divide into portions.

**parched** adj. 1 dried out with heat. 2 inf. very thirsty.
▷ SYNS DRY, baked, arid, scorched, desiccated, dehydrated.

**parchment** n. 1 writing material made from animal skin. 2 paper resembling this.

**pardon** n. forgiveness.
• v. (**pardoned**, **pardoning**) forgive or excuse.
■ pardonable adj.
▷ SYNS n. 1 FORGIVENESS, absolution. 2 AMNESTY, reprieve, exoneration, acquittal, release, discharge. • v. 1 FORGIVE, absolve, excuse. 2 EXONERATE, acquit, reprieve, release; inf. let off.

**pare** v. 1 trim the edges of. 2 gradually reduce.

**parent** n. a father or mother.
■ parental adj. parenthood n.

**parentage** n. the identity and origins of your parents.
▷ SYNS ORIGINS, extraction, birth, family, ancestry, lineage, heritage, descent.

**parenthesis** n. (pl. **parentheses**) 1 a word or phrase inserted as an explanation or aside. 2 a pair of round brackets ().

**pariah** n. an outcast.
▷ SYNS OUTCAST, persona non grata, leper, undesirable.

**parish** n. 1 an area with its own church and clergy. 2 the smallest unit of local government in rural areas.
■ parishioner n.

**parity** n. equality.

**park** n. 1 a public garden in a town. 2 the enclosed land of a country house. 3 an area for a specified purpose: *a science park.* **4** an area for parking vehicles. • v. temporarily leave a vehicle somewhere.

**parka** n. a hooded windproof jacket.

**Parkinson's disease** n. a disease causing trembling and muscular rigidity.

**parlance** n. a way of speaking.

**parley** n. (pl. **-eys**) a discussion to settle a dispute.

**parliament** n. an assembly that makes a country's laws. ■ parliamentarian adj. & n. parliamentary adj.
▷ SYNS LEGISLATIVE ASSEMBLY, congress, senate, chamber, house.

**parlour** (US **parlor**) n. **1** dated a sitting room. **2** a shop providing particular goods or services.

**parlous** adj. precarious.

**Parmesan** n. a hard Italian cheese.

**parochial** adj. **1** of a church parish. **2** having a narrow outlook.

**parody** n. (pl. **-ies**) an imitation using exaggeration for comic effect. • v. (**parodied, parodying**) produce a parody of.
▷ SYNS n. SATIRE, lampoon, pastiche, caricature, imitation, mockery; inf. spoof, take-off, send up.

**parole** n. the early release of a prisoner on condition of good behaviour. • v. release on parole.

**paroxysm** n. an outburst of emotion; a sudden attack of pain, coughing, etc.

**parquet** n. flooring of wooden blocks arranged in a pattern.

**parrot** n. a tropical bird with brightly coloured feathers, able

to mimic human speech.
• v. (**parroted, parroting**) repeat without thought or understanding.

**parry** v. **1** ward off a blow. **2** evade a question.
▷ SYNS WARD OFF, fend off, deflect, block, counter, repel, repulse.

**parsimonious** adj. mean or stingy. ■ parsimony n.

**parsley** n. a herb with crinkly leaves.

**parsnip** n. a vegetable with a large yellowish tapering root.

**parson** n. a parish priest.

**parsonage** n. a rectory or vicarage.

**part** n. **1** a piece combining with others to make up a whole. **2** some but not all of something. **3** a person's contribution to a situation. **4** an acting role.
• v. **1** separate or be separated. **2** (**part with**) give up possession of. • adv. partly. □ part of speech a word's grammatical class (e.g. noun, adjective, or verb). part-time for only part of the usual working day or week. take part join in.
▷ SYNS n. **1** PIECE, portion, section, segment, fraction. **2** COMPONENT, bit, constituent, element, unit. **3** ROLE, involvement, contribution, hand. • v. DIVIDE, separate, split, break up.

**partake** v. (**partook, partaken, partaking**) **1** join in an activity. **2** eat or drink.

**partial** adj. **1** favouring one side in a dispute. **2** not complete or total. **3** (**partial to**) liking something. ■ partiality n. partially adv.
▷ SYNS **1** PART, limited, incomplete, fragmentary. **2** BIASED, prejudiced, partisan, one-sided,

discriminatory, preferential, unfair.

**participate** v. take part in something. ■ **participant** n. **participation** n.
▷ SYNS TAKE PART, join in, engage, contribute, share.

**participle** n. Grammar a word formed from a verb (e.g. *burnt*, *burning*, *frightened*, *frightening*) and used as an adjective or noun (as in *burnt toast*).

**particle** n. a tiny portion of matter.
▷ SYNS BIT, piece, speck, spot, atom, molecule.

**particular** adj. 1 relating to an individual member of a group or class. 2 more than is usual. 3 very careful or concerned about something. • n. a detail. □ in particular especially.
▷ SYNS adj. 1 SPECIFIC, individual, precise. 2 *particular care:* SPECIAL, especial, exceptional, unusual, uncommon, remarkable. 3 *particular about something:* FASTIDIOUS, discriminating, selective, fussy, painstaking, meticulous, punctilious, demanding, finicky; inf. pernickety, picky.

**particularly** adv. 1 especially or very. 2 in particular.
▷ SYNS 1 *particularly good:* ESPECIALLY, very, extremely, exceptionally, singularly, unusually, remarkably. 2 *ask for him particularly:* SPECIFICALLY, in particular, explicitly, expressly, specially.

**parting** n. 1 an act of leaving someone. 2 a line of scalp visible when hair is combed in different directions.

**partisan** n. 1 a strong supporter. 2 a guerrilla. • adj. prejudiced.
▷ SYNS n. 1 GUERRILLA, resistance fighter. 2 SUPPORTER, adherent, devotee, backer, follower, disciple.

**partition** n. division into parts; a structure dividing a space into separate parts. • v. divide into parts or by a partition.
▷ SYNS v. DIVIDE, subdivide, separate, screen off, fence off.

**partly** adv. not completely but to some extent.
▷ SYNS IN PART, partially, half, somewhat, fractionally, slightly.

**partner** n. each of two people sharing with another or others in an activity; each of a pair; the person with whom you have an established relationship. • v. be the partner of.

**partnership** n. 1 the state of being a partner or partners. 2 an association of two or more people as partners.
▷ SYNS COOPERATION, association, collaboration, alliance, union, coalition.

**partridge** n. a game bird.

**party** n. 1 a social gathering. 2 an organized political group. 3 a group taking part in an activity or trip. 4 one side in an agreement or dispute. □ party wall a wall shared by two adjoining houses or rooms.
▷ SYNS 1 CELEBRATION, function, reception, gathering, festivity, soirée; inf. bash, do. 2 FACTION, group, alliance, camp.

**pass** v. 1 move or go onward, past, through, or across. 2 change from one state to another. 3 transfer. 4 kick, hit, or throw the ball to a teammate. 5 (of time) go by. 6 spend time.

**7** be successful in an exam.
**8** declare satisfactory. **9** approve
a proposal by voting. • **n. 1** an act
of passing. **2** a success in an
exam. **3** a permit to enter a
place. **4** a route over or through
mountains. **5** inf. a sexual
advance. □ **pass away** die. **pass
out** become unconscious.
**passport** an official document
certifying the holder's identity
and citizenship and entitling
them to travel abroad.
**password** a secret word or
phrase used to gain admission.
▷ SYNS **v. 1** GO, move, proceed,
progress, travel. **2** TRANSFER,
hand over, give. **3** *the hours
passed slowly:* GO BY, proceed,
advance, elapse. **4** *pass the time:*
SPEND, occupy, fill, use, employ,
while away. **5** *pass exams:*
SUCCEED IN, get through. **6** *pass
the motion:* VOTE FOR, accept,
approve, adopt, authorize,
ratify. • **n.** PERMIT, warrant,
licence.

**passable** adj. **1** just satisfactory.
**2** able to be travelled along or
on.
▷ SYNS **1** ADEQUATE, all right,
acceptable, satisfactory,
average, tolerable, fair, mediocre, unexceptional. **2** OPEN,
clear, navigable.

**passage** n. **1** the passing of
someone or something; the
right to pass through. **2** a way
through or across; a journey by
sea or air. **3** an extract from a
book etc. ■ **passageway** n.
▷ SYNS **1** PASSING, progress, course.
**2** JOURNEY, voyage, trek,
crossing, trip, tour. **3** PASSAGE-
WAY, corridor, hall, hallway.
**4** EXTRACT, excerpt, quotation,
citation, verse.

**passé** adj. old-fashioned.

**passenger** n. a person travelling in a car, bus, train, ship, or
aircraft, other than the driver,
pilot, or crew.

**passer-by** n. (pl. **passers-by**) a
person who happens to be going
past.

**passing** adj. not lasting long;
casual.

**passion** n. **1** strong emotion.
**2** great enthusiasm. **3** sexual
love. **4** (**the Passion**) Jesus's
suffering on the cross.
▷ SYNS **1** INTENSITY, enthusiasm,
emotion, fervour, ardour, zeal,
vigour, spirit. **2** FASCINATION,
obsession, fixation, addiction,
mania.

**passionate** adj. involving
intense emotion, enthusiasm,
or sexual love.
▷ SYNS **1** *a passionate plea:*
IMPASSIONED, ardent, intense,
fervent, vehement, emotional,
heartfelt. **2** *a passionate lover:*
AMOROUS, sexy, ardent, sensual,
lustful.

**passive** adj. **1** accepting what
happens without resistance.
**2** (of a verb) in which the
subject undergoes the action of
the verb. ■ **passivity** n.
▷ SYNS INACTIVE, submissive,
compliant, acquiescent,
unresisting.

**Passover** n. a Jewish festival
commemorating the escape of
the Israelites from slavery in
Egypt.

**past** adj. **1** gone by in time and
no longer existing. **2** (of time)
that has gone by. • **n. 1** a past
period or the events in it. **2** a
person's previous experiences.
• **prep. 1** to or on the further side
of. **2** in front of or from one side
to the other of. **3** beyond the

scope or power of. • adv. going past or beyond.
▷ SYNS adj. 1 GONE, over, bygone, olden, long ago. 2 PREVIOUS, former, erstwhile, one-time, sometime.

**pasta** n. dough formed in various shapes and cooked in boiling water.

**paste** n. 1 a soft, moist substance. 2 a glue. 3 a hard glassy substance used in imitation gems. • v. coat or stick with paste.

**pastel** n. 1 a chalk-like crayon. 2 a pale shade of colour. • adj. (of a colour) pale.
▷ SYNS adj. PALE, soft, delicate, muted.

**pasteurize** (or **-ise**) v. sterilize by heating.

**pastiche** n. a work in the style of another artist.

**pastille** n. a small sweet or lozenge.

**pastime** n. a recreational activity.
▷ SYNS HOBBY, leisure activity, recreation, diversion, amusement, entertainment, distraction, relaxation.

**pastor** n. a clergyman in charge of a church or congregation.

**pastoral** adj. 1 of country life. 2 (of a farm etc.) keeping sheep and cattle. 3 of spiritual and moral guidance.

**pastrami** n. seasoned smoked beef.

**pastry** n. (pl. **-ies**) a dough made of flour, fat, and water, used for making pies etc.; an individual item of food made with this.

**pasture** n. grassy land suitable for grazing cattle. • v. put animals to graze.
▷ SYNS n. FIELD, meadow, grazing.

**pasty**[1] n. (pl. **-ies**) a small savoury pie baked without a dish.

**pasty**[2] adj. 1 of or like paste. 2 unhealthily pale.

**pat** v. (**patted**, **patting**) touch gently with the flat of the hand. • n. 1 an act of patting. 2 a small mass of a soft substance. • adj. & adv. unconvincingly quick and simple. □ off pat known by heart.

**patch** n. 1 a piece of material used to mend or strengthen. 2 a small area differing from its surroundings. 3 a plot of land. 4 inf. a period of time. • v. mend with a patch. □ patch up 1 repair. 2 settle a dispute. patchwork needlework in which small pieces of cloth are joined to make a pattern.
▷ SYNS n. patch of ground: PLOT, area, piece, tract. • v. MEND, repair, cover, fix.

**patchy** adj. (**-ier**, **-iest**) 1 existing in small isolated areas. 2 uneven in quality.

**pâté** n. a savoury paste made from meat etc.

**patella** n. the kneecap.

**patent** adj. 1 obvious. 2 made or sold under a patent. • v. obtain a patent for. • n. an official right to be the sole maker or user of an invention. □ patent leather glossy varnished leather.
■ patently adv.

**paternal** adj. of or like a father; related through the father.
■ paternally adv.

**paternity** n. fatherhood.

**path** n. 1 a way by which people pass on foot; a line along which a person or thing moves. 2 a course of action.

▷ syns **1** PATHWAY, footpath, footway, track, trail. **2** COURSE, route, circuit, track, orbit, trajectory.

**pathetic** adj. arousing pity or sadness; very inadequate. ■ **pathetically** adv.
▷ syns **1** PITIFUL, moving, touching, poignant, heart-breaking, sad, mournful. **2** LAMENTABLE, deplorable, miserable, feeble, poor, in-adequate, unsatisfactory.

**pathology** n. the study of disease. ■ **pathological** adj. **pathologist** n.

**pathos** n. a pathetic quality.

**patience** n. **1** calm endurance. **2** a card game for one player.
▷ syns **1** CALM, composure, equanimity, serenity, tranquillity, restraint, tolerance, forbearance, stoicism, fortitude. **2** PERSEVERANCE, persistence, endurance, tenacity, assiduity, staying power.

**patient** adj. showing patience. • n. a person receiving medical treatment.
▷ syns adj. UNCOMPLAINING, serene, calm, composed, tranquil, tolerant, accommodating, forbearing, stoical.

**patina** n. a sheen on a surface produced by age or use.

**patio** n. (pl. **-os**) a paved area outside a house.

**patriarch** n. the male head of a family or tribe. ■ **patriarchal** adj. **patriarchy** n.

**patricide** n. the killing by someone of their own father; someone guilty of this.

**patrimony** n. (pl. **-ies**) heritage.

**patriot** n. a person who strongly supports their country. ■ **patriotism** n.

**patriotic** adj. devoted to and vigorously supporting your country.
▷ syns NATIONALIST, nationalistic, loyal, flag-waving; derog. jingoistic.

**patrol** v. (**patrolled**, **patrolling**) walk or travel regularly through an area to see that all is well. • n. patrolling; a person or group patrolling.
▷ syns v. POLICE, guard, monitor. • n. **1** WATCH, guard, monitoring. **2** SENTRY, guard, watchman, watch.

**patron** n. **1** a person giving financial or other support to a cause. **2** a regular customer. □ **patron saint** a saint regarded as a protector. ■ **patronage** n.
▷ syns **1** SPONSOR, backer, benefactor, promoter. **2** CUSTOMER, client, shopper, regular.

**patronize** (or **-ise**) v. **1** treat someone as if they are naive or foolish. **2** be a regular customer of.
▷ syns **1** LOOK DOWN ON, condescend to, treat contemptuously. **2** FREQUENT, shop at, buy from, do business with, trade with.

**patronizing** adj. condescending or superior.
▷ syns CONDESCENDING, supercilious, superior, disdainful; inf. high and mighty.

**patter** v. make a repeated light tapping sound. • n. **1** a pattering sound. **2** fast continuous talk.

**pattern** n. **1** a decorative design. **2** a regular sequence of events. **3** a model, design, or set of instructions for making something. **4** an example to follow. ■ **patterned** adj.

▷ SYNS **1** DESIGN, decoration, motif. **2** DESIGN, model, guide, blueprint, plan, template.

**paucity** n. lack or scarcity.

**paunch** n. a large protruding stomach.

**pauper** n. a very poor person.

**pause** n. a temporary stop. • v. stop temporarily.

▷ SYNS n. BREAK, interruption, lull, respite, hiatus, gap, interval; inf. breather. • v. STOP, halt; rest, wait, hesitate.

**pave** v. cover a surface with flat stones.

**pavement** n. a raised path at the side of a road.

**pavilion** n. **1** a building on a sports ground for use by players and spectators. **2** an ornamental building.

**paw** n. a foot of an animal that has claws. • v. feel or scrape with a paw or hoof.

**pawn** n. **1** a chess piece of the smallest size and value. **2** a person used by others for their own purposes. • v. leave with a pawnbroker as security for money lent. □ **pawnbroker** a person licensed to lend money in exchange for an item left with them.

**pawpaw** n. a papaya.

**pay** v. **1** give someone money for work or goods. **2** give what is owed. **3** be profitable or worthwhile. **4** suffer as a result of your actions. **5** give attention etc. to. • n. wages. □ **payroll** a list of a company's employees and their wages. ■ **payable** adj.

▷ SYNS v. **1** REMUNERATE, reward, reimburse, recompense. **2** SPEND, expend, lay out; discharge, settle pay off, clear. • n. WAGES, salary, payment,

earnings, remuneration, fee, stipend.

**payee** n. a person to whom money is paid or due.

**payment** n. **1** the action of paying. **2** an amount paid.

▷ SYNS **1** REMITTANCE, settlement, discharge, clearance. **2** *monthly payments:* INSTALMENT, premium.

**PC** abbr. **1** police constable. **2** personal computer. **3** politically correct; political correctness.

**PDF** n. an electronic file which can be sent by any system and displayed on any computer.

**PE** abbr. physical education.

**pea** n. an edible round seed growing in pods.

**peace** n. freedom from war or disturbance.

▷ SYNS **1** PEACEFULNESS, accord, harmony, concord. **2** SERENITY, calm, rest, quiet, calmness, repose. **3** *a lasting peace:* TREATY, truce, armistice, ceasefire.

**peaceable** adj. avoiding conflict; peaceful.

▷ SYNS PEACE-LOVING, non-violent, placid, mild, good-natured, even-tempered, amiable, pacific, pacifist.

**peaceful** adj. free from war or disturbance; not involving violence. ■ **peacefully** adv.

▷ SYNS TRANQUIL, restful, quiet, calm, still, undisturbed, serene, composed, placid, untroubled.

**peacemaker** n. a person who brings about peace.

▷ SYNS ARBITRATOR, mediator, conciliator, appeaser, pacifier.

**peach** n. a round juicy fruit with a rough stone; a pinkish-yellow colour.

**peacock** n. a large colourful bird with a long fan-like tail.

**peahen** n. the female of the peacock.

**peak** n. a pointed top, esp. of a mountain; a stiff brim at the front of a cap; the point of highest value, intensity, etc. • v. reach a highest point. • adj. maximum. ■ **peaked** adj.
▷ SYNS n. **1** TOP, summit, crest, pinnacle. **2** HEIGHT, climax, culmination, zenith, acme.

**peaky** adj. looking pale and sickly.

**peal** n. the sound of ringing bells; a set of bells; a loud burst of thunder or laughter. • v. ring or sound loudly.

**peanut** n. **1** an oval edible seed that develops in a pod underground. **2** (**peanuts**) inf. a small sum of money.

**pear** n. a rounded fruit tapering towards the stalk.

**pearl** n. a round creamy-white gem formed within the shell of an oyster. ■ **pearly** adj.

**peasant** n. (esp. in the past) a poor smallholder or agricultural labourer. ■ **peasantry** n.

**peat** n. decomposed plant matter formed in damp areas.

**pebble** n. a small smooth round stone. ■ **pebbly** adj.

**pecan** n. a smooth pinkish-brown nut.

**peccadillo** n. (pl. **-os**) a small sin or fault.

**peck** v. **1** strike, bite, or pick up with the beak. **2** kiss lightly and hastily. • n. an act of pecking.

**peckish** adj. inf. hungry.

**pectin** n. a substance found in fruits which makes jam set.

**pectoral** adj. relating to the chest or breast.

**peculiar** adj. **1** strange or odd. **2** (**peculiar to**) belonging only to.
▷ SYNS STRANGE, odd, unusual, funny, curious, bizarre, weird, eccentric, queer, abnormal, unconventional, outlandish.

**peculiarity** n. an unusual or distinctive feature or habit.
▷ SYNS CHARACTERISTIC, feature, quality, property, trait, attribute.

**pedal** n. a lever operated by the foot. • v. (**pedalled, pedalling**; US **pedaled**) ride a bicycle by using its pedals.

**pedantic** adj. excessively concerned with minor details or rules. ■ **pedant** n. **pedantry** n.

**peddle** v. sell goods by going from house to house.

**peddler** = PEDLAR.

**pedestal** n. a base supporting a column or statue etc.
▷ SYNS BASE, support, stand, pillar, plinth.

**pedestrian** n. a person walking. • adj. dull.
▷ SYNS adj. DULL, unimaginative, uninspired, plodding, flat, mundane, humdrum, run-of-the-mill, mediocre.

**pediatrics** US sp. of PAEDIATRICS.

**pedicure** n. cosmetic treatment of the feet and toenails.

**pedigree** n. recorded ancestry; a line of descent. • adj. (of an animal) descended from a known line of animals of the same breed.

**pedlar** (or **peddler**) n. a person who peddles goods; a seller of illegal drugs.

**peek** v. peep or glance. • n. a peep.

**peel** n. the skin or rind of a fruit or vegetable. • v. remove the peel from; strip off an outer covering; (of skin etc.) come off in flakes or layers.

**peep** v. look quickly or surreptitiously; show slightly. • n. a brief or surreptitious look. □ peephole a small hole in a door through which callers can be seen.

**peer**[1] v. look with difficulty or concentration.

**peer**[2] n. 1 a member of the nobility. 2 a person who is your equal in age, social status, etc.
▷ SYNS 1 NOBLE, nobleman, noblewoman, aristocrat, lord, lady. 2 EQUAL, coequal, fellow.

**peerage** n. peers as a group; the rank of peer or peeress.

**peeress** n. a female peer; a peer's wife.

**peerless** adj. better than all others.
▷ SYNS INCOMPARABLE, matchless, unrivalled, unsurpassed, unparalleled, superlative, second to none.

**peevish** adj. irritable.

**peg** n. 1 a pin or bolt used as a fastening or to hang things on. 2 a clip for holding clothes on a line. • v. (pegged, pegging) 1 fix or mark with pegs. 2 fix a price etc. at a particular level. □ off the peg (of clothes) ready-made.

**pejorative** adj. expressing disapproval.

**Pekinese** n. a small dog with long hair and a snub nose.

**pelican** n. a waterbird with a large pouch in its bill. □ pelican crossing a pedestrian crossing with lights operated by the pedestrians.

**pellet** n. a small round mass of a substance; a piece of small shot.

**pell-mell** adj. & adv. in a confused or rushed way.

**pellucid** adj. very clear.

**pelmet** n. a border of cloth or wood above a window.

**pelt** v. hurl missiles at. • n. an animal skin. □ at full pelt as fast as possible.

**pelvis** n. the bony frame at the base of the spine. ■ pelvic adj.

**pen** n. 1 a device for writing with ink. 2 a small enclosure for farm animals. • v. (penned, penning) 1 write or compose. 2 shut in a restricted space. □ penfriend a person with whom one forms a friendship by exchanging letters. pen name a writer's pseudonym.

**penal** adj. of or involving punishment.

**penalize** (or -ise) v. inflict a penalty on; put at a disadvantage.
▷ SYNS PUNISH, discipline, fine.

**penalty** n. (pl. -ies) a punishment for breaking a law, rule, etc.
▷ SYNS PUNISHMENT, fine, forfeit.

**penance** n. an act done as a punishment for wrongdoing.
▷ SYNS ATONEMENT, reparation, amends.

**pence** pl. of PENNY.

**penchant** n. a strong liking.
▷ SYNS LIKING, fondness, preference, taste, partiality, predilection.

**pencil** n. an instrument containing graphite, used for drawing or writing.
• v. (pencilled, pencilling; US penciled) write or draw with a pencil.

**pendant** n. an ornament hung from a chain round the neck. • adj. (also **pendent**) hanging.

**pending** adj. waiting to be decided or settled. • prep. while waiting for.

**pendulous** adj. hanging loosely.

**pendulum** n. a weight hung from a fixed point and swinging freely, used to regulate the mechanism of a clock.

**penetrate** v. 1 force a way into or through. 2 understand something complex. 3 (**penetrating**) (of a sound) clearly heard above other sounds. ■ penetration n. ▷ SYNS 1 PIERCE, enter, perforate, stab, gore. 2 UNDERSTAND, comprehend, fathom, grasp.

**penguin** n. a flightless Antarctic seabird.

**penicillin** n. an antibiotic.

**peninsula** n. a piece of land almost surrounded by water. ■ peninsular adj.

**penis** n. the male organ used for urinating and having sex.

**penitent** adj. feeling or showing regret for having done wrong. • n. a penitent person. ■ penitence n. penitential adj. ▷ SYNS adj. REPENTANT, contrite, regretful, remorseful, sorry, apologetic, rueful, ashamed.

**penitentiary** n. (pl. **-ies**) US a prison.

**pennant** n. a long tapering flag.

**penniless** adj. having no money. ▷ SYNS IMPECUNIOUS, penurious, impoverished, indigent, poor, poverty-stricken, destitute.

**penny** n. (pl. **pennies** for separate coins, **pence** for a sum of money) a British bronze coin worth one hundredth of £1; a former coin worth one twelfth of a shilling. □ penny-pinching stingy.

**pension** n. an income paid by the state, an ex-employer, or a private fund to a person who is retired, disabled, etc. • v. (**pension off**) dismiss with a pension. ■ pensioner n.

**pensive** adj. deep in thought. ▷ SYNS THOUGHTFUL, reflective, contemplative, meditative, ruminative.

**pentagon** n. a geometric figure with five sides.

**pentagram** n. a five-pointed star.

**pentathlon** n. an athletic event involving five activities.

**Pentecost** n. Whit Sunday.

**penthouse** n. a flat on the top floor of a tall building.

**pent-up** adj. not expressed or released.

**penultimate** adj. last but one.

**penumbra** n. the partially shaded outer part of a shadow.

**penury** n. extreme poverty. ■ penurious adj. ▷ SYNS POVERTY, impoverishment, destitution.

**people** pl.n. 1 human beings. 2 the ordinary citizens of a country. 3 (pl. **peoples**) the members of a particular nation or ethnic group. • v. populate or fill with people. ▷ SYNS pl.n. 1 HUMAN BEINGS, humans, mortals, individuals. 2 CITIZENS, subjects, inhabitants, population, populace. 3 ETHNIC GROUP, race, tribe.

**pep** inf. n. liveliness. • v. (**pepped**, **pepping**) (**pep up**) make livelier. □ pep talk a talk intended to encourage confidence and effort.

**pepper** n. 1 a hot-tasting seasoning made from peppercorns. 2 a capsicum. • v. 1 sprinkle with pepper. 2 scatter on or over. 3 hit repeatedly with small missiles. ■ **peppery** adj.

**peppercorn** n. a dried berry, ground to make pepper.

**peppermint** n. 1 a plant producing an aromatic oil. 2 a sweet flavoured with this.

**pepperoni** n. beef and pork sausage seasoned with pepper.

**peptic** adj. of digestion.

**per** prep. 1 for each. 2 in accordance with.

**perambulate** v. formal walk through or round.

**per annum** adv. for each year.

**per capita** adv. & adj. for each person.

**perceive** v. 1 become aware of through the senses. 2 understand or interpret in a particular way.
▷ SYNS 1 SEE, discern, observe, notice, spot, catch sight of, glimpse, make out. 2 REGARD, look on, view, consider, think of, judge.

**per cent** adv. in or for every hundred.

**percentage** n. 1 a rate or amount per hundred. 2 a proportion or share.

**perceptible** adj. able to be perceived. ■ **perceptibly** adv.

**perception** n. perceiving; the ability to perceive.
▷ SYNS 1 DISCERNMENT, appreciation, awareness, recognition, consciousness, knowledge, grasp, understanding, comprehension, apprehension, notion, conception, idea, sense. 2 PERSPICACITY, discernment, understanding, discrimination, insight.

**perceptive** adj. having or showing sensitive insight.
▷ SYNS INSIGHTFUL, discerning, sensitive, intuitive, penetrating, perspicacious, astute, shrewd.

**perch**¹ n. a branch or bar on which a bird rests or roosts; a high seat. • v. sit or rest somewhere; balance something on a narrow support.

**perch**² n. (pl. **perch**) an edible freshwater fish.

**percolate** v. filter, esp. through small holes; prepare in a percolator.

**percolator** n. a coffee-making pot in which boiling water is circulated through ground coffee in a perforated drum.

**percussion** n. instruments played by being struck or shaken.

**peregrinations** pl.n. old use travels.

**peregrine** n. a falcon.

**peremptory** adj. imperious; insisting on obedience.
▷ SYNS IMPERIOUS, high-handed, overbearing, autocratic, dictatorial, domineering.

**perennial** adj. lasting a long or infinite time; (of plants) living for several years. • n. a perennial plant. ■ **perennially** adv.

**perestroika** n. (in the former USSR) reform of the economic and political system.

**perfect** adj. 1 without faults or defects. 2 complete or total: a perfect stranger. • v. make

perfect. ■ **perfection** n.
**perfectly** adv.
▷ SYNS **adj. 1** FLAWLESS, faultless,
impeccable, immaculate,
pristine; exemplary, ideal.
**2** EXACT, precise, accurate,
faithful.

**perfectionist** n. a person who
seeks perfection.

**perfidious** adj. treacherous or
disloyal. ■ **perfidy** n.

**perforate** v. pierce and make
holes in. ■ **perforation** n.

**perform** v. **1** carry out a task
etc. **2** function. **3** present
entertainment to an audience.
■ **performance** n.
▷ SYNS **1** DO, carry out, execute,
discharge, complete.
**2** FUNCTION, work, operate,
run, go. **3** ACT, play, appear.

**performer** n. a person who
performs.
▷ SYNS ACTOR/ACTRESS, player,
entertainer, artist, artiste,
musician, singer, dancer.

**perfume** n. **1** a scented liquid
for applying to the body. **2** a
pleasant smell. • v. give a
pleasant smell to.
▷ SYNS **n.** SCENT, fragrance,
cologne; aroma, smell, bouquet.

**perfunctory** adj. done without
thought, effort, or enthusiasm.
▷ SYNS CURSORY, superficial, desultory, brief, hasty, hurried, rapid,
casual.

**pergola** n. an arched structure
covered in climbing plants.

**perhaps** adv. possibly.

**peril** n. serious danger.
▷ SYNS DANGER, jeopardy, risk,
hazard, menace, threat.

**perilous** adj. full of danger or
risk.
▷ SYNS DANGEROUS, hazardous,
risky, precarious.

**perimeter** n. the boundary or
outer edge of an area.
▷ SYNS BOUNDARY, border, limits,
edge, margin, periphery.

**period** n. **1** a length or portion of
time; a lesson in a school. **2** an
occurrence of menstruation. **3** a
full stop. • adj. (of dress or furniture) belonging to a past age.
▷ SYNS **n.** TIME, spell, interval,
term, stretch, span, age, era,
epoch, aeon.

**periodic** adj. happening at
intervals.
▷ SYNS PERIODICAL, recurrent,
recurring, repeated, regular;
intermittent, occasional,
infrequent, sporadic.

**periodical** adj. periodic.
• n. a magazine etc. published
at regular intervals.
■ **periodically** adv.

**peripatetic** adj. going from
place to place.

**peripheral** adj. **1** on the outer
limits of something. **2** of
secondary importance.
▷ SYNS **1** OUTER, outlying,
surrounding. **2** SECONDARY,
subsidiary, lesser, minor,
unimportant.

**periphery** n. (pl. -ies) the outer
limits of an area; the fringes of
a subject.

**periscope** n. a tube attached to
a set of mirrors, enabling you to
see things above them and
otherwise out of sight.

**perish** v. **1** die. **2** be destroyed.
**3** rot.

**perishable** adj. liable to decay
or go bad in a short time.

**peritoneum** n. (pl. -neums
or -nea) the membrane lining
the abdominal cavity.

**peritonitis** n. inflammation of
the peritoneum.

**perjure** v. (**perjure yourself**) lie under oath.

**perjury** n. the crime of lying under oath.

**perk** n. inf. a benefit to which an employee is entitled. • v. (**perk up**) make or become more cheerful or lively.

**perky** adj. (**-ier, -iest**) lively and cheerful.

**perm** n. a treatment giving hair a long-lasting curly style. • v. treat hair with a perm.

**permafrost** n. permanently frozen subsoil in arctic regions.

**permanent** adj. lasting indefinitely. ■ permanence n.
▷ SYNS LASTING, enduring, continuing, perpetual, everlasting, eternal, abiding, constant, irreparable, irreversible, lifelong, indissoluble, indelible.

**permeable** adj. allowing liquid or gases to pass through.

**permeate** v. spread throughout.
▷ SYNS SPREAD THROUGH, pervade, saturate, fill, perfuse, steep, charge.

**permissible** adj. allowable.
▷ SYNS PERMITTED, allowable, acceptable, authorized, sanctioned, legal, lawful, legitimate.

**permission** n. consent or authorization.
▷ SYNS AUTHORIZATION, sanction, leave, licence, dispensation, consent, assent, go-ahead, agreement, approval, approbation.

**permissive** adj. tolerant, esp. in social and sexual matters.
▷ SYNS LIBERAL, tolerant, broad-minded, open-minded, easy-going, indulgent, lenient.

**permit** v. **1** allow to do something. **2** make possible. • n. an official document giving permission.
▷ SYNS v. ALLOW, let, authorize, sanction, grant, license, consent to, assent to, agree to; tolerate, stand for.

**permutation** n. each of several possible arrangements of a number of things.

**pernicious** adj. harmful.

**pernickety** adj. inf. fussy or over-fastidious.

**peroxide** n. a chemical used as a bleach or disinfectant.

**perpendicular** adj. at an angle of 90° to a line or surface. • n. a perpendicular line.

**perpetrate** v. carry out a bad or illegal action. ■ perpetrator n.

**perpetual** adj. **1** never ending or changing. **2** very frequent. ■ perpetually adv.
▷ SYNS **1** EVERLASTING, eternal, never-ending, unending, endless, undying, permanent, lasting, abiding, enduring. **2** INCESSANT, unceasing, ceaseless, non-stop, continuous, unbroken, unremitting, interminable.

**perpetuate** v. cause to continue indefinitely.
▷ SYNS PRESERVE, conserve, sustain, maintain, continue.

**perpetuity** n. the state of lasting forever.

**perplex** v. puzzle or baffle. ■ perplexity n.
▷ SYNS PUZZLE, baffle, mystify, stump, bewilder, confuse, nonplus, disconcert.

**perquisite** n. formal a special privilege or benefit.

**per se** adv. intrinsically.

**persecute** v. treat badly over a long period; harass.
■ **persecution** n. **persecutor** n.
▷ SYNS OPPRESS, tyrannize, abuse, mistreat, maltreat, ill-treat, torment, victimize.

**persevere** v. continue in spite of difficulties. ■ **perseverance** n.
▷ SYNS PERSIST, keep on, keep going, continue, carry on, press on.

**persist** v. continue to do something despite difficulty or opposition; continue to exist.
■ **persistence** n.

**persistent** adj. **1** continuing to do something in spite of difficulty or opposition. **2** continuing or recurring for a long time.
▷ SYNS **1** TENACIOUS, determined, persevering, resolute, dogged, indefatigable, unflagging, stubborn, obstinate. **2** CONSTANT, continual, continuous, interminable, incessant, unceasing, relentless.

**person** n. **1** an individual human being. **2** a person's body. **3** Grammar one of the three classes of personal pronouns and verb forms, referring to the speaker, the person spoken to, or a third party. □ **in person** physically present.
▷ SYNS INDIVIDUAL, human (being), creature, living soul, mortal.

**persona** n. (pl. **-nas** or **-nae**) the aspect of someone's character that is presented to others.

**personable** adj. attractive in appearance or manner.
▷ SYNS PLEASANT, agreeable, amiable, affable, likeable, charming; attractive, good-looking.

**personage** n. a person of importance or high status.

**personal** adj. **1** belonging to, affecting, or done by a particular person. **2** concerning a person's private life. **3** of a person's body. ■ **personally** adv.
▷ SYNS **1** *a personal style:* PERSONALIZED, individual, idiosyncratic, characteristic, unique. **2** *personal reasons:* PRIVATE, confidential, secret.

**personality** n. **1** the qualities that form a person's character. **2** lively or interesting personal qualities. **3** a celebrity.
▷ SYNS **1** NATURE, disposition, character, temperament, make-up. **2** CELEBRITY, household name, star, luminary, leading light.

**personalize** (or **-ise**) v. **1** design to suit or identify as belonging to a particular individual. **2** cause a discussion etc. to be concerned with personalities rather than abstract topics.

**personification** n. a person or thing embodying a quality or concept.
▷ SYNS EMBODIMENT, incarnation, epitome, essence, quintessence.

**personify** v. (**personified**, **personifying**) represent in human form or as having human characteristics; be an example of a particular quality etc.

**personnel** n. employees or staff.
▷ SYNS STAFF, employees, workers, workforce, manpower.

**perspective** n. **1** the art of drawing so as to give an effect of solidity and relative distance. **2** a particular point of view. **3** understanding of the relative importance of things.

▷ SYNS OUTLOOK, view, viewpoint, point of view, standpoint, stance, angle, slant, attitude.

**perspex** n. trademark a tough transparent plastic.

**perspicacious** adj. showing great insight. ■ perspicacity n.

**perspire** v. sweat.
■ perspiration n.

**persuade** v. use reasoning or argument to make someone believe or do something.
▷ SYNS PREVAIL ON, induce, convince, win over, talk into, bring round, influence, sway, inveigle, cajole, wheedle.

**persuasion** n. 1 persuading. 2 a belief or set of beliefs.

**persuasive** adj. able to persuade people.
▷ SYNS CONVINCING, cogent, compelling, forceful, weighty, telling.

**pert** adj. attractively lively or cheeky.

**pertain** v. be relevant or related.

**pertinacious** adj. persistent.
■ pertinacity n.

**pertinent** adj. relevant.
■ pertinence n.

**perturb** v. make anxious or uneasy.
▷ SYNS DISTURB, worry, trouble, upset, disquiet, disconcert, unsettle.

**peruse** v. read carefully.
■ perusal n.

**pervade** v. spread throughout.
▷ SYNS PERMEATE, spread through, fill, suffuse, perfuse, infuse.

**pervasive** adj. spreading widely through an area or group of people.
▷ SYNS PREVALENT, extensive, ubiquitous, omnipresent, rife, widespread.

**perverse** adj. deliberately behaving unreasonably or unacceptably; contrary to reason or expectation.
■ perversity n.
▷ SYNS AWKWARD, contrary, uncooperative, unhelpful, obstructive, disobliging, recalcitrant, stubborn, obstinate.

**pervert** v. 1 distort the form or meaning of. 2 corrupt or lead astray. • n. a person whose sexual behaviour is abnormal or unacceptable. ■ perversion n.
▷ SYNS v. 1 DISTORT, twist, bend, abuse, misapply, falsify. 2 CORRUPT, lead astray, warp; deprave, debase.

**perverted** adj. sexually abnormal or unacceptable.
▷ SYNS DEPRAVED, corrupt, deviant, abnormal, warped, twisted, unhealthy, immoral, evil; inf. sick.

**pervious** adj. permeable; penetrable.

**pessimism** n. lack of hope or confidence in the future.
■ pessimist n.

**pessimistic** adj. lacking hope or confidence in the future.
▷ SYNS GLOOMY, negative, cynical, defeatist, fatalistic, bleak, despairing.

**pest** n. 1 an insect or animal that attacks crops etc. 2 inf. an annoying person or thing.

**pester** v. annoy with persistent requests or questions.
▷ SYNS BADGER, hound, harass, plague, annoy, bother, persecute; inf. hassle.

**pesticide** n. a substance used to destroy harmful insects etc.

**pestilence** n. a deadly epidemic disease.

**pestle** n. a club-shaped instrument for grinding things to powder.

**pesto** n. a sauce of basil, olive oil, Parmesan cheese, and pine nuts.

**pet** n. **1** a tame animal kept for company and pleasure. **2** a favourite. • adj. favourite. • v. (**petted, petting**) stroke or pat; kiss and caress.
▷ SYNS n. FAVOURITE, darling, idol, apple of your eye; inf. blue-eyed boy/girl. • v. STROKE, caress, fondle, pat.

**petal** n. one of the coloured outer parts of a flower head.

**peter** v. gradually come to an end.
▷ SYNS (**peter out**) FADE, wane, ebb, diminish, taper off, die out, fizzle out.

**petite** adj. small and dainty.

**petition** n. a formal written request signed by many people. • v. present a petition to.

**petrel** n. a seabird.

**petrify** v. **1** change into a stony mass. **2** paralyse with fear.
▷ SYNS TERRIFY, frighten, horrify, scare to death.

**petrochemical** n. a chemical obtained from petroleum or natural gas. • adj. relating to petroleum or natural gas.

**petrol** n. refined petroleum used as fuel in vehicles.

**petroleum** n. an oil found in layers of rock and refined to produce fuels.

**petticoat** n. a woman's undergarment in the form of a skirt.

**pettifogging** adj. petty or trivial.

**petty** adj. (**-ier, -iest**) **1** unimportant; trivial.

**2** small-minded. **3** minor.
□ **petty cash** money kept in an office for small payments.
■ pettiness n.

**petulant** adj. sulky or irritable.
■ petulance n.
▷ SYNS QUERULOUS, peevish, fretful, cross, irritable, fractious, grumpy, sulky.

**petunia** n. a plant with white, purple, or red funnel-shaped flowers.

**pew** n. a long bench-like seat in a church.

**pewter** n. a grey alloy of tin with copper and antimony.

**pH** n. a measure of acidity or alkalinity.

**phallus** n. (pl. **-luses** or **-li**) a penis. ■ phallic adj.

**phantom** n. a ghost.
▷ SYNS GHOST, apparition, spectre, wraith; inf. spook.

**pharaoh** n. a ruler in ancient Egypt.

**pharmaceutical** adj. relating to medicinal drugs.

**pharmacist** n. a person skilled in pharmacy.

**pharmacology** n. the study of the uses and effects of drugs.

**pharmacy** n. (pl. **-ies**) **1** a place where medicinal drugs are prepared or sold. **2** the preparation and dispensing of these drugs.

**pharynx** n. the cavity at the back of the nose and throat.

**phase** n. a distinct period in a process of change or development. • v. **1** carry something out in stages. **2** (**phase in or out**) bring gradually into or out of use.

**PhD** abbr. Doctor of Philosophy.

**pheasant** n. a large, long-tailed game bird.

**phenomenal** adj. remarkable or outstanding. ■ **phenomenally** adv.
▷ SYNS REMARKABLE, exceptional, extraordinary, amazing, astonishing, astounding, sensational, outstanding, unprecedented.

**phenomenon** n. **1** a fact or situation observed to exist or happen. **2** a remarkable person or thing.
▷ SYNS **1** OCCURRENCE, event, happening, fact, experience, incident. **2** MARVEL, sensation, wonder, prodigy.

**pheromone** n. a chemical substance released by an animal and causing a response in others of its species.

**phial** n. a small bottle.

**philanderer** n. a man who has many casual sexual relationships. ■ **philandering** n. & adj.
▷ SYNS WOMANIZER, ladies' man, flirt, Lothario, Casanova, Don Juan.

**philanthropic** adj. generous and benevolent.
▷ SYNS CHARITABLE, generous, public-spirited, benevolent, magnanimous, munificent, bountiful, open-handed.

**philanthropy** n. the practice of helping people in need. ■ **philanthropist** n.

**philately** n. stamp collecting. ■ **philatelist** n.

**philistine** n. an uncultured person.

**philosophical** adj. **1** of philosophy. **2** bearing misfortune calmly. ■ **philosophically** adv.

**philosophy** n. **1** the study of the fundamental nature of knowledge, reality, and existence. **2** a set or system of beliefs. ■ **philosopher** n.
▷ SYNS **1** REASONING, thinking, thought. **2** BELIEFS, credo, convictions, ideology, ideas, doctrine, principles.

**phlegm** n. mucus in the nose and throat.

**phlegmatic** adj. not excitable or emotional.
▷ SYNS CALM, composed, serene, tranquil, placid, impassive, stolid, imperturbable.

**phobia** n. an extreme or irrational fear. ■ **phobic** adj. & n.
▷ SYNS FEAR, dread, horror, terror, aversion, antipathy, revulsion.

**phoenix** n. a mythical bird said to burn itself and be born again from its ashes.

**phone** n. a telephone. • v. make a telephone call. □ **phonecard** a prepaid card allowing calls to be made on a public telephone. **phone-in** a broadcast during which listeners or viewers join in by telephone.

**phonetic** adj. of or representing speech sounds. • n. (**phonetics**) the study of speech sounds. ■ **phonetically** adv.

**phoney** (or **phony**) inf. adj. not genuine. • n. a phoney person or thing.

**phosphate** n. a compound of phosphorous.

**phosphorescent** adj. luminous. ■ **phosphorescence** n.

**phosphorus** n. a non-metallic element which glows in the dark.

**photo** n. (pl. **-os**) a photograph. □ **photo finish** a finish of a race so close that the winner has to

be decided from a photograph.
**photofit** a picture of a person
made up of separate
photographs of facial features.
**photogenic** looking attractive in
photographs. **photosensitive**
responding to light.

**photocopy** n. (pl. **-ies**) a
photographic copy of a
document. • v. (**-copied,**
**-copying**) make a photocopy of.
■ **photocopier** n.

**photograph** n. a picture made
with a camera. • v. take a
photograph of. ■ **photographer**
n. **photographic** adj.
**photography** n.
▷ SYNS n. PHOTO, snap, snapshot,
picture, shot, print, slide, transparency.

**photostat** n. trademark a
photocopier; a photocopy.

**photosynthesis** n. the process
by which green plants use
sunlight to convert carbon
dioxide and water into
nutrients. ■ **photosynthesize** v.

**phrase** n. **1** a group of words
forming a unit. **2** a unit in a
melody. • v. express in words.
■ **phrasal** adj.
▷ SYNS n. EXPRESSION, term, idiom,
saying.

**phraseology** n. (pl. **-ies**) a form
of words used to express
something.

**physical** adj. **1** of the body. **2** of
things that can be seen, heard,
or touched. **3** of physics or the
operation of natural forces.
□ **physical education** instruction in physical exercise
and games. ■ **physically** adv.
▷ SYNS **1** BODILY, corporeal,
corporal, carnal, fleshly.
**2** MATERIAL, concrete, tangible,
palpable, visible, real.

**physician** n. a person qualified
to practise medicine.
▷ SYNS DOCTOR, GP, specialist,
consultant.

**physics** n. the study of the
nature and properties of matter
and energy. ■ **physicist** n.

**physiognomy** n. (pl. **-ies**) the
features of a person's face.

**physiology** n. the study of the
bodily functions of living
organisms. ■ **physiological** adj.
**physiologist** n.

**physiotherapy** n. treatment
of an injury etc. by massage and
exercise. ■ **physiotherapist** n.

**physique** n. the shape and size
of a person's body.
▷ SYNS BODY, build, shape, frame,
figure.

**pi** n. the ratio of a circle's
circumference to its diameter
(about 3.14).

**pianissimo** adv. Music very
softly.

**piano** n. (pl. **-os**) a musical
instrument with strings struck
by hammers when keys are
pressed. • adv. Music softly.
■ **pianist** n.

**pianoforte** n. formal a piano.

**piazza** n. a public square or
marketplace.

**picador** n. a mounted bullfighter with a lance.

**picaresque** adj. (of fiction)
recounting the adventures of a
roguish hero.

**piccalilli** n. a pickle of chopped
vegetables and hot spices.

**piccolo** n. (pl. **-os**) a small flute.

**pick** v. **1** take hold of and remove
from its place. **2** select. • n. **1** an
act of selecting. **2** the best of a
group. **3** a pickaxe. □ **pickaxe** a
tool with a pointed iron bar at

right angles to its handle, for breaking ground etc. **pick on** single out for unfair treatment. **pickpocket** a person who steals from people's pockets. **pickup 1** a small truck with low sides. **2** an act of picking up. **3** a device converting sound vibrations into electrical signals for amplification. **pick up 1** go to collect. **2** improve or increase. **3** casually become acquainted with.
▷ SYNS v. **1** LIFT, take, scoop, gather. **2** SELECT, choose, single out, opt for, plump for, decide on, settle on, fix on. • n. BEST, choice, prime, cream, flower.

**picket** n. **1** people stationed outside a workplace to dissuade others from entering during a strike. **2** a pointed stake set in the ground. • v. (**picketed**, **picketing**) form a picket outside a workplace.

**pickings** pl.n. profits or gains.

**pickle** n. **1** vegetables preserved in vinegar or brine. **2** inf. a difficult situation. • v. preserve in vinegar or brine.

**picnic** n. an informal outdoor meal. • v. (**picnicked**, **picnicking**) have a picnic.
■ **picnicker** n.

**pictograph** n. a pictorial symbol used as a form of writing.

**pictorial** adj. having to do with or expressed in pictures.

**picture** n. a painting, drawing, or photograph; a mental image; the cinema. • v. represent in a picture; imagine.
▷ SYNS n. PAINTING, drawing, sketch, watercolour, print, canvas, portrait, illustration, likeness. • v. **1** IMAGINE, call to

mind, visualize, see. **2** PAINT, draw, depict, portray, illustrate.

**picturesque** adj. attractive in a quaint or charming way.
▷ SYNS BEAUTIFUL, pretty, lovely, attractive, scenic, charming, quaint, pleasing, delightful.

**pidgin** n. a simplified form of a language with elements taken from local language.

**pie** n. a baked dish of ingredients topped with pastry. □ **pie chart** a diagram representing quantities as sections of a circle.

**piebald** adj. (of a horse) having irregular patches of white and black.

**piece** n. **1** a portion or part **2** an item in a set. **3** a musical, literary, or artistic work. **4** a small object used in board games. □ **piecemeal** done in a gradual and inconsistent way. **piece together** assemble from individual parts. **piecework** work paid for according to the amount produced.
▷ SYNS PART, bit, section, segment, lump, hunk, wedge; fragment, shard, shred; share, slice, portion, quota, percentage.

**pied** adj. having two or more different colours.

**pied-à-terre** n. (pl. **pieds-à-terre**) a small house for occasional use.

**pier** n. **1** a structure built out into the sea, used as a landing stage or a promenade. **2** a pillar supporting an arch or bridge.
▷ SYNS JETTY, quay, wharf, dock, landing stage.

**pierce** v. **1** make a hole in something with a sharp object. **2** force or cut a way through.
▷ SYNS PENETRATE, puncture, perforate, prick, stab, spike.

**piercing** adj. very sharp, cold, or high-pitched.
▷ SYNS **1** SHRILL, ear-splitting, high-pitched, loud. **2** BITTER, biting, cutting, raw, cold, freezing, glacial, arctic. **3** *his piercing gaze:* SEARCHING, probing, penetrating, shrewd, sharp, keen.

**piety** n. being religious or reverent.

**pig** n. **1** an animal with a short, curly tail and a flat snout. **2** inf. a greedy or unpleasant person. □ **pig-headed** obstinate. **pigsty** an enclosure for pigs. **pigtail** a length of hair worn in a plait at the back or on each side of the head. ■ **piglet** n.
▷ SYNS HOG, boar, sow, porker, swine, piglet.

**pigeon** n. a bird of the dove family.

**pigeonhole** n. a small compartment where letters etc. may be left. • v. place in a particular category.

**piggy** adj. like a pig. □ **piggyback** a ride on someone's back and shoulders. **piggy bank** a money box shaped like a pig.

**pigment** n. colouring matter. ■ **pigmentation** n.

**pigmy** = PYGMY.

**pike** n. **1** a spear with a long wooden shaft. **2** (pl. **pike**) a large voracious freshwater fish.

**pilaster** n. a rectangular column.

**pilchard** n. a small sea fish.

**pile** n. **1** a number of things lying one on top of another. **2** inf. a large amount. **3** a heavy post driven into the ground to support foundations. **4** the surface of a carpet or fabric with many small projecting threads. **5** (**piles**) haemorrhoids. • v. **1** place in a pile. **2** (**pile up**) accumulate.
▷ SYNS n. HEAP, stack, mound, mass, collection, accumulation, stockpile, hoard. • v. **1** HEAP, stack. **2** (**pile up**) ACCUMULATE, grow, mount up, escalate, increase, accrue, build up.

**pile-up** n. a collision of several vehicles.
▷ SYNS CRASH, collision, smash, accident.

**pilfer** v. steal small items of little value.

**pilgrim** n. a person who travels to a sacred place for religious reasons. ■ **pilgrimage** n.

**pill** n. a small piece of solid medicine for swallowing whole; a contraceptive pill. □ **pillbox 1** a small round hat. **2** a small, partly underground concrete fort.
▷ SYNS TABLET, capsule, lozenge.

**pillage** n. & v. plunder.

**pillar** n. a vertical structure used as a support for a building. □ **pillar box** a postbox.

**pillion** n. a passenger seat behind a motorcyclist.

**pillory** n. (pl. **-ies**) hist. a wooden frame with holes for the head and hands, in which offenders were locked as a punishment. • v. (**pilloried**, **pillorying**) ridicule publicly.

**pillow** n. a cushion for supporting the head in bed.

**pilot** n. **1** a person who flies an aircraft; a person qualified to steer ships into or out of a harbour. **2** something done or produced as a test or experiment. • v. **1** act as pilot of an aircraft or ship. **2** test a project etc. □ **pilot light** a small

burning jet of gas, used to fire a boiler.
▷ SYNS n. **1** AIRMAN/AIRWOMAN, aviator, flyer. **2** NAVIGATOR, steersman, helmsman. • v. FLY, drive, navigate, steer, manoeuvre.

**pimiento** n. a sweet pepper.

**pimp** n. a man who controls prostitutes and takes a percentage of their earnings.

**pimple** n. a small inflamed spot on the skin. ■ **pimply** adj.
▷ SYNS SPOT, pustule; inf. zit.

**PIN** abbr. personal identification number.

**pin** n. **1** a thin pointed piece of metal with a round head, used as a fastener. **2** a short metal rod or peg. • v. **1** fasten or attach with pins. **2** hold someone so they are unable to move. **3** (**pin down**) force to be specific.
□ **pinball** a game in which small balls are propelled across a sloping board to strike targets. **pins and needles** a tingling sensation. **pinstripe** a very narrow pale stripe in dark cloth. **pin-up** a poster of an attractive person.
▷ SYNS v. **1** ATTACH, fasten, fix, join, nail. **2** PINION, hold, restrain.

**pinafore** n. **1** an apron. **2** a sleeveless dress worn over a blouse or jumper.

**pince-nez** n. a pair of glasses that clip on to the nose.

**pincer** n. **1** (**pincers**) a metal tool with blunt jaws for gripping things. **2** a front claw of a lobster etc.

**pinch** v. **1** squeeze tightly between your finger and thumb. **2** inf. steal. • n. **1** an act of pinching. **2** a small amount.
□ **feel the pinch** experience financial hardship.

**pine** v. **1** become weak from grief etc. **2** miss someone intensely. • n. an evergreen tree with needle-shaped leaves.

**pineapple** n. a large juicy tropical fruit.

**ping** n. & v. (make) a short sharp ringing sound. □ **ping-pong** table tennis.

**pinion** n. **1** a bird's wing. **2** a small cogwheel. • v. tie or hold someone's arms or legs.

**pink** adj. pale red. • n. **1** a pink colour. **2** a garden plant with fragrant flowers. **3** (**the pink**) inf. the best condition. • v. cut a zigzag edge on fabric.

**pinnacle** n. a high pointed rock; a small ornamental turret; the most successful moment.
▷ SYNS PEAK, height, culmination, high point, acme, zenith, climax, summit, apex, apogee.

**pinpoint** v. locate exactly.
▷ SYNS IDENTIFY, determine, discover, distinguish, locate, home in on, put your finger on.

**pint** n. a measure for liquids, one-eighth of a gallon (0.568 litre).

**pioneer** n. a person who is one of the first to explore a new region or subject. • v. be the first to explore, use, or develop.
▷ SYNS n. **1** SETTLER, colonist, explorer. **2** DEVELOPER, innovator, groundbreaker, trailblazer. • v. DEVELOP, introduce, launch, initiate, institute, originate, create, break new ground.

**pious** adj. devoutly religious; making a hypocritical display of virtue.
▷ SYNS **1** RELIGIOUS, holy, godly, churchgoing, devout, reverent, God-fearing, righteous.
**2** SANCTIMONIOUS, hypocritical,

self-righteous, holier-than-thou, goody-goody.

**pip** n. **1** a small seed in fruit. **2** a short high-pitched sound.
• v. (**pipped**, **pipping**) inf. narrowly defeat.

**pipe** n. **1** a tube through which something can flow. **2** a narrow tube with a bowl at one end for smoking tobacco. **3** a wind instrument. **4** (**pipes**) bagpipes.
• v. **1** convey liquid through a pipe. **2** play music on a pipe. **3** utter in a shrill voice. ◻ **pipe dream** an unrealistic hope or scheme. **piping hot** very hot.
▷ SYNS n. **1** TUBE, cylinder, conduit, main, duct, channel, pipeline, drainpipe.

**pipeline** n. a long pipe for conveying petroleum etc. over a distance.

**pipette** n. a thin tube for transferring or measuring small amounts of liquid.

**piquant** adj. pleasantly sharp in taste or smell. ▪ **piquancy** n.
▷ SYNS SPICY, peppery, tangy, tasty, savoury, sharp.

**pique** n. a feeling of hurt pride.
• v. **1** hurt the pride of. **2** stimulate curiosity etc.

**piranha** n. a fierce tropical freshwater fish.

**pirate** n. a person who attacks and robs ships at sea. • v. reproduce a film etc. for profit without permission. ▪ **piracy** n.

**pirouette** v. & n. (perform) a spin on one leg in ballet.

**pistachio** n. (pl. **-os**) a type of nut.

**piste** n. a ski run.

**pistil** n. the seed-producing part of a flower.

**pistol** n. a small gun.

**piston** n. a sliding disc or cylinder inside a tube, esp. as part of an engine or pump.

**pit** n. **1** a hole in the ground. **2** a coal mine. **3** a sunken area. **4** an area where racing cars are refuelled etc. • v. **1** (**pit against**) test in a contest with. **2** make a hollow in.
▷ SYNS n. **1** HOLE, trough, hollow, excavation, cavity, crater, pothole. **2** mine, colliery, quarry, shaft.

**pitch** n. **1** an area of ground marked out for an outside game. **2** the degree of highness or lowness of a sound; the level of intensity of something. **3** the steepness of a slope. **4** a form of words used when trying to sell something. **5** a place where a street trader or performer is stationed. **6** a dark tarry substance. • v. **1** throw. **2** set up a tent. **3** set your voice, a piece of music, etc. at a particular pitch; aim at a particular market, level of understanding, etc. **4** (of a ship) plunge forward and back alternately. **5** make a roof slope at a particular angle. ◻ **pitch-black** (or **pitch-dark**) completely dark. **pitched battle** a battle whose time and place are decided beforehand. **pitchfork** a long-handled fork for lifting hay.
▷ SYNS n. **1** FIELD, ground, stadium, arena, playing field. **2** LEVEL, point, degree, height, extent, intensity. • v. **1** THROW, fling, hurl, toss, lob; inf. chuck, bung. **2** *pitch a tent*: PUT UP, set up, erect, raise. **3** FALL, tumble, topple, plunge.

**pitcher** n. a large jug.

**piteous** adj. deserving or arousing pity.

▷ SYNS PITIFUL, pathetic, distressing, moving, sad, heart-rending, plaintive, poignant, touching.

**pitfall** n. an unsuspected danger or difficulty.
▷ SYNS TRAP, hazard, peril, danger, difficulty, snag, catch, stumbling block.

**pith** n. **1** spongy tissue in stems or fruits. **2** the essence of something. ■ **pithy** adj.

**pitiful** adj. **1** deserving or arousing pity. **2** very small or inadequate. ■ **pitifully** adv.

**pitta** n. a flat bread which is hollow inside.

**pittance** n. a very small allowance or wage.

**pituitary gland** n. a gland at the base of the brain, influencing growth and development.

**pity** n. **1** a feeling of sorrow for another's suffering. **2** a cause for regret. • v. (**pitied**, **pitying**) feel pity for.
▷ SYNS n. **1** COMPASSION, commiseration, condolence, sympathy, fellow feeling, understanding. **2** *it's a pity:* SHAME, misfortune. • v. FEEL SORRY FOR, commiserate with, sympathize with, feel for.

**pivot** n. a central point or shaft on which a thing turns or swings. • v. (**pivoted**, **pivoting**) turn on a pivot.
▷ SYNS n. AXIS, fulcrum, axle, swivel.

**pivotal** adj. vitally important.

**pixel** n. any of the minute illuminated areas making up the image on a VDU screen.

**pixie** n. a small supernatural being in fairy tales.

**pizza** n. a round, flat piece of dough baked with a savoury topping.

**pizzeria** n. a pizza restaurant.

**pizzicato** adv. plucking the strings of a violin etc. instead of using the bow.

**placard** n. a poster or similar notice.

**placate** v. make less angry. ■ **placatory** adj.
▷ SYNS CALM, pacify, soothe, appease, conciliate, mollify.

**place** n. **1** a particular position or location; a particular town, district, building, etc. **2** a chance to study on a course, belong to a team, etc.; a position in a sequence. • v. **1** put in a particular position or situation; find a home, job, etc. for. **2** identify or classify. **3** make an order for goods. □ **take place** occur.
▷ SYNS n. LOCATION, site, spot, setting, position, situation, area, locale, venue; country, state, region, locality, district. • v. **1** PUT, position, set, deposit, rest, settle, station, situate. **2** ORDER, rank, grade, class, classify, categorize, bracket.

**placebo** n. (pl. **-os**) a substance prescribed for the patient's psychological benefit rather than for any physical effect.

**placement** n. putting someone or something in a place or home; posting someone temporarily in a workplace for experience.

**placenta** n. (pl. **-tae** or **-tas**) the organ in the womb that nourishes the fetus.

**placid** adj. not easily upset. ■ **placidity** n.

▷ SYNS CALM, composed, self-possessed, serene, tranquil, equable, even-tempered, peaceable, easy-going, unperturbed, imperturbable, stolid, phlegmatic.

**placket** n. an opening in a garment for fastenings or access to a pocket.

**plagiarize** (or **-ise**) v. copy another person's writings and present them as your own. ■ **plagiarism** n.

**plague** n. **1** a deadly contagious disease. **2** an infestation. • v. cause continual trouble to; annoy or pester.
▷ SYNS v. AFFLICT, torment, bedevil, trouble, beset; pester, harass, badger, bother, persecute, hound.

**plaice** n. (pl. **plaice**) an edible flatfish.

**plaid** n. fabric woven in a tartan or chequered design.

**plain** adj. **1** simple or ordinary. **2** not patterned. **3** easy to see or understand. **4** frank or direct. **5** not attractive. • n. a large area of level country. □ **plain clothes** ordinary clothes rather than uniform. **plain sailing** smooth and easy progress. ■ **plainness** n.
▷ SYNS adj. **1** CLEAR, obvious, evident, apparent, manifest, transparent, patent, unmistakable. **2** STRAIGHT-FORWARD, uncomplicated, comprehensible, intelligible, understandable, lucid. **3** SIMPLE, basic, ordinary, unsophisticated. **4** UNATTRACTIVE, ugly, unprepossessing, ill-favoured.

**plaintiff** n. a person bringing an action in a court of law.

**plaintive** adj. sounding sad.

▷ SYNS MOURNFUL, doleful, melancholy, sad, sorrowful, wistful, pitiful.

**plait** n. a length of hair or rope made up of strands woven together. • v. form into a plait.

**plan** n. **1** a proposed means of achieving something. **2** an intention. **3** a map or diagram. • v. **1** intend. **2** work out the details of an intended action. **3** draw a plan of. ■ **planner** n.
▷ SYNS n. **1** SCHEME, proposal, proposition; system, method, procedure, strategy, stratagem, formula; way, means, measure, tactic. **2** BLUEPRINT, drawing, diagram, sketch, layout. • v. **1** ARRANGE, organize, work out, map out, schedule. **2** INTEND, aim, propose, mean; contemplate, envisage.

**plane** n. **1** an aeroplane. **2** a level surface; a level of thought or development. **3** a tool for smoothing wood or metal by paring shavings from it. **4** a tall spreading tree with broad leaves. • v. smooth or pare a surface with a plane. • adj. level.
▷ SYNS adj. FLAT, level, horizontal, even, flush, smooth.

**planet** n. a large round mass in space orbiting round a star. ■ **planetary** adj.

**planetarium** n. (pl. **-ria** or **-riums**) a room with a domed ceiling on which lights are projected to show the positions of the stars and planets.

**plangent** adj. loud and melancholy.

**plank** n. a long flat piece of timber.

**plankton** n. minute life forms floating in the sea, rivers, etc.

**plant** n. **1** a living organism such as a tree, grass, etc., with neither the power of movement nor special organs of digestion. **2** a factory; its machinery. **3** someone placed in a group as an informer. • v. place in soil for growing; place in position.
▷ SYNS n. **1** FLOWER, vegetable, herb, shrub, weed. **2** FACTORY, works, foundry, mill, workshop.

**plantain** n. **1** a tropical banana-like fruit. **2** a herb.

**plantation** n. an estate on which cotton, tobacco, tea, etc. is cultivated; an area planted with trees.

**plaque** n. **1** a commemorative plate fixed on a wall. **2** a deposit that forms on teeth.

**plasma** n. **1** the colourless fluid part of blood. **2** a kind of gas.

**plaster** n. **1** a mixture of lime, sand, water, etc. used for coating walls. **2** a sticky strip of material for covering cuts. • v. cover with plaster; coat thickly. □ **plasterboard** board made of plaster set between two sheets of paper, used to line interior walls and ceilings. **plaster of Paris** a white paste made from gypsum, used for making moulds or casts.
▷ SYNS v. COVER THICKLY, smother, spread, coat, smear.

**plastic** n. a synthetic substance that can be moulded to a permanent shape. • adj. **1** made of plastic. **2** easily moulded. □ **plastic surgery** surgery performed to reconstruct or repair parts of the body.
■ **plasticity** n.

**plasticine** n. trademark a soft modelling material.

**plate** n. **1** a flat dish for holding food. **2** articles of gold, silver, or other metal. **3** a flat thin sheet of metal, glass, etc. **4** an illustration on special paper in a book. • v. cover or coat with metal. □ **plate glass** thick glass for windows etc.
▷ SYNS n. **1** DISH, platter, salver. **2** SHEET, panel, layer, pane, slab. **3** ILLUSTRATION, picture, photograph, print, lithograph.

**plateau** n. (pl. **-teaux** or **-teaus**) **1** an area of level high ground. **2** a state of little change following rapid progress.

**platelet** n. a small disc in the blood, involved in clotting.

**platen** n. a plate in a printing press holding the paper against the type; the roller of a typewriter or printer.

**platform** n. a raised level surface or area on which people or things can stand; a raised structure beside a railway track at a station.
▷ SYNS DAIS, rostrum, podium, stage, stand.

**platinum** n. a precious silvery-white metallic element.

**platitude** n. a commonplace remark. ■ **platitudinous** adj.
▷ SYNS TRUISM, commonplace, banality.

**platonic** adj. involving affection but not sexual love.

**platoon** n. a subdivision of a military company.

**platter** n. a large flat serving dish.

**platypus** n. (pl. **-puses**) an Australian animal with a duck-like beak, which lays eggs.

**plaudits** pl.n. praise; applause.

**plausible** adj. seeming probable; persuasive but

deceptive. ■ **plausibility** n.
**plausibly** adv.
▷ SYNS BELIEVABLE, credible,
persuasive, likely, feasible,
conceivable.

**play** v. **1** take part in games for
enjoyment. **2** take part in a
sport or contest. **3** compete
against another player or
team. **4** act the role of. **5** perform
on a musical instrument.
**6** move a piece in a game.
**7** make a CD, tape, etc.
produce sounds. • n. **1** games
taken part in for enjoyment.
**2** the performing of a sports
match. **3** a dramatic work.
**4** freedom of movement.
□ **playboy** a wealthy man
who spends his time seeking
pleasure. **playgroup** a regular
play session for preschool
children. **playhouse** a theatre.
**playing card** each of a set of
pieces of card used in games.
**playmate** a friend with
whom a child plays. **playpen**
a portable enclosure for a young
child to play in. **playwright** a
person who writes plays.
▷ SYNS v. **1** AMUSE YOURSELF, entertain yourself, enjoy yourself,
have fun; frolic, romp, caper.
**2** TAKE PART IN, participate in,
join in. **3** COMPETE AGAINST,
take on, challenge. **4** ACT,
perform, portray, represent.
• n. AMUSEMENT, enjoyment,
recreation, pleasure, fun.

**player** n. **1** a person taking part
in a sport or game. **2** a person
who plays a musical instrument.
**3** an actor.
▷ SYNS **1** COMPETITOR, contestant,
participant. **2** MUSICIAN,
performer, instrumentalist.
**3** PERFORMER, actor, entertainer,
artist, thespian.

**playful** adj. full of fun; light-
hearted. ■ **playfully** adv.
▷ SYNS **1** FUN-LOVING, high-
spirited, frisky, lively,
exuberant, mischievous,
impish. **2** LIGHT-HEARTED,
joking, humorous, jocular,
facetious, tongue-in-cheek.

**plaza** n. a public square.

**plc** (or **PLC**) abbr. public limited
company.

**plea** n. **1** an emotional request.
**2** a defendant's answer to a
charge in a law court.
▷ SYNS APPEAL, entreaty, supplication, petition.

**plead** v. **1** put forward a case in a
law court. **2** make an appeal or
entreaty. **3** present as an excuse.
▷ SYNS APPEAL TO, beg, entreat,
beseech, implore, request.

**pleasant** adj. enjoyable;
friendly and likeable.
▷ SYNS **1** PLEASING, pleasurable,
agreeable, enjoyable,
entertaining, amusing, delightful. **2** FRIENDLY, amiable,
affable, genial, likeable,
charming, engaging.

**pleasantry** n. (pl. **-ies**) a
friendly or humorous remark.

**please** v. **1** give pleasure to.
**2** wish or desire. **3** (**please
yourself**) do as you choose.
• adv. a polite word of request.
▷ SYNS v. **1** GLADDEN, delight,
charm, divert, entertain, amuse.
**2** do as you please: WANT, wish,
see fit, like, desire, be inclined.

**pleased** adj. feeling or showing
pleasure and satisfaction.
▷ SYNS HAPPY, glad, delighted,
thrilled; contented, satisfied,
gratified.

**pleasurable** adj. enjoyable.
■ **pleasurably** adv.

**pleasure** n. a feeling of happy satisfaction and enjoyment; a source of this.
▷ SYNS HAPPINESS, delight, joy, enjoyment, entertainment, amusement, diversion, satisfaction, gratification, fulfilment, contentment.

**pleat** n. a flat fold of cloth.
• v. make pleats in.

**plebeian** adj. of the lower social classes; uncultured or vulgar.

**plebiscite** n. a referendum.

**plectrum** n. (pl. -trums or -tra) a small piece of plastic etc. for plucking the strings of a musical instrument.

**pledge** n. 1 a solemn promise; something deposited as a guarantee that a debt will be paid etc. 2 a token of something. • v. commit by a promise; give as a pledge.
▷ SYNS n. 1 PROMISE, word of honour, vow, assurance, commitment, undertaking, oath. 2 SECURITY, surety, guarantee, collateral. • v. PROMISE, give your word, vow, undertake, swear.

**plenary** adj. entire; attended by all members.

**plenipotentiary** adj. & n. (pl. -ies) (an envoy) with full powers to take action.

**plenitude** n. abundance; completeness.

**plentiful** adj. existing in large amounts.
▷ SYNS ABUNDANT, copious, ample, profuse, lavish, generous.

**plenty** pron. enough or more than enough. • n. a situation where necessities are available in large quantities.
■ plenteous adj.

▷ SYNS n. (**plenty of**) ENOUGH, sufficient, a great/good deal of, masses of; inf. lots of, heaps of, stacks of, piles of.

**plethora** n. an oversupply or excess.
▷ SYNS OVERABUNDANCE, excess, superfluity, surplus, surfeit, glut.

**pleurisy** n. inflammation of the membranes around the lungs.

**pliable** adj. flexible; easily influenced. ■ pliability n.
▷ SYNS 1 FLEXIBLE, bendable, bendy, pliant, elastic, supple. 2 MALLEABLE, compliant, biddable, tractable.

**pliant** adj. pliable.

**pliers** pl.n. pincers with flat surfaces for gripping things.

**plight** n. a predicament.

**plimsoll** n. a canvas sports shoe.

**plinth** n. a slab forming the base of a column or statue etc.

**plod** v. (plodded, plodding) trudge; work slowly but steadily.

**plonk** inf. n. cheap wine. • v. set down heavily or carelessly.

**plop** n. a sound like something small dropping into water with no splash.

**plot** n. 1 a secret plan to do something wrong or illegal. 2 the story in a play, novel, or film. 3 a small piece of land. • v. 1 secretly plan a wrong or illegal action. 2 mark a route etc. on a map. ■ plotter n.
▷ SYNS n. 1 CONSPIRACY, intrigue, machinations. 2 STORYLINE, story, scenario. • v. 1 PLAN, scheme, conspire, intrigue. 2 MAP, chart, mark.

**plough** (US **plow**) n. an implement for turning over soil.

• v. **1** turn over earth with a plough. **2** make your way laboriously.

**ploy** n. a cunning manoeuvre.
▷ syns **RUSE**, tactic, scheme, trick, stratagem, gambit, manoeuvre, move.

**pluck** v. pull out or off; pick a flower etc.; strip a bird of its feathers. • n. courage.
■ plucky adj.

**plug** n. **1** a piece of solid material that tightly blocks a hole. **2** a device with metal pins that fit into holes in a socket to make an electrical connection.
• v. (**plugged**, **plugging**) **1** block or fill with a plug. **2** (**plug in**) connect an appliance to an electric socket. **3** inf. promote a product by mentioning it publicly.

**plum** n. **1** an oval fruit with a pointed stone. **2** reddish purple.
• adj. inf. highly desirable.

**plumage** n. a bird's feathers.

**plumb** n. a heavy weight hung on a cord (**plumb line**), used for testing depths or verticality.
• adv. exactly. • v. **1** measure the depth of water; get to the bottom of. **2** install a bath, washing machine, etc.

**plumber** n. a person who fits and repairs plumbing.

**plumbing** n. a system of water and drainage pipes etc. in a building.

**plume** n. a long, soft feather; something resembling this.

**plummet** v. (**plummeted**, **plummeting**) fall steeply or rapidly.
▷ syns **FALL** (**HEADLONG**), plunge, hurtle, nosedive, dive, drop.

**plump** adj. full or rounded in shape; rather fat. • v. **1** make

more full or rounded. **2** (**plump for**) decide on.
▷ syns **adj.** CHUBBY, rotund, buxom, stout, fat, fleshy, portly, roly-poly; inf. tubby, podgy.

**plunder** v. rob. • n. plundering; goods etc. stolen.
▷ syns **v.** ROB, pillage, loot, raid, ransack, rifle. • n. LOOT, booty, spoils; inf. swag.

**plunge** v. **1** jump or dive; fall suddenly; decrease rapidly. **2** push or go forcefully into something. • n. an act of plunging.
▷ syns **v. 1** THRUST, stick, jab, push, drive. **2** DIVE, nosedive, plummet, drop, fall, pitch.

**plunger** n. a long-handled suction cup used to unblock pipes.

**pluperfect** adj. Grammar (of a tense) referring to action completed before some past point of time, e.g. *we had arrived.*

**plural** adj. **1** more than one in number. **2** Grammar (of a word or form) referring to more than one. • n. Grammar a plural word or form. ■ plurality n.

**plus** prep. with the addition of.
• adj. **1** (before a number) above zero. **2** more than the amount indicated: *twenty plus.* • n. **1** the sign (+). **2** an advantage.

**plush** n. cloth with a long soft nap. • adj. **1** made of plush. **2** inf. luxurious.

**plutocrat** n. a wealthy, powerful person.

**plutonium** n. a radioactive metallic element used in nuclear weapons and reactors.

**ply**¹ n. (pl. **plies**) a thickness or layer of wood, cloth, etc.

□ **plywood** board made of layers of wood glued together.

**ply²** v. (**plied**, **plying**) **1** use a tool etc.; work at a trade. **2** (of a ship etc.) travel regularly over a route. **3** continually offer food etc. to.

**p.m.** abbr. after noon.

**pneumatic** adj. filled with or operated by compressed air.

**pneumonia** n. inflammation of the lungs.

**PO** abbr. **1** Post Office. **2** postal order.

**poach** v. **1** cook by simmering in a small amount of liquid. **2** take game or fish illegally. ■ **poacher** n.

**pocket** n. **1** a small bag sewn into or on clothing for carrying things. **2** an isolated group or area. **3** an opening at the corner or side of a billiard table. • v. **1** put into your pocket. **2** take dishonestly. □ **pocket money** money given regularly to a child by their parents.

**pockmarked** adj. (of the skin) marked by hollow scars.

**pod** n. a long narrow seed case.

**podcast** n. a digital recording of a radio broadcast, made available on the Internet for downloading to a personal audio player. ■ **podcasting** n.

**podgy** adj. inf. rather fat.

**podium** n. (pl. **-diums** or **-dia**) a pedestal or platform.

**poem** n. a piece of imaginative writing in verse.

**poet** n. a person who writes poems.

**poetic** (or **poetical**) adj. of or like poetry. ■ **poetically** adv.

**poetry** n. poems; a poet's work.

**po-faced** adj. inf. serious and disapproving.

**pogrom** n. an organized massacre.

**poignant** adj. evoking sadness. ■ **poignancy** n.
▷ SYNS TOUCHING, moving, sad, pitiful, piteous, heart-rending, tear-jerking, plaintive.

**point** n. **1** a tapered, sharp end. **2** a particular place or moment. **3** an item, detail, or idea. **4** the advantage or purpose of something. **5** a feature or quality. **6** a unit of scoring. **7** a dot. **8** a promontory. **9** an electrical socket. **10** a junction of two railway lines. • v. **1** direct attention by extending your finger. **2** aim or face in a particular direction. **3** fill in joints of brickwork with mortar. □ **beside the point** irrelevant. **point-blank 1** at very close range. **2** in a blunt way. **point of view** an attitude or opinion.
▷ SYNS n. **1** TIP, end, extremity, prong, spike, tine. **2** PLACE, position, location, site, spot; time, juncture, stage, period, moment, instant. **3** *what's the point of this?*: PURPOSE, aim, object, objective, goal, intention; use, sense, value, advantage. **4** *good points*: CHARACTERISTIC, trait, attribute, quality, feature, property.
• v. DIRECT, aim, level, train.

**pointed** adj. **1** tapering to a point. **2** (of a remark or look) expressing a clear message.

**pointer** n. a thing that points to something; a dog that faces stiffly towards game it has scented.

**pointless** adj. having no purpose or meaning.

▷ SYNS FUTILE, useless, in vain, unavailing, fruitless, senseless.

**poise** n. graceful bearing; self-assurance. • v. cause to be balanced.
▷ SYNS n. COMPOSURE, equanimity, self-possession, aplomb, self-assurance, calmness, serenity, dignity.

**poison** n. a substance that causes death or injury when swallowed or absorbed.
• v. 1 harm or kill with poison. 2 put poison on or in. 3 have a harmful effect on.
▷ SYNS n. VENOM, toxin. • v. CONTAMINATE, pollute, blight, taint.

**poisonous** adj. 1 (of an animal) producing poison. 2 (of a substance) causing death or illness if taken into the body.
▷ SYNS VENOMOUS, deadly, lethal, toxic, noxious.

**poke** v. 1 prod with your finger, a stick, etc. 2 search or pry. □ poke fun at ridicule.
▷ SYNS JAB, prod, dig, elbow, nudge, push, thrust.

**poker** n. 1 a stiff metal rod for stirring up a fire. 2 a gambling card game.

**poky** adj. (-ier, -iest) small and cramped.
▷ SYNS CRAMPED, narrow, small, tiny, confined.

**polar** adj. 1 of or near the North or South Pole. 2 of magnetic or electrical poles. 3 (of opposites) extreme, absolute. □ polar bear a white bear of Arctic regions.

**polarize** (or **-ise**) v. 1 restrict the vibrations of a light wave to one direction. 2 give magnetic poles to. 3 set at opposite extremes of opinion.

**Polaroid** n. trademark 1 a material that polarizes light passing through it, used in sunglasses. 2 a camera that prints a photograph as soon as it is taken.

**pole** n. 1 a long rod or post. 2 the north (**North Pole**) or south (**South Pole**) end of the earth's axis. 3 one of the opposite ends of a magnet or terminals of an electric cell or battery. □ poles apart having nothing in common.
▷ SYNS POST, pillar, stanchion, stake, stick, support, prop, rail, rod.

**polecat** n. a small animal of the weasel family.

**polemic** n. a verbal attack on a belief or opinion.
■ polemical adj.

**police** n. a civil force responsible for keeping public order.
• v. keep order in a place by means of police. □ police state a country where political police supervise and control citizens' activities. ■ policeman n. policewoman n.

**policy** n. 1 a general plan of action. 2 an insurance contract.
▷ SYNS PLANS, strategy, stratagem, approach, system, programme, procedure.

**polio** (or **poliomyelitis**) n. an infectious disease causing temporary or permanent paralysis.

**polish** v. 1 make smooth and shiny by rubbing. 2 refine or improve. 3 (**polish off**) finish off. • n. 1 a substance used to polish something. 2 shininess. 3 refinement or elegance.
▷ SYNS v. 1 BUFF, rub, burnish, shine. 2 PERFECT, refine, improve, hone.

**polished** adj. **1** shiny. **2** refined and sophisticated. **3** accomplished and skilful.
▷ SYNS **1** SHINY, glossy, gleaming, lustrous, burnished. **2** REFINED, cultivated, civilized, well bred, polite, urbane, suave, sophisticated. **3** EXPERT, accomplished, masterly, skilful, adept.

**polite** adj. having good manners; civilized or well bred.
■ politeness n.
▷ SYNS **1** WELL MANNERED, courteous, civil, respectful, deferential, well behaved, well bred; tactful, diplomatic. **2** *polite society:* CIVILIZED, refined, cultured, genteel, urbane, sophisticated.

**politic** adj. showing good judgement.
▷ SYNS WISE, prudent, sensible, advisable, judicious, expedient, shrewd, astute.

**political** adj. of the government and public affairs of a country; of or promoting a particular party. □ political correctness avoidance of language or behaviour that may be considered discriminatory. ■ politically adv.

**politician** n. a person holding an elected government post.

**politics** n. the science and art of government; political affairs or life; political principles.

**polka** n. a lively dance for couples.

**poll** n. **1** the votes cast in an election. **2** an estimate of public opinion made by questioning people. • v. record the opinions or votes of; receive a specified number of votes. □ poll tax hist. a tax on each member of the population.

▷ SYNS n. VOTE, ballot, referendum, plebiscite.

**pollard** v. cut off the top and branches of a tree to encourage new growth.

**pollen** n. a fertilizing powder produced by flowers. □ pollen count a measurement of the amount of pollen in the air.

**pollinate** v. fertilize with pollen. ■ pollination n.

**pollster** n. a person conducting an opinion poll.

**pollute** v. make dirty or poisonous. ■ pollutant n. pollution n.
▷ SYNS CONTAMINATE, infect, taint, poison, dirty, foul.

**polo** n. a game like hockey, played on horseback. □ polo neck a high turned-over collar on a sweater.

**poltergeist** n. a ghost said to throw objects about.

**polyester** n. a synthetic resin or fibre.

**polygamy** n. a system of having more than one wife or husband at a time. ■ polygamist n. polygamous adj.

**polygon** n. a geometric figure with many sides.

**polygraph** n. a lie-detecting machine.

**polymath** n. a person with knowledge of many subjects.

**polymer** n. a substance whose molecular structure is formed from many identical small molecules.

**polyp** n. **1** a simple organism with a tube-shaped body. **2** a small lump projecting from a mucous membrane.

**polystyrene** n. a light synthetic material.

**polythene** n. a tough light plastic.

**polyunsaturated** adj. (of fat) not associated with the formation of cholesterol in the blood.

**polyurethane** n. a synthetic resin used in paint etc.

**pomander** n. a ball of mixed sweet-smelling substances.

**pomegranate** n. a tropical fruit with many seeds.

**pommel** n. a knob on the hilt of a sword; an upward projection on a saddle.

**pomp** n. the splendid clothes, customs, etc. that are part of a grand ceremony.
▷ SYNS CEREMONY, pageantry, show, spectacle, splendour, grandeur, magnificence, majesty.

**pompom** n. a small woollen ball as a decoration on a garment.

**pompous** adj. full of ostentatious dignity and self-importance. ■ **pomposity** n.
▷ SYNS SELF-IMPORTANT, puffed up, imperious, overbearing, arrogant, haughty, proud.

**poncho** n. (pl. **-os**) a cloak like a blanket with a hole for the head.

**pond** n. a small area of still water.

**ponder** v. be deep in thought; think over.
▷ SYNS THINK ABOUT, consider, reflect on, mull over, contemplate, meditate on, ruminate on, muse on.

**ponderous** adj. heavy or unwieldy; laborious.

**pong** inf. n. & v. stink.

**pontiff** n. the Pope.

**pontificate** v. speak pompously and at length.

**pontoon** n. **1** a flat-bottomed boat supporting a temporary bridge; such a bridge. **2** a card game.

**pony** n. (pl. **-ies**) a small breed of horse. □ **ponytail** a hairstyle in which the hair is drawn back and tied at the back of the head.

**poodle** n. a dog with a curly coat.

**pool** n. **1** a small area of still water. **2** a swimming pool. **3** a puddle. **4** a shared fund or supply. **5** a game resembling snooker. **6** (**the pools**) a form of gambling on the results of football matches. • v. put into a common fund; share.

**poop** n. a raised deck at the back of a ship.

**poor** adj. **1** having little money. **2** of a low quality or standard. **3** deserving sympathy.
▷ SYNS **1** POVERTY-STRICKEN, penniless, impoverished, needy, destitute; inf. hard up. **2** SUB-STANDARD, inferior, below par, imperfect, bad, deficient, unsatisfactory, inadequate. **3** *you poor thing:* UNFORTUNATE, unlucky, luckless, hapless, ill-fated, ill-starred, wretched.

**poorly** adv. badly. • adj. unwell.

**pop** v. (**popped, popping**) **1** make a sudden short explosive sound. **2** go or put somewhere quickly. • n. **1** a sudden short explosive sound. **2** a fizzy drink. **3** (or **pop music**) modern popular music with a strong melody and beat. • adj. **1** of pop music. **2** made intellectually accessible to the general public. □ **popcorn** maize kernels heated until they burst open.

**pope** n. the head of the Roman Catholic Church.

**poplar** n. a tall slender tree.

**poplin** n. a plain woven cotton fabric.

**poppadom** n. a round piece of savoury Indian bread fried until crisp.

**poppy** n. (pl. **-ies**) a plant with bright flowers on tall stems.

**poppycock** n. inf. nonsense.

**populace** n. the general public.
▷ SYNS THE (GENERAL) PUBLIC, the (common) people, the population, the masses.

**popular** adj. **1** liked by many people. **2** of or for the general public. ■ popularity n.
▷ SYNS **1** WELL LIKED, fashionable, all the rage, hot, in demand, sought-after. **2** WIDESPREAD, general, common, current, prevalent, prevailing.

**popularize** (or **-ise**) v. **1** make generally liked. **2** present in an understandable non-technical form.

**populate** v. fill with a population.

**population** n. the inhabitants of an area.
▷ SYNS INHABITANTS, residents, community, people, citizenry, populace, society.

**populous** adj. thickly populated.

**porcelain** n. fine china.

**porch** n. a roofed shelter over the entrance of a building.

**porcupine** n. an animal covered with protective spines.

**pore** n. a tiny opening on the skin or on a leaf. □ pore over study closely.
▷ SYNS OPENING, orifice, hole, outlet.

**pork** n. the flesh of a pig as food.

**pornography** n. writings or pictures intended to stimulate erotic feelings by portraying sexual activity. ■ pornographic adj.

**porous** adj. letting through fluid or air.

**porpoise** n. a small whale.

**porridge** n. a food made by boiling oats or oatmeal in water or milk.

**port** n. **1** a harbour. **2** a town with a harbour. **3** an opening for loading a ship or firing a gun from a tank etc. **4** a socket in a computer network into which a device can be plugged. **5** strong, sweet red wine. **6** the left-hand side of a ship or aircraft. □ porthole a small window in the side of a ship or aircraft.
▷ SYNS HARBOUR, docks, marina.

**portable** adj. able to be carried.

**portal** n. a large and impressive doorway or gate.

**portcullis** n. a vertical grating lowered to block the gateway to a castle.

**portend** v. foreshadow.

**portent** n. an omen. ■ portentous adj.

**porter** n. **1** a person employed to carry luggage or goods. **2** a doorkeeper of a large building.

**portfolio** n. (pl. **-os**) **1** a case for loose sheets of paper. **2** a set of investments. **3** the position and duties of a government minister.

**portico** n. (pl. **-oes** or **-os**) a roof supported by columns forming a porch or similar structure.

**portion** n. a part or share; an amount of food for one person.

• v. divide; distribute portions of.
▷ SYNS n. SHARE, quota, part, allocation, slice; piece, bit, section; helping, serving.

**portly** adj. rather fat.

**portmanteau** n. (pl. **-teaus** or **-teaux**) a travelling bag opening into two equal parts.

**portrait** n. a picture of a person or animal; a description.
▷ SYNS PAINTING, picture, drawing, likeness.

**portray** v. make a picture of; describe; represent in a play etc.
■ portrayal n.
▷ SYNS **1** PAINT, draw, sketch, depict, represent. **2** DESCRIBE, characterize.

**pose** v. **1** constitute or present a problem etc. **2** adopt or place in a particular position, esp. to be painted, photographed, etc.; pretend to be someone or something. • n. **1** an attitude in which someone is posed. **2** a pretence.
▷ SYNS v. **1** pose problems: CONSTITUTE, present, create, cause, produce, give rise to. **2** posing at the bar: STRIKE A POSE, attitudinize, put on airs; inf. show off.
• n. **1** POSTURE, stance, position, attitude. **2** ACT, pretence, facade, front, masquerade, affectation.

**poser** n. **1** a puzzling problem. **2** a poseur.

**poseur** n. a person who behaves in a way intended to impress.

**posh** adj. inf. **1** very elegant or luxurious. **2** upper-class.

**posit** v. put forward as a basis for argument.

**position** n. **1** a place where something is situated. **2** a way in which someone or something is placed or arranged. **3** a situation. **4** a job. **5** a person's status. **6** a point of view.
• v. place or arrange.
▷ SYNS n. **1** LOCATION, place, situation, spot, site, area, locality. **2** an upright position: POSTURE, stance, attitude, pose. **3** his financial position: SITUATION, state, condition, circumstances. **4** a secretarial position: POST, job, appointment. **5** his position in the class: LEVEL, place, rank, status, standing.
• v. PLACE, locate, situate, put, set, station.

**positive** adj. **1** indicating agreement or support; hopeful or encouraging; (of the results of a test) showing the presence of something. **2** definite; convinced. **3** (of a battery terminal) through which electric current enters. **4** (of a quantity) greater than zero. • n. a positive quality. □ **positive discrimination** the policy of favouring members of groups often discriminated against when appointing to jobs etc.
▷ SYNS adj. **1** CONFIDENT, optimistic, cheerful, hopeful, sanguine; inf. upbeat. **2** GOOD, favourable, promising, encouraging, heartening. **3** DEFINITE, conclusive, incontrovertible, indisputable, irrefutable. **4** CERTAIN, sure, convinced, satisfied.

**positron** n. a particle with a positive electric charge.

**posse** n. inf. **1** a group or gang. **2** hist. a body of law enforcers.

**possess** v. **1** have or own. **2** dominate the mind of.
■ possessor n.
▷ SYNS OWN, have, be blessed with, enjoy.

**possession** n. **1** the state of owning something. **2** something owned.
▷ SYNS (**possessions**) BELONGINGS, things, property, effects, worldly goods.

**possessive** adj. **1** jealously guarding your possessions; demanding someone's total attention. **2** Grammar indicating possession.

**possibility** n. **1** a thing that is possible. **2** the state of being possible.
▷ SYNS CHANCE, likelihood, probability; risk, danger.

**possible** adj. capable of existing, happening, being done, etc. ■ **possibly** adv.
▷ SYNS **1** FEASIBLE, practicable, doable, attainable, achievable. **2** LIKELY, potential, conceivable, probable.

**possum** n. inf. an opossum.

**post** n. **1** the official system for delivering letters etc. **2** letters etc. sent or delivered. **3** an upright piece of timber or metal used as a support or marker. **4** a place of duty. **5** a job. • v. **1** send via the postal system. **2** put up a notice. **3** send to a place to take up a job or duty. □ **postbox** a large public box into which letters are put for sending by post. **postcard** a card for sending a message by post without an envelope. **postcode** a group of letters and numbers in a postal address to assist the sorting of mail. **postman** (or **postwoman**) a person employed to deliver or collect post. **postmark** an official mark stamped on a letter or parcel, giving the date of posting. **post office** a building where postal business is carried on.

▷ SYNS n. POLE, stake, upright, prop, support, picket, strut, pillar, stanchion. • v. PUT UP, stick up, pin up, attach, fix, fasten.

**post-** pref. after.

**postage** n. a charge for sending something by post.

**postal** adj. of or sent by post.

**post-date** v. put a date on a cheque etc. that is later than the actual date.

**poster** n. a large picture or notice used for decoration or as an advertisement.
▷ SYNS PLACARD, notice, bill, advertisement.

**posterior** adj. near or at the back. • n. the buttocks.

**posterity** n. future generations.

**postgraduate** n. a student studying for a higher degree.

**post-haste** adv. with great speed.

**posthumous** adj. happening, appearing, etc. after a person's death.

**post-mortem** n. an examination of a body to determine the cause of death; an analysis of something that has happened.

**post-natal** adj. after childbirth.

**postpone** v. cause an event to take place later than was originally planned. ■ **postponement** n.
▷ SYNS DEFER, put off/back, delay, hold over, adjourn.

**postscript** n. an additional paragraph at the end of a letter etc.

**postulate** v. assume to be true as a basis for reasoning.

**posture** n. the way a person stands, walks, etc. • v. assume a posture, esp. for effect.

▷ SYNS n. POSITION, pose, attitude, stance; bearing, carriage.

**posy** n. (pl. **-ies**) a small bunch of flowers.

**pot** n. **1** a rounded container used for storage or cooking. **2** inf. cannabis. • v. (**potted**, **potting**) **1** plant in a flowerpot. **2** preserve food in a pot. **3** (**potted**) in a short, understandable form. **4** (in billiards or snooker) send a ball into a pocket. □ **pot belly** a large protuberant belly. **pot luck** whatever is available. **potshot** a shot aimed at random.

**potassium** n. a soft silvery-white metallic element.

**potato** n. (pl. **-oes**) a vegetable with starchy white flesh that grows underground as a tuber.

**potent** adj. very powerful.
■ **potency** n.
▷ SYNS POWERFUL, strong, mighty, formidable, influential, forceful; convincing, cogent, compelling, persuasive.

**potentate** n. a monarch or ruler.

**potential** adj. capable of being developed or used. • n. an ability or capacity for development.
■ **potentiality** n. **potentially** adv.
▷ SYNS adj. POSSIBLE, likely, probable, prospective; latent.
• n. PROMISE, possibilities, potentiality, prospects, ability, capability.

**pothole** n. a deep underground cave; a hole in a road surface.
□ **potholing** exploring potholes as a sport. ■ **potholer** n.

**potion** n. a liquid medicine or drug.
▷ SYNS DRINK, brew, concoction, mixture.

**potpourri** n. (pl. **-rris**) **1** a scented mixture of dried petals and spices. **2** any mixture.

**potter**[1] n. a maker of pottery.

**potter**[2] v. work on trivial tasks in a leisurely way.

**pottery** n. (pl. **-ies**) articles made of baked clay; a potter's work or workshop.

**potty** inf. adj. **1** mad or stupid. **2** enthusiastic. • n. (pl. **-ies**) a bowl used as a toilet by a young child.

**pouch** n. **1** a small bag. **2** a pocket of skin in which certain animals carry their young.

**pouffe** n. a padded stool.

**poultice** n. a moist dressing used to reduce inflammation.

**poultry** n. domestic fowls.

**pounce** v. swoop down and seize or attack. • n. an act of pouncing.
▷ SYNS v. JUMP, spring, swoop, attack, ambush.

**pound** n. **1** a measure of weight, 16 oz. avoirdupois (0.454 kg) or 12 oz. troy (0.373 kg). **2** the basic unit of money of the UK. **3** a place where stray dogs or illegally parked vehicles are kept until claimed. • v. **1** hit heavily again and again. **2** beat or throb. **3** run heavily.
▷ SYNS n. COMPOUND, enclosure, pen, yard. • v. **1** BEAT, strike, hit, batter, thump, pummel, punch. **2** THROB, pulsate, pulse, hammer, race.

**pour** v. **1** flow or cause to flow. **2** rain heavily. **3** come or go in large numbers.
▷ SYNS GUSH, rush, stream, flow, course, jet, spurt.

**pout** v. push out your lips. • n. a pouting expression.

**poverty** n. **1** the state of being very poor. **2** lack or scarcity.
▷ SYNS PENNILESSNESS, destitution, impoverishment, penury, hardship, neediness.

**powder** n. **1** a mass of fine dry particles. **2** a cosmetic in this form. • v. cover or sprinkle with powder. ■ **powdery** adj.

**power** n. **1** the ability to do something. **2** influence or control. **3** right or authority. **4** a country with international influence and military strength. **5** strength or force. **6** mechanical or electrical energy. **7** a product of a number multiplied by itself a given number of times. • v. supply with mechanical or electrical power.
□ **power station** a building where electrical power is generated.
▷ SYNS n. **1** ABILITY, capability, capacity, potential, faculty. **2** CONTROL, command, authority, dominance, supremacy, ascendancy, mastery, dominion, sway. **3** STRENGTH, force, might, vigour.

**powerful** adj. having power. ■ **powerfully** adv.
▷ SYNS **1** STRONG, sturdy, strapping, stout, robust, vigorous, tough. **2** INFLUENTIAL, dominant, authoritative, commanding, forceful, strong, vigorous, potent. **3** COGENT, compelling, convincing, persuasive, eloquent.

**powerless** adj. without power.
▷ SYNS WEAK, feeble, impotent, helpless, defenceless.

**pp** abbr. **1** (**pp.**) pages. **2** per procurationem (used when signing a letter on someone else's behalf).

**PR** abbr. **1** public relations. **2** proportional representation.

**practicable** adj. able to be done. ■ **practicability** n.
▷ SYNS FEASIBLE, realistic, possible, viable, workable, doable.

**practical** adj. **1** involving activity rather than study or theory. **2** likely to be successful or useful. **3** skilled at making or doing things. □ **practical joke** a humorous trick played on someone. ■ **practicality** n. **practically** adv.
▷ SYNS **1** practical knowledge: APPLIED, empirical, hands-on, actual. **2** FEASIBLE, realistic, viable, possible, reasonable. **3** REALISTIC, sensible, down-to-earth, businesslike, hard-headed.

**practice** n. **1** repeated exercise to improve skill. **2** action as opposed to theory. **3** a custom or habit. **4** a doctor's or lawyer's business.
▷ SYNS **1** put into practice: ACTION, operation, application, effect, exercise, use. **2** TRAINING, preparation, study, exercise, drill, workout, rehearsal. **3** standard practice: PROCEDURE, method, system, usage, tradition, convention.

**practise** (US **practice**) v. **1** do something repeatedly or habitually. **2** be working in a particular profession.
▷ SYNS **1** CARRY OUT, perform, do, execute, follow, pursue, observe. **2** WORK AT, run through, go over, rehearse, polish.

**practitioner** n. a professional worker, esp. in medicine.

**pragmatic** adj. a realistic and sensible attitude or approach.
■ **pragmatically** adv.

**prairie** n. (in North America) a large treeless area of grassland.

**praise** v. 1 express approval or admiration of. 2 express thanks to or respect for God. • n. approval expressed in words.
▷ SYNS v. 1 APPLAUD, acclaim, compliment, congratulate, pay tribute to, laud, eulogize. 2 *praise God:* WORSHIP, glorify, honour, exalt. • n. APPROVAL, acclaim, approbation, plaudits, compliments, congratulations, commendation.

**praiseworthy** adj. deserving approval and admiration.
▷ SYNS COMMENDABLE, laudable, admirable, meritorious, deserving, creditable.

**praline** n. a sweet substance made by crushing sweetened nuts.

**pram** n. a four-wheeled conveyance for a baby.

**prance** v. move springily.
▷ SYNS LEAP, spring, jump, skip, cavort, caper, gambol.

**prank** n. a mischievous act.
▷ SYNS TRICK, practical joke, hoax, caper, stunt.

**prattle** v. chatter in a childish way. • n. childish chatter.

**prawn** n. an edible shellfish like a large shrimp.

**pray** v. 1 say a prayer. 2 hope earnestly.

**prayer** n. 1 a request for help or expression of thanks to God or a god. 2 an earnest hope.

**pre-** pref. before; beforehand.

**preach** v. 1 deliver a sermon. 2 recommend a course of action.

3 moralize in a pompous way.
■ **preacher** n.

**preamble** n. an opening statement.

**prearrange** v. arrange beforehand.

**precarious** adj. not safe or secure.
▷ SYNS RISKY, hazardous, perilous, dangerous, touch-and-go.

**precaution** n. something done to avoid problems or danger.
■ **precautionary** adj.
▷ SYNS SAFEGUARD, preventative/preventive measure, provision.

**precede** v. come or go before in time, order, etc.

**precedence** n. being more important than someone or something else.

**precedent** n. a previous case serving as an example to be followed.

**precept** n. a command or rule of conduct.

**precinct** n. 1 an enclosed area around a place or building. 2 an area closed to traffic in a town.

**precious** adj. 1 of great value. 2 beloved. 3 affectedly refined.
▷ SYNS 1 VALUABLE, costly, expensive, dear, priceless, rare. 2 VALUED, cherished, prized, treasured, beloved.

**precipice** n. a very steep face of a cliff or rock.

**precipitate** v. 1 cause to happen suddenly or prematurely; cause to move suddenly and uncontrollably. 2 cause a substance to be deposited in solid form from a solution. • adj. rash, hasty. • n. a substance precipitated from a solution.

▷ SYNS V. HASTEN, accelerate, expedite, speed up, push forward, bring on, trigger.

**precipitation** n. rain or snow.

**precipitous** adj. very steep.

**precis** n. (pl. **precis**) a summary. • v. summarize.

**precise** adj. **1** clear and detailed. **2** accurate over details. **3** particular. ■ **precisely** adv. **precision** n.
▷ SYNS EXACT, accurate, correct, specific, detailed, explicit.

**preclude** v. prevent from happening.
▷ SYNS PREVENT, prohibit, rule out, debar, bar, hinder, impede.

**precocious** adj. having developed earlier than is usual.

**preconceived** adj. (of an idea) formed beforehand.

**preconception** n. an idea or opinion that is formed before full knowledge or evidence is available.
▷ SYNS PRECONCEIVED IDEA, assumption, presupposition, presumption, prejudgement, prejudice.

**precondition** n. a condition that must be fulfilled beforehand.

**precursor** n. a forerunner.

**predator** n. an animal that hunts and kills others for food. ■ **predatory** adj.

**predecessor** n. a person who held an office, job, etc. before the current holder.
▷ SYNS PRECURSOR, forerunner, antecedent, ancestor, forefather, forebear.

**predestination** n. the doctrine that everything has been determined in advance.

**predicament** n. a difficult situation.
▷ SYNS DIFFICULT SITUATION, plight, tight corner, mess, emergency, crisis, dilemma, quandary, trouble; inf. jam, hole, fix, pickle, scrape, tight spot.

**predicate** n. Grammar the part of a sentence that says something about the subject (e.g. *is short* in *life is short*).

**predict** v. foretell. ■ **predictable** adj. **prediction** n. **predictor** n.
▷ SYNS FORECAST, foretell, prophesy, foresee, anticipate.

**predilection** n. a special liking.
▷ SYNS LIKING, fondness, preference, partiality, taste, penchant.

**predispose** v. make likely to do, be, or think something. ■ **predisposition** n.

**predominant** adj. **1** present as the main part. **2** having the greatest power. ■ **predominance** n. **predominantly** adv. **predominate** v.

**pre-eminent** adj. better than all others. ■ **pre-eminence** n.
▷ SYNS OUTSTANDING, leading, foremost, chief, excellent, distinguished, prominent, eminent, important.

**pre-empt** v. take action to prevent an occurrence; forestall someone. ■ **pre-emptive** adj.

**preen** v. (of a bird) smooth its feathers with its beak. □ **preen yourself** attend to your appearance; feel self-satisfied.

**prefabricated** adj. (of a building) made in sections that can be assembled on site.

**preface** n. an introductory statement. • v. **1** introduce with a preface. **2** lead up to an event.
▷ SYNS N. INTRODUCTION, foreword, preamble, prologue, prelude.

**prefect** n. **1** a senior school pupil with some authority over other pupils. **2** an administrative official in certain countries.

**prefer** v. (**preferred**, **preferring**) like better than another or others. ■ **preferable** adj. **preferably** adv.
▷ SYNS FAVOUR, incline towards, choose, select, pick, opt for, go for.

**preference** n. preferring; something preferred; favour shown to one person over others.
▷ SYNS LIKING, partiality, predilection, fondness, taste, inclination, penchant.

**preferential** adj. favouring a particular person or group. ■ **preferentially** adv.

**preferment** n. promotion.

**prefix** n. a letter or group of letters placed at the beginning of a word to alter its meaning.

**pregnant** adj. **1** having a child or young developing in the womb. **2** full of meaning. ■ **pregnancy** n.
▷ SYNS **1** EXPECTING, with child; inf. in the family way. **2** a pregnant pause: MEANINGFUL, significant, suggestive, expressive.

**prehensile** adj. (of an animal's tail) able to grasp things.

**prehistoric** adj. of the period before written records were made. ■ **prehistorically** adv.

**prejudge** v. form a judgement before knowing all the facts.

**prejudice** n. a preconceived and irrational opinion; hostility and injustice based on this.
• v. **1** cause to have a prejudice. **2** cause harm to.

▷ SYNS n. BIAS, discrimination, partisanship, partiality, chauvinism, bigotry, intolerance, racism, sexism.

**prejudicial** adj. harmful to rights or interests.
▷ SYNS DETRIMENTAL, unfavourable, damaging, injurious, harmful, hurtful, inimical; formal deleterious.

**prelate** n. a clergyman of high rank.

**preliminary** adj. preceding a main action or event. • n. (pl. -ies) a preliminary action or event.
▷ SYNS adj. INTRODUCTORY, prefatory, prior, precursory, opening, initial, preparatory.

**prelude** n. an action or event leading up to another; an introductory part or piece of music.
▷ SYNS **1** OVERTURE, opening, introduction, start, beginning. **2** INTRODUCTION, preface, prologue, preamble.

**premarital** adj. before marriage.

**premature** adj. coming or done before the usual or proper time.
▷ SYNS EARLY, untimely, unseasonable.

**premeditated** adj. planned beforehand.
▷ SYNS PLANNED, prearranged, intentional, intended, deliberate, calculated, wilful.

**premenstrual** adj. occurring before a menstrual period.

**premier** adj. first in importance, order, or time. • n. a prime minister or other head of government.

**premiere** n. the first public performance of a play etc.

**premise** (or **premiss**) n. a statement on which reasoning is based.

**premises** pl.n. a house or other building and its grounds.

**premium** n. **1** an amount to be paid for an insurance policy. **2** a sum added to a usual price or charge. □ **at a premium 1** above the usual price. **2** scarce and in demand.

**premonition** n. a feeling that something will happen.
▷ SYNS FOREBODING, presentiment, intuition, feeling, hunch.

**preoccupy** v. completely fill someone's thoughts.
■ **preoccupation** n.
▷ SYNS ENGROSS, absorb, distract, obsess, occupy, prey on someone's mind.

**preparation** n. **1** preparing; something done to make ready. **2** a substance prepared for use.
▷ SYNS **1** ARRANGEMENTS, plans, provisions; groundwork, spadework. **2** MIXTURE, compound, concoction, potion.

**preparatory** adj. preparing for something. □ **preparatory school** a private school for pupils between seven and thirteen.

**prepare** v. make ready for use; get ready to do or deal with something. □ **prepared to** willing to.
▷ SYNS GET READY, arrange, develop, put together, draw up, produce, construct, compose, concoct.

**preponderance** n. the state of being greater in number.
■ **preponderant** adj. **preponderate** v.

**preposition** n. Grammar a word used with a noun or pronoun to show place, time, or method, e.g. '*after* dinner' or 'we went *by* train'.

**prepossessing** adj. attractive.

**preposterous** adj. utterly absurd or outrageous.
▷ SYNS ABSURD, ridiculous, ludicrous, farcical, laughable, outrageous.

**prerequisite** n. something that is required before something else can happen.

**prerogative** n. a right or privilege.

**presage** v. be an omen of. • n. omen.

**Presbyterian** adj. & n. (a member) of a Church governed by elders of equal rank.

**prescient** adj. having knowledge of events before they happen. ■ **prescience** n.

**prescribe** v. **1** advise the use of a medicine etc. **2** state officially that something should be done.

**prescription** n. a doctor's written instruction stating that a patient may be issued a medicine.

**prescriptive** adj. stating what should be done.

**presence** n. being present; a person or thing that is present without being seen; an impressive manner or bearing. □ **presence of mind** ability to act sensibly in a crisis.
▷ SYNS **1** EXISTENCE, being; attendance, appearance. **2** *a woman of presence:* MAGNETISM, aura, charisma, personality.

**present**[1] adj. **1** being in the place in question. **2** existing or being dealt with now. • n. the time occurring now.
▷ SYNS adj. **1** EXISTING, existent, extant. **2** PRESENT-DAY, current,

contemporary. **3** IN ATTENDANCE, available, at hand. • n. TODAY, now, here and now.

**present²** n. a gift. • v. **1** formally give something to someone; cause trouble or difficulty. **2** introduce a broadcast; represent in a particular way. □ **present itself** become apparent. ■ **presentation** n. **presenter** n.
▷ SYNS n. GIFT, donation, offering, contribution, gratuity. • v. **1** GIVE, hand over, confer, bestow, award, grant, accord. **2** INTRODUCE, announce.

**presentable** adj. clean or smart enough to be seen in public.

**presentiment** n. a foreboding.
▷ SYNS FOREBODING, premonition, intuition, feeling, hunch.

**presently** adv. **1** soon. **2** now.

**preservative** n. a substance that preserves perishable food.

**preserve** v. keep safe, unchanged, or in existence; treat food to prevent it decaying. • n. **1** interests etc. regarded as one person's domain. **2** (also **preserves**) jam. ■ **preservation** n.
▷ SYNS v. CONSERVE, protect, safeguard, defend, guard, care for, keep, save, maintain, uphold, keep alive.

**preside** v. be in authority or control.
▷ SYNS BE IN CHARGE OF, control, direct, run, conduct, supervise, govern, rule.

**president** n. the head of an organization; the head of a republic. ■ **presidency** n. **presidential** adj.

**press** v. **1** (cause to) move into contact with something by applying force; push

downwards or inwards; squeeze or flatten; iron clothes. **2** urge; try hard to persuade or influence; insist on a point. **3** move in a specified direction by pushing. **4** (**press on**) continue with what you are doing. **5** bring into use as a makeshift measure. • n. **1** a device for flattening or squeezing. **2** a machine for printing. **3** (**the press**) newspapers or journalists as a whole. □ **press conference** an interview given to a number of journalists. **press-gang** force to do something. **press stud** a small fastener with two parts that are pressed together. **press-up** an exercise involving lying on the floor and pressing down with your hands to raise your body.
▷ SYNS v. **1** DEPRESS, push down. **2** IRON, smooth out, flatten. **3** URGE, entreat, exhort, implore, pressurize, force, compel, coerce. • n. NEWSPAPERS, the media, Fleet Street.

**pressing** adj. urgent.

**pressure** n. **1** steady force applied to an object by something in contact with it. **2** influence or persuasion of an oppressive kind; stress. • v. pressurize a person. □ **pressure cooker** a pan for cooking things quickly by steam under pressure. **pressure group** an organized group seeking to exert influence by concerted action.
▷ SYNS n. **1** FORCE, weight, compression. **2** COMPULSION, coercion, constraint, duress. **3** STRAIN, stress, tension, burden, load.

**pressurize** (or **-ise**) v. **1** try to compel into an action. **2** maintain constant artificially raised pressure in an aircraft cabin etc.

**prestige** n. respect resulting from good reputation or achievements.
▷ SYNS STATUS, standing, stature, reputation, repute, fame, renown, honour, esteem, importance, influence, eminence; kudos, cachet.

**prestigious** adj. having or bringing respect and admiration.
▷ SYNS IMPORTANT, prominent, impressive, high-ranking, reputable, respected, esteemed, eminent, distinguished, well known, celebrated, illustrious, renowned, famous.

**presto** adv. Music very quickly.

**prestressed** adj. (of concrete) strengthened by wires within it.

**presumably** adv. it may be presumed.

**presume** v. **1** suppose to be true. **2** be presumptuous. **3** (**presume on**) take advantage of someone's kindness etc.
■ presumption n.
▷ SYNS ASSUME, take it, suppose, believe, think, imagine, judge, guess, surmise, conjecture.

**presumptuous** adj. behaving too self-confidently.
▷ SYNS OVERCONFIDENT, cocksure, arrogant, bold, forward, impertinent, impudent, cocky.

**presuppose** v. require as a precondition; assume at the beginning of an argument.
■ presupposition n.

**pretence** (US **pretense**) n. **1** pretending. **2** a claim to have or be something.

▷ SYNS SHOW, semblance, appearance, false front, guise, facade, masquerade.

**pretend** v. **1** speak or behave so as to make something seem to be the case when it is not. **2** claim to have a skill, title, etc.
■ pretender n.
▷ SYNS PUT ON AN ACT, act, play-act, put it on, sham, feign, fake, dissimulate, dissemble, make believe.

**pretension** n. **1** a claim to have or be something. **2** pretentiousness.

**pretentious** adj. trying to appear more important, intelligent, etc., than is the case.
▷ SYNS AFFECTED, ostentatious, showy, grandiose, elaborate, extravagant.

**pretext** n. a false reason used to justify an action.

**prettify** v. (**prettified**, **prettifying**) try to make something look pretty.

**pretty** adj. (**-ier**, **-iest**) attractive.
• adv. to a moderate extent.
■ prettiness n.
▷ SYNS adj. LOVELY, attractive, good-looking, personable, appealing, cute; Scot. & N. Engl. bonny.

**pretzel** n. a salty knot-shaped biscuit.

**prevail** v. **1** be stronger. **2** be widespread or current. **3** (**prevail on**) persuade.
▷ SYNS WIN, triumph, carry the day, conquer, overcome.

**prevalent** adj. widespread or common. ■ prevalence n.
▷ SYNS WIDESPREAD, prevailing, frequent, usual, common, current, popular, general, universal; endemic, rampant, rife.

**prevaricate** v. speak or act evasively or misleadingly. ■ prevarication n.
▷ SYNS EQUIVOCATE, shilly-shally, hum and haw, hedge, beat about the bush, play for time.

**prevent** v. keep from happening; make unable to do something. ■ prevention n.
▷ SYNS PUT A STOP TO, halt, arrest, avert, fend off, stave off, ward off, hinder, impede, hamper, obstruct, baulk, foil, thwart, frustrate, forestall, prohibit, bar.

**preventive** (or **preventative**) adj. designed to prevent something.

**previous** adj. coming before in time or order. ■ previously adv.
▷ SYNS 1 FORMER, ex-, past, erstwhile. 2 PRECEDING, foregoing, earlier, prior.

**prey** n. an animal hunted or killed by another for food; a victim. □ **bird of prey** a bird that kills and eats birds and mammals. **prey on 1** kill and eat. **2** distress or worry.

**price** n. 1 the amount of money for which something is bought or sold. 2 something unwelcome that must be done to achieve something. • v. decide the price of.
▷ SYNS n. COST, charge, fee, levy; amount, figure, sum.

**priceless** adj. invaluable.

**prick** v. 1 pierce slightly. 2 cause a slight prickling feeling. • n. a mark, hole, or pain caused by pricking.
▷ SYNS v. PIERCE, puncture, perforate, stab, nick, spike.

**prickle** n. 1 a small thorn or spine. 2 a tingling feeling. • v. have a tingling feeling.

**prickly** adj. 1 having prickles. 2 easily offended.

**pride** n. 1 pleasure or satisfaction gained from achievements, qualities, or possessions. 2 a source of this. 3 self-respect. 4 a group of lions. □ **pride of place** the most prominent position. **pride yourself on** be proud of.
▷ SYNS 1 SATISFACTION, gratification, pleasure, joy, delight. 2 CONCEIT, vanity, arrogance, self-importance, hubris, narcissism. 3 SELF-ESTEEM, dignity, self-respect, self-worth.

**priest** n. 1 a member of the clergy. 2 (fem. **priestess**) a person who performs ceremonies in a non-Christian religion. ■ priesthood n.

**prig** n. a self-righteous person.

**priggish** adj. self-righteously moralistic and superior.
▷ SYNS SELF-RIGHTEOUS, holier-than-thou, sanctimonious, prudish, puritanical, prim, strait-laced, narrow-minded.

**prim** adj. very formal and correct and disapproving of anything rude.
▷ SYNS PROPER, demure, strait-laced, prudish, prissy, priggish, puritanical.

**prima ballerina** n. a chief ballerina.

**primacy** n. pre-eminence.

**prima donna** n. 1 the chief female singer in an opera. 2 a temperamental and self-important person.

**prima facie** adj. & adv. accepted as correct until proved otherwise.

**primal** adj. 1 primitive or primeval. 2 fundamental.

**primary** adj. 1 first in time, order, or importance. 2 (of a school or education) for children below the age of 11. • n. (pl. **-ies**) (in the US) a preliminary election to choose delegates or candidates. □ **primary colour** each of the colours blue, red, and yellow, from which all other colours can be obtained by mixing.
■ **primarily** adv.
▷ SYNS **adj. 1** PRIME, chief, main, principal, leading, predominant, paramount, basic, fundamental, essential. **2** EARLIEST, original, initial, first, opening.

**primate** n. 1 an animal belonging to the group that includes monkeys, apes, and humans. 2 an archbishop.

**prime** adj. 1 most important. 2 excellent. • n. a state or time of greatest strength, success, excellence, etc. • v. prepare for use or action; provide with information in preparation for something. □ **prime minister** the head of a government. **prime number** a number that can be divided only by itself and one.
▷ SYNS **adj. 1** see **PRIMARY** (1). **2** TOP-QUALITY, best, first-class, choice, select.

**primer** n. 1 a substance painted on a surface as a base coat. 2 an elementary textbook.

**primeval** adj. of the earliest times of the world.

**primitive** adj. of or at an early stage of evolution or civilization; simple or crude.
▷ SYNS **1** ANCIENT, earliest, primeval, primordial, primal. **2** CRUDE, simple, rudimentary, rough, unsophisticated. **3** UN-CIVILIZED, barbarian, barbaric, savage.

**primordial** adj. primeval.

**primrose** n. a pale yellow spring flower.

**prince** n. a son or other close male relative of a king or queen.

**princely** adj. of or appropriate to a prince; (of a sum of money) generous.

**princess** n. 1 a daughter or other close female relative of a monarch. 2 a prince's wife or widow.

**principal** adj. first in rank or importance. • n. 1 the most important person in an organization; the head of a school or college; a leading performer in a play, concert, etc. 2 a sum of money lent or invested, on which interest is paid.
■ **principally** adv.
▷ SYNS **adj.** MAIN, chief, primary, leading, foremost, first, dominant, key, crucial, vital, essential, basic, prime, central; premier, paramount, major, overriding.

**principality** n. (pl. **-ies**) a country ruled by a prince.

**principle** n. a law, rule, or theory that something is based on; beliefs governing your actions and personal behaviour; a scientific law applying across a wide field. □ **in principle** in theory. **on principle** because of your moral principles.
▷ SYNS DOCTRINE, belief, creed, credo, rule, criterion, tenet, code, ethic, dictum, canon, law.

**print** v. 1 produce a book etc. by a process involving the transfer of words or pictures to paper. 2 write words without joining the letters. 3 produce a photographic print from a negative. • n. printed words in a book etc.; a mark where something has pressed a surface; a printed picture or design. □ **printout** a page of printed material from a computer's printer. ■ **printer** n.

**prior** adj. coming before in time, order, or importance. • n. (fem. **prioress**) **1** a person next in rank below an abbot or abbess. **2** the head of a priory.

**prioritize** (or **-ise**) v. treat as more important than other things; arrange in order of importance.

**priority** n. (pl. **-ies**) something regarded as more important than others; being treated as more important than others; the right to proceed before other traffic.

**priory** n. (pl. **-ies**) a monastery or nunnery governed by a prior or prioress.

**prise** (US **prize**) v. force open or apart.

**prism** n. **1** a transparent object with triangular ends that separates white light into colours. **2** a solid geometric shape whose ends are equal and parallel. ■ **prismatic** adj.

**prison** n. a building where criminals are kept as a punishment.
▷ SYNS JAIL, gaol, lock-up; inf. nick.

**prisoner** n. **1** a person kept in prison. **2** a person in confinement.
▷ SYNS CONVICT, captive, detainee, internee; inf. jailbird.

**prissy** adj. prim or prudish.

**pristine** adj. in its original and unspoilt condition.
▷ SYNS UNMARKED, unblemished, spotless, immaculate, clean, in mint condition.

**privacy** n. being undisturbed or unobserved.

**private** adj. **1** belonging to a particular person or group; confidential; secluded. **2** not provided or owned by the state; not holding public office. • n. a soldier of the lowest rank.
▷ SYNS adj. **1** CONFIDENTIAL, secret, unofficial, off-the-record, hush-hush. **2** PERSONAL, intimate, secret. **3** RESERVED, retiring, self-contained, uncommunicative, secretive.

**privation** n. shortage of food etc.; hardship.
▷ SYNS DEPRIVATION, disadvantage, poverty, hardship, indigence, destitution.

**privatize** (or **-ise**) v. transfer from state to private ownership. ■ **privatization** n.

**privet** n. a bushy evergreen shrub.

**privilege** n. a special right granted to a person or group; a great honour. ■ **privileged** adj.
▷ SYNS ADVANTAGE, benefit; prerogative, entitlement, right.

**privy** n. (pl. **-ies**) an outside toilet. • adj. (**privy to**) sharing knowledge of a secret.

**prize** n. an award for victory or superiority; something that can be won. • adj. **1** winning a prize. **2** excellent. • v. **1** value highly. **2** US sp. of PRISE.
▷ SYNS n. TROPHY, medal, award, accolade, reward, honour.
• v. VALUE, treasure, cherish, hold dear.

**pro** n. (pl. **pros**) inf. a professional. □ **pros and cons** arguments for and against something.

**proactive** adj. gaining control by taking the initiative.

**probability** n. (pl. **-ies**) the extent to which something is probable; a probable event.

**probable** adj. likely to happen or be true. ■ **probably** adv.
▷ SYNS LIKELY, odds-on, expected, anticipated, predictable, on the cards.

**probate** n. the official process of proving that a will is valid.

**probation** n. 1 the release of an offender from prison on condition of good behaviour under supervision. 2 a period of training and testing a new employee. ■ **probationer** adj.

**probe** n. 1 a blunt surgical instrument for examining the body. 2 an investigation. 3 an unmanned exploratory spacecraft. • v. 1 examine with a probe. 2 conduct an inquiry.
▷ SYNS v. INVESTIGATE, scrutinize, inquire into, examine, study, research, analyse.

**probity** n. honesty.

**problem** n. something difficult to deal with or understand.
▷ SYNS DIFFICULTY, complication, trouble, mess, predicament, plight, dilemma, quandary.

**problematic** adj. difficult to deal with or understand.
▷ SYNS DIFFICULT, hard, troublesome, complicated, knotty, thorny, tricky.

**proboscis** n. 1 a mammal's long flexible snout. 2 the long thin mouthpart of some insects.

**procedure** n. a series of actions done to accomplish something, esp. an established or official one. ■ **procedural** adj.
▷ SYNS COURSE/PLAN OF ACTION, policy, system, method, methodology, modus operandi, technique, means, practice, strategy.

**proceed** v. 1 begin a course of action. 2 go on to do. 3 continue. 4 move forward.
▷ SYNS 1 BEGIN, get going, move, start. 2 GO, make your way, advance progress, carry on.

**proceedings** pl.n. an event or series of actions; a lawsuit.
▷ SYNS 1 ACTIVITIES, events, goings-on, doings, happenings. 2 CASE, lawsuit, litigation, trial.

**proceeds** pl.n. the profit from a sale, performance, etc.
▷ SYNS TAKINGS, profits, returns, receipts, income, earnings.

**process** n. 1 a series of actions to achieve an end. 2 a natural series of changes. • v. 1 perform a series of actions to change or preserve something. 2 deal with using an established procedure. ■ **processor** n.
▷ SYNS n. METHOD, system, technique, means, practice, approach, way; procedure, operation.

**procession** n. a number of people or vehicles going along in an orderly line.
▷ SYNS PARADE, march, column, file, train, cortège, cavalcade, motorcade.

**proclaim** v. announce publicly. ■ **proclamation** n.
▷ SYNS ANNOUNCE, declare, pronounce, advertise, publish, broadcast, promulgate.

**proclivity** n. (pl. **-ies**) a tendency.
▷ SYNS TENDENCY, inclination, leaning, propensity, bent, penchant, predisposition, weakness.

**procrastinate** v. postpone action. ■ **procrastination** n.
▷ SYNS DELAY, stall, temporize, play for time, drag your feet.

**procreate** v. produce young.
■ procreation n.

**procurator fiscal** n. (in Scotland) a public prosecutor and coroner.

**procure** v. obtain.
■ procurement n.
▷ SYNS OBTAIN, acquire, get, secure.

**prod** v. 1 poke. 2 stimulate to action. • n. 1 a poke; a pointed object like a stick. 2 a stimulus.
▷ SYNS v. POKE, jab, dig, elbow, butt, push, shove.

**prodigal** adj. wasteful or extravagant.

**prodigious** adj. impressively large.

**prodigy** n. (pl. -ies) a young person with exceptional abilities.
▷ SYNS GENIUS, wonder, marvel, sensation.

**produce** v. 1 make or manufacture. 2 cause to happen or exist. 3 present for inspection. 4 administer the staging, financing, etc. of a film or play.
• n. things produced or grown.
■ producer n. production n.
▷ SYNS v. MAKE, manufacture, construct, build, fabricate, put together, assemble, create.

**product** n. 1 a thing produced. 2 an amount obtained by multiplying one number by another.
▷ SYNS COMMODITY, artefact; goods, wares, merchandise.

**productive** adj. producing or achieving a great deal.
■ productivity n.
▷ SYNS FERTILE, fruitful, rich, high-yielding, prolific.

**profane** adj. 1 not sacred. 2 irreverent or blasphemous.
• v. treat with a lack of respect.
■ profanity n.

**profess** v. 1 claim that something is true. 2 declare your faith in a religion.
▷ SYNS DECLARE, maintain, announce, proclaim, assert, state, affirm, avow.

**profession** n. 1 a job requiring special training and formal qualifications. 2 the people engaged in this. 3 a declaration.
▷ SYNS 1 CAREER, occupation, vocation, calling, métier, line of work, job, business. 2 DECLARATION, assertion, avowal, claim, protestation.

**professional** adj. 1 of or belonging to a profession. 2 paid rather than amateur. 3 competent or skilful.
• n. a professional person.
■ professionally adv.
▷ SYNS adj. SKILLED, skilful, proficient, expert, masterly, adept, competent, efficient, experienced.

**professor** n. a university teacher of the highest rank.

**proffer** v. offer.
▷ SYNS OFFER, tender, present, give, submit, volunteer, suggest, propose.

**proficient** adj. competent; skilled. ■ proficiency n.

**profile** n. 1 a side view, esp. of the face. 2 a short account of a person's character or career. 3 the extent to which someone attracts attention.
▷ SYNS 1 OUTLINE, silhouette, contour, lines, shape, form, figure. 2 SHORT BIOGRAPHY, sketch, thumbnail sketch, portrait, vignette.

**profit** n. financial gain; an advantage or benefit. • v. (**profited, profiting**) make money; benefit

someone. ■ **profitability** n.
**profitably** adv.
▷ SYNS n. 1 TAKINGS, proceeds, gain, yield, return, receipts, income, earnings, winnings. 2 GAIN, benefit, advantage, good, value, use, avail.

**profitable** adj. 1 making a profit. 2 useful.
▷ SYNS 1 MONEYMAKING, commercial, remunerative, lucrative. 2 REWARDING, productive, valuable, useful, beneficial, worthwhile.

**profiteering** n. the making of a large profit in an unfair way.

**profligate** adj. wasteful or extravagant; dissolute.

**profound** adj. 1 very great. 2 showing or needing great insight. ■ **profundity** n.
▷ SYNS 1 DEEP, intense, great, extreme, sincere, earnest, heartfelt, wholehearted, fervent. 2 INTELLIGENT, discerning, penetrating, perceptive, astute, thoughtful, insightful.

**profuse** adj. plentiful. ■ **profusion** n.
▷ SYNS ABUNDANT, copious, plentiful, prolific.

**progenitor** n. an ancestor.

**progeny** n. offspring.

**progesterone** n. a hormone that stimulates the uterus to prepare for pregnancy.

**prognosis** n. (pl. **-noses**) a forecast, esp. of the course of a disease.

**programme** (US **program**) n. 1 a planned series of future events or actions. 2 a sheet giving details about a play, concert, etc. 3 a radio or television broadcast. 4 (**program**) a series of software instructions for a computer. • v. 1 (**program**) provide a computer with a program. 2 make or arrange in a particular way or according to a plan.
▷ SYNS n. 1 AGENDA, calendar, schedule, timetable; syllabus, curriculum. 2 PRODUCTION, show, performance, broadcast.

**progress** n. forward movement; development. • v. move forwards; develop.
■ **progression** n.
▷ SYNS n. HEADWAY, advance, advancement, progression, development, growth. • v. MAKE YOUR WAY, advance, go, continue, proceed, forge ahead.

**progressive** adj. 1 favouring reform or new ideas. 2 proceeding gradually or in stages.
▷ SYNS MODERN, advanced, radical, innovative, revolutionary, forward-looking, avant-garde.

**prohibit** v. (**prohibited**, **prohibiting**) forbid.
■ **prohibition** n.
▷ SYNS FORBID, ban, bar, proscribe, veto, interdict, outlaw; rule out, preclude.

**prohibitive** adj. 1 (of a price) too high. 2 forbidding something.
▷ SYNS EXORBITANT, steep, extortionate, excessive, preposterous.

**project** n. a plan or undertaking; a piece of work involving research. • v. 1 estimate; plan. 2 stick out beyond something else. 3 cause light or an image to fall on a surface or screen; present yourself to others in a particular way.
▷ SYNS n. SCHEME, plan, programme, enterprise, undertaking, venture, campaign.

• v. JUT OUT, protrude, extend, stick out, stand out.

**projectile** n. a missile.

**projection** n. **1** an estimate of future situations based on a study of present ones. **2** the projection of an image etc. **3** something sticking out from a surface.

**projector** n. an apparatus for projecting images on to a screen.

**prolapse** n. a condition in which an organ of the body slips forward out of place.

**proletariat** n. working-class people. ■ **proletarian** adj. & n.

**proliferate** v. increase or reproduce rapidly. ■ **proliferation** n.
▷ SYNS INCREASE, multiply, extend, expand, burgeon, accelerate, escalate, rocket, snowball, mushroom.

**prolific** adj. producing things abundantly.

**prologue** n. an introduction to a play, poem, etc.

**prolong** v. lengthen in extent or duration.
▷ SYNS LENGTHEN, draw out, drag out, protract, spin out.

**prom** n. inf. **1** a promenade. **2** a promenade concert.

**promenade** n. a paved public walk, esp. by the sea. □ **promenade concert** a concert of classical music at which part of the audience stands.

**prominent** adj. **1** famous or important. **2** sticking out. **3** conspicuous. ■ **prominence** n.
▷ SYNS **1** IMPORTANT, famous, renowned, well known, eminent, distinguished, illustrious, celebrated. **2** PROTRUDING, protuberant, jutting

out. **3** CONSPICUOUS, noticeable, eye-catching, obtrusive.

**promiscuous** adj. having many sexual relationships.
■ **promiscuity** n.

**promise** n. **1** an assurance that you will do something or that something will happen. **2** potential excellence. • v. **1** make a promise. **2** give reason to expect.
▷ SYNS n. **1** WORD, assurance, pledge, vow, guarantee, oath, commitment, undertaking. **2** POTENTIAL, talent, ability, aptitude. • v. SWEAR, vow, pledge, undertake, guarantee.

**promising** adj. likely to turn out well.
▷ SYNS ENCOURAGING, hopeful, favourable, auspicious, propitious, optimistic, bright.

**promontory** n. (pl. **-ies**) high land jutting out into the sea.
▷ SYNS HEADLAND, head, point, cape; cliff.

**promote** v. **1** help the progress of. **2** publicize a product. **3** raise to a higher rank or office.
■ **promoter** n. **promotion** n. **promotional** adj.
▷ SYNS **1** ADVANCE, further, foster, aid, develop, boost. **2** ADVERTISE, publicize; inf. push, plug, hype. **3** ELEVATE, upgrade.

**prompt** v. **1** cause to happen or do. **2** supply forgotten words to an actor. • adj. done or acting without delay. • adv. exactly or punctually.
▷ SYNS v. CAUSE, make, move, induce, impel, spur on, motivate, stimulate, inspire, provoke. • adj. IMMEDIATE, instant, swift, rapid, speedy, quick, fast, early.

**promulgate** v. make widely known.

**prone** adj. **1** lying face downwards. **2** likely to do or suffer something.

**prong** n. each of the pointed parts of a fork.

**pronoun** n. a word used instead of a noun to indicate someone or something already mentioned or known, e.g. *I*, *this*, *it*.

**pronounce** v. **1** utter a sound or word distinctly or in a certain way. **2** declare or announce.
■ pronouncement n. pronunciation n.

**pronounced** adj. noticeable.
▷ SYNS MARKED, noticeable, distinct, obvious, conspicuous, striking, unmistakable.

**proof** n. **1** evidence that something is true or exists. **2** a copy of printed material for correction. • adj. resistant to: *damp-proof*. ◻ proofread read printed proofs and mark any errors.
■ proofreader n.
▷ SYNS n. EVIDENCE, substantiation, corroboration, confirmation, verification, authentication, validation.

**prop** n. **1** a pole or beam used as a temporary support. **2** inf. a portable object used on a play or film set. • v. (**propped**, **propping**) support with or as if with a prop.
▷ SYNS n. POLE, post, support, upright, buttress, strut.
• v. (**prop up**) HOLD UP, shore up, bolster up, buttress, support, brace, underpin.

**propaganda** n. information intended to persuade or convince people.

**propagate** v. **1** grow a new plant from a parent plant.

**2** spread or transmit news etc.
■ propagation n.

**propane** n. a hydrocarbon fuel gas.

**propel** v. (**propelled**, **propelling**) push forwards or onwards.
■ propellant n. & adj.
▷ SYNS MOVE, push, drive, thrust, force, impel.

**propeller** n. a revolving device with blades, for propelling a ship or aircraft.

**propensity** n. (pl. **-ies**) a tendency or inclination.

**proper** adj. **1** genuine. **2** appropriate or correct. **3** very respectable. ◻ proper name (or proper noun) the name of a person, place, or organization.
■ properly adv.
▷ SYNS **1** RIGHT, correct, accepted, conventional, established, appropriate, suitable. **2** RESPECTABLE, decorous, seemly, refined, genteel.

**property** n. **1** something owned. **2** a building and its land. **3** a quality or characteristic.
▷ SYNS **1** POSSESSIONS, belongings, goods, effects, chattels. **2** QUALITY, attribute, characteristic, feature, power.

**prophecy** n. (pl. **-ies**) a prediction of future events.
▷ SYNS PREDICTION, forecast, prognostication.

**prophesy** v. (**prophesied**, **prophesying**) predict that something will happen.
▷ SYNS PREDICT, foretell, forecast, foresee.

**prophet** n. **1** a person who foretells events. **2** a religious teacher inspired by God.
■ prophetic adj.
▷ SYNS SEER, soothsayer, oracle.

**prophylactic** adj. intended to prevent disease.

**propitiate** v. win or regain the favour of.

**propitious** adj. favourable.

**proponent** n. a person putting forward a proposal.
▷ SYNS ADVOCATE, supporter, backer, promoter, champion.

**proportion** n. a part or share of a whole; a ratio; the correct relation in size or degree; dimensions. ■ **proportional** (or **proportionate**) adj.
▷ SYNS **1** RATIO, distribution. **2** PORTION, part, segment, amount, quantity, share, percentage.

**proposal** n. **1** the proposing of something; a plan or suggestion. **2** an offer of marriage.
▷ SYNS SCHEME, plan, idea, project, motion, proposition, suggestion, recommendation.

**propose** v. **1** put forward an idea etc. for consideration; nominate for a position. **2** make an offer of marriage to someone.
▷ SYNS **1** PUT FORWARD, advance, offer, present, submit, suggest. **2** INTEND, mean, plan, have in mind, aim.

**proposition** n. **1** a statement or assertion. **2** a suggested plan. **3** a project considered in terms of the likelihood of success. • v. inf. offer to have sex with someone.

**propound** v. put forward an idea etc. for consideration.

**proprietary** adj. **1** of an owner or ownership. **2** (of a product) marketed under a registered trade name.

**proprietor** n. the owner of a business. ■ **proprietorial** adj.

**propriety** n. correctness of behaviour.

**propulsion** n. the process of propelling or being propelled.

**pro rata** adj. proportional. • adv. proportionally.

**prosaic** adj. ordinary and unimaginative. ■ **prosaically** adv.
▷ SYNS UNIMAGINATIVE, ordinary, uninspired, commonplace, dull, tedious, boring, humdrum, mundane, pedestrian.

**proscenium** n. (pl. **-ums** or **-ia**) the part of a theatre stage in front of the curtain.

**proscribe** v. forbid.

**prose** n. ordinary written or spoken language.

**prosecute** v. **1** take legal proceedings against someone for a crime. **2** continue a course of action. ■ **prosecution** n. **prosecutor** n.

**proselyte** n. a recent convert to a religion.

**prospect** n. the likelihood of something's occurring; chances of success. • v. explore in search of something. ■ **prospector** n.
▷ SYNS n. LIKELIHOOD, odds, chance(s), probability, possibility.

**prospective** adj. expected or likely to happen.
▷ SYNS FUTURE, to-be, intended, expected, potential, possible, likely.

**prospectus** n. (pl. **-tuses**) a document giving details of a school, business, etc.

**prosper** v. succeed or thrive.
▷ SYNS DO WELL, thrive, flourish, succeed, get ahead, make good.

**prosperous** adj. financially successful. ■ **prosperity** n.

▷ SYNS WELL OFF, well-to-do, affluent, wealthy, rich, successful.

**prostate** n. the gland round the neck of the bladder in male mammals.

**prosthesis** n. (pl. **-theses**) an artificial body part.

**prostitute** n. a person who has sex for money. • v. put your talents to an unworthy use. ■ prostitution n.

**prostrate** adj. **1** face downwards; lying horizontally. **2** overcome or exhausted. • v. cause to be prostrate. ■ prostration n.
▷ SYNS adj. PRONE, flat, stretched out, horizontal.

**protagonist** n. **1** the chief person in a drama, story, etc. **2** an important person in a real event.

**protean** adj. variable; versatile.

**protect** v. keep from harm or injury. ■ protector n.
▷ SYNS **1** KEEP SAFE, save, safeguard, shield, preserve, defend, shelter, secure. **2** GUARD, defend, watch over, look after, take care of.

**protection** n. **1** the action of protecting or the state of being protected. **2** a thing that protects.
▷ SYNS **1** DEFENCE, preservation, security, safe keeping, safety. **2** BARRIER, buffer, shield, bulwark, screen, cover.

**protectionism** n. a policy of protecting home industries from competition by taxes etc.

**protective** adj. giving protection.

**protectorate** n. a country that is controlled and protected by another.

**protégé** n. a person who is guided and supported by another.

**protein** n. an organic compound forming an essential part of humans' and animals' food.

**protest** n. a statement or action indicating disapproval. • v. **1** express disapproval. **2** declare firmly: *protested her innocence.* ■ protestation n. protester n.
▷ SYNS n. OBJECTION, complaint, remonstration, fuss, outcry. • v. OBJECT, take exception, complain, demur, remonstrate, make a fuss, inveigh against; inf. kick up a fuss.

**Protestant** n. a member of any of the western Christian Churches that are separate from the Roman Catholic Church.

**protocol** n. the system of rules governing formal occasions; accepted behaviour in a situation.
▷ SYNS ETIQUETTE, conventions, formalities, customs, proprieties.

**proton** n. a subatomic particle with a positive electric charge.

**prototype** n. an original example from which others are developed.

**protozoan** n. (pl. **-zoa** or **-zoans**) a one-celled microscopic animal.

**protracted** adj. lasting for a long time.

**protractor** n. an instrument for measuring angles.

**protrude** v. project or stick out. ■ protrusion n.

**protuberance** n. a bulging part.

**protuberant** adj. sticking out or bulging.
▷ SYNS STICKING OUT, protruding, prominent, jutting out, bulging, bulbous.

**proud** adj. 1 feeling pride. 2 giving cause for pride. 3 slightly sticking out from a surface.
▷ SYNS 1 PLEASED, glad, happy, satisfied, gratified. 2 ARROGANT, conceited, vain, self-important, haughty; inf. high-and-mighty.

**prove** v. 1 demonstrate to be true. 2 turn out to be.
■ **proven** adj.
▷ SYNS ESTABLISH, demonstrate, substantiate, corroborate, verify, validate, authenticate, confirm.

**provenance** n. a place of origin.

**proverb** n. a short well-known saying.
▷ SYNS SAYING, adage, maxim, saw, axiom, aphorism.

**proverbial** adj. 1 referred to in a proverb. 2 well known.

**provide** v. 1 make available to someone. 2 (**provide for**) supply with necessities; make preparations for.
▷ SYNS SUPPLY, give, furnish, equip, issue, come up with, contribute.

**provided** (or **providing**) conj. on condition that.

**providence** n. 1 God's or nature's protection. 2 being provident.

**provident** adj. careful in preparing for the future.

**providential** adj. happening very luckily.

**province** n. 1 an administrative division of a country. 2 (**the provinces**) all parts of a country outside its capital city.

**provincial** adj. 1 of a province or provinces. 2 unsophisticated or narrow-minded. • n. an inhabitant of a province.
▷ SYNS adj. 1 LOCAL, small-town, rural. 2 UNSOPHISTICATED, parochial, small-minded, insular, inward-looking, narrow-minded.

**provision** n. 1 the process of providing things. 2 a stipulation in a treaty or contract etc.

**provisional** adj. arranged temporarily. ■ **provisionally** adv.
▷ SYNS TEMPORARY, interim, stopgap, transitional; to be confirmed, tentative.

**provisions** pl.n. food and drink.
▷ SYNS SUPPLIES, food and drink, stores, groceries, foodstuffs, provender.

**proviso** n. (pl. **-os**) a condition attached to an agreement.
▷ SYNS CONDITION, stipulation, provision, rider, qualification, restriction.

**provoke** v. 1 make angry. 2 rouse to action; produce as a reaction. ■ **provocation** n. **provocative** adj.
▷ SYNS 1 ANNOY, anger, incense, enrage, irritate, exasperate, infuriate, vex, gall. 2 AROUSE, produce, cause, give rise to, engender, result in, lead to, trigger.

**provost** n. the head of a college.

**prow** n. a projecting front part of a ship.

**prowess** n. skill or expertise.
▷ SYNS SKILL, expertise, ability, talent, genius, aptitude, proficiency, know-how.

**prowl** v. move about restlessly or stealthily. ■ **prowler** n.
▷ SYNS SLINK, skulk, steal, sneak, creep.

**proximity** n. nearness.

**proxy** n. (pl. **-ies**) a person authorized to represent or act for another.
▷ SYNS REPRESENTATIVE, deputy, substitute, agent, delegate, surrogate.

**prude** n. a person who is easily shocked by matters relating to sex.

**prudent** adj. showing thought for the future. ■ **prudence** n.
▷ SYNS WISE, judicious, sage, shrewd, sensible, far-sighted, politic, circumspect, cautious, careful.

**prudish** adj. easily shocked by sexual matters.
▷ SYNS PRIM, priggish, prissy, puritanical, strait-laced.

**prune** n. a dried plum. • v. trim a tree etc. by cutting away dead or unwanted parts.

**prurient** adj. showing excessive interest in sexual matters.
■ **prurience** n.

**pry** v. (**pries**, **pried**, **prying**) inquire too inquisitively about someone's private affairs.

**PS** abbr. postscript.

**psalm** n. a sacred song.

**pseudo** adj. fake.

**pseudonym** n. a fictitious name used esp. by an author.

**psyche** n. the human soul, mind, or spirit.

**psychedelic** adj. 1 (of a drug) producing hallucinations. 2 having vivid colours or abstract patterns.

**psychiatry** n. the study and treatment of mental illness.
■ **psychiatric** adj. **psychiatrist** n.

**psychic** adj. 1 of or having apparently supernatural powers. 2 of the mind. • n. a person claiming psychic powers.

**psychoanalyse** (US **-yze**) v. treat by psychoanalysis.

**psychoanalysis** n. a method of treating mental disorders by investigating the unconscious elements of the mind.
■ **psychoanalyst** n.

**psychology** n. the scientific study of the mind; the way in which someone thinks or behaves. ■ **psychological** adj. **psychologically** adv. **psychologist** n.

**psychopath** n. a person suffering from a severe mental illness resulting in antisocial or violent behaviour.
■ **psychopathic** adj.

**psychosis** n. (pl. **psychoses**) a mental disorder in which a person's perception of reality is severely distorted.
■ **psychotic** adj.

**psychosomatic** adj. (of illness) caused or made worse by mental stress.

**psychotherapy** n. treatment of mental disorder by psychological rather than medical means.
■ **psychotherapist** n.

**PT** abbr. physical training.

**Pt** abbr. 1 Part. 2 (**pt**) pint. 3 (**pt.**) point.

**PTA** abbr. parent-teacher association.

**pterodactyl** n. an extinct reptile with wings.

**PTO** abbr. please turn over.

**pub** n. a building in which beer and other drinks are served.
▷ SYNS PUBLIC HOUSE, bar, tavern, inn.

**puberty** n. the period during which adolescents reach sexual maturity.

**pubescence** n. the time when puberty begins. ■ **pubescent** adj.

**pubic** adj. of the lower abdomen.

**public** adj. of, for, or known to people in general. • n. **1** ordinary people in general. **2** a group with a particular interest. □ **public address system** a system of loudspeakers amplifying sound for an audience. **public house** a pub. **public relations** the business of keeping a good public image by an organization or famous person. **public school** (in the UK) a private fee-paying school. **public sector** the part of the economy that is controlled by the state. ■ **publicly** adv.
▷ SYNS adj. **1** *public awareness*: POPULAR, general, common, universal, widespread. **2** *public figures*: PROMINENT, well known, important, eminent, respected, influential, prestigious, famous. • n. PEOPLE, population, country, nation, community, citizens, citizenry, populace, the masses.

**publican** n. the owner or manager of a pub.

**publication** n. publishing; a published book, newspaper, etc.
▷ SYNS BOOK, newspaper, magazine, periodical, journal, booklet, brochure, leaflet, pamphlet.

**publicity** n. attention given to someone or something by the media; material used in publicizing something.

**publicize** (or **-ise**) v. make widely known; promote or advertise. ■ **publicist** n.

▷ SYNS **1** MAKE PUBLIC, announce, broadcast, publish, spread, distribute, promulgate. **2** PROMOTE, advertise, push; inf. hype, plug.

**publish** v. **1** produce a book etc. for public sale. **2** make generally known. ■ **publisher** n.

**puce** adj. & n. brownish purple.

**puck** n. a hard rubber disc used in ice hockey.

**pucker** v. contract into wrinkles. • n. a wrinkle.

**pudding** n. **1** a sweet cooked dish; the dessert course of a meal. **2** a savoury dish containing flour, suet, etc.

**puddle** n. a small pool of rainwater or other liquid.

**puerile** adj. childish.

**puff** n. **1** a short burst of breath or wind; smoke, etc., blown out by this. **2** a light pastry case with a filling. • v. **1** emit or send out in puffs; breathe heavily. **2** (cause to) swell. □ **puffball** a ball-shaped fungus. **puff pastry** light flaky pastry.
▷ SYNS n. GUST, waft, breath, flurry, breeze, draught. • v. **1** PANT, blow, gasp. **2** SWELL, distend, inflate, dilate, bloat.

**puffin** n. a seabird with a short striped bill.

**puffy** adj. (**-ier**, **-iest**) puffed out or swollen.

**pug** n. a small breed of dog with a flat nose and wrinkled face.

**pugilist** n. a boxer.

**pugnacious** adj. eager to argue or fight. ■ **pugnacity** n.
▷ SYNS BELLIGERENT, bellicose, combative, aggressive, antagonistic, argumentative, quarrelsome.

**puke** inf. v. & n. vomit.

**pukka** adj. real or genuine.

**pull** v. 1 apply force to something so as to move it towards yourself. 2 move steadily or with effort. 3 strain a muscle. • n. 1 an act of pulling. 2 a force or attraction. 3 a deep drink or draw on a cigarette etc. □ pull out withdraw. pull through get through an illness.
▷ SYNS v. 1 HAUL, drag, draw, trail, tow, tug, heave, yank. 2 *pull a muscle:* STRAIN, sprain, wrench.

**pullet** n. a young hen.

**pulley** n. (pl. **-eys**) a wheel over which a rope etc. passes, used in lifting things.

**pullover** n. a knitted garment for the upper body.

**pulmonary** adj. of the lungs.

**pulp** n. a soft, wet mass of crushed material; the soft moist part of fruit. • v. crush to pulp. ■ pulpy adj.

**pulpit** n. a raised enclosed platform from which a preacher speaks.

**pulsate** v. expand and contract rhythmically. ■ pulsation n.
▷ SYNS BEAT, throb, pulse, palpitate, pound, thud, thump, drum.

**pulse** n. 1 the rhythmical beat of the blood as it is pumped around the body. 2 a single beat, throb, or vibration. 3 the edible seed of beans, peas, lentils, etc. • v. pulsate.

**pulverize** (or **-ise**) v. crush to powder.

**puma** n. a large brown American wild cat.

**pumice** n. solidified lava used for scouring or polishing.

**pummel** v. (**pummelled**, **pummelling**; US **pummeled**) strike repeatedly with the fists.

**pump** n. 1 a machine for moving liquid, gas, or air. 2 a plimsoll. • v. 1 force air etc. in a particular direction using a pump; inflate or empty using a pump. 2 move vigorously up and down.

**pumpkin** n. a large round orange-coloured fruit.

**pun** n. a joke that uses a word or words with more than one meaning.

**punch** v. 1 strike with the fist. 2 cut a hole in something. 3 press a key on a machine. • n. 1 a blow with the fist. 2 a device for cutting holes or impressing a design. 3 a drink made of wine or spirits mixed with fruit juices etc. □ punchline the final part of a joke, providing the humour.
▷ SYNS v. STRIKE, hit, thump, pummel; inf. wallop, whack, clout.

**punctilious** adj. showing great attention to detail or correct behaviour.

**punctual** adj. arriving or doing things at the appointed time. ■ punctuality n. punctually adv.
▷ SYNS ON TIME, on the dot, prompt, in good time.

**punctuate** v. 1 insert the appropriate marks in written material to separate sentences etc. 2 interrupt at intervals. ■ punctuation n.

**puncture** n. a small hole caused by a sharp object. • v. make a puncture in.
▷ SYNS V. PERFORATE, pierce, prick, penetrate.

**pundit** n. an expert.

**pungent** adj. having a strong sharp taste or smell.
- ■ pungency n.
- ▷ SYNS SHARP, strong, acid, sour, bitter, tart; spicy, piquant.

**punish** v. impose a penalty on someone for an offence.
- ■ punishment n.
- ▷ SYNS DISCIPLINE, penalize, correct, teach someone a lesson.

**punitive** adj. inflicting or intended as a punishment.

**punk** (also **punk rock**) n. a loud aggressive form of rock music.

**punnet** n. a small container for fruit etc.

**punt**[1] n. a long narrow, flat-bottomed boat, moved forward with a long pole. • v. travel in a punt.

**punt**[2] v. kick a dropped football before it touches the ground.

**punter** n. inf. **1** a person who gambles. **2** a customer.

**puny** adj. (-ier, -iest) small and weak.
- ▷ SYNS WEAK, weakly, frail, feeble, undersized, stunted, small, slight, little.

**pup** n. a young dog; a young wolf, rat, or seal.

**pupa** n. (pl. **pupae**) a chrysalis.

**pupate** v. become a pupa.

**pupil** n. **1** a person who is taught by another. **2** the opening in the centre of the iris of the eye.

**puppet** n. a kind of doll made to move as an entertainment; a person etc. controlled by another.

**puppy** n. (pl. **-ies**) a young dog.

**purchase** v. buy. • n. **1** buying; something bought. **2** a firm hold or grip.
- ▷ SYNS v. See BUY. n. **1** BUY, acquisition, investment. **2** GRIP, hold, foothold, footing, toehold, leverage.

**purdah** n. the Muslim or Hindu system of screening women.

**pure** adj. **1** not mixed with any other substance. **2** innocent or good. **3** complete; nothing but. **4** theoretical rather than practical: *pure mathematics.*
- ■ purely adv. purity n.
- ▷ SYNS **1** UNADULTERATED, unmixed; flawless, perfect, genuine, real. **2** CLEAN, clear, fresh, unpolluted, uncontaminated. **3** VIRTUOUS, moral, good, innocent; chaste, virginal, undefiled, unsullied. **4** SHEER, utter, absolute, out-and-out, complete, total.

**purée** n. pulped fruit or vegetables etc. • v. make into a purée.

**purgative** n. a laxative.

**purgatory** n. a place or condition of suffering, esp. (in RC belief) in which souls undergo purification before going to heaven.

**purge** v. **1** empty the bowels by taking a laxative. **2** rid of undesirable people or things. • n. the process of purging.

**purify** v. make pure.
- ■ purification n.
- ▷ SYNS CLEAN, cleanse, decontaminate, disinfect, sterilize, sanitize, fumigate.

**purist** n. a stickler for correctness.

**puritan** n. a person with strong moral beliefs who is critical of others' behaviour.

**puritanical** adj. having a very strict or critical attitude towards self-indulgent behaviour.

▷ SYNS MORALISTIC, strait-laced, prudish, prim, priggish, austere, ascetic, abstemious.

**purl** n. a knitting stitch. • v. make this stitch.

**purlieus** n. the area around or near a place.

**purloin** v. steal.

**purple** adj. & n. (of) a colour made by mixing red and blue.

**purport** n. meaning. • v. appear or claim to be or do.

**purpose** n. the intended result of an action etc.; a feeling of determination. • v. intend. □ on purpose intentionally.
■ purposely adv.
▷ SYNS n. **1** REASON, point, basis, motivation, cause, justification. **2** AIM, intention, object, objective, goal, end, target, ambition, aspiration, desire, wish, hope.

**purposeful** adj. determined.
▷ SYNS DETERMINED, resolute, single-minded, firm, committed, dedicated, persistent, dogged.

**purr** n. a low vibrant sound that a cat makes when pleased; any similar sound. • v. make this sound.

**purse** n. **1** a small pouch for carrying money. **2** US a handbag. **3** money available for use. • v. pucker the lips.

**purser** n. a ship's officer in charge of accounts.

**pursue** v. **1** follow; try to catch or attain. **2** continue along a route; engage in an activity.
▷ SYNS **1** GO AFTER, follow, chase, hunt, stalk, track, trail, shadow; inf. tail. **2** pursue a career: ENGAGE IN, work at, practise.

**pursuit** n. **1** the act of pursuing. **2** a leisure activity.

**purvey** v. supply food etc. as a business. ■ purveyor n.

**pus** n. thick yellowish matter produced from an infected wound.

**push** v. **1** apply force to something so as to move it away from yourself. **2** move forward by using force. **3** urge to greater effort. **4** inf. sell an illegal drug. • n. **1** an act of pushing. **2** a great effort. □ pushchair a folding chair on wheels, in which a young child can be pushed along.
▷ SYNS v. **1** SHOVE, thrust, propel, drive, ram, elbow, jostle. **2** URGE, press, force, coerce, spur on, prod, goad, dragoon.

**pushy** adj. (-ier, -iest) very self-assertive or ambitious.
▷ SYNS ASSERTIVE, overbearing, domineering, aggressive, forceful, ambitious.

**pusillanimous** adj. cowardly.

**pussy** (or **puss**) n. inf. a cat. □ pussyfoot act cautiously.

**pustule** n. a pimple or blister.
■ pustular adj.

**put** v. **1** move or bring to a particular position or state. **2** express or phrase. **3** throw a shot or weight as a sport. □ put down **1** suppress. **2** kill a sick animal. put off **1** postpone. **2** discourage. put up with tolerate.
▷ SYNS **1** PLACE, lay, set, deposit, position, rest, stand, situate, settle. **2** EXPRESS, word, phrase, frame; state, say, utter.

**putative** adj. generally considered to be.

**putrefy** v. (**putrefied, putrefying**) rot. ■ putrefaction n.

**putrid** adj. rotten and foul-smelling.

**putt** v. hit a golf ball gently so that it rolls into or near a hole. • n. this stroke. ■ **putter** n.

**putty** n. a soft paste that sets hard, used for fixing glass in frames, filling holes, etc.

**puzzle** v. **1** confuse or bewilder. **2** think hard about a problem. • n. a game, toy, or problem designed to test mental skills or knowledge.
▷ SYNS v. CONFUSE, bewilder, perplex, baffle, mystify; inf. flummox, stump.

**puzzling** adj. confusing or mysterious.
▷ SYNS BAFFLING, perplexing, bewildering, confusing, mysterious, obscure, incomprehensible, impenetrable, cryptic.

**PVC** abbr. polyvinyl chloride, a sort of plastic.

**pygmy** (or **pigmy**) n. (pl. **-ies**) a member of a black African people of very short stature; a very small person or thing.

**pyjamas** (US **pajamas**) pl.n. a loose jacket and trousers for sleeping in.

**pylon** n. a tall metal structure carrying electricity cables.

**pyramid** n. a structure with triangular sloping sides that meet at the top.

**pyre** n. a pile of wood for burning a dead body.

**pyromaniac** n. a person with an uncontrollable impulse to set things on fire.

**pyrotechnics** pl.n. a firework display, or the art of staging these.

**pyrrhic** adj. (of a victory) gained at too great a cost to be worthwhile.

**python** n. a large snake that crushes its prey.

# Qq

**QC** abbr. Queen's Counsel.

**quack** n. **1** a duck's harsh cry. **2** a person who falsely claims to have medical skill. • v. (of a duck) make its harsh cry.

**quad** n. **1** a quadrangle. **2** a quadruplet.

**quadrangle** n. a four-sided courtyard bordered by large buildings.

**quadrant** n. a quarter of a circle or of its circumference.

**quadraphonic** (or **quadrophonic**) adj. (of sound reproduction) using four channels.

**quadratic** adj. Math. involving the second and no higher power of an unknown quantity.

**quadrilateral** n. a geometric figure with four sides.

**quadruped** n. a four-footed animal.

**quadruple** adj. **1** having four parts or elements. **2** four times as much. • v. multiply by four.

**quadruplet** n. one of four children born at one birth.

**quaff** v. drink heartily.

**quagmire** n. a bog or marsh.
▷ SYNS BOG, marsh, swamp, morass, mire, fen.

**quail** n. a small game bird.
• v. feel or show fear.
▷ SYNS v. FLINCH, shrink, recoil, cower, cringe, shiver, tremble, quake, blanch.

**quaint** adj. attractively strange or old-fashioned.

**quake** v. shake or tremble, esp. with fear.

**Quaker** n. a member of the Society of Friends, a Christian movement rejecting set forms of worship.

**qualification** n. 1 the act of qualifying. 2 a pass in an exam etc. 3 a statement limiting the meaning of another statement.
▷ SYNS 1 CERTIFICATE, diploma, degree, licence. 2 MODIFICATION, limitation, reservation, stipulation; condition, proviso, caveat.

**qualified** adj. officially recognized as able to do a particular job.
▷ SYNS CERTIFICATED, chartered, licensed, professional; trained, proficient, skilled, experienced, expert.

**qualify** v. (qualified, qualifying) 1 meet the necessary standard or conditions to be entitled to something. 2 become officially recognized as able to do a particular job. 3 limit the meaning of a statement.
■ qualifier n.

**qualitative** adj. of or concerned with quality.

**quality** n. 1 the standard of something as measured against other similar things. 2 a distinctive feature. 3 excellence.
▷ SYNS 1 STANDARD, class, calibre, condition, value, grade, rank. 2 FEATURE, trait, attribute, characteristic, aspect, point.

**qualm** n. a feeling of doubt or unease.
▷ SYNS DOUBT, misgiving, concern, anxiety; scruple, hesitation, reluctance, apprehension, unease.

**quandary** n. (pl. -ies) a state of uncertainty.

**quango** n. (pl. -os) an organization that works independently but with support from the government.

**quantify** v. (quantified, quantifying) express or measure the quantity of.
■ quantifiable adj.

**quantitative** adj. of or concerned with quantity.

**quantity** n. 1 an amount or number. 2 a large number or amount. □ quantity surveyor a person who measures and prices building work.
▷ SYNS AMOUNT, total, aggregate, sum, quota, weight, mass, volume, bulk.

**quantum leap** n. the minimum amount of energy that can take part in a physical process.

**quarantine** n. a period of time when an animal or person that may have a disease is kept in isolation. • v. put into quarantine.

**quark** n. a component of elementary particles.

**quarrel** n. 1 an angry argument. 2 a reason for disagreement.
• v. (quarrelled, quarrelling; US quarreled) engage in a quarrel.
■ quarrelsome adj.

▷ SYNS n. ARGUMENT, row, fight, disagreement, dispute, squabble, altercation, wrangle; inf. tiff. • v. ARGUE, row, fight, squabble, bicker, wrangle, fall out.

**quarry** n. **1** an animal or person that is hunted or chased. **2** a place where stone etc. is dug out of the earth. • v. (**quarried, quarrying**) obtain stone etc. from a quarry.
▷ SYNS n. PREY, victim.

**quart** n. a quarter of a gallon (two pints or 1.13 litres).

**quarter** n. **1** each of four equal parts of something. **2** three months. **3** fifteen minutes. **4** a US or Canadian coin worth 25 cents. **5** (**quarters**) accommodation. **6** mercy shown to an opponent. • v. **1** divide into quarters. **2** put into lodgings. □ **quarterdeck** the part of a ship's upper deck near the stern. **quarter-final** a match preceding the semi-final of a competition. **quartermaster** an army officer in charge of accommodation and supplies.

**quarterly** adj. & adv. produced or occurring once in every quarter of a year. • n. (pl. **-ies**) a quarterly periodical.

**quartet** n. **1** a group of four instruments or voices. **2** music for these.

**quartz** n. a hard mineral.

**quasar** n. a kind of galaxy which gives off enormous amounts of energy.

**quash** v. **1** declare invalid. **2** put an end to.
▷ SYNS **1** CANCEL, reverse, revoke, rescind, repeal, withdraw, overrule, overturn. **2** STOP,

crush, stamp out, squash, quell, suppress.

**quasi-** comb. form seeming to be but not really so.

**quatrain** n. a stanza or poem of four lines.

**quaver** v. (of a voice) tremble. • n. **1** a trembling sound. **2** a musical note equal to half a crotchet. ■ **quavery** adj.
▷ SYNS v. QUIVER, tremble, shake.

**quay** n. a platform in a harbour for loading and unloading ships. ■ **quayside** n.

**queasy** adj. (**-ier, -iest**) feeling sick. ■ **queasiness** n.
▷ SYNS SICK, nauseous, nauseated, bilious, ill.

**queen** n. **1** the female ruler of a country. **2** a king's wife. **3** the best or most important woman or thing. **4** a playing card ranking next below king. **5** a piece in chess. **6** a reproductive bee, ant, etc. ■ **queenly** adj.

**queer** adj. **1** strange or odd. **2** derog. (of a man) homosexual. • n. a homosexual man.
▷ SYNS adj. ODD, strange, peculiar, unusual, extraordinary, funny, curious, weird, bizarre, uncanny; unconventional, unorthodox, atypical, anomalous, abnormal.

**quell** v. suppress.

**quench** v. **1** satisfy thirst. **2** put out a fire.
▷ SYNS **1** SATISFY, slake, sate, satiate. **2** EXTINGUISH, put out, blow out, douse.

**querulous** adj. complaining peevishly.

**query** n. (pl. **-ies**) a question. • v. (**queried, querying**) ask a question.

**quest** n. a long search.

**question** n. **1** a sentence requesting information. **2** a matter needing to be dealt with. **3** doubt. • v. **1** ask questions of. **2** express doubt about. □ out of the question not possible. question mark a punctuation mark (?) placed after a question.
▷ SYNS n. **1** QUERY, enquiry. **2** ISSUE, problem, matter, concern, subject. • v. **1** INTERROGATE, cross-examine, quiz, interview; inf. grill, pump. **2** QUERY, challenge, dispute, doubt, suspect.

**questionable** adj. open to doubt.

**questionnaire** n. a list of questions seeking information.

**queue** n. a line of people or vehicles waiting their turn for something. • v. (**queued**, **queuing** or **queueing**) wait in a queue.
▷ SYNS n. LINE, row, column, file, chain, string.

**quibble** n. a minor objection. • v. raise a minor objection.
▷ SYNS n. CRITICISM, complaint, objection, niggle. • v. OBJECT, complain, cavil, split hairs; inf. nit-pick.

**quiche** n. a baked flan with a savoury filling.

**quick** adj. **1** moving fast. **2** taking a short time. **3** intelligent. • n. the sensitive flesh below the nails. □ quicksand loose wet sand that sucks in anything resting on it. quicksilver mercury. quickstep a fast foxtrot. quick-tempered easily angered. ■ quickly adv.
▷ SYNS adj. **1** FAST, rapid, speedy, swift, fleet. **2** BRIEF, fleeting, momentary, hasty, hurried, cursory, perfunctory.

**quicken** v. make or become quicker.
▷ SYNS SPEED UP, accelerate, hurry, hasten.

**quid** n. (pl. **quid**) inf. one pound in money.

**quid pro quo** n. (pl. **quid pro quos**) a favour given in return for another.

**quiet** adj. **1** making little noise. **2** calm and tranquil. **3** discreet. • n. absence of noise or disturbance.
▷ SYNS adj. **1** SILENT, hushed, noiseless, soundless; low, muted, inaudible. **2** PEACEFUL, sleepy, tranquil, calm, restful.

**quieten** v. make or become quiet and calm.
▷ SYNS SILENCE, hush, shush, quiet, calm; inf. shut up.

**quiff** n. an upright tuft of hair.

**quill** n. **1** a large feather. **2** a pen made from this. **3** a spine of a porcupine or hedgehog.

**quilt** n. a padded bed covering. • v. line with padding and fix with lines of stitching.

**quin** n. inf. a quintuplet.

**quince** n. a hard yellow fruit.

**quinine** n. a bitter-tasting drug used to treat malaria.

**quintessence** n. the perfect or most typical example. ■ quintessential adj. quintessentially adv.
▷ SYNS EXEMPLAR, epitome, embodiment, ideal.

**quintet** n. **1** a group of five instruments or voices. **2** music for these.

**quintuple** adj. **1** having five parts or elements. **2** five times as much.

**quintuplet** n. one of five children born at one birth.

**quip** n. a witty remark.
• v. (**quipped**, **quipping**) make a witty remark.

**quirk** n. **1** a peculiar habit. **2** a strange thing that happens by chance. ■ **quirky** adj.

**quisling** n. a traitor who collaborates with occupying forces.

**quit** v. **1** leave a place. **2** resign from a job. **3** inf. stop.
▷ SYNS **1** LEAVE, depart, resign, walk out. **2** GIVE UP, stop, cease, leave off, refrain from, desist from.

**quite** adv. **1** to a certain extent. **2** completely. • exclam. exactly.
▷ SYNS **adv. 1** COMPLETELY, entirely, totally, wholly, absolutely. **2** FAIRLY, relatively, moderately, reasonably, to some extent, rather, somewhat.

**quits** adj. on even terms after retaliation or repayment.

**quiver** v. slightly shake or vibrate. • n. **1** a quivering movement or sound. **2** a case for holding arrows.
▷ SYNS **v.** TREMBLE, shiver, vibrate, quaver, quake, shudder, pulsate, convulse.

**quixotic** adj. idealistic and impractical.

**quiz** n. (pl. **quizzes**) a competition in which people answer questions to test their knowledge. • v. (**quizzed**, **quizzing**) interrogate.

**quizzical** adj. showing mild or amused puzzlement.
■ **quizzically** adv.
▷ SYNS QUESTIONING, puzzled, perplexed, baffled, mystified; amused, teasing.

**quoit** n. a ring thrown to encircle a peg in the game of **quoits**.

**quorate** adj. having a quorum present.

**quorum** n. a minimum number of people that must be present for a valid meeting.

**quota** n. **1** a quantity allowed. **2** a share that is expected or needed.
▷ SYNS SHARE, allowance, allocation, ration, portion, slice; inf. cut, whack.

**quotation** n. a passage or price quoted. □ **quotation marks** punctuation marks (' ' or " ") enclosing words quoted.
▷ SYNS **1** CITATION, quote, excerpt, extract, selection, passage, line. **2** ESTIMATE, quote, price, charge, figure.

**quote** v. **1** repeat something spoken or written by another person. **2** give an estimated price. ■ **quotable** adj.
▷ SYNS REPEAT, recite; mention, cite, refer to, name, instance, allude to.

**quotidian** adj. daily.

**quotient** n. the result of a division sum.

**q.v.** abbr. used to direct a reader to another part of a book.

# Rr

**R** abbr. **1** Regina or Rex. **2** river.

**rabbi** n. a Jewish religious leader.

**rabbit** n. a burrowing animal with long ears and a short tail.

**rabble** n. a disorderly crowd.

**rabid** adj. **1** fanatical. **2** having rabies.

**rabies** n. a contagious disease of dogs etc., that can be transmitted to humans.

**raccoon** (or **racoon**) n. a small American mammal with a striped tail.

**race** n. **1** a contest of speed. **2** each of the major divisions of humankind. **3** a subdivision of a species. • v. **1** compete in a race. **2** go at full or excessive speed. □ **racecourse** a ground or track for horse or dog racing. **racetrack 1** a racecourse. **2** a track for motor racing.
▷ SYNS n. CONTEST, competition, chase, pursuit, relay. • v. RUN, sprint, dash, bolt, speed, hare, fly, tear, zoom.

**racial** adj. of or based on race. ■ **racially** adv.

**racism** (or **racialism**) n. **1** the belief that certain races are better than others. **2** hostility to or discrimination towards other races. ■ **racist** adj. & n.
▷ SYNS RACIALISM, xenophobia, chauvinism, bigotry.

**rack** n. **1** a framework for hanging or placing things on. **2** hist. an instrument of torture on which people were tied and stretched. • v. (also **wrack**) cause suffering to. □ **rack and ruin** destruction.

**racket** n. **1** (or **racquet**) a stringed bat used in tennis and similar games. **2** a loud noise. **3** inf. a fraudulent business or scheme.

**racketeer** n. a person who operates a fraudulent business etc.

**raconteur** n. a skilled storyteller.

**racoon** = RACCOON.

**racy** adj. lively and exciting.

**radar** n. a system for detecting objects by means of radio waves.

**radial** adj. having spokes or lines etc. that radiate from a central point.

**radiant** adj. **1** shining or glowing brightly. **2** showing joy or health. **3** (of heat) transmitted by radiation. ■ **radiance** n.
▷ SYNS **1** SHINING, bright, illuminated, brilliant, glowing, luminous, lustrous. **2** JOYFUL, elated, ecstatic, euphoric, happy, delighted.

**radiate** v. **1** (of energy) be emitted in rays or waves. **2** spread out from a central point.
▷ SYNS SEND OUT, give off/out, emit, emanate, scatter, diffuse, cast, shed.

**radiation** n. energy sent out as electromagnetic waves or atomic particles.

**radiator** n. **1** a device for heating a room, usu. filled with hot water pumped in through pipes. **2** an engine-cooling device in a vehicle.

**radical** adj. **1** of the basic nature of something; fundamental. **2** supporting complete political or social reform. **3** departing from tradition; new.
• n. someone holding radical views. ■ **radically** adv.
▷ SYNS adj. **1** THOROUGH, complete, total, comprehensive, exhaustive, sweeping, far-reaching, profound. **2** FUNDAMENTAL, basic, essential, deep-seated. **3** EXTREMIST, extreme, militant, fanatic; revolutionary.

**radii** pl. of **RADIUS**.

**radio** n. (pl. **-os**) **1** the sending and receiving of electro-magnetic waves carrying sound messages. **2** broadcasting in sound. **3** a device for receiving or sending radio signals.
• v. (**radioed**, **radioing**) send by radio.

**radioactive** adj. giving out harmful radiation or particles. ■ **radioactivity** n.

**radiocarbon** n. a radioactive form of carbon used in carbon dating.

**radiography** n. the production of X-ray photographs.

**radiology** n. a study of X-rays and similar radiation, e...c. of their use in medicine.

**radiotherapy** n. the treatment of disease by X-rays or similar radiation.

**radish** n. a plant with a crisp, hot-tasting root, eaten in salads.

**radium** n. a radioactive metallic element.

**radius** n. (pl. **-dii** or **-diuses**) **1** a straight line from the centre to the edge of a circle. **2** the thicker long bone of the forearm.

**RAF** abbr. Royal Air Force.

**raffia** n. fibre from the leaves of a palm tree, used for making hats, mats, etc.

**raffish** adj. slightly disreputable in appearance.

**raffle** n. a lottery with an object as the prize. • v. offer as the prize in a raffle.
▷ SYNS n. LOTTERY, draw, sweepstake, tombola.

**raft** n. a flat structure used as a boat or floating platform.

**rafter** n. one of the sloping beams forming the framework of a roof.

**rag** n. **1** a piece of old cloth. **2** (**rags**) old torn clothes. **3** a programme of entertainments by students in aid of charity.

**ragamuffin** n. a person in ragged dirty clothes.

**rage** n. violent anger. • v. **1** show violent anger. **2** continue with great force. □ **all the rage** very popular.
▷ SYNS n. FURY, anger, wrath, ire.
• v. BE FURIOUS, be enraged, seethe, be beside yourself, rant, rave, storm, fume.

**ragged** adj. **1** old and torn. **2** rough or irregular.
▷ SYNS **1** TATTERED, torn, ripped, frayed, threadbare. **2** JAGGED, uneven, rough, irregular, serrated, craggy.

**ragtime** n. an early form of jazz, played esp. on the piano.

**raid** n. **1** a sudden attack. **2** a surprise visit by police to arrest suspects or seize illegal goods.
• v. make a raid on.

▷ SYNS n. ATTACK, assault, onslaught, incursion, sortie. • v. **1** ATTACK, assault, assail, storm, rush, set upon. **2** PLUNDER, pillage, loot, ransack.

**rail** n. **1** a horizontal bar. **2** each of the two metal bars forming a railway track. **3** the railway system. • v. **1** enclose or provide with a rail. **2** complain strongly. □ **railing** a fence made of rails. **railway 1** a track made of rails along which trains run. **2** a transport system using trains and tracks.
▷ SYNS v. PROTEST, fulminate, inveigh, rage.

**rain** n. atmospheric moisture falling as drops. • v. **1** fall as rain. **2** fall in large quantities. □ **rainbow** an arch of colours in the sky, caused by the sun shining through water droplets in the atmosphere. **raincoat** a coat made from water-resistant fabric. **rainfall** the amount of rain falling. **rainforest** a dense tropical forest with consistently heavy rainfall. ■ **rainy** adj.
▷ SYNS n. RAINFALL, precipitation, drizzle, shower, cloudburst, torrent, downpour, deluge. • v. POUR, teem, pelt down, tip down; drizzle.

**raise** v. **1** move or lift upwards or to an upright position. **2** increase the amount or level of. **3** cause to be heard, felt, or considered. **4** bring up a child. **5** collect money.
▷ SYNS v. **1** LIFT, elevate, uplift, hoist, hold up. **2** INCREASE, put up; heighten, augment, amplify, intensify; inf. hike, jack up. **3** PROPOSE, bring up, advance, suggest, present, broach. **4** BRING UP, rear, nurture, educate.

**raisin** n. a dried grape.

**raison d'être** n. (pl. **raisons d'être**) the most important reason for someone or something's existence.

**rake** n. **1** a tool with prongs for gathering leaves, smoothing soil, etc. **2** a fashionable but immoral man. • v. **1** gather or smooth with a rake. **2** scratch with a sweeping movement. **3** sweep with gunfire etc. **4** search through.

**rakish** adj. dashing but slightly disreputable.

**rally** v. **1** bring or come together (again) for a united effort. **2** revive; recover strength. • n. **1** a mass meeting held as a protest or in support of a cause. **2** a long-distance driving competition over public roads. **3** a recovery. **4** a series of strokes in tennis etc.
▷ SYNS v. **1** COME TOGETHER, assemble, group, convene; summon, round up, muster, marshal, mobilize. **2** RECOVER, recuperate, revive, get better, improve, perk up. • n. MEETING, gathering, assembly, convention, convocation.

**ram** n. **1** an adult male sheep. **2** a striking or plunging device. • v. (**rammed, ramming**) strike or push heavily. □ **ramrod** a rod formerly used to ram down the charge of a firearm.
▷ SYNS v. **1** FORCE, thrust, plunge, push, cram, stuff, jam. **2** STRIKE, hit, run into, crash into, collide with.

**Ramadan** n. the ninth month of the Muslim year, when Muslims fast from dawn to sunset.

**ramble** n. a walk taken for pleasure. • v. **1** take a ramble. **2** talk at length in a confused way. ■ **rambler** n.

▷ SYNS v. WALK, hike, wander, stroll, amble, roam, rove.

**rambling** adj. lengthy and confused.

▷ SYNS LONG-WINDED, verbose, wordy, prolix, lengthy; wandering, roundabout, circuitous, disconnected, disjointed.

**ramifications** pl.n. complex results of an action or event.

▷ SYNS CONSEQUENCES, results, effects, outcome, upshot, aftermath.

**ramp** n. a slope joining two levels.

**rampage** v. behave or race about violently. • n. violent behaviour.

▷ SYNS v. RUN RIOT, run amok, go berserk.

**rampant** adj. **1** flourishing uncontrollably. **2** (of an animal in heraldry) standing on one hind leg with its forefeet in the air.

▷ SYNS OUT OF CONTROL, unrestrained, unchecked, unbridled, widespread, rife.

**rampart** n. a broad-topped defensive wall.

**ramshackle** adj. tumbledown or rickety.

**ran** past of RUN.

**ranch** n. a large cattle farm in America.

**rancid** adj. smelling or tasting of stale fat.

**rancour** (US **rancor**) n. bitterness or resentment. ■ **rancorous** adj.

**random** adj. done or occurring without method, planning, etc.

▷ SYNS HAPHAZARD, arbitrary, indiscriminate, sporadic, casual, unsystematic, disorganized, unplanned; chance, accidental.

**randy** adj. (**-ier, -iest**) inf. sexually aroused.

**rang** past of RING.

**range** n. **1** a set of similar or related things. **2** the limits between which something operates or varies. **3** the distance over which a thing can travel or be effective. **4** a large open area for grazing or hunting. **5** a place with targets for shooting practice. **6** a series of mountains or hills. • v. **1** vary or extend between specified limits. **2** place in rows or in order. **3** travel over a wide area.

▷ SYNS n. **1** SCOPE, compass, limits, bounds, confines, span, gamut, reach, sweep, extent, area, field, orbit. **2** ASSORTMENT, variety, selection, array, collection. • v. EXTEND, stretch, reach, cover, go, run; fluctuate, vary.

**ranger** n. an official in charge of a park or forest.

**rangy** adj. tall, slim, and long-limbed.

**rank** n. **1** a position in a hierarchy, esp. in the armed forces; high social position. **2** a line of people or things. **3** (**the ranks**) ordinary soldiers, not officers. • v. give a rank to; have a specified rank; arrange in ranks. • adj. **1** foul-smelling. **2** growing too thickly. **3** complete: *a rank amateur*. □ **rank and file** the ordinary members of an organization.

▷ SYNS n. GRADE, level, echelon, stratum, class, status, position, station. • v. CLASSIFY, class, categorize, grade.

**rankle** v. cause lasting resentment.

**ransack** v. go quickly through a place stealing or searching for things.

**ransom** n. a price demanded or paid for the release of a captive. • v. demand or pay a ransom for.

**rant** v. make a violent speech.

**rap** n. 1 a quick sharp blow. 2 a type of popular music in which words are spoken rhythmically over an instrumental backing. • v. (**rapped**, **rapping**) strike with a quick sharp blow.

**rapacious** adj. very greedy. ■ rapacity n.
▷ SYNS GRASPING, greedy, acquisitive, avaricious, covetous.

**rape**[1] v. have sex with someone against their will. • n. an act of raping. ■ rapist n.

**rape**[2] n. a plant with oil-rich seeds.

**rapid** adj. very quick. • pl.n. part of a river where the water flows very fast. ■ rapidity n.
▷ SYNS adj. QUICK, fast, swift, speedy, fleet, hurried, hasty, prompt, precipitate.

**rapier** n. a thin, light sword.

**rapport** n. a harmonious understanding or relationship.
▷ SYNS AFFINITY, bond, empathy, sympathy, understanding.

**rapprochement** n. a resumption of friendly relations.

**rapt** adj. fascinated.

**rapture** n. intense delight. ■ rapturous adj.

**rare** adj. 1 not occurring or found very often. 2 unusually good. 3 (of meat) only lightly cooked. ■ rarely adv. rarity n.
▷ SYNS 1 INFREQUENT, scarce, few and far between, uncommon, odd. 2 UNUSUAL, uncommon, out of the ordinary, exceptional, atypical, singular, remarkable, unique.

**rarebit** see **WELSH RABBIT**.

**rarefied** adj. 1 (of air) of lower pressure than usual. 2 esoteric.

**raring** adj. inf. very eager.

**rascal** n. a dishonest or mischievous person.
▷ SYNS 1 SCALLYWAG, imp, scamp, mischief-maker. 2 VILLAIN, scoundrel, rogue, blackguard, ne'er-do-well.

**rash** n. an eruption of spots or patches on the skin. • adj. acting or done without due consideration of the risks.
▷ SYNS adj. RECKLESS, impetuous, hasty, impulsive, madcap, audacious, foolhardy, foolish, incautious, headstrong, careless, heedless, thoughtless, imprudent, hare-brained.

**rasher** n. a slice of bacon.

**rasp** n. 1 a harsh, grating noise. 2 a coarse file. • v. 1 make a harsh, grating sound. 2 scrape.

**raspberry** n. an edible red berry.

**Rastafarian** (or **Rasta**) n. a member of a Jamaican religious movement.

**rat** n. a rodent like a large mouse. • v. (**ratted**, **ratting**) (**rat on**) inf. inform on. ☐ rat race a fiercely competitive way of life.

**ratatouille** n. a dish of stewed onions, courgettes, tomatoes, etc.

**ratchet** n. a bar or wheel with notches in which a device engages to prevent backward movement.

**rate** n. 1 a quantity, frequency, etc., measured against another. 2 a speed. 3 a fixed price or

charge. **4** (**rates**) a local tax on land and buildings paid by a business. • v. **1** estimate the value of. **2** judge to be of a certain quality. **3** be worthy of.
▷ SYNS n. **1** PERCENTAGE, ratio, proportion, scale, standard. **2** PACE, speed, tempo, velocity. **3** CHARGE, price, cost, tariff. • v. **1** ASSESS, appraise, evaluate, estimate, judge, weigh up, grade, rank. **2** REGARD AS, consider, deem, reckon.

**rather** adv. **1** by preference: *I'd rather not.* **2** to a certain extent. **3** on the contrary; more precisely. **4** instead of.
▷ SYNS **1** SOONER, preferably, more readily. **2** QUITE, fairly, a bit, slightly, somewhat.

**ratify** v. (**ratified, ratifying**) confirm an agreement etc. formally. ■ **ratification** n.
▷ SYNS CONFIRM, endorse, sign, sanction, authorize, validate.

**rating** n. **1** the level at which a thing is rated. **2** a sailor without a commission.

**ratio** n. (pl. **-ios**) the relationship between two amounts, reckoned as the number of times one contains the other.
▷ SYNS PROPORTION, correlation, relationship, percentage, fraction, quotient.

**ration** n. a fixed allowance of food etc. • v. limit to a ration.
▷ SYNS n. ALLOWANCE, quota, allocation, portion, share, amount, helping, proportion, percentage. • v. LIMIT, restrict, control.

**rational** adj. able to think sensibly; based on reasoning. ■ **rationally** adv.
▷ SYNS SENSIBLE, reasonable, reasoned, logical, sound, intelligent, judicious, prudent, astute, shrewd.

**rationale** n. the reasons for an action or belief.

**rationalism** n. treating reason as the basis of belief and knowledge. ■ **rationalist** n.

**rationalize** (or **-ise**) v. **1** invent a rational explanation for. **2** make more efficient.
▷ SYNS **1** EXPLAIN, account for, justify, defend, excuse. **2** STREAMLINE, reorganize, modernize.

**rattan** n. thin, pliable stems of a palm, used in furniture making.

**rattle** v. **1** (cause to) make a rapid series of short, hard sounds. **2** inf. make nervous or irritable. • n. a rattling sound; a toy that makes this. □ **rattlesnake** an American viper with horny rings on the tail that make a rattling sound.
▷ SYNS v. CLATTER, clank, jangle, clink, clang.

**raucous** adj. loud and harsh.
▷ SYNS STRIDENT, piercing, shrill, screeching, harsh, grating, discordant; loud, noisy.

**raunchy** adj. (**-ier, -iest**) inf. sexually provocative.

**ravage** v. do great damage to. • pl.n. damage.
▷ SYNS v. DEVASTATE, lay waste, ruin, destroy, despoil.

**rave** v. **1** talk in a wild or angry way. **2** speak or write about enthusiastically. • n. a large event with dancing to fast, electronic music.
▷ SYNS v. **1** RANT, rage, storm, fume, shout. **2** ENTHUSE, rhapsodize, eulogize, gush, wax lyrical.

**raven** n. a large black crow. • adj. (of hair) glossy black.

**ravenous** adj. very hungry.

▷ SYNS STARVING, starved, famished.

**ravine** n. a deep narrow gorge.

**ravioli** n. small square pasta cases containing a savoury filling.

**ravish** v. 1 dated rape. 2 (**ravishing**) very beautiful.

**raw** adj. 1 not cooked. 2 not yet processed. 3 (of the skin) red and painful from being rubbed. 4 inexperienced. 5 (of an emotion or quality) strong and undisguised. 6 (of weather) cold and damp. □ **raw deal** unfair treatment.

▷ SYNS 1 UNCOOKED, fresh. 2 UNPROCESSED, untreated, unrefined, crude. 3 COLD, chilly, freezing, bitter, bleak.

**ray** n. 1 a line or narrow beam of light or other radiation. 2 a trace of something. 3 a large, flat sea fish.

▷ SYNS BEAM, shaft, streak, stream, gleam.

**rayon** n. a synthetic fabric made from viscose.

**raze** v. tear down a building.

**razor** n. a sharp-edged instrument used for shaving.

**razzmatazz** n. inf. extravagant publicity and display.

**RC** abbr. Roman Catholic.

**re** prep. concerning.

**reach** v. 1 stretch out a hand to touch or grasp something. 2 be able to touch. 3 arrive at; get as far as. 4 achieve. 5 make contact with. • n. 1 the distance over which someone or something can reach. 2 a section of a river.

▷ SYNS v. 1 STRETCH, extend, hold, thrust, stick. 2 GET TO, arrive at, come to. 3 CONTACT, get in touch with, get through to, get hold of. • n. AUTHORITY,

influence, power; scope, range, compass, ambit.

**react** v. respond in a particular way. ■ **reactive** adj.

▷ SYNS RESPOND, behave, act, conduct yourself.

**reaction** n. 1 a response to a stimulus, event, etc. 2 a bad physical response to a drug. 3 a process in which substances interact causing chemical or physical change.

**reactionary** adj. & n. (pl. -ies) (a person) opposed to progress and reform.

▷ SYNS CONSERVATIVE, right-wing, traditionalist, diehard.

**reactor** n. an apparatus for the production of nuclear energy.

**read** v. 1 understand the meaning of written or printed words or symbols. 2 speak such words aloud. 3 have a particular wording. 4 discover by reading. 5 interpret in a particular way. 6 (of an instrument) show a measurement. ■ **reader** n.

▷ SYNS 1 PERUSE, study, scrutinize, pore over, scan. 2 INTERPRET, construe, take to mean.

**readable** adj. 1 able to be read. 2 enjoyable to read.

▷ SYNS 1 LEGIBLE, decipherable, clear, intelligible, comprehensible. 2 ENJOYABLE, entertaining, interesting, gripping, enthralling.

**readership** n. the readers of a newspaper etc.

**readily** adv. without hesitation.

▷ SYNS WILLINGLY, gladly, happily, cheerfully, eagerly.

**readjust** v. adjust again; adapt to a changed situation.

**ready** adj. 1 prepared for an activity or situation. 2 available. 3 willing. 4 quick or easy.

• v. (**readied**, **readying**) prepare.
■ **readiness** n.
▷ SYNS **adj. 1** PREPARED, (all) set, organized, arranged; completed, finished, done; inf. psyched up, geared up. **2** WILLING, eager, pleased, disposed, happy, glad.

**reagent** n. a substance used to produce a chemical reaction.

**real** adj. **1** actually existing or occurring. **2** not artificial; genuine. □ **real estate** US land or housing.
▷ SYNS **1** ACTUAL, factual, true, material, physical, tangible, concrete. **2** *real gold:* GENUINE, authentic, proper, bona fide. **3** *real feelings:* SINCERE, heartfelt, earnest, unfeigned.

**realism** n. the accurate and true representation of things.
■ **realist** n.

**realistic** adj. **1** sensible and practical. **2** true to life.
■ **realistically** adv.
▷ SYNS **1** PRACTICAL, pragmatic, rational, down-to-earth, matter-of-fact, sensible, common-sensical, level-headed. **2** LIFELIKE, true-to-life, true, faithful, naturalistic.

**reality** n. **1** the state of things as they actually exist. **2** a thing that is experienced or seen.
▷ SYNS *harsh realities:* FACT, actuality, truth.

**realize** (or **-ise**) v. **1** become aware of a fact. **2** fulfil a hope or plan. **3** convert an asset into money; be sold for.
■ **realization** n.
▷ SYNS **1** UNDERSTAND, grasp, take in, comprehend, apprehend, recognize, see, perceive, discern. **2** FULFIL, achieve, accomplish, bring off, actualize. **3** MAKE, clear, gain, earn.

**really** adv. **1** in fact. **2** thoroughly.
• exclam. expressing interest, surprise, etc.

**realm** n. **1** a kingdom. **2** a field of activity or interest.
▷ SYNS KINGDOM, country, land, dominion, nation.

**ream** n. **1** 500 sheets of paper. **2** (**reams**) a large quantity.

**reap** v. **1** cut grain etc. as harvest. **2** receive as the result of actions.
▷ SYNS **1** CUT, harvest, gather in. **2** RECEIVE, obtain, get, acquire, secure, realize.

**rear** n. the back part. • adj. at the back. • v. **1** bring up children; breed animals. **2** (of a horse) raise itself on its hind legs. **3** extend to a great height. □ **rear admiral** the naval rank above commodore. **rearguard** a body of troops protecting the rear of the main force.
■ **rearward** adj. & adv. **rearwards** adv.
▷ SYNS **n.** BACK, back part, hind part, tail, tail end. • v. BRING UP, raise, care for, nurture, parent; educate.

**rearm** v. arm again.
■ **rearmament** n.

**reason** n. **1** a motive, cause, or justification. **2** the ability to think and draw logical conclusions; sanity. • v. **1** think and draw logical conclusions. **2** (**reason with**) persuade by logical argument.
▷ SYNS **n. 1** GROUNDS, cause, basis, motive, motivation, rationale; explanation, justification, argument. **2** defence, vindication, excuse. **2** REASONING, rationality, logic, cognition; good sense, judgement, wisdom; sagacity. • v. THINK, cogitate; calculate, conclude, deduce, judge.

**reasonable** adj. **1** fair and sensible; appropriate. **2** fairly good. ■ **reasonably** adv.
▷ SYNS **1** SENSIBLE, fair, fair-minded, rational, logical, just, equitable; level-headed, realistic, practical, commonsensical. **2** WITHIN REASON, practicable, appropriate, suitable. **3** TOLERABLE, passable, acceptable, average; inf. OK.

**reassure** v. restore confidence to. ■ **reassurance** n.
▷ SYNS PUT SOMEONE'S MIND AT REST, put at ease, encourage, hearten, cheer up.

**rebate** n. a partial refund.

**rebel** v. (**rebelled**, **rebelling**) refuse to obey the government or ruler; oppose authority or convention. • n. a person who rebels.
▷ SYNS v. MUTINY, riot, revolt, rise up. • n. REVOLUTIONARY, insurgent, mutineer.

**rebellion** n. an act of rebelling against a government or ruler.
▷ SYNS UPRISING, revolt, insurrection, mutiny, revolution, insurgence.

**rebellious** adj. rebelling or wanting to rebel.
▷ SYNS **1** REBEL, revolutionary, insurgent, mutinous. **2** DEFIANT, disobedient, unruly, insubordinate, recalcitrant.

**rebound** v. **1** spring back after impact. **2** (**rebound on**) have an unpleasant effect on. • n. a ball or shot that rebounds. □ **on the rebound** while still upset about a failed relationship.
▷ SYNS v. **1** BOUNCE BACK, recoil, ricochet, boomerang. **2** MISFIRE, backfire.

**rebuff** v. reject ungraciously. • n. a snub.

▷ SYNS v. REJECT, refuse, turn down, spurn, snub, slight. • n. SNUB, rejection, slight; inf. brush-off.

**rebuke** v. reprove. • n. a reproof.
▷ SYNS v. REPRIMAND, tell off, scold, chide, admonish, reproach, reprove, berate, upbraid, castigate, take to task; inf. tick off.

**rebut** v. (**rebutted**, **rebutting**) declare or show to be false. ■ **rebuttal** n.

**recalcitrant** adj. obstinately disobedient.
▷ SYNS INTRACTABLE, refractory, unmanageable, disobedient, insubordinate, defiant, rebellious, wayward.

**recall** v. **1** summon to return. **2** remember; remind someone of. • n. recalling or being recalled.

**recant** v. withdraw a former opinion or belief.

**recap** v. (**recapped**, **recapping**) recapitulate.

**recapitulate** v. give a summary of. ■ **recapitulation** n.

**recce** n. inf. a reconnaissance.

**recede** v. move back from a position; diminish; slope backwards.

**receipt** n. the act of receiving; a written acknowledgement that something has been received or paid.

**receive** v. **1** acquire, accept, or take in. **2** experience or meet with. **3** greet on arrival.
▷ SYNS **1** BE GIVEN, get, gain, acquire; be sent, accept. **2** UNDERGO, experience, meet with, sustain, be subjected to. **3** WELCOME, greet.

**receiver** n. **1** a person or thing that receives something. **2** the earpiece of a telephone; an

apparatus that converts broadcast electrical signals into sound or images. **3** (also **official receiver**) an official who handles the affairs of a bankrupt company.
■ receivership n.

**recent** adj. happening in a time shortly before the present.
■ recently adv.
▷ SYNS NEW, fresh, latest, modern, contemporary, current, up to date.

**receptacle** n. a container.
▷ SYNS CONTAINER, holder, repository.

**reception** n. **1** an act of receiving; a reaction to something. **2** a formal social occasion to welcome guests. **3** an area in a hotel, office, etc. where guests and visitors are greeted. **4** the quality of broadcast signals received.

**receptionist** n. a person employed to greet and deal with clients or guests.

**receptive** adj. quick to receive ideas.

**receptor** n. a nerve ending that responds to a stimulus such as light.

**recess** n. **1** a part or space set back from the line of a wall or room etc. **2** a temporary cessation from business. • v. fit a light etc. in a recess.
▷ SYNS n. **1** ALCOVE, niche, nook, corner, bay. **2** BREAK, interval, rest, holiday, vacation.

**recession** n. a temporary decline in economic activity.

**recessive** adj. (of a gene) remaining latent when a dominant gene is present.

**recidivist** n. a person who constantly commits crimes.

**recipe** n. **1** instructions for preparing a dish. **2** something likely to lead to a particular outcome.

**recipient** n. a person who receives something.

**reciprocal** adj. given or done in return; affecting two parties equally. ■ reciprocally adv. reciprocity n.
▷ SYNS MUTUAL, shared, common, joint, give-and-take, corresponding.

**reciprocate** v. respond to an action or emotion with a similar one.

**recital** n. **1** a musical performance. **2** a long account of a series of facts, events, etc.
▷ SYNS **1** PERFORMANCE, concert, show. **2** ACCOUNT, report, description; litany, list, catalogue.

**recite** v. **1** repeat aloud from memory. **2** state facts in order.
■ recitation n.
▷ SYNS **1** SAY, repeat, declaim, quote, deliver. **2** LIST, enumerate, reel off, recount, relate, describe.

**reckless** adj. wildly impulsive.
▷ SYNS RASH, impulsive, careless, thoughtless, heedless, madcap, wild, precipitate, headlong, hasty, irresponsible, harebrained, foolhardy, imprudent, unwise.

**reckon** v. **1** calculate. **2** have as your opinion. **3** (**reckon on**) rely on.
▷ SYNS **1** THINK, be of the opinion, believe, suppose, dare say. **2** COUNT, calculate, work out, add up, compute.

**reclaim** v. **1** take action to recover possession of. **2** make land usable. ■ reclamation n.

**recline** v. lie back in a relaxed position.
▷ SYNS LIE, rest, repose, loll, lounge, sprawl, stretch out.

**recluse** n. a person who avoids contact with other people.
■ reclusive adj.
▷ SYNS HERMIT, lone wolf, loner.

**recognition** n. **1** the act of recognizing. **2** appreciation or acknowledgement.

**recognize** (or **-ise**) v. **1** identify or know again from previous experience. **2** acknowledge as genuine, valid, or worthy.
■ recognizable adj.
▷ SYNS **1** KNOW, identify, place, remember, recall. **2** ACKNOWLEDGE, accept, admit, concede; be aware of, perceive, discern, appreciate.

**recoil** v. spring or shrink back in fear or disgust; rebound. • n. the act of recoiling.
▷ SYNS v. DRAW BACK, spring back, shrink, shy away, flinch.

**recollect** v. remember.
■ recollection n.

**recommend** v. suggest as suitable for a purpose or role; (of a quality etc.) make something appealing or desirable.
▷ SYNS ADVOCATE, commend, put in a good word for, speak well of, endorse, vouch for; suggest, put forward, propose.

**recompense** v. **1** compensate. **2** pay for work. • n. compensation.

**reconcile** v. **1** restore friendly relations between. **2** make compatible. **3** persuade to accept something unwelcome.
■ reconciliation n.
▷ SYNS REUNITE, pacify, appease, placate, mollify.

**reconnaissance** n. military observation of an area to gain information.
▷ SYNS SURVEY, exploration, inspection, observation; inf. recce.

**reconnoitre** (US **reconnoiter**) v. (**reconnoitred**, **reconnoitring**) make a reconnaissance of.
▷ SYNS SURVEY, explore, investigate, scrutinize, inspect, observe; inf. check out.

**reconsider** v. consider again, with a view to changing.

**reconstitute** v. reconstruct; restore dried food to its original form.

**reconstruct** v. **1** rebuild after damage. **2** enact a past event.
■ reconstruction n.

**record** n. **1** an account kept for evidence or information. **2** a plastic disc carrying recorded sound. **3** facts known about a person's past. **4** the best performance or most remarkable event of its kind.
• v. **1** make a record of. **2** convert sound etc. into permanent form for later reproduction. □ off the record unofficially.
▷ SYNS n. **1** ACCOUNT, document, documentation, data, file, evidence, report; chronicle, annals, archives; register, log. **2** DISC, album, single, LP, recording. • v. WRITE DOWN, take down, note, enter, log, document.

**recorder** n. **1** a person or thing that records. **2** a simple woodwind instrument.

**recount**[1] v. describe in detail.
▷ SYNS DESCRIBE, relate, tell, report, detail, list.

**recount**[2] v. count again. • n. a second or subsequent counting.

**recoup** v. recover a loss.

**recourse** n. a source of help to which someone may turn.

**recover** v. 1 return to health. 2 regain possession or control of. ■ recovery n.
▷ SYNS 1 GET BETTER, recuperate, convalesce, improve, rally, revive, pull through. 2 RETRIEVE, regain, get back, recoup, reclaim.

**recreation** n. enjoyable leisure activity. ■ recreational adj.
▷ SYNS 1 RELAXATION, leisure, amusement, entertainment, enjoyment. 2 ACTIVITY, pastime, hobby.

**recrimination** n. an accusation in response to another.

**recruit** n. a new member, esp. of the armed forces. • v. enlist someone as a recruit. ■ recruitment n.
▷ SYNS n. NEW MEMBER, initiate, beginner, learner, trainee, novice. • v. ENLIST, call up, draft, conscript.

**rectangle** n. a flat shape with four right angles and four sides, two of which are longer than the others. ■ rectangular adj.

**rectify** v. (**rectified**, **rectifying**) put right.
▷ SYNS PUT RIGHT, right, correct, amend, remedy, repair, fix, make good.

**rectitude** n. morally correct behaviour.
▷ SYNS RIGHTEOUSNESS, virtue, honour, integrity, principle, probity, honesty.

**rector** n. 1 a priest in charge of a parish. 2 the head of certain schools, colleges, and universities.

**rectory** n. (pl. **-ies**) the house of a rector.

**rectum** n. the last section of the large intestine. ■ rectal adj.

**recumbent** adj. lying down.

**recuperate** v. recover from illness; regain. ■ recuperation n.

**recur** v. (**recurred**, **recurring**) happen again or repeatedly. ■ recurrence n.

**recurrent** adj. happening often or repeatedly.
▷ SYNS REPEATED, recurring, periodic, cyclical, perennial, regular, frequent.

**recycle** v. convert waste into a reusable form. ■ recyclable adj.

**red** adj. 1 of the colour of blood or fire. 2 flushed, esp. with embarrassment. 3 (of hair) reddish brown. 4 inf. communist. • n. 1 a red colour or thing. 2 a communist. □ red-blooded virile and healthy. red carpet privileged treatment for an important visitor. redcurrant a small edible red berry. red-handed in the act of doing something wrong. redhead a person with red hair. red herring a misleading clue. red-hot so hot it glows red. red-light district an area with many brothels. red tape complicated official rules. redwood a giant coniferous tree with reddish wood. ■ redden v.
▷ SYNS adj. 1 SCARLET, ruby, vermilion, crimson, carmine. 2 FLUSHED, blushing; florid, ruddy.

**redeem** v. 1 make up for the faults of. 2 save from sin. 3 pay a debt. 4 exchange a coupon for goods or money. 5 fulfil a promise. ■ redemption n.

**redeploy** v. send to a new place or task. ■ redeployment n.

**redolent** adj. 1 strongly reminiscent of. 2 smelling strongly of.
▷ SYNS 1 EVOCATIVE, suggestive, reminiscent. 2 SWEET-SMELLING, fragrant, scented, aromatic.

**redouble** v. increase or intensify.

**redoubtable** adj. formidable.

**redound** v. (**redound to**) formal be to someone's credit.

**redress** v. set right.
• n. reparation or amends.

**reduce** v. 1 make or become less. 2 (**reduce to**) bring to a particular state or condition.
■ **reducible** adj. **reduction** n.
▷ SYNS 1 LESSEN, lower, bring down, decrease, cut, curtail, contract, shorten, abbreviate; moderate, alleviate, ease. 2 BRING TO, bring to the point of, drive to.

**redundant** adj. 1 no longer needed or useful. 2 no longer employed. ■ **redundancy** n.
▷ SYNS UNNECESSARY, unneeded, surplus, superfluous.

**reed** n. 1 a water or marsh plant with tall hollow stems. 2 a vibrating part which produces sound in certain wind instruments.

**reedy** adj. (of a voice) having a thin high tone.

**reef** n. 1 a ridge of rock or coral just above or below the surface of the sea. 2 a part of a sail that can be drawn in when there is a high wind. • v. shorten a sail.

**reek** n. a strong unpleasant smell. • v. smell strongly.

**reel** n. 1 a cylinder on which something is wound. 2 a lively Scottish or Irish folk dance.
• v. 1 wind on or off a reel. 2 stagger. 3 (**reel off**) recite rapidly.

▷ SYNS v. STAGGER, lurch, sway, stumble, totter, wobble.

**refectory** n. (pl. **-ies**) the dining room in an educational or religious institution.

**refer** v. (**referred, referring**) mention; turn to for information; pass to someone else for help or decision. ■ **referral** n.
▷ SYNS (**refer to**) 1 CONSULT, turn to, look at, have recourse to. 2 PASS, hand on, send, transfer. 3 MENTION, allude to, touch on, speak of, cite.

**referee** n. 1 an umpire, esp. in football and boxing. 2 a person willing to provide a reference for someone applying for a job.
• v. (**refereed, refereeing**) be a referee of.
▷ SYNS n. UMPIRE, judge, adjudicator.

**reference** n. 1 a mention or allusion. 2 the use of a source of information. 3 a letter giving information about someone's suitability for a new job. □ **with reference to** concerning.
▷ SYNS 1 MENTION, allusion, comment, remark. 2 SOURCE, citation, authority, credit. 3 TESTIMONIAL, recommendation, credentials.

**referendum** n. (pl. **-dums** or **-da**) a vote by the people of a country on a single political issue.

**refine** v. 1 remove impurities or defects from. 2 make small improvements to.
▷ SYNS 1 PURIFY, clean, cleanse, filter. 2 IMPROVE, perfect, polish.

**refined** adj. well educated and elegant.
▷ SYNS CULTIVATED, cultured, polished, stylish, elegant,

sophisticated, urbane, gracious, well mannered, well bred, gentlemanly, ladylike, genteel.

**refinement** n. the quality of being well educated, elegant, and having good taste.
▷ SYNS CULTIVATION, taste, discrimination, grace, style, elegance, finesse, sophistication, urbanity, good breeding, good manners, gentility.

**refinery** n. (pl. **-ies**) a place where crude substances are refined.

**reflect** v. 1 throw back light, heat, or sound. 2 show an image of. 3 think deeply. 4 (**reflect well/badly on**) give a good or bad impression of. ■ reflector n.
▷ SYNS 1 THROW BACK, send back; mirror, echo. 2 THINK, contemplate, consider, mull over, ponder, meditate.

**reflection** n. 1 reflecting or being reflected. 2 a reflected image. 3 serious thought. 4 a sign of something's true nature; a source of discredit.
▷ SYNS 1 IMAGE, mirror image, likeness. 2 THOUGHT, thinking, consideration, contemplation, meditation, rumination, cogitation.

**reflective** adj. 1 reflecting light etc. 2 thoughtful.

**reflex** n. an action done without conscious thought in response to a stimulus. ● adj. 1 done as a reflex. 2 (of an angle) more than 180°.
▷ SYNS adj. AUTOMATIC, involuntary, spontaneous; inf. knee-jerk.

**reflexive** adj. Grammar referring back to the subject of a clause or verb, e.g. *himself* in *he washed himself*.

**reflexology** n. the massaging of points on the feet as a treatment for stress etc.

**reform** v. 1 improve by making changes. 2 cause to improve behaviour. ● n. reforming.
■ reformation n.
▷ SYNS v. 1 IMPROVE, make better, ameliorate, amend, change, adapt, reorganize. 2 MEND YOUR WAYS, turn over a new leaf.

**refract** v. (of water, air, or glass) make a ray of light change direction when it enters at an angle. ■ refraction n.

**refractory** adj. stubborn or unmanageable.

**refrain** v. stop yourself from doing something. ● n. the part of a song repeated at the end of each verse.
▷ SYNS v. DESIST, abstain, forbear, avoid, eschew, stop, give up, quit.

**refresh** v. 1 give new energy to. 2 prompt someone's memory.
■ refreshingly adv.
▷ SYNS INVIGORATE, revitalize, revive, restore, fortify, enliven, stimulate, energize, rejuvenate.

**refreshing** adj. 1 giving new energy or strength. 2 pleasantly new or different.
▷ SYNS INVIGORATING, reviving, bracing, stimulating, exhilarating, energizing.

**refreshment** n. 1 a snack or drink. 2 the giving of new energy.

**refrigerate** v. make food or drink cold to keep it fresh.
■ refrigeration n.

**refrigerator** n. an appliance in which food and drink are stored at a low temperature.

**refuge** n. a shelter from danger or trouble.

▷ SYNS SHELTER, safety, security, protection, asylum, sanctuary; haven, retreat.

**refugee** n. a person who has left their country because of war or persecution.

**refund** v. pay back money to. • n. a repayment of money.
▷ SYNS V. REPAY, return, pay back; reimburse, compensate.

**refurbish** v. redecorate and improve a building etc. ■ refurbishment n.

**refuse¹** v. say that you are unwilling to do or accept something. ■ refusal n.
▷ SYNS TURN DOWN, decline, pass up; reject, spurn, rebuff.

**refuse²** n. rubbish.

**refute** v. prove a statement or person to be wrong. ■ refutation n.
▷ SYNS PROVE WRONG, disprove, rebut, invalidate.

**regain** v. obtain again after loss; reach again.
▷ SYNS GET BACK, win back, recover, recoup, retrieve, reclaim, repossess.

**regal** adj. like or fit for a king or queen. ■ regally adv.

**regale** v. feed or entertain well.

**regalia** pl.n. emblems of royalty or rank.

**regard** v. 1 think of in a particular way. 2 look steadily at. • n. 1 concern or care. 2 respect or high opinion. 3 a steady gaze. 4 (**regards**) best wishes. □ with regard to concerning.
▷ SYNS V. 1 LOOK ON, view, consider, see, think of, deem, judge. 2 WATCH, look at, gaze at, stare at, observe, study, scrutinize, eye. • n. 1 CARE, consideration, heed, attention, thought.

2 RESPECT, esteem, admiration, approval, approbation. 3 LOOK, gaze, stare, observation, scrutiny. 4 (**regards**) BEST WISHES, respects, greetings, salutations.

**regarding** prep. with reference to.

**regardless** adv. 1 despite what is happening. 2 (**regardless of**) without regard for.

**regatta** n. boat races organized as a sporting event.

**regency** n. (pl. -ies) a period of government by a regent.

**regenerate** v. 1 bring new life or strength to. 2 grow new tissue. ■ regeneration n.
▷ SYNS RENEW, restore, revitalize, revive, revivify, rejuvenate.

**regent** n. a person appointed to rule while the monarch is too young or unfit to rule, or is absent.

**reggae** n. a style of popular music originating in Jamaica.

**regicide** n. the killing or killer of a king.

**regime** n. 1 a government. 2 a system of doing things.

**regimen** n. a prescribed course of treatment etc.

**regiment** n. a permanent unit of an army. • v. organize very strictly. ■ regimental adj.

**Regina** n. the reigning queen.

**region** n. an area; an administrative division of a country; a part of the body. ■ regional adj.
▷ SYNS AREA, province, territory, division, section, sector, zone, quarter, part.

**register** n. 1 an official list. 2 a range of a voice or musical instrument; a level of formality in language. • v. 1 enter in a register; express or convey an

opinion or emotion. **2** (of a measuring instrument) show a reading; become aware of. □ **register office** a place where marriages are performed and births, marriages, and deaths are recorded. ■ **registration** n.
▷ SYNS n. LIST, roll, roster, index, directory, catalogue.
• v. **1** RECORD, enter, write down, put in writing, note, log. **2** READ, record, indicate, show. **3** DISPLAY, exhibit, express, evince, betray, reveal, reflect.

**registrar** n. **1** an official responsible for keeping written records. **2** a hospital doctor training to be a specialist.

**registry** n. (pl. **-ies**) **1** a place where registers are kept. **2** registration. □ **registry office** a register office.

**regress** v. relapse to an earlier or less advanced state.
■ **regression** n.
▷ SYNS REVERT, relapse, lapse, backslide, degenerate, retrogress.

**regret** n. a feeling of sorrow, annoyance, or repentance.
• v. (**regretted**, **regretting**) feel regret about.
▷ SYNS n. SORROW, remorse, contrition, repentance, compunction, ruefulness, penitence. • v. **1** FEEL SORRY ABOUT, feel contrite about, repent, rue. **2** LAMENT, bemoan, mourn, grieve over; deplore.

**regretful** adj. feeling or showing regret.
■ **regretfully** adv.
▷ SYNS SORRY, remorseful, apologetic, contrite, repentant, rueful, penitent, conscience-stricken.

**regrettable** adj. unfortunate or undesirable. ■ **regrettably** adv.

▷ SYNS DEPLORABLE, reprehensible, blameworthy, disgraceful; unfortunate, unwelcome, ill-advised.

**regular** adj. **1** following or arranged in a pattern. **2** done, happening, or doing something frequently. **3** following an accepted standard. **4** belonging to a country's permanent armed forces. **5** even or symmetrical.
• n. a regular customer, soldier etc. ■ **regularity** n.
▷ SYNS adj. **1** *regular breathing*: RHYTHMIC, steady, even, constant, unchanging. **2** *his regular route*: USUAL, normal, customary, habitual, routine, typical, accustomed. **3** *the regular channels*: OFFICIAL, established, conventional, proper, orthodox, standard, usual, traditional. **4** EVEN, uniform, consistent, fixed, symmetrical.

**regulate** v. control the rate or speed of a machine or process; control by rules. ■ **regulator** n. **regulatory** adj.
▷ SYNS **1** CONTROL, adjust. **2** SUPERVISE, police, monitor; manage, direct, guide, govern.

**regulation** n. a rule; regulating.
▷ SYNS RULE, ruling, order, directive, act, law, decree, statute, edict.

**regurgitate** v. bring swallowed food up again to the mouth.

**rehabilitate** v. restore to a normal life or good condition.
■ **rehabilitation** n.

**rehash** v. reuse old ideas or material.

**rehearsal** n. a trial performance of a play or other work for later public performance.

▷ SYNS PRACTICE, run-through; inf. dry run.

**rehearse** v. practise a play etc. for later performance; state points again.
▷ SYNS PRACTISE, try out, run through, go over.

**reign** n. a sovereign's period of rule. • v. rule as a sovereign; be supreme.

**reimburse** v. repay money to.

**rein** n. **1** long straps attached to a bridle, used to control a horse. **2** the power to direct and control. • v. **1** control with reins. **2** restrain.
▷ SYNS v. RESTRAIN, check, curb, constrain, hold back, control.

**reincarnation** n. the rebirth of a soul in another body after death.

**reindeer** n. (pl. **-deer** or **-deers**) a deer of Arctic regions.

**reinforce** v. strengthen with additional people, material, or quantity. ■ reinforcement n.
▷ SYNS STRENGTHEN, fortify, bolster up, shore up, buttress, prop up, support; augment, increase, add to, supplement.

**reinstate** v. restore to a previous position.

**reiterate** v. say again or repeatedly. ■ reiteration n.

**reject** v. refuse to accept. • n. a person or thing rejected. ■ rejection n.
▷ SYNS v. **1** REFUSE, turn down, decline. **2** REBUFF, spurn, snub, discard, abandon, desert, forsake, cast aside.

**rejig** v. (**rejigged**, **rejigging**) rearrange.

**rejoice** v. feel or show great joy.

**rejoin** v. **1** join again. **2** retort.

**rejoinder** n. a reply or retort.

**rejuvenate** v. make more lively or youthful. ■ rejuvenation n.

**relapse** v. fall back into a previous state; become worse after improvement. • n. relapsing.
▷ SYNS v. LAPSE, regress, retrogress, revert, backslide, degenerate.

**relate** v. **1** narrate. **2** show to be connected. **3** (**relate to**) have to do with; feel sympathy with.
▷ SYNS **1** RECOUNT, tell, narrate, report, impart, communicate, recite, chronicle. **2** CONNECT, associate, link, correlate. **3** (**relate to**) APPLY TO, be relevant to, concern, refer to, pertain to.

**related** adj. belonging to the same family, group, or type.
▷ SYNS CONNECTED, associated, linked, allied, affiliated, concomitant; akin, kindred.

**relation** n. **1** the way in which people or things are connected or related. **2** (**relations**) the way in which people or groups behave towards each other. **3** a relative.
▷ SYNS **1** CONNECTION, association, link, tie-in, correlation, alliance, bond, relationship, inter-relation. **2** RELATIVE, kinsman, kinswoman.

**relationship** n. the relation or relations between people or things; an emotional and sexual association between two people.
▷ SYNS **1** see **RELATION** (1). **2** (LOVE) AFFAIR, romance, liaison.

**relative** adj. considered in relation to something else; true only in comparison with something else. • n. a person connected to another by descent or marriage.
■ relatively adv.

▷ SYNS **adj. 1** COMPARATIVE, comparable, respective, correlative, parallel, corresponding. **2** PROPORTIONATE, in proportion, commensurate. **n.** see **RELATION** (2).

**relativity** n. **1** Physics a description of matter, energy, space, and time according to Albert Einstein's theories. **2** absence of absolute standards.

**relax** v. make or become less tense; rest; make a rule less strict.
▷ SYNS **1** LOOSEN, slacken, weaken, lessen. **2** UNWIND, loosen up, ease up/off, take it easy; rest, unbend; inf. chill out.

**relaxation** n. the state of being free from tension and worry.
▷ SYNS RECREATION, enjoyment, amusement, entertainment, pleasure, leisure.

**relay** n. **1** a group of workers etc., relieved after a fixed period by another group; a race between teams in which each person in turn covers part of the total distance. **2** a device activating an electrical circuit. **3** a device which receives and retransmits a signal. • v. receive and pass on or retransmit.
▷ SYNS v. PASS ON, communicate, send, transmit, spread, circulate.

**release** v. **1** set free; remove from a fixed position. **2** make information, or a film or recording, available to the public. • n. **1** releasing. **2** a film or recording released.
▷ SYNS v. **1** SET FREE, free, let go/out, liberate; deliver, emancipate; untie, loose, unleash. **2** MAKE PUBLIC, make known, issue, break, announce, reveal, divulge, disclose, publish, broadcast, circulate, disseminate.

**relegate** v. consign to a lower rank or position. ■ **relegation** n.

**relent** v. **1** abandon or moderate a harsh intention or cruel treatment. **2** become less intense.
▷ SYNS SOFTEN, capitulate, yield, give way/in, come round.

**relentless** adj. oppressively constant; harsh or inflexible.
▷ SYNS **1** HARSH, ruthless, merciless, pitiless, implacable, cruel, hard, strict, severe, obdurate, unyielding, inflexible, unbending. **2** UNRELENTING, unremitting, persistent, incessant, unceasing, constant, ceaseless, non-stop.

**relevant** adj. related to the matter in hand. ■ **relevance** n.
▷ SYNS APPLICABLE, pertinent, apposite, material, to the point, germane.

**reliable** adj. able to be relied on. ■ **reliability** n. **reliably** adv.
▷ SYNS DEPENDABLE, trustworthy, trusty, true, faithful, devoted, steadfast, staunch, constant, unfailing.

**reliance** n. dependence on or trust in someone or something. ■ **reliant** adj.

**relic** n. something that survives from earlier times.

**relief** n. **1** a feeling of relaxation after anxiety. **2** alleviation of pain. **3** a break in monotony or tension. **4** help given to those in need. **5** a person replacing another on duty. **6** a carving in which the design stands out from the surface.
▷ SYNS **1** ALLEVIATION, mitigation, reduction, lessening. **2** AID, help, assistance, succour.

**3** RESPITE, break, variation, diversion; inf. let-up.

**relieve** v. give or bring relief to; release from a task, burden, or duty; raise the siege of.
▷ SYNS **1** ALLEVIATE, mitigate, assuage, allay, soothe, soften, ease, dull, reduce, lessen, diminish. **2** AID, help, assist, rescue, save, succour.

**religion** n. belief in and worship of a God or gods; a system of faith and worship.

**religious** adj. **1** of or believing in a religion. **2** very careful and regular.
▷ SYNS **1** *religious festivals:* HOLY, divine, theological, scriptural, spiritual. **2** *religious people:* CHURCHGOING, godly, God-fearing, pious, devout.

**relinquish** v. give up.
▷ SYNS GIVE UP, renounce, resign, abdicate, surrender.

**reliquary** n. (pl. **-ies**) a receptacle for holy relics.

**relish** n. **1** great enjoyment. **2** a strong-tasting pickle or sauce. • v. enjoy greatly.
▷ SYNS n. ENJOYMENT, delight, pleasure, satisfaction, gratification, zest, gusto. • v. ENJOY, delight in, love, adore, revel in, savour.

**relocate** v. move to a different place. ■ **relocation** n.

**reluctant** adj. unwilling.
■ **reluctance** n.
▷ SYNS UNWILLING, disinclined, unenthusiastic, grudging, loath, averse.

**rely** v. (**relied, relying**) have confidence in; depend on for help etc.
▷ SYNS DEPEND ON, count on, bank on, trust in, swear by.

**remain** v. stay; be left or left behind; continue in the same condition.
▷ SYNS **1** STAY, continue, carry on, last, persist, endure, prevail. **2** BE LEFT (OVER), survive.

**remainder** n. the remaining people or things; a quantity left after subtraction or division.
▷ SYNS REMNANT, residue, rest, balance; surplus, excess.

**remains** pl.n. things that remain or are left; a dead body.
▷ SYNS **1** REMNANTS, leftovers, leavings; residue, rest. **2** RELICS, antiquities. **3** CORPSE, body, cadaver, carcass.

**remand** v. send a defendant to wait for their trial, either on bail or in jail. □ **on remand** remanded.

**remark** v. **1** say as a comment. **2** notice. • n. a comment.
▷ SYNS v. MENTION, comment, say, state, declare, pronounce, observe. • n. COMMENT, observation, statement, utterance, reflection.

**remarkable** adj. striking or extraordinary. ■ **remarkably** adv.
▷ SYNS EXTRAORDINARY, unusual, singular, notable, noteworthy, memorable, exceptional, outstanding, striking, impressive, phenomenal, wonderful, marvellous.

**remedial** adj. **1** providing a remedy. **2** provided for children with learning difficulties.

**remedy** n. (pl. **-ies**) something that cures a condition or puts a matter right. • v. (**remedied, remedying**) set right.
▷ SYNS n. **1** CURE, treatment, medicine, medication, medicament, antidote. **2** SOLUTION, answer, panacea. • v. **1** CURE,

heal, treat, counteract.
**2** RECTIFY, solve, put right,
redress, fix, sort out.

**remember** v. **1** have in or bring
to the mind someone or
something from the past.
**2** keep something to be done in
mind. ■ **remembrance** n.
▷ SYNS RECALL, call to mind,
recollect, think of, reminisce,
look back on.

**remind** v. cause to remember.
■ **reminder** n.

**reminisce** v. think or talk about
the past.

**reminiscence** n. an account of
something remembered; the
enjoyable remembering of past
events.

**reminiscent** adj. tending to
remind you of something.
▷ SYNS EVOCATIVE, suggestive,
redolent.

**remiss** adj. negligent.
▷ SYNS NEGLIGENT, neglectful,
irresponsible, lax, slack,
slipshod, careless.

**remission** n. **1** cancellation of a
debt or penalty. **2** the reduction
of a prison sentence; a temporary recovery from an illness.

**remit** v. (**remitted, remitting**)
**1** cancel a debt or punishment.
**2** send money. **3** refer a matter
to an authority. • n. a task
assigned to someone.

**remittance** n. the sending of
money; money sent.

**remnant** n. a small remaining
quantity or piece.
▷ SYNS **1** REMAINDER, residue, rest,
remains, leftovers. **2** PIECE,
fragment, scrap.

**remonstrate** v. make a protest.

**remorse** n. deep regret for your
wrongdoing.

▷ SYNS REGRET, sorrow, contrition,
penitence, repentance, guilt,
ruefulness, compunction.

**remorseful** adj. filled with
regret or guilt.
▷ SYNS SORRY, regretful, apologetic, contrite, penitent,
repentant.

**remorseless** adj. pitiless;
relentless.

**remote** adj. **1** far away in place
or time; not close; aloof or unfriendly. **2** (of a possibility)
very slight.
▷ SYNS **1** DISTANT, far (off), out of
the way, outlying, inaccessible,
off the beaten track, isolated,
secluded, lonely. **2** UNLIKELY,
improbable, implausible,
doubtful, dubious, slight, slim,
small. **3** ALOOF, distant,
detached, withdrawn, reserved,
uncommunicative,
unapproachable, stand-offish,
unfriendly.

**removal** n. the act of removing;
the transfer of furniture etc.
when moving house.

**remove** v. take off or away;
dismiss from office; get rid of.
• n. a degree of remoteness or
difference. ■ **removable** adj.
▷ SYNS v. **1** TAKE AWAY, move, shift,
transfer, carry away. **2** DISMISS,
discharge, oust, dislodge,
depose; inf. sack, fire. **3** TAKE OFF,
pull off, doff. **4** GET RID OF,
abolish, eliminate, axe, do away
with, eradicate.

**remunerate** v. pay or reward
for services. ■ **remuneration** n.
**remunerative** adj.

**Renaissance** n. **1** a revival of
art and learning in Europe in
the 14th–16th centuries. **2** (**renaissance**) any similar revival.

**renal** adj. of the kidneys.

**rend** v. (**rent, rending**) tear.

**render** v. **1** provide a service, help, etc. **2** present for inspection, payment, etc. **3** cause to become. **4** perform music or drama. **5** melt down fat.

**rendezvous** n. (pl. **rendezvous**) a prearranged meeting or meeting place.
▷ SYNS APPOINTMENT, date, meeting, assignation.

**rendition** n. the way something is rendered or performed.

**renegade** n. a person who deserts a group, cause, etc.
▷ SYNS DEFECTOR, deserter, turncoat, traitor.

**renege** v. fail to keep a promise or agreement.
▷ SYNS GO BACK ON YOUR WORD, break your promise, default, back out, pull out.

**renew** v. resume an interrupted activity; replace something broken or worn out; extend the validity of a licence etc.; give fresh life or vigour to.
■ renewal n.

**rennet** n. curdled milk, used in making cheese.

**renounce** v. give up formally; reject.
▷ SYNS **1** GIVE UP, relinquish, abandon, abdicate, surrender, waive, forego. **2** REJECT, repudiate, disown, wash your hands of, spurn.

**renovate** v. repair or restore to good condition. ■ renovation n.
▷ SYNS MODERNIZE, refurbish, overhaul, restore, revamp, repair, redecorate; inf. do up.

**renown** n. fame.
■ renowned adj.

**rent**[1] n. regular payment made for the use of property or land.
• v. pay or receive rent for.

▷ SYNS V. LEASE, hire, charter; let.

**rent**[2] past & p.p. of REND.
• n. a tear in a piece of fabric.

**rental** n. rent; renting.

**renunciation** n. an act of giving up a right or possession.

**reoccur** v. (**reoccurring, reoccurred**) occur again or repeatedly. ■ reoccurrence n.

**reorganize** (or **-ise**) v. organize in a new way.
■ reorganization n.

**rep** n. inf. **1** a representative. **2** repertory.

**repair** v. **1** restore to a good condition. **2** formal go to a place.
• n. **1** the process of repairing. **2** condition for use: *in good repair.*
▷ SYNS V. MEND, fix, put right, restore, patch up.

**reparation** n. **1** the making of amends for a wrong. **2** (**reparations**) compensation for war damage paid by a defeated state.

**repartee** n. an exchange of witty remarks.

**repast** n. formal a meal.

**repatriate** v. send someone back to their own country.
■ repatriation n.

**repay** v. (**repaid, repaying**) pay back. ■ repayment n.
▷ SYNS PAY BACK, refund, reimburse, recompense, compensate.

**repeal** v. cause a law to be no longer valid. • n. the repealing of a law.
▷ SYNS V. REVOKE, rescind, abrogate, annul, nullify, set aside, cancel, reverse.

**repeat** v. **1** say or do again. **2** (**repeat yourself**) say the same thing again. **3** (**repeat itself**)

occur again in the same way.
• n. something that recurs or is repeated.
▷ SYNS V. SAY AGAIN, restate, reiterate, recapitulate, recap; recite, quote, parrot, duplicate, replicate.

**repel** v. (**repelled, repelling**) drive away or back; disgust.
▷ SYNS **1** REPULSE, fight off, drive back, force back, ward off, fend off, keep at bay. **2** REVOLT, disgust, sicken, nauseate, turn someone's stomach.

**repellent** adj. causing disgust.
• n. a substance used to keep away pests or to make something impervious to water etc.
▷ SYNS adj. REPULSIVE, revolting, disgusting, sickening, nauseating, repugnant, abhorrent, offensive, obnoxious, loathsome, vile, nasty, abominable, horrible, horrid, foul.

**repent** v. feel regret about a wrong or unwise action.
■ repentance n.

**repentant** adj. feeling regret about a wrong or unwise action.
▷ SYNS PENITENT, remorseful, apologetic, regretful, contrite, rueful, ashamed, guilt-ridden.

**repercussions** pl.n. the consequences of an event or action.
▷ SYNS CONSEQUENCES, results, effects, reverberations, aftermath, fallout, backlash.

**repertoire** n. the material known or regularly performed by a person or company.

**repertory** n. (pl. **-ies**) **1** the performance by a company of various plays etc. at regular intervals. **2** a repertoire.

**repetition** n. repeating; an instance of this.

**repetitious** adj. repetitive.

**repetitive** adj. having too much repetition.
▷ SYNS RECURRENT, unchanging, unvaried, monotonous, dreary, tedious, boring, mechanical, automatic.

**replace** v. **1** put back in place. **2** provide or be a substitute for.
■ replacement n.
▷ SYNS **1** PUT BACK, return, restore. **2** TAKE THE PLACE OF, succeed, supersede, supplant; substitute for, stand in for, fill in for, cover for.

**replay** v. play a recording again; play a match again.
• n. something replayed.

**replenish** v. refill.

**replete** adj. full; well supplied.
▷ SYNS FULL (UP), satiated, sated, glutted, gorged, stuffed, well fed.

**replica** n. an exact copy.
▷ SYNS COPY, duplicate, facsimile, model, reproduction, imitation.

**replicate** v. make a replica of.

**reply** v. (**replied, replying**) answer. • n. (pl. **-ies**) an answer.
▷ SYNS V. ANSWER, respond, rejoin, retort, come back, counter.
• n. ANSWER, response, rejoinder, retort, riposte, comeback.

**report** v. **1** give an account of. **2** make a formal complaint about. **3** present yourself on arrival; be responsible to a superior. • n. **1** a spoken or written account; a written assessment of a pupil's progress. **2** an explosive sound.
▷ SYNS V. **1** ANNOUNCE, communicate, give an account of, describe, outline, detail, reveal,

divulge, disclose. **2** TELL ON, inform on; inf. grass on, rat on. **3** PRESENT YOURSELF, arrive, turn up, clock on/in. • n. **1** ACCOUNT, statement, record. **2** ARTICLE, piece, story, communiqué, dispatch, bulletin. **3** EXPLOSION, bang, blast, crack.

**reporter** n. a person who reports news for a newspaper or broadcasting company.
▷ SYNS JOURNALIST, correspondent, columnist; inf. hack.

**repose** n. a state of peace or calm. • v. rest.
▷ SYNS n. REST, relaxation, ease, peace, inactivity; sleep, slumber.

**repository** n. (pl. -ies) a storage place.

**repossess** v. take back goods etc. when payments are not made. ■ repossession n.

**reprehensible** adj. deserving condemnation.
▷ SYNS DEPLORABLE, disgraceful, despicable, culpable, blameworthy, bad, shameful, discreditable, dishonourable, indefensible, unjustifiable, inexcusable.

**represent** v. **1** speak or act on behalf of. **2** be an example of. **3** amount to. **4** describe in a particular way. **5** depict in a work of art. **6** symbolize.
▷ SYNS **1** STAND FOR, symbolize, personify, epitomize, typify, embody. **2** DEPICT, portray, render, delineate, illustrate, picture. **3** ACT FOR, speak for.

**representation** n. representing or being represented; a picture, diagram, etc.
▷ SYNS DEPICTION, portrayal, portrait, illustration, picture, painting, drawing, sketch, image, model.

**representative** adj. **1** typical of a group or class. **2** consisting of people chosen to act or speak on behalf of a wider group.
• n. an agent of a firm who visits potential clients to sell its products; a person chosen to represent others.
▷ SYNS adj. **1** TYPICAL, archetypal, characteristic, illustrative, indicative. **2** ELECTED, elective, democratic. • n. SPOKESMAN, spokeswoman, agent; mouthpiece.

**repress** v. subdue, restrain, or control. ■ repression n. repressive adj.
▷ SYNS RESTRAIN, hold back, subdue, control, suppress, keep in check, bottle up, stifle, curb.

**reprieve** n. a postponement or cancellation of punishment; a temporary relief from trouble.
• v. give a reprieve to.
▷ SYNS n. STAY OF EXECUTION, remission, pardon, amnesty.

**reprimand** v. formally express strong disapproval to.
• n. a formal statement of disapproval.

**reprint** v. print again. • n. a book reprinted.

**reprisal** n. an act of retaliation.
▷ SYNS RETALIATION, revenge, vengeance, retribution, an eye for an eye.

**reproach** v. express disapproval of. • n. an act of reproaching.

**reproachful** adj. expressing disapproval or disappointment.
▷ SYNS DISAPPROVING, reproving, critical, censorious, accusatory.

**reprobate** n. an immoral or unprincipled person.

**reproduce** v. produce again; produce a copy of; produce young or offspring.
▷ SYNS **1** COPY, duplicate, replicate, recreate, imitate, emulate, mirror, simulate. **2** BREED, procreate, bear young, multiply, propagate.

**reproduction** n. **1** the act of reproducing. **2** a copy of a work of art. ■ **reproductive** adj.
▷ SYNS COPY, duplicate, replica, facsimile, print.

**reproof** n. an expression of condemnation for a fault.

**reprove** v. give a reproof to.

**reptile** n. a cold-blooded animal of a class that includes snakes, lizards, and tortoises.

**republic** n. a country in which the supreme power is held by the people's representatives, not by a monarch.

**republican** adj. of or advocating a republic. • n. a person advocating republican government.

**repudiate** v. refuse to accept; deny the truth of.
■ **repudiation** n.
▷ SYNS DISOWN, reject, abandon, forsake, desert, renounce, turn your back on, wash your hands of.

**repugnant** adj. very distasteful.

**repulse** v. drive back by force; reject or rebuff.

**repulsion** n. a feeling of extreme distaste.
■ **repulsive** adj.

**reputable** adj. having a good reputation.
▷ SYNS RESPECTABLE, respected, of good repute, well thought of, prestigious; reliable, dependable, trustworthy.

**reputation** n. what is generally believed about a person or thing.
▷ SYNS REPUTE, standing, name, character, position, status.

**repute** n. reputation. • v. (**be reputed**) be said or thought to be. ■ **reputedly** adv.

**request** n. an act of asking for something; something asked for. • v. ask for; ask someone to do something.
▷ SYNS n. APPEAL, entreaty, petition, plea, application, call.
• v. ASK FOR, appeal for, call for, solicit, seek, apply for, put in for; beg, entreat.

**requiem** n. a Christian Mass for the souls of the dead; music for this.

**require** v. **1** need; depend on for success or fulfilment. **2** order or oblige.
▷ SYNS **1** NEED, be in need of. **2** CALL FOR, demand, necessitate, involve, entail.

**requirement** n. a need.
▷ SYNS NEED, wish, demand, want, necessity, prerequisite, stipulation.

**requisite** adj. required or needed. • n. something needed.
▷ SYNS adj. NECESSARY, required, prerequisite, essential, needed.

**requisition** n. an official order laying claim to the use of property or materials. • v. take possession of by such an order.

**rescind** v. repeal or cancel a law etc.

**rescue** v. save from danger or distress. • n. rescuing.
▷ SYNS v. SAVE, come to the aid of; free, set free, release, liberate.

**research** n. study and investigation to establish facts.
• v. carry out research into a subject.
▷ SYNS n. EXPERIMENTATION, study, tests, investigation, fact-finding, testing, exploration.
• v. INVESTIGATE, inquire into, look into, probe, explore, analyse, study, examine.

**resemblance** n. the fact of resembling; a way in which things resemble each other.
▷ SYNS LIKENESS, similarity, similitude, sameness, correspondence, comparability.

**resemble** v. be like.
▷ SYNS BE LIKE, look like, be similar to, take after, remind you of.

**resent** v. feel bitter towards or about.
▷ SYNS BEGRUDGE, grudge, be annoyed/angry at, dislike.

**resentful** adj. feeling bitter or angry about something.
▷ SYNS AGGRIEVED, indignant, irritated, piqued, disgruntled, bitter, embittered.

**resentment** n. bitterness or anger.
▷ SYNS BITTERNESS, indignation, pique, disgruntlement, hard feelings, ill will, animosity.

**reservation** n. **1** the act of reserving. **2** reserved accommodation etc. **3** doubt. **4** an area of land set aside for a purpose.
▷ SYNS DOUBT, qualm, scruple, misgivings, scepticism, unease, hesitation.

**reserve** v. put aside for future or special use; order or set aside for a particular person; have or keep a right or power. • n. **1** a supply of something available for use if required; a military force for use in an emergency; a substitute player in a sports team. **2** land set aside for special use, esp. the protection of wildlife. **3** lack of friendliness or warmth.
▷ SYNS v. **1** PUT ASIDE, put away, keep, save, retain. **2** BOOK, engage, charter, hire.
• n. **1** STORE, stock, supply, pool, cache, stockpile, hoard.
**2** PRESERVE, reservation, sanctuary, park. **3** RETICENCE, detachment, distance, remoteness, formality, coolness.

**reserved** adj. slow to reveal emotion or opinions.
▷ SYNS RETICENT, aloof, detached, remote, formal, undemonstrative, cool, uncommunicative, unsociable, unfriendly, unresponsive, unforthcoming, quiet, private.

**reservoir** n. a lake used as a store for a water supply; a container for a supply of fluid.

**reshuffle** v. reorganize.
• n. a reorganization.

**reside** v. live permanently.

**residence** n. residing; the place where a person lives.
▷ SYNS HOUSE, home, dwelling, domicile, quarters, lodgings.

**resident** n. a long-term inhabitant; a guest in a hotel.
• adj. living somewhere on a long-term basis.
▷ SYNS n. INHABITANT, occupant, occupier, householder, denizen.

**residential** adj. designed for living in; lived in; providing accommodation.

**residue** n. what is left over.
■ residual adj.
▷ SYNS REMAINDER, remnant, rest, surplus, extra, excess, remains, leftovers.

**resign** v. **1** give up a job or position of office. **2** (**resign yourself**) accept something undesirable but inevitable.
▷ SYNS GIVE NOTICE, hand in your notice, leave, quit.

**resignation** n. **1** an act of resigning. **2** a letter stating an intention to resign. **3** acceptance of something bad but inevitable.

**resilient** adj. springing back when bent, pressed, etc.; readily recovering from shock or distress. ■ **resilience** n.
▷ SYNS **1** ELASTIC, springy, flexible, pliant, supple, pliable. **2** TOUGH, strong, hardy; irrepressible.

**resin** n. a sticky substance produced by some trees; a similar substance made synthetically, used in plastics.

**resist** v. oppose strongly or forcibly; withstand; refrain from accepting or yielding to.
▷ SYNS **1** WITHSTAND, be proof against, weather. **2** OPPOSE, fight against, defy; obstruct, impede, hinder, block, thwart, frustrate. **3** REFRAIN, forbear, stop/restrain yourself.

**resistance** n. **1** the act of resisting or the ability to resist. **2** a secret organization that fights against an occupying enemy. **3** the degree to which a material or device resists the passage of an electric current. ■ **resistant** adj.

**resistor** n. a device that resists the passage of an electric current.

**resolute** adj. determined.
▷ SYNS DETERMINED, resolved, decided, single-minded, purposeful, firm, staunch, steadfast, unwavering, unfaltering, unswerving, tenacious, dogged, persevering, persistent, unshakeable, strong-willed.

**resolution** n. **1** a firm decision; determination; a formal statement of a committee's opinion. **2** solving a problem etc. **3** the degree to which detail is visible in an image.
▷ SYNS **1** DETERMINATION, resolve, will power, firmness, purposefulness, doggedness, perseverance, persistence, tenacity, staying power. **2** DECISION, resolve, commitment, promise, pledge.

**resolve** v. **1** find a solution to. **2** decide firmly on a course of action. **3** separate into constituent parts.
• n. determination.
▷ SYNS v. **1** DECIDE, make up your mind, determine. **2** SOLVE, settle, sort out, fix, deal with, put right, rectify.

**resonant** adj. (of sound) deep, clear, and ringing. ■ **resonance** n.

**resonate** v. be filled with a deep, clear, ringing sound.

**resort** n. **1** a popular holiday destination. **2** a strategy or course of action. • v. turn to for help; adopt as a measure.
▷ SYNS n. RECOURSE, expedient, course (of action), alternative, option, possibility, hope.
• v. FALL BACK ON, turn to, have recourse to, make use of, use, avail yourself of.

**resound** v. be filled with a ringing, booming, or echoing sound.

**resource** n. **1** a supply of an asset to be used when needed. **2** a strategy for dealing with difficulties; the ability to find such strategies.

**resourceful** adj. clever at finding ways of doing things.

**resources** pl.n. available assets.
▷ SYNS ASSETS, funds, money, capital; supplies, reserves, stocks.

**respect** n. **1** admiration or esteem. **2** a particular aspect or point. **3** consideration for others' rights and feelings. • v. feel or show respect for. ■ **respectful** adj. **respectfully** adv.
▷ SYNS n. **1** ESTEEM, regard, high opinion, admiration, veneration, reverence, deference, honour. **2** ASPECT, facet, feature, way, sense, particular, point, detail. • v. ESTEEM, think highly of, admire, look up to, revere, honour.

**respectable** adj. **1** regarded as proper or correct. **2** adequate or acceptable. ■ **respectability** n. **respectably** adv.
▷ SYNS REPUTABLE, upright, honest, honourable, trustworthy, good, well bred, proper.

**respective** adj. belonging to each as an individual.
▷ SYNS INDIVIDUAL, separate, personal, own, particular, specific.

**respectively** adv. for each separately in the order mentioned.

**respiration** n. breathing.

**respirator** n. **1** a device worn over the face to prevent the inhalation of smoke etc. **2** a device that enables someone to breathe artificially.

**respiratory** adj. of respiration.

**respite** n. rest or relief from something difficult or unpleasant.

▷ SYNS REST, break, breathing space, lull, relief; inf. breather, let-up.

**resplendent** adj. brilliant with colour or decorations.

**respond** v. answer or react.

**respondent** n. a defendant in a lawsuit.

**response** n. an answer or reaction.
▷ SYNS ANSWER, reply, rejoinder, retort, comeback.

**responsibility** n. being responsible; a duty resulting from your job or position.
▷ SYNS **1** DUTY, task, role, job. **2** BLAME, fault, guilt, culpability, liability, accountability.

**responsible** adj. **1** obliged to do something or care for someone; being the cause of something and so deserving blame or credit for it. **2** able to be trusted. **3** (of a job) involving important duties etc. **4** (**responsible to**) having to report to a senior person. ■ **responsibly** adv.
▷ SYNS **1** IN CHARGE, in control, accountable, liable, answerable; to blame, at fault, guilty, culpable. **2** TRUSTWORTHY, sensible, level-headed, reliable, dependable.

**responsive** adj. responding readily to an influence.

**rest** v. **1** stop working or moving in order to relax or recover strength. **2** place or be placed for support; remain or be left in a specified condition. **3** depend or be based on. • n. **1** a period of resting. **2** a prop or support for an object. ☐ **the rest** the remaining part, people, or things.

▷ SYNS v. **1** RELAX, unwind, put your feet up, take it easy; sleep, take a nap, catnap, doze. **2** LIE ON, lean on, stand on, sit on. • n. **1** REPOSE, relaxation, leisure, time off; sleep, slumber. **2** BREAK, interval, interlude, intermission, lull, respite, breathing space.

**restaurant** n. a place where meals can be bought and eaten.

**restaurateur** n. a restaurant keeper.

**restful** adj. soothing and relaxing.
▷ SYNS QUIET, calm, tranquil, relaxing, peaceful, soothing.

**restitution** n. **1** the restoring of a thing to its proper owner or original state. **2** compensation.

**restive** adj. restless.

**restless** adj. unable to rest or relax.
▷ SYNS **1** SLEEPLESS, wakeful, tossing and turning, fitful. **2** UNEASY, ill at ease, on edge, fidgety, agitated.

**restorative** adj. able to restore health or strength.

**restore** v. bring back to a previous condition, place, or owner; repair a building, work of art, etc.; bring back a previous practice, situation, etc.
  ■ **restoration** n.
▷ SYNS **1** RENOVATE, repair, fix, mend, refurbish, rebuild, revamp, redecorate; inf. do up. **2** RETURN, give back, hand back. **3** RE-ESTABLISH, reinstitute, reinstate, bring back.

**restrain** v. **1** keep under control. **2** stop from moving or acting freely.
▷ SYNS CONTROL, check, curb, suppress, repress, contain, smother, stifle, bottle up, rein in.

**restraint** n. **1** the act of restraining. **2** something that restrains. **3** self-controlled behaviour.
▷ SYNS **1** CONSTRAINT, check, curb, control, restriction, limitation, rein. **2** SELF-RESTRAINT, self-control, self-discipline, moderation.

**restrict** v. **1** put a limit on. **2** stop from moving or acting freely.
  ■ **restrictive** adj.
▷ SYNS **1** LIMIT, regulate, control, moderate, curb. **2** HINDER, impede, hamper, obstruct.

**restriction** n. **1** a limiting condition or measure. **2** the act of restricting.
▷ SYNS LIMITATION, constraint, control, check, curb.

**result** n. **1** a thing caused or produced by something else. **2** information obtained by experiment or calculation. **3** a final score or mark in a contest or exam. • v. **1** occur as a result. **2** (**result in**) have a particular outcome.
▷ SYNS n. CONSEQUENCE, outcome, upshot, effect, reaction, repercussion. • v. **1** FOLLOW, ensue, develop, stem, spring, evolve, occur, happen, come about. **2** (**result in**) END IN, culminate in, finish in, terminate in.

**resultant** adj. occurring as a result.

**resume** v. begin again or continue after a pause.
  ■ **resumption** n.
▷ SYNS CARRY ON, continue, recommence, begin again, reopen.

**résumé** n. a summary.

**resurgent** adj. rising or arising again. ■ **resurgence** n.

**resurrect** v. bring back to life or into use. ■ **resurrection** n.

**resuscitate** v. restore to consciousness. ■ **resuscitation** n.

**retail** n. the sale of goods to the public. • v. sell or be sold by retail. ■ **retailer** n.

**retain** v. keep possession of; absorb and hold; hold in place.
▷ SYNS KEEP, keep hold of, hold/hang on to, preserve, maintain.

**retainer** n. a fee paid to a barrister to secure their services.

**retaliate** v. repay an injury, insult, etc. by inflicting one in return. ■ **retaliation** n.

**retard** v. hold back the development or progress of.

**retarded** adj. offens. less developed mentally than is usual at a certain age.

**retch** v. strain your throat as if vomiting.

**retention** n. the act of retaining.

**retentive** adj. able to retain things.

**reticent** adj. not revealing your thoughts or feelings. ■ **reticence** n.

**retina** n. (pl. **-nas** or **-nae**) a membrane at the back of the eyeball, sensitive to light.

**retinue** n. attendants accompanying an important person.

**retire** v. 1 stop working because of age. 2 withdraw. 3 go to bed. ■ **retirement** n.
▷ SYNS 1 STOP WORKING, be pensioned off. 2 WITHDRAW, leave, retreat, decamp, go. 3 GO TO BED, go to sleep, turn in.

**retiring** adj. shy.

▷ SYNS SHY, diffident, self-effacing, unassuming, reserved, reticent, quiet, timid.

**retort** v. make a sharp or witty reply. • n. 1 a reply of this kind. 2 a glass container used for distilling liquids and heating chemicals.

**retrace** v. go back over or repeat a route.

**retract** v. pull back; withdraw an allegation etc. ■ **retractable** adj. **retraction** n.
▷ SYNS 1 DRAW IN, pull in/back. 2 TAKE BACK, withdraw, recant, disclaim, disavow, backtrack on.

**retreat** v. withdraw after defeat or from an uncomfortable situation; move back.
• n. 1 retreating. 2 a quiet or secluded place.
▷ SYNS v. 1 WITHDRAW, pull back, back off, give way/ground, retire, turn tail. 2 GO BACK, recede, ebb. • n. 1 WITHDRAWAL, evacuation. 2 REFUGE, haven, shelter, sanctuary, hideaway, hideout.

**retrench** v. reduce costs or spending.

**retribution** n. deserved punishment.
▷ SYNS REPRISAL, retaliation, revenge, vengeance, punishment, justice, requital, an eye for an eye, tit for tat.

**retrieve** v. 1 get or bring back; extract information stored in a computer. 2 improve a bad situation. ■ **retrieval** n.
▷ SYNS GET BACK, recover, regain, recoup, salvage, rescue.

**retriever** n. a breed of dog used to retrieve game.

**retrograde** adj. going backwards; reverting to an inferior state.

**retrospect** n. (**in retrospect**) when looking back on a past event.

**retrospective** adj. looking back on the past; taking effect from a date in the past.

**retsina** n. a Greek resin-flavoured white wine.

**return** v. 1 come or go back. 2 give, send, or put back. 3 give a verdict. 4 yield a profit. 5 elect to office. • n. 1 an act of returning. 2 a profit. 3 a ticket allowing travel to a place and back again.
▷ SYNS v. 1 GO BACK, come back, recur, reoccur, reappear. 2 GIVE BACK, repay, pay back; put back, replace, restore, reinstall. • n. 1 HOMECOMING; reappearance, recurrence. 2 PROFIT, yield, gain, interest, dividend.

**reunion** n. a gathering of people who have not seen each other for some time.

**reunite** v. bring or come together again.

**reuse** v. use again.

**Rev.** (or **Revd**) abbr. Reverend.

**rev** inf. n. a revolution of an engine. • v. (**revved**, **revving**) cause an engine to run faster.

**revamp** v. alter so as to improve.

**reveal** v. make visible by uncovering; make known.
▷ SYNS 1 SHOW, bring to light, uncover, lay bare, expose, unveil. 2 DISCLOSE, divulge, tell, let slip, give away, release, leak, make known/public, broadcast, publicize.

**reveille** n. a military waking signal.

**revel** v. 1 celebrate in a lively, noisy way. 2 (**revel in**) take

great pleasure in. • pl.n. lively, noisy celebrations. ■ **reveller** n. **revelry** n.
▷ SYNS v. 1 CELEBRATE, make merry, party, carouse. 2 (**revel in**) DELIGHT IN, love, adore, relish, savour, lap up.

**revelation** n. revealing; a surprising thing revealed.

**revenge** n. retaliation for an injury or wrong. • v. avenge.
▷ SYNS n. VENGEANCE, retaliation, retribution, reprisal, an eye for an eye.

**revenue** n. the income received by an organization, or by a government from taxes.
▷ SYNS INCOME, profits, returns, receipts, proceeds, takings.

**reverberate** v. be repeated as an echo; continue to have effects. ■ **reverberation** n.
▷ SYNS RESOUND, echo, ring, resonate.

**revere** v. respect or admire deeply.
▷ SYNS RESPECT, admire, esteem, think highly of, look up to.

**reverence** n. deep respect.

**reverend** adj. a title given to Christian ministers.

**reverent** adj. showing deep respect.
▷ SYNS RESPECTFUL, reverential, admiring, awed, deferential.

**reverie** n. a daydream.

**reverse** v. move backwards; cancel; convert to its opposite; turn inside out or upside down etc. • adj. opposite in direction, nature, order, etc. • n. 1 a change of direction; the opposite side. 2 a setback. ■ **reversal** n. **reversible** adj.
▷ SYNS v. CHANGE, alter; set aside, cancel, overturn, revoke, repeal, rescind, annul, nullify,

invalidate. • n. **1** OPPOSITE, contrary, converse, antithesis. **2** OTHER SIDE, back, underside, flip side. **3** SETBACK, upset, failure, misfortune, mishap, blow, disappointment.

**revert** v. return to a previous state, practice, etc. ■ **reversion** n.

**review** n. **1** a general survey of events or a subject; revision or reconsideration; a critical report on a book, play, etc. **2** a ceremonial inspection of troops etc. • v. make or write a review of. ■ **reviewer** n.
▷ SYNS n. **1** STUDY, analysis, evaluation, survey, examination, assessment, appraisal. **2** CRITICISM, critique, notice. • v. ANALYSE, examine, study, survey, scrutinize, assess, appraise, evaluate.

**revile** v. criticize scornfully.

**revise** v. **1** re-examine and alter or correct. **2** reread work already done in preparation for an exam. ■ **revision** n.
▷ SYNS **1** AMEND, emend, correct, alter, change, edit, rewrite. **2** GO OVER, reread; inf. swot/mug up on.

**revival** n. **1** an improvement in condition, strength, or popularity. **2** a new production of an old play.
▷ SYNS RENAISSANCE, restoration, resurrection, rebirth, regeneration.

**revivalism** n. the promotion of a return to religious faith. ■ **revivalist** n.

**revive** v. come or bring back to life, consciousness, or strength; restore interest in or use of.
▷ SYNS **1** BRING ROUND, resuscitate. **2** REFRESH, restore, energize, regenerate, enliven, revitalize.

**revoke** v. withdraw a decree, law, etc. ■ **revocation** n.

**revolt** v. **1** rebel against an authority. **2** cause strong disgust in. • n. rebellion or defiance.
▷ SYNS v. **1** RISE UP, take up arms, rebel, mutiny. **2** REPEL, disgust, sicken, nauseate, turn someone's stomach.

**revolution** n. **1** the forcible overthrow of a government and installation of a new one; a complete change in methods etc. **2** a single, complete movement around a central point.
▷ SYNS **1** REBELLION, revolt, insurrection, uprising, rising, insurgence, coup. **2** METAMORPHOSIS, sea change, upheaval, transformation.

**revolutionary** adj. **1** involving great change. **2** of or engaged in political revolution.
▷ SYNS **1** NEW, pioneering, original, innovative, progressive. **2** REBELLIOUS, rebel, insurgent, mutinous, seditious, subversive, extremist.

**revolutionize** (or **-ise**) v. change completely.

**revolve** v. move in a circle around a central point; be centred on.
▷ SYNS GO ROUND, turn round, rotate, spin, circle, orbit.

**revolver** n. a type of pistol.

**revue** n. a theatrical show consisting of a series of items.

**revulsion** n. strong disgust.

**reward** n. something given or received in return for service or merit. • v. give a reward to.

▷ SYNS n. RECOMPENSE, award, payment, bonus, present, gift.

**rewarding** adj. providing satisfaction.
▷ SYNS SATISFYING, gratifying, fulfilling, beneficial, worthwhile, valuable.

**Rex** n. a reigning king.

**rhapsodize** (or **-ise**) v. talk or write about something very enthusiastically.

**rhapsody** n. (pl. **-ies**) 1 an expression of great enthusiasm. 2 a romantic musical composition. ■ **rhapsodic** adj.

**rheostat** n. a device for varying the resistance to electric current.

**rhesus factor** n. a substance in red blood cells which can cause disease in a newborn baby.

**rhesus monkey** n. a small southern Asian monkey.

**rhetoric** n. the art of using words impressively; impressive language.

**rhetorical** adj. 1 expressed so as to sound impressive. 2 (of a question) asked for effect rather than to obtain an answer. ■ **rhetorically** adv.
▷ SYNS POMPOUS, grandiose, high-flown, oratorical, bombastic, grandiloquent, turgid.

**rheumatism** n. a disease causing pain in the joints and muscles. ■ **rheumatic** adj.

**rhinestone** n. an imitation diamond.

**rhino** n. (pl. **rhino** or **rhinos**) inf. a rhinoceros.

**rhinoceros** n. (pl. **rhinoceros** or **rhinoceroses**) a large thick-skinned animal with one horn or two on its nose.

**rhododendron** n. an evergreen shrub with large clusters of flowers.

**rhombus** n. a diamond-shaped figure. ■ **rhomboid** adj. & n.

**rhubarb** n. a plant with thick red stems cooked and eaten as fruit.

**rhyme** n. 1 a word that has or ends with the same sound as another. 2 similarity of sound between words. 3 a short poem with rhyming lines. • v. have or end with the same sound.

**rhythm** n. 1 a strong, regular, repeated pattern of movement or sound. 2 a regularly recurring sequence of events.
■ **rhythmic** adj. **rhythmically** adv.
▷ SYNS BEAT, cadence, tempo, time, metre.

**rib** n. one of the curved bones round the chest; a structural part resembling this.

**ribald** adj. humorous in a coarse or irreverent way.
▷ SYNS BAWDY, risqué, coarse, earthy, rude, naughty, racy, suggestive.

**riband** n. a ribbon.

**ribbon** n. a decorative narrow strip of fabric; a long, narrow strip.

**riboflavin** n. vitamin $B_2$.

**rice** n. grains of a cereal plant grown for food on wet land in hot countries.

**rich** adj. 1 having a lot of money or assets. 2 abundant. 3 having or producing something in large amounts. 4 (of soil) fertile. 5 (of food) containing much fat or sugar. 6 (of colour, sound, or smell) pleasantly deep and strong. • pl.n. wealth.
▷ SYNS adj. 1 WEALTHY, affluent, well off, well-to-do, prosperous,

moneyed; *inf.* well heeled, loaded. **2** PLENTIFUL, abundant, ample, profuse, copious, lavish. **3** FERTILE, productive, fecund, fruitful. • *pl.n.* WEALTH, affluence, money, capital, assets, resources.

**richly** *adv.* fully or thoroughly; elaborately.

**rick** n. **1** a stack of hay etc. **2** a slight sprain or strain. • v. sprain or strain slightly.

**rickets** n. a bone disease caused by vitamin D deficiency.

**rickety** adj. shaky or insecure.

**rickshaw** n. a two-wheeled vehicle pulled along by a person.

**ricochet** v. (ricocheted, ricocheting) rebound from a surface after striking it with a glancing blow. • n. a rebound of this kind.

**rid** v. **1** free from something unpleasant or unwanted. **2** (get rid of) be freed or relieved of.
▷ SYNS **1** CLEAR, free, scourge. **2** (get rid of) DISPOSE OF, throw away/out, clear out, discard, do away with; destroy, eliminate.

**riddance** n. (good riddance) expressing relief at being rid of someone or something.

**riddle** n. **1** a cleverly worded question, asked as a game; something puzzling or mysterious. **2** a coarse sieve. • v. make many holes in; permeate.
▷ SYNS PUZZLE, poser, conundrum, brain-teaser, problem, enigma, mystery.

**ride** v. (rode, ridden, riding) sit on and control the movements of a horse, bicycle, etc.; travel in a vehicle; be carried or supported by. • n. a spell of riding; a roller coaster or

similar fairground amusement; a path for horse riding.

**rider** n. **1** a person who rides a horse etc. **2** an additional statement or condition.

**ridge** n. a long narrow hilltop; a narrow raised strip; a line where two upward slopes meet.
■ **ridged** adj.

**ridicule** n. contemptuous mockery. • v. make fun of.
▷ SYNS n. DERISION, mockery, scorn, jeering, jeers, taunts, satire, sarcasm. • v. DERIDE, mock, laugh at, scoff at, scorn, jeer at, jibe at, make fun of, taunt.

**ridiculous** adj. deserving to be laughed at.
▷ SYNS ABSURD, laughable, farcical, ludicrous, risible, stupid, foolish, half-baked, inane, fatuous, senseless, silly; preposterous, outrageous.

**rife** adj. widespread; full of.
▷ SYNS WIDESPREAD, common, prevalent, general, extensive, ubiquitous, universal, endemic.

**riff** n. a short repeated phrase in jazz etc.

**riff-raff** n. disreputable people.

**rifle** n. a gun with a long barrel. • v. search hurriedly through.
▷ SYNS v. RUMMAGE, search, hunt; ransack.

**rift** n. **1** a crack, split, or break. **2** a serious break in friendly relations.
▷ SYNS **1** SPLIT, crack, break, fissure, cleft, crevice, cranny. **2** DISAGREEMENT, breach, split, division, estrangement, schism, fight, row, quarrel, conflict, feud.

**rig** v. **1** fit sails and rigging on a boat; set up a device or structure. **2** manage or run fraudulently. • n. **1** an apparatus

for a particular purpose: *a lighting rig.* **2** a piece of equipment for extracting oil or gas from the ground.
▷ SYNS v. MANIPULATE, engineer, tamper with, misrepresent, distort, falsify.

**rigging** n. the ropes and chains supporting a ship's masts.

**right** adj. **1** on or towards the side which is to the east when facing north. **2** morally good or justified. **3** factually correct. **4** most appropriate. **5** satisfactory, sound, or normal. • adv. **1** on or to the right-hand side. **2** completely. **3** exactly; directly. **4** correctly. • n. **1** what is morally good. **2** an entitlement to have or do something. **3** the right-hand side or direction. **4** a party or group favouring conservative views and capitalist policies. • v. **1** restore to a normal or upright position. **2** make amends for. ☐ **right angle** an angle of 90°.
▷ SYNS adj. **1** JUST, fair, equitable, good, proper, moral, ethical, honourable, honest, lawful, legal. **2** CORRECT, accurate, unerring, exact, precise; inf. spot on. **3** SUITABLE, appropriate, fitting, correct, desirable, ideal. • n. **1** LAWFULNESS, legality, righteousness, virtue, integrity, rectitude, propriety, justice, fairness, equity. **2** PREROGATIVE, privilege, authority, power, licence, permission, entitlement. • v. RECTIFY, put to rights, sort out, fix, remedy, repair.

**righteous** adj. morally right. ■ **righteousness** n.
▷ SYNS GOOD, virtuous, upright, moral, ethical, law-abiding, honest, honourable, high-minded.

**rightful** adj. having a right to something; just or legitimate. ■ **rightfully** adv.

**rigid** adj. **1** unable to bend. **2** strict or inflexible. ■ **rigidity** n.
▷ SYNS **1** STIFF, hard, taut, unbendable, inelastic. **2** STRICT, severe, stern, stringent, rigorous, inflexible, uncompromising.

**rigmarole** n. a long complicated procedure.

**rigor mortis** n. stiffening of the body after death.

**rigorous** adj. **1** very thorough or accurate. **2** (of a rule etc.) strictly applied or followed. **3** harsh or severe. ■ **rigorously** adv.
▷ SYNS METICULOUS, painstaking, thorough, scrupulous, conscientious, punctilious, careful, accurate, precise.

**rigour** (US **rigor**) n. **1** the quality of being thorough or severe. **2** (**rigours**) demanding conditions.

**rile** v. inf. annoy.

**rill** n. a small stream.

**rim** n. an edge or border, esp. of something circular. • v. (**rimmed**, **rimming**) provide with a rim.
▷ SYNS n. BRIM, edge, lip, border, margin, brink.

**rime** n. frost.

**rind** n. a tough outer layer on fruit, cheese, bacon, etc.
▷ SYNS PEEL, skin.

**ring**[1] n. **1** a small circular band worn on a finger. **2** a circular object or mark. **3** an enclosed area for a sport etc. **4** a group working together illegally or secretly: *a drug ring.* • v. **1** surround. **2** draw a circle round. ☐ **ringleader** a person

who leads others in crime or causing trouble. **ringlet** a corkscrew-shaped curl of hair. **ringtone** a sound made by a mobile phone when an incoming call is received. **ringworm** a skin disease causing small circular itchy patches.
▷ SYNS n. **1** BAND, circle, halo, disc. **2** ARENA, enclosure, stadium. **3** GANG, syndicate, cartel, association, organization. • v. CIRCLE, encircle, surround, enclose, hem in, fence in, seal off.

**ring²** v. **1** make a clear resonating sound. **2** echo with a sound. **3** call by phone. **4** call for attention by sounding a bell. • n. **1** an act or sound of ringing. **2** a quality conveyed by words: *a ring of truth*. **3** a telephone call.
▷ SYNS v. **1** CHIME, peal, sound, toll, clang. **2** CALL, telephone, phone.

**rink** n. an enclosed area of ice for skating, ice hockey, etc.

**rinse** v. wash out soap etc. from. • n. an act of rinsing; a liquid for colouring the hair.
▷ SYNS v. WASH, clean, sluice, flush.

**riot** n. **1** a violent disturbance by a crowd of people. **2** a large and varied display. • v. take part in a riot. □ **run riot** behave in an unrestrained way. ■ **rioter** n.
▷ SYNS n. UPROAR, commotion, disturbance, tumult, melee, fracas, fray, brawl; violence, fighting. • v. RUN RIOT, go on the rampage, run wild/amok.

**riotous** adj. **1** involving public disorder. **2** involving wild and uncontrolled behaviour.
▷ SYNS **1** *a riotous crowd:* UNRULY, disorderly, uncontrollable, unmanageable, wild, violent, lawless, anarchic. **2** *a riotous party:* UPROARIOUS, lively, loud, noisy, boisterous.

**RIP** abbr. rest in peace.

**rip** v. (**ripped**, **ripping**) tear or become torn; pull forcibly away. • n. a torn place. □ **ripcord** a cord pulled to open a parachute. **rip-off** inf. a very overpriced article. **rip off** inf. cheat; steal.

**ripe** adj. ready for harvesting and eating; matured; (of age) advanced. ■ **ripen** v.
▷ SYNS MATURE, full grown, mellow, juicy, luscious, tender, sweet.

**riposte** n. a quick reply.

**ripple** n. a small wave; a gentle sound that rises and falls. • v. form ripples.

**rise** v. **1** come or go up; get up from lying or sitting. **2** increase in quantity, intensity, pitch, etc.; slope upwards. **3** rebel. **4** (of a river) have its source. • n. an act of rising; a pay increase; an upward slope. □ **give rise to** cause.
▷ SYNS v. **1** MOVE UP, arise, ascend, climb. **2** RISE UP, tower, soar, rear up. **3** INCREASE, soar, rocket, escalate, shoot up. **4** STAND UP, get to your feet, get up. • n. INCREASE, hike, escalation, upsurge, upswing.

**risible** adj. ridiculous.

**rising** n. a revolt.

**risk** n. a possibility of meeting danger or suffering harm; a person or thing that causes this. • v. expose to danger or loss.
▷ SYNS n. DANGER, possibility, chance, peril, threat, jeopardy. • v. ENDANGER, imperil, jeopardize, hazard, put at risk, gamble with.

**risky** adj. involving risk.
▷ SYNS DANGEROUS, hazardous, perilous, unsafe, precarious, uncertain; inf. dicey.

**risotto** n. (pl. -os) a dish of rice with meat, vegetables, etc.

**risqué** adj. slightly indecent.

**rissole** n. a mixture of minced meat formed into a flat shape and fried.

**rite** n. a ritual.
▷ SYNS RITUAL, ceremony, service, sacrament, liturgy, act, practice, tradition.

**ritual** n. a set series of actions used in a religious or other ceremony. • adj. done as a ritual. ■ **ritually** adv.

**rival** n. a person or thing that competes with or can equal another. • v. (**rivalled**, **rivalling**; US **rivaled**) be comparable to.
▷ SYNS n. OPPONENT, adversary, antagonist, competitor, challenger, contender. • v. COMPETE WITH, vie with, match, equal, measure up to, compare with.

**rivalry** n. (pl. -ies) a situation in which two people are competing for the same thing.

**riven** adj. torn apart.

**river** n. a large natural flow of water.

**rivet** n. a short metal pin or bolt for holding together two metal plates. • v. (**riveted**, **riveting**) **1** fasten with a rivet. **2** attract and hold the attention of.

**rivulet** n. a small stream.

**RN** abbr. Royal Navy.

**RNA** abbr. ribonucleic acid, a substance in living cells which carries instructions from DNA.

**road** n. a prepared track along which vehicles may travel; a way to achieving a particular outcome. □ **road rage** violent anger caused by conflict with the driver of another vehicle. **roadworks** repairs to roads or to pipes under roads. **roadworthy** (of a vehicle) fit to be used on the road.
▷ SYNS STREET, thoroughfare, highway.

**roam** v. wander.

**roan** adj. (of a horse) having a dark coat sprinkled with white hairs.

**roar** n. a loud, deep sound made or like that made by a lion; a loud sound of laughter. • v. give a roar.
▷ SYNS v. BELLOW, yell, bawl, shout, howl; inf. holler.

**roast** v. cook food in an oven; make or become very warm. • adj. (of food) having been roasted. • n. a joint of meat that has been roasted.

**rob** v. (**robbed**, **robbing**) steal from; deprive unfairly of something.
▷ SYNS STEAL FROM, burgle, hold up, break into, mug, defraud, swindle, cheat; inf. rip off.

**robber** n. a person who commits robbery.
▷ SYNS BURGLAR, thief, mugger, housebreaker; bandit, highwayman.

**robbery** n. the action of robbing a person or place.
▷ SYNS BURGLARY, theft, stealing, housebreaking, larceny; mugging, hold-up, break-in, raid.

**robe** n. a long loose garment. • v. dress in a robe.

**robin** n. a small bird with a red breast.

**robot** n. a machine able to carry out a complex series of actions automatically. ■ **robotic** adj.
▷ SYNS AUTOMATON, android, machine.

**robust** adj. sturdy; healthy; forceful.
▷ SYNS HEALTHY, strong, vigorous, muscular, powerful, tough, rugged, sturdy, strapping, brawny, burly.

**rock** n. **1** the hard part of the earth's crust; a projecting mass of this; a large stone. **2** a hard sweet made in sticks. **3** loud popular music with a heavy beat. **4** a rocking movement. • v. **1** move to and fro or from side to side. **2** shock greatly. ☐ **rock and roll** rock music with elements of blues. **rock bottom** the lowest possible level.
▷ SYNS n. BOULDER, stone. • v. MOVE TO AND FRO, swing, sway, roll, lurch, pitch.

**rocker** n. a curved piece of wood on the bottom of a rocking chair.

**rockery** n. (pl. **-ies**) an arrangement of rocks in a garden with plants growing between them.

**rocket** n. **1** a missile or spacecraft propelled by a stream of burning gases. **2** a firework that shoots into the air and explodes. • v. (**rocketed, rocketing**) move rapidly upwards or away.

**rocky** adj. **1** of or like rock; full of rocks. **2** unstable.
▷ SYNS **1** STONY, pebbly. **2** UNSTEADY, unstable, shaky, teetering, wobbly.

**rococo** adj. in a highly ornate style of decoration.

**rod** n. a slender straight bar of wood, metal etc.; a long stick with a line and hook, for catching fish.
▷ SYNS BAR, stick, pole, baton, staff.

**rode** past of RIDE.

**rodent** n. an animal with strong front teeth for gnawing things.

**rodeo** n. (pl. **-eos**) a competition or exhibition of cowboys' skill.

**roe**[1] n. a mass of eggs in a female fish's ovary.

**roe**[2] n. (pl. **roe** or **roes**) a small deer.

**rogue** n. **1** a dishonest or mischievous person. **2** an elephant living apart from the herd. ■ **roguish** adj.
▷ SYNS VILLAIN, scoundrel, rascal, reprobate, wretch, cad, blackguard, ne'er-do-well; inf. rotter, bounder.

**role** n. an actor's part; a person's or thing's function.
▷ SYNS **1** PART, character. **2** CAPACITY, function, position, job, post, office.

**roll** v. **1** move by turning over and over; move on wheels. **2** turn something flexible over on itself to form a ball or cylinder. **3** sway from side to side; (of a deep sound) reverberate. **4** flatten with a roller. • n. **1** a cylinder formed by rolling flexible material. **2** an act of rolling. **3** a reverberating sound of thunder etc. **4** a small individual loaf of bread. **5** an official list or register. ☐ **roll-call** the calling of a list of names to check that all are present. **rolling pin** a roller for flattening dough. **rolling stock** railway engines, carriages, etc.
▷ SYNS v. **1** GO ROUND, turn, rotate, revolve, spin, whirl, wheel. **2** FURL, coil, fold. **3** TOSS, rock, pitch, lurch, sway, reel. • n. **1** SPOOL, reel, bobbin, cylinder. **2** REGISTER, list, index, directory, catalogue.

**roller** n. **1** a cylinder rolled over things to flatten or spread them, or on which something is wound. **2** a long swelling wave. □ **roller coaster** a switchback at a fair. **roller skate** a boot with wheels, for gliding across a hard surface.

**rollicking** adj. full of boisterous high spirits.

**roly-poly** n. a pudding of suet pastry spread with jam and rolled up. • adj. plump.

**Roman** adj. of Rome or its ancient empire. • n. **1** an inhabitant of Rome. **2** (**roman**) plain upright type. □ **Roman Catholic** a member of the Christian Church which has the Pope as its head. **Roman numeral** each of the letters representing numbers in the ancient Roman system.

**romance** n. a feeling of excitement associated with love; a love affair or love story; a feeling of exciting mystery and remoteness from everyday life. • v. try to win the love of.
▷ SYNS **1** LOVE AFFAIR, affair, liaison, courtship. **2** MYSTERY, glamour, excitement, exoticism, mystique.

**Romanesque** adj. of or in a style of architecture common in Europe about 900–1200.

**romantic** adj. having to do with love; viewing or showing life in an idealized way. • n. a romantic person. ■ **romantically** adv.
▷ SYNS adj. **1** LOVING, amorous, affectionate, tender, sentimental. **2** UNREALISTIC, idealistic, impractical, starry-eyed, fairy-tale. • n. DREAMER, idealist, sentimentalist.

**romanticize** (or **-ise**) v. view or represent as better or more beautiful than is the case.

**Romany** n. (pl. **-ies**) a gypsy; the language of the gypsies.

**romp** v. play about in a lively way.

**roof** n. (pl. **roofs**) the upper covering of a building, car, cavity, etc. • v. cover with a roof.

**rook** n. **1** a bird of the crow family. **2** a chess piece with a top shaped like battlements.

**rookery** n. (pl. **-ies**) a colony of rooks.

**room** n. **1** a division of a building, separated off by walls. **2** space for occupying or moving in; scope to act or happen.
▷ SYNS **1** SPACE, elbow room; area, expanse, extent. **2** SCOPE, capacity, margin, leeway, latitude, freedom, opportunity.

**roomy** adj. (**-ier**, **-iest**) having plenty of space.

**roost** n. a place where birds perch or rest. • v. perch, esp. for rest.

**rooster** n. a male domestic fowl.

**root** n. **1** the part of a plant that grows into the earth and absorbs nourishment from the soil; the embedded part of a hair, tooth, etc. **2** the basis or origin of something. **3** a number in relation to another which it produces when multiplied by itself a specified number of times. **4** (**roots**) a person's family or origins. • v. **1** cause to take root; cause to stand fixed and unmoving. **2** (of an animal) turn up ground with its snout in search of food; rummage.
▷ SYNS n. **1** RADICLE, rhizome, tuber. **2** SOURCE, origin, genesis, starting point, basis,

foundation, beginnings. v. (**root out**) ERADICATE, get rid of, weed out, do away with, eliminate, abolish, destroy.

**rope** n. a strong thick cord.
• v. fasten or secure with rope.
▷ SYNS n. CORD, cable, line, strand, hawser.

**ropy** (or **ropey**) adj. inf. poor in quality or health.

**rosary** n. (pl. **-ies**) a set series of prayers; a string of beads for keeping count in this.

**rose**[1] n. 1 a fragrant flower with prickly stems. 2 a soft pink colour. □ **rose hip** the fruit of the rose.

**rose**[2] past of RISE.

**rosé** n. a light pink wine.

**rosemary** n. a shrub with fragrant leaves used as a herb.

**rosette** n. a round badge or ornament made of ribbons.

**roster** n. a list showing people's turns of duty etc.

**rostrum** n. (pl. **-tra** or **-trums**) a platform for standing on to make a speech, conduct an orchestra, etc.

**rosy** adj. (**-ier, -iest**) 1 deep pink. 2 promising or hopeful.

**rot** v. (**rotted, rotting**) gradually decay. • n. 1 rotting. 2 inf. nonsense.
▷ SYNS v. 1 DECOMPOSE, decay, crumble, disintegrate, perish. 2 GO BAD, go off, spoil, putrefy, fester. • n. DECOMPOSITION, decay, putrefaction, mould, blight.

**rota** n. a list of duties to be done or people to do them in rotation.

**rotate** v. revolve round an axis; arrange, occur, or deal with in a

recurrent series. ■ **rotary** adj. **rotation** n.
▷ SYNS 1 REVOLVE, go round, turn, spin, whirl, swivel, wheel, gyrate. 2 ALTERNATE, take turns.

**rote** n. regular repetition of something to be learned.

**rotisserie** n. a revolving spit for roasting meat.

**rotor** n. a rotating part of a machine.

**rotten** adj. 1 decayed. 2 corrupt. 3 inf. very bad.
▷ SYNS 1 DECAYING, bad, off, mouldy, rancid, decomposing, putrid, putrescent, festering. 2 CORRUPT, immoral, dishonourable, contemptible, despicable, bad, wicked, villainous, evil.

**Rottweiler** n. a large powerful breed of dog.

**rotund** adj. rounded and plump.

**rotunda** n. a round, domed building or hall.

**rouge** n. a red powder or cream for colouring the cheeks.

**rough** adj. 1 not smooth or level; not gentle; difficult and unpleasant. 2 (of weather or the sea) wild and stormy; harsh in sound or taste; unsophisticated, plain, or basic. 3 not worked out in every detail. • n. 1 a basic draft. 2 longer grass at the edge of a golf course. □ **rough-and-ready** crude or simple but effective. ■ **roughen** v. **roughly** adv.
▷ SYNS adj. 1 UNEVEN, irregular, bumpy, rutted, rocky, stony, rugged, craggy. 2 COARSE, bristly, scratchy; shaggy, hairy, bushy. 3 STORMY, squally, wild, tempestuous, turbulent, choppy. 4 HARSH, severe, hard, tough, difficult, unpleasant, arduous. 5 PRELIMINARY, hasty,

quick, cursory, incomplete, rudimentary, basic. **6** APPROXIMATE, inexact, imprecise, vague.

**roughage** n. dietary fibre.

**roughshod** adj. (**ride roughshod over**) treat inconsiderately or arrogantly.

**roulette** n. a gambling game in which a ball is dropped on to a revolving wheel.

**round** adj. **1** shaped like a circle, sphere, or cylinder; having a curved surface. **2** (of a number) expressed in convenient units rather than exactly. • n. **1** a circular shape or piece. **2** a tour of visits or inspection; a recurring sequence of activities; one of a sequence of actions or events; one section of a competition. **3** a song for several voices starting the same tune at different times. **4** the amount of ammunition needed for one shot. • adv. **1** in a circle or curve; so as to surround someone or something; so as to cover a whole area or group. **2** so as to face in a different direction; facing in a particular way: *the wrong way round.* **3** so as to reach a new place or position. • prep. **1** so as to surround, enclose, or cover. **2** from or on the other side of. • v. **1** pass and go round. **2** (**round up** or **down**) alter a number for convenience. **3** make rounded. □ **round trip** a journey to a place and back again. **round up** gather into one place.
▷ SYNS adj. CIRCULAR, ring-shaped, cylindrical, spherical, globular, bulbous, convex, curved. • n. **1** SUCCESSION, sequence, series, cycle. **2** STAGE, level; heat, game.

**roundabout** n. **1** a revolving platform at a funfair, with

model horses etc. to ride on. **2** a road junction at which traffic moves in one direction round a central island. • adj. indirect or circuitous.
▷ SYNS adj. INDIRECT, circuitous, meandering, tortuous; oblique, circumlocutory, periphrastic.

**rounders** n. a team game played with bat and ball, in which players have to run round a circuit.

**Roundhead** n. hist. a supporter of the Parliamentary party in the English Civil War.

**roundly** adv. in a firm or thorough way.

**rouse** v. wake; cause to become active or excited.
▷ SYNS **1** WAKE (UP), awaken. **2** STIR UP, excite, electrify, galvanize, stimulate, inspire, arouse.

**rout** n. a complete defeat; a disorderly retreat. • v. defeat completely and force to retreat.
▷ SYNS v. DEFEAT, trounce, beat hollow; inf. thrash, annihilate.

**route** n. a course or way from a starting point to a destination.
▷ SYNS COURSE, way, itinerary, road, path.

**routine** n. a standard procedure; a set sequence of movements. • adj. in accordance with routine.
▷ SYNS n. PATTERN, procedure, practice, custom, habit, programme, schedule, formula, method, system. • adj. USUAL, normal, everyday, common, ordinary, typical, customary, habitual, conventional, standard.

**roux** n. (pl. **roux**) a mixture of heated fat and flour as a basis for a sauce.

**rove** v. wander.

**row**¹ n. people or things in a line.
▷ SYNS LINE, column, queue, procession, chain, string, crocodile.

**row**² v. propel a boat using oars.

**row**³ n. a loud noise; an angry
argument. • v. quarrel angrily.

**rowan** n. a tree with clusters of
red berries.

**rowdy** adj. (-ier, -iest) noisy and
disorderly. ■ rowdily adv.
rowdiness n.
▷ SYNS UNRULY, disorderly, noisy,
boisterous, loud, wild, rough,
unrestrained, riotous.

**rowlock** n. a device on the side
of a boat for holding an oar.

**royal** adj. of or suited to a king
or queen. □ royal blue deep,
vivid blue. ■ royally adv.
▷ SYNS REGAL, kingly, queenly,
princely, sovereign.

**royalist** n. a person supporting
or advocating monarchy.

**royalty** n. (pl. -ies) 1 the
members of a royal family;
royal status or power. 2 payment
to an author, patentee, etc. for
each copy, performance, or use
of their work.

**RSPCA** abbr. Royal Society for
the Prevention of Cruelty to
Animals.

**RSVP** abbr. please reply (short
for French *répondez s'il vous
plaît*).

**rub** v. (rubbed, rubbing) move
your hand, a cloth, etc. over a
surface while pressing down
firmly; polish, clean, dry, or
make sore in this way; erase
marks with a rubber. • n. an act
of rubbing; an ointment to be
rubbed on.
▷ SYNS v. 1 MASSAGE, knead, stroke.
2 SCRUB, scour, polish, clean.
3 (rub out) ERASE, efface,
obliterate, expunge, remove.

**rubber** n. a tough elastic
substance made from the juice
of certain plants or synthetically; a piece of this for erasing
pencil marks. ■ rubbery adj.

**rubbish** n. waste or discarded
material; nonsense.
▷ SYNS 1 WASTE, refuse, litter,
lumber, junk, debris, detritus;
US garbage, trash. 2 see
NONSENSE.

**rubble** n. rough fragments of
stone, brick, etc.

**rubella** n. a disease with
symptoms like mild measles.

**rubric** n. words put as a heading
or note of explanation.

**ruby** n. (pl. -ies) a red precious
stone; a deep red colour. □ ruby
wedding a 40th wedding
anniversary.

**ruche** n. a decorative frill of
fabric.

**ruck** v. crease or wrinkle. • n. 1 a
crease or wrinkle. 2 a tightly
packed crowd.

**rucksack** n. a bag carried on the
back.

**ructions** pl.n. inf. unpleasant
arguments or protests.

**rudder** n. a vertical piece of
metal or wood hinged to the
stern of a boat, used for
steering.

**ruddy** adj. (-ier, -iest) having a
reddish colour.

**rude** adj. 1 offensively impolite
or bad-mannered. 2 referring to
sex etc. in an offensive way.
3 (of health) good.
▷ SYNS 1 ILL-MANNERED, bad-
mannered, impolite, dis-
courteous, impertinent,
insolent, impudent, cheeky,
disrespectful, curt, brusque,
blunt, offhand. 2 VULGAR,
coarse, indelicate, smutty, dirty,

naughty, risqué, blue, ribald, bawdy.

**rudimentary** adj. **1** basic or elementary. **2** not highly developed.
▷ SYNS **1** ELEMENTARY, basic, fundamental. **2** PRIMITIVE, crude, simple, rough-and-ready, unsophisticated.

**rudiments** pl.n. the fundamental principles or elements; an undeveloped form of something.
▷ SYNS BASICS, fundamentals, essentials, foundation; inf. nuts and bolts.

**rue** v. regret deeply. ■ **rueful** adj.

**ruff** n. a pleated frill worn round the neck; a ring of feathers or fur round a bird's or animal's neck.

**ruffian** n. a violent lawless person.

**ruffle** v. disturb the calmness or smoothness of; annoy. • n. a gathered frill.
▷ SYNS v. RUMPLE, dishevel, tousle, disarrange, disorder, mess up; inf. muss up.

**rug** n. a small carpet; a thick woollen blanket.

**rugby** (or **rugby football**) n. a team game played with an oval ball which may be kicked or carried.

**rugged** adj. **1** having a rocky surface. **2** (of a man) strong-featured.
▷ SYNS **1** ROUGH, uneven, bumpy, rocky, stony, craggy. **2** STRONG-FEATURED, rough-hewn; strong, tough, sturdy, vigorous, brawny, robust, muscular; inf. hunky.

**rugger** n. inf. rugby.

**ruin** v. completely spoil or destroy; reduce to bankruptcy.
• n. destruction; the complete loss of a person's money or property; the damaged remains of a building etc. ■ **ruination** n. **ruinous** adj.
▷ SYNS v. **1** DESTROY, devastate, lay waste, demolish, wreck, spoil. **2** BANKRUPT, impoverish.
• n. **1** DESTRUCTION, devastation, wreckage, demolition, disintegration. **2** RUINATION, bankruptcy, insolvency, penury, impoverishment.

**rule** n. **1** a statement or principle governing behaviour or describing a regular occurrence in nature etc.; a dominant custom; government or control. **2** a ruler used by carpenters etc.
• v. **1** govern; keep under control; give an authoritative decision. **2** (**rule out**) exclude. **3** draw a line using a ruler.
▷ SYNS n. **1** RULING, law, regulation, statute, order, decree, edict, commandment, directive, act. **2** PRINCIPLE, precept, standard, axiom, maxim. **3** GOVERNMENT, administration, jurisdiction, reign, authority, command, power, dominion. • v. **1** PRESIDE OVER, govern, control, run, administer, manage. **2** ORDER, decree, pronounce, ordain, lay down; decide, determine, resolve.

**ruler** n. **1** a person who rules. **2** a straight strip used in measuring or for drawing straight lines.

**ruling** n. an authoritative decision.
▷ SYNS JUDGEMENT, decision, adjudication, finding, verdict, decree, pronouncement, resolution.

**rum** n. an alcoholic spirit made from sugar cane.

**rumba** n. a ballroom dance.

**rumble** n. & v. (make) a low continuous sound.

**rumbustious** adj. inf. boisterous.

**ruminant** n. an animal that chews the cud, such as a cow or sheep.

**ruminate** v. 1 think deeply. 2 chew the cud.

**rummage** v. search clumsily. • n. an untidy search through a number of things.

**rummy** n. a card game.

**rumour** (US **rumor**) n. an un-confirmed story spread among a number of people. □ **be rumoured** be spread as a rumour.
▷ SYNS GOSSIP, hearsay, talk; report, story, whisper.

**rump** n. the buttocks.

**rumple** v. make less neat and tidy.

**rumpus** n. a noisy disturbance.

**run** v. 1 move with quick steps with always at least one foot off the ground; move around hurriedly. 2 move smoothly in a particular direction; flow. 3 travel regularly along a route. 4 be in charge of; function; continue, operate, or proceed. 5 stand as a candidate in an election; compete in a race. 6 smuggle drugs. • n. 1 a spell of running; a running pace; a journey. 2 a point scored in cricket or baseball. 3 a continuous spell or sequence. 4 unrestricted use of a place. 5 an enclosed area where domestic animals can range. 6 a ladder in stockings or tights. □ **rundown** a brief summary. **run-down** weak or exhausted. **runway** a strip of hard ground where aircraft take off and land.
▷ SYNS v. 1 RACE, rush, hasten, hurry, dash, sprint, bolt, dart, career, tear, charge, speed; jog, lope; inf. hare. 2 MOVE, glide, slide, roll, flow, course. 3 CONTINUE, extend, stretch, reach. 4 MANAGE, be in charge of, control, head, lead, direct, administer, supervise, super-intend, oversee. • n. 1 JOG, sprint, dash. 2 DRIVE, ride, trip, outing, excursion, jaunt, journey; inf. spin. 3 SPELL, spate; sequence, series, succession; streak, chain, string.

**rune** n. a letter of an ancient Germanic alphabet.

**rung**¹ n. a crosspiece of a ladder etc.

**rung**² p.p. of RING².

**runner** n. 1 a person or animal that runs; a messenger. 2 a shoot that grows along the ground and can take root. 3 a groove, strip, or roller etc. for a thing to move on. 4 a long narrow rug. □ **runner-up** a competitor who comes second.

**runny** adj. (-ier, -iest) semi-liquid; producing mucus.

**run-of-the-mill** adj. ordinary.
▷ SYNS ORDINARY, average, un-exceptional, unremarkable, commonplace, standard, conventional, dull.

**runt** n. the smallest animal in a litter.

**rupture** n. a break or breach; an abdominal hernia. • v. burst or break; cause a hernia in.
▷ SYNS n. BREAK, fracture, crack, split, burst, fissure.

**rural** adj. of, in, or like the countryside.

▷ SYNS PASTORAL, rustic, bucolic; agricultural, agrarian.

**ruse** n. a deception or trick.

**rush**[1] v. move or act with great speed; produce, deal with, or transport hurriedly; force into hasty action; make a sudden assault on. • n. a sudden quick movement; a very busy state or period; a sudden flow or surge. □ **rush hour** one of the times of the day when traffic is busiest.
▷ SYNS v. HURRY, hasten, run, race, dash, sprint, bolt, dart, career, tear, charge, speed, scurry, scamper. • n. **1** SURGE, flow, gush, spurt, stream, flood. **2** HURRY, haste, speed, urgency, rapidity.

**rush**[2] n. a water plant with a slender pithy stem.

**rusk** n. a dry biscuit.

**russet** adj. soft reddish brown.

**rust** n. a brownish flaky coating forming on iron exposed to moisture. • v. make or become rusty.

**rustic** adj. of or like country life; charmingly simple and unsophisticated.

**rustle** v. **1** make a sound like paper being crumpled. **2** steal horses or cattle. • n. a rustling sound. ■ **rustler** n.

**rusty** adj. affected by rust; deteriorating through lack of use.

**rut**[1] n. **1** a deep track made by wheels. **2** a habitual dull pattern of behaviour.
▷ SYNS **1** FURROW, groove, track, trough, ditch, hole, pothole. **2** *stuck in a rut*: TREADMILL, dead end, boring routine.

**rut**[2] n. the periodic sexual excitement of a male deer, goat, etc. • v. (**rutted**, **rutting**) be affected with this.

**ruthless** adj. having no pity.
▷ SYNS MERCILESS, pitiless, cruel, heartless, hard-hearted, cold-blooded, harsh, callous, remorseless, implacable; barbarous, inhuman, brutal, savage, sadistic.

**rye** n. a cereal; whisky made from this.

# Ss

**S** abbr. **1** South or Southern. **2** (s) seconds.

**sabbath** n. a day for rest and religious worship.

**sabbatical** n. a period of paid leave for study or travel.

**sable** adj. black.

**sabotage** n. wilful damage to machinery, materials, etc.

• v. commit sabotage on. ■ **saboteur** n.
▷ SYNS n. DAMAGE, destruction, vandalism, disruption. • v. DAMAGE, destroy, wreck, ruin, incapacitate, cripple, vandalize, disrupt.

**sabre** (US **saber**) n. a curved sword.

**sac** n. a hollow bag-like structure.

**saccharin** n. an artificial sweetener.

**sachet** n. a small bag or sealed pack.

**sack** n. **1** a large strong bag. **2** (**the sack**) inf. dismissal from employment. • v. **1** inf. dismiss. **2** plunder a captured town. □ **sackcloth** a coarse fabric woven from flax or hemp.
▷ SYNS n. BAG, pack, pouch. • v. DISMISS, discharge; inf. fire, kick out, give someone their cards, boot out.

**sacrament** n. any of the symbolic Christian religious ceremonies.

**sacred** adj. connected to a god or goddess and greatly revered; to do with religion.
▷ SYNS HOLY, blessed, hallowed, consecrated, sanctified; religious, spiritual.

**sacrifice** n. the slaughter of a victim or presenting of a gift to win a god's favour; this victim or gift; the giving up of a valued thing for the sake of something else. • v. offer as a sacrifice. ■ **sacrificial** adj.
▷ SYNS n. OFFERING, gift, oblation. • v. **1** GIVE UP, forgo, renounce, abandon, surrender, relinquish. **2** OFFER (UP), immolate.

**sacrilege** n. disrespect to a sacred thing. ■ **sacrilegious** adj.
▷ SYNS DESECRATION, profanity, blasphemy, impiety, irreverence, disrespect.

**sacrosanct** adj. too important or precious to be changed.

**sacrum** n. (pl. **-crums** or **-cra**) the triangular bone at the base of the spine.

**sad** adj. (**sadder**, **saddest**) feeling or causing sorrow. ■ **sadden** v. **sadness** n.

▷ SYNS **1** UNHAPPY, sorrowful, depressed, downcast, miserable, despondent, wretched, glum, gloomy, doleful, melancholy, mournful, woebegone, heartbroken; inf. blue, down in the mouth/dumps. **2** TRAGIC, sorry, pitiful, distressing, heartbreaking, heart-rending.

**saddle** n. **1** a seat for a rider. **2** a joint of meat from the back of an animal. • v. put a saddle on a horse; burden with a task.

**sadism** n. enjoyment derived from inflicting pain on others. ■ **sadist** n. **sadistic** adj.

**safari** n. an expedition to observe or hunt wild animals.

**safe** adj. **1** protected from risk or danger. **2** not leading to harm. **3** giving security. • n. a strong lockable cabinet for valuables. ■ **safely** adv.
▷ SYNS adj. **1** SECURE, protected, sheltered, guarded, defended, out of harm's way. **2** UNHARMED, unhurt, unscathed, out of danger; inf. OK. • n. STRONGBOX, safety-deposit box.

**safeguard** n. a means of protection. • v. protect.
▷ SYNS n. PROTECTION, defence, precaution, security; surety. • v. PROTECT, preserve, guard, secure.

**safety** n. freedom from risk or danger. □ **safety belt** a seat belt. **safety pin** a pin with a point held in a guard when closed.
▷ SYNS PROTECTION, security, shelter, sanctuary, refuge.

**saffron** n. a yellow spice.

**sag** v. (**sagged**, **sagging**) gradually droop or sink.
▷ SYNS SINK, droop, subside, slump.

**saga** n. a long story.

▷ SYNS EPIC, chronicle, legend, history.

**sagacious** adj. wise.

**sage** n. **1** a herb. **2** an old and wise man. • adj. wise.

**sago** n. the starchy pith of the sago palm, used in puddings.

**said** past and p.p. of **SAY**.

**sail** n. **1** a piece of fabric spread to catch the wind and drive a boat along. **2** a journey by boat. **3** the arm of a windmill. • v. **1** travel by water. **2** move smoothly.

**sailor** n. a member of a ship's crew.

▷ SYNS SEAMAN, seafarer, mariner, boatman; inf. salt, sea dog.

**saint** n. a holy person, esp. one venerated by the RC or Orthodox Church; a very good person. ■ **sainthood** n.

**saintly** adj. very holy or good.

▷ SYNS HOLY, godly, pious, religious, devout, spiritual, virtuous, righteous, good, God-fearing, innocent, pure.

**sake** n. (**for the sake of**) **1** so as to achieve. **2** out of consideration for.

**salacious** adj. containing too much sexual detail.

**salad** n. a cold dish of raw vegetables etc.

**salamander** n. a newt-like animal.

**salami** n. a strongly flavoured sausage, eaten cold.

**salary** n. (pl. **-ies**) a fixed regular payment made to an employee. ■ **salaried** adj.

▷ SYNS PAY, wages, earnings, remuneration, fee, emolument, stipend.

**sale** n. **1** the exchange of something for money. **2** a period in which goods are sold at reduced prices. **3** an event at which goods are sold. □ **salesman** (or **saleswoman** or **salesperson**) a person whose job is to sell goods. ■ **saleable** adj.

**salient** adj. most noticeable or important.

**saline** adj. containing salt.

**saliva** n. the watery liquid that forms in the mouth.

**salivate** v. produce saliva.

**sallow** adj. (of the complexion) yellowish.

**sally** n. **1** a sudden charge from a besieged place. **2** a witty reply. • v. (**sallied, sallying**) set out.

**salmon** n. (pl. **salmon**) a large fish with pinkish flesh.

**salmonella** n. a germ causing food poisoning.

**salon** n. **1** a place where a hairdresser, beautician, etc. works. **2** a reception room in a large house.

**saloon** n. **1** a car with a separate boot. **2** a public lounge on a ship.

**salsa** n. **1** a type of Latin American dance music. **2** a spicy sauce.

**salt** n. **1** sodium chloride used to flavour and preserve food. **2** a chemical compound formed by the reaction of an acid with a base. • adj. containing or treated with salt. • v. season or preserve with salt. □ **salt cellar** a container for salt. ■ **salty** adj.

**salubrious** adj. health-giving.

**salutary** adj. producing a good effect.

**salutation** n. a greeting.

**salute** n. **1** a gesture of respect or acknowledgement. **2** a raising of a hand to the head, made as a formal military gesture of respect. • v. make a salute to.

▷ SYNS v. **1** GREET, hail, welcome, acknowledge, address. **2** PAY TRIBUTE TO, pay homage to, honour.

**salvage** v. **1** save from being lost or destroyed. **2** rescue a ship or its cargo from loss at sea. • n. **1** the act of salvaging. **2** salvaged cargo.

▷ SYNS v. RESCUE, save, recover, retrieve, reclaim.

**salvation** n. the saving of someone from harm or sin.

**salve** n. a soothing ointment; something that reduces feelings of guilt. • v. reduce feelings of guilt.

**salver** n. a small tray.

**salvo** n. (pl. **-oes** or **-os**) a simultaneous discharge of guns; a sudden series of aggressive statements or acts.

**Samaritan** n. a charitable or helpful person.

**samba** n. a Brazilian dance.

**same** adj. exactly alike. • pron. the one already mentioned. • adv. in the same way.

▷ SYNS adj. **1** IDENTICAL, selfsame, very same. **2** MATCHING, alike, twin, indistinguishable, interchangeable, corresponding, equivalent.

**samovar** n. a Russian tea urn.

**sample** n. a small part intended to show what the whole is like. • v. **1** take a sample of. **2** try out.

▷ SYNS n. SPECIMEN, example, taste, taster.

**sampler** n. a piece of embroidery showing various stitches.

**samurai** n. (pl. **samurai**) hist. a Japanese army officer.

**sanatorium** n. (pl. **-riums** or **-ria**) **1** a place for treating chronic diseases or convalescents. **2** a room for sick pupils in a school.

**sanctify** v. (**sanctified, sanctifying**) make holy or sacred.

▷ SYNS CONSECRATE, bless, hallow.

**sanctimonious** adj. ostentatiously pious.

▷ SYNS SELF-RIGHTEOUS, smug, holier-than-thou, pious, hypocritical; inf. goody-goody.

**sanction** n. **1** a penalty for disobeying a law. **2** official permission. • v. give permission for.

▷ SYNS n. **1** PENALTY, punishment, deterrent; embargo, ban, boycott. **2** AUTHORIZATION, permission, consent, approval, endorsement; inf. thumbs up, green light, OK. v. see **AUTHORIZE**.

**sanctity** n. sacredness or holiness.

**sanctuary** n. **1** a place of refuge; a place where wildlife is protected. **2** a sacred place.

▷ SYNS **1** REFUGE, haven, shelter, retreat, hideout, hideaway. **2** HOLY PLACE, temple, shrine, sanctum.

**sanctum** n. a sacred place; a private place.

**sand** n. **1** very fine loose fragments of crushed rock. **2** (**sands**) a wide area of sand. • v. smooth with sandpaper or a sander. □ **sandbag** a bag of sand, used to protect against floods etc. **sandbank** a raised bank of sand in the sea or a river. **sandblast** roughen or clean with a jet of sand. **sandcastle** a model castle built out of sand. **sandpaper** paper with a coating of sand or another rough substance, for smoothing surfaces. **sandstone** rock formed from compressed sand. **sandstorm** a strong desert wind carrying clouds of sand.

**sandal** n. a light shoe with straps.

**sander** n. a power tool for smoothing surfaces.

**sandwich** n. two slices of bread with a filling between. • v. put between two other people or things.

**sandy** adj. (-ier, -iest) **1** like sand; covered with sand. **2** yellowish brown.

**sane** adj. **1** not mad. **2** sensible.
▷ SYNS **1** OF SOUND MIND, in your right mind, compos mentis, rational, lucid. **2** SENSIBLE, practical, reasonable, prudent, wise.

**sang** past of SING.

**sanguine** adj. optimistic.

**sanitary** adj. of sanitation; hygienic. □ **sanitary towel** a pad worn to absorb menstrual blood.

**sanitation** n. arrangements to protect public health, esp. drainage and disposal of sewage.

**sanitize** (or -ise) v. make hygienic; alter to make more acceptable.

**sanity** n. the condition of being sane.

**sank** past of SINK.

**sap** n. the food-carrying liquid in plants. • v. (**sapped, sapping**) exhaust gradually.
▷ SYNS **v.** DRAIN, enervate, exhaust, weaken, enfeeble, debilitate.

**sapling** n. a young tree.

**sapphire** n. a blue precious stone; its colour.

**sarcasm** n. the use of irony to mock or convey contempt.
▷ SYNS IRONY, derision, mockery, ridicule, scorn.

**sarcastic** adj. showing or expressing sarcasm.
▷ SYNS IRONIC, sardonic, derisive, scornful, mocking, caustic, trenchant.

**sarcophagus** n. (pl. **-phagi**) a stone coffin.

**sardine** n. a small herring-like fish.

**sardonic** adj. humorous in a mocking way.

**sari** n. a length of cloth draped round the body, worn by Indian women.

**sarong** n. a strip of cloth wrapped round the body and tucked at the waist.

**sartorial** adj. of tailoring, clothing, or style of dress.

**sash** n. **1** a strip of cloth worn round the waist or over one shoulder. **2** a frame holding the glass in a window.

**sat** past and p.p. of SIT.

**Satan** n. the devil.

**satanic** adj. relating to or typical of Satan.
▷ SYNS DIABOLICAL, fiendish, devilish, demonic, wicked, evil, hellish, sinful.

**satanism** n. the worship of Satan. ■ **satanist** n. & adj.

**satchel** n. a bag for school books, hung over the shoulder.

**sated** adj. fully satisfied.

**satellite** n. **1** a heavenly or artificial body revolving round a planet. **2** a country that is dependent on another. □ **satellite television** television in which the signals are broadcast via satellite.

**satiate** v. satisfy fully.

**satin** n. a smooth, glossy fabric.

**satire** n. **1** the use of humour, irony, etc. to criticize or ridicule. **2** a novel, play, etc. using satire.
▷ SYNS PARODY, burlesque, caricature, lampoon; inf. spoof, send-up.

**satirical** adj. using humour, irony, or exaggeration to mock or criticize.
▷ SYNS MOCKING, ironic, sarcastic; sardonic, caustic, trenchant, mordant.

**satirize** (or **-ise**) v. mock or criticize using satire.
▷ SYNS MOCK, ridicule, deride, make fun of, parody, lampoon, caricature; inf. send up.

**satisfaction** n. **1** pleasure arising from having what you want or need. **2** a satisfactory way of dealing with an injustice, complaint, etc.
▷ SYNS CONTENTMENT, content, pleasure, gratification, fulfilment, enjoyment, happiness, pride.

**satisfactory** adj. acceptable.
■ satisfactorily adv.
▷ SYNS ADEQUATE, all right, acceptable, fine, sufficient, competent, passable; inf. OK.

**satisfy** v. **1** please someone by meeting their expectations, needs, or desires. **2** meet a demand, desire, or need.
▷ SYNS **1** FULFIL, gratify, meet, appease, assuage, quench, slake, satiate. **2** CONVINCE, assure, reassure, put someone's mind at rest.

**satsuma** n. a small variety of orange.

**saturate** v. **1** soak thoroughly. **2** supply a market beyond the limits of demand.
■ saturation n.
▷ SYNS **1** SOAK, drench, wet through. **2** FLOOD, oversupply, overfill, overload.

**Saturday** n. the day following Friday.

**satyr** n. a woodland god in classical mythology, with a goat's ears, tail, and legs.

**sauce** n. a liquid food added for flavour. □ saucepan a deep cooking pan with a long handle.

**saucer** n. a shallow curved dish on which a cup stands.

**saucy** adj. (**-ier**, **-iest**) cheeky; sexually suggestive.
■ saucily adv.

**sauerkraut** n. chopped pickled cabbage.

**sauna** n. a hot room for cleaning and refreshing the body.

**saunter** v. stroll. • n. a stroll.
▷ SYNS v. STROLL, amble, wander, meander, walk, promenade; inf. mosey.

**sausage** n. a tube of minced meat encased in a skin.

**sauté** adj. fried quickly in shallow oil.

**savage** adj. wild and fierce; cruel and vicious; primitive and uncivilized. • n. a primitive or uncivilized person; a brutal person. • v. fiercely attack and maul. ■ savagery n.
▷ SYNS adj. **1** VICIOUS, brutal, cruel, sadistic, violent, murderous, bloodthirsty, barbarous. **2** FIERCE, ferocious, wild, untamed, undomesticated, feral. **3** PRIMITIVE, uncivilized.
• v. MAUL, lacerate, tear to pieces, attack.

**savannah** n. a grassy plain in hot regions.

**save** v. **1** rescue from harm or danger. **2** store for future use. **3** avoid or guard against. **4** prevent the scoring of a goal. • n. an act of saving in football etc.
▷ SYNS v. **1** RESCUE; set free, free, liberate, bail out. **2** PRESERVE, protect, safeguard, keep safe. **3** PUT/SET ASIDE, put by, keep, reserve, conserve, stockpile, store, hoard.

**savings** pl.n. money saved.
▷ SYNS CAPITAL, assets, reserves, funds, nest egg.

**saviour** (US **savior**) n. a person who rescues people from harm.
▷ SYNS RESCUER, knight in shining armour, good Samaritan, friend in need.

**savoir faire** n. the ability to act appropriately in social situations.

**savour** (US **savor**) n. flavour; smell. • v. enjoy fully or thoroughly.
▷ SYNS v. ENJOY, appreciate, delight in, relish, revel in.

**savoury** (US **savory**) adj. salty or spicy rather than sweet; morally respectable.

**saw**[1] past of SEE.

**saw**[2] n. **1** a cutting tool with a jagged blade. **2** a saying. • v. (**sawed**, **sawn**, **sawing**) cut with a saw.

**saxophone** n. a brass wind instrument with finger-operated keys.

**say** v. **1** utter words; express, convey, or state; have written or shown on the surface. **2** suppose as a possibility. • n. the opportunity to state your opinion.
▷ SYNS v. **1** SPEAK, utter, voice, pronounce. **2** STATE, declare,

remark, announce, observe, comment, mention, opine; claim, maintain, assert. **3** ESTIMATE, judge, guess, predict, speculate, conjecture, surmise. **4** SUPPOSE, assume, imagine, presume.

**saying** n. a well-known phrase or proverb.
▷ SYNS PROVERB, maxim, aphorism, axiom, adage, epigram, saw; platitude, cliché.

**scab** n. a crust forming over a cut as it heals.

**scabbard** n. the sheath of a sword etc.

**scabies** n. a contagious skin disease.

**scaffold** n. **1** a platform for the execution of criminals. **2** a structure of scaffolding.
▷ SYNS **1** GALLOWS, gibbet. **2** SCAFFOLDING, framework, gantry.

**scaffolding** n. poles and planks providing platforms for people working on buildings etc.

**scald** v. burn with hot liquid or steam; clean or peel using boiling water. • n. an injury by scalding.

**scale** n. **1** a range of values for measuring or grading something. **2** relative size or extent. **3** (**scales**) an instrument for weighing. **4** a fixed series of notes in a system of music. **5** each of the overlapping plates protecting the skin of fish and reptiles. **6** a deposit formed in a kettle etc. by hard water. **7** tartar on teeth. • v. **1** climb. **2** represent in proportion to the size of the original. **3** remove scale(s) from. ■ **scaly** adj.
▷ SYNS n. **1** SEQUENCE, series, succession; hierarchy, ladder, ranking, pecking order.

**2** EXTENT, size, scope, magnitude, dimensions. • v. CLIMB, ascend, clamber up, mount.

**scallop** n. **1** an edible shellfish with two hinged fan-shaped shells. **2** (**scallops**) semicircular curves as an ornamental edging. ■ **scalloped** adj.

**scallywag** n. a rascal.

**scalp** n. the skin of the head excluding the face. • v. cut the scalp from.

**scalpel** n. a small sharp-bladed knife used by a surgeon.

**scamp** n. a rascal.

**scamper** v. run with quick, light steps.

**scampi** pl.n. the tails of large prawns, fried in breadcrumbs.

**scan** v. **1** read quickly. **2** move a detector or beam across. **3** convert a document etc. into digital form for storing or processing on a computer. **4** (of verse) follow metrical rules. • n. scanning. ■ **scanner** n.
▷ SYNS v. STUDY, examine, scrutinize, inspect, survey, look through, cast your eye over, leaf through, thumb through.

**scandal** n. an action or event causing outrage.
▷ SYNS **1** WRONGDOING, impropriety, misconduct. **2** DISGRACE, shame, outrage, injustice.

**scandalize** (or **-ise**) v. shock.

**scandalous** adj. causing outrage by being wrong or unacceptable.
▷ SYNS DISGRACEFUL, shocking, outrageous, monstrous, criminal, wicked, shameful, deplorable.

**Scandinavian** adj. of the countries of Scandinavia, esp. Norway, Sweden, and Denmark.

**scant** adj. barely enough.
▷ SYNS LITTLE, minimal, limited, insufficient, inadequate, deficient.

**scanty** adj. (**-ier**, **-iest**) too small in size or amount. ■ **scantily** adv.
▷ SYNS MEAGRE, scant, sparse, minimal, small, paltry, negligible, insufficient, inadequate, deficient, limited, restricted.

**scapegoat** n. a person blamed for the wrongdoings of others.

**scapula** n. (pl. **-lae** or **-las**) the shoulder blade.

**scar** n. the mark where a wound has healed. • v. (**scarred, scarring**) mark with a scar.
▷ SYNS n. MARK, blemish, discoloration, disfigurement, cicatrix.

**scarce** adj. not enough to supply a demand; rare. ■ **scarcity** n.
▷ SYNS IN SHORT SUPPLY, meagre, scant, scanty, sparse, insufficient, deficient, inadequate, lacking, at a premium, rare, few and far between, uncommon, unusual.

**scarcely** adv. only just; only a short time before; surely or probably not.

**scare** v. frighten or be frightened. • n. **1** a fright. **2** general alarm. □ scarecrow a figure set up to scare birds away from crops. scaremongering the spreading of alarming rumours.
▷ SYNS v. FRIGHTEN, alarm, startle, terrify, terrorize, petrify.

**scarf** n. (pl. **scarves** or **scarfs**) a length of fabric worn around the neck or head.

**scarlet** adj. & n. brilliant red. □ scarlet fever an infectious fever producing a scarlet rash.

**scarp** n. a very steep slope.

**scary** adj. (**-ier**, **-iest**) inf. frightening.

**scathing** adj. severely critical.
▷ SYNS WITHERING, searing, savage, fierce, stinging, biting, mordant, trenchant, caustic, scornful, harsh, sharp.

**scatter** v. throw in various random directions; (cause to) move off in different directions. □ **scatterbrained** (or **scatty**) disorganized and forgetful.
▷ SYNS 1 DISSEMINATE, spread, sow, sprinkle, strew, broadcast, fling, toss, throw. 2 BREAK UP, disperse, disband, separate.

**scavenge** v. search for usable objects among rubbish etc.; (of animals) search for decaying flesh as food. ■ **scavenger** n.

**scenario** n. 1 the script or summary of a film or play. 2 a possible or hypothetical sequence of events.
▷ SYNS PLOT, outline, synopsis, storyline, plan, sequence of events.

**scene** n. 1 the place where an incident occurs. 2 a view of a place. 3 an incident. 4 a piece of continuous action in a play or film. 5 a display of emotion or anger.
▷ SYNS 1 PLACE, location, site, position, spot, locale. 2 EVENT, incident, happening, episode. 3 FUSS, exhibition, commotion, to-do, tantrum.

**scenery** n. 1 a landscape considered in terms of its appearance. 2 the background used to represent a place on a stage or film set.
▷ SYNS 1 LANDSCAPE, countryside, country; view, vista, panorama. 2 SET, stage set, backdrop.

**scenic** adj. picturesque.
▷ SYNS PICTURESQUE, pretty, beautiful, pleasing.

**scent** n. 1 a pleasant smell. 2 perfume. 3 a trail left by an animal, indicated by its smell. • v. 1 make fragrant. 2 detect by smell. 3 sense that something is about to happen.
▷ SYNS n. AROMA, perfume, fragrance, smell.

**sceptic** (US **skeptic**) n. a sceptical person. ■ **scepticism** n.

**sceptical** adj. not easily convinced; having doubts.
■ **sceptically** adv.
▷ SYNS DOUBTING, doubtful, dubious, distrustful, mistrustful, suspicious, disbelieving, unconvinced, cynical.

**sceptre** (US **scepter**) n. a staff carried by a monarch.

**schedule** n. a programme or timetable of events. • v. plan for a particular time. □ **scheduled flight** a regular public flight rather than a specially chartered one.
▷ SYNS n. PLAN, programme, timetable, diary, calendar, itinerary, agenda.

**scheme** n. 1 a plan for achieving something. 2 a plot. 3 a system or pattern. • v. plot.
▷ SYNS n. 1 PLAN, project, programme, strategy, tactic. 2 PLOT, intrigue, conspiracy, ruse, ploy, machinations.
• v. PLOT, conspire, intrigue, manoeuvre, plan.

**schism** n. a disagreement or division within an organization.
▷ SYNS DIVISION, split, rift, breach, rupture, break, separation, severance.

**schizophrenia** n. a mental disorder whose symptoms include a withdrawal from reality into fantasy.
■ **schizophrenic** adj. & n.

**schnapps** n. a strong alcoholic spirit.

**scholar** n. 1 a person studying at an advanced level. 2 the holder of a scholarship.
▷ SYNS ACADEMIC, intellectual; authority, expert; inf. egghead.

**scholarly** adj. devoted to academic studies.
▷ SYNS LEARNED, erudite, academic, well read, intellectual, literary, studious, bookish.

**scholarship** n. 1 academic work. 2 a grant made to a student to help pay for their education.

**scholastic** adj. of schools or education.

**school** n. 1 an educational institution. 2 a group of artists, philosophers, etc. sharing similar ideas. 3 a group of fish or sea mammals. • v. educate or train.
▷ SYNS n. ACADEMY, college, seminary. • v. TRAIN, teach, educate, instruct, tutor, coach.

**schooner** n. 1 a sailing ship. 2 a glass for sherry.

**science** n. study or knowledge of the physical or natural world, based on observation and experiment; a particular branch of this. ■ **scientific** adj. **scientist** n.

**scimitar** n. a short curved oriental sword.

**scintillating** adj. sparkling; lively, witty, or exciting.
▷ SYNS SPARKLING, dazzling, effervescent, lively, vivacious, animated, brilliant, witty, clever.

**scissors** pl.n. a cutting instrument with two pivoted blades.

**scoff** v. 1 speak scornfully. 2 inf. eat greedily.

▷ SYNS MOCK, ridicule, deride, jeer, sneer, jibe, taunt, laugh, belittle, scorn.

**scold** v. rebuke angrily.

**sconce** n. a candle holder attached to a wall.

**scone** n. a soft flat cake, eaten buttered.

**scoop** n. 1 a spoon-like implement; a short-handled deep shovel. 2 inf. an item of news published by one newspaper before its rivals. • v. lift or hollow with (or as if with) a scoop.

**scooter** n. 1 a lightweight motorcycle. 2 a child's toy consisting of a footboard on wheels, propelled by the foot and steered by a long handle.

**scope** n. 1 opportunity. 2 the range of a subject, activity, etc.
▷ SYNS 1 OPPORTUNITY, freedom, latitude, capacity. 2 EXTENT, range, reach, sweep, span, area, sphere, realm, compass, orbit.

**scorch** v. burn or become burnt on the surface.
▷ SYNS BURN, singe, char, sear, blacken.

**score** n. 1 the number of points, goals, etc. gained in a contest. 2 a set of twenty. 3 the written music for a composition.
• v. 1 gain a point, goal, etc. in a contest; keep a record of the score. 2 cut a line or mark into. 3 arrange a piece of music.
▷ SYNS n. RESULT, outcome, total, tally. • v. 1 WIN, gain, achieve, chalk up, notch up. 2 SCRATCH, cut, notch, scrape, nick, chip, gouge.

**scorn** n. open contempt.
• v. 1 express scorn for. 2 reject with scorn.

▷ SYNS n. CONTEMPT, disdain, derision, mockery. • v. **1** DERIDE, mock, scoff at, sneer at.
**2** SPURN, rebuff, reject, shun.

**scornful** adj. contemptuous.
▷ SYNS CONTEMPTUOUS, derisive, mocking, withering, scathing, snide, supercilious, disdainful.

**scorpion** n. a creature related to spiders, with pincers and a sting in its long tail.

**Scotch** n. whisky distilled in Scotland.

**scotch** v. put an end to a rumour.

**scot-free** adv. without injury or punishment.

**Scots** adj. Scottish. • n. the form of English used in Scotland.

**Scottish** adj. of Scotland or its people.

**scoundrel** n. a dishonest person.

**scour** v. **1** clean by rubbing.
**2** search thoroughly.
▷ SYNS **1** SCRUB, rub, clean, cleanse, abrade, wash, polish. **2** SEARCH, comb, hunt through, leave no stone unturned.

**scourge** n. **1** a whip. **2** a cause of great suffering. • v. flog.
▷ SYNS n. BANE, curse, affliction, plague, burden, cross to bear.

**scout** n. a person sent to gather information. • v. act as a scout.

**scowl** n. & v. (make) a bad-tempered frown.
▷ SYNS FROWN, glower, glare, grimace.

**scrabble** v. scratch or search busily with the hands, paws, etc.

**scraggy** adj. thin and bony.

**scramble** v. **1** move hastily or awkwardly. **2** make a transmission unintelligible except by means of a special receiver;

cook beaten eggs in a pan.
• n. **1** an act of scrambling. **2** a motorcycle race over rough ground.
▷ SYNS v. **1** CLAMBER, climb, crawl, scrabble. **2** HURRY, hasten, rush, race, scurry.

**scrap** n. **1** a small piece or amount. **2** (**scraps**) uneaten food left after a meal.
**3** discarded metal suitable for reprocessing. **4** inf. a fight.
• v. **1** discard as useless. **2** inf. fight. □ **scrapbook** a book for sticking cuttings etc. in.
▷ SYNS n. **1** FRAGMENT, piece, bit, snippet, shred, remnant.
**2** (**scraps**) LEFTOVERS, leavings, remains, remnants. **3** WASTE, junk, rubbish, scrap metal.
• v. THROW AWAY/OUT, get rid of, discard, dispose of, abandon, jettison; inf. chuck out, ditch.

**scrape** v. **1** clean, smooth, or damage by passing a hard edge across a surface. **2** just manage to achieve. • n. **1** a scraping movement or sound. **2** inf. a difficult situation.
▷ SYNS v. **1** SCOUR, rub, scrub, file, rasp. **2** GRAZE, scratch, abrade, skin, cut, bark.

**scratch** v. **1** mark or wound with a something sharp. **2** rub with the fingernails to relieve itching. **3** withdraw from a competition. • n. a mark or wound made by scratching. □ **from scratch** from the very beginning. **up to scratch** up to the required standard.
▷ SYNS v. SCRAPE, abrade, graze, skin, cut, lacerate, bark.
• n. GRAZE, abrasion, cut, laceration, wound.

**scrawl** v. write in a hurried, untidy way. • n. scrawled handwriting.

**scrawny** adj. thin and bony.
▷ SYNS THIN, bony, skinny, scraggy, gaunt.

**scream** v. give a piercing cry, esp. of fear or pain. • n. a screaming cry or sound.
▷ SYNS V. SHRIEK, howl, shout, cry out, yell, screech, bawl; inf. holler.

**scree** n. a mass of loose stones on a mountainside.

**screech** n. & v. (make) a harsh scream.

**screed** n. a tiresomely long piece of writing or speech.

**screen** n. 1 an upright partition used to divide a room or hide something. 2 the front surface of a television or computer monitor, on which images and data are displayed. 3 a blank surface on to which films are projected. • v. 1 conceal or protect. 2 show or broadcast a film or television programme. 3 test for the presence or absence of a disease.
□ **screenplay** the script of a film. **screen saver** a computer program which replaces an unchanging screen display with a moving image.
▷ SYNS N. PARTITION, divider; protection, shield, shelter, guard, buffer. • v. 1 PARTITION, divide; conceal, hide; protect, shelter, shield, guard.
2 CHECK, test, examine, investigate, vet.

**screw** n. 1 a metal pin with a spiral thread, twisted into a surface to join things together. 2 a propeller. • v. 1 fasten or tighten with screws. 2 rotate so as to attach or remove.
□ **screwdriver** a tool for turning screws.

**scribble** v. write or draw hurriedly or carelessly.
• n. something scribbled.

**scribe** n. hist. a person who copied out documents.

**scrimp** v. economize.
▷ SYNS SKIMP, economize, tighten your belt.

**script** n. 1 the text of a play, film, or broadcast. 2 handwriting.
▷ SYNS 1 TEXT, screenplay, lines, words. 2 HANDWRITING, writing, hand, calligraphy.

**scripture** (or **scriptures**) n. the sacred writings of Christianity or another religion.

**scroll** n. a roll of paper or parchment. • v. move displayed data up or down on a computer screen.

**Scrooge** n. a person who is mean with money.

**scrotum** n. (pl. **-ta** or **-tums**) the pouch of skin enclosing the testicles.

**scrounge** v. cadge.
■ **scrounger** n.
▷ SYNS BEG, borrow; inf. cadge, sponge, freeload.

**scrub** v. (**scrubbed**, **scrubbing**) rub hard to clean. • n. 1 an act of scrubbing. 2 land covered with bushes and small trees.
▷ SYNS V. BRUSH, scour, rub, clean, wash.

**scruff** n. the back of the neck.

**scruffy** adj. (**-ier**, **-iest**) shabby and untidy.
▷ SYNS UNTIDY, unkempt, dishevelled, shabby, down at heel, ragged, tattered, messy, tatty.

**scrum** n. 1 a formation in rugby in which players push against each other with their heads down and struggle for possession of the ball. 2 inf. a disorderly crowd.

**scruple** n. a feeling of doubt as to whether an action is morally right. • v. hesitate because of scruples.
▷ SYNS n. (**scruples**) QUALMS, compunction, hesitation, reservations, second thoughts, doubts, misgivings, uneasiness, reluctance.

**scrupulous** adj. very careful and thorough.
▷ SYNS CAREFUL, meticulous, painstaking, thorough, rigorous, strict, conscientious, punctilious.

**scrutinize** (or **-ise**) v. examine carefully.
▷ SYNS EXAMINE, study, inspect, survey, peruse; investigate, probe, inquire into.

**scrutiny** n. (pl. **-ies**) careful examination.

**scuba-diving** n. swimming underwater using an aqualung.

**scud** v. (**scudded**, **scudding**) move quickly, driven by the wind.

**scuff** v. mark a shoe by scraping it against something.

**scuffle** n. a short, confused fight or struggle. • v. take part in a scuffle.

**scull** n. 1 each of a pair of small oars used by a single rower. 2 a light boat for a single rower. • v. row with sculls.

**scullery** n. (pl. **-ies**) a room for washing dishes and similar work.

**sculpt** v. carve or shape.

**sculpture** n. 1 the art of carving or shaping wood, stone, etc. 2 a work made in this way. • v. make by sculpture. ■ **sculptor** n. (fem. **sculptress**)
▷ SYNS n. STATUE, statuette, bust, figure, figurine.

**scum** n. 1 a layer of dirt or froth on the surface of a liquid. 2 inf. a worthless person.

**scupper** v. 1 inf. thwart. 2 sink a ship deliberately.

**scurf** n. flakes of skin.

**scurrilous** adj. insulting or slanderous.
▷ SYNS INSULTING, offensive, disparaging, defamatory, slanderous, gross, scandalous.

**scurry** v. (**scurried**, **scurrying**) run with short, quick steps.

**scurvy** n. a disease caused by lack of vitamin C.

**scuttle** n. a box or bucket for fetching and holding coal. • v. 1 scurry. 2 sink a ship by letting in water.

**scythe** n. a tool with a curved blade, for cutting long grass.

**SE** abbr. south-east or south-eastern.

**sea** n. 1 the salt water surrounding the continents. 2 an area of sea. 3 a vast expanse. □ **sea change** a great or remarkable change. **seafaring** travelling by sea. **seafood** shellfish and sea fish as food. **seagull** a gull. **sea horse** a small fish with a horse-like head. **sea lion** a large seal. **seaman** a sailor. **seaplane** an aircraft designed to land on and take off from water. **seasick** feeling nausea caused by the motion of a ship. **seaside** a beach area or holiday resort. **sea urchin** a sea animal with a round spiny shell. **seaweed** large algae growing in the sea.

**seal** n. 1 a device used to join things or close something firmly. 2 a piece of wax with a design stamped into it, attached to a document. 3 a confirmation

or guarantee. **4** a sea mammal with flippers. • v. **1** close or fasten securely. **2** coat so as to prevent fluid passing through. **3** make definite.
▷ SYNS n. EMBLEM, symbol, insignia, badge, crest.
• v. **1** FASTEN, secure, shut, close. **2** CLINCH, settle, conclude, complete.

**seam** n. **1** a line where two pieces of fabric are sewn together. **2** a layer of coal etc. in the ground.
▷ SYNS **1** JOIN, stitching. **2** LAYER, stratum, vein, lode.

**seamless** adj. with no obvious joins; smooth and continuous. ■ seamlessly adv.

**seamstress** n. a woman who sews, esp. for a living.

**seamy** adj. (-ier, -iest) immoral or sordid.

**seance** n. a meeting where people try to make contact with the dead.

**sear** v. scorch or burn.
▷ SYNS BURN, singe, scorch, char.

**search** v. **1** try to find. **2** examine thoroughly so as to find. • n. an act of searching. □ search engine a computer program that searches the Internet for web pages containing a specific item. searchlight a powerful outdoor light with a movable beam.
▷ SYNS v. HUNT, look, seek, rummage, scour; ransack, rifle, comb, turn upside down.
• n. HUNT, look, quest.

**season** n. **1** one of the four divisions of the year. **2** a part of the year when a particular activity takes place. • v. **1** add salt etc. to food. **2** dry wood for use as timber. □ season ticket a ticket allowing travel or admission within a particular period.

**seasonable** adj. suitable for the season.

**seasonal** adj. of a season or seasons; varying with the seasons. ■ seasonally adv.

**seasoned** adj. experienced.
▷ SYNS EXPERIENCED, practised, well versed, established; veteran.

**seasoning** n. a substance used to enhance the flavour of food.

**seat** n. **1** a thing made or used for sitting on. **2** a site or location. **3** a country house. **4** a place in an elected parliament or council. **5** the buttocks. • v. **1** cause to sit. **2** have enough seats for. □ seat belt a strap securing a person to a seat in a vehicle or aircraft.
▷ SYNS n. **1** CHAIR, bench, settle, stool, stall. **2** HEADQUARTERS, base, centre, hub, heart; location, site. • v. **1** POSITION, place, put, ensconce, install. **2** HAVE ROOM FOR, hold, take, accommodate.

**sebaceous** adj. producing oil or fat.

**secateurs** pl.n. pruning clippers.

**secede** v. withdraw from membership. ■ secession n.
▷ SYNS WITHDRAW, break away, split, pull out, disaffiliate, resign.

**secluded** adj. (of a place) sheltered and private.
▷ SYNS SHELTERED, concealed, hidden, private, unfrequented, off the beaten track.

**seclusion** n. privacy.
▷ SYNS PRIVACY, solitude, retreat, retirement, withdrawal,

isolation, concealment, hiding, secrecy.

**second¹** adj. **1** next after the first. **2** inferior or subordinate. • n. **1** a second highest grade in an exam. **2** an attendant at a duel or boxing match. **3** (**seconds**) goods of inferior quality. • v. formally support a proposal etc. □ **second-class** next or inferior to first class in quality etc. **second-hand** having had a previous owner; heard from another person. **second-rate** of poor quality. **second sight** the supposed ability to foretell the future. **second thoughts** a change of opinion after reconsideration. **second wind** a renewed capacity for effort.
▷ SYNS adj. **1** NEXT, following, subsequent. **2** SECONDARY, lower, subordinate, lesser, inferior. • v. SUPPORT, back, approve, endorse.

**second²** n. a sixtieth part of a minute.

**second³** v. transfer temporarily to another job or department. ■ **secondment** n.

**secondary** adj. **1** coming after, or less important than, something else. **2** (of education) for children from the age of 11 to 16 or 18.
▷ SYNS LESSER, subordinate, ancillary, subsidiary, peripheral, minor, incidental.

**secret** adj. kept from or not known by others. • n. **1** something secret. **2** a means of achieving something: *the secret of success.* ■ **secrecy** n.
▷ SYNS adj. **1** CONFIDENTIAL, private, classified, under wraps; inf. hush-hush. **2** HIDDEN, concealed, disguised;

clandestine, covert, furtive, undercover, underground, surreptitious, stealthy, cloak-and-dagger.

**secretariat** n. a government office or department.

**secretary** n. (pl. **-ies**) **1** a person employed to type letters, keep records, etc. **2** the chief assistant of a UK government minister. ■ **secretarial** adj.

**secrete** v. **1** (of a cell, gland, etc.) produce and discharge a substance. **2** hide. ■ **secretion** n.
▷ SYNS **1** PRODUCE, discharge, emit, excrete. **2** HIDE, conceal, cover up; inf. stash away.

**secretive** adj. inclined to conceal feelings or information.
▷ SYNS RETICENT, uncommunicative, unforthcoming, reserved, silent, quiet; inf. cagey.

**sect** n. a group with different religious beliefs from those of a larger group.

**sectarian** adj. of a sect or sects.
▷ SYNS FACTIONAL, separatist, partisan; extreme, fanatical, doctrinaire, inflexible.

**section** n. **1** a distinct part. **2** a subdivision. **3** a cross-section. • v. divide into sections.
▷ SYNS n. PART, segment, division, component, piece, portion, bit, unit.

**sector** n. a distinct area or part.
▷ SYNS **1** PART, division, branch, department, arm, field. **2** ZONE, quarter, district, area, region.

**secular** adj. not religious or spiritual.
▷ SYNS LAY, non-religious; temporal, worldly, earthly.

**secure** adj. **1** safe. **2** fixed or fastened so as not to give way or become loose. **3** confident.

• v. **1** make secure. **2** succeed in obtaining.

▷ SYNS **adj. 1** SAFE, protected, out of harm's way, invulnerable. **2** FASTENED, fixed, closed, shut, locked. **3** CONFIDENT, unworried, at ease, relaxed.
• v. **1** FASTEN, close, shut, lock, bolt, chain, seal. **2** OBTAIN, acquire, gain, get, get hold of.

**security** n. (pl. **-ies**) **1** being secure. **2** precautions taken against espionage, theft, etc. **3** something offered as a guarantee of the repayment of a loan.

**sedate** adj. calm and unhurried.
• v. give a sedative to.

▷ SYNS **adj. 1** SLOW, unhurried, dignified, relaxed, leisurely. **2** CALM, placid, quiet, uneventful, dull.

**sedative** n. a drug that makes you calm or sleepy.

**sedentary** adj. involving or taking little exercise.

**sediment** n. solid matter that settles to the bottom of a liquid.

▷ SYNS DREGS, lees, grounds, deposit, residue, precipitate.

**sedition** n. words or actions inciting rebellion. ■ **seditious** adj.

**seduce** v. **1** persuade to have sex. **2** persuade to do something unwise. ■ **seduction** n.

▷ SYNS ATTRACT, lure, tempt, entice, beguile, inveigle.

**seductive** adj. tempting and attractive.

▷ SYNS ATTRACTIVE, alluring, tempting, provocative, exciting, sultry, sexy.

**see¹** v. **1** perceive with the eyes. **2** experience or witness. **3** realize or deduce. **4** think of in a particular way. **5** meet. **6** guide or lead to a place.

▷ SYNS **1** DISCERN, perceive, spot, notice, catch sight of, glimpse, make out, spy. **2** UNDERSTAND, grasp, comprehend, follow, realize, recognize.

**see²** n. a bishop's or archbishop's district or position.

**seed** n. **1** a small object produced by a plant from which a new plant may grow. **2** the origin of something. **3** any of the stronger competitors in a sports tournament, who are kept from playing each other in the early rounds. **4** dated semen. • v. **1** sow with seeds. **2** remove seeds from. **3** make a competitor a seed in a tournament.

**seedling** n. a very young plant.

**seedy** adj. (**-ier, -iest**) sordid or disreputable.

**seek** v. **1** try to find or obtain. **2** try or want to do.

▷ SYNS **1** SEARCH FOR, look for, be after, hunt for. **2** ASK FOR, request, solicit, appeal for.

**seem** v. give the impression of being. ■ **seemingly** adv.

▷ SYNS APPEAR TO BE, look, sound, come across as.

**seemly** adj. socially appropriate.

**seen** p.p. of SEE¹.

**seep** v. ooze slowly through a substance.

▷ SYNS OOZE, leak, exude, drip, trickle, percolate.

**seer** n. a prophet.

**see-saw** n. a long board balanced on a central support, so that children sitting on each end can ride up and down.
• v. repeatedly change between two states or positions.

**seethe** v. **1** be very angry. **2** boil or churn.

**segment** n. each of the parts into which something is divided. ■ **segmented** adj.
▷ SYNS SECTION, part, division, piece, portion, slice.

**segregate** v. separate from others. ■ **segregation** n.
▷ SYNS SEPARATE, set apart, isolate, cut off.

**seismic** adj. of earthquakes.

**seize** v. **1** take hold of forcibly or suddenly. **2** take possession of by force or by right. **3** (**seize on**) take eager advantage of. **4** (**seize up**) become jammed.
▷ SYNS **1** GRAB, grasp, snatch, take hold of, grip, clutch. **2** CONFISCATE, impound, commandeer, appropriate. **3** ABDUCT, take captive, kidnap.

**seizure** n. **1** the act of seizing. **2** a stroke or an epileptic fit.

**seldom** adv. not often.
▷ SYNS RARELY, hardly ever, infrequently; inf. once in a blue moon.

**select** v. carefully choose from a group. • adj. **1** carefully chosen. **2** exclusive. ■ **selector** n.
▷ SYNS v. CHOOSE, pick, single out, opt for, decide on, settle on. • adj. **1** CHOICE, prime, first-class, top-quality. **2** EXCLUSIVE, elite, privileged.

**selection** n. selecting; things selected; things from which to choose.
▷ SYNS **1** CHOICE, pick, option. **2** VARIETY, range, array; assortment, anthology, miscellany, collection.

**selective** adj. choosing carefully.
▷ SYNS PARTICULAR, discriminating, discerning; fussy, fastidious; inf. choosy.

**self** n. (pl. **selves**) a person's essential nature and individuality.

**self-assured** adj. confident. ■ **self-assurance** n.

**self-centred** adj. thinking only of yourself and your own affairs.

**self-confidence** n. confidence in your own worth and abilities. ■ **self-confident** adj.
▷ SYNS SELF-ASSURANCE, confidence, self-possession, poise, aplomb.

**self-conscious** adj. nervous or awkward because worried about what others think of you.
▷ SYNS AWKWARD, nervous, uncomfortable, embarrassed, shy.

**self-contained** adj. **1** complete in itself. **2** not needing or influenced by others.

**self-determination** n. the right or ability of a country to manage its own affairs.

**self-evident** adj. obvious.

**self-important** adj. having an exaggerated sense of your own importance.
▷ SYNS POMPOUS, vain, conceited, arrogant, full of yourself, swollen-headed, egotistical, presumptuous, overbearing.

**selfish** adj. concerned mainly with your own needs and wishes.
▷ SYNS EGOCENTRIC, egotistic, self-seeking, self-centred, self-absorbed.

**selfless** adj. unselfish.

**self-made** adj. having become successful by your own efforts.

**self-possessed** adj. confident and controlled.

**self-raising** adj. (of flour) having baking powder already added.

**self-respect** n. pride and confidence in yourself.

**self-righteous** adj. complacent about your own virtue.
▷ SYNS SANCTIMONIOUS, self-satisfied, holier-than-thou, smug, pious, complacent; inf. goody-goody.

**selfsame** adj. the very same.

**self-satisfied** adj. smugly pleased with yourself.

**self-service** adj. (of a shop etc.) where customers select goods and pay at a checkout.

**self-sufficient** adj. not needing outside help.

**sell** v. 1 exchange or offer for money. 2 (of goods) be sold. 3 persuade someone of the merits of.
▷ SYNS PUT UP FOR SALE, put on the market, vend, auction, trade in, deal in, traffic in, peddle, hawk.

**seller** n. a person who sells.
▷ SYNS VENDOR, retailer, trader, merchant, dealer; shopkeeper, pedlar, hawker.

**Sellotape** n. trademark transparent adhesive tape.

**semantic** adj. of meaning in language.

**semaphore** n. a system of signalling with the arms.

**semblance** n. an outward appearance or form.
▷ SYNS APPEARANCE, show, air, guise, pretence, facade, front, veneer.

**semen** n. the sperm-bearing fluid produced by males.

**semester** n. a half-year course or university term.

**semibreve** n. a note in music, equal to two minims or half a breve.

**semicircle** n. half of a circle.
■ semicircular adj.

**semicolon** n. a punctuation mark (;).

**semiconductor** n. a substance that conducts electricity in certain conditions.

**semi-detached** adj. (of a house) joined to another on one side.

**semi-final** n. a match or round in a contest, preceding the final.

**seminal** adj. 1 strongly influencing later developments. 2 of semen.

**seminar** n. a small class for discussion and research.

**semi-precious** adj. (of gems) less valuable than those called precious.

**semitone** n. half a tone in music.

**semolina** n. hard grains left after flour is milled, used to make puddings.

**senate** n. the upper house of certain parliaments; the governing body of certain universities.

**senator** n. a member of a senate.

**send** v. 1 cause to go or be taken to a destination. 2 cause to move sharply or quickly. 3 put in a specified state.
▷ SYNS 1 DISPATCH, mail, post, forward. 2 PROPEL, project, eject, discharge, shoot.

**senile** adj. losing mental faculties because of old age.
■ senility n.

**senior** adj. 1 of older people. 2 high or higher in status. 3 of schoolchildren above the age of about 11. • n. a senior person.
□ senior citizen an elderly person. ■ seniority n.

**sensation** n. **1** a feeling produced by stimulation of a sense organ or of the mind. **2** excited interest; a person or thing producing this.
▷ SYNS **1** FEELING, sense, awareness, consciousness, perception, impression. **2** STIR, excitement, commotion, furore, scandal.

**sensational** adj. causing great public interest or excitement.
▷ SYNS SPECTACULAR, exciting, thrilling, startling, staggering, dramatic, amazing, shocking, scandalous, lurid.

**sensationalism** n. deliberate use of sensational stories etc.
□ **sensationalist** adj.

**sense** n. **1** any of the powers (sight, hearing, smell, taste, touch) by which the body perceives things. **2** a feeling that something is the case. **3** awareness or sensitivity. **4** a sensible and practical attitude. **5** a meaning. • v. **1** perceive by a sense. **2** be vaguely aware of.
▷ SYNS n. **1** FEELING, sensation, faculty. **2** APPRECIATION, awareness, understanding, sensitivity. **3** COMMON SENSE, wisdom, sagacity, reason, wit, intelligence, nous. **4** MEANING, definition, nuance, drift, gist. • v. FEEL, be aware of, perceive, discern, intuit.

**senseless** adj. foolish.

**sensibility** n. (pl. **-ies**) the ability to understand emotion or art.

**sensible** adj. having or showing common sense. ■ **sensibly** adv.
▷ SYNS PRACTICAL, realistic, reasonable, rational, logical, down-to-earth, no-nonsense, level-headed, wise.

**sensitive** adj. **1** quick to detect or be affected by slight changes. **2** appreciating the feelings of others. **3** easily offended or upset. **4** secret or controversial.
■ **sensitivity** n.
▷ SYNS **1** RESPONSIVE, reactive, susceptible, vulnerable. **2** TACTFUL, careful, thoughtful, diplomatic. **3** TOUCHY, over-sensitive, thin-skinned, defensive, temperamental.

**sensitize** (or **-ise**) v. make sensitive or aware.

**sensor** n. a device for detecting a particular physical property.

**sensory** adj. of the senses or sensation.

**sensual** adj. relating to or arousing the physical senses as a source of pleasure.
▷ SYNS PHYSICAL, carnal, bodily, fleshly, sensuous; hedonistic, sybaritic.

**sensuous** adj. of the senses rather than the intellect; affecting the senses pleasantly.

**sent** past and p.p. of SEND.

**sentence** n. **1** a set of words making a single complete statement. **2** a punishment decided by a law court. • v. pass sentence on an offender.
▷ SYNS n. PRISON TERM, punishment; inf. time. • v. CONDEMN, punish, convict.

**sentient** adj. able to feel things.

**sentiment** n. **1** an opinion or feeling. **2** sentimentality.
▷ SYNS **1** FEELING, view, thought, attitude, opinion, belief. **2** SENTIMENTALITY, sentimentalism.

**sentimental** adj. full of exaggerated or self-indulgent feelings of tenderness or nostalgia. ■ **sentimentality** n.

▷ SYNS EMOTIONAL, romantic, nostalgic, affectionate, loving, tender; mawkish; inf. soppy.

**sentinel** n. a sentry.

**sentry** n. (pl. **-ies**) a soldier keeping watch or guard on something.

▷ SYNS GUARD, lookout, watch, watchman, sentinel.

**separate** adj. **1** forming a unit by itself. **2** different; distinct. • v. **1** move or come apart. **2** stop living together as a couple. **3** divide. ■ **separable** adj. **separation** n.

▷ SYNS adj. UNCONNECTED, unrelated, distinct, different, detached, discrete, independent. • v. **1** DISCONNECT, detach, disengage; sever, split. **2** BREAK UP, split up, part, divorce. **3** DIVIDE, come between, keep apart, partition.

**sepia** n. a reddish-brown colour.

**September** n. the ninth month.

**septet** n. a group of seven musicians.

**septic** adj. infected with bacteria. □ **septic tank** a tank in which sewage decomposes.

▷ SYNS INFECTED, festering, putrefying, putrid.

**septicaemia** (US **septicemia**) n. blood poisoning.

**sepulchral** adj. gloomy.

**sepulchre** (US **sepulcher**) n. a tomb.

**sequel** n. what follows, esp. as a result; a novel or film etc. continuing the story of an earlier one.

▷ SYNS FOLLOW-UP, development, result, consequence, outcome, upshot.

**sequence** n. an order in which related items follow one another; a set of things that

follow each other in a particular order. ■ **sequential** adj.

▷ SYNS CHAIN, course, cycle, series, progression, succession, order, pattern.

**sequester** v. **1** isolate. **2** sequestrate.

**sequestrate** v. take legal possession of assets until a debt has been paid. ■ **sequestration** n.

**sequin** n. a small shiny disc sewn on clothes for decoration. ■ **sequinned** adj.

**seraph** n. (pl. **-phim** or **-phs**) a member of the highest order of angels.

**serenade** n. music played for a lover, outdoors and at night. • v. perform a serenade for.

**serendipity** n. the fortunate occurrence of events by chance. ■ **serendipitous** adj.

▷ SYNS CHANCE, luck, good fortune, fortuitousness, happy accident.

**serene** adj. calm and peaceful. ■ **serenity** n.

▷ SYNS CALM, composed, tranquil, peaceful, placid, still, quiet, unperturbed, unruffled; inf. unflappable.

**serf** n. a medieval farm labourer tied to working on a particular estate.

**serge** n. strong woollen fabric.

**sergeant** n. a non-commissioned army officer; a police officer ranking just below inspector.

**serial** n. a story presented in a series of instalments. • adj. repeatedly committing the same offence or doing the same thing: *a serial killer*.

**serialize** (or **-ise**) v. produce as a serial.

**series** n. (pl. **series**) a number of similar things coming one after another; a set of related television or radio programmes.
▷ SYNS SUCCESSION, sequence, chain, course, string, run, cycle, set, row; spate, wave.

**serious** adj. **1** dangerous or severe. **2** needing careful thought or action. **3** solemn or thoughtful. **4** sincere.
▷ SYNS **1** SEVERE, grave, bad, critical, acute, grievous, dangerous. **2** IMPORTANT, significant, momentous, weighty, far-reaching, consequential. **3** SOLEMN, earnest, grave, sombre, unsmiling, dour, poker-faced.

**sermon** n. a talk on a religious or moral subject.
▷ SYNS HOMILY, address, oration, lecture.

**serpent** n. a large snake.

**serpentine** adj. twisting like a snake.

**serrated** adj. having a jagged, sawlike edge.

**serried** adj. placed or standing close together.

**serum** n. (pl. **-ra** or **-rums**) a thin fluid left when blood has clotted.

**servant** n. a person employed to do domestic work.
▷ SYNS ATTENDANT, retainer, domestic, maid, charwoman, cleaner; menial, drudge, lackey; inf. skivvy.

**serve** v. **1** perform duties or services for. **2** be employed in the armed forces. **3** spend a period in a job or in prison. **4** present food or drink to. **5** attend to a customer. **6** fulfil a purpose. **7** hit the ball in tennis

etc. to begin play. • n. an act of serving in tennis etc.
▷ SYNS v. **1** serve food: DISH UP, give out, distribute; supply, provide. **2** serve a customer: ATTEND TO, deal with, see to; help, assist.

**server** n. a computer or program which controls or supplies information to a computer network.

**service** n. **1** the act of serving. **2** a period of employment in an organization. **3** help or advice. **4** a religious ceremony. **5** a system supplying a public need. **6** a department run by the state. **7** (**the services**) the armed forces. **8** a routine inspection and maintenance of a vehicle etc. **9** a matching set of crockery. **10** a serve in tennis etc. • v. **1** perform maintenance on. **2** provide services for. □ serviceman (or **servicewoman**) a member of the armed forces. **service station** a garage selling petrol etc.
▷ SYNS n. **1** WORK, employment, labour. **2** GOOD TURN, favour, kindness. **3** CEREMONY, ritual, rite, sacrament. • v. OVERHAUL, check, go over, maintain, repair.

**serviceable** adj. functioning; hard-wearing.
▷ SYNS **1** FUNCTIONAL, utilitarian, practical, durable, hard-wearing, tough, strong. **2** FUNCTIONING, usable, operational, working.

**serviette** n. a table napkin.

**servile** adj. excessively willing to serve others.
▷ SYNS SUBSERVIENT, obsequious, sycophantic, fawning, submissive, toadying.

**serving** n. a quantity of food for one person.

**servitude** n. slavery; being subject to someone more powerful.

**sesame** n. a tropical plant grown for its oil-rich seeds.

**session** n. 1 a meeting or meetings for discussing something. 2 a period spent in a particular activity.
▷ SYNS 1 MEETING, sitting, assembly, conference, discussion. 2 PERIOD, time, spell, stretch.

**set** v. 1 put in a specified place, position, or state. 2 give a task to. 3 decide on or fix a time, value, etc. 4 establish as an example or record. 5 adjust a device as required. 6 prepare a table for a meal. 7 harden into a solid, semi-solid, or fixed state. 8 (of the sun etc.) appear to move towards and below the earth's horizon. • n. 1 a number of people or things grouped together. 2 the way something is set. 3 a radio or television receiver. 4 a group of games forming a unit in a tennis match. 5 scenery for a play or film. □ **set square** a right-angled triangular drawing instrument.
▷ SYNS v. 1 PUT, place, lay, deposit, position; inf. stick, park, plonk. 2 *set a date:* ARRANGE, schedule, fix, decide on, choose, agree on, determine, designate, appoint, name, specify, stipulate. 3 *set your watch:* ADJUST, regulate, synchronize, calibrate, correct. 4 *set the table:* LAY, prepare, arrange. 5 *the concrete set slowly:* SOLIDIFY, harden, stiffen, thicken, gel, cake, congeal, coagulate. • n. COLLECTION, group, series, batch, array, assortment, selection.

**setback** n. a problem that delays progress.

▷ SYNS PROBLEM, difficulty, complication, hitch, hold-up, delay.

**sett** n. a badger's burrow.

**settee** n. a sofa.

**setter** n. a long-haired breed of dog.

**setting** n. 1 the way or place in which something is set. 2 a set of cutlery or crockery laid for one person.
▷ SYNS ENVIRONMENT, surroundings, position, situation, background, location, place, site.

**settle**¹ v. 1 resolve a problem or dispute. 2 come to live in a new place. 3 adopt a more steady lifestyle. 4 become or make calmer. 5 become at ease in new situation. 6 pay a debt. 7 sit or rest comfortably or securely. 8 (**settle for**) accept something less than satisfactory. ■ **settler** n.
▷ SYNS 1 RESOLVE, sort out, clear up, work out, put right, reconcile. 2 SET UP HOME, put down roots, move to. 3 CALM, quieten, soothe, relax.

**settle**² n. a wooden seat with a high back and arms.

**settlement** n. 1 the act of settling. 2 a place where people establish a community. 3 an agreement intended to settle a dispute.
▷ SYNS 1 COMMUNITY, colony, encampment, outpost, post. 2 RESOLUTION, agreement, deal, bargain, pact.

**seven** adj. & n. one more than six; 7. ■ **seventh** adj. & n.

**seventeen** adj. & n. one more than sixteen; 17. ■ **seventeenth** adj. & n.

**seventy** adj. & n. seven times ten; 70. ■ **seventieth** adj. & n.

**sever** v. cut or break off.
▷ SYNS **1** CUT OFF, chop off, hack off, detach, sunder; amputate, dock. **2** BREAK OFF, discontinue, suspend, end, terminate, cease.

**several** pron. more than two but not many. • adj. separate.

**severe** adj. **1** strict or harsh; extreme or intense. **2** very plain in style or appearance.
  ■ **severity** n.
▷ SYNS **1** HARSH, strict, rigorous, unsparing, relentless, merciless, ruthless; sharp, caustic, biting, cutting, scathing, withering. **2** *a severe shortage:* ACUTE, serious, grave, critical, dire, dangerous. **3** *severe storms:* FIERCE, strong, violent, intense, powerful. **4** *a severe test:* DEMANDING, taxing, exacting, tough, difficult, hard, arduous, punishing. **5** *a severe expression:* STERN, grim, austere, forbidding, dour, unsmiling, sombre, sober. **6** *a severe style:* AUSTERE, stark, spartan, ascetic, plain, simple, unadorned, unembellished.

**sew** v. (**sewed**, **sewn** or **sewed**, **sewing**) make, join, or repair by making stitches with a needle and thread. ■ **sewing** n.
▷ SYNS STITCH, embroider, mend, darn.

**sewage** n. liquid waste drained from houses etc. for disposal.

**sewer** n. an underground channel for carrying sewage.

**sex** n. **1** either of the two main groups (male and female) into which living things are divided. **2** the fact of being male or female. **3** sexual intercourse.
▷ SYNS SEXUAL INTERCOURSE, lovemaking, making love, copulation, coitus, mating, fornication.

**sexism** adj. prejudice or discrimination on the basis of sex.
  ■ **sexist** adj. & n.

**sextant** n. an instrument for measuring angles and distances.

**sextet** n. a group of six musicians; music for these.

**sexual** adj. **1** of sex. **2** of the sexes. **3** (of reproduction) involving the fusion of male and female cells. ◻ **sexual intercourse** sexual contact involving the insertion of a man's penis into a woman's vagina.
  ■ **sexually** adv.

**sexuality** n. **1** capacity for sexual feelings. **2** a person's sexual preference.

**sexy** adj. **1** sexually attractive or exciting. **2** sexually aroused. **3** inf. exciting or interesting.
▷ SYNS SEDUCTIVE, desirable, alluring; erotic, titillating, arousing, exciting.

**shabby** adj. **1** worn out or scruffy. **2** unfair. ■ **shabbily** adv.
▷ SYNS WORN, worn-out, threadbare, ragged, frayed, tattered, scruffy, tatty, the worse for wear.

**shack** n. a roughly built hut.

**shackle** n. one of a pair of metal rings joined by a chain, for fastening a prisoner's wrists or ankles. • v. put shackles on; restrict or limit.

**shade** n. **1** darkness and coolness caused by shelter from direct sunlight. **2** a colour. **3** a lampshade. • v. **1** screen from direct light. **2** cover or reduce the light of. **3** darken parts of a drawing etc.
▷ SYNS **1** SHADINESS, shadow, shelter, cover. **2** COLOUR, hue, tone, tint. • v. SCREEN, cover, shelter.

**shadow** n. **1** a dark area produced by an object coming between light and a surface. **2** partial darkness. **3** a slight trace. • v. **1** cast a shadow over. **2** follow and watch secretly. ■ **shadowy** adj.

▷ SYNS n. **1** see SHADE (1). **2** SILHOUETTE, outline, shape. **3** *a shadow of doubt:* TRACE, scrap, shred; hint, suggestion, suspicion.

**shady** adj. **1** situated in or giving shade. **2** of doubtful honesty.

▷ SYNS **1** SHADED, shadowy, dark, dim; leafy. **2** SUSPICIOUS, suspect, questionable, dubious, untrustworthy, disreputable, dishonest, shifty.

**shaft** n. **1** a long, slender, straight handle etc.; an arrow or spear; a ray or beam; a long rotating rod transmitting power in a machine; each of the two poles between which a horse is harnessed to a vehicle. **2** a vertical or sloping passage or opening.

▷ SYNS **1** POLE, stick, rod, staff, stem, handle, hilt. **2** RAY, beam, gleam, streak, pencil. **3** PASSAGE, duct, tunnel, well, flue.

**shag** n. coarse tobacco. • adj. (of a carpet) with a long rough pile.

**shaggy** adj. (**-ier**, **-iest**) (of hair or fur) long, thick, and untidy; having shaggy hair or fur.

**shah** n. a title of the former ruler of Iran.

**shake** v. **1** tremble or vibrate. **2** move quickly up and down or to and fro. **3** shock or astonish. • n. an act of shaking. □ **shake hands** clasp right hands in greeting, parting, or agreement.

▷ SYNS v. **1** VIBRATE, tremble, quiver, quake, shudder, shiver, judder, wobble, rock, sway. **2** JIGGLE, joggle, agitate, waggle;

brandish. **3** SHOCK, alarm, worry, distress, upset.

**shaky** adj. (**-ier**, **-iest**) shaking; not safe or certain. ■ **shakily** adv.

▷ SYNS **1** TREMBLING, tremulous, quivering, unsteady, wobbly, weak, tottering, teetering. **2** FAINT, dizzy, giddy, lightheaded. **3** UNRELIABLE, questionable, dubious, doubtful, tenuous, flimsy.

**shale** n. stone that splits easily.

**shall** v.aux. **1** used with *I* and *we* to express future tense. **2** expressing determination or an order.

**shallot** n. a small onion-like plant.

**shallow** adj. of little depth; superficial. • n. a shallow area in a river etc.

▷ SYNS adj. SUPERFICIAL, facile, simplistic; lightweight, trifling, trivial, empty, frivolous, foolish, silly.

**sham** n. a pretence; something that is not genuine. • adj. not genuine. • v. (**shammed**, **shamming**) pretend.

▷ SYNS n. PRETENCE, fake, forgery, counterfeit, simulation. • adj. PRETEND, feigned, fake, artificial, put-on, simulated, affected, insincere, false, bogus; inf. phoney, pseudo.

**shamble** v. walk in a shuffling or lazy way.

**shambles** n. a state of great disorder.

▷ SYNS CHAOS, muddle, mess, confusion, disorder, disarray, disorganization.

**shame** n. **1** embarrassment or distress aroused by having done something wrong or foolish. **2** loss of respect. **3** a cause of shame. **4** a cause of regret.

• v. cause to feel shame.
■ **shameless** adj.
▷ SYNS n. **1** HUMILIATION, embarrassment, mortification; guilt, remorse, contrition. **2** DISGRACE, dishonour, discredit, disrepute, infamy.

**shamefaced** adj. showing shame.
▷ SYNS ASHAMED, abashed, sheepish, guilty, conscience-stricken, contrite, penitent, embarrassed, remorseful.

**shameful** adj. causing shame.
▷ SYNS DISGRACEFUL, deplorable, despicable, dishonourable, discreditable, contemptible, reprehensible, ignoble, shabby.

**shampoo** n. a liquid used to wash hair; a preparation for cleaning upholstery etc.; the process of shampooing.
• v. wash or clean with shampoo.

**shamrock** n. a clover-like plant.

**shandy** n. (pl. **-ies**) beer mixed with lemonade.

**shank** n. the lower part of the leg.

**shanty** n. (pl. **-ies**) **1** a shack. **2** a traditional song sung by sailors. □ **shanty town** a settlement where poor people live in roughly built shacks.

**shape** n. **1** an area or form with a definite outline; well-defined structure or arrangement. **2** a particular condition or shape. • v. **1** give a shape to; influence the nature of. **2** (**shape up**) develop or happen in a particular way.
■ **shapeless** adj.
▷ SYNS n. **1** FORM, figure, configuration, formation, structure, contour, outline, silhouette, profile. **2** GUISE, appearance, likeness, semblance, image.

**3** CONDITION, state, health, trim, fettle.

**shapely** adj. having an attractive shape.
▷ SYNS WELL PROPORTIONED, voluptuous, curvaceous, curvy.

**shard** n. a broken piece of pottery.

**share** n. **1** a part given to one person out of something divided among several; an amount that someone is entitled to or required to have. **2** one of the equal parts forming a business company's capital and entitling the holder to a proportion of the profits. • v. give or have a share of; have or use jointly. □ **shareholder** an owner of shares in a company.
▷ SYNS n. ALLOWANCE, ration, allocation, quota, portion, part, measure, helping; inf. cut, slice, whack. • v. **1** DIVIDE, split, go halves; inf. go fifty-fifty, go Dutch. **2** DIVIDE UP, allocate, apportion, parcel out, ration out.

**shark** n. **1** a large voracious sea fish. **2** inf. an unscrupulous swindler.

**sharp** adj. **1** having a cutting or piercing edge or point; (of a remark etc.) hurtful. **2** clear and definite. **3** sudden and noticeable. **4** quick to understand, notice, etc. **5** (of a taste or smell) intense and piercing. **6** above the correct or normal pitch in music. • adv. precisely. • n. (a sign indicating) a note raised by a semitone. □ **sharp practice** dishonest business dealings. **sharpshooter** a person skilled in shooting.
▷ SYNS adj. **1** RAZOR-EDGED, keen, cutting, sharpened, honed. **2** *a sharp pain:* INTENSE, acute,

severe, stabbing, shooting, excruciating. **3** *sharp words:* HARSH, bitter, hard, cutting, scathing, caustic, barbed, acrimonious, trenchant, venomous, malicious, vitriolic, hurtful, cruel. **4** *a sharp increase:* SUDDEN, abrupt, rapid, steep, unexpected. **5** *her sharp mind:* INTELLIGENT, bright, clever, smart, shrewd, astute, canny, discerning, perceptive, quick-witted.

**sharpen** v. make or become sharp.
▷ SYNS HONE, whet, strop, grind.

**shatter** v. **1** break violently into small pieces. **2** destroy; distress greatly.
▷ SYNS **1** SMASH, break, splinter, fracture, pulverize, crush, crack. **2** DESTROY, wreck, ruin, dash, devastate.

**shave** v. **1** remove hair by cutting it off close to the skin with a razor. **2** cut a thin slice from something. • n. an act of shaving. ■ **shaven** adj. **shaver** n.

**shaving** n. a thin strip cut off a surface.

**shawl** n. a large piece of soft fabric worn round the shoulders or wrapped round a baby.

**she** pron. the female previously mentioned.

**sheaf** n. (pl. **sheaves**) a bundle of corn stalks; a similar bundle.

**shear** v. (**sheared, shorn** or **sheared, shearing**) **1** cut or trim with shears. **2** break because of strain. • pl.n. (**shears**) a large cutting instrument shaped like scissors.

**sheath** n. a cover for the blade of a knife or tool; a condom.

▷ SYNS SCABBARD; cover, covering, case, casing, envelope, sleeve.

**sheathe** v. put into a sheath; encase in a tight covering.

**shed** n. a simple building used for storage. • v. **1** lose leaves etc. naturally. **2** get rid of. **3** give off light. **4** drop or spill.
▷ SYNS n. HUT, outhouse, lean-to, shack. • v. **1** SLOUGH OFF, cast off, moult. **2** DROP, spill, scatter.

**sheen** n. gloss or lustre.
▷ SYNS SHINE, lustre, gloss, polish, patina.

**sheep** n. (pl. **sheep**) a mammal with a woolly coat. □ **sheepdog** a dog trained to guard and herd sheep. **sheepskin** a sheep's skin with the wool on.

**sheepish** adj. feeling shy or foolish.
▷ SYNS EMBARRASSED, ashamed, shamefaced, abashed, hangdog, mortified, chastened.

**sheer** adj. **1** not mixed or qualified. **2** very steep. **3** (of fabric) very thin. • v. swerve from a course.
▷ SYNS adj. **1** UTTER, complete, total, pure, absolute, downright, out-and-out. **2** STEEP, abrupt, precipitous, perpendicular. **3** DIAPHANOUS, transparent, see-through, gauzy.

**sheet** n. **1** a piece of cotton or other fabric used to cover a bed. **2** a large thin piece of glass, metal, paper, etc. **3** an expanse of water, flame, etc.
▷ SYNS **1** *a sheet of glass:* PANE, panel, plate. **2** *a sheet of paper:* LEAF, page, folio. **3** *sheets of water:* EXPANSE, area, stretch, sweep.

**sheikh** n. a Muslim or Arab leader.

**shelf** n. (pl. **shelves**) a flat piece of wood etc. fastened to a wall etc. for things to be placed on; a ledge of rock.

**shell** n. **1** the hard outer covering of eggs, nut kernels, and of animals such as snails and tortoises; the outer structure or form of something, esp. when hollow. **2** a metal case filled with explosive, fired from a large gun. • v. **1** remove the shells of. **2** fire explosive shells at. □ **shellfish** an edible water animal that has a shell. **shell shock** psychological disturbance resulting from exposure to battle conditions.
▷ SYNS n. **1** CARAPACE, case, casing, husk, pod, integument. **2** BULLET, cartridge, shot; shrapnel. • v. BOMB, bombard, strafe, fire on.

**shelter** n. a structure that shields against danger, wind, rain, etc.; protection. • v. provide with shelter; take shelter.
▷ SYNS n. PROTECTION, cover, screen; safety, security, refuge, sanctuary, asylum. • v. PROTECT, shield, screen, cover, save, guard, defend.

**sheltered** adj. protected from the more unpleasant aspects of life.
▷ SYNS *a sheltered life:* PROTECTED, secluded, cloistered, isolated, withdrawn, reclusive, quiet.

**shelve** v. **1** put on a shelf. **2** postpone or cancel. **3** slope.

**shenanigans** pl.n. inf. high-spirited or underhand behaviour.

**shepherd** n. a person who tends sheep. • v. guide or direct. □ **shepherd's pie** a pie of minced meat topped with mashed potato.

▷ SYNS v. ESCORT, conduct, usher, guide, direct, steer.

**sherbet** n. a sweet powder made into an effervescent drink.

**sheriff** n. **1** the Crown's chief executive officer in a county. **2** a judge in Scotland. **3** US the chief law-enforcing officer of a county.

**sherry** n. (pl. **-ies**) a fortified wine.

**shibboleth** n. a long-standing belief or principle held by a group of people.

**shield** n. **1** a broad piece of armour held for protection. **2** any source of protection. • v. protect.

**shift** v. move or change from one position to another; transfer blame etc. • n. **1** a slight change in position etc. **2** a set of workers who start work when another set finishes; the time for which they work.
▷ SYNS v. MOVE, carry, transfer, switch, reposition, rearrange.

**shiftless** adj. lazy and inefficient.

**shifty** adj. inf. seeming untrustworthy.

**shilly-shally** v. (**-shallied**, **-shallying**) be indecisive.

**shimmer** v. & n. (shine with) a soft quivering light.
▷ SYNS GLISTEN, glint, flicker, twinkle, sparkle, gleam, glow.

**shin** n. the front of the leg below the knee. • v. (**shinned**, **shinning**) (**shin up**) climb quickly.

**shine** v. **1** (**shone, shining**) give out or reflect light; be excellent or outstanding. **2** (**shined, shining**) polish. • n. brightness.
▷ SYNS v. **1** GLEAM, glow, glint, sparkle, twinkle, glitter, glisten,

shimmer, flash, beam, radiate. **2** POLISH, burnish, buff, wax, gloss. • n. **1** LIGHT, brightness, gleam, glow, glint, sparkle, twinkle, glitter, shimmer, flash, glare, beam, radiance, illumination. **2** see SHEEN.

**shingle** n. **1** a mass of small pebbles on a beach etc. **2** a wooden roof tile. **3** (**shingles**) a disease causing a rash of small blisters.

**shiny** adj. reflecting light.
▷ SYNS SHINING, polished, burnished, gleaming, glossy, satiny, lustrous.

**ship** n. a large seagoing vessel. • v. (**shipped**, **shipping**) transport on a ship. □ **shipment** the act of transporting goods; an amount of goods shipped. **shipping** ships as a whole. **shipshape** orderly and neat. **shipwreck** the sinking or breaking up of a ship at sea. **shipwrecked** having suffered a shipwreck. **shipyard** a place where ships are built and repaired.

**shire** n. a county. □ **shire horse** a heavy, powerful breed of horse.

**shirk** v. avoid work or a duty.
▷ SYNS AVOID, evade, dodge, get out of; inf. skive off.

**shirt** n. a garment for the upper part of the body, with a collar and sleeves.

**shirty** adj. inf. annoyed.

**shiver** v. tremble slightly, esp. with cold or fear. • n. a shivering movement. ■ **shivery** adj.
▷ SYNS v. TREMBLE, quiver, shake, shudder, quaver, quake.

**shoal** n. **1** a large number of fish swimming together. **2** a shallow place; an underwater sandbank.

**shock** n. **1** a sudden upsetting or surprising experience. **2** sudden surprise and distress. **3** a medical condition caused by loss of blood, severe injury, etc. **4** a violent impact or tremor. **5** a sudden discharge of electricity through the body. **6** a thick mass of hair. • v. **1** surprise and upset. **2** outrage and disgust.
▷ SYNS n. BLOW, upset, surprise, revelation, bolt from the blue, eye-opener. • v. APPAL, horrify, outrage, scandalize, disgust, traumatize; distress, upset, disturb, stun.

**shocking** adj. **1** causing outrage or disgust. **2** inf. very bad.
■ **shockingly** adv.

**shoddy** adj. badly made or done.
▷ SYNS POOR-QUALITY, inferior, second-rate, trashy, cheap, cheapjack; inf. tacky.

**shoe** n. **1** a covering for the foot. **2** a horseshoe. • v. (**shod**, **shoeing**) fit with a shoe or shoes. □ **on a shoestring** with only a very small amount of money. **shoehorn** a curved implement for easing the heel into a shoe.

**shone** past and p.p. of SHINE.

**shoo** int. a sound uttered to frighten animals away.

**shook** past of SHAKE.

**shoot** v. **1** kill or wound with a bullet or arrow. **2** fire a gun. **3** move swiftly and suddenly. **4** aim a ball at a goal. **5** film or photograph. **6** (of a plant) send out shoots. • n. **1** a young branch or new growth of a plant. **2** an occasion when game is shot for sport. □ **shooting star** a small meteor seen to move rapidly. **shooting stick** a walking stick with a handle that unfolds to form a seat.

▷ SYNS v. 1 GUN DOWN, mow down, hit, pick off, bag, fell, kill. 2 FIRE, discharge, launch, let fly. 3 RACE, dash, sprint, charge, dart, fly, hurtle, bolt, streak, run, speed. • n. BUD, offshoot, scion, sucker, sprout, tendril, sprig.

**shop** n. 1 a building where goods are sold. 2 a workshop. • v. (**shopped**, **shopping**) buy things from shops. □ **shop floor** the place in a factory where things are made. **shop-soiled** dirty or damaged from being on display in a shop. **shop steward** a trade union official elected by workers as their spokesman.
■ **shopper** n.

▷ SYNS n. STORE, boutique, emporium; supermarket, superstore.

**shoplifter** n. a person who steals goods from a shop.
■ **shoplifting** n.

**shore** n. the land along the edge of the sea or a lake. • v. prop with a length of timber.

▷ SYNS n. SEASHORE, seaside, beach, coast, strand.

**shorn** p.p. of SHEAR.

**short** adj. 1 of small length in space or time. 2 small in height. 3 not having enough of. 4 rude and abrupt. 5 (of pastry) crumbly. • adv. not going far enough. • n. 1 a small drink of spirits. 2 (**shorts**) trousers reaching only to the knee or thigh. • v. have a short circuit. □ **shortbread** (or **shortcake**) a rich, crumbly biscuit. **short-change** cheat, esp. by giving insufficient change. **short circuit** a fault in an electrical circuit when the current flows along a

shorter route than normal. **short cut** a quicker route or method. **shortfall** an amount by which something is less than what is required. **shorthand** a method of rapid writing using abbreviations and symbols. **shortlist** a list of selected candidates from which a final choice is made. ■ **shorten** v. **shortness** n.

▷ SYNS adj. 1 CONCISE, brief, succinct, to the point, pithy, abridged. 2 BRIEF, fleeting, short-lived, momentary, passing, quick, rapid. 3 SMALL, little, tiny, petite, diminutive; Scot. wee; inf. pint-sized. 4 SCARCE, scant, meagre, sparse, insufficient, deficient, lacking, inadequate.

**shortage** n. a lack of something.

▷ SYNS DEARTH, scarcity, lack, deficiency, paucity, deficit, shortfall, want.

**shortcoming** n. a fault or defect.

▷ SYNS DEFECT, fault, flaw, imperfection, failing, drawback, weakness.

**shortly** adv. 1 soon. 2 curtly.

**short-sighted** adj. 1 unable to see things unless they are close to your eyes. 2 lacking foresight.

▷ SYNS 1 MYOPIC, nearsighted. 2 ILL-CONSIDERED, ill-advised, misguided, unwise, unimaginative, hasty.

**shot**¹ n. 1 a firing of a gun etc. 2 (in sport) a hit, stroke, or kick of the ball as an attempt to score. 3 inf. an attempt. 4 a photo. 5 inf. a measure of spirits. 6 inf. an injection. 7 ammunition. 8 a heavy ball thrown in the sport of shot put. □ **shotgun** a

gun for firing small shot at short range. **shot put** an athletic contest in which a heavy round ball is thrown as far as possible.
▷ SYNS **1** CRACK, bang, blast; gunfire. **2** PHOTOGRAPH, photo, snapshot, picture.

**shot²** past & p.p. of **SHOOT**.

**should** v.aux. used to express duty or obligation, a possible or expected future event, or (with *I* and *we*) a polite statement or a conditional clause.

**shoulder** n. the joint between the upper arm and the main part of the body. • v. **1** take on a responsibility. **2** push with your shoulder. □ **shoulder blade** the large flat bone of the shoulder.

**shout** n. a loud cry or call.
• v. speak or call out loudly.
▷ SYNS v. CRY OUT, call out, yell, roar, bellow, scream, bawl; inf. holler.

**shove** n. a rough push. • v. push roughly; place carelessly.
▷ SYNS v. PUSH, thrust, force, ram, shoulder, elbow.

**shovel** n. a spade-like tool for moving sand, snow, etc.
• v. (**shovelled, shovelling**; US **shoveled**) shift or clear with a shovel.

**show** v. **1** be or make visible. **2** offer for inspection or viewing. **3** present an image of. **4** guide or lead. **5** treat in a particular way. **6** demonstrate or prove. • n. **1** a theatrical performance or light entertainment programme. **2** an outward display, esp. when misleading. □ **show business** the entertainment profession. **showdown** a final confrontation intended to settle a dispute. **showjumping** the sport of riding horses over a

course of obstacles in an arena. **show off** try to impress people. **showroom** a room where goods for sale are displayed.
▷ SYNS v. **1** *show his grief:* DISPLAY, exhibit, manifest, reveal, convey, express, betray. **2** *show them to their seats:* ESCORT, accompany, usher, conduct, attend, guide, lead, direct, steer. **3** *show them what to do:* DEMONSTRATE, explain, describe, teach, instruct. • n. **1** DISPLAY, exhibition, presentation, exposition, spectacle; performance, production.
**2** APPEARANCE, guise, semblance, pretence, pose, affectation.

**showcase** n. **1** an occasion for presenting something favourably. **2** a glass display case.
• v. put on display.

**shower** n. **1** a brief fall of rain or snow. **2** a large number of things that arrive together. **3** a device spraying water over someone's body; a wash in this. • v. **1** (cause to) fall in a shower; give a number of things to. **2** wash in a shower.
■ **showery** adj.

**show-off** n. a person who tries to impress others.
▷ SYNS EXHIBITIONIST, extrovert, swaggerer, boaster; inf. poser.

**showy** adj. very bright or colourful; ostentatious or gaudy.
▷ SYNS OSTENTATIOUS, ornate, flamboyant, elaborate, fancy, gaudy, garish, flashy; inf. bling-bling.

**shrank** past of **SHRINK**.

**shrapnel** n. pieces of metal scattered from an exploding bomb.

**shred** n. **1** a small strip torn or cut from something. **2** a very small amount. • v. (**shredded**, **shredding**) tear or cut into shreds.

▷ SYNS n. **1** STRIP, ribbon, rag, fragment. **2** SCRAP, bit, iota, whit, particle, jot, trace.

**shrew** n. a small mouse-like animal.

**shrewd** adj. showing good judgement.

▷ SYNS ASTUTE, sharp, clever, intelligent, smart, perceptive, wise, sagacious, canny; cunning, crafty, wily.

**shriek** n. & v. (make) a piercing cry.

▷ SYNS SCREAM, screech, squeal, squawk, howl, yelp.

**shrill** adj. piercing and high-pitched in sound.

▷ SYNS HIGH-PITCHED, high, sharp, piercing, penetrating, ear-splitting, screechy.

**shrimp** n. a small edible shellfish.

**shrine** n. a place connected with a holy person or event.

**shrink** v. **1** make or become smaller. **2** draw back in fear or disgust. ■ **shrinkage** n.

▷ SYNS **1** GET SMALLER, contract, diminish, lessen, reduce, dwindle, decline, shrivel. **2** DRAW BACK, recoil, retreat, flinch, cringe.

**shrivel** v. (**shrivelled**, **shrivelling**; US **shriveled**) shrink and wrinkle from lack of moisture.

▷ SYNS WITHER, wilt, dry up, shrink, wrinkle.

**shroud** n. a cloth in which a dead body is wrapped for burial; a thing that conceals. • v. wrap in a shroud; conceal.

▷ SYNS v. COVER, envelop, cloak, blanket, veil, screen, conceal, hide.

**shrub** n. a woody plant smaller than a tree.

**shrubbery** n. (pl. **-ies**) an area planted with shrubs.

**shrug** v. (**shrugged**, **shrugging**) raise your shoulders as a gesture of indifference or lack of knowledge. • n. this movement.

**shrunken** adj. having shrunk.

**shudder** v. shiver or shake violently. • n. this movement.

**shuffle** v. **1** walk without lifting your feet clear of the ground. **2** rearrange. • n. **1** a shuffling movement or walk. **2** a rearrangement.

**shun** v. (**shunned**, **shunning**) avoid.

▷ SYNS AVOID, evade, steer clear of, shy away from, keep your distance from, cold-shoulder.

**shunt** v. move a train to a side track; move to a different position.

**shut** v. (**shut**, **shutting**) move something into position to block an opening; keep in or out of a place by blocking an opening; close a book, curtains, etc.; (of a shop etc.) stop operating for business. ◻ **shut up** inf. be quiet.

▷ SYNS CLOSE, pull to, fasten, lock, secure, seal.

**shutter** n. a screen that can be closed over a window; a device that opens and closes the aperture of a camera.

**shuttle** n. **1** a form of transport travelling frequently between places. **2** a device carrying the weft thread in weaving. • v. move, travel, or send to and fro. ◻ **shuttlecock** a light cone-shaped object, struck with rackets in badminton.

**shy** adj. nervous or timid around other people. • v. **1** (of a horse) turn aside in fright. **2** avoid through nervousness.
▷ SYNS adj. BASHFUL, diffident, timid, reserved, introverted, nervous, self-effacing, withdrawn.

**SI** abbr. Système International, the international system of units of measurement.

**Siamese** adj. of Siam (the former name for Thailand). ▫ **Siamese cat** a breed of cat with pale fur and darker face, paws, and tail. **Siamese twins** twins whose bodies are joined at birth.

**sibling** n. a brother or sister.

**sic** adv. written exactly as it stands in the original.

**sick** adj. **1** ill. **2** wanting to vomit. **3** bored by or annoyed with. **4** inf. macabre or morbid.
▷ SYNS **1** ILL, unwell, poorly, ailing, indisposed. **2** NAUSEOUS, nauseated, queasy, bilious, green about the gills. **3** FED UP, bored, tired, weary. **4** MORBID, macabre, ghoulish, perverted.

**sicken** v. **1** become ill. **2** disgust.
▷ SYNS NAUSEATE, turn someone's stomach, revolt, disgust, repulse.

**sickle** n. a curved blade used for cutting corn etc.

**sickly** adj. **1** often ill. **2** causing nausea.
▷ SYNS UNHEALTHY, in poor health, delicate, frail, weak.

**sickness** n. **1** an illness or disease. **2** nausea or vomiting.
▷ SYNS **1** ILLNESS, disease, ailment, complaint, infection, infirmity, indisposition; inf. bug. **2** NAUSEA, queasiness, biliousness, vomiting.

**side** n. **1** a position to the left or right of an object, place, or central point. **2** either of the halves into which something is divided. **3** a surface of an object. **4** a part near the edge. **5** one of two opposing groups or teams. **6** a particular aspect. **7** a bounding line of a plane figure. • adj. additional or less important. ▫ **sideboard** a piece of furniture with cupboards and drawers for crockery, glasses, etc. **sideboards** (or **sideburns**) a strip of hair growing down each side of a man's face. **side effect** a secondary, usu. unwelcome effect. **side-saddle** (of a rider) sitting with both feet on the same side of the horse. **sideshow** a small show or stall at a fair etc. **sidestep** avoid by stepping sideways; avoid dealing with or discussing. **sidetrack** distract. **sidewalk** US a pavement. **sideways** to, towards, or from the side.
▷ SYNS n. **1** EDGE, border, verge, margin, fringe, flank, boundary, bank, perimeter, periphery. **2** *the east side of the city*: DISTRICT, quarter, area, neighbourhood, sector. **3** *his side of the argument*: POINT OF VIEW, viewpoint, opinion, angle, aspect, standpoint, position, slant. **4** FACTION, camp, party, wing.

**sideline** n. **1** something done in addition to your main activity. **2** either of the two lines along the longer sides of a football pitch etc. • v. remove from an influential position. ▫ **on/from the sidelines** watching something but not involved in it.

**sidelong** adj. to or from one side; sideways.

▷ SYNS INDIRECT, oblique, sideways; furtive, covert, sly.

**siding** n. a short track by the side of a railway, used in shunting.

**sidle** v. walk in a furtive or timid way.

**siege** n. a military operation in which forces surround a town and cut off its supplies.

**siesta** n. an afternoon nap or rest.

**sieve** n. a utensil with a mesh through which liquids or fine particles can pass. • v. put through a sieve.
▷ SYNS n. STRAINER, filter, colander, riddle.

**sift** v. 1 sieve. 2 examine carefully and select or analyse.

**sigh** v. let out a long deep breath expressing sadness, relief, etc. • n. an act of sighing.

**sight** n. 1 the ability to see. 2 seeing. 3 the distance within which you can see. 4 a thing seen or worth seeing. 5 inf. an unsightly thing. 6 a device looked through to aim or observe with a gun or telescope etc. • v. see. ■ **sighted** adj. **sightless** adj.
▷ SYNS n. 1 EYESIGHT, vision. 2 VIEW, glimpse, look. 3 LANDMARK, monument, spectacle.

**sightseeing** n. visiting places of interest. ■ **sightseer** n.

**sign** n. 1 an indication that something exists, is occurring, or may occur. 2 a signal, gesture, or notice giving information or an instruction. 3 a symbol or word representing something in algebra, music, etc. 4 any of the twelve divisions of the zodiac.

• v. 1 write your name on something. 2 make a sign. □ **signpost** a sign on a post, giving the direction and distance to a place.
▷ SYNS n. 1 INDICATION, symptom, mark, pointer, manifestation, token. 2 NOTICE, placard, signpost. 3 SYMBOL, figure, emblem, character.

**signal** n. 1 a sign or gesture giving information or a command; an apparatus indicating whether a railway line is clear. 2 an electrical impulse or radio wave sent or received.
• v. (**signalled**, **signalling**; US **signaled**) make a signal; indicate by means of a signal.
• adj. noteworthy.
▷ SYNS n. SIGN, gesture, cue; indication, evidence, pointer.
• v. GESTURE, indicate, beckon, motion, gesticulate, nod, sign.

**signatory** n. (pl. **-ies**) a person who has signed an agreement.

**signature** n. a person's name written in a distinctive way, used in signing something. □ **signature tune** a tune announcing a particular radio or television programme.

**signet ring** n. a ring with an engraved design.

**significance** n. 1 importance. 2 the meaning of something.
▷ SYNS 1 IMPORTANCE, consequence, magnitude, seriousness. 2 MEANING, sense, import, signification, point, gist, essence.

**significant** adj. 1 important or large enough to have an effect. 2 having a particular or secret meaning. ■ **significantly** adv.
▷ SYNS 1 IMPORTANT, of consequence, weighty, momentous, serious, notable, noteworthy.

**2** MEANINGFUL, eloquent, expressive, pregnant, knowing.

**signify** v. (**signified, signifying**) indicate; mean; be important.
▷ SYNS **1** INDICATE, be a sign of, be evidence of, point to, betoken. **2** MEAN, denote, represent, symbolize, stand for.

**Sikh** n. a follower of a religion that developed from Hinduism. ■ Sikhism n.

**silage** n. green fodder stored and fermented in a silo.

**silence** n. complete lack of sound or speech. • v. make silent.
▷ SYNS n. QUIET, quietness, hush, still, stillness, peace, peacefulness, tranquillity. • v. QUIET, quieten, hush, muffle.

**silencer** n. a device to reduce the noise made by a gun, exhaust, etc.

**silent** adj. **1** without sound. **2** not speaking. **3** unspoken.
▷ SYNS **1** QUIET, hushed, still, noiseless, soundless. **2** SPEECHLESS, dumb, mute, taciturn, uncommunicative, tight-lipped. **3** UNSPOKEN, wordless, tacit, implicit, understood.

**silhouette** n. a dark shadow or outline seen against a light background. • v. show as a silhouette.
▷ SYNS n. OUTLINE, contour, profile, form, shape.

**silica** n. a compound of silicon occurring as quartz and in sandstone etc.

**silicon** n. a chemical element that is a semiconductor.
□ silicon chip a microchip.

**silicone** n. a synthetic substance made from silicon.

**silk** n. a fine, soft fibre produced by silkworms, made into thread or fabric. □ silkworm a caterpillar that spins a silk cocoon. ■ silken adj.

**silky** adj. smooth and shiny like silk.
▷ SYNS SILKEN, smooth, sleek, glossy, satiny.

**sill** n. a shelf or slab at the base of a doorway or window.

**silly** adj. (**-ier, -iest**) lacking common sense. ■ silliness n.
▷ SYNS FOOLISH, stupid, idiotic, mindless, brainless, senseless, misguided, unwise, imprudent, thoughtless, foolhardy, irresponsible, mad, hare-brained, absurd, fatuous, vacuous, inane, asinine, immature, childish; inf. daft, crazy.

**silo** n. (pl. **silos**) **1** a pit or airtight structure for holding silage. **2** a pit or tower for storing grain. **3** an underground place where a missile is kept ready for firing.

**silt** n. sediment deposited by water in a channel or harbour etc. • v. fill or block with silt.

**silver** n. a shiny, whitish precious metal; articles made of this; coins made of an alloy resembling it; the colour of silver. □ silver jubilee the 25th anniversary of a significant event. silver wedding a 25th wedding anniversary.
■ silvery adj.

**SIM card** n. a smart card in a mobile phone carrying an identification number and storing personal data.

**simian** adj. of or like a monkey or ape.

**similar** adj. alike but not identical. ■ similarly adv.

▷ SYNS LIKE, alike, comparable, corresponding, analogous, parallel, equivalent; kindred.

**similarity** n. the state or fact of being similar.
▷ SYNS RESEMBLANCE, likeness, comparability, correspondence, similitude, parallel, equivalence, uniformity.

**simile** n. a phrase that compares one thing to another, using *as* or *like*.

**simmer** v. 1 (cause to) boil very gently. 2 be full of barely suppressed anger or excitement.

**simper** v. smile in an affected way. • n. an affected smile.

**simple** adj. 1 easily done or understood. 2 plain and basic. 3 composed of a single element. 4 of very low intelligence. ■ simplicity n. simply adv.
▷ SYNS 1 EASY, uncomplicated, straightforward, elementary; inf. a piece of cake. 2 CLEAR, plain, lucid, comprehensible, understandable. 3 PLAIN, basic, unadorned, understated.

**simpleton** n. a person with low intelligence.

**simplify** v. (simplified, simplifying) make easier or less complex. ■ simplification n.

**simplistic** adj. treating complex issues as more simple than they really are.

**simulate** v. imitate; pretend to feel; produce a computer model of. ■ simulation n. simulator n.

**simultaneous** adj. occurring at the same time.
▷ SYNS CONCURRENT, contemporaneous, concomitant, coinciding, coincident, synchronous.

**sin** n. an act that breaks a religious or moral law.
• v. (sinned, sinning) commit a sin. ■ sinner n.
▷ SYNS n. WRONG, wrongdoing, crime, offence, misdeed, transgression; trespass.
• v. TRANSGRESS, go astray, do wrong, trespass, fall from grace.

**since** prep. from a specified time or event until the present. • conj. 1 from the time that. 2 because. • adv. from that time or event.

**sincere** adj. without pretence or deceit. ■ sincerity n.
▷ SYNS GENUINE, real, true, honest, unfeigned, unaffected, bona fide, wholehearted, heartfelt, earnest, profound.

**sine** n. (in a right-angled triangle) the ratio of the side opposite an angle to the hypotenuse.

**sinecure** n. a paid job which requires little or no effort.

**sinew** n. tough fibrous tissue joining muscle to bone.

**sinful** adj. wicked and immoral.
▷ SYNS IMMORAL, wicked, evil, wrong, bad, iniquitous, unrighteous, corrupt, criminal.

**sing** v. (sang, sung, singing) make musical sounds with the voice; perform a song; make a whistling sound. ■ singer n.
▷ SYNS CAROL, croon, chant; trill, warble.

**singe** v. (singed, singeing) burn slightly. • n. a slight burn.
▷ SYNS v. SCORCH, burn, sear, char.

**single** adj. 1 one only. 2 designed for one person. 3 not in a romantic or sexual relationship. 4 consisting of one part. 5 (of a ticket) valid for an outward journey only. • n. a single person or thing. ◻ single-handed

without help. **single-minded** determined to pursue a particular goal. **single out** choose or distinguish from others. **single parent** a person bringing up a child or children without a partner.
■ **singly** adv.
▷ SYNS **adj. 1** ONE, sole, lone, solitary. **2** INDIVIDUAL, particular, separate, distinct. **3** UNMARRIED, unwed, unattached, (fancy) free.

**singlet** n. a sleeveless vest.

**singleton** n. a single person or thing.

**singular** adj. **1** exceptional or remarkable. **2** (of a word or form) referring to just one person or thing. • n. Grammar the singular form of a word.
▷ SYNS **adj.** EXTRAORDINARY, exceptional, rare, unusual, remarkable, unique, outstanding, notable, noteworthy, striking, signal.

**sinister** adj. seeming evil or dangerous.
▷ SYNS **1** MENACING, ominous, threatening, forbidding, frightening; inf. scary. **2** EVIL, wicked, bad, criminal, corrupt, nefarious, villainous.

**sink** v. **1** go down below the surface of liquid; move slowly downwards; gradually penetrate the surface of; decline. **2** (**sink in**) be realized or understood. **3** invest money. • n. a fixed basin with taps and a drainage pipe.
▷ SYNS **v. 1** GO UNDER, submerge, founder, capsize; scuttle, scupper. **2** FALL, drop, descend, go down, plunge, plummet.

**sinuous** adj. curving or undulating.

▷ SYNS WINDING, curving, twisting, meandering, undulating, serpentine.

**sinus** n. a cavity in the bones of the face that connects with the nostrils.

**sinusitis** n. inflammation of a sinus.

**sip** v. (**sipped**, **sipping**) drink in small mouthfuls. • n. an amount sipped.

**siphon** n. a tube used to move liquid from one container to another. • v. draw off through a siphon.

**sir** n. **1** a polite form of address to a man. **2** used as the title of a knight or baronet.

**sire** n. an animal's male parent. • v. be the male parent of.

**siren** n. a device that makes a loud prolonged warning sound.

**sirloin** n. the best part of a loin of beef.

**sissy** n. (pl. **-ies**) inf. a weak or timid person.

**sister** n. **1** a daughter of the same parents as another person. **2** a female colleague. **3** a nun. **4** a senior female nurse.
□ **sister-in-law** the sister of your wife or husband; the wife of your brother. ■ **sisterly** adj.

**sit** v. **1** take or be in a position with the body resting on the buttocks; be in a particular position or state; pose for a portrait. **2** serve as a member of a council, jury, etc.; (of a committee etc.) hold a session; take an exam.
▷ SYNS **1** SIT DOWN, take a seat, settle down, be seated, take a pew. **2** BE PLACED, be situated, rest, perch.

**sitar** n. a guitar-like Indian lute.

**sitcom** n. inf. a situation comedy.

**site** n. the place where something is located or happens. • v. locate.
▷ SYNS LOCATION, situation, position, place, locality, setting.

**sitting** n. a period of posing for a portrait; a session of a committee etc.; a scheduled period for a group to be served in a restaurant. □ **sitting room** a room for sitting and relaxing in. **sitting tenant** a tenant already in occupation.

**situate** v. put in a particular place.
▷ SYNS LOCATE, position, place, put, site, establish.

**situated** adj. in a specified position or condition.

**situation** n. **1** the location and surroundings of a place. **2** a set of circumstances. **3** a job. □ **situation comedy** a comedy series in which the same characters are involved in amusing situations.
▷ SYNS **1** PLACE, position, location, site, setting, environment. **2** CIRCUMSTANCES, affairs, condition, state. **3** POST, position, place, job, employment.

**six** adj. & n. one more than five; 6. ■ **sixth** adj. & n.

**sixteen** n. one more than fifteen; 16. ■ **sixteenth** adj. & n.

**sixty** adj. & n. six times ten; 60. ■ **sixtieth** adj. & n.

**size**[1] n. the overall measurements or extent of something; one of a series of standard measurements in which things are made and sold. • v. assess.
▷ SYNS n. DIMENSIONS, measurements, proportions, magnitude, bulk, area, expanse, extent.

**size**[2] n. a gluey solution used to glaze paper or stiffen textiles.

**sizeable** (or **sizable**) adj. fairly large.

**sizzle** v. make a hissing sound like that of frying.

**skate** n. **1** a boot with a blade or wheels attached, for gliding over ice or a hard surface. **2** an edible flatfish. • v. move on skates. □ **skateboard** a narrow board with wheels fixed to the bottom, for riding on while standing.

**skein** n. a loosely coiled bundle of yarn.

**skeletal** adj. **1** of the skeleton. **2** very thin.

**skeleton** n. the bones and cartilage forming the supporting structure of an animal body; a supporting or basic framework or structure. • adj. referring to a minimum number of people: *a skeleton staff.* □ **skeleton key** a key designed to fit many locks.

**skeptic** US sp. of **sceptic**.

**sketch** n. **1** a rough drawing or painting. **2** a short scene in a comedy show. **3** a brief account. • v. make a sketch of.
▷ SYNS n. **1** DRAWING, outline, diagram, plan. **2** SKIT, act, scene. **3** OUTLINE, account, rundown, summary, synopsis. • v. DRAW, rough out, outline.

**sketchy** adj. not detailed or thorough.
▷ SYNS INCOMPLETE, patchy, rough, cursory, perfunctory, superficial, vague, imprecise, hurried, hasty.

**skew** v. change direction; make biased. □ **skewbald** (of a horse) having patches of white and brown.

**skewer** n. a pin to hold pieces of food together while cooking. • v. pierce with a skewer.

**ski** n. one of a pair of long narrow strips of wood etc. fixed under the feet for travelling over snow. • v. (**skis, skied, skiing**) travel on skis. ■ **skier** n.

**skid** v. (**skidded, skidding**) slide uncontrollably off course. • n. a skidding movement.

**skilful** (US **skillful**) adj. having or showing skill. ■ **skilfully** adv.
▷ SYNS SKILLED, able, good, accomplished, adept, competent, efficient, adroit, deft, dexterous, masterly, expert, experienced, trained, practised, professional, proficient, talented.

**skill** n. ability to do something well. ■ **skilled** adj.
▷ SYNS EXPERTISE, skilfulness, ability, adeptness, competence, adroitness, deftness, dexterity, aptitude, finesse, prowess, proficiency, talent.

**skillet** n. a frying pan.

**skim** v. (**skimmed, skimming**) 1 take matter from the surface of a liquid. 2 glide. 3 read quickly. □ **skimmed milk** milk from which the cream has been removed.

**skimp** v. supply or use less than what is necessary.

**skimpy** adj. (**-ier, -iest**) scanty.

**skin** n. the tissue forming the outer covering of the body; the skin of a dead animal used for clothing etc.; the outer layer of fruits etc. • v. (**skinned, skinning**) strip the skin from. □ **skin diving** swimming under water with flippers and an aqualung. **skinflint** inf. a miser. **skinhead** a young person of a group with very short shaved hair.
▷ SYNS n. 1 EPIDERMIS, cuticle, derma. 2 COMPLEXION, colouring. 3 HIDE, pelt, fleece. 4 PEEL, rind. 5 FILM, coating, coat, layer.

**skinny** adj. (**-ier, -iest**) very thin.
▷ SYNS THIN, lean, scraggy, scrawny, emaciated, skeletal, skin and bone.

**skint** adj. inf. very short of money.

**skip**[1] v. (**skipped, skipping**) move lightly with a hopping or bouncing step; jump repeatedly over a rope turned over the head and under the feet; omit or move quickly over. • n. a skipping movement.
▷ SYNS v. 1 BOUND, jump, leap, spring, hop, bounce, dance, caper, prance, gambol, frisk. 2 OMIT, leave out, miss out, pass over.

**skip**[2] n. a large open container for builders' rubbish etc.

**skipper** n. inf. a captain.

**skirmish** n. & v. (take part in) a minor fight or conflict.
▷ SYNS BATTLE, fight, clash, conflict, encounter, confrontation, tussle, fracas.

**skirt** n. a woman's garment hanging from the waist and covering the lower body and legs. • v. form or go along the edge of; avoid dealing with. □ **skirting board** a wooden board along the base of the wall of a room.
▷ SYNS v. 1 GO ROUND, walk round, circle. 2 EVADE, avoid, dodge, sidestep.

**skit** n. a short parody or comedy sketch.

**skittish** adj. lively and unpredictable.

**skittle** n. one of the wooden pins set up to be bowled down with a ball in the game of skittles.

**skive** v. inf. dodge a duty; play truant. ■ skiver n.

**skulduggery** n. trickery.

**skulk** v. loiter stealthily.

**skull** n. the bony framework of the head. □ skullcap a small cap without a peak.

**skunk** n. a black and white animal able to spray a foul-smelling liquid.

**sky** n. (pl. **skies**) the upper atmosphere. □ skydiving the sport of parachuting from an aircraft. skylark a lark that sings while in flight. skylight a window set in a roof. skyscraper a very tall building.
▷ SYNS THE HEAVENS, the firmament, the blue yonder.

**slab** n. a broad flat piece of something solid.
▷ SYNS HUNK, piece, chunk, lump, slice, wedge.

**slack** adj. **1** not tight. **2** not busy; lazy or negligent. • n. **1** a slack piece of rope. **2** (**slacks**) casual trousers. • v. work slowly or lazily. ■ slacken v.
▷ SYNS adj. **1** LOOSE, limp; flaccid, sagging, saggy. **2** SLOW, quiet, sluggish. **3** LAX, negligent, remiss, careless, slapdash, slipshod, sloppy, lackadaisical.

**slag** n. solid waste left when metal has been smelted. □ slag off inf. criticize rudely.

**slain** p.p. of SLAY.

**slake** v. satisfy thirst.
▷ SYNS SATISFY, quench, assuage, relieve.

**slalom** n. a skiing or canoeing race following a winding course marked out by poles.

**slam** v. (**slammed, slamming**) shut forcefully and noisily; put or hit forcefully. • n. a slamming noise.
▷ SYNS v. BANG, crash, smash, dash, fling, throw.

**slander** n. the crime of making false statements that damage a person's reputation. • v. make such statements about.
▷ SYNS n. DEFAMATION, misrepresentation, libel, vilification, disparagement, denigration. • v. DEFAME, libel, cast aspersions on, malign, vilify, smear, denigrate, run down.

**slanderous** adj. containing slander.
▷ SYNS DEFAMATORY, disparaging, libellous, pejorative, false, malicious, scurrilous.

**slang** n. very informal words and phrases used by a particular group of people.
▷ SYNS COLLOQUIALISMS, jargon, patois, argot, cant; inf. lingo.

**slant** v. **1** slope. **2** present news etc. from a particular point of view. • n. **1** a slope. **2** a point of view.
▷ SYNS v. **1** SLOPE, tilt, lean, dip, shelve, list. **2** BIAS, distort, twist, skew. • n. **1** SLOPE, tilt, gradient, incline. **2** POINT OF VIEW, viewpoint, standpoint, stance, angle, perspective.

**slap** v. (**slapped, slapping**) strike with the open hand or a flat object; place forcefully or carelessly. • n. an act or sound of slapping. □ slapdash hurried and careless. slapstick comedy based on deliberately clumsy actions.
▷ SYNS v. SMACK, strike, hit, cuff, spank; inf. wallop, clout, whack.

**slash** v. cut with a violent sweeping stroke. • n. **1** a cut made by slashing. **2** an oblique line (/) used between alternatives.

**slat** n. a narrow strip of wood, metal, etc.

**slate** n. rock that splits easily into flat plates; a piece of this used as roofing material.

**slaughter** v. kill animals for food; kill ruthlessly or in great numbers. • n. killing in this way. □ **slaughterhouse** a place where animals are killed for food.
▷ SYNS v. KILL, butcher, massacre, murder, slay. • n. MASSACRE, murder, butchery, killing, carnage.

**slave** n. **1** hist. a person owned by another and forced to obey them. **2** a person influenced or controlled by something. • v. work very hard. □ **slave-driver** a person who makes others work very hard.
▷ SYNS v. TOIL, labour, drudge, slog, graft, work your fingers to the bone.

**slaver** v. have saliva flowing from the mouth.
▷ SYNS SLOBBER, drool, dribble, salivate.

**slavery** n. **1** the state of being a slave. **2** the practice of owning slaves.
▷ SYNS ENSLAVEMENT, bondage, servitude, subjugation, thrall.

**slavish** adj. excessively submissive or imitative.
▷ SYNS SERVILE, subservient, obsequious, sycophantic, fawning.

**slay** v. (**slew**, **slain**, **slaying**) kill.

**sleaze** n. inf. immoral or dishonest behaviour.

**sleazy** adj. (**-ier**, **-iest**) sordid or squalid.

**sledge** (US **sled**) n. a cart on runners for travelling over snow. • v. travel or convey in a sledge.

**sledgehammer** n. a large, heavy hammer.

**sleek** adj. smooth and glossy; looking well fed and thriving.
▷ SYNS SMOOTH, glossy, shiny, lustrous, silken, silky, satiny.

**sleep** n. a state of rest in which the eyes are closed and the mind unconscious. • v. **1** be asleep. **2** have sleeping accommodation for. **3** (**sleep with**) have sex with. □ **sleeping bag** a warm padded bag for sleeping in. **sleepover** a night spent by children at another person's house. **sleepwalk** walk around while asleep.
▷ SYNS n. NAP, catnap, doze, siesta; inf. snooze, kip, forty winks, shut-eye. • v. BE ASLEEP, slumber, doze, drowse; inf. snooze, kip.

**sleeper** n. **1** a railway coach fitted for sleeping in. **2** a beam on which the rails of a railway rest. **3** a ring worn in a pierced ear to keep the hole from closing.

**sleepy** adj. needing or ready for sleep.
▷ SYNS DROWSY, tired, somnolent, languorous, lethargic, sluggish.

**sleet** n. hail or snow and rain falling together.

**sleeve** n. the part of a garment covering the arm; the cover for a record.

**sleigh** n. a sledge drawn by horses or reindeer.

**sleight** n. (**sleight of hand**) skilful use of the hands when performing conjuring tricks.

**slender** adj. **1** slim and graceful. **2** barely enough.

▷ syns **SLIM**, thin, slight, lean, svelte, willowy, sylphlike.

**slept** past and p.p. of **SLEEP**.

**sleuth** n. inf. a detective.

**slew**¹ past of **SLAY**.

**slew**² v. turn or swing round.

**slice** n. **1** a thin, broad piece of food cut from a larger portion; a portion. **2** a sliced stroke.
• v. **1** cut into slices. **2** strike a ball so that it spins away from the direction intended.
▷ syns n. **PIECE**, portion, wedge, chunk, slab.

**slick** adj. **1** efficient and effortless; glib. **2** smooth and glossy or slippery. • n. a patch of oil.
• v. make sleek.
▷ syns adj. **1** **SMOOTH**, well organized, efficient, effortless, polished. **2** **GLIB**, fluent, plausible, smooth-talking.

**slide** v. (**slid, sliding**) move along a smooth surface, always remaining in contact with it; move or pass smoothly. • n. **1** a structure with a smooth slope for children to slide down. **2** a piece of glass for holding an object under a microscope. **3** a picture for projecting on to a screen. **4** a hinged clip to hold hair in place.
▷ syns v. **SLIP**, skid, slither, skate, skim, glide.

**slight** adj. not great or large; trivial; slender. • v. insult by treating with lack of respect
• n. a snub. ■ **slightly** adv.
▷ syns adj. **1** **SMALL**, tiny, minute, modest, negligible, insignificant, minimal, trivial.
**2** **SLIM**, slender, petite, diminutive. • v. **SNUB**, insult, rebuff, cold-shoulder, scorn.
• n. **INSULT**, snub, affront, rebuff.

**slim** adj. **1** gracefully thin.
**2** small in width. **3** very small.
• v. (**slimmed, slimming**) become thinner.
▷ syns adj. **1** **SLENDER**, thin, lean, trim, slight, svelte, willowy. **2** *a slim chance:* **SLIGHT**, small, faint, remote.

**slime** n. an unpleasant thick liquid substance.

**slimy** adj. **1** like or covered by slime. **2** insincerely flattering.
▷ syns **SLIPPERY**, greasy, mucky, wet, sticky.

**sling** n. **1** a loop of fabric used to support or raise a hanging object. **2** a looped strap used to throw a stone etc. • v. (**slung, slinging**) **1** hang or carry with a sling or strap. **2** inf. throw.

**slink** v. (**slunk, slinking**) move in a stealthy way.
▷ syns **SIDLE**, sneak, creep, steal, slip, slide.

**slinky** adj. **1** close-fitting.
**2** graceful and sensuous.

**slip** v. **1** lose your balance and slide. **2** fall or slide out of place. **3** gradually worsen. **4** move or place quietly and quickly. **5** get free from. • n. **1** an act of slipping. **2** a slight mistake. **3** a petticoat. **4** a small piece of paper. □ **slipped disc** a displaced disc in the spine that presses on nerves and causes pain. **slip road** a road for entering or leaving a motorway. **slipshod** careless or disorganized. **slipstream** a current of air or water driven back by a propeller or jet engine. **slip up** inf. make a mistake. **slipway** a slope leading into water, for launching or landing boats.
▷ syns v. **1** **SLIDE**, skid, slither, fall.
**2** **SNEAK**, creep, steal, slink, sidle. • n. **MISTAKE**, error,

blunder, miscalculation, oversight.

**slipper** n. a light indoor shoe.

**slippery** adj. **1** difficult to hold or stand on because smooth or wet. **2** untrustworthy.
▷ SYNS GREASY, oily, slimy, icy, glassy, smooth.

**slit** n. a narrow straight cut or opening. • v. (**slit**, **slitting**) cut a slit in.
▷ SYNS n. CUT, split, slash, gash, rip, incision, tear, rent, fissure, opening.

**slither** v. slide unsteadily.

**sliver** n. a small thin strip.

**slob** n. inf. a lazy, untidy person.

**slobber** v. slaver.

**sloe** n. a small wild plum.

**slog** v. (**slogged**, **slogging**) **1** work hard. **2** hit hard. • n. a spell of hard work or tiring walking.

**slogan** n. a phrase used in advertising or politics.
▷ SYNS CATCHPHRASE, jingle, motto.

**slop** v. (**slopped**, **slopping**) spill or overflow. • n. (**slops**) **1** unappetizing liquid food. **2** liquid refuse.

**slope** n. a surface with one end at a higher level than another. • v. slant up or down.
▷ SYNS n. GRADIENT, slant, incline, angle, pitch, tilt; hill, hillock, bank. • v. SLANT, incline, lean, tilt, dip, drop.

**sloppy** adj. (**-ier**, **-iest**) **1** wet and slushy. **2** careless. **3** too sentimental.

**slot** n. **1** a narrow opening into which something may be inserted. **2** a place in a schedule etc. • v. (**slotted**, **slotting**) fit into a slot. □ **slot machine** a machine operated by putting coins into a slot.
▷ SYNS n. **1** SLIT, crack, hole, opening, aperture. **2** PLACE, spot, time, space, period.

**sloth** n. **1** laziness. **2** a slow-moving animal of tropical America. ■ **slothful** adj.

**slouch** v. stand, sit, or move in a lazy way. • n. a slouching posture.

**slough**[1] n. a swamp.

**slough**[2] v. shed old or dead skin.

**slovenly** adj. careless and untidy.
▷ SYNS SCRUFFY, untidy, messy, unkempt, dishevelled, bedraggled.

**slow** adj. **1** not moving quickly. **2** taking a long time. **3** (of a clock) showing an earlier time than the correct one. **4** not quick to understand or learn. • v. reduce speed. □ **slow-worm** a snake-like lizard. ■ **slowly** adv.
▷ SYNS adj. **1** UNHURRIED, leisurely, sedate, measured; ponderous, plodding, sluggish. **2** LENGTHY, time-consuming, protracted, long-drawn-out, prolonged. • v. **1** REDUCE SPEED, decelerate, brake. **2** HOLD BACK/UP, delay, retard, set back.

**sludge** n. thick mud.

**slug** n. **1** a small creature like a snail without a shell. **2** a small amount of a drink. **3** a bullet. • v. (**slugged**, **slugging**) inf. hit hard.

**sluggish** adj. slow-moving; not energetic or alert.
▷ SYNS INACTIVE, inert, lifeless, listless, lethargic, torpid, indolent, lazy, slothful, drowsy, sleepy, enervated.

**sluice** n. a sliding gate controlling a flow of water; a channel carrying off water. • v. rinse with water.

**slum** n. a run-down city area.

**slumber** v. & n. sleep.

**slump** n. a sudden great fall in prices or demand. • v. 1 undergo a slump. 2 sit down heavily and limply.
▷ SYNS n. DROP, fall, nosedive, collapse, downturn, slide, decline, decrease. • v. 1 PLUMMET, nosedive, fall, drop, go down, slide. 2 COLLAPSE, sink, fall, flop.

**slung** past and p.p. of SLING.

**slunk** past and p.p. of SLINK.

**slur** v. (slurred, slurring) speak in an unclear way. • n. a damaging allegation.
▷ SYNS n. INSULT, slight, slander, libel, allegation, smear, stain.

**slurp** v. & n. (make) a noisy sucking sound.

**slurry** n. a semi-liquid mixture of water and manure, cement, etc.

**slush** n. partly melted snow.

**slut** n. a slovenly or immoral woman. ■ sluttish adj.

**sly** adj. cunning and deceitful.
▷ SYNS 1 CUNNING, crafty, wily, artful, conniving, scheming, devious, underhand, deceitful. 2 ROGUISH, mischievous, arch, knowing.

**smack** n. 1 a slap; the sound of this. 2 a loud kiss. 3 a single-masted boat. • v. 1 slap. 2 close and part the lips noisily. 3 (smack of) taste of; suggest.

**small** adj. 1 of less than normal size. 2 not great in amount, power, or importance. □ small-holding a small area of leased agricultural land. small hours the period soon after midnight. smallpox a viral disease with

blisters that leave permanent scars. small talk polite conversation on unimportant subjects.
▷ SYNS 1 LITTLE, tiny, short, petite, diminutive, minute, miniature; Scot. wee; inf. pint-sized. 2 SLIGHT, minor, unimportant, trifling, trivial, insignificant, inconsequential.

**smarmy** adj. inf. excessively and insincerely friendly.

**smart** adj. 1 neat and elegant; well dressed. 2 inf. intelligent. 3 brisk. • v. give a sharp, stinging pain; feel upset and annoyed. ■ smarten v.
▷ SYNS adj. WELL DRESSED, fashionable, stylish, elegant, chic, neat, spruce, trim, dapper; inf. natty. • v. STING, burn, hurt.

**smash** v. break noisily into pieces; hit or collide with forcefully; destroy or ruin. • n. an act or sound of smashing.
▷ SYNS v. 1 BREAK, shatter, splinter, crack. 2 COLLIDE WITH, crash into, hit, strike, run into. 3 DESTROY, ruin, shatter, devastate, wreck, dash.

**smashing** adj. inf. excellent.

**smattering** n. a slight knowledge; a small amount.

**smear** v. 1 spread with a greasy or dirty substance. 2 damage the reputation of. • n. 1 a mark made by smearing. 2 a slander.
▷ SYNS v. 1 SPREAD, daub, rub, slather, plaster. 2 SMUDGE, streak, mark, soil. 3 SULLY, tarnish, blacken, damage, taint, stain, defame, slander, libel.

**smell** n. 1 the ability to sense things with the nose. 2 an odour. 3 an act of smelling. • v. 1 sense the smell of. 2 give off a smell.

▷ SYNS n. ODOUR, scent, aroma, perfume, fragrance, bouquet; stink, stench, reek; inf. pong.
• v. 1 SCENT, sniff. 2 STINK, reek; inf. pong.

**smelly** adj. having a strong or unpleasant smell.
▷ SYNS FOUL-SMELLING, stinking, rank, malodorous, fetid; lit. noisome.

**smelt** v. extract metal from its ore by heating and melting it.

**smidgen** n. inf. a tiny amount.

**smile** n. a facial expression indicating pleasure or amusement, with the corners of the mouth upturned. • v. give a smile.
▷ SYNS v. BEAM, grin; smirk, simper.

**smirk** n. & v. (give) a smug smile.

**smite** v. (**smote, smitten, smiting**) 1 old use hit hard. 2 (**be smitten**) be strongly attracted to someone.

**smith** n. 1 a worker in metal. 2 a blacksmith.

**smithereens** n.pl. inf. small fragments.

**smithy** n. (pl. **-ies**) a blacksmith's workshop.

**smock** n. a loose shirt-like garment; a loose overall.

**smog** n. fog or haze made worse by atmospheric pollution.

**smoke** n. 1 visible vapour given off by a burning substance. 2 an act of smoking tobacco.
• v. 1 give out smoke. 2 breathe smoke from a cigarette etc. in and out. 3 preserve meat or fish by exposure to smoke.
□ **smokescreen** a thing intended to disguise motives. ■ **smoker** n. **smoky** adj.

**smooch** v. inf. kiss and cuddle.

**smooth** adj. 1 having an even surface; not harsh in sound or taste; moving evenly without bumping; free from difficulties. 2 charming but perhaps insincere. • v. make smooth.
▷ SYNS adj. 1 smooth surfaces: EVEN, level, flat, plane, unwrinkled; glossy, sleek, silky, polished. 2 smooth waters: CALM, still, tranquil, glassy, undisturbed. 3 smooth progress: STEADY, regular, rhythmic, uninterrupted, unbroken, fluid; easy, effortless, trouble-free. 4 a smooth young man: SUAVE, urbane, sophisticated, debonair, courteous, gracious, glib, slick; inf. smarmy.

**smoothie** n. 1 a drink made of fruit puréed with milk, yogurt, or ice cream. 2 inf. a charming and confident man.

**smote** past of SMITE.

**smother** v. 1 suffocate or stifle. 2 cover thickly.
▷ SYNS 1 SUFFOCATE, stifle, asphyxiate, choke. 2 SMEAR, spread, cover, plaster.

**smoulder** (US **smolder**) v. 1 burn slowly with smoke but no flame. 2 show silent or suppressed anger etc.

**SMS** abbr. Short Message Service, used to send and receive text messages on mobile phones.

**smudge** n. a dirty or blurred mark. • v. make or become blurred or smeared.
▷ SYNS n. MARK, spot, smear, streak, stain, blotch, splotch.

**smug** adj. (**smugger, smuggest**) irritatingly pleased with yourself.
▷ SYNS SELF-SATISFIED, complacent, pleased with yourself, superior.

**smuggle** v. convey goods illegally into or out of a country; convey secretly. ■ **smuggler** n.

**smut** n. **1** a small flake of soot or dirt. **2** indecent pictures, stories, etc. ■ **smutty** adj.

**snack** n. a small or casual meal.

**snag** n. **1** a problem. **2** a jagged projection; a tear caused by this. • v. (**snagged**, **snagging**) catch or tear on a snag.
▷ SYNS n. CATCH, drawback, hitch, stumbling block, obstacle, disadvantage, inconvenience, problem, complication.

**snail** n. a soft-bodied creature with a shell.

**snake** n. a reptile with a long narrow body and no legs. • v. move in a winding course.

**snap** v. (**snapped**, **snapping**) break with a sharp sound; (of an animal) make a sudden bite; open or close briskly or with a sharp sound; speak suddenly and irritably. • n. **1** a snapping sound or movement. **2** a snapshot. • adj. done or happening at short notice. □ **snapshot** an informal photo.
▷ SYNS v. **1** BREAK, fracture, splinter, crack. **2** BARK, snarl, growl; inf. jump down someone's throat.

**snappy** adj. (**-ier**, **-iest**) inf. **1** irritable. **2** neat and stylish. **3** quick.

**snare** n. a trap with a loop of wire that pulls tight. • v. catch or trap.
▷ SYNS n. TRAP, wire, noose. • v. TRAP, ensnare, catch.

**snarl** v. **1** growl with bared teeth; say aggressively. **2** become entangled. • n. an act of snarling.

**snatch** v. seize quickly or eagerly. • n. an act of snatching; a fragment of music or talk.
▷ SYNS v. SEIZE, grab, take hold of, pluck, clutch at.

**snazzy** adj. (**-ier**, **-iest**) inf. stylish.

**sneak** v. **1** move, convey, or obtain furtively. **2** inf. report another's wrongdoings. • n. a telltale. ■ **sneakily** adv. **sneaky** adj.
▷ SYNS v. **1** CREEP, steal, tiptoe, slip, slide, slink, sidle. **2** TELL TALES, inform; inf. tell, rat, grass.

**sneaker** n. a soft shoe worn for sports or casual occasions.

**sneaking** adj. **1** secret. **2** (of a feeling) staying in the mind.
▷ SYNS **1** SECRET, private, hidden, concealed, undisclosed, unexpressed. **2** *a sneaking suspicion*: NIGGLING, nagging, lingering, persistent.

**sneer** n. a scornful smile or remark. • v. smile or speak scornfully.
▷ SYNS v. SMIRK, snigger; scoff, scorn, disdain, mock, jeer at, ridicule, deride, insult.

**sneeze** n. & v. (give) a sudden involuntary expulsion of air through the nose.

**snide** adj. sneering slyly.

**sniff** v. **1** draw air audibly through the nose. **2** (**sniff around**) inf. investigate secretly. **3** (**sniff out**) inf. discover. • n. an act of sniffing.

**sniffle** v. sniff slightly or repeatedly. • n. this act or sound.

**snigger** v. & n. (give) a sly giggle.
▷ SYNS TITTER, giggle; sneer, smirk.

**snip** v. (**snipped**, **snipping**) cut with small quick strokes. • n. **1** an act of snipping. **2** inf. a bargain.

**snipe** n. (pl. **snipe** or **snipes**) a wading bird. • v. fire shots from a hiding place; make sly critical remarks. ■ **sniper** n.

**snippet** n. a small piece.
▷ SYNS BIT, piece, scrap, fragment, particle, shred; excerpt, extract.

**snivel** v. (**snivelled, snivelling**; US **sniveled**) cry; complain in a whining way.
▷ SYNS WHIMPER, whine, weep, cry, sob; inf. grizzle, blub, blubber.

**snob** n. a person with an exaggerated respect for social position or wealth.
■ **snobbery** n.

**snobbish** adj. typical of a snob.
▷ SYNS ELITIST, snobby, superior, supercilious; arrogant, haughty, disdainful, condescending; pretentious, affected; inf. snooty, stuck-up, hoity-toity.

**snood** n. a hairnet worn at the back of a woman's head.

**snooker** n. a game played on a table, with 21 balls to be pocketed in a set order.

**snoop** v. inf. investigate secretly.

**snooty** adj. (**-ier, -iest**) inf. snobbishly contemptuous.

**snooze** inf. n. & v. (take) a nap.

**snore** n. a snorting sound made during sleep. • v. make such sounds.

**snorkel** n. a tube for a swimmer to breathe through while under water. ■ **snorkelling** (US **snorkeling**) n.

**snort** n. & v. (make) an explosive sound made by forcing breath through the nose.

**snout** n. an animal's long projecting nose or nose and jaws.

**snow** n. frozen water vapour in the atmosphere that falls in light white flakes. • v. 1 fall as snow. 2 (**be snowed under**) be overwhelmed with work etc. □ **snowboarding** the sport of sliding downhill over snow on a single short, broad ski. **snowdrift** a bank of deep snow heaped up by the wind. **snowdrop** a plant bearing drooping white flowers in late winter. **snowman** a human figure made of compressed snow. **snowplough** (US **snowplow**) a device or vehicle for clearing roads of snow. ■ **snowy** adj.

**snowball** n. a ball of packed snow. • v. increase in size or intensity.

**snub** v. (**snubbed, snubbing**) reject or ignore contemptuously. • n. an act of snubbing. • adj. (of the nose) short and turned up at the end.
▷ SYNS v. IGNORE, shun, rebuff, spurn, cut, slight, cold-shoulder, insult, affront.

**snuff** n. powdered tobacco for sniffing up the nostrils. • v. put out a candle.

**snuffle** v. breathe with a noisy sniff. • n. a snuffling sound.

**snug** adj. 1 cosy. 2 close-fitting. • n. a small cosy room in a pub.
▷ SYNS adj. 1 COSY, comfortable, warm, homely; inf. comfy. 2 CLOSE-FITTING, tight, skintight.

**snuggle** v. settle into a warm, comfortable position.
▷ SYNS NESTLE, cuddle, curl up, nuzzle.

**so** adv. 1 to such a great extent. 2 to the same extent. 3 similarly. 4 thus. • conj. 1 therefore. 2 with the aim or result that. □ **so-and-so** 1 a person whose name you

**soak → sociology**

do not know. **2** a disliked person. **so-called** wrongly called by the term or name specified. **so-so** mediocre.

**soak** v. place or lie in liquid so as to become thoroughly wet; (of liquid) penetrate; absorb.
▷ SYNS **1** DRENCH, wet through, saturate. **2** STEEP, immerse, souse, marinate. **3** PERMEATE, penetrate, seep into.

**soaking** adj. very wet.
▷ SYNS DRENCHED, soaked, sodden, saturated, sopping, wringing.

**soap** n. **1** a substance used for washing things. **2** inf. a soap opera. • v. wash with soap. □ **soap opera** a television or radio serial dealing with the daily lives of a group of characters. ∎ **soapy** adj.

**soar** v. rise high, esp. in flight.
▷ SYNS **1** FLY, take flight, take off, ascend, climb, rise. **2** RISE, increase, rocket, spiral.

**sob** v. (**sobbed**, **sobbing**) cry with loud gasps. • n. a sound of sobbing.
▷ SYNS v. WEEP, cry, snivel, howl, bawl; inf. blub, blubber.

**sober** adj. **1** not drunk. **2** serious. **3** (of colour) not bright. • v. make or become sober. ∎ **sobriety** n.
▷ SYNS adj. **1** CLEAR-HEADED; teetotal, abstinent; inf. on the wagon. **2** SERIOUS, solemn, sensible, staid, grave, level-headed, down-to-earth. **3** SOMBRE, dark, subdued; drab, plain.

**soccer** n. football.

**sociable** adj. fond of company; friendly and welcoming.
▷ SYNS FRIENDLY, affable, cordial, neighbourly, companionable, gregarious, convivial, communicative, genial, outgoing.

**social** adj. **1** of society. **2** needing the company of others. **3** (of an activity) in which people meet each other for pleasure. **4** (of animals) living in organized communities. • n. a social gathering. □ **social security** money provided by the state for people with little or no income. **social services** welfare services provided by the state. **social worker** a person trained to help people with social problems.

**socialism** n. the theory that a country's resources, industries, and transport should be owned and managed by the state. ∎ **socialist** n.

**socialite** n. a person prominent in fashionable society.

**socialize** (or **-ise**) v. mix with other people for pleasure.
▷ SYNS MIX, mingle, fraternize, consort, hobnob.

**society** n. **1** an ordered community; a particular system of ordering the community. **2** an organization or club. **3** wealthy and fashionable people. **4** company.
▷ SYNS **1** MANKIND, humanity, civilization, the public, the people, the population, the community. **2** COMMUNITY, culture, civilization. **3** HIGH SOCIETY, aristocracy, gentry, nobility, upper classes, elite, beau monde; inf. upper crust. **4** ASSOCIATION, club, group, circle, fraternity, league, union, alliance.

**sociology** n. the study of human society. ∎ **sociological** adj. **sociologist** n.

**sock** n. **1** a knitted garment for the foot. **2** inf. a hard blow. • v. inf. hit hard.

**socket** n. a hollow into which something fits.

**sod** n. turf; a piece of this.

**soda** n. **1** (also **soda water**) carbonated water. **2** a compound of sodium.

**sodden** adj. very wet.

**sodium** n. a soft silver-white metallic element.

**sodomy** n. anal intercourse.

**sofa** n. a long upholstered seat with a back.

**soft** adj. **1** easy to mould, cut, compress, or fold. **2** not rough in texture. **3** quiet and gentle. **4** subtle. **5** not strict. **6** (of drinks) non-alcoholic. **7** (of a drug) unlikely to cause addiction. □ **software** computer programs.
▷ SYNS **1** PLIABLE, pliant; squashy, spongy, pulpy, doughy. **2** SMOOTH, velvety, fleecy, downy, furry, silky, silken. **3** soft light/voices: LOW, dim, faint, subdued, muted; hushed, whispered, murmured, quiet.

**soften** v. make or become soft or softer.
▷ SYNS ALLEVIATE, ease, relieve, soothe, cushion, temper, mitigate, assuage, moderate, diminish, blunt, calm, deaden.

**soggy** adj. (**-ier**, **-iest**) very wet and soft.

**soil** n. **1** the upper layer of the earth. **2** a nation's territory. • v. make dirty.
▷ SYNS n. EARTH, ground, loam, dirt, turf. • v. DIRTY, stain, muddy, smear, smudge.

**soirée** n. an evening social gathering.

**sojourn** n. a temporary stay. • v. stay temporarily.

**solace** v. & n. (give) comfort in distress.

**solar** adj. of or from the sun. □ **solar plexus** a network of nerves at the pit of the stomach. **solar system** the sun together with the planets etc. in orbit around it.

**solarium** n. (pl. **-riums** or **-ria**) a room equipped with sunbeds.

**sold** past and p.p. of SELL.

**solder** n. a soft alloy used for joining metals. • v. join with solder.

**soldier** n. a member of an army. • v. **1** serve as a soldier. **2** (**soldier on**) inf. persevere doggedly.

**sole** n. **1** the underside of a foot. **2** the underside of a shoe etc. **3** an edible flatfish. • adj. **1** one and only. **2** belonging or restricted to one person or group. • v. put a sole on a shoe. ■ **solely** adv.

**solemn** adj. **1** formal and dignified. **2** serious. ■ **solemnity** n.
▷ SYNS **1** DIGNIFIED, ceremonial, stately, formal, majestic, imposing, grand. **2** SERIOUS, grave, sober, sombre, unsmiling. **3** SINCERE, genuine, earnest, honest, heartfelt.

**solemnize** v. perform a ceremony; mark with a ceremony.

**solenoid** n. a coil of wire magnetized by electric current.

**solicit** v. **1** try to obtain. **2** (of a prostitute) approach someone.

**solicitor** n. a lawyer who advises clients and instructs barristers.

**solicitous** adj. anxious about a person's well-being.
■ **solicitude** n.
▷ SYNS CONCERNED, caring, attentive, considerate; anxious, worried.

**solid** adj. **1** firm and stable in shape. **2** strongly built. **3** not hollow. **4** consisting of the same substance throughout. **5** (of time) uninterrupted. **6** three-dimensional. **7** reliable. • n. a solid substance, object, or food.
■ **solidity** n.
▷ SYNS adj. **1** FIRM, hard, solidified, set. **2** WELL BUILT, sound, substantial, strong, sturdy, durable. **3** WELL FOUNDED, sound, valid, reliable, reasonable, logical, cogent, convincing.

**solidarity** n. unity resulting from common aims or interests etc.
▷ SYNS UNITY, unanimity, like-mindedness, camaraderie, team spirit, harmony.

**solidify** v. make or become solid.
▷ SYNS HARDEN, set, thicken, congeal, cake.

**soliloquy** n. (pl. **-ies**) a speech made aloud to yourself.

**solitaire** n. **1** a gem set by itself. **2** a game for one person played on a board with pegs.

**solitary** adj. alone; isolated; single.
▷ SYNS **1** LONELY, friendless, alone, on your own; reclusive, cloistered. **2** REMOTE, out of the way, isolated, cut-off, unfrequented, in the middle of nowhere. **3** LONE, single, sole, by itself.

**solitude** n. being solitary.

**solo** n. (pl. **-os**) music for a single performer; an unaccompanied

performance etc. • adj. & adv. for or done by one person.
■ **soloist** n.

**solstice** n. either of the times (about 21 June and 22 Dec.) when the sun reaches its highest or lowest point in the sky at noon.

**soluble** adj. **1** able to be dissolved. **2** able to be solved.

**solution** n. **1** a liquid containing something dissolved; the process of dissolving. **2** a way of solving a problem; the answer found.
▷ SYNS ANSWER, result, resolution, panacea, way out, key, explanation.

**solve** v. find the answer to.
▷ SYNS RESOLVE, answer, find the key to, work out, fathom, decipher, clear up, get to the bottom of, unravel.

**solvent** adj. having more money than you owe. • n. a liquid used for dissolving something.
■ **solvency** n.

**sombre** (US **somber**) adj. dark or gloomy.
▷ SYNS **1** DARK, dull, drab, sober, funereal. **2** GLOOMY, depressed, sad, melancholy, doleful, mournful, lugubrious, solemn, serious, sober.

**sombrero** n. (pl. **-os**) a hat with a very wide brim.

**some** adj. **1** an unspecified quantity or number of; unknown or unspecified: approximate. **2** considerable. **3** remarkable. • pron. some people or things. □ **somebody** someone. **somehow** in an unknown or unspecified way. **someone** an unknown or unspecified person; a person of importance. **something** an unspecified or unknown thing or amount. **sometime** at an unspecified or unknown time; former. **somewhat** to some extent. **somewhere** in or to an unspecified or unknown place.

**somersault** n. a leap or roll turning your body upside down and over. • v. move in this way.

**sometimes** adv. occasionally.
▷ SYNS OCCASIONALLY, now and then, from time to time, once in a while, every so often.

**somnolent** adj. sleepy.

**son** n. a male in relation to his parents. □ **son-in-law** the husband of your daughter.

**sonar** n. a device for detecting objects under water by reflection of sound waves.

**sonata** n. a musical composition for one instrument, usu. in several movements.

**song** n. a set of words to be sung; singing. □ **songbird** a bird with a musical song.

**sonic** adj. of sound waves.

**sonnet** n. a poem of 14 lines.

**sonorous** adj. deep and resonant.
▷ SYNS DEEP, rich, full, resonant, clear, ringing.

**soon** adv. **1** in or after a short time. **2** (**sooner**) rather.
▷ SYNS SHORTLY, in the near future, before long, in a minute/moment.

**soot** n. a black powdery substance produced by burning. ■ **sooty** adj.

**soothe** v. calm; ease pain or distress. ■ **soothing** adj.
▷ SYNS EASE, assuage, alleviate, allay, moderate, mitigate, palliate, soften, lessen, reduce.

**soothsayer** n. a prophet.

▷ SYNS SEER, prophet, oracle.

**sop** n. a concession to pacify an angry person. • v. (**sopped, sopping**) soak up liquid.

**sophisticated** adj. **1** experienced in matters of culture or fashion. **2** highly developed and complex. ■ **sophistication** n.
▷ SYNS **1** WORLDLY-WISE, worldly, experienced, suave, urbane, cultured, cultivated, polished, refined, elegant, stylish, cosmopolitan. **2** ADVANCED, modern, state-of-the-art.

**sophistry** n. clever but misleading arguments. ■ **sophist** n.

**soporific** adj. causing drowsiness or sleep.

**sopping** adj. drenched.

**soppy** adj. inf. too sentimental.

**soprano** n. (pl. **-os**) the highest singing voice.

**sorbet** n. a water ice.

**sorcerer** n. (fem. **sorceress**) a magician.
▷ SYNS MAGICIAN, wizard, warlock, necromancer, magus.

**sorcery** n. the use of magic.
▷ SYNS MAGIC, black arts, witchcraft, wizardry, spells.

**sordid** adj. dishonest or immoral; dirty.
▷ SYNS SLEAZY, seedy, unsavoury, tawdry, cheap, degenerate, dishonourable, disreputable, discreditable, contemptible, ignominious, shameful, immoral.

**sore** adj. painful or aching. • n. a sore place. ■ **soreness** n.
▷ SYNS adj. PAINFUL, aching, hurting, tender, inflamed, raw, smarting, throbbing, bruised, wounded, injured. • n. WOUND, scrape, abrasion, cut, laceration,

graze, boil, abscess, lesion, swelling.

**sorely** adv. very much; severely.

**sorrow** n. deep distress caused by loss, disappointment, etc.; a cause of this. • v. grieve.
■ sorrowful adj.
▷ SYNS n. **1** SADNESS, unhappiness, grief, misery, distress, heartache, heartbreak, anguish, wretchedness, dejection, depression, mourning. **2** TROUBLE, woe, misfortune, affliction, trial, tribulation.

**sorry** adj. **1** feeling sympathy. **2** feeling regret. **3** wretched or pitiful.
▷ SYNS **1** SYMPATHETIC, full of pity, compassionate, moved. **2** REGRETFUL, apologetic, repentant, penitent, remorseful, contrite, ashamed, shamefaced. **3** SAD, distressed, sorrowful, upset.

**sort** n. **1** a kind or category. **2** inf. a person of a specified nature. • v. **1** arrange in groups. **2** (**sort out**) solve a problem.
▷ SYNS n. KIND, type, variety, class, category, style, genre, breed, make, brand. • v. **1** CLASSIFY, class, categorize, catalogue, grade, rank, group, arrange, order, organize, systematize. **2** RESOLVE, settle, clear up, solve, fix, deal with.

**sortie** n. an attack by troops from a besieged place; a flight by an aircraft on a military operation.
▷ SYNS SALLY, foray, charge, raid, attack.

**SOS** n. an international distress signal; an urgent appeal for help.

**sotto voce** adv. in an undertone.

**soufflé** n. a light dish made with beaten egg white.

**sought** past and p.p. of SEEK.

**souk** n. a market in Muslim countries.

**soul** n. **1** the spiritual or immortal element of a person. **2** a person's inner nature. **3** emotional energy or power. **4** someone embodying a quality: *the soul of discretion.* **5** a person. **6** a kind of music with elements of gospel and rhythm and blues.
▷ SYNS **1** SPIRIT, psyche, inner self. **2** EMBODIMENT, personification, incarnation, essence, epitome.

**soulful** adj. showing deep feeling.

**soulless** adj. lacking interest or individuality; lacking feeling.

**sound** n. **1** vibrations in the air sensed by the ear. **2** a thing that can be heard. **3** a narrow stretch of water. • v. **1** make a sound. **2** give a specified impression. **3** (**sound off**) express opinions forcefully. **4** (**sound out**) ask someone what they think. **5** test the depth of water. • adj. **1** in good condition. **2** (of reasoning) valid. **3** (of sleep) deep. □ **sound barrier** the point at which an aircraft reaches the speed of sound. **sound bite** a short memorable extract from a speech. **soundtrack** the sound accompaniment to a film.
■ soundly adv. soundproof adj.
▷ SYNS **1** RESOUND, reverberate, resonate. **2** *sound the alarm:* OPERATE, set off, ring. **3** *sounds like it:* APPEAR, seem, strike you as. • adj. **1** HEALTHY, fit, in good shape; solid, substantial, sturdy, well built, undamaged. **2** WELL FOUNDED, valid, reasonable, logical, weighty, reliable.

**sounding** n. **1** a measurement of the depth of water. **2** (**soundings**) information found out before action is taken.

**soup** n. liquid food made from meat, vegetables, etc.

**sour** adj. **1** tasting sharp. **2** unpleasantly stale. **3** resentful or angry. • v. make or become sour.
▷ SYNS adj. **1** ACID, tart, bitter, sharp, vinegary. **2** BAD, off, stale, rancid, curdled. **3** EMBITTERED, resentful, bitter, bad-tempered, disagreeable, angry.

**source** n. **1** the place from which something comes or is obtained. **2** a river's starting point. **3** a person, book etc. supplying information.
▷ SYNS ORIGIN, derivation, start, beginning, root, author, originator.

**souse** v. **1** soak. **2** (**soused**) pickled.

**south** n. **1** the point or direction to the right of a person facing east. **2** the southern part of a place. • adj. & adv. **1** towards or facing the south. **2** (of wind) from the south. ■ **southerly** adj. & adv. **southward** adj. & adv. **southwards** adv.

**south-east** n. the point or direction midway between south and east. ■ **south-easterly** adj. & n. **south-eastern** adj.

**southern** adj. of or in the south.

**southerner** n. a person from the south of a region.

**south-west** n. the point or direction midway between south and west. ■ **south-westerly** adj. & n. **south-western** adj.

**souvenir** n. a thing kept as a reminder of a person, place, or event.

**sou'wester** n. a waterproof hat with a broad flap at the back.

**sovereign** n. **1** a king or queen who is the supreme ruler of a country. **2** a former British coin worth one pound. • adj. supreme; (of a state) independent. ■ **sovereignty** n.
▷ SYNS n. RULER, monarch, king, queen, emperor, empress, tsar, potentate. • adj. **1** SUPREME, absolute, unlimited; chief, principal, dominant, predominant, ruling. **2** INDEPENDENT, self-ruling, self-governing, autonomous.

**sow**¹ v. **1** plant seed by scattering it on the earth. **2** spread something unwelcome.
▷ SYNS PLANT, scatter, disperse, strew, distribute.

**sow**² n. an adult female pig.

**soya bean** n. an edible bean that is high in protein.

**soy sauce** n. a sauce made with fermented soya beans.

**spa** n. **1** a place with a health-giving mineral spring. **2** a place offering health and beauty treatments.

**space** n. **1** an unoccupied area. **2** the universe beyond the earth's atmosphere. **3** the whole expanse in which all things exist and move. **4** an interval of time. • v. arrange with gaps in between. □ **spacecraft** a vehicle for travelling in space. **spaceship** a manned spacecraft.
▷ SYNS n. **1** ROOM, capacity, area, volume, expanse, extent, scope, latitude, margin, leeway. **2** OUTER SPACE, the universe, the galaxy, the solar system.

**spacious** adj. providing plenty of space.
▷ SYNS ROOMY, commodious, capacious, sizeable, large, big, ample; extensive, sweeping, rolling.

**spade** n. a tool for digging, with a broad metal blade on a handle.
□ spadework hard preparatory work.

**spaghetti** pl. n. pasta made in long strings.

**spam** n. unwanted email sent to many people. • v. (**spamming**, **spammed**) send unwanted email to many people. .

**span** n. 1 extent from side to side. 2 duration. 3 a part of a bridge between the uprights.
• v. (**spanned, spanning**) extend across or over.
▷ SYNS n. 1 EXTENT, length, reach, stretch, spread, distance. 2 TIME, duration, period, space, interval. • v. BRIDGE, cross, traverse, pass over.

**spangle** n. a small piece of decorative glittering material.
• v. cover with spangles.

**spaniel** n. a dog with drooping ears and a silky coat.

**spank** v. slap on the buttocks.

**spanner** n. a tool for gripping and turning a nut or bolt.

**spar** v. (**sparred, sparring**) 1 practice boxing. 2 argue. • n. a strong pole used to support a ship's sails.

**spare** adj. 1 additional to what is needed. 2 not in use or occupied. 3 thin. • n. an extra thing kept in reserve. • v. 1 let someone have. 2 refrain from killing or harming.
▷ SYNS adj. EXTRA, additional, supplementary, auxiliary, reserve; surplus, superfluous. • v. 1 GIVE,

part with, provide, afford, do without. 2 PARDON, let off, reprieve, release, have mercy.

**sparing** adj. economical.
■ sparingly adv.
▷ SYNS ECONOMICAL, frugal, thrifty, careful, prudent, parsimonious.

**spark** n. 1 a fiery particle. 2 a flash of light produced by an electrical discharge. 3 a trace.
• v. give off sparks. □ spark plug a device which ignites the fuel in an engine.

**sparkle** v. 1 shine with flashes of light. 2 be lively or witty. 3 (**sparkling**) (of drink) fizzy.
• n. a sparkling light.
▷ SYNS v. GLITTER, glint, glisten, twinkle, flicker, flash, shimmer.

**sparkler** n. a hand-held firework that gives out sparks.

**sparrow** n. a small brownish-grey bird.

**sparse** adj. thinly scattered.
▷ SYNS SCANTY, scattered, meagre, scarce, few and far between, in short supply.

**spartan** adj. not comfortable or luxurious.
▷ SYNS AUSTERE, harsh, frugal, stringent, rigorous, strict, severe, ascetic, abstemious.

**spasm** n. a strong involuntary contraction of a muscle; a sudden brief spell of activity or emotion etc.
▷ SYNS 1 CONTRACTION, convulsion, cramp, twitch. 2 FIT, paroxysm, attack, bout, seizure, burst.

**spasmodic** adj. occurring in brief irregular bursts.
■ spasmodically adv.
▷ SYNS INTERMITTENT, fitful, irregular, sporadic, erratic, periodic.

**spastic** offens. adj. of cerebral palsy. • n. a person with cerebral palsy.

**spat¹** past & p.p. of **SPIT**.

**spat²** n. inf. a petty quarrel.

**spate** n. a number of similar things coming one after another.
▷ SYNS SERIES, succession, run, string, epidemic, outbreak, wave.

**spatial** adj. of or existing in space. ■ spatially adv.

**spatter** v. scatter with or fall in small drops. • n. a spray or splash.

**spatula** n. a knife-like tool with a broad blunt blade.

**spawn** n. the eggs of fish, frogs, etc. • v. 1 deposit spawn. 2 generate.

**spay** v. sterilize a female animal by removing the ovaries.

**speak** v. 1 say something. 2 communicate or be able to communicate in a particular language.
▷ SYNS 1 SAY, utter, state, voice, express, pronounce, articulate, enunciate. 2 TALK, converse, communicate, chat, gossip.

**speaker** n. 1 a person who speaks. 2 a loudspeaker.
▷ SYNS SPEECH-MAKER, lecturer, orator.

**spear** n. a weapon with a long shaft and pointed tip; a pointed shoot or stem. • v. pierce with a spear or other pointed object. ☐ spearhead a person or group leading an attack or movement; lead an attack or movement.
▷ SYNS n. JAVELIN, lance, pike, assegai, harpoon.

**spearmint** n. a type of mint used in cooking.

**special** adj. 1 better than or different from usual. 2 for a particular purpose or person. ■ specially adv.
▷ SYNS 1 EXCEPTIONAL, unusual, remarkable, out of the ordinary, outstanding, unique. 2 SPECIFIC, particular, individual, distinctive, distinct.

**specialist** n. an expert in a particular branch of a subject.
▷ SYNS EXPERT, authority, professional, connoisseur, master.

**speciality** n. (pl. -ies) a skill or subject in which someone is an expert; a product for which a person or region is famous.

**specialize** (or -ise) v. 1 be or become a specialist. 2 adapt for a particular purpose.

**species** n. (pl. **species**) a group of similar animals or plants which can interbreed.
▷ SYNS SORT, kind, type, variety, class, category, group, genus, breed, genre.

**specific** adj. particular; precise and clear. • n. a precise detail. ■ specifically adv.
▷ SYNS adj. 1 PARTICULAR, specified, fixed, set, distinct, definite. 2 CLEAR-CUT, unambiguous, unequivocal, exact, precise, explicit, express, detailed.

**specification** n. specifying; details describing a thing to be made or done.

**specify** v. (**specified, specifying**) identify precisely; include in specifications.
▷ SYNS STATE, name, stipulate, identify, define, set out, itemize, detail, list, spell out, enumerate.

**specimen** n. a part or individual taken as an example or for examination or testing.

▷ SYNS SAMPLE, example, illustration, instance; model, prototype, pilot.

**specious** adj. seeming reasonable, but in fact wrong.

**speck** n. a small spot or particle.
▷ SYNS SPOT, fleck, dot, speckle; particle, bit, atom, iota, grain, trace.

**speckle** n. a small patch of colour. ■ **speckled** adj.

**spectacle** n. 1 a visually striking performance or display. 2 (**spectacles**) a pair of lenses in a frame, worn in front of the eyes to correct vision.
▷ SYNS 1 SIGHT, vision, scene, picture. 2 DISPLAY, show, exhibition, pageant, parade, extravaganza.

**spectacular** adj. very impressive or striking. • n. a spectacular performance.
▷ SYNS adj. IMPRESSIVE, magnificent, splendid, breathtaking, glorious, dazzling, sensational, stunning, dramatic, remarkable; striking, picturesque.

**spectator** n. a person who watches a game, incident, etc.
▷ SYNS VIEWER, observer, onlooker, watcher, witness.

**spectre** (US **specter**) n. a ghost; a haunting fear.

**spectrum** n. (pl. **-tra**) bands of colour or sound forming a series according to their wavelengths; an entire range of ideas etc.

**speculate** v. 1 form opinions by guessing. 2 buy in the hope of making a profit. ■ **speculation** n. **speculator** n.
▷ SYNS CONJECTURE, theorize, hypothesize, guess, surmise; reflect, think, wonder, muse.

**speculative** adj. based on theory or guesswork rather than knowledge.
▷ SYNS CONJECTURAL, theoretical, hypothetical, academic, tentative, unproven.

**speech** n. 1 speaking or the ability to speak. 2 a formal talk given to an audience.
▷ SYNS 1 SPEAKING, talking, communication, conversation, dialogue. 2 DICTION, articulation, enunciation, elocution, pronunciation. 3 TALK, lecture, address, discourse, oration, sermon.

**speechless** adj. unable to speak due to shock or emotion.

**speed** n. 1 rate of movement or operation. 2 a fast rate. • v. 1 move quickly. 2 (**speed up**) accelerate. 3 drive at an illegal speed. □ **speedboat** a fast motorboat. **speedometer** a device in a vehicle indicating its speed. **speedway** a form of motorcycle racing on a dirt track. ■ **speedy** adj.
▷ SYNS n. RATE, tempo, momentum, velocity, pace; rapidity, swiftness, haste, hurry, alacrity, promptness.

**spell** v. 1 give the letters forming a word in correct order. 2 mean or have as a result. 3 (**spell out**) state explicitly. • n. 1 a short period of time. 2 words spoken to make a piece of magic work.
▷ SYNS n. 1 PERIOD, interval, stretch, run, patch. 2 CHARM, incantation, magic formula; magic, sorcery.

**spellbound** adj. entranced.
▷ SYNS ENTHRALLED, entranced, riveted, rapt, transfixed, captivated, bewitched, mesmerized.

**spend** v. **1** pay money to buy something. **2** pass time. **3** use up. □ **spendthrift** a person who spends money irresponsibly.
▷ SYNS **1** PAY OUT, expend, disburse; inf. splurge. **2** PASS, occupy, fill, take up, while away.

**sperm** n. (pl. **sperms** or **sperm**) **1** semen. **2** a spermatozoon.

**spermatozoon** n. (pl. **-zoa**) the fertilizing cell of a male animal.

**spermicide** n. a contraceptive substance that kills sperm.

**spew** v. **1** pour out. **2** inf. vomit.

**sphere** n. **1** a perfectly round solid figure or object. **2** an area of activity or interest.
■ **spherical** adj.
▷ SYNS **1** GLOBE, ball, orb, globule. **2** AREA, field, range, scope, extent, compass.

**sphincter** n. a ring of muscle controlling an opening in the body.

**sphinx** n. an ancient Egyptian statue with a lion's body and human or animal head.

**spice** n. **1** a strong-tasting substance for flavouring food. **2** interest or excitement.
• v. flavour with spice.
▷ SYNS n. FLAVOURING, seasoning, condiment.

**spick and span** adj. neat and clean.

**spicy** adj. strongly flavoured with spice.
▷ SYNS PIQUANT, tangy, hot, peppery, spiced, seasoned, tasty, strong.

**spider** n. an eight-legged insect-like animal. ■ **spidery** adj.

**spiel** n. inf. a glib persuasive speech.

**spigot** n. a small peg or plug.

**spike** n. a thin, pointed piece of metal, wood, etc. • v. **1** impale on a spike. **2** inf. secretly add alcohol to a drink. ■ **spiky** adj.

**spill** v. (**spilt** or **spilled**, **spilling**) cause or allow to run over the edge of a container; spread outside an allotted space. • n. **1** an amount spilled. **2** a thin strip of wood or paper for lighting a fire.
■ **spillage** n.
▷ SYNS v. POUR, flow, overflow, run, slop, slosh.

**spin** v. **1** turn rapidly on an axis. **2** draw out and twist into threads; make yarn in this way. **3** (**spin out**) prolong. • n. **1** a spinning movement. **2** inf. a short drive for pleasure. **3** a favourable slant given to a news story. □ **spin doctor** a person employed to give a favourable interpretation of events to the media. **spin-off** an incidental benefit.
▷ SYNS v. REVOLVE, rotate, turn, circle, whirl, gyrate.

**spina bifida** n. a condition in which part of the spinal cord is exposed, often causing paralysis.

**spinach** n. a vegetable with green leaves.

**spinal** adj. of the spine.

**spindle** n. **1** a rod used in spinning. **2** a rod around which something revolves.

**spindly** adj. long or tall and thin.

**spine** n. **1** the backbone. **2** the part of a book where the pages are hinged. **3** a needle-like projection on a plant or animal.
■ **spiny** adj.
▷ SYNS **1** BACKBONE, spinal column, vertebrae. **2** NEEDLE, spike, barb, quill.

**spineless** adj. having no spine; lacking determination.

**spinney** n. (pl. **-eys**) a thicket.

**spinster** n. an unmarried woman.

**spiral** adj. forming a continuous curve round a central point or axis. • n. **1** a spiral line or thing. **2** a continuous, usu. harmful, increase or decrease. • v. **1** move in a spiral course. **2** increase or decrease continuously.

▷ SYNS adj. COILED, corkscrew, winding, twisting, whorled, helical. • n. COIL, twist, whorl, corkscrew, helix.

**spire** n. a tall pointed structure on a church tower.

**spirit** n. **1** a person's character and feelings, thought to survive after death. **2** a ghost. **3** typical character or quality. **4** a person's mood. **5** courage and determination. **6** the intended meaning of a law etc. **7** strong distilled alcoholic drink. • v. (**spirited**, **spiriting**) take away rapidly and secretly. □ **spirit level** a sealed glass tube containing a bubble in liquid, used to test that a surface is level.

▷ SYNS n. **1** SOUL, psyche, inner self, mind. **2** GHOST, phantom, spectre, apparition. **3** *the spirit of the age:* ETHOS, essence, quintessence; atmosphere, mood, feeling.

**spirited** adj. courageous and determined.

▷ SYNS COURAGEOUS, brave, valiant, heroic, plucky, determined, resolute, vigorous, lively, vivacious, animated, energetic.

**spiritual** adj. **1** of the human spirit or soul. **2** of religion or religious belief. • n. a religious song associated with black Christians of the southern US.
■ **spirituality** n. **spiritually** adv.

▷ SYNS adj. **1** NON-MATERIAL, incorporeal, ethereal, intangible, other-worldly. **2** RELIGIOUS, sacred, divine, holy, ecclesiastic, devotional.

**spiritualism** n. attempted communication with spirits of the dead. ■ **spiritualist** n.

**spit** v. **1** eject saliva, food, etc. from the mouth. **2** (of rain) fall lightly. • n. **1** saliva; an act of spitting. **2** a metal spike holding meat while it is roasted. **3** a narrow strip of land projecting into the sea.

▷ SYNS v. EXPECTORATE, hawk. • n. SPITTLE, saliva, sputum.

**spite** n. malicious desire to hurt or annoy someone. • v. hurt or annoy from spite. □ **in spite of** not being prevented by.

▷ SYNS n. MALICE, ill will, malevolence, venom, hostility, resentment, rancour, vengefulness, vindictiveness.

**spiteful** adj. deliberately hurtful. ■ **spitefully** adv.

▷ SYNS MALICIOUS, malevolent, venomous, malign, hostile, resentful, snide, rancorous, vengeful, vindictive, inf. bitchy, catty.

**spittle** n. saliva.

**splash** v. **1** cause liquid to fall on something in scattered drops; move or fall with such drops. **2** (**splash out**) spend extravagantly. • n. **1** splashing. **2** a patch of colour; a small quantity of liquid.

▷ SYNS v. **1** SPATTER, sprinkle, spray, shower, splatter, squirt, slosh, slop. **2** PADDLE, wade, wallow.

**3** BLAZON, display, plaster, publicize, broadcast, trumpet.

**splatter** v. splash or spatter.

**splay** v. spread out wide apart.

**spleen** n. **1** an organ involved in maintaining the proper condition of the blood. **2** bad temper.

**splendid** adj. very impressive; excellent.

▷ SYNS MAGNIFICENT, imposing, superb, grand, sumptuous, resplendent, opulent, luxurious, plush, de luxe, palatial, rich, costly, lavish, ornate, gorgeous, glorious, dazzling, elegant, handsome.

**splendour** (US **splendor**) n. a splendid appearance.

▷ SYNS MAGNIFICENCE, grandeur, sumptuousness, opulence, luxury, luxuriousness, richness, elegance.

**splenetic** adj. bad-tempered.

**splice** v. join by interweaving or overlapping the ends.

**splint** n. a rigid support for a broken bone.

**splinter** n. a thin, sharp piece of broken wood etc. • v. break into splinters. □ **splinter group** a small breakaway group.

▷ SYNS SLIVER, fragment, shiver, shard, chip, shred, piece, bit.

**split** v. (**split**, **splitting**) break into parts by force; divide or share; separate. • n. a split thing or place; (**the splits**) a seated position with the legs stretched fully apart.

▷ SYNS v. **1** BREAK, chop, hew, lop, cleave, splinter; rend, rip, tear, slash, slit. **2** DIVIDE, separate. **3** SHARE (OUT), divide up, apportion, distribute, dole out, parcel out, allot, allocate; inf. divvy up. **4** BREAK UP, separate, part; divorce. • n. **1** BREAK, cut, rent,

rip, tear, slash, slit, crack, fissure, breach. **2** DIVISION, rift, schism, rupture, separation, break-up, alienation, estrangement.

**splodge** n. a spot, splash, or smear.

**splutter** v. make a rapid series of spitting sounds; speak or utter incoherently. • n. a spluttering sound.

**spoil** v. **1** make less good or pleasant; (of food) become unfit for eating. **2** harm the character of a child by being indulgent. • n. stolen goods.

▷ SYNS v. **1** DAMAGE, impair, mar, blemish, disfigure, deface, injure, harm, ruin, destroy, wreck. **2** PAMPER, overindulge, mollycoddle, cosset, coddle, baby. **3** GO BAD/OFF, turn, rot, decompose, perish, decay.

**spoiler** n. a device that slows down an aircraft by interrupting the air flow; a similar device on a vehicle, preventing it from being lifted off the road at speed.

**spoilsport** n. a person who spoils others' enjoyment.

▷ SYNS KILLJOY, dog in the manger, misery; inf. wet blanket, party-pooper.

**spoke**¹ n. any of the bars connecting the hub to the rim of a wheel.

**spoke**² past of SPEAK.

**spokesman** (or **spokeswoman**) n. a person who speaks on behalf of a group.

**sponge** n. **1** a sea creature with a soft porous body. **2** a piece of a light absorbent substance used for washing, padding, etc. **3** a light cake. • v. **1** clean with a sponge. **2** inf. live at the expense of others.

**spongy** adj. porous, absorbent, or compressible.

▷ SYNS SOFT, squashy, cushiony, springy, resilient, elastic; porous, absorbent.

**sponsor** n. **1** a person who provides funds for an artistic or sporting event etc.; a person who promises to give money to a charity if another person completes a task or activity. **2** a person who proposes a new law. • v. be a sponsor for. ■ sponsorship n.

▷ SYNS n. PATRON, backer, promoter, guarantor, supporter. • v. FINANCE, back, fund, subsidize; promote, support; inf. bankroll.

**spontaneous** adj. not caused by outside influences; not rehearsed. ■ spontaneity n.

▷ SYNS UNPLANNED, unpremeditated, unrehearsed, impromptu, extempore, spur-of-the-moment, extemporaneous; voluntary, unforced, unprompted; inf. off-the-cuff.

**spoof** n. inf. a parody.

**spook** n. inf. a ghost. ■ spooky adj.

**spool** n. a reel on which something is wound.

**spoon** n. an eating and cooking utensil with a rounded bowl and a handle. • v. transfer with a spoon. □ spoon-feed feed with a spoon; give excessive help to.

**sporadic** adj. occurring at irregular intervals or in a few places. ■ sporadically adv.

▷ SYNS IRREGULAR, intermittent, scattered, random, infrequent, occasional, isolated, spasmodic.

**spore** n. one of the tiny reproductive cells of fungi, ferns, etc.

**sporran** n. a pouch worn in front of a kilt.

**sport** n. a competitive activity involving physical effort and skill. • v. **1** wear or display prominently. **2** play. □ sports car a small, fast car. sports jacket a man's jacket for informal wear. sportsman (or **sportswoman**) a person who takes part in a sport; a fair and generous person.

▷ SYNS n. **1** GAMES, physical exercise, physical activity, physical recreation. **2** AMUSEMENT, entertainment, diversion, fun, pleasure, enjoyment.

**sporting** adj. **1** concerning or interested in sport. **2** fair and generous.

**spot** n. **1** a round mark. **2** a pimple. **3** a place or position. • v. **1** notice. **2** mark with spots. □ on the spot **1** at once. **2** at the scene of an event. spot check a random check. ■ spotter n. spotty adj.

▷ SYNS n. **1** MARK, dot, fleck, smudge, stain, blotch, patch. **2** PIMPLE, pustule, blackhead, blemish. **3** PLACE, site, position, situation, setting, location. • v. SEE, notice, observe, catch sight of, detect, make out, discern, recognize.

**spotless** adj. completely clean or pure.

▷ SYNS **1** CLEAN, pristine, immaculate, shining, gleaming. **2** PURE, flawless, faultless, unsullied, untainted, blameless, above reproach.

**spotlight** n. **1** a lamp projecting a strong beam of light on a small area. **2** intense public attention.

▷ SYNS PUBLIC EYE, limelight, glare of publicity, public attention.

**spouse** n. a husband or wife.
▷ SYNS HUSBAND/WIFE, partner, consort; inf. better/other half.

**spout** n. a projecting tube or lip through which liquid is poured or conveyed; a jet of liquid.
• v. **1** come or send out in a stream. **2** utter or speak lengthily.
▷ SYNS v. **1** SPURT, gush, spew, squirt, jet, spray, emit, erupt, disgorge, pour, stream, flow. **2** HOLD FORTH, sound off; inf. mouth off, spiel.

**sprain** v. injure by wrenching violently. • n. this injury.

**sprang** past of SPRING.

**sprat** n. a small edible fish.

**sprawl** v. **1** sit, lie, or fall with arms and legs spread out. **2** spread out irregularly. • n. the disorganized expansion of a city.
▷ SYNS v. **1** STRETCH OUT, lounge, loll, slump, flop.

**spray** n. **1** liquid dispersed in tiny drops. **2** a liquid or device for spraying. **3** a branch with leaves and flowers. **4** a bunch of cut flowers. • v. **1** apply a spray of liquid to. **2** scatter over an area.
▷ SYNS n. **1** SHOWER, jet, mist, squirt, foam, froth. **2** AEROSOL, vaporizer, atomizer, sprinkler.
• v. JET, spout, gush; sprinkle, shower.

**spread** v. **1** open out fully; extend over a wide area or specified period of time. **2** apply in an even layer. **3** (cause to) affect or be known by increasing numbers. • n. **1** spreading; the extent to which something spreads; a range. **2** a paste for spreading on bread. **3** an article etc. covering several pages of a newspaper. **4** inf. a lavish meal.
□ **spreadeagled** with the arms and legs extended. **spreadsheet** a computer program in which figures in a grid are used in calculations.
▷ SYNS v. **1** STRETCH, extend, open out, unfurl, unroll, fan out. **2** COVER, coat, daub, apply, smear, plaster, slather. **3** DISSEMINATE, circulate, put about, make public, broadcast, publicize, propagate, promulgate.
• n. EXTENT, stretch, span, reach, compass, sweep.

**spree** n. a period of unrestrained activity.
▷ SYNS BOUT, orgy; inf. binge, splurge.

**sprig** n. a twig or shoot.

**sprightly** adj. lively and energetic.

**spring** v. **1** jump. **2** move or do suddenly. **3** arise or originate. • n. **1** the season between winter and summer. **2** a spiral coil that returns to its former shape after being pressed or pulled. **3** a jump. **4** a place where water flows from an underground source. **5** elasticity. □ **springboard** a flexible board from which a diver or gymnast jumps to gain more power. **spring-clean** clean thoroughly. ■ **springy** adj.
▷ SYNS v. **1** JUMP, leap, bound, vault, hop. **2** ORIGINATE, derive, stem, arise, emanate.

**springbok** n. a southern African gazelle.

**sprinkle** v. scatter small drops or particles over a surface; fall in this way. ■ **sprinkler** n.
▷ SYNS SPRAY, shower, splash, spatter, scatter, strew.

**sprint** v. run at full speed. • n. a fast run; a short, fast race.

**sprite** n. an elf or fairy.

**sprocket** n. a projection on a wheel, engaging with links on a chain etc.

**sprout** v. begin to grow or appear; produce shoots. • n. **1** a plant's shoot. **2** a Brussels sprout.
▷ SYNS v. BUD, germinate, burgeon; shoot up, spring up, grow, develop, appear.

**spruce** adj. neat and smart. • v. make smarter. • n. a fir tree.
▷ SYNS adj. NEAT, well groomed, smart, trim, dapper, elegant; inf. natty.

**sprung** p.p. of **SPRING**. • adj. fitted with springs.

**spry** adj. active or lively.

**spud** n. inf. a potato.

**spume** n. froth.

**spun** past and p.p. of **SPIN**.

**spur** n. **1** a spiked device worn on a rider's heel. **2** an encouragement. **3** a projection. • v. **1** encourage. **2** urge a horse on with spurs. □ **on the spur of the moment** on impulse.
▷ SYNS n. STIMULUS, incentive, encouragement, inducement, impetus. • v. STIMULATE, encourage, prompt, prod, impel, motivate.

**spurious** adj. not genuine or authentic.
▷ SYNS BOGUS, fake, fraudulent, sham, feigned, specious; inf. phoney, pseudo.

**spurn** v. reject contemptuously.
▷ SYNS REJECT, turn down, rebuff, snub, slight, cold-shoulder, disdain, scorn.

**spurt** v. gush out; increase speed suddenly. • n. a sudden gush; a sudden burst of activity or speed.
▷ SYNS v. GUSH, squirt, shoot, surge, jet, spring, pour, stream, spout. • n. **1** GUSH, spout, jet, spray. **2** BURST, outburst, fit, surge.

**sputum** n. mixed saliva and mucus.

**spy** n. (pl. **spies**) a person who secretly watches or gathers information. • v. **1** be a spy. **2** watch secretly. **3** see.
▷ SYNS v. NOTICE, observe, see, spot, sight, catch sight of, glimpse.

**sq.** abbr. square.

**squabble** n. a noisy and petty quarrel. • v. have a squabble.
▷ SYNS n. QUARREL, row, dispute, disagreement, argument, altercation; inf. tiff. • v. QUARREL, row, argue, bicker, have words; inf. scrap.

**squad** n. a small group working together.

**squadron** n. a unit of an air for████████████arships.

**squalid** adj. dirty and unpleasant; very immoral or dishonest. ■ squalor n.
▷ SYNS **1** DIRTY, filthy, dingy, grubby, grimy, seedy, sordid, sleazy; inf. grotty. **2** SORDID, unsavoury, base, corrupt, dishonest, dishonourable, disgraceful, contemptible, shameful.

**squall** n. a sudden storm or wind.

**squander** v. spend wastefully.
▷ SYNS WASTE, dissipate, fritter away, run through; inf. blow.

**square** n. **1** a flat shape with four equal sides and four right angles; an area or object shaped like this. **2** the product of a number multiplied by itself.

**3** an instrument for testing right angles. • adj. **1** of square shape. **2** right-angled; level or parallel. **3** of or using units expressing the measure of an area. **4** fair or honest. **5** inf. old-fashioned. • adv. directly; straight. • v. **1** make square. **2** mark with squares. **3** multiply a number by itself. **4** make or be compatible; settle a bill or debt. □ **square dance** a dance in which four couples face inwards from four sides.
▷ SYNS n. **1** PIAZZA, plaza, quadrangle. **2** FOGEY, conservative, traditionalist; inf. stick-in-the-mud, fuddy-duddy. • adj. **1** EQUAL, even, level pegging, drawn. **2** FAIR, just, equitable, honest, straight, upright, above board, ethical; inf. on the level. **3** OLD-FASHIONED, behind the times, conservative, traditionalist, conventional, conformist, bourgeois, strait-laced, stuffy; inf. fuddy-duddy.

**squash** v. **1** ▃▃▃▃▃▃▃▃ **2** force into a restricted space. **3** suppress or reject. • n. **1** a state of being squashed. **2** a fruit-flavoured drink. **3** a game played with rackets and a small ball in a closed court. **4** a vegetable like a marrow.
▷ SYNS v. **1** CRUSH, squeeze, mash, pulp, flatten, compress. **2** FORCE, cram, jam, squeeze, wedge, pack.

**squat** v. **1** sit on your heels. **2** unlawfully occupy an uninhabited place. • n. **1** a squatting posture. **2** a place occupied unlawfully. • adj. short and wide. ■ **squatter** n.

**squawk** n. & v. (make) a loud harsh cry.

**squeak** n. & v. (make) a short high-pitched cry or sound. ■ **squeaky** adj.
▷ SYNS SQUEAL, peep, cheep, yelp, whimper.

**squeal** n. & v. (make) a long shrill cry or sound.

**squeamish** adj. easily sickened or disgusted.

**squeeze** v. **1** press firmly; extract liquid from something by doing this. **2** hug; move or force into or through a tight space. • n. an act of squeezing; an embrace.
▷ SYNS v. **1** COMPRESS, crush, squash, mash, pulp. **2** GRIP, clutch, pinch, press. **3** CROWD, cram, pack, jam, squash, wedge.

**squelch** v. & n. (make) a sound like someone treading in thick mud.

**squid** n. a sea creature with ten tentacles.

**squiggle** n. a short curly line. ■ **squiggly** adj.

**squint** n. a condition in which one eye looks in a different direction from the other. • v. have a squint affecting one eye; look with partly closed eyes.

**squire** n. a country gentleman.

**squirm** v. wriggle; feel embarrassed.
▷ SYNS WRIGGLE, wiggle, writhe, twist, turn.

**squirrel** n. a small tree-climbing animal with a bushy tail.

**squirt** v. force liquid out of a small opening in a thin jet; wet with a jet of liquid. • n. a jet of liquid.

**St** abbr. **1** Saint; Street. **2** (**st**) stone (in weight).

**stab** v. (**stabbed**, **stabbing**) pierce, wound, or kill with

something pointed; poke. • n. 1 a stabbing thrust; a sudden sharp sensation. 2 *inf.* an attempt.
▷ SYNS v. KNIFE, run through, skewer, impale, spear, slash. • n. 1 PUNCTURE, gash, slash, incision. 2 PANG, twinge, ache, throb, spasm.

**stabilize** (or **-ise**) v. make or become stable. ■ **stabilizer** n.

**stable** n. a building in which horses are kept; an establishment for training racehorses. • v. put or keep in a stable. • adj. firmly fixed or established. ■ **stability** n.
▷ SYNS adj. 1 FIRM, solid, steady, secure, fixed, fast, immovable. 2 STRONG, steadfast, established, long-lasting, long-term, unwavering, abiding, durable, enduring, lasting. 3 WELL BALANCED, balanced, steady, sensible, responsible, down-to-earth, sane.

**staccato** adv. *Music* with each sound sharply distinct.

**stack** n. 1 an orderly pile or heap. 2 *inf.* a large quantity. 3 a chimney. • v. arrange in a stack.
▷ SYNS n. HEAP, pile, tower, mound, mountain.

**stadium** n. a sports ground surrounded by tiers of seats for spectators.

**staff** n. 1 a stick used as a support or weapon. 2 the people employed by an organization. 3 a stave in music. • v. provide with a staff of people.
▷ SYNS n. 1 STICK, cane, crook, rod, pole, baton, mace, sceptre. 2 EMPLOYEES, workers, workforce, personnel.

**stag** n. a fully grown male deer. □ **stag night** an all-male party for a man about to marry.

**stage** n. 1 a point reached in a process, journey, etc. 2 a raised platform for theatrical performances etc.; acting as a profession. • v. present on the stage; organize and carry out. □ **stagecoach** a horse-drawn vehicle formerly used to carry passengers along a regular route. **stage fright** nervousness before or during a performance.
▷ SYNS n. 1 POINT, period, step, juncture, time, phase, level. 2 LAP, leg, stretch. 3 PLATFORM, dais, rostrum, podium. • v. PUT ON, produce, direct, perform, mount, present.

**stagger** v. 1 move or go unsteadily. 2 astonish. 3 arrange so as not to coincide exactly.
▷ SYNS 1 REEL, sway, teeter, totter, wobble, lurch. 2 AMAZE, astound, dumbfound, astonish, flabbergast, shock, stupefy, stun.

**stagnant** adj. (of water) not moving and having a stale smell; not active or developing. ■ **stagnate** v.
▷ SYNS 1 STILL, motionless, standing; stale, dirty, brackish. 2 SLUGGISH, slow-moving, quiet, inactive, static.

**staid** adj. steady and serious.
▷ SYNS SEDATE, quiet, serious, solemn, sober, respectable, proper, decorous, stiff, stuffy.

**stain** v. mark or discolour with dirty patches; dye. • n. a mark caused by staining; a disgrace or blemish. □ **stainless steel** a steel alloy not liable to rust or tarnish.
▷ SYNS v. SOIL, mark, discolour, dirty, smudge, smear, spatter, splatter. • n. 1 MARK, spot, blotch, smudge, smear. 2 BLEMISH, injury, taint, blot, stigma, disgrace.

**stair** n. **1** each of a set of fixed steps. **2** (**stairs**) a flight of these. □ **staircase** (or **stairway**) a set of stairs and its surrounding structure. **stairwell** a shaft in which a staircase is built.

**stake** n. **1** a pointed post driven into the ground. **2** a sum of money gambled. **3** a share or interest in a business etc. • v. **1** support with a stake. **2** gamble.
▷ SYNS n. **1** POST, pole, stick, spike, upright. **2** BET, wager, ante. **3** SHARE, interest, investment, involvement. • v. BET, wager, gamble, risk.

**stalactite** n. a deposit of calcium carbonate hanging like an icicle.

**stalagmite** n. a deposit of calcium carbonate standing like a pillar.

**stale** adj. not fresh; no longer new or interesting.
▷ SYNS **1** *stale food:* OLD, off, dry, hard, mouldy, musty, rancid. **2** *stale air:* STUFFY, musty, fusty. **3** *stale jokes:* HACKNEYED, tired, worn-out, banal, trite, un-original; inf. corny, old hat.

**stalemate** n. **1** a situation in which progress is impossible. **2** a position counting as a draw in chess.
▷ SYNS DEADLOCK, impasse, stand-off; draw, tie.

**stalk** n. a stem or similar supporting part. • v. **1** pursue stealthily; follow and harass. **2** walk in a stiff or proud manner. ■ **stalker** n.
▷ SYNS n. STEM, shoot, twig, branch, trunk. • v. **1** PURSUE, follow, shadow, trail, hunt; inf. tail. **2** STRIDE, march, flounce, strut.

**stall** n. **1** a booth or stand for the sale of goods. **2** a compartment in a stable, toilet, etc. **3** (**stalls**) the ground floor seats in a theatre. **4** a seat in a chancel. • v. **1** (of an engine) stop running. **2** stop making progress. **3** be obstructive or evasive. **4** (of an aircraft) move too slowly to be controlled effectively.
▷ SYNS n. STAND, table, counter, booth, kiosk. • v. DELAY, play for time, hedge, drag your feet, stonewall.

**stallion** n. an uncastrated male horse.

**stalwart** adj. loyal and hard-working. • n. a stalwart person.

**stamen** n. the pollen-bearing part of a flower.

**stamina** n. the ability to withstand long physical or mental strain.
▷ SYNS ENDURANCE, staying power, resilience, fortitude, strength, energy, determination, grit.

**stammer** v. speak with involuntary pauses or repetitions of a syllable. • n. this act or tendency.

**stamp** v. **1** bring your foot down heavily. **2** press a mark or pattern on a surface. **3** (**stamp out**) suppress by force. • n. **1** a small adhesive label stuck to a posted item to record payment of postage. **2** an instrument for stamping a mark. **3** this mark. **4** a distinctive quality. **5** an act of stamping the foot.
▷ SYNS v. **1** TRAMPLE, step, tread; crush, squash, flatten. **2** IMPRINT, inscribe, engrave, emboss, mark. **3** (**stamp out**) QUASH, suppress, put down, quell, crush, extinguish, put an end to, eradicate, eliminate. • n. MARK,

hallmark, indication, sign, characteristic, quality.

**stampede** n. a sudden rush of animals or people. • v. take part in a stampede.

**stance** n. **1** the way in which someone stands. **2** a standpoint.
▷ SYNS **1** POSTURE, pose. **2** STAND, standpoint, position, attitude, angle, slant, viewpoint, point of view, opinion.

**stanch** = STAUNCH.

**stanchion** n. an upright post or support.

**stand** v. **1** be or become upright, supported by the feet. **2** place or be situated in a particular position. **3** remain valid or unchanged. **4** tolerate. **5** be in a specified condition. **6** be a candidate in an election. • n. **1** an attitude towards an issue. **2** resistance to attack. **3** a structure for holding or displaying something. **4** a raised structure for spectators. **5** a platform. **6** a stall. □ **standby 1** readiness for action. **2** a person or thing ready to be used in an emergency. **3** (of tickets) sold only at the last minute. **stand down** resign or withdraw. **stand-offish** inf. distant and cold. **standpoint** an attitude towards a particular issue. **standstill** a situation without movement or activity. **stand up for** speak in support of.
▷ SYNS v. **1** RISE, get to your feet, get up. **2** BE SITUATED, be located, be positioned. **3** REMAIN IN FORCE, remain valid, hold, apply, be unchanged. **4** TOLERATE, put up with, endure, bear, take, abide.

**standard** n. **1** a measure or model used to make comparisons; a level of quality

or achievement. **2** a principle of conduct. **3** a flag. • adj. used or accepted as normal or average. □ **standard lamp** a tall lamp placed on the floor.
▷ SYNS n. **1** QUALITY, level, grade, calibre. **2** YARDSTICK, benchmark, measure, criterion, guide, guideline, norm, touchstone, model, pattern, example, exemplar. **3** PRINCIPLE, ideal; (**standards**) code of behaviour, morals, ethics. **4** FLAG, banner, pennant, streamer, ensign, colours. • adj. USUAL, ordinary, average, normal, common, regular, stock, typical, set, fixed, conventional.

**standardize** (or **-ise**) v. cause to conform to a standard.

**standing** n. **1** status. **2** duration or length.
▷ SYNS STATUS, rank, social station, footing, place.

**standpoint** n. an attitude towards a particular issue.
▷ SYNS POINT OF VIEW, viewpoint, perspective, angle, attitude, stance, opinion.

**stank** past of STINK.

**stanza** n. a verse of poetry.

**staple** n. **1** a piece of wire used to fasten papers together; a piece of bent metal used as a fastening. **2** a main or standard food or product etc. • adj. main or important. • v. secure with a staple or staples. ∎ **stapler** n.
▷ SYNS adj. CHIEF, primary, main, principal, basic, fundamental, essential.

**star** n. **1** a huge mass of burning gas visible as a glowing point in the night sky. **2** a shape representing a star. **3** a famous person. • v. **1** have as a leading performer. **2** have a leading role. □ **starfish** a star-shaped sea animal. **starry-eyed** full of unrealistic hopes. **star sign** a sign of the zodiac. ■ **stardom** n. **starry** adj.

▷ SYNS n. CELEBRITY, superstar, VIP, leading light, personality.

**starboard** n. the right-hand side of a ship or aircraft.

**starch** n. **1** a carbohydrate occurring in cereals, potatoes, etc. **2** a preparation for stiffening fabrics. • v. stiffen with starch. ■ **starchy** adj.

**stare** v. gaze fixedly. • n. a staring gaze.

▷ SYNS v. GAZE, gape, goggle, glare; inf. gawp.

**stark** adj. **1** desolate or bare. **2** sharply evident; downright. • adv. completely.

▷ SYNS adj. DESOLATE, bare, barren, arid, empty, godforsaken, bleak, depressing, grim.

**starlet** n. inf. a promising young female film star etc.

**starling** n. a bird with glossy black speckled feathers.

**start** v. **1** begin to do, happen, or operate. **2** cause to happen or operate. **3** set out on a journey. **4** jerk from surprise. • n. **1** a beginning, or the point at which something begins. **2** an advantage given at the beginning of a race. **3** a jerk of surprise. ■ **starter** n.

▷ SYNS v. **1** BEGIN, commence, get going, get under way; inf. get the ball rolling, kick off. **2** ESTABLISH, set up, found, create, institute, initiate, inaugurate, open, launch. **3** SET OUT/OFF, depart, leave; inf. hit the road. **4** JUMP, jerk, twitch, flinch. • n. BEGINNING, commencement, opening,

inception, inauguration, dawn, birth; inf. kick-off.

**startle** v. shock or surprise.

▷ SYNS SHOCK, scare, frighten, alarm, surprise, astonish.

**startling** adj. very surprising or remarkable.

▷ SYNS SURPRISING, astonishing, amazing, unexpected, unforeseen, staggering, shocking, extraordinary, remarkable.

**starve** v. **1** die or suffer from hunger. **2** cause to starve. **3** inf. feel very hungry. ■ **starvation** n.

**starving** adj. **1** suffering from starvation. **2** inf. very hungry.

▷ SYNS UNDERNOURISHED, malnourished; VERY HUNGRY, ravenous; inf. famished, starved.

**stash** v. inf. store secretly.

**state** n. **1** the condition that someone or something is in. **2** a country considered as an organized political unit. **3** civil government. **4** inf. an agitated condition. **5** grandeur or ceremony. • v. express in words. □ **statesman** (or **stateswoman**) an experienced and respected political figure.

▷ SYNS n. **1** CONDITION, shape, position, situation, circumstances, state of affairs. **2** COUNTRY, nation, land, realm, kingdom, republic. • v. EXPRESS, voice, utter, declare, announce, make known, air.

**stately** adj. dignified or grand.

▷ SYNS CEREMONIAL, dignified, solemn, majestic, royal, regal, magnificent, grand, glorious, splendid, elegant, imposing, impressive, august.

**statement** n. a clear expression of something; an official account of an event; a written report of a financial account.

▷ SYNS DECLARATION, affirmation, assertion, announcement, utterance, communication, proclamation; account, testimony, report.

**static** adj. **1** not moving or changing. **2** (of an electric charge) acquired by objects that cannot conduct a current. • n. static electricity; crackling or hissing on a telephone, radio, etc.
▷ SYNS adj. UNMOVING, unchanging, constant, stable, steady, invariable; motionless, immobile.

**station** n. **1** a place where trains stop for passengers to get on and off. **2** a place where a particular activity is carried on. **3** a broadcasting channel. **4** a place where someone stands, esp. on duty; a person's status. • v. assign to a station.
▷ SYNS n. **1** *a railway station:* TERMINUS, terminal, depot. **2** *the police station:* BASE, office, headquarters. **3** *the lookout's station:* POST, place, position.

**stationary** adj. not moving.
▷ SYNS UNMOVING, motionless, immobile, at a standstill.

**stationer** n. a seller of stationery.

**stationery** n. paper and other materials needed for writing.

**statistic** n. **1** an item of information obtained by studying numerical data. **2** (**statistics**) the collection and analysis of numerical information.
■ **statistical** adj. **statistician** n.

**statue** n. a sculptured, cast, or moulded figure.
▷ SYNS STATUETTE, sculpture, effigy, figure, figurine, bust, head.

**statuesque** adj. attractively tall and dignified.
▷ SYNS DIGNIFIED, stately, majestic, imposing, impressive, regal.

**statuette** n. a small statue.

**stature** n. bodily height; importance or reputation.
▷ SYNS **1** HEIGHT, tallness, size. **2** STATUS, reputation, importance, standing, eminence, prominence, note, renown.

**status** n. **1** a person's position or rank in relation to others; high rank or prestige. **2** the situation at a particular time. □ **status quo** the existing state of affairs.
▷ SYNS STANDING, rank, level, position, place; importance, stature, prominence, prestige.

**statute** n. a written law.

**statutory** adj. required or permitted by law.

**staunch** adj. very loyal. • v. stop the flow of blood from a wound.
▷ SYNS adj. LOYAL, faithful, committed, devoted, dedicated, reliable, stalwart, dependable, constant, steadfast, unwavering.

**stave** n. **1** a vertical wooden post; one of the strips of wood forming the side of a cask or tub. **2** a set of five horizontal lines on which music is written. • v. (**stove** or **staved**, **staving**) **1** dent or break a hole in. **2** (**stave off**) ward off.

**stay** v. **1** remain in the same place; live temporarily; continue in the same state. **2** stop or postpone. • n. **1** a period of staying somewhere. **2** a postponement.
▷ SYNS v. **1** REMAIN, wait, stay put, continue, linger, tarry. **2** LODGE, room; visit, sojourn, holiday. **3** CHECK, curb, arrest, stop,

delay, hold, prevent, hinder, impede, obstruct. • n. **1** VISIT, sojourn, stop, stopover, holiday, vacation. **2** POSTPONEMENT, suspension, adjournment, deferment, delay.

**stead** n. (**in someone's/something's stead**) instead of someone or something.

**steadfast** adj. not changing in your attitudes or aims.

**steady** adj. **1** firmly fixed; not shaking. **2** regular and even. **3** sensible and reliable. • v. (**steadied, steadying**) make steady. ■ **steadily** adv. **steadiness** n.
▷ SYNS adj. **1** FIRM, fixed, stable, secure, immovable. **2** STILL, motionless, unmoving, unwavering. **3** UNIFORM, even, regular, rhythmic, consistent. **4** WELL BALANCED, sensible, level-headed, rational, down-to-earth, calm, reliable, dependable, responsible. • v. **1** STABILIZE, secure, balance, brace, support. **2** CALM, settle, compose, quieten, control, get a grip on.

**steak** n. a thick slice of meat (esp. beef) or fish.

**steal** v. **1** take dishonestly. **2** move stealthily.
▷ SYNS **1** THIEVE, take, appropriate, misappropriate, pilfer, purloin, filch, embezzle; plagiarize; inf. pinch, nick, swipe, rip off. **2** SLIP, slide, tiptoe, sneak, creep, slink, sidle.

**stealth** n. caution and secrecy.

**stealthy** adj. cautious and surreptitious.
▷ SYNS SURREPTITIOUS, furtive, cautious, secret, clandestine, covert, sly.

**steam** n. vapour into which water is changed by boiling;

power derived from steam under pressure; momentum. • v. **1** give off steam; become misted over with steam. **2** cook or treat with steam; travel under steam power. □ **steam-roller** a heavy, slow vehicle with a roller, used in road construction. ■ **steamer** n. **steamy** adj.

**steed** n. lit. a horse.

**steel** n. a very strong alloy of iron and carbon. • v. mentally prepare yourself for something difficult.

**steep** adj. **1** sloping sharply. **2** (of a rise or fall) very large or rapid. • v. soak in liquid; permeate thoroughly.
▷ SYNS adj. **1** SHEER, abrupt, precipitous, perpendicular, vertical. **2** *a steep rise:* SHARP, rapid, sudden, precipitate.

**steeple** n. a church tower and spire. □ **steeplechase** a race for horses or athletes, with fences to jump. **steeplejack** a person who repairs tall structures such as chimneys or steeples.
▷ SYNS SPIRE, tower, belfry, minaret.

**steer**[1] v. direct the course of; guide.
▷ SYNS GUIDE, navigate, drive, pilot, manoeuvre; lead, direct, conduct, usher, shepherd.

**steer**[2] n. a bullock.

**stellar** adj. of a star or stars.

**stem** n. **1** the supporting part of a plant; a long, thin supporting section. **2** the root or main part of a word. • v. (**stemmed, stemming**) **1** stop the flow of. **2** (**stem from**) have as its source.

**stench** n. a foul smell.

**stencil** n. a sheet of card etc. with a cut-out design, painted

over to produce the design on the surface below.
• v. (**stencilled**, **stencilling**; US **stenciled**) decorate with a stencil.

**stenographer** n. US a shorthand typist.

**step** v. (**stepped**, **stepping**) lift and set down a foot or alternate feet. • n. **1** a movement of a foot and leg in stepping; the distance covered in this way. **2** a level surface to place the foot on in climbing. **3** a level or grade; a measure or action. □ **stepladder** a short free-standing folding ladder. **stepping stone** a raised stone for stepping on when crossing a stream; a stage in progress towards a goal.
▷ SYNS v. WALK, tread, stride, pace, move. • n. **1** STRIDE, pace, footstep, footfall, tread. **2** WALK, gait. **3** RUNG, stair, tread. **4** COURSE OF ACTION, move, act, action, measure, manoeuvre, procedure. **5** STAGE, level, grade, rank, degree.

**step-** comb. form related by remarriage of a parent, as *stepmother*, *stepson*, etc.

**steppe** n. a grassy plain, esp. in SE Europe and Siberia.

**stereo** n. (pl. **-os**) **1** stereophonic sound. **2** a stereo music player.

**stereophonic** adj. (of sound reproduction) using two transmission channels so as to give the effect of sound from more than one source.

**stereoscopic** adj. (of a photo) taken with a special device to give a three-dimensional effect.

**stereotype** n. an oversimplified idea of the typical characteristics of a person or thing. • v. view as a stereotype.
■ **stereotypical** adj.

**sterile** adj. **1** unable to produce fruit or offspring. **2** free from bacteria. ■ **sterility** n.
▷ SYNS **1** INFERTILE, barren, unproductive. **2** STERILIZED, antiseptic, disinfected, aseptic, sanitary, hygienic.

**sterilize** v. **1** make free from bacteria. **2** make infertile.
▷ SYNS **1** DISINFECT, decontaminate, sanitize, clean, purify. **2** NEUTER, castrate, spay, geld.

**sterling** n. British money. • adj. of standard purity; excellent.

**stern** adj. strict or severe. • n. the rear of a ship.
▷ SYNS adj. **1** STRICT, harsh, hard, rigorous, stringent, rigid, exacting, demanding, unsparing, inflexible, authoritarian. **2** SEVERE, forbidding, frowning, serious, unsmiling, sombre, sober, dour, austere.

**sternum** n. the breastbone.

**steroid** n. any of a group of organic compounds that includes certain hormones.

**stethoscope** n. a medical instrument for listening to a patient's heart or breathing.

**stew** v. cook slowly in a closed pot. • n. a dish made by stewing meat etc.
▷ SYNS n. CASSEROLE, hotpot, ragout, fricassée, goulash.

**steward** n. **1** a person employed to manage an estate etc. **2** (fem. **stewardess**) a passengers' attendant on a ship or aircraft. **3** an official at a race meeting or show etc.

**stick** v. **1** push a pointed object into or through something. **2** cling or adhere. **3** (**be stuck**) be unable to move or to make

progress. **4** (**stick out**) be prominent or conspicuous. **5** inf. put quickly or carelessly. • **n. 1** a thin piece of wood or other material. **2** an implement used to propel the ball in hockey, polo, etc.
▷ SYNS v. **1** PUSH, insert, jab, poke; pierce, penetrate, puncture, prick, spear, stab, run through, impale. **2** GLUE, paste, gum, tape, fasten, attach, fix; cling, adhere. **3** JAM, get jammed, catch, get caught, get trapped. **4** (**stick out**) PROTRUDE, jut out, project, stand out. • n. CANE, staff, crook, pole, post, upright; club.

**sticker** n. an adhesive label or sign.

**stickleback** n. a small fish with sharp spines on its back.

**stickler** n. a person who insists on something.

**sticky** adj. **1** sticking to what is touched. **2** humid.
▷ SYNS **1** ADHESIVE; gummy, gluey, glutinous, viscous, tacky. **2** HUMID, close, muggy, sultry, oppressive.

**stiff** adj. **1** not bending or moving easily; formal in manner. **2** severe or strong; difficult. ■ **stiffen** v.
▷ SYNS **1** RIGID, inflexible, inelastic, firm, hard. **2** DIFFICULT, hard, arduous, tough, laborious, exacting, demanding, formidable, challenging, tiring, exhausting. **3** *stiff punishment:* SEVERE, harsh, stringent, rigorous, drastic. **4** *a stiff manner:* FORMAL, reserved, unfriendly, cold, austere; inf. starchy, stand-offish.

**stifle** v. feel or cause to feel unable to breathe; suppress.

▷ SYNS **1** SUFFOCATE, smother, asphyxiate, choke. **2** SUPPRESS, check, restrain, hold back, choke back, muffle, curb.

**stigma** n. a mark of shame.
▷ SYNS SHAME, disgrace, dishonour, stain, taint.

**stigmata** n.pl. marks corresponding to the marks of the Crucifixion on Christ's body.

**stigmatize** (or **-ise**) v. regard or treat as shameful.

**stile** n. steps or bars for people to climb over a fence.

**stiletto** n. (pl. **-os**) **1** a thin, high heel on a woman's shoe. **2** a dagger with a narrow blade.

**still** adj. **1** not moving. **2** (of drinks) not fizzy. • n. **1** silence and calm. **2** a photograph taken from a cinema film. **3** a distilling apparatus. • adv. **1** continuing the same up to the present or the time mentioned. **2** nevertheless. **3** even. □ **stillborn** born dead. **still life** a picture of inanimate objects.
▷ SYNS adj. **1** MOTIONLESS, unmoving, immobile, inert, stock-still, stationary, static. **2** QUIET, silent, hushed, soundless, noiseless, tranquil, undisturbed. • n. QUIETNESS, quiet, silence, hush, calm, tranquillity, peace, serenity.

**stilt** n. either of a pair of poles with footrests, for walking raised above the ground; each of a set of posts supporting a building.

**stilted** adj. stiffly formal.
▷ SYNS STIFF, unnatural, wooden, strained, forced, laboured, constrained, awkward.

**stimulant** n. something that stimulates.

**stimulate** v. **1** make active or excited. **2** cause a reaction in the body. ■ **stimulation** n.

▷ SYNS ENCOURAGE, spur on, motivate, prompt, trigger, galvanize, inspire, excite.

**stimulating** adj. arousing interest or enthusiasm.

▷ SYNS **2** INTERESTING, exciting, stirring, thought-provoking, inspiring, intriguing, provocative.

**stimulus** n. (pl. **-uli**) something that stimulates.

▷ SYNS INCENTIVE, fillip, spur, boost, encouragement, impetus, stimulant; inf. shot in the arm.

**sting** n. a sharp wounding part of an insect; a wound made by this; a sharp tingling sensation. • v. (**stung, stinging**) wound with a sting; produce a stinging sensation; hurt or upset.

▷ SYNS v. **1** SMART, burn, hurt. **2** HURT, wound, distress, grieve, upset, pain, mortify.

**stingy** adj. (**-ier, -iest**) mean.

▷ SYNS MEAN, miserly, parsimonious, niggardly, tight-fisted, cheese-paring, penny-pinching.

**stink** n. an offensive smell. • v. (**stank** or **stunk, stinking**) give off a stink.

**stint** n. a period of work. • v. (**stint on**) provide or use in a frugal way.

**stipend** n. a salary.

**stipulate** v. demand or specify as part of an agreement. ■ **stipulation** n.

▷ SYNS SPECIFY, set down, set out, lay down, demand, require, insist.

**stir** v. **1** mix a substance by moving a spoon round in it. **2** move; arouse or stimulate. • n. **1** an act of stirring. **2** a commotion.

▷ SYNS v. **1** MIX, blend, beat, whip. **2** MOVE, disturb, agitate, rustle. **3** STIMULATE, excite, arouse, awaken, waken, kindle, quicken, inspire. **4** ROUSE, spur, prompt, encourage, motivate, drive; incite, provoke, inflame, goad. • n. EXCITEMENT, commotion, disturbance, fuss, uproar, to-do, brouhaha.

**stirring** adj. causing great excitement or strong emotion.

▷ SYNS EXCITING, thrilling, rousing, stimulating, moving, inspiring, passionate, impassioned.

**stirrup** n. a support for a rider's foot, hanging from the saddle.

**stitch** n. **1** a loop of thread made by a single pass of the needle in sewing or knitting; a method of making a stitch. **2** a sudden pain in the side. • v. make or mend with stitches.

**stoat** n. a weasel-like animal.

**stock** n. **1** a supply of goods or materials available for sale or use. **2** livestock. **3** a business company's capital; a portion of this held by an investor. **4** liquid made by stewing bones etc. **5** ancestry; reputation. **6** the trunk or stem of a tree or shrub. **7** the handle of a rifle. **8** (**stocks**) a wooden structure in which criminals were formerly locked as a public punishment. • adj. common or conventional. • v. keep in stock; provide with a supply. □ **stockbroker** a broker who buys and sells shares for clients. **stock exchange** (or **stock market**) a place where stocks and shares are bought and sold. **stocktaking** the recording of the amount of stock held by a business.

▷ SYNS n. **1** STORE, supply, stockpile, reserve, reservoir,

accumulation, hoard, cache.
**2** SUPPLIES, goods, merchandise,
wares. **3** ANIMALS, livestock,
cattle, sheep. **4** SHARES,
investment, holding, money.
**5** DESCENT, lineage, ancestry,
extraction, family, parentage,
pedigree. • adj. **1** *stock sizes:*
STANDARD, regular, average.
**2** *stock responses:* USUAL,
routine, conventional, traditional, stereotyped, clichéd,
hackneyed, formulaic.

**stockade** n. a protective fence.

**stocking** n. a close-fitting
covering for the foot and leg.

**stockist** n. a firm that stocks
certain goods.

**stockpile** v. gather together a
large stock of things.
▷ SYNS STORE UP, amass, accumulate, stock up on, collect, put by,
hoard, save; inf. salt away, stash
away.

**stocky** adj. (**-ier, -iest**) short and
sturdy.
▷ SYNS THICKSET, sturdy, chunky,
burly, brawny, solid, strapping,
hefty.

**stodge** n. inf. heavy, filling food.
■ **stodgy** adj.

**stoic** n. a calm and uncomplaining person. ■ **stoicism** n.

**stoical** adj. enduring pain and
hardship without complaint.
▷ SYNS LONG-SUFFERING,
uncomplaining, patient,
forbearing, tolerant, resigned,
phlegmatic, philosophical.

**stoke** v. tend and put fuel on a
fire etc.

**stole**¹ n. a woman's long scarf or
shawl.

**stole**², **stolen** past and p.p. of
STEAL.

**stolid** adj. not excitable.

▷ SYNS IMPASSIVE, phlegmatic,
unemotional, cool, calm,
placid, unexcitable.

**stomach** n. the internal organ
in which the first part of digestion occurs; the abdomen; appetite. • v. endure or tolerate.
▷ SYNS n. ABDOMEN, belly, paunch,
pot belly; inf. tummy, gut.
• v. STAND, put up with, bear,
take, tolerate, abide, endure.

**stomp** v. tread heavily.

**stone** n. **1** a piece of rock; stones
or rock as a substance or material. **2** a gem. **3** the hard case
round the kernel of certain
fruits. **4** (pl. **stone**) a unit of
weight equal to 14 lb. • v. **1** pelt
with stones. **2** remove stones
from fruit. ▢ **Stone Age** the prehistoric period when tools were
made of stone. **stonewall** delay
or block by giving evasive
replies.
▷ SYNS **1** PEBBLE, rock, boulder.
**2** PRECIOUS STONE, jewel, gem.
**3** KERNEL, pit, seed, pip.

**stony** adj. **1** full of stones. **2** cold
and unfeeling.
▷ SYNS **1** ROCKY, pebbly, gravelly,
shingly. **2** COLD, chilly, frosty,
hard, stern, severe, unfriendly,
unfeeling, uncaring, un-
sympathetic, insensitive,
callous, heartless.

**stood** past and p.p. of STAND.

**stooge** n. a comedian's assistant; a person working for and
controlled by others.
▷ SYNS UNDERLING, lackey,
henchman, minion;
inf. dogsbody, sidekick.

**stool** n. **1** a seat without arms or
a back. **2** (**stools**) faeces.

**stoop** v. bend forwards and
down; lower yourself morally.
• n. a stooping posture.

▷ SYNS **v. 1** BEND, lean, crouch.
**2** SINK, descend, lower yourself, resort.

**stop v. 1** come or bring to an end. **2** prevent. **3** cease moving. **4** block a hole. • **n. 1** an act of stopping. **2** a place where a bus stops regularly. **3** a thing preventing movement. **4** a set of organ pipes. □ **stopcock** a valve regulating the flow in a pipe. **stopgap** a temporary substitute. **stop press** late news added to a newspaper. **stopwatch** a watch that can be started and stopped, used to time races. ■ **stoppage** n.
▷ SYNS **v. 1** END, halt, finish, terminate, wind up, discontinue, cut short, interrupt. **2** *he stopped smoking:* CEASE, refrain from, desist from, give up, cut out; inf. quit, pack in. **3** PREVENT, obstruct, impede, block, bar. • **n. 1** HALT, end, finish, cessation, close, conclusion, termination, standstill. **2** BREAK, stopover, stay, visit.

**stopper** n. a plug for closing a bottle etc.

**storage** n. storing; a space for this.

**store** n. **1** a supply of something available for use; a storehouse. **2** a large shop. • v. keep for future use.
▷ SYNS **n. 1** SUPPLY, stock, stockpile, reserve, bank, cache, reservoir. **2** STOREROOM, storehouse, warehouse, repository, depository. **3** SHOP, supermarket, retail outlet, emporium. • v. STOCKPILE, collect, accumulate, amass, put aside/away, hoard, keep; inf. squirrel away, salt away, stash away.

**storey** n. (pl. **-eys** or **-ies**) a particular level of a building.

**stork** n. a long-legged bird with a long bill.

**storm** n. a disturbance of the atmosphere with strong winds and rain or snow; an uproar or controversy. • v. **1** move angrily and violently; be angry. **2** suddenly attack and capture.
▷ SYNS **n.** GALE, hurricane, cyclone, tempest, squall, typhoon.

**stormy** adj. affected by a storm.
▷ SYNS BLUSTERY, windy, gusty, squally, rainy, wild, tempestuous, turbulent.

**story** n. (pl. **-ies**) an account of an incident (true or invented).
▷ SYNS **1** TALE, narrative, anecdote; fable, myth, legend; inf. yarn. **2** NEWS ITEM, article, feature, scoop.

**stout** adj. **1** fat; thick and strong. **2** brave and determined. • n. a strong dark beer.
▷ SYNS **adj. 1** FAT, plump, portly, tubby, dumpy, corpulent, rotund, stocky, thickset, burly. **2** STRONG, heavy, solid, substantial, sturdy, durable, robust, tough. **3** BRAVE, courageous, valiant, valorous, gallant, fearless, intrepid, bold, doughty, determined, resolute, staunch, steadfast, unyielding.

**stove**¹ past & p.p. of STAVE.

**stove**² n. a device for cooking or heating.

**stow** v. **1** pack or store away. **2** (**stow away**) hide on a ship, aircraft, etc. to travel secretly. □ **stowaway** a person who stows away.
▷ SYNS PLACE, put, pack, store, load; inf. stash.

**straddle** v. sit or stand with one leg on each side of; extend across.

**strafe** v. attack with gunfire from the air.

**straggle** v. grow or spread untidily; lag behind others.
■ **straggler** n. **straggly** adj.

**straight** adj. **1** extending or moving in one direction, without a curve or bend; level or even; tidy or orderly. **2** honest and direct. **3** in continuous succession. **4** undiluted. • adv. in a straight line or manner; without delay. □ **straight away** immediately.
■ **straighten** v.
▷ SYNS adj. **1** DIRECT, undeviating. **2** SUCCESSIVE, consecutive, in a row, running. **3** IN ORDER, orderly, neat, tidy, shipshape, spick and span. **4** HONEST, sincere, frank, candid, truthful, forthright, straightforward; inf. upfront.

**straightforward** adj. **1** simple or uncomplicated. **2** frank.
▷ SYNS **1** UNCOMPLICATED, easy, simple, elementary, effortless, undemanding, plain sailing. **2** FRANK, honest, candid, direct, forthright, plain-speaking; inf. upfront.

**strain** v. **1** make an intense effort. **2** injure by overexertion. **3** make great or excessive demands on. **4** sieve to separate solids from liquid. • n. **1** a force stretching something. **2** an injury from straining. **3** a severe demand on strength or resources. **4** the sound of a piece of music. **5** a variety or breed of animal etc. **6** a tendency in a person's character. ■ **strainer** n.
▷ SYNS v. OVERTAX, overwork, overextend, overdo it, exhaust. • n. **1** TENSION, tightness, tautness. **2** PRESSURE, demands, stress; tension, exhaustion, fatigue.

**strained** adj. (of manner etc.) not relaxed.
▷ SYNS **1** FORCED, artificial, unnatural, false, constrained, stiff. **2** AWKWARD, uneasy, uncomfortable, tense, edgy, embarrassed.

**strait** n. **1** (also **straits**) a narrow stretch of water connecting two seas. **2** (**straits**) trouble or difficulty. □ **strait-laced** very prim and proper.

**straitjacket** (or **straightjacket**) n. a strong garment used to restrain the arms of a violent person.

**strand** n. **1** a single thread, esp. one woven or plaited with others; one element in a complex whole. **2** a shore. • v. run aground; leave in difficulties.
▷ SYNS n. **1** THREAD, fibre, filament, length. **2** ELEMENT, component, theme.

**stranded** adj. **1** abandoned or helpless. **2** driven or left aground.
▷ SYNS **1** HELPLESS, alone, abandoned, left in the lurch. **2** BEACHED, grounded, shipwrecked, wrecked, marooned.

**strange** adj. **1** unusual or odd. **2** not seen or met before.
▷ SYNS **1** UNUSUAL, odd, curious, peculiar, funny, queer, bizarre, weird, uncanny. **2** UNFAMILIAR, unknown, new, novel.

**stranger** n. a person you do not know; a person who does not live in or know a place.
▷ SYNS NEWCOMER, visitor, foreigner.

**strangle** v. kill by squeezing the throat; prevent from developing. □ **stranglehold** a strangling grip; complete control.
▷ SYNS **1** THROTTLE, choke, garrotte. **2** SUPPRESS, inhibit, repress, check, restrain, hold back, curb, stifle.

**strangulation** n. strangling.

**strap** n. a strip of flexible material used for fastening, carrying, or holding on to. • v. (**strapped**, **strapping**) secure or fasten with a strap.
▷ SYNS n. BAND, belt, thong, cord, tie. • v. FASTEN, secure, tie, bind, lash.

**strapping** adj. tall and robust.

**stratagem** n. a cunning plan or scheme.
▷ SYNS PLAN, scheme, manoeuvre, tactic, ploy, trick, ruse, plot, machination, subterfuge.

**strategic** adj. **1** of strategy. **2** (of weapons) for use against enemy territory rather than in battle.
■ **strategically** adv.

**strategy** n. (pl. **-ies**) the planning and directing of military activity in a war etc.; a plan for achieving a major goal.
■ **strategist** n.
▷ SYNS MASTER PLAN, game plan, policy, programme, plan of action, scheme, tactics.

**stratify** v. (**stratified**, **stratifying**) arrange in strata.

**stratosphere** n. a layer of the atmosphere about 10–50 km above the earth's surface.

**stratum** n. (pl. **strata**) one of a series of layers or levels.
▷ SYNS LAYER, seam, vein, lode.

**straw** n. **1** dry cut stalks of corn etc.; a single piece of this. **2** a narrow tube for sucking up liquid to drink. □ **straw poll** an unofficial test of public opinion.

**strawberry** n. a soft edible red fruit with seeds on the surface.

**stray** v. move aimlessly from a group or from the right course or place. • adj. having strayed. • n. a stray animal.
▷ SYNS v. **1** WANDER, go astray, drift. **2** DIGRESS, deviate, get sidetracked, go off at a tangent. • adj. **1** HOMELESS, lost, abandoned. **2** *a stray bullet*: RANDOM, chance, freak, unexpected, isolated, lone, single.

**streak** n. **1** a thin line or mark. **2** a continuous period of luck etc. **3** an element in someone's character. • v. **1** mark with streaks. **2** move very rapidly. **3** inf. run naked in a public place.
■ **streaker** n. **streaky** adj.
▷ SYNS n. **1** LINE, band, strip, stripe, bar; smear, smudge, mark. **2** ELEMENT, vein, trace, touch; trait, characteristic. **3** SPELL, period, run, stretch.

**stream** n. **1** a small river; a flow of liquid, things, or people. **2** a group in which schoolchildren of the same level of ability are placed. • v. **1** move in a continuous flow; float in the wind. **2** run with liquid. **3** arrange schoolchildren in streams.
▷ SYNS n. **1** RIVER, brook, rivulet, rill, beck; Scot. burn; US creek. **2** FLOW, rush, gush, surge, jet, current, cascade. • v. FLOW, run, pour, course, spill, gush, surge, flood, cascade, well.

**streamer** n. a long narrow strip of material used for decoration.

**streamlined** adj. **1** having a shape presenting little resistance to a flow of air or water. **2** efficient.

▷ SYNS **1** AERODYNAMIC, smooth, sleek. **2** EFFICIENT, smooth-running, well run, well-organized, slick.

**street** n. a public road lined with buildings.
▷ SYNS ROAD, thoroughfare, avenue, boulevard.

**strength** n. **1** being strong. **2** a good or advantageous quality. **3** the total number of people making up a group.
■ strengthen v.
▷ SYNS **1** POWER, might, force, brawn, muscle, muscularity, sturdiness, robustness, vigour, toughness, stamina. **2** FORTI-TUDE, courage, bravery, pluck, backbone; inf. grit, guts. **3** ADVAN-TAGE, asset, strong point, forte.

**strenuous** adj. making or re-quiring great effort.
▷ SYNS **1** ARDUOUS, laborious, taxing, demanding, difficult, hard, tough, uphill, heavy, exhausting, tiring. **2** VIGOROUS, energetic, zealous, forceful, strong, spirited, determined, resolute, tenacious, tireless, dogged.

**stress** n. **1** pressure; mental or emotional strain. **2** emphasis; extra force given to a syllable or note. • v. **1** emphasize. **2** subject to pressure. ■ stressful adj.
▷ SYNS n. **1** STRAIN, pressure, tension, worry, anxiety. **2** EMPHASIS, priority, import-ance, weight; accent, accentu-ation. • v. EMPHASIZE, accentuate, underline, underscore, point up, highlight, press home.

**stretch** v. **1** pull out tightly or to a greater extent; become longer or wider without breaking; extend part of the body to its full length. **2** extend over an

area or period. **3** make demands on. • n. **1** an act of stretching. **2** the ability to be stretched. **3** a continuous area or period.
▷ SYNS v. **1** EXTEND, elongate, lengthen, expand, draw out, pull out. **2** STRAIN, overtax, over-extend, drain, sap. • n. **1** EXPANSE, area, tract, belt, extent, sweep. **2** PERIOD, time, spell, term, run, stint.

**stretcher** n. a long framework used for carrying a sick or injured person.

**strew** v. (**strewed**, **strewn** or **strewed**, **strewing**) scatter over a surface; cover with scattered things.

**stricken** adj. afflicted by an illness, shock, or grief.

**strict** adj. requiring obedience to rules; following rules or beliefs exactly.
▷ SYNS **1** a strict interpretation: PRECISE, exact, literal, faithful. **2** strict parents: STERN, severe, harsh, uncompromising, authoritarian, firm, austere, rigorous, hard, tough. **3** strict confidence: ABSOLUTE, utter, complete, total.

**stricture** n. **1** severe criticism. **2** a restriction.

**stride** v. (**strode**, **stridden**, **striding**) walk with long steps. • n. a single long step; progress.
▷ SYNS v. STEP, pace, walk, stalk, march.

**strident** adj. loud and harsh. ■ stridency n.
▷ SYNS HARSH, raucous, rough, grating, jarring, shrill, loud, screeching.

**strife** n. quarrelling or conflict.

**strike** v. **1** hit; come into forcible contact with. **2** attack suddenly; afflict; come suddenly into the mind of. **3** stop work in protest. **4** ignite a match by friction. **5** indicate the hour by chiming. **6** reach an agreement. **7** unexpectedly discover. • *n*. **1** a refusal by employees to work. **2** a sudden attack.

▷ SYNS v. **1** HIT, slap, smack, beat, thrash, thump, punch, cuff, rap, cane; *inf.* wallop, belt, clout, whack, bash, clobber. **2** RUN INTO, knock into, bang into, bump into, collide with. **3** ATTACK, afflict, affect, hit. **4** GO ON STRIKE, take industrial action, down tools, walk out. • *n.* INDUSTRIAL ACTION, walkout.

**striker** *n.* **1** a worker on strike. **2** (in football) a forward.

**striking** *adj.* noticeable; impressive.

▷ SYNS **1** NOTICEABLE, obvious, conspicuous, distinct, marked, unmistakable, remarkable, extraordinary, incredible, amazing. **2** IMPRESSIVE, imposing, grand, splendid, magnificent, superb, marvellous, wonderful.

**string** *n.* **1** a narrow cord. **2** a length of catgut or wire on a musical instrument, which is vibrated to produce notes. **3** (**strings**) stringed instruments. **4** a sequence of similar items or events. **5** (**strings**) *inf.* conditions or restrictions. • *v.* (**strung**, **stringing**) **1** arrange on a string. **2** (**string out**) spread out on a line. **3** fit strings on an instrument etc.

**stringent** *adj.* (of regulations etc.) strict. ■ **stringency** *n.*

▷ SYNS STRICT, firm, rigid, rigorous, severe, harsh, tough,

exacting, inflexible, hard and fast.

**stringy** *adj.* like string; (of food) tough and fibrous.

**strip** *v.* (**stripped**, **stripping**) remove clothes or coverings from; undress; deprive of property, rank, etc. • *n.* **1** an act of undressing. **2** the identifying outfit of a sports team. **3** a long, narrow piece or area. □ **strip light** a tubular fluorescent lamp. **striptease** an entertainment in which a performer gradually undresses.

▷ SYNS v. **1** UNDRESS, disrobe. **2** TAKE AWAY, dispossess of, deprive of, confiscate. • *n.* PIECE, bit, band, belt, ribbon, slip, shred.

**stripe** *n.* a long narrow band on a surface, differing in colour or texture from its surroundings. ■ **striped** *adj.* **stripy** *adj.*

▷ SYNS STRIP, band, belt, bar.

**stripling** *n.* a youth.

**stripper** *n.* **1** a device for stripping something. **2** a striptease performer.

**strive** *v.* **1** make great efforts. **2** struggle.

▷ SYNS TRY, attempt, endeavour, make an effort, exert yourself, do your best, labour, strain, struggle.

**strobe** *n.* a bright light which flashes rapidly.

**strode** past of STRIDE.

**stroke** *v.* gently move your hand over. • *n.* **1** an act of hitting; the sound of a striking clock. **2** an act of stroking. **3** a mark made by a movement of a pen, paintbrush, etc. **4** a style of swimming. **5** a loss of consciousness due to an interruption in the supply of blood to the brain.

▷ SYNS v. CARESS, fondle, pat, pet, touch, rub, massage. • n. THROMBOSIS, embolism, seizure.

**stroll** v. walk in a leisurely way. • n. a leisurely walk.

▷ SYNS v. SAUNTER, amble, wander, meander, ramble, promenade, take the air; inf. mosey.

**strong** adj. 1 able to move heavy weights or resist great pressure; having skills, qualities, or numbers assisting survival or victory; (of an argument) persuasive; able to bear distress. 2 intense; concentrated; containing much alcohol. 3 having a specified number of members: *fifty strong*. □ **stronghold** a place strengthened against attack; a place of strong support for a cause or political party. **strongroom** a room designed for the safe storage of valuable items. ■ **strongly** adv.

▷ SYNS 1 POWERFUL, brawny, muscular, strapping, sturdy, burly, robust, vigorous, tough, hardy, lusty. 2 *a strong character:* DETERMINED, forceful, assertive, tough, tenacious, formidable, redoubtable. 3 *strong doors/ material:* SOLID, well built, secure, well fortified, impregnable; heavy-duty, sturdy, durable, hard-wearing, long-lasting. 4 *strong feelings:* INTENSE, vehement, passionate, fervent, fervid. 5 *a strong supporter:* KEEN, eager, enthusiastic, dedicated, staunch, loyal, steadfast. 6 *a strong argument:* PERSUASIVE, cogent, compelling, convincing, potent, weighty, sound, valid, well founded.

**stroppy** adj. inf. bad-tempered or awkward.

**strove** past of STRIVE.

**struck** past & p.p. of STRIKE.

**structure** n. the way a thing is constructed or organized; a thing's supporting framework or essential parts; a complex whole. ■ **structural** adj.

▷ SYNS 1 BUILDING, edifice, construction, erection, pile. 2 CONSTRUCTION, form, configuration, shape, constitution, composition, make-up, organization, system, arrangement, design, framework.

**strudel** n. flaky pastry filled with apple etc.

**struggle** v. move violently to get free; progress with difficulty. • n. a spell of struggling; a difficult task.

▷ SYNS v. 1 STRIVE, try, endeavour, exert yourself, do your best, battle, labour, toil, strain. 2 FIGHT, grapple, wrestle, scuffle.

**strum** v. (**strummed**, **strumming**) play a guitar or similar instrument.

**strung** past and p.p. of STRING.

**strut** n. 1 a bar of wood or metal supporting something. 2 a strutting walk. • v. (**strutted**, **strutting**) walk proudly and confidently.

▷ SYNS v. SWAGGER, swank, parade, flounce; US inf. sashay.

**strychnine** n. a bitter highly poisonous substance.

**stub** n. 1 a short stump. 2 a counterfoil of a cheque, ticket, etc. • v. (**stubbed**, **stubbing**) 1 strike your toe against a hard object. 2 extinguish a cigarette by pressure. ■ **stubby** adj.

**stubble** n. **1** short stiff hairs growing after shaving. **2** the cut stalks of cereal plants left in the ground after harvesting.
■ **stubbly** adj.

**stubborn** adj. obstinate or unyielding. ■ **stubbornness** n.
▷ SYNS OBSTINATE, mulish, pigheaded, wilful, strong-minded, perverse, recalcitrant, unyielding, inflexible, immovable, intransigent, uncompromising, persistent, tenacious.

**stucco** n. plaster used for coating walls or moulding into decorations. ■ **stuccoed** adj.

**stuck** past & p.p. of STICK.
□ **stuck-up** conceited and snobbish.

**stud** n. **1** a piece of metal with a large head that projects from a surface. **2** a fastener consisting of two buttons joined with a bar. **3** a small piece of jewellery for a pierced ear etc. **4** an establishment where horses etc. are kept for breeding. • v. (**studded**, **studding**) cover with studs or other small objects.

**student** n. a person studying at a university, college, or school.
▷ SYNS UNDERGRADUATE, scholar, pupil, schoolchild.

**studied** adj. done with careful effort.
▷ SYNS DELIBERATE, careful, conscious, calculated, intentional; affected, forced, strained, artificial.

**studio** n. (pl. **-os**) the workroom of a painter, photographer, etc.; premises where cinema films are made; a room from which television or radio programmes are broadcast. □ **studio flat** a flat containing one main room.

**studious** adj. spending much time in study; deliberate and careful.
▷ SYNS SCHOLARLY, academic, intellectual, bookish, serious, earnest.

**study** n. **1** time and effort spent in learning. **2** a detailed analysis. **3** a room for reading and writing. **4** a piece of art. • v. **1** learn about or investigate. **2** look at closely.
▷ SYNS v. **1** WORK, revise; inf. swot, cram, mug up. **2** INVESTIGATE, inquire into, research, look into, examine, analyse.

**stuff** n. material, objects, etc. of a particular or unspecified kind. • v. **1** fill tightly or hastily. **2** fill the skin of a dead animal to make it lifelike.
▷ SYNS n. **1** MATERIAL, fabric, matter, substance. **2** THINGS, objects, articles, items, belongings, possessions, paraphernalia. • v. FILL, pad, pack; shove, thrust, cram, squeeze, force, jam.

**stuffing** n. **1** a mixture put inside meat etc. before cooking. **2** padding used to fill cushions etc.

**stuffy** adj. **1** lacking fresh air. **2** narrow-minded.
▷ SYNS AIRLESS, close, muggy, fuggy, musty, stale.

**stultify** v. (**stultified**, **stultifying**) cause to lose enthusiasm or energy.

**stumble** v. trip and lose your balance; walk unsteadily; make mistakes in speaking etc. • n. an act of stumbling. □ **stumbling block** an obstacle.
▷ SYNS v. **1** TRIP, slip, lose your balance; stagger, totter, teeter. **2** STAMMER, stutter, hesitate, falter.

**stump** n. 1 the base of a tree left in the ground when the rest has gone; a remaining piece. 2 one of the uprights of a wicket in cricket. • v. baffle. ■ **stumpy** adj.

**stun** v. (**stunned, stunning**) knock unconscious; astonish.
▷ SYNS 1 DAZE, stupefy, knock out, lay out. 2 SHOCK, astound, dumbfound, stupefy, devastate, stagger, amaze, astonish; inf. flabbergast, knock for six.

**stung** past and p.p. of **STING**.

**stunk** past and p.p. of **STINK**.

**stunning** adj. very impressive.
▷ SYNS SENSATIONAL, wonderful, marvellous, magnificent, glorious, impressive, splendid, beautiful, lovely, gorgeous.

**stunt** n. an action displaying skill and daring; something done to attract attention. • v. hinder the growth or development of.

**stupefy** v. (**stupefied, stupefy-ing**) make unable to think properly. ■ **stupefaction** n.

**stupendous** adj. amazingly large or good.

**stupid** adj. 1 lacking intelligence. 2 dazed. ■ **stupidity** n.
▷ SYNS UNINTELLIGENT, foolish, dense, obtuse, idiotic, slow, simple-minded, brainless, mindless; silly, senseless, ludicrous, ridiculous, laughable, fatuous, asinine; inf. thick, dim, dumb, dopey.

**stupor** n. a dazed condition.

**sturdy** adj. (**-ier, -iest**) strongly built or made.
▷ SYNS WELL BUILT, muscular, athletic, strong, strapping, powerful, robust, tough, hardy, lusty; solid, substantial, well made, durable.

**sturgeon** n. a large fish from whose roe caviar is made.

**stutter** v. speak with difficulty; stammer. • n. a stammer.

**sty** n. (pl. **sties**) 1 a pigsty. 2 (also **stye**) an inflamed swelling on the edge of the eyelid.

**style** n. 1 a way of doing something; a particular design, appearance, or arrangement. 2 elegance. • v. design, shape, or arrange in a particular way.
▷ SYNS n. 1 TECHNIQUE, method, methodology, approach, manner, way, mode, system. 2 KIND, type, variety, sort, genre. 3 STYLISHNESS, elegance, poise, sophistication, chic, flair, dash, panache. 4 FASHION, trend, vogue, mode.

**stylish** adj. fashionably elegant.
▷ SYNS FASHIONABLE, smart, sophisticated, elegant, chic, modern, up to date; inf. trendy, natty, classy.

**stylist** n. a fashion designer; a hairdresser.

**stylistic** adj. of literary or artistic style.

**stylized** (or **-ised**) adj. represented non-realistically.

**stylus** n. (pl. **-luses** or **-li**) a needle-like device for cutting or following a groove in a record.

**stymie** v. (**stymied, stymieing** or **stymying**) inf. obstruct or thwart.

**suave** adj. charming, confident, and elegant.

**sub** n. inf. 1 a submarine. 2 a subscription. 3 a substitute.

**subatomic** adj. smaller than an atom; occurring in an atom.

**subconscious** adj. & n. (of) our own mental activities of which we are not aware.

**subcontinent** n. a large land mass forming part of a continent.

**subcutaneous** adj. under the skin.

**subdivide** v. divide a part into smaller parts. ■ subdivision n.

**subdue** v. bring under control; make quieter or less intense.
▷ SYNS **1** CONQUER, defeat, vanquish, overcome, subjugate, triumph over, crush, quash. **2** CONTROL, curb, restrain, check, hold back, repress, suppress, stifle, quell.

**subdued** adj. **1** quiet and thoughtful or depressed. **2** (of colour or lighting) soft; muted.
▷ SYNS **1** SOMBRE, low-spirited, downcast, dejected, depressed, gloomy, despondent, dispirited. **2** DIM, muted, soft, subtle.

**subedit** v. check and correct text before printing.
■ subeditor n.

**subject** n. **1** a person or thing being discussed or dealt with. **2** a branch of knowledge studied or taught. **3** a citizen in a monarchy. **4** Grammar the word in a sentence naming the person or thing performing the action of the verb. • adj. **1** able to be affected by. **2** dependent on. **3** under the authority of. • v. cause to undergo.
■ subjection n.
▷ SYNS n. **1** TOPIC, theme, question, subject matter; substance, gist. **2** BRANCH OF KNOWLEDGE, discipline. **3** CITIZEN, national. • adj. **1** SUSCEPTIBLE TO, liable to, prone to, vulnerable to. **2** CONDITIONAL ON, contingent on, dependent on.

**subjective** adj. dependent on personal taste or views etc.

**subjugate** v. bring under control by force. ■ subjugation n.
▷ SYNS CONQUER, vanquish, defeat, crush, quash, enslave, subdue, suppress.

**subjunctive** n. Grammar (of a verb) expressing what is imagined, wished, or possible.

**sublet** v. (**sublet**, **subletting**) let property etc. that you are already renting to someone else.

**sublimate** v. transform into a purer or idealized form.
■ sublimation n.

**sublime** adj. **1** of great excellence. **2** extreme.
▷ SYNS EXALTED, noble, lofty, awe-inspiring, majestic, magnificent, glorious, superb, wonderful, marvellous.

**subliminal** adj. below the level of conscious awareness.

**sub-machine gun** n. a hand-held lightweight machine gun.

**submarine** n. a vessel that can operate under water. • adj. under the surface of the sea.

**submerge** v. go or cause to be under water. ■ submersion n.
▷ SYNS **1** DIVE, sink, plummet. **2** IMMERSE, dip, plunge, duck, dunk. **3** FLOOD, inundate, deluge, engulf, swamp.

**submission** n. the submitting of something; a proposal etc. submitted.

**submissive** adj. meek and obedient.
▷ SYNS COMPLIANT, yielding, acquiescent, unassertive, passive, obedient, biddable, dutiful, docile, meek; inf. under someone's thumb.

**submit** v. **1** give in to authority or power. **2** present for consideration.

▷ SYNS **1** YIELD, give way/in, back down, capitulate, surrender; accept, comply, conform. **2** PUT FORWARD, present, offer, proffer, tender, propose, suggest.

**subordinate** adj. of lesser importance or rank. • n. a subordinate person. • v. treat as less important than something else. ■ subordination n.

▷ SYNS adj. LOWER-RANKING, junior, lower; lesser, minor, secondary, subsidiary, ancillary, auxiliary. • n. JUNIOR, assistant, second, deputy, aide.

**subpoena** n. a writ commanding a person to appear in a law court.

**subscribe** v. **1** pay in advance to receive a publication etc. regularly; contribute to a fund. **2** (**subscribe to**) agree with an idea or proposal. ■ subscriber n. subscription n.

▷ SYNS (**subscribe to**) AGREE WITH, accept, believe in, endorse, back, support.

**subsequent** adj. occurring after something. ■ subsequently adv.

▷ SYNS FOLLOWING, ensuing, succeeding, later, future, next.

**subservient** adj. completely obedient. ■ subservience n.

▷ SYNS SUBMISSIVE, deferential, compliant, obedient, meek, biddable, docile, passive, downtrodden; inf. under someone's thumb.

**subside** v. sink to a lower or normal level; become less intense. ■ subsidence n.

▷ SYNS ABATE, let up, moderate, ease, quieten, calm, slacken, die out, peter out, lessen, dwindle, recede.

**subsidiary** adj. of secondary importance; (of a company) controlled by another. • n. (pl. **-ies**) a subsidiary company.

**subsidize** (or **-ise**) v. pay a subsidy to or for.

▷ SYNS CONTRIBUTE TO, back, support, invest in, sponsor, finance, fund, underwrite.

**subsidy** n. (pl. **-ies**) a sum of money given to help keep the price of a product or service low.

▷ SYNS GRANT, contribution, backing, support, sponsorship, finance, funding.

**subsist** v. keep yourself alive. ■ subsistence n.

▷ SYNS SURVIVE, live, exist, support yourself.

**subsoil** n. soil lying below the surface layer.

**substance** n. **1** a solid, liquid, or gas with particular properties. **2** the matter of which a thing consists. **3** solid basis in reality. **4** importance. **5** the most important or essential part or meaning.

▷ SYNS **1** MATTER, material, stuff, mass. **2** MATERIAL, compound, matter, stuff. **3** SIGNIFICANCE, importance, weight, validity.

**substantial** adj. **1** strongly built or made; of considerable size, importance, or value. **2** concerning the essence of something. ■ substantially adv.

▷ SYNS **1** SOLID, sturdy, strong, well built, durable. **2** CONSIDERABLE, real, significant, important, notable, major, valuable, useful; sizeable, large, appreciable. **3** ESSENTIAL, basic, fundamental.

**substantiate** v. support with evidence.

**substitute** n. a person or thing that acts or serves in place of another. • v. use or serve as a substitute. ■ **substitution** n.

▷ SYNS n. REPLACEMENT, deputy, relief, proxy, reserve, surrogate, stand-in, locum.

**subsume** v. include or absorb in a larger group.

**subterfuge** n. deceit used to achieve an aim.

▷ SYNS TRICKERY, guile, cunning, intrigue, deviousness, deceit, duplicity, deception.

**subterranean** adj. underground.

**subtext** n. an underlying theme.

**subtitle** n. 1 a caption displayed on a cinema or television screen to translate dialogue. 2 a subordinate title. • v. provide with subtitle(s).

**subtle** adj. (**subtler**, **subtlest**) so slight or delicate as to be hard to analyse or identify; making fine distinctions; ingenious. ■ **subtlety** n. **subtly** adv.

▷ SYNS 1 DELICATE, faint, understated, low-key, muted. 2 *a subtle distinction:* FINE, fine-drawn, nice, slight.

**subtotal** n. the total of part of a group of figures.

**subtract** v. remove a part, quantity, or number from a greater one. ■ **subtraction** n.

**suburb** n. a residential area outside the central part of a town. ■ **suburban** adj.

**suburbia** n. suburbs and their inhabitants.

**subversive** adj. trying to undermine an established system or institution.

▷ SYNS SEDITIOUS, disruptive, troublemaking, inflammatory, revolutionary.

**subvert** v. undermine the authority of a system or institution. ■ **subversion** n.

▷ SYNS UNDERMINE, destabilize, disrupt, destroy, damage, weaken, overthrow, overturn, sabotage.

**subway** n. a tunnel under a road, used by pedestrians; an underground railway.

▷ SYNS UNDERGROUND, metro, tube.

**succeed** v. 1 achieve your aim or wish. 2 take the place previously filled by; come next in order.

▷ SYNS 1 TRIUMPH, achieve success, do well, thrive, make it. 2 BE SUCCESSFUL, work (out), come off; inf. do the trick. 3 FOLLOW, replace, take the place of, supersede.

**success** n. 1 the attainment of an aim. 2 the gaining of wealth or status. 3 a successful person or thing.

**successful** adj. 1 having achieved an aim. 2 having achieved wealth or status.

▷ SYNS 1 FLOURISHING, thriving, booming, profitable, money-making, lucrative. 2 PROSPEROUS, affluent, wealthy; famous, eminent, top.

**succession** n. a number of people or things following one after the other; succeeding to a throne or other position.

▷ SYNS SEQUENCE, series, progression, course, run, cycle, chain, train.

**successive** adj. following one another or following others.

**successor** n. a person or thing that succeeds another.

▷ SYNS HEIR, inheritor, next-in-line.

**succinct** adj. concise and clear.

**succour** (US **succor**) v. & n. help.

**succulent** adj. juicy; (of plants) having thick fleshy leaves. • n. a succulent plant. ■ **succulence** n.
▷ SYNS adj. JUICY, moist, luscious, mouth-watering.

**succumb** v. give way to pressure or temptation.
▷ SYNS YIELD, give in/way, submit, surrender, capitulate.

**such** adj. **1** of the type previously mentioned or about to be mentioned. **2** to so high a degree.

**suck** v. **1** draw into the mouth by tightening the lips and breathing in. **2** hold in the mouth and pull at with the mouth muscles. **3** pull in a particular direction. **4** (**suck up to**) inf. try to please to gain advantage. • n. an act of sucking.

**sucker** n. **1** an organ or device that can stick to a surface by suction. **2** inf. a person who is easily fooled. **3** a shoot springing from the base of a plant.

**suckle** v. feed at the breast.

**suckling** n. an unweaned child or animal.

**sucrose** n. sugar.

**suction** n. the force produced when a partial vacuum is created by the removal of air.

**sudden** adj. happening or done quickly and unexpectedly. ■ **suddenly** adv. **suddenness** n.
▷ SYNS UNEXPECTED, unforeseen, unlooked-for; immediate, instantaneous, instant, abrupt, rapid, swift.

**sudoku** n. a puzzle in which numbers are inserted into a grid consisting of nine squares each subdivided into a further nine squares.

**suds** pl.n. a froth of soap and water.

**sue** v. (**sued, suing**) take legal proceedings against.

**suede** n. leather with a velvety nap on one side.

**suet** n. hard white fat from round an animal's kidneys, used in cooking.

**suffer** v. **1** experience something bad. **2** be affected by a disease. **3** dated tolerate. ■ **suffering** n.
▷ SYNS EXPERIENCE, undergo, sustain, endure, face, meet with.

**sufferance** n. (**on sufferance**) tolerated but only grudgingly.

**suffice** v. be enough.

**sufficient** adj. enough. ■ **sufficiency** n.
▷ SYNS ENOUGH, adequate, plenty of, ample.

**suffix** n. a part added on to the end of a word.

**suffocate** v. die or cause to die from lack of air. ■ **suffocation** n.
▷ SYNS SMOTHER, stifle, asphyxiate.

**suffrage** n. the right to vote in political elections.

**suffragette** n. hist. a woman who campaigned for the right to vote.

**suffuse** v. spread throughout or over.
▷ SYNS PERMEATE, pervade, cover, spread over, imbue, bathe.

**sugar** n. a sweet crystalline substance obtained from the juices of various plants.
• v. sweeten or sprinkle with sugar □ **sugar beet** a type of beet from which sugar is obtained. **sugar cane** a tropical plant from which sugar is obtained. ■ **sugary** adj.

**suggest** v. 1 propose for consideration. 2 imply; cause someone to think of.
▷ SYNS 1 PROPOSE, put forward, submit, recommend, advocate. 2 INDICATE, hint, imply, intimate, insinuate.

**suggestible** adj. easily influenced.

**suggestion** n. 1 suggesting; something suggested. 2 a slight trace.
▷ SYNS 1 PROPOSAL, proposition, motion, submission, recommendation. 2 HINT, trace, touch, suspicion. 3 INSINUATION, hint, implication, intimation.

**suggestive** adj. conveying a suggestion; suggesting something indecent.
▷ SYNS PROVOCATIVE, titillating, indecent, indelicate, improper, ribald, risqué, vulgar, smutty, lewd, salacious.

**suicide** n. the action of killing yourself intentionally; a person who does this. ■ suicidal adj.

**suit** n. 1 a set of clothes to be worn together, esp. a jacket and trousers or skirt. 2 any of the four sets into which a pack of cards is divided. 3 a lawsuit. • v. 1 be right or good for. 2 (of clothes etc.) enhance the appearance of. □ suitcase a case with a handle and a hinged lid for carrying clothes.
▷ SYNS n. 1 OUTFIT, ensemble. 2 LAWSUIT, court case, action, proceedings. • v. BECOME, look good on, flatter.

**suitable** adj. right for the purpose or occasion.
■ suitability n. suitably adv.
▷ SYNS APPROPRIATE, acceptable, satisfactory, fitting, fit, right, befitting, in keeping.

**suite** n. 1 a set of rooms or furniture. 2 a set of musical pieces.

**suitor** n. a man who is seeking to marry a woman.

**sulk** v. be silently bad-tempered or resentful. • n. a period of sulking. ■ sulkily adv.

**sulky** adj. silent and bad-tempered.
▷ SYNS SULLEN, moody, petulant, disgruntled, grumpy, ill-humoured, in a bad mood, bad-tempered, surly.

**sullen** adj. silent and bad-tempered.
▷ SYNS SURLY, sulky, sour, morose, resentful, moody, gloomy, grumpy, bad-tempered; unresponsive, uncommunicative, unfriendly.

**sully** v. (sullied, sullying) stain or blemish.

**sulphur** (US sulfur) n. a pale yellow chemical element. □ sulphuric acid a strong corrosive acid. ■ sulphurous adj.

**sultan** n. a Muslim king or ruler.

**sultana** n. 1 a seedless raisin. 2 a sultan's wife.

**sultry** adj. hot and humid; suggesting passion and sensuality.
▷ SYNS 1 CLOSE, airless, stuffy, stifling, oppressive, muggy, humid, sticky, hot. 2 SENSUAL, sexy, voluptuous, seductive, erotic.

**sum** n. 1 an amount of money. 2 a total. 3 an arithmetical calculation. • v. summarize.
▷ SYNS n. AMOUNT, total, tally, aggregate.

**summarize** (or -ise) v. give a summary of.
▷ SYNS SUM UP, give a synopsis of, precis, encapsulate, abridge,

condense, outline, put in a nutshell.

**summary** n. (pl. **-ies**) a brief statement of the main points of something. • adj. **1** without unnecessary detail. **2** without legal formalities. ■ **summarily** adv.
▷ SYNS n. SYNOPSIS, precis, résumé, abstract, abridgement, digest, outline. • adj. IMMEDIATE, instant, instantaneous, prompt, rapid, sudden, abrupt, peremptory.

**summer** n. the warmest season of the year. ■ **summery** adj.

**summit** n. **1** the top of a mountain; the highest point. **2** a conference between heads of states.
▷ SYNS **1** TOP, peak, crest, crown, apex. **2** PEAK, height, pinnacle, zenith, acme, culmination, climax.

**summon** v. send for; order to appear in a law court; call to a meeting; produce a reaction or quality.
▷ SYNS **1** SEND FOR, call for. **2** ORDER, convene, assemble, convoke, muster, rally.

**summons** n. a command summoning a person; a written order to appear in a law court.
▷ SYNS WRIT, subpoena.

**sumo** n. Japanese wrestling.

**sumptuous** adj. splendid, lavish, and costly.
▷ SYNS LAVISH, luxurious, de luxe, opulent, magnificent, splendid.

**sun** n. the star around which the earth travels; the light or warmth from this; any fixed star. • v. (**sunned**, **sunning**) expose to the sun. □ **sunbathe** sit or lie in the sun to get a suntan. **sunbed** a device with ultraviolet lamps for acquiring an artificial suntan. **sunburn** inflammation of the skin caused by too much exposure to the sun. **sunburnt** (or **sunburned**) suffering from sunburn. **sundial** a device showing the time by the shadow cast by a pointer. **sunflower** a tall plant with large yellow flowers. **sunshine** sunlight unbroken by cloud. **sunstroke** illness caused by excessive exposure to the sun. **suntan** a golden-brown skin colouring caused by exposure to the sun.

**sundae** n. a dish of ice cream and fruit, nuts, syrup, etc.

**Sunday** n. the day after Saturday. □ **Sunday school** a class held on Sundays to teach children about Christianity.

**sunder** v. lit. split apart.

**sundry** adj. various. • n.pl. (**sundries**) various small items.

**sung** p.p. of SING.

**sunk** p.p. of SINK.

**sunken** adj. **1** having sunk. **2** lower than the surrounding area.

**sunny** adj. (**-ier**, **-iest**) **1** full of sunshine. **2** cheerful.

**sunrise** n. the time when the sun rises.
▷ SYNS DAWN, daybreak, first light, early morning; lit. cockcrow.

**sunset** n. **1** the time when the sun sets. **2** the colours in the sky at sunset.
▷ SYNS NIGHTFALL, twilight, dusk, evening; lit. gloaming.

**super** adj. inf. excellent.

**superannuation** n. an employee's pension.

**superb** adj. of the most impressive or splendid kind.

▷ SYNS SUPERLATIVE, excellent, first-rate, first-class, outstanding, remarkable, brilliant, marvellous, magnificent, wonderful, splendid, fantastic, fabulous.

**supercharger** v. a device that makes an engine more efficient by forcing extra air or fuel into it. ■ **supercharged** adj.

**supercilious** adj. haughty and superior.

▷ SYNS ARROGANT, haughty, conceited, proud, disdainful, scornful, condescending, superior, patronizing, imperious, snobbish, snobby; inf. hoity-toity, snooty, stuck-up.

**superficial** adj. of or on the surface; lacking the ability to think deeply. ■ **superficiality** n. **superficially** adv.

▷ SYNS 1 SURFACE, exterior, external, outer, slight. 2 CURSORY, perfunctory, hasty, hurried, casual, sketchy, desultory. 3 SHALLOW, empty-headed, trivial, frivolous, silly, lightweight.

**superfluous** adj. more than is required.

▷ SYNS SPARE, surplus, extra, unneeded, excess, unnecessary, redundant.

**superhuman** adj. having exceptional ability or powers.

**superimpose** v. place on top of something else.

**superintend** v. oversee.

**superintendent** n. 1 a supervisor. 2 a senior police officer.

**superior** adj. 1 higher in status, quality, or power. 2 arrogant and conceited. • n. a person of higher rank or status.
■ **superiority** n.

▷ SYNS adj. 1 HIGHER, higher-ranking, senior. 2 BETTER, higher-grade, finer, greater. 3 HAUGHTY, disdainful, condescending, supercilious, patronizing, snobbish, snobby; inf. high-and-mighty, hoity-toity, snooty, stuck-up.

**superlative** adj. 1 of the highest quality. 2 of the grammatical form expressing 'most'.

▷ SYNS EXCELLENT, magnificent, wonderful, marvellous, supreme, best, consummate, outstanding, remarkable, first-rate, first-class, premier, prime, unsurpassed, unparalleled, unrivalled.

**supermarket** n. a large self-service store selling food and household goods.

**supernatural** adj. not able to be explained by the laws of nature.

▷ SYNS UNEARTHLY, otherworldly, spectral, ghostly, phantom, magical, magic, mystic, occult, paranormal, psychic.

**supernova** n. (pl. **-novas** or **-novae**) a star that suddenly increases in brightness because of an explosion.

**supernumerary** adj. extra.

**superpower** n. an extremely powerful nation.

**superscript** adj. written just above and to the right of a word etc.

**supersede** v. take the place of.

▷ SYNS TAKE THE PLACE OF, replace, take over from, displace, succeed, supplant.

**supersonic** adj. of or flying at speeds greater than that of sound.

**superstition** n. a belief in magical and similar influences;

an idea or practice based on this. ■ **superstitious** adj.

**superstore** n. a large supermarket.

**superstructure** n. a structure that rests on something else; the upper parts of a ship or building.

**supervise** v. direct and inspect workers etc. ■ **supervision** n. **supervisory** adj.
▷ SYNS OVERSEE, be in charge of, direct, manage, run, superintend, keep an eye on, watch, observe.

**supervisor** n. a person who supervises.
▷ SYNS MANAGER, overseer, controller, superintendent, governor, chief, head; foreman.

**supine** adj. 1 lying face upwards. 2 passive or lazy.

**supper** n. a light or informal evening meal.

**supplant** v. take the place of.
▷ SYNS TAKE THE PLACE OF, replace, displace, supersede, oust, usurp, overthrow, remove, unseat.

**supple** adj. bending easily.
▷ SYNS 1 LITHE, lissom, loose-limbed, limber. 2 PLIANT, pliable, soft, flexible, malleable, elastic.

**supplement** n. something added as an extra part or to make up for a deficiency. • v. provide or be a supplement to.
▷ SYNS n. 1 ADDITION, extra, add-on, adjunct. 2 SURCHARGE, increase. • v. ADD TO, augment, increase, top up, boost.

**supplementary** adj. completing or improving something.
▷ SYNS ADDITIONAL, extra, more, further; add-on, subsidiary.

**supplicate** v. ask humbly for something. ■ **supplicant** n. **supplication** n.

**supply** v. (**supplied, supplying**) provide; make available to. • n. (pl. **-ies**) a stock to be used; supplying; necessary goods provided.
▷ SYNS v. 1 PROVIDE, give, furnish, contribute, donate, grant; inf. fork out, shell out. 2 SATISFY, meet, fulfil. • n. 1 STOCK, store, reserve, reservoir, stockpile, hoard, cache. 2 (**supplies**) PROVISIONS, stores, rations, food, foodstuffs, produce.

**support** v. 1 bear the weight of. 2 assist financially; encourage, help, or approve of; confirm or back up. • n. the act of supporting; a person or thing that supports.
▷ SYNS v. 1 BEAR, carry, hold up, prop up, brace, shore up, underpin, buttress. 2 MAINTAIN, provide for, sustain, take care of, look after. 3 COMFORT, encourage, buoy up, hearten, fortify. 4 BACK UP, substantiate, bear out, corroborate, confirm, verify, validate, authenticate, endorse, ratify. 5 BACK, champion, help, assist, aid, side with, vote for, stand up for; advocate, promote, espouse, defend; subsidize, finance, fund; inf. stick up for. • n. 1 BASE, foundations, pillar, post, prop, underpinning, substructure, brace, buttress. 2 KEEP, maintenance, sustenance, subsistence. 3 ENCOURAGEMENT, succour, comfort, help, assistance, backing; tower of strength, prop, mainstay.

**supporter** n. a person who supports a sports team, political party, etc.

▷ SYNS **1** ADVOCATE, backer, adherent, promoter, champion, defender, apologist; helper, ally, voter. **2** CONTRIBUTOR, donor, sponsor, patron, benefactor, well-wisher. **3** FAN, follower, enthusiast, devotee.

**supportive** adj. providing encouragement or emotional help.
▷ SYNS ENCOURAGING, positive, helpful, sympathetic, reassuring, understanding, caring, concerned.

**suppose** v. assume or think; take as a hypothesis; presuppose. □ **be supposed to** be required or expected to.
■ **supposedly** adv.
▷ SYNS **1** ASSUME, dare say, take as read, presume, expect, imagine, believe, think, fancy, suspect, guess, surmise, reckon, conjecture. **2** HYPOTHESIZE, postulate, posit.

**supposition** n. a belief not based on proof or certainty.
▷ SYNS BELIEF, conjecture, speculation, assumption, presumption, theory, hypothesis.

**suppress** v. **1** put an end to. **2** keep from being known.
■ **suppression** n.
▷ SYNS **1** CRUSH, quash, conquer, stamp out, extinguish, put down, put an end to. **2** RESTRAIN, stifle, hold back, control, keep in check, curb, bottle up. **3** KEEP SECRET, conceal, hide, hush up, withhold, cover up.

**suppurate** v. form pus.

**supremacy** n. the state of being superior to all others.
▷ SYNS ASCENDANCY, predominance, dominion, authority, mastery, control, power, rule, sovereignty, dominance, superiority.

**supreme** adj. highest in authority; greatest or most important.
■ **supremely** adv.
▷ SYNS **1** HIGHEST-RANKING, highest, leading, chief, foremost, principal. **2** EXTREME, greatest, utmost, uttermost, maximum, extraordinary, remarkable.

**supremo** n. (pl. **-os**) inf. a person in overall charge of something.

**surcharge** n. an additional charge.

**sure** adj. **1** completely confident. **2** reliable; certainly true or correct. **3** (**sure to**) certain to receive, do, etc. • adv. certainly.
■ **surely** adv.
▷ SYNS adj. **1** CERTAIN, definite, positive, convinced, confident, assured; unhesitating, unwavering. **2** GUARANTEED, unfailing, infallible, unerring, tested, tried and tested, foolproof; inf. sure-fire. **3** RELIABLE, dependable, trusted, trustworthy, trusty, loyal, faithful, steadfast.

**surety** n. (pl. **-ies**) a guarantee; a guarantor of a person's promise.

**surf** n. the breaking of waves on a seashore etc. • v. ride on the crest of a wave on a surfboard; move between sites on the Internet. □ **surfboard** a long, narrow board used in surfing.
■ **surfer** n.

**surface** n. the outside or uppermost layer of something; the top or upper limit; an outward appearance. • v. **1** come to the surface of water etc.; become apparent. **2** put a specified surface on.
▷ SYNS n. **1** OUTSIDE, exterior, top. **2** APPEARANCE, facade.
• v. APPEAR, come to light,

emerge, materialize, arise, crop up.

**surfeit** n. an excessive amount, esp. of food or drink.

**surge** v. move forward in or like waves; increase in volume or intensity. • n. a surging movement or increase.
▷ SYNS V. GUSH, rush, stream, flow, pour, cascade.

**surgeon** n. a doctor qualified to perform surgical operations.

**surgery** n. (pl. **-ies**) **1** treatment by cutting open the body and repairing or removing parts. **2** a doctor's or dentist's consulting room. ■ **surgical** adj.

**surly** adj. bad-tempered and unfriendly.
▷ SYNS BAD-TEMPERED, grumpy, crotchety, grouchy, cantankerous, irascible, testy, gruff, abrupt, brusque, churlish, morose, sullen, sulky.

**surmise** v. guess or suppose. • n. a guess.
▷ SYNS V. GUESS, conjecture, suspect, deduce, assume, presume, gather, suppose, think, believe, imagine.

**surmount** v. overcome a difficulty or obstacle; be on top of.
▷ SYNS GET OVER, overcome, conquer, triumph over, beat, get the better of.

**surname** n. a family name.

**surpass** v. outdo; excel.
▷ SYNS EXCEL, exceed, transcend, outdo, outshine, outstrip, beat, overshadow, eclipse.

**surplice** n. a white robe worn by clergy and choristers.

**surplus** n. an amount left over. • adj. excess.
▷ SYNS n. EXCESS, surfeit, glut; remainder, residue. • adj. EXCESS, leftover, superfluous,

unwanted, unused, remaining, extra, spare.

**surprise** n. **1** a feeling caused by something sudden or unexpected. **2** an unexpected thing. • v. **1** cause to feel surprise. **2** come on or attack unexpectedly.
▷ SYNS n. **1** ASTONISHMENT, amazement, disbelief, wonder. **2** SHOCK, bolt from the blue, bombshell, eye-opener.
• v. **1** ASTONISH, amaze, take aback, startle, astound, stun, stagger; inf. bowl over, flabbergast. **2** TAKE BY SURPRISE, catch unawares, catch off guard, catch red-handed.

**surprising** adj. astonishing or unexpected.
▷ SYNS ASTONISHING, amazing, startling, astounding, staggering, incredible, extraordinary; unexpected, unforeseen.

**surreal** adj. bizarre or dreamlike.

**surrender** v. give in to an opponent; hand over. • n. surrendering.
▷ SYNS V. **1** GIVE IN, give yourself up, yield, submit, capitulate, lay down your arms, raise the white flag, throw in the towel. **2** RELINQUISH, renounce, forgo, cede, waive, hand over, deliver up, sacrifice.

**surreptitious** adj. done stealthily.
▷ SYNS STEALTHY, clandestine, secret, sneaky, sly, furtive, covert.

**surrogate** n. a deputy. □ **surrogate mother** a woman who bears a child on behalf of another. ■ **surrogacy** n.

**surround** v. be all round something. • n. a border.

▷ SYNS V. ENCIRCLE, enclose, encompass, ring, fence in, hem in, confine.

**surroundings** pl.n. things or conditions around a person or place.
▷ SYNS ENVIRONMENT, setting, background, milieu, vicinity, locality, habitat.

**surtax** n. an additional tax.

**surveillance** n. close observation.
▷ SYNS OBSERVATION, watch, scrutiny, reconnaissance, spying, espionage.

**survey** v. look at and take a general view of; examine and report on the condition of a building; measure and map out. • n. a general view, examination, or description; a report or map produced by surveying.
■ surveyor n.
▷ SYNS V. LOOK AT/OVER, observe, view, contemplate, regard, examine, inspect, scan, study, consider, scrutinize, take stock of, size up. • n. 1 STUDY, consideration, review, overview, examination, inspection, scrutiny. 2 INVESTIGATION, inquiry, probe, questionnaire, census.

**survival** n. surviving; something that has survived from an earlier time.

**survive** v. continue to live or exist; not be killed by; remain alive after the death of.
■ survivor n.
▷ SYNS 1 LIVE ON, continue, remain, last, persist, endure, go on, carry on. 2 OUTLIVE, outlast.

**susceptible** adj. easily affected or influenced. ■ susceptibility n.
▷ SYNS 1 IMPRESSIONABLE, credulous, gullible, naive,

innocent, ingenuous. 2 (**susceptible to**) OPEN TO, receptive to, vulnerable to, defenceless against.

**sushi** n. a Japanese dish of balls of cold rice with raw fish etc.

**suspect** v. 1 feel that something may exist or be true. 2 believe someone to be guilty without proof. 3 doubt the genuineness of. • n. a person suspected of a crime etc. • adj. possibly dangerous or false.
▷ SYNS V. 1 FEEL, have a feeling, be inclined to think, fancy, surmise, guess, conjecture, have a hunch, suppose, believe, think, conclude. 2 DOUBT, have misgivings about, distrust, mistrust.

**suspend** v. 1 halt temporarily. 2 temporarily bar from a job or from attending school. 3 (**suspended**) (of a sentence) not enforced as long as no further offence is committed. 4 hang up.
▷ SYNS ADJOURN, interrupt, cut short, break off, discontinue.

**suspender** n. an elastic strap to hold up a stocking.

**suspense** n. anxious uncertainty about what may happen.
▷ SYNS UNCERTAINTY, tension, doubt, anticipation, expectation, expectancy, excitement, anxiety, nervousness, apprehension.

**suspension** n. 1 suspending. 2 the means by which a vehicle is supported on its axles.
□ suspension bridge a bridge suspended by cables running between towers.

**suspicion** n. 1 an unconfirmed belief; a feeling that someone is guilty; distrust. **2** a slight trace.

▷ SYNS **1** DOUBT, misgiving, qualm, scepticism, distrust, mistrust. **2** FEELING, intuition, impression, inkling, hunch, fancy, belief, notion, idea.

**suspicious** adj. **1** feeling suspicion. **2** apparently dishonest or dangerous.

▷ SYNS **1** DOUBTFUL, sceptical, distrustful, mistrustful, disbelieving, unsure, wary. **2** SUSPECT, dubious, disreputable, unsavoury; inf. shifty, shady.

**sustain** v. **1** support; give strength to; keep alive or in existence. **2** suffer something unpleasant.

▷ SYNS **1** BEAR, support, carry, prop up, shore up. **2** COMFORT, help, assist, encourage, buoy up, cheer up, hearten, succour. **3** KEEP ALIVE, maintain, preserve, feed, nourish.

**sustainable** adj. (of development etc.) able to be continued without damage to the environment.

**sustained** adj. continuing for a long period.

▷ SYNS CONTINUOUS, ongoing, steady, constant, prolonged, persistent; relentless, unremitting.

**sustenance** n. food or nourishment.

▷ SYNS FOOD, nourishment, nutriment, provisions, victuals, rations, provender.

**suture** n. a stitch or thread used in the stitching of a wound or cut.

**svelte** adj. slender and graceful.

**SW** abbr. south-west or south-western.

**swab** n. a pad for cleaning wounds or taking specimens; a specimen taken with this.
• v. (**swabbed**, **swabbing**) clean with a swab.

**swaddle** v. wrap in garments or a cloth.

**swag** n. inf. loot.

**swagger** v. walk or behave very arrogantly or confidently. • n. a swaggering walk or manner.

▷ SYNS v. STRUT, parade; inf. sashay.

**swallow** v. **1** cause to pass down the throat. **2** absorb or engulf. **3** believe. • n. **1** an act of swallowing. **2** a fast-flying bird with a forked tail.

▷ SYNS v. EAT, drink, gulp down, consume, devour; inf. scoff, swill, swig.

**swam** past of SWIM.

**swamp** n. a marsh. • v. flood with water; overwhelm with a mass of things.

▷ SYNS n. MARSH, bog, quagmire, mire, morass, fen. • v. **1** FLOOD, inundate, deluge, soak, drench, saturate. **2** OVERWHELM, engulf, snow under, overload, besiege, beset.

**swan** n. a large, white, long-necked waterbird. □ swansong a person's last performance or achievement.

**swank** v. inf. show off.

**swanky** adj. (**-ier**, **-iest**) inf. luxurious and expensive.

**swap** (also **swop**) v. (**swapped**, **swapping**) exchange or substitute. • n. an act of swapping.

▷ SYNS v. EXCHANGE, trade, barter, switch, change, replace.

**swarm** n. a large group of insects, people, etc. • v. **1** move in a swarm. **2** be crowded. **3** (**swarm up**) climb by gripping with the arms and legs.

▷ SYNS n. CROWD, horde, mob, throng, mass, army, herd, pack.
• v. FLOCK, crowd, throng, stream, surge.

**swarthy** adj. having a dark complexion.

**swashbuckling** adj. having daring and romantic adventures.

**swastika** n. a symbol formed by a cross with ends bent at right angles.

**swat** v. (**swatted, swatting**) hit hard with something flat.

**swatch** n. a sample of cloth etc.

**swathe**[1] (US **swath**) n. a strip cut in one sweep or passage by a scythe or mower.

**swathe**[2] v. wrap with layers of coverings.

**sway** v. 1 move gently to and fro. 2 influence someone. • n. 1 a swaying movement. 2 influence or control.
▷ SYNS v. 1 SWING, shake, undulate, rock. 2 INFLUENCE, affect, persuade, prevail on, bring round, win over, manipulate.
• n. JURISDICTION, rule, government, sovereignty, dominion, control, command, power, authority, ascendancy, domination, mastery.

**swear** v. 1 state or promise on oath; state emphatically. 2 use a swear word.
▷ SYNS 1 PROMISE, pledge, vow, give your word. 2 INSIST, avow, declare, assert, maintain. 3 CURSE, blaspheme, use bad language.

**swear word** n. an offensive or obscene word.
▷ SYNS EXPLETIVE, oath, curse, obscenity, profanity.

**sweat** n. moisture given off by the body through the pores as a result of heat, effort, or anxiety.
• v. give off sweat; work hard.
□ **sweatshirt** a loose cotton sweater. **sweatshop** a place employing workers for long hours in poor conditions.
■ **sweaty** adj.

**sweater** n. a pullover.

**swede** n. a large variety of turnip.

**sweep** v. 1 clean by brushing away dirt etc. 2 move quickly or forcefully. 3 (**sweeping**) wide in range or effect. 4 (**sweeping**) (of a statement) too general.
• n. 1 an act of sweeping. 2 a long curving movement. 3 a long expanse of land etc. 4 a person who cleans soot from chimneys. □ **sweepstake** a form of gambling in which all the stakes are divided among the winners.

**sweet** adj. 1 having the pleasant taste of sugar. 2 having a pleasant smell or sound. 3 pleasant and kind. 4 charming and endearing. • n. 1 a small piece of confectionery made with sugar. 2 a sweet dish forming a course of a meal. □ **sweetcorn** a variety of maize with sweet kernels eaten as a vegetable. **sweet-talk** inf. persuade by using flattery or charm. ■ **sweeten** v.
▷ SYNS adj. 1 SWEETENED, sugary, sugared, syrupy, saccharine. 2 FRAGRANT, aromatic, perfumed, scented. 3 MELODIOUS, musical, tuneful, mellifluous, harmonious, silvery. 4 GOOD-NATURED, amiable, pleasant, agreeable, friendly, kindly, charming, likeable. 5 CUTE, loveable, adorable, endearing, charming, appealing. • n. 1 CONFECTIONERY,

bonbon; US candy. **2** DESSERT, pudding; inf. afters.

**sweetener** n. **1** a sweetening substance. **2** inf. a bribe.

**sweetheart** n. a girlfriend or boyfriend.
▷ SYNS GIRLFRIEND, boyfriend, lover, love; suitor, admirer.

**swell** v. **1** become larger. **2** increase in strength or amount. • n. **1** a rounded form. **2** a gradual increase. **3** the movement of the sea.
▷ SYNS v. **1** EXPAND, bulge, distend, inflate, dilate, bloat, puff up, balloon. **2** INCREASE, grow, rise, mount, escalate, multiply, proliferate, snowball, mushroom.

**swelling** n. a swollen place on the body.
▷ SYNS BUMP, lump, bulge, blister, inflammation, protuberance.

**swelter** v. be uncomfortably hot.

**sweltering** adj. uncomfortably hot.
▷ SYNS HOT, stifling, humid, sultry, sticky, muggy, close; torrid, tropical; inf. boiling, baking.

**swept** past and p.p. of SWEEP.

**swerve** v. turn aside from a straight course. • n. a swerving movement.
▷ SYNS v. VEER, skew, deviate, sheer, go off course.

**swift** adj. quick or prompt. • n. a fast-flying bird with narrow wings.
▷ SYNS adj. FAST, rapid, quick, fleet, brisk, prompt, immediate, instantaneous, speedy, sudden, abrupt, hasty.

**swig** v. (**swigging**, **swigged**) inf. drink quickly.

**swill** v. rinse; (of liquid) swirl round in a container.

• n. kitchen refuse mixed with water and fed to pigs.

**swim** v. (**swam**, **swum**, **swimming**) **1** move through water using the arms and legs. **2** be covered with liquid. **3** be dizzy. • n. a period of swimming. ■ **swimmer** n.

**swimmingly** adv. easily and satisfactorily.

**swindle** v. cheat someone in order to get money. • n. a piece of swindling. ■ **swindler** n.
▷ SYNS v. DEFRAUD, cheat, trick, dupe, deceive, fleece; inf. do, con, diddle, rip off, pull a fast one on.

**swine** n. **1** (pl. **swine**) a pig. **2** inf. a contemptible person.

**swing** v. **1** move to and fro while suspended or on an axis. **2** move by grasping a support and jumping; move in a smooth curve. **3** change from one mood or opinion to another; influence decisively. • n. **1** a swinging movement. **2** a hanging seat for swinging on. **2** a change in opinion etc.
▷ SYNS v. **1** SWAY, move to and fro, flutter, flap; hang, dangle. **2** CURVE, veer, turn, bend, wind, twist. **3** CHANGE, fluctuate, oscillate, shift, waver, see-saw, yo-yo.

**swingeing** adj. severe; extreme.

**swipe** v. **1** hit with a swinging blow. **2** inf. steal. **3** pass a swipe card through an electronic reader. • n. a swinging blow. □ **swipe card** a plastic card carrying coded information which is read when the card is slid through an electronic device.

**swirl** v. move in a spiralling pattern.

▷ SYNS WHIRL, eddy, circulate, revolve, spin, twist, churn.

**swish** v. move with a soft hissing sound. • n. this sound.

**switch** n. **1** a device operated to turn electric current on or off. **2** a change or exchange. **3** a flexible shoot cut from a tree. • v. **1** change in position or direction. **2** exchange. **3** turn an electrical device on or off. □ **switchback** a road with alternate sharp ascents and descents. **switchboard** a device for routing phone calls.

▷ SYNS n. CHANGE, move, shift, transition, reversal, turnaround, U-turn. • v. EXCHANGE, interchange, trade, swap.

**swivel** n. a link or pivot enabling one part to revolve without turning another. • v. (**swivelled**, **swivelling**; US **swiveled**) turn on or as if on a swivel.

**swollen** p.p. of SWELL.

**swoon** v. faint.

**swoop** v. make a sudden downward rush; make a sudden attack. • n. an act of swooping.

**swop** = SWAP.

**sword** n. a weapon with a long blade and a hilt. □ **swordfish** an edible sea fish with a sword-like snout.

**swore** past of SWEAR.

**sworn** p.p. of SWEAR. • adj. bound by an oath.

**swot** inf. v. (**swotted**, **swotting**) study hard. • n. a person who studies hard.

**swum** p.p. of SWIM.

**swung** past and p.p. of SWING.

**sycamore** n. a large tree of the maple family.

**sycophant** n. a person who tries to win favour with someone by flattery.

**sycophantic** adj. obsequious and ingratiating.

▷ SYNS OBSEQUIOUS, servile, unctuous, subservient, ingratiating, toadying, flattering; inf. smarmy.

**syllable** n. a unit of sound in a word.

**syllabus** n. (pl. **-buses** or **-bi**) the subjects to be covered by a course of study.

**syllogism** n. reasoning in which a conclusion is drawn from two propositions.

**sylph** n. a slender girl or woman.

**symbiosis** n. (pl. **-oses**) a relationship between two organisms living in close, mutually beneficial association. ■ **symbiotic** adj.

**symbol** n. **1** a thing representing something else. **2** a character with a fixed meaning. ■ **symbolism** n.

▷ SYNS **1** REPRESENTATION, token, sign, emblem, figure, image. **2** SIGN, character, mark, letter.

**symbolic** adj. **1** acting as a symbol. **2** involving the use of symbols or symbolism.

▷ SYNS **1** EMBLEMATIC, representative, indicative, suggestive. **2** FIGURATIVE, allegorical, metaphorical, allusive.

**symbolize** (or **-ise**) v. be a symbol of; represent by means of a symbol.

▷ SYNS STAND FOR, represent, exemplify, denote, signify, mean; typify, personify, epitomize.

**symmetrical** adj. showing symmetry.

▷ SYNS BALANCED, proportional, regular, even, harmonious, uniform, consistent.

**symmetry** n. the exact match in size or shape between two halves, parts, or sides of something.

**sympathetic** adj. **1** feeling or showing sympathy. **2** pleasing or likeable. ■ **sympathetically** adv.
▷ SYNS **1** COMPASSIONATE, caring, concerned, solicitous, empathetic, understanding, sensitive; comforting, supportive, considerate, kind. **2** LIKEABLE, pleasant, pleasing, agreeable, congenial, friendly, genial.

**sympathize** (or **-ise**) v. feel or express sympathy.
▷ SYNS COMMISERATE WITH, pity, offer your condolences, feel (sorry) for, identify with, empathize with.

**sympathy** n. (pl. **-ies**) sorrow at someone else's misfortune; understanding between people; support or approval.
▷ SYNS **1** COMPASSION, caring, concern, solicitude; commiseration, pity, condolence, comfort, solace, support, kindness. **2** RAPPORT, fellow feeling, affinity, empathy, harmony, accord, compatibility, fellowship.

**symphony** n. (pl. **-ies**) an elaborate musical composition for a full orchestra. ■ **symphonic** adj.

**symposium** n. (pl. **-siums** or **-sia**) a meeting for discussing a particular subject.

**symptom** n. a sign of the existence of a condition, esp. a disease. ■ **symptomatic** adj.
▷ SYNS SIGN, indication, signal, mark, characteristic, feature, token, evidence, demonstration, manifestation.

**synagogue** n. a building for public Jewish worship.

**synchronize** (or **-ise**) v. cause to happen or operate at the same time or the same rate.

**syncopate** v. change the accents in music so that weak beats become strong and vice versa. ■ **syncopation** n.

**syndicate** n. a group of people or firms combining to achieve a common interest. • v. control or manage by a syndicate; arrange publication in many newspapers etc. simultaneously.

**syndrome** n. a set of medical symptoms which tend to occur together.

**synergy** n. cooperation of two or more things to produce a combined effect greater than the sum of their separate effects.

**synod** n. an official meeting of Church ministers and members.

**synonym** n. a word or phrase meaning the same as another in the same language. ■ **synonymous** adj.

**synopsis** n. (pl. **-opses**) a brief summary.

**syntax** n. the arrangement of words to form sentences. ■ **syntactic** adj.

**synthesis** n. **1** combining. **2** the production of chemical compounds from simpler substances.
▷ SYNS COMBINATION, union, blend, amalgam, fusion, composite, mixture, compound.

**synthesize** (or **-ise**) v. **1** make by chemical synthesis. **2** combine into a coherent whole.

**synthesizer** (or **-iser**) n. an electronic musical instrument able to produce a great variety of sounds.

**synthetic** adj. made by synthesis; not genuine.
▷ SYNS IMITATION, man-made, fake, artificial, mock, ersatz.

**syphilis** n. a venereal disease.

**syringe** n. a tube with a nozzle and piston, for sucking in and ejecting liquid. • v. clean with liquid from a syringe.

**syrup** n. a thick sweet liquid.
■ syrupy adj.

**system** n. a set of connected things that form a whole or work together; an organized scheme or method; orderliness.
▷ SYNS **1** STRUCTURE, organization, network, arrangement, set-up. **2** METHOD, methodology, technique, process, procedure, approach, practice, means, way, modus operandi. **3** METHOD, order, orderliness, planning, logic.

**systematic** adj. methodical.
■ systematically adv.
▷ SYNS METHODICAL, organized, orderly, planned, systematized, logical, efficient, businesslike.

# Tt

**tab** n. a small projecting flap or strip.

**tabby** n. (pl. **-ies**) a cat with grey or brown fur and dark stripes.

**tabernacle** n. (in the Bible) a portable shrine; a place of worship for some religions.

**table** n. **1** a piece of furniture with a flat top supported on one or more legs. **2** a list of facts or figures arranged in columns. • v. present for discussion at a meeting. □ tablespoon a large spoon for serving food. table tennis a game played with bats and a small hollow ball on a table.
▷ SYNS n. CHART, diagram, figure, graph, plan; list, index. • v. SUBMIT, put forward, propose, suggest.

**tableau** n. (pl. **-leaux**) a silent motionless group arranged to represent a scene.

**tablet** n. **1** a slab bearing an inscription etc. **2** a pill in the shape of a disc or cylinder.
▷ SYNS **1** SLAB, panel, stone. **2** PILL, capsule, lozenge.

**tabloid** n. a small-sized newspaper, often sensational in style.

**taboo** n. a ban or prohibition made by religion or social custom. • adj. prohibited by a taboo.
▷ SYNS adj. FORBIDDEN, prohibited, banned, proscribed.

**tabular** adj. arranged in a table or list.

**tabulate** v. arrange in tabular form.

**tacit** adj. understood or suggested without being spoken.
▷ SYNS IMPLICIT, understood, implied, unstated, unspoken, silent, wordless.

**taciturn** adj. saying little.
▷ SYNS UNFORTHCOMING, uncommunicative, reticent, tight-lipped, quiet, silent.

**tack** n. **1** a small broad-headed nail. **2** a long stitch as a temporary fastening. **3** a change of course in sailing; an approach to a problem. **4** equipment used in horse riding. • v. **1** fasten or fix with tacks. **2** change course by turning a boat into the wind; do this repeatedly. **3** (**tack on**) casually add.
▷ SYNS n. **1** DRAWING PIN, nail, pin, staple, rivet. **2** COURSE OF ACTION, method, approach, way, strategy.

**tackle** n. **1** a set of ropes and pulleys for lifting etc. **2** equipment for a task or sport. **3** an act of tackling in football etc. • v. **1** start to deal with; confront. **2** try to take the ball from an opponent in football etc.
▷ SYNS n. GEAR, equipment, apparatus, tools, implements, accoutrements, paraphernalia, trappings. • v. UNDERTAKE, address, apply yourself to, get to grips with, embark on, take on; confront, face up to.

**tacky** adj. (**-ier**, **-iest**) **1** (of paint, glue, etc.) not quite dry. **2** inf. tasteless.

**tact** n. sensitivity and skill in dealing with others.
■ **tactless** adj.
▷ SYNS DIPLOMACY, discretion, sensitivity, thoughtfulness, consideration, delicacy, finesse.

**tactful** adj. having or showing tact.
▷ SYNS DIPLOMATIC, sensitive, delicate, subtle, discreet, perceptive, thoughtful, considerate.

**tactic** n. an action to achieve a particular end; the organization of military forces during a war.
▷ SYNS MANOEUVRE, expedient, stratagem, trick, scheme, plan, ploy, course of action, method, approach, tack.

**tactical** adj. of tactics; (of weapons) for use in a battle or at close quarters. □ **tactical voting** voting for the candidate most likely to defeat the leading candidate.
■ **tactically** adv.
▷ SYNS STRATEGIC, politic, shrewd, skilful, adroit, clever, cunning.

**tactile** adj. of or using the sense of touch.

**tadpole** n. the larva of a frog or toad, at the stage when it has gills and a tail.

**taffeta** n. a crisp shiny fabric.

**tag** n. **1** a label; an electronic device attached to someone to monitor their movements. **2** a metal point on a shoelace etc. **3** a much-used phrase or quotation. • v. (**tagged**, **tagging**) **1** attach a tag to. **2** (**tag on**) add at the end. **3** (**tag along**) follow without being invited.

**tagliatelle** n. pasta in ribbon-shaped strips.

**tail** n. **1** the part sticking out at the rear of an animal. **2** the rear or end of something. **3** (**tails**) the side of a coin without the image of a head on it. **4** (**tails**) inf. a tailcoat. • v. **1** inf. follow and observe. **2** (**tail off**) become smaller or weaker. □ **tailback** a long queue of traffic. **tailcoat** a man's formal coat with a long divided flap at the back. **tailgate 1** the door at the back of an estate or hatchback car. **2** a hinged flap at the back of

a truck. **tailplane** a small wing at the tail of an aircraft. **tailspin** a spinning dive by an aircraft. **tailwind** a wind blowing from behind.
▷ SYNS n. BACK, rear, end, extremity.

**tailor** n. a maker of men's clothes. • v. **1** make clothes as a tailor. **2** make or adapt for a special purpose. ■ **tailor-made** adj.
▷ SYNS n. OUTFITTER, dressmaker, couturier, clothier, costumier. • v. CUSTOMIZE, adapt, adjust, modify, change, alter, mould, fit, cut, shape.

**taint** n. a trace of an undesirable quality. • v. contaminate or spoil.

**take** v. **1** reach for and hold. **2** occupy a place or position. **3** carry or bring with you. **4** remove. **5** require or use up. **6** accept or receive. **7** react to or interpret. **8** experience or endure. **9** perform an action, etc. **10** study or teach a subject. • n. **1** a sequence of film or sound recorded at one time. **2** an amount gained. □ **take after** resemble a parent etc. **takeaway 1** a restaurant or shop selling cooked food to be eaten elsewhere. **2** a meal of such food. **take in 1** realize fully. **2** deceive. **take off 1** become airborne. **2** mimic. **takeover** an act of taking over. **take over** take control of. **take part** join in. **take place** occur.
▷ SYNS v. **1** GET/LAY HOLD OF, grasp, grip, clutch. **2** GET, receive, obtain, gain, acquire, secure, procure, come by, win. **3** SEIZE, capture, arrest, abduct. **4** STEAL, appropriate, filch, pilfer, purloin; inf. pinch, nick. **5** *it takes an hour:* REQUIRE, need,

necessitate. **6** *take it with you:* CARRY, bring, transport, convey. **7** *take her home:* ESCORT, accompany, conduct, guide, lead, usher. **8** *the room takes 100 people:* HOLD, contain, accommodate.

**takings** pl.n. money taken in business.
▷ SYNS PROCEEDS, receipts, earnings, winnings, profit, gain, income, revenue.

**talc** n. talcum powder; a soft mineral.

**talcum powder** n. a light powder used to make skin feel smooth and dry.

**tale** n. a story.
▷ SYNS STORY, narrative, anecdote, legend, fable, myth, parable, allegory, saga; inf. yarn.

**talent** n. a special ability.
▷ SYNS GIFT, flair, aptitude, facility, knack, bent, ability, faculty.

**talented** adj. having talent.
▷ SYNS GIFTED, skilled, skilful, accomplished, brilliant, expert, able, capable, deft, adept, proficient.

**talisman** n. (pl. **-mans**) an object supposed to bring good luck.

**talk** v. **1** speak so as to give information or express ideas or feelings. **2** be able to speak. • n. **1** conversation. **2** an speech or lecture.
▷ SYNS v. SPEAK, converse, communicate; confer, consult, parley; chat, chatter, gossip; inf. natter. • n. **1** CONVERSATION, chat, discussion, dialogue. **2** LECTURE, speech, address, discourse, oration.

**talkative** adj. talking very much.
▷ SYNS LOQUACIOUS, garrulous, voluble, chatty.

**tall** adj. of great or specified height. □ **tall order** a difficult task. **tall story** an unlikely account.
▷ SYNS BIG, high, lofty, towering, soaring, sky-high.

**tallow** n. animal fat used to make candles and soap.

**tally** n. (pl. **-ies**) a current score or amount. • v. (**tallied, tallying**) agree or correspond.
▷ SYNS n. COUNT, record, total, reckoning. • v. AGREE, correspond, accord, concur, coincide, match, conform.

**talon** n. a curved claw.

**tambourine** n. a percussion instrument with jingling metal discs.

**tame** adj. (of an animal) not dangerous or frightened of people; unexciting. • v. make tame or manageable.
▷ SYNS adj. 1 DOMESTICATED, domestic, docile. 2 UNEXCITING, uninteresting, uninspired, dull, bland, insipid, pedestrian, humdrum, boring, tedious. • v. 1 DOMESTICATE, break in, train. 2 SUBDUE, discipline, curb, control, master, overcome, suppress, repress.

**tamper** v. meddle or interfere.
▷ SYNS MEDDLE, interfere, mess about, tinker, fiddle.

**tampon** n. a plug of absorbent material inserted into the vagina to absorb menstrual blood.

**tan** v. (**tanned, tanning**) 1 make or become brown by exposure to sun. 2 convert animal skin into leather. • n. 1 a suntan. 2 yellowish brown.

**tandem** n. a bicycle for two riders, one behind another. □ **in tandem** together or at the same time.

**tandoori** adj. (of Indian food) cooked in a clay oven.

**tang** n. a strong taste or smell.
■ **tangy** adj.

**tangent** n. 1 a straight line that touches a curve without intersecting it. 2 Math. (in a right-angled triangle) the ratio of the sides opposite and adjacent to an angle. 3 a completely different line of thought etc. ■ **tangential** adj.

**tangerine** n. a small orange.

**tangible** adj. able to be perceived by touch; real.
■ **tangibly** adv.
▷ SYNS 1 TOUCHABLE, palpable, corporeal, physical. 2 *tangible proof*: CONCRETE, real, actual, definite, clear.

**tangle** v. twist into a knotted mass. • n. a tangled mass or condition.

**tangled** adj. 1 matted and intertwined. 2 confused and intricate.
▷ SYNS 1 ENTANGLED, twisted, knotted, knotty, matted, messy, snarled. 2 CONFUSED, jumbled, mixed-up, chaotic, complicated, intricate, complex.

**tango** n. (pl. **-os**) a ballroom dance.

**tank** n. 1 a large container for liquid or gas. 2 an armoured fighting vehicle moving on a continuous metal track.

**tankard** n. a large beer mug.

**tanker** n. a ship, aircraft, or vehicle for carrying liquid in bulk.

**tannin** n. a bitter-tasting substance found in tea, grapes, etc.

**tannoy** n. trademark a public address system.

**tantalize** (or **-ise**) v. torment by the sight of something desired but kept out of reach or withheld.
▷ SYNS TEASE, torment, torture, tempt, entice, lure, allure, excite, titillate.

**tantamount** adj. equivalent.

**tantrum** n. an outburst of bad temper.

**tap** n. **1** a device controlling a flow of liquid or gas from a pipe or container. **2** a light blow. • v. (**tapped**, **tapping**) **1** knock gently. **2** draw liquid from a barrel etc. **3** fit a device to a phone to listen secretly to conversations. ▫ **on tap** readily available. **tap dancing** dancing performed in shoes with metal pieces on the toes and heels.

**tapas** pl.n. small Spanish savoury dishes.

**tape** n. **1** a narrow strip of material for tying, fastening, or labelling things. **2** magnetic tape. **3** a cassette or reel containing this. • v. **1** record on magnetic tape. **2** fasten with tape. ▫ **tape measure** a strip of tape marked for measuring length. **tape recorder** an apparatus for recording and reproducing sounds on magnetic tape. **tapeworm** a ribbon-like worm living as a parasite in intestines.

**taper** n. a thin candle. • v. **1** reduce in thickness towards one end. **2** (**taper off**) gradually lessen.

**tapestry** n. (pl. **-ies**) a piece of thick fabric with a woven or embroidered design.

**tapioca** n. starchy grains obtained from cassava, used in making puddings.

**tapir** n. a piglike animal with a flexible snout.

**tar** n. a thick, dark liquid distilled from coal etc.; a similar substance formed by burning tobacco. • v. (**tarred**, **tarring**) coat with tar.

**taramasalata** n. a dip made from fish roe.

**tarantula** n. a very large hairy spider.

**tardy** adj. (**-ier**, **-iest**) late; slow.

**target** n. a person, object, or place that is the aim of an attack; an objective. • v. (**targeted**, **targeting**) aim at; direct.
▷ SYNS n. **1** OBJECTIVE, goal, object, aim, end, intention. **2** BUTT, victim, object, subject.

**tariff** n. a list of fixed charges; a tax to be paid.
▷ SYNS TAX, duty, toll, excise, levy.

**tarmac** n. trademark broken stone mixed with tar; an area surfaced with this. ■ **tarmacked** adj.

**tarnish** v. cause metal to become stained; spoil a reputation. • n. a stain on metal.
▷ SYNS v. SULLY, besmirch, blacken, stain, blemish, blot, taint.

**tarot** n. a pack of cards used for fortune telling.

**tarpaulin** n. a waterproof canvas.

**tarragon** n. an aromatic herb.

**tart** n. **1** a small pie or flan with a sweet filling. **2** inf. a woman who has many sexual partners. • adj. sour in taste; sharp and sarcastic.
▷ SYNS n. PASTRY, tartlet, pie, strudel. • adj. SHARP, sour, acid, tangy, piquant.

**tartan** n. a checked pattern; cloth marked with this.

**tartar** n. a hard deposit forming on teeth.

**tartare sauce** n. a cold savoury sauce.

**task** n. a piece of work to be done. □ **take to task** rebuke. **task force** a group organized for a special task. **taskmaster** a person who makes others work hard.

▷ SYNS JOB, duty, chore, assignment, commission, mission, undertaking.

**tassel** n. an ornamental bunch of hanging threads.

**taste** n. **1** the sensation of flavour perceived in the mouth on contact with a substance. **2** the sense by which taste is perceived. **3** a small sample of food or drink. **4** a brief experience. **5** a liking. **6** the ability to judge what is good quality or appropriate. • v. **1** perceive or test the flavour of. **2** have a particular flavour. **3** experience briefly.

▷ SYNS n. **1** FLAVOUR, savour, tang. **2** MORSEL, bit, mouthful, sample, sip, soupçon. **3** LIKING, love, fondness, fancy, penchant, partiality, inclination, appetite, thirst, hunger. **4** DISCRIMINATION, discernment, judgement; refinement, elegance, grace, style. • v. SAMPLE, test, try.

**tasteful** adj. showing good judgement of quality.
■ **tastefully** adv.

▷ SYNS IN GOOD TASTE, aesthetic, artistic, elegant, graceful, refined, stylish, chic.

**tasteless** adj. **1** having no flavour. **2** showing poor judgement of quality.

▷ SYNS **1** FLAVOURLESS, bland, insipid, watery, unappetizing, uninteresting. **2** VULGAR, crude,

tawdry, garish, gaudy, loud, flashy, showy, cheap.

**tasty** adj. (**-ier**, **-iest**) having a pleasant flavour.

▷ SYNS DELICIOUS, appetizing, palatable, delectable, mouth-watering.

**tattered** adj. ragged.

**tatters** pl.n. torn pieces.

**tattle** n. & v. gossip.

**tattoo** n. **1** a permanent design made on the skin with a needle and ink. **2** a military display. **3** a rhythmic tapping. • v. mark with a tattoo.

**tatty** adj. (**-ier**, **-iest**) inf. worn and shabby.

**taught** past and p.p. of TEACH.

**taunt** v. jeer at provocatively. • n. a taunting remark.

▷ SYNS v. JEER AT, sneer at, insult, tease, torment, provoke, goad, ridicule, deride, mock, poke fun at.

**taut** adj. stretched tightly.

▷ SYNS TIGHT, stretched, rigid, flexed, tensed.

**tautology** n. saying the same thing again in different words.
■ **tautological** adj.

**tavern** n. old use an inn or pub.

**tawdry** adj. showy but cheap or tasteless.

▷ SYNS SHOWY, gaudy, flashy, garish, loud, tasteless.

**tawny** adj. orange-brown.

**tax** n. money compulsorily paid to the state. • v. impose a tax on; make heavy demands on. □ **tax return** a form declaring income for a particular year, used for tax assessment. ■ **taxation** n.

▷ SYNS n. LEVY, charge, duty, toll, excise, tariff. • v. STRAIN, stretch, overburden, overload, try, wear out, exhaust, sap, drain.

**taxi** n. a vehicle which transports fare-paying passengers to their chosen destination. • v. (**taxied, taxiing**) (of an aircraft) move along the ground.

**taxidermy** n. the process of stuffing and mounting the skins of animals in lifelike form. ■ **taxidermist** n.

**TB** abbr. tuberculosis.

**tea** n. **1** a drink made by infusing the dried leaves of an Asian shrub in boiling water. **2** these leaves. **3** an afternoon or evening meal. □ **tea bag** a porous sachet of tea leaves. **teacake** a currant bun. **teaspoon** a small spoon for stirring tea etc. **tea towel** a cloth for drying washed crockery etc.

**teach** v. **1** give lessons in a subject to a class or pupil. **2** show how to do something. ▷ SYNS INSTRUCT, educate, school, tutor, coach, train, drill.

**teacher** n. a person who teaches. ▷ SYNS TUTOR, instructor; lecturer, professor, don; coach, trainer; guide, mentor, guru.

**teak** n. strong heavy wood from an Asian evergreen tree.

**team** n. a group of players forming one side in a competitive sport; a set of people or animals working together. • v. combine into a team or set. □ **teamwork** organized effort as a group. ▷ SYNS n. GROUP, band, company, gang, crew, troupe, squad, side, line-up.

**tear**[1] v. **1** pull forcibly apart or to pieces; make a hole or split in; become torn. **2** inf. move hurriedly. • n. a hole etc. torn.

□ **tearaway** a wild or reckless person. ▷ SYNS v. RIP, split, rend, rupture.

**tear**[2] n. a drop of liquid forming in and falling from the eye. □ **tear gas** a gas causing severe irritation to the eyes. ■ **tearfully** adv. ▷ SYNS RIP, split, hole, rent, run, rupture.

**tearful** adj. crying or about to cry. ▷ SYNS IN TEARS, crying, weeping, sobbing, lachrymose.

**tease** v. **1** playfully make fun of or attempt to provoke. **2** pick into separate strands. • n. a person who teases. ▷ SYNS v. MAKE FUN OF, poke fun at, taunt, bait, goad; mock, ridicule, deride; inf. pull someone's leg, wind up.

**teat** n. a nipple on an animal's udder; a plastic nipple-shaped device for sucking milk from a bottle.

**technical** adj. **1** of a particular subject, craft, etc. **2** of the practical use of machinery and methods in science and industry. **3** requiring specialized knowledge. **4** according to a strict legal interpretation. ■ **technically** adv.

**technicality** n. (pl. **-ies**) a small formal detail in a set of rules.

**technician** n. **1** a person employed to look after technical equipment. **2** a person skilled in the technique of an art, science, craft, or sport.

**Technicolor** n. trademark a process of producing cinema films in colour.

**technique** n. **1** a special way of doing something. **2** a person's level of skill in a particular field.

▷ SYNS **1** METHOD, system, procedure, approach, way, strategy, means. **2** SKILL, proficiency, expertise, mastery, artistry, ability.

**technology** n. (pl. **-ies**) the application of scientific knowledge in industry etc.; equipment developed in this way. ■ **technological** adj.

**tectonic** adj. of the earth's crust.

**teddy** (or **teddy bear**) n. (pl. **-ies**) a soft toy bear.

**tedious** adj. too long, slow, or dull. ■ **tedium** n.

▷ SYNS WEARISOME, tiresome, tiring, dull, boring, uninteresting, soporific, dreary, uninspired, flat, monotonous, humdrum.

**tee** n. **1** a place from which a golf ball is struck at the start of play. **2** a small peg for supporting this ball. • v. (**teed, teeing**) **1** place a ball on a tee. **2** (**tee off**) make the first stroke in golf.

**teem** v. be full of; (of water or rain) pour.

**teenager** n. a person in their teens. ■ **teenage** adj.

**teens** pl.n. the years of age from 13 to 19.

**teepee** = TEPEE.

**tee shirt** n. a T-shirt.

**teeter** v. balance or move unsteadily.

**teeth** pl. of TOOTH.

**teethe** v. (of a baby) develop first teeth. □ **teething troubles** problems in the early stages of an enterprise.

**teetotal** adj. abstaining completely from alcohol.
■ **teetotaller** n.

**telecommunications** pl.n. communication by telephone, radio, cable, etc.

**telegram** n. a message sent by telegraph.

**telegraph** n. a system or apparatus for sending messages from a distance along wires. • v. send by telegraph.

**telekinesis** n. the supposed ability to move things without touching them.

**telepathy** n. supposed communication by means other than the senses. ■ **telepathic** adj.

**telephone** n. a device for transmitting speech by wire or radio. • v. contact by telephone.
▷ SYNS V. CALL, phone, ring, dial.

**telephonist** n. an operator of a telephone switchboard.

**telephoto lens** n. a photographic lens producing a large image of a distant object.

**teleprinter** n. a device for transmitting telegraph messages as they are keyed.

**telescope** n. an optical instrument for making distant objects appear larger. • v. make or become shorter by sliding each section inside the next; condense or combine to occupy less space or time.
■ **telescopic** adj.

**teletext** n. an information service transmitted to televisions.

**televise** v. transmit by television.

**television** n. **1** a system for transmitting visual images with sound and displaying them electronically on a screen. **2** televised programmes. **3** an apparatus for receiving these.
■ **televisual** adj.

**telex** n. a system of telegraphy using teleprinters and public transmission lines. • v. send by telex.

**tell** v. **1** communicate information to. **2** order or instruct. **3** express in words. **4** determine or establish. **5** be able to recognize a difference. **6** have a noticeable effect. □ **tell off** inf. reprimand.
▷ SYNS **1** INFORM, apprise, notify, brief, fill in. **2** INSTRUCT, order, command, direct, call on, require; formal enjoin. **3** RELATE, recount, narrate, report, recite, describe; utter, voice, state, declare, communicate, impart, divulge. **4** DISTINGUISH, differentiate, discriminate.

**teller** n. **1** a narrator. **2** a person appointed to count votes. **3** a bank cashier.

**telling** adj. having a noticeable effect.
▷ SYNS REVEALING, significant, important, meaningful, influential, striking, potent, powerful, compelling.

**telltale** adj. revealing something. • n. a person who reveals secrets.

**telly** n. inf. television.

**temerity** n. audacity or boldness.

**temp** inf. n. a temporary employee. • v. work as a temp.

**temper** n. **1** a person's state of mind. **2** a fit of anger.
• v. **1** reheat and cool metal to increase its strength and elasticity. **2** moderate or neutralize. □ **keep** (or **lose**) **your temper** remain (or fail to remain) calm under provocation.
▷ SYNS n. **1** MOOD, humour, frame of mind. **2** BAD MOOD, fury, rage, tantrum, pet; inf. paddy, strop.
• v. MODERATE, soften, modify, mitigate, alleviate, allay, lessen, weaken.

**temperament** n. a person's nature as it controls their behaviour.
▷ SYNS DISPOSITION, nature, character, personality, make-up, constitution, mind.

**temperamental** adj. relating to temperament; liable to unreasonable changes of mood.
■ **temperamentally** adv.
▷ SYNS EXCITABLE, emotional, volatile, mercurial, capricious, erratic, unpredictable, touchy, moody, highly strung, neurotic.

**temperance** n. total abstinence from alcohol.

**temperate** adj. **1** (of a climate) without extremes. **2** self-restrained.
▷ SYNS MODERATE, mild, gentle, clement, balmy.

**temperature** n. **1** the degree of heat or cold. **2** a body temperature above normal.

**tempest** n. a violent storm.
■ **tempestuous** adj.

**template** n. a piece of material used as a pattern for cutting shapes etc.

**temple** n. **1** a building for worship. **2** the flat part between the forehead and the ear.
▷ SYNS PLACE OF WORSHIP, shrine, sanctuary, house of God.

**tempo** n. (pl. **-pos** or **-pi**) the speed of a piece of music; the rate of motion or activity.
▷ SYNS BEAT, rhythm, cadence, time, speed.

**temporal** adj. **1** secular. **2** relating to time.
▷ SYNS SECULAR, worldly, material, earthly.

**temporary** adj. lasting for a limited time. ■ **temporarily** adv.
▷ SYNS **1** SHORT-TERM, interim, provisional. **2** BRIEF, fleeting, passing, momentary, short-lived.

**temporize** (or **-ise**) v. delay making a decision.

**tempt** v. try to persuade someone to do something appealing but wrong. ■ **temptation** n. **temptress** n.
▷ SYNS ENTICE, persuade, inveigle, induce, cajole, coax, lure, attract, appeal to, seduce, tantalize.

**ten** adj. & n. one more than nine; 10. ■ **tenth** adj. & n.

**tenable** adj. able to be defended or held.
▷ SYNS JUSTIFIABLE, defensible, defendable, supportable, credible, reasonable, rational, sound, viable.

**tenacious** adj. holding firmly to something. ■ **tenacity** n.

**tenant** n. a person who rents land or property from a landlord. ■ **tenancy** n.

**tend** v. **1** take care of. **2** have a specified tendency.
▷ SYNS LOOK AFTER, take care of, care for, attend to, minister to.

**tendency** n. (pl. **-ies**) an inclination to act in a particular way.
▷ SYNS INCLINATION, disposition, predisposition, proclivity, propensity, penchant.

**tendentious** adj. controversial.

**tender** adj. **1** not tough or hard; delicate; painful when touched. **2** gentle and loving. • n. **1** a formal offer to supply goods or carry out work at a stated price. **2** a boat used to ferry people and supplies to and from a ship. **3** a truck attached to a steam locomotive to carry fuel and water. • v. offer formally; make a tender for a piece of work. ■ **tenderness** n.
▷ SYNS adj. **1** FRAGILE, frail, delicate, sensitive. **2** LOVING, affectionate, compassionate, soft-hearted, kind, warm, caring, gentle, solicitous, generous. **3** SORE, painful, aching, smarting, throbbing, inflamed, raw, bruised.

**tendon** n. a strip of strong tissue connecting a muscle to a bone.

**tendril** n. a threadlike part by which a climbing plant clings; a slender curl of hair.

**tenement** n. a building divided into flats.

**tenet** n. a firm belief or principle.

**tennis** n. a game in which players use rackets to strike a soft ball over a net on an open court.

**tenor** n. **1** general meaning or character. **2** the highest ordinary male singing voice.

**tense** adj. stretched tightly; nervous and anxious. • v. make or become tense. • n. any of the forms of a verb that indicate the time of the action.
▷ SYNS adj. **1** TIGHT, taut, rigid, stretched. **2** NERVOUS, keyed up, worked up, overwrought, anxious, uneasy, worried, apprehensive, agitated, jumpy, edgy, on edge; inf. uptight.

**tensile** adj. of tension; capable of being stretched.

**tension** n. **1** being stretched tight; strain caused by forces working in opposition; electromagnetic force. **2** mental or emotional strain.

▷ SYNS **1** TIGHTNESS, tautness, rigidity. **2** STRAIN, stress, pressure, anxiety, worry, suspense, uncertainty.

**tent** n. a portable shelter made of canvas etc.

**tentacle** n. a slender flexible part of certain animals, used for feeling or grasping.

**tentative** adj. hesitant.
▷ SYNS **1** SPECULATIVE, conjectural, exploratory, trial, provisional. **2** HESITANT, faltering, uncertain, unsure, cautious.

**tenterhooks** pl.n. (**on tenterhooks**) in a state of nervous suspense.

**tenuous** adj. very slight; very thin.
▷ SYNS SLIGHT, flimsy, weak, insubstantial, shaky, doubtful, dubious.

**tenure** n. the holding of an office or of land or accommodation etc.

**tepee** (or **teepee**) n. a conical tent used by American Indians.

**tepid** adj. lukewarm.

**tequila** n. a Mexican liquor.

**term** n. **1** a fixed or limited period; a period of weeks during which a school etc. is open. **2** a word or phrase; each quantity or expression in a mathematical series or ratio etc. **3** (**terms**) conditions offered or accepted; relations between people: *on good terms*. □ **come to terms with** reconcile yourself to.
▷ SYNS **1** WORD, expression, phrase, name, title, denomination, designation. **2** PERIOD, time, spell, interval, stretch.

**terminal** adj. **1** of or forming an end. **2** (of a disease) leading to death. • n. **1** a terminus. **2** a

building where air passengers arrive and depart. **3** a point of connection in an electric circuit. **4** a keyboard and screen joined to a central computer system. ■ **terminally** adv.
▷ SYNS adj. FATAL, deadly, mortal, lethal; incurable. • n. **1** TERMINUS, depot. **2** WORKSTATION, visual display unit, VDU.

**terminate** v. come or bring to an end. ■ **termination** n.
▷ SYNS END, conclude, finish, stop, wind up, discontinue.

**terminology** n. (pl. **-ies**) the technical terms of a subject. ■ **terminological** adj.
▷ SYNS LANGUAGE, phraseology, vocabulary, nomenclature, jargon, terms, expressions, words; inf. lingo.

**terminus** n. (pl. **-ini** or **-inuses**) the end; the last stopping place on a rail or bus route.

**termite** n. a small insect that is destructive to timber.

**tern** n. a seabird.

**terrace** n. **1** a raised level place; a patio. **2** a row of houses built in one block. ■ **terraced** adj.

**terracotta** n. brownish-red unglazed pottery; its colour.

**terrain** n. land with regard to its natural features.

**terrapin** n. a freshwater turtle.

**terrestrial** adj. of the earth; of or living on land; (of television broadcasting) not using a satellite.

**terrible** adj. extremely bad, serious, or unpleasant. ■ **terribly** adv.
▷ SYNS **1** BAD, poor, incompetent, useless, hopeless, atrocious. **2** DREADFUL, terrifying, frightening, frightful,

horrifying, horrible, horrific, horrendous, harrowing, hideous, grim, unspeakable, appalling, awful, gruesome, ghastly.

**terrier** n. a small dog.

**terrific** adj. **1** very great or intense. **2** inf. excellent.
■ **terrifically** adv.
▷ SYNS **1** TREMENDOUS, huge, massive, colossal, great, mighty, considerable, intense, extreme, prodigious. **2** see **EXCELLENT**.

**terrify** v. (**terrified, terrifying**) fill with terror.
▷ SYNS FRIGHTEN, horrify, petrify, scare.

**terrine** n. a mixture of chopped meat, fish, etc. pressed into a container and served cold.

**territorial** adj. of, having, or defending a territory.
□ Territorial Army (in the UK) a military reserve of volunteers.

**territory** n. **1** an area under the control of a ruler or state. **2** an area in which someone has rights, responsibilities, or knowledge.
▷ SYNS REGION, area, enclave, state, region, dependency, colony; ground, terrain.

**terror** n. **1** extreme fear. **2** a cause of this.
▷ SYNS FRIGHT, fear, dread, horror.

**terrorism** n. the unofficial use of violence and intimidation in the attempt to achieve political aims. ■ **terrorist** n.

**terrorize** (or **-ise**) v. threaten and scare over a period of time.
▷ SYNS PERSECUTE, victimize, torment, tyrannize, menace, threaten, bully; scare, frighten, terrify, petrify.

**terse** adj. concise or curt.

▷ SYNS **1** CONCISE, succinct, compact, brief, laconic, short, crisp, pithy. **2** ABRUPT, curt, brusque, blunt, clipped.

**tertiary** adj. third in order or level.

**test** n. **1** a procedure to discover the quality, performance, presence, etc. of something. **2** a short exam. **3** (also **test match**) an international cricket or rugby match. • v. subject to a test. □ **test tube** a thin glass tube used to hold material in laboratory tests.
▷ SYNS n. TRIAL, experiment, examination, check, assessment, evaluation, appraisal, investigation, analysis, study. • v. EXAMINE, check, try out, trial, assess, evaluate, appraise, investigate.

**testament** n. **1** a will. **2** evidence or proof. **3** (**Testament**) each of the two divisions of the Bible.

**testate** adj. having made a will before dying.

**testicle** n. a male organ that produces sperm. ■ **testicular** adj.

**testify** v. (**testified, testifying**) **1** give evidence in court. **2** serve as evidence or proof.

**testimonial** n. **1** a formal statement of a person's good character and qualifications. **2** a public tribute.

**testimony** n. **1** a formal statement, esp. under oath. **2** evidence or proof.
▷ SYNS EVIDENCE, attestation, sworn statement, affidavit.

**testosterone** n. a male sex hormone.

**testy** adj. irritable.

**tetanus** n. a disease causing muscular spasms and rigidity.

**tetchy** adj. bad-tempered and irritable. ■ **tetchily** adv.

**tête-à-tête** n. a private conversation between two people.

**tether** v. fasten an animal to a post etc. • n. a rope or chain used to tether an animal.

**tetrahedron** n. (pl. **-hedra** or **-hedrons**) a solid with four triangular faces.

**Teutonic** adj. German.

**text** n. 1 a written or printed work. 2 the main body of a book as distinct from illustrations etc. 3 a text message. • v. send someone a text message. □ **textbook** a book used for the study of a subject. **text message** an electronic message sent and received via mobile phone. ■ **textual** adj.
▷ SYNS n. 1 TEXTBOOK, book, publication, work. 2 WORDS, content, body, wording, copy.

**textile** n. a woven or knitted fabric.

**texture** n. the feel or consistency of a substance. ■ **textural** adj.
▷ SYNS FEEL, touch; appearance, surface, grain.

**thalidomide** n. a sedative drug, found to cause fetal malformations when taken by pregnant women.

**than** conj. & prep. used to introduce the second part of a comparison.

**thank** v. express gratitude to. □ **thanksgiving** the expression of gratitude to God. **Thanksgiving** a national holiday held in the autumn in North America. **thank you** a polite expression of gratitude.

**thankful** adj. feeling or expressing gratitude.

▷ SYNS GRATEFUL, pleased, relieved, glad.

**thankfully** adv. 1 in a thankful way. 2 fortunately.

**thankless** adj. unpleasant and unappreciated.

**thanks** pl.n. 1 an expression of gratitude. 2 thank you.
▷ SYNS GRATITUDE, gratefulness, acknowledgement, appreciation, recognition.

**that** adj. & pron. (pl. **those**) referring to a person or thing seen or heard or already mentioned or known, or the more distant of two things. • pron. introducing a clause defining or identifying something. • adv. to such a degree. • conj. introducing a statement or suggestion.

**thatch** n. a roof made of straw or reeds etc. • v. cover with thatch.

**thaw** v. 1 make or become unfrozen. 2 become friendlier. • n. a period of warm weather that melts ice and snow.
▷ SYNS v. MELT, defrost, soften, liquefy.

**the** adj. used to refer to one or more people or things already mentioned or understood; the definite article.

**theatre** (US **theater**) n. 1 a place in which plays are performed. 2 the writing and production of plays. 3 a room where specific activities are done: *an operating theatre.*
▷ SYNS 1 PLAYHOUSE, auditorium, amphitheatre. 2 ACTING, the stage, drama, show business.

**theatrical** adj. 1 of acting, actors, or the theatre. 2 exaggerated for effect.
▷ SYNS 1 DRAMATIC, stage, thespian; show-business;

inf. showbiz. **2** EXAGGERATED, ostentatious, melodramatic, overdone, showy, affected.

**thee** pron. old use you (as the singular object of a verb or preposition).

**theft** n. stealing.
▷ SYNS STEALING, robbery, thieving, burglary, larceny, embezzlement.

**their** adj. of or belonging to them.

**theirs** poss.pron belonging to them.

**them** pron. the objective case of *they*.

**theme** n. **1** a subject being discussed. **2** a melody which is repeated in a musical piece. ▢ **theme park** an amusement park based around a particular idea. ■ **thematic** adj.
▷ SYNS **1** SUBJECT, topic, thesis, argument, text. **2** MELODY, tune; motif, leitmotif.

**themselves** pron. the emphatic and reflexive form of *they* and *them*.

**then** adv. **1** at that time. **2** after that. **3** in that case.

**thence** adv. formal from that place or source.

**theology** n. (pl. **-ies**) **1** the study of God. **2** a system of religious beliefs. ■ **theologian** n. **theological** adj.

**theorem** n. a scientific or mathematical statement that can be proved by reasoning.

**theoretical** adj. concerning or based on theory rather than practice. ■ **theoretically** adv.
▷ SYNS HYPOTHETICAL, conjectural, speculative, suppositional, notional.

**theorize** (or **-ise**) v. form theories.

**theory** n. **1** a set of ideas intended to explain something. **2** the principles on which an activity is based.
▷ SYNS HYPOTHESIS, thesis, conjecture, supposition, speculation, postulation, proposition; opinion, view, belief.

**therapeutic** adj. **1** of the curing of disease. **2** having a good effect on the body or mind. ■ **therapeutically** adv.

**therapy** n. (pl. **-ies**) treatment for a physical or mental disorder. ■ **therapist** n.

**there** adv. **1** in, at, or to that place. **2** on that issue. ▢ **thereabouts** near that place, time, or figure. **thereafter** after that time. **thereby** by that means. **thereupon** formal immediately after that.

**therefore** adv. for that reason.
▷ SYNS CONSEQUENTLY, so, as a result, accordingly, hence; formal thus.

**thermal** adj. **1** of or using heat. **2** made of a special insulating fabric. • n. an upward current of warm air.

**thermodynamics** n. the science of the relationship between heat and other forms of energy.

**thermometer** n. an instrument for measuring temperature.

**Thermos** n. trademark a vacuum flask.

**thermostat** n. a device that regulates temperature automatically.

**thesaurus** n. a dictionary of synonyms.

**these** pl. of THIS.

**thesis** n. **1** a theory put forward and supported by reasoning.

**2** a long essay written as part of a university degree.
▷ SYNS **1** THEORY, hypothesis, contention, argument, proposition, premise, postulation. **2** DISSERTATION, essay, paper, treatise, study, monograph, disquisition.

**thespian** adj. of the theatre.
• n. an actor or actress.

**they** pron. **1** the people already referred to. **2** people in general.

**thiamine** (or **thiamin**)
n. vitamin $B_1$.

**thick** adj. **1** with opposite sides or surfaces relatively far apart. **2** made up of many closely packed elements. **3** dense or difficult to see through. **4** relatively firm in consistency. **5** inf. stupid. • n. the busiest or most intense part. □ **thickset** heavily or solidly built. **thick-skinned** not sensitive to criticism or insults. ■ **thickness** n.
▷ SYNS adj. **1** BROAD, wide, large, big, bulky, sturdy, chunky, solid, substantial. **2** *a thick paste:* FIRM, stiff, semi-solid; clotted, coagulated, viscous, gelatinous. **3** *thick mists:* DENSE, heavy, opaque, impenetrable, soupy, murky.

**thicken** v. make or become thick or thicker.
▷ SYNS STIFFEN, set, solidify, congeal, clot, coagulate.

**thicket** n. a dense group of shrubs or small trees.

**thief** n. (pl. **thieves**) a person who steals.
▷ SYNS ROBBER, burglar, housebreaker, shoplifter, pickpocket, mugger.

**thieve** v. steal.

**thigh** n. the upper part of the leg.

**thimble** n. a hard cap worn to protect the end of the finger in sewing.

**thin** adj. **1** not thick. **2** lean. **3** (of a sound) faint and high-pitched. **4** lacking substance.
• v. (**thinned**, **thinning**) make or become thinner.
▷ SYNS adj. **1** SLIM, slender, lean, slight; skinny, gaunt, scrawny, scraggy, bony, skeletal, emaciated, underweight. **2** FINE, light, delicate, flimsy, diaphanous, sheer, gauzy, filmy. **3** INSUBSTANTIAL, weak, feeble, lame, poor.

**thine** adj. & poss.pron old use your or yours.

**thing** n. **1** an inanimate object. **2** an unspecified object, activity, action, etc. **3** (**things**) belongings.
▷ SYNS **1** OBJECT, article, item, artefact. **2** (**things**) BELONGINGS, possessions, stuff, property, worldly goods, effects, bits and pieces.

**think** v. **1** have a belief or opinion. **2** use the mind to form ideas, solve problems, etc.
• n. an act of thinking. □ **think tank** a body of experts providing advice and ideas.
▷ SYNS v. **1** BELIEVE, consider, hold, suppose, deem, expect, presume, imagine, guess; inf. reckon. **2** PONDER, reflect, deliberate, contemplate, muse, ruminate, concentrate, meditate, brood.

**third** adj. next after second.
• n. **1** a third thing, class, etc. **2** one of three equal parts. □ **the third degree** long and severe questioning. **third-degree burn** a burn of the most severe kind. **third party** a person besides the two main ones involved in a situation; (of insurance)

covering injury suffered by a person other than the insured.

**third-rate** of very poor quality.

**Third World** the developing countries of Asia, Africa, and Latin America.

**thirst** n. 1 a feeling of needing or wanting to drink. 2 a strong desire. • v. have a strong desire for.

**thirsty** adj. feeling or causing thirst.
▷ SYNS LONGING FOR A DRINK, dehydrated, dry; inf. parched, gasping.

**thirteen** adj. & n. one more than twelve; 13. ■ **thirteenth** adj. & n.

**thirty** adj. three times ten; 30. ■ **thirtieth** adj. & n.

**this** adj. & pron. (pl. **these**) the person or thing near, mentioned, or indicated. • adv. to the degree or extent indicated.

**thistle** n. a prickly plant.

**thither** adv. old use to or towards that place.

**thong** n. 1 a strip of leather used as a fastening, lash, etc. 2 a G-string.

**thorax** n. (pl. **-aces** or **-axes**) the part of the body between the neck and the abdomen. ■ **thoracic** adj.

**thorn** n. 1 a small sharp projection on a plant. 2 a thorny bush or tree.

**thorny** adj. 1 having many thorns. 2 causing distress or difficulty.
▷ SYNS 1 PRICKLY, spiky, barbed, spiny, sharp. 2 *a thorny issue:* see **DIFFICULT** (2).

**thorough** adj. 1 complete in every way. 2 detailed and careful. □ **thoroughbred** an animal of pure breed.

**thoroughfare** a road or path between two places. ■ **thoroughly** adv.
▷ SYNS IN-DEPTH, exhaustive, complete, comprehensive, thoroughgoing, intensive, extensive, widespread, sweeping, all-embracing, all-inclusive, detailed, meticulous, scrupulous, assiduous, conscientious, painstaking, punctilious, methodical, careful.

**those** pl. of **THAT**.

**thou** pron. old use you.

**though** conj. despite the fact that. • adv. however.

**thought** past & p.p. of **THINK**. • n. 1 an idea. 2 the process of thinking. 3 careful consideration.
▷ SYNS n. 1 IDEA, notion, view, theory, opinion. 2 THINKING, contemplation, consideration, reflection, meditation, rumination.

**thoughtful** adj. 1 thinking deeply. 2 considerate. 3 thought out carefully. ■ **thoughtfully** adv.
▷ SYNS 1 PENSIVE, reflective, introspective, meditative, contemplative, ruminative. 2 CONSIDERATE, attentive, caring, solicitous, helpful, kind, neighbourly, compassionate, charitable, unselfish.

**thoughtless** adj. 1 inconsiderate. 2 without thinking of the consequences.
▷ SYNS 1 INCONSIDERATE, insensitive, tactless, undiplomatic, unkind. 2 UNTHINKING, heedless, absent-minded, careless, imprudent, unwise, foolish, silly, reckless, rash.

**thousand** adj. & n. ten hundred; 1,000. ■ **thousandth** adj. & n.

**thrall** n. the state of being in another's power.

**thrash** v. 1 beat violently and repeatedly. 2 move in a violent or uncontrolled way. 3 inf. defeat heavily.

**thread** n. 1 a thin strand of cotton or wool etc. 2 the spiral ridge of a screw. 3 the theme of a story, argument, etc. • v. 1 pass a thread through. 2 move between obstacles.
▷ SYNS n. COTTON, yarn; strand, filament, fibre.

**threadbare** adj. worn and tattered with age.
▷ SYNS WORN, old, holey, thin, frayed, tattered, ragged, shabby.

**threat** n. 1 a stated intention to harm someone. 2 a person or thing likely to cause harm or danger.
▷ SYNS 1 WARNING, ultimatum. 2 DANGER, peril, risk, hazard.

**threaten** v. make or be a threat to.
▷ SYNS 1 MENACE, intimidate, browbeat, bully, terrorize. 2 ENDANGER, jeopardize, imperil, put at risk.

**three** adj. & n. one more than two; 3. □ **three-dimensional** having or appearing to have length, breadth, and depth. **threesome** a group of three people.

**thresh** v. separate grains of corn from the rest of the plant.

**threshold** n. 1 a piece of wood or stone forming the bottom of a doorway. 2 a level or point marking the start of something.

▷ SYNS 1 DOORWAY, doorstep, entrance. 2 START, beginning, brink, verge, dawn, opening.

**threw** past of THROW.

**thrice** adv. old use three times.

**thrift** n. economical management of resources.

**thrifty** adj. careful with money.
▷ SYNS ECONOMICAL, careful, frugal, sparing, parsimonious, penny-pinching.

**thrill** n. 1 a sudden feeling of excitement. 2 an exciting experience. 3 a wave of emotion. • v. excite.
■ **thrilling** adj.
▷ SYNS n. EXCITEMENT, exhilaration, pleasure, delight, joy; inf. buzz, kick. • v. EXCITE, stimulate, arouse, stir, electrify, intoxicate.

**thriller** n. an exciting story or film etc.

**thrive** v. 1 grow or develop well. 2 prosper.
▷ SYNS FLOURISH, prosper, bloom, burgeon, succeed, boom.

**throat** n. 1 the passage from the back of the mouth to the oesophagus or lungs. 2 the front of the neck.

**throaty** adj. (-ier, -iest) deep and husky.

**throb** v. 1 beat or pulsate with a strong rhythm. 2 feel regular bursts of pain. • n. a regular pulsation.
▷ SYNS v. BEAT, pulse, pulsate, palpitate, pound.

**throes** pl.n. severe or violent pains.

**thrombosis** n. (pl. -oses) the formation of a blood clot in a blood vessel or the heart.

**throne** n. **1** a ceremonial seat for a monarch or bishop. **2** the power or rank of a monarch.

**throng** n. a crowded mass of people. • v. gather somewhere in large numbers.
▷ SYNS n. CROWD, horde, mob, mass, host, multitude, swarm, flock, pack, herd, drove.

**throttle** n. a device controlling the flow of fuel or power to an engine. • v. strangle.
▷ SYNS v. STRANGLE, choke, garrotte.

**through** prep. & adv. **1** from end to end or side to side of. **2** from start to finish. **3** by means of. • adj. **1** (of public transport) continuing to the final destination. **2** passing straight through a place. **3** having passed to the next stage of a competition. □ throughout all the way through. throughput the amount of material processed.

**throve** past of THRIVE.

**throw** v. **1** send through the air from the hand. **2** move or place hurriedly or roughly. **3** project or direct in a particular direction. **4** send suddenly into a particular state. **5** confuse. • n. **1** an act of throwing. **2** a light cover for furniture. □ throw away get rid of. throwback a person or thing that resembles someone or something that existed in the past. throw up vomit.
▷ SYNS v. **1** HURL, toss, sling, fling, pitch, lob, propel, launch, cast; inf. heave, chuck. **2** DISCONCERT, discomfit, fluster, astonish, surprise, dumbfound, confuse.

**thrush** n. a songbird with a speckled breast.

**thrust** v. (**thrust**, **thrusting**) push suddenly or forcibly. • n. a thrusting movement or force.
▷ SYNS v. PUSH, shove, ram, drive, force, propel.

**thud** n. a dull, heavy sound. • v. (**thudded**, **thudding**) move or fall with a thud.

**thug** n. a violent person.
■ thuggery n.
▷ SYNS RUFFIAN, hooligan, bully boy, hoodlum, criminal, villain, gangster.

**thumb** n. the short, thick first digit of the hand. • v. **1** turn over pages with the thumb. **2** ask for a lift in a passing vehicle by signalling with the thumb.

**thump** v. **1** hit heavily. **2** (of the heart) beat rapidly. • n. a heavy blow or noise.

**thunder** n. **1** a loud rumbling or crashing noise heard after lightning. **2** a loud, deep noise. • v. **1** make the sound of thunder. **2** speak loudly or angrily. □ thunderbolt a flash of lightning with a crash of thunder. thunderclap a crash of thunder. ■ thunderous adj. thundery adj.

**Thursday** n. the day after Wednesday.

**thus** adv. formal **1** as a result of this. **2** in this way.

**thwart** v. prevent from accomplishing something.
▷ SYNS FRUSTRATE, foil, check, block, stop, prevent, defeat, impede, obstruct, hinder, hamper; inf. stymie.

**thy** adj. old use your.

**thyme** n. a fragrant herb.

**thyroid** n. a large gland in the neck, secreting a growth hormone.

**tiara** n. a jewelled semicircular headdress.

**tibia** n. (pl. **tibiae**) the inner shin bone.

**tic** n. an involuntary muscular twitch.

**tick** n. 1 a regular clicking sound, as made by a clock or watch. 2 a mark (✓) used to show that an answer is correct or an item on a list has been dealt with. 3 a bloodsucking mite or parasitic insect. 4 inf. a moment.
• v. 1 make regular ticking sounds. 2 mark with a tick. 3 (**tick over**) (of an engine) run in neutral. 4 (**tick off**) inf. reprimand.

**ticket** n. 1 a piece of card or paper entitling the holder to enter or travel somewhere etc. 2 a label. 3 notification of a traffic offence.

**ticking** n. strong fabric used to cover mattresses.

**tickle** v. 1 touch lightly so as to cause a slight tingling sensation. 2 amuse or appeal to. • n. the act or sensation of tickling. ■ **tickly** adj.

**ticklish** adj. 1 sensitive to tickling. 2 requiring careful handling.

**tidal** adj. of or affected by tides.

**tiddler** n. inf. a small fish.

**tiddlywinks** pl.n. a game in which small counters are flicked into a cup.

**tide** n. 1 the sea's regular rise and fall. 2 a surge of feeling or trend of events. • v. (**tide over**) help temporarily.

**tidings** pl.n. lit. news.

**tidy** adj. (**-ier, -iest**) neat and orderly. • v. (**tidied, tidying**) make tidy. ■ **tidily** adv. **tidiness** n.

▷ SYNS adj. 1 NEAT, orderly, in order, spruce, shipshape, spick and span. 2 ORGANIZED, methodical, systematic, businesslike.
• v. CLEAR UP, put in order, straighten, spruce up, neaten.

**tie** v. 1 attach or fasten with string, cord, etc. 2 form into a knot or bow. 3 restrict or limit. 4 link or connect. 5 achieve the same score as another competitor. • n. 1 a thing that ties. 2 a strip of cloth worn round a collar and knotted at the front. 3 an equal score in a game or match. 4 a sports match in which the winners proceed to the next round. □ **tie-break** a means of deciding a winner when competitors have tied.
▷ SYNS v. 1 FASTEN, attach, fix, bind, secure, tether, moor, lash. 2 DRAW, be equal, be even.

**tied** adj. (of a house) for occupation only by a person working for its owner.

**tiepin** n. an ornamental pin for holding a tie in place.

**tier** n. any of a series of rows or levels placed one above the other. ■ **tiered** adj.
▷ SYNS ROW, rank, bank, line; layer, level.

**tiff** n. inf. a petty quarrel.

**tiger** n. a large striped wild cat.

**tight** adj. 1 closed or fastened firmly. 2 close-fitting. 3 stretched taut. 4 leaving little room. 5 strictly imposed. 6 (of money or time) limited. • adv. closely or firmly. • pl. n. a close-fitting stretchy garment covering the legs, hips, and bottom. □ **tightrope** a rope or wire stretched high above the ground, on which acrobats balance. ■ **tighten** v.

▷ SYNS adj. **1** FIRM, fast, secure, fixed. **2** TAUT, rigid, stiff, tense, stretched. **3** SMALL, narrow, limited, restricted, cramped, constricted. **4** STRICT, rigorous, stringent, tough.

**tigress** n. a female tiger.

**tilde** n. an accent (~) put over a letter to mark a change in its pronunciation.

**tile** n. a thin slab of baked clay etc. used for covering roofs, walls, or floors. • v. cover with tiles.

**till¹** prep. & conj. until.

**till²** n. a cash register or drawer for money in a shop etc.

**till³** v. prepare land for crops.

**tiller** n. a bar by which the rudder of a boat is turned.

**tilt** v. move into a sloping position. • n. a sloping position. □ at full tilt at full speed or force.

▷ SYNS v. SLOPE, tip, lean, list, slant, incline.

**timber** n. wood prepared for use in building or carpentry.

**timbre** n. the quality of a voice or musical sound.

**time** n. **1** the continuing progress of existence and events in the past, present, and future. **2** a period of time. **3** a point of time measured in hours and minutes. **4** an instance of something happening or being done. **5** (**times**) expressing multiplication. **6** rhythm in music. • v. **1** arrange a time for. **2** measure the time taken by. □ behind the times out of date. time bomb a bomb that can be set to explode at a set time. time-honoured respected because of antiquity. timepiece a clock or watch. timeshare an arrangement in which joint owners use a property as a holiday home at different times.

▷ SYNS n. **1** AGE, era, epoch, period. **2** WHILE, spell, stretch, stint. **3** MOMENT, point, instant, occasion, juncture. **4** RHYTHM, tempo, beat; measure, metre. • v. SCHEDULE, arrange, fix, set, timetable, organize.

**timeless** adj. not affected by the passage of time.

**timely** adj. occurring at a good time.

▷ SYNS OPPORTUNE, well timed, convenient, appropriate, seasonable, felicitous.

**timetable** n. a list of times at which events are scheduled to take place.

▷ SYNS SCHEDULE, programme, agenda, calendar.

**timid** adj. lacking courage or confidence. ■ timidity n.

▷ SYNS FEARFUL, afraid, faint-hearted, timorous, nervous, scared, frightened, cowardly; shy, diffident.

**timorous** adj. timid.

**timpani** (or **tympani**) pl.n. kettledrums.

**tin** n. **1** a silvery-white metal. **2** a metal container. **3** a sealed metal container for preserving food. • v. (**tinned**, **tinning**) seal food in a tin.

**tincture** n. a solution of a medicinal substance in alcohol.

**tinder** n. any dry substance that catches fire easily.

**tine** n. a prong or point of a fork etc.

**tinge** n. a slight trace of a colour, feeling, or quality. • v. (**tinged**, **tingeing**) give a tinge to.

**tingle** n. a slight prickling or stinging sensation. • v. have or cause a tingle.
▷ SYNS v. PRICKLE, prick, sting, tickle; quiver, tremble.

**tinker** v. casually try to repair or improve. • n. a travelling mender of pots and pans.
▷ SYNS v. FIDDLE, adjust, play about.

**tinkle** v. make a light, clear ringing sound. • n. a light, clear ringing sound.

**tinnitus** n. ringing or buzzing in the ears.

**tinny** adj. 1 having a thin, metallic sound. 2 made of thin or inferior metal.

**tinsel** n. glittering decorative metallic strips or threads.

**tint** n. a shade of colour.
• v. colour slightly.
▷ SYNS n. SHADE, colour, tone, tinge, hue.

**tiny** adj. (-ier, -iest) very small.
▷ SYNS MINUTE, small, little, diminutive, miniature, minuscule, infinitesimal, microscopic; insignificant, trifling, negligible, inconsequential.

**tip** n. 1 the end of something thin or tapering. 2 a small sum of money given for good service etc. 3 a piece of advice. 4 a place where rubbish is left. 5 a prediction of a likely winner.
• v. 1 overbalance and fall over. 2 empty the contents of a container by holding it at an angle. 3 give a tip for good service. 4 name as a likely winner. 5 (**tip off**) inf. give secret information to.
▷ SYNS n. POINT, end, extremity, top, head. • v. 1 TILT, lean, list, slant, topple, overturn, fall over, capsize. 2 POUR, empty, drain, unload, dump.

**tipple** n. inf. an alcoholic drink.
• v. drink alcohol regularly.

**tipster** n. a person who gives tips, esp. about likely winners in racing.

**tipsy** adj. slightly drunk.

**tiptoe** v. (tiptoed, tiptoeing) walk very quietly with your heels raised.

**tirade** n. a long angry speech.
▷ SYNS DIATRIBE, harangue, rant, lecture.

**tire** v. 1 make or become tired. 2 become bored. • n. US sp. of TYRE. ■ **tiring** adj.
▷ SYNS v. EXHAUST, wear out, fatigue, drain, weary, enervate; flag, droop.

**tired** adj. 1 in need of sleep or rest. 2 (**tired of**) bored with.
▷ SYNS EXHAUSTED, worn out, weary, fatigued, drained, enervated; inf. done in, all in, knackered.

**tireless** adj. not tiring easily.
▷ SYNS VIGOROUS, energetic, industrious, determined, resolute, dogged, untiring, indefatigable, unflagging.

**tiresome** adj. annoying or tedious.
▷ SYNS 1 WEARISOME, laborious, tedious, boring, monotonous, dull, uninteresting, unexciting, humdrum, routine. 2 TROUBLESOME, irksome, vexatious, irritating, annoying, exasperating, trying.

**tissue** n. 1 a substance forming an animal or plant body. 2 a disposable paper handkerchief. □ **tissue paper** very thin, soft paper.

**tit** n. a small songbird.

**titanic** adj. enormous.

**titanium** n. a silver-grey metal.

**titbit** n. a small choice bit of food or item of information.

**tithe** n. one-tenth of income or produce, formerly paid to the Church.

**titillate** v. excite or stimulate, esp. sexually.
▷ SYNS EXCITE, arouse, stimulate, thrill, tantalize.

**titivate** v. inf. make smarter or more attractive.

**title** n. 1 the name of a book, picture, film, etc. 2 a word indicating position or job, or used in speaking to someone with a particular rank or job. 3 the position of champion in a sporting contest. □ title deed a legal document showing a person's right to own a property.
▷ SYNS NAME, designation, form of address; rank, office, position; inf. moniker.

**titled** adj. having a title indicating high rank.

**titter** n. a short, quiet laugh.
• v. give a titter.

**tittle-tattle** v. & n. gossip.

**titular** adj. having a title but no real power.

**TNT** abbr. trinitrotoluene, a powerful explosive.

**to** prep. 1 in the direction of. 2 so as to reach a particular state. 3 indicating the person or thing affected. 4 indicating that a verb is in the infinitive. • adv. into a closed position. □ to and fro backwards and forwards.

**toad** n. a short, stout, tailless amphibian.

**toadstool** n. a fungus with a rounded cap on a stalk.

**toady** n. (pl. -ies) a person who is ingratiating or obsequious.

• v. (**toadied, toadying**) behave in this way.

**toast** n. 1 bread heated until brown and crisp. 2 an act of drinking together in honour of someone. 3 a respected or admired person. • v. 1 make bread brown and crisp by heating it. 2 drink a toast to.
■ toaster n.

**tobacco** n. the dried leaves of a plant, used for smoking.

**tobacconist** n. a shopkeeper selling cigarettes etc.

**toboggan** n. a small sledge for sliding downhill.

**today** adv. 1 on this present day. 2 at the present time. • n. 1 this present day. 2 the present time.

**toddle** v. (of a young child) walk with short unsteady steps.
■ toddler n.

**toe** n. any of the digits at the end of the foot. • v. touch with the toes. □ toehold a small foothold.

**toffee** n. a sweet made with heated butter and sugar.

**tofu** n. a food made from mashed soya beans.

**tog** n. 1 (**togs**) inf. clothes. 2 a unit for measuring the warmth of duvets or clothing.

**toga** n. a loose outer garment worn by men in ancient Rome.

**together** adv. 1 with or near to another person. 2 so as to touch or combine. 3 regarded as a whole. 4 at the same time.

**toggle** n. a short piece of wood etc. passed through a loop to fasten a garment.

**toil** v. work or move laboriously.
• n. laborious work.

**toilet** n. 1 a bowl for urinating or defecating into. 2 the process

of washing and grooming yourself. □ **toilet water** a light perfume.
▷ SYNS LAVATORY, WC, bathroom, convenience, urinal, latrine, privy; inf. loo.

**toiletries** pl.n. articles used in washing and grooming.

**token** n. **1** a thing representing a feeling, fact, or quality. **2** a voucher that can be exchanged for goods. **3** a disc used to operate a machine. • adj. done just for the sake of appearances.
▷ SYNS n. SYMBOL, sign, emblem, badge, representation, indication, mark, expression, demonstration. • adj. PERFUNCTORY, superficial, nominal, slight, minimal.

**told** past & p.p. of TELL.

**tolerable** adj. **1** endurable. **2** fairly good. ▪ **tolerably** adv.
▷ SYNS **1** ENDURABLE, bearable, supportable. **2** PASSABLE, adequate, satisfactory, acceptable, fair, average, not bad; inf. OK.

**tolerance** n. **1** the ability to tolerate something. **2** an allowable variation in the size of a machine part.

**tolerant** adj. showing tolerance.
▷ SYNS FORBEARING, open-minded, broad-minded, liberal, unprejudiced, unbiased; patient, understanding, lenient, indulgent, permissive, easygoing.

**tolerate** v. **1** allow to exist or happen without protest. **2** endure patiently.
▪ **toleration** n.
▷ SYNS **1** ALLOW, permit, condone, accept, countenance. **2** ENDURE, put up with, bear, take, stand, abide, stomach.

**toll** n. **1** a charge paid for the use of certain roads or bridges. **2** the number of casualties arising from a disaster. **3** a single ring of a bell. • v. (of a bell) ring with slow strokes, esp. to mark a death.
▷ SYNS n. **1** CHARGE, fee, payment, levy, tariff. **2** NUMBER, count, tally, reckoning, total.

**tom** (or **tomcat**) n. a male cat.

**tomahawk** n. a light axe formally used by American Indians.

**tomato** n. (pl. **-oes**) a red fruit used as a vegetable.

**tomb** n. a stone structure forming a burial place.
□ **tombstone** a flat inscribed stone marking a grave.
▷ SYNS BURIAL CHAMBER, sepulchre, mausoleum, vault, crypt, catacomb, grave.

**tombola** n. a game in which tickets for prizes are drawn at random from a revolving drum.

**tomboy** n. a girl who enjoys rough and noisy activities.

**tome** n. a large book.

**tomfoolery** n. silly behaviour.

**tomorrow** adv. **1** on the day after today. **2** in the near future. • n. **1** the day after today. **2** the near future.

**tom-tom** n. a drum beaten with the hands.

**ton** n. **1** a measure of weight, either 2,240 lb (**long ton**) or 2,000 lb (**short ton**) or 1,000 kg (**metric ton**). **2** a unit of volume in shipping. **3** inf. a large number or amount.

**tone** n. **1** the quality of a musical sound. **2** the feeling or mood expressed in a person's voice. **3** general character. **4** a basic interval in music, equal to two

semitones. **5** a shade of colour. **6** firmness of muscles. • v. **1** give firmness to muscles. **2** (**tone down**) make less harsh or extreme. □ **tone deaf** unable to hear differences in musical pitch. ■ **tonal** adj. **tonality** n.
▷ SYNS n. **1** SOUND, pitch, timbre, colour. **2** MOOD, air, feel, attitude, character, spirit, vein.

**toner** n. **1** a liquid applied to the skin to reduce oiliness. **2** a powder used in photocopiers.

**tongs** pl.n. a tool with two arms used for grasping things.

**tongue** n. **1** the muscular organ in the mouth, used in tasting and speaking. **2** a language. **3** a strip of leather etc. under the laces of a shoe. □ **tongue-in-cheek** not seriously meant. **tongue-tied** too nervous to speak.

**tonic** n. **1** a drink taken to increase energy and well-being; something invigorating. **2** (also **tonic water**) a fizzy soft drink with a bitter flavour.
▷ SYNS RESTORATIVE, stimulant; inf. pick-me-up.

**tonight** adv. on the present evening or night. • n. the evening or night of the present day.

**tonnage** n. **1** weight in tons. **2** a ship's carrying capacity measured in tons.

**tonne** n. a metric ton.

**tonsil** n. either of two small masses of tissue in the throat.

**tonsillitis** n. inflammation of the tonsils.

**tonsure** n. a circular area on a monk's head where the hair is shaved off.

**too** adv. **1** more than is desirable. **2** also.

**took** past of TAKE.

**tool** n. an implement used for a particular task. • v. impress a design on leather.
▷ SYNS n. IMPLEMENT, instrument, utensil, device, apparatus, gadget, appliance, machine, contrivance, contraption.

**toot** n. a short sound made by a horn or whistle. • v. make a toot.

**tooth** n. (pl. **teeth**) each of the hard white structures in the jaws, used in biting and chewing. □ **toothpaste** a paste for cleaning the teeth. **toothpick** a thin, pointed piece of wood etc. for removing food stuck between the teeth.

**top** n. **1** the highest or uppermost point, part, or surface. **2** a thing placed on or covering the upper part of something. **3** the utmost degree. **4** a garment for the upper part of the body. **5** a toy that spins its point when set in motion. • adj. highest in position or rank etc. • v. **1** be more than. **2** be at the highest place or rank in. **3** reach the top of. **4** put a top or topping on. □ **topcoat 1** an overcoat. **2** an outer coat of paint. **top hat** a man's tall formal black hat. **top-heavy** unstable because too heavy at the top. **topknot** a knot of hair arranged on the top of the head. **topsoil** the top layer of soil.
▷ SYNS n. **1** SUMMIT, peak, pinnacle, crest, crown, tip, apex, vertex, apogee. **2** CAP, lid, stopper, cork, cover. • adj. **1** HIGHEST, uppermost, topmost. **2** FOREMOST, leading, principal, pre-eminent, greatest, finest. **3** MAXIMUM, greatest, utmost.

**topaz** n. a precious stone of various colours, esp. yellow.

**topiary** n. the art of clipping shrubs into ornamental shapes.

**topic** n. the subject of a text, speech, etc.
▷ SYNS SUBJECT, theme, issue, question, argument, thesis.

**topical** adj. of or dealing with current affairs. ■ topically adv.
▷ SYNS CURRENT, up to date, contemporary, recent, relevant.

**topless** adj. having the breasts uncovered.

**topography** n. the arrangement of the physical features of an area. ■ topographical adj.

**topping** n. a layer of food poured or spread over another food.

**topple** v. overbalance and fall.
▷ SYNS 1 FALL OVER, tip over, keel over, overturn, overbalance. 2 OVERTHROW, oust, unseat, bring down.

**topsy-turvy** adv. & adj. 1 upside down. 2 in disorder.

**tor** n. a hill or rocky peak.

**Torah** n. (in Judaism) the law of God as revealed to Moses.

**torch** n. 1 a portable electric lamp. 2 a burning piece of wood etc. carried as a light.

**tore** past of TEAR¹.

**toreador** n. a bullfighter.

**torment** n. 1 great suffering. 2 a cause of this. • v. 1 cause to suffer greatly. 2 tease or annoy. ■ tormentor n.
▷ SYNS n. AGONY, suffering, torture, pain, anguish, misery, distress, trauma. • v. TORTURE, rack, afflict, harrow, plague.

**torn** p.p. of TEAR¹.

**tornado** n. (pl. -oes or -os) a violent destructive whirlwind.

**torpedo** n. (pl. -oes) an explosive underwater missile.

• v. (**torpedoed**, **torpedoing**) attack or destroy with a torpedo.

**torpid** adj. sluggish and inactive. ■ torpor n.

**torque** n. a force causing rotation.

**torrent** n. 1 a fast and powerful stream of liquid. 2 an outpouring: *a torrent of abuse*. ■ torrential adj.
▷ SYNS FLOOD, deluge, cascade, rush, stream.

**torrid** adj. 1 very hot and dry. 2 passionate.

**torsion** n. the state of being twisted.

**torso** n. (pl. -os) the trunk of the human body.

**tortellini** n. stuffed pasta parcels rolled into small rings.

**tortilla** n. a thin, flat maize pancake.

**tortoise** n. a slow-moving reptile with a hard shell. □ tortoiseshell 1 the mottled brown and yellow shell of certain turtles, used to make ornaments. 2 a cat with markings resembling tortoiseshell.

**tortuous** adj. 1 full of twists and turns. 2 complex.
▷ SYNS TWISTING, winding, serpentine, zigzag; convoluted, complicated, complex.

**torture** n. 1 the infliction of pain as a punishment or means of coercion. 2 great suffering. • v. inflict torture on. ■ torturer n.
▷ SYNS n. 1 ABUSE, ill-treatment, maltreatment, persecution. 2 AGONY, suffering, pain, torment, anguish, misery, distress. • v. 1 ABUSE, ill-treat,

mistreat, persecute; torment, rack, afflict, harrow, plague.

**Tory** n. (pl. **-ies**) a member or supporter of the British Conservative Party.

**toss** v. throw lightly; roll about from side to side; shake or turn food in liquid to coat it lightly. • n. an act of tossing. □ **toss-up** a situation where two outcomes are equally likely.
▷ SYNS v. **1** THROW, hurl, cast, sling, pitch, lob, propel, launch; inf. chuck. **2** ROLL, sway, pitch, rock, lurch.

**tot** n. **1** a small child. **2** a small drink of spirits. • v. (**totted**, **totting**) (**tot up**) add up.

**total** adj. **1** being the whole number or amount. **2** complete. • n. a total amount. • v. **1** amount to. **2** calculate the total of.
■ **totality** n. **totally** adv.
▷ SYNS adj. **1** ENTIRE, complete, whole, full, comprehensive, combined, aggregate, overall. **2** *a total disaster:* UTTER, absolute, complete, downright, out and out, outright, unmitigated, unqualified. • n. SUM, aggregate, whole, entirety, totality. • v. **1** ADD UP TO, come to, amount to. **2** ADD UP, count, tot up.

**totalitarian** adj. of a regime in which no rival parties or loyalties are permitted.
▷ SYNS AUTOCRATIC, authoritarian, despotic, dictatorial, tyrannical, undemocratic, oppressive.

**totalizator** (or **totalisator**) n. a device showing the number and amount of bets staked on a race.

**tote** inf. n. a system of betting using a totalizator. • v. carry.

**totem** n. a natural object adopted as a tribal emblem.

□ **totem pole** a pole decorated with totems.

**totter** v. move in an unsteady way.
▷ SYNS TEETER, wobble, stagger, stumble, reel, sway, lurch.

**toucan** n. a tropical American bird with a very large beak.

**touch** v. **1** come into or be in physical contact with. **2** feel or stroke. **3** harm or interfere with. **4** affect. **5** arouse sympathy or gratitude in. • n. **1** an act of touching. **2** the ability to perceive things through physical contact. **3** a small amount. **4** a detail. **5** a way of dealing with something. □ **touch-and-go** (of an outcome) possible but very uncertain. **touch down** (of an aircraft) land. **touchline** the boundary line on each side of a rugby or football field. **touchstone** a standard by which something is judged.
▷ SYNS v. **1** MEET, converge, adjoin, abut. **2** FEEL, stroke, tap, brush, graze, pat, fondle, caress. **3** AFFECT, move, influence, have an effect on. • n. BIT, trace, suggestion, hint, tinge; dash, taste, spot, drop, soupçon.

**touché** exclam. an acknowledgement of a valid criticism.

**touching** adj. arousing pity, affection, or gratitude.
▷ SYNS MOVING, affecting, heart-warming, emotional, emotive, poignant.

**touchy** adj. easily offended.
▷ SYNS SENSITIVE, hypersensitive, oversensitive, thin-skinned, tetchy, testy, irritable, peevish, querulous, bad-tempered, short-tempered.

**tough** adj. **1** strong enough to withstand wear and tear; hard to chew. **2** (of a person) resilient. **3** difficult or unfair; strict; prone to violence.
• n. a rough or violent person.
■ **toughen** v.
▷ SYNS adj. **1** STRONG, durable, resilient, sturdy, robust, solid, stout, hard-wearing. **2** CHEWY, leathery, gristly, stringy, fibrous. **3** DIFFICULT, hard, arduous, onerous, laborious, strenuous, exacting, taxing, gruelling, demanding. **4** STRICT, stern, severe, rigorous, harsh, hard-hitting, unsentimental.

**toupee** n. a small wig.

**tour** n. a journey, visiting one place after another. • v. make a tour of.
▷ SYNS n. TRIP, excursion, journey, expedition, jaunt, outing, peregrination. • v. TRAVEL ROUND/THROUGH, journey through, explore, holiday in, visit.

**tourism** n. the commercial organization of holidays and services for tourists.

**tourist** n. a person visiting a place for pleasure.
▷ SYNS VISITOR, sightseer, holiday-maker, tripper.

**tournament** n. a sporting contest consisting of a series of matches.
▷ SYNS COMPETITION, contest, meeting, event, fixture.

**tourniquet** n. a strip of material pulled tightly round a limb to stop the flow of blood from an artery.

**tousle** v. ruffle someone's hair.

**tout** v. try to sell. • n. a person who buys tickets for popular events and resells them at high prices.
▷ SYNS v. ASK FOR, solicit, seek, petition for, appeal for, beg for.

**tow** v. use one vehicle etc. to pull another along behind.
□ **towpath** a path beside a river or canal, originally for horses towing barges.
▷ SYNS PULL, draw, drag, haul, tug, lug.

**towards** (or **toward**) prep. **1** in the direction of. **2** in relation to. **3** as a contribution to.

**towel** n. a piece of absorbent material for drying things.
• v. (**towelled**, **towelling**; US **toweled**) rub with a towel.

**towelling** (US **toweling**) n. fabric for towels.

**tower** n. a tall narrow building; a tall pile or structure. • v. be very tall. □ **tower block** a tall building with many storeys.

**town** n. a collection of houses, shops, etc. larger than a village. □ **town hall** the building containing local government offices. **township** (in South Africa) a suburb or city mainly inhabited by black people.

**toxic** adj. **1** poisonous. **2** of or caused by poison. ■ **toxicity** n.
▷ SYNS POISONOUS, virulent, noxious; dangerous, harmful.

**toxin** n. a poison produced by a living organism.

**toy** n. a thing to play with. • adj. (of a breed of dog) very small.
• v. (**toy with**) fiddle with idly; casually consider. □ **toy boy** inf. a woman's much younger male lover.

**trace** v. **1** find or follow by careful investigation. **2** copy a design etc. by drawing over it on transparent paper. **3** draw

an outline. • n. 1 a mark or other sign of the existence or passing of something. 2 a very small amount. 3 a slight indication.
▷ SYNS v. TRACK DOWN, find, discover, detect, unearth. • n. 1 MARK, sign, vestige, indication, evidence, remains, remnant. 2 BIT, touch, hint, suggestion, suspicion, tinge.

**trachea** n. the windpipe.

**track** n. 1 a rough path or road; a railway line; a racecourse. 2 marks left by a moving person or thing; a course followed. 3 a section on a CD, tape, etc. 4 a continuous band round the wheels of a tank, tractor, etc. • v. follow the trail or course of; find after a thorough search. □ **tracksuit** an outfit consisting of a loose sweatshirt and trousers.
▷ SYNS n. 1 PATH, pathway, footpath, way. 2 MARK, trace, footprint, trail, spoor. 3 COURSE, orbit, route, trajectory. • v. FOLLOW, pursue, trail, trace, tail, stalk.

**tract** n. 1 a large area of land. 2 a major passage in the body. 3 a pamphlet on a religious or political theme.

**tractable** adj. easy to deal with or control.

**traction** n. 1 the act of pulling a thing along a surface. 2 a way of treating a broken bone by gradually pulling it back into position. 3 the grip of a tyre on the road.

**tractor** n. a powerful vehicle for pulling farm equipment.

**trade** n. 1 the buying and selling of goods and services. 2 a job requiring special skills. • v. 1 buy and sell. 2 exchange.

□ **trademark** a symbol, word, or words chosen to represent a company or product. **trade-off** a compromise. **tradesman** a person engaged in trading or a trade. **trade union** an organized association of employees formed to protect their rights.
▷ SYNS n. 1 COMMERCE, buying and selling, dealing, traffic, business. 2 LINE OF WORK, occupation, job, career, profession, craft, vocation, calling, work, employment. • v. 1 DEAL, traffic, market. 2 SWAP, exchange, barter, switch.

**trader** n. a person who trades goods, currency, or shares.
▷ SYNS DEALER, merchant, buyer, seller, vendor, supplier, trafficker.

**tradition** n. a belief or custom handed down from one generation to another; a long-established procedure.
▷ SYNS CUSTOM, practice, convention, ritual, observance, habit, institution, usage.

**traditional** adj. relating to or following tradition.
▷ SYNS ESTABLISHED, customary, time-honoured, accustomed, conventional, usual, habitual, set, routine, ritual, age-old.

**traduce** v. misrepresent in an unfavourable way.

**traffic** n. 1 vehicles, ships, or aircraft moving along a route. 2 trading. • v. (**trafficked**, **trafficking**) trade in something illegal. □ **traffic lights** a set of automatically operated lights for controlling the flow of traffic. ■ **trafficker** n.

**tragedian** n. a writer of tragedies; an actor in tragedy.

**tragedy** n. (pl. **-ies**) a serious play with an unhappy ending; a very sad event or situation.
▷ SYNS DISASTER, calamity, catastrophe, misfortune, affliction, adversity.

**tragic** adj. extremely sad; of dramatic tragedy. ▪ **tragically** adv.
▷ SYNS **1** DISASTROUS, calamitous, catastrophic, devastating, fatal, terrible, dreadful, appalling, awful. **2** SAD, unhappy, pathetic, moving, distressing, heart-rending, pitiful, piteous.

**tragicomedy** n. (pl. **-ies**) a drama with elements of both tragedy and comedy.

**trail** n. **1** a series of signs left behind by a person etc. in passing. **2** a line of people or things. **3** a path. ▪ v. **1** draw or be drawn along behind someone or something. **2** follow the trail of. **3** walk or move slowly or wearily.
▷ SYNS n. **1** TRACK, scent, spoor, traces, marks, signs, footprints. **2** PATH, pathway, footpath, way, route. ▪ v. **1** DRAG, sweep, dangle, hang down, droop. **2** FOLLOW, pursue, track, trace, tail, shadow, stalk.

**trailer** n. **1** an unpowered vehicle pulled by another vehicle. **2** a short extract from a film etc., used to advertise it.

**train** n. **1** a joined set of railway vehicles. **2** a line of pack animals or vehicles; a sequence of events. **3** part of a long robe, trailing behind the wearer.
▪ v. **1** teach a particular skill to; practise and exercise to become physically fit. **2** cause a plant to grow in a particular direction. **3** aim a gun etc.
▷ SYNS n. PROCESSION, line, file, column, convoy, cavalcade, caravan. ▪ v. **1** INSTRUCT, teach, coach, tutor, school, ground, drill. **2** EXERCISE, work out. **3** AIM, point, focus, direct, level.

**trainee** n. a person being trained.

**trainer** n. **1** a person who trains people or animals. **2** a soft shoe for sports or casual wear.

**traipse** v. walk wearily or reluctantly.

**trait** n. a characteristic.
▷ SYNS CHARACTERISTIC, attribute, feature, quality, property, idiosyncrasy, peculiarity, quirk.

**traitor** n. a person who betrays their country, organization, etc. ▪ **traitorous** adj.
▷ SYNS TURNCOAT, renegade, defector, deserter, double agent, quisling, fifth columnist.

**trajectory** n. (pl. **-ies**) the path followed by a moving object.

**tram** (or **tramcar**) n. a passenger vehicle powered by electricity and running on rails laid in the road.

**trammel** v. (**trammelled**, **trammelling**; US **trammeled**) hamper or restrain.

**tramp** v. walk with heavy footsteps; go on foot across an area. ▪ n. **1** a vagrant. **2** the sound of heavy footsteps. **3** a long walk.

**trample** v. tread on and crush.
▷ SYNS TREAD ON, step on, stamp on, squash, crush, flatten.

**trampoline** n. a sheet of canvas attached by springs to a frame, used for jumping on in acrobatic leaps.

**trance** n. a sleeplike or dreamy state.
▷ SYNS DAZE, stupor, dream.

**tranquil** adj. peaceful and untroubled. ■ **tranquillity** n. **tranquilly** adv.
▷ SYNS PEACEFUL, restful, calm, quiet, still, serene, placid, undisturbed.

**tranquillize** (or **-ise**; US **tranquilize**) v. give a sedative drug to.

**tranquillizer** (or **-iser**; US **tranquilizer**) n. a drug used to reduce anxiety and tension.

**transact** v. perform or carry out business.

**transaction** n. **1** an instance of buying or selling. **2** the action of conducting business.
▷ SYNS DEAL, undertaking, arrangement, bargain, negotiation.

**transcend** v. go beyond the range or limits of; surpass. ■ **transcendence** n. **transcendent** adj.
▷ SYNS EXCEED, surpass, outdo, outstrip, outclass, outshine, eclipse.

**transcendental** adj. of a spiritual or non-physical realm.

**transcribe** v. put into written form; write out notes in full. ■ **transcription** n.

**transcript** n. a written version of a broadcast.

**transept** n. a part lying at right angles to the nave in a church.

**transfer** v. (**transferred**, **transferring**) move from one position etc. to another.
• n. transferring; a conveyance of property from one person to another; a design for transferring from one surface to another. ■ **transference** n.
▷ SYNS V. **1** CONVEY, move, shift, remove, take, carry, transport. **2** MAKE OVER, sign over, hand over, pass on, consign.

**transfigure** v. transform into something nobler or more beautiful. ■ **transfiguration** n.

**transfix** v. **1** pierce or impale. **2** make motionless with fear or astonishment.

**transform** v. change completely or strikingly.
▷ SYNS CHANGE, alter, convert, transfigure, transmogrify; revolutionize, reconstruct, rebuild, reorganize, rework.

**transformation** n. a marked change in nature, form, or appearance.
▷ SYNS CHANGE, alteration, conversion, metamorphosis, transfiguration, transmogrification.

**transformer** n. an apparatus for changing the voltage of an electric current.

**transfusion** n. an injection of blood or other fluid into a blood vessel.

**transgress** v. go beyond what is morally or legally acceptable. ■ **transgression** n. **transgressor** n.

**transient** adj. lasting only for a short time. ■ **transience** n.
▷ SYNS TRANSITORY, brief, short-lived, impermanent, momentary, ephemeral, fleeting, passing.

**transistor** n. **1** a device able to amplify or rectify electric currents. **2** a portable radio using transistors.

**transit** n. the process of travelling or conveying someone or something across an area.
▷ SYNS MOVEMENT, transport, transportation, haulage, conveyance; travel, passage.

**transition** n. the process of changing from one state to another. ■ **transitional** adj.

▷ SYNS CHANGE, transformation, conversion, metamorphosis, shift, switch, progression, progress, passage.

**transitive** adj. (of a verb) used with a direct object.

**transitory** adj. lasting only briefly.

**translate** v. express words or text in another language. ■ **translation** n. **translator** n.

**translucent** adj. partly transparent. ■ **translucence** n.

**transmission** n. 1 transmitting; a broadcast. 2 the gear transmitting power from engine to axle in a motor vehicle.

**transmit** v. 1 pass on from one person, place, or thing to another. 2 send out an electrical signal or a radio or television programme. ■ **transmitter** n.

▷ SYNS **1** TRANSFER, pass on, communicate, convey, impart, dispatch, relay, disseminate, spread, circulate. **2** BROADCAST, send out, air, televise.

**transmogrify** v. (**transmogrified, transmogrifying**) change into something completely different.

**transmute** v. change in form or substance. ■ **transmutation** n.

**transparency** n. (pl. **-ies**) 1 being transparent. 2 a photographic slide.

**transparent** adj. 1 able to be seen through. 2 obvious or evident.

▷ SYNS CLEAR, see-through, translucent, pellucid, crystalline, limpid, glassy.

**transpire** v. 1 become known; happen. 2 (of plants) give off vapour from leaves etc. ■ **transpiration** n.

▷ SYNS COME ABOUT, happen, occur, take place, befall.

**transplant** v. transfer to another place or situation; transfer living tissue to another body or part of the body. • n. transplanting of tissue; something transplanted. ■ **transplantation** n.

**transport** v. convey from one place to another. • n. 1 a means of conveying people or goods; the process of transporting. 2 (**transports**) extremely strong emotions. ■ **transportation** n.

▷ SYNS V. CONVEY, take, transfer, move, shift, carry, send, deliver; ship, ferry. • n. TRANSPORTATION, conveyance; transit, carriage, freight.

**transpose** v. 1 cause two or more things to change places. 2 put music into a different key. ■ **transposition** n.

▷ SYNS INTERCHANGE, exchange, switch, swap, reverse, invert.

**transverse** adj. crosswise.

**transvestite** n. a person who likes to dress in clothes worn by the opposite sex.

**trap** n. 1 a device for capturing an animal. 2 a scheme for tricking or catching someone. 3 a two-wheeled horse-drawn carriage. • v. (**trapped, trapping**) catch or hold in a trap. □ **trapdoor** a hinged or removable panel in a floor, ceiling, or roof.

▷ SYNS n. SNARE, net, gin; pitfall, booby trap. • v. **1** SNARE, ensnare, entrap; capture, catch, corner. **2** TRICK, dupe, deceive, lure, inveigle, beguile.

**trapeze** n. a hanging horizontal bar used by acrobats.

**trapezium** n. a quadrilateral with only two opposite sides parallel.

**trapper** n. a person who traps animals, esp. for furs.

**trappings** pl.n. accessories; symbols of status.
▷ SYNS ACCESSORIES, accoutrements, appurtenances, appointments, trimmings, paraphernalia, equipment, apparatus, gear.

**trash** n. waste or worthless material. ■ trashy adj.

**trauma** n. a physical injury; emotional shock following a stressful event. ■ traumatize v.

**traumatic** adj. deeply distressing.
▷ SYNS DISTURBING, distressing, upsetting, shocking, painful, agonizing, hurtful.

**travail** n. & v. old use labour.

**travel** v. 1 go from one place to another. 2 journey along or through. • n. 1 the act of travelling. 2 (**travels**) journeys.
▷ SYNS v. JOURNEY, tour, voyage, wander, ramble, roam, rove.

**traveller** (US **traveler**) n. 1 a person who travels. 2 a gypsy.
□ traveller's cheque a cheque for a fixed amount, able to be cashed in other countries.
▷ SYNS TRIPPER, tourist, holiday-maker, sightseer, globetrotter.

**travelogue** n. a book or film about someone's travels.

**traverse** v. travel or extend across.

**travesty** n. (pl. **-ies**) a shocking misrepresentation.

**trawl** n. a large wide-mouthed fishing net. • v. fish with a trawl; search thoroughly.

**trawler** n. a boat used in trawling.

**tray** n. a flat board with a rim, used for carrying small articles.

**treacherous** adj. guilty of or involving betrayal or deception; having hidden or unpredictable dangers. ■ treachery n.
▷ SYNS 1 TRAITOROUS, double-crossing, renegade, perfidious; duplicitous, disloyal, faithless. 2 HAZARDOUS, dangerous, perilous, risky.

**treacle** n. a thick sticky liquid produced when sugar is refined. ■ treacly adj.

**tread** v. (**trod, trodden, treading**) walk in a specified way; walk on or along; press or crush with the feet. • n. 1 the manner or sound of walking. 2 a horizontal surface of a stair. 3 the part of a tyre that touches the ground.
□ treadmill a large wheel turned by the weight of people or animals treading on steps fitted into it, formerly used to drive machinery; a tiring or boring job. tread water keep upright in water by making treading movements.
▷ SYNS v. WALK, step, stride, pace, march, tramp; trample, crush, squash, flatten.

**treadle** n. a lever worked by the foot to operate a machine.

**treason** n. the crime of betraying your country. ■ treasonable adj.
▷ SYNS TREACHERY, betrayal, disloyalty, faithlessness, sedition, subversion, mutiny, rebellion.

**treasure** n. a collection of precious metals or gems; a highly valued object or person. • v. value highly; look after carefully.

▷ SYNS n. RICHES, valuables, wealth, fortune, jewels, gems, gold, silver. • v. VALUE, prize, hold dear, cherish.

**treasurer** n. a person in charge of the funds of an institution.

**treasury** n. (pl. **-ies**) the revenue of a state, institution, etc.; the government department in charge of the economy.

**treat** v. **1** behave towards or deal with in a specified way; give medical treatment to; subject to a chemical or other process. **2** buy something for someone in order to give pleasure. • n. something special that gives pleasure.

▷ SYNS v. **1** DEAL WITH, handle, tackle. **2** REGARD, consider, view, look on. **3** MEDICATE, nurse, care for, attend to, tend; cure, heal, remedy. • n. LUXURY, indulgence, extravagance; titbit, delicacy; present, gift.

**treatise** n. a written work dealing with one subject.

▷ SYNS DISCOURSE, exposition, disquisition, dissertation, thesis, study, essay, paper, monograph, tract, pamphlet.

**treatment** n. **1** a way of behaving towards someone or dealing with something. **2** medical care for an illness or injury.

▷ SYNS **1** BEHAVIOUR, conduct, handling, dealings. **2** MEDICAL CARE, therapy, nursing; medication, drugs.

**treaty** n. (pl. **-ies**) a formal agreement between states.

▷ SYNS AGREEMENT, settlement, pact, deal, covenant, contract, concordat, entente.

**treble** adj. three times as much or as many. • n. **1** a treble

quantity or thing. **2** a high-pitched voice.

**tree** n. a large woody plant with a main stem and a number of branches.

**trek** n. a long arduous journey. • v. (**trekked**, **trekking**) make a trek.

▷ SYNS n. EXPEDITION, trip, journey, hike, march. • v. TRAMP, hike, trudge, march, slog, footslog.

**trellis** n. a light framework of crossing strips of wood.

**tremble** v. shake or shiver; be very frightened. • n. a trembling movement.

▷ SYNS v. SHAKE, quiver, quaver; shudder, judder, teeter, totter, wobble, rock.

**tremendous** adj. immense; excellent.

▷ SYNS **1** GREAT, huge, enormous, immense, massive, vast, colossal, prodigious, stupendous, gigantic, gargantuan, mammoth. **2** *a tremendous player:* see **EXCELLENT**.

**tremor** n. a slight trembling movement; a sudden feeling of fear or excitement.

**tremulous** adj. trembling or quivering.

**trench** n. a deep ditch.

**trenchant** adj. expressed strongly and clearly.

**trend** n. a general tendency; a fashion. □ **trendsetter** a person leading the way in fashion or ideas.

▷ SYNS **1** TENDENCY, drift, course, direction, current, inclination. **2** FASHION, vogue, style, mode, look, craze.

**trendy** adj. (**-ier**, **-iest**) inf. fashionable.

**trepidation** n. nervousness.

**trespass** v. enter land or property unlawfully; intrude. • n. the act of trespassing. ■ **trespasser** n.
▷ SYNS v. INTRUDE, encroach, infringe, invade.

**tress** n. a lock of hair.

**trestle** n. a framework consisting of a horizontal bar on sloping legs, used in pairs to support a surface such as a table top.

**triad** n. a group of three.

**trial** n. 1 an examination of evidence in a law court to decide if someone is guilty of a crime. 2 a test of quality or performance. 3 something that tries your patience.
▷ SYNS 1 COURT CASE, hearing, inquiry, tribunal. 2 TEST, dry run, try-out, check, experiment. 3 NUISANCE, pest, bother, annoyance, irritant.

**triangle** n. a geometric figure with three sides and three angles. ■ **triangular** adj.

**triathlon** n. an athletic contest involving three different events.

**tribe** n. a social group in a traditional society consisting of linked families. ■ **tribal** adj.

**tribulation** n. trouble or suffering.

**tribunal** n. a group of people appointed to settle disputes.

**tributary** n. (pl. **-ies**) a river or stream flowing into a larger river or lake.

**tribute** n. 1 something said or done as a mark of respect. 2 hist. payment made by a state to a more powerful one.
▷ SYNS ACCOLADE, commendation, testimonial, paean, eulogy, panegyric, praise, homage, congratulations, compliments, bouquets.

**trice** n. (**in a trice**) in a moment.

**triceps** n. (pl. **triceps**) the large muscle at the back of the upper arm.

**trick** n. 1 something done to deceive or outwit someone. 2 a clever act performed for entertainment. 3 a mannerism. • v. deceive or outwit. ■ **trickery** n.
▷ SYNS 1 STRATAGEM, ploy, ruse, dodge, wile, manoeuvre, deceit, deception, subterfuge. 2 KNACK, art, technique, skill. 3 HOAX, (practical) joke, prank, jape. • v. DECEIVE, delude, mislead, take in, cheat, hoodwink, fool, dupe, hoax, defraud, swindle; inf. con.

**trickle** v. flow in a thin stream; come or go gradually. • n. a trickling flow.
▷ SYNS v. DRIP, dribble, leak, ooze, seep.

**tricky** adj. (**-ier**, **-iest**) difficult.
▷ SYNS DIFFICULT, problematic, awkward, delicate, sensitive, ticklish, thorny, knotty.

**tricolour** (US **tricolor**) n. a flag with three colours in stripes.

**tricycle** n. a three-wheeled pedal-driven vehicle.

**trident** n. a three-pronged spear.

**trifle** n. 1 something of little value or importance; a very small amount. 2 a cold dessert of sponge cake and fruit with layers of custard, jelly, and cream. • v. (**trifle with**) treat without seriousness or respect.

**trifling** adj. trivial.

**trigger** n. a lever for releasing a spring, esp. to fire a gun; an event that causes something to happen. • v. cause to happen.

◻ **trigger-happy** apt to shoot on the slightest provocation.

**trigonometry** n. a branch of mathematics dealing with the relationship of sides and angles of triangles.

**trilby** n. (pl. **-ies**) a man's soft felt hat.

**trill** n. & v. (make) a high vibrating sound.

**trillion** n. **1** a million million. **2** dated a million million million.

**trilobite** n. a fossil marine creature.

**trilogy** n. (pl. **-ies**) a group of three related books, plays, etc.

**trim** v. **1** cut untidy edges from; shorten and neaten. **2** decorate. **3** adjust a sail. • n. **1** decoration. **2** an act of cutting. **3** good condition. • adj. (**trimmer**, **trimmest**) neat and smart.
▷ SYNS v. CUT, clip, snip, shear, prune, pare, neaten, tidy up.

**trimaran** n. a boat like a catamaran, with three hulls.

**trimming** n. **1** decoration or accompaniment. **2** (**trimmings**) small pieces trimmed off.

**trinity** n. (pl. **-ies**) **1** (**the Trinity**) (in Christian belief) the three persons (Father, Son, and Holy Spirit) that make up God. **2** a group of three.

**trinket** n. a small ornament or piece of jewellery.

**trio** n. (pl. **-os**) a group or set of three; a group of three musicians.

**trip** v. **1** catch your foot on something and fall. **2** (**trip up**) make a mistake. **3** move with quick light steps. **4** activate a mechanism. • n. **1** a journey or excursion. **2** an act of stumbling. **3** inf. a hallucinatory experience caused by taking a drug.
▷ SYNS v. STUMBLE, lose your footing, stagger, slip, fall, tumble. • n. EXCURSION, tour, expedition, voyage, jaunt, outing.

**tripartite** adj. consisting of three parts.

**tripe** n. **1** the stomach of a cow or sheep as food. **2** inf. nonsense.

**triple** adj. having three parts or members; three times as much or as many. • v. increase by three times its amount.

**triplet** n. each of three children born at one birth; a set of three.

**triplicate** adj. existing in three copies or examples.

**tripod** n. a three-legged stand.

**tripper** n. a person who goes on a pleasure trip.

**triptych** n. a picture or carving on three panels.

**trite** adj. unoriginal and dull.

**triumph** n. a great victory or achievement; joy resulting from this. • v. be successful or victorious. ∎ **triumphal** adj.
▷ SYNS n. **1** CONQUEST, victory, win, success, achievement. **2** EXULTATION, jubilation, elation, delight, joy, glee, pride. • v. WIN, succeed, come first, carry the day.

**triumphant** adj. **1** having won a battle or contest. **2** joyful after a victory or achievement.
▷ SYNS **1** VICTORIOUS, successful, winning, undefeated, unbeaten. **2** EXULTANT, jubilant, elated, joyful, gleeful, proud.

**triumvirate** n. a group of three powerful people.

**trivet** n. a metal stand for a kettle or hot dish.

**trivia** pl.n. unimportant things.

**trivial** adj. of little value or importance. ▪ **triviality** n. **trivialize** v. **trivially** adv.

▷ SYNS UNIMPORTANT, insignificant, inconsequential, insubstantial, petty, minor, negligible, paltry, trifling.

**trod**, **trodden** past and p.p. of TREAD.

**troll** n. (in stories) an ugly giant or dwarf.

**trolley** n. (pl. **-eys**) a basket on wheels for transporting goods; a small table on wheels.

**trollop** n. a promiscuous woman.

**trombone** n. a large brass wind instrument with a sliding tube. ▪ **trombonist** n.

**troop** n. 1 (**troops**) soldiers or armed forces. 2 a group of people or animals. • v. move in a group.

▷ SYNS n. (**troops**) SOLDIERS, forces, servicemen/women, services, army, military.

**trooper** n. 1 a soldier in a cavalry or armoured unit. 2 US a state police officer.

**trophy** n. (pl. **-ies**) an object awarded as a prize; a souvenir of an achievement.

**tropic** n. 1 a line of latitude 23˚ 26' north or south of the equator. 2 (**the tropics**) the region between these, with a hot climate. ▪ **tropical** adj.

**trot** n. a horse's pace faster than a walk; a moderate running pace. • v. (**trotted**, **trotting**) move at a trot.

**trotter** n. a pig's foot.

**troubadour** n. a medieval travelling poet.

**trouble** n. 1 difficulty or inconvenience; a cause of this; an unfortunate situation. 2 public unrest. • v. 1 cause distress or inconvenience to. 2 make the effort to do something. □ **troubleshooter** a person who investigates and solves problems in an organization.

▷ SYNS n. 1 PROBLEMS, bother, inconvenience, worry, anxiety, distress, stress, harassment, unpleasantness; inf. hassle. 2 MISFORTUNE, difficulty, trial, tribulation, burden, pain, woe, grief, heartache, misery, affliction, suffering. 3 DISEASE, illness, sickness. 4 DISTURBANCE, disorder, unrest, fighting, fracas. • v. 1 WORRY, bother, concern, disturb, upset, agitate, distress, perturb, annoy, irritate, vex, irk; inconvenience. 2 TAKE THE TIME, bother, make the effort, exert yourself.

**troublemaker** n. a person who causes trouble.

▷ SYNS MISCHIEF-MAKER, rabble-rouser, firebrand, agitator; inf. stirrer.

**troublesome** adj. causing difficulty or annoyance.

▷ SYNS ANNOYING, irritating, exasperating, maddening, infuriating, irksome, bothersome, tiresome, worrying, upsetting; difficult, awkward, trying, unmanageable.

**trough** n. 1 a long, open receptacle for animals' food or water. 2 a region of low atmospheric pressure.

**trounce** v. defeat heavily.

▷ SYNS DEFEAT, beat hollow, rout, thrash, crush, overwhelm.

**troupe** n. a touring group of entertainers.

**trouper** n. **1** a member of a troupe. **2** a reliable person.

**trousers** pl.n. a two-legged outer garment that covers the body from the waist down.

**trousseau** n. (pl. **-eaux** or **-eaus**) clothes etc. collected by a bride for her marriage.

**trout** n. (pl. **trout** or **trouts**) an edible freshwater fish.

**trowel** n. a small garden tool for digging; a similar tool for spreading mortar etc.

**troy** n. a system of weights used for precious metals and gems.

**truant** n. a pupil who stays away from school without permission. • v. stay away as a truant. ▪ **truancy** n.
▷ SYNS V. PLAY TRUANT, malinger; inf. skive, play hookey, bunk off.

**truce** n. an agreement to cease hostilities temporarily.
▷ SYNS CEASEFIRE, armistice, peace, respite.

**truck** n. **1** a lorry. **2** an open railway wagon.

**truculent** adj. defiant and aggressive.

**trudge** v. walk laboriously.

**true** adj. **1** in accordance with fact. **2** real or actual. **3** accurate. **4** loyal. ▪ **truly** adv.
▷ SYNS **1** CORRECT, accurate, right, verifiable; literal, factual, unvarnished. **2** REAL, genuine, authentic, actual, bona fide, proper. **3** LOYAL, faithful, trustworthy, reliable, dependable, staunch, steadfast, constant, devoted, dedicated.

**truffle** n. **1** an underground fungus eaten as a delicacy. **2** a soft chocolate sweet.

**trug** n. a shallow wooden basket.

**truism** n. a statement that is obviously true and says nothing new.

**trump** n. (in card games) a card of the suit chosen to rank above the others. • v. (**trump up**) invent a false accusation.

**trumpet** n. a brass musical instrument with a flared end; something shaped like this.
• v. (**trumpeted, trumpeting**) proclaim loudly; (of an elephant) make a loud sound through its trunk.
▪ **trumpeter** n.

**truncate** v. shorten by cutting off the end. ▪ **truncation** n.

**truncheon** n. a short thick stick carried as a weapon.

**trundle** v. move or roll slowly and heavily.

**trunk** n. **1** a tree's main stem. **2** the body apart from the head and limbs. **3** a large box for transporting or storing articles. **4** an elephant's long flexible nose. **5** US the boot of a car. **6** (**trunks**) men's shorts for swimming. □ **trunk road** an important main road.

**truss** n. a framework supporting a roof; a surgical support for a hernia. • v. tie up securely.

**trust** n. **1** firm belief in the reliability, truth, or ability of someone or something. **2** responsibility for someone or something. **3** an arrangement whereby someone manages property for the benefit of others. **4** an organization managed by trustees. • v. **1** have trust in. **2** entrust. **3** hope.
▪ **trustful** adj.
▷ SYNS n. **1** FAITH, confidence, belief, conviction, credence, assurance, certainty, reliance.

**2** RESPONSIBILITY, duty, obligation. • v. HOPE, assume, presume, expect, believe, take it.

**trustee** n. a person given legal powers to manage property for the benefit of others.

**trustworthy** adj. honest, truthful, and reliable.
▷ SYNS RELIABLE, honest, dependable, honourable, upright, principled, responsible.

**trusty** adj. (-ier, -iest) reliable or faithful.

**truth** n. the quality of being true; something that is true.
▷ SYNS **1** VERACITY, truthfulness, sincerity, candour, honesty; accuracy, correctness. **2** REALITY, actuality, factuality.

**truthful** adj. habitually telling the truth; accurate or realistic. ■ **truthfully** adv.
▷ SYNS **1** HONEST, sincere, trustworthy, genuine; candid, frank, open, forthright, straight. **2** TRUE, accurate, correct, factual, faithful, reliable; unvarnished, unembellished, veracious.

**try** v. **1** attempt. **2** (also **try out**) test something new or different. **3** (**try on**) put on a garment to see if it fits. **4** be a strain on. **5** subject to a legal trial. • n. **1** an attempt. **2** a touchdown in rugby, entitling the player's side to a kick at goal.
▷ SYNS v. **1** ATTEMPT, aim, endeavour, exert yourself, strive, seek. **2** TRY OUT, test, put to the test, appraise, evaluate, assess; sample.

**trying** adj. annoying.
▷ SYNS TROUBLESOME, bothersome, tiresome, irksome, vexatious,

annoying, irritating, exasperating.

**tryst** n. a meeting between lovers.

**tsar** (or **czar**) n. an emperor of Russia before 1917.

**tsetse** n. an African blood-sucking fly that transmits diseases.

**T-shirt** (or **tee shirt**) n. a short-sleeved casual top.

**tub** n. a low, wide, open round container for liquids etc.; a small container for food.

**tuba** n. a large low-pitched brass wind instrument.

**tubby** adj. inf. short and fat.

**tube** n. **1** a long, hollow glass or metal cylinder; a similarly shaped container. **2** (**the Tube**) trademark the underground railway system in London.

**tuber** n. a short thick rounded root or underground stem from which shoots will grow.

**tuberculosis** n. a serious infectious disease, affecting esp. the lungs. ■ **tubercular** adj.

**tubular** adj. tube-shaped.

**tuck** n. **1** a flat fold stitched in a garment etc. **2** dated snacks eaten by children at school. • v. **1** push, fold, or turn between two surfaces; hide or put away neatly. **2** (**tuck in**) inf. eat heartily.

**Tuesday** n. the day after Monday.

**tuft** n. a bunch of threads, grass, hair, etc., held or growing together at the base.

**tug** v. (**tugged, tugging**) pull hard or suddenly. • n. **1** a vigorous pull. **2** a small, powerful boat for towing others. □ **tug of war** a contest in which two

teams pull at opposite ends of a rope.
▷ SYNS v. PULL, drag, lug, draw, haul, heave, tow.

**tuition** n. teaching or instruction.

**tulip** n. a garden plant with a cup-shaped flower.

**tumble** v. fall headlong; move in an uncontrolled way. • n. **1** a fall. **2** an untidy mass or state.
□ tumble-dryer a machine for drying washing in a heated rotating drum.
▷ SYNS v. FALL, topple, lose your footing, stumble, trip up.

**tumbledown** adj. dilapidated.
▷ SYNS DILAPIDATED, ramshackle, decrepit, neglected, derelict, ruined, rickety.

**tumbler** n. **1** a drinking glass with no handle or stem. **2** an acrobat. **3** a pivoted piece in a lock, holding the bolt.

**tumescent** adj. swollen.

**tummy** n. (pl. **-ies**) inf. the stomach.

**tumour** (US **tumor**) n. an abnormal growth of tissue in the body.

**tumult** n. a loud, confused noise; confusion or disorder.
▷ SYNS DIN, uproar, commotion, racket, hubbub, hullabaloo, clamour, shouting, yelling, pandemonium, babel, bedlam.

**tumultuous** adj. **1** very loud or uproarious. **2** excited, confused, or disorderly.
▷ SYNS **1** LOUD, deafening, thunderous, uproarious, noisy, clamorous. **2** DISORDERLY, rowdy, unruly, turbulent, riotous, wild.

**tuna** n. (pl. **tuna** or **tunas**) a large edible sea fish.

**tundra** n. a vast, flat Arctic region where the subsoil is permanently frozen.

**tune** n. a melody; correct musical pitch. • v. **1** adjust a musical instrument to the correct pitch. **2** adjust a radio or television to a particular frequency. **3** adjust an engine to run smoothly.
■ tuneful adj.
▷ SYNS n. MELODY, air, song.

**tuner** n. **1** a person who tunes pianos. **2** a radio receiver as part of a hi-fi system.

**tungsten** n. a heavy grey metallic element.

**tunic** n. a close-fitting jacket worn as part of a uniform; a loose garment reaching to the knees.

**tunnel** n. an underground passage. • v. (**tunnelled, tunnelling**; US **tunneled**) make a passage underground or through something.
▷ SYNS n. UNDERPASS, subway; burrow, subway; • v. DIG, burrow, mine, drill.

**tunny** n. (pl. **-ies**) = TUNA.

**turban** n. a long length of material worn wound round the head by Muslim and Sikh men.

**turbid** adj. (of a liquid) muddy or cloudy.

**turbine** n. a machine or motor driven by a wheel that is turned by a flow of water or gas.

**turbo** n. (pl. **turbos**) = TURBOCHARGER.

**turbocharger** n. a supercharger driven by a turbine powered by the engine's exhaust gases.
■ turbocharged adj.

**turbot** n. a large edible flatfish.

**turbulent** adj. full of disorder or confusion; (of air or water) moving unevenly or violently. ■ **turbulence** n. ▷ SYNS **1** TEMPESTUOUS, stormy, rough, choppy, wild. **2** ROWDY, unruly, disorderly, restless, agitated, wild, violent.

**tureen** n. a deep covered dish from which soup is served.

**turf** n. (pl. **turfs** or **turves**) short grass and the soil just below it; a piece of this. • v. **1** cover with turf. **2** (**turf out**) inf. force to leave.

**turgid** adj. swollen; (of language) pompous.

**turkey** n. (pl. **-eys**) a large bird bred for food.

**Turkish** n. the language of Turkey. • adj. of Turkey. □ **Turkish bath** a period of sitting in a room filled with very hot air or steam, followed by washing and massage. **Turkish delight** a sweet of flavoured gelatin coated in icing sugar.

**turmeric** n. a bright yellow spice.

**turmoil** n. a state of great disturbance or confusion. ▷ SYNS AGITATION, ferment, confusion, disorder, upheaval, chaos, pandemonium, bedlam, tumult.

**turn** v. **1** move around a central point. **2** move so as to face or go in a different direction. **3** make or become: *she turned pale*. **4** shape wood on a lathe. • n. **1** an act of turning. **2** a bend in a road. **3** the time when a member of a group must or is allowed to do something. **4** a time when one period ends and another begins. **5** a change in a situation. **6** a brief feeling of illness. **7** a short performance. **8** a short walk. □ **in turn** in succession. **turncoat** a person who changes sides in a dispute etc. **turn down** reject. **turnout** the number of people attending or taking part in an event. **turnover 1** the amount of money taken by a business. **2** the rate at which employees leave or goods are sold and are replaced. **3** a small pie made of pastry folded over a filling. **turnstile** a revolving gate allowing only one person at a time to pass through. **turntable** a circular revolving platform. **turn-up** the end of a trouser leg folded upwards.
▷ SYNS v. **1** ROTATE, revolve, circle, roll, spin, wheel, whirl, twirl, gyrate, swivel, pivot. **2** BEND, curve, wind, twist, meander. **3** BECOME, grow, get, go. • n. **1** ROTATION, revolution, circle, spin, whirl, twirl, gyration, swivel. **2** TURNING, bend, corner; junction. **3** *you'll get your turn in a minute*: OPPORTUNITY, chance; stint, spell, time; try, attempt, go.

**turning** n. a point where a road branches off another. □ **turning point** a moment at which a decisive change takes place.

**turnip** n. a plant with an edible round white root.

**turpentine** n. oil used to thin paint and clean brushes.

**turpitude** n. formal wickedness.

**turps** n. inf. turpentine.

**turquoise** n. a bluish-green semi-precious stone; its colour.

**turret** n. a small tower; a revolving tower for a gun on a warship or tank. ■ **turreted** adj.

**turtle** n. a sea creature like a tortoise. □ **turn turtle** capsize. **turtle dove** a small dove with a soft purring call. **turtleneck** a high, round, close-fitting neckline.

**tusk** n. a long pointed tooth projecting from the mouth of an elephant, walrus, etc.

**tussle** n. a struggle or scuffle.

**tutor** n. a private teacher; a teacher at a university. • v. act as tutor to.

**tutorial** n. a period of tuition given by a tutor. • adj. of a tutor.

**tutu** n. a dancer's short, stiff skirt.

**tuxedo** n. (pl. **-os** or **-oes**) a dinner jacket.

**TV** abbr. television.

**twang** n. **1** a sharp vibrating sound. **2** a nasal intonation. • v. make a twang.

**tweak** v. **1** pull or twist sharply. **2** inf. make fine adjustments to. • n. a sharp pull.

**twee** adj. affectedly pretty or sentimental.

**tweed** n. a thick woollen fabric.

**tweet** v. & n. (give) a chirp.

**tweezers** pl.n. small pincers for handling very small things.

**twelve** adj. & n. one more than eleven; 12. ■ **twelfth** adj. & n.

**twenty** adj. & n. twice ten; 20. ■ **twentieth** adj. & n.

**twice** adv. two times; in double amount or degree.

**twiddle** v. fiddle with aimlessly. □ **twiddle your thumbs** have nothing to do.

**twig** n. a small shoot growing from a branch or stem.

**twilight** n. light from the sky after sunset; a period or state of gradual decline.
▷ SYNS DUSK, sunset, nightfall; Scot. gloaming.

**twill** n. a fabric with a slightly ridged surface.

**twin** n. each of two children born at the same birth; a thing that is exactly like another. • v. (**twinned**, **twinning**) link or combine as a pair.
▷ SYNS n. DOUBLE, lookalike, image, duplicate, clone; inf. spitting image, dead ringer.

**twine** n. strong thread or string. • v. twist or wind.

**twinge** n. a slight or brief pang.
▷ SYNS PAIN, spasm, pang, ache, throb; cramp, stitch.

**twinkle** v. shine with a flickering light. • n. a twinkling light.

**twirl** v. spin round lightly or rapidly. • n. a twirling movement.

**twist** v. **1** bend, curl, or distort. **2** force out of the natural position. **3** have a winding course. **4** deliberately change the meaning of. • n. **1** an act of twisting. **2** a spiral shape. **3** an unexpected development.
▷ SYNS v. **1** CONTORT, misshape, deform, distort. **2** WRENCH, turn, sprain, rick. **3** *the path twisted:* WIND, curve, swerve, bend, zigzag, meander, snake. **4** *twist their words:* DISTORT, pervert, misinterpret, garble, misrepresent, falsify, change, alter.

**twit** n. inf. a silly person.

**twitch** v. make a short jerking movement. • n. a twitching movement.

**twitter** v. make light chirping sounds. • n. a twittering sound.

**two** adj. & n. one more than one; 2. □ **two-dimensional** having or appearing to have length and breadth but no depth. **twosome** a set of two people. **two-time** be unfaithful to a spouse or lover.

**two-faced** adj. insincere or deceitful.
▷ SYNS DECEITFUL, insincere, hypocritical, false, untrustworthy, duplicitous, disloyal.

**tycoon** n. a wealthy, influential industrialist.

**tying** present participle of TIE.

**tympani** = TIMPANI.

**tympanum** n. (pl. **-pana** or **-panums**) the eardrum.

**type** n. **1** a kind or category. **2** inf. a person of a specified nature. **3** printed characters or letters. • v. write using a typewriter or computer. □ **typecast** (of an actor) repeatedly cast in the same type of role. **typeface** a particular design of printed type. **typescript** a typed copy of a text. **typesetter** a person or machine that arranges type for printing. **typewriter** a machine with keys for producing print-like characters. ■ **typist** n.
▷ SYNS n. KIND, sort, variety, class, category, order, set, genre, strain, species, ilk.

**typhoid** n. a serious infectious fever.

**typhoon** n. a tropical storm.

**typhus** n. an infectious disease transmitted by parasites.

**typical** adj. having the distinctive qualities of a particular type of person or thing.
■ **typically** adv.
▷ SYNS **1** REPRESENTATIVE, classic, quintessential, archetypal, model, stereotypical. **2** NORMAL, average, ordinary, standard, regular, routine, run-of-the-mill, conventional, unremarkable, unexceptional.

**typify** v. (**typified**, **typifying**) be a typical example of.
▷ SYNS EPITOMIZE, exemplify, characterize, personify, represent, embody.

**typography** n. the process or style of printing. ■ **typographer** n. **typographical** adj.

**tyrannical** adj. exercising power in a cruel and unfair way.
▷ SYNS DESPOTIC, autocratic, dictatorial, oppressive, authoritarian, high-handed, harsh, strict, severe, cruel.

**tyrannize** (or **-ise**) v. rule in a cruel way.

**tyrannosaurus rex** n. a large flesh-eating dinosaur.

**tyranny** n. (pl. **-ies**) cruel and oppressive government or rule. ■ **tyrannous** adj.

**tyrant** n. a cruel and oppressive ruler.
▷ SYNS DESPOT, autocrat, dictator, martinet, slave-driver, hard taskmaster, bully.

**tyre** (US **tire**) n. a rubber covering that fits round a wheel.

# Uu

**ubiquitous** adj. found everywhere.
▷ SYNS EVERYWHERE, omnipresent, pervasive, universal.

**udder** n. a bag-like milk-producing organ of a cow, goat, etc.

**UFO** abbr. unidentified flying object.

**ugly** adj. **1** unpleasant to look at. **2** threatening or hostile.
■ ugliness n.
▷ SYNS UNATTRACTIVE, unsightly, hideous, ill-favoured, plain, unprepossessing; misshapen, deformed.

**UK** abbr. United Kingdom.

**ukulele** n. a small four-stringed guitar.

**ulcer** n. an open sore on the body. ■ ulcerated adj.

**ulna** n. (pl. **-nae** or **-nas**) the thinner long bone of the forearm.

**ulterior** adj. beyond what is obvious or admitted.

**ultimate** adj. **1** final. **2** best or most extreme. **3** fundamental.
▷ SYNS LAST, final, concluding, terminal, end.

**ultimatum** n. (pl. **-tums** or **-ta**) a final warning that action will be taken unless demands are met.

**ultrasonic** adj. above the range of normal human hearing.

**ultrasound** n. ultrasonic waves.

**ultraviolet** adj. of or using radiation with a wavelength shorter than that of visible light rays.

**umbilical** adj. of the navel.
□ umbilical cord a flexible tube by which a fetus is nourished while in the womb.

**umbrage** n. (**take umbrage**) be offended.

**umbrella** n. a folding device used as a protection against rain.

**umlaut** n. a mark (¨) over a vowel indicating a change in pronunciation, used esp. in Germanic languages.

**umpire** n. a person who supervises a sporting contest to ensure that rules are observed.
• v. act as umpire in.
▷ SYNS n. ADJUDICATOR, arbitrator, judge, referee.

**umpteen** adj. inf. very many.

**UN** abbr. United Nations.

**unacceptable** adj. not satisfactory or allowable.
▷ SYNS INTOLERABLE, inadmissible, inappropriate, unsuitable, unreasonable; inf. out of order.

**unaccompanied** adj. having no companion or escort.
▷ SYNS ALONE, on your own, by yourself, solo, lone, solitary.

**unaccountable** adj. **1** not explicable. **2** not having to justify your actions.
■ unaccountably adv.

**unadulterated** adj. not mixed or diluted.

**unanimous** adj. with everyone's agreement. ■ **unanimity** n.
▷ SYNS IN AGREEMENT, of one mind, in harmony, in accord, united.

**unarmed** adj. without weapons.

**unassailable** adj. unable to be attacked or defeated.

**unassuming** adj. not arrogant or pretentious.

**unattended** adj. not supervised or looked after.

**unavoidable** adj. unable to be avoided or prevented.
▷ SYNS INESCAPABLE, inevitable, inexorable, ineluctable, certain, assured.

**unaware** adj. not aware of something. • adv. unexpectedly.
▷ SYNS adj. UNKNOWING, unconscious, ignorant, heedless, unmindful, oblivious, uninformed, unenlightened, unwitting; inf. in the dark.

**unbalanced** adj. mentally or emotionally unstable.

**unbeknown** adj. (**unbeknown to**) without the knowledge of.

**unbelievable** adj. 1 unlikely to be true. 2 extraordinary.
▷ SYNS INCREDIBLE, inconceivable, unthinkable, unimaginable, unconvincing, far-fetched, implausible, improbable.

**unbending** adj. strict and inflexible.

**unbidden** adj. without having been invited.

**unbounded** adj. without limits.

**unbridled** adj. unrestrained.

**unburden** v. (**unburden yourself**) reveal your thoughts and feelings.

**uncalled** adj. (**uncalled for**) undesirable or unnecessary.

**uncanny** adj. strange or mysterious. ■ **uncannily** adv.

**unceremonious** adj. rude or abrupt. ■ **unceremoniously** adv.

**uncertain** adj. 1 not known, reliable, or definite. 2 not completely sure.
▷ SYNS 1 UNKNOWN, undetermined, unsettled, in the balance. 2 UNSURE, doubtful, dubious, undecided, irresolute, hesitant, wavering, vacillating, ambivalent, in two minds.

**uncivilized** adj. 1 not having developed a modern culture or way of life. 2 not behaving in accordance with accepted moral standards.
▷ SYNS 1 BARBAROUS, primitive, savage, wild. 2 UNCOUTH, coarse, rough, boorish, vulgar, philistine, uneducated, unsophisticated.

**uncle** n. a brother or brother-in-law of your father or mother.

**uncomfortable** adj. not comfortable; uneasy or awkward.
▷ SYNS UNEASY, awkward, nervous, tense, edgy, embarrassed.

**uncommon** adj. unusual. ■ **uncommonly** adv.

**uncompromising** adj. inflexible or unwilling to compromise.
▷ SYNS INFLEXIBLE, unbending, unyielding, hard-line, determined, obstinate, obdurate, tenacious, inexorable, intransigent, intractable.

**unconditional** adj. not subject to conditions.
▷ SYNS COMPLETE, total, entire, full, absolute, utter, unequivocal, unquestioning, unlimited.

**unconscious** adj. **1** not conscious. **2** done without you realizing. **3** not aware.
■ **unconsciousness** n.
▷ SYNS **1** COMATOSE, knocked out; inf. out cold. **2** SUBCONSCIOUS, instinctive, involuntary; unintentional, unintended, unthinking. **3** UNAWARE, oblivious, ignorant, heedless.

**unconventional** adj. not following what is generally done or believed.
▷ SYNS UNORTHODOX, unusual, uncommon, out of the ordinary, atypical, different, original, eccentric, idiosyncratic, odd, strange, extraordinary, nonconformist, bohemian.

**uncouth** adj. lacking good manners.
▷ SYNS ROUGH, coarse, uncivilized, uncultured, uncultivated, unrefined, unsophisticated, crude, loutish, boorish, oafish, rude, impolite, discourteous, bad-mannered, ill-bred, vulgar.

**uncover** v. remove a covering from; reveal or expose.

**unction** n. anointing with oil, esp. as a religious rite.

**unctuous** adj. excessively polite or flattering.
▷ SYNS SYCOPHANTIC, ingratiating, obsequious, fawning, servile.

**undecided** adj. not having made a decision; not resolved.

**undeniable** adj. undoubtedly true. ■ **undeniably** adv.

**under** prep. **1** extending below. **2** at a lower level or grade than. **3** governed or controlled by; undergoing. **4** in accordance with rules. • adv. in or to a position directly below something. ☐ **under way** making progress.

**underarm** adj. & adv. done with the arm or hand below shoulder level.

**undercarriage** n. an aircraft's landing wheels and their supports.

**underclass** n. the lowest and poorest social class in a country.

**undercoat** n. a layer of paint used under a finishing coat.

**undercover** adj. done or doing things secretly.

**undercurrent** n. an underlying feeling, influence, or trend.

**undercut** v. (**undercut**, **undercutting**) **1** offer goods or services for a lower price than a competitor. **2** weaken or undermine.

**underdog** n. a competitor thought unlikely to win.

**underdone** adj. not thoroughly cooked.

**underestimate** v. make too low an estimate of.

**underfoot** adv. **1** on the ground. **2** getting in the way.

**undergo** v. (**undergoes**, **underwent**, **undergone**, **undergoing**) experience; be subjected to.
▷ SYNS EXPERIENCE, sustain, endure, bear, be subjected to, stand, withstand, weather.

**undergraduate** n. a university student who has not yet taken a degree.

**underground** adj. & adv. under the surface of the ground; secretly. • n. an underground railway.

**undergrowth** n. thick growth of shrubs and bushes under trees.

**underhand** adj. done or doing things slyly or secretly.

▷ SYNS DECEITFUL, dishonest, dishonourable; devious, sneaky, furtive, covert.

**underlay** n. material laid under a carpet.

**underlie** v. (**underlay, underlain, underlying**) be the cause or basis of.

**underline** v. 1 draw a line under. 2 emphasize.

**underling** n. a subordinate.

**undermine** v. weaken gradually; weaken the foundations of.

▷ SYNS WEAKEN, impair, damage, injure, threaten, subvert, sabotage.

**underneath** prep. & adv. below; so as to be concealed by.

**underpants** pl.n. an undergarment for the lower part of the body.

**underpass** n. a road passing under another.

**underpin** v. (**underpinned, underpinning**) support a structure from below.

**underprivileged** adj. not having the normal standard of living or rights.

▷ SYNS DISADVANTAGED, deprived, in need, needy, poor, impoverished.

**underrate** v. underestimate.

**underscore** v. underline.

**undersell** v. (**undersold, underselling**) sell at a lower price than a competitor.

**undersigned** n. the person or people who have signed a particular document.

**underskirt** n. a petticoat.

**understaffed** adj. having too few members of staff.

**understand** v. 1 grasp the meaning, nature, or cause of; see the significance of. 2 infer; assume without being told; interpret in a particular way.

▷ SYNS 1 COMPREHEND, apprehend, grasp, see, take in, follow, fathom; inf. get the hang of, figure out. 2 APPRECIATE, recognize, accept, sympathize, empathize. 3 GATHER, hear, be informed, learn, believe.

**understandable** adj. able to be understood; natural, reasonable, or forgivable.
  ■ **understandably** adv.

**understanding** adj. showing insight or sympathy. • n. 1 ability to understand; sympathetic insight. 2 an agreement.

▷ SYNS adj. COMPASSIONATE, sympathetic, sensitive, considerate, kind, thoughtful, tolerant, patient. • n. 1 COMPREHENSION, apprehension, grasp, appreciation. 2 COMPASSION, sympathy, empathy, sensitivity, insight. 3 AGREEMENT, arrangement, bargain, pact, deal.

**understate** v. represent as smaller, less good, etc., than is the case. ■ **understatement** n.

▷ SYNS DOWNPLAY, play down, make light of, minimize.

**understated** adj. pleasingly subtle.

**understudy** n. (pl. **-ies**) an actor who studies another's part in order to be able to take their place if necessary. • v. (**understudied, understudying**) be an understudy for.

**undertake** v. (**-took, -taken, -taking**) begin an activity; formally promise to do something.

▷ SYNS TAKE ON, set about, tackle, begin, start, commence, embark on, attempt, try.

**undertaker** n. a person whose business is to organize funerals.

**undertaking** n. **1** work etc. undertaken. **2** a formal promise.

**undertone** n. **1** a low or subdued tone. **2** an underlying quality or feeling.
▷ SYNS **1** MURMUR, whisper. **2** UNDERCURRENT, suggestion, intimation, atmosphere, aura, tenor, flavour.

**underwater** adj. & adv. situated or occurring below the surface of water.

**underwear** n. clothing worn under other clothes, next to the skin.

**underwent** past of **UNDERGO**.

**underworld** n. **1** a part of society habitually involved in crime. **2** (in mythology) the home of the dead, under the earth.

**underwrite** v. (**underwrote**, **underwritten**, **underwriting**) accept legal responsibility for an insurance policy; undertake to finance. ■ **underwriter** n.

**undesirable** adj. harmful or unpleasant.

**undisguised** adj. (of a feeling) not disguised or concealed.
▷ SYNS OPEN, obvious, evident, patent, manifest, transparent, overt, unmistakable.

**undo** v. (**undoes**, **undid**, **undone**, **undoing**) **1** unfasten. **2** cancel the effect of. **3** cause disaster to. **4** (**undoing**) a person's ruin or downfall.

**undoubted** adj. not disputed.
▷ SYNS UNDISPUTED, unquestioned, not in doubt, not in question, certain, unquestionable, indubitable, incontrovertible, irrefutable.

**undress** v. take clothes off.

**undue** adj. excessive.
■ **unduly** adv.

▷ SYNS UNWARRANTED, unjustified, unreasonable, inappropriate; excessive, immoderate, disproportionate.

**undulate** v. move with a wave-like motion; have a wavy shape. ■ **undulation** n.

**undying** adj. everlasting.

**unearth** v. uncover or bring out from the ground; find by searching.

**uneasy** adj. (**-ier**, **-iest**) troubled or uncomfortable. ■ **unease** n. **uneasily** adv.
▷ SYNS ILL AT EASE, troubled, perturbed, worried, anxious, apprehensive, agitated, nervous, on edge, edgy, restless, unsettled, uncomfortable, awkward; inf. jittery.

**unemotional** adj. not having or showing strong feelings.
▷ SYNS DETACHED, dispassionate, reserved, impassive, undemonstrative, cool, cold, unfeeling.

**unemployed** adj. without a paid job. ■ **unemployment** n.
▷ SYNS JOBLESS, out of work, redundant, laid off; inf. on the dole.

**unending** adj. endless.

**unequal** adj. **1** not equal in quantity, size, or value. **2** not fair or evenly balanced.
▷ SYNS **1** DIFFERENT, dissimilar, uneven, irregular, varying. **2** UNFAIR, unjust, inequitable; uneven, one-sided, ill-matched.

**unequalled** (US **unequaled**) adj. better or greater than all others.

**unequivocal** adj. leaving no doubt. ■ **unequivocally** adv.
▷ SYNS UNAMBIGUOUS, clear, clear-cut, plain, explicit, unqualified, categorical, direct, straightforward, blunt.

**unerring** adj. making no mistake. ■ **unerringly** adv.

**uneven** adj. not level or smooth; not regular. ■ **unevenness** n.
▷ SYNS **1** ROUGH, bumpy, lumpy, potholed. **2** IRREGULAR, asymmetrical, unbalanced, lopsided.

**uneventful** adj. not marked by interesting or exciting events.
▷ SYNS UNINTERESTING, dull, monotonous, boring, tedious, humdrum, routine, ordinary, run-of-the-mill.

**unexceptionable** adj. not open to objection.

**unexceptional** adj. not unusual.

**unexpected** adj. not expected or thought likely to happen.
▷ SYNS UNFORESEEN, unanticipated, unpredicted; sudden, abrupt, surprising, out of the blue.

**unfailing** adj. constant; never stopping or going wrong.
■ **unfailingly** adv.

**unfair** adj. not fair or just.
▷ SYNS UNJUST, inequitable, partisan, prejudiced, biased, one-sided; undeserved, unmerited, uncalled-for, unreasonable, unjustifiable.

**unfaithful** adj. not loyal; having committed adultery.
▷ SYNS **1** DISLOYAL, faithless, perfidious, treacherous, traitorous. **2** ADULTEROUS; inf. two-timing.

**unfashionable** adj. not fashionable or popular.
▷ SYNS OUT OF FASHION, outdated, old-fashioned, outmoded, dated, passé; inf. uncool.

**unfit** adj. **1** unsuitable. **2** not in good physical condition.

**unflappable** adj. inf. calm in a crisis.

**unfold** v. **1** open or spread out. **2** reveal or be revealed.

**unforeseen** adj. not predicted.

**unforgettable** adj. impossible to forget.

**unfortunate** adj. having bad luck; regrettable.
■ **unfortunately** adv.
▷ SYNS UNLUCKY, out of luck, luckless, ill-starred, ill-fated, star-crossed, hapless, wretched, poor.

**unfounded** adj. with no basis.

**unfriendly** adj. not friendly.
▷ SYNS HOSTILE, antagonistic, aggressive, unpleasant, disagreeable, inhospitable, aloof, cold, cool, frosty, distant.

**unfurl** v. unroll or spread out.

**ungainly** adj. clumsy or awkward.

**unguarded** adj. **1** not guarded. **2** incautious.

**unguent** n. an ointment or lubricant.

**ungulate** n. a hoofed animal.

**unhappy** adj. **1** not happy. **2** unfortunate. ■ **unhappily** adv. **unhappiness** n.
▷ SYNS SAD, miserable, sorrowful, dejected, despondent, disconsolate, down, downcast, dispirited, depressed, melancholy, blue, gloomy, glum, mournful, woebegone.

**unhealthy** adj. (-ier, -iest) not healthy; harmful to health.
■ **unhealthily** adv.
▷ SYNS **1** IN POOR HEALTH, unwell, ill, ailing, sick, sickly, poorly, infirm. **2** HARMFUL, detrimental, injurious, damaging.

**unheard** adj. previously unknown.

**unhinged** adj. mentally unbalanced.

**unicorn** n. a mythical horse-like animal with one straight horn on its forehead.

**uniform** n. distinctive clothing worn by members of the same organization or school.
• adj. always the same; not varying. ■ **uniformed** adj. **uniformity** n. **uniformly** adv.
▷ SYNS n. LIVERY, regalia, dress, costume. • adj. SAME, like, identical, similar, equal; constant, consistent, steady, invariable, unchanging, stable, regular, even.

**unify** v. (**unified**, **unifying**) unite. ■ **unification** n.

**unilateral** adj. done by or affecting only one person or group. ■ **unilaterally** adv.

**unimportant** adj. lacking in importance.
▷ SYNS INSIGNIFICANT, inconsequential, of no account, immaterial, irrelevant, minor, trivial, petty.

**uninhibited** adj. expressing yourself or acting freely.
▷ SYNS UNSELFCONSCIOUS, free and easy, relaxed, unreserved, outgoing, extrovert.

**unintentional** adj. not done on purpose.
▷ SYNS UNINTENDED, accidental, inadvertent, unwitting, unthinking, unconscious.

**uninterested** adj. not interested or concerned.
▷ SYNS INDIFFERENT, unconcerned, uninvolved, apathetic, unresponsive.

**uninterrupted** adj. continuous.
▷ SYNS UNBROKEN, continuous, continual, constant, steady, sustained.

**uninviting** adj. unattractive or unpleasant.

**union** n. uniting or being united; a whole formed by uniting parts; an association; a trade union. □ **Union Jack** the national flag of the UK.
▷ SYNS 1 JOINING, junction, merger, fusion, amalgamation, blend, combination, synthesis, coalition. 2 ASSOCIATION, league, consortium, syndicate, guild, confederation, federation.

**unionist** n. 1 a member of a trade union. 2 a person in favour of the union of Northern Ireland with Great Britain.

**unionize** (or **-ise**) v. make or become members of a trade union.

**unique** adj. 1 the only one of its kind; belonging only to one place, person, etc. 2 remarkable.
▷ SYNS ONLY, single, sole, lone, solitary, exclusive.

**unisex** adj. suitable for people of either sex.

**unison** n. the fact of two or more things happening or being said at the same time.

**unit** n. 1 an individual thing, person, or group, esp. as part of a complex whole. 2 a fixed quantity used as a standard of measurement. 3 a piece of furniture or equipment; part of an institution, having a specialized function.
▷ SYNS COMPONENT, part, element, constituent, subdivision, segment, module, item.

**Unitarian** n. a person who believes that God is one being and rejects the idea of the Trinity.

**unitary** adj. single; of a single whole.

**unite** v. join together; make or become one.

▷ SYNS **1** JOIN, unify, link, connect, combine, amalgamate, fuse, blend, mix, merge. **2** JOIN FORCES, band together, cooperate, collaborate.

**unity** n. (pl. **-ies**) the state of being united or coherent; a complex whole.
▷ SYNS AGREEMENT, harmony, accord, unanimity, consensus, togetherness, solidarity.

**universal** adj. of, for, or done by all. ■ **universally** adv.
▷ SYNS GENERAL, all-inclusive, all-embracing, comprehensive, across the board, worldwide, global, widespread, common, ubiquitous.

**universe** n. the whole of space and everything in it.

**university** n. (pl. **-ies**) an educational institution for advanced learning and research.

**unkempt** adj. looking untidy or neglected.
▷ SYNS UNTIDY, dishevelled, disordered, tousled, rumpled, wind-blown, scruffy.

**unkind** adj. not caring or kind. ■ **unkindness** n.
▷ SYNS MEAN, spiteful, malicious, malevolent, unsympathetic, un-feeling, callous, hard-hearted, heartless, uncharitable, nasty.

**unknown** adj. not known. • n. an unknown person or thing.
▷ SYNS UNIDENTIFIED, unnamed, nameless, anonymous, incognito, unheard of, obscure.

**unleaded** adj. (of petrol) without added lead.

**unleash** v. release or let loose.

**unleavened** adj. (of bread) made without yeast.

**unless** conj. except when; if not.

**unlike** prep. not like; uncharacteristic of. • adj. different.

**unlikely** adj. not likely to happen or be true.
▷ SYNS IMPROBABLE, doubtful, dubious, implausible, unconvincing, incredible, unbelievable.

**unlimited** adj. not limited; very great in number.
▷ SYNS **1** UNRESTRICTED, unconstrained, unrestrained, uncontrolled, unchecked, untrammelled. **2** LIMITLESS, boundless, inexhaustible, immeasurable, incalculable, untold, infinite.

**unmask** v. expose the true nature of.

**unmentionable** adj. too shocking to be spoken of.

**unmistakable** adj. not able to be mistaken for anything else. ■ **unmistakably** adv.

**unmitigated** adj. total or absolute.

**unmoved** adj. not affected by emotion or excitement.

**unnatural** adj. not natural or normal. ■ **unnaturally** adv.
▷ SYNS **1** UNUSUAL, abnormal, strange, queer, odd, bizarre. **2** AFFECTED, artificial, feigned, false, contrived, studied, strained, forced.

**unnecessary** adj. not needed; excessive. ■ **unnecessarily** adv.
▷ SYNS NEEDLESS, unneeded, in-essential, uncalled for, gratuit-ous, dispensable, expendable, redundant, unwanted.

**unnerve** v. cause to lose courage or determination.

**unobtrusive** adj. not conspicuous or attracting attention.

**unpack** v. take things out of a suitcase, bag, etc.

**unparalleled** adj. never yet equalled.

**unpick** v. undo the stitching of.

**unpleasant** adj. causing distaste or distress.
▷ SYNS DISAGREEABLE, unpalatable, unsavoury, unappetizing, objectionable, obnoxious, disgusting, repugnant, revolting, nasty, nauseating.

**unpopular** adj. not liked or popular. ■ **unpopularity** n.
▷ SYNS DISLIKED, friendless, unloved, unwanted, unwelcome, rejected, out of favour.

**unprecedented** adj. never done or known before.

**unpredictable** adj. changeable or unreliable.
▷ SYNS CHANGEABLE, variable, unreliable, erratic; capricious, mercurial, volatile, unstable.

**unprepared** adj. not ready or equipped for something.

**unprepossessing** adj. unattractive.

**unpretentious** adj. modest or unassuming.
▷ SYNS SIMPLE, plain, modest; unassuming, unaffected, natural, straightforward.

**unprincipled** adj. without moral principles.

**unprofessional** adj. contrary to professional standards of behaviour. ■ **unprofessionally** adv.

**unprompted** adj. spontaneous.

**unqualified** adj. **1** not having the necessary qualifications. **2** complete.

**unravel** v. (**unravelled, unravelling**; US **unraveled**) disentangle or become disentangled; solve.

**unreal** adj. strange and not seeming real.
▷ SYNS IMAGINARY, make-believe, fictitious, mythical, fanciful, hypothetical, non-existent, illusory.

**unrealistic** adj. not having a sensible understanding of what can be achieved.
▷ SYNS IMPRACTICAL, unfeasible, unworkable, unreasonable, silly, foolish, fanciful.

**unreasonable** adj. not based on good sense; unfair or excessive. ■ **unreasonably** adv.
▷ SYNS UNACCEPTABLE, outrageous, preposterous, irrational, illogical; excessive, immoderate, undue, inordinate, disproportionate.

**unrelenting** adj. not becoming less intense, severe, or strict.

**unreliable** adj. not able to be relied on.
▷ SYNS UNDEPENDABLE, untrustworthy, irresponsible, unpredictable, erratic, fickle.

**unremitting** adj. not ceasing.

**unrequited** adj. (of love) not given in return.

**unreserved** adj. without reservations or doubts; complete. ■ **unreservedly** adv.

**unrest** n. disturbance or disorder; dissatisfaction.
▷ SYNS DISSATISFACTION, discontent; dissent, discord, strife, protest, rebellion, uprising, disturbance, trouble.

**unrivalled** (US **unrivaled**) adj. having no equal.

**unruly** adj. disorderly or difficult to control. ■ **unruliness** n.
▷ SYNS DISORDERLY, undisciplined, disobedient, obstreperous, recalcitrant, refractory,

uncontrollable, wild, wilful, wayward.

**unsavoury** (US **unsavory**) adj. disagreeable to the taste or smell; not respectable.
▷ SYNS UNPLEASANT, disagreeable, unpalatable, distasteful, nasty, disgusting; disreputable, degenerate, dishonest, dishonourable, immoral.

**unscathed** adj. without suffering any injury.

**unscrupulous** adj. lacking moral scruples or principles.
▷ SYNS UNPRINCIPLED, unethical, amoral, immoral, shameless, corrupt, dishonest, dishonourable, devious.

**unseat** v. cause to fall from a saddle; remove from a position of power.

**unselfish** adj. not selfish.
▷ SYNS ALTRUISTIC, selfless, self-sacrificing, philanthropic, public-spirited, charitable, generous, kind.

**unsettle** v. make anxious or uneasy.

**unsettled** adj. changeable; anxious or uneasy; not yet resolved.

**unshakeable** (or **unshakable**) adj. firm.

**unsightly** adj. ugly.

**unskilled** adj. not having or needing special skill or training.

**unsociable** adj. disliking company.

**unsocial** adj. (of working hours) not falling within the normal working day.

**unsolicited** adj. not requested.

**unsophisticated** adj. simple and natural or naive.
▷ SYNS UNWORLDLY, naive, simple, innocent, inexperienced, childlike, artless, guileless, ingenuous, natural, unaffected, unpretentious.

**unspeakable** adj. too bad to be described in words.

**unstable** adj. not stable; mentally or emotionally unbalanced.
▷ SYNS UNSTEADY, rickety, shaky, wobbly, tottery, insecure, precarious.

**unstinting** adj. given freely and generously.

**unsuccessful** adj. not successful.
▷ SYNS FAILED, abortive, ineffective, fruitless, vain, futile, useless, unproductive, unprofitable.

**unsuitable** adj. not right or suitable for a particular purpose or occasion.
▷ SYNS INAPPROPRIATE, inapt, inapposite, unacceptable, unfitting, out of place, ill-chosen, ill-judged.

**unsung** adj. not celebrated or praised.

**unswerving** adj. not changing or becoming weaker.

**untenable** adj. not able to be maintained or defended against criticism etc.

**unthinkable** adj. impossible to imagine or accept.

**unthinking** adj. thoughtless.

**untidy** adj. (**-ier, -iest**) in disorder; not keeping things neat. ■ **untidily** adv. **untidiness** n.
▷ SYNS DISORDERED, in disarray, messy, disarranged, disorganized, chaotic, cluttered, muddled, jumbled, topsy-turvy, at sixes and sevens, higgledy-piggledy.

**until** prep. & conj. up to the point in time or the event mentioned.

**untimely** adj. happening at an unsuitable time; premature.

**unto** prep. old use to.

**untold** adj. **1** not told. **2** too much or too many to be counted.

**untoward** adj. unexpected and inconvenient.

**unusual** adj. **1** not usual. **2** exceptional. ■ **unusually** adv.
▷ SYNS **1** UNCOMMON, atypical, abnormal, singular, odd, strange, curious, queer, bizarre, weird, surprising, unexpected, different, unconventional, unwonted, unorthodox, irregular. **2** EXTRAORDINARY, exceptional, singular, rare, remarkable, outstanding.

**unveil** v. remove a veil or covering from; reveal or make known.

**unwaged** adj. not doing paid work.

**unwarranted** adj. not justified.
▷ SYNS UNJUSTIFIABLE, unjustified, indefensible, inexcusable, unforgivable, unpardonable, uncalled-for, gratuitous.

**unwell** adj. ill.

**unwieldy** adj. awkward to move or control because of its size, shape, or weight.
▷ SYNS CUMBERSOME, unmanageable, awkward, clumsy, hefty, bulky.

**unwilling** adj. reluctant. ■ **unwillingly** adv. **unwillingness** n.
▷ SYNS RELUCTANT, disinclined, unenthusiastic, grudging, averse, loath.

**unwind** v. (**unwound**, **unwinding**) undo something that has been wound or twisted; relax after work or tension.

**unwise** adj. foolish.

**unwitting** adj. unaware; unintentional. ■ **unwittingly** adv.
▷ SYNS UNAWARE, unconscious, unintentional, unintended, inadvertent.

**unwonted** adj. not customary or usual.

**unworldly** adj. not aware of the realities of life.

**unwritten** adj. (of a rule etc.) based on custom not statute.

**up** adv. **1** to, in, or at a higher place or position; to a higher level or value. **2** out of bed. **3** towards or as far as a stated place, position, etc. **4** so as to be closed or finished. **5** inf. amiss: *what's up?* • prep. from a lower to a higher point of. • adj. moving or directed upwards. • v. (**upped**, **upping**) raise or increase. □ **ups and downs** alternate good and bad fortune.

**upbeat** adj. inf. cheerful and optimistic.

**upbraid** v. reproach.

**upbringing** n. the way in which a child is taught and looked after.

**update** v. bring up to date.

**upend** v. set on end or upside down.

**upgrade** v. raise to a higher standard or grade.

**upheaval** n. a sudden violent change or movement.
▷ SYNS DISRUPTION, disturbance, disorder, confusion, turmoil, chaos.

**uphill** adj. & adv. going or sloping upwards.

**uphold** v. (**upheld**, **upholding**) support.
▷ SYNS SUPPORT, back, stand by, champion, defend, maintain, sustain.

**upholster** v. provide furniture with a soft, padded covering. ■ upholstery n.

**upkeep** n. the process or cost of keeping something in good condition.

**uplift** v. make more hopeful or happy.

**upload** v. transfer data to a larger computer system.

**upmarket** adj. expensive or of high quality.

**upon** prep. on.

**upper** adj. higher in place, position, or rank. • n. the part of a shoe above the sole. □ the upper hand advantage or control. **upper case** capital letters. **upper class** the social group with the highest status. ■ uppermost adj. & adv.

**uppity** adj. inf. self-important.

**upright** adj. 1 in a vertical position. 2 strictly honest or honourable. • n. a vertical part or support.
▷ SYNS adj. 1 ERECT, on end, vertical, perpendicular; rampant. 2 HONEST, honourable, upstanding, decent, respectable, worthy, good, virtuous, righteous, law-abiding, moral.

**uprising** n. a rebellion.

**uproar** n. an outburst of noise and excitement or anger.
▷ SYNS TUMULT, turmoil, disorder, confusion, commotion, mayhem, pandemonium, bedlam, din, noise, clamour, hubbub, racket.

**uproarious** adj. noisy and lively; very funny.

**uproot** v. pull a tree etc. out of the ground; force someone to leave their home.

**upset** v. 1 make unhappy or disappointed. 2 knock over; disrupt or disturb. • n. a state of being upset. • adj. unhappy, disappointed, or disturbed.
▷ SYNS v. 1 OVERTURN, knock/push over, upend, tip over, topple, capsize. 2 DISTURB, unsettle, dismay, disquiet, trouble, worry, agitate, fluster, distress, hurt, grieve.

**upshot** n. an outcome.

**upside down** adv. & adj. with the upper part where the lower part should be; in or into great disorder.

**upstage** adv. & adj. at or towards the back of a theatre stage. • v. draw attention away from someone.

**upstairs** adv. & adj. to or on a higher floor.

**upstanding** adj. honest and respectable.

**upstart** n. a person newly risen to a high position, esp. one who behaves arrogantly.

**upstream** adj. & adv. towards the source of a stream or river, against the current.

**upsurge** n. an increase.

**uptight** adj. inf. nervously tense or angry.

**up to date** adj. modern or fashionable.
▷ SYNS MODERN, contemporary, new, state-of-the-art, present-day; fashionable, voguish.

**upturn** n. an improvement or upward trend.

**upward** adj. & adv. towards a higher level ■ upwards adv.

**upwind** adj. & adv. into the wind.

**uranium** n. a radioactive metallic element used as fuel in nuclear reactors.

**urban** adj. of a city or town.

**urbane** adj. (of a man) sophisticated and courteous. ■ **urbanity** n.
▷ SYNS SUAVE, sophisticated, debonair, worldly, cultivated, cultured, courteous, polite.

**urchin** n. a poor, raggedly dressed child.

**Urdu** n. a language of Pakistan and India.

**ureter** n. the duct from the kidney to the bladder.

**urethra** n. the duct which carries urine from the body.

**urge** v. 1 encourage or advise strongly. 2 recommend strongly. • n. a strong desire or impulse.
▷ SYNS v. 1 ENCOURAGE, exhort, press, enjoin, implore, entreat, appeal, beg, plead; egg on, spur, push. 2 ADVISE, recommend, counsel, advocate, suggest. • n. DESIRE, need, compulsion, longing, yearning, wish; impulse.

**urgent** adj. needing or calling for immediate attention or action. ■ **urgency** n.
▷ SYNS IMPERATIVE, vital, crucial, critical, top-priority, acute, pressing, serious, grave.

**urinal** n. a receptacle in a public toilet into which men urinate.

**urinate** v. pass urine from the body. ■ **urination** n.

**urine** n. waste liquid which collects in the bladder and is passed out of the body. ■ **urinary** adj.

**URL** abbr. uniform (or universal) resource locator, the address of a World Wide Web page.

**urn** n. 1 a container for holding a cremated person's ashes. 2 a large metal container with a tap, for keeping water etc. hot.

**us** pron. used by a speaker to refer to himself or herself and one or more other people.

**USA** (or **US**) abbr. United States (of America).

**usable** adj. able to be used.

**usage** n. the using of something.

**use** v. 1 cause to serve your purpose or achieve your ends; treat in a specified way; exploit unfairly. 2 (**use up**) consume the whole of. 3 (**used**) second-hand. • n. the using of something; the power to control and use something; a purpose for which something is used. □ **used to 1** was accustomed to. 2 familiar with.
▷ SYNS v. 1 MAKE USE OF, utilize, employ, work, operate, wield, ply, avail yourself of. 2 CONSUME, get through, exhaust, deplete, expend, spend. • n. USEFULNESS, good, advantage, benefit, service, help, gain, profit, avail; purpose, point.

**useful** adj. able to be used for a practical purpose. ■ **usefully** adv.
▷ SYNS 1 OF USE, functional, utilitarian, of service, practical, convenient. 2 BENEFICIAL, advantageous, helpful, worthwhile, profitable, rewarding, productive, valuable.

**useless** adj. serving no purpose; hopelessly incompetent.
▷ SYNS VAIN, in vain, to no avail, unavailing, unsuccessful, futile, fruitless, unprofitable, unproductive.

**user** n. a person who uses something. □ **user-friendly** easy for people to use or understand.

**usher** n. a person who shows people to their seats in a

theatre etc. or in church.
• v. lead or escort.

**usherette** n. a woman who ushers people to seats in a theatre etc.

**USSR** abbr. hist. Union of Soviet Socialist Republics.

**usual** adj. happening or done typically, regularly, or frequently.
▷ SYNS HABITUAL, customary, accustomed, wonted, normal, regular, routine, everyday, established, set, familiar, typical, ordinary, average, standard, stock.

**usually** adv. generally speaking; as a rule.
▷ SYNS GENERALLY, as a rule, normally, in the main, mainly, mostly, for the most part.

**usurp** v. seize power or a position wrongfully or by force.
▷ SYNS TAKE OVER, seize, commandeer.

**usury** n. the lending of money at excessively high rates of interest.

**utensil** n. a tool or container, esp. for domestic use.

**uterus** n. the womb.
■ uterine adj.

**utilitarian** adj. useful rather than decorative.

**utility** n. (pl. **-ies**) 1 the state of being useful. 2 a company supplying water, gas, electricity, etc. to the public. □ utility room a room for large domestic appliances.

**utilize** (or **-ise**) v. make use of.

**utmost** adj. furthest or most extreme. • n. the furthest point or degree etc.

**Utopia** n. an imagined perfect place. ■ utopian adj.

**utter¹** adj. complete or absolute.
■ utterly adv.

**utter²** v. make a sound or say something.
▷ SYNS SAY, speak, voice, express, articulate, pronounce, enunciate.

**utterance** n. a word, statement, or sound uttered.
▷ SYNS REMARK, comment, statement, observation, word.

**U-turn** n. the turning of a vehicle in a U-shaped course so as to face the opposite way; a complete change of policy.

# Vv

**V** (or **v**) n. (as a Roman numeral) 5. • abbr. 1 volts. 2 versus.

**vacancy** n. 1 an unoccupied position, job, room, etc. 2 empty space.
▷ SYNS OPENING, position, post, job, opportunity.

**vacant** adj. 1 empty or unoccupied. 2 showing no interest or understanding.
▷ SYNS 1 UNOCCUPIED, unfilled, free, empty, available, uninhabited, untenanted.
2 BLANK, expressionless,

glassy, emotionless; vacuous, inane.

**vacate** v. cease to occupy.
▷ SYNS LEAVE, quit, move out of, evacuate.

**vacation** n. **1** an interval between terms in universities and law courts. **2** US a holiday.

**vaccinate** n. inoculate with a vaccine. ■ vaccination n.

**vaccine** n. a substance used to stimulate the production of antibodies and so give immunity against a disease.

**vacillate** v. keep changing your mind. ■ vacillation n.
▷ SYNS DITHER, shilly-shally, waver, hesitate, equivocate; inf. hum and haw.

**vacuous** adj. showing a lack of thought or intelligence.

**vacuum** n. **1** a space from which air has been removed. **2** a gap.
□ **vacuum cleaner** an electrical machine that sucks up dust. **vacuum flask** a container for keeping liquids hot or cold.
▷ SYNS EMPTINESS, void, empty space, nothingness.

**vagabond** n. a wanderer or vagrant.

**vagary** n. (pl. **-ies**) an unpredictable change or action.
▷ SYNS CHANGE, variation, quirk, caprice, whim, fancy.

**vagina** n. the passage leading from the vulva to the womb. ■ vaginal adj.

**vagrant** n. a person without a settled home. ■ vagrancy n.
▷ SYNS TRAMP, beggar, itinerant, nomad, vagabond.

**vague** adj. **1** not certain or definite. **2** not expressing yourself clearly.
▷ SYNS **1** INDISTINCT, indeterminate, ill-defined, unclear,

nebulous, amorphous, shadowy, hazy, fuzzy, blurry. **2** IMPRECISE, inexact, loose, generalized, ambiguous, hazy, woolly.

**vain** adj. **1** excessively proud of your appearance, abilities, etc. **2** useless or futile. □ **in vain** without success.
▷ SYNS **1** CONCEITED, narcissistic, self-admiring, proud, arrogant, boastful, cocky. **2** UNSUCCESSFUL, futile, useless, unavailing, to no avail, ineffective, fruitless, unproductive, abortive.

**valance** n. a short curtain or hanging frill.

**vale** n. a valley.

**valediction** n. a farewell.
■ valedictory adj.

**valency** (or **valence**) n. the combining power of an atom as compared with that of the hydrogen atom.

**valentine** n. a romantic greetings card sent on St Valentine's Day (14 Feb.); a person to whom you send such a card.

**valet** n. a man's personal male attendant. • v. (**valeted**, **valeting**) clean a car as a professional service.

**valiant** adj. brave.

**valid** adj. **1** legally binding or acceptable. **2** logically sound.
■ validity n.
▷ SYNS SOUND, well founded, reasonable, logical, justifiable, defensible, bona fide; effective, cogent, powerful, convincing, credible, forceful.

**validate** v. make or show to be valid. ■ validation n.
▷ SYNS RATIFY, legalize, legitimize, authorize, sanction, warrant, approve, endorse.

**valley** n. (pl. **-eys**) a low area between hills.
▷ SYNS DALE, dell, vale; Scot. glen.

**valour** (US **valor**) n. bravery.

**valuable** adj. of great value or worth. • pl.n. valuable things.
▷ SYNS adj. **1** COSTLY, expensive, priceless, precious. **2** USEFUL, helpful, beneficial, advantageous, worthwhile.

**valuation** n. an estimate of the worth of something.

**value** n. **1** the amount of money that something is worth. **2** importance or usefulness. **3** (**values**) standards of behaviour. • v. **1** consider precious. **2** estimate the value of. □ value added tax a tax on the amount by which goods rise in value at each stage of production.
▷ SYNS n. **1** COST, price. **2** WORTH, usefulness, advantage, benefit, gain, profit, good, avail; importance, significance. • v. RATE HIGHLY, appreciate, esteem, think highly of, set store by, respect; prize, cherish, treasure.

**valve** n. **1** a device controlling flow through a pipe. **2** a structure allowing blood to flow in one direction only.

**vampire** n. (in stories) a dead person who leaves their grave to drink the blood of living people. □ vampire bat a blood-sucking tropical bat.

**van** n. **1** a covered vehicle for transporting goods etc. **2** a railway carriage for luggage or goods. **3** the leading part.

**vandal** n. a person who damages things wilfully. ■ vandalism n. vandalize v.

**vane** n. a broad blade forming part of a windmill, propeller, etc.

**vanguard** n. the foremost part of an advancing army etc.
▷ SYNS ADVANCE GUARD, forefront, front, front line, van.

**vanilla** n. a flavouring obtained from the pods of a tropical plant.

**vanish** v. disappear completely.

**vanity** n. **1** conceit. **2** futility.
▷ SYNS CONCEIT, narcissism, self-love, pride, arrogance, boastfulness.

**vanquish** v. conquer.

**vantage point** (or **vantage point**) n. a position giving a good view.

**vapid** adj. insipid or uninteresting.
▷ SYNS INSIPID, flat, lifeless, colourless, bland, uninteresting.

**vaporize** (or **-ise**) v. convert or be converted into vapour.

**vapour** (US **vapor**) n. moisture suspended in air, into which certain liquids or solids are converted by heating.
■ vaporous adj.

**variable** adj. changeable. • n. a part or element liable to change. ■ variability n.

**variance** n. (**at variance**) disagreeing.

**variant** n. a form of something differing from others or from a standard.

**variation** n. **1** a change or slight difference. **2** a variant. **3** a new but still recognizable version of a musical theme.
▷ SYNS CHANGE, alteration, modification; difference, dissimilarity.

**varicose** adj. (of veins) permanently swollen.

**varied** adj. involving a number of different types or elements.

▷ SYNS DIVERSE, assorted, miscellaneous, mixed, heterogeneous.

**variegated** adj. having irregular patches of colours.

**variety** n. **1** not being uniform or monotonous; a selection of different things of the same type. **2** a sort or kind. **3** light entertainment involving singing, dancing, and comedy.
▷ SYNS **1** VARIATION, diversification, diversity, change, difference. **2** ASSORTMENT, selection, miscellany, range, mixture, medley. **3** see SORT.

**various** adj. **1** of different kinds or sorts. **2** several.
■ **variously** adv.
▷ SYNS VARYING, diverse, different, differing, varied, assorted, sundry, mixed, miscellaneous, heterogeneous.

**varnish** n. a liquid that dries to form a shiny transparent coating. • v. coat with varnish.

**vary** v. (**varied**, **varying**) make or be or become different.
▷ SYNS **1** DIFFER, be different, be dissimilar. **2** CHANGE, alter, fluctuate.

**vase** n. a container for holding cut flowers.

**vasectomy** n. (pl. **-ies**) a surgical removal of part of the ducts that carry semen from the testicles, as a means of sterilization.

**vassal** n. a person or country subordinate to another.

**vast** adj. very great in area or size.

**VAT** abbr. value added tax.

**vat** n. a large tank for liquids.

**vault** n. **1** an arched roof. **2** an underground storage room; a burial chamber. **3** an act of vaulting. • v. jump using your hands or a pole.
▷ SYNS n. CELLAR, basement; crypt, tomb. • v. JUMP, leap, spring, bound.

**VC** abbr. Victoria Cross.

**VCR** abbr. video cassette recorder.

**VDU** abbr. visual display unit.

**veal** n. calf's flesh as food.

**vector** n. **1** a quantity (e.g. velocity) that has both magnitude and direction. **2** the carrier of a disease or infection.

**veer** v. change direction.
▷ SYNS TURN, swerve, swing, sheer, wheel.

**vegan** n. a person who eats no meat or animal products.

**vegetable** n. a plant grown for food.

**vegetarian** n. a person who does not eat meat or fish. • adj. eating or including no meat or fish.

**vegetate** v. live an uneventful life.

**vegetation** n. plants.

**vehement** adj. showing strong feeling. ■ **vehemence** n.
▷ SYNS PASSIONATE, ardent, impassioned, fervent, strong, forceful, powerful, intense, zealous.

**vehicle** n. a car, lorry, or other thing used for transporting people or goods. ■ **vehicular** adj.

**veil** n. a piece of fabric concealing or protecting the face; something that conceals. • v. cover with or as if with a veil.
▷ SYNS v. HIDE, conceal, cover, mask, screen.

**vein** n. **1** any of the blood vessels conveying blood towards the

heart. **2** a narrow streak or stripe; a narrow layer of ore etc. **3** a mood or style. ∎ **veined** adj.
▷ SYNS **1** BLOOD VESSEL, capillary. **2** LODE, seam, stratum. **3** STREAK, stripe, line, thread.

**Velcro** n. trademark a fastener consisting of two strips of fabric which cling together when pressed.

**veld** (or **veldt**) n. open grassland in southern Africa.

**velocity** n. (pl. **-ies**) speed.

**velour** n. a plush fabric resembling velvet.

**velvet** n. a fabric with a soft, thick, short pile on one side.

**venal** adj. susceptible to bribery.

**vend** v. sell. ◻ **vending machine** a slot machine that dispenses small articles. ∎ **vendor** n.

**vendetta** n. a feud.

**veneer** n. a thin covering layer of fine wood; a superficial show of a quality.
▷ SYNS **1** FACING, covering, coat, finish. **2** FACADE, false front, show, appearance, semblance, guise, mask, pretence.

**venerable** adj. given great respect because of age, wisdom, etc.
▷ SYNS VENERATED, respected, revered, honoured, esteemed, hallowed.

**venerate** v. respect deeply. ∎ **veneration** n.

**venereal disease** n. a disease caught by having sex with an infected person.

**Venetian** adj. of Venice. • n. a person from Venice. ◻ **venetian blind** a window blind consisting of adjustable horizontal slats.

**vengeance** n. retaliation or revenge.

▷ SYNS REVENGE, retribution, retaliation, reprisal, an eye for an eye.

**vengeful** adj. seeking vengeance.

**venial** adj. (of a sin) pardonable.

**venison** n. meat from a deer.

**venom** n. **1** a poisonous fluid secreted by snakes etc. **2** bitter feeling or language.
▷ SYNS POISON, toxin.

**venomous** adj. producing venom.
▷ SYNS POISONOUS, toxic, lethal, deadly, fatal.

**vent** n. **1** an opening allowing gas or liquid to pass through. **2** a slit in a garment. • v. express a strong emotion.
▷ SYNS n. OPENING, outlet, aperture, hole, duct, flue. • v. GIVE VENT TO, express, air, utter, voice, verbalize.

**ventilate** v. cause air to enter or circulate freely in. ∎ **ventilation** n.
▷ SYNS AIR, aerate, oxygenate, freshen.

**ventilator** n. **1** a device for ventilating a room etc. **2** a respirator.

**ventricle** n. a cavity, esp. in the heart or brain.

**ventriloquist** n. an entertainer who can make their voice seem to come from elsewhere. ∎ **ventriloquism** n.

**venture** n. a risky undertaking. • v. dare to do something risky; dare to say something bold.
▷ SYNS n. ENTERPRISE, undertaking, project, scheme, gamble.

**venue** n. an appointed place for a meeting, concert, etc.

**veracious** adj. truthful. ∎ **veracity** n.

**veranda** n. a roofed terrace.

**verb** n. a word indicating an action or occurrence.

**verbal** adj. **1** of or in words. **2** spoken. **3** of a verb.
■ **verbally** adv.
▷ SYNS ORAL, spoken, said, stated; unwritten.

**verbatim** adv. & adj. in exactly the same words.
▷ SYNS WORD FOR WORD, literal, exact, faithful, precise.

**verbiage** n. excessively long or detailed speech or writing.

**verbose** adj. using more words than are needed.
▷ SYNS WORDY, loquacious, garrulous, voluble; long-winded, prolix, lengthy, tautological.

**verdant** adj. (of grass etc.) green.

**verdict** n. a decision reached by a jury; a decision or opinion reached after testing something.
▷ SYNS DECISION, judgement, adjudication, finding, conclusion, ruling.

**verdure** n. green vegetation.

**verge** n. the extreme edge or brink; a grass edging of a road etc. • v. come close to being.
▷ SYNS N. EDGE, border, margin, rim, brink, boundary, perimeter. • v. (**verge on**) APPROACH, border on, be close to.

**verger** n. a church caretaker.

**verify** v. (**verified**, **verifying**) check the truth or correctness of. ■ **verifiable** adj. **verification** n.
▷ SYNS CONFIRM, substantiate, prove, corroborate, attest to, testify to, validate, authenticate.

**verisimilitude** n. the appearance of being true.

**veritable** adj. genuine.

**vermicelli** n. pasta made in slender threads.

**vermilion** adj. & n. bright red.

**vermin** n. (pl. **vermin**) an animal or insect regarded as a pest.

**vernacular** n. the ordinary language of a country or district.

**vernal** adj. of or occurring in spring.

**verruca** n. an infectious wart on the foot.

**versatile** adj. able to do or be used for many different things.
■ **versatility** n.
▷ SYNS ADAPTABLE, flexible, resourceful; adjustable, handy, multi-purpose, all-purpose.

**verse** n. poetry; a group of lines forming a unit in a poem or hymn; a numbered division of a Bible chapter.
▷ SYNS **1** STANZA, canto, couplet. **2** POEM, lyric, sonnet, ode, ballad.

**versed** adj. (**versed in**) skilled or experienced in.

**version** n. a particular form of something, differing from others; an account of events from a particular viewpoint.
▷ SYNS **1** ACCOUNT, report, story, rendering, interpretation, understanding, reading, impression. **2** VARIANT, form, type, kind, sort.

**verso** n. (pl. **versos**) the left-hand page of an open book; the back of a loose document.

**versus** prep. against.

**vertebra** n. (pl. **-brae**) any of the small bones forming the backbone.

**vertebrate** n. an animal having a backbone.

**vertical** adj. perpendicular to a horizontal line or surface. • n. a vertical line or surface.
■ **vertically** adv.

**vertigo** n. dizziness caused by looking down from a height.
▷ SYNS DIZZINESS, giddiness, light-headedness.

**verve** n. enthusiasm and vigour.
▷ SYNS ENTHUSIASM, vigour, energy, vitality, vivacity, liveliness, animation, spirit, life, brio, fervour, gusto, passion.

**very** adv. to a high degree.
• adj. **1** actual or precise: *this very moment.* **2** mere: *the very thought.*
▷ SYNS adv. EXTREMELY, exceedingly, exceptionally, uncommonly, unusually, decidedly, particularly, eminently, remarkably, really, truly, terribly; inf. awfully, jolly.

**vessel** n. **1** a ship or boat. **2** a tubelike structure conveying fluid in the body, or in a plant. **3** a container for liquids.
▷ SYNS **1** SHIP, boat, craft, barque. **2** CONTAINER, receptacle.

**vest** n. an undergarment worn on the upper part of the body.
• v. give power or property to.
□ **vested interest** a personal reason for wanting something to happen.

**vestibule** n. an entrance hall; a porch.

**vestige** n. a small amount or trace. ■ **vestigial** adj.

**vestment** n. a ceremonial garment worn by clergy or members of a church choir.

**vestry** n. (pl. **vestries**) a room in a church, used as an office and for changing into ceremonial robes.

**vet** n. **1** a veterinary surgeon. **2** US a military veteran.
• v. (**vetted, vetting**) examine critically for faults etc.

**veteran** n. a person with long experience, esp. in the armed forces.

**veterinary** adj. of or for the treatment of diseases and injuries of animals. □ **veterinary surgeon** a person qualified to treat diseased or injured animals.

**veto** n. (pl. **-oes**) an authoritative rejection of something proposed; the right to make this. • v. (**vetoed, vetoing**) reject by a veto.
▷ SYNS n. REJECTION, prohibition, proscription, embargo, ban.
• v. REJECT, turn down, prohibit, forbid, proscribe, disallow, embargo, ban.

**vex** v. annoy. □ **vexed question** a problem that is much discussed.
■ **vexation** n.

**VHF** abbr. very high frequency.

**via** prep. by way of; through.

**viable** adj. capable of working successfully, or of living or surviving. ■ **viability** n.
▷ SYNS WORKABLE, feasible, practicable, practical, possible.

**viaduct** n. a long bridge carrying a road or railway over a valley.

**vial** n. a small bottle.

**vibrant** adj. full of energy and enthusiasm; resonant; bright.
■ **vibrancy** n.
▷ SYNS **1** LIVELY, energetic, spirited, animated, sparkling, vivacious, dynamic. **2** VIVID, bright, strong, striking.

**vibrate** v. **1** move rapidly and continuously to and fro. **2** (of a

sound) resonate. ■ **vibration** n. **vibrator** n.
▷ SYNS SHAKE, oscillate, pulsate, tremble, quiver, throb; reson-ate, resound, reverberate, ring.

**vibrato** n. (in music) a rapid slight fluctuation in the pitch of a note.

**vicar** n. a minister in charge of a parish.

**vicarage** n. a vicar's house.

**vicarious** adj. experienced in the imagination rather than directly.
▷ SYNS INDIRECT, second-hand, surrogate.

**vice** n. **1** wicked or immoral be-haviour. **2** criminal activities in-volving sex or drugs. **3** a bad habit. **4** (US **vise**) a tool with two jaws for holding an object firmly.
▷ SYNS **1** IMMORALITY, corruption, wickedness, evil, iniquity, depravity, degeneracy; sin. **2** FAILING, flaw, fault, defect, weakness, shortcoming.

**vice-** comb. form next in rank to.

**viceroy** n. a person governing a colony etc. as the sovereign's representative.

**vice versa** adv. reversing the order of the items just mentioned.

**vicinity** n. (pl. **-ies**) the surrounding district.
▷ SYNS SURROUNDING AREA, neighbourhood, locality, area, district, region, environs, precincts.

**vicious** adj. **1** cruel or violent. **2** wild and dangerous. □ **vicious circle** a situation in which one problem leads to another, which then makes the first one worse.

▷ SYNS FIERCE, ferocious, savage, dangerous, violent, brutal, cruel, inhuman, barbarous, barbaric, fiendish, sadistic.

**victim** n. a person harmed or killed.

**victimize** (or **-ise**) v. single out for cruel or unfair treatment. ■ **victimization** n.
▷ SYNS PERSECUTE, terrorize, pick on, discriminate against.

**victor** n. a winner.
▷ SYNS WINNER, champion, conqueror.

**victorious** adj. having won a victory.
▷ SYNS CONQUERING, triumphant, winning, successful, prize-winning, top, first.

**victory** n. (pl. **-ies**) an act of defeating an opponent.

**video** n. (pl. **-os**) **1** a system of recording and reproducing moving images on magnetic tape. **2** a film on magnetic tape. • v. (**videoed, videoing**) make a video of. □ **video recorder** a machine for recording television programmes and playing videos. **videotape 1** magnetic tape for recording images and sound. **2** a cassette of this.

**vie** v. (**vied, vying**) compete eagerly for something.
▷ SYNS COMPETE, contend, contest, struggle, strive.

**view** n. **1** the ability to see something or to be seen from a particular position. **2** something seen from a particular position, esp. natural scenery. **3** an atti-tude or opinion. • v. **1** look at or inspect. **2** regard as. □ **view-finder** a device on a camera showing what will appear in the picture. **viewpoint 1** a position giving a good view. **2** an opinion. ■ **viewer** n.

▷ SYNS n. **1** SIGHT, perspective, vision, visibility. **2** OUTLOOK, prospect, scene, scenery, vista, panorama, landscape. **3** OPINION, viewpoint, belief, conviction, attitude, thinking, idea, feeling, sentiment. • v. LOOK AT, watch, observe, contemplate, regard, survey, inspect, scrutinize.

**vigil** n. a period of staying awake to keep watch or pray.

**vigilant** adj. watchful. ■ **vigilance** n.

▷ SYNS WATCHFUL, on the lookout, observant, sharp-eyed, eagle-eyed, attentive, alert, on your guard, careful, wary.

**vigilante** n. a member of a group undertaking crime prevention and punishment without legal authority.

**vignette** n. a brief vivid description.

**vigorous** adj. **1** strong, healthy, and full of energy. **2** involving effort, energy, or determination.

▷ SYNS **1** ROBUST, healthy, strong, fit, tough. **2** ENERGETIC, strenuous, spirited, determined, passionate, fervent.

**vigour** (US **vigor**) n. physical or mental strength; forcefulness.

**Viking** n. an ancient Scandinavian trader and pirate.

**vile** adj. extremely unpleasant or wicked.

▷ SYNS FOUL, nasty, horrid, horrible, offensive, obnoxious, odious, repulsive, repellent, revolting, repugnant, disgusting, loathsome, hateful, nauseating, sickening, dreadful, abominable, monstrous.

**vilify** v. (**vilified**, **vilifying**) speak or write about in an unjust and unpleasant way. ■ **vilification** n.

▷ SYNS DEFAME, run down, revile, denigrate, disparage, speak ill of, cast aspersions on, malign, slander, libel.

**villa** n. a house in a residential district; a rented holiday home.

**village** n. a community in a rural area that is smaller than a town. ■ **villager** n.

**villain** n. a wicked person. ■ **villainous** adj. **villainy** n.

▷ SYNS ROGUE, scoundrel, blackguard, wretch, cad, reprobate, wrongdoer, miscreant.

**villein** n. hist. a feudal tenant subject to a lord.

**vinaigrette** n. a salad dressing of oil and vinegar.

**vindicate** v. clear of blame; justify. ■ **vindication** n.

▷ SYNS ACQUIT, clear, absolve, exonerate.

**vindictive** adj. showing a strong or excessive desire for vengeance.

▷ SYNS VENGEFUL, revengeful, avenging, unforgiving, resentful, spiteful, rancorous, venomous, malicious, malevolent.

**vine** n. a climbing plant on which grapes grow. □ **vineyard** a plantation of vines producing grapes for winemaking.

**vinegar** n. a sour liquid made from wine, cider, or beer, used as a seasoning or for pickling. ■ **vinegary** adj.

**vintage** n. **1** the year in which a wine was produced. **2** wine of high quality from a particular year. **3** the time that something was produced. • adj. (of something from the past) of high quality.

▷ SYNS **adj.** CLASSIC, ageless, enduring, prime, choice, select, superior, best.

**vintner** n. a wine merchant.

**vinyl** n. a type of strong plastic.

**viola** n. an instrument like a violin but of lower pitch.

**violate** v. break a rule, promise, etc.; treat with disrespect; rape. ■ **violation** n.
▷ SYNS **1** BREAK, breach, infringe, contravene, transgress, disobey, disregard. **2** DESECRATE, profane, defile.

**violence** n. actions using physical force intended to hurt, damage, or kill; great force or intensity.
▷ SYNS FORCE, brute force, roughness, ferocity, brutality, savagery.

**violent** adj. **1** using or involving violence. **2** very intense. ■ **violently** adv.
▷ SYNS **1** BRUTAL, vicious, destructive, savage, fierce, ferocious, bloodthirsty, homicidal, murderous. **2** STRONG, powerful, uncontrolled, unrestrained, unbridled, uncontrollable, un-governable, wild, passionate, intense, extreme, vehement.

**violet** n. **1** a small plant with purple or blue flowers. **2** a bluish-purple colour.

**violin** n. a musical instrument with four strings of treble pitch, played with a bow. ■ **violinist** n.

**violoncello** n. (pl. **-cellos**) a cello.

**VIP** abbr. very important person.

**viper** n. a poisonous snake.

**viral** adj. of a virus.

**virgin** n. **1** a person who has never had sex. **2** (**the Virgin**) Mary, the mother of Jesus. • adj. **1** not yet used or spoilt. **2** having had no sexual experience. ■ **virginal** adj. **virginity** n.

**virile** adj. (of a man) having strength and a strong sex drive. ■ **virility** n.

**virtual** adj. **1** almost as described, but not completely. **2** of or using virtual reality. ☐ **virtual reality** a system in which images that look like real, three-dimensional objects are created by computer. ■ **virtually** adv.

**virtue** n. **1** behaviour showing high moral standards. **2** a good or useful quality. **3** dated chastity.
▷ SYNS **1** GOODNESS, righteousness, morality, integrity, rectitude, honour, decency, respectability. **2** GOOD POINT, asset, advantage, merit, strength.

**virtuoso** n. (pl. **-osos** or **-osi**) an expert performer. ■ **virtuosity** n.

**virtuous** adj. having high moral standards.
▷ SYNS RIGHTEOUS, good, moral, ethical, upright, upstanding, honest, honourable, decent, respectable.

**virulent** adj. (of poison or dis-ease) extremely strong or violent; bitterly hostile. ■ **virulence** n. **virulently** adv.
▷ SYNS **1** POISONOUS, toxic, venom-ous, deadly, lethal, fatal. **2** HOSTILE, spiteful, venomous, vicious, vindictive, malicious, malevolent, vitriolic, bitter, rancorous, scathing.

**virus** n. **1** a minute organism which can cause disease.

**2** a destructive code introduced secretly into a computer system.

**visa** n. an official mark on a passport, permitting the holder to enter a specified country.

**visage** n. lit. a person's face.

**vis-à-vis** prep. in relation to.

**viscera** pl.n. the internal organs of the body. ■ visceral adj.

**viscose** n. a fabric made from cellulose.

**viscount** n. a nobleman ranking between earl and baron.

**viscountess** n. a woman holding the rank of viscount; a viscount's wife or widow.

**viscous** adj. thick and sticky. ■ viscosity n.

**visibility** n. the state of being visible; the distance you can see under certain weather conditions etc.

**visible** adj. able to be seen or noticed. ■ visibly adv.
▷ syns PERCEPTIBLE, apparent, evident, noticeable, recognizable, manifest, plain, clear, obvious, patent, unmistakable, distinct.

**vision** n. **1** the ability to see. **2** the ability to think about the future with imagination or wisdom. **3** a mental image, dream, or apparition.
▷ syns **1** SIGHT, eyesight, view, perspective. **2** APPARITION, dream, hallucination, mirage, illusion.

**visionary** adj. thinking about the future with imagination or wisdom. • n. (pl. -ies) a visionary person.
▷ syns adj. INSPIRED, imaginative, wise; idealistic, quixotic.

**visit** v. **1** go to see a person or place. **2** view a website or webpage. **3** inflict something harmful or unpleasant on someone. • n. an act of visiting. ■ visitor n.
▷ syns v. call on, look in on, stop by; stay with.

**visitation** n. **1** an official visit or inspection. **2** trouble regarded as divine punishment.

**visor** (or **vizor**) n. a movable front part of a helmet, covering the face; a screen for protecting the eyes from light.

**vista** n. a pleasing view.

**visual** adj. of or used in seeing. □ visual display unit a device displaying information from a computer on a screen. ■ visually adv.

**visualize** (or **-ise**) v. form a mental picture of.
▷ syns ENVISAGE, conjure up, picture, envision, imagine.

**vital** adj. **1** absolutely necessary. **2** essential for life. **3** full of energy. ■ vitally adv.
▷ syns **1** ESSENTIAL, necessary, indispensable, key, imperative, critical, crucial, all-important. **2** LIVELY, animated, spirited, vivacious, dynamic, energetic, vigorous.

**vitality** n. the state of being strong and active.
▷ syns ENERGY, liveliness, spirit, vivacity, animation, vibrancy, zest, dynamism, vigour.

**vitamin** n. an organic compound present in food and essential for normal nutrition.

**vitiate** v. make imperfect or ineffective.

**vitriol** n. savagely hostile remarks. ■ vitriolic adj.

**viva**[1] exclam. long live!

**viva**[2] (or **viva voce**) n. an oral university exam.

**vivacious** adj. lively and high-spirited. ∎ **vivacity** n.
▷ SYNS LIVELY, full of life, animated, effervescent, bubbly, ebullient, sparkling, spirited, high-spirited, vibrant, dynamic, vital.

**vivid** adj. bright or intense; clear; (of imagination) lively.
▷ SYNS **1** STRONG, intense, colourful, rich, glowing, bright, brilliant, clear. **2** GRAPHIC, dramatic, striking, lively, stirring, powerful, realistic, memorable.

**viviparous** adj. giving birth to live young.

**vivisection** n. performance of experiments on living animals.

**vixen** n. a female fox.

**vizor** = VISOR.

**vocabulary** n. (pl. **-ies**) the words known by a person, or used in a particular language or activity; a list of words and their meanings.

**vocal** adj. **1** of or for the voice. **2** expressing opinions freely. ∙ n. a piece of sung music. ∎ **vocally** adv.

**vocalist** n. a singer.

**vocalize** (or **-ise**) v. utter.

**vocation** n. **1** a strong belief that you ought to pursue a particular career. **2** a career or occupation. ∎ **vocational** adj.
▷ SYNS CALLING, life's work, profession, occupation, career, job, trade, craft.

**vociferous** adj. expressing opinions in a loud and forceful way.

**vodka** n. a clear Russian alcoholic spirit.

**vogue** n. the current fashion or style.

**voice** n. sounds formed in the larynx and uttered by the mouth as speech or song. ∙ v. express in words. ▫ **voicemail** an electronic system for storing messages from phone callers.
▷ SYNS V. PUT INTO WORDS, express, utter, articulate, vocalize, air, give vent to.

**void** adj. **1** not valid. **2** empty. ∙ n. an empty space. ∙ v. **1** discharge. **2** declare invalid.
▷ SYNS adj. **1** INVALID, ineffective, non-viable, useless, worthless. **2** EMPTY, vacant, blank, bare, clear, free.

**voile** n. a thin, semi-transparent fabric.

**volatile** adj. **1** evaporating rapidly. **2** liable to change quickly and unpredictably. ∎ **volatility** n.
▷ SYNS **1** CAPRICIOUS, mercurial, unpredictable, changeable, inconstant, erratic, unstable. **2** EXPLOSIVE, charged, tense, strained.

**vol-au-vent** n. a small puff pastry case filled with a savoury mixture.

**volcano** n. (pl. **-oes**) a mountain with a vent through which lava is forced. ∎ **volcanic** adj.

**vole** n. a small rodent.

**volition** n. the exercise of a person's will.

**volley** n. (pl. **-eys**) **1** a number of missiles etc. fired at one time; a rapid series of questions, insults, etc. **2** a return of the ball in tennis etc. before it touches the ground. ∙ v. send in a volley. ▫ **volleyball** a game for two teams in which a ball is hit by hand over a net.

**volt** n. a unit of electromotive force.

**voltage** n. electromotive force expressed in volts.

**volte-face** n. a complete change of attitude or policy.

**voluble** adj. talking easily and at length.
▷ SYNS TALKATIVE, loquacious, garrulous, chatty; eloquent, forthcoming, fluent, glib.

**volume** n. 1 a book. 2 the amount of space held or occupied by a container or object; the amount or quantity of something. 3 the loudness of a sound.
▷ SYNS 1 BOOK, publication, tome. 2 SPACE, bulk, capacity. 3 LOUDNESS, sound, amplification.

**voluminous** adj. (of clothing) loose and full.
▷ SYNS CAPACIOUS, roomy, ample, full, big, billowing.

**voluntary** adj. 1 done, given, or acting by choice. 2 working or done without payment.
■ **voluntarily** adv.
▷ SYNS OF YOUR OWN FREE WILL, of your own accord; optional, discretionary, elective, non-compulsory.

**volunteer** n. a person who offers to do something; a person who works for no pay; a person who freely joins the armed forces. • v. offer without being asked.

**voluptuous** adj. 1 (of a woman) curvaceous and sexually attractive. 2 giving sensual pleasure.
▷ SYNS CURVY, curvaceous, shapely, full-figured, buxom.

**vomit** v. (**vomited**, **vomiting**) bring up food from the stomach through the mouth. • n. vomited food.

▷ SYNS V. BE SICK, spew, heave, retch, gag; inf. puke, throw up.

**voodoo** n. a religious cult involving sorcery and possession by spirits.

**voracious** adj. 1 wanting or eating great quantities of food. 2 very eager and enthusiastic.
■ **voracity** n.
▷ SYNS 1 GREEDY, gluttonous, ravenous. 2 INSATIABLE, compulsive, enthusiastic, eager.

**vortex** n. (pl. **-texes** or **-tices**) a whirlpool or whirlwind.

**vote** n. 1 a formal choice between two or more candidates or options. 2 the right to participate in an election. • v. give or register a vote.
▷ SYNS n. BALLOT, poll, election, referendum, plebiscite.

**vouch** v. guarantee the accuracy or reliability of.
▷ SYNS (**vouch for**) ATTEST TO, bear witness to, answer for, be responsible for, guarantee.

**voucher** n. a piece of paper that may be exchanged for goods or services.

**vouchsafe** v. give or grant.

**vow** n. a solemn promise. • v. solemnly promise.
▷ SYNS n. PROMISE, pledge, oath, bond, covenant, commitment, word of honour. • v. SWEAR, pledge, promise, undertake, give your word, commit yourself.

**vowel** n. a letter or the alphabet representing a speech sound made without audible stopping of the breath, e.g. a or e.

**voyage** n. a journey by water or in space. • v. make a voyage.
▷ SYNS n. JOURNEY, trip, expedition, crossing, cruise, passage.

**voyeur** n. a person who gets sexual pleasure from watching others having sex or undressing.

**vs** abbr. versus.

**vulcanize** (or **-ise**) v. strengthen rubber by treating it with sulphur.

**vulgar** adj. **1** referring inappropriately to sex or bodily functions. **2** lacking refinement or good taste. □ **vulgar fraction** a fraction shown by numbers above and below a line, not decimally. ■ **vulgarity** n.

▷ SYNS **1** RUDE, indecent, indecorous, indelicate, crude, coarse, offensive, off colour, ribald, bawdy, obscene, salacious, smutty, dirty, filthy; inf. raunchy. **2** TASTELESS, crass, tawdry, ostentatious, showy, flashy, gaudy.

**vulnerable** adj. exposed to being attacked or harmed. ■ **vulnerability** n.

▷ SYNS EXPOSED, unprotected, unguarded, defenceless, helpless, weak.

**vulture** n. a large bird of prey that feeds on dead animals.

**vulva** n. the female external genitals.

**vying** present participle of **VIE**.

# Ww

**W** abbr. **1** West; Western. **2** watts.

**wacky** adj. (**-ier, -iest**) inf. mad or eccentric.

**wad** n. **1** a pad of soft material. **2** a bundle of papers or banknotes. • v. (**wadded, wadding**) compress into a pad.

▷ SYNS n. **1** PAD, lump, mass, ball, plug. **2** BUNDLE, roll.

**waddle** v. walk with short swaying steps. • n. a waddling gait.

**wade** v. **1** walk through water or mud. **2** (**wade through**) read ~mething very long or boring.
~ADDLE, ford, cross.

1 a long-legged
~ (**waders**) high
~oots.

~hin, light biscuit.

**waffle** n. **1** inf. lengthy but vague or trivial talk or writing. **2** a small batter cake eaten hot with butter or syrup. • v. inf. talk or write waffle.

**waft** v. pass gently through the air.

**wag** v. (**wagged, wagging**) move briskly to and fro. • n. **1** a wagging movement. **2** inf. a witty person.

▷ SYNS v. SWING, swish, shake, twitch, wave, wiggle, waggle.

**wage** n. a fixed regular payment for work. • v. carry on a war.

▷ SYNS n. PAY, salary, earnings, payment, fee, remuneration, stipend, emolument.

**wager** n. a bet. • v. make a bet.

▷ SYNS n. BET, gamble, stake; inf. flutter. • v. BET, gamble, lay odds, put money on, speculate.

**waggle** v. wag.

**wagon** (or **waggon**) n. **1** a vehicle, esp. a horse-drawn one, for transporting goods. **2** a railway vehicle for carrying goods in bulk.

**waif** n. a poor, helpless person, esp. a child.

**wail** v. & n. (give) a long sad cry.
▷ SYNS HOWL, bawl, yowl, weep, cry, sob, moan, whine, lament.

**waist** n. **1** the part of the body between ribs and hips. **2** a narrow middle part. □ **waistcoat** a close-fitting, waist-length garment with no sleeves or collar. **waistline** the measurement around a person's waist.

**wait** v. **1** stay in a place or delay action until a particular time or event. **2** be delayed or deferred. **3** (**wait on**) act as an attendent to. **4** act as a waiter or waitress. • n. an act or period of waiting.
▷ SYNS v. STAY, remain, rest, stop, linger; delay, hold back, bide your time, hang fire, mark time; inf. hang around, sit tight, hold your horses. • n. DELAY, hold-up, interruption, interval.

**waiter** (or **waitress**) n. a person who serves customers in a restaurant etc.
▷ SYNS SERVER, steward, stewardess, attendant.

**waive** v. refrain from insisting on a right etc. ■ **waiver** n.
▷ SYNS RELINQUISH, renounce, give up, abandon, surrender, yield, forgo.

**wake**[1] v. **1** (also **wake up**) stop sleeping. **2** stir; rouse. • n. **1** a party held after a funeral. **2** a watch kept beside the body of a dead person.

▷ SYNS v. **1** AWAKE, awaken, waken, wake up, stir, come to, get up; formal arise. **2** ROUSE, evoke, stir up, activate, stimulate. • n. VIGIL, watch; funeral.

**wake**[2] n. a trail of disturbed water left by a ship. □ **in the wake of** following.
▷ SYNS WASH, backwash, slipstream, trail, path.

**waken** v. wake.

**walk** v. **1** move on foot at a fairly slow pace. **2** travel over on foot. **3** accompany on foot. **4** (**walk out**) leave suddenly or angrily. • n. **1** a journey on foot. **2** a way of walking. **3** a path for walking. □ **walking stick** a stick used for support when walking. **walkout** a sudden angry departure as a protest or strike. **walkover** an easy victory. ■ **walker** n.
▷ SYNS v. **1** STROLL, saunter, amble, plod, trudge, hike, tramp, trek, march, stride, step. **2** ACCOMPANY, escort, see, take. **3** (**walk out on**) DESERT, abandon, forsake, leave, leave in the lurch, run away from, throw over, jilt; inf. chuck, dump.
• n. **1** STROLL, saunter, promenade, ramble, hike, tramp, march, airing; dated constitutional. **2** PATH, pathway, footpath, track, avenue, walkway, promenade, pavement.

**walkie-talkie** n. a portable two-way radio.

**wall** n. **1** a continuous upright structure forming one side of a building or room or enclosing an area of land. **2** a barrier. **3** the outer layer or lining of a body organ or cavity.
• v. surround or enclose with a wall. □ **wallflower 1** a garden plant. **2** inf. a girl who has no

to dance with at a party.
**wallpaper** decorative paper for covering the interior walls of a room.

▷ SYNS n. **1** PARTITION, screen, divider, separator. **2** BARRIER, barricade, obstacle.

**wallaby** n. (pl. **-ies**) a marsupial like a small kangaroo.

**wallet** n. a small folding case for money, credit cards, etc.

▷ SYNS PURSE, notecase; US pocketbook, billfold.

**wallop** inf. v. (**walloped, walloping**) hit hard. • n. a heavy blow.

**wallow** v. **1** roll in mud or water etc. **2** indulge in. • n. an act of wallowing.

▷ SYNS v. **1** LOLL AROUND, lie around, roll around, splash around. **2** LUXURIATE, bask, indulge (yourself), delight, revel, glory; enjoy.

**walnut** n. an edible nut with a wrinkled shell.

**walrus** n. a large sea mammal with long tusks.

**waltz** n. **1** a ballroom dance. **2** the music for this. • v. **1** dance a waltz. **2** inf. move in a casual, confident way.

**wan** adj. pale and ill-looking.

▷ SYNS PALE, pallid, ashen, white; anaemic, colourless, bloodless, waxen, washed out, pasty, peaky.

**wand** n. a slender rod, esp. used for casting magic spells.

▷ SYNS BATON, stick, staff, bar, rod.

**wander** v. go from place to place casually or aimlessly; stray. • n. wandering. □ **wanderlust** a strong desire to travel.

▷ SYNS v. **1** STROLL, saunter, walk, ramble, roam, meander, rove, range, drift; inf. mosey, mooch.

**2** STRAY, depart, diverge, veer, swerve, deviate, digress.

**wane** v. become weaker; (of the moon) appear to decrease in size.

▷ SYNS DECREASE, decline, diminish, dwindle, shrink, taper off, subside, sink, ebb, dim, fade away, vanish, die out, peter out.

**wangle** v. inf. obtain by trickery or scheming.

**want** v. desire to have or do; lack; (of a suspected criminal) sought by the police. • n. a desire; a lack or need.

▷ SYNS v. **1** DESIRE, wish for, long for, hope for, yearn for, pine for, fancy, crave, hanker after, hunger for, thirst for, lust after, covet, need; inf. have a yen for. **2** NEED, be in need of, require, call for, demand, cry out for. • n. **1** LACK, absence, unavailability; dearth, deficiency, inadequacy, insufficiency, paucity, shortage, scarcity. **2** NEED, privation, poverty, destitution, penury. **3** WISH, desire, longing, yearning, fancy, craving, hankering, hunger, thirst.

**wanting** adj. lacking or deficient.

▷ SYNS DEFICIENT, inadequate, lacking, insufficient, imperfect, disappointing, unacceptable, flawed, faulty, defective, substandard, inferior, second-rate.

**wanton** adj. **1** deliberate or unprovoked. **2** sexually immoral. ■ **wantonly** adv.

▷ SYNS **1** DELIBERATE, unprovoked, wilful, malicious, spiteful, wicked, arbitrary, unjustified, needless, unnecessary, uncalled for, gratuitous, senseless, pointless. **2** PROMISCUOUS, immoral, shameless, fast, lascivious, licentious, libertine, dissolute; dated loose, of easy virtue.

**WAP** abbr. Wireless Application Protocol, a means of enabling mobile phones to access the Internet.

**war** n. armed conflict, esp. between countries; open hostility; a long contest or campaign. • v. (**warred, warring**) engage in war. □ **warfare** the activity of fighting a war. **warhead** the explosive head of a missile. **warmonger** a person who seeks to bring about war.
▷ SYNS n. WARFARE, hostilities, combat, fighting, struggle, armed conflict, battle, fight, campaign.

**warble** v. sing with a gentle trilling note.

**ward** n. **1** a room for patients in a hospital. **2** an administrative division of a city or town. **3** a child under the care of a guardian or court. □ **ward off** prevent from doing harm.
▷ SYNS **1** ROOM, department, unit, area. **2** DISTRICT, constituency, division, quarter, zone, parish. **3** CHARGE, dependant, protégé.

**warden** n. an official with supervisory duties.

**warder** n. a prison officer.
▷ SYNS PRISON OFFICER, guard, warden, jailer; inf. screw.

**wardrobe** n. a large cupboard for hanging clothes in; a stock of clothes etc.

**ware** n. pottery of a specified type; articles for sale.
▷ SYNS (**wares**) GOODS, products, commodities, merchandise, produce, stock.

**warehouse** n. a large building for storing goods.

▷ SYNS STOREROOM, depot, depository, stockroom; inf. lock-up.

**warlike** adj. hostile.
▷ SYNS AGGRESSIVE, hostile, belligerent, bellicose, pugnacious, combative, militaristic, militant.

**warm** adj. **1** moderately hot. **2** affectionate, kind, or enthusiastic. **3** providing warmth. • v. make or become warm. □ **warm-blooded** maintaining a constant body temperature. **warm up** prepare for exercise.
▷ SYNS adj. **1** HOT, cosy, snug; tepid, lukewarm, heated. **2** KIND, friendly, enthusiastic, amiable, affectionate, loving, sympathetic, tender, caring, sincere, genuine.

**warmth** n. the quality of being warm; enthusiasm, affection, or kindness.

**warn** v. **1** inform about a possible danger or problem. **2** advise not to do something; order to keep away.
▷ SYNS **1** INFORM, notify, give notice, tell, let know, forewarn; inf. tip off, put wise. **2** ADVISE, exhort, urge, counsel, caution.

**warning** n. **1** advance notice of something. **2** advice against wrong or foolish actions. **3** something indicating a possible danger or problem.
▷ SYNS **1** ADVANCE NOTICE, notification, forewarning, alert, hint; inf. tip-off. **2** CAUTION, advice, exhortation, counselling. **3** OMEN, portent, signal, sign, token.

**warp** v. make or become bent or twisted; distort or pervert. • n. **1** a distortion in shape. **2** the lengthwise threads in a loom.

**warrant** n. a document giving legal authorization for an action; justification. • v. justify; guarantee.
▷ SYNS n. AUTHORIZATION, consent, sanction, permission, licence. • v. JUSTIFY, vindicate, excuse, account for, be a reason for.

**warranty** n. (pl. **-ies**) a guarantee of repair or replacement of a purchased article.

**warren** n. a series of burrows where rabbits live.

**warrior** n. a person who fights in a battle.

**wart** n. a small, hard growth on the skin. □ **warthog** an African wild pig with warty lumps on its face.

**wary** adj. (**-ier, -iest**) cautious or suspicious. ■ **warily** adv. **wariness** n.
▷ SYNS CAREFUL, cautious, circumspect, chary, suspicious, distrustful, leery, on your guard, on the alert, attentive, heedful, watchful.

**wash** v. 1 clean with water and soap etc. 2 flow past, against, or over. 3 coat thinly with paint. • n. 1 an act of washing; clothes etc. to be washed; a cleansing solution. 2 water disturbed by a moving ship. 3 a thin coating of paint. □ **washbasin** a basin used for washing one's hands and face. **washed out** pale and tired. **washout** inf. a disappointing failure. **wash up** wash dishes etc. after use.
▷ SYNS v. 1 WASH YOURSELF, bath, bathe, shower. 2 CLEAN, cleanse, sponge, scrub, launder, shampoo. 3 SPLASH, dash, break, beat. • n. BATH, shower, ablutions; clean, cleaning.

**washer** n. a small flat ring fixed between a nut and bolt.

**washing** n. clothes etc. to be washed or that have just been washed.

**wasp** n. a stinging insect with a black and yellow striped body.

**waspish** adj. sharply irritable.

**wassail** old use n. revelry with a lot of drinking. • v. celebrate in this way; sing carols.

**wastage** n. an amount wasted; loss of employees by retirement or resignation.

**waste** v. 1 use carelessly or extravagantly; fail to make use of. 2 become thinner and weaker. • adj. discarded because not wanted; (of land) unfit for use. • n. 1 an instance of wasting; material that is not wanted. 2 a large expanse of barren land.
▷ SYNS v. SQUANDER, dissipate, fritter away, misspend, misuse, throw away, go through; inf. blow. • adj. 1 LEFTOVER, unused, superfluous, unwanted, worthless, useless. 2 DESERT, barren, uncultivated, unproductive, arid, bare, desolate, uninhabited, unpopulated, wild, bleak, cheerless. • n. 1 SQUANDERING, dissipation, misuse, prodigality. 2 RUBBISH, refuse, debris, dross, dregs, leavings, garbage, trash.

**wasteful** adj. extravagant. ■ **wastefully** adv.
▷ SYNS EXTRAVAGANT, prodigal, profligate, thriftless, spendthrift, lavish.

**watch** v. look at attentively; observe; be cautious about; look out for; be careful. • n. 1 a small timepiece worn on your wrist. 2 an instance or spell of watching. 3 a shift worked by

firefighters or police officers.
□ **watchdog** a dog kept to guard private property; a group monitoring the practices of companies. **watchman** a man employed to guard an empty building. **watchtower** a tower built as a high observation point. **watchword** a word or phrase expressing a central aim or belief.

▷ SYNS **v. 1** LOOK AT, observe, view, eye, gaze at, stare at, contemplate, behold, inspect, scrutinize, survey, scan, examine. **2** KEEP WATCH ON, keep in sight, spy on; inf. keep tabs on. **3** MIND, take care of, look after, supervise, superintend, tend, guard, protect, keep an eye on.
• **n. 1** WRISTWATCH, pocket watch, timepiece, chronometer, stopwatch. **2** GUARD, vigil.

**watchful** adj. alert to possible difficulty and danger.

▷ SYNS OBSERVANT, alert, vigilant, attentive, heedful, sharp-eyed, wary, circumspect, cautious.

**water** n. **1** the liquid which forms the seas, lakes, rivers, and rain. **2** (**waters**) an area of sea controlled by a particular country. **3** a watery secretion.
• **v. 1** sprinkle water over; provide with water. **2** produce tears or saliva. **3** (**water down**) dilute; make less forceful.
□ **water cannon** a device ejecting a powerful jet of water to disperse a crowd. **water closet** a toilet flushed by water. **watercolour** artists' paint mixed with water rather than oil; a picture painted with watercolours. **watercourse** a brook, stream, or artificial water channel. **watercress** a cress which grows in running water. **waterfront** a part of a town alongside a body of water. **watering can** a container with a spout for watering plants. **water lily** a plant that grows in water, with large floating leaves. **waterline** the level normally reached by the water on the side of a ship. **waterlogged** saturated with water. **watermark** a faint design made in some paper, visible when held against the light. **water meadow** a meadow periodically flooded by a stream. **watermelon** a melon with watery red pulp. **watermill** a mill worked by a waterwheel. **waterproof** unable to be penetrated by water. **watershed 1** an area of land separating two river systems. **2** a turning point in a state of affairs. **waterskiing** the sport of skimming over water on skis while towed by a motor boat. **waterspout** a column of water formed by a whirlwind over the sea. **water table** the level below which the ground is saturated with water. **waterway** a river, canal, or other route for travel by water.

▷ SYNS **n. 1** $H_2O$, Adam's ale. **2** SEA, river, lake, loch, pool, reservoir.
• **v. 1** SPRINKLE, moisten, dampen, wet, douse, hose, spray, drench, saturate, flood. **2** (**water down**) DILUTE, thin, weaken, adulterate.

**waterfall** n. a stream of water falling from a height.

▷ SYNS FALLS, cascade, cataract, rapids.

**watertight** adj. **1** not allowing water to pass through. **2** unable to be questioned.

▷ SYNS **1** IMPERMEABLE, impervious, hermetically sealed, waterproof.

**2** INDISPUTABLE, unquestionable, incontrovertible, irrefutable, unassailable, flawless.

**watery** adj. **1** of or like water. **2** containing too much water. **3** weak or pale.

▷ SYNS **1** LIQUID, fluid, aqueous. **2** WET, damp, moist, sodden, soggy, squelchy, saturated, waterlogged, marshy, boggy. **3** THIN, runny, weak, diluted, tasteless, flavourless, insipid.

**watt** n. a unit of electric power.

**wattage** n. an amount of electric power expressed in watts.

**wattle** n. **1** interwoven sticks used as material for fences, walls, etc. **2** a fold of skin hanging from the neck of a turkey and some other birds.

**wave** n. **1** a moving ridge of water on the sea's surface. **2** an act of waving your hand. **3** a slight curl in hair. **4** a sudden increase in a phenomenon or emotion. **5** a wave-like motion by which heat, light, sound, or electricity is transmitted. • v. move your hand or arm to and fro as a greeting or signal; move to and fro or up and down. □ **waveband** a range of wavelengths. **wavelength 1** the distance between successive crests of a wave of sound, light, etc. **2** a person's way of thinking.

▷ SYNS n. **1** BREAKER, roller, ripple, billow, white horse, swell, surf. **2** CURL, undulation, kink. **3** SPATE, surge, upsurge, rush, outbreak, rash. • v. **1** SHAKE, move up and down, waggle, wag. **2** GESTURE, gesticulate, signal, sign, beckon, indicate. **3** RIPPLE, undulate, stir, flutter, flap, sway, swing.

**waver** v. be unsteady; be undecided.

▷ SYNS **1** FALTER, flicker, wobble. **2** HESITATE, be indecisive, dither, equivocate, hem and haw, vacillate; inf. shilly-shally, pussyfoot around.

**wavy** adj. (**-ier, -iest**) having waves or curves.

▷ SYNS CURLY, undulating, squiggly, rippled, curving, winding.

**wax** n. a soft solid used for polishing, making candles, etc. • v. **1** coat or polish with wax. **2** (of the moon) appear to gradually increase in size. **3** become stronger. **4** lit. speak or write in a specified way. □ **waxwork** a lifelike dummy modelled in wax. ■ **waxy** adj.

**way** n. **1** a method or manner of doing something. **2** a road or path. **3** a direction: *go the other way.* **4** a distance: *a long way to go.* **5** a respect or aspect: *wrong in every way.* □ **have your way** get what you want. **in the way** forming an obstacle. **make way** allow someone to pass. **wayfarer** lit. a traveller. **wayside** the edge of a road.

▷ SYNS **1** METHOD, means, course of action, process, procedure, technique, system, plan, scheme, manner, mode, modus operandi. **2** HABIT, custom, wont, practice, conduct, behaviour, manner, style, nature, disposition, characteristic, trait, attribute, mannerism, peculiarity, idiosyncrasy. **3** DIRECTION, route, course, path. **4** DISTANCE, length, journey.

**waylay** v. (**waylaid, waylaying**) lie in wait for.

▷ SYNS AMBUSH, attack, lie in wait for, hold up; accost, intercept.

**wayward** adj. unpredictable and hard to control.
▷ SYNS WILFUL, self-willed, headstrong, stubborn, obstinate, perverse, contrary, uncooperative, refractory, recalcitrant, unruly, ungovernable, unmanageable, incorrigible, disobedient.

**WC** abbr. water closet.

**we** pron. used by a person referring to himself or herself and another or others; people in general.

**weak** adj. **1** lacking strength or energy. **2** lacking power, influence, or ability. **3** very diluted.
▷ SYNS **1** FRAIL, fragile, delicate, feeble, infirm, sickly, debilitated, incapacitated, puny. **2** UNCONVINCING, untenable, unsatisfactory, feeble, flimsy, lame.

**weaken** v. make or become weak.
▷ SYNS **1** ENFEEBLE, debilitate, incapacitate, sap, tire, exhaust. **2** DECREASE, dwindle, diminish, ebb, lessen.

**weakling** n. a weak person or animal.
▷ SYNS MILKSOP, namby-pamby, coward; inf. wimp, sissy, drip, doormat.

**weakness** n. being weak; a fault; something you cannot resist.
▷ SYNS **1** FRAILTY, fragility, delicacy, feebleness, infirmity, debility, incapacity, indisposition, enervation, fatigue. **2** COWARDLINESS, spinelessness, timidity, impotence. **3** FAULT, flaw, weak point, failing, defect, shortcoming, imperfection, Achilles' heel.

**weal** n. a red swollen mark left on flesh by a blow or pressure.

**wealth** n. **1** a large amount of money, property, etc.; the state of being rich. **2** a large amount.
▷ SYNS **1** AFFLUENCE, riches, fortune, means, assets, possessions, resources, funds, money, cash, capital, treasure, property, holdings, wherewithal. **2** ABUNDANCE, profusion, plethora, mine, cornucopia.

**wealthy** adj. rich.
▷ SYNS RICH, affluent, moneyed, well off, well-to-do, prosperous; inf. well heeled, rolling in it, loaded.

**wean** v. accustom a baby to food other than its mother's milk; cause to give up something gradually.

**weapon** n. a thing used to inflict harm or damage; a means of gaining an advantage or defending oneself.
■ weaponry n.

**wear** v. **1** have on the body as clothing or ornament. **2** damage by friction or use. **3** (**wear out**) exhaust. **4** (**wear off**) stop being effective or strong. • n. **1** clothes of a particular type. **2** damage caused by friction or use.
▷ SYNS v. **1** HAVE ON, be dressed in, be clothed in, sport. **2** ERODE, corrode, abrade. **3** (**wear out**) FATIGUE, tire, weary, exhaust, drain, sap, prostrate, enervate. **4** (**wear off**) FADE, diminish, dwindle, decrease, lessen, disappear, subside, ebb, wane.

**wearisome** adj. causing weariness.

**weary** adj. **1** very tired. **2** tiring or tedious. • v. (**wearied, wearying**) make or become

weary. ■ **wearily** adv.
**weariness** n.
▷ SYNS adj. **1** TIRED, fatigued, exhausted, drained, worn out, spent, enervated, prostrate; inf. dead beat, dog-tired, knackered. **2** TIRING, exhausting, fatiguing, draining, demanding, taxing, arduous, gruelling.

**weasel** n. a small, slender carnivorous wild mammal.

**weather** n. the state of the atmosphere in terms of sunshine, rain, wind, etc. • v. **1** wear away or change by exposure to the weather. **2** come safely through. □ **weathervane** a revolving pointer to show the direction of the wind.
▷ SYNS V. SURVIVE, come through, ride out, withstand, surmount, overcome, resist.

**weave** v. **1** make fabric by interlacing long threads with others. **2** compose a story etc. **3** move from side to side, esp. to get round obstacles.
▷ SYNS **1** ENTWINE, interlace, intertwine, twist, braid, plait. **2** INVENT, make up, fabricate, construct, create, contrive.

**web** n. **1** a network of fine strands made by a spider etc.; a complex system of interconnected elements. **2** (**the Web**) the World Wide Web. **3** skin between the toes of ducks, frogs, etc. □ **weblog** a website used for personal opinions or experiences. **web page** a document that can be accessed via the Internet. **website** a location on the Internet that maintains one or more web pages.
■ **webbed** adj.
▷ SYNS LACEWORK, mesh, lattice, latticework, net, netting.

**wed** v. (**wedded, wedding**) marry; unite or combine. □ **wedlock** the state of being married.
▷ SYNS MARRY, get married, become man and wife; inf. get hitched, tie the knot.

**wedding** n. a marriage ceremony.
▷ SYNS MARRIAGE, nuptials.

**wedge** n. a piece of wood, metal, etc. with a thick end that tapers to a thin edge. • v. force apart or fix in position with a wedge; force into a narrow space.
▷ SYNS V. SQUEEZE, cram, jam, thrust, stuff, ram, force.

**Wednesday** n. the day after Tuesday.

**wee** adj. Scot. little.

**weed** n. **1** a wild plant growing where it is not wanted. **2** a thin or weak person. • v. **1** remove weeds from. **2** (**weed out**) remove as unwanted.
■ **weedy** adj.

**week** n. a period of seven successive days; the five days from Monday to Friday. □ **weekday** a day of the week other than Sunday or Saturday. **weekend** Saturday and Sunday. ■ **weekly** adj. & adv.

**weep** v. (**wept, weeping**) shed tears; (of a sore etc.) exude liquid. • n. a spell of weeping.
▷ SYNS CRY, sob, wail, snivel, whimper, lament, grieve, mourn, keen; inf. blubber, blub.

**weepy** adj. (**-ier, -iest**) tearful.

**weevil** n. a small beetle.

**weft** n. the crosswise threads in weaving.

**weigh** v. **1** find how heavy someone or something is; have a specified weight. **2** assess the

nature or importance of; have influence. **3** (**weigh down**) be a burden to.
▷ SYNS (**weigh up**) CONSIDER, contemplate, think over, mull over, ponder, deliberate over, muse on, reflect on.

**weight** n. **1** the heaviness of a person or thing; a unit or system of units for expressing this; a piece of metal of known weight used in weighing; a heavy object or load. **2** influence. • v. **1** make heavier or hold down with a weight. **2** arrange so as to give one party an advantage.
▷ SYNS n. **1** HEAVINESS, load, poundage, tonnage, avoirdupois. **2** BURDEN, load, onus, millstone, albatross, trouble, worry, strain. **3** INFLUENCE, force, importance, significance, consequence, value, substance; inf. clout.

**weighting** n. extra pay or allowances given in special cases.

**weighty** adj. (**-ier, -iest**) heavy; serious, important, or influential.

**weir** n. a small dam built to regulate the flow of a river.

**weird** adj. uncanny or bizarre.
▷ SYNS **1** UNCANNY, eerie, unnatural, unearthly, ghostly, strange, queer, mysterious; inf. spooky, creepy. **2** BIZARRE, outlandish, eccentric, odd, strange, peculiar, queer, freakish, offbeat.

**welcome** n. an instance or way of greeting someone; a pleased reaction. • v. **1** greet in a polite or friendly way. **2** be glad to receive. • adj. gladly received; much wanted or needed.

▷ SYNS n. GREETING, salutation, reception. • v. **1** GREET, receive, meet, usher in. **2** APPROVE OF, be pleased by, embrace. • adj. PLEASING, agreeable, gratifying, cheering, wanted, appreciated, popular, desirable.

**weld** v. unite pieces of metal by heating or pressure; unite into a whole. • n. a welded joint.
■ **welder** n.

**welfare** n. **1** well-being. **2** organized help given to people in need. □ **welfare state** a system under which the state provides pensions, health care, etc.
▷ SYNS **1** WELL-BEING, health, happiness, comfort, security, prosperity, success, fortune. **2** SOCIAL SECURITY, state benefit, income support.

**well¹** adv. **1** in a good, appropriate, or advantageous way. **2** kindly or favourably. **3** thoroughly; extremely. **4** very probably; with good reason. • adj. in good health; satisfactory. • exclam. used to express surprise, anger, resignation, etc. □ **well-being** good health, happiness, and security. **well disposed** having a sympathetic or friendly attitude. **well read** having read much literature. **well spoken** having an educated and refined voice. **well-to-do** wealthy.
▷ SYNS adj. **1** HEALTHY, fit, strong, robust, hale and hearty, thriving. **2** SATISFACTORY, all right, fine; inf. OK.

**well²** n. a shaft sunk into the ground to obtain water, oil, etc.; an enclosed shaft-like space. • v. (of liquid) rise to the surface.
▷ SYNS n. **1** SPRING, borehole, waterhole. **2** SOURCE, supply,

wellspring, fount, reservoir, mine.

**well built** adj. strong and sturdy.
▷ SYNS STURDY, strapping, brawny, burly, hefty, muscular, strong; inf. beefy.

**wellington** n. a knee-length waterproof boot.

**well off** adj. wealthy.
▷ SYNS WEALTHY, rich, affluent, well-to-do, moneyed, prosperous; inf. well heeled, rolling in it, made of money, loaded, quids in.

**Welsh** adj. & n. (the language) of Wales. □ **Welsh rabbit** (or **rarebit**) melted cheese on toast.

**welt** n. **1** a leather rim to which the sole of a shoe is attached. **2** a weal.

**welter** n. a large disordered number of items.

**welterweight** n. a boxing weight between lightweight and middleweight.

**wend** v. (**wend your way**) go.

**went** past of GO.

**wept** past and p.p. of WEEP.

**werewolf** n. (in myths) a person who at times turns into a wolf.

**west** n. the direction in which the sun sets; the western part of a place. • adj. & adv. towards or facing the west; (of a wind) from the west. ■ **westerly** adj. & adv. **westerner** a person from the west of a region. **westward** adj. & adv. **westwards** adv.

**western** adj. of or in the west. • n. a film or novel about cowboys in western North America.

**westernize** (or **-ise**) v. bring under the influence of Europe and North America.

**wet** adj. (**wetter**, **wettest**) soaked or covered with liquid; rainy; (of paint etc.) not yet dry. • v. (**wetted**, **wetting**) make wet. • n. wet weather; wetness. □ **wet blanket** someone who spoils other people's pleasure by being gloomy. **wet nurse** a woman employed to breastfeed another's child. **wetsuit** a rubber garment worn for warmth in water sports or diving.
▷ SYNS adj. **1** DAMP, moist, soaked, drenched, saturated, sopping, dripping, soggy, waterlogged. **2** RAINY, raining, pouring, showery, drizzling, damp. • v. DAMPEN, damp, moisten, sprinkle, spray, douse. • n. WETNESS, damp, moisture, condensation, humidity.

**wether** n. a castrated ram.

**whack** inf. v. strike forcefully. • n. a sharp blow.

**whale** n. a very large sea mammal.

**whaler** n. a whaling ship; a sailor engaged in whaling.

**whaling** n. the hunting and killing of whales.

**wharf** n. (pl. **wharfs** or **wharves**) a landing stage where ships load and unload.
▷ SYNS QUAY, pier, jetty, dock, landing stage.

**what** adj. **1** asking for information about something. **2** used to emphasize something great or remarkable. • pron. **1** what thing or things: *what is it?* **2** the thing that: *just what I need.* • adv. to what extent? □ **whatever** everything or anything that; at all; of any kind.

**wheat** n. a cereal crop whose grain is ground to make flour.

**wheedle** v. coax.

**wheel** n. a disc or circular frame that revolves on a shaft passing through its centre, used to move a vehicle, as part of a machine, etc.; a turn or rotation. • v. **1** push or pull a vehicle with wheels. **2** turn; move in circles or curves. □ **wheelbarrow** a small cart with a single wheel at the front and two handles at the rear, used to move small loads. **wheelbase** the distance between a vehicle's front and rear axles. **wheelchair** a chair on wheels for an invalid or disabled person.

**wheeze** v. breathe with a hoarse whistling sound. • n. this sound. ■ **wheezy** adj.
▷ SYNS v. GASP, rasp, whistle, hiss, cough.

**whelk** n. a shellfish with a spiral shell.

**whelp** n. a puppy. • v. give birth to puppies.

**when** adv. **1** at what time? **2** at which time or in which situation. • conj. **1** at the time that. **2** whenever. **3** and just then. **4** although. □ **whenever 1** at whatever time. **2** every time that.

**whence** adv. & conj. formal from where? from which?

**where** adv. **1** in or to what place? **2** in what direction or respect? **3** at, in, or to which. **4** in or to a place or situation in which. □ **whereabouts 1** where or approximately where? **2** the place where someone or something is. **whereas** in contrast with the fact that. **whereby** by which. **whereupon** immediately after which. **wherever 1** in or to whatever place. **2** in every case when. **wherewithal** the money etc. needed for a particular purpose.

**whet** v. (**whetted, whetting**) sharpen a knife etc.; stimulate appetite or interest.
▷ SYNS SHARPEN, hone, strop, file, grind.

**whether** conj. introducing a choice between alternatives.

**whey** n. the watery liquid left when milk forms curds.

**which** adj. & pron. specifying a particular member or members of a set; introducing further information about something just referred to. □ **whichever** any which; that or those which; regardless of which.

**whiff** n. a puff of air or odour.

**while** conj. **1** during the time that; at the same time as. **2** although; whereas. • n. a period of time. □ **while away** pass time in an interesting way.

**whilst** conj. while.

**whim** n. a sudden desire.
▷ SYNS IMPULSE, desire, urge, notion, fancy, caprice, vagary, inclination.

**whimper** v. & n. (make) a feeble crying sound.
▷ SYNS WHINE, cry, sob, sniffle, snivel, moan.

**whimsical** adj. playfully fanciful; capricious. ■ **whimsically** adv.
▷ SYNS **1** FANCIFUL, playful, mischievous, waggish, quaint. **2** CAPRICIOUS, fickle, volatile, changeable, unpredictable.

**whimsy** n. playfully unusual behaviour or humour.

**whine** n. a long, high complaining cry or similar shrill sound. • v. give or make a whine; complain peevishly.

▷ SYNS v. WHIMPER, cry, wail, moan; inf. grizzle.

**whinge** v. inf. complain peevishly.

**whinny** n. (pl. **-ies**) a gentle neigh. • v. (**whinnied**, **whinnying**) neigh gently.

**whip** n. **1** a cord or strip of leather on a handle, used for striking a person or animal. **2** a dessert made from cream etc. beaten into a frothy mass. **3** an official maintaining discipline in a political party. • v. **1** strike with a whip. **2** beat into a froth. **3** move or take out quickly. □ whiplash injury caused by a severe jerk to the head.
▷ SYNS n. LASH, scourge, cat-o'-nine-tails, crop. • v. FLOG, lash, scourge, flagellate, cane, thrash, beat, belt, tan the hide of.

**whippet** n. a small, slender breed of dog.

**whirl** v. spin round and round; move with bewildering speed. • n. a whirling movement; busy or confused activity.
▷ SYNS v. SPIN, rotate, revolve, wheel, turn, circle, twirl, swirl, gyrate.

**whirlpool** n. a current of water whirling in a circle.
▷ SYNS EDDY, vortex, maelstrom.

**whirlwind** n. a column of air rotating rapidly. • adj. very quick and unexpected.
▷ SYNS n. TORNADO, hurricane, typhoon. • adj. RAPID, swift, quick, speedy, headlong.

**whirr** n. & v. (make) a low, continuous regular sound.

**whisk** v. **1** move or take out suddenly and quickly. **2** beat into a froth. • n. **1** a utensil for beating eggs etc. **2** a bunch of twigs etc. for brushing or flicking things.

**whisker** n. **1** a long stiff hair growing from the face of a cat etc. **2** (**whiskers**) hairs growing on a man's cheek.

**whisky** (Irish & US **whiskey**) n. a spirit distilled from malted grain.

**whisper** v. speak very softly. • n. a very soft tone; a whispered remark.
▷ SYNS v. MURMUR, mutter, speak softly. • n. MURMUR, mutter, hushed tone, undertone.

**whist** n. a card game usu. for two pairs of players.

**whistle** n. a shrill sound made by forcing breath between the lips or teeth; a similar sound; a device for producing this. • v. make such a sound; produce a tune in this way. □ whistle-stop very fast and with only brief pauses.

**Whit** adj. Whitsun. □ Whit Sunday the seventh Sunday after Easter.

**whit** n. a very small part or amount.
▷ SYNS BIT, scrap, shred, jot, iota, mite.

**white** adj. **1** of the colour of milk or fresh snow; relating to people with light-coloured skin; very pale. **2** (of coffee or tea) with milk. • n. **1** a white colour or thing; a white person. **2** the transparent substance round egg yolk; the pale part of the eyeball around the iris. □ white-collar relating to work in an office. white elephant a useless possession. white lie a harmless lie told to avoid hurting someone's feelings. White Paper (in the UK) a government report giving information on an issue. white spirit light petroleum used as paint thinner or solvent. ■ **whiten** v.

▷ SYNS **adj.** PALE, wan, pallid, ashen, bloodless, waxen, pasty, peaky.

**whitebait** n. very small fish used as food.

**whitewash** n. 1 a liquid containing lime or powdered chalk, used for painting walls white. 2 deliberate concealment of mistakes. • v. 1 paint with whitewash. 2 conceal mistakes.

**whither** adv. old use to what place.

**whiting** n. (pl. **whiting**) a small sea fish used as food.

**Whitsun** (or **Whitsuntide**) n. the weekend or week including Whit Sunday.

**whittle** v. carve wood by cutting thin slices from it; gradually reduce.

**whizz** v. (**whizzed**, **whizzing**) move quickly through the air with a hissing sound; move or go fast.

**who** pron. 1 what or which person or people? 2 introducing more information about someone just mentioned. □ **whodunnit** (US **whodunit**) inf. a detective story or play. **whoever** any person who; regardless of who.

**whoa** exclam. a command to a horse to stop or slow down.

**whole** adj. complete or entire; in one piece. • n. the full amount; a complete system made up of parts. □ **on the whole** considering everything; in general. **wholefood** food that has been processed as little as possible. **wholemeal** made from the whole grain of wheat.

▷ SYNS **adj.** 1 ENTIRE, complete, full, unabridged, uncut. 2 INTACT, in

one piece, undamaged, unharmed, unhurt.

**wholehearted** adj. completely sincere and committed.

▷ SYNS COMPLETE, unreserved, unqualified, full, total, absolute, sincere, earnest.

**wholesale** n. the selling of goods in large quantities to be sold to the public by others.
• adj. & adv. 1 being sold in such a way. 2 on a large scale. ■ **wholesaler** n.

▷ SYNS **adj. & adv.** EXTENSIVE, widespread, wide-ranging, indiscriminate, mass, total, comprehensive.

**wholesome** adj. 1 good for health or well-being. 2 morally good.

▷ SYNS 1 HEALTHY, nutritious, nourishing, good for you. 2 MORAL, innocent, decent, clean, improving, edifying.

**wholly** adv. entirely or fully.

▷ SYNS COMPLETELY, totally, fully, entirely, utterly, thoroughly, in every respect.

**whom** pron. used instead of *who* as the object of a verb or preposition.

**whoop** v. & n. (make) a loud cry of excitement. □ **whooping cough** an infectious disease marked by violent convulsive coughs.

**whopper** n. inf. 1 something very large. 2 a blatant lie.

**whore** n. a prostitute.

**whorl** n. each of the turns of a spiral or coil; a spiral or coil; a ring of leaves or petals.

**whose** pron. & adj. belonging to whom or to which.

**why** adv. for what reason or purpose; on account of which.

• **exclam.** expressing surprise, annoyance, etc.

**wick** n. a length of thread in a candle or lamp etc. which carries liquid fuel to the flame.

**wicked** adj. **1** morally bad; evil or sinful. **2** playfully mischievous. ■ **wickedness** n.
▷ SYNS EVIL, sinful, immoral, bad, wrong, villainous, base, vile, foul, corrupt, iniquitous, nefarious, heinous, abhorrent, monstrous, atrocious, abominable, despicable, hateful, odious, criminal, lawless, dastardly.

**wicker** n. twigs interwoven to make furniture, baskets, etc. ■ **wickerwork** n.

**wicket** n. a set of three stumps with two bails across the top, used in cricket; a small door or gate.

**wide** adj. **1** of great width; having a particular width. **2** including a variety of people or things. **3** far from the target. • adv. to the full extent; far from the target. □ **wide awake** fully awake.
▷ SYNS adj. **1** BROAD, extensive, spacious. **2** EXTENSIVE, broad, large, vast, wide-ranging, comprehensive, catholic.

**widen** v. make or become wider.
▷ SYNS BROADEN, expand, extend, enlarge, open up/out.

**widespread** adj. spread among a large number or over a large area.
▷ SYNS GENERAL, extensive, universal, common; prevalent, rife, pervasive.

**widow** n. a woman whose husband has died and who has not remarried. • v. (**be widowed**) become a widow or widower.

**widower** n. a man whose wife has died and who has not remarried.

**width** n. **1** the extent of something from side to side. **2** wide range or extent.
▷ SYNS **1** BREADTH, broadness, span, diameter. **2** SCOPE, breadth, range, extent, extensiveness.

**wield** v. hold and use a tool etc.; have and use power.
▷ SYNS **1** BRANDISH, flourish, wave, swing, use, ply. **2** EXERCISE, exert, have, hold, possess.

**wife** n. (pl. **wives**) the woman a man is married to.

**wig** n. a covering of hair worn on the head.

**wiggle** v. move repeatedly from side to side. • n. an act of wiggling. ■ **wiggly** adj.

**wigwam** n. a conical tent formerly lived in by some North American Indian peoples.

**wild** adj. **1** not domesticated or tame. **2** not cultivated or inhabited. **3** uncontrolled. **4** inf. very enthusiastic. **5** inf. very angry. **6** random: *a wild guess.* • n. desolate places. □ **wildcat** (of a strike) sudden and unofficial. **wildfowl** game birds. **wild goose chase** a useless search. **wildlife** the native animals of a region.
▷ SYNS adj. **1** UNTAMED, undomesticated, feral, savage, fierce, ferocious. **2** UNCULTIVATED, native, indigenous. **3** PRIMITIVE, uncivilized; savage, barbarous. **4** STORMY, tempestuous, turbulent, blustery, squally. **5** UNCONTROLLED, unrestrained, out of control, undisciplined, rowdy, unruly, riotous, disorderly.

**wildebeest** n. a gnu (a kind of antelope).

**wilderness** n. an uncultivated, uninhabited area.
▷ SYNS WILDS, wastes; desert.

**wiles** pl.n. cunning plans.
▷ SYNS TRICKS, ruses, ploys, schemes, subterfuges, stratagems.

**wilful** (US **willful**) adj. **1** deliberate. **2** stubbornly self-willed.
■ wilfully adv.
▷ SYNS **1** DELIBERATE, intentional, conscious, premeditated, planned, calculated.
**2** HEADSTRONG, obstinate, stubborn, pig-headed, self-willed, recalcitrant, uncooperative.

**will¹** v.aux. used with *I* and *we* to express promises or obligations, and with other words to express a future tense.

**will²** n. **1** your power to decide on something and take action; a desire or intention. **2** (also **will power**) determination used to achieve something. **3** a legal document with instructions for the disposal of someone's property after their death.
• v. **1** exercise your will; influence by doing this.
**2** bequeath in a will. □ **at will** whenever you like.
▷ SYNS n. **1** VOLITION, choice, option, decision, prerogative.
**2** DESIRE, wish, preference, inclination. **3** DETERMINATION, will power, resolution, resolve, single-mindedness, doggedness, tenacity.

**willing** adj. ready to do what is asked; given or done readily.
■ willingness n.
▷ SYNS PREPARED, ready, disposed, minded, happy, glad; inf. game.

**willingly** adv. readily.
▷ SYNS VOLUNTARILY, of your own free will, of your own accord, readily, without reluctance, gladly.

**will-o'-the-wisp** n. **1** a faint flickering light seen on marshy ground. **2** a hope or aim that can never be fulfilled.

**willow** n. a tree with flexible branches and narrow leaves.

**willowy** adj. tall and slim.

**willy-nilly** adv. whether you like it or not.

**wilt** v. droop through heat or lack of water; feel tired and weak.
▷ SYNS DROOP, sag, wither, shrivel, languish.

**wily** adj. cunning.
▷ SYNS SHREWD, clever, sharp, astute, canny; cunning, crafty, artful, sly.

**wimp** n. inf. a feeble or timid person.

**win** v. **1** defeat an opponent in a contest; gain as the result of a contest etc., or by effort. **2** (**win over**) gain someone's agreement. • n. a victory in a game or contest.
▷ SYNS v. **1** COME FIRST, be victorious, carry the day, succeed, triumph, prevail. **2** SECURE, gain, pick up, carry off; inf. land, bag.

**wince** v. & n. (make) a slight movement from pain or embarrassment etc.

**winch** n. a hauling or lifting device consisting of a cable winding round a rotating drum.
• v. hoist or haul with a winch.

**wind¹** n. **1** a natural current of air; breath as needed for exertion. **2** gas in the stomach or intestines. **3** an orchestra's wind instruments. • v. cause to be out of breath. □ **windbag** inf. a person who talks at unnecessary length. **windbreak** a screen providing shelter from the wind. **windfall** fruit blown off a tree by the wind; a piece of unexpected good fortune. **wind instrument** a musical instrument played by blowing a current of air into it. **windmill** a building with sails or vanes that turn in the wind and generate power to grind corn etc. **windpipe** the tube carrying air down the throat to the lungs. **windscreen** (or US **windshield**) the glass screen at the front of a vehicle. **windsock** a light, flexible cone mounted on a mast to show the direction and strength of the wind. **windsurfing** the sport of riding on water on a sailboard. **windswept** exposed to strong winds. ■ **windward** adj. & adv.

▷ SYNS n. 1 BREEZE, air current, gust; gale, hurricane; lit. zephyr. 2 BREATH; inf. puff.

**wind²** v. (**wound, winding**) 1 move in a twisting or spiral course. 2 wrap something repeatedly around something else or round on itself. 3 operate by turning a key, handle, etc. □ **wind up** bring or come to an end.

▷ SYNS TWIST, curve, bend, loop, snake, zigzag.

**window** n. 1 an opening in a wall, filled with glass to let in light. 2 a framed area on a computer screen for viewing information. □ **window-shop** spend time looking at goods in shop windows.

**windy** adj. marked by or exposed to strong winds.

▷ SYNS BREEZY, blowy, blustery, gusty; stormy, wild, squally.

**wine** n. an alcoholic drink made from fermented grape juice. □ **wine bar** a bar or small restaurant that specializes in serving wine.

**winery** n. (pl. **-ies**) a place where wine is made.

**wing** n. 1 a projecting part enabling a bird, insect, or bat to fly. 2 a projection on both sides of an aircraft, supporting it in the air. 3 a part of a large building. 4 a group within an organization. 5 (**wings**) the sides of a theatre stage. 6 the part of a soccer or rugby field close to the sidelines. 7 the bodywork above the wheel of a car. • v. 1 fly, or move very quickly. 2 wound in the wing or arm. □ **wingspan** the measurement from tip to tip of the wings of a bird etc. ■ **winged** adj.

**winger** n. an attacking player on the wing in soccer etc.

**wink** v. rapidly close and open one eye as a signal; shine intermittently. • n. an act of winking.

▷ SYNS v. 1 BLINK, flutter, bat. 2 SPARKLE, twinkle, shine, flash, glitter, gleam.

**winkle** n. an edible sea snail. □ **winkle out** extract or prise out.

**winner** n. a person or thing that wins.

▷ SYNS VICTOR, champion, conqueror.

**winning** adj. charming. • pl.n. money won by gambling etc.

▷ SYNS adj. 1 VICTORIOUS, successful, triumphant, conquering. 2 ENGAGING, charming, endearing, sweet, cute, disarming, winsome, fetching.

**winnow** v. fan or toss grain to free it of chaff.

**winsome** adj. appealing.

**winter** n. the coldest season of the year. • v. spend the winter in a particular place.

**wintry** adj. cold and bleak.
▷ SYNS BLEAK, cold, chilly, frosty, freezing, icy, snowy, glacial, bitter.

**wipe** v. **1** rub a surface to clean or dry it. **2** erase data from a computer, video, etc. • n. an act of wiping; a piece of material for wiping with. □ **wipe out** completely destroy or eliminate. ■ **wiper** n.
▷ SYNS v. RUB, mop, sponge, swab; clean, dry.

**wire** n. a strand of metal; a length of this used for fencing, conducting electric current, etc. • v. **1** install electric wires in. **2** fasten or strengthen with wire.

**wireless** adj. using radio, microwaves, etc. (as opposed to wires) to transmit signals. • n. dated a radio.

**wiring** n. a system of electric wires in a building, vehicle, etc.

**wiry** adj. like wire; thin but strong.
▷ SYNS **1** SINEWY, tough, athletic; lean, spare, thin. **2** COARSE, rough; curly.

**wisdom** n. the quality of being wise; knowledge and experience. □ **wisdom tooth** a molar tooth at the back of the mouth, usu. appearing at about the age of 20.
▷ SYNS SAGACITY, intelligence, knowledge, discernment, perception, insight, sense, common sense, shrewdness, astuteness, prudence, judiciousness.

**wise** adj. having or showing experience, knowledge, and good judgement. □ **wisecrack** inf. a joke or witty remark.
▷ SYNS SAGE, sagacious, clever, intelligent, learned, knowledgeable, discerning, perceptive, insightful, sensible, prudent, judicious, shrewd, canny, astute, smart.

**wish** n. a desire or hope; a thing desired or hoped for; expressions of friendly feeling. • v. feel a desire; desire or express a desire for something to happen to someone. □ **wishbone** a forked bone between the neck and breast of a bird.
▷ SYNS n. DESIRE, longing, hope, yearning, craving, hunger, thirst, hankering, want, aspiration, inclination, urge, whim. • v. DESIRE, want, long for, hope for, yearn for, fancy, crave, hunger for, thirst for, lust after, covet, set your heart on, hanker after, have a yen for.

**wishful** adj. based on impractical wishes rather than facts: *wishful thinking.*

**wishy-washy** adj. feeble or bland.
▷ SYNS **1** FEEBLE, weak, ineffectual, effete, spineless, weak-kneed. **2** WATERY, weak; bland, tasteless, flavourless, insipid.

**wisp** n. a small, thin bunch or strand. ■ **wispy** adj.

**wisteria** n. a climbing shrub with bluish-lilac flowers.

**wistful** adj. full of sad or vague longing. ■ **wistfully** adv.
▷ SYNS NOSTALGIC, yearning, longing; plaintive, regretful, rueful, forlorn, melancholy; pensive, reflective.

**wit** n. amusing ingenuity in expressing words or ideas; a person who has this; intelligence. □ **at your wits' end** worried and not knowing what to do.
▷ SYNS **1** WITTINESS, humour, drollery; repartee, badinage, banter, raillery. **2** COMEDIAN, humorist, wag, comic; inf. card.

**witch** n. a woman who practises witchcraft. □ **witch doctor** a person believed to have magic powers that cure illness. **witch hazel** a shrub used to make an astringent lotion. **witch-hunt** a campaign against a person who holds unpopular views.
▷ SYNS SORCERESS, enchantress, hex.

**witchcraft** n. the practice of magic.
▷ SYNS SORCERY, magic, black magic, witchery, wizardry.

**with** prep. **1** accompanied by; in the same direction as. **2** having; characterized by. **3** using. **4** in relation to. **5** indicating opposition or separation. **6** affected by.

**withdraw** v. **1** remove or take away; take money from a bank account; take back a statement etc. **2** go away from a place. ▪ **withdrawal** n.
▷ SYNS **1** REMOVE, extract, take away, take out, pull out. **2** RETRACT, take back, unsay. **3** LEAVE, pull out, retreat, depart.

**withdrawn** adj. very shy or reserved.
▷ SYNS RESERVED, quiet, uncommunicative, introverted, unsociable, inhibited, retiring; shy, timid.

**wither** v. make or become dry and shrivelled; scornful.

▷ SYNS SHRIVEL, dry up/out, wilt, droop, die.

**withhold** v. (**withheld**, **withholding**) refuse to give; suppress a reaction etc.
▷ SYNS **1** HOLD BACK, keep back, retain, refuse to give. **2** SUPPRESS, repress, restrain, hold back, check, control.

**within** prep. inside; not beyond the limit or scope of; in a time no longer than. • adv. inside.

**without** prep. not having; in the absence of; not doing a specified action.

**withstand** v. (**withstood**, **withstanding**) endure successfully.
▷ SYNS RESIST, hold out against, endure, weather, survive, stand, tolerate, bear.

**witless** adj. stupid.

**witness** n. a person who sees or hears something; a person who gives evidence in a law court; a person who watches the signing of a document and signs to confirm this. • v. be a witness of.
▷ SYNS n. EYEWITNESS, observer, spectator, onlooker; bystander. • v. SEE, observe, view, watch; be present at, attend.

**witticism** n. a witty remark.
▷ SYNS JOKE, quip, jest, pun, bon mot; inf. wisecrack, crack, one-liner.

**witty** adj. (**-ier**, **-iest**) clever, inventive, and funny. ▪ **wittily** adv.
▷ SYNS AMUSING, funny, humorous, droll, facetious, waggish, comic, clever, sparkling, scintillating.

**wives** pl. of **WIFE**.

**wizard** n. a man with magical powers; a person with great skill in a particular field. ▪ **wizardry** n.

▷ SYNS SORCERER, warlock, magician, magus.

**wizened** adj. shrivelled or wrinkled with age.
▷ SYNS WRINKLED, lined, gnarled, withered, shrivelled, weather-beaten, shrunken.

**woad** n. a plant whose leaves were formerly used to make blue dye.

**wobble** v. stand or move unsteadily; (of the voice) quiver. • n. a wobbling movement or sound. ■ **wobbly** adj.
▷ SYNS v. ROCK, teeter, sway, see-saw, shake.

**woe** n. sorrow or distress; troubles. □ **woebegone** sad or miserable.
▷ SYNS 1 MISERY, sorrow, distress, wretchedness, sadness, unhappiness, grief, anguish, pain, suffering, despair, gloom, melancholy. 2 (**woes**) TROUBLES, problems, misfortunes, trials, tribulations, difficulties.

**woeful** adj. 1 very sad. 2 very bad. ■ **woefully** adv.

**wok** n. a large bowl-shaped frying pan used in Chinese cookery.

**woke** past of WAKE.

**woken** p.p. of WAKE.

**wold** n. an area of high, open country.

**wolf** n. (pl. **wolves**) a wild animal of the dog family. • v. eat quickly and greedily. □ **cry wolf** raise false alarms. ■ **wolfish** adj.

**woman** n. (pl. **women**) an adult human female. □ **womankind** women as a group.
■ **womanhood** n. **womanly** adj.
▷ SYNS 1 LADY, girl, female; inf. bird, chick; US inf. dame. 2 GIRLFRIEND, sweetheart, partner, lover; wife, spouse.

**womanize** (or **-ise**) v. (of a man) have many casual affairs with women. ■ **womanizer** n.

**womb** n. the organ in female mammals in which the young develop before birth.

**wombat** n. a burrowing Australian marsupial like a small bear.

**won** past and p.p. of WIN.

**wonder** n. a feeling of surprise and admiration; a person or thing that evokes this. • v. 1 feel curiosity. 2 feel surprise and admiration.
▷ SYNS n. 1 AWE, admiration, fascination; surprise, astonishment, amazement. 2 MARVEL, phenomenon, miracle, spectacle, beauty. • v. 1 PONDER, think, speculate, conjecture, muse, reflect, ask yourself. 2 MARVEL, be amazed, stand in awe.

**wonderful** adj. extremely good or remarkable.
■ **wonderfully** adv.
▷ SYNS MARVELLOUS, magnificent, superb, excellent, glorious, lovely; inf. super, fantastic, great, terrific, tremendous, sensational, fabulous, incredible, awesome, brilliant.

**wondrous** adj. inspiring wonder.

**wont** formal adj. accustomed to do something. • n. your usual behaviour.

**woo** v. seek to marry; seek the favour of.

**wood** n. 1 the tough fibrous substance of a tree. 2 (also **woods**) a small forest.
□ **woodcut** a print made from a design cut in a block of wood. **woodland** land covered with trees. **woodlouse** a small

insect-like animal with a segmented body. **woodpecker** a bird with a strong bill that pecks at tree trunks to find insects. **woodwind** wind instruments other than brass instruments. **woodwork** the wooden parts of a room; the activity of making things from wood. **woodworm** the larva of a kind of beetle, that bores into wood. ■ **woody** adj.

▷ SYNS **1** FOREST, woodland, trees; copse, coppice, grove. **2** TIMBER, logs, planks; US lumber.

**wooded** adj. covered with trees.

**wooden** adj. **1** made of wood. **2** showing no emotion.

**woof** n. a dog's gruff bark.
• v. bark.

**wool** n. **1** the soft hair forming the coat of a sheep or goat. **2** yarn or fabric made from this.

**woollen** (US **woolen**) adj. made of wool. • pl.n. (**woollens**) woollen garments.

**woolly** adj. **1** covered with wool; made of or like wool. **2** vague or confused. • n. (pl. **-ies**) a woollen garment.

▷ SYNS adj. **1** WOOLLEN, wool. **2** FLEECY, fluffy, shaggy. **3** VAGUE, hazy, unclear, imprecise, confused, muddled.

**word** n. a unit of language which has meaning and is used with others to form sentences; a remark; news or a message; a promise; a command.
• v. express in a particular style.
□ **word processor** a computer or program for producing and storing text.

▷ SYNS n. **1** TERM, expression, name. **2** PROMISE, word of honour, pledge, assurance, guarantee, undertaking, vow,

oath. **3** NEWS, information, communication, message, report.
• v. PHRASE, express, couch, put.

**wording** n. the way something is worded.

**wordy** adj. using too many words.

▷ SYNS LONG-WINDED, verbose, prolix, rambling; garrulous, voluble.

**wore** past of WEAR.

**work** n. **1** the use of bodily or mental power in order to do or make something; such activity as a means of earning money; a task to be done. **2** a thing or things done or made. **3** (**works**) a factory; the mechanism of a clock or other machine. • v. **1** do work as your job. **2** function properly; operate a machine etc. **3** have the desired result; bring about or accomplish: *working miracles*. **4** shape or produce.
□ **workhouse** a former public institution in which poor people were housed and fed in return for work. **workout** a session of vigorous exercise. **workstation** a desktop computer that is part of a network. **worktop** a flat surface for working on in a kitchen. **work-to-rule** a refusal to do extra work or overtime as a form of protest.

▷ SYNS n. **1** LABOUR, toil, slog, effort, exertion, sweat, drudgery, industry; lit. travail. **2** TASK, job, duty, assignment; chore. **3** EMPLOYMENT, occupation; job, profession, career, trade, vocation, calling. • v. **1** BE EMPLOYED, have a job, earn your living. **2** TOIL, labour, slog, exert yourself, slave; inf. plug away. **3** FUNCTION, go, operate, run. **4** OPERATE, use, control, handle, manipulate. **5** SUCCEED, work out, inf. come off.

**workaday** adj. ordinary.

**worker** n. a person who works; a neuter bee or ant etc. that does the basic work of the hive or colony.
▷ SYNS EMPLOYEE, hand, workman, labourer, operative; wage-earner.

**working** adj. **1** having paid employment; doing manual work. **2** used as a basis for work or discussion. • n. **1** a mine or part of a mine. **2** (**workings**) the way in which a system operates. □ **working class** the social group consisting largely of people who do manual or industrial work.

**workman** n. a man employed to do manual work. □ **workman-like** showing efficient skill.

**workmanship** n. the skill with which something is made or done.
▷ SYNS CRAFTSMANSHIP, artistry, craft, art, handiwork; expertise, skill.

**workshop** n. **1** a room or building in which goods are made or repaired. **2** a meeting for discussion and activity on a particular subject or project.
▷ SYNS **1** WORKROOM, studio, factory, works, plant. **2** STUDY GROUP, seminar, class.

**world** n. **1** the earth with all its countries and peoples. **2** all that belongs to a particular region, period, or area of activity. □ **worldwide** throughout the world. **World Wide Web** a system of linked and cross-referenced documents for accessing information on the Internet.

▷ SYNS **1** EARTH, globe, planet. **2** SPHERE, society, milieu, realm, domain, province.

**worldly** adj. of or concerned with material rather than spiritual things; sophisticated.
▷ SYNS **1** EARTHLY, terrestrial, temporal, secular, material, carnal, fleshly, corporeal, physical. **2** SOPHISTICATED, worldly-wise, urbane, experienced, knowing, cosmopolitan.

**worm** n. **1** a creature with a long soft body and no backbone or limbs. **2** (**worms**) internal parasites. • v. **1** move by crawling or wriggling. **2** insinuate yourself. **3** obtain by clever persistence. □ **worm cast** a small spiral of earth cast up by a burrowing worm. **wormwood** a woody shrub with a bitter taste.

**worn** adj. thin or damaged as a result of wear. □ **worn out** exhausted; damaged by use.
▷ SYNS **1** SHABBY, worn out, threadbare, tattered, in tatters, ragged, frayed. **2** HAGGARD, drawn, strained, careworn; weary, tired.

**worried** adj. feeling, showing, or expressing anxiety.
▷ SYNS ANXIOUS, perturbed, troubled, bothered, distressed, concerned, upset, distraught, uneasy, fretful, agitated, nervous, edgy, on edge, tense, apprehensive, fearful, afraid, frightened; inf. uptight.

**worry** v. **1** feel or cause to feel anxious; annoy or disturb. **2** (of a dog) repeatedly push at and bite something. • n. (pl. **-ies**) anxiety or unease; a source of anxiety.
▷ SYNS v. **1** FRET, brood, be anxious. **2** TROUBLE, disturb, bother,

distress, upset, concern, disquiet, unsettle. • n. 1 ANXIETY, perturbation, distress, concern, unease, disquiet, fretfulness, agitation, edginess, apprehension. 2 NUISANCE, pest, trial, trouble, problem, headache.

**worse** adj. & adv. less good or well. • n. something worse.

**worsen** v. make or become worse.
▷ SYNS 1 AGGRAVATE, exacerbate, intensify, increase, heighten. 2 DETERIORATE, degenerate, decline; inf. go downhill.

**worship** n. reverence and respect paid to a god; adoration of or devotion to a person or thing. • v. (**worshipped**, **worshipping**; US **worshiped**) honour as a god; take part in an act of worship; idolize.
■ **worshipper** n.
▷ SYNS n. REVERENCE, veneration, homage, honour, adoration, devotion, praise, glorification, exaltation. • v. 1 REVERE, venerate, pay homage to, honour, adore, praise, pray to, glorify, exalt. 2 ADORE, idolize, heroworship, lionize.

**worst** adj. & adv. most bad or badly. • n. the worst part, feature, event, etc.

**worth** adj. having a specified value; deserving to be treated in a particular way. • n. value or merit; the amount that a specified sum will buy.
■ **worthless** adj.
▷ SYNS n. 1 VALUE, price, cost. 2 BENEFIT, value, use, advantage, virtue, service, gain, profit, help.

**worthless** adj. having no real value or use; having no good qualities.

▷ SYNS 1 VALUELESS, cheap, shoddy, gimcrack. 2 USELESS, no use, ineffective, fruitless, unavailing, pointless. 3 GOOD-FOR-NOTHING, ne'er-do-well, useless, feckless.

**worthwhile** adj. worth the time or effort spent.
▷ SYNS VALUABLE, useful, of use, beneficial, advantageous, helpful, profitable, productive, constructive.

**worthy** adj. (**-ier**, **-iest**) having great merit; deserving. • n. (pl. **-ies**) a worthy person.
▷ SYNS adj. VIRTUOUS, good, moral, upright, upstanding, righteous, honest, principled, decent, honourable, respectable, reputable.

**would** v.aux. used in senses corresponding to *will*[1] in the past tense, conditional statements, questions, polite requests and statements, and to express probability or something that happens from time to time.

**wound**[1] n. an injury to the body caused by a cut, blow, etc.; injury to feelings. • v. inflict a wound on.
▷ SYNS n. INJURY, lesion, cut, graze, scratch, gash, laceration. • v. INJURE, hurt, cut, graze, scratch, gash, lacerate, tear, puncture, slash.

**wound**[2] past & p.p. of WIND[2].

**wove** past of WEAVE.

**woven** p.p. of WEAVE.

**wow** inf. exclam. expressing astonishment.

**WPC** abbr. woman police constable.

**wrack** n. seaweed. • v. = RACK.

**wraith** n. a ghost.

**wrangle** n. a long dispute or argument. • v. engage in a wrangle.

**wrap** v. (**wrapped**, **wrapping**) enclose in paper or soft material; encircle or wind round. • n. a shawl. □ **wrapped up in** absorbed by. ■ **wrapper** n. **wrapping** n.
▷ SYNS v. **1** SWATHE, envelop, enfold, swaddle, cloak. **2** WRAP UP, parcel up, do up, gift-wrap.

**wrath** n. anger. ■ **wrathful** adj.
▷ SYNS ANGER, rage, fury, outrage, annoyance, exasperation.

**wreak** v. cause damage; exact revenge.

**wreath** n. a decorative ring of flowers or leaves.

**wreathe** v. encircle; twist into a wreath; wind or curve.
▷ SYNS **1** ENCIRCLE, surround; garland, festoon, adorn, deck, decorate. **2** SPIRAL, twist, wind, coil, curl.

**wreck** n. the destruction of a ship at sea; a ship that has suffered this; something destroyed or dilapidated; a person in a very bad state. • v. cause a ship to sink; destroy or ruin.
▷ SYNS n. **1** SHIPWRECK, sunken ship. **2** WRECKAGE, debris, remains, ruins. • v. **1** DEMOLISH, smash up, damage, destroy, write off; vandalize. **2** RUIN, destroy, devastate, shatter, undo, spoil, dash.

**wreckage** n. the remains of something wrecked.

**wren** n. a very small bird.

**wrench** v. twist or pull violently round; damage or injure by twisting. • n. **1** a violent twist or pull. **2** an adjustable spanner-like tool.
▷ SYNS v. TWIST, pull, tug, yank, wrest, jerk, tear, force.

**wrest** v. wrench away; obtain by force or effort.

**wrestle** v. fight (esp. as a sport) by grappling with and trying to throw down an opponent; struggle with a task or problem. ■ **wrestler** n.

**wretch** n. an unfortunate person; a despicable person.

**wretched** adj. **1** very unhappy. **2** of poor quality. **3** infuriating.
▷ SYNS MISERABLE, unhappy, sad, broken-hearted, sorrowful, distressed, desolate, dejected, despairing, depressed, melancholy, gloomy, mournful, woebegone, doleful, forlorn, abject.

**wriggle** v. **1** move with short twisting movements. **2** (**wriggle out of**) avoid doing. • n. a wriggling movement.
▷ SYNS v. SQUIRM, twist, writhe, wiggle, flail; snake, worm, slither.

**wring** v. (**wrung**, **wringing**) twist and squeeze, esp. to remove liquid; squeeze someone's hand firmly or forcibly; obtain with effort or difficulty.
▷ SYNS **1** TWIST, squeeze. **2** EXTRACT, force, exact, wrest, wrench.

**wrinkle** n. a small line or fold, esp. in fabric or a person's skin. • v. make or cause wrinkles on. ■ **wrinkly** adj.
▷ SYNS n. CREASE, fold, pucker, furrow, ridge, line, crinkle, crow's foot.

**wrist** n. the joint connecting the hand and forearm.

**writ** n. a formal command issued by a court etc.

**write** v. (**wrote**, **written**, **writing**) **1** make letters or other symbols on a surface with a pen, pencil, etc. **2** compose a text or musical work. **3** write and send a letter to someone. **4** write the necessary details on a cheque etc. □ **write-off** a vehicle too damaged to be worth repairing. **write-up** a newspaper review.

▷ SYNS **1** WRITE DOWN, put in writing, jot down, note, record, list, inscribe, scribble, scrawl. **2** COMPOSE, draft, pen, dash off.

**writer** n. a person who has written something, or who writes as an occupation.

▷ SYNS AUTHOR, wordsmith, penman, novelist, essayist, biographer, journalist, columnist, scriptwriter, playwright; inf. hack.

**writhe** v. twist or squirm in pain or embarrassment.

▷ SYNS SQUIRM, twist and turn, toss and turn, wriggle, thrash, flail, struggle.

**writing** n. handwriting; literary works. □ **in writing** in written form.

▷ SYNS **1** HANDWRITING, hand, penmanship, script, calligraphy; scribble, scrawl. **2** WORKS, oeuvre, books, publications.

**wrong** adj. **1** not true or correct; mistaken. **2** unjust, dishonest, or immoral. **3** unsuitable or undesirable. • adv. **1** mistakenly or incorrectly. **2** unjustly. • n. an immoral or unjust action. • v. treat unjustly. ■ **wrongly** adv.

▷ SYNS adj. **1** INCORRECT, inaccurate, in error, erroneous, mistaken, inexact, wide of the mark, off target; inf. off beam. **2** ILLEGAL, unlawful, illicit,

criminal, dishonest, unethical, immoral, bad, wicked, sinful, blameworthy; inf. crooked. **3** INAPPROPRIATE, unsuitable, inapt, inapposite, infelicitous. **4** AMISS, awry, out of order, faulty, defective. • n. **1** IMMORALITY, sin, sinfulness, wickedness, crime, villainy, wrongdoing. **2** MISDEED, offence, crime, transgression, sin. • v. **1** ILL-USE, mistreat, abuse, harm, hurt. **2** MALIGN, misrepresent, impugn, defame, slander, libel.

**wrongdoer** n. a person who commits illegal or dishonest acts.

▷ SYNS OFFENDER, lawbreaker, criminal, delinquent, culprit, villain, miscreant.

**wrongdoing** n. illegal or dishonest behaviour.

**wrongful** adj. not fair, just, or legal. ■ **wrongfully** adv.

▷ SYNS UNFAIR, unjust, improper, unjustified, unwarranted, unlawful, illegal.

**wrote** past of WRITE.

**wrought** adj. (of metals) shaped by hammering. □ **wrought iron** tough iron suitable for forging or rolling.

**wrung** past and p.p. of WRING.

**wry** adj. **1** (of humour) dry or mocking. **2** (of the face) contorted in disgust or disappointment.

▷ SYNS **1** IRONIC, sardonic, mocking, sarcastic, dry, droll, witty. **2** TWISTED, contorted, crooked.

**WWW** abbr. World Wide Web.

# Xx

**X** n. (as a Roman numeral) ten.
□ **X-ray** a photograph made by using electromagnetic radiation (**X-rays**) that can penetrate solids.

**xenon** n. a gaseous element, present in air.

**xenophobia** n. a strong dislike or fear of people from other countries. ■ **xenophobic** adj.

**Xerox** n. trademark **1** a photocopying machine. **2** a photocopy. • v. (**xerox**) photocopy.

**Xmas** n. inf. Christmas.

**xylophone** n. a musical instrument with flat wooden bars struck with small hammers.

# Yy

**yacht** n. **1** a medium-sized sailing boat. **2** a powered boat equipped for cruising.
■ **yachting** n.

**yak** n. a long-haired Asian ox.

**yam** n. the edible tuber of a tropical plant.

**yang** n. (in Chinese philosophy) the active male force in the universe.

**yank** inf. v. pull sharply. • n. **1** a sharp pull. **2** (**Yank**) an American.

**yap** n. a shrill bark. • v. (**yapped**, **yapping**) bark shrilly.

**yard** n. **1** a unit of length equal to 3 feet (0.9144 metre). **2** a piece of enclosed ground next to a building. **3** a pole slung from a mast to support a sail.

**yardstick** n. a standard for comparison.

▷ SYNS STANDARD, measure, gauge, scale, guide, criterion, benchmark.

**yarmulke** (or **yarmulka**) n. a skullcap worn by Jewish men.

**yarn** n. **1** any spun thread. **2** inf. a story.

**yashmak** n. a veil worn by Muslim women in certain countries.

**yawn** v. **1** open your mouth wide and inhale deeply due to tiredness or boredem. **2** (**yawning**) wide open. • n. an act of yawning.

**yd** abbr. yard.

**year** n. **1** the period of 365 days (or 366 in leap years) from 1 Jan. to 31 Dec. **2** any consecutive period of twelve months. **3** ~~the time taken by the earth to go once around the sun.~~

□ **yearling** an animal between one and two years old.

**yearly** adv. & adj. happening or produced once a year or every year.
▷ SYNS ANNUALLY, per annum, once a year, every year.

**yearn** v. feel great longing.
▷ SYNS LONG, pine, crave, desire, wish for, hanker after, ache, hunger for, thirst for.

**yeast** n. a fungus used to cause fermentation in making beer and wine and as a raising agent in making bread.

**yell** n. & v. (give) a shout or scream.
▷ SYNS SHOUT, cry, howl, scream, shriek, screech, roar; inf. holler.

**yellow** adj. 1 of the colour of egg yolks or ripe lemons. 2 inf. cowardly. • n. a yellow colour. • v. turn yellow. ■ **yellowish** adj.

**yelp** n. & v. (make) a shrill bark or cry.

**yen** n. 1 (pl. **yen**) the basic monetary unit in Japan. 2 inf. a longing or yearning.
▷ SYNS HANKERING, desire, wish, fancy, longing, craving, hunger, thirst.

**yeoman** n. hist. a man who owned and farmed a small estate.

**yes** exclam. & n. 1 expressing agreement or assent. 2 used as a response to someone who is trying to attract your attention.

**yesterday** adv. on the day before today. • n. 1 the day before today. 2 the recent past.

**yet** adv. 1 up until now or then. 2 this soon. 3 from now into the future. 4 still; even. • conj. nevertheless.

**yeti** n. a large manlike animal said to live in the Himalayas.

**yew** n. an evergreen tree with dark needle-like leaves.

**Y-fronts** pl.n. trademark men's underpants with a Y-shaped seam at the front. ·

**Yiddish** n. the language used by Jews from eastern Europe.

**yield** v. 1 produce or provide a natural or industrial product. 2 produce a result. 3 give way to demands or pressure. 4 give up possession of. • n. an amount yielded or produced.
▷ SYNS v. 1 PRODUCE, provide, supply, give, return, bring in, earn. 2 SURRENDER, capitulate, submit, admit defeat, give in. 3 RELINQUISH, surrender, cede, give up, part with.

**yin** n. (in Chinese philosophy) the passive female presence in the universe.

**yob** n. inf. a rude, aggressive young man.

**yodel** v. (**yodelled, yodelling**; US **yodeled**) sing with a quickly alternating change of pitch. • n. a yodelling cry. ■ **yodeller** n.

**yoga** n. a system involving breathing exercises and the holding of particular body positions, based on Hindu philosophy.

**yogurt** (or **yoghurt**) n. food made from milk that has been thickened by the action of bacteria.

**yoke** n. 1 a piece of wood fastened over the necks of two animals pulling a plough etc. 2 something that restricts freedom or is a burden. 3 a part of a garment fitting over the shoulders. 4 a frame fitting over the shoulders, used to carry buckets. • v. 1 join with a yoke. 2 bring into a close relationship.

**yokel** n. an unsophisticated country person.
▷ SYNS RUSTIC, peasant, country bumpkin, provincial; US inf. hillbilly.

**yolk** n. the yellow part in the middle of an egg.

**yonder** adj. & adv. old use over there.

**yonks** pl.n. inf. a long time.

**yore** n. (of yore) lit. long ago.

**Yorkshire pudding** n. a baked batter pudding eaten with roast beef.

**you** pron. 1 the person or people addressed. 2 any person in general.

**young** adj. having lived or existed for only a short time. • n. an animal's offspring.
▷ SYNS adj. 1 YOUTHFUL, juvenile, junior, adolescent. 2 NEW, recent, undeveloped, fledgling, in the making.

**youngster** n. a young person.
▷ SYNS CHILD, youth, juvenile, teenager, adolescent, boy, girl, lad, lass; inf. kid.

**your** adj. of or belonging to you.

**yours** poss.pron belonging to you.

**yourself** pron. (pl. -selves) the emphatic and reflexive form of *you*.

**youth** n. 1 the period between childhood and adult age. 2 the state or quality of being young.
3 a young man. 4 young people. □ **youth club** a club providing leisure activities for young people. **youth hostel** a place providing cheap accommodation for young people.
▷ SYNS 1 YOUNG DAYS, teens, adolescence, boyhood, girlhood, childhood. 2 BOY, lad, youngster, juvenile, teenager, adolescent; inf. kid.

**youthful** adj. 1 young. 2 characteristic of young people.
▷ SYNS YOUNG, active, vigorous, spry, sprightly; boyish, girlish.

**yowl** v. & n. (make) a loud wailing cry.

**yo-yo** n. (pl. -yos) trademark a disc-shaped toy that can be made to rise and fall on a string that winds round in a groove. • v. (yo-yoed, yo-yoing) move up and down rapidly.

**yucca** n. a plant with sword-like leaves and spikes of white flowers.

**yuck** (or **yuk**) exclam. inf. an expression of disgust. ■ **yucky** adj.

**Yuletide** (or **Yuletide**) n. old use Christmas.

**yummy** adj. (-ier, -iest) inf. delicious.

**yuppie** (or **yuppy**) n. inf. a young middle-class professional person who earns a great deal of money.

# Zz

**zany** adj. (**-ier**, **-iest**) crazily funny.

**zap** inf. v. (**zapped**, **zapping**) **1** destroy. **2** move or propel suddenly.

**zeal** n. great energy, enthusiasm, and commitment.
▷ SYNS PASSION, energy, enthusiasm, commitment, ardour, fervour, eagerness, keenness, gusto; fanaticism.

**zealot** n. a person who is fanatical in support of a cause.

**zealous** adj. showing great enthusiasm for a cause or aim.
▷ SYNS ARDENT, fervent, fervid, passionate, enthusiastic, eager, keen, energetic; fanatical.

**zebra** n. an African horse-like animal with black and white stripes. □ **zebra crossing** a pedestrian road crossing marked with broad white stripes.

**zeitgeist** n. the characteristic spirit or mood of a particular period.

**Zen** n. a form of Buddhism.

**zenith** n. **1** the point of greatest power or success. **2** the point in the sky directly overhead.
▷ SYNS HIGHEST POINT, height, top, peak, pinnacle.

**zephyr** n. lit. a soft gentle wind.

**zero** n. **1** the figure 0; nought. **2** a temperature of 0°C (32°F).
▷ SYNS NOUGHT, nothing, nil, 0; inf. zilch.

**zest** n. **1** keen enjoyment or interest. **2** orange or lemon peel as flavouring.

▷ SYNS RELISH, appetite, enjoyment, gusto, enthusiasm, eagerness, energy.

**zigzag** n. a line having sharp alternate right and left turns.
• adj. & adv. in a zigzag.
• v. (**zigzagged**, **zigzagging**) move in a zigzag.

**zilch** n. inf. nothing.

**zinc** n. a white metallic element.

**zing** inf. n. vigour. • v. move swiftly.

**Zionism** n. a movement for the development of a Jewish nation in Israel. ■ Zionist n.

**zip** n. (also **zipper**) a fastener with teeth that interlock when brought together by a sliding tab. • v. (**zipped**, **zipping**) **1** fasten with a zip. **2** inf. move at high speed.

**zircon** n. a brown or semi-transparent mineral.

**zit** n. inf. a spot on the skin.

**zither** n. a stringed instrument played with the fingers.

**zodiac** n. (in astrology) a band of the sky divided into twelve equal parts (**signs of the zodiac**) each named after a constellation.

**zombie** n. **1** (in stories) a corpse that has been brought back to life by magic. **2** inf. a completely unresponsive person.

**zone** n. an area having particular characteristics or a particular use. • v. divide into zones.
■ zonal adj.

▷ SYNS **n.** AREA, sector, section, belt, district, region, province.

**zoo** n. a place where wild animals are kept for display, conservation, and study.

**zoology** n. the scientific study of animals. ■ **zoological** adj. **zoologist** n.

**zoom** v. **1** move very quickly. **2** (of a camera) change smoothly from a long shot to a close-up or vice versa. □ **zoom lens** a lens allowing a camera to zoom.

**zucchini** n. (pl. **-ini** or **-inis**) US a courgette.

**zygote** n. a cell formed by the union of two gametes.